PSYCHOLOGY TODAY
FOURTH EDITION

PSYCHOLOGY TODAY
AN INTRODUCTION

FOURTH EDITION

J. JAY BRAUN
Arizona State University

DARWYN E. LINDER
Arizona State University

With Chapter Introductions by
ISAAC ASIMOV

RANDOM HOUSE/NEW YORK

Fourth Edition
9876543

Library of Congress Cataloging in Publication Data
Braun, Jay, 1938-
Psychology today.
First-3d editions entered under title.
Bibliography: p.
Includes index.
1. Psychology. I. Linder, Darwyn E., joint author.
II. Title.
BF121.P85 1979   150   78-26633
ISBN 0-394-32066-2

Manufactured in the United States of America. Composed
by Typothetae, Palo Alto, California. Printed and bound by
R. R. Donnelley & Sons Co., Willard, Ohio.

Cover design: Doug Fornuff
Text design: James L. McGuire
Picture research: Abigail Solomon & Associates

PREFACE

In planning the fourth edition of *Psychology Today,* our aim was to retain the currency, comprehensiveness, and flair of the first three editions while articulating more clearly the fundamental principles of psychology and the relationships among the various subdisciplines. To that end, rather than enlist the aid of a large team of authors of individual chapters, consultants, and advisors (as was done for the earlier editions), this revision was done under the expert guidance of two highly respected psychologists: Jay Braun and Darwyn E. Linder, both professors in the Department of Psychology at Arizona State University.

Professor Braun, an experimental physiological psychologist, holds a Ph.D. from Ohio State University and taught at Yale University for eight years. He is a consulting editor for *Behavioral Biology* and has published thirty articles in professional journals. Professor Linder, an experimental social psychologist, holds a Ph.D. from the University of Minnesota and taught at Duke University for seven years. He has served as editor of the *Journal Supplement Abstract Service* for the American Psychological Association, is a Fellow of the American Psychological Association, and has published twenty-five articles in professional journals.

Professors Braun and Linder take equal responsibility for the content and the approach of this revision. With their guidance, we have made important modifications in the book, which can be summarized as follows:

TABLE OF CONTENTS. Although the text still consists of twenty-eight chapters, it is now divided into eight parts, as against seven in the third edition: Part Four of the third edition is now Parts Four and Five. The sequence and content of some chapters have also been rearranged in order to achieve a more logical flow of topics and to permit greater flexibility in using the book.

Four of the chapters are new to this edition: "The Brain and Behavior" (11), "Human Sexuality" (17),

"Adjustment to the Problems of Life" (21), and Conflict and Cooperation" (28). *Psychology Today,* is one of the first of the major introductory psychology textbooks to devote a full chapter to human sexuality. The thorough, well-illustrated discussion of the structures and functions of the brain in Chapter 11 is of great importance to students' understanding of behavior. Likewise, we think that students will benefit from a chapter-length discussion of the adjustments that ordinary people make in the course of their lives from adolescence to old age. Chapter 28 uses aggression and altruism to illuminate the human dilemma of conflict versus cooperation, demonstrating how that dilemma is central to such contemporary social problems as resource management and the energy crisis.

While the entire text has been reintegrated and updated, the following revisions are especially noteworthy:

- Inclusion of new findings on the competency of newborn infants (Chapter 7)
- Discussions of theoretical orientations, in addition to Jean Piaget's, toward cognitive development, using a life-span approach (Chapter 8)
- A life-span approach to social and personality development, with discussions of gender role and sex role development, as well as moral development, as parts of the maturation process (Chapter 10)
- Special attention to pain and pain research (Chapter 12)
- New material on nonverbal communication of emotion, on stress, and on psychosomatic illness (Chapter 15)
- Clear discussions of personality theorists, with expanded coverage of social learning theory and a new section on the work of Karen Horney (Chapters 18 and 19)
- Reorganized discussion of major theories of abnormality, with expanded coverage of the social learning and biological approaches (Chapter 23)

- Broader coverage of reinforcement and cognitive theories of attitude formation and change (Chapter 25)
- New material on the causes of romantic love and expanded coverage of attribution theory (Chapter 26)

SPECIAL FEATURES. Twenty chapters in this edition contain two-page illustrated essays, or "special features," which highlight an aspect of the chapter topic that is of particular importance and interest to student readers. The subjects of these special features range from "Learning to Learn Better" (Chapter 4) to "Why Do People Take Unnecessary Risks?" (Chapter 16) to "Sexism and Racism as Attitudes" (Chapter 25) to "Extrasensory Perception" (Chapter 13).

PEDAGOGICAL AIDS. Each chapter is followed by a summary, in which the main points of the chapter are recapitulated and important terms are set in bold type and defined. After each summary is an annotated list of recommended readings. At the back of the book are a glossary, which refers readers to the pages of the text on which terms are defined; a reference list, which students should find valuable as a resource for their own research; an index

of names; and a carefully prepared thorough index of subjects.

ILLUSTRATIONS. In illustrating this edition, we have kept the best of the CRM graphics from the previous edition and added many new color and black-and-white photographs, diagrams, and charts. The photographs have been chosen for their inherent high quality as well as for their value in stimulating thought and illuminating the text. The diagrams and charts have been designed to make abstract concepts and research findings readily understandable to students.

ASIMOV INTRODUCTIONS. For each chapter the noted author Isaac Asimov has prepared a light but thought-provoking introductory essay. Many of these are new to this edition.

Taken together, these innovations and improvements make for the soundest, best-integrated, and most readable edition yet of *Psychology Today*. We invite student readers to embark on their introduction to psychology in the full confidence that they will find the experience enjoyable and rewarding.

Barry R. Fetterolf

Editor in Chief of Special Publications

A NOTE OF ACKNOWLEDGMENT We wish to thank the many people who assisted us in the preparation of this edition of *Psychology Today*. We must begin by acknowledging the many outstanding psychologists whose contributions to earlier editions provided the foundation and framework for the present edition. Next, our warmest thanks go to the consultants, listed, whose recommendations helped us shape the blueprint for revising the text. Special gratitude goes to the critical readers, also listed, who reviewed the chapters of the new edition and whose comments and suggestions were invaluable.

Three of the consultants who aided us deserve special mention: Antoinette Zeiss, who prepared extensive material for the chapter on human sexuality; Nancy Eisenberg-Berg, who made indispensable contributions to the chapter on personality and social development; and Harry Kauffman, who aided us in revising the chapter on person perception. It is also a genuine pleasure to acknowledge our indebtedness to our colleagues in the Department of Psychology at Arizona State University who gave unstintingly of their time and expertise as we asked them endless questions about their special areas of knowledge. We are especially grateful to our department chairman, Leonard Goodstein, who provided encouragement and an atmosphere in which a project of this scope could be nurtured and completed. We also thank the staff members, who provided excellent support, especially Joyce Evans and Deborah Rhoads. Their willingness to translate barely legible drafts into neatly typed copy and to search out obscure references under short deadlines is deeply appreciated.

Random House editorial staff members deserve thanks for their work on the revision: Paul Shensa, the editor who recruited us for the exciting task of constructing this edition; Barry R. Fetterolf, who supervised the entire project with insight and enthusiasm; Mary Schieck, who did an excellent job of shaping us to our task; Cele Gardner, our project editor, who coordinated the effort with truly unusual patience, good humor, and a meticulous concern for the quality of the text; Marilyn Miller, the project editor who supervised the copy-editing process and the illustration program with relentless energy and perceptive judgment; Suzanne Thibodeau and Stephanie Wald, who made extensive editorial contributions to the first two sections of the book; Jan Carney, who coordinated a great deal of the communication with the reviewers; and Richard Dresser and Dorchen Leidholdt, whose assistance with the manuscript and proofs is greatly appreciated.

The production team at Random House has also earned our gratitude for their excellent work in turning our manuscript into a handsome book: Kathy Grasso, production supervisor; James L. McGuire and Sheila Granda, designers; and R. Lynn Goldberg, photo editor.

We thank the writers who helped us to transform ideas into words, especially James Cassidy, Paula Franklin, Vicki Goldberg, Susan Hajjar, Virginia Joyner, Martha Leff, Ann Levine, Roberta Bauer Meyer, Linda Rosen, and Roslyn Siegel.

Finally, we must acknowledge our continuing indebtedness to Joe and Felicia, Ferne and Els.

For Mary and Marie,

JJB
DEL

CONTENTS

CONTENTS

PART ONE

ABOUT PSYCHOLOGY

All organisms behave, and psychology is the study of behavior. Behind this deceptively simple statement lies a century of growth and change in the theories and techniques of the young science of psychology. In studying behavior, psychologists have extended the boundaries of their discipline until it now encompasses all aspects of behavior—human and animal, normal and abnormal, individual and social, instinctual and purposeful, physical and mental. In the various parts of this book we present an overview of the major areas of psychology. We begin in Part One with an introduction to psychology as a science and to the methods employed by psychologists.

In Chapter 1, "Understanding Psychology: Introduction," we examine the emergence of psychology as an independent discipline, looking at some of the major ideas about its basic nature that have been set forth over the years; we then enumerate the fields of specialization within modern psychology and the educational requirements for various careers in psychology. Chapter 2, "Doing Psychology: Methodology," provides insight into how psychologists do research: the methods they use to gather data, the statistical tools with which they analyze those data, and some of the problems their methods of investigation may present. The chapter concludes with a discussion of the ethical principles to which psychologists adhere in conducting their studies.

CHAPTER ONE

UNDERSTANDING PSYCHOLOGY: INTRODUCTION

I have a feeling that the difficulty with understanding psychology is that too many people already understand it—or think they do.

In such fields of science as chemistry, physics, geology, astronomy, paleontology (you name it), the subject matter is far removed from the common experience of life. The great majority of the population can live their lives without making any personal contact with these studies and yet in no way feel the poorer for it. They are content to leave these subjects to the few experts and students in the field, and they have no hesitation in saying, "I don't know anything about that."

Not so with psychology. Insofar as psychology deals with how human beings behave, people generally seem convinced they understand it. After all, they themselves are behaving all the time, and all the people around them are behaving, too. They have to deal with the behavior of others and so guide their own behavior as to make things go as nearly their own way as possible.

Naturally, everyone gains a certain rule-of-thumb proficiency at keeping out of trouble and at getting along; and very few people can do that and not feel certain that they are keen psychologists. If they've learned a few terms that are associated with psychology, such as "inferiority complex" and "introvert," they trot them out at every opportunity. All this pseudo-knowledge, of course, must stand in the way of real knowledge.

Worse, this pseudo-knowledge automatically leads to a certain distrust and even fear of professional psychologists. If a professional knows more about psychology than you do, and if you are such a great psychologist, then the professional must be a veritable miracle worker, who knows all about you and can make you do anything.

My wife, for instance, is a psychiatrist, and when this fact comes out in general conversation, there is usually a nervous stir. Although she's a sweet, kind, and gentle woman, sidelong glances are directed at her and statements become terribly guarded, as if designed to give her no handle for "psychoanalyzing" the speaker.

Sometimes a person will draw me aside and ask if she psychoanalyzes me all the time. That's at about the level of supposing that because I'm a chemist, I'm constantly analyzing the chemical content of the dinners she prepares. Besides, she's no dummy—she wouldn't psychoanalyze me for less than her full fee.

And come to think of it, I'm no better than anyone else. Here I am, psychologizing at you and I don't know any psychology. But then, I have this advantage over most people: I *know* I don't know any psychology.

Isaac Asimov

3

What does the term **psychology** mean to you? Does it conjure up images of a man or woman in a starched white lab coat, intent on the movements of a rat through a maze? Or do you picture an inscrutable, bearded man, listening to a patient on a couch pouring out his or her anguish? These are common preconceptions. How accurate are they? Psychology does indeed involve both laboratory experiments with animals and therapy for the emotionally disturbed, but these are only parts of the picture. In fact, psychology is concerned with an almost endless array of basic research problems and with a broad range of applied, or practical, matters.

How, then, can we define psychology? It is surprisingly difficult to provide a concise, formal definition that satisfies everyone who practices psychology. Most psychologists would agree that psychology is the study of behavior—and then become embroiled in arguments about the definition of behavior and about the specific kinds of behavior they should be concerned with. (Indeed, psychologists have not yet agreed on the basic question of the extent to which behavior is governed by the mind and by the body; see the accompanying special feature.) These and other controversies (which we will examine as we go along) are but one measure of the broad and diverse scope of psychology. The study of behavior in all its complexity leads psychologists to investigate everything from how flatworms learn to how a symphony is created, from the seemingly undifferentiated howls of a hungry infant to the obviously complex reactions of an adult to the death of a spouse. Biology and physiology, child and adult development, learning, thinking, perception, emotions, motivation, personality, and social behavior—all are parts of psychology.

Although different psychologists may define the subject differently, their combined efforts have made it what it is—truly, the study of *all* behavior. Psychology has something to say about virtually every aspect of our lives. All our behavior—from the moment of conception to the moment of death—raises relevant and indeed pressing issues for psychological investigation.

THE GROWTH OF PSYCHOLOGY

Psychology has not always been so broadly interpreted. In fact, it has grown tremendously in the hundred years since it first broke away from philoso-

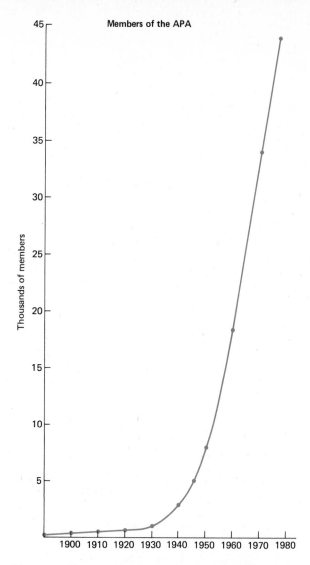

Figure 1.1 The growth of membership in the American Psychological Association over the past fifty years. (After Daniel, 1975)

phy and physiology, in which it had its origins, and emerged as a separate discipline (see Figure 1.1). The growth of this young and fertile discipline has been marked by a series of expansions in both subject matter and research methodology. The tremendous growth of psychology is perhaps best portrayed by examining a few of the major ideas about its fundamental nature as they have been elaborated over the years.

PSYCHOLOGY AS THE STUDY OF CONSCIOUS EXPERIENCE Wilhelm Wundt, who founded the first psychological laboratory in Leipzig, Germany, in 1879 and is generally thought to be responsible for the formal beginnings of psychology (Boring, 1957), quite stringently limited the subject to the study of conscious experience. Wundt believed that all our complex conscious experiences are merely intricate combinations of elemental sensations—that is, intellectual towers made of sensory building blocks. In much the same way that a chemist uses certain processes to discover the basic elements composing all the complex substances in the world, Wundt attempted to use introspection to find the basic sensations. He trained people carefully in the technique of introspection, teaching them to observe and report the "content" or "elements" of awareness in a particular situation. Wundt also tried to discover the principles—the "mental chemistry"—by which those sensations combine to become our conscious experience. In essence, Wundt's approach to establishing a discipline of psychology was confined to analyzing detailed descriptions of how people perceive things in the world. Psychology, then, was formally defined as the study of conscious experience.

PSYCHOLOGY AS THE STUDY OF UNCONSCIOUS PROCESSES
For Sigmund Freud, a physician who practiced in Vienna until 1938, conscious experiences were only the tip of the iceberg. Beneath the surface, he believed, lay primitive biological urges that seek expression but are in conflict with the requirements of society and morality. According to Freud, these unconscious motivations and conflicts are powerful influences on our conscious thoughts and actions; they thus are responsible for much human behavior, including many of the physical symptoms that troubled Freud's patients (R. Watson, 1963, pp. 423–425).

Since unconscious processes could not be directly studied through introspection, Freud developed a new method for indirectly studying them by interpreting overt behavior. In this technique, known as **free association**, a patient said everything that came to mind—no matter how absurd or irrelevant it sounded—without attempting to produce logical, meaningful statements; lack of restraint was essential. Freud's role, that of psychoanalyst, was completely passive; he merely sat and listened, then interpreted the associations. Free associations, Freud believed, reveal the operation of unconscious processes. Freud also believed that dreams are expressions of the most primitive unconscious urges.

To learn more about these urges he developed dream analysis—basically an extension of free association—whereby the patient free-associated to his or her dreams (Freud, 1940).

While working out his ideas, Freud took meticulous, extensive notes on all his patients and treatment sessions. He used these records, or case studies, to develop and illustrate a comprehensive theory of personality—that is, of the total, functioning person (Hall and Lindzey, 1978). Freud's theory of personality will be discussed in Chapter 18.

In many areas of psychology today Freud's view of unconscious motivation remains a powerful and controversial influence. Modern psychologists may support, alter, or attempt to refute it—but most have a strong opinion about it. (Freud's theories are discussed in Chapters 10, 18, and 23.) The technique of free association is still employed by numerous psychoanalysts, and the method of intensive case study still is a tool for investigating behavior.

According to Freud, human beings have both a conscious and an unconscious self, and the latter is a powerful influence on our behavior.

The Mind and the Body:
A Manner of Speaking

The Mind as Machine

Scientists often use metaphorical explanations of natural phenomena when they cannot understand them directly; they say things are "like" something else. At one time, for example, atoms were characterized as miniature solar systems: The nucleus of the atom was "like" the sun, and the whirling electrons were "like" its planets. Psychologists are especially likely to use metaphorical explanations because many of the processes they seek to understand cannot be viewed directly. Thoughts, emotions, motives, attention, memory—these have always seemed suspiciously spiritual and unusually resistant to scientific analysis, so psychologists begin by saying, for example, that memory is "like a library."

The popular metaphors in psychology have changed periodically in response to technological progress. Hundreds of years ago, when European clockmakers, just for fun, designed springs and gears to move the parts of realistic dolls, writers began to use phrases like "the springs of action" and "wound up," and we still find these in our vocabulary today.

Later, when the steam engine came along, writers and psychologists saw certain similarities between steam-powered machines and human beings. The machines "ate" coal or wood and turned the resulting energy into steam pressure, which in turn could be channeled through pipes and pistons to create a wide variety of actions. Sigmund Freud's psychoanalytic theory (described in Chapter 18) is sometimes said to be "hydraulic" because he spoke of psychic energy that "flowed" through channels, got blocked and repressed, and "leaked out," or expressed itself, in unexpected forms (such as dreams and slips of the tongue).

Not long after Freud developed the energy metaphor, American behaviorist psychologists (whose view of learning is presented in Chapter 4) adopted the "switchboard" metaphor. They likened human behavior—which they explained in terms of a stimulus followed by a response—to the plugging in of a switch on a telephone switchboard and the immediate ringing of a phone.

Today a new breed of machines is available—computers—and, true to form, psychologists and popular writers now describe people in terms of these machines. People sometimes express their failure to comprehend something by saying that it "doesn't compute" or is "difficult to process."

The Mind-Body Problem

These metaphorical explanations of human behavior rest on—and reflect—one of the central issues of psychology: the mind-body problem. To what extent, psychologists and other scientists ask, is the human organism indeed a kind of machine, displaying predictable, albeit complex, patterns of behavior? And to what extent is behavior governed by that subtle, mysterious faculty known as the human mind? In short, what is the relationship between mind and body?

There is no doubt that that relationship is a complex one. Consider psychosomatic illnesses—bodily disorders that have no apparent physical basis, but appear to be psychological in origin. (Familiar examples are ulcers, high blood pressure, migraine headaches, and asthma.) How are psychological complaints, such as emotional stress and unhappiness, translated into physical symptoms? Nobody knows for sure. Nevertheless, it is not uncommon for a physician to tell a patient who is shown by tests to be in excellent health but who complains of headaches, dizziness, or other symptoms that his or her problems are "psychosomatic." A doctor who does this is assuming the *independence* of mind and body. What the doctor is saying, in effect, is, "There is nothing physically wrong with you, it's all mental—all in your head." But what does this mean? For many psychologists the word "mental" is simply a label for the functions of the brain, and the brain is part of the nervous system, interconnected with all other areas of the body. Thus if something is wrong with a person "mentally," it is also wrong physically (Graham, 1967).

According to this *interactionist* view, there is nothing about human behavior that cannot ultimately be explained, through experimentation, on the basis of straightforward physical and chemical laws of nature. Human beings are incredible machines, but they are machines all the same. The way to explain behavior is to discover how the machine works. There is no need to invoke mental or psychological principles, no need to attribute behavior to emotions and to conscious or unconscious motives.

This mechanistic approach to

human behavior has its roots in the seventeenth century. Before then, Western thinkers had regarded the mind and body as separate and qualitatively different. The body was viewed as a mere puppet; the mind was the puppeteer, exercising complete control. French philosopher René Descartes (1596–1650) broke with tradition to propose that mind and body interact, each influencing the other.

Today, although psychologists continue to speak of the mind and the body as separate entities for convenience of discussion, most acknowledge that mind and body are intimately entwined. But even now, three hundred years after Descartes, no one knows exactly how, or how intimately.

So the mind-body problem refuses to go away, and stubbornly resists a definitive solution. As food for your own thoughts about this issue, consider the following instances—just a few among many—of the mind and body working on each other to influence human lives.

According to the interactionalist view, mind and body are one; thus sexual desire cannot be separated from the physiological changes that occur simultaneously with it.

- Severe depression, schizophrenia, and manic-depressive psychosis (discussed in Chapter 22) are often referred to as ''psychological disorders'' or ''mental illnesses''—terms that, in effect, assign these problems exclusively to the mind and divorce them from the body. Yet these and other ailments can occasionally be treated with drugs (see Chapter 24), which suggests that they may indeed have an organic, or physical, component. No one knows for sure whether they do, because nearly all these drugs were discovered by accident and, amazingly, no one knows exactly how they work.

- Recently Dr. René Mastrovito (cited in Schmeck, 1974) conducted a personality study of thirty women who had cancers of the reproductive tract. He found a striking similarity among the personalities of his subjects: all were responsible, idealistic, and highly restrained.

- Anthropologists and physicians working among primitive groups have reported many cases in which healthy people lay down and died when an enemy cast a voodoo spell on them (Cannon, 1942). Are the belief in witchcraft, and the fear a curse inspires, really powerful enough to kill?

What makes each person unique? The nineteenth-century English physiologist Francis Galton studied the biological determinants of individual differences and concluded that genius is hereditary.

clusion was premature. Galton did not consider the obvious possibility that the tendency of genius to run in eminent families might be a result of the exceptional environments and numerous socioeconomic advantages that also tend to "run" in such families.

The data Galton used were based on his study of biographies. However, not content to limit his inquiry to indirect accounts, Galton went on to invent procedures for directly testing the abilities and characteristics of a wide range of people. These tests were the primitive forebears of the modern personality and intelligence tests that virtually everyone who reads this book has taken at some time. Galton also devised statistical techniques, notably the correlation coefficient, that are still in use today (see Chapter 2).

Although Galton began his work shortly before psychology emerged as an independent discipline, his theories and techniques quickly became central aspects of the new science. In 1883 he published a book, *Inquiries into Human Faculty and Its Development*, that is regarded as having defined the beginnings of individual psychology. Galton's writings raised the issue of whether behavior is determined by heredity or environment—a subject that has become the focus of heated controversy, especially in recent years (see Chapters 3 and 20). Galton's influence can also be seen in the current widespread use of psychological tests, in the continuing controversy over their use, and in the statistical methods employed to evaluate their findings (all discussed in Chapter 20).

PSYCHOLOGY AS THE STUDY OF INDIVIDUAL DIFFERENCES

Sir Francis Galton, a nineteenth-century English physiologist, was concerned with the biological determinants of individual differences—that is, with the way in which biology decides how one person's abilities, character, and behavior differ from those of other people. Galton (1869) traced the ancestry of various eminent people and found that greatness runs in families. (This was appropriate, as Galton himself was considered a genius and his family included at least one towering intellectual figure—a cousin named Charles Darwin.) Galton therefore concluded that genius or eminence is a hereditary trait. Of course, this con-

PSYCHOLOGY AS THE STUDY OF OBSERVABLE BEHAVIOR

The pioneering work of Russian physiologist Ivan Pavlov, who won the Nobel Prize in 1904, charted another new course for psychological investigation. In a now-famous experiment Pavlov rang a bell each time he gave a dog some meat powder. The dog, of course, would salivate the moment it saw the meat powder. After Pavlov repeated the procedure many times, the dog would salivate when it heard the bell, even if no food appeared.

The concept of the conditioned reflex—a response (salivation) elicited by a stimulus (the bell) other than the one that first produced it (food)—provided psychologists with a new tool, a means of exploring the development of behavior. Using this tool, they could begin to account for behavior as the product of prior experience. This enabled them to explain that certain behavior and certain differences among individuals were the result of learning.

Psychologists involved in investigating observable behavior became known as **behaviorists**. Their position, as formulated by American psychologist John B. Watson (1924), was that psychology should concern itself *only* with the observable facts of behavior. Watson further contended that all behavior—even in its apparently instinctive aspects—is the result of conditioning, and occurs because the appropriate stimulus is present in the environment.

Watson did not succeed in restricting psychology to the study of observable behavior. In fact, he expanded the field considerably by extending the range of problems and phenomena with which psychologists could deal. In this sense his emphasis on the mechanisms of learning and on the significance of the environment in developing and maintaining behavior were major contributions. In addition, by using conditioned reflexes and other techniques for the study of learning processes, Watson contributed to the development of such areas of psychological investigation as learning (Chapter 4), memory (Chapter 5), and problem solving (Chapter 6).

Though it was Watson who defined and solidified the behaviorist position, it is B. F. Skinner, the contemporary American psychologist, who has refined and popularized it. Skinner has both narrowed the specific predictive claims of behaviorism and has broadened its social implications.

Skinner has sought to show how, in principle, his laboratory techniques might be applied to society as a whole. His classic, still widely read novel *Walden Two* (1949) portrays what is no doubt his idea of Utopia—a small town in which conditioning, through rewarding those who display behavior that is considered desirable, rules every conceivable facet of life.

Skinner has exerted great influence on both the general public and the science of psychology. His face is familiar to nationwide television audiences, and his book *Beyond Freedom and Dignity* (1971) became a runaway bestseller. A number of Walden Two communities have been formed in various parts of the country, and many people toilet-train their children, lose weight, quit smoking, and overcome phobias by using Skinner-inspired methods.

Skinner has been widely criticized, for many are convinced he seeks to limit personal freedom with his "manipulative" conditioning techniques; he has been heartily applauded as a social visionary for the very same reason. In any event, his theories and methods have permeated psychology. Behaviorist-inspired techniques are vying with more traditional psychotherapy for primacy in the treatment of various psychological disorders. The techniques of reinforcement, or controlled reward and punishment, have become increasingly popular in education, and Skinner's teaching machine was the forerunner of modern programmed instruction. Moreover, a vast number of today's psychologists use Skinner's research methodology to obtain precise findings in their laboratory experiments (Herrnstein, 1977).

In this section we have seen how psychology has expanded from an infant discipline characterized by a focus on conscious experience to a vast, nearly undefinable modern science that embraces the study of *all* behavior. We have seen how the list of clinical and research methods has grown from simple introspection to the broad range of techniques in use today. Of course, the brief survey we have presented is not intended as a comprehensive history. We have touched on a few of the most important contributions to the scope, substance, and methodology of psychological investigation—and must leave more extensive and detailed discussions to the historians.

PSYCHOLOGY TODAY

The modern science of psychology is based on developments that occurred in many countries over many years. In fact, we can trace its roots back to ancient Greece, although, as we have seen, only one hundred years have passed since psychology emerged as an independent discipline. Today psychology flourishes in many countries of the world: in Germany, where Wundt established his laboratory; in England, where Galton worked; in Russia, where Pavlov discovered the conditioned reflex; in Japan, where the discipline is still relatively new; and in numerous other countries. There have been significant developments in psychology on virtually every continent. However, it is in the United States that psychology has achieved its highest level of support for research, its greatest degree of popular acceptance, and its greatest diversity. This diversity can perhaps be best illustrated by looking at the many fields of specialization in which American psychologists engage.

FIELDS OF SPECIALIZATION The American Psychological Association (APA), located in Washington, D.C., is the national professional organization for psychologists. In 1978, the APA had more than 47,000 members, most of whom belonged to one or more of thirty-four specialized divisions. Figure 1.2 lists the seventeen divisions of the APA that have more than 1,000 members. The list includes some overlap, because a psychologist may belong to several divisions if he or she wishes, but it gives some idea of the variety of psychological specialties and the range of psychologists' interests.

The rest of this book can be said to be about the specialties listed in Figure 1.2, of course, but brief descriptions of some of the major specialties here will serve to demonstrate the current diversity of psychology as a science and a profession.

DEVELOPMENTAL PSYCHOLOGY **Developmental psychology** encompasses all aspects of the development of behavior over the entire life span, from before birth to old age. Every psychological concept—learning, memory, motivation, perception, personality, thinking, and so on—can be examined from the standpoint of how it develops and changes through life. Some developmental psychologists specialize in studying the capacities of the newborn human infant. Others concern themselves with the

Figure 1.2 Membership in the seventeen most populous divisions of the American Psychological Association in 1977. Note that a psychologist might be a member of more than one division. Psychotherapists and clinicians, for example are likely also to be members of the Personality and Social Division.

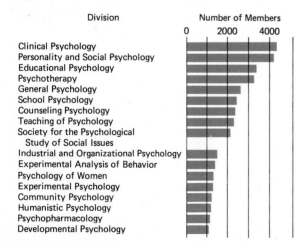

development of these capacities in the child, and still others focus on changes through adulthood.

Historically, developmental psychology has roots in the major traditions of psychology: in Freud's insistence on the importance of one's early experiences (Freud traced many of the problems of his adult patients to circumstances that prevailed during their childhood); in the behaviorists' insistence that all human behavior is learned (Watson boldly asserted that he could take any newborn child and mold it, using principles of learning and conditioning, to follow any kind of career); and in the concern with individual differences, which gave rise to a number of tests and measures designed to evaluate the nature and meaning of the various ways in which children develop. In recent years developmental psychology has become a particularly active specialty, an upsurge in interest inspired largely by the research and theories of the brilliant Swiss psychologist Jean Piaget, whose studies of the development of children's thinking have made him one of the most influential psychologists today (see Chapter 8).

Developmental psychologists work in a wide variety of settings: as consultants to children's television programs; in federal programs such as Head Start; in private practice; in institutions, where they may do psychotherapy with emotionally disturbed children; in industry, where they may try to determine how an employee's attitude to work changes with age; and in schools, where they may work with children who have learning problems. Most of them, however, are found in university settings conducting research on developmental processes. Fascinating and sometimes surprising information has come from such research. In recent years, for example, it has been shown that newborn human infants, despite their helpless appearance, are amazingly adept at dealing with their environment. They can apparently perceive different colors, tones, tastes, and smells, and they quickly learn to discriminate between familiar and unfamiliar voices. By the age of three weeks, they even appear to be capable of rudimentary imitative behavior. These findings and many others are discussed in some detail in Chapters 7 through 10, on human development.

EXPERIMENTAL PSYCHOLOGY **Experimental psychology** is the application of the experimental, scientific method to the study of behavioral processes. The image of the researcher in a white coat,

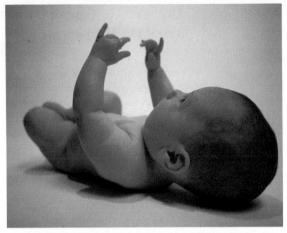

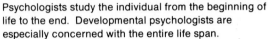
Psychologists study the individual from the beginning of life to the end. Developmental psychologists are especially concerned with the entire life span.

running rats through mazes, captures the stereotype of the experimental psychologist, but very narrowly. Experimental psychologists are identified not so much by *what* they study as by *how* they do it. They receive special training in research design, methodology, and the logic of the scientific approach in formulating theories of behavior. As we will see throughout this book, any concept or question in psychology can be approached by the experimentalist: What is the basis for the love between an infant and its mother? Does acupuncture work? Can one learn while one sleeps? Can animals think? What

is the role of the brain in memory? These are some of the questions that might determine the work of an experimental psychologist. Obviously, the experimentalist who can provide answers to such questions contributes greatly to the more "practical" areas of psychology. As Figure 1.2 shows, a relatively small number of psychologists associate themselves with experimental psychology per se, but it should be pointed out that all the special fields of psychology include individuals who could be labeled "experimental" because they do research on psychological questions.

Figure 1.3 Do animals think?

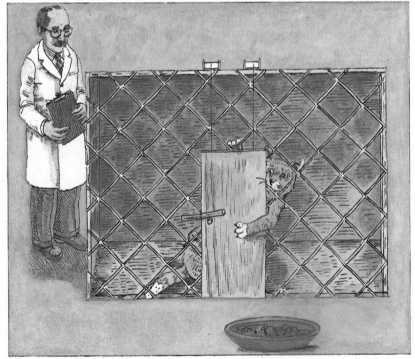

The experimental research tradition in psychology stems from the laboratory orientation of Wilhelm Wundt, whose contributions we have already described. But this tradition can be traced back even further, to pioneers such as Gustave Fechner, a nineteenth-century German physicist and psychologist who founded **psychophysics**, the study of the relationship between the physical world and the perceived world (see Chapter 12). Psychophysics is currently an influential and active subdiscipline of experimental psychology.

John Watson's behaviorism also had a tremendous impact on the development and refinement of the experimental approach to psychology. This impact is indicated by the number of experimental psychologists in the Experimental Analysis of Behavior division of the APA (see Figure 1.2); this division is composed principally of the intellectual descendants of the behaviorist view, as formulated by Watson and enriched and broadened by Skinner.

In experimental psychology, the three basic areas currently of greatest interest to researchers are the laws of learning, the basic processes of perception, and the nature of thinking and consciousness; experimental psychologists seek to uncover the fundamental laws governing these processes. Because of the generally abstract nature of their work and interests, most experimental psychologists work in academic settings, which can nurture basic research that does not necessarily have a direct concern with solving "practical" problems.

However, many people trained as experimental psychologists are hired to work in business and industry, where they may be called **industrial psychologists**, another major specialty. For someone who enjoys practical and creative problem solving, this is a particularly interesting field. An industrial psychologist may work with an engineer to design airplane controls that will increase a pilot's effectiveness, or may arrange rewards and incentives to increase productivity in an office or a factory.

In addition, because of the special training in mathematics and computer sciences received nowadays by most experimental psychologists, the rapidly growing computer industry has been hiring many holders of advanced degrees in psychology. **Psychopharmacologists** constitute another group of experimental psychologists who sometimes work in industry. Many are employed by pharmaceutical companies to assess the psychological effects of drugs that are under development. Using various standardized behavioral testing procedures, a psychopharmacologist might examine the effects of a particular drug on an organism's learning ability, perception, reaction time, emotions, or sleep and waking cycles.

PERSONALITY PSYCHOLOGY Our relatives, friends, and acquaintances recognize each of us as a unique person. Each of us is known for having a specific set of characteristics, ways of behaving, ways of getting along in the world, ways of interacting with others. The combination of traits that makes

Break time in a factory. Industrial psychologists study and work clinically in business and industry.

each of us unique, different from all others, and at the same time consistent in our behavior in a variety of situations, we call our personality. **Personality psychology** is characterized by the development of theories about what makes up human personality and by the measurement of personality characteristics or traits.

Thinkers since at least the time of ancient Greece have speculated about what we would now call the nature of personality, its structure and its dynamics. The dominant historical figure, though, in the development of personality theory is Sigmund Freud. Freud's theories about personality structure and dynamics have been challenged by many critics in the past century, and by now many theories of personality are available as alternatives to Freud's, as we will see in Chapters 18 and 19.

One of the more fascinating developments in personality psychology came recently in the form of a challenge to the concepts of masculinity and femininity. Research (Bem, 1975; Spence and Helmreich, 1978) has shown that rather than characterizing masculinity and femininity as a bipolar dimension—that is, rather than saying that each person is either masculine or feminine—it is more fruitful to think of masculinity and femininity as sets of behavior or of capacities that are not mutually exclusive within an individual. In other words, each person may be androgynous, exhibiting behavior that is considered either masculine or feminine, depending on which is more appropriate to the situation (Bem, 1975). If masculinity and femininity can coexist within a single person, and if they are merely sets of behavior, rather than fundamental dimensions of personality, the implication is that we should not be so tightly tied to definitions of particular roles as masculine or feminine. This research is of course closely related to the issues of sex-role stereotypes and to the women's movement.

SOCIAL PSYCHOLOGY **Social psychology** deals with the behavior of people in groups. Each of us is enmeshed in a network of social relationships with people we encounter at work, at school, in the neighborhood, and within our family. Social psychologists study the ways in which these relationships develop. They want to know who likes whom—and why. They are interested in the attitudes that people have toward social issues and in the way those attitudes are formed and changed by our society. For example, when children become teenagers, their attitudes about the use of drugs like

Today, traditional ideas of suitable jobs for women are being redefined.

marijuana may differ from the attitudes of their parents. There may be a great deal of discussion in the family about the use of such drugs, and attitudes may alter as information is exchanged.

Social psychology began to emerge as a specialty in the United States in the 1920s. At first the major emphasis was the study of attitudes and changes in attitudes. The horizons of social psychology were, however, greatly broadened with Kurt Lewin's arrival in this country in the 1930s. Lewin founded the study of group dynamics, and much of the subsequent research that has been done on person perception, social influence, and group behavior stems from his impact on his students and followers. Social psychology has now become an extremely wide-ranging part of psychology; though research still is conducted on attitudes and attitude change, social psychologists now study friendship formation, romantic attraction, perception of other persons, behavior in groups, and bargaining and conflict, to mention only a few topics. (These and other aspects of social psychology are discussed in Chapters 25 through 28.)

Social psychologists are now attempting to assess the effect that violence in the mass media has on ag-

Today, because of social pressures, more and more men are doing work that has been traditionally defined, and frequently devalued, as "feminine."

pressed or may show other symptoms that prompt them to seek help from clinical psychologists.

The study of abnormal behavior and the formulation of theories about the causes of abnormality have a long history, as we will see in Chapter 22. Clinical psychologists attempt to study the basis of disorder, looking at the biological, biochemical, educational, and environmental causes of abnormal behavior. They also attempt to develop effective treatments for disorders.

Clinical psychology has developed in part from Freudian analytic theory and in part from the tradition of psychiatry started by Emil Kraepelin, who developed the first system of diagnosis and classification of mental disorder (discussed in Chapter 22). Clinical assessment of abnormal behavior has developed in part from psychological assessment and the measurement of individual differences as initiated by Sir Francis Galton.

In the last three decades clinical psychology has been very heavily influenced by the behaviorists. Thus, a large number of clinical psychologists now view abnormal behavior as a learned or conditioned response and view the treatment of abnormality as a matter of helping the disturbed person to unlearn the unwanted response and to learn new, more appropriate responses. One of the most striking advances in the use of behavioral techniques to treat abnormal behavior has been in alleviating phobias (irrational fears). Recent research (Bandura, Adams, and Beyer, 1977) has shown that treatment in which the client is carefully guided through a series of steps to overcome the phobia can have dramatic effects. The subjects in this study had strong snake phobias, but showed a marked reduction of phobic behavior after only one treatment session that averaged about ninety minutes. This and other approaches to the treatment of mental disorder are discussed in detail in Chapter 24.

gressive behavior, especially in young viewers. For example, studies conducted in several countries have demonstrated that a steady diet of media violence does seem to increase the aggressive behavior of juvenile delinquents (Parke et al., 1977). Delinquent boys who were shown aggressive or violent movies such as *Bonnie and Clyde* and *The Dirty Dozen* engaged in more acts of physical aggression after seeing these movies than did boys who watched such "neutral" movies as *Lili* or *Daddy's Fiancée*.

CLINICAL PSYCHOLOGY **Clinical psychology** is concerned with the study of abnormal behavior, with the measurement and diagnosis of mental disorder, and with the treatment of disturbed individuals. It is certainly possible that you or a member of your family may need the services of a clinical psychologist at some time in life. Children who develop behavioral problems or whose parents find them unmanageable are often seen by clinical psychologists. Adults whose attempts to cope with the stresses of life are unsuccessful may become anxious or de-

PSYCHOLOGY: BASIC AND APPLIED SCIENCE After this brief look at a few specializations in contemporary psychology, it should be apparent that psychology is both a basic and an applied science. In **basic science**, knowledge is acquired for its own sake, in order to make possible a fuller understanding of the nature of things; the "usefulness" of the knowledge is not an issue. In **applied science**, certain findings of basic science are used to accomplish practical goals. To illustrate, most biologists

The stresses of contemporary city life can cause people to become anxious or depressed enough to seek aid from clinical psychologists.

and physicists practice basic science; most physicians and engineers practice applied science. Psychologists may practice either. For instance, a developmental psychologist who studies the ability of young infants to perceive patterns is doing basic research. She is not directly concerned with the implications her findings may have for the design of crib toys, but a psychologist who does applied science (perhaps a psychological consultant to a toy manufacturer) is. Similarly, a social psychologist who studies the friendships among a group of office workers—who likes whom, how much, and why—is doing basic science. If he discovers that one member of the group has no friends at all and another has so many friends he hardly has time to work, the psychologist might try to understand and explain the situation, but he would not try to alter it. He would leave that to a practitioner of applied psychology, such as a clinical or industrial psychologist.

Sometimes, students who have been in their first psychology course for only a few weeks ask about the relation of psychology to everyday life, and they do so in a challenging tone of voice. Psychology, they imply, is not telling them what they want to know; it is not doing what it ought to be doing. One student may object because psychology is too slow, too painstaking, too plodding. All those intricate studies, many of them conducted with animals by researchers who are rigorously, infuriatingly objective, are *boring*. "Where," this student may ask, "is the insight into the nature of humanity that I enrolled in the course for?" Another student may object because psychology is too *abstract*, too remote—grandiose theories, animal studies (again), experi-

Abnormal behavior is studied and treated by clinical psychologists.

ments on such arcane matters as the smallest change in the brightness of a light that a person can perceive. "What," this student may say, "is the *use* of it all? What good will it do me to learn all this?"

The person who finds the scientific approach incompatible with his or her own way of looking at things might still find psychology worth looking into, as a complement to the literary and the philosophical views of human nature. As for the second student, the one more interested in the applications of psychological knowledge, he or she may, without too much effort, be able to develop an interest in psychology as a basic science as well. For example, students who find mnemonic (memory-jogging) devices useful may begin to wonder why they work; if so, they probably will be interested in what psychologists know about the way memories are organized in the human brain. People who use a token economy with their children—rewarding them with something for showing desired behavior—may be-

come curious about the principles of learning on which such economies are based. People who think they need psychotherapy may want to know not only what type would be best for them but why any therapy is effective; they may also want to know what psychologists have discovered about the causes of mental disorders.

PSYCHOLOGY AS A VOCATION

Psychology is practiced by men and women in a number of professions that have differing educational requirements. Many people use the terms psychologist, psychiatrist, and psychoanalyst interchangeably. They are not the same, and it is important to distinguish among them, especially if one is considering a career in these disciplines. Psy-

Traditionally, the drama of human life has been interpreted by writers, artists, and musicians. Today, however, psychologists also contribute insights into our understanding of what is human.

chiatrists are physicians with specialized training in the treatment of mental disorders. Psychiatrists first earn an M.D. and complete a medical internship, as other physicians do. Then, during a three-year residency program in psychiatry, nearly always in a hospital, they receive specific training in the treatment of mental disorders. As physicians, they may prescribe drugs and use other medical procedures, as well as conduct psychotherapy.

Some psychiatrists wish to become psychoanalysts. Psychoanalysis (which was developed by Freud) is a specialized form of treatment within psychiatry. Basically, it involves free association by the client and occasional interpretations by the psychoanalyst to help the client bring unconscious conflicts into consciousness and resolve them (see Chapters 18 and 24). To become a psychoanalyst, a psychiatrist must engage in an extensive study of psychoanalytic theory, undergo psychoanalysis himself or herself, and conduct psychoanalysis with clients, under the supervision of an experienced analyst. Psychoanalytic institutes that provide such training have been established in a number of major American cities.

The majority of psychologists have earned a Ph.D. in the discipline of psychology. As we have seen, some are engaged in basic research to uncover the fundamental laws of behavior; some in applied research to solve specific problems (for example, problems that arise in schools or industry); and some, like psychiatrists, in providing counseling and therapy to people suffering from psychological problems.

To earn a Ph.D., a psychologist must participate for four to six years in a graduate program in a department of psychology at a university. Typically, this program includes broad exposure to the theories and findings of psychology, a special focus on a subdiscipline (for example, developmental or social psychology), and extensive training in research methods. Each Ph.D. candidate must complete an original research project of fairly wide scope, under the direction of experienced researchers on the graduate faculty, and must then submit the findings as a doctoral dissertation.

Students who want to become clinical or counseling psychologists must meet all the requirements for the Ph.D. and must also complete specialized training in diagnosis and psychotherapy. In addition, they must complete an additional year of training at an institution that has an internship program accredited by the American Psychological Association.

Clinical psychologists generally work in hospitals or in private practice. Social, developmental, and experimental psychologists are usually based at a university, where they combine research with teaching. Many psychologists, especially industrial, organizational, and educational psychologists, serve as part-time or full-time consultants for government agencies, school systems, and private industry.

What of the student who does not want or cannot afford graduate training? In the last ten years or so, psychology has become one of the most popular majors in the college curriculum. According to Judith Cates of the American Psychological Association, 37,000 B.A.s in psychology were awarded in 1970–1971, and the number is supposed to double by 1980–1981. The few surveys that are available reveal that between one-third and two-thirds of those who major in psychology do not go on to graduate school. A survey of 1969 and 1970 B.A.s (Cates, 1973) showed that 29 percent expected to do graduate work in psychology; 24 percent planned to do graduate work in other fields (most often, law or medicine); and 47 percent had no immediate plans for further education. To a considerable extent, psychology has become a "general major," like English or history—fascinating, informative, worthwhile, and indirectly related to many careers and interests.

LOOKING AHEAD

Reading this book and taking a course will not make you a skilled psychological researcher or qualify you to conduct psychotherapy. But you will learn a good deal about the ways in which behavior is shaped by biological, environmental, and psychological factors.

Chapter 2 introduces the methods psychologists use in research. Part Two considers the basic aspects of behavior, with special emphasis on learning, memory, and problem solving (topics of immediate interest to all students). Part Three traces human development in all its complexity: physical, cognitive, and language development, and the foundations of personality and social behavior. The brain, the senses, and perception are the subjects of Part Four. Part Five explores human consciousness, motivation, emotion, and sexuality. Part Six describes theories of personality and the assessment of personality and intelligence. Adjustment, behavior disorders, and approaches to treatment are the subjects of Part Seven. Finally, in Part Eight, we look at social behavior and what psychology can tell us about, and do for, society.

We hope this book will sharpen your taste for further exploration in psychology. For those who do choose to go on in the field, we hope it will provide a solid foundation for future studies. For those who do not, we hope it will enrich your understanding of some of the forces that influence your life.

You have already spent a good deal of time studying behavior, of course. You could not function as a human being if you were not able to predict how people will react in certain situations; if you did not have theories about why people behave as they do; if you did not, on occasion, manipulate other people's behavior. But look for a moment at the accompanying box. How many of these statements seem true? All? Most? Research by psychologists has shown them *all* to be *false*. As you will discover again and again, much common sense about human behavior turns out to be nonsense. Therefore, it is very likely that this book will challenge many of your assumptions and even change your outlook on many aspects of your life.

True or False?

1. For the first week of life, a baby sees nothing but a gray blur regardless of what he or she "looks at."
2. A child learns to talk more quickly if the adults around him habitually repeat the word he is trying to say, using proper pronunciation.
3. The best way to get a chronically noisy schoolchild to settle down and pay attention is to punish him or her.
4. Slow learners remember more of what they learn than fast learners.
5. Highly intelligent people—"geniuses"—tend to be physically frail and socially isolated.
6. On the average, you cannot predict from a person's grades at school and college whether he or she will do well in a career.
7. A third or more of the people suffering from severe mental disorders are potentially dangerous.
8. The more severe the disorder, the more intensive the therapy required to cure it; for example, schizophrenics usually respond best to psychoanalysis.
9. Quite a few psychological characteristics of men and women appear to be inborn; in all cultures, for example, women are more emotional and sexually less aggressive than men.
10. The only way to get people to like you is to be nice to them all the time.
11. A hypnotic trance is very similar to a light stage of sleep.

RECOMMENDED READINGS

AMERICAN PSYCHOLOGICAL ASSOCIATION. *Careers in Psychology.* Washington, D.C.: American Psychological Association, 1976. Prepared by the major national organization of psychologists, this booklet describes the subdisciplines and various career opportunities within psychology.

BORING, EDWIN G. *A History of Experimental Psychology.* 2nd ed. New York: Appleton-Century-Crofts, 1950. The classic comprehensive presentation of the history of psychology from antiquity to the twentieth century.

COHEN, IRA S. (ed.). *Perspectives on Psychology: Introductory Readings.* New York: Praeger, 1975. A well-chosen collection of readings by major contributors to psychology, providing a broad sample of issues and perspectives in psychology.

EYSENCK, HANS J., W. ARNOLD, and RICHARD MEILI (eds.). *Encyclopedia of Psychology.* New York: Herder and Herder, 1972. 3 volumes. An alphabetical listing of definitions and articles covering important psychological terms and concepts, written by psychologists from all over the world.

HILGARD, ERNEST R. (ed.). *American Psychology in Historical Perspective*. Washington, D.C.: American Psychological Association, 1978. An historical record of American psychology from 1892 to the present, based on addresses delivered by presidents of the American Psychological Association.

MARX, MELVIN H., and WILLIAM A. HILLIX. *Systems and Theories in Psychology*. 2nd ed. New York: McGraw-Hill, 1973. An historically oriented discussion of major psychological systems and theories, comprehensive but primarily experimental in emphasis.

SCHULTZ, DUANE. *A History of Modern Psychology*. 2nd ed. New York: Academic Press, 1975. Focuses on the past century of development in psychology and includes brief biographies of major historical figures.

WOLMAN, BENJAMIN B. (ed.). *Handbook of General Psychology*. Englewood Cliffs, N.J.: Prentice-Hall, 1973. A collection of forty-five articles that reveals both the diversity of psychologists' interests and the unifying nature of psychology's philosophical and methodological foundations.

CHAPTER TWO

DOING PSYCHOLOGY: METHODOLOGY

I once served as a sample of one in a psychology study. I was seventeen and undersized, a junior in college, and making a little money toward my tuition by working for a professor of psychology.

I was in his office one day when one of his graduate students came in and asked me if I would help him. He didn't know who I was, but I was young and skinny and looked stupid and that was enough.

It seemed he was devising a maze that he intended to use to test students for some dark purpose of his own. He had a board with innumerable nailheads on it. If you touched any one of the nailheads with a wired metal stylus, a circuit would be completed. Some nailheads would light a green light and some a red light. The trick was to try to go from one end of the board to the other, lighting only the green lights. Naturally, you had to begin hit-or-miss, but each time you repeated the attempt, you got it more nearly right. In the end you could follow the winding path of the green lights rapidly and surely.

The student timed me and when I had learned the path, he decided that if a stupid kid could do it that quickly, it was too easy. He added winds and twists, then brought it back and timed me again. Then he added more winds and twists until he judged, from the time it took me to solve the maze, that it was difficult enough for the average college student.

And when the professor came in, just then, the student showed him the maze. The professor studied the wiring in astonishment and said, "Why is it so complicated?"

"It has to be," said the student, "or it's solved much too easily."

"Did you check it on someone?"

"Certainly."

"On whom?"

The student pointed to me, where I sat looking as stupid as ever. "On him."

The professor knew me, however. He clicked his tongue in exasperation and said, "Here, take it back, start all over, and use somebody else to test it on so that you'll end up with something fairly reasonable."

I gathered at once that the poor fellow had made a sampling error. After he left, I said, "I'm sorry, sir. If I had known he was looking for an average student, I'd have told him I was above average."

"It's all right," said the professor. "You're below average in plenty of other ways." And I guess he was right. You can't fool a psychologist.

Isaac Asimov

This chapter is about research methods in psychology. Are you looking forward to reading it? Not very much, probably. Most people are considerably more interested in what psychologists know than in how they find it out—or in the larger question of what it means, among psychologists, to "know" something. People would rather watch a basketball game than read the rules of the game. They prefer reading a sonnet to studying the poetic conventions that govern the writing of sonnets. They would also rather be told *what* a study demonstrates than learn *how* it was conducted.

This propensity, though understandable, is regrettable. The methods and statistical techniques available to psychologists to a large extent determine both the questions that can and cannot be answered and the kinds of answers that are obtained—definitive or suggestive, precise or not so precise, comprehensive or limited. The more people know about those methods and techniques, the better able they are to understand and evaluate what psychologists say. Possibly you suspect that the details of psychological studies, like the intricacies of American economic policy, are too complicated for anyone but a specialist to be able to follow; but in psychology, as in politics, "leaving it to the experts" is not a very good idea. For one thing, the experts sometimes disagree, and a knowledge of methodology can help you determine which position is supported by the best evidence. For another, the matters they deal with often have social and political as well as scientific significance. Child care, education, race relations, mental health, sex differences, poverty, behavioral engineering—these are only a few of the many topics with social and political implications that psychologists study and, sometimes, express themselves on publicly. You will be much better able to assess both the meaning and the validity of what they say about these matters if you know something about the methods used in the studies they cite to support their assertions.

It may help you develop an interest in methodology if you think of a question you hope this course will answer. Perhaps you are wondering whether mental disorder is inherited. Perhaps you are curious about why some people do so well in competitive situations, such as exams, while others do so poorly. Maybe you want to know why people fall in love. Keep your question in mind as you read this chapter, and perhaps after you have finished it, you will be able to begin to design a psychological study to help answer your question.

The general procedure psychologists use when conducting studies can be simply described. First, they decide what kind of data would give a meaningful answer to the question they are investigating; next, they gather the data by means of one or more methods; then, they analyze the data, usually by means of statistical techniques.

GATHERING THE DATA: METHODS
Which method psychologists choose to use in a particular study depends, not surprisingly, on the na-

ture of the question they want to answer. For example: A social psychologist studying attitudes may conduct a survey. A psychotherapist interested in formulating a new theory of personality may begin with case studies, the intensive observation of a few individuals. A developmental psychologist who wants to assess continuities in behavior from childhood to adulthood may design a longitudinal study, collecting data from the same individuals on several occasions during their lives. A physiological psychologist studying relationships between the brain and behavior will probably conduct a laboratory experiment.

As you read about the various methods, give some thought to the kind of information each of them yields. The basic goal of psychology, broadly stated, is to understand behavior. Specifically, the goals of psychology are to describe, explain and predict behavior. The method used in a particular study determines, in part, which goal is attained. For example, naturalistic observation usually allows description of behavior but does not allow the researcher to manipulate the circumstances or the surrounding situation so as to be able to control the behavior. Likewise, test scores may permit the prediction but not the explanation of behavior; that is, intelligence tests may predict how well you will do in college, but differences in test scores do not *explain* why people earn different grades in college. A laboratory experiment often makes it possible to predict and control behavior and may allow the psychologist to explain the behavior on the basis of experimental variables; but the experiment may not lead to a sufficient understanding of the behavior as it occurs under natural conditions. In many areas of research, all of these methods complement one another, leading to more adequate descriptions, explanations, and predictions of behavior.

SAMPLING No matter what method researchers use in gathering data, it is almost certain that they will have to collect only a **sample**—a selected segment—of the data pertaining to the hypothesis. Almost no questions permit the gathering of *all* the relevant data, but the sample must be of adequate size to reflect the universe of information it is meant to represent. For example, an opinion poll meant to reflect the opinions of all Democrats in the United States could not have as its sample only six people. Given the great number of people who can be identified as Democrats, such a small sample is too likely

Suppose you graduated a few years ago from a large high school and the organizer of your class reunion asked you to prepare a general description of what happened to your class. Are most of your classmates married? Did most of them stay in the same region? What types of occupations did they enter? Since it would be out of the question to find and interview all of your classmates, you decide that a sample of 10 percent will have to do. How would you go about selecting your sample?

to produce bias. If, by chance, four of the six people in the sample come from Mississippi and Alabama, the findings of this poll would probably be biased toward the views of Southern Democrats (which are often opposed to those of Northern Democrats). The principal requirement of a sample is that it be representative of the population under consideration. A sample can be representative on the basis of being a **random sample**; that is, every member of the population has an equal chance of being included in the sample. If you wanted to take a random sample of the members of your psychology class, you could put the name of each class member on a slip of paper, throw all the slips into a hat, mix them up well, and draw out a certain number of names at random. Depending on the number of people in the class, if you drew out 10 to 20 percent of the names, chances are this sample would be representative of the class along many dimensions—height, weight, political opinion, religion, and so on.

In some instances, where the population being sampled has some known characteristics, a **representative sample** may be specified in terms of the proportions of certain kinds of people who must appear in the sample. In public opinion polling, a sample is constructed in such a way that a certain proportion will come from both sexes, from each ethnic minority in the population, from each age group, and so on. For example, the proportion of black women in the population between the ages of twenty and twenty-nine may be specified; then a certain number of black women are randomly selected for inclusion in the public opinion poll. Random sampling and representative sampling will

under most circumstances lead to an adequate representation of the characteristic of the population that is of interest. Haphazard sampling—that is, simply examining the most convenient or first members of the population encountered—will usually not lead to an adequate representation of characteristics of the population.

THE SURVEY A **survey** is an attempt to estimate the opinions, characteristics, or behavior of an entire population. Because it is usually impossible to survey an entire population, a representative sample is drawn. The data of interest are then collected through the use of interviews, questionnaires, or, sometimes, public records. If the sample has been carefully constructed to be representative, the results of the survey may be used to characterize the entire population.

Probably the most famous survey of recent years is the one that resulted in the Kinsey reports, published in 1948 and 1953. Alfred Kinsey and his staff interviewed more than ten thousand men and women about their sexual behavior and attitudes—as radical a thing to do at the time as the Masters and Johnson studies were about fifteen years later, when subjects performed sexual intercourse in the laboratory (see Chapter 17). Kinsey found, among other things, that behaviors that had been considered "abnormal," such as masturbation, homosexuality, and oral-genital sex, were much more common than most people had supposed. Some of his findings on masturbation appear in Table 2.1.

Table 2.1 Kinsey's Survey Data About Masturbation

	In Females	In Males
Relation to Age and Marital Status		
Accumulative incidence		
Total: experience	62%	93%
Total: with orgasm	58%	92%
By age 12	12%	21%
By age 15	20%	82%
By age 20	33%	92%
Active incidence to orgasm	Increases to middle age	Decreases after teens
Frequency (active median) to orgasm	Uniform to mid-fifties	Steady decrease after teens
Average, unmarried groups	0.3–0.4 per week	0.4–1.8 per week
Average, married groups	0.2 per week	0.1–0.2 per week
Individual variation	Very great	Less
Percentage of total outlet		
In unmarried groups	37–85%	31–70%
In married groups	About 10%	4–6%
In previously married groups	13–44%	8–18%
Relation to Educational Level		
Accumulative incidence to orgasm		
Grade school group	34%	89%
High school group	59%	95%
College group	57%	96%

Source: Adapted from Alfred C. Kinsey *et al., Sexual Behavior in the Human Female.* Philadelphia: Saunders, 1953, pp. 173–175.

Surveys can be oral (interviews) or written (questionnaires). Interviews have the advantage of letting the investigators see the subjects; they also allow them to modify the questions if it seems advisable. Questionnaires take less time to administer and so are particularly useful in gathering information from a large number of people.

In conducting a survey of either sort, investigators must try to ensure that the sample is truly representative of the group being studied. In 1936, a poll by *Literary Digest* magazine predicted a massive victory for Republican candidate Alf Landon over Democratic incumbent Franklin D. Roosevelt, but Roosevelt won by a landslide. The problem was that the magazine had polled people whose names appeared on lists of telephone subscribers and automobile owners. In those Depression days, people who had telephones and cars tended to be quite wealthy, and, then as now, wealthy people were more likely to be Republicans. Thus the population sampled in the survey was not the voting population as a whole, and the results of the survey were very misleading.

Social psychologists often use surveys to gather data on people's attitudes and beliefs. In doing this,

one problem they encounter is that people sometimes give misleading answers, either deliberately or accidentally. Some people answer "yes" whenever they can, just to be agreeable; others seem to have a built-in tendency to say "no." If a survey concerns a touchy area, such as sex, money, or race relations, people are especially likely to claim that they *do* believe whatever they think they *ought* to believe. The psychologist conducting a survey can often control for this problem by including several differently worded questions on the same topic. Thus a person might say in answer to one question that he or she has no objection to a certain sexual practice and then, in answer to another, that he or she has never engaged in the practice and certainly never intends to. In such a case, the psychologist would suspect that the subject's attitude toward the practice was somewhat less positive than the first answer seems to have suggested.

THE CASE STUDY   A **case study** is an intensive

investigation of one or a few individuals, usually with reference to a single psychological phenomenon. Case studies provide a wealth of descriptive information about the phenomenon as it is demonstrated by the person or persons being studied. They allow for considerable depth of analysis and may imply the existence of certain behavioral laws; however, they do not *prove* that any law is really operating.

There are two important principles in the use of case studies. The first is the observation of regularity, lawfulness, or patterning of behavior that indicates that the behavior is organized around some principle. The second is the need for subsequent case studies to replicate the pattern of behavior observed and again show the operation of laws of behavior developed in earlier case studies.

been observed over long periods of time to determine the impact that the injury has had on psychological functioning and to observe the way in which some psychological functions are gradually recovered. The reason the case-study method is useful in these studies, of course, is that it would be unethical to inflict such injuries deliberately or to withhold medical treatment in order to observe the effects of brain injury.

While the case-study method does not allow for the definitive proof of psychological laws or principles, it is an extremely valuable method for obtaining insights into the regularity and patterning of behavior. The example of schizophrenic language in the boxed insert provides an insight into schizophrenia that a general description could not. In the hands of a brilliant psychologist, the case-

---

"My Sin Is Also a Perfume"

This passage is a small part of a diary written by a young man while he was in a deeply disturbed mental state. A document like this is not an easy piece of data to categorize or treat statistically, and one cannot be sure how representative it is of the behavior of all schizophrenics. But it is an accurate record of one person's behavior and probably gives the observer the most direct contact with schizophrenia that he could have without becoming schizophrenic himself.

Pride want of Money wordly gane who we are God help us to make the right move With God help we can over come the sin

of the world. God help us to do our best. curcomseion [circumcision] *5,000 cases per day* Dear God help me to forget some things. I am sorry I done some thing and will try to do better The part of the brain is much bigger than a dime. And is oppsite from which hand you write with The part is smaller yet that has to do with vision The nerves like telegraph wires to all parts of our body called cranial nerves A baby get it personality from its envirment. How long has it been sence you talked with the lord. And told him your hearts hiden secrets. Why don't our Churches Practice the brotherhood they preach. Billy Graham We need more prayer life. A few min. in prayer help's us so much. We ate like a bunch

of cattle going thorough a shoot prepairing for market.

My sin cause Christ to be hurt My sin is also a perfume

We can sin by Using our eye's. We should watch what we see with our eye's.

3 nerves control 1. muscles 2. skin 3. organs inside of us God sure knew what he wasdoing when he made mankind My love for women has been turned from women to men be caus I couldn't make over them. The devil know our week points better than we do. Freind ship How to wind friend

(From Bert Kaplan, ed., *The Inner World of Mental Illness,* New York: Harper & Row, 1964.)

Case-study methodology is especially useful in instances where it would be impossible or unethical to conduct the research by means of an experiment in which subjects are randomly assigned to different treatments. For example, the study of recovery of function from brain damage has been conducted primarily through case studies. Individuals who have suffered severe head injuries in accidents have

study method can be a powerful tool indeed. Sigmund Freud's theory of personality development, described in Chapter 18, is based on case studies of the patients who came to him for treatment. Jean Piaget's theory of intellectual development, described in Chapter 8, began with intensive observations of the behavior of his own three children as they were growing up.

Figure 2.1 Naturalistic observation, sometimes done through a one-way window, is a useful technique for studying such matters as teaching methods and classroom interactions. The teacher of a class is usually too involved in what is happening to be an objective observer; and the presence of the researcher in the classroom would probably distract the students and cause them to alter their behavior.

NATURALISTIC OBSERVATION The cardinal rule of **naturalistic observation** is that the investigator should stay out of the way—for example, by observing animals from inside a camouflaged enclosure or children from behind a one-way window—because the purpose of the method is to find out how behavior occurs under natural conditions, without interference or distraction from an outsider (see Figure 2.1). Naturalistic observation is commonly used by ethologists as a first step in studying the behavior of an animal species. A social psychologist might use naturalistic observation to study leadership roles within a commune or a therapy group. A developmental psychologist might use it to study the way four-year-olds interact at a preschool. An experimental psychologist might use it to study the organization of a species' behavior before, say, designing an experiment meant to find out what kinds of problems members of that species can solve and how they go about it.

Psychologists sometimes use **participant observation**, in which members of a research team actually join an existing group in order to record events and impressions that are accessible only to group members. For example, three social psychologists, Leon Festinger, H. W. Riecken, Jr., and Stanley Schachter (1956), joined a secretive doomsday group that had predicted the end of the world in a great flood on a certain date and at a certain time. By becoming members of the group, the psychologists were able to be present when the fateful moment came and went and to observe the way in which the disconfirmation of the prophecy influenced the behavior of group members. Contrary to what might be expected, the group members became much less secretive after the disconfirmation, and engaged in a great deal of activity aimed at publicizing their views and attracting new members.

In observational research it is very important to develop ways of recording the data that avoid the problems of completely subjective interpretation. How do we know the doomsday group became less secretive after the disconfirmation? Because the researchers kept a careful record of their observations. By examining such data, other psychologists can determine whether the conclusions are reasonable. The record of observations can be kept as a set of notes, as tape recordings, or as ratings on forms used for such studies. The important principle is that the data can be examined directly by researchers other than the original observer. Thus the observer's possible biases and idiosyncratic interpretations can be detected.

THE CROSS-CULTURAL COMPARISON A **cross-cultural comparison**, as the name implies, is used to compare the behavior patterns of people in different countries or cultures. Sometimes these studies reveal interesting differences. For example, W. Hudson (1960) found that Bantus and other native Africans, when shown the pictures reproduced in Figure 2.2, were unable to identify the objects' locations in depth, whereas people in Western cultures have no difficulty doing so. Hudson concluded that it is necessary to have undergone specific educational processes in order to be able to interpret the depth cues drawn, such as the converging lines. Other cross-cultural studies demonstrate apparently universal behavior patterns; for example, Lawrence Kohlberg (1963) has found that children in several different cultures seem to go through the same stages of moral development in the same order, as described in Chapter 10.

THE LONGITUDINAL STUDY

In a **longitudinal study**, the same group of people is studied from time to time over a period of years. Longitudinal studies, although time-consuming to conduct, are the best method available to assess consistencies and incon-

Figure 2.2 Individuals of the Bantu of Africa were asked to identify spatial relationships in this series of pictures. They were asked, for example, whether the man was trying to spear the elephant or the antelope. Western adults make no errors in tasks of this kind. The Bantus' performance, however, depended considerably on whether they had been to school or not. This cross-cultural comparison suggested that perception of depth in pictures is separate from ordinary depth perception. (After Hudson, 1960.)

sistencies in behavior over time. As an illustration, suppose that you wanted to know whether characteristically dependent children turn out to be dependent adults. One way to find out would be to select a group of adults, assess their dependency, and then try to discover, by reconstructing their biographies, how dependent they were as children. A more reliable way would be to do a longitudinal study: to select a group of children, assess their dependency, and then assess it again every few years as the children grow up and become adults. Jerome Kagan and Howard Moss (1962) have performed such a study. Following their subjects from birth through early adulthood, they assessed the continuity not only of dependency but of various other behaviors. Some of their findings are shown in Figure 2.3.

Longitudinal studies have in some instances provided evidence quite different from that collected using cross-sectional studies. In cross-sectional studies of intelligence, for example, the intelligence of a cross-section of people of various ages is measured at one time using group tests. The outcome of such studies had once led investigators to conclude that the high point of development of intelligence was somewhere between eighteen and twenty years of age, after which intelligence consistently declined. But those data had resulted from cross-sectional studies, and the older individuals in the samples had, of course, very different educations and different life experiences. A thirty-six-year longitudinal study (Bailey, 1970) indicated that intelligence increased steadily until about age twenty-six, after which it leveled off and did not show decreases, at least until the age of thirty-six. Another study, by David Campbell (1965), assessed the intelligence of a sample of persons twenty-five years after graduation from college. Campbell's data showed that rather than declining, the measured intelligence of these individuals had significantly increased.

THE EXPERIMENT

Many psychologists regard the experiment as "the method of choice"; that is, they consider the experiment to be more definitive regarding cause-and-effect relationships than any other method, and they use it in their research whenever the question they are investigating allows them to. An **experiment** differs from the other research methods we have described in that the psychologist actively controls the presence, absence, or intensity of those factors thought to affect the be-

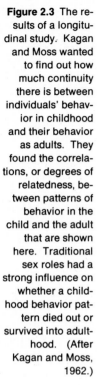

Figure 2.3 The results of a longitudinal study. Kagan and Moss wanted to find out how much continuity there is between individuals' behavior in childhood and their behavior as adults. They found the correlations, or degrees of relatedness, between patterns of behavior in the child and the adult that are shown here. Traditional sex roles had a strong influence on whether a childhood behavior pattern died out or survived into adulthood. (After Kagan and Moss, 1962.)

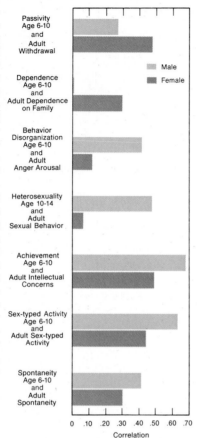

family, and friends about how one *should* act in various situations.)

The condition they set up to achieve anonymity was a perfectly dark room. The volunteer **subjects** (university students between eighteen and twenty-five years of age) were told only that they would be in the room for an hour with other people and that there were no rules about what to do or what not to do. The subjects were told that each would be escorted from the room alone after the hour and that there would be no chance of subsequently meeting the other subjects. This group of subjects is the **experimental group**.

The researchers also selected participants for a **control group**. These are subjects who have the same characteristics as the experimental subjects except that the experimental treatment is not applied to them. The control group was given instructions identical to the first group's but was ushered into a lighted room.

The researchers tape-recorded conversation during the hour each group remained in the lighted or darkened rooms; took photographs to record seating arrangements and the like (using infrared cameras for the unlighted room); and, directly after the experiment, asked the subjects to write down their impressions of the experience.

In an experiment, the word **variable** is used to refer to any factor that is capable of change. In this experiment the variables were amount of light and amount of talking and touching. The variable that the experimenter deliberately manipulates is called the **independent variable**; in this case, the researchers manipulated the amount of light. The variable that the researcher thinks will change when the independent variable changes is called the **dependent variable**—in this experiment, the amount of talking and touching.

It may help you keep these terms straight if you remember that the words "independent" and "dependent" refer to the relationship between the variables. Changes in the independent variable (amount of light, in this case) are controlled or manipulated by the experimenter. Changes in the dependent variable *depend* on changes in the independent variable if the experimenter's **hypothesis**—the proposition or belief being tested—is correct. It is also helpful to know that the hypothesis can always be rephrased into an "if/then" statement: If a perfectly dark room produces a feeling of anonymity, then under these conditions social interaction—touching and talking—will differ from interactions that are governed by social norms. The

havior of interest, and holds all other factors constant. The main advantage of the experiment over other data-gathering methods is that it permits the experimenter to control the conditions of the study and thus to rule out all influences on the subjects' behavior except the factors being examined. Its main disadvantage is that ruling out extraneous influences occasionally creates such an unnatural situation that one is forced to wonder how closely the behavior exhibited during the experiment actually resembles its real-life counterpart.

The essential characteristics of an experiment can be illustrated by citing a relatively simple one conducted by social psychologists Kenneth Gergen, Mary Gergen, and William Barton (1973). These researchers wondered how a group of people would interact under conditions of perfect anonymity (see Figure 2.4 on page 30). They formulated a hypothesis that people under such conditions would act in ways different from those dictated by social norms. (Norms are the expectations of one's society,

variable that follows the word "if" is the independent variable; the variable that follows the word "then" is the dependent variable.

Part A of Table 2.2 sets out the components of the experiment. Part B of the table gives some of the **data**, or results, the researchers obtained. In the lighted room, people kept a conversation going for the entire hour; they remained seated (usually three feet away from any other subject); and no one touched anyone else. In the dark room, conversation slacked off after the first half hour; subjects moved about a great deal; and touched each other both accidentally and on purpose. In fact, 50 percent of these subjects hugged another person. Because the experimenters were able to control the independent variable and manipulate it at will, the direction of causality of these effects is clear: The changes in lighting caused the changes in the behavior of the subjects. Thus, the researchers' hypothesis was supported.

Table 2.2   Components of the Experiment by Gergen, Gergen, and Barton*

A

Theoretical interest: The behavior of the de-individuated person, the person who is anonymous or not likely to be identified by others.

Experimental hypothesis: A group of strangers will interact differently in total darkness than they will in ordinary lighting.

Participants: 46 college students between the ages of eighteen and twenty-five, solicited by advertisement, telephone, or personal contact, gathered in groups of between seven and nine with approximately equal numbers of males and females in each group.

Experimental chamber: A soundproof, double-doored room measuring 10 by 12 by 18½ feet, with a carpeted floor and padded walls, and equipped with ventilating fan, microphone, one-way glass, infrared lighting, and ordinary lighting.

Procedure: 1. All participants upon arrival at the laboratory taken to a small room alone where given time-consuming task to do until arrival of other participants. 2. All participants given written instructions informing them of freedom to relate in any manner wished during experimental session and asking them to remove shoes, watches, earrings, rings, glasses, and contents of pockets until after the session. 3. All participants led one by one to experimental chamber. 4. Participants in Black Room Condition (experimental group) left for one hour with no visible illumination except pinpoint of blue light over door. Confederate of experimenter present in case of emergency. Participants in White Room Condition (control group) left for one hour with illumination from normal overhead lighting. 5. All participants led one at a time from the experimental chamber back to original small room and given lengthy questionnaire to fill out.

*Note that a complete account of the experiment includes the theoretical thinking that led up to the formation of a specific experimental hypothesis, a description of all the conditions to which the subjects were exposed from beginning to end, and an explanation of how the different variables were controlled and measured. Note also that the results given here are summaries of the data, not a list of every behavior of every subject.

B

Results: Observations of behavior in the experimental chamber:

	Black Room	White Room
Movement	50% change of position every five minutes.	10% change of position during whole session.
Verbal communication	High during first half-hour, then low.	High throughout session.

Percent of subjects reporting selected behaviors and experiences in questionnaire:

	Black Room	White Room
Talked small talk	96	100
Introduced self by first name	92	100
Laughed or giggled	80	100
Felt close to other person	92	75
Felt suspended—beyond normal time and space	80	65
Touched accidentally	100	5
Felt sexually aroused	75	30
Lay on floor	64	50
Found self in middle of room	84	10
Touched purposefully	88	0
Hugged	48	0
Prevented self from being touched	16	0

Figure 2.4 Drawings of the dark and lighted rooms used in Gergen, Gergen, and Barton's experiment (1973) to discover how people would act when they were placed in a situation in which they were completely anonymous. The experimenters hypothesized that darkness would encourage strangers to relax social inhibitions. The experimental group was placed in a dark room (darkness is the independent variable), and the amount of talking, moving, and touching was recorded. A control group was placed in an identical room, but with normal lighting. Again talking, moving, and touching were measured.

Another essential feature of the experiment is the random assignment of subjects to conditions. That is, when a subject agreed to participate in this experiment, he or she was assigned at random to the lighted room or the darkened room. Because of this random assignment, there is no reason to suspect that the people who were in the darkened room were just naturally less talkative and more inclined to engage in touching and hugging. In short, the random assignment of subjects rules out explanations that would be based on systematic differences that existed between the groups of subjects prior to the experiment. These two features—the control of experimental conditions by the experimenter and random assignment of subjects to various experimental conditions—make the experiment a valid way of establishing the existence of cause-and-effect relationships between independent and dependent variables.

CORRELATIONAL RESEARCH Sometimes, for practical or ethical reasons, a cause-and-effect question cannot be studied by means of an experiment. For example, a psychologist might suspect that normal development of vision in human beings depends not only on physical maturation but also on experience in seeing. The ideal way to test that possibility would be to raise an experimental group of newborn babies in total darkness for six months or a year, preventing them from acquiring any visual experience. Then their visual abilities would be compared to those of a control group of infants treated exactly the same as those in the experimental group except that they were raised under normal light conditions. As with the brain-damage study mentioned earlier, such an experiment would be completely unethical. What the psychologist might do instead is conduct this experiment on newborn animals rather than on newborn human infants.

Often, however, conducting an experiment with animal instead of human subjects is not feasible because the behavior to be studied occurs only in human beings. Suppose, for instance, that a psychologist thinks that the ability to hear spoken language is necessary for normal language development—that is, that deafness will cause deficits in the way a child uses language, even if the child is given special training in an effort to compensate for deafness. In such a case, an animal experiment would be of no use. Instead, the psychologist can conduct a **correlational study** to assess the strength of the relationship between deafness and certain language deficits. Although such a study cannot establish that deafness *causes* the deficits, it can establish that deafness and certain language deficits have a strong tendency to occur in the same people.

A **correlation** is an indication of the degree of relatedness between two variables. In some instances, the relationship between the two variables turns out to be close and positive, meaning that a high rank on one measure is usually accompanied by a high rank on another measure. For example, there is a strong **positive correlation** between IQ scores and academic performance: people who score high on IQ tests tend to get high grades; people who score low on IQ tests tend to get low grades. In other instances, the relationship between the two variables is close and negative, meaning that a high rank on one measure is usually accompanied by a low rank on the other. For example, there is a strong **negative correlation** between musical ability and tone deafness (inability to distinguish the pitch of musical notes); the more tone-deaf a person is, the less likely it is that he or she will be able to play an instrument well or compose music that people will want to listen to. In still other instances, there is little or no relationship, either positive or negative, between the two variables; for example, there is no relationship between eye color and academic success or between hair color and tone deafness. Correlation as a statistical tool is discussed in a later section of this chapter.

A problem with correlations is that people often misinterpret them. Instead of seeing a correlation as indicating merely that two things tend to occur together, they see it as indicating cause and effect. Suppose you were told that there is a positive correlation between the number of Popsicles sold by ice-cream vendors at swimming pools and the number of people admitted to hospitals for heat stroke. Would you conclude that Popsicles cause heat stroke?

Correlations do not indicate cause and effect; what they do is allow you to make *predictions* about events. If you know that a person has a high IQ, you can predict that she is likely to get good grades, or vice versa; if you know that a person is very tone-deaf, you can predict that he is not likely to compose a piece of music you would care to hear, or vice versa. Note that in either case your prediction could be wrong. Very few events are perfectly correlated.

TESTS, PSYCHOPHYSIOLOGICAL MEASURES, AND RATINGS Tests, psychophysiological measures, and ratings are grouped together here because they all can be used to measure individual behavior. One use of intelligence tests, for example, is to predict how well a given child is likely to do at school; personality tests may be used to assess an individual's emotional maturity, interests, and values, and so on. (Intelligence and personality tests are discussed in detail in Chapter 20.)

Psychophysiological measures are used to study psychological events, such as emotional arousal and sleep, which are known to be associated with measurable physiological change. The great value of such measures is that they provide objective, quantitative data on phenomena that are hard to assess precisely in other ways. An electroencephalogram (EEG) of the electrical activity of the brain, for example, makes it possible for psychologists doing sleep research to determine which of several stages of sleep a subject is in. Similarly, psychologists studying emotional arousal can learn more about the strength of an emotion if they measure changes in a subject's heart rate, respiration rate, and galvanic skin response, or GSR (a measure of the electrical conductivity of the skin, which increases when a person perspires), than they can if they rely only on the subject's outward behavior (such as weeping) or subjective impressions (see Figure 2.5).

Subjective impressions are valuable too: one way they can be studied is in the form of ratings. In an interesting study of fear in skydivers, Walter Fenz and Seymour Epstein (1967) asked novice and experienced sports parachutists to rate the intensity of their subjective fear at various points in the jump sequence. Fenz and Epstein then compared these self-ratings with physiological measures of emotional arousal. The results are shown in Figure 2.6.

Figure 2.5 Polygraph, or "lie detector," recordings. Note that there are four pen tracings: Abdominal and chest breathing is recorded from rubber tubes fastened around the subject's middle; blood pressure is recorded from a rubber cuff fastened tightly around the upper arm; and galvanic skin response is recorded from a pair of electrodes pasted to the fingertips. The record at the left shows the subject's reaction when he was suddenly asked, "What is nine times seven?" He seemed to regard this as a threatening challenge: All physiological measures show marked changes. The record at the right was made previously while the subject was being asked routine questions about his age, occupation, and so forth.

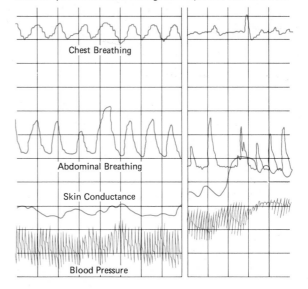

Chest Breathing

Abdominal Breathing

Skin Conductance

Blood Pressure

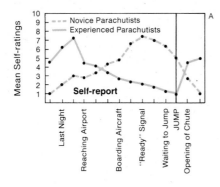

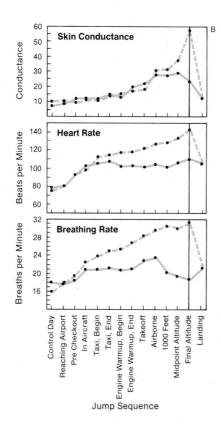

Figure 2.6 (A) When asked to assign numbers to their feelings of fear (with 1 meaning the time of least fear and 10 meaning the time of most fear), novice parachutists reported most fear at the "ready" signal just before the jump. Experienced parachutists said their fear was nearly at its lowest at this time. (B) Physiological measures indicated that both groups became more aroused right up to the time of the jump. Fenz and Epstein suggest that the experienced parachutists had learned to inhibit their experience of fear in response to the first signs of physiological arousal. (After Fenz and Epstein, 1967.)

ANALYZING THE DATA: STATISTICAL TOOLS

After you have collected some data (whether in an experiment or other type of study), how do you find out what the data mean? Usually researchers collect their data in a form that can be analyzed by statistics—mathematical methods for analyzing, interpreting, and presenting the data in summary form. There are two main kinds of statistics: descriptive and inferential.

DESCRIPTIVE STATISTICS Descriptive statistics are used to reduce a mass of data to a form that is more manageable and understandable. Using descriptive statistics, investigators are able to say something meaningful about their findings with a few words and figures.

DESCRIBING DISTRIBUTIONS OF SCORES Suppose psychologists are studying anxiety in various occupational groups. They have made up a questionnaire containing forty-seven questions that can be answered "yes" or "no"—for example, "I am often anxious during social contacts with my co-workers"; "I am often anxious while eating in restaurants." They give the questionnaire to a group of fifty gas-station attendants, and then add up each of the scores. They find that some of the attendants worry about many things and some worry about few things. But no one worries about more than 36 things, and no one worries about fewer than 11. The **range** of the scores is therefore 25 (that is, 36−11 = 25). The researchers can now construct a **histogram** of the scores, as shown in Figure 2.7A. A histogram is a graph of a **frequency distribution**, which is an arrangement of data that shows the number of instances, or the frequencies, of each class or value of a variable.

Next, the researchers give the questionnaire to a group of fifty dentists, and they want to compare anxiety in the two groups. They add up the dentists' scores and construct a histogram for them (Figure 2.7B). Then they choose a method for comparing the responses of the two groups. One way is to compare the central tendencies of the two

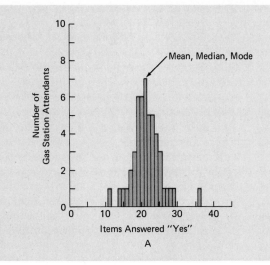

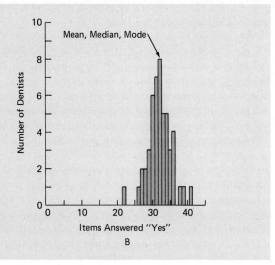

Figure 2.7 Two frequency distributions. In each figure, the vertical scale shows the frequency with which a score on the horizontal scale was observed. (A) The distribution of the scores from an imaginary group of gas-station attendants on an imaginary questionnaire. (B) The distribution of the scores of an imaginary group of dentists on the same test. Note that these distributions are similar in range but different in their averages. Also note that mean, median, and mode—the three measures of central tendency—are the same in both of these normal, symmetrical distributions.

distributions. A **central tendency** is some kind of middle value of a set of scores. There are several ways to measure—and thus to express—central tendency, and which **measure of central tendency** is used depends partly on how a group of scores is distributed.

One measure of central tendency is the **arithmetic mean**. To find the arithmetic mean, you merely add up all the scores and then divide by the number of people who took the test. As Figures 2.7A and B show, the mean score for the gas-station attendants was about 21; for the dentists, it was about 32. The other two measures of central tendency indicated in Figures 2.7A and B are the median and the mode. The **median** is the score that falls in the exact middle of a distribution of numbers that are arranged from highest to lowest. For example, the median of the following set of numbers—86, 84, 78, 77, 70—which represent the height, in inches, of five players on a hypothetical basketball team, is 78. The **mode** is the score that is most frequently obtained in a distribution.

In the two examples shown in Figures 2.7A and B, the mean, the median, and the mode are equal. These examples are symmetrical distributions, and equivalence of mean, median, and mode is a defining characteristic of symmetrical distributions.

Many kinds of distributions of scores are symmetrical and have a characteristic shape; that is, when they are plotted in a histogram (as in Figures 2.7A and B), the resulting curve has a characteristic "bell" shape. This is called a **normal distribution**.

When a very large sample of scores is plotted, the result tends to look like the normal distribution shown in Figure 2.8.

Remember, then, that in a normal distribution the three major measures of central tendency are equal. But remember too that the normal curve is an ideal. Few distributions, if any, ever exactly match the bell shape of the normal curve. Consider the distribution shown in Figure 2.9: This represents the distribution of salaries at a plastics company. Suppose someone told you that the mean income of the fifty people employed there was $18,000 a year; what would that indicate to you? Look at the distribution: the president of the company earns $70,000 a year; he pays three executives $40,000 and four ex-

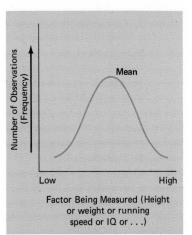

Figure 2.8 The "bell" shape of an ideal normal distribution of frequencies. The highest point of the normal curve represents the mean.

ecutives $30,000; there are six managers who earn $20,000 and six salespeople who earn $15,000. It turns out that the remaining thirty people, who run the machines, all earn $12,666 or less. The mean of all fifty salaries is indeed $18,000, but this measure of central tendency is not a fair representation of the actual distribution of salaries.

In this case, a better measure of central tendency would be the median, the score that has the same number of individuals scoring above and below it. In the plastics company, the median income is $12,666. The mode, or most frequent score, is only $6,333 a year: more people make that than make any other salary.

You can see that it is extremely important for a researcher to know and take account of how scores are distributed. Even when the mean, the median, and the mode are all the same, as in symmetrical distributions (see Figures 2.7A and B) the range of scores in these distributions could be different. For this reason, psychologists need an additional descriptive statistic that tells them how the scores vary around the mean.

VARIABILITY AND STANDARD DEVIATION The measures that tell a researcher how closely clustered or how widely spread out the distribution of scores is are called measures of variability. Range, discussed

Figure 2.9 The distribution of incomes in an imaginary plastics company. Note that the shape of this distribution is completely different from the shapes in Figure 2.7. Note also that the mean, median, and mode are not identical in this distribution. Frequency distributions of this kind—and of many other kinds—occur in psychology, but normal distributions are the most common.

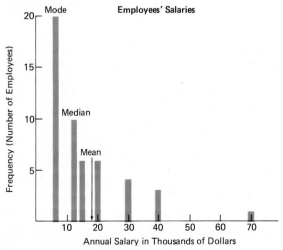

above, is one measure of variability, but variability is usually expressed in terms of the **standard deviation**—a number that indicates the extent to which figures in a given set of data vary from the mean.

Look at the two distributions of history quiz scores shown in Figures 2.10A and B. The mean for both sets of scores is 58, but the standard deviation for the scores in 2.10A is about 10; that for 2.10B is about 2. By knowing the standard deviation, you know whether the actual scores in the set of scores varied widely or only a little around the mean.

Calculating the standard deviation is not difficult, although it is tedious unless one has the assistance of a computer or electronic calculator. Here are the steps: (1) calculate the mean of all the scores you have obtained; (2) subtract the mean from each score and, in each case, square the difference; (3) add all the squares together; (4) divide the sum by the total number of scores you are dealing with; and (5) take the square root of that value. Figures 2.10A and 2.10B illustrate this procedure as it was used to calculate the standard deviations for the distributions shown.

If you were to measure almost any trait in a large group of people—height, weight, IQ, friendliness—you would find that the largest number of people fall near the mean, while fewer and fewer people would fall at each level on either side of the mean. You would find, in other words, that measurements of most traits form a normal distribution. Any normal distribution can be completely described by the mean and the standard deviation. And normal distributions can easily be compared when these descriptive statistics are given. The mean tells you the location of each distribution on the dimension you have measured and allows you to see any differences in central tendency. The standard deviation allows you to compare the variability of scores within a given distribution with the variability of scores within other distributions.

CORRELATION COEFFICIENTS Correlational research was discussed earlier in this chapter. Psychologists who wish to assess the strength of a correlation (the degree of relatedness between measures of two variables) make use of a statistical tool called the **correlation coefficient**. A correlation coefficient is a number ranging from −1, which indicates a perfect negative correlation between the two variables, through 0, which indicates no correlation, to +1, which indicates a perfect positive correlation. Thus the closer a correlation coefficient is

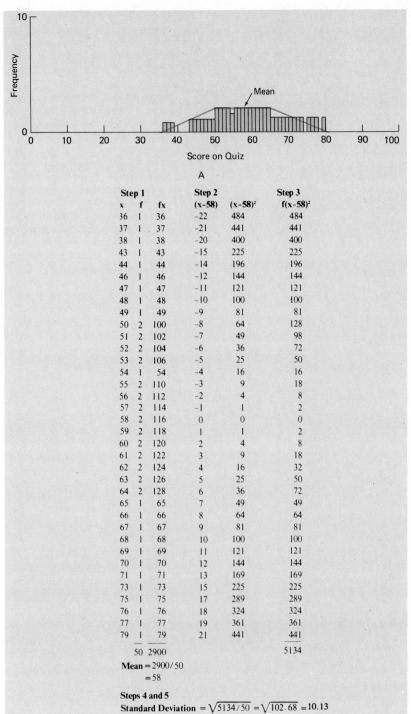

Score on Quiz

A

Step 1			Step 2		Step 3
x	f	fx	(x–58)	(x–58)²	f(x–58)²
36	1	36	–22	484	484
37	1	37	–21	441	441
38	1	38	–20	400	400
43	1	43	–15	225	225
44	1	44	–14	196	196
46	1	46	–12	144	144
47	1	47	–11	121	121
48	1	48	–10	100	100
49	1	49	–9	81	81
50	2	100	–8	64	128
51	2	102	–7	49	98
52	2	104	–6	36	72
53	2	106	–5	25	50
54	1	54	–4	16	16
55	2	110	–3	9	18
56	2	112	–2	4	8
57	2	114	–1	1	2
58	2	116	0	0	0
59	2	118	1	1	2
60	2	120	2	4	8
61	2	122	3	9	18
62	2	124	4	16	32
63	2	126	5	25	50
64	2	128	6	36	72
65	1	65	7	49	49
66	1	66	8	64	64
67	1	67	9	81	81
68	1	68	10	100	100
69	1	69	11	121	121
70	1	70	12	144	144
71	1	71	13	169	169
73	1	73	15	225	225
75	1	75	17	289	289
76	1	76	18	324	324
77	1	77	19	361	361
79	1	79	21	441	441
	50	2900			5134

Mean = 2900/50
= 58

Steps 4 and 5
Standard Deviation = $\sqrt{5134/50}$ = $\sqrt{102.68}$ = 10.13

Figure 2.10A A frequency distribution with high variability, and the calculation of its mean and standard deviation. Compare this distribution with the distribution in Figure 2.10B. Note that the means of these distributions are exactly the same and that both distributions have the "bell" shape (indicated by the colored curves) of the theoretical normal distribution. In the calculations, the letter x stands for the values of various scores. The letter f stands for the frequency with which a score occurred. Note that the total of all the scores is computed in Step 1 by multiplying each score, x, by the number of times it occurred, f, and adding up the resulting products. Note that the sum of the squares in Step 3 is computed similarly. (See page 36 for Figure 2.10B.)

to +1 or –1, the stronger the relationship—positive or negative—between the correlated variables. This means that a correlation coefficient of, say, –.65 between two variables is just as strong as a correlation coefficient of +.65. This is an important point about correlation coefficients, and it is one that confuses many people: the estimate of the *strength* of a relationship between two variables is determined without regard to the sign (+ or –) of the correlation. Rather, it is based on how closely the correlation coefficient approaches +1 or –1. Consider the following example: If at some university a correlation of –.42 is found between grade-point averages (GPA) of the students and number of traffic violations, and a correlation of +.26 is found between grade-point averages and some measure of athletic

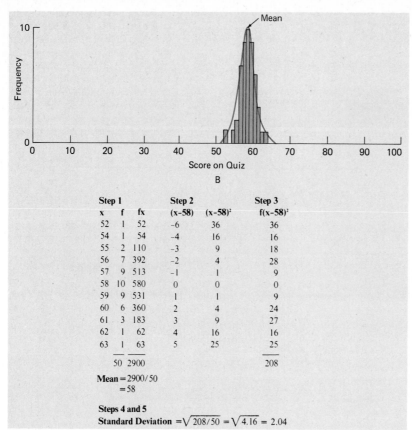

Figure 2.10B A frequency distribution with low variability, and the computation of its mean and standard deviation. Compare this distribution with the one in Figure 2.10A. Also compare the computations in each figure. The standard deviation is a measure of the degree to which individual scores differ from the central tendency of all the scores. In Step 1 the central tendency, the mean, is computed. In Steps 2 and 3 the difference between the mean and each individual score is computed and squared, so that positive and negative differences are both given positive weight in the measurement of variability. Finally, the average of these squared differences is computed and the square root is taken in order to bring the result back to the scale of the original scores.

Step 1			Step 2		Step 3
x	f	fx	(x-58)	(x-58)²	f(x-58)²
52	1	52	-6	36	36
54	1	54	-4	16	16
55	2	110	-3	9	18
56	7	392	-2	4	28
57	9	513	-1	1	9
58	10	580	0	0	0
59	9	531	1	1	9
60	6	360	2	4	24
61	3	183	3	9	27
62	1	62	4	16	16
63	1	63	5	25	25
	50	2900			208

Mean = 2900/50
= 58

Steps 4 and 5
Standard Deviation = $\sqrt{208/50} = \sqrt{4.16} = 2.04$

ability, such as running speed, a stronger relationship has been demonstrated between traffic violations and GPA than between athletic ability and GPA. In other words, in this fictitious example, traffic violations would be a better predictor of student grades than athletic ability. A minus sign in front of a correlation coefficient simply indicates that as one variable gets bigger, the other tends to get smaller—like the relationship between the length and the thickness of a rubber band as it is stretched, which probably would be found to have close to a perfect correlation of –1.

In most psychological studies, the correlations identified are relatively weak. For example, the correlation between the height of a parent and the height of his or her same-sex child is about .50; the correlation between IQ scores and school grades is about .45; the correlation between physical punishment by a mother and physical aggression by her child is about .20. See Figure 2.11 for two examples of the "scatter plot," a method of organizing data to discover the existence of correlations.

INFERENTIAL STATISTICS Inferential statistics provide ground rules or conventions for determining what conclusions can legitimately be drawn from data. Remember that researchers begin with a hypothesis—a conjecture that, under certain circumstances, people (or animals) will behave in a certain way. They collect data about how a sample of people do behave under those specific circumstances—data that are in a form that can be treated statistically (scores, ratings, and so on). They then summarize their data using descriptive statistics like those discussed in the preceding section. Now they must make use of *inferential* statistics so that they can *infer* (draw a reasonable conclusion as to) whether their original hypothesis was clearly supported by the data. Were the experimental results due primarily to chance, or do the data indeed show a significant pattern or relationship?

PROBABILITY Say you toss a coin a hundred times. If it lands heads up fifty-three times, is the coin biased? What if it lands heads up seventy-nine times? Statisticians have worked out methods for determining the probability of obtaining any given result with any given number of tosses of an unbiased coin. More exactly, if the probability of heads is .50, there are tables to indicate how often in,

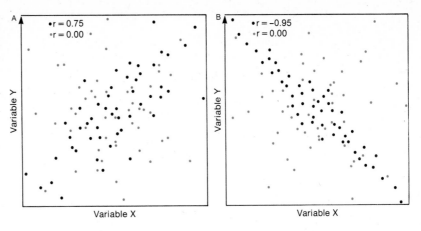

Figure 2.11 Data that are being examined for the existence of correlations are often plotted in the manner shown here. These "scatter plots" reveal visually the degree to which two variables are related. In both of these plots the set of lighter points shows a zero correlation. The darker-colored set of points in A represents a moderate positive correlation. The darker points in B represent a strong negative correlation.

say, one hundred tosses one can expect to obtain twenty-eight, fifty-three, seventy-nine, or any other number of heads from zero to one hundred.

Probability is a complex area of mathematics; our intuitions about "what the chances are" are not always correct. For example, assume that you have tossed a coin ten times and that it has landed heads up each time. You are about to toss it again. Reflect for a moment on what you would predict will occur on this next toss. There are three possible predictions: (1) another head will turn up; (2) a tail will turn up; or (3) the odds are still .50, so it's impossible to tell. If you predicted that a tail would turn up, you committed a common error known as the "gambler's fallacy." The reason it is a fallacy is that there is no reason to expect that the probability of a tail turning up is any higher than .50 at this point. Indeed, the prediction that probably has the most merit at this point is that another head will turn up, for it appears that the coin you have been dealing with is, for some reason, a biased one.

The odds of getting a head on any given toss of an unbiased coin are 50-50; that is, a head will turn up half the time. To find the odds of getting two heads in a row, you multiply the odds for getting one event (one head) by the odds for getting the second (another head): ½ x ½ is ¼. For four heads in a row, the odds would be ¹⁄₁₆ that such an event would occur by chance alone (½ x ½ x ½ x ½). The probability that a coin will come up heads ten times in a row is ½ raised to the tenth power, which is ¹⁄₁,₀₂₄; that is, the odds against this event's occurring by chance with a fair coin are 1,024 to 1, which is why you might begin to suspect in such a case that the coin is biased and that your coin-tossing results are not a matter of chance (see Figure 2.12). This is exactly the kind of logic used in inferential statistics. That is, when psychologists conduct a study, they want to be able to make a judgment of how likely it is that the results did not occur by chance: they want to know how significant their results are.

STATISTICAL SIGNIFICANCE Suppose that an experimental group of rats has been given an injection of caffeine, the stimulant in coffee. On the average, these rats learn to run a maze in thirty trials. A control group of animals is injected with a **placebo** (a substance that has no physiological effect), to ensure that the two groups will not perform differently merely because one has received an injection and the other has not. The control group learns to run the same maze in an average of thirty-eight trials. Is the difference between thirty and thirty-eight trials large enough for the experimenter to conclude that the caffeine increased the speed with which the experimental animals learned the maze, or might these results have been obtained merely by chance?

Psychologists and other scientists have adopted an arbitrary convention for making such decisions. By various methods they calculate the probability that the outcome of the study could have occurred

Figure 2.12 A frequency distribution of the outcomes of two hundred tosses of ten pennies at a time. Each tally represents the occurrence of a particular number of heads and tails among the ten pennies on one toss. (Note that if this distribution is looked at sideways, it has a "normal" shape. The most common outcome in this demonstration was five heads and five tails, but an eight-to-two ratio also occurred a number of times. Suppose you had tossed the coins just once and obtained nine tails and one head. Would you have been justified in judging the coins to be biased?

```
all heads
9 heads
1 tail
8 heads
2 tails    JHT JHT
7 heads
3 tails    JHT JHT JHT JHT
6 heads
4 tails    JHT JHT JHT JHT JHT JHT JHT III
5 heads
5 tails    JHT JHT JHT JHT  JHT JHT JHT JHT  JHT III
4 heads
6 tails    JHT JHT JHT JHT JHT JHT JHT I
3 heads
7 tails    JHT JHT JHT JHT JHT JHT JHT
2 heads
8 tails    JHT JHT I
1 head
9 tails    II
all tails
```

by chance alone. By comparing the distributions of scores obtained by the experimental group with those obtained by the control group, in the example above, the investigator can calculate the probability of obtaining that large a difference by chance. "Chance" in this case means that the caffeine had no effect on learning and the results occurred because of sampling differences between the two groups. If the probability that the experimental group learned that much faster just by chance is quite low, say .05 (or 20 to 1 odds), the investigator may say that the "chance" explanation of the difference can be rejected and the difference in learning must be due to the experimental treatment.

The levels of **statistical significance** are conventions for deciding when to reject the chance hypothesis. If an outcome could occur only once in twenty times by chance, the probability of that outcome is .05 and an investigator would summarize the findings by saying that the results had attained the ".05 level of statistical significance." Some investigators choose more stringent levels, say .01 (or 100 to 1 odds). In each case, however, the investigator computes the probability that the results occurred solely by chance. Only if that probability

is low does the researcher assert that the results supported the hypothesis.

SELECTED METHODOLOGICAL PROBLEMS

In describing the methods and statistical techniques that psychologists commonly use, we have, for the sake of clarity, greatly simplified the process of conducting a research study. To give a more accurate picture, it is necessary to survey a few of the problems and pitfalls that can invalidate the interpretation of a psychological study unless they are coped with successfully.

THE SELF-FULFILLING PROPHECY The term **self-fulfilling prophecy** refers to the fact that the expectations of investigators can influence their findings. In psychology, as in other fields, people tend to find what they are looking for. For example, if in-

Figure 2.13 This researcher will probably find that females are more sociable under the conditions of his experiment than males are. His finding will be correct in principle, but will he include his own smile in his account of the experimental conditions? He is probably unconscious of subtle variations in his own behavior and will mistakenly attribute the male–female differences he observes to some other factor. If his experimental hypothesis has to do with male–female differences, he may have made a self-fulfilling prophecy.

Setting:
A psychologist is seated at his desk. There is a knock on his office door.

Psychologist:
Come in.
(A male student enters)
Sit down, please.

I am going to read you a set of instructions. I am not permitted to say anything which is not in the instructions nor can I answer any questions about this experiment.

After the student has completed the experiment, he leaves.
There is another knock at the door.

Psychologist:
Come in.
(A female student enters)
Sit down, please.
(The psychologist smiles)
I am going to read you a set of instructions. I am not permitted to say anything which is not in the instructions nor can I answer any questions about this experiment. OK? We are developing a test of . . .

The only difference between the two episodes is the smile!
Can a smile affect the results of an experiment?

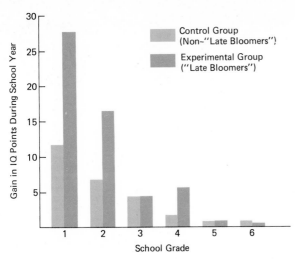

Figure 2.14 Teachers in each of the six grades of an elementary school were led to believe that certain of their pupils had been discovered to be "late bloomers" on the basis of a special test and would show great academic gains during the year. In fact, the pupils were selected at random. Intelligence tests were given both at the beginning and at the end of the school year. This histogram shows the relative IQ gains during the year of the control group (pupils not expected to be "late bloomers" by their teachers) and the experimental group (pupils who were expected to be "late bloomers"). Both groups gained in the lower grades, but the experimental group gained more. However, in the upper grades there was little effect, perhaps because the teachers already had strong expectations about the pupils based on their performances in earlier grades. (After Rosenthal, 1966.)

vestigators are conducting a study in which they interview subjects face to face, they can affect a subject's responses by unwittingly communicating positive or negative feelings, as by smiling when the subject's responses corroborate the theory and frowning when they contradict it (see Figure 2.13).

Consider this example: Robert Rosenthal (1966) told a group of elementary school teachers that some of their pupils had obtained high scores on some special tests and were sure to show unusual intellectual development during the school year. Actually, these pupils were no different from others not identified to the teachers as potential "bloomers." Later in the year, the teachers rated the "bloomers" as more interested, more curious, and happier than other students. And when all the children were given IQ tests at the end of the year, the "bloomers" showed a significantly greater gain in IQ than did the "nonbloomers," as Figure 2.14 shows. This effect was strong in the early grades—among first-graders, the "bloomers" gained an average of 15 IQ points more than did the control "nonbloomers"—but the difference in IQ gains did not appear in the fifth and sixth grades. Presumably, the teachers of

younger children were particularly susceptible to outside suggestions about the students' abilities because they had not yet had a chance to get to know them or about them.

One way for a researcher to avoid self-fulfilling prophecies is to employ a procedure called the **double-blind technique**, in which neither the experimenter nor the subjects know which subjects belong to the experimental group and which belong to the control group. (This procedure can be compared to the single-blind technique, in which the experimenter knows who is in which group but the subjects do not.) In an experiment testing the effects of a tranquilizing drug, for example, the experimental group would be given the tranquilizer and the control group would receive a placebo, perhaps in the form of a sugar pill. Only some outside party, such as the pharmacist who supplied the pills, would know which group received which kind of pill. The pharmacist would not give that information to the experimenter until after the effects of drug and placebo on the two groups of subjects had been recorded. In nonexperimental studies, a similar technique can be used. For example, psychologists looking for a possible positive (or negative) correlation between IQ and psychological adjustment might assess psychological adjustment partly through interviews; it would be important that they not know their subjects' IQ scores until after they had interviewed them and recorded their conclusions concerning their adjustment.

PROBLEMS OF MEASUREMENT When psychologists set out to measure IQ, they know that the way to do it is to use an IQ test. There are standard ways to measure certain other psychological phenomena, too; for example, two ways to assess the maze-running ability of a rat are to see how much time it takes the rat to run the maze on successive trials and to see how many trials are needed before the rat can run the maze without error. In other cases, however, deciding how to measure the thing one is trying to measure can be a major methodological problem.

DO THE EXPERIMENTAL AND CONTROL CONDITIONS REALLY DIFFER? It occasionally happens that experimenters inadvertently create no meaningful differences between their experimental and control conditions. The independent variable that they think they are manipulating in fact remains the same for both groups. Needless to say, the results of such an experiment may be interpreted improperly.

Here is a case in point. You have probably seen advertisements for devices that allow you to "learn while you sleep." Such a device might consist of a tape recorder, several tapes on which to record material you want to memorize, and a small loudspeaker to be placed under your pillow at night. The fantasies of effortless achievement that can be built around sleep learning are limitless. But can any of them be realized?

You might suppose that a study testing whether sleep learning actually occurs could be done by creating an experimental group in which sleeping subjects are presented with factual material to learn and a control group in which subjects who are awake are given the same material to listen to. By testing both groups after training, you could find out (1) whether the sleeping subjects learned anything at all, and (2) how effective sleep learning is compared to learning while awake. Some studies, done just this way, seemed to have established a definite learning effect in the sleeping subjects.

The problem is, how do you know for sure that the subjects in the experimental group were asleep? In some early sleep-learning studies, the experimenters merely looked at the subjects; if their eyes were closed, it was assumed that they were sleeping. But having one's eyes closed, even while dozing, is not the same thing as being asleep (see Figure 2.15).

Fortunately, as we mentioned earlier, it is known that sleep and wakefulness can be assessed by taking EEG recordings of brain waves; in addition, instruments can be used to measure eye movements and muscle tension. The EEG helps to define accurately the state a person is in: awake, dozing, sleeping lightly, sleeping deeply, or dreaming.

In a sleep-learning study using EEG recordings as the criteria of sleep, Charles Simon and William Emmons (1956) presented subjects with ninety-six questions and answers concerning unfamiliar but easily learned material. For example, one item was "Question: In what kind of store did Ulysses S. Grant work before the Civil War? Answer: A hardware store." Simon and Emmons gave the questions and answers to groups of subjects in different states of sleep, drowsiness, and wakefulness, and then tested the subjects shortly after they awakened the next morning by asking the questions again. The results did not support the findings of the earlier studies or the claims of the manufacturers of sleep-learning machines. If the subjects were asleep, as indicated by the EEG recordings, they did not learn. The subjects who did learn were either dozing lightly or awake, and the more awake they were, the more they learned. Thus, when appropriate measurements demonstrated that the experimental and control conditions really differed, sleep learning was not shown to take place.

Figure 2.15 Is he sleeping? Only the EEG chart shows for sure.

IS THE MEASURE SENSITIVE ENOUGH? In 1973, Harriet Rheingold and Carol Eckerman reported a study that seemed to deny the existence of stranger anxiety in infants between six months and a year old—a phenomenon that most developmental psychologists, and most parents, had firmly believed in. Rheingold and Eckerman reported that infants in their study smiled at strangers and generally gave no overt indication of distress in their presence.

It now seems clear that their conclusions resulted from the use of a single, not very sensitive measure of infant distress. Rheingold and Eckerman measured how often the infants smiled at strangers, but they did not measure, for instance, how long it took each infant to smile; perhaps the infants smiled only after a period of wariness. Furthermore, recent studies (including one by Joseph Campos, 1976), which used several different measures, indicate that stranger anxiety does exist in nine-month-olds. The studies show, for one thing, that the heart rates of nine-month-old infants tend to speed up (indicating defensiveness) when they are approached by a stranger, whereas the heart rates of five-month-old infants slow down (indicating interest). Second, when infants are given a choice, they show a strong preference to be away from strangers, even though they may not cry in a stranger's presence. Third, after nine-month-old infants have been taught to press a lever in order to get a glimpse of their mothers or a glimpse of a female stranger, they press the lever more quickly when doing so lets them see their mothers.

HOW CAN STATES OF CONSCIOUSNESS BE MEASURED? As we have noted, EEG recordings of the brain's electrical activity provide a direct, objective indication of whether a person is sleeping and, if so, how deeply, but direct and objective ways of studying other states of consciousness have proved hard to find. Instead, psychologists have to rely on indirect measures and, sometimes, on extremely ingenious experimental designs.

One of the claims made by the proponents of hypnosis is that hypnotized subjects can be made to experience no pain or to lose their sense of hearing, sight, and so on. Usually, these claims are assessed by examining behavior over which the hypnotized person has at least some voluntary control. For example, a hypnotist will put a person into a trance, suggest that she has lost her sense of hearing, and then sound a loud noise. When asked, the subject typically says that she heard nothing; moreover, she

does not jump or flinch in response to the noise.

Even jumping in response to an unexpected, loud noise is subject to some voluntary control, however. J. P. Sutcliffe (1961) therefore devised a different test of hypnotically induced deafness. Earlier research had shown that if a person hears a playback of his own voice approximately a fifth of a second after he has spoken (a procedure called delayed auditory feedback), his speech is disrupted (Broadbent, 1952). If a person is deaf, delayed auditory feedback should have no effect. Sutcliffe's subjects were deeply hypnotized, told that they were now deaf, and then given a delayed auditory feedback test. Their performance deteriorated. Thus, even though the subjects reported not being able to hear, the feedback test indicated that they could.

Researching pain perception entails difficulties similar to those encountered in designing studies to research hysterical symptoms and hypnotic states. Whether given drug anesthesia, hypnosis, placebos, or acupuncture, many subjects report a substantial reduction of pain. Yet such verbal reports alone are not sufficient to indicate that the intensity of the pain has been reduced. A striking example of the difference between the verbal reports of people undergoing a painful experience and other kinds of measures is offered in a study by Carl T. Javert and James D. Hardy (1951). These researchers tested two groups of pregnant women for pain sensitivity while the women were in labor and about to give birth (see Figure 2.16). One group had been trained in a natural-childbirth technique and, when asked how much pain they felt, tended to minimize their sensations. The second group had not been so trained, and reported considerable pain. The psychologists then asked the women to adjust the intensity of a point of light focused on their skin so as to indicate the amount of pain they were experiencing from their labor contractions at the moment. Surprisingly, both groups of women set the lights to the same average intensity. Evidently both groups underwent the same amount of pain, even though the group trained in natural-childbirth techniques *reported* experiencing less pain.

We have described these studies to illustrate a few of the more interesting ways psychologists have found to assess subjective states, not to convince you that hysterical symptoms, hypnotic phenomena, and pain reduction through natural-childbirth techniques are "unreal." Reaching a decision on the question of their "reality" is very difficult, because there is a good deal of apparently reliable evidence on both sides. It may be that some sort of

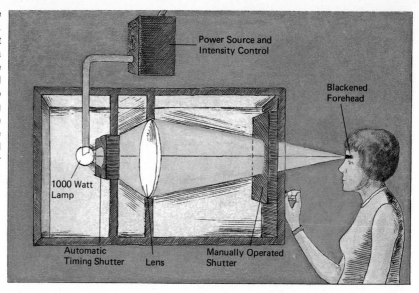

Figure 2.16 A technique for the measurement of sensitivity to pain. A beam of radiation from a heat lamp is directed by a lens through a timing shutter and onto the subject's forehead. The forehead has been blackened with ink to provide a uniformly absorbing surface. Javert and Hardy (1951) asked their subjects to adjust the intensity of the light until it matched the discomfort they felt from labor pains.

Power Source and Intensity Control

Blackened Forehead

1000 Watt Lamp

Automatic Timing Shutter

Lens

Manually Operated Shutter

compromise reflects the actual state of affairs—that a person experiencing hypnotic deafness, though in some sense able to hear, does not hear consciously, or that a woman using natural-childbirth techniques, though aware of a fairly high level of pain, does not experience the pain as intensely as a woman who is not using the techniques.

THE REPLICATION REQUIREMENT During the course of their training, psychologists are taught to anticipate and avoid methodological errors, for example by using the double-blind technique when there is a danger that a self-fulfilling prophecy may affect their findings. Despite all an investigator's training and efforts, however, errors sometimes do occur. The need to bring such errors to light is one reason for the requirement that the findings of a scientific study be replicated—that is, duplicated by at least one other psychologist at a different laboratory—before they are accepted by the profession.

Sometimes, a second psychologist attempts to reproduce all the conditions of the original study. At other times, the second investigator modifies some condition of the original study, for instance by using adults from the general population as subjects instead of using college students, in order to assess the generality of the first psychologist's findings. When the results of either type of replication study do not agree with those of the original study, psychologists go back and try to figure out why.

A series of studies on the effects of rhythmic stimulation on infant development illustrates the increased accuracy and understanding that can result from the type of replication process whereby certain conditions of the original study are modified. In 1962, a pediatrician named Lee Salk reported a study on the relation between an infant's prenatal experience and its behavior after birth. Salk's hypothesis was that an unborn child, in the uterus, hears its mother's heart beating and, by the learning process called imprinting (described in Chapter 3), comes to associate that sound with the security and comfort that unborn infants are assumed to experience in the womb. If his hypothesis was correct, Salk reasoned, then newborn infants should find heartbeat sounds soothing: they should cry less, sleep more, and gain weight faster than infants who have no opportunity to hear heartbeat sounds.

Salk placed two groups of newborn infants in separate nurseries and played an amplified heartbeat sound in one nursery. He found that the babies in the nursery with the heartbeat sound did cry less, sleep more, and gain weight faster than the babies in the other nursery. He concluded that his hypothesis was confirmed.

Other researchers, however, were not satisfied. Just what characteristics of a heartbeat, they wanted to know, do newborns find so soothing? Is it the *quality* of the sound—the particular "thud-thump" that a beating heart emits—as Salk believed, or is it perhaps the *rhythmicity* of the sound? Yvonne Brackbill and several colleagues (1966) tested the latter possibility by presenting groups of newborn infants with three different rhythmic sounds: a beating heart, a metronome, and a lullaby. As it turned out, all three sounds were equally effective in quieting the babies. This finding cast a certain amount of doubt on Salk's conclusions regarding the possibility that the infants had imprinted on the heartbeat sounds. Associations that are learned through imprinting are very specific, and although imprinting might account for an association between the sound of a heartbeat and a feeling of comfort, it would be unlikely to account for a more general association between rhythmic sounds and comfort.

Furthermore, Brackbill thought, the crucial factor might not be the rhythmicity of the sound at all. Beating hearts, metronomes, and lullabies are not only rhythmic but also constant and monotonous. Brackbill (1971) decided to find out what effect other kinds of monotonous stimulation would have on newborns: not only heartbeat sounds but also constant light, increased heat, and snug swaddling, which has been used with babies in a number of different cultures. Using different groups of infants, she assessed the effects of these stimuli singly and in various combinations. Her results were clear: The more types of constant stimulation the infants received, the quieter and more contented they seemed. A comparison of the behavior of the four infant groups that received only one kind of stimulation showed that the single most effective procedure in the study was not the heartbeat sound but swaddling (see Figure 2.17).

This result has different practical implications from Salk's findings, as well as different implications for psychologists interested in the effects of prenatal experience. The practical question of how best to soothe a young baby is by no means trivial, as anyone who has spent any time with a restless infant knows. Salk's study suggested that hospital nurseries and the homes of newborn babies should be equipped with recordings of heartbeat sounds.

Brackbill's 1971 study indicates that snug swaddling, perhaps supplemented by other kinds of monotonous stimulation, will do the job better. One result of this series of studies is that the staffs of many hospitals have stopped telling new mothers to wrap their babies loosely so that they can exercise and have started teaching mothers how to wrap their babies tightly.

The sequence of events just described is a very common one. A researcher conducts a study and obtains findings that are widely recognized as interesting, significant, and provocative. Other researchers study the study and find something about it questionable; in this instance, Brackbill questioned Salk's interpretation of his results as confirming his imprinting hypothesis. The other researchers therefore formulate and test hypotheses of their own, which differ in some way from those of the original experimenter. Ideally, these later investigations clarify, correct, and extend the findings of the first study, so that some point about behavior (in this case, that newborn infants find constant, monotonous stimulation soothing) can be regarded as having been conclusively demonstrated.

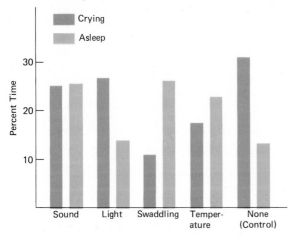

Figure 2.17 Percentage of time babies spent crying (while awake) and sleeping under various conditions of stimulation. The graph does not include time spent quietly awake or drowsy. (After Brackbill, 1971.)

ETHICAL PRINCIPLES IN PSYCHOLOGICAL RESEARCH

At several points in this chapter we have said that a research project could not be conducted because it would be "unethical." For example, we noted that raising a group of infants in total darkness to determine the effect of lack of stimulation on the development of vision would be unethical. It is obvious that such a procedure could cause irreparable harm; therefore, ethical considerations demand that such research never be conducted with human participants, regardless of the potential significance of the outcome. The great bulk of psychological research involves no risk to participants at all, and no ethical question is raised; but other cases are not so clearcut.

While psychologists have an ethical obligation to protect the dignity and welfare of the people who participate in research, they are also obligated to try to find answers to important scientific, psychological questions. At times these obligations are in conflict. In order to conduct important studies, psychologists may have to use procedures that involve some risk of physical or psychological harm to some of the participants. These questions then arise: How great is the risk, and how important is the knowledge that may be gained? Neither question can be answered fully *before* a study is conducted. How, then, can the researcher decide whether or not to undertake the study.

In 1973 the American Psychological Association issued ten principles, shown in Table 2.3, to guide the conduct of research that involves human subjects. These broad guidelines are applied to specific research proposals by a review panel established at each research institution under the authority of the Office for Protection from Research Risks of the De-

partment of Health, Education, and Welfare. Federal regulations require that all research sponsored by U.S. government grants be reviewed and approved by such a panel. Recent interpretations of federal guidelines have caused most universities to require that *all* research involving human participants receive the approval of a review panel. The decision as to whether a particular study can be conducted according to ethical standards is a complex one, in which the investigator and a panel of qualified people assess the potential risk to participants and the possible benefits to be gained from the research.

Table 2.3   Ethical Principles in the Conduct of Research with Human Participants

---

The decision to undertake research should rest upon a considered judgment by the individual psychologist about how best to contribute to psychological science and to human welfare. The responsible psychologist weighs alternative directions in which personal energies and resources might be invested. Having made the decision to conduct research, psychologists must carry out their investigations with respect for the people who participate and with concern for their dignity and welfare.

1. In planning a study the investigator has the personal responsibility to make a careful evaluation of its ethical acceptability, taking into account these Principles for research with human beings. To the extent that this appraisal, weighing scientific and humane values, suggests a deviation from any Principle, the investigator incurs an increasingly serious obligation to seek ethical advice and to observe more stringent safeguards to protect the rights of the human research participant.

2. Responsibility for the establishment and maintenance of acceptable ethical practice in research always remains with the individual investigator. The investigator is also responsible for the ethical treatment of research participants by collaborators, assistants, students, and employees, all of whom, however, incur parallel obligations.

3. Ethical practice requires the investigator to inform the participant of all features of the research that reasonably might be expected to influence willingness to participate and to explain all other aspects of the research about which the participant inquires. Failure to make full disclosure gives added emphasis to the investigator's responsibility to protect the welfare and dignity of the research participant.

4. Openness and honesty are essential characteristics of the relationship between investigator and research participant. When the methodological requirements of a study necessitate concealment or deception, the investigator is required to ensure the participant's understanding of the reasons for this action and to restore the quality of the relationship with the investigator.

5. Ethical research practice requires the investigator to respect the individual's freedom to decline to participate in research or to discontinue participation at any time. The obligation to protect this freedom requires special vigilance when the investigator is in a position of power over the participant. The decision to limit this freedom increases the investigator's responsibility to protect the participant's dignity and welfare.

6. Ethically acceptable research begins with the establishment of a clear and fair agreement between the investigator and the research participant that clarifies the responsibilities of each. The investigator has the obligation to honor all promises and commitments included in that agreement.

7. The ethical investigator protects participants from physical and mental discomfort, harm, and danger. If the risk of such consequences exists, the investigator is required to inform the participant of that fact, secure consent before proceeding, and take all possible measures to minimize distress. A research procedure may not be used if it is likely to cause serious and lasting harm to participants.

8. After the data are collected, ethical practice requires the investigator to provide the participant with a full clarification of the nature of the study and to remove any misconceptions that may have arisen. Where scientific or

humane values justify delaying or withholding information, the investigator acquires a special responsibility to assure that there are no damaging consequences for the participant.

9. Where research procedures may result in undesirable consequences for the participant, the investigator has the responsibility to detect and remove or correct these consequences, including, where relevant, long-term aftereffects.

10. Information obtained about the research participants during the course of an investigation is confidential. When the possibility exists that others may obtain access to such information, ethical research practice requires that this possibility, together with the plans for protecting confidentiality, be explained to the participants as a part of the procedure for obtaining informed consent.

Source: American Psychological Association. *Ethical Principles in the Conduct of Research with Human Participants*. Washington, D.C.: American Psychological Association, 1973, pp. 1–2.

In many instances research that cannot be done with human participants is performed on animals: rats, cats, pigeons, monkeys, and many other species. For example, a psychologist may study the importance of visual experience by raising one group of rats in complete darkness and another group under normal lighting conditions. But while researchers may use procedures with animals that would be unethical to use with humans, there are also stringent standards governing the use of animals in research. State and federal regulations specify procedures and standards for animal care—that is, housing, feeding, and cleaning. Ethical standards prohibit the researcher from inflicting unnecessary pain. Here, too, the importance of the research is weighed against the potential for harm to the participants, the animals involved. Thus the use of all the research methods discussed in this chapter is guided by ethical and humane standards of treatment for both human and animal participants.

SUMMARY

1. The general procedure psychologists use to conduct studies involves deciding what kind of data would give a meaningful answer to the question they are investigating, gathering the data by means of one or more methods, and analyzing the data, usually by means of statistical techniques. The method of gathering data used in a particular study depends on the nature of the question the psychologist wants to answer.

   A. Regardless of what method researchers use in gathering data, they will have to collect a **sample,** or selected segment, of the data pertaining to the hypothesis. The sample must be large enough to be representative of the population under consideration.

      1. In a **random sample** every member of the population has an equal chance of being included.

      2. In a **representative sample** people who are known to possess certain characteristics are included in proportion to their numbers in the population being sampled.

   B. A **survey** is an attempt to estimate the opinions, characteristics, or behavior of an entire population. The estimate is usually based on a representative sample of the population. Data may be collected through the use of interviews, questionnaires, or public records.

   C. A **case study** is an intensive investigation of one or a few individuals, usually with reference to a single psychological phenomenon. This kind of study may imply the existence of certain behavioral laws, but it does not prove that any law is operating. Case-study methodology is useful in instances where it would be impossible or unethical to conduct the research by means of an experiment in which subjects are randomly assigned to different treatments.

   D. The purpose of **naturalistic observation** is to find out how behavior occurs under natural conditions without interference or distraction from an outsider. It is commonly used by ethologists as a first step in studying the behavior of an animal species. In **participant**

observation researchers join an existing group in order to record events and impressions that are accessible only to group members.

E. A **cross-cultural comparison** is used to compare the behavior patterns of people in different countries or cultures.

F. In a **longitudinal study** the same group of people is studied from time to time over a period of years. Longitudinal studies are the best method available to assess consistencies and inconsistencies in behavior over time.

G. In an **experiment** the psychologist actively controls the presence, the absence, or the intensity of those factors thought to affect the behavior being studied, and holds all other factors constant. Many psychologists consider the experiment to be more definitive regarding cause-and-effect relationships than any other method of gathering data. The main disadvantage of the experiment is that by ruling out extraneous influences, the researcher may create a very unnatural situation.

1. Subjects in an experiment are assigned to experimental conditions at random. The **experimental group** consists of those subjects who undergo the experimental treatment. The **control group** consists of those subjects who have the same characteristics as the experimental group except that the experimental treatment is not applied to them.

2. A **variable** is any factor in the experiment that is capable of change. The variable that the experimenter deliberately manipulates is the **independent variable**. The variable that the experimenter thinks will change when the independent variable changes is the **dependent variable**.

3. The **hypothesis** is the proposition or belief being tested.

4. The **data** are the observations (scores, ratings, etc.) obtained in the experiment.

H. **Correlational research** indicates the degree of relatedness between two variables. In a **positive correlation**, a high rank on one variable is usually accompanied by a high rank on the other. In a **negative correlation**, a high rank on one variable is usually accompanied by a low rank on the other. Correlational research is often used when, for practical or ethical reasons, a cause-and-ef-

fect question cannot be studied by means of an experiment. While a correlation does not indicate cause and effect, it does allow one to make predictions about the likelihood that two things will occur together.

I. Tests, psychophysiological measures, and ratings can be used to measure individual behavior. Tests can be used to measure intelligence and personality. Psychophysiological measures provide objective, quantitative data on phenomena, such as brain activity, that are hard to assess precisely in other ways. Ratings are used to assess a participant's subjective impressions.

2. Researchers usually collect their data in a form that can be analyzed by statistics. The two main kinds of statistics are descriptive and inferential.

A. Descriptive statistics are used to reduce a mass of data to a more manageable and understandable form.

1. Test scores (to take just one kind of research data) can be compared by describing how they are distributed.

a. The **range** of a set of scores is the difference between the highest and the lowest scores.

b. Another means of describing a group of scores is their **central tendency**. There are three measures of central tendency.

1. The **arithmetic mean** is computed by adding up all the scores and then dividing by the number of people who took the test.

2. The **median** is the score that falls in the exact middle of a distribution of scores that are arranged from highest to lowest.

3. The **mode** is the score that is most frequently obtained in a distribution.

The equivalence of the mean, the mode, and the median is a defining characteristic of a symmetrical or **normal distribution**.

2. Measures of variability indicate how closely clustered the distribution of scores is. The most commonly used measure of variability is the **standard deviation**, which is a number that indicates the extent to which figures in a given set of data vary from the mean. Any normal distribution can be described completely by the

mean and the standard deviation.

3. **Correlation coefficients** are used to describe the strength of a relationship between two variables. A correlation coefficient is a number ranging from -1 (a perfect negative correlation) through 0 (no correlation) to $+1$ (a perfect positive correlation).

B. Inferential statistics are used to draw a reasonable conclusion as to whether the original hypothesis was clearly supported by the data or whether the research results were due primarily to chance.

1. Probability is a complex area of mathematics that deals with the likelihood of certain results occurring.

2. The concept of **statistical significance** is a convention for deciding when to reject the chance hypothesis. Psychologists use various methods to calculate the probability that the outcome of the study could have occurred by chance alone.

3. There are a number of methodological problems that can invalidate the interpretation of a psychological study unless they are dealt with successfully.

A. The term **self-fulfilling prophecy** refers to the fact that the expectations of investigators can influence their findings. One way for a researcher to avoid self-fulfilling prophecies is to employ a procedure called the **double-blind technique,** in which neither the experimenter nor the subjects know which subjects belong to the experimental group and which belong to the control group.

B. Deciding how to measure the thing one is trying to measure can be a major methodological problem.

1. The experimenter may fail to create a meaningful difference between the experimental and control conditions. The results of such an experiment are likely to be interpreted improperly.

2. If the measure of data in an experiment is not sensitive enough, the results of the experiment may be misleading.

3. Psychologists must rely on indirect measures and ingenious experimental designs to study different states of consciousness.

C. Before the findings of a scientific study are accepted by the profession, they must be replicated in a study by at least one other psychologist at a different laboratory, in order to reveal any possible errors in the original study. The second investigator may either modify or attempt to reproduce the conditions of the original study.

4. Certain psychological studies may involve some risk of physical or psychological harm to some of the participants.

A. The American Psychological Association has developed a set of ten principles to guide the conduct of researchers.

B. A review panel established at each research institution under the authority of the Office for Protection from Research Risks of the Department of Health, Education and Welfare applies these guidelines to specific research proposals.

C. In many instances research that cannot ethically be done with human participants is performed on animals. State and federal regulations specify standards for the use of animals in research and procedures for their care.

RECOMMENDED READINGS

AMERICAN PSYCHOLOGICAL ASSOCIATION. *Ethical Principles in the Conduct of Research with Human Participants.* Washington, D.C.: American Psychological Association, 1973. A presentation of ethical guidelines in human experimentation.

BRONFENBRENNER, URIE. "The Structure and Verification of Hypotheses," in Urie Bronfenbrenner (ed.), *Influences on Human Development.* Hinsdale, Ill.: Dryden Press, 1972. One of the few extremely clear and readable descriptions of the logic of inference in psychology.

HAYS, WILLIAM L. *Statistics for Psychologists.* New York: Holt, Rinehart and Winston, 1963. An advanced treatment of statistical methods and probability theory for the social scientist.

KERLINGER, FRED. *Foundations of Behavioral Research.* New York: Holt, Rinehart and Winston, 1964. A very thorough coverage of many facets of behavioral research and fallacies to be avoided.

MONTE, CHRISTOPHER F. *Psychology's Scientific Endeavor.* New York: Praeger, 1975. A brief but informative presentation of the logic of scientific methods in psychology.

SPENCE, JANET T., JOHN W. COTTON, BENTON J. UNDERWOOD, and CARL P. DUNCAN. *Elementary Statistics.* 3rd ed. Englewood Cliffs, N.J.: Prentice-Hall, 1976. An accurate and easy-to-read presentation of the basic methods of statistical analysis and inference that are most often used by psychologists.

TURNER, MERLE B. *Philosophy and the Science of Behavior.* New York: Appleton-Century-Crofts, 1967. This prize-winning book is a fascinating discussion of psychological method and theory and their philosophical underpinnings.

PART TWO

LEARNING AND COGNITION

Many psychologists consider learning to be the most important topic in psychology. As these psychologists point out, all aspects of human culture depend on the capacity to learn. We begin our study of learning by discussing the processes by which organisms experience and adapt to their environments. Thus Chapter 3, "Perspectives on Behavior," examines the history of animal-behavior studies; major influences on behavior—heredity, environment, and learning; and approaches to interpreting behavior.

Chapter 4, "Learning," focuses on the ways in which learning takes place. After reviewing the basic processes of classical conditioning and operant conditioning, we turn to a consideration of the processes by which behavior is controlled and conclude with a discussion of the relationship between learning and cognition (thinking and reasoning).

Chapter 5, "Memory," deals with the ways in which the human mind takes in, stores, organizes, retrieves, and in some cases forgets items of information.

In Chapter 6, "Thinking and the Problem-Solving Process," we discuss a number of views of thinking and problem solving; a variety of strategies for problem solving; impediments to problem solving; considerations involved in making decisions; and computer models of human thinking processes.

CHAPTER THREE

PERSPECTIVES ON BEHAVIOR

The nature-nurture problem has been with us for quite a while, and it pops up when you least expect it. At this time, cloning is much in the news, and those who talk about it seem to assume that nature is all and nurture nothing. If the clone has your gene pattern, then he or she is *you,* or, at the very least, your identical twin brother or sister and practically you.

Of course, the cloned nucleus develops within the cytoplasm of an ovum produced by a woman who is not *your* biological mother and within a womb that was not the womb that sheltered *you*—but never mind that. Let's consider nonbiological influences.

I have, as of now, written two hundred books. That would seem enough to weary the world and reduce the demand for more to a muted whisper, but let us suppose my readers clamor for two thousand. What is to be done? Why, they might take up a subscription to finance the cloning of me and, eventually, fifty identical twins with Isaac's gene pattern (we'll assume no mutations) will be assaulting typewriters and turning out perfect Asimovian books.

But will they? Do I turn out books entirely because of my gene pattern?

I grew up in poverty at a time when there was no television, no comic books, very little radio. My father had a candy store, but he would not allow me to read "cheap magazines." I was forced to go to the library for reading material, and, without guidance, I read eclectically.

My clones, growing up decades later, are bound to be subjected to other cultural influences. At the very least, there will be television.

Then, too, I knew in my youth that if I didn't find a better way of making a living, I would inherit the candy store, and I desperately did not want to do that. I went to college in order to do something more notorious with my life, and I began to write in order to help pay my tuition. My clones, however, are not likely to be running scared.

Even if a life were manufactured for them that was as nearly like mine as possible (at enormous expense), there would still be the fact that when I began to write, I was utterly free. *Anything* I wrote was an "Asimov story."

My clones? If something they wrote was good, but not "Asimovian," it would be a failure.

Undoubtedly, not one of the clones would become a writer under such conditions, and since, aside from my writing, it is dubious whether or not I am worth much to anybody, it would all end up as fifty wastes of effort, gene pattern or no gene pattern.

Isaac Asimov

The study of animal behavior has contributed to the development of some major concepts in psychology and has broadened scientific perspectives on human behavior. By looking at a wide range of behavioral capabilities in different animals, we have gotten a better view of what is special about human behavior. This information serves as a basis for exploring how and why these special characteristics evolved in the first place.

A good way to begin to understand a complex system is to compare it with a simpler one that shares some of its features. Many aspects of the behavior or lower animals are similar to human behavior; in a number of cases what we learn about animals can be generalized to human beings. For example, techniques for developing elementary language ability in chimpanzees (discussed in Chapter 9) are being used to help children with language problems to speak.

In addition, knowledge of how various animals relate to their environment and to the behavior patterns of other species within the same environment gives us an appreciation of the delicate, ecological balance of life. The chain of life is, in many respects, a chain of intertwined behavioral relationships of which we human beings are an integral part.

The most basic psychological concept that has emerged from studies of animals is that behavior is an expression of inherited and environmental factors *working together*. The inheritance of hands or fins, lungs or gills, for example, plus a nervous system compatible with such structures, helps to determine how an animal behaves. Environment and experience also affect behavior. A hungry frog that gobbles up a bee the first time it sees one quickly learns that bees should be excluded from its diet. A major purpose of this chapter is to show how hereditary and environmental factors operate together to bring about some behavior that traditionally has been considered "instinctive" and some behavior that has been regarded as "learned."

The discussion that follows reviews some of the fundamental principles, observations, and general rules of behavior study. It also points out some problems involved in applying information about animal behavior to human beings. Our emphasis in this book is on human behavior, but throughout it we will be discussing issues that have been raised or clarified by studies of animals other than humans, issues that are a large part of our attempts to know ourselves.

ANIMAL STUDIES: THE HISTORICAL BACKGROUND

Contributions to our knowledge of animal behavior have come mainly from two disciplines, European ethology and American comparative psychology. These two disciplines overlap substantially now, but originally they were quite different.

ETHOLOGY AND COMPARATIVE PSYCHOLOGY Ethology was developed by European zoologists who sought to explain animal behavior in evolutionary and physiological terms. They turned for their principal source to Charles Darwin, who in such works as *On the Origin of Species* (1859) and *The Expression of the Emotions in Man and Animals* (1872) furnished evidence that behavioral traits evolve according to many of the same principles as do anatomical and physiological traits. Ethologists came to believe that certain patterns of behavior are inherited (instinctive), and they regarded those patterns as a product of evolution. They held that the evolution of form (body structure and physiology) and function (behavior) are interdependent and that the form and functions of any species are inherited adaptations to its environment.

Ethologists asked an important question about behavior: What is its **adaptive significance** for the animal? That is, how does an animal's behavior help it to survive and reproduce successfully? To answer this question, ethologists observed the way animals in their natural habitat behave in social, predatory, migratory, maternal, and other situations. An animal's behavior then was analyzed to determine its role in the animal's survival. Although ethologists recognized that animals are capable of learning, they viewed this ability to learn as narrowly limited by inherited factors.

Comparative psychologists working in the United States after World War II focused primarily on the role of learning in the determination of behavior. They compared the behavior of different species of animals, hoping to find certain underlying similarities that would suggest general "laws of behavior." Largely ignoring animal behavior in natural habitats, the comparative psychologists relied on laboratory experiments, in which the life histories, the environmental experiences, and sometimes the genetic histories of the animals could be carefully controlled and examined.

Today the interests of ethology and comparative psychology have merged to a great extent (Mason and Lott, 1976). Their initial separation, however, was reflected both in their principal methodologies—field research versus laboratory research—and in the species they most frequently studied. Ethologists concentrated on birds, fish, and insects; comparative psychologists concentrated on rats, monkeys, and humans. Given these differences, it is perhaps not surprising that ethologists emphasized the instinctive causes of animal behavior and comparative psychologists the role of learning and experience. Though the contributions of both views have now been incorporated into general psychology, their different emphases were at one point the focus of a major debate among psychologists.

Would a researcher such as the man shown here be more likely to be a comparative psychologist or an ethologist?

THE NATURE VERSUS NURTURE ISSUE Although it is obvious to us today that an animal's behavior is the product of its heredity and environment, psychologists have not always thought so. In the early part of this century there were vigorous debates over whether certain behavior could be considered "instinctive" (inborn) or "learned" (environmentally determined). The debates were particularly vigorous over the issue of human behavior. At one extreme were psychologists such as William McDougall (1908), who considered human behavior to be essentially instinctive. At the other extreme was the "radical" view, held by John B. Watson (1930), that for the most part human behavior is learned. Watson likened the newborn human infant to a "blank slate" ready to be "inscribed" by its experience with its environment.

The controversy between psychologists holding one or the other of these opinions became known as the **"nature versus nurture"** issue. Those like McDougall who believed that there is no fundamental difference between animals and human beings argued that human behavior reflects basic natural instincts for survival, just as the behavior of other animals can be said to reflect their instinct for survival. Those like Watson who believed that human beings are fundamentally different from lower animals argued that human behavior is principally a product of the way the individual has been nurtured from infancy through adulthood: that experience with the environment is the major determinant of human behavior. Central to this controversy was the problem of defining "instinct."

Psychologists thought of instinctive behavior as different from reflexes on the one hand and from learned behavior on the other. Instinctive behavior was a concept used to describe patterns of unlearned, organized behavior involving the entire animal. It applied to activities that move the animal toward the attainment of a goal. Feeding, mating, and aggression are some examples of instinctive behavior. Reflexes were viewed as components of instincts, having a relationship to instinctive behavior like the relationship individual notes of a melody have to the entire musical composition. To be considered instinctive, a behavior pattern had to develop separately from any opportunity to practice it; it had to occur in its full form at the first opportunity for it to appear.

In his classic essay "The Descent of Instinct" (1955) Frank Beach pointed out the futility of attempting to characterize animal behavior as either instinctive or not instinctive. Using the example of nest building in the pregnant female rat, Beach pointed out that this complex behavior seems to fit the criteria for "instinctive" behavior. Pregnant female rats build nests in a standard manner the first time they become pregnant. They do so even if they have been raised in isolation, which would eliminate the opportunity to learn about nest building by watching other rats do it. However, if they are raised from birth in cages that contain no objects the rats can carry, and thus are prevented from gaining experience in carrying things around, when they later become pregnant they will not build nests, even if nesting materials are available (Lehrman, 1953). Apparently, the early, indirect experience of manipulating materials in the environment is necessary for the proper development of nesting behavior in later life.

Should nest building in the rat then be considered as noninstinctive? And if so, what does this add to our understanding of nesting in rats? Beach concluded that classification of this kind adds nothing more than arbitrary labels to behavior. Naming is not explaining. To explain any behavior properly one must know how it develops, what causes it to occur, and how it may be changed or modified by experience.

SPECIES-SPECIFIC BEHAVIOR Because of these problems in defining instinct, the expression "species-specific behavior" has come to replace it in psychological terminology. The term is from ethology. Instead of asking whether behavior is or is not innate, modern psychologists attempt to provide an account of both hereditary and environmental factors that are responsible for it. **Species-specific behavior** is defined as behavior that is typical of a particular species, the members of which share two major characteristics: (1) a common inheritance and (2) a common environment that has provided them with similar influences and experiences. The concept of species-specific behavior integrates the two major influences on behavior, rather than viewing them in an either-or fashion.

Contemporary research in animal behavior often combines ethology's field approach with comparative psychology's laboratory approach. A good example of how this is done is in the analysis of the species-specific behavior of singing in birds.

In the first nine months after it hatches, the wild chaffinch, a member of the sparrow family, pro-

gresses from producing only simple food-begging calls to singing the notes and the "syllables" that will make up its final song. But these notes and trills are not sung in any distinct order. During the tenth month a characteristic song pattern begins to form, and by the time the chaffinch is twelve months old its singing crystallizes into the specific song that the bird will sing for the rest of its life. Field studies give us the basic description of the development of this behavior as well as the observation that the song is most vigorously sung during nesting season. This suggests that the principal function of the song is related to identifying other members of the species and to selecting mates.

The laboratory studies of W. H. Thorpe (1961) give us additional insight into the development of the chaffinch's species-specific behavior. Thorpe isolated young chaffinches from other birds as soon as they hatched and kept each of them isolated for a year. These birds grew up to produce abnormal songs—they did not develop the song of a mature chaffinch. However, if tape recordings of normal chaffinch songs were played for them during the first four months of isolation, the young birds developed virtually normal songs at the usual age of about twelve months. It is apparent from this that the early experience of hearing the chaffinch song is essential for the normal development of singing. In addition, the young birds apparently "learn" the song in the early months even though they are unable to reproduce it accurately until months later. Furthermore, Thorpe found that if the birds are exposed to an electronically rearranged form of the song, they will later reproduce the rearranged version instead of the normal one. They will not, however, learn the songs of species that are very different from chaffinches. Figure 3.1 shows some spectrographic recordings of the songs of chaffinches raised under various conditions. These laboratory studies reveal that the form of the song is flexible within certain limits, and that it is determined by the experience of hearing other chaffinches sing during what is called a **sensitive period** of development. This is a relatively restricted interval during which an animal is especially susceptible to particular influences that may bring about enduring behavior changes or behavioral effects.

INFLUENCES ON BEHAVIOR

As the chaffinch example illustrates, no one influ-

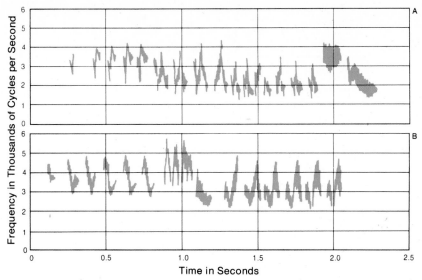

Figure 3.1 Sound spectographs of two chaffinches. (A) The song of a normal adult. (B) The song of a chaffinch reared in isolation and exposed during a sensitive period to a tape recording of a normal song spliced in such a way that the ending came in the middle. This bird's song reflects both learned and innate influences. It sings with the "splice" heard on the tape, but it also sings with the overall broadening and deepening trend of the normal song. It would not sing in this way if it were merely mimicking the tape. (After Thorpe, 1961)

ence can account for a particular behavior pattern. We must consider genetic, developmental, environmental, and life-experience factors taken together. In this section we will review some basic research that shows how we can gain insight into particular behavior patterns of a species by examining the roles of inheritance, environment, and learning.

INHERITANCE Inherited, or genetic, factors obviously influence the nature of an organism's physical traits, sensory systems, and the organization of its brain. These physiological features help in turn to determine the behavioral capacities of a given species of animal. To illustrate the role of inheritance in behavior we will look at some specialized sensory capacities; some fixed, stereotyped patterns

of behavior; and the results of experiments in which animals have been selectively bred to display specific behavior.

SENSORY CAPACITIES Animals experience the world quite differently from the way we do, and examining their sensory capacities can provide valuable insight as to how and why a certain behavior occurs. As Karl Von Frisch (1950, 1967) showed in a series of experiments, we can begin to understand how honeybees find their way unerringly from distant locations back to the hive by knowing that they can perceive polarized light. This inherited perceptual ability enables them to identify the position of the sun even on overcast days and then use its position as a navigational guide as they go to and from the hive to forage for

This bee has not accidentally alighted on this flower. Because of their sensitivity to differences in ultra-violet light, bees can discriminate between flowers that simply look white to human beings.

At night, without a light on, we crash into chairs, a bed, maybe even stub a toe. But bats do not have such problems. Their ability to localize objects around them by responding to echoes of their own sounds, emitted while flying, prevents crashes.

nectar, often over long distances. In addition, by knowing that bees are visually sensitive to differences in ultraviolet light, we can better understand how they are capable of discriminating, at a distance, between flowers that simply look white to us.

Similarly, by understanding that bats have the capacity to localize objects in space by responding to the echoes of high-frequency sounds that they continuously emit while flying, we can appreciate how they avoid crashing into obstacles. This capacity also explains how, in the dark, bats are capable of intercepting small insects in flight.

Salmon, after having spent several years traveling thousands of miles in the ocean, return to spawn in the same stream where they were born. How do they manage this complicated navigational problem? Studies of the migration patterns of these homing salmon (Hasler and Larson, 1955) have shed some light on this mystery. Salmon have a sense of smell that can discriminate among subtle chemical differences in the water of different streams. Moreover, they are able to remember these differences. Apparently the salmon remember the stream of their birth by its odor. When they have reached sexual maturity after several years in the ocean, they go back to the coastal regions (we still do not know why), swim up the coast until they encounter the familiar home-stream odor, and then "follow their noses" home. When the salmon's nose is plugged up, it becomes incapable of swimming up the proper stream or tributary.

It would be amazing if a friend of yours were to say, "This is the room where I was born; I remember the odor of the lilac tree by the window." Yet salmon perform a similar feat: After several years of life, using their sense of smell, they locate the stream where they were born.

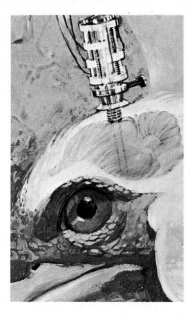

Figure 3.2 A pair of electrodes has been implanted in the brain of this chicken and is held in place by an apparatus through which electrical stimulation may be delivered.

Thus homing salmon have two unusual abilities: the sensory capability to smell subtle differences in the chemical composition of water and the ability to remember and recognize the odor of the stream of their birth. Although there is no evidence to support the suggestion that salmon somehow inherit an "ancestral memory" of the way back home, as earlier instinct theorists suggested, they do inherit the special sensory and brain mechanisms that provide an important foundation for this amazing behavior.

We may ask why such an intricate specialized mechanism evolved in the first place. Why don't the salmon just swim up any old stream to spawn when they become sexually mature? The answer to this question can only be inferred, as human beings were not around to witness the evolution of the salmon. However, we do know that some streams dry up seasonally; others have the wrong temperature for the proper nurturing of salmon eggs; and in others the salmon are in great danger from predators. The salmon's return to the stream of its birth would appear to ensure that breeding will occur in a place where the continuance of the cycle has been successful at least once before.

FIXED ACTION PATTERNS Careful observation of any animal shows that much of its species-specific behavior consists of relatively stereotyped and often-repeated patterns of movements, known as **fixed action patterns.** These may range from simple behavior such as pecking to the more complex patterns of courtship. We do not know how these patterns develop because, as we have seen, they usually appear in full form the first time they are performed. We do know, however, that these patterns are somehow "wired" into the animal's nervous system.

An animal can be made to perform fixed action patterns by stimulating its brain electrically. Erich von Holst and Ursula von St. Paul (1962) used this technique in a study of chickens. The area of the brain von Holst and von St. Paul stimulated is called the brain stem. As shown in Figure 3.2, they placed electrodes at various places in the brain stem; in some places, stimulation produced a specific behavior pattern, and different places often yielded different patterns. With a large number of electrodes, a large number of patterns could be elicited. Stimulating some areas produced simple actions—the chicken would stand up or sit down or turn its head to one side. Other areas elicited more complex patterns—grooming, attack behavior, fleeing behavior, eating, or courtship.

Once von Holst and von St. Paul had specified exactly which fixed action patterns were produced by stimulating certain areas, they began to examine the relationships among the patterns. To do this, they simultaneously stimulated two different areas that would normally evoke two different fixed action patterns. Then they observed how the two patterns interacted.

In a natural setting, triggering two fixed action patterns simultaneously sometimes produces **displacement activity.** Suppose, for example, that a bird is sitting on a nest containing eggs. When it sees a man approaching, the bird begins to vacillate between escaping and staying on the nest with the

Figure 3.3 In situations where two or more fixed action patterns are released at high intensity, displacement activities often appear. The gull on the left, undergoing conflict between the fixed action patterns of fighting or fleeing from the attacking gull on the right, is making nesting movements, which are wholly irrelevant to the situation. (After Tinbergen, 1951.)

eggs. At some point the bird is likely to stop vacillating and carry out a fixed action pattern that appears to be irrelevant to the situation: it preens its feathers. Similarly, when one herring gull is confronted by another gull on the attack, as shown in Figure 3.3, the first gull will, for a while, vacillate between running away and fighting; then it may show displacement activity: it carries out nest-building movements. The word "displacement" was originally used to suggest that energy was displaced from the conflicting forms of behavior (escaping harm versus protecting eggs, for example) onto a seemingly irrelevant activity (such as preening). This "energy" interpretation has been called into question by many investigators, however. It is best to think of the term "displacement" merely as indicating the occurrence of an activity that seems irrelevant to the situation.

When von Holst and von St. Paul stimulated simultaneously an area that produces aggressive pecking and an area that produces fleeing with feathers smoothed down close to the body, the hen ran excitedly back and forth giving piercing cries—a displacement activity. This displacement activity is similar to the behavior that occurs naturally when a hen has a conflict between protecting its nest and escaping from a dangerous enemy.

Von Holst and von St. Paul elicited other simultaneous fixed action patterns as well. Stimulation of one area in the brain stem causes a chicken to stretch out its neck and flatten its feathers; stimulation of another area makes it fluff up its feathers. When both areas were stimulated simultaneously, the animal would stretch out its neck and flatten its feathers; after the stimulation stopped, it would fluff its feathers. That is, it showed first one fixed action pattern and then the other. In other instances, both action patterns occurred at once. Furthermore, simultaneous stimulation of the area that produces looking to the left and the area that evokes sitting led the hen to sit and look to the left at the same time.

These examples of how brain stimulation was used to elicit fixed action patterns suggest that the forms of behavior produced are the result of characteristic patterns of brain organization. Animals other than birds also display behavior typical of their species when certain parts of their brains are stimulated. Laboratory-raised cats that have never seen a rat or killed another animal will kill a rat when the appropriate part of the brain is electrically stimulated (Flynn et al., 1970). The cats display a form of attack that is almost identical to the form

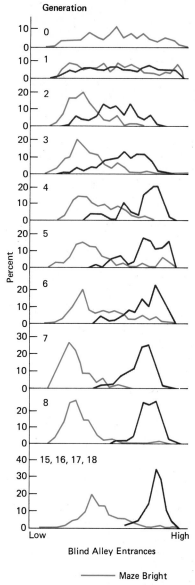

Figure 3.4 Progress of selection in rats for low and high errors in a seventeen-unit maze. By the eighth generation of selection the maze-bright and maze-dull lines were well separated, and further selection resulted in no improvement. (After Tryon, 1940c)

seen in the wild when experienced cats attack and kill prey (Berntson, Hughes, and Beattie, 1976). These observations strongly indicate that inherited brain mechanisms underlie species-specific behavior.

SELECTIVE BREEDING EXPERIMENTS The most compelling illustrations of heredity's role in behavior have come from the results of selectively breeding animals to display particular behavioral traits. We are all aware that dogs display a great variety of behavioral specialties that have been deliberately fostered over centuries of selective breeding. German shepherds have been bred to display ferocious protectiveness; retrievers have been bred to exhibit a willingness and ability to retrieve such objects as game birds and rabbits.

In the laboratory, experiments with fruit flies have likewise shown that certain behavioral tendencies are heritable. For example, if fruit flies are put into a long glass tube that has a light at one end and is dark at the other, some of the flies will move to the light end of the tube while others will stay in the dark. Movement toward the light in this situation is called *phototaxis.* Experiments have shown that the behavioral trait of phototaxis will become more prevalent in a fly population by selectively breeding together the flies that display it (Hirsch and Boudreau, 1958). This indicates that the difference in behavior between moving and not moving toward a light clearly has a genetic foundation. Perhaps some flies, genetically, are more sensitive than others to light. In similar experiments it has been shown that learning ability, too, is heritable.

Individual members of a species may differ in their learning ability in different situations. Noting this, R. C. Tryon (1940a, b) conducted a series of experiments to test whether these differences could be emphasized through selective breeding. He trained a large group of rats, using food as a reward, to find their way through a complicated maze. Each rat ran the maze every day for nineteen consecutive days. The measure of learning ability was the total number of errors (wrong turns) made by a rat during trials two to nineteen. The rats displayed wide variations in initial learning ability, as shown in the top graph (marked Generation 0) in Figure 3.4. Tryon then selected the fastest learners and bred them together; he bred the slowest learners together as well. When the offspring matured, he trained them in the maze and then selectively bred, again, bright to bright and dull to dull, repeating this process through twenty-five generations over a period of fifteen years. By the eighth generation, as shown in Figure 3.4, the two repeatedly selected stocks of rats were quite distinct in their ability to learn the maze: the brightest slow learners were about equivalent in maze performance to the dullest fast learners.

Maze-learning ability in rats was thus shown to be heritable. Although later studies (Searle, 1949) showed that the superiority of the rats who learned the maze well did not always generalize to other learning situations (for example, when escape from water was the measure of learning, the "maze-dull" rats were superior), it did clearly demonstrate that inheritance contributes to the capacity to learn in a specific situation.

In these experiments selective breeding increased the heritability of the trait being studied. This raises an important point: the fact that a trait has high heritability does not mean that every member of a given population or species will inherit the trait; rather, it means that there is a high *probability* that the trait, when it does appear in an individual, is the result of genetic rather than environmental factors. Thus, **heritability** is the extent to which observed individual variation of a trait can be attributed to genetic differences among members of a particular population in a particular environment. The heritability of a trait can change if the genetic factors that produce the trait change. Thus, selective breeding involves manipulation of the factors that produce such traits as phototaxis and maze brightness.

A change in the environmental factors that produce a trait can also affect the heritability of that trait. The heritability of blindness, for example, has increased markedly since 1800 as a result of the elimination of smallpox and other communicable diseases that are potential environmental causes of blindness. In other words, because there are fewer *environmental* factors contributing to blindness, a greater percentage of this trait's occurrence in the population is now attributable to *genetic* differences among individuals. (This does not mean that the *incidence* of blindness in the population has increased—only that its *heritability* has.)

ENVIRONMENTAL STIMULI Behavioral scientists have long understood that specific stimuli in the environment often seem to serve as signals for fixed action patterns as well as for more complex kinds of behavior. In fact, such stimuli determine whether or not the behavior will occur at all.

SIGN STIMULI The European naturalist Jakob von Uexküll (1921) gave us a vivid picture of the behavior of the female tick, which for a meal will climb into the branches of a bush and wait for weeks, if necessary, for a mammal to pass directly beneath

Motionless, this tick is waiting for a meal. Only the distinctive odor of a mammal's skin glands leads the tick to fall off its leaf and onto its host.

her. As she waits, the tick seems unresponsive to the barrage of sights, sounds, and odors about her. Only one stimulus will elicit a response. The distinctive odor of a mammal's skin glands (caused by butyric acid) signals an approaching meal and leads the tick to drop onto her host. The odor is thus identified as a **sign stimulus** that releases the fixed action pattern of feeding in the tick.

The red underside of several species serves as a sign stimulus to its predators or enemies. Niko

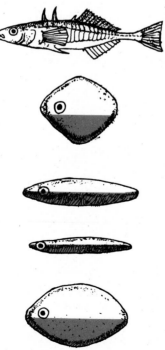

Figure 3.5 Tinbergen found that a male stickleback will attack any of the bottom four of these models before it will attack the top one, which closely resembles a stickleback in everything but the red belly. The red belly acquired by male sticklebacks during the mating season is a sign for attack that outweighs all other stimuli.

Tinbergen (1951) reported that the male stickleback fish will attack a crude model of another stickleback if the model has a red belly. The general shape of the model is unimportant as long as it has a red belly. The stickleback ignores models that seem very fishlike to human beings, like the one shown at the top of Figure 3.5, but it quickly attacks the other models shown, which seem unfishlike but have a red underside. For a male robin protecting its territory, red breast feathers on another bird are a sign stimulus for attack.

Although color is a key element in many sign stimuli, it is not always important. Many sign stimuli elicit a response only if they are the right size. Tinbergen reported a remarkable example in which a herring gull, offered an egg several times larger than one of its own eggs, preferred the larger egg to its own—even when the substitute egg was so large that the bird could not assume a normal brooding position, as shown in the accompanying photograph.

SEQUENTIAL STIMULI By trying to determine which stimuli appear to be most closely associated with the onset of behavior, we can begin to gain some insight into very complex behavioral patterns, such as the flight north made by some birds in spring. These seasonal migrations are examples of patterns of behavior that are triggered by **sequential stimuli** in the environment. William Rowan (1931) found that the migration northward of some species of snowbirds and crows is associated with the gradual lengthening of the day as spring approaches. He captured a number of these birds and

A herring gull attempting to brood an egg many times the size of the egg it lays. For this species and for a number of other birds, size is a key element of the sign stimulus that elicits brooding behavior.

placed them in a room with artificial illumination that could be altered daily. If they received gradually increasing amounts of illumination, mimicking the lengthening of daylight time as spring draws near, they tended to fly north when they were released even if it happened to be the dead of winter. When they were subjected to gradually decreasing amounts of illumination, as occurs with the approach of winter, these birds tended to fly south when released. Apparently, increases and decreases in the amount of light are critical stimuli in determining the onset and direction of migration in the birds.

It also seems that gradual increases or decreases in the amount of daylight time provoke corresponding increases and decreases in the size of the sex glands of these birds: they increase in size as summer waxes and decrease as summer wanes. Under artificial illumination the same changes in the sex glands can be induced even in the wrong season. This observation tells us still more about the chain of causality that results in migratory and, eventually, mating behavior. Gradually increasing amounts of daylight somehow elicit an increase in sex-gland activity. Such activity causes changes in blood chemistry resulting from the circulating hormones, and this in turn contributes to the birds' undertaking their migration to the north.

Daniel Lehrman (1964) showed in his studies of ring doves that the chain of stimuli leading to reproduction can be quite a long one. Each step in the process—courting, mating, nest building, and caring for the young—requires distinctive stimuli before it can be taken. These stimuli provoke hormonal changes in the birds. These hormonal changes produce behavioral changes that serve in part as further stimuli for the next link in the chain.

LEARNING One fruitful way to study species-specific behaviors is to observe their development from studies of animals (especially those that are young). In this way, we have discovered that (1) the ability of an animal to learn is itself species-specific to some degree; and (2) many species-specific behaviors must be learned. The following discussions will illustrate these conclusions.

SPECIES-SPECIFIC LEARNING Animals vary considerably in their species-specific learning capacities and in the flexibility of behavior they bring to bear on a new situation. Some species will learn one behavior pattern very readily and yet be extremely inflexible when a new pattern is needed. As Tinbergen observed (1951), the hunting wasp digs a nest, flies once or twice around the site, and then heads off and ranges widely in search of food. Figure 3.6 shows that the wasp can find its way back

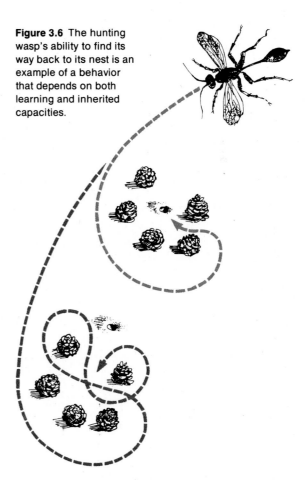

Figure 3.6 The hunting wasp's ability to find its way back to its nest is an example of a behavior that depends on both learning and inherited capacities.

Imprinting. A few hours after they were hatched (during a sensitive period), these goslings saw Konrad Lorenz instead of their mother. Thereafter they followed him around as if he were the real mother.

to the nest easily, something that many human beings would not be able to do in a new place. The wasp obviously learns landmarks extremely rapidly. If the landmarks are moved a little, however, as shown in the figure, the wasp becomes hopelessly disoriented, even if the nest is in plain view.

We know that an animal's ability to learn the relationships between things is related to its particular sensory or motor capabilities. Rats, for example, readily learn to solve quite complex problems involving odor discrimination; they do poorly by comparison, however, when they try to learn to solve the same problems by visual means.

A series of experiments by John Garcia and his colleagues (1966, 1972, 1974) has shown how powerful, and yet how limited, some kinds of learning via the senses can be. For example, taste learning is very powerful in rats. Thus even when several hours intervene between food intake and illness, rats who ate a small amount of a distinctively flavored toxic food that made them ill avoided that kind of food thereafter. They made this association between taste and illness even when hours separated the intake of the food from the experience of illness. In fact, they made this association even when the illness was actually caused not by the food but by a drug or X-rays, administered several hours after the rats ate the flavored food. Other studies have shown that rats who experienced motion sickness when rotated on a turntable after they drank distinctively flavored water "blamed" the sickness on the fla-

vored water rather than on the dizzying rotation (Braun and McIntosh, 1973). This kind of taste aversion learning is much more powerful in rats than learning relationships between other kinds of sensory events; for example, they do not learn to associate a light or tone with a shock to the feet, if these two events occur even a few minutes apart.

IMPRINTING Studies of bird songs have shown that, for some species, exposure to their song is necessary very early in life before this species-specific behavior can occur in its mature form. Chickens have no such requirement and will produce a normal song even if they are deafened as soon as they hatch. As we have seen, however, chaffinches will produce an abnormal song if they are prevented from hearing other members of their species during the first year of life. Additional research with other animals supports the observation that there are certain times in the lives of animals called **sensitive periods,** when they are especially susceptible to certain kinds of learning. The now-classic example of such a sensitive period is the phenomenon of **imprinting,** the process by which some species of birds and mammals form early social attachments. Konrad Lorenz (1965) first found that a newly hatched duckling or gosling will form an attachment, or "imprint," to the first moving object it encounters and will then follow it. In the wild that first object is usually its mother. In the laboratory the baby bird can be exposed to something other than its mother and become imprinted inappropriately; it can be made to follow a human being (see the accompanying photograph), a box on wheels, a bird of a different species.

The length of the sensitive period during which imprinting can occur is fairly restricted. A slightly older duckling or gosling (sometimes only a few hours older) will not form these attachments. The time in the young bird's life when the sensitive period for attachment occurs seems to depend on two factors, as shown in Figure 3.7. The sensitive period cannot begin until the animal can walk well enough to be able to follow the stimulus. And it must end when the animal develops a fear of novel stimuli, as it does after it has had time to become familiar with a certain environment.

It is not difficult to see the importance of these attachments for young birds. Early attachments to moving objects—in the wild, usually other birds of the infant's own species—seem to be the first stage of participation in social systems of many birds. In other words, imprinting seems to be a primary mechanism for the development of the social bonds that are a necessary part of a bird's life with others of the same species. These bonds can be highly resistant to change. Lorenz described an extreme case, a barnyard goose that he raised. The goose not only followed him but, when it reached sexual maturity, attempted to mate with him.

Imprinting clearly demonstrates our earlier conclusions about the relationship between learning and species-specific behavior. First, the species of birds that show imprinting are exhibiting a species-specific ability to learn; in this example, they learn attachment during a sensitive period. Second, imprinting demonstrates the role that learning can play in the development of species-specific behavior. In many species (for example, sheep, dogs, cats, birds, and possibly even humans) the learning that occurs during sensitive periods seems to be essential to the development of normal species-specific social behavior (Scott, 1962).

LIFE EXPERIENCES Most nonscientists would agree that cats will "instinctively" kill rats. Behavioral scientists would agree that the cat's predatory behavior is species-specific because it is common among wild cats and because it can be produced by brain stimulation, as we saw earlier. They would disagree, however, about the inevitability of rat killing by cats.

In a classic series of studies concerning the genesis

of the cat's response to the rat, Zing Yang Kuo (1930) found the relationships between these two "natural enemies" to be quite flexible. The cats displayed a range of responses to rats, from congeniality to fear to killing, depending upon what their experience had taught them about rats when they were kittens. Kittens raised in the same cages with rats did not kill them. But the majority of kittens raised with a rat-killing mother eventually killed rats.

Other groups of kittens, raised in isolation from rats and also from the experience of observing a rat-killing mother, did not automatically kill rats when they were given the opportunity. But they became rat killers after observing other cats kill rats. However, kittens that were reared with rats did not develop rat-killing behavior even after they watched other cats kill rats. As a final demonstration of the role of learning in the cat's behavior toward the rat, Kuo used classical conditioning techniques: he presented a rat to a cat and then punished the cat; when the cat was confronted with a rat later, the cat ran away.

That the cat's predatory behavior depends on learning and experience is quite clear from this study. As Kuo concluded, "Our study has shown that kittens can be made to kill a rat, to love it, to hate it, to fear it or to play with it: it depends on the life history of the kitten" (1930, p. 34).

INTERPRETING BEHAVIOR

Humans inevitably observe and describe behavior from their own point of view. We tend to look for purpose or intent in the behavior of animals, to attribute human values and motives to animals, and to make unjustified and simplistic generalizations from one species of animal to another. This section offers some guidelines and some questions to ask to help us avoid these inappropriate tendencies.

WHAT IS THE ADAPTIVE SIGNIFICANCE OF A TRAIT? One of the assumptions guiding the study of animal behavior is that any trait consistently displayed by a species of animal in its normal habitat must have some sort of adaptive significance for the animal. In evolutionary theory, the **adaptive significance** of a trait refers to the way in

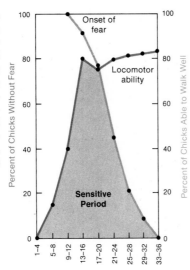

Figure 3.7 The period during which a chick may be easily imprinted is limited by an early inability to run after the stimulus, and a later tendency to fear and avoid novel stimuli. (After Hess, 1973)

Onset of fear

Locomotor ability

Sensitive Period

Percent of Chicks Without Fear

Percent of Chicks Able to Walk Well

Age in Hours

1–4 5–8 9–12 13–16 17–20 21–24 25–28 29–32 33–36

100 80 60 40 20 0

100 80 60 40 20 0

which it helps a species to survive in its ecological niche—its special part of the environment. For example, nest-building behavior can be viewed as increasing the probability of survival of offspring, and hence of the species, because it helps ensure that the offspring will mature to a breeding age and thus perpetuate the species. Sometimes the adaptive significance of a trait is obvious, as in most instances of feeding behavior, but in other cases it is obscure.

Anybody who has ever wondered about the tendency of some moths to fly to their death in a candle flame has really been asking what possible advantage such self-destructive behavior could have for the moth. Moths usually forage at night, when the light that attracts them is provided mainly by the moon. Presumably this tendency to move toward a light source (the moon) helps to disperse the moths throughout a foraging area, for no matter how far they fly, they will obviously never reach or pass the moon. From this, one might deduce that over the thousands of years of their evolution there was little danger that moths would get close to the light that attracted them—until humans invented candles.

Sometimes laboratory experiments must be performed to determine the adaptive significance of a behavior trait. For example, some moths and butterflies have evolved striking and highly colorful circular patterns on their wings, as the photograph of the Io moth at the bottom of this page shows. When the resting moth is touched or startled, it will suddenly throw open its wings without taking off. What is the possible adaptive significance of this behavior? Are the wing pattern and the behavior related? One might guess that the pattern is related to protective coloration (camouflage), except that the sudden wing flicking is bound to attract the attention of a predator. One might also guess that the pattern aids in mate selection (in the same way as do the brilliant feathers of the peacock), except that this colorful pattern and the moth's attention-getting behavior seem to make it so vulnerable.

Alternatively, one might suggest that the circular patterns often resemble eyes, and their sudden display to a potential predator, such as a bird, may frighten the predator off. A clever laboratory experiment (Blest, 1957a, b) showed that this indeed appears to be the case: sudden exposure of the wing patterns is likely to inhibit predation. Birds displayed reluctance to eat a meal worm that had eye-like spots projected on either side of it; they showed no such hesitation toward one that had some other kind of projected pattern (crosses or parallel lines). This example of the adaptive significance of wing-displaying behavior in some moths is compelling because it shows how simple behavior in one animal can be related to or dependent upon the behavior of another animal. Presumably, avoiding large and widely spaced eye-like patterns has its own adaptive significance for the birds.

An Io moth. The circular pattern on its wings has an unexpected adaptive significance for the moth—and for its predators.

HOW PURPOSIVE IS BEHAVIOR? It is often tempting to talk about the adaptive significance of some behavioral characteristic as though the behavior represented some "purpose" intended by the animal. We may say, for example, that the frog's purpose in striking at flies is to get food. We would be less inclined, however, to interpret the ensnarement of a fly by the Venus flytrap plant as being anything other than the reflexive closing of the leaves of the plant triggered by the stimulus of a fly moving about on them. The relationship of the behavior in each case to survival—that is, its adaptive significance (food getting)—is obvious. But can we say that the frog or the flytrap in any way perceives the consequence of ensnaring a fly? Or is fly catching simply an automatic reaction that contributes to the survival of these two organisms?

The more similar an animal is to human beings, the more inclined we are to interpret the behavior as having some motive or purpose, as human behavior usually does. To ascribe purpose to behavior, in the sense of saying that it is caused by some perception by the animal of the consequences of the behavior, makes explanations of animal behavior unnecessarily complex. And, as the following example suggests, such explanations can be unjustified.

At the beginning of this chapter we described how pregnant female rats that have been raised normally will build a nest the first time they become pregnant. Why do they do this? It would be tempting to describe the nest-building behavior of the pregnant rats as having the purpose of providing warmth and seclusion for the offspring yet to be born. Newborn rats are unable to maintain their body temperature adequately, and the nest site and insulating nesting material help to keep them warm. They also help to keep them contained in one place, where their mother can protect them from predators.

However, closer observation of this behavior reveals that any rat will carry materials and construct a nest if it gets cold. One of the side effects of pregnancy in the female rat is a lowering of body temperature, which is promoted by changes in the blood chemistry of the pregnant rat. It would appear that the nest-building behavior of the female rat is a simple response to getting cold, that it has nothing to do directly with intentional preparation for the arrival of the offspring. If the temperature of the nesting areas of laboratory rats is kept warm enough, they will be less likely to build nests. Nest building in the pregnant female rat does have the result of providing a warm brooding area when the litter is born, and such behavior for a warm-blooded animal like the rat is certainly adaptive. But this result is fortuitous. The stimulus of lowered body temperature alone is sufficient to trigger the nest-building behavior of the rat, whether or not the rat is pregnant.

The example of nest building in the pregnant rat illustrates application of the **principle of parsimony** to the interpretation of animal behavior. Years ago, the naturalist Lloyd Morgan proposed this conservative principle (which has since been labeled "Morgan's Canon") in reaction to the anthropomorphic interpretations that naturalists at the time applied to animal behavior. (Anthropomorphism is the attribution of human characteristics to animals and objects.) As Morgan (1894) stated the principle, "In no case may we interpret an action as the outcome of the exercise of a higher psychical faculty, if it can be interpreted as the outcome of the exercise of one which stands lower in the psychological scales." In other words, he was suggesting that we need not make our interpretations of animal behavior overly—and sometimes misleadingly—complex in order to understand the behavior.

GENERALIZING TO HUMAN BEHAVIOR In the nineteenth century it was a common practice to interpret animal behavior anthropomorphically—that is, to ascribe to it human values and motivation. In recent years it has been popular to do the opposite—to account for human behavior, in a simplistic way, as similar to the behavior of animals. Julian Edney (1974) has labeled this approach the "beastopomorphic" interpretation. He cited studies of human and animal territoriality to illustrate this.

According to the "beastopomorphic" view, said Edney, humans share with other animals the drive to claim, defend, and compete for territory, and this drive is inherited and irrevocable. But despite the similarities between animals and human beings, there are very significant differences. According to Edney, in animals the use of space tends to follow stereotypical, fixed patterns, but among humans its use is highly variable (for example, nomadic or sedentary, hunting and gathering or farming). This wide range of different ways of using space suggests that human territoriality is largely based on cultural traditions. For animals, territoriality serves primarily physiological needs, such as providing food and shelter; for human beings it serves a far

Sociobiology:
Is Social Behavior All in the Genes?

Ever since parents first told their children to behave themselves, it has been widely assumed that behavior in general is the product of early training. But social scientists know better: animal behaviors, and at least some human behaviors, are major evolutionary achievements, the products of centuries of evolutionary selection (Mason and Lott, 1976). Behaviors represent modes of adapting to the environment: by singing, birds announce their territories, and monkeys go through elaborate rituals before or instead of fighting; it is assumed that those behaviors have proved, over many generations, to have adaptive significance for these animals in their natural habitats.

A new discipline is studying the hereditary basis of behavior in animals and humans, trying to determine whether various social behaviors are, like anatomical and physiological characteristics, an inheritance from remote ancestors. This science, known as **sociobiology**, synthesizes the findings of biology, anthropology, and psychology. In 1975, Harvard zoologist Edward O. Wilson published *Sociobiology: The New Synthesis*, in which he defined the new discipline as "the systematic study of the biological basis of all social behavior" (1975a, p. 595).

Sociobiologists hope to develop general laws concerning the evolution and biology of social behaviors and to identify a hereditary origin for many forms of human social behavior, such as aggression and self-sacrifice. The study involves extensive comparison of human and animal behavior, especially the behavior of primates, like monkeys and apes.

Sociobiologists regard their discipline as the last phase of the revolution begun by Charles Darwin. It tries to fill a major gap in Darwin's theory of natural selection: nature's goal is individual survival and reproduction, yet several behavioral traits of humans and other animals seem to work directly against this goal. Soldier ants will fight to the death, thus contributing to saving their group from invaders. A bird will often call out a warning to other birds that a predator is nearby, though the warning call itself alerts the enemy to that particular bird's whereabouts and risks the bird's life. Dolphins have been known to band together and support a stricken companion on the surface of the water where it can breathe (Wilson, 1975b). And of course among humans, parents die rescuing their children from fires, and soldiers throw themselves suicidally upon grenades to save their buddies.

Sociobiologists fit all these acts of self-sacrifice into nature's economy. They explain that altruism itself favors genetic gain: the individual risks itself, but the result of this behavior is that other individuals who share its genes may survive. The soldier ant, which is sterile, protects its queen, which then lives to produce more of the soldier ant's kind. The bird who calls a warning in effect also protects its kind, and this increases the chance that its genes will survive, as does the behavior of the mother who saves her baby. The battlefield hero dies confident that the nation will keep his family safe to reproduce—and thus to perpetuate his own genes. The noted British biologist J. B. S. Haldane once joked that he would give his life for his two brothers, each of whom shares about half his genes, or for eight cousins (cited in *Time*, August 1, 1977).

Sociobiology seeks to explain other social behaviors, even aggression, in terms of genetic advantage. The bully who kicks sand in the ninety-seven-pound weakling's face is actually sending a message to the weakling's girl friend: "I have good genes. You ought to mate with me."

The idea that genes determine human social behavior has been so controversial that Wilson has even been picketed. Some critics, notably Richard Lewontin, Steven Gould, and other members of the Harvard-based Sociobiology Study Group, have expressed fear that sociobiology may be seen as an endorsement of the political, economic, and legal status quo, which, according to the logic of sociobiology, must have been determined by our genes (reported in Wade, 1976). One commentator has also noted that Wilson's book stresses ex-amples of altruism among vertebrates, whereas the examples from the social insects show far more self-sacrificial altruism, and the latter are made possible by the fact that genetic competition has been *eliminated*: thus, "a cowardly soldier [ant] has no more offspring than a brave soldier that sacrifices her life in battle, for both are sterile" (Campbell, 1975, p. 1113).

Other critics of sociobiology point out that there is no hard evidence that specific genes exist for altruism, aggression, or other social behaviors, but only theories and guesswork (Washburn, 1978). They also point out that animals may behave very selfishly indeed. Among the lions of the Serengeti Plain in East Africa, lionesses have been observed driving their own cubs away from food if the catch was small; many of these cubs have died of starvation. Of 1,400 herring gull chicks studied during one period, 23 percent were killed by attacks from adults of their own species as they strayed from the nest (Marler, 1976).

Along the same lines, anthropologists have repeatedly contested the popular belief that human males are innately aggressive and dominant over females, having inherited genes for these traits from their primate forebears. The supporters of this argument often cite studies of baboons which document male aggression and dominance over females. Opponents of the argument point out that the baboons observed in these studies were in a game park, an abnormal environment that exposed them to a heavy concentration of predators (especially human ones) and to a high level of tension. Among baboon troops that live undisturbed in the forest, however, it is female baboons that determine the troop's movements, and males exhibit very little aggression and few male dominance patterns (Pilbeam, 1972).

If baboon behavior can vary so widely in different environments, it is even more likely that human behavior will do so. Genes may very well be an important component of human social behavior, but they cannot entirely determine it. If the children of two great athletes are never permitted to exercise, their genes will never make them athletes. Indeed, the flexibility of human social behavior, the extreme differences manifested in various cultures and in different contexts, is almost uniquely human (Pilbeam, 1972). Only human beings construct cultures, passing on large and growing accumulations of learning from generation to generation and thereby to a certain extent overcoming the slow process of genetic evolution.

The question of the extent to which heredity does determine human social behavior is far from settled. But Wilson and some other sociobiologists believe that genetic inclinations need not always be obeyed and sometimes should not be. Evolution takes place so slowly that we may still be inheriting behavior patterns which were adaptive in prehistoric times but which are no longer useful. When humans lived in hunter-gatherer societies, it might have been necessary to wage war against all foreigners in order to survive; now war could mean the end of humankind (Wilson, 1975b). The major contribution of sociobiology has been to remind us that genes do count, but that human beings have the capacity to learn an extraordinarily flexible range of behaviors.

greater range of needs, such as privacy, status, and ideology. This example shows how animal analogies fall far short of accounting for human behavior.

Similarly, many writers, from Freud to Lorenz, have suggested that aggression is an inescapable part of our basic animal inheritance. This view too has been sharply criticized (Pilbeam, 1972), not only because it promotes what its critics believe is an unnecessarily pessimistic view of human nature but also because it runs counter to much of the evidence. We know that human aggression can be modified to take many forms, some of which are less destructive than others. We also know that just as cats appear to learn to control their species-specific predatory behavior, humans can learn to suppress, control, and rechannel aggressive behavior. (For further discussion of this issue, see the accompanying special feature.)

Given these cautions against direct analogies between human and animal behavior, how is our understanding of ourselves enriched by the vast amount of information we have gathered about other animals? For one thing, some analytic tools borrowed from animal studies have been valuable in clarifying human behavior. For example, the concept of species-specific behavior has been used to study the development of human language (Marler, 1970; Lenneberg, 1967). In order to speak, a child needs the vocal apparatus and the brain organization to control it. Language ability is, in this respect, inherited. But it is also environmentally determined, in the sense that its expression is shaped by experience with a particular language. Language is neither strictly innate nor strictly learned; it is a product of both factors. Without the inherited capacity or the experience, a child could not develop a formal language.

Another value of animal research is that in many cases (even though we are cautious about the use of direct analogies) the results do appear to be applicable to humans. This conclusion will be evident throughout the rest of the book, especially in the next chapter, on learning, in which fundamental principles derived mainly from studies of lower animals have been successfully applied to the control and understanding of human learning.

SUMMARY

1. The study of animal behavior has contributed to the development of some major concepts in psychology and has broadened scientific perspectives on human behavior. The most basic concept that has emerged from studies of animals is that behavior is an expression of inherited and environmental factors working together. Contributions to the knowledge of animal behavior have come primarily from European ethology and American comparative psychology. These two disciplines were initially quite separate, but they have merged to a great extent.
   A. European ethology is based on Darwin's work on the evolution of behavioral traits. Ethologists believed that the evolutions of form (body structure and physiology) and function (behavior) are interdependent and that both are inherited adaptations by a particular species to its environment; they thought that learning is narrowly limited by inherited factors. Their major concern with behavior was its **adaptive significance**—its importance in helping the animal to survive and reproduce successfully. Ethologists re-

lied heavily on field research for their data.
   B. American comparative psychology was concerned primarily with the influences of environmental factors, especially learning, on the determination of behavior. Comparative psychologists compared the behavior of different species of animals in an attempt to determine general "laws of behavior." They relied mainly on laboratory experiments for their data so that they could control the life histories, the environment, and sometimes the genetic histories of the animals.
   C. The debate over whether certain behavior could be considered as "instinctive" (inborn) or "learned" (environmentally determined) became known as the **"nature versus nurture"** issue. Instinctive behavior was defined as unlearned, organized patterns of behavior involving the animal in some sort of goal-oriented action such as feeding, mating, or aggression. Reflexes were viewed as components of instincts.
      1. William McDougall was among those who believed that human behavior re-

flects basic natural instincts for survival.

2. John B. Watson represented the "radical" view that for the most part human behavior is learned. He believed that experience with the environment is the major factor accounting for human behavior.

3. Frank Beach used the example of nest building in the pregnant female rat to point out the futility of trying to characterize animal behavior as either instinctive or not instinctive. He believed that to explain any behavior requires knowledge of how it develops, what causes it to occur, and how it may be modified by experience.

D. The concept of species-specific behavior has replaced the classical notion of instinct. This permits psychologists to attempt to account for both hereditary and environmental factors in behavior. **Species-specific behavior** is behavior that is typical of a particular species, the members of which share two major characteristics:
   1. a common inheritance and
   2. a common environment that has provided them with similar influences and experiences.

Contemporary research on animal behavior often combines the field approach of ethology with the laboratory approach of comparative psychology.

2. The behavior pattern of a species is influenced by genetic, developmental, environmental, and life-experience factors. These factors must be considered together in order to account for behavior.

A. Inherited, or genetic, factors influence physical traits, sensory systems, and the organization of the brain. These physiological features help to determine the behavioral capacities of a given species of animal.
   1. An examination of animals' sensory capacities can provide insight into how and why some behavior occurs. Studies of sensory capacities include Karl Von Frisch's experiments on the visual capacities of honeybees and Hasler and Larson's studies of salmon migration.
   2. **Fixed action patterns** are relatively stereotyped and frequently repeated patterns of movements. These patterns appear in full form the first time they are performed and are somehow "wired" into the animal's nervous system. Electrical

stimulation of the animal's brain can elicit both fixed action patterns and **displacement activity,** behavior that seems irrelevant to the situation. Experiments by Erich von Holst and Ursula von St. Paul, who used this technique on chickens, suggest that fixed action patterns represent characteristic patterns of brain organization.

3. The selective breeding of animals to display particular behavioral traits illustrates the importance of heredity to behavior. **Heritability** is the extent to which observed individual variation of a trait can be attributed to genetic differences among members of a particular population in a particular environment.
   a. Experiments have shown that the behavior trait of phototaxis can be made more prevalent in a fruit fly population by selective breeding. This indicates that the difference in behavior between the flies who move toward a light and those who do not is based on genetic factors.
   b. Tryon's selective breeding of rats showed that maze-learning ability in rats is heritable. This indicates that inheritance contributes to the capacity to learn in a specific situation.

B. Specific stimuli in the environment often seem to serve as signals for fixed action patterns as well as for more complex kinds of behavior.
   1. A **sign stimulus** is an element of the environment that releases a fixed action pattern in an animal. A sign stimulus may be a particular odor, color, or shape.
   2. Some complex behavioral patterns in animals are associated with **sequential stimuli** in the environment.
      a. Rowan's experiments with snowbirds showed that increases and decreases in amounts of daylight stimulate the birds' migration and influence the size of their sex glands and, ultimately, their mating behavior.
      b. Lehrman's studies of ring doves showed that there is a long chain of stimuli leading to reproduction. Each step in the process—courting, mating, nest building, and caring for the

young—requires distinctive stimuli.

C. Developmental studies of species-specific behavior in young animals have led to two conclusions: the ability of an animal to learn is itself species-specific to some degree, and learning is essential for the development of much species-specific behavior.

1. Animals vary in their species-specific learning capacities and in their flexibility of behavior in new situations. The particular relationships that an animal can learn are related to its sensory or motor systems. John Garcia's experiments with rats have shown the powerful yet limited nature of some kinds of learning.

2. **Sensitive periods** are certain times in the lives of animals when they are especially susceptible to particular kinds of learning. **Imprinting** is the process by which some species of birds and mammals form early social attachments. The experiments of Konrad Lorenz suggest that imprinting is a primary mechanism for the development of the social bonds that are a necessary part of a bird's life with others of the same species.

3. The importance of life experiences in the development of species-specific behavior was illustrated by Zing Yang Kuo's studies. Kuo found that a cat's response to a rat depended on what the cat had learned about rats as a kitten.

3. Certain assumptions guide our interpretation of data about animal behavior.

A. Any trait consistently displayed by a species of animal in its normal habitat must have some adaptive significance for the animal. Sometimes laboratory experiments are necessary to determine the adaptive significance

of a particular trait. Blest's experiments with moths showed how simple behavior in one animal can be related to or dependent upon the behavior of another.

B. Ascribing purpose to an animal's behavior, in the sense of saying that it is caused by some perception by the animal of the consequences of the behavior, makes explanations of that behavior unnecessarily complex. The **principle of parsimony,** proposed by Lloyd Morgan, suggests that whenever possible, we should interpret animal behavior as the result of the exercise of a lower rather than a higher mental faculty.

C. The interpretation of animal behavior in anthropomorphic terms in the nineteenth century has given way to what Julian Edney has called a "beastopomorphic" interpretation—accounting for human behavior, in a simplistic way, as similar to the behavior of animals.

1. Edney disagreed with the beastopomorphic view. He noted that in regard to territoriality, for example, the use of space among animals tends to follow stereotypical fixed patterns, while among humans its use is highly variable.

2. David Pilbeam has criticized the view of many writers (including Freud and Lorenz) that aggression is a fundamental and inescapable part of the animal inheritance of human beings. He contended that such a view runs counter to much evidence and is overly pessimistic.

D. Concepts borrowed from studies of lower animals, such as the concept of species-specific behavior, have contributed to the analysis and understanding of human behavior.

RECOMMENDED READINGS

ALCOCK, JOHN. *Animal Behavior: An Evolutionary Approach.* Sunderland, Mass.: Sinauer, 1975. A broad, biologically oriented discussion of animal behavior processes; thorough and well-written.

DARWIN, CHARLES. *The Descent of Man* (1871). Philadelphia: West, 1902. The evolutionary case for the idea that humans and some other mammals are descended from common ancestors.

DE THIER, VINCENT G. *To Know a Fly.* San Francisco: Holden Day, 1962. A delightful, readable account of the behavior of flies.

DEWSBURY, DONALD A. *Comparative Animal Behavior.* New York: McGraw-Hill, 1978. A comprehensive, up-to-date textbook on animal behavior from the perspective of a comparative psychologist.

EIBL-EIBESFELDT, IRENÄUS. *Ethology: The Biology of Behavior.* New York: Holt, Rinehart and Winston (2nd ed.), 1975. A useful introductory survey of the field of ethology, written by a student and colleague of Konrad Lorenz.

LORENZ, KONRAD. *King Solomon's Ring.* New York: Crowell, 1952. A light, easy-to-read book of essays about Lorenz's many interesting experiences with animals.

TINBERGEN, NIKO. *Animal Behavior.* New York: Time-Life Books, 1965. A beautifully illustrated book on animal behavior for the general public, with an excellent running narrative by one of the world's leading ethologists.

VAN LAWICK-GOODALL, JANE. *In the Shadow of Man.* Boston: Houghton Mifflin, 1971. A very readable account of what Van Lawick-Goodall learned during the several years that she studied and lived with wild chimpanzees in Africa.

CHAPTER FOUR

LEARNING

Most people seem to fear and resent behaviorist ideas of how learning takes place and of how human behavior is controlled. They seem to think that behaviorism involves, in effect, finding the buttons on other people and pressing them in such a way as to get others to respond as you wish. To many people, this seems to deny human beings their freedom of will and makes of them only so many machines. But if so many people dread these supposed implications of behaviorism, why was it that Dale Carnegie made a fortune out of his book *How to Win Friends and Influence People*? And why do so many politicians seem confident that they can get what they want with a pleasant smile and an empty phrase? I think the answer is that everyone is eager to learn how to manipulate *other* people, but everyone gets nervous at the prospect of being manipulated *by* others.

Personally, I consider myself to be very predictable. I know my own buttons, and I don't care that they are there. For instance, I respond favorably to praise. It has an extraordinary reinforcing effect on me. All my publishers and

editors find this out at once. It is part of their job, of course, to study the weaknesses of writers and to use those weaknesses to manipulate those writers. So they carefully begin to praise the quickness with which I complete my work; the speed with which I read galleys and prepare indexes; the cooperativeness with which I make (reasonable) revision; and so on.

All this I lap up with avidity; no one has ever dished me up more praise than I can swallow. What's more, in order to get still more of it, I complete my work more quickly than ever, read galleys and do indexes with still greater speed, make (reasonable) revisions with at least a trace of a smile, and the result is that over the last eight years I have averaged a book a month.

I once knew an editor who didn't understand this. He ran a marvelous magazine, and published top-notch stories. He encouraged writers to strike out in new directions, sometimes with the best results. But there was one catch. When he was forced to reject a story, he grew bitter and would frame the rejection in vitriolic language. No writer who got one of that editor's rejection letters was likely to

forget the experience. The writer came out of the ordeal battered and bleeding—and wondering if he or she ought to send any more stories in that direction. After getting two or three rejections of that type, the writer wondered no more. And as more and more writers decided not to work under such conditions, the editor stopped getting stories.

This was the only successful writers' strike I've ever known of. Eventually, getting desperate for stories to publish, the editor was forced to send letters to his writers, promising to refrain from sending out insulting rejection letters. Apparently he had learned something that I have always suspected to be true. I have buttons that need pushing, and so does everyone else. I try to get them pushed and I pout and quit if they aren't pushed, and so does everyone else. Maybe the most effective "push" is a smile and a kind word—in behaviorist terms, a reinforcement rather than a punishment. Could the behaviorists basically be saying that it's love that makes the world go round?

Isaac Asimov

Of all the animals, human beings are unmatched in the complexity, richness, and flexibility of their behavior. In order to understand human behavior, it is essential to understand how human beings learn. For this reason, psychological research has emphasized the study of learning and has tried to discover the basic principles of learning. This concern will become increasingly apparent throughout this book: the emphasis on learning underlies contemporary approaches to such psychological processes as motivation, perception, and thinking, and learning theories form the basis for much of the practice of education and rehabilitation today. Major theories of child development, of behavior adjustment and maladjustment, of social behavior, of neurosis and some forms of psychosis—all emphasize the important influence of learning. In addition, principles of learning are used to help explain and treat such varied problems as drug addiction, obesity, phobias (irrational fears), and sexual dysfunctions.

This chapter describes basic features of the learning process and how learning shapes and changes our behavior.

LEARNING ABOUT LEARNING

If a physicist had to account for the "behavior" of a frisbee when it is thrown, two major kinds of factors would have to be considered: the specific frisbee (its weight, diameter, degree of curvature, and depth) and the forces acting on the frisbee (the force of the throw, angle of attack, wind velocity and direction). Similarly, in accounting for the behavior of animals, the psychologist considers the features of the specific animal and the environmental forces that act on the animal.

Given precise enough measurements, the physicist could come up with a good account of the frisbee's flight pattern and could accurately predict where the frisbee would land following a throw. Constant flight conditions would produce a highly consistent flight pattern. A change in any of the variables acting on the frisbee would result in a predictable change in the flight pattern. Now, imagine the problem that would confront the physicist if the frisbee could "learn"—if its flight patterns changed with its "experience," even though the flight conditions remained constant.

This is the essence of the problem confronting the psychologist who tries to predict human behavior. To varying degrees, the behavior of living creatures tends to change with their experience. The reasons for these changes are not at all obvious, and processes other than learning may account for some of them. For instance, physical growth produces some changes in behavior. Behavior is also affected by muscle fatigue and is motivated by emotions such as fear. Thus, not all behavioral changes resulting from environmental experience can be defined as due to learning. For this reason, we will define **learning** as a relatively permanent change in behavioral potential which accompanies experience, but which is not the result of simple growth factors or of reversible influences such as fatigue or hunger (Kimble, 1961).

LEARNING AND PERFORMANCE Learning is not something that can be seen. Rather, we know it has happened by its result: a specific kind of change in an organism's *performance*. Learning is an inferred change in behavioral potential; it cannot be measured directly. Performance, however, is both observable and measurable. An experimenter can set up various situations conducive to learning and then measure the performance of animals in those situations. To the degree that the learning situation is carefully controlled, changes in performance should reflect differences in learning.

Inferring changes in learning from changes in performance is not as simple as it may seem, though. Performance may be influenced by many factors other than learning; we have already noted the importance of growth, fatigue, and emotions. Thus, improvements in performance are not always the result of more thorough learning. For example, a football player may have played better this week than last week for a variety of reasons. He may have had a cold last week, or he may have had a fight with his wife, or this week's game may have been especially important to him. Even if he had learned a new play in the intervening week's practice sessions, we cannot be certain that his improved performance resulted only from this new knowledge.

Similarly, we cannot be sure that if performance changes for the worse, it is because something that was learned has been forgotten. For instance, a hungry rat can be taught to run a maze for a food reward. If it runs the maze faster on trial 20 than on trial 1, the experimenter can tentatively conclude

Although during a season a jockey's performance may improve, we would be unable to say that this change is simply the result of learning.

that learning has taken place. If the rat never saw the maze before, the experimenter is likely to attribute increases in the efficiency of its performance to learning. By trial 40, however, the rat may have eaten its fill and its performance may begin to decline. While performance may be impaired, what has been learned will probably be retained. When the rat is hungry again, it will demonstrate the response it learned as diligently as it had before. So performance can vary even though learning remains constant. The point to remember is that learning, as inferred from performance, is a *relatively permanent* change in behavior potential that accompanies experience.

TWO VIEWS OF LEARNING What is the fundamental nature of the learning process? Many theories, some complementary and others contradictory, have been suggested. Here we will be concerned with two major schools of thought: the S-R **associationist school,** which views the learning process as the development of associations between stimuli and responses; and the **cognitive school,** which emphasizes the role of thinking and reasoning, complex intellectual processes, in learning.

Edwin Thorndike (1898) was the first proponent of what has come to be called stimulus-response (S-R) association theory. Thorndike studied the behavior of cats confined in puzzle boxes. The cats were required to perform several manipulations in order to escape from their confinement. According to Thorndike's description, the cats' initial behavior was essentially trial-and-error: they would scramble around in the box and eventually make the right combination of moves that released the door to the box. As the cats were put back into the same puzzle box time and again, they gradually became more proficient at escaping. Thorndike explained that this increased agility at escaping was caused by the strengthening of stimulus-response associations, with the stimuli being the manipulative components of the box and the responses being those that allowed the cat to escape. Thorndike concluded that those stimuli that were related to a successful response would, with practice, become increasingly effective at eliciting that response. To account for the strengthening (and weakening) of S-R associations, Thorndike formulated the **Law of Effect.** This law says, in essence, that responses that bring "satisfaction" tend to strengthen stimulus-response associations, while responses that produce "discomfort" tend to weaken them. In formulating the Law of Effect, Thorndike anticipated later studies of the effects of reward and punishment on learning. Two models of the learning process discussed in this chapter, classical conditioning and operant conditioning, are related to the associationist view conceived by Thorndike.

The cognitive (or "thinking") approach to understanding the learning process can be traced to Edward Tolman (1932). Tolman also studied animal learning, which he ascribed to certain thought processes that intervene between a stimulus and the making of a response to it. To Tolman, Thorndike's formulation was too rigid and inflexible. Tolman was convinced that learning is not simply the establishment of a series of S-R connections in the brain, as Thorndike argued. Learning, as Tolman

Observational learning.

viewed it, is systematic and purposeful rather than based on random trial-and-error responses. It is a rational process involving the thought processes of the learner. Types of learning that correspond to this view are **observational learning,** in which an individual learns simply by observing the behavior of others, and **latent learning,** in which an individual learns a new behavior without repeatedly practicing it and without manifesting it until an incentive to do so arises.

CLASSICAL CONDITIONING

Classical conditioning (sometimes called Pavlovian conditioning) involves reflex behavior. A simple reflex is an involuntary response that is elicited (brought on) by a specific stimulus. For example, a sharp puff of air on the eye elicits a blink of the eyelid; a tap on the tendon under the kneecap produces a knee jerk; the prick of a thorn or the heat of a flame causes the immediate withdrawal of a hand or foot. In classical conditioning, what basically happens is that a neutral simulus, when it is repeatedly presented with another stimulus that

normally evokes a reflexive response, comes to elicit that response when presented by itself. For example, if a tone is sounded just before a puff of air is directed at the eye, and this is done several times in succession, the subject will probably learn to blink at the sound of the tone, as though in anticipation of the air puff. Thus, the eyeblink reflex has become associated with a new stimulus that does not normally evoke that reflex; the reflex can be said to have been "classically conditioned." And the eyeblink to the tone is known as a "conditioned response."

The Nobel prize-winning Russian physiologist Ivan Pavlov (1849–1936) accidentally discovered classical conditioning while conducting studies on the physiology of digestion. Pavlov had been interested in how the reflexes of the stomach prepare it for food when food is placed in the mouth. In a series of experiments with dogs (1927), he found that the mouth also prepares itself, by secreting saliva, when food is merely seen or smelled. Pavlov called these secretions "psychic secretions" because they occurred in anticipation of the food, before it was actually presented to the dog. When an animal first sees an unfamiliar food, it does not salivate. However, once the animal learns that particular sights or odors (or other stimuli) are associated with a desirable food, it will salivate at these stimuli in anticipation of the food.

ESTABLISHING A CONDITIONED RESPONSE

The salivary reflex, like other reflexes, is evoked by a **stimulus**—food in a dog's mouth—that elicits a **response**—salivation. Other stimuli, such as ringing bells or flashing lights, do not normally cause salivation. So far as salivation is concerned, they are neutral. However, Pavlov found that if a previously neutral stimulus, such as the sound of a bell, regularly occurs just before food is placed in a dog's mouth, the bell itself gradually comes to elicit the salivation response. In Pavlov's terms, the food in the mouth is the **unconditioned stimulus.** It elicits the **unconditioned response** (or **unconditioned reflex**) of salivation. The term "unconditioned" is used because the response usually does not depend on the organism's previous experience with the stimulus—it does not have to be learned. The new stimulus that comes to elicit salivation is called the **conditioned stimulus.** The animal's salivation response to the conditioned stimulus is called the **conditioned response** (or **conditioned reflex**). It is

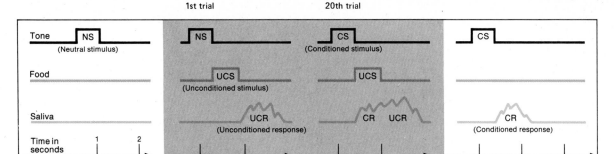

1st trial   20th trial

Tone — NS (Neutral stimulus) | NS — UCS | CS — UCS (Conditioned stimulus) | CS — CR (Conditioned response)

Food — (Unconditioned stimulus)

Saliva — UCR (Unconditioned response) — CR UCR — CR

Time in seconds 1 2

Figure 4.1 The relationship of events in classical conditioning (from left to right). *Before*—A stimulus such as a tone that elicits no salivary response can be described as a neutral stimulus (NS) with respect to salivation. This stimulus, the tone, is paired with an unconditioned stimulus (US) food, which elicits the unconditioned response (UCR) of salivation. *During conditioning*—Repeated pairing of the tone and the food begin to elicit salivation in response to the tone as well as to the food. Because the previously neutral tone is no longer neutral, but capable of calling forth salivation, the tone itself becomes a conditioned stimulus (CS) and the salivation it elicits now becomes a conditioned response (CR). *After*—Finally, a test with the tone alone is sufficient to elicit salivation.

conditioned by the animal's experience of the constant pairing of the unconditioned stimulus with the new, conditioned stimulus, the bell. In other words, classical conditioning occurs when a previously neutral stimulus comes to produce a response similar to that produced by an unconditioned stimulus, as shown in Figure 4.1. Pavlov found that a large number of stimuli can serve as conditioned stimuli for salivation: the sound of a metronome, a flash of a light, a brush on the skin.

Pavlov's experimental apparatus is illustrated in Figure 4.2. Before the experiments began, each dog underwent minor surgery; a tube was inserted in its cheek so that saliva would flow from the duct in the dog's salivary gland into a glass container. The mechanical device on the far left of the drawing kept track of the number of drops secreted. In front of the dog was a food tray from which the animal could eat when food was made available.

In a typical classical conditioning study, the experimenter presented a stimulus—say, a light—and several seconds later food was dropped into the dog's tray. The dog picked up the food (also known as the reward or the reinforcer) and salivated as a result of the food in its mouth; this was the unconditioned response. As the pairing of the light and food continued, the previously neutral stimulus, the light, began to elicit salivation. This salivation to the light was the conditioned response. Once every few trials, the light was presented alone, without food. As Figure 4.3A shows, the light alone eventually elicited salivation.

Pavlov used similar procedures to condition reflexes other than salivation. For example, an elec-

Figure 4.2 The apparatus used in early studies of classical conditioning. Saliva dropping from a tube inserted into the dog's cheek strikes a lightly balanced arm, and the resulting motion is transmitted hydraulically to a pen that traces a record on a slowly revolving drum. Pavlov's discovery of conditioned salivation was an accidental by-product of his researches into the activity of the digestive system.

Figure 4.3 (A) Acquisition of a conditioned response. (A) On early test trials—with light alone—there is little salivation. Later in the series the light alone (CS) elicits considerable salivation. A conditioned response (CR) has been acquired. (B) Extinction of a conditioned response. When the light-food pairings are eliminated, the amount of salivation (CR) to the light alone (CS) drops steadily until the relationship between the CS and the CR is destroyed.

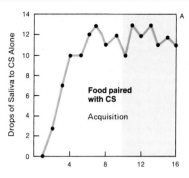

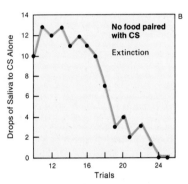

tric shock to a dog's forepaw elicited a withdrawal response—the dog pulled its paw away from the stimulus. If the unconditioned stimulus of shock was regularly preceded by some previously neutral stimulus, such as the ticking of a metronome, the dog soon learned to pull its paw away in response to the sound alone.

This tendency to react to the neutral stimulus, or CS, as though it were the UCS, Pavlov called **stimulus substitution.** In the examples cited, his dogs responded to a light or bell as if it were food and to the ticking of a metronome as if it were an electric shock. In much the same way, a student may respond to the announcement that there will be a test next week (the CS) with an accelerated heart rate, as if the actual test (or, in this case, the UCS) were being presented immediately.

CS–UCS RELATIONSHIPS A classically conditioned response can be established and maintained only if certain requirements are met. One important requirement is the **contingency,** or predictableness of the time relationship, between the conditioned and the unconditioned stimuli (Res-

corla, 1967). In a typical conditioning experiment, the CS and the UCS consistently occur close together in time, with the onset of the CS slightly preceding the onset of the UCS. For example, Pavlov presented the light (CS) five seconds before the food (UCS), and in some cases the light remained on until the food was given. If, however, the food was presented before the light, the animal was not likely to learn to salivate at the light because the light did not predict the occurrence of food. In fact, it signaled the opposite. This presentation of the UCS before the CS is called **backward conditioning,** and it is an ineffective procedure for establishing classically conditioned responses.

A learned relationship between CS and UCS also will be weak or will not develop at all if these two events are presented randomly and independently in time. When there is no consistent relationship between them, it is difficult to establish a clear conditioned response. If the light is presented five seconds before the food, then five seconds after the food, and then ten seconds before the food, and so on, the animal "learns" that the light signal is not related to food in any systematic fashion. In fact, this may make it difficult to establish conditioning to the same CS in later experiments, since the animal will have already learned that this CS has not been related systematically to other events in the past (Rescorla, 1967).

Pavlov also found that his dogs displayed an "orienting reflex" when a new CS was introduced into the experimental situation. Early in his work, he had called this the "what-is-it reflex" or the "reflex of curiosity." It refers to the tendency to pay attention to any novel stimulus, regardless of its significance. However, if the new CS is presented repeatedly without anything else happening (no UCS), the orienting reflex will gradually disappear. Since the CS does not signal anything, the animal learns to ignore it. This phenomenon, referred to as **habituation,** is a simple form of learning. It means that the repeated presentation of a stimulus results in a decrease in behavior in response to that stimulus. We stop responding to stimuli that do not signal anything of importance, as we learn that such stimuli are irrelevant. For example, the familiar sound of the refrigerator's motor "kicking in" will probably elicit no orienting reflex. In fact, we become habituated to the sound so completely that our attention is alerted only if the refrigerator develops a strange new sound. Through the process of habituation, we learn which recurrent events in the environment can safely be ignored.

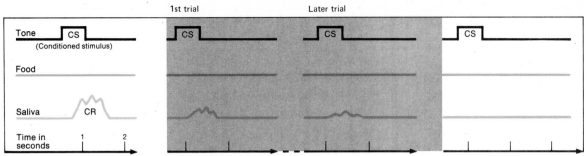

Figure 4.4 The relationship of events in the extinction of a classically conditioned response. The CS is presented repeatedly without the UCS. As a result, the CR gradually diminishes until it is no stronger than it was before conditioning.

EXTINCTION OF A CLASSICALLY CONDITIONED RESPONSE Once a classically conditioned response has been established, can we expect it to be maintained for the life of the organism? Pavlov found that a conditioned response will continue if the conditioned stimulus is presented in conjunction with the unconditioned stimulus at least occasionally. If this occasional pairing does not occur, the conditioned response will gradually disappear. For example, if a dog has been trained to salivate in response to a light paired with food, and then the light is repeatedly presented without the food, the number of drops of saliva will gradually decline toward zero, as shown in Figure 4.3B. This slow disappearance is called **extinction**: the conditioned response decreases in strength until it is extinguished (see Figure 4.4).

THE BEHAVIORIST INTERPRETATION Pavlov's findings have had an enormous impact on American psychology in general and on behaviorism in particular. John B. Watson, the founder of American behaviorism, was so impressed by Pavlov's work that he based most of his analysis of behavior on it. All learning, Watson argued, can be explained within the framework of classical conditioning. He pointed out, for example, that fear can be classically conditioned, and he demonstrated his point in a famous experiment involving an eleven-month-old boy named Albert (see Figure 4.5). Watson and his colleague Rosalie Rayner (1920) showed Albert a white rat. Albert showed no signs of fear and even tried to play with the rat. Then Watson and Rayner began their classical conditioning procedure: at regular intervals they pre-

Figure 4.5 In a classic experiment Watson and Rayner (1920) conditioned an eleven-month-old baby to be afraid of a rat. At first the child showed no fear response to the animal and enjoyed playing with it (NS). Later the presence of the rat was paired with a loud, disturbing noise which caused an instinctive fear reaction in the child (UCS). Over repeated pairings of the noise and the presence of the rat, the child became more and more afraid of the animal. Finally, the presence of the rat alone was sufficient to elicit the fear response. The rat thus became the CS, and the fear response, which had originally been an UCR, now became a CR. What do you think might happen if the child was next presented with a white rabbit? How do you think this learned fear response could be extinguished?

79

sented the rat and simultaneously sounded a loud noise just behind the child's ear. The noise made Albert cry and become upset, and gradually he began to show conditioned fear whenever he saw the rat, even if the noise was not sounded. In fact, Albert's conditioned fear generalized to other furry objects and animals—a rabbit, a dog, and even a piece of fur.

Watson also studied the ways in which conditioned fears, like Albert's, can be reduced or eliminated. The most successful technique described by Watson (1924) was what he called "unconditioning": when furry animals were paired with food and with special attention from adults, instead of with a loud noise, the fear response gradually disappeared. This technique is similar to those used very successfully today· for treating phobias in children and adults.

Although few behaviorists today agree with Watson's notion that all learning can be explained through classical conditioning, virtually no one questions its importance in many types of learning.

OPERANT CONDITIONING

In the 1930s B. F. Skinner in the United States and Jerzy Konorski and Stefan Miller in Poland described a second type of conditioning called **operation conditioning,** or **instrumental conditioning.** There are a number of differences between classical and operant conditioning. One of the most basic differences is that classical conditioning applies to reflexes, while operant conditioning applies to what is usually called voluntary behavior. Reflexes are sometimes called **respondent behavior,** in order to point up the contrast with voluntary, or **operant behavior.** For example, when an animal salivates in response to food in its mouth, the salivation is a reflex (a "respondent"). From a behavioral standpoint, the reflex response is elicited from the organism by a specific stimulus. Operant behavior, on the other hand, is said to be emitted spontaneously by the organism. It is behavior that "operates" on or has an effect on the environment. It is not associated with an obvious stimulus. For instance, no particular stimulus is necessary to induce a rat to sniff and move about its cage. Such behavior is to a rat as flying is to a bird and swinging through trees is to a monkey. In the same way, the babbling of a human infant is operant behavior.

Though operant behavior is not elicited by obvious specific stimuli in the environment, it is *influenced* by environmental factors—in particular, by rewards and punishments. In other words, operant behavior is affected by its consequences. Generally, operant behavior that results in the appearance or attainment of something that is liked will be repeated, and operant behavior that results in something that is disliked will not be repeated. This relationship was originally formulated by Thorndike in his Law of Effect, and it is what operant conditioning depends on. In operant conditioning, behavior is made to increase in response to a particular stimulus because the behavior is followed by a positive consequence.

Figure 4.6 The relationship of events in operant conditioning (from left to right). Before conditioning, some particular response occurs infrequently. Then a food reinforcer is introduced as an immediate consequence of that response. The subsequent rate of responding increases markedly until the response occurs at a very high rate. If the food reinforcer is later stopped, responding will still continue, but only for a short period of time.

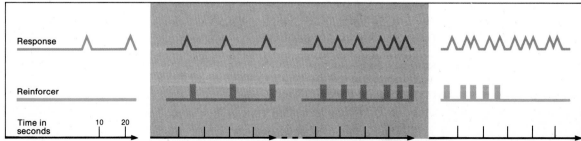

"The bird behaves as if there were a causal relation between its behavior and the presentation of food. A few accidental connections between a ritual and favorable consequence suffice to set up and maintain the behavior in spite of many unreinforced instances. The bowler who has released the ball down the alley but continues to behave as if he were controlling it by twisting and turning his arm and shoulder is (a) case in point. These behaviors have no real effect upon one's luck or upon the ball . . . just as food would appear as often if the pigeon did nothing––or, strictly speaking, did something else."
(B. F. Skinner, 1948)

Figure 4.7 The conditioning of superstitious behavior. Note the sense of continuity Skinner draws between the behavior of the pigeon and that of human beings.

REINFORCEMENT The consequences of behavior can be classified according to their effects on behavior. If a consequence produces a repetition or increase in frequency of the behavior that produced it, this consequence is called **reinforcement,** or **reward.** If, on the other hand, the consequence of behavior results in the suppression or decrease in frequency of that behavior, this is called **punishment.** Whether a consequence is a reward or a punishment can vary for different individuals. For example, some people play tennis every day because the vigorous exercise involved brings them the reinforcement of feeling fit; other people, however, regard the exhaustion that results from chasing a fuzzy ball around in the hot sun as a punishment not to be endured.

Reinforcement can be classified as either positive or negative, but either way it always means that some response is strengthened (see Figure 4.6). In **positive reinforcement,** the frequency of a response increases because the response is followed by a reward, such as food when one is hungry. In **negative reinforcement,** the frequency of the response increases because the response removes or enables one to avoid a negative (painful or unpleasant) stimulus.

Sometimes, behavior is strengthened because by chance it happens to precede reinforcement. Although the relationship between the behavior and the reinforcer is accidental (*not* contingent), the individual mistakenly assumes that the behavior *causes* the reinforcement, and so the response increases. This kind of behavior change is called **superstitious behavior.**

Young children who have not developed mature reasoning abilities can be particularly susceptible to false assumptions about the relationships between what they do and what happens. For example, a child may happen to press the button on a school water fountain at the startling instant the school bell rings. The child may then conclude that pressing the button makes the school bell ring. If the child avoids drinking from the fountain in the future, this can be called superstitious behavior.

Skinner (1948) was able to produce superstitious behavior in pigeons by systematically presenting a food reinforcer to them on some time schedule, say every two minutes, regardless of what the pigeon was doing at the time. That is to say, reinforcement was not made contingent on any specific type of operant behavior. In the absence of a clear contingency (as defined by the experimenter) between behavior and reinforcement, the pigeons after a few hours began to develop ritualistic, stereotyped behavior patterns such as head bobbing, turning in circles, and hopping from side to side. This behavior had initially happened to coincide with the presentation of a reward; now, it occurred in the intervals between reinforcements. The pigeons seemed to be acting as though there were an explicit relationship between their behavior and the reward, even though there was none. Although reinforcement was presented on schedule regardless of the pigeons' behavior, it nevertheless had an *effect* on their behavior, as shown in Figure 4.7. Skinner (1961) concluded that the results of these experiments strongly support the Law of Effect.

Intelligence does not protect us from acquiring

Rat in Skinner box.

frequency. The workings of operant conditioning can be studied in any situation in which it is possible to control the presentation of reinforcement, as the following discussion will illustrate.

THE APPARATUS Psychologists have used many devices to carry out operant conditioning. The best-known apparatus was developed by B. F. Skinner (1938) and has come to be called the **Skinner box.** The Skinner box provides a controlled setting in which a rat, pigeon, or other animal may be trained to press a bar for a reward in much the same way a person pulls a lever or knob to obtain food from a vending machine. In studying operant conditioning, the experimenter can use this apparatus to vary the number of times the subject has to press the bar to obtain various reinforcers.

Another apparatus used to study operant behavior is the **maze,** examples of which are shown in Figure 4.8. In a maze a hungry or thirsty animal learns to run along the path that leads to a reinforcement—food or water.

The **jump stand** is another apparatus that is used for the study of operant conditioning (Figure 4.9). It was invented by the late Karl Lashley, an eminent physiological psychologist, who used it to train a rat to distinguish between vertical and horizontal stim-

superstitious behavior. To consider just one example, if a golfer shoots unusually well on a day when he is wearing a new sweater, he may continue to wear that sweater every time he plays golf. He probably would not state that his attire causes him to play better, but he is superstitiously attached to his "lucky sweater."

ESTABLISHING OPERANTLY CONDITIONED RESPONSES Operant behavior, as we have noted, is emitted by the organism rather than elicited by an obvious stimulus. Operant conditioning can make this behavior increase greatly in

Figure 4.8 Floor plans of various kinds of learning mazes used for operant conditioning. The crucial variable involved in maze learning is the speed and/or accuracy of the run from the start box to the end, or goal box (i.e. the expanded areas at the end of each maze).

The runway sets the simplest learning task; the animal has only to learn that food is available in the goal box. "Y" and "T" mazes are used for discrimination problems; the animal has to learn that food or some other reward is available in only one particular goal box. The "U" maze presents the same problem, but the goal boxes are not in view at the choice point. The multiple "Y" maze presents a series of choice points rather than just one.

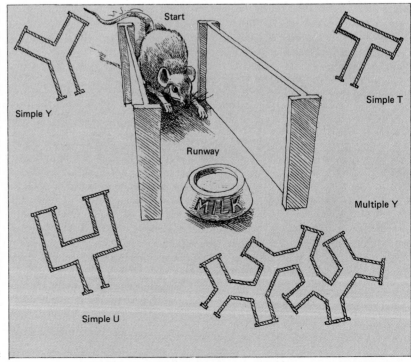

Figure 4.9 A rat makes the correct choice in a trial on the Lashley jump stand. A puff of air from the tube leading up to the jumping platform forces the rat to make a choice. Learning is rapid in this apparatus because a correct choice produces food and safety whereas an incorrect choice produces aversive consequences: The rat bumps its nose on the closed door (horizontally striped in this case) and falls into the net below.

uli (1960). In a jump stand, a rat is forced to jump through a door marked with a particular stimulus—for instance, vertical bars. Behind the "correct" door, the rat finds food or some other reinforcement. The other door, marked with horizontal bars, is locked, so that when the rat jumps incorrectly, it is punished by bumping its nose and falling down into a net. To avoid the possibility that the rat is learning a position preference—right or left—rather than learning to discriminate between vertical and horizontal stimuli, the experimenter randomly switches the two stimuli from side to side. Also, on most trials, some pressure has to be exerted on the rat—perhaps a puff of air on its back—to get it to jump at all.

SHAPING In operant conditioning experiments, one of the most frequently studied responses is bar pressing by rats; it is a well-defined act, easy for the rat to perform, and easy to record automatically. However, although an untrained rat has in its repertoire of behavior all the operant behavior necessary for bar pressing, this behavior rarely occurs in the correct sequence. In order to press the bar, the rat must approach it, rise up on its hind legs, put its front paws on the bar, and push it down toward the floor. The rat will rarely execute the sequence spontaneously. Instead of waiting for the rat to stumble on the correct response, the experimenter uses a procedure called **shaping,** in which the animal is reinforced for displaying closer and closer approximations of the desired behavior. The shaping process, developed by Skinner, is effective only if the animal is hungry or thirsty or otherwise motivated to work for reinforcement.

Shaping begins by reinforcing the first response that shows the rat is on the right track—in this case, approaching the bar. After a few reinforcements, the rat begins to interrupt its other behavior in order to approach the bar. Now, reinforcement is withheld until the rat not only approaches the bar but also rises slightly off the floor in front of the bar. At first, the rat may be rewarded for the mere lifting of one paw off the floor; gradually, the experimenter reinforces it only if both paws are lifted high enough to reach the bar. Finally, the experimenter withholds the reward until the bar is actually pressed, thus concluding the shaping process. This is illustrated in Figure 4.10. Students often wonder whether this somewhat laborious shaping procedure can be hastened by simply placing the rat's paws on the bar and pushing. While this rather direct technique may seem appealing, the animal is usually far too frightened to learn anything from it.

Shaping, then, is a form of operant conditioning based on the reinforcement of ever-closer approximations of a desired behavior. Each successive approximation must be only a small step beyond what the subject was previously doing. If the steps are too large, the procedure fails.

The same technique can also be used in training performing animals to do complicated tricks. Dolphins, for example, can be taught to leap from the water on cue, and elephants can be taught to dance. Shaping procedures can also be used to modify human behavior. For instance, the focus of the popular book *Toilet Training in Less Than a Day* (Azrin & Foxx, 1974) is the use of shaping and reward to produce desirable behavior. Likewise, shaping procedures provide an important foundation for modern behavioral therapy and have

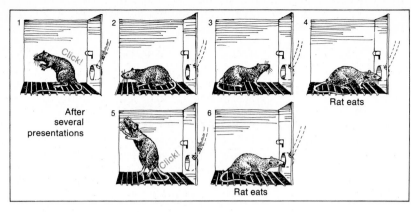

Figure 4.10 Shaping, the bar-press response. A clicking noise first cues the rat to orient itself toward the food box and the bar. The rat is rewarded at first for any movements in the general vicinity of the bar; later only if it rises on its hind legs; and finally only when it places its forepaws on the bar. The weight of the paws activates an electric circuit which automatically dispenses food (reinforcer). The shaping process is now complete.

proven to be highly effective in treating a number of behavior disorders in adults (Lanyon and Lanyon, 1978).

MAINTAINING OPERANTLY CONDITIONED RESPONSES

Once an operant response—say, bar pressing—has been established through shaping, how does the experimenter ensure that the animal will continue to emit this behavior? The key to maintaining operant behavior is reinforcement. By altering the relationship between behavior and reinforcement, the experimenter can influence many aspects of the animal's response.

SCHEDULES OF REINFORCEMENT A man who hires himself out to plow fields can generally be paid in one of three ways: by the hour, by the number of acres plowed per day, or by a percentage of the farm's profits (by the yield). It is not difficult to imagine that the relationship between work and pay will have a powerful influence on how this man works. For instance, if he is paid by the hour, he may work relatively slowly, especially if there is only a limited amount of work available. If paid by the acre, he may set his plow shallowly so that he can work faster, and he may tend to space his furrows farther apart. If paid a percentage of the profits, he may try to maximize his pay by taking time to cultivate the land as effectively as possible, perhaps by plowing the soil deeply to produce plants with a higher yield. In each situation, our plowman alters his behavior to produce reinforcement (money) most efficiently. In psychological terminology, each method of payment represents a different **schedule of reinforcement.** In the same way, the behavior of people in school and on the job and the behavior of animals in a laboratory can be subjected to a considerable amount of control through the manipulation of schedules of reinforcement.

In the laboratory, new operant behavior usually is firmly established by providing reinforcement

Shaping is often used to teach circus elephants tricks such as this one.

each time it occurs. This is called a **continuous reinforcement schedule;** each bar press yields a food pellet. Once the behavior has been established, however, the best way to maintain it is to use a **partial reinforcement schedule.** This will, paradoxically, result in more behavior per unit of reward.

One schedule of partial reinforcement is called a **fixed-ratio schedule.** On this schedule, the organism is rewarded each time it makes a specified number of responses. For example, a rat would be reinforced with a food pellet for every twenty bar presses. This is analogous to the plowman being paid by the number of acres plowed. The rat performing on a fixed-ratio schedule tends to press the bar at a more rapid rate than if it were rewarded continuously. The relationship between the work and the reward is direct and explicit; the faster the rat works, the more it eats.

Another schedule of partial reinforcement is called a **fixed-interval** schedule. In this situation, the rat is rewarded for bar pressing at the end of a fixed interval of time, say one minute, regardless of the number of responses made. This is analogous to an hourly wage, and the rat, like the plowman, learns to work the minimum amount necessary to obtain reinforcement. Thus, immediately following a reward, the rat will tend to ignore the bar for a while and then will gradually increase its bar pressing as the fixed interval comes to an end. This schedule yields a relatively low response output because of the fixed time relationship between the behavior and the reward.

Both the fixed-interval and the fixed-ratio schedules of reinforcement are based on regular and predictable relationships between behavior and reinforcement. In using these partial schedules, the experimenter is able to induce the animal to emit the desired behavior more than once to get a single reward. By the same token, partial reinforcement schedules that are irregular or unpredictable are even more efficient in inducing behavior than those that are fixed.

Variable-ratio and **variable-interval** schedules provide reinforcement on highly unpredictable and irregular bases. For example, a reward may be provided an *average* of once every ten responses (variable ratio) or an *average* of once per minute (variable interval). In a variable-ratio schedule, because the reward occurs randomly, at times it may occur after every response and at other times only after twenty to thirty responses. Using a variable-interval schedule, rewards may randomly

follow one another after ten seconds or after ten minutes. Because the unpredictability of these schedules requires the subject always to be alert to the possibility of reward, irregular schedules tend to result in high rates of response.

The persistent behavior of an animal on a variable schedule is analogous to the actions of a person who is "addicted" to slot machines. Slot machines are designed to make money, not lose it, and most people are aware that in the long run the player is bound to lose. Yet, because the amount of reinforcement and the reinforcement schedule are highly varied, slot machines have a compelling effect on the behavior of the person pulling the handle. If the machine were programmed to operate on a fixed schedule, it would soon become monotonously apparent to the player that, on the average, for every dollar invested somewhat less than a dollar is returned. However, since the machine pays out random amounts at random times, the player may continue to harbor a hope that the next pull will bring the big jackpot.

The power of irregular schedules to maintain behavior is such that it is easy to maintain undesirable responses unintentionally. For example, new parents often find "crying behavior" very difficult to deal with in their baby. So they rush to soothe the crying infant. But it is easy to reinforce crying with parental attention. The child soon learns that

If slot machines were operated on fixed schedules, it would be unlikely that anyone would play them.

The Quest for More Efficient Learning

The job of educational psychologists is to apply the concepts of learning theory discussed in this chapter in order to promote more efficient learning. Focusing on the classroom—where most formal learning takes place—these psychologists evaluate many different teaching and learning techniques. In approaching the problem of learning efficiency, they may concentrate on the material to be learned, on the psychological state of the learner, on learning strategies, or on new methods of presenting information, such as programmed instruction.

The Material to Be Learned

Research shows that *meaningfulness* is an important variable affecting learning. The more meaningful the material—that is, the more it relates to what we already know—the more readily it "sinks in." Test yourself with the following lists of syllables. Study each list in turn for one minute, then see how many of the five items you remember.

1	2	3
boy	mas	zoj
tan	pul	vaf
car	tal	zyt
dip	fer	jyz
hut	dod	giw

(Based on Glaze, 1928)

You probably found list 1 the easiest to learn, because it contains real words that were already familiar to you. For the same reason, the nonsense syllables in list 2, which resemble English words, should have given you less trouble than the completely unfamiliar syllables in list 3.

How do educational psychologists apply the principle of meaningfulness to actual learning situations? One technique is to present new material in stages, making sure the learner has mastered one stage—has made that material meaningful—before moving on to the next. Another technique is to present information in such a way that it is relevant to the learner's personal experience.

A second variable that affects learning efficiency is *novelty*. This variable may either increase or decrease the efficiency of learning. Suppose that you are presented with the following information: The animal with the longest gestation period is the elephant, which carries its young for twenty-two months. The novelty of this fact, as presented in the context of a psychology textbook, will probably enable you to remember it quite easily. However, if the same statement were presented in a textbook on elephant physiology, it would be just one novel statement about elephants among many, and it would be quite difficult to recall. Thus, too much novelty may hinder learning, but a small amount engages the learner's attention and thereby increases learning efficiency. The student can structure some novelty into the learning situation, perhaps by studying with friends or at the library instead of alone or at home.

Organizational principles are another factor in learning efficiency. Students generally find it easier to learn new information by rules than by rote—by studying the "forest" rather than the "trees." Try memorizing the following words by rote. You will probably find yourself doing a good deal of tedious repeating.

bad dab bag gab ban nab bat tab

Now see if you can discover some pattern that relates these words to one another. If you have noticed that each word begins with the final letter of the preceding word, that *a* is always the middle letter, and that reversal and alphabetical order are also involved, then you have no doubt found the list quite easy to learn. In addition, you will probably remember the list longer than you would if you had simply learned it by rote.

The Learner

In general, extremely high and extremely low levels of *anxiety* affect performance adversely, while a moderate level seems beneficial. That is, the student who is in terror of flunking out and the student who couldn't care less are not likely to do as well on an exam as their moderately anxious classmates (Sarason, Mandler, and Craighill, 1952).

Motivation appears to have a similar effect on performance. The poorly motivated student will probably perform poorly, and the overly motivated one may have difficulty because of high emotional arousal. Rewards are often useful in raising low levels of motivation.

Although punishment may also be used to motivate the student and to structure the learning situation, this approach has its drawbacks. Punishment may decrease the frequency of incorrect responses, but it does little to teach correct ones. Furthermore, the threat of punishment may arouse the learner emotionally and thus interfere with performance.

Learning Strategies

We all have our own strategies for optimizing learning efficiency. Since these are usually based on our individual strengths and weaknesses, they differ from person to person. There are, however, certain techniques that seem almost universally effective.

Rehearsal is one such strategy. The more we practice something, the better we will remember it.

Rehearsal is especially effective when it is active. Instead of passively reading and rereading the material you want to learn, try writing summaries from time to time or asking yourself questions about what you have read. Such techniques force us to organize information, and this organization should make learning easier.

When we rehearse a skill or fact more than is necessary for immediate performance, we are said to *overlearn* it. Overlearning is what makes it possible for people to ride a bicycle or type or recite the Pledge of Allegiance many years after they last did so. While overlearning and cramming all night for an exam may produce similar grades, overlearned facts will probably remain available to the student long after the exam, while "crammed" facts tend to be forgotten almost immediately after the test.

Although cramming remains a popular study technique, research has shown that such "massed practice" is generally less efficient than "distributed practice," or study that is spread out over time. If you do have to cram, take a short break every hour. Increased efficiency will more than compensate for the time lost.

Programmed Instruction

As we have seen, ability, motivation, and learning strategies differ greatly from person to person. Traditional instruction, with one teacher for thirty or forty or even two hundred students, cannot possibly take such individual differences into account. However, programmed instruction—by means of special textbooks, teaching machines, or even computers—allows students to work individually.

Programmed instruction provides immediate feedback by testing the student on each new segment of information and proceeding only after he or she demonstrates comprehension. Since this technique keeps each person at a level he or she can master, everyone receives assurance of competency, and no one is overwhelmed by meaningless material. The frequent successes in each individualized program minimize feelings of failure—and the attendant frustration, boredom, and withdrawal—that the slow learner so often experiences in the traditional classroom.

Programmed instruction incorporates the principle of active rehearsal. Usually, the program requires the student to answer a question, repeat a fact, or restate a principle before proceeding. The program may also promote overlearning by presenting the same information in several different ways and with numerous examples.

There are several methods for presenting programmed instruction. Perhaps the most common is the programmed textbook. Another is the teaching machine, developed by B. F. Skinner in the 1950s. The most sophisticated method of programmed teaching is computer-assisted instruction (CAI). This method has several advantages over earlier techniques. Instead of proceeding in linear fashion from step A to step B, the computer can branch off into remedial or supplementary step A1 or A2 if this will improve the student's comprehension. The computer can also be programmed to jump back to the start of a sequence that is causing difficulty or to jump forward to a new sequence for the fast learner. Finally, the computer can maintain a record of each student's progress and use this information to structure subsequent work.

While programmed instruction seems to have many advantages over traditional teaching, it does have some drawbacks. Students may dislike working with machines for long periods of time and may miss certain stimulating aspects of classroom instruction—for example, the human interaction, the exchange of ideas, and even the competition. For these reasons, it seems most sensible to use programmed instruction as a supplement to traditional classes rather than as a substitute for them. Finally, the expense of installing and maintaining a computerized system will probably limit the availability of this method of instruction.

crying is a sure means of bringing its parents to its side. Most parents, realizing this, try to avoid reinforcing "unnecessary" crying by ignoring it. The child, in an effort to regain their attention, may intensify its crying behavior. When this happens, the parents may reach the point where they "can't stand it any longer" and attend to the infant, thus reinforcing the even louder crying. Eventually, the infant's crying behavior may be maintained by frustrated parents who provide reinforcement on an increasingly strained but effective irregular partial reinforcement schedule. The only way to halt such behavior is to consistently refuse to reward attention-getting crying. However, the parents must first learn to distinguish between crying for "legitimate" reasons, such as hunger or wet diapers, and crying for attention. Most infants eventually learn that only under certain conditions is crying reinforced.

STIMULUS CONTROL Besides controlling the vigor and pattern of operant responses, reinforcement has another important effect. It relates behavior to stimuli that are present during or are associated with the learning situation. The stimuli provided by the Skinner box and the bar, for example, become associated both with reinforcement and with the behavior of bar pressing, possibly through a process of classical conditioning (Rescorla and Solomon, 1967).

Here is a commonplace example of stimulus control. No doubt you have had the experience of taking a shower in a building with inadequate plumbing. Because the cold water pressure is often low, the sound of a toilet flushing has caused you to flee from the shower stall. What has happened, psychologically? In this situation, a classically conditioned response—fear—develops from the pairing of the sound of the toilet flushing (the CS) with the scalding water (the UCS) that comes out of the shower when the cold water pressure drops. When you, as the shower taker, become attuned to toilet flushing, you quickly learn to display the operant behavior of "flight from the shower stall" to this stimulus, and the behavior is reinforced when you avoid painful stimulation. This provides a good example of how classical and operant conditioning may be related in a simple learning situation.

EXTINCTION OF OPERANTLY CONDITIONED RESPONSES When an operantly conditioned response is no longer reinforced, the frequency of the response gradually decreases over time, and eventually it dies out. This extinction process is illustrated in Figure 4.11. For the crying child, the withdrawal of parental attention may eventually result in a decrease in crying. For the rat in a Skinner box, bar pressing will die out when food pellets are no longer presented. But this learned behavior is not extinguished easily. Although the behavior may occur less frequently, during the initial phases of extinction it tends to be executed more forcefully and in a wider variety of ways. For example, if a pigeon who has been reinforced for pecking at a light has that reinforcement withdrawn, then it becomes agitated and upset and tends to exaggerate the response that had formerly brought rewards. Similarly, the child whose cries are ignored will probably cry even louder before this response is finally extinguished.

This exaggeration of previously reinforced behavior upon withdrawal of the reward is common in adult behavior as well. For example, suppose a

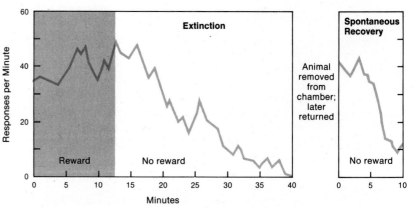

Figure 4.11 Extinction of an operantly conditioned response. Initially the animal's responding is reinforced. After 12½ minutes reinforcement is withheld, and responding steadily declines. After 40 minutes the animal is removed from the chamber. When it is returned, its response begins again at nearly the original rate, even though there is *no* reinforcement. This spontaneous recovery may result from an association between the chamber and being rewarded.

front door that usually works well does not open one day. The previously reinforced response of grasping the knob and turning it is no longer rewarded by the opening of the door. Before giving up on the door, however, the behavior of the person who is trying to open it may become more variable and forceful—he or she may rattle the door, pound it, or kick it before finally going to another door.

Some time after the frustrated door opener has given up on that front door, he or she is likely to approach it again for one more try. In the same way, if an animal is removed from the experimental chamber for a while after a response has been extinguished and then is put back in again, the response will reappear. This phenomenon is called **spontaneous recovery.** During the rest period outside the experimental chamber, the animal seems to recover spontaneously from the effects of extinction. It may be that the behavior reappears because the animal is responding once more to the stimuli associated with the chamber. In the past it had been reinforced for a certain behavior when it had been placed in the chamber; why not this time?

COMPARISON OF CLASSICAL AND OPERANT CONDITIONING

Psychologists use classical and operant conditioning procedures to investigate learning. As we have seen, there are several basic distinctions between the two types of conditioning procedures. Table 4.1 summarizes these differences. To review, the classical conditioning psychologist tends to concentrate on reflexive behavior, while the operant conditioning psychologist explores the relationship between voluntary behavior and reward or punishment. Although both types of conditioning involve the establishment of a relationship between stimuli and responses, the relationship that the experimenter imposes between the response and reinforcement differs in the two types. In classical conditioning the reinforcer or UCS compels the response to occur—for example, food in the mouth causes reflex salivation. The opposite relationship characterizes operant conditioning; here, the appropriate response causes reinforcement to occur—a bar press results in food. In the classical conditioning situation behavior is determined by what happens *before* a response is produced; in operant conditioning, the reinforcement that occurs *after* the response determines future behavior.

Although classical and operant conditioning have been presented as two distinct forms of learning, some psychologists argue that these processes are really two sides of the same coin. For example, Hearst and Jenkins (1974) pointed out that the *outcome* of both kinds of learning is the same: In both cases, the time sequence is

Stimulus $\longrightarrow$ Response $\longrightarrow$ Reinforcement

In classical conditioning, the sequence involves a conditioned stimulus (a bell, for example), which produces a conditioned response (such as salivation) and is followed by the reinforcer or unconditioned stimulus (food in the mouth). In operant conditioning the sequence of events involves, say, the inside of a Skinner box with the bar as stimulus, which leads to bar-press responses, which are followed by food reinforcers. In both cases, after training, certain stimuli (the bell, the Skinner box) dispose the animal to behave in certain ways (sal-

---

Table 4.1   Distinctions Between Classical Conditioning and Operant Conditioning

Classical Conditioning	Operant Conditioning
Behavior affected is usually experienced as *involuntary*—for example, reflexes (knee jerk, salivation, eyeblink), feelings (fear, anxiety).	Behavior affected is usually experienced as *voluntary*—for example, actions (bar press), thoughts (plans for action).
Key events (unconditioned and conditioned stimuli) are *presented* to the organism.	Key events (reinforcement and punishment) are *produced* by the organism's behavior.
Those events *elicit* the behavior; that is, they directly evoke it.	Those events *control* the behavior; that is, they determine how often the organism emits it.
In the absence of key stimuli, the behavior *does not occur.*	In the absence of specific stimuli, the behavior *does occur;* the effect of discriminative stimuli is to alter its frequency.

ivating or bar pressing). Finally, in both cases the removal of the reinforcer leads to the eventual extinction of the learned behavior.

See the accompanying special feature for a discussion of various learning strategies, many of which involve application of the principles of both classical and operant conditioning.

BEHAVIOR CONTROL

Thus far, we have discussed some of the ways in which reinforcement can produce behavior control in both classical and operant conditioning procedures. We know that a reinforcer is necessary both to elicit reflexive behavior in the classical model and to maintain operant behavior. Further, we know that behavior learned under either of these conditions will extinguish if reinforcement is removed. Finally, we know that the schedule of reinforcement—the relationship between behavior and reward—will influence both the rate and the persistence of the learned response. However, this does not exhaust the possibilities of behavior control. In this section, we will describe other factors and techniques that have been shown to influence the performance of learned behavior.

DISCRIMINATION AND GENERALIZATION

Suppose that we have successfully trained a dog to salivate at the sound of a bell? Can we also expect this animal to salivate if it hears a gong, a ringing telephone, or a high-pitched voice? Conversely, can we train this dog to salivate only when it hears a *particular* bell and to ignore all other bell stimuli? The first process is called **generalization**—the application of a learned response to a number of similar stimuli. The second process is called **discrimination**—learning to make a particular response only to a particular stimulus. Both processes are important aspects of behavior control.

Precise stimulus control can be easily established through a procedure called **discrimination training.** Suppose that by operant conditioning we have trained a rat to press a bar for food reinforcement. In order to establish a light as a controlling stimulus, we would continue to reinforce the animal only when the light is on. During the periods when the light is turned off, the rat would not be rewarded for

a bar-press response. If we alternated light-on and light-off periods, the rat would soon learn to respond only when the light is on. In this way, the processes of reinforcement and extinction could be used together to bring behavior under the control of a specific stimulus (here, the light). A parallel procedure would be used in the classical conditioning situation. If a particular bell was always followed by food, and another bell was never followed by food, the dog would soon learn to salivate only at the sound of the one bell.

In these examples, the light and bell are **discriminative stimuli;** that is, their presence controls the specific behavior because they provide the animal with additional information about reinforcement. For discrimination training to be successful, the animal obviously must have the sensory capacity to discriminate the reinforced stimulus from all other stimuli. For example, the rat must be able to distinguish between light-on and light-off conditions, and the dog must be able to hear the difference between two different bells. Figure 4.12 shows the sequence of events in operant discrimination training.

What happens when the stimulus is altered, but still somewhat recognizable? For example, how will a pigeon that has been trained to peck at a yellow key respond when it is presented with a green key? Normally, it will peck at the green key as well, but to a lesser degree than at the original stimulus. When an organism responds in this way to a stimulus different from the stimulus with which it was originally conditioned, psychologists say that **stimulus generation** has occurred.

Stimulus generalization is common in everyday life. It occurs in situations analogous to both operant and classical conditioning models. For example, Watson's famous baby Albert generalized his conditioned fear of white rats to other white, furry animals and objects. A young child who has just learned to call the family dog "doggie" will probably call a lot of other animals by the same name—not only other dogs, but cats and perhaps even cows and horses. Similarly, an adult who has just learned to drive a standard-shift car will often try to depress the nonexistent clutch pedal when driving a car with an automatic transmission.

To limit the extent of generalization, discrimination-training procedures can be used, similar to the ones described for training the rat to press the bar only when the light is on. Let us continue with the example of the pigeon that has been conditioned to peck at a yellow light key. In discrimination train-

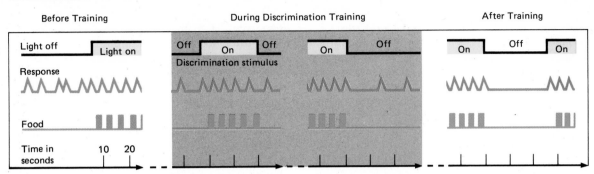

Before Training   During Discrimination Training   After Training

Figure 4.12 The course of discrimination training. Early in the procedure the animal responds as frequently to the presence as to the absence of light. Responses, however, are reinforced only when the positive stimulus, or "light on" condition is present. As the alternations of "light on" and "light off" are continued, behavior is reinforced in one condition and not the other. In this way, behavior gradually comes under control of the positively reinforced "light on", stimulus.

ing, the yellow light alternates with the green light, but only responses to the yellow light are rewarded. Pecking the green light key, the response that is being extinguished, decreases as training proceeds.

To test how effective this discrimination training is in limiting generalization, let us compare the behavior of this pigeon with the behavior of a second pigeon that has not been trained to discriminate yellow from green. Each pigeon is given a test consisting of a series of different-colored lights, including the yellow and green ones. During the generalization test, no responses at all are reinforced. Eventually, all responses will cease. The psychologist measures the number of responses each pigeon makes to the lights before extinction is complete (e. g. Guttman and Kalish, 1956). Figure 4.13 shows the results of a typical experiment of this kind; the amount of responding is plotted along the

vertical axis. The resulting curve is called a **generalization gradient.** The peak of the generalization gradients for both pigeons is for the yellow light; that is, the less similar the stimulus is to the yellow light, the less either bird responds. However, the pigeon that did not receive discrimination training produces a wider and flatter generalization gradient than does the bird that was trained. In other words, the one without discrimination training responds more to lights other than the yellow light. This points up an important and well-documented finding: the effect of discrimination training is to sharpen and strengthen stimulus control.

CONDITIONED REINFORCERS Stimulus generalization enables an animal to perform behavior it

Figure 4.13 Graph showing generalization gradients for two pigeons in a test of color generalization. One pigeon had previously received discrimination training; the other had been rewarded for pecking a yellow light but had seen no other colored lights before the generalization test. Discrimination training results in a much more sharply peaked generalization gradient. That is, the pigeon that had received discrimination training treats the colors as more distinct than does the pigeon without this training. Color difference exerts more control over its behavior.

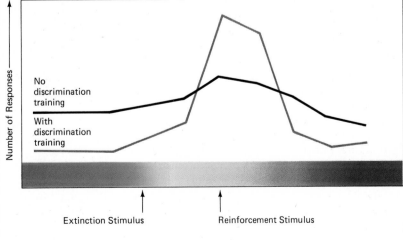

Number of Responses

No discrimination training

With discrimination training

Extinction Stimulus   Reinforcement Stimulus

has learned, even though the stimulus is not the one to which the animal was trained to respond. An animal may also perform behavior it has learned even though the reinforcers are different from the original reinforcers, or **primary reinforcers** (such as food) that initially established the response. In such a situation, the power of the primary reinforcer has generalized to **secondary reinforcers,** or **conditioned reinforcers.** A conditioned reinforcer is a stimulus that acts as a signal that the primary reinforcer will arrive soon. For example, the clicking sound of food being released into a food cup of a Skinner box signals that the primary reinforcer, the food, is on its way. If this signal consistently precedes the arrival of the food, it may acquire the power to elicit the learned behavior.

In the world outside the laboratory, it is rare that a learned behavior is immediately followed by a primary reinforcer. Usually, the time gap between response and reinforcement is bridged by a signal that reinforcement is forthcoming. For example, most people are paid for their work with money, a secondary reinforcer that can later be exchanged for primary and essential reinforcers, such as food and shelter. If a currency should lose its value, however, it will also lose its power to maintain behavior. This is precisely what happened in Europe during the economic depression of the 1930s; when currency became worthless for purchasing essential goods, people quickly stopped working for money and instead insisted on being paid directly in essential goods and services.

The power of conditioned reinforcers is suggested by a series of experiments with chimpanzees that was carried out by John Wolfe (1936). Wolfe showed that chimpanzees could be trained to perform tasks in order to obtain tokens that the chimpanzees used to buy food from a vending machine called a Chimp-O-Mat. (See Figure 4.14.) The most important conclusion stemming from research with the Chimp-O-Mat is that conditioned reinforcers—the tokens—will bridge very long delays between the performance of a task and the arrival of a primary reinforcer, such as food. Without the tokens, even small delays between the performance of the task and the arrival of food made the chimpanzees reluctant to continue performing the task.

Although the effectiveness of conditioned reinforcement is most obvious in the operant conditioning model, it can also be used to control behavior acquired through classical conditioning. For example, suppose a dog has been trained to salivate at the

sound of a bell (CS), which is always followed by food (the UCS or primary reinforcer). Pavlov called this **first-order conditioning.** Then the sound of the bell is paired with the stimulus of a flashing light; in other words, the bell is used as a secondary reinforcer to establish the salivation response to the flashing light. In time, the animal will produce a salivation response when the flashing light alone is presented. Pavlov called this **second-order conditioning.** For a human example of second-order conditioning, let us return to the example of the shower taker who flees at the sound of a flushing toilet. If that sound is often preceded by the sound of the bathroom door being slammed (by someone coming in to use the toilet), the shower taker may soon learn to flee the shower whenever the new

Figure 4.14 A powerful conditioned reinforcer in daily human life is money. Wolfe showed in an important series of experiments that chimpanzees, too, could learn to use "money." Chimps could be conditioned to pull down a heavily weighted handle in order to obtain tokens (poker chips), which could then be inserted into a machine that vended peanuts or bananas. The value of the tokens to the chimps was evident from the fact that they would work for them and save them—and would sometimes try to steal them from each other. (After Wolfe, 1936.)

sound is heard, to avoid being scalded when the toilet is flushed.

In addition to bridging the time gap between response and primary reinforcement, conditioned reinforcers can also be used in the establishment of new behavior. In other words, a conditioned reinforcer may generalize to new learning situations. For instance, the tokens used to maintain a chimpanzee's bar-pulling behavior will also be effective in establishing a new response, such as bell ringing. In the same way, money is an effective conditioned reinforcer for a wide variety of human behavior. Further, a person will work for money to satisfy a great number of needs—hunger, shelter, comfort, and variety. As long as money can be used to meet any of these needs, it will continue to motivate human behavior as a conditioned reinforcer.

Long sequences of behavior can be effectively maintained by conditioned reinforcers. The chimpanzee working for tokens carries out at least three separate responses in sequence, and the first two of these responses are maintained by conditioned reinforcers. The chimp first pulls a handle to obtain a token from the token-dispensing machine, then operates the Chimp-O-Mat with the token to obtain food, and finally eats the food.

AVERSIVE CONDITIONING Most of the techniques for behavior control described so far have relied on positive reinforcers—food, money, or similar rewards that increase the frequency of the behavior that precedes them. Another method of controlling behavior involves the use of unpleasant, or aversive, stimuli. The two principal techniques used in aversive conditioning are negative reinforcement and punishment.

NEGATIVE REINFORCEMENT AND PUNISHMENT In positive reinforcement, as we have seen, the frequency of a response increases because it is followed by a positive event. In **negative reinforcement,** the frequency of a response increases because the response removes some aversive stimulation, such as electric shock. The contrast between the two types of reinforcement can be illustrated by the following example. A little boy throws a temper tantrum because his parents do not want him to play in the mud. His parents give in and permit him to play in the mud; they have positively reinforced his tantrum in that his response has resulted in the desired event—he can play in the mud. At the same time, the child has negatively reinforced the parents' giving in; that is, their giving in has removed the aversive event, the temper tantrum, so their action has been reinforced.

This example highlights an important distinction between two concepts that are frequently confused: negative reinforcement and punishment. Negative reinforcement is *not* a synonym for punishment. In negative reinforcement, the response increases in frequency because it removes something unpleasant. In **punishment,** the effect on responding is the opposite: the response *decreases* because it produces an unpleasant stimulus or event.

Although negative reinforcement and punishment are two completely different processes, they are often categorized (as here) under aversive conditioning because they both involve aversive stimulation; that is, there must be some aversive stimulus, either before the response (negative reinforcement) or after it (punishment). For example, the parents' giving in is negatively reinforced by the removal of the aversive event, the temper tantrum. But at the same time, their attempt to prevent their son from playing in the mud is punished by the tantrum. In

Figure 4.15 The relationship of events in positive reinforcement, negative reinforcement, and punishment. Reinforcement always means that some response is *strengthened,* or increased in rate. In positive reinforcement the consequence that strengthens a response is the *onset* of some pleasant event. In negative reinforcement the consequence that strengthens the response is the *removal* of some unpleasant event. In punishment, the effect on responding is the opposite; responding decreases because the response produces the onset of an unpleasant event.

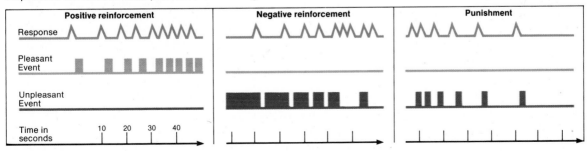

this way, the child uses punishment to decrease the frequency of the parents' attempts to keep him from playing in the mud. This increases the likelihood that they will give in to future temper tantrums, which are negative reinforcement. (Figure 4.15 on page 93 diagrams the sequence of events in positive reinforcement, negative reinforcement, and punishment.)

PUNISHMENT AND ITS SIDE EFFECTS There are many kinds of punishment—spanking children,

The effectiveness of punishment is widely questioned in our society.

flunking students, jailing lawbreakers—and punishment can be a useful means of controlling behavior. Certainly "accidental" punishments can very effectively suppress the repetition of a particular behavior: a child has to touch a hot stove only once.

Although punishment can quickly eliminate undesirable behavior, or at least reduce its frequency, it can also create undesirable side effects. Because punishment is intrinsically unpleasant, it sometimes creates emotional disturbances, which can interfere with learning. Then, too, punishment may only temporarily discourage some behavior and may do so only when the punisher is present. In addition, punishment can readily result in the punisher becoming an "aversive stimulus," to be escaped from or avoided; and this can interfere with learning. In a school that uses punishment as a primary technique to induce learning, children may become truant, and thus never learn the skills that the school is supposed to teach them.

Other methods for eliminating undesirable behavior do not have these side effects. For example, a psychologist can determine which reinforcer is maintaining some undesirable behavior; then by eliminating the reinforcer, he or she can see to it that the behavior is extinguished. Another technique is the use of positive reinforcement to condition behavior that is incompatible with the unwanted behavior. Thus, instead of attempting to eliminate stuttering by punishing it, a parent or teacher can reinforce smooth speech. Still another method is to try to avoid the need to punish incorrect behavior by ensuring from the start that only correct behavior occurs. This technique, commonly used by animal trainers, usually requires careful initial shaping of behavior and the elimination of opportunities to carry out an undesirable response. A clever experiment with pigeons (Terrace, 1963) provides a good demonstration of what can be called errorless learning. The pigeons had previously been trained extensively to peck at a red key, but not at a green one, for a food reward (operant discrimination). Then, when the pigeons were performing perfectly on this red-green discrimination, the experimenter trained them to discriminate a vertical stripe from a horizontal stripe in the following manner: the vertical stripe was put on the red key (the rewarded key), and the horizontal stripe was put on the green one (the unrewarded key). Then, as the pigeons continued to perform perfectly on the red-green discrimination, without once pecking at the green key, the researcher gradually faded out the colored lights over a series of trials,

Figure 4.16 The principle of errorless learning via the technique of fading was grasped by Abbé Sicard in the eighteenth century. Lane (1976) reports how ingeniously the Abbé taught a deaf-mute to read. The written word for an object was placed inside an outline drawing of that object. The strength of the outline was then gradually diminished, while the strength of the word inside was gradually increased until only the word itself remained.

until both keys were colorless (but the stripes were still present). The pigeons continued to ignore the unrewarded key with the horizontal stripe on it. Apparently, as the color stimuli gradually diminished in visibility, the pigeons picked up the stripe stimuli in an incidental fashion and continued to respond without error on this new discrimination. See Figure 4.16 for another example of errorless learning.

LEARNING AND COGNITION

In the preceding sections, we have discussed learning in terms of an association between stimulus and response. According to the traditional S-R school, an association will not be established unless it is reinforced. In the past, many psychologists attempted to explain all facets of the learning process in this manner. However, in recent years there has been a growing recognition that some types of learning are better understood using concepts developed by cognitive psychologists. **Cognition** is not a very precise term; generally, it refers to any mental process by which a person acquires knowledge about the world. Cognitive psychologists believe that learning can occur in the absence of obvious reinforcement, and they believe that no specific overt effort is required for the learning to occur. Accordingly, they focus on how knowledge is used and manipulated in the learning process rather than on the role specific reinforcement might play.

LATENT LEARNING   One form of learning that occurs without immediate reinforcement is **latent learning.** As we mentioned earlier, this kind of learning is called latent because the organism does not demonstrate what it has learned until some later time, when reinforcement is available. While an animal may learn about its environment without being reinforced, it will not demonstrate the learned behavior until some reward is provided.

Tolman and Honzik (1930) studied the behavior of rats that were permitted to explore a maze in the absence of any reward. When half of the rats were given food at the end of the maze, they rapidly decreased their time and error scores in running the maze, compared with the unfed rats. However, when food was subsequently given to the unfed group, their error and time scores quickly fell to the same level as the first group's; in fact, the second group seemed to have learned more quickly than the first group. Tolman and Honzik concluded that the unfed group had profited by their early exploration trials, but that the learning remained "latent" until reward was introduced into the situation. In other words, the rats could learn about the maze without being rewarded, but they would not demonstrate this knowledge unless they were reinforced (see Figure 4.17). This type of experiment provided support for Tolman's notion that learning is a result of cognition, rather than of simple association between stimulus and response that is stamped in by reinforcement.

Similarly, people can find their way from one part of a strange city to another, without error, on the basis of verbal instructions. Reinforcement and repeated practice are not essential for learning the specific route. The verbal instructions are stored until the time comes to translate them into action.

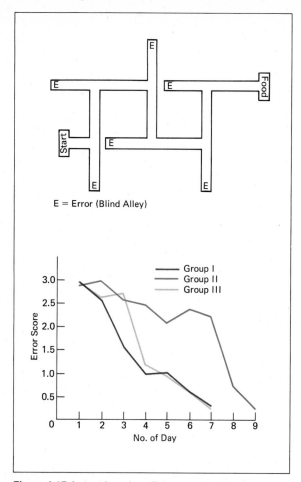

E = Error (Blind Alley)

Figure 4.17 Latent learning. Tolman and colleagues argued that learning was a result of cognition—a thinking process which involves more than just the association of stimuli and responses through reinforcement. Support for this idea came from a series of experiments like the one shown here (Blodgett 1929). Rats in Group I were put in the complex maze once a day for 9 consecutive days; they always found food at the maze's end. Group II rats were also put in the maze, but they were not rewarded on their first six trials; reward was introduced on the 7th day. Group III found their first reward on day 3. Rats in II and III began by making many errors, but these dropped profoundly on the day *after* reward was first introduced. Thus during *non-rewarded* trials the rats had been learning more than they had exhibited; reward improved performance, but did not determine it.

OBSERVATIONAL LEARNING A great deal of our information about the world is obtained by observing the behavior of others. This process of learning through observation is variously called **modeling, imitative learning,** or **observational learning.** It can occur in the absence of reinforcement, and, as with latent learning, the new behavior may not be demonstrated until a later time. We may store information about a modeled behavior in our memory—how to perform the latest dance steps, how our roommate gets dates; the consequences of writing a best-seller—and use this information to structure our behavior in the future. We may imitate the behavior of our friends, or we may model our behavior on that of people we will never meet—movie stars, fictional characters, athletes, or other media heroes and heroines. Through observational learning, more than just overt behavior is acquired; a full range of attitudes, emotions, and social styles is also learned. In addition to learning what to do, people also learn what *not* to do. For example, a little girl who sees her brother being punished for writing on the walls learns an important fact about her home environment—writing on the walls is a punishable offense and is to be avoided, or at least must be performed discretely.

Observational learning is not restricted to humans, and experiments have shown that a wide variety of animals—birds, rats, cats, monkeys, apes—are also able to benefit from modeling. The following descriptions in a classic experimental paper provide some instances of modeling that should be familiar to most readers—especially those who have younger brothers or sisters or who are parents:

> Most of Viki's imitation occurs in play. At about 16 months of age, she began to imitate such bits of household routine as dusting furniture and washing clothes and dishes. Before she was two years old, . . . some of her play was . . . complex and precise. For instance, she appropriated a lipstick, stood on the wash-basin, looked in the mirror, and applied the cosmetic—not at random, but to her mouth. She then pressed her lips together and smoothed the color with her finger, just as she had seen the act performed.
> (Hayes and Hayes, 1952, p. 415)

What is particularly interesting about the above observations is that they are not descriptions of the behavior of an active human child; Viki is a chimpanzee. The Hayeses raised her like a child in order to study the intellectual and social development of this most humanlike animal under such conditions. The study compared in detail the imitative behavior of the chimpanzee to that of human children, and the Hayeses concluded that the three-year-old chimpanzee reared in a human environment displayed imitative behavior very similar to that displayed by three-year-old human children.

At this point, it seems clear that observational

learning is very widespread and that cognitive models of learning have great relevance to both human and animal behavior. Cognition is an obvious part of human experience, and learning theories that do not consider the role of mental activity and knowledge seem to ignore a crucial facet of this experience. Cognitive models of learning contribute to many areas of psychology, including personality and social development, psychopathology, and psychotherapy. This theoretical approach to human behavior will reappear in many of the following chapters; it provides the major foundation for the next chapter, on memory.

Summary

1. **Learning** can be described as a relatively permanent change in behavior potential that accompanies experience. Learning is not something that can be seen; it must be inferred from precise observations and measurements of changes in an organism's performance. There are two main, opposing schools of thought on the nature of the learning process. The **associationist school** views learning as the development of associations between stimuli and responses. The **cognitive school** focuses on the role of thinking and reasoning in the learning process.
   A. Edwin Thorndike's **Law of Effect** states that responses bringing "satisfaction" tend to strengthen stimulus-response associations, while responses producing "discomfort" tend to weaken them. The classical conditioning and operant conditioning models of learning stem from this associationist view.
   B. Edward Tolman believed that learned behavior is purposeful and involves the rational thought processes of the learner. Types of learning that support this cognitive view are **observational learning** and **latent learning.**

2. **Classical conditioning,** discovered by Ivan Pavlov, involves reflex behavior. A simple reflex is an involuntary response that is elicited by a specific stimulus.
   A. Pavlov found that a **stimulus**—in his experiments, food in a dog's mouth—elicited the **response** of salivation. Food in the mouth is the **unconditioned stimulus** (UCS) in this example, and salivation is the **unconditioned response** (UCR). The word "unconditioned" means that the response does not depend on any learned relationship or prior experience with the stimulus. When a previously neutral stimulus, such as the sound of a bell, regularly occurs just before food is placed in the dog's mouth, it will eventually elicit the salivation response even when it is presented alone. The bell is then called the **conditioned stimulus** (CS). Salivation that occurs to the conditioned stimulus is called the **conditioned response** (CR).
   B. There must be a **contingency,** or predictable time relationship, between the conditioned and unconditioned stimuli in order for a classically conditioned response to be established.
      1. Normally, the CS is presented just a few seconds before the UCS. Unless the CS consistently signals that food or another UCS will follow, a learned relationship between the two stimuli will be very weak or will not develop at all.
      2. Pavlov also noticed that his dogs tended to pay attention to any novel stimulus. He called this the "orienting reflex." If a new stimulus, however, is presented repeatedly without anything happening afterward, **habituation** takes place: the animal ignores the stimulus, and the orienting response gradually disappears.
   C. A classically conditioned response will not persist for long unless the CS and UCS are presented in conjunction with each other every once in a while. If this occasional pairing does not occur, the conditioned response will eventually disappear; that is, **extinction** will take place.
   D. Pavlov's work had a profound effect on behavioral psychology. John B. Watson maintained that the principles of classical conditioning can account for all learning.

3. While classical conditioning primarily involves reflexes, or **respondent behavior, operant conditioning,** or **instrumental conditioning,** primarily

involves voluntary, or **operant, behavior.** Operant behavior is emitted spontaneously by the organism, is not associated with an obvious stimulus, and generally has an effect on the environment. Although operant behavior is not elicited by a specific stimulus, as in classical conditioning, it is influenced by environmental rewards and punishments brought about by the behavior.

A. A consequence of behavior that causes an increase in or repetition of the behavior that produced it is called a **reinforcement,** or **reward.** If, however, the consequence of behavior produces a decrease in the occurrence of that behavior, it is called **punishment.** Reinforcement may be positive or negative, but it always produces a strengthening of some behavior or response. In **positive reinforcement,** a particular response is followed by a reward, which causes an increase in the frequency of the response. In **negative reinforcement,** a response is followed by the removal of a negative (unpleasant or painful) stimulus, which also causes an increase in the frequency of the response.

B. Operant conditioning can be studied in any situation that permits a controlled presentation of reinforcements.

1. In order to speed up the learning of a particular response, psychologists use a procedure called **shaping,** in which an animal or human is reinforced for exhibiting closer and closer approximations of the desired behavior.

C. An operantly conditioned response, once established, can be maintained by various schedules of reinforcement and by stimulus control.

1. The emission of desired behavior is affected by the types and frequency of reinforcement, or **schedules of reinforcement.** Providing reinforcement each time behavior occurs is called **continuous reinforcement;** it is an effective means for establishing a new operant behavior. Once the behavior has been established, the best way to maintain it is through a **partial reinforcement** schedule. There are a variety of partial reinforcement schedules.

   a. On a **fixed-ratio** schedule of partial reinforcement, the organism is rewarded after it has made a specified number of responses. On a **fixed-interval** schedule, the organism is rewarded after a fixed interval of time has elapsed, regardless of the number of responses made.

   b. Partial reinforcement schedules that are irregular or unpredictable are even more efficient in maintaining behavior. A **variable-ratio** schedule *randomly* provides reinforcement after an average *number* of responses. A **variable-interval** schedule *randomly* rewards responses that occur after an average amount of *time* has elapsed.

2. Control of the stimulus is also essential in maintaining an operantly conditioned response. This involves using reinforcement to induce the organism to associate a particular behavior with a particular stimulus.

D. As in classical conditioning, when an operantly conditioned response is no longer reinforced, the response gradually decreases and eventually is extinguished altogether. However, during the initial phases of extinction, the behavior is often emitted even more forcefully than usual. Some time after a response has been extinguished in one setting, if the organism is placed in the same situation, the response will usually reappear temporarily. This phenomenon is known as **spontaneous recovery.**

4. Several distinctions exist between classical and operant conditioning procedures. The focus in classical conditioning is on reflexive behavior, while in operant conditioning the emphasis is on the relationship between voluntary behavior and reward or punishment. Behavior that is conditioned classically is determined by what happens *before* the response is produced, while operantly conditioned behavior is determined by the reinforcement that occurs *after* a particular response. Some psychologists believe that classical and operant conditioning are not distinctly different, but are two sides of the same coin.

5. Several other factors and techniques play a part in behavior control.

A. When an organism is trained to produce a particular response to a particular stimulus, but later learns to produce the same response to another stimulus, **stimulus generalization** has occurred. Conversely, **stimulus discrimi-**

nation involves emitting a specific response only to one particular stimulus. Precise stimulus control can be established through **discrimination training.** This involves the use of reinforcement and extinction together. **A discriminative stimulus** signals the organism that reinforcement will be obtained only while it is present. Discrimination training, therefore, inhibits generalization.

B. The phenomenon of generalization applies not only to stimuli, but also to reinforcers. Although a **primary reinforcer,** such as food, may have originally established a particular response, the effects of a primary reinforcer may generalize to **secondary reinforcers,** or **conditioned reinforcers.**

C. Like positive reinforcers, aversive conditioning techniques can also be used to control behavior. Negative reinforcement and punishment are the two major types of aversive conditioning.

   1. In **negative reinforcement,** the frequency of a response is *increased* because the response produces the *removal* of an aversive (unpleasant) stimulus. **Punishment,** however, produces a *decrease* in the response, because the response causes the *occurrence* of an aversive stimulus.

   2. Although punishment can be an effective technique in suppressing the occurrence of certain behavior, it also produces several undesirable side effects. It may create emotional disturbances, which can interfere with learning. It may also discourage some behavior only temporarily or only in the presence of the punisher.

6. The associationist school relies on the establishment of stimulus-response connections through reinforcement. Cognitive psychologists, however, believe that learning can occur without obvious reinforcement, and the focus of their research is on how knowledge is used and manipulated in the learning process, rather than on the role of reinforcement.

A. **Latent learning** occurs without immediate reinforcement. The organism does not exhibit what it has learned until some later time, when reinforcement is available.

B. Another form of learning that occurs in the absence of reinforcement is called **modeling, imitative learning,** or **observational learning.** This type of learning results simply from observing the behavior of others. Newly learned behavior may occur immediately after observation of a model, or it may not be demonstrated until a later time (as in the case of latent learning).

RECOMMENDED READINGS

HINTZMAN, DOUGLAS L. *The Psychology of Learning and Memory.* San Francisco: Freeman, 1978. A very readable, up-to-date broad survey of basic learning and memory processes.

LANYON, RICHARD I., and BARBARA P. LANYON. *Behavior Therapy: A Clinical Introduction.* Reading, Mass.: Addison-Wesley, 1978. A primer of the application of learning principles to a wide range of psychological problems.

SELIGMAN, MARTIN E. P., and JOANNE L. HAGER. *Biological Boundaries of Learning.* Englewood Cliffs, N.J.: Prentice-Hall, 1972. An excellent collection of important papers that deal with a number of learning phenomena and that are at the cutting edge of contemporary research in learning. Em-

phasizes important relationships between behaviorist and ethological traditions.

SKINNER, B. F. *Walden Two.* New York: Macmillan, 1949. A novel outlining a utopian society where behavior is programmed according to Skinner's analysis of learning by reinforcement.

SKINNER, B. F. *Beyond Freedom and Dignity.* New York: Knopf, 1971. Skinner's controversial book that argues for a program of psychological engineering in society and against the meaningfulness of such concepts as freedom and dignity.

WALTERS, GARY C., and JOAN E. GRUSEC. *Punishment.* San Francisco: Freeman, 1977. A fine synthesis of child-development and learning research concerning procedures and effects of punishment.

CHAPTER FIVE

MEMORY

Memory has a good press. It is considered a great thing to have a good memory, and a constant annoyance to be prone to forget. To remember trivial things is often considered a sign of great intelligence, and in the 1950s, game shows on television offered huge sums of money and vast public respect for people who could remember batting averages of ball players and middle names of Presidents. Newspaper and magazine reports of investigations into the machinery of memory always seem to be about ways and means for making memory more extensive and intensive, and yet. . . .

In all the fuss, is there no one to raise a voice in praise of forgetting? Is there no one who is willing to point out that if memory has its uses, so has forgettery?

For instance, when I was seventeen, my younger brother was eight, and I was in charge of him when my hard-working parents couldn't be. At one time he was playing assiduously and noisily with a rubber ball, and my mother wanted him to stop. He wouldn't, so my mother looked at me and made a gesture that indicated I was to take care of it. I approached my younger brother with a friendly grin and said, "Hey, Stan, throw me the ball and I'll show you a trick." He threw me the ball and I instantly tossed it over the roof. The ball was gone, and that effectively stopped his playing.

But he looked at me with shock and horror, then hung his head and walked away, and that look went through me like an ice pick. I had betrayed him and taken advantage of his trust, and I cannot adequately describe what a mean dog I felt myself to be at that moment.

For years afterward, Stanley's eight-year-old face would rise before me, hurt and disillusioned, and each time I squirmed. Nothing I could do would wipe it out. It was always there, as clear and fresh as in the beginning, any time I chose to look at it. At this very moment, as I write, I feel the bitter shame.

In adulthood, Stan and I rarely had the chance to talk to each other alone, but one of those rare occasions came a couple of years ago. On impulse, I decided to cleanse myself of the burden. I told Stanley the story and then apologized and asked for forgiveness. But Stanley looked at me, puzzled, and said, "I don't remember a thing about it."

The incident hadn't bothered him for more than an hour or two, but thanks to my inefficient forgettery, it has made me writhe for over thirty years!

Isaac Asimov

We have at our disposal a seemingly limitless quantity of facts about our past (Where did you go to kindergarten? Who was your second-grade teacher? Who was your best friend when you were twelve?). We can also recall innumerable facts about our environment (Who is President of the United States? What does a red traffic light mean?). Most of us remember our telephone number, social security number, address, birth date, and thousands of other such facts.

Memory also includes information from each of the senses. For example, visual memories enable us to recognize pictures, places we have visited, and the faces of people we have met. With our memory for sounds, we can recall the melody of a song (Hum "The Star-Spangled Banner") and the tone of people's voices. We can also recognize odors (How does the air smell after it rains?) and tactile sensations (How does velvet feel?). The capacity of memory seems almost infinite, and it is difficult to imagine leading a normal life without this ability to call upon past experience.

Memory is a crucial part of the learning process, for without it, experiences would be lost as soon as they became part of the past. Each experience would be completely novel. There would be no means of using past experiences to shape our behavior, and the same information would have to be learned again and again.

In a sense, memory and learning are two sides of the same coin. We could not learn without memory, and conversely, memory would have no content if we were not learning from the environment. Memory gives learning some permanence and also influences the ways in which we learn. Past learning experiences, retained as memories, alter our perspectives in new learning situations. For example, the memory of having failed an exam because class notes were ignored will probably result in an intensive effort to learn those notes for the next exam. At the same time, new learning often modifies our memories of the past. A teacher who is disliked for his strictness may be recalled with more kindness if new experiences prove that his advice was correct. Learning and memory continually interact in this way, each providing fuel and direction for the other.

WHAT IS MEMORY?

Memory is the retention of experience, the foundation of a person's knowledge about the world. It is memory that allows us to greet a new day knowing more than we did on the previous one. The central mystery of memory is how experience is encoded, or registered, by the brain. Numerous analogies have been proposed to account for this phenomenon.

Following Richard Caton's discovery of electrical brain activity in 1875, it was suggested that memories are represented by unique patterns of electrical activity in the brain. Almost a century later, E. Roy

John (1967) summarized a number of experiments which indicated that consistent changes in the patterns of electrical brain activity do take place as an animal learns to perform and remember some task. It has also been shown, however, that learned behavior can occur in the absence of these changes, and that these changes can even occur without the appropriate behavior being displayed (Chow, Dement, and John, 1957; Schuckman and Battersby, 1965). In addition, experiments in which strips of tantalum wire were implanted in the brains of monkeys (under the assumption that unique patterns of electrical activity would be short-circuited by the wire) indicated that memories for specific tasks were not disrupted by this procedure (Sperry, Miner, and Myers, 1955). Thus, memory does not appear to be based on obvious changes in the electrical activity of the brain.

The associationist school of thought (introduced in Chapter 4) has hypothesized that memory, like learning, is represented by the associations formed (presumably in the brain) between stimuli and responses: the stronger an association, the more likely we are to remember a particular sequence of movements (such as swinging a tennis racket) or a certain perceptual experience (such as the image of someone's face). Associationists concentrated on studying the conditions that strengthen or weaken memory processes. They described the organization of memory in various ways: as analogous to a large set of "storage bins," each holding separate memories, or to a telephone switchboard in which dialing a certain number (the stimulus) activates a particular line (the association link), which results in the ringing of a specific phone (the response).

The switchboard analogy was based on what associationists called a "connectionist theory" of learning, which held that the strengthening of a stimulus-response link occurs within a limited and special set of connections in the brain. The connectionist theory does not appear to be correct. If memory were based on specific connections in the brain, then it should be possible to find certain brain areas, damage to which would lead to the loss of specific memories. In a lifetime of research devoted to examining the relationships among memory, learning, and the brain, an eminent physiological psychologist, Karl S. Lashley, was unable to identify areas for specific memories in animal subjects (see Chapter 11). In fact, surveying the results of his extensive experiments, Lashley (1950) said that he was tempted to conclude that learning was impossible! And yet learning and memory do occur, at least as defined by the research of experimental psychologists and by the everyday experiences of anybody who pauses to think about it.

While the specific nature of memory encoding by the brain remains a mystery, two explanations for the process seem most likely: changes in the anatomical structure and changes in the chemistry of brain cells. Neuroscientists and physiological psychologists are currently exploring these two possibilities. Though they are still unable to explain the physiological bases of memory, psychologists who study cognition (the process of knowing) have made substantial progress in defining the nature of memory processes as they are reflected in behavior.

Cognitive psychologists became convinced that many facets of human memory cannot be understood by analyzing stimulus-response associations (why, for example, are some memories inaccessible at one time but accessible at another?). After all, instead of automatically responding to a particular "stimulus," humans tend to evaluate their options, to think about them, and then to select the best one. An experiment (Carmichael, Hogan, and Walter, 1932) demonstrated how "thought" can bias a person's memory for visual material (see Figure 5.1). In this experiment, the way people reproduced figures shown to them was determined to a large degree by how the figures were described: a figure consisting of two circles connected by a short, straight line was reproduced quite differently depending on whether it was labeled "eyeglasses" or "dumbbell."

So the cognitive psychologists discarded the concepts of stimulus and response and replaced them with those of knowledge and mental activity. They also portrayed humans as active organizers of information, rather than as passive recipients of the stimuli that produce automatic responses. This approach focuses on the activities that occur in a person's mind between the time it is presented with information and the time it recalls or responds to it.

Researchers who study memory usually focus on three closely related but separable processes: **attention, memory storage,** and **memory retrieval.** Attention refers to the ability to deal with limited amounts of information from the environment at any one time; storage refers to the process by which certain information is retained; and retrieval refers to the means used to gain access to the stored information. These three components of memory are easily recognized in everyday life. Everyone has had the frustrating experience of learning a particular fact—a name, place, or date—and then being unable to produce that fact when it is needed. For example, information that has been memorized for an exam may stubbornly refuse to appear when it is required, but then become available when the exam is over. In this situation, the grade on the exam reflects a failure of the retrieval process, but the grade does not serve as an accurate measure of what

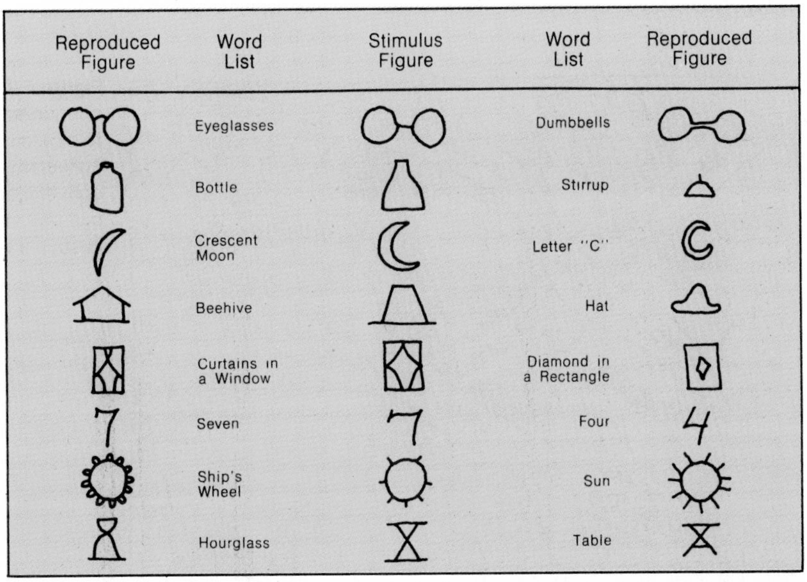

Figure 5.1 Carmichael, Hogan, and Walter designed an experiment to study the influence of set on perception. Subjects were shown the line patterns in the middle column of this figure, and these stimuli were described as drawings of various objects. Later, when the subjects were asked to reproduce from memory the patterns they had seen, they made the drawings shown in the right and left columns. You can see how the naming of the patterns influenced their drawings. (After Carmichael, Hogan, and Walter, 1932.)

Reproduced Figure	Word List	Stimulus Figure	Word List	Reproduced Figure
	Eyeglasses		Dumbbells	
	Bottle		Stirrup	
	Crescent Moon		Letter "C"	
	Beehive		Hat	
	Curtains in a Window		Diamond in a Rectangle	
	Seven		Four	
	Ship's Wheel		Sun	
	Hourglass		Table	

has been attended to and stored in memory. While memory is a function of all three components, each phase of the memory process can be described and studied individually.

MEMORY AND ATTENTION

Storing information in memory and retrieving it at a later time depend a great deal on **attention,** the ability to focus on certain information from the environment while ignoring other information.

Attention is a crucial concept for understanding why only some information enters into memory storage. Our senses are constantly being bombarded by the environment—sights, sounds, odors, tactile sensations are all present simultaneously. But there are limitations on the amount of information that can be attended to at one time. While listening to music, for example, a person may be unaware of the discomfort of a tight pair of shoes. If the irritation were to grow more intense, however, it would probably become difficult to concentrate on the music. Likewise, if you were instructed to count and remember the number of vowels from a passage in this book, you would probably recall very little of the meaning conveyed in that passage. Conversely, when you read for content, you are unlikely to notice the number of vowels in the passage.

Past experiences can also influence which environmental information we attend to. We are likely to be more attentive to information about driving safety if we remember a previous automobile accident. The present also influences memory, though: when information is retrieved from memory, it is often because we are devoting attention to a situation—such as an exam or a problem-solving task—that demands the information. One of the goals of psychologists who study memory is to determine how attention operates to select what information gets stored in and summoned from memory.

SENSORY GATING The brain monitors incoming sensory information to some extent, directing attention to one type of sensory input while putting a damper on information that is less important. For example, while attending to a visual stimulus, the brain reduces the volume of information coming from other sensory channels. Thus, when examining a painting, a person usually is less aware of the surrounding sounds and odors. This selective turning to one kind of input while reducing others is called **sensory gating.** It cuts down extraneous "noise" in the environment, permitting attention to be focused in one place. Sensory gating does not completely eliminate information from the damped-down senses, however. If a strange sound—or an unexpected silence—is detected, attention will probably shift from what is being seen to what is being heard. This indicates that information in the tuned-down sensory systems is still processed to

Figure 5.2 The "cocktail party phenomenon" refers to the ability to pick out and listen to one conversation in the midst of several conversations. How is it that we can pay attention to only one voice in such a babble?

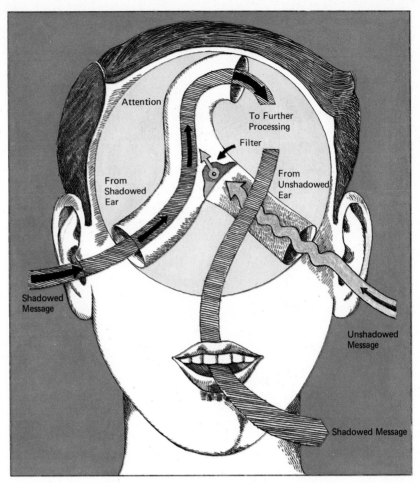

Figure 5.3 The "filter model" of how we listen to the input to only one ear at a time during shadowing. (After Broadbent, 1958.)

some extent, thus enabling us to know when to shift our attention.

SELECTIVE ATTENTION   A more complex form of information selection can occur within a *single* sensory channel. When we carry on a conversation at a crowded cocktail party, for example, our ears receive a great deal of extraneous information. In addition to hearing the person we are speaking with, we may also hear the din of other conversations, the clink of glasses, the sounds of music. Despite the confusion of sounds, we somehow manage to follow our partner's conversation, the message being attended to (see Figure 5.2). It may seem that this is accomplished by completely ignoring all other sounds, but in fact, research indicates that the sounds seemingly not attended to are given an elementary form of attention. In the same way that sensory gating does not completely eliminate information from the other senses, **selective attention**

permits some processing of information within the same sensory channel that is not at the focus of attention.

Psychologists have studied this "cocktail party phenomenon" of hearing. One researcher (Cherry, 1953) used a **dichotic listening** technique, in which a subject wearing a set of earphones heard two different messages played simultaneously one in each ear. The subject was instructed to "shadow" the message coming into one ear. To shadow a message is to repeat it aloud as it is received; the subject's voice, like a shadow, trails along immediately behind the recorded message. Later, the subject was asked to recognize or recall material from the nonshadowed message, the one coming into the other ear. If the nonshadowed message had been completely ignored, the subject would have been unable to remember anything about it. This was not the case. Under most conditions, people detected the broad characteristics of the nonshadowed message. They could report whether a voice was present and whether it changed midway from male to female, but they generally did not remem-

Figure 5.4 An experiment by Triesman showed that if a message switches from one ear to the other suddenly, the listener may fail to shadow one ear consistently. (After Triesman, 1964.)

Speech bubbles: "I SAW THE GIRL/Song was wishing . . ." ". . . me that bird/JUMPING IN THE STREET." "I SAW THE GIRL JUMPING . . ."

ber the content of the message or the language in which it was spoken. They did not even notice the difference between speech and nonsense sounds. However, people did hear their own names in the unattended channel, as well as information that was relevant to the shadowed message.

One researcher postulated that selective attention is based on our analysis of the physical aspects of information coming in through different sensory channels (Broadbent, 1958). When we attend to something we hear in one ear at the expense of information coming into the other ear (as in the shadowing experiments), we have become attuned to the difference in the location of the two messages (right and left); this physical difference guides our attention to one of them and allows it to be maintained there while the other message is filtered out (see Figure 5.3 on page 105). Some experiments have shown that a person's attention can flip back and forth between separate channels to follow the meaning of a message (Triesman, 1960). When a subject followed a message in one ear and the message jumped to the other ear, the subject's attention also jumped to follow the message. This

happened despite instructions to stay with the original channel no matter what (see Figure 5.4). That the sound was a message—that is to say, it had *meaning*—seems to have been an important factor in selective attention. Attention may first operate on the basis of the physical characteristics of the message (where it comes from, what the voice quality is), but this can yield to the meaning or content of a message when enough information has been gathered to make sense of it (Triesman, 1964).

MEMORY STORAGE

Once an item of information has been attended to, it must be stored or retained if it is to have any future usefulness. **Memory storage** refers to the ability to retain the lessons of experience for later application. This storage ability cannot be observed directly; instead, psychologists make inferences about storage by examining the performance of subjects on memory retrieval tasks.

Figure 5.5 When exposed to this array of unrelated items for a brief period, people typically recall no more than nine of them. But if subjects are signaled immediately after the exposure to recall just one of the lines, they can always recall all four items correctly. This evidence suggests that people "read" the information from some sort of complete sensory image of the stimulus, which fades in the time it takes to say the names of a few of the letters and numbers in the image.

Memory storage ability seems to take three forms. **Sensory storage** refers to the momentary persistence of sensory information after the stimulation has ceased; we can store a great deal of information in this memory system, but only for an instant. **Short-term memory** is the memory of events that have just taken place; this storage system holds only a small amount of information, but can keep it available for several seconds. **Long-term memory** stores information indefinitely, to be used over and over again; its capacity is thought to be limitless.

SENSORY STORAGE   When the pattern of letters and numbers in Figure 5.5 is presented very briefly, most people are able to remember between five and nine of the twelve items. People who try this task usually believe, immediately after the presentation, that they will recall more than eight or nine, but by the time they have reported six or so, the other items seem to have evaporated from their memory. Are the subjects correct in saying that they remembered more items before they began to report them? In 1960 George Sperling devised a technique to answer this question. He flashed an array like the one in Figure 5.5 to subjects and followed it by sounding a high, medium, or low tone to indicate which line they should report. Under these conditions, the subjects displayed almost perfect recall, indicating that immediately after the presentation of a stimulus, all the symbols *are* available in memory. During the span of time it took to report about six symbols, however, the remaining symbols seem to have been lost from memory.

Sensory storage appears to be **modality specific**—that is, the storage occurs within the sensory system that received the information, not at some central location. Additional information coming in the same sensory path immediately disrupts the storage. If, shortly after the array in Figure 5.5 is presented, a second visual stimulus—say a set of X's—is flashed, people's memory for the initial array may be lost. However, if the second stimulus is a sound or an odor, it does not interfere with memory for the visual array. Moreover, memory for the visual array is even better if the stimulus is made brighter during presentation or if the presentation is preceded and followed by darkness.

Sensory storage is not limited to the visual system. As another example, if several of a person's finger joints are touched simultaneously by air jets, it is difficult for that person to report more than three touch locations correctly. However, if the finger joints are classified into three sets—upper, middle, and lower (analogous to Sperling's three tones)—memory is significantly improved, indicating that most of the pressure information was stored for at least a moment.

The "shadowing" study discussed earlier (Cherry, 1953) provides an example of sensory storage in the auditory system. The shadowed material, remember, had to be stored long enough to be repeated aloud. However, when subjects who performed this task were questioned about the shadowed, and therefore attended to, message, they were usually able to repeat only the last three or four words of the message. Apparently, the process of shadowing the incoming message actually interfered with instating it into memory. Even though the information was processed in sensory storage (going into the ear and out the mouth, as it were), this did not ensure that it would become a part of permanent memory.

What sensory storage seems to be able to provide is a second or so during which information that warrants further processing can be selected. Usually we are not aware of the existence of this very brief memory, but special circumstances can make us aware of it. For instance, in today's movies the action seems smooth and realistic because the time lapse between frames is extremely small. The time lapse is within the limits of sensory information storage, so that successive images blend together smoothly, giving the illusion of continuous motion. When movies made early in this century are shown with a modern projector, however, the action seems jerky and unnatural. The reason for the jerkiness is that too much time is left between frames, which permits the sensory image of one frame to begin to fade from sensory storage before the next frame appears.

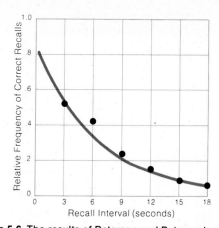

Figure 5.6 The results of Peterson and Peterson's experiment to measure the length of time that short-term memory lasts without the aid of rehearsal. Subjects were shown a three-consonant combination (CPQ, for example) that they were to remember; immediately after they saw it, they began to count backward by threes from some number supplied by the experimenter. The longer the experimenter let them count before asking them to recall the combination, the less likely the subjects were to recall it correctly.

SHORT-TERM MEMORY If memory ability were limited to sensory storage, where images fade within about a second, we would have a fragile foundation for storing experiences. However, information does remain in memory long enough to be useful. After we look up a telephone number in the local directory, we can certainly remember it longer than a second—otherwise we would be unable to dial it. However, most of us probably dial quickly, knowing that we will not remember the number very long without some special effort. Often, we must repeat or rehearse the number—either aloud or mentally—several times before it is dialed. If we get distracted for a few seconds and rehearsal stops, we will probably be forced to consult the directory again. This example illustrates two basic features of **short-term memory** (STM). First, the information entering short-term memory is lost within seconds unless the individual regards it as important enough to renew it by **rehearsal,** or repetition. Second, because only a limited amount of information can be rehearsed at one time, the capacity of short-term memory is quite limited.

The rehearsal process seems to require some kind of speech—either overt, as in repeating the telephone number aloud, or implicit, as in rehearsing the number mentally. Rehearsal seems to maintain information in short-term memory in the following way: the subject says the information either aloud or silently, hears what is being said, and then re-stores this information. This cycle is repeated until it is time to use the information. In the rehearsal, items are maintained in memory acoustically—that is, the *sounds* of the items are repeated and stored. Although rehearsal can also be visual, acoustic rehearsal (especially implicit) seems to be faster (Weber and Castleman, 1970). Yet it is easily disrupted by either external distractions—for in-

stance, the sounds of someone talking—or internal events—such as thinking about one's own telephone number while trying to remember the new number.

How long does an item stay in short-term memory without rehearsal? Various experiments have yielded figures under twenty seconds. When subjects are given a short series of letters—say CPQ—to remember and then are asked to count backwards by threes from say, 270 (267. . . 264. . . 261, and so on), they are likely to forget the letters within about fifteen seconds. The backward counting is an interfering task, a device used by psychologists to keep subjects from rehearsing the letters. If the subjects could secretly rehearse CPQ while appearing to take a deep breath between counts, their memory for CPQ would probably last longer than fifteen seconds. The duration varies from situation to situation, depending on the information to be remembered, the type of interfering task, and the amount of rehearsal allowed (Peterson and Peterson, 1959).

What is the capacity of short-term memory? In other words, how much information will it hold? In 1956, George Miller published a paper entitled "The Magical Number Seven, Plus or Minus Two: Some Limits on Our Capacity for Processing Information." In in 1956, Miller summarized the results of many experiments, all indicating that a majority of humans can hold between five and nine items in memory. Although the magical number has never been pinned down precisely, everyone agrees that it is near the range specified by Miller. If anything, his estimate may have been a bit too high.

Miller was puzzled by the ability of humans, despite their limited short-term memory capacity, to process large amounts of information. He concluded that we expand our relatively small capacity by chunking information. If we could process only seven letters at a time, our thoughts would be limited indeed. Instead, however, we can arrange letters into words (chunk them) and then group words into familiar phrases (larger chunks), which permits us to hold about seven phrases in memory. By chunking phrases into sentences, we can further expand the capacity of short-term memory.

The process of chunking actually makes use of already established memory stores to categorize or encode new information. For example, the number "1492" is easier to recall than the number "2568" if we remember the year that Columbus landed in America. By using this "old" information, we reduce our memory load to one date instead of four numbers. In this fashion, we could conceivably recall a string of twenty-eight numbers if the numbers could be chunked into seven familiar dates.

Information can also be chunked by using a rule that organizes it. Consider the following number sequence: 149162536496481100121. While the sequence contains twenty-one numbers, it can be recalled as only one chunk of information. All we need do is to remember to square, in succession, the numbers 1 through 11 ($1^2 = 1$; $2^2 = 4$; $3^2 = 9$; $4^2 = 16$, and so on). In this way, chunking allows us to bypass the seven-item "bottleneck" that seems to characterize short-term memory.

Chunks need not be verbal; in fact, some of the most useful ones are visual. Study the chessboard shown in Figure 5.7A for about five seconds, then turn the page and see how many pieces you can draw correctly on the empty board there (Figure 5.7B). If you are unfamiliar with the game of chess, you will probably be limited to the "magical" range of about seven pieces. You may well recall even fewer than seven pieces, because the position of each piece requires several chunks of information: what the piece looks like and the row and column of its location. It may surprise you to know that excellent chess players are able to reproduce the entire board after a five-second exposure. At one time, this kind of performance led people to believe that master chess players had unusually good memories. However, experiments have shown that this amazing memory is lost if the pieces are arranged in

Figure 5.7A Study this arrangement of chess pieces for five seconds. Then turn to the empty chess board on the next page and try to reproduce the arrangement. The amount you are able to recall correctly represents approximately seven of the chunks you have developed for processing information about chess games.

a random pattern that is unlikely to occur in games between good players. In such cases, the masters' memory range is no greater than anyone else's. Thus, the masters' superiority has something to do with recognizing familiar visual configurations or chunks, and is not a sign of unusual intelligence or memory capacity.

Research on chess masters suggest that they can identify 25,000 to 100,000 visual chunks. Although this sounds like an astronomical number, it seems plausible when we consider that the educated speaker of English has a vocabulary that is about the same size. When we realize that the chess master probably starts playing the game in early childhood and is likely to devote more time to the game than anything else, the large number of chunks does not seem so unreasonable.

LONG-TERM MEMORY A few pages back we discussed the process of looking up a telephone number and holding it in short-term memory. The number remains available only as long as we repeat it to ourselves, and if we are distracted for several seconds we are likely to forget it. If this were the entire capacity of our memory, we would be forced to spend our day continuously repeating our own telephone number, and we would never be able to learn anyone else's number. Obviously, there is more to memory than this short-term "holding pattern."

Long-term memory (LTM) can be considered the repository of our permanent knowledge. The amount of information in long-term memory is

Figure 5.7B Turn to Figure 5.7A on the preceding page, if you have not already looked at it, and study it for five seconds. Then try to reproduce the arrangement shown there on this empty chess board. Your success in doing so will depend heavily on your experience with the game of chess.

almost beyond comprehension. There are some theorists (for example, Penfield, 1959) who suggest that every fact that enters this long-term storage remains there in some form throughout a person's life.

How information is transferred from short-term to long-term memory is not completely understood. It is generally believed that the transfer depends on the amount of time the information has remained in the rehearsal cycle: the longer the time, the more likely the transfer. Once information begins to enter long-term storage, still more time is needed for consolidation processes to firmly fix it there. According to this consolidation theory, unless the initial physiological change, or **memory trace,** caused by the new information has time to become stable and firm, new information coming in may interfere with or obliterate it. The longer the consolidation processes operate, the more durable the memory. Although we cannot observe these transfer and consolidation processes directly, there is increasing evidence to support their existence. Figure 5.8 shows one such theory of memory.

FREE-RECALL EXPERIMENTS Bennet Murdock (1962) reported a series of memory experiments that seem to indicate the effects of rehearsal and consolidation time on short-and long-term memory. Subjects listened to a list of twenty words presented at a rate of one per second. At the end of the list the subjects were given a minute and a half to recall as many words as they could. After a short break, a new list of twenty words was read, followed by

another recall test. The results of the experiment, averaged over several subjects and many trials, are summarized in Figure 5.9A, a **serial position curve,** which shows the percentage of words recalled at each of the twenty positions on the list. It indicates that memory was excellent for the last few words on the list; these are thought to have been stored in short-term memory and still were being rehearsed when the subject was asked to recall them. Memory was next best for items at the beginning of the list; these items are believed to have been stored in long-term memory because there was more time for the rehearsal and consolidation processs to operate. Memory was weakest for items in the middle of the list.

Figure 5.9B shows that when more time was allowed between items, making longer rehearsal and consolidation possible, long-term memory for these items improved, while short-term memory for items on the later part of the list was not affected. However, when subjects were asked to count backward by threes as soon as the last word was presented, the upturn at the end of the curve was destroyed, as shown in Figure 5.9C; short-term memory was eliminated by preventing rehearsal, but long-term memory of items from the beginning of the list remained the same.

ANTEROGRADE AMNESIA The most striking studies of transfer and consolidation processes have involved epileptics who had undergone certain kinds of brain surgery to prevent seizures. These patients obtained relief from their epilepsy, but they sometimes suffered an unfortunate side effect: they could no longer transfer information from short-term to long-term memory; that is, they could no longer learn from and retain new experiences. This condition is called **anterograde amnesia** because the patient's memory for events that occurred *before* brain surgery remains unaffected.

Brenda Milner (1962) analyzed a number of such cases of anterograde amnesia. According to Milner, it is damage to the part of the brain called the hippocampus that is responsible for the disruption of memory, but this does not cause any other impairments in intellectual functioning. She described a twenty-seven-year-old man who had undergone radical brain surgery to prevent severe seizures. When Milner interviewed him two years after the operation, he still reported his age to be twenty-seven. He retained little memory of the operation, and kept repeating, "It is as though I am

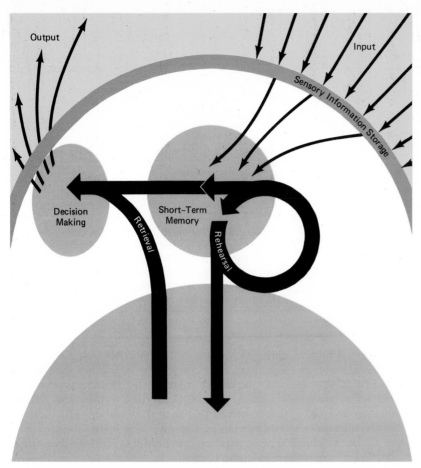

Figure 5.8 According to one theory of memory, input to the senses is stored temporarily, and some of it is passed on into short-term memory. There it decays rapidly, but a limited amount of information can be refreshed continually by rehearsal. Information can also be "coded" for storage in long-term memory. Items from either type of memory can be used in decision making, which in turn results in behavior of some kind, or "output."

just waking up from a dream; it seems as though it has just happened." He had little, if any, memory of events since the operation; he did slightly better on an IQ test than he had done before the surgery, and his memory for events before the operation was completely intact. Because he could not memorize new information he faced enormous problems in his day-to-day life. For instance, when his family moved to a new house, he was unable to learn his address and kept returning to his old house. He would reread magazines without finding their contents familiar. He would forget where household articles were kept. It appeared that he could retain items in short-term memory, but the moment he became distracted and shifted his attention, the memories would be lost.

Anterograde amnesia can also be caused by certain diseases of the brain. For example, severe chronic alcoholism can lead to general brain damage and a group of symptoms called Korsakov's Syndrome (after the nineteenth-century Russian physician who first described it). The patient with Korsakov's Syndrome has problems of memory that are very similar to those described by Milner—that

is, new information is no longer transferred to permanent storage, although old information usually remains available.

RETROGRADE AMNESIA The transfer of information from short- to long-term memory can also be impaired by head injuries (Russell and Nathan, 1946). The patient may be unable to recall the events immediately preceding the injury, or the memory loss may extend back over days or even years. This condition is called **retrograde amnesia** because the memory deficit includes only the past, and memory for new events is normal.

Retrograde amnesia, though most commonly produced by head injuries, may also result from other types of damage to the brain. For instance, the patient undergoing electroconvulsive shock therapy usually experiences memory loss, as may the victim of carbon monoxide poisoning. The extent of the memory loss appears to be related to the severity of the damage to the brain. One explanation of retrograde amnesia suggests that the consolidation period is disrupted by the brain

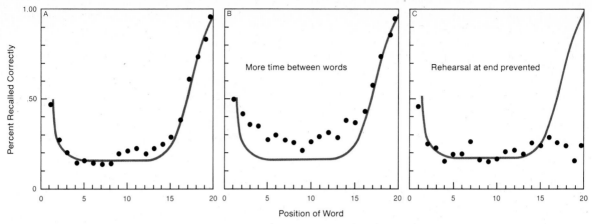

Figure 5.9 The results of a series of experiments by Murdock (A and B) and by Postman and Phillips (C) that elegantly demonstrate the separate contributions of short-term memory (STM) and long-term memory (LTM) to the serial position curve. The black dots show the percentage of correct recalls as a function of the position of the word in the list. The colored line in A represents the idealized form of the data there and is repeated in B and C for purposes of comparison. Note that in B, LTM's contribution has been enhanced by the allowance of more rehearsal and organization time between words, but STM's contribution is unaffected. In C, the contribution of STM has been completely eliminated by the prevention of rehearsal, but LTM's contribution is unchanged.

injury, so the new memory does not get firmly recorded. Thus, the victim of an automobile accident may remember nothing of the events that immediately preceded the crash because a head injury disrupted the consolidation of those events into permanent memory. Recent memories immediately preceding an injury appear to be more fragile than older ones.

Recovery from retrograde amnesia may occur in a few minutes or over a period of years, depending on the severity of the injury. Memory return is usually gradual. With recovery, the span of time covered by the retrograde amnesia begins to lessen. Usually, memories of the distant past are the first to reappear; sometimes, memory of events that occurred immediately before the injury happened never is recovered.

DRUG FACILITATION Although brain injuries can impair the transfer of information to long-term memory, certain drugs can increase transfer and consolidation. For instance, Breen and McGaugh (1961) reported that low doses of the neural stimulant strychnine sulfate, injected into rats just after a learning trial, result in better memory of the task at some later date when the drug is no longer present in the animal's system.

In another study, of rats learning to perform a maze-running task, Breen and McGaugh used the neural stimulant pictrotoxin. Rats receiving the highest doses after their trials made significantly fewer errors in future trials than rats given lower dosages, and all the rats given the drug performed better than a control group that was given saline injections. The researchers concluded that pictrotoxin facilitates memory by enhancing the consolidation process. According to this view, the rat that receives this neural stimulant after a trial remembers more of what was learned on the trial because the stimulant produces greater than normal consolidation activity.

MEMORY RETRIEVAL

Retrieving stored information is in some ways the key property of memory. Individuals can retrieve a vast number of facts when presented with a specified topic (How much do you know about cars? What does your bedroom look like?) and can recall relevant information in a very short time. The speed and efficiency of retrieval from human memory are astounding. Consider how this is reflected in our reading ability: the average person can follow and comprehend from 300 to 600 words per minute—five to ten words per second!

RECOGNITION AND RECALL Retrieval takes two basic forms: recognition and recall. In **recognition,** we are presented with something and asked if we have seen or heard it before. We can look at a face or an object and know almost immediately whether it is familiar. The process seems to occur automatically and is usually accurate. In **recall,** we are asked to retrieve specific pieces of information, usually on the basis of certain cues, and this often requires an active search of our memory stores (What is your mother's family name?).

Recognition is easier than recall. If we pass someone on the street whom we knew in elementary school, we may recognize the face but be unable to recall the name. In recognition, we need only decide if the person, object, experience, sound, or word before us is the one we are seeking. An experiment (Haber and Standing, 1969) showed that recognition for visual memories seems to be practically limitless. Subjects were shown 2,560 photographs of various scenes, each shown for ten seconds. On a subsequent day, the subjects were able to recognize between 85 and 95 percent of these pictures!

Recall is often a quite difficult type of retrieval. In this method we must recover information on the basis of cues that are sometimes quite sparse. When recall does occur, it generally tends to be accurate. The most common recall failure is the inability to retrieve anything, as when people stumble in speaking, trying to find the word they want, or fail to remember a name they thought they knew. False recalls are rare. When they do occur, it is usually possible to explain them in terms of strong, familiar associations. For example, parents sometimes call one of their children by another's name, an error that is especially easy for us to understand in large families.

RELEARNING Sometimes, memory is so poor that information cannot be recalled or even recognized with certainty. Nevertheless, we may be able to **relearn** the information in less time than the original learning required. Even though the information is no longer accessible, it apparently leaves a trace that can facilitate new storage and retrieval.

This subtle trace can be revealed by means of the **relearning score,** or **savings score,** a measurement devised by Hermann Ebbinghaus in 1885 (see Figure 5.10). Using himself as a subject, Ebbinghaus recorded the number of repetitions needed to learn a list of unrelated items accurately. Then he waited some time (presumably without thinking about the list) and relearned the list, again recording the number of repetitions needed for him to be able to repeat it accurately from memory. The difference in the number of trials between the original and the second learning session he called the savings score. The results showed that the shorter the time period between the first and second sessions, the fewer the trials needed for relearning and the higher the savings score.

REMEMBERING AS RECONSTRUCTING Most of us can readily recite the alphabet or the days of the week. But how fast can we say the alphabet backwards? How rapidly can we give the days of the week in alphabetical order? The fact that our retrieval system breaks down when faced with these requests indicates something very important about how memory is organized and how the retrieval system operates. Items are stored in memory in a very specific, sometimes even rigid, fashion. Large groups of items tend to be structured in the way that they are most frequently practiced or the context in which they most frequently occur. Thus, retrieval is most efficient when the memory search strategy parallels the original memory storage strategy.

If you live in a college dormitory, you are

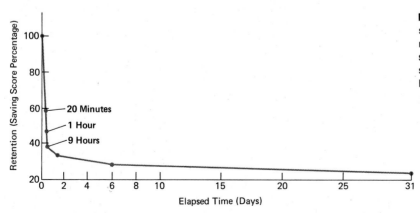

Figure 5.10 Relearning. The saving score (time saved in relearning a set of nonsense syllables) as a function of time since the first learning. (After Ebbinghaus, 1885.)

probably familiar with the names and faces of the other students who share that living space. Still, if you were spending your summer vacation traveling in Europe and spotted one of those familiar faces in a London pub, you might well have some difficulties matching the face with a name. But should your former dorm-mate approach you and say, "We shared a bathroom in our freshman year," this information could help to focus your memory. Once you have placed the face in its **context,** or setting, it becomes easier to retrieve the missing name. You can begin by reconstructing the scene where the face was familiar. Where did you live in your freshman year? What did the bathroom look like? Whom did you see at the time you took your morning shower? By reconstructing the scene, you direct your attention to the right "area" of your memory.

Retrieval can be viewed as a problem-solving task in which the correct answer comes from asking the correct question (Lindsay and Norman, 1972). Suppose you were asked to recall what you were wearing exactly one month ago. Your initial reaction to such a question probably would be that it is impossible to answer. However, you probably could answer it if you broke it down into smaller subproblems—for instance, "What day of the week was it? What classes do I have on that day? What was the weather like? By solving each of these subproblems, you probably could reconstruct the day in question, eventually hitting upon the cue that would lead directly to your memory of what you wore that day. In this example, successful retrieval depends not on attacking the problem directly, but rather on actively searching memory stores and narrowing down the alternatives until the correct memory is pinpointed. You can test your retrieval by trying one of the problems in Figure 5.11.

CONFABULATION Motivation affects retrieval, as it does most human activities. A person offered a thousand dollars to remember the name of his first-grade teacher is more likely to come up with it than is the person who is offered a dime. But under conditions of high motivation, we often commit a memory error called **confabulation:** If unable to retrieve a certain item from memory, we may manufacture something else that seems appropriate. For some time, psychologists were impressed by the apparent ability of people in deep states of hypnosis to give detailed reports of events that

> In the rooms you live in, how many windows are there?
>
> What were you doing on Monday afternoon in the third week of September two years ago?
>
> Can pigeons fly airplanes?

Figure 5.11 Retrieval problems that demonstrate the reconstructive nature of memory. If, at first glance, any of these questions seems impossible to answer, try anyway. You may be surprised at what you can recall if you put your mind to it. (After Lindsay and Norman, 1972.)

occurred during childhood. The hypnotist would ask the subject to describe, for instance, his sixth birthday. Typically, the subject, if in a deep trance, would give a lengthy and quite impressive account of a birthday party complete with cake, candles, presents, and guests. He would seem absolutely convinced that the report was accurate, but objective evidence usually contradicted him. It could almost always be shown that the subject had confabulated—that he had combined several birthday parties and invented missing details; even under further questioning, the subject could not distinguish the true parts of the story from the imaginary parts.

STATE-DEPENDENT MEMORY Successful retrieval can sometimes depend on the state an individual was in when the memory was originally stored. Consider the plight of Charlie Chaplin in his movie *City Lights*. Chaplin plays the role of a tramp befriended by an alcoholic millionaire who invites him to live in his mansion. Unfortunately, on the rare occasions when the millionaire is sober, he has no memory of who Chaplin is, and throws him out of the mansion. But as soon as the millionaire gets drunk again, Chaplin once more becomes an honored guest (see Figure 5.12).

Although Chaplin's friend depicts an extreme form of state-dependent memory, a number of drugs, including alcohol, have been shown to be capable of producing various degrees of memory **dissociation**—that is, a separation between the storage and retrieval processes. What happens is that information learned while one is under the influence of certain drugs may not be retrieved well without the drug, but may be retrieved much better when the drug condition is restored.

In one study of dissociation, Donald Overton (1964) trained rats to run a maze while they were under the influence of the drug sodium pentobarbital (a barbiturate drug sometimes used in sleeping pills). Later, half the rats were drugged again and tested for memory of the maze, while the other half were tested in a nondrug state. The group tested in the drug state remembered the maze much better than the group tested in the nondrug state. In one experiment the dissociation was so extreme that Overton was able to teach the rats one solution in the drug state and the opposite solution in the nondrug state, with no interference between the two states.

State-dependent memory has also been demonstrated in people under the influence of alcohol and marijuana, although the results are far from clearcut. One study (Goodwin, Crane, and Guze, 1969) showed that memory loss was greater for subjects going from the alcohol to the nonalcohol state than for those going from nonalcohol to alcohol. In the same way, subjects who learned while under the influence of marijuana and were tested while drug-free, showed greater memory loss than subjects who learned while drug-free and were tested while under the influence of marijuana (Darley et al., 1973). These findings suggest that some commonly used drugs may alter the storage of new information but may have a lesser effect on the retrieval of previously stored information.

IMAGERY We have already seen how remarkable our capacity for visual memory is. Research has shown that people can remember verbal materials better if they hook them to a visual image of some kind (Bower and Clark, 1969; Paivio, 1971). Many popular **mnemonic,** or memory-assisting, devices rely on visual imagery (see Figure 5.13). For example, to recall the French word for snail—*escargot*—we may think of a giant snail carrying a cargo of S's on its back, leaving us with an image of "S-cargo." Other mnemonic devices are discussed in the accompanying special feature.

Imagery is most helpful to verbal memory when the items to be remembered are concrete rather than abstract. For example, compare the word combinations "steamship–canary" and "dissonance–republic." The first pair of words, both concrete nouns, immediately suggests specific images, while the second pair, both abstract nouns, either suggests no images at all or suggests images that are not uniquely tied to the words to be remembered. For instance, the word "republic" may suggest an image of the American flag, but later, when this image is recalled, the word "democracy" rather than "republic" may come to mind.

Memory for visual images is further improved if we can weave the images into some sort of scene. Examine, for a moment, the two parts of Figure 5.14. An experiment (Horowitz, Lampel, and Takanishi, 1969) showed that the top part—the

Figure 5.12 State-dependent behavior: the drunken millionaire does not seem to be the same person as the sober millionaire.

Mnemonic Devices

For thousands of years, forgetful humans have wished they could improve their memories. Through a tragic accident, the Greek poet Simonides found one way. As Cicero tells the story, Simonides was attending a banquet when he was called away to see two visitors. While he was gone, the roof of the banquet hall collapsed, killing all the guests and mutilating them so badly that the victims' relatives could not identify them. Simonides found that he could help. By picturing the banquet in his mind, the poet easily remembered where each guest had been sitting. He could then identify the bodies just by their location in the hall.

Simonides' discovery was the first of many techniques that have been developed for organizing information so that it can be more easily remembered. These techniques are called **mnemonic devices** (Loftus and Loftus, 1976, pp. 64–65).

All mnemonic systems follow the same basic principles. The purpose of all of them is to organize information, and they all make use of information already stored in memory. Although some material may be learned by sheer repetition, it is much more efficient to group and structure new material in some way, making maximum use of already familiar and organized information.

Major Mnemonic Devices

Method of Loci

The mnemonic device used by Simonides is called the **method of loci**. It involves the use of a series of *loci*, or places, that are already firmly imprinted in memory. Simonides visualized the banquet hall and then "saw" each guest in his proper place.

You can use this technique yourself. Suppose, for example, that you must learn the names of the Presidents of the United States in chronological order. You simply visualize a familiar place—say, the house in which you grew up—and imagine each President in a particular location—George Washington greeting you at the front door, John Adams and Thomas Jefferson talking in the entrance hall, James Madison playing backgammon with John Quincy Adams on the stairway, and so on until you find Jimmy Carter sunning himself on the roof. Thus, you will be able to visualize and recall the Presidents by taking a mental journey through the house along the same route. You could use the same loci to recall information about each of Shakespeare's plays or the chemical reactions involved in photosynthesis.

Imagery

The method of loci is a mnemonic device that is based on imagery. The principle behind imagery as a mnemonic device is that you will remember something if you can picture it in some way. The image you create need not be unusual or bizarre—an ordinary scene will work just as well. But it is helpful to imagine a scene with a strong positive or negative emotional impact. In one study designed to test the effectiveness of images in remembering (Sadalla and Loftness, 1972), subjects were shown lists of noun pairs. They were instructed to form neutral, positive, or negative images about the words that would help them to recall the missing word in each pair. Neutral images were to be vivid, but without emotional content; positive images were to evoke very pleasant feelings; and negative images were to be "horrifying" and "uncomfortable to think about." Subjects found that positive and negative images helped them recall the missing words far better than did neutral images. Interestingly, it did not matter whether the images were positive or negative—any strong emotion associated with an image was better than none.

Rhymes

One of the simplest mnemonic schemes organizes the material to be learned into a rhyme: "I before E except after C"; "Thirty days hath September, April, June, and November . . ."; and so on. The rhyme system takes advantage of the fact that we have no difficulty remembering the individual items (the letters or the months); the problem is remembering something about them (order, number of days). The rhyme helps because it imposes an external constraint on memory: if we remember incorrectly, the rhyme does not work.

Acronyms

If you take the first letter of each word in a series that you are trying to remember and make a word from them, you have created an acronym. "ROY G. BIV," for example, represents the order of the colors of the spectrum: *R*ed, *O*range, *Y*ellow, *G*reen, *B*lue, *I*ndigo, *V*iolet.

The Key-Word System

Another popular mnemonic device is the key-word system,

or peg system. This method requires that you memorize a list of simple words or sentences such as these:

One is a bun.
Two is a shoe.
Three is a tree.
Four is a door.
Five is a hive.
Six is sticks.
Seven is heaven.
Eight is a gate.
Nine is a line.
Ten is a hen.

This list is easy to learn because the words associated with the numbers are concrete, easily visualized nouns that rhyme with the numbers. You can use the list to remember either numbers or ordered lists of objects. As a simple example, suppose that you wish to remember the number 4391. Say: "4-3-9-1, door, tree, line, bun; I see a little door in a big tree, and when I open the door, there is a line leading to a bun." Though this may sound silly, it works. If you want to remember a list of objects rather than numbers, you might imagine the first object inside a bun, the second in shoes, the third up a tree, and so on.

The Mind of a Mnemonist

Even with all these mnemonic devices, you may still forget things that you want to remember. If so, you may find some consolation in the story of a man who had the opposite problem: he remembered everything.

In the 1920s, a Russian psychologist, Aleksandr Luria, met a newspaper reporter, "S." Luria was told of the man's superior memory and, curious to see how good it really was, began to study S in his laboratory. Luria was quickly astonished: it seemed that S had an unlimited

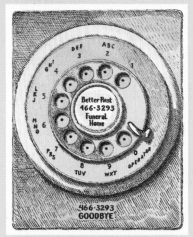

The telephone dial can be used as a mnemonic. If you have trouble remembering a seven-digit phone number, you can use the letters accompanying each number on the dial to make a word. Some agencies and commercial establishments try to get a phone number that will make a word identifying them. The example here, however, is a purely mythical one.

ability to remember things. Long lists of words or nonsense syllables were quickly memorized and easily recalled. Time did not interfere with S's memory: he had perfect recall of long word lists fifteen years after he had learned them.

Like Simonides, S found that imagery was a key element in his feats of memory. In his book *The Mind of a Mnemonist* (1968), Luria described S at a session fifteen years after their original meetings:

S. would sit with his eyes closed, pause, then comment: "Yes, yes . . . This was a series you gave me once when we were in your apartment . . . You were sitting at the table and I in the rocking chair . . . You were wearing a gray suit and you looked at me like this . . . Now, then, I can see you saying . . ." And with that he would reel off the series precisely as I had given it to him at the earlier sessiol. (p. 12)

At this point, you are probably thinking that you could breeze through college with a memory like S's. In fact, you probably couldn't. The mechanism that helped S to remember—imagery—hindered him greatly when he tried to read. Instead of thinking as he read, as most people do, S would imagine whole scenes. His mind would become so filled with images that he could not zero in on what was important in the text. His graphic mode of thinking interfered with his understanding of both prose and poetry because he found it difficult to interpret or analyze what he read by isolating the important points. In short, S had trouble thinking in abstract terms because he remembered all the concrete particulars: he literally "could not see the forest for the trees."

To make matters worse, S's mental images tended to combine with one another to form still more images. Thus he would be led far astray from the original material.

S's phenomenal memory carried with it one other ability that the average person can barely conceive of: because S could remember everything, *he could not forget anything*. Virtually everything S had ever seen, done, read, and heard—pleasant and unpleasant, trivial and important, from his earliest childhood to his old age—stayed in his memory, shifting, combining, piling up. This mnemonic overload seems as much a curse as a blessing, and the thought of it is probably enough to make most of us grateful to have an ordinary memory that lets us remember almost everything we want or need to and lets us forget almost everything we don't.

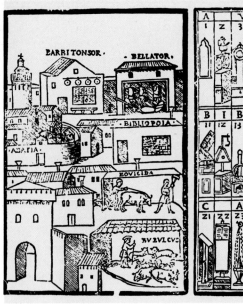
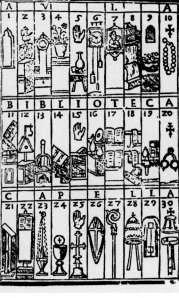

Figure 5.13 Technical aids to memory have a long history, beginning with the use of the method of loci by Greek and Roman orators. These woodcuts are from a text explaining the method of loci that was written in the sixteenth century by a Dominican monk for the benefit of such professionals as jurists, confessors, and ambassadors. At the left is a set of loci, an abbey and its associated buildings. At the right are objects that can be placed in these loci and so remembered. Note that each row on the right corresponds to one of the abbey buildings (top row, the courtyard; middle row, the library; bottom row, the chapel). Note also that every fifth place in each row is marked by a hand and every tenth by a cross. As the memorizer mentally moves through the abbey, he or she can "tick off" the items that are being recalled on the fingers of each hand.

rabbit *in* the cart—was remembered much better than the bottom part—the rabbit and the cart.

Why imagery is such a powerful tool of memory is not completely understood. It may not be because images are inherently memorable but because imagery is processed in the nonlinguistic systems of the brain. According to this line of reasoning, we are more likely to remember words plus images than words alone for the same reason that it is better to have two reminder notes for ourselves—one at home and one in our pockets—than to have only one. The two kinds of "notes"—verbal and visual—make it twice as likely that we will remember the message.

A very small percentage of the human population possesses a unique ability known as **eidetic imagery.** While most of us maintain visual images that are more or less vague, people with eidetic imagery can visualize a scene with almost photographic clarity. Research with children indicates that only about 5 percent have this ability, and this figure drops even lower after adolescence (Haber, 1969). Though the eidetic child can describe in detail many of the elements of a complex picture, this ability does not seem to aid long-term memory processes. For instance, if an eidetic child is asked to describe a picture while in the act of viewing it, the eidetic image is not formed. It seems that verbal processes interfere with the formation of an eidetic image, and that the eidetic child is no more skilled than other children in storing verbal information.

Some recent research done with subjects who were totally blind from birth indicates that imagery can be used as a memory-improving device even in people who have never had visual experience. In one experiment (Jonides, Kahn, and Rozin, 1975),

both sighted and congenitally blind adults showed improved memory when they were given word pairs such as "locomotive–dishtowel" and told to imagine a relationship between the words of each pair—for example, the locomotive wrapped in the dishtowel (see Figure 5.15). The fact that the imagery instructions improved the memory of blind subjects as well as sighted ones indicates that the imagery effect does not rely on vision. The researchers were puzzled as to how to explain this imagery effectiveness; attempts to relate it to other sensory channels, such as hearing or touch, were unsuccessful.

Figure 5.14 Drawings shown to subjects by Horowitz, Lampel, and Takanashi (1969). Which one is likely to be recalled better—the rabbit in the cart or the rabbit and the cart?

Figure 5.15 A visualization that might aid a person to remember the word pair *locomotive–towel*.

The notion that memories "fade" with time has a certain poetic appeal and may well fit in with some of our subjective experiences. For instance, our memory of a movie seen last week is probably stronger and more detailed than of a movie seen last year. However, there are many long-term memory phenomena that cannot be explained by decay theory. Motor skills tend to be remembered over long periods of time without practice; for example, an adult who has not ridden a bicycle for twenty years usually has little trouble demonstrating the skill for a child. A senile person who cannot remember what happened yesterday may readily recall childhood experiences. Also, research has demonstrated that people forget substantially less if they sleep for several hours after learning something than if they stay awake (see Figure 5.16). These facts are difficult to explain if we assume that memories simply decay with the passage of time.

F ORGETTING

We have concentrated until now on successes of the memory system—information gets in, is stored, and is retrieved. When something goes wrong with the process of memory retrieval, forgetting occurs.

There are three major explanations of forgetting: decay, interference, and motivated forgetting. Though these explanations conflict with one another at several important points, they are not entirely incompatible. A comprehensive account of forgetting will probably include all of them.

DECAY OF MEMORY TRACES   Perhaps the oldest theory of forgetting states that memories wear away, or **decay,** with the passage of time. Decay theory presumes that when a new fact is learned or a new experience occurs, a physiological change or memory trace is formed in the brain. With time, the trace decays and may disappear altogether—the information is forgotten. The only way to increase the strength of the memory trace is to make use of, or practice, the stored information. Decay theory appears to account for the transience of the more fragile sensory and short-term memory stores, but the application of decay theory to long-term memory is open to question.

INTERFERENCE   Another explanation of forgetting attributes it to **interference**—other material blocks out the memory. This explanation would say that the apparent "decay" of our memory of last year's movie is caused by interference from all the events, including movies we had seen. Had we seen no other movies, perhaps the memory would have faded much less over the same period of time. Although interference probably does not explain all forgetting, it does account for the experimental

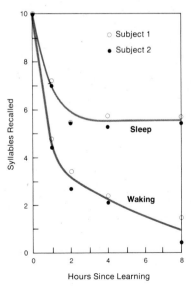

Figure 5.16 Two subjects were given lists of non-sense syllables to learn (BIK, QAJ, NIC, for example) and were tested after various periods of time. When the subjects were allowed to sleep during the time interval between learning and recall, they remembered much more than they did if they had stayed awake. (After Jenkins and Dallenbach, 1924.)

results presented in Figure 5.16. People who learned something, then went to sleep and were not subject to interference, were better able to recall what they learned than were people who continued their waking activities; the subjects who remained awake remembered only about 10 percent of the material after eight hours; those who slept recalled about 60 percent (Jenkins and Dallenbach, 1924).

We have already seen that near the beginning of the storage process, interference from extraneous material can prevent new information from passing into long-term memory. Suppose we are asked to memorize list A of the adjectives shown in Table 5.1 and then asked to memorize list B.

TABLE 5.1   Lists of Adjectives Used in Testing Long-Term Memory

List A	List B	List C
happy	gay	58
big	large	22
hard	solid	18
funny	humorous	19
thin	slender	33
calming	soothing	71
neat	tidy	45

If in the future we are asked to recall list A, we will probably find that we have forgotten some of the list A words. We may hesitate, recall some of the list A items, and add some words from list B. When material memorized later (list B) interferes with remembering material memorized earlier (list A), psychologists say that **retroactive interference** has taken place. "Retro" means backward, indicating that the interference has moved backward from list B to list A. Suppose we are asked to recall items from list B but mistakenly include some of the words from list A. This is called **proactive interference**—"pro" means forward, with the interference moving forward from list A to list B.

Now suppose that after we memorize list A, we are given list C instead of list B to learn. It is likely that list C will interfere very little with our memory of list A. Some researchers did experiments with this type of material (McGeoch, 1942). Their results indicated that the greater the similarity between the materials to be memorized, the greater the interference during recall. Because lists A and B contain very similar material, list B creates more interference with list A than does list C. Similarly, if list B were translated into French, this would reduce

its interference with list A, because it would be easier to distinguish between the two lists.

These findings can be applied to your own study habits to minimize the effects of interference. For example, it may be wise not to study highly similar subjects—such as math and physics, or psychology and sociology—close together in time. By separating the study of similar kinds of material, you give yourself time to consolidate new information and reduce both proactive and retroactive interference between the subjects. Sleep provides the best protection from interference, for when you sleep you are not absorbing new information that can interfere with the material you have studied already. Students rarely have time to nap between studying subjects, though, so a more practical suggestion is to study dissimilar material—like chemistry and anthropology—in the same study session.

MOTIVATED FORGETTING   The failure to retrieve an item from memory is not always caused by decay or interference. Sometimes, forgetting occurs without any actual memory loss. This kind of forgetting is a matter of **suppression** or **repression,** a conscious or unconscious decision to "forget" unpleasant or disturbing memories. Although the material has not disappeared from storage, the person has arranged things so that the retrieval mechanism bypasses the path to the repressed memory. However, indications that the apparently forgotten material is still available usually show up in the person's behavior—he or she may pause or fumble for words when discussing events related to the critical memory, and there may be other signs of anxiety, such as sweating or blushing.

AN OVERVIEW OF MEMORY PROCESSES

Let us conclude this chapter by briefly reviewing the memory processes we have been discussing. Figure 5.17 shows how those processes fit together. The box represents the individual, and the elements within the box—attention, consolidation, memory, remembering, and forgetting—are not directly observable, but are inferred from performance. Outside the box are elements that can be manipulated, controlled, and measured in memory experiments:

sensory information, rehearsal, and performance. Though the processes of storage and retrieval are presented within separate brackets, there is some overlap in the areas covered by these brackets. This indicates that although storage and retrieval are discussed as distinct processes, there is not always a clear boundary between them.

The model illustrates the relationships among a series of memory processes. For example:

1. A large amount of *sensory information,* represented by the arrows, is impinging on the "organism." Only a limited amount of that information actually enters the memory system. The single arrow that breaks through the box represents that small amount of information that actually receives our attention. At the same time, the information already stored in memory directs our attention to important, novel, or relevant sensory information from the external environment.

2. *Rehearsal* is portrayed as a "looping" process that bridges the gap between instatement and storage of information in memory. The rehearsal loop is necessary if information is to be transferred from short-term to long-term storage. Although rehearsal takes place within the individual, the model shows the rehearsal loop partially outside the organism because it can be observed and controlled externally.

3. *Consolidation* is a "reverbatory" process that we assume occurs in the brain when permanent memories are established. It is portrayed as cyclical, connecting the attention and storage processes. The longer the consolidation cycle, the more durable the stored memory will be.

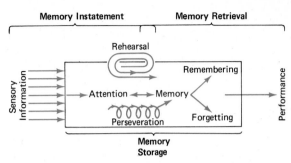

Figure 5.17 Memory processes.

4. *Memory* refers to the three forms of storage—sensory, short-term, long-term. It includes all categories of stored information: visual, verbal, auditory, tactile, and so on.

5. *Remembering* and *forgetting* are both aspects of the process of retrieving information from storage. The solid line to remembering indicates that an item may be successfully retrieved from storage; the broken line to forgetting illustrates that retrieval may be partially or completely unsuccessful. When forgetting takes place, the organism is likely to scan memory storage again in search of a new pathway to the lost information.

6. *Performance* is portrayed by an arrow extending out from the box, for performance is behavior that is observable. It is determined both by what is remembered and by what is forgotten. Performance is also influenced by such factors as motivation, emotional state, and drug use.

SUMMARY

1. Memory is the capacity to retain information. The study of memory cannot be clearly separated from the study of learning. Learning provides the substance, or content, of memory. In turn, memory of past experiences and their consequences provides the basis for learning in future situations of a similar nature. One of the main questions addressed in memory research is how new information is encoded, or registered, by the brain.

   A. As yet, the physiological bases of memory remain a mystery. Researchers are investigating possible anatomical or chemical changes that may occur in brain cells when specific memories are encoded.

   B. Cognitive psychologists believe that humans actively organize their experiences and information. Their cognitive approach to memory research emphasizes the mental activities that occur between the presentation of information and its later recall or recognition.

   C. Most researchers have focused on three related yet distinct memory processes: attention, memory storage, and memory retrieval.

      1. **Attention** is the ability to focus on specific

information from the environment.

2. **Memory storage** refers to the process of information retention.

3. **Memory retrieval** refers to the methods by which access to the stored information is achieved.

2. Attention plays a critical role in determining which information will enter into memory storage. Our senses are continually bombarded with information, but we are limited in the amount of information we can attend to at any one time. Past experience may influence which information we attend to.

A. **Sensory gating** is a process that directs attention to information coming in through one sensory channel, while decreasing the attention paid to information coming in through other sensory channels.

B. **Selective attention** is a somewhat more complex phenomenon that occurs within a *single* sensory channel. It allows us to attend to some information coming in on a channel, while muting the extraneous information that comes in on that channel at the same time. In both sensory gating and selective attention, some processing of information does occur in the channel that is not the primary focus of attention.

3. There seem to be three forms of memory storage: sensory storage, short-term memory, and long-term memory.

A. **Sensory storage** describes our ability to retain a great deal of sensory information for an instant (less than one second) after the stimulus is no longer present. This type of memory storage seems to be **modality specific,** meaning that the sensory system that receives the information is the same one that stores it. When additional information comes in on the same sensory path, it disrupts the storage of the earlier information. If, however, the first stimulus is received by one sensory system (say, vision) and the second stimulus is received by another (say, hearing or smell), the original (visual) memory is not disrupted. The purpose of sensory storage seems to be to provide a brief moment during which certain information is selected for further processing.

B. Memory for events for a short while after they have occurred is called short-term memory. This type of storage system retains a small amount of information for several seconds. Short-term memory (STM) has two basic characteristics. First, information entering STM is lost within seconds unless it is *rehearsed*, or repeated. Second, the amount of information that can be stored in STM is very limited. George Miller summarized experiments indicating that most people can hold between five and nine items in STM. Information can, however, be chunked to form larger units, thereby increasing the amount of information that can be stored.

C. **Long-term memory** (LTM) refers to the storage of our permanent knowledge; its capacity is thought to be boundless. The actual process by which information is transferred from short-term to long-term memory is not completely understood. It is generally believed, however, that the longer a piece of information has been rehearsed, the more likely the transfer. When information first enters long-term storage, a certain amount of additional time is necessary to stabilize or consolidate the memory trace (initial physiological change) produced by the new information.

1. Experiments using a free-recall technique have yielded data that formed what is known as the **serial position curve.** Items from the end of a list were remembered best (thought to be stored in STM); items at the beginning of a list (thought to be stored in LTM) were less well remembered; and items from the middle of a list were not well remembered at all.

2. The transfer of new information into LTM can be impaired by certain types of brain injuries. Some epileptics who had undergone brain surgery to prevent severe seizures developed **anterograde amnesia:** they could not retain new experiences, although their memory for events prior to surgery remained intact.

3. Another type of memory disturbance known as **retrograde amnesia** may be brought on by head injuries. In this type of amnesia, the patient may not remember events that occurred before the injury; memory for new events, however, often occurs normally.

4. The transfer of information to LTM and its consolidation can be enhanced by certain drugs.

4. The two basic methods of information retrieval are **recognition** and **recall** of material. In recognition, we need only decide if a stimulus is one we have encountered before. Recall, however, involves being able to recover and actually produce information, often on the basis of sparse cues.

   A. There are times when memory is so severely impaired that information cannot be recalled or even recognized. However, a subtle trace of the information seems to be retained, since we are able to **relearn** information in less time than the original learning required. The difference in the number of trials it takes to learn a list perfectly between the original and subsequent learning sessions is called the **savings score.**

   B. Retrieval occurs most efficiently when the strategies for memory search coincide with the strategies for memory storage. Also, by placing objects or people in **context,** we can more easily retrieve the information about them that we want.

   C. Motivation can affect memory retrieval; we remember things more easily if we have a reason to do so. When motivation is very high, however, a memory error called **confabulation** may occur. Confabulation involves inventing information that seems appropriate, to fill in a memory gap.

   D. The retrieval of information may depend on the state an individual was in when the memory was stored. Several drugs, including alcohol, can produce memory **dissociation,** a separation between the storage and retrieval processes.

   E. Research suggests that memory for verbal materials can be improved by associating the verbal stimulus with a visual image. Many **mnemonic** devices rely on visual imagery. Most people produce visual images that are somewhat vague. A few people, however, possess an ability known as **eidetic imagery,** which enables them to visualize a scene with almost the same detail and clarity found in a photograph.

5. **Forgetting** reflects a failure of the memory retrieval system. There are three major explanations of forgetting: decay, interference, and motivated forgetting. A comprehensive account of forgetting will probably include all three.

   A. Perhaps the oldest theory of forgetting states that memories **decay,** or wear away, with the passage of time; the only way to retain a memory trace is to use or practice the stored information. This theory does not adequately explain the presence of many long-term memory phenomena, such as knowing how to ride a bicycle after not having practiced for many years.

   B. Another theory states that forgetting occurs as a result of **interference**—when other material blocks out the memory.

      1. When material memorized later (list B) interferes with remembering material memorized earlier (list A), this is called **retroactive interference.**

      2. When material memorized earlier (list A) interferes with remembering material memorized later (list B), this is called **proactive interference.**

      3. Other research suggests that the greater the similarity of materials to be memorized, the greater the interference during recall.

   C. Failure to retrieve an item from memory may occur without being caused by decay or interference. In these cases, "forgetting" is due to **suppression** or **repression,** a conscious or unconscious decision to "forget" certain disturbing memories.

RECOMMENDED READINGS

BADDELEY, ALAN D. *The Psychology of Memory.* New York: Basic Books, 1976. An excellent, comprehensive textbook on memory.

KLATZKY, ROBERTA. *Human Memory: Structure and Processes.* San Francisco: Freeman, 1975. An introduction to memory from a cognitive perspective.

MEYER, BONNIE A. F. *The Organization of Prose and Its Effects on Memory.* New York: Oxford American Elsevier, 1975. An intriguing discussion of how the organization of language influences our memory for written works.

NORMAN, DONALD. *Memory and Attention: An Introduction to Human Information Processing.* 2nd ed. New York: Wiley, 1976. An up-to-date analysis of the processes of memory and attention.

CHAPTER SIX

THINKING AND THE PROBLEM-SOLVING PROCESS

Everyone must solve a problem of some sort at almost every moment of his or her life—even if it is a simple one, such as, Where did I put my glasses? It is the mathematician and the scientist, however, who are usually considered *the* problem solvers. It is their profession to consider and solve, if possible, the deepest problems posed by the universe. How do they do it?

One could never find out by reading the learned papers in which they describe their discoveries. These are dry, straight-line, logical expositions, prepared after the fact of discovery. Such papers are very likely to contain not one hint of the actual manner in which the solution of some problem was arrived at.

Here is a case in point. Back in the 1850s a German chemist, Friedrich August Kekulé von Stradonitz, had worked out a system for representing the arrangements of the atoms in molecules. He connected their symbols with little dashes according to a small number of simple rules. The formulas that were pro-duced in this fashion could be used to explain the ways in which particular molecules behaved. They could even be used to predict new ways in which they would behave under special circumstances. The formulas helped guide chemists to the synthesis of new and remarkable substances that did not exist in nature.

There remained one important substance, benzene, that did not seem to fit. Kekulé tried to work out a formula for its atoms (six carbon atoms and six hydrogen atoms in each molecule) but could not do it. He arranged the carbon atoms in the different kinds of chains that worked for other molecules, but none made sense of the way in which benzene behaved. If the benzene problem were not solved, his whole system might break down.

One day in 1865, he was in Ghent, Belgium, on a public bus. He was tired, and, lulled by the droning beat of the horses' hooves on the cobblestones, he fell into a comatose half-sleep. In that sleep, the overwhelming preoccupa-tion with the problem of molecular structure took over. He seemed to see a vision of atoms attaching themselves to each other in chains that moved about. And then one chain twisted in such a way that head and tail joined, forming a ring—and Kekulé came to full wakefulness with a start.

That was it! He arranged the six carbon atoms of the benzene molecule in a ring and found that he could now account for its properties. It was that semicomatose vision that established his system, and although chemists have deepened and broadened that system in the century since then, they have never departed from it. When Kekulé came to describe the new addition to his system, he said nothing of his dream. He merely advanced evidence and reasoning in the driest possible way—as though that were how he had worked it out. We only know of the dream because he described it in a letter to a friend during another moment of relaxation long afterward.

Isaac Asimov

Any kind of mental activity, from idle daydreaming to planning a menu to developing a way of landing a vehicle on Mars, can be called "thinking." There are many kinds of thinking, but the kind that psychologists have devoted the most study to is the thinking related to solving problems. There are two reasons for this emphasis. First, thinking is, for the most part, a very private affair. It is best witnessed and studied by observing, in a controlled, experimental situation, the thinker's visible attempts to solve a problem. These attempts can be measured, and the measurements can be used to gain some understanding of how thinking works. Second, much human endeavor can be viewed as a process of identifying and solving problems—from deciding which of several equally attractive cars to buy to determining the cause of cancer. Psychologists who study problem solving hope that the more we understand about the thought processes underlying it, the easier and more effective problem solving will become.

TWO VIEWS OF PROBLEM SOLVING

To solve any problem, we must, to some extent, call on past learning and memory. Even when we are faced with a completely novel problem, we must use many levels of prior knowledge to reach a solution to it. For many years, two major schools of psychology engaged in considerable debate about the degree to which past experience "explained" the thinking process. The different emphases of the cognitive and associationist views of behavior have been described in Chapters 4 and 5, on learning and memory. You will recall that associationist psychologists considered learning to be the result of reinforced associations between stimulus and response, while cognitive psychologists emphasized the use and manipulation of acquired knowledge in learning. The two schools also applied these emphases to their studies of problem-solving processes.

The classic associationist view emphasized the role of practice and experience. According to the associationists, the organism faced with a new problem comes to it possessing a repertoire of stimulus-response associations (habits). These associations are available to the organism because they are stored in its memory. In order to solve the new problem, the organism applies these old habits in trial-and-error fashion until a particular strategy is

rewarded. In this view of problem solving, thinking is hardly an organized and directed process; rather, it is essentially a hit-or-miss application of old associations, perhaps in various new combinations, until a solution is finally found. Furthermore, the associationists presumed that these associations are tested through overt behavior rather than mentally. John B. Watson, in fact, held the extreme view that human thinking is based on the practice of "sub-vocal speech"—that we formulate our problem-solving strategies by talking to ourselves.

The extreme view of problem solving as a trial-and-error process was based, to a great extent, on the early research of Edward Thorndike (1911), described in Chapter 4. From his experimental work with animals, Thorndike concluded that non-human animals are incapable of higher mental processes. He based this conclusion mainly on studies of cats in a puzzle box: a hungry cat was placed inside a closed box. Food was available just outside the box. In order to reach the food, the cat had to manipulate a latch connected to a mechanism that released the door of the box. Cats seemed to solve this problem in trial-and-error fashion when an accidental body movement released the latch. This led Thorndike to view problem solving by animals as poorly directed, essentially trial-and-error behavior.

Originally, the cognitive perspective was represented by what has been called the **Gestalt school** of psychology. These psychologists were first interested in uncovering the laws governing the organization of the perceptual world. They were impressed with the orderly and well-structured nature of human perception—the ability we have to sort out particular objects and events against the textured backdrop of our environment. This ability, they believed, is a result of the way the brain is organized. Unlike the associationists, the Gestalt psychologists discerned a genuine quality of "mind" at work as a person engages in the process of problem solving. The mind, they argued, aids in solving problems by organizing and restructuring the problem-solving situation. Thinking allows successive mental reorganizations of a problem situation, eliminating the need for much trial-and-error behavior, until a tentative solution appears to the thinker. The associationists believed that when a tentative solution appears, an organism then merely organizes its overt behavior to apply that solution. Gestalt psychologists were certain that problem solving is not accomplished solely by hit-and-miss trials in acts of specific behavior.

Whereas Thorndike viewed successful problem solving as *following* the correct response, Gestalt psychologists viewed it as *preceding* the correct response.

It is problem solving through *insight* that provides what is perhaps the most famous example in support of the Gestalt position. Some of the earliest research on the insight phenomenon was performed by Wolfgang Köhler, using chimpanzees as subjects. In his work *The Mentality of Apes* (1925), Köhler reflected the Gestalt focus on perception and problem solving rather than on learning as such.

In one of Köhler's experiments, a banana was suspended from the ceiling of the chimpanzee's cage, out of the animal's reach. The cage also contained one or more boxes which the chimp could stack under the banana in order to reach it. This problem—how to get the banana—was relatively difficult for most of the chimpanzees; it required that they turn away from the banana to move the boxes into the correct position. Another of Köhler's experiments required the chimpanzee to assemble interlocking sticks to rake in food that was placed outside the cage; the food could not be reached without assembling the sticks and using them as tools.

In both the box problem and the stick problem the chimpanzees' initial efforts at a solution usually involved fruitless attempts to reach the goal without any tools. When this direct approach failed, a chimpanzee often paused for a long time, as though studying the situation. Suddenly, the chimpanzee appeared to "see" the value of the box or stick as a tool to reach the food. Once the chimpanzee had reorganized its perceptions in this way, it had little difficulty in solving similar types of problems that were presented to it subsequently. Köhler called this the **insight** experience: the solution to the problem was reached when the value of the stick or box as a tool was perceived. The relationship between the food and the tool was not discovered through random trial and error, but rather by a sudden perception, or insight, that the available objects could be used as tools.

While the insight phenomenon does not seem to be based on trial-and-error behavior, there is evidence that past experience plays an important role in learning by insight. H. G. Birch (1945) repeated Köhler's stick experiment, with one important variation: he used chimpanzees that had no experience playing with sticks, and found that none of them could solve the problem. Next, the chimpanzees were given the opportunity to play with sticks for a

Köhler's classic work with chimpanzees. In this instance, the chimp seemed to have an "Aha!" experience when it realized the value of using objects as tools to achieve a goal. In this photo Grande builds a four-story structure out of boxes in order to obtain food that is hung out of immediate reach.

long time with no food present. After the play period ended and the food was introduced, all of them solved the problem of how to reach the food within twenty seconds. Thus, it appeared to Birch that past experience can have a major effect on insightful behavior.

As with many scientific controversies, then, there seems to be some truth to both the associationist and the cognitive views of problem solving. For instance, we may learn by strict rote association that 9 × 7 = 63, but in order to solve the problem 99 × 77, we must add certain conceptual rules to our rote association. George Mandler (1962) suggested that the cognitive and associationist perspectives are not incompatible, that they actually work together to explain problem solving. According to Mandler, knowledge brought to a new situation, in the form of previously acquired associations, provides the rules and symbols that become part of the foundation for thinking. Thus, cognitive processes such as insight may develop from associationist processes such as experience. In the case of Birch's experiment with chimpanzees, the associations formed during the play period with the sticks clearly contributed to the ease with which insight produced a solution.

REPRODUCTIVE AND CREATIVE THINKING

The problems we face daily vary greatly in their complexity and in the effort required for solving them. Problems can be roughly categorized as to complexity according to whether they require reproductive or creative thinking. **Reproductive thinking** is the direct application of previous knowledge to a new problem. For example, if we have to convert a temperature reading from the Fahrenheit to the Celsius scale, we simply reproduce the formula for making this conversion and apply it to the problem. In **creative thinking,** previously learned rules are either unavailable or do not apply

directly. We have to generate new rules based on other stores of information. This would be the case if we were asked to convert the scale of a temperature reading, but did not know the formula for making this conversion. Then we would have to use previously acquired knowledge—for instance, the freezing and boiling points of the two temperature scales—in order to come up with a formula that would be new in our experience, which we could apply to the problem. Figure 6.1 depicts a problem that requires creative—or, in psychologist Edward de Bono's terms, lateral—thinking.

Perhaps because creative thinking involves the development of innovative solutions and discoveries, it is the most intriguing kind to psychologists. At the extreme, it is represented by such events as Einstein's formulation of the laws of relativity and by Kekulé's "insightful" solution to the problem of benzene's molecular structure, described by Isaac Asimov at the beginning of this chapter. However, creative thinking is also the kind of thinking that is least accessible to scientific analysis. Great artists and scientists are usually at a loss to explain how they accomplish their work, often recalling that brilliant advances came in a dream or just simply "appeared" (Ghiselin, 1952).

n old money-lender offered to cancel a merchant's debt and keep him from going to prison if the merchant would give the money-lender his lovely daughter. Horrified yet desperate, the merchant and his daughter agreed to let Providence decide. The money-lender said he would put a black pebble and a white pebble in a bag and the girl would draw one. The white pebble would cancel the debt and leave her free. The black one would make her the money-lender's, although the debt would be canceled. If she refused to pick, her father would go to prison. From the pebble-strewn path they were standing on, the money-lender picked two pebbles and quickly put them in the bag, but the girl saw he had picked up two black ones. What would you have done if you were the girl?

Figure 6.1 Psychologist Edward de Bono uses the terms vertical and lateral thinking to distinguish between what we have broadly labeled reproductive and creative thinking, respectively. The problem shown in this figure requires a more flexible, generative, lateral type of thinking. Try to solve the dilemma yourself, and then check your solution with that described in Figure 6.17. (The problem is taken from *New Think*, written by Edward de Bono, the originator of the concept of lateral thinking. © 1967, 1968 Edward de Bono, Basic Books, Inc., Publishers, New York.)

Research (for example, Barron, 1958) has shown that creative people tend to prefer complexity in their environment, are accepting of their own internal complexities, and tend to be interested in abstract thinking and in the meaning of facts rather than the facts themselves. Although these observations help to characterize the creative person, they do not reveal the nature of creative thought processes. It has been suggested (Nisbett and Wilson, 1977) that not only are we unaware of how we reach creative solutions, but generally we are not even aware of our own unawareness.

We have discussed the importance of **insight,** in which components from one or more previously experienced problems recombine suddenly to produce a solution to a new problem. Many cognitive psychologists are interested in the role of insight in creativity. When insight occurs, it usually is with problems that are resistant to more routine problem-solving efforts. For instance, many people find the following analogy puzzling at first; those who solve it usually do so through insight.

Whale: Cry = Son:
Study   Chair   Pattern   Star

Once they have solved this analogy, there is little difficulty in transferring the rule to similar analogies, such as the one presented here:

Reed: Book = Sea:
Man   Picture   Marsh   Car

The second analogy requires no new insight because it requires no new combinations. (If you have not yet attained the insight necessary to solve the analogy, pay less attention to the spelling of the words and more attention to their sound.)

Although we often act in creative ways, with little understanding or thought about how we accomplish these acts, the behavior of problem solvers who have used certain problem-solving strategies has, on occasion, been described. We will examine some of these strategies in the following section.

PROBLEM-SOLVING STRATEGIES

All problem situations have certain conceptual elements in common: an individual is prevented by a barrier, either physical or psychological, from reaching some goal, and an effort must be made to circumvent or surmount the barrier. Because there are many different types of problems, each demanding a particular combination of reproductive and creative thought, there are probably also optimal strategies for surmounting the barriers that keep us from solving these different types of problems. In order to study problem solving, then, we must analyze both the impediments presented by a particular problem and the strategies that seem the most appropriate for overcoming those kinds of impediments.

PHASES IN PROBLEM SOLVING Karl Duncker (1945) used a technique that shed light on the general approach that people appear to take in solving unique (non-recurring) problems. Duncker would present someone with a complex problem and ask that person to "think out loud" while trying to reach a solution. Duncker used the following problem:

> A person has an inoperable stomach tumor. He can be treated with radiation, but radiation of sufficient intensity will destroy healthy tissue as well as the tumor. How can radiation be used to eliminate the tumor without destroying the healthy tissue surrounding it?

Figure 6.2 is a diagram of the attempts at a solution by one person who thought of an unusually large number of possibilities. The experimenter provided the general conceptualization of the problem shown at the top of the diagram. From this the subject analyzed the problem, breaking it down into several general outlines or possibilities for solution; then, each outline was further analyzed to reach several possible means of solution. Finally, from some of these posssible means the subject constructed possible specific solutions to the problem. The specific solutions that were not the "best solution" were rejected, leaving the "best solution" shown in the lower right-hand corner of the diagram.

Duncker observed that the general possibilities for a solution are formulated early in the problem-solving process, with more concrete possibilities for a solution developing out of the general ones later on. Therefore, he suggested that problem solving be viewed as an ordered series of phases leading to a specific solution. This is a useful general description of some of our behavior when we are faced with a problem. A closer look at the process, however, reveals that other strategies can also be identified.

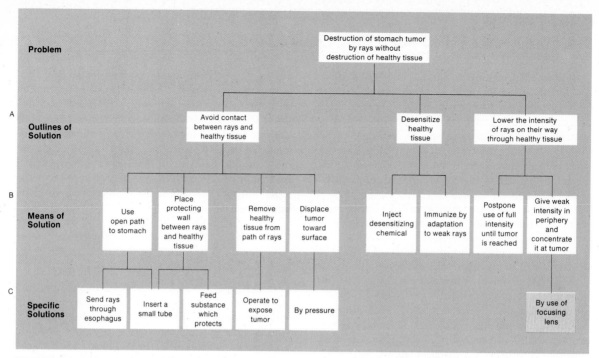

Figure 6.2 A diagram of the attempts made by one subject to solve the problem posed by Duncker. Note that the subject's thoughts (spoken aloud, as Duncker requested) can be interpreted in terms of a hierarchy—from extremely general syntheses at the top to highly specific analyses at the bottom. The technique of requiring a subject to "think out loud" has since been used repeatedly in studies of problem solving. It is a method that you can use with yourself as subject, with the aid of a tape recorder or pencil and paper. (After Duncker, 1945.)

HYPOTHESIS TESTING Hypothesis testing is a strategy that is commonly used by scientists to solve problems. It involves the formulation and testing of ideas about the manner in which a goal can be reached. For instance, if our goal is travel to a friend's house and the problem is that our car is not running, we may generate several possible hypotheses to surmount the barrier—call a taxi, borrow a car, walk to our friend's home, and so on. As we generate each of these possible solutions, we test it in our mind or in reality—we have no money for a cab, no one's car is available to borrow, it is too cold to walk to our friend's home. We continue to develop and test hypotheses about how to solve our problem until an acceptable solution is reached.

Edward Tolman (1948) and David Krech (1932), two early formulators of **hypothesis-testing theory,** showed that in problem-solving or learning situations even rats often act as if they are testing hypotheses. In one set of experiments Krech used a maze like the one shown in Figure 6.3, in which two alleys were equipped with lights that the experimenter could turn on and off. At each choice point in the maze, the rat could turn either right or left and toward an alley that was either lighted or dark. Although Krech adjusted the apparatus from trial

to trial so that left-right and dark-light cues did not always lead to the end of the maze, the rats behaved as though they were testing a series of hypotheses. First, they might choose mostly left turns; when that did not work, they might choose mostly right turns; when that did not work, they might choose only lighted alleys; and so on.

Later investigators have generally accepted the notion that problem solving involves the use of hypotheses and have tried to specify more precisely how hypotheses are selected and how they are related to each other in complex tasks like playing checkers or solving problems in logic, which involve numerous interrelated hypotheses. In Krech's maze there were only a few possible hypotheses, because a turn at each point of choice could only be toward the right or left and toward a lighted or dark alley. But a checkers player about to begin a game could never even consider all the 10^{40} play sequences (hypotheses) that are possible during the course of a game of checkers. Even if a player could evaluate three hypotheses every micromillisecond (one millionth of one thousandth of a second), it would take 10^{21} (one billion trillion) centuries to consider all the alternatives (Samuel, 1959). Clearly, the way the checkers player conceptualizes the play sequences

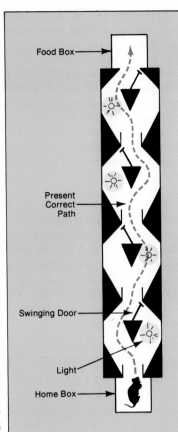

Figure 6.3 The maze used by Krech. At each of the four choice points (triangular blocks) a rat could take either the left or the right path, one of which was lighted and the other not. Because the lights and the swinging doors were changed from trial to trial, the rat could not find a single solution that would reliably lead to the food. The rat would try one possible solution over several trials—for example, choosing the right-hand paths—and then reject it for another possibility until it successfully navigated the maze. (After Krech, 1932.)

Food Box

Present Correct Path

Swinging Door

Light

Home Box

and chooses one or another must involve some general strategy that allows many hypotheses to be discarded at a glance.

HEURISTICS AND ALGORITHMS In the 1950s Allen Newell, J. C. Shaw, and Herbert Simon (1958) developed a computer model of problem solving; it was a computer program called the **General Problem Solver** (GPS) that has since solved diverse problems in logic, algebra, and chess. In part, the program was developed to show more precisely how people use hypotheses. The basic premise of the GPS program is that all goal-directed thinking is influenced by a small number of procedures called heuristics.

A **heuristic** is any strategy for discovery or investigation; it may be thought of as any rule of thumb that provides a general direction for solving problems. Heuristic strategies rely on familiarity with

the task or some parts of it. While a heuristic approach does not guarantee that one will solve a problem, it can increase the possibility of success. For example, a beekeeper's problem may be to remove honey from a hive without being stung. A heuristic strategy, based on the beekeeper's experience, produces several tactics for doing this: open the hive in the middle of the day when most bees are out foraging; wear white rather than colored clothing; select a windless, sunny day. While these rules of thumb do not ensure success, they do increase its probability. You may want to apply heuristic strategies to the problem posed in Figure 6.4.

Newell and his colleagues tried to identify the heuristics that people most commonly use in solving problems; then they programmed the computer to use them, either singly or in combination. They

Figure 6.4 Match your skill against that consummate expert in deductive problem solving, Sherlock Holmes. The case of Hilton and Elsie Cubitt began when client Hilton handed Sherlock the first hieroglyphic fragment. Several days later Sherlock received three more samples; shortly afterward the last example came. Sherlock rushed into action after seeing the last fragments. Why? What message did these last figures contain? How would you solve this puzzle of the "dancing men"? What heuristics, or rules of thumb, might be helpful? Check your solution with the one explained in the caption for Figure 6.17.

found that the one heuristic that the computer (and perhaps human problem solvers as well) relied on heavily is **subgoal analysis** (see Figure 6.5). In a subgoal analysis the General Problem Solver divides a difficult problem into a series of smaller problems, or subgoals, which it has a better chance of solving. Faced with a chess problem, for example, GPS first sees if the king is safe from attack (subgoal 1). If the king is in danger, GPS concentrates on moves that will protect it or remove it from the danger zone (subgoal 2). If the king is safe, GPS goes on to its next most important subgoal, which is to ensure that other pieces are not in danger (subgoal 3). If the other pieces do not need defending, GPS works through a series of offensive subgoals. In this way, GPS uses subgoal analysis to divide a difficult problem—how to win the game—into a number of related subproblems, each of which constitutes a problem in its own right.

Figure 6.5 Subgoal analysis. The overall problem—putting the opponent's king in checkmate—is divided into a series of smaller, more manageable goals. Each subgoal has its own heuristic or strategy which, if followed, can increase (but not guarantee) the probability of success. Here such analysis indicates that what is needed is the defensive strategy of advancing a pawn to block the opponent's bishop from seizing the knight.

Subgoal I—be sure king is safe; it's OK.

Subgoal II—protect king; not necessary now.

Subgoal III—be sure other pieces safe; Oops, his bishop threatens my knight.

Subgoal IV—correct III. I'll move this pawn to stop his bishop.

Subgoal V—gain control of central regions; I'll keep this in mind . . . .

Heuristics can be contrasted with another problem-solving method called algorithmics. An **algorithm** is a precisely stated set of rules that works for solving all instances of a particular type of problem. For example, the rules for long division or subtraction work for all division and subtraction problems regardless of the particular numbers that compose the problems; these rules ensure "success" if they are followed (see Figure 6.6). Though it is sometimes possible to solve a long-division or subtraction problem with a heuristic short cut, following the longer algorithmic procedure will produce more consistent success.

It is not always practical to use algorithms, because some problems have more possible solutions than can reasonably be tested in a short span of time. For instance, the algorithmic checkers player would have 10^{40} possible combinations of moves to evaluate, and a chess player would have some 10^{120} play sequences to consider. Presumably, the only way to play chess or checkers successfully is to use heuristic strategies.

LEARNING TO LEARN Problem-solving strategies, like those described above, are learned when an organism is exposed repeatedly to the same types of problems. Harry Harlow has called the acquisition of strategies of this sort **learning to learn.**

Harlow (1949) gave monkeys the problem of finding a raisin that had been placed under one of two lids or cups. In one version of the task, a monkey was first presented with one red lid and one green lid, with the raisin always placed under the green lid. The experimenter kept changing the position of the two lids, so the monkey was forced, after several tries, to learn that color and not position was the important cue for finding the raisin. After the monkey had mastered this problem, Harlow switched to triangular and circular lids, but continued to change the position of the lid with the raisin under it. As before, it took several tries for the monkey to realize that the shape of the lid and not its position or color provided the cues for solving the problem (see Figure 6.7). After doing hundreds of problems like these, in which the significant characteristics of the lids were changed for each problem, the monkeys learned that the appearance of the lids, not their position, was always the key to the solution. They also learned that each new problem was completely independent of the previous ones; although a particular shape or

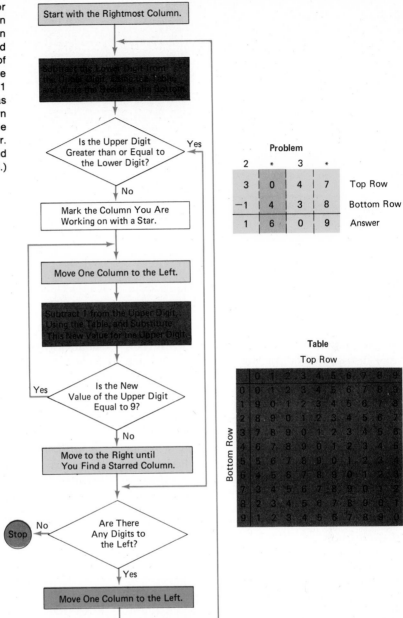

Figure 6.6 An algorithm for subtraction of whole numbers. An infinite number of subtraction problems can be correctly solved by following this precise set of rules. To use the algorithm to solve the sample problem, begin at step 1 and continue down the chart, as directed. Try making up your own subtraction problem and using the algorithm to get the answer. (Adapted from Lewis and Papadimitriou, 1978.)

color may have been rewarded in past problems, this was irrelevant to the new ones. Eventually, they could solve these problems with, at most, one error; they had learned a strategy of ignoring position and paying attention only to the characteristics of the lids.

Harlow and Margaret Harlow (1949) called this strategy a **learning set** and suggested that learning sets provide an organizing principle for higher mental processes. They regarded a learning set as a pattern of responses that develops in response to a particular problem situation. The learning set does not provide the specific answer to a problem, but it does enable the organism to search efficiently for a correct solution. Learning sets, they concluded, are built up as we gain experience with the environment. As experience increases, we learn to discard inefficient and unproductive strategies in favor of strategies that work well. Eventually, we learn to combine simple learning sets into complex patterns. According to Harlow and Harlow, the development and use of learning sets is actually a process of learning how to think: "Thinking does not develop spontaneously as an expression of innate abilities; it is the end result of a long learning process" (1949, p. 6). Without this ability to use

Figure 6.7 Learning to learn. The monkey is first presented with two differently shaped objects, under one of which he will always find food. Over subsequent trials the position of the rewarded object is shifted so that the monkey must learn that shape, not position, is the cue for reward. New problems with different objects which required the same discrimination between shape and position were then presented. At first learning was slow, but as more and more problems of the same type were solved, the monkeys' behavior became increasingly efficient. (After Harlow and Harlow, 1949.)

experience to develop more efficient learning strategies, we would be limited to the relatively slow trial-and-error method.

We should keep in mind that Harlow's studies of the learning to learn process differ in several ways from insight studies. In Harlow's experiments, a very specific strategy was learned and transferred to conceptually identical problems. In contrast, in the insight experiments conducted by Birch, the animals were provided with general knowledge about sticks that contributed to a creative solution to a novel problem. Although both learning sets and insight are related to past experience, learning to learn is a gradual process, one based on knowledge that is closely related to the specific problem, while insight seems to occur suddenly and without previous direct experience with the specific problem situation.

Learning to learn forms the basis for hypothesis testing, heuristics, algorithmics, and other problem-solving strategies. That is, the more familiar each of these strategies becomes, the more easily and efficiently it can be used to solve problems. Sometimes, however, a high degree of competence in a particular strategy can actually interfere with efficient problem solving because it may prevent us from seeing a simpler route around a barrier to a goal.

Psychologists have long recognized the importance of **transfer of training** in problem solving and learning. Transfer of training occurs when something learned in performing one task affects an organism's performance on a second task. In **positive transfer** the solution of one problem facilitates a subject's performance on a subsequent problem, as shown in Harlow's experiments. For instance, someone who has learned to play the clarinet well usually has a relatively easy time learning to play the saxophone, because it is possible to transfer

clarinet-playing skill to saxophone playing. In **negative transfer** the solution to one problem interferes with the solution to a second problem. For instance, the clarinet player may find that the motions learned while playing the clarinet actually make it more difficult to learn to play the guitar.

IMPEDIMENTS TO PROBLEM SOLVING

There are three major factors that can produce negative transfer or otherwise interfere with successful problem solving. Two—fixation and learned helplessness—are related to past experience. The third—the emotional or motivational state of the problem solver—is related more closely to the immediate problem-solving situation.

FIXATION Sometimes we automatically apply a strategy that is inappropriate to the problem at hand and rigidly cling to it, despite its lack of utility. This tendency is known as **fixation,** and it can powerfully inhibit or prevent successful problem solving.

How a simple problem can be made difficult by a perceptual fixation was described by Martin Scheerer (1963). He presented subjects with nine dots arranged in a square (see Figure 6.8A) and asked them to connect all the dots by drawing four straight lines without lifting the pencil from the paper. Most subjects perceived the nine dots as a square and assumed that the pencil lines had to be drawn within the boundaries of the square. Actually, the only way to solve the problem is to draw

Figure 6.8 Two mind-teasers designed by Martin Scheerer (1963). (A) Nine dots are arranged in a square. The problem is to connect them by drawing four continuous straight lines without lifting pencil from paper. (B) Six matches must be assembled to form four congruent equilateral triangles each side of which is equal to the length of the matches. (If you don't have matches, any six objects equal in length will do.) Check your answers with those given in Figure 6.9b.

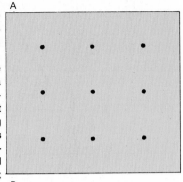

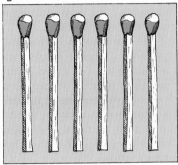

lines that extend beyond the perceptual boundaries of the square (see Figure 6.9A). Thus, subjects who fixated on the dots as representing a square found that this limited frame or reference led to a faulty assumption about the rules and blocked their ability to solve the problem.

Research by Abraham Luchins (1946) demonstrated how strong the fixation of newly acquired habits or sets can be. Luchins gave his subjects—thousands of them, under many different conditions—a series of six arithmetic problems (Figure 6.10). All but one of the problems could be solved most simply in the same way: Fill Jar B and dump its contents into another container, then use Jar A once and Jar C twice to bail out the extra water. This method can be stated as a formula: B − A − 2C.

What about the sixth problem? Luchins found that almost all the subjects could solve this problem if they had not already fixated on the set that developed from solving the other five problems. Roughly two-thirds of the subjects who had solved the first five problems persisted in using the B − A − 2C formula although it was inappropriate for the sixth problem. Their fixation was so strong that many either got the wrong answer and gave up or staunchly maintained that the formula did work,

insisting that 76 − 28 − 3 − 3 equals 25.

Another type of fixation involves the inability to use a familiar object in an unfamiliar way. Duncker termed this hindrance **functional fixedness** and demonstrated it by the candle problem shown in the photograph on page 137. A subject was given a box of candles, matches, tacks, and string and asked to mount a candle vertically on a wooden wall using any of the objects available. The candles and matches were given to the subject in their boxes, which emphasized the boxes as containers and so encouraged the problem solver to fix upon this familiar function. Thus the problem solver might easily overlook another possible function of the boxes: they could be used as candleholders.

Duncker's concept of functional fixedness was further explored by H. G. Birch and H. S. Rabinowitz (1951). These researchers used the "two-string" problem. Two cords were suspended from the ceiling, and the subject's task was to tie the cords together. However, the cords were set up far enough apart that the subject could not reach one while holding onto the other. The solution to the problem required tying a weight to the end of one of the cords, then swinging it like a pendulum until it could be caught while the subject held the other cord. In the experimental room Birch and Rabinowitz placed two objects that could be used as weights: a switch and a relay. The subjects were divided into three groups. Group S was given a pretest problem that involved wiring the switch into an electrical circuit, thus "fixing" its function as an electrical switch; Group R was also given a pretest problem, this one requiring the use of the relay as an electrical relay; and a control group was given no prior experience with the two objects. After the pretest period the subjects were presented with the "two-string" problem, and the experimenters observed whether the subjects used the relay or the switch to solve the problem. They found that all the subjects in Group R—that is, those subjects who had solved their pretest problem by using a relay—selected the switch to create a pendulum. In contrast, most of the subjects in Group S selected the relay. Subjects in the control group were equally likely to use the switch or the relay. From these results it is clear that subjects displayed functional fixedness; their prior experience with either of the weighted objects "set" them to see those objects in a certain way, and thus interfered with their ability to assign the new function of "pendulum weight" to the objects.

All types of fixation demonstrate essentially the

Figure 6.9 Solutions to the mind-teasers in Figure 6.8. The principal impediment in both of these problems is perceptual fixation. (A) The dot problem is solved by extending the lines beyond the dots; most people assume that they must stay within the perceived square structure. (B) The match problem is solved by building a three-dimensional pyramid; most people assume that the matches must lie flat, as they were first perceived.

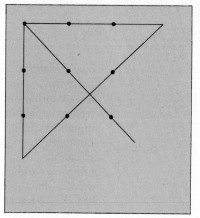
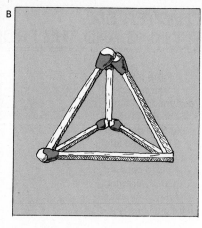

same phenomenon: counterproductive behavior results when a problem solver inappropriately transfers previously acquired knowledge to a new situation or when previous knowledge prevents the problem solver from finding an obvious solution because familiar items have to be viewed in a novel manner. For further discussion of the importance of flexibility in problem solving, see the accompanying special feature on pages 138–139.

LEARNED HELPLESSNESS

Learned helplessness is an interesting example of the negative effects of previous experience. This is a condition in which an organism that has previously been unable to avoid some kind of trauma (a painful or otherwise unpleasant experience) passively accepts the trauma in the future, even when escape is possible. Martin Seligman (1975) described this type of behavior in dogs that were exposed to inescapable electric shock in a Pavlovian conditioning situation. When these same dogs were placed in a box and given the opportunity to learn to avoid shock by crossing a barrier, they did not do so. Instead, they exhibited learned helplessness—a passive acceptance of shock with no attempt to escape.

This same pattern of behavior was demonstrated in human subjects (Miller and Seligman, 1975). Three groups were exposed to an escapable loud noise, an inescapable loud noise, or no loud noise. They were then given a simple card-sorting task in which their successes and failures were prearranged by the experimenters. When those subjects who had been helpless to escape the noise were asked how they thought they would perform on the next trial of the task, they made their estimates without reference to their performance on the last trial. It was as though these subjects did not believe that the outcome of the task was under their control. In contrast, those subjects who had been able to escape

the noise by altering their behavior varied their estimates of the next trial depending on the last trial's success or failure.

Thus it seemed to Miller and Seligman that the experience of being helpless in a situation could have a negative effect on future problem solving. From these results one can speculate that individuals who have been raised in environments in which the relationship between what they do and what happens to them is ambiguous may later have difficulty learning that their behavior can change their situations.

Figure 6.10 Luchins' classic demonstration of set in problem solving. In each of the problems in this series you must work out how you could measure out the quantities of liquid indicated on the right by using jars with the capacities shown on the left. Try the series yourself before reading on. After solving the first five problems, nearly two-thirds of Luchins' subjects were unable to solve the sixth. The sixth problem actually requires a simpler strategy than the first five, and it would be easily solved were it not for the set established by the first five.

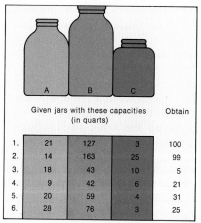

	A	B	C	Obtain
	Given jars with these capacities (in quarts)			Obtain
1.	21	127	3	100
2.	14	163	25	99
3.	18	43	10	5
4.	9	42	6	21
5.	20	59	4	31
6.	28	76	3	25

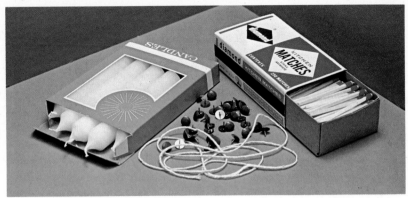

A problem used by Duncker to demonstrate functional fixedness: He gave subjects the materials shown and asked them to mount a candle on a wall so that it could be used to give light. Try to solve the problem yourself. (The use of the term "functional fixedness" gives you a clue to the solution of the problem that Duncker's subjects did not have.) The solution is given in Figure 6.17.

MOTIVATIONAL LEVEL The effects of past experience on problem solving may often be long-lived and stable. In contrast, the emotional and motivational states of the problem solver are relatively short-term. The effect of motivation on problem solving should be familiar to most college students. Most of us have had the experience of performing poorly on a test because we were not motivated to study for it. The opposite experience is also common: we have been so hypermotivated to prepare for a test that it actually interfered with our test performance. A number of studies have validated these experiences. Research has indicated that there is an optimal motivational level for efficient problem solving and that the optimal level appears to vary with the type of problem.

One experiment performed by Birch (1945) investigated the role of motivation in the problem-solving behavior of chimpanzees. Birch varied his subjects' motivational levels by depriving them of food for from two to forty-eight hours. The task, using sticks as tools to reach food, was similar to the one in Köhler's insight experiments. Birch found that the most efficient problem-solving behavior was demonstrated by the subjects that were deprived of food for a moderate amount of time—that is, by those subjects who had developed moderate motivational levels. Animals in a low-motivation condition (those who were not especially hungry) were easily diverted from the task, as they were not strongly interested in obtaining food. Animals in a high-motivation condition (those who were extremely hungry) also had difficulty in solving the problem, although the difficulty was of a different type. They concentrated upon the goal—food—to the extent of ignoring the objects that would enable them to reach the food. They also had a variety of emotional responses—frustration, tantrums, screaming, and so on—that interfered with problem solving. From these results, it appeared to Birch that very high motivation levels tend to produce fixation on unsuccessful strategies and to obstruct

the flexibility necessary for solutions based on insight.

Motivational effects are not restricted to "insight" problems. Research has also shown that performance on reaction-time tasks, maze learning, and a variety of other problem-solving tasks is affected by the level of motivation. At low levels of motivational arousal, performance is poor; as motivation increases, performance improves, but only up to a point. After a certain point, called the **optimal arousal level,** further increases in motivation cause performance to deteriorate. This relationship, diagrammed in Figure 6.11, is often called the **Yerkes-Dodson law,** after the two psychologists who first wrote about it in 1908. The results obtained by

Figure 6.11 The relationship between motivational arousal and the effectiveness of performance may be represented as an inverted "U." For a given task there is an optimal amount of arousal; a greater or a lesser degree of activation will result in less efficient behavior. This result is known as the Yerkes-Dodson law. The peak of the curve varies with the nature of the task: Optimal arousal for a complex, intricate task such as repairing an electron microscope may be far below the optimal arousal for a simple physical task like washing dishes. (After Yerkes and Dodson, 1908.)

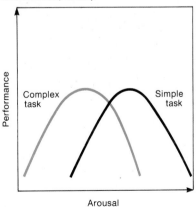

Flexibility and Creative Thinking

An anecdote that circulated during World War II had to do with a bomber whose pilot, flying home from a mission, found the controls of his plane becoming less and less responsive. The problem was traced to a leak in the aircraft's hydraulic system. The plane carried no spare hydraulic fluid. But someone managed to come up with a substitute in time to prevent a crash: the members of the crew refilled the system with their urine. Not an elegant solution, perhaps, but more than adequate under the circumstances—and a good example of flexible, creative thinking at its most practical.

Just what is "creative" thinking? Where does it originate? How does it work? The observation has been made more than once that creativity involves an ability to see con-

nections between seemingly unrelated things. It might not have occurred to many intelligent people to use urine in a hydraulic system, for instance, because the two things would normally be thought of (if at all) in entirely different contexts. A number of psychologists, noting that some individuals are more prone to rigidity of thought than others, have suggested that flexible thinking and creativity go together.

To examine this possibility, psychologists have developed a variety of "creativity tests" with the aim of measuring flexibility, posing such unconventional questions as, "How many uses can you find for a bicycle tire?" One test of this sort, the Remote Associates Test, focuses on the capacity to perceive connections between words. Studies by Sarnoff Mednick and

Martha Mednick, the originators of the Remote Associates Test (1961), and Arthur Staats (1957) have revealed some correlation between high scores on the test and creativity in other areas. In one study, for example, architects rated as highly creative by their peers turned out to have higher scores than architects who had not been rated as especially creative. Granted that the significance of an ability to make remote associations between words is not at all clear—and granted, too, that standardized tests are a less than ideal way to measure something as unstandard as creativity—it seems reasonable to conclude that highly creative people tend to be more flexible than most in their associative skills.

Vertical Thinking
Taking the flexibility argument

Creativity may be seen as the ability to see things in another way than is usual. These children have used a sheet in a creative manner.

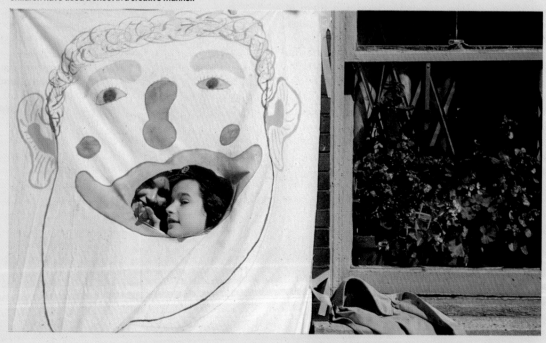

a step further, Edward de Bono in his book *New Think* (1967) differentiates between two general types of thinking, referring to them as ''vertical'' and ''lateral'' thinking. Vertical thinking is uncreative and not very flexible—roughly the equivalent of what we call logic. De Bono readily concedes, of course, that logic is essential to the solution of many problems. But it can also lead to ingrained and often mechanical patterns of thinking that hinder, rather than aid, our ability to size up new situations. An interesting test of analytical habits involves four cards like those shown in the accompanying figure. Each of them has a circle on one side and a triangle on the other; every circle and triangle is either red or blue. The problem is to find out whether or not all cards with a red triangle on one side have a blue circle on the other. Which of the cards do you need to turn over to determine the answer?

Most people give one of two answers: they say that you need to turn over only the card with the red triangle showing; or they say that you need to turn over the cards showing the red triangle and the blue circle. Both answers are wrong. The correct answer is that you must turn over the cards showing the red triangle and the red circle. What is intriguing about this problem is not only that most people reach a logically incorrect answer (and usually feel quite confident as they do so) but also that the way they reach it seems to be firmly ingrained. Most people have difficulty understanding why the correct solution should be to turn over both the red-triangle and the red-circle cards. An especially frequent source of error is the supposition that if all the cards with red triangles on one side

have blue circles on the other, then all the cards with blue circles on one side must have red triangles on the other—an assumption that arises only from habitual patterns of thinking, not from the information given with the problem.

In de Bono's view, vertical thinking is based on such assumptions—dominant ideas, as he calls them, to which people believe they must adhere faithfully. He offers a portrait of the ultimate vertical thinker. A man has cut a small opening in the door to save himself the trouble of opening it every time his cat wants to come in or go out—logical enough. Now the cat has had a kitten. The man carries his dominant idea a step further and cuts a second, smaller opening in the door.

Lateral Thinking

It is the essence of de Bono's lateral thinking to identify and

reduce the dominance of fixed ideas, and to try instead to observe things from as many viewpoints as possible. De Bono draws an analogy between the two types of thinking and the digging of holes:

> Logic is the tool that is used to dig holes deeper and bigger, to make them altogether better holes. But if the hole is in the wrong place, then no amount of improvement is going to put it in the right place. No matter how obvious this may seem to every digger, it is still easier to go on digging in the same place than to start all over again in a new place. Vertical thinking is digging the same hole deeper; lateral thinking is trying again elsewhere. (1967)

The ability to ''try again elsewhere'' resulted in one of the landmarks of medical history, when Edward Jenner decided to give up trying to figure out why people got smallpox and concentrate on a different question—why dairy maids didn't get it. As he learned, they usually contracted a harmless case of cowpox, which apparently made them immune to the deadly smallpox—a discovery that led Jenner to the concept of vaccination, which has resulted in the virtual eradication of the disease.

Despite such examples of the value of lateral thinking, vertical thinking is so deeply entrenched in our culture that to question it is to risk being considered odd, or even somehow subversive. De Bono argues that education, in particular, almost invariably stresses vertical thinking at the expense of lateral abilities, leaving the latter largely untapped and undeveloped. Creativity thus continues to be viewed too often as a rare and mysterious gift, rather than as part of the standard equipment of the human mind.

Birch fit well into the relationship between level of motivation and problem-solving behavior developed by Robert Yerkes and J. D. Dodson.

A PROBLEM TO SOLVE

Let us see now if we can apply our knowledge of problem solving to solving an actual problem. Work on the problem presented below and keep in mind the general strategies of problem solving, as well as the impediments, so that you can appreciate your own attempts to reach a solution.

A bear, starting from point P, walked one mile due south. Then he changed direction and walked one mile due east. Then he turned again to the left and walked one mile due north, and arrived exactly at the point P he started from. What color was the bear? (Polya, 1975)

At first glance, this may seem to be a ridiculous problem, but don't give up. If you cannot reach a solution, use the hints below. Seriously consider each hint before you go on to the next.

1. What colors can bears be?
2. In which parts of the world do bears of each color live?
3. Where in the world could a bear walk three miles in the manner described and return to its starting point?

Here is the solution: the bear is white. Point P must be the North Pole—the only place on the globe where it is possible to walk due south, then due east, then due north, and end up at the starting point (the South Pole is eliminated by question 2, because no bears live there). Once you know this, you can deduce that the bear must be white, since all polar bears are white.

This problem illustrates several aspects of the problem-solving process: each hint is a *subgoal* that will be of use to direct the problem solver's efforts in the right direction. Most people fall into the perceptual trap of envisioning the bear on a flat plain, in which case it is impossible to explain how the bear could make its journey. If you avoid this perceptual *fixation* by viewing the world as a globe, it becomes relatively easy to locate the bear's habitat. In the

process of reaching this conclusion, you may have tested and discarded a number of alternative *hypotheses*—for instance, that the bear was on a treadmill. You may well have reached the correct solution with a sudden flash of *insight* when you reorganized your perception of the world from a flat map to a spherical globe. You probably used your past *experience* with the world, applying *heuristics* to limit the number of possible alternatives and refining each solution until you could test its correctness.

D ECISION MAKING

Making the right decisions is fundamental to the problem-solving process. In Duncker's tumor-radiation problem cited earlier, for instance, subjects typically derived several alternative solutions and then decided that one of those solutions was the best possible answer. Thus, it is conceivable that a subject could have arrived at the correct solution but failed to recognize it and so decided to discard it. It is not uncommon, however, for people to recognize a solution as correct and yet to reject that solution. Our discussion of problem-solving strategies, aids, and impediments has not explained why people do not always make the most rational decisions, even when all the relevant information is available to them.

A number of studies have shown that people will often ignore important information when making decisions. For instance, research on consumer behavior indicates that too much information about price and quantity may confuse the shopper, sometimes leading to the purchase of relatively expensive items. Even when unit prices are posted below the shelf that holds a particular item, shoppers sometimes have difficulty in selecting the most economical product (Russo, Krieser, and Miyashita, 1975). People often make irrational decisions on more serious issues in their lives, too. For example, residents of flood-plain areas tend to ignore the hazards of their living sites, refusing to purchase flood insurance and rebuilding homes destroyed by flood in exactly the same locations (Slovic, Kunreuther, and White, 1974).

A great deal of research has been directed at decision making. Recent bibliographies have listed well over a thousand references to books and articles on this subject in business, government, ecology, laws, and, of course, psychology (Barron, 1974;

Kleiter, Gachowetz, and Huber, 1976). Particular attention has been devoted to analyzing the limitations of human decision making, the way people estimate their probability of success, and the role played by the expectations and behavior of the decision maker.

UTILITY AND PROBABILITY Suppose you are faced with the following decision: your friends are about to leave on a weekend skiing trip, but you have an exam scheduled for early Monday morning. You have already studied for the exam, but you are not sure how difficult it will be. At the same time, it is early in the ski season and you are not sure if there will be enough snow for good skiing. Should you go? According to psychologists, there are two sets of variables that will determine your decision. First, you will examine the utility of your options: How valuable is a weekend in the mountains versus a weekend in the library? Second, you will examine the probabilities involved: How likely is it that there will be enough snow, and what are the chances that your exam will be easy? Your decision will be based on your evaluation of these factors.

UTILITY Each decision we make entails a certain amount of risk; optimal decision making involves choosing the alternative with the least risk and the most gain. A number of studies have shown that our perception of risk depends on our estimate of the relative **utility** of the various possible results of a choice. That is, we place a value on our choices according to how useful we think they may be.

In relatively simple decision making, we can categorize the potential results as shown in Figure 6.12. In this decision matrix, there are four possible results related to the decision of the doctor and the condition of the patient. If the doctor judged the patient to be alive when he was dead, this would be called a "false alarm"; if the patient were alive, the doctor's decision would be a "hit." If the doctor judged the patient to be dead when he was indeed dead, this would be a "correct rejection"; if the patient were alive, her judgment would be a "miss." In this situation, the consequences of a miss would be very severe—the death of the patient—while the consequences of a false alarm would be far less serious. Therefore, the doctor's perception of the utility of her choices would probably bias her toward the decision that posed the lesser risk—that is, behaving as though the patient were still alive even when most of the physiological signs indicated otherwise.

PROBABILITY ESTIMATES We tend to display certain consistent errors when we estimate the **probability** of events in specific situations. Often, our estimates are very different from the rational estimates that can be derived from mathematical calculations (see Figure 6.13). For instance, we can calculate that the probability of the number 13 coming up on a roulette wheel is 1 in 38. However, even when we are aware of this probability, we often commit the "gambler's fallacy" (mentioned in Chapter 2)—that is, many of us assume that if 13 has not come up on the wheel after numerous spins, then the "law of averages" makes it likely that 13 will come up soon. Of course, this fallacy ignores the mathematical fact that each spin of the wheel is completely independent of the last spin. The wheel has no memory, and the probability of any number coming up will not be affected by the numbers that

A   Dead   IN ACTUAL FACT   Alive

DECISION

"He's Dead"

Correct Rejection   HE'S DEAD.   Miss   HE'S DEAD.

"He's Alive"

False Alarm   HE'S ALIVE!   Hit   HE'S ALIVE!

Figure 6.12 A matrix of possible outcomes in deciding whether a patient is dead or alive. To maximize chances for a successful solution, the doctor must estimate the utility of her possible choices. If she decides that the patient is dead when he is really alive (Miss), the consequences are obviously more severe than if she incorrectly decides that he is alive (False Alarm). Thus in making her decision the doctor relies on selection of the course of action that will potentially be more useful to the patient.

Figure 6.13 An exaggerated probability error (see below). While this example is so extreme as to be funny, probability errors are commonly made and affect our decision-making success.

when we use the most sophisticated problem-solving strategies, we are still subject to the judgmental biases that are part of being human (see Figure 6.14).

Some of these biases have been studied in jury situations. Clyde Hendrick and David Shaffer (1975) reported that jurors tend to infer guilt when a defendant pleads the Fifth Amendment, refusing to testify for fear of self-incrimination. Other research on jurors' behavior has demonstrated that judgments of guilt or innocence are often based on such factors as the way the defendant dresses, the order in which evidence is presented, and how the jurors perceive the character of the defendant. Thus, there are many psychological variables that affect judgments and choices. It is important that we recognize and understand that such variables influence our decision making so that we may make our choices more positive and logical. There is evidence that behavioral decision theory is beginning to have an impact on industrial, medical, military, and meteorological decision making (Slovic, Fischhoff, and Lichtenstein, 1977).

have come up in the last hundred, or even thousand, spins, unless the wheel is rigged.

We tend to overestimate low-probability events and underestimate high-probability events. For instance, though there is a much greater chance of drowning in the sea than of being attacked by a shark, most people experience far more concern about the shark. In the same way, we know that, statistically, airplane travel is considerably safer than journeys by car, but many people think that a plane trip is more dangerous. Conversely, we tend to underestimate some high-probability events. For example, when a hurricane is forecast, many people in the area refuse to leave their homes because they make poor estimates about the likelihood that the storm will affect them.

DECISION MAKING AND THE FUTURE In a recent review of behavioral decision theory, Paul Slovic, Baruch Fischhoff, and Sarah Lichtenstein (1977) emphasized the importance of making rational choices in our complex, modern world. We cannot rely solely on habit or instinct to make our decisions, and we rarely have the time for trial-and-error approaches to our problems. However, even

COMPUTER MODELS OF THINKING

The first "generation" of modern digital computers, developed about forty years ago, were designed to aid human problem solving. At that time, scientists were concerned with transforming the manual desk calculator into a fully automatic machine that could store information and make mathematical calculations quickly and accurately. These machines were called "computers" because their job was, in fact, to compute mathematical tables.

In the second generation, the computer's "memory" capacity was expanded so that it could operate as a giant file cabinet, holding vast amounts of information that could be recycled on command. In the third generation, computers were equipped with devices analogous to human sense organs; now the computer could obtain its data directly from the external environment via a battery of sensors. Furthermore, computers could pass on their information to a human operator directly, with the use of some sort of visual display. Thus we have computers that can obtain their own information, transform and sort data, and present facts to a human operator in a variety of forms (Miller, 1967). Though today's computers can appropria-

© 1970 United Feature Syndicate, Inc.

Next time, Snoopy should:

1. thoroughly canvass a wide range of alternative courses of action;
2. survey the full range of objectives to be fulfilled and the values implicated by the choice;
3. carefully weigh whatever he knows about the costs and risks of negative consequences, as well as the positive consequences, that could flow from each alternative;
4. intensively search for new information relevant to further evaluation of the alternatives;
5. correctly assimilate and take account of any new information or expert judgment to which he is exposed, even when the information or judgment does not support the course of action he initially prefers;
6. reexamine the positive and negative consequences of all known alternatives, including those originally regarded as unacceptable, before making a final choice;
7. make detailed provisions for implementing or executing the chosen course of action, with special attention to contingency plans that might be required if various known risks were to materialize.

Figure 6.14 Snoopy needs some help, and that's what Irving Janis and Leon Mann (1977) provide. The suggestions they offer for rational decision making were synthesized from a large body of literature on effective decision making. Notice how their suggestions incorporate the notions of utility and probability. But think, too, of the rational difficulties one might encounter at each step and of any not-so-rational factors that might interfere with sound decision making.

tely be called "information-processing machines," since they do far more than simply compute, are they also "thinking machines"?

Computers can now perform in ways that astound all but the most sophisticated of computer specialists; however, we cannot say that computers "think" in the same sense that humans think. In order to design a computer that mimics human thought processes, we would require a far better understanding of human thinking than we actually have. We know that computers can outperform humans in solving many types of problems, especially reproductive ones; at the same time, there are some aspects of human cognitive performance that cannot be matched by a computer—for instance, computers will generally lose a chess match with a master chess player.

Cognitive psychologists have added a function to the computer's original problem-solving role: they now look to the computer as a model and standard of comparison for human cognitive processes. In fact, much of the specialist's vocabulary for human problem solving is derived from computer terminology: information processing, input and output, programs, and so on. In the attempt to design computer programs that match human capacities, scientists hope to gain some insight into human thinking. They are taking two approaches in their comparison of human and mechanical information processing: computer simulation and artificial-intelligence research.

COMPUTER SIMULATION AND ARTIFICIAL-INTELLIGENCE RESEARCH

In **computer simulation,** psychologists construct computer programs that act as much like people as possible. The purpose of this is to find precise explanations of particular processes and to make predictions that can be tested experimentally with human subjects. The computer program is, in fact, the theory, and it is an especially clear form of theory: each logical step is completely specified, and precise predictions can be made by running the program under various conditions to see what it does. As a theory, the program predicts that humans will act just as *it* does. Such predictions are tested by observing the behavior of human subjects as they perform under the same conditions as specified in the program.

In the second approach, called **artificial-intelligence (AI) research,** scientists and engineers attempt to build machines that perform human functions. However, they make no special effort to use the same processes as those found in humans. In fact, often their goal is to find novel methods that will enable machines to work better and faster than humans. For instance, AI researchers want to build a voice-operated typewriter that may, in some ways, replace and outperform a human secretary. They have no particular interest in making the machine work the way a human being works, as long as it performs efficiently. Although AI research may seem less relevant to the concerns of psychologists than does computer simulation, many programming techniques and mechanical devices invented by AI researchers have proved useful to simulation psychologists. For example, when an AI researcher programs a machine to perform an operation previously performed only by humans, simulation psychologists study the machine to try to gain insight into how humans function.

COMPARISONS BETWEEN COMPUTERS AND HUMAN BEINGS

A few complex computer programs serve as models of small facets of human cognition; for example, a program exists that can test the correctness of logical propositions better than the most outstanding mathematicians can. Computers can play a fairly skilled game of chess, as well as a variety of other games. In many ways, however, computers have failed to approach human abilities. For one thing, the capacity of human memory is far greater than the capacity of even the most impressive computer, and our ability to retrieve facts from memory has not been duplicated in computer programs.

There are other characteristics of human thinking that are not reproduced in the current generation of computers. First, computers are rigid (see Figure 6.15). They do not estimate or improvise as humans do. They are unbelievably single-minded and do not discover a solution to one kind of problem while searching for the solution to a different kind. This limitation seems to be caused, in part, by the sequential nature of computer programs; a computer solves problems by proceeding through a predetermined list of instructions in some sequence. Although high-level human cognitive processes also seem to be more or less sequential, they are built on a foundation of parallel processes. For instance, if we need a screwdriver but none is available, we will substitute makeshift tools—a dime, a knife blade, or a piece of stiff paper. After a little thought, we will reject some of the substitutes as unsuitable; we may then try others and either accept or reject them. The evaluation process is sequential and computerlike, but the creative or associative stage is not. Thus, computers are incapable of insight and creativity; while Köhler's chimpanzees employed insight to see that a stick could be used as a tool to reach food, a computer would be unable to make this novel connection unless it had been programmed to do so. The sudden reorganization of the elements of a problem, so common in human experience, cannot yet be accomplished by a computer. The number of associative links needed in a mind that provides creative solutions to new problems every day is astronomical—greater than anything we can imagine being put into a present-day computer's memory.

Second, computers are not emotional. We know that many human cognitive processes are influenced by emotions; as we have seen, motiviation, arousal, and anxiety play a role in problem solving. We work harder and faster when we want to meet an important deadline. We pay particular attention to novel, surprising, or dangerous stimuli, and we remember some things better than others because they are important to us. In addition, our

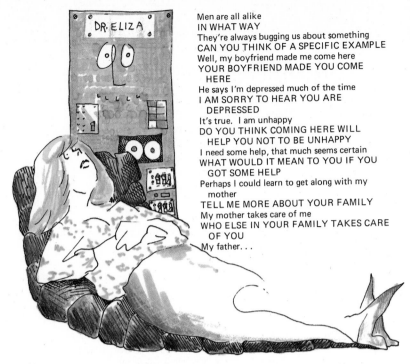

Men are all alike
IN WHAT WAY
They're always bugging us about something
CAN YOU THINK OF A SPECIFIC EXAMPLE
Well, my boyfriend made me come here
YOUR BOYFRIEND MADE YOU COME
    HERE
He says I'm depressed much of the time
I AM SORRY TO HEAR YOU ARE
    DEPRESSED
It's true. I am unhappy
DO YOU THINK COMING HERE WILL
    HELP YOU NOT TO BE UNHAPPY
I need some help, that much seems certain
WHAT WOULD IT MEAN TO YOU IF YOU
    GOT SOME HELP
Perhaps I could learn to get along with my
    mother
TELL ME MORE ABOUT YOUR FAMILY
My mother takes care of me
WHO ELSE IN YOUR FAMILY TAKES CARE
    OF YOU
My father...

Figure 6.15 Can a computer do personal problem solving? Joseph Weizenbaum's work suggests that it might help. He programmed a computer to act like a therapist, as this actual conversation illustrates. At first glance, ELIZA appears to be a good, nondirective therapist. But its effectiveness is limited. If the "client" suddenly shifted linguistic modes by using words symbolically, ELIZA could not follow suit. It would reply to the client's words but would actually miss their meaning. And if the client should utter a nonsensical sentence such as 'Please dance on a noun,' ELIZA would not recognize that as an absurdity and might instead respond, 'AND HOW DO YOU FEEL ABOUT NOUNS?' Thus computer thinking is constrained; unlike humans, computers cannot assume the perspective of another nor deal adequately with problems of meaning.   (After Weizenbaum, 1966.)

decision making is often biased by our emotions; we tend to make certain decisions with our "heart" rather than our "head," consistently overestimating or underestimating the probabilities of some events. In contrast, computer decisions are based solely on facts. Although rudimentary computer models of emotion and personality have been constructed, they are not very realistic or complete.

Third, computers have not yet been successfully programmed to view the world from a uniquely personal perspective. Endel Tulving (1972) has called this **episodic memory,** the memory for particular events in one's life as these were experienced from one's own point of view. This is in contrast to **semantic memory,** the recall of specific facts. A person can know that a canary is yellow, that the sun sets in the west, and that all humans are mortal; and a computer can "know" these facts too. But a person can also report on when and where canaries have been seen, how certain sunsets looked, and which emotions accompanied the death of a friend. There is no reason why a computer cannot be programmed to keep a record of its own dealings; in fact, many do this to some extent already. But the relationship between episodic and semantic memory in humans is not well understood, and some-

Figure 6.16 Despite their limitations, computers can do some remarkable things, as shown by this block-world of the computer program written by artificial intelligence researcher Terry Winograd. The pictures here were simulated on a high-resolution cathode-ray-tube screen connected to the computer, but the program could in principle be used to control a real robot. One major achievement of this program is its ability to understand and produce (via a computer-controlled typewriter) sentences that accurately describe its block-world. Note the difference in kind and precision of expression in the dialogue between Winograd and his computer and that discussed in Figure 6.15.   (After Winograd, 1974.)

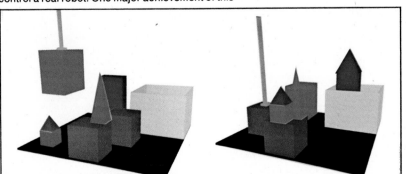

Will you please stack up both of the red blocks and either a green cube or a pyramid?
OK

Which cube is sitting on the table?
THE LARGE GREEN ONE WHICH SUPPORTS THE RED PYRAMID

Is there a large block behind a pyramid?
YES, THREE OF THEM: A LARGE RED ONE, A LARGE GREEN ONE AND THE BLUE ONE

Put a small one onto the green cube which supports a pyramid.
OK

thing like a "sense of identity" is even further from being included in a formal program. It will be some time before these human qualities will be simulated by a computer.

Fourth, computers do not develop or change themselves in dramatic ways, although some do learn a few things. Jean Piaget and other developmental psychologists argue that abstract thinking develops only after long experience with physical actions. If this is the case, can abstract thinking and, especially, cognitive development be simulated by a computer that can have no experience with actions, does not move around to get new perspectives on its environment, does not manipulate objects, and does not come into conflict with people whose perspectives differ from its own?

Finally, can a computer really understand anything? Artificial-intelligence researchers have had considerable difficulty in building a machine that can translate one human language into another, the way human translators do at the United Nations. After many failures they began to realize that the machine could not work effectively unless it understood the meaning of the message it was translating.

There is no way to translate from one language to another without understanding the message being transmitted. A language is more than a set of rules for combining words; it has subtleties of meaning and nuances of expression that are extremely complex, and an adequate translation of a language requires an understanding of what is being said.

Although no one knows at the moment how to solve the problems raised by human meaning, movements, and development, an artificial-intelligence researcher named Terry Winograd (1972) did develop an interesting computer program to control a robot. The program was meant to fit in with a television camera "eye" and a mechanical arm, thus creating a more realistic input-output system than had been seen in previous computer models of human behavior. A dialogue between Winograd and the program is shown in Figure 6.16 on page 145. Although not as emotional and complex as See-Threepio, the fictional computerized robot in the movie *Star Wars*, Winograd's program represents considerable progress. No doubt further progress will, indirectly at least, shed new light on the ways in which people think.

Figure 6.17 (A) Answer to the problem shown in Figure 6.4: "Having recognized . . . that the symbols stood for letters, and having applied the rules which guide us in all forms of writing, the solution was easy enough. The first message was so short that it was impossible to do more than say that the symbol ⅄ stood for E. As you are aware, E is the most common letter in the English Alphabet . . . [so] it was reasonable to set this down as E . . . in some cases, [this] figure was bearing a flag, but it was probable, from the way in which distributed, that they were used to break the sentence up into words. I accepted this as a hypothesis. . . . I waited for fresh material. . . . [Now] I got the two E's coming second and fourth in a word of five letters. It might be 'sever' or 'level' or 'never'. . . . The latter as a reply to an appeal is far the most probable. . . . Accepting it as correct, we are now able to say that the symbols ⅄ ⊣ Ɤ stand respectively for N, V and R." And so on. The last fragment was a threat of murder against Mrs. Cubitt: ELSIE. PREPARE TO MEET THY GOD." (A. Conan Doyle. *The Return of Sherlock Holmes,* "The Adventure of the Dancing Men." New York: Ballantine Books, © 1975.) (B) The answer to the problem shown in Figure 6.1. (C) The answer to the problem shown in the photograph on page 137.

Summary

1. All problem solving is based, to some extent, on past learning and memory. In explaining how we think, two major schools of psychology have differed in what they considered the most important aspects of the process of thought.

   A. The associationists emphasized the role of experience. In their view, thinking was hardly an organized process; it was regarded as a hit-or-miss application of old associations. These associations were presumed to be tested through some form of specific experience rather than by merely thinking about them. This view of problem solving was based largely on the research of Edward Thorndike.

   B. The cognitive psychologists, as represented by the Gestalt school, insisted that the mind contributes to problem solving by organizing and restructuring the problem-solving situation. Gestalt psychologists believed that a tentative solution to a problem appears to the thinker without much trial-and-error behavior.

   C. The **insight experience** occurs when the solution to a problem is discovered by a sudden perception. The research of Wolfgang Köhler supported the Gestalt view by discounting the role of trial-and-error behavior. The experiments of H. G. Birch suggested the importance of past experience in learning through insight. George Mandler postulated that the associationist and cognitive perspectives may work together to explain problem solving.

2. Problems can be categorized as to complexity according to whether they require reproductive or creative thinking. **Reproductive thinking** is the direct application of previous knowledge to a new problem. In **creative thinking,** previously learned rules are either unavailable or do not apply directly. Creative thinking is the kind of thinking that is least accessible to scientific analysis. People often act in creative ways, with little understanding or thought about how they accomplish these acts.

3. All problem situations have certain conceptual elements in common. In order to study problem solving, both the impediments presented by a particular problem and the strategies most appropriate for overcoming those impediments must be analyzed.

   A. Karl Duncker studied problem solving by presenting a subject with a complex problem and asking that the problem be thought through out loud. Duncker concluded that problem solving may be viewed as an ordered series of phases leading to a specific solution.

   B. Hypothesis testing involves the formulation and testing of ideas about the manner in which a goal can be reached. Edward Tolman and David Krechevsky, formulators of American **hypothesis-testing theory,** showed that rats often act as if they are testing hypotheses in problem-solving or learning situations. Investigators have generally accepted the notion that problem solving involves the use of hypotheses and have tried to specify more precisely how hypotheses are selected and how they are related to each other in complex tasks.

   C. It is often useful to apply strategies that enable one to discard many hypotheses at a glance. Two such strategies are heuristics and algorithms.

      1. The **General Problem Solver** is a computer model of problem solving. The premise of the General Problem Solver is that all goal-directed thinking is influenced by a small number of procedures called heuristics. A **heuristic** is any strategy that provides a general direction for solving problems. Heuristic strategies rely on familiarity with the task or some parts of it, and they can increase the possibility of success. The one heuristic strategy that a computer relies on heavily is **subgoal analysis,** by which a difficult problem is divided into a series of smaller problems.

      2. An **algorithm** is a precisely stated set of rules that works for all instances of a particular type of problem. It is not always practical to use algorithms because of the number of possible solutions that some problems have.

D. The acquisition of problem-solving strategies after repeated exposure to the same types of problems is called **learning to learn.**

1. A **learning set** is a pattern of responses that develops in response to a particular problem situation. Learning to learn forms the basis for other problem-solving strategies.

2. **Transfer of training** occurs when something learned on one task affects an organism's performance on a second task. In **positive transfer** the solution of one problem facilitates one's performance on a second problem; in **negative transfer** the solution to one problem interferes with finding a solution to the second.

4. There are three major factors that can produce negative transfer or otherwise interfere with successful problem solving.

A. **Fixation** occurs when a person automatically applies a strategy that is inappropriate to the problem at hand and rigidly clings to it. **Functional fixedness** is a type of fixation involving the inability to use a familiar object in an unfamiliar way.

B. **Learned helplessness** is a phenomenon in which an organism that has previously been unable to avoid some kind of trauma will passively accept the trauma in the future, even when escape from it is possible.

C. Research indicates that the optimal motivational level for efficient problem solving appears to vary with the type of problem. After the optimal arousal level is reached, further increases in arousal cause performance to deteriorate. This relationship is called the **Yerkes-Dodson law.**

5. Making the right decisions is fundamental to problem solving. Studies have shown that people often ignore important information when making decisions.

A. Researchers suggest that there are two sets of variables that determine a decision: the utility of the options and the probabilities involved.

1. Optimal decision making involves choosing the alternative with the least risk and the most gain. Our estimate of the **utility** of a choice is based on how useful we perceive it to be to us.

2. We tend to display certain consistent errors when we estimate the **probability** of events in specific situations. We tend to overestimate low-probability events and to underestimate high-probability events.

B. Even when we use the most sophisticated problem-solving strategies, we are still subject to judgmental biases. Some of these biases have been studied in jury situations.

6. Cognitive psychologists are using computers as a model and standard of comparison for human cognitive processes.

A. In **computer simulation,** psychologists construct computer programs that act as much like people as possible. The purpose of this is to find precise explanations of particular processes and to make predictions that can be tested experimentally with human subjects.

B. In **artificial-intelligence research,** scientists attempt to build machines that perform human functions (but that do not necessarily use the same processes as those found in humans).

C. Though computers can perform certain tasks better than humans, they do not match human capabilities in many other ways.

RECOMMENDED READINGS

ADAMS, J. L. *Conceptual Block-Busting.* San Francisco: Freeman, 1974. An entertaining analysis of problem-solving strategies that can be applied to everyday situations.

BRUNNER, JEROME S. *Beyond the Information Given.* New York: Norton, 1973. Selected papers by one of the most influential cognitive psychologists, including some of his papers on hypothesis theory and on modularization of skills.

LINDSAY, PETER H., AND DONALD A. NORMAN. *Human Information Processing: An Introduction to Psychol-* ogy. 2nd ed. New York: Academic Press, 1977. A thorough and easy-to-read introduction to psychology from an information-processing point of view.

NEWELL, ALLEN, AND HERBERT A. SIMON. *Human Problem Solving.* Englewood Cliffs, N. J.: Prentice-Hall, 1971. A good reasonable statement of the authors' thoughts on problem-solving research.

RAPHAEL, BERTRAM. *The Thinking Computer: Mind Inside Matter.* San Francisco: Freeman, 1976. A very readable introduction to computer functioning.

PART THREE

HUMAN DEVELOPMENT

The development of a human being is a truly remarkable process. In a matter of nine months, a single microscopic cell transforms itself into a fully formed human infant who has surprisingly well-developed perceptual and cognitive capabilities. Six years later, this newborn has grown into an accomplished first-grader, as proficient in language as many adults and ready to begin mastering such complex skills as reading and arithmetic. From there it is a relatively short step to social and sexual maturation in adolescence, and then to such adult roles as worker, wife or husband, and parent.

The branch of psychology that seeks to explain this complex process of growth and change is called developmental psychology. Developmental psychologists explore how physical growth takes place, how intellectual and social behavior develop and change over time, and how these aspects of development relate to one another. Recognizing that human development does not end with young adulthood, developmental psychologists are concerned with the entire human life span from conception to death.

In Chapter 7, "Early Development," we begin our study of human development by considering the patterns of change that occur in the human infant before birth and in the first few months of life. Chapter 8, "Cognitive Development," then focuses on the ways in which the intellectual skills of thinking and reasoning develop in the human being from infancy to adulthood, with emphasis on the brilliant work of developmental psychologist Jean Piaget. In Chapter 9, "Language Development," we consider how humans acquire language. Chapter 10, "Personality and Social Development," explains the processes by which we become unique individuals and members of society.

CHAPTER SEVEN

EARLY DEVELOPMENT

Psychologists have developed experimental techniques of the utmost ingenuity for measuring the abilities and competency of babies. They have had to, for babies are fascinating little mammals with whom direct communication is impossible. If we could only *remember* what babies were like—or one baby, at any rate, the one we used to be. Yet every human being was once a baby, and one-way communication with earlier growth stages of one's self is possible across time. It is called memory.

Since I am rather proud of my own memory, I have tried now and then to remember as far back as I could and to identify my earliest clear memory.

I remember, distinctly, a particular book. I recall sitting in a chair, turning the pages of the book and loving the pictures in it. Then I recall wanting the book again and looking about for it, but not finding it and wondering where it was. The feeling of loss was keen and persistent, and I remember that feeling to this day.

Eventually, I described the memory to my mother in an effort to place it in time. My mother had no trouble. She said, "I remember the book. You were two years old at the time and were crazy about it."

I said, "But what happened to it? I remember turning the pages, and then I couldn't find it."

"Sure," she said, "because every page you turned you tore out."

From this I deduce that when infants are destructive, they don't mean to be.

Another memory, one that may be even earlier and that certainly antedates my ability to speak, is that of being handed by my father to a strange woman. My father then took up something which, as I look back on it, must have been the harness, or part of the harness, of a horse. I suppose he had to go somewhere, presumably with my mother, and was leaving me with a grandmother or aunt.

I objected to this arrangement. I remember crying strenuously, while the strange woman kept me clutched to her ample bosom and took me off somewhere. The point is that I remember my emotions exactly. I was not frightened. I was not angry. What I wanted to get across was simply, "Hey, I want to be with my father!"

Since I didn't know how to say that, I made the only emphatic sound I knew how to make, the one that most frequently got me the results I wanted. I wailed.

The memory of that episode has soothed me a bit when I had wailing children of my own, and has encouraged me to take the wailing as mere comment on the situation.

Isaac Asimov

This chapter describes what psychologists know about the interaction of heredity and environment in the earliest months of life. We will begin with the process of human development: an orderly sequence of events from childhood into old age, directed by heredity but constantly influenced by environment. Then we will look at prenatal development and at the crucial role environmental factors play in a baby's development before it is born. Finally, we will focus on the human newborn: With what abilities are humans equipped at birth, and how quickly do they begin to acquire the cognitive and social traits characteristic of their species? Recent findings suggest that the newborn infant is remarkably competent.

THE PROCESS OF DEVELOPMENT

In examining the process of human development, psychologists generally ask two closely related questions: How do individuals change—physically, mentally, and socially—as they grow older? And why do these observable patterns of change occur as they do? These two basic questions—the how and the why of human development—are explored in this section.

DEVELOPMENTAL SEQUENCES: THE QUESTION OF HOW Anyone who has watched children grow knows that many changes in their behavior are neither accidental nor random. There

is an orderly sequence to the development of a young person's motor skills, language, cognitive capacities, and social behavior. Nor are such developmental sequences limited to childhood. Throughout young and middle adulthood, and on into old age, sequential patterns of development and change can be observed in all human beings.

Perhaps the most familiar example of a developmental sequence is the series of stages associated with motor development during infancy. Figure 7.1 shows some of the milestones in the first two years of life. By the time babies are about two months old, they are able to raise their head and chest while lying on their stomach—a feat that enables them to scan the world beyond their crib. Between the fourth and seventh months, hand–eye coordination has improved enough to enable them to reach out and grasp almost any object within range—mother's glasses, father's nose, the mobile dangling overhead. By seven months, they usually can sit up without support, and a few months later they are able to hoist themselves into a standing position while holding on to furniture. At age ten months, most babies are accomplished crawlers, capable of wreaking havoc on all low-lying areas of the house. And fi-

Developmental psychologists are interested in the process of human development throughout the life span; specifically, they want to know how and why people

change. These two babies grew up to be prominent. Can you guess who they are? The answer appears upside-down below.

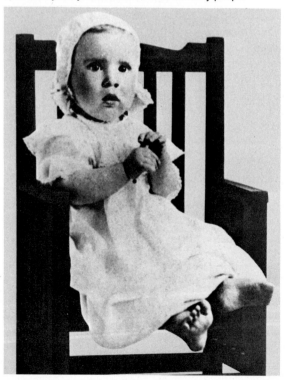

(left) Richard Nixon; (right) Marlon Brando.

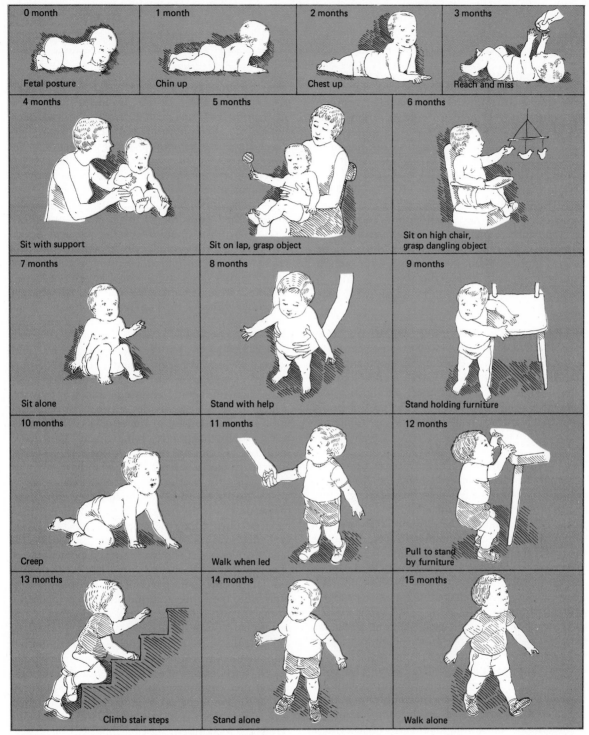

Figure 7.1 The sequence of motor development. The age given for the appearance of each skill is approximate; there is a wide range of individual differences. (Adapted from Shirley, 1933.)

nally, usually around the first birthday, infants take their first solo step—an event that opens a whole new realm of experience.

It is important to note that this sequence of an infant's motor development, like all such descriptions, consists of averages or norms, established after observing a large number of babies. This description does not tell us what the *ideal* behavior is, but merely what the mathematically calculated "average" baby does. In fact, there are wide variations in the age at which normal infants master motor skills. Some perfectly normal babies, for example, never crawl, but go directly from sitting and standing to taking their first steps. Walking may begin as early as eight months or as late as twenty. Such individual variations can be seen in all the other developmental sequences. Still, the concept of developmental sequences is a useful one because it emphasizes the important fact that human development is not random: the progression through the sequences is orderly and predictable.

DETERMINANTS OF DEVELOPMENT: THE QUESTION OF WHY

As we have just seen, every person goes through similar developmental sequences. Yet, individual rates of development differ. What accounts for these similarities and differences among individuals? The answer lies in two interrelated factors: heredity and environment.

HEREDITARY FACTORS Every person begins life as a single cell that is formed when a male germ cell, or sperm, penetrates a female germ cell, or egg. Unlike all other cells in the human body, which contain paired chromosomes, these germ cells contain twenty-three *single* chromosomes—coiled, threadlike structures that carry genes, the units of hereditary information. The germ cell is formed in a process called **meiosis**, in which the twenty-three chromosome pairs of a single cell are split apart, rearranged, and distributed to two germ cells having twenty-three single chromosomes each. At conception, the twenty-three chromosomes from the mother's germ cell pair with the twenty-three from the father's to make a complete set of genetic instructions for a new human being. Meiosis and fertilization guarantee variety. For each egg and sperm combination, there are over 8 million (2_{23}) possible combinations of chromosomes. Each individual (with the exception of identical twins, who come from the same egg and sperm) is genetically unique.

How exactly do the genes carried by the chromosomes influence development? It is only within the last several decades that scientists have pieced together an answer to this question. Chromosomes are composed primarily of long strands of a complex

substance called DNA (deoxyribonucleic acid). A gene is a small portion of a DNA molecule that either contains the code for producing one of the many proteins from which the body is built or specifies the plan for combining proteins to form the organ systems and general physical properties of the body. Genes, in other words, are the chemical "instructions" for the development and maintenance of a living organism.

Every organism has, to some extent, a genetically programmed timetable for its physical maturation. Under normal circumstances, the physical development of an individual's muscles, organs, and nervous system will unfold at a certain pace. Since we are all human, we share similar (though not identical) maturational timetables. Heredity, then, has a threefold influence on human development: it influences physical form, behavioral capacities, and the rate of physical maturation.

Does this mean that genes *determine* the rate and pattern of certain developmental sequences? To answer this question, researchers have turned to studies of identical twins. Identical twins are born when a single fertilized egg divides in two, each half having a full complement of the same genetic instructions. Although separate, these twins are genetically identical. (Fraternal twins, in contrast, develop from two separately fertilized eggs and are no more alike than other brothers and sisters.) Because identical twins are genetically identical, researchers have believed that differences between them that emerged during their development could be taken as evidence of the influence of environmental factors. Conversely, if one twin received a certain kind of stimulation from its environment that the other did not, but the twins nevertheless developed at the same rate, then this could be taken as evidence of strong genetic influence on the development of a certain behavior sequence.

For many years, scientists believed that motor development was controlled almost exclusively by genes. Early experiments with identical twins suggested that environmental differences—giving only one of the twins special training, for example—had little effect. Both twins mastered basic motor skills (crawling, walking) at the same age. In one experiment (Gesell, 1929), a set of twins developed the ability to climb stairs at virtually the same time, even though one had been given repeated assisted practice in stair climbing, while the other had not. Similarly, two other twins developed the ability to crawl and then to walk at the same time, even though one had been carefully exercised in these

Studies of identical twins have been important in evaluating the respective roles of heredity and environment in influencing development.

skills and the other had been denied opportunities to practice (McGraw, 1935, 1939a). Thus, it appeared that the sequences of early motor development were heavily influenced by heredity.

Early cross-cultural studies (studies of children in different cultures) tended to confirm this belief. Although different cultures give babies different opportunities and encouragement to practice motor skills, records from five of Europe's largest cities showed that most infants took their first steps within a few months of one another. Even Hopi Indian infants, who spent their first year bound to cradleboards which severely restricted their movements, walked at about the same age as infants in other cultures who had had far more practice in muscular coordination (Dennis and Dennis, 1940). Thus, the logical assumption at the time was that environmental differences seemed to have little influence on when basic motor skills emerged. Future research, however, was to suggest a somewhat different kind of conclusion.

ENVIRONMENTAL FACTORS Scientists now know that heredity is never the sole influence on development. Environment is necessarily an important factor in any developmental process. An organism cannot even begin to grow without material from the environment (food) to build its cells and tissues, and the environment continues to influence its development throughout life. Psychologists now realize that motor development can be accelerated or retarded by the presence or absence of environmental stimulation. Apparently, the ranges of the environmental variations in the earlier studies, mentioned above, had been too limited to reveal this.

We know now that a severe lack of social and intellectual stimulation accompanied by little opportunity for physical activity can cause a marked decline in motor development. In a foundling home in Lebanon, for example, where children spent most of their first year lying on their back in bare cribs, virtually ignored by adults, motor skills were so retarded that some infants over a year old could not sit up (Dennis and Sayegh, 1965). However, a simple program of environmental therapy produced dramatic positive changes. When infants were propped into sitting positions and allowed to play for as little as an hour each day with such ordinary objects as fresh flowers, pieces of colored sponge, and colored plastic disks strung on a chain, their rate of motor development accelerated enormously.

While an impoverished environment retards development, motor skills can be encouraged by giving a child extra experience and stimulation, provided they are appropriate to the baby's age. Consider early practice of the infant's "walking" reflex. When a newborn baby is held upright, with its feet just touching a flat surface, the infant will march along as if walking, even though it cannot yet support its own weight. Normally, this reflexive stepping motion is not practiced and disappears by the second month. But one study has shown that when babies are trained to use their walking reflex regularly, they not only do not lose the behavior in later infancy, but they begin to walk at a significantly earlier age (about one to two months earlier) than most other infants (Zelazo, Zelazo, and Kolb, 1972). There are clear limits to this enhancement of motor development, however. Thus, no six-month-old can be enabled to walk, no matter how much exercise it is given. Although infants who receive

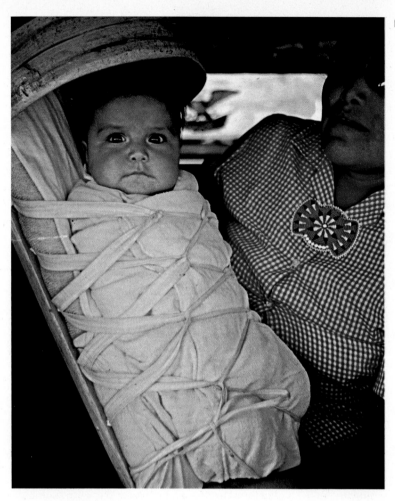

Hopi Indian infant.

practice began walking at a significantly earlier age than those who do not, the average difference is small—ten months compared to twelve months. This is well within the range of individual differences. Moreover, we do not know whether this acceleration is caused by more rapid development of muscle strength or by more rapid learning. The important point is that, within limits, developmental sequences respond to environmental manipulation.

Like the repeated practice of specific skills, generalized stimulation can also lead to accelerated development. This has been demonstrated with premature infants. Nurses and parents tend to regard premature babies as especially fragile and so avoid fondling them as they do normal babies. But physical stimulation may be exactly what these infants need. One researcher (Rice, 1975) encouraged a group of mothers to stroke and gently massage their premature babies for fifteen minutes, then to rock and cuddle them for five minutes, four times a day. At the end of four months, the stimulated babies showed significant gains in weight, motor reflexes, and even mental functioning over a control group of premature babies who did not receive this handling.

This study suggests that stimulation from the environment not only enhances muscle strength but also facilitates the development of the nervous system, as indicated by the stimulated premature infants' gains in motor reflexes. A number of experiments with animals support the conclusion that environmental stimulation can have specific, measurable effects on brain development. For example, studies of rats have shown that enriched and stimulating environments are associated with chemical and physical changes in the brain (Rosenzweig, Bennett, and Diamond, 1972). In one study, rats placed in bare cages within larger enriched environments—where they could see other rats climbing on equipment and manipulating objects but were unable to participate themselves—showed no more brain change than did isolated rats completely removed from the enriched environment, whereas the rats participating in the enriched environment underwent significant brain changes. (Ferchmin, Bennett, and Rosenzweig, 1975). Clearly, an organism must *participate* in an enriched environment to be affected by it; merely being exposed to the environment is not enough. (It is important to bear in mind also that these were captive rats. The "enrichment" condition might actually have provided the captive rats with no more varied stimulation than the natural environment would have provided. Therefore, one might argue that the isolated rats' development was retarded rather than that the "enriched" rats' development was accelerated.)

All this is not to say that surrounding infants with all sorts of toys and giving them constant attention will guarantee parents a precocious child. While severe environmental deprivation can result in serious retardation of development (see Figure 7.2), healthy development can proceed in many different environments (Kagan, 1978). The development of most infants who experience normal freedom of movement and the opportunity to interact with the varied environment found in most homes seems to be only modestly affected by extra enrichment. As one researcher (White, 1967, 1971) has pointed out, there may be an optimal amount of stimulation for optimal development, but it must be appropriate to the baby's age and abilities. Too much stimulation before the baby is ready for it may be merely irritating or confusing.

SENSITIVE PERIODS OF DEVELOPMENT The phenomenon of sensitive periods (sometimes called optimal or critical periods) of development illustrates the relationship between the hereditary and environmental determinants of behavior particularly well. A **sensitive period**, as we saw in Chapter 3, is a time during development when an organism is especially susceptible to certain kinds of environmental influences. The same experience before or after this period may have little or no impact. The "readiness" depends on genetically guided maturation; the outcome depends on the environment. The best-known example of a sensitive period is imprinting. As we noted in Chapter 3, some baby birds and other animals appear to establish permanent social bonds with members of their own or another species only if they are exposed to them during a critical time span. The sensitive period in which to socialize dogs to humans, for example, extends from three to twelve weeks of age. If puppies are not exposed to people during this period, they are not likely to become attached to a human master later in life (Scott, Stewart, and De Ghett, 1974).

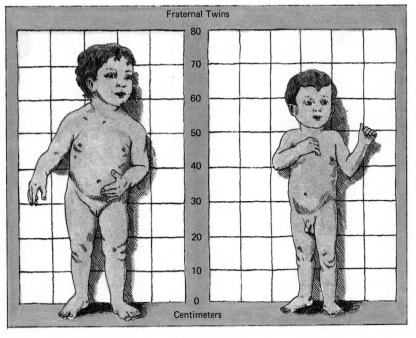

Figure 7.2 Deprivation dwarfism. In one study, the effects of emotional deprivation were observed in a pair of fraternal twins. This drawing, based on photographs taken when the children were almost thirteen months old, shows that the female was normal in weight and stature, but her brother was the size of a seven-month-old. Shortly after the twins were born, the father lost his job and left home. Hurt and angry, the mother displaced her hostility toward the father to the son, and soon the boy's growth rate began to decline. It is thought that emotional stress affects the pituitary gland, depressing the secretion of growth hormone and thus stunting growth. When the father eventually returned home and the emotional climate of the household improved, the boy began to grow again. (After Gardner, 1972.)

In our culture, we tend to want our children to have "everything."

Are there sensitive periods in human development? Some psychologists (for example, Hess, 1970) believe that there are. The optimal period for rapid language development, for example, seems to be between two and thirteen years. (Think how difficult it is to learn a second language in high school or college.) John Bowlby (1958) suggested that there are sensitive periods in human social and emotional development as well. He argued that babies seem to have an innate drive to establish a "love" relationship with a parent or caretaker, and that love objects selected later in life resemble that person. Though many psychologists reject the notion of imprinting in humans, most agree that children must reach a level of maturational readiness before they can profit from certain kinds of experiences. Moreover, there seem to be periods when certain kinds of experiences will have the greatest impact on future behavior.

The basic point of this section—indeed, of this entire chapter—is that hereditary and environmental influences are two sides of the same coin. Although it is useful to distinguish between them, they can never be entirely separated. Figure 7.3 shows an analogy for the interaction between heredity and environment in development. As we stressed in Chapter 3, a child cannot even begin to develop without heredity, just as that child cannot begin to live without interacting with the environment. This close collaboration between "nature" and "nurture"

applies even to developmental disorders for which a specific genetic "cause" can be identified (see the accompanying special feature). We will see more evidence of the interaction between heredity and environment in the sections that follow.

Figure 7.3 Geneticist Conrad Waddington's graphic analogy for the interaction of heredity and environment in development. The landscape represents the possibilities determined by genetic factors, and the path of the rolling ball represents the actual course of development. Such forces on the ball as cross-winds represent environmental factors. The ball can roll down different valleys, depending on the forces that are brought to bear on it, but it cannot easily change from one valley to another once it has started. The analogy is useful in helping us understand how genetic and environmental factors interact to produce different personality traits or different degrees of intellectual ability. (After Waddington, 1957.)

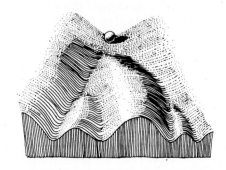

PRENATAL DEVELOPMENT

A new human being begins developing as soon as a sperm and an egg unite. In approximately thirty-eight weeks, the growing organism is transformed from a single cell to a living, functioning newborn baby. This period of remarkable growth and change has been studied in great detail.

PRENATAL GROWTH AND BEHAVIOR Development during the nine months in the womb is more rapid than during any other period in human life. From the fertilized egg, the fetus increases in size hundreds of thousands of times. This rapid growth represents the first major developmental sequence in an individual's existence. It unfolds in a predictable manner, triggered and guided by both genetic and environmental factors. During prenatal development, behavioral potential, as well as structural complexity, increases. This entire span of development can be divided into three basic periods: the germinal, the embryonic, and the fetal.

THE GERMINAL PERIOD Almost immediately after fertilization, the egg begins the process of cell division that will eventually produce a human body made up of many billions of cells. At first the multiplying cells are all identical; there is no differentiation between nerve cells, for example, and muscle cells, or between blood cells and bone cells. But by the end of the first two weeks, the cells have begun to differentiate into three primary layers from which the various tissues and organs will be produced. Exactly what triggers this process is still something of a mystery, but scientists believe that the answer may lie in subtle differences in the chemical environments to which different cells are exposed as the cell mass increases in size.

THE EMBRYONIC PERIOD Within four weeks after conception, the organism, called an **embryo**, is already about one-fifth of an inch long, 10,000 times larger than the original fertilized egg. In appearance it is nearly all head, with a tiny heart which pumps blood through microscopic veins and arteries. There are also the beginnings of a brain, kidneys, a liver, and a digestive tract, plus indentations in the head region that will eventually become jaws, eyes, and ears. By the end of this period, about the eighth week, the embryo is almost an inch long and is clearly human.

THE FETAL PERIOD For the next thirty weeks, until its birth, the developing organism is known as a **fetus**. By sixteen weeks, the fetus is six to seven inches long and weighs about four ounces. The lower part of the body has grown so that the head now is only about one-fourth of the total body size. The sixteen-week-old fetus looks like a miniature baby. Its face is obviously a human face. Hair may appear on its head. Bones can be distinguished. The ears, eyes, nose, and mouth approximate the appearance they will have at birth. All the major internal organs have attained their typical shape and plan, although they are not yet capable of maintaining the fetus outside the uterus. At this stage, the mother may first feel the fetus move.

By twenty-three weeks, the fetus has become quite active. It sleeps and wakes as a newborn baby does, and even has a favorite position for its naps. Studies of prematurely delivered babies (Hooker, 1952) have shown that by twenty-four weeks a fetus can cry, open and close its eyes, and look up, down, and sideways. It has also developed a grasping reflex. It may even hiccup. During the final eight or nine weeks, the actions of the fetus become increasingly restricted by its snug fit in the womb. Fat forms over its entire body, smoothing out its wrinkled skin and rounding out contours. The fetus usually gains about half a pound a week during the last eight or nine weeks in the uterus. At birth, the average full-term baby is about twenty inches long and weighs a little more than seven pounds.

ENVIRONMENTAL INFLUENCES The stages of prenatal growth just discussed have, of course, a genetic foundation. Yet, even within the uterus the fetus is not immune from external influences on its development. Perhaps the most important is the diet of the mother, from whom the fetus receives its nourishment. Diets deficient in calcium, phosphorus, iodine, and vitamins B, C, and D are associated with high frequencies of malformed fetuses. Studies with animals suggest that a maternal protein deficiency may cause an irreversible reduction in brain weight, number of brain cells, and learning

Controlling Genetic Defects
Through Environmental Change

With the realization that all developmental sequences can be heavily influenced by environment, scientists have made significant advances in the prevention and alleviation of certain developmental disorders, including some caused by genetic defects once thought to be impervious to environmental control. Such research is tremendously important: five out of every hundred children born have a genetic defect or malformation of some kind (Etzioni, 1973). To illustrate the progress that has been made in this area, let us consider two hereditary disorders with effects that until recently were believed to be impossible to prevent or control: phenylketonuria and Down's syndrome.

DOWN'S SYNDROME (TANDEM G/G TRANSLOCATION)

SEX CHROMOSOMES

Phenylketonuria

Since the mid-1960s, delivery-room attendants have pricked the heels of more than 10 million American babies shortly after birth and taken a few drops of blood for analysis. This procedure has saved 1,000 babies from the severe mental retardation caused by the genetic disorder called phenylketonuria, or PKU.

PKU is caused by a defect in the gene that codes for the body's use of phenylalanine, a protein present in milk and many other foods. The defective gene results in the lack of a liver enzyme needed to convert phenylalanine into another protein (tyrosine). The unconverted phenylalanine builds up and changes to a toxic substance that attacks the cells of the nervous system and causes progressive mental retardation.

Thus, a single defective gene can produce, through several

steps, a number of observable features and behavioral traits. Children with PKU appear normal at birth, but their intelligence stops developing during the first year. Without treatment, one-third of PKU victims never learn to walk, and two-thirds never learn to talk. Children with PKU have lighter pigmentation of skin and hair, shorter stature, and greater irritability than normal children. The disorder afflicts approximately one in 20,000 whites, and is extremely rare among blacks.

The series of biochemical steps between a genetic code and an observable feature or trait is called a gene action pathway. Few of these pathways are clearly understood, but with PKU, scientists have been able to break the tragic chain of developmental events that would otherwise begin with the defective gene. The drops

of blood taken from the newborn baby's heel are analyzed for the presence of phenylalanine. An abnormally high level indicates the presence of the defective gene, and the baby is immediately started on a diet low in phenylalanine. Simply by adjusting one minor aspect of the infant's internal environment—the level of phenylalanine in the body—doctors can prevent the devastating effects of the faulty gene.

Down's Syndrome

Another genetic disorder that responds to environmental intervention—but in this case intervention with the *external* environment—is Down's syndrome (or "mongolism"). Afflicting one child out of every 600 born, Down's syndrome causes a brain malformation leading to mental retardation that is usually severe: IQ levels average below 50 (a person with an IQ of 100 is considered to be of average intelligence). Victims have poor muscle tone, short stature, protruding tongues, small ears, stubby fingers, and a fold of skin at the inner corners of the eyes (the last of which gives them a vaguely Asiatic appearance that inspired the term "mongolism").

Down's syndrome results from a chromosomal abnormality. Instead of having the usual twenty-three pairs of chromosomes, for a total of forty-six, children born with the syndrome have an extra chromosome in the twenty-first pair, for a total of forty-seven chromosomes (see the accompanying photograph). It is this extra chromosome that causes the trouble.

As yet, nothing can be done to prevent the formation of the extra chromosome, but doctors can detect its presence quite early in pregnancy. Using a technique called **amniocentesis**, the doctor withdraws some of the fetal cells that are sloughed off into the amniotic fluid that surrounds the fetus in the womb (see the accompanying photograph) and then tests those cells for the presence of abnormal chromosomes.

The effects of Down's syndrome cannot be prevented by manipulating the body's chemical environment, as with PKU. But research indicates that environmental therapy of a different kind can be very helpful in alleviating at least some of its effects. In a normal baby, the rate of motor development is about twice that of an infant with Down's syndrome; by age two the average Down's-syndrome child has developed the motor skills of a typical one-year-old. In one study, however, a group of two-year-olds with Down's syndrome were given eighteen months of intensive practice in a number of sensorimotor tasks. The result: by age three and a half, they had overcome the lag, performing as well on these tasks as normal children the same age (Rynders, 1975).

Although we do not yet know how enduring the results of such special environmental stimulation can be, these preliminary findings have given new cause for optimism.

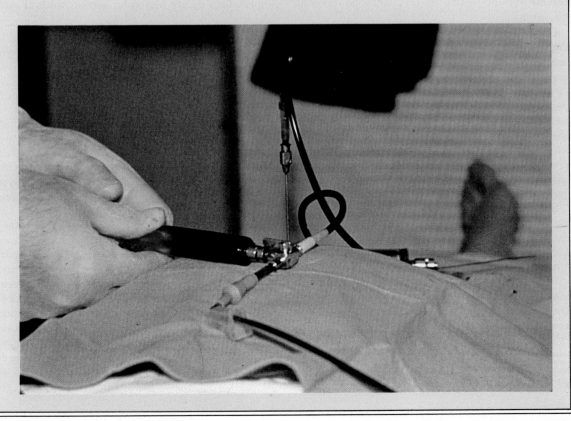

ability in offspring (Winick and Noble, 1966). More disturbing still is the finding that female rats born to protein-deficient mothers may bear learning disabled offspring, even if the mothers receive perfectly well-balanced diets during pregnancy (Bresler, Ellison, and Zamenhof, 1975). The reason appears to be that the mothers are unable to form a normal placenta, the network of blood vessels through which their developing young are nourished. These findings may well apply to humans. If so, malnutrition during pregnancy may have negative effects not only on a woman's children but on her grandchildren.

Various drugs can also adversely affect fetal development. Babies born to alcoholic mothers, for example, may be born addicted to alcohol themselves. A golden rule of obstetric practice today is to advise women to take as little medication during pregnancy as possible. The thalidomide tragedies of the early 1960s, when many European women who took the sedative thalidomide during the early weeks of pregnancy produced babies with severely deformed arms and legs, vividly illustrates the terrible consequences of using certain drugs. More recently, cancer has been found in many young women whose mothers had taken the drug diethylstilbestrol (DES) early in pregnancy to prevent miscarriage.

Cigarette smoking can also affect the fetus. Women who smoke during pregnancy give birth to babies who are, on the average, lighter and smaller than normal (Butler and Goldstein, 1973). The reasons for this are not clear. The tar and nicotine in cigarettes may have direct effects on fetal development. It has been found, for example, that when pregnant women who are nonsmokers inhale cigarette smoke, the fetal heart rate increases. However, it is possible that heavy smokers also do not eat properly and that this dietary deficiency, rather than smoking itself, retards fetal development.

Because most of the basic organ systems are taking form in the first **trimester**, or third, of pregnancy, maternal malnutrition and drug use are likely to have their greatest impact on the fetus at this time. This is also the time that fetal development is most susceptible to the effects of rubella, or German measles. If a pregnant woman contracts this seemingly minor disease during the first trimester, her baby may suffer such major birth defects as blindness. Thus, the time of occurrence is often a crucial factor in determining whether an environmental influence will produce abnormality in a developing fetus. The first trimester appears to be an

WHY START A LIFE UNDER A CLOUD?

Smoking is harmful to your baby's health. Quit for both of you. For help call your American Cancer Society.

Although it is not clear how cigarette smoking affects the fetus, it is known that women who smoke tend to have lighter and smaller babies than nonsmokers.

especially sensitive period for certain kinds of birth defects.

THE COMPETENCY OF THE NEWBORN

Looking at the animal kingdom as a whole, there are wide variations in the degree of sensory and motor development at birth. Some animals are born with impressive motor coordination and highly acute sensory capabilities. Newborn horses, calves, and guinea pigs, for example, are extremely precocious and can see, hear, stand, walk, even run within a few hours after birth. Because of this, they are classified as **precocial** species. Others are born almost completely helpless. Cats, mice, and sparrows, for instance, come into the world blind and physically feeble, totally dependent on their parents for survival. These are classified as **altricial** species.

Newborn humans are both altricial and precocial—a peculiar mix of incapacity and competence. Most human babies are physically weak and helpless at birth; most are not even capable of holding up their own heads. Yet when we look at the sensory development of the newborn human, we

An infant's earliest behaviors are reflexive; objects put into its hand are automatically grasped, and objects put into its mouth are automatically sucked. In this photograph, a baby is beginning to experiment with and expand these primitive ways of knowing and understanding the world.

find remarkably mature and well-integrated systems. All the human senses, in fact, are capable of functioning even before birth (Gottlieb, 1976). Thus, newborn humans may not be capable of navigating in their environment, but they are certainly capable of perceiving and being influenced by that environment from the moment they are born.

REFLEXES AND MOTOR SKILLS Most babies appear quite helpless at birth because of their limited motor capacity. Relatively weak for many months, they are completely dependent on their caretakers. Yet the newborn quickly masters certain essential motor skills, such as feeding, which requires the coordination of three separate activities: sucking, swallowing, and breathing. The newborn also comes equipped with a set of reflexes that can be elicited by specific stimuli. Some of these reflexes

are adaptive and may help the baby survive in its new surroundings. Others are simply manifestations of neurological pathways in the baby that will later come under voluntary control or will be integrated into more mature patterns of behavior, such as stepping movements of the legs (Minkowski, 1967). Still others may be remnants of traits possessed by prehuman ancestors.

One of the most familiar reflexes is the rooting reflex, the baby's tendency to turn its head in the direction of any object that gently stimulates its cheek or the corner of its mouth. This reflex has obvious adaptive significance for feeding: it helps the baby locate the nipple with its mouth.

In the first few weeks of life a baby also has a strong grasping reflex. If one places a one-week-old baby on its back and inserts a finger into its hand, it is likely to grasp the finger firmly. Sometimes a grasping newborn can literally hang by one hand. The meaning and purpose of this grasping reflex is

Figure 7.4 These drawings represent three phases in the development of aquatic behavior in infants. (A) Reflex swimming movements. (B) Disorganized behavior. (C) Voluntary or deliberate movements. These drawings were obtained by tracing successive frames of 16mm movie film illustrating the quality of consecutive movements at different chronological or developmental stages. (McGraw, 1939.)

not entirely clear. It has been suggested that this is a vestige from our prehuman past. If our early ancestors carried their young around on their backs or undersides, as do many apes and monkeys, the ability to cling tightly to the fur or skin of the mother would have obvious survival value for the offspring (Prechtl, 1965).

Another reflex observed in newborns is the "swimming" reflex. If a baby only a few weeks old is placed facedown in a pool of water, it will move its arms and legs in a remarkably well-coordinated pattern that closely resembles crawling and that can propel the baby a short distance through the water. Moreover, if the infant's head is submerged, another reflex inhibits breathing, preventing water from entering the lungs. The infantile swimming reflex lasts only a short time. When four-month-old babies are placed in water, they thrash about, coughing and gasping if their head slips under the water. Interestingly, at about the beginning of the second year babies again show a tendency to make rhythmic swimming motions. These motions, first described by Myrtle McGraw (1939b), are quite different from the early, reflexive movements (see Figure 7.4). They appear more deliberate and purposeful. Yet these, too, disappear. At age five or six, children struggle vainly to hold themselves in a horizontal position in water. They have to be painstakingly "taught" to swim, a skill they once performed easily.

Why does swimming behavior appear, disappear, then reappear in a different form? McGraw believed that the initial reflex is lost after the development of brain structures that allow voluntary control over muscle coordination. The fact that many infant response patterns (such as walking and reaching) take this "repetitive" course of appearance, loss, and reappearance may support this view. However, T. G. R. Bower (1976) has suggested that the apparent loss occurs because infants are not given continuous opportunity to practice this behavior. As we noted earlier, early practice of the walking reflex may hasten the onset of actual walking. Early practice of reaching and grasping behavior may accelerate reappearance of this behavior as well. But practice does not affect all repetitive behavior (Bower, 1976). So the precise reasons why certain abilities emerge, disappear, then reappear remains a mystery.

SENSORY AND PERCEPTUAL ABILITIES

How do newborn infants, lying in a hospital nursery, perceive the world? Do they see a roomful of stable objects and hear distinct sounds? Or is the sensory world of newborns an ever-changing chaos of meaningless shapes and noises—as William James put it, "one great blooming, buzzing confusion"?

These are obviously difficult questions to answer. How does one measure the sensory and perceptual capabilities of newborn infants who can neither speak nor understand the questions of curious psychologists? One reasonable approach is to take advantage of the things babies *can* do. And what they can do is suck, turn their heads, look at things, cry, smile, and show signs of surprise or fright. The vigor of a baby's sucking, the patterns of eye movements, and expressions of pleasure and displeasure are all closely tied to how the baby is being stimulated. By measuring these behaviors while stimulating the baby in different ways, it is possible to infer how the infant perceives the world. For example, infants spend less time looking at out-of-focus movies than they do looking at the same movies in focus. Moreover, infants quickly learn to suck vigorously on a pacifier attached to the focusing mechanism of a movie projector in order to cause an out-of-focus picture to become more sharply defined. This suggests that babies are attuned to distinct edges; if the visual world were a blurry confusion for infants, they would not care that a movie was slightly blurry (Kalnins and Bruner, 1973).

In recent years a great amount of research has been devoted to assessing the newborn infant's perceptions. These investigations have refuted the notion that the world is essentially disorganized and chaotic to a baby. Here we will examine some of these very interesting findings.

VISION Can a newborn human perceive depth, the third dimension of space? This question was once at the heart of a debate over whether or not basic perceptual abilities are learned. On one side of the issue were the so-called environmentalists, who argued that a baby must learn to perceive three-dimensional space. Others, called nativists, asserted that babies' brains are constructed in such a way that they see depth the first time they open their eyes—in other words, that babies are born with depth perception. The truth has been found to be somewhere in between: infants seem to have a fairly well-organized perceptual world shortly after birth, but through learning they increase and refine their capacity to relate to the perceptual world.

Nonetheless, the degree of perceptual organization that humans possess at birth is truly remarkable. Though the world is represented two-dimensionally on the retina of its eye, a baby can respond appropriately to the third dimension. For example, when a newborn is held upright and an object is moved toward its face, the infant protects itself, as shown in Figure 7.5, by raising its hands and pulling back its head (Bower, Broughton, and Moore, 1971). Moreover, newborns seem capable of making the fine distinction between an approaching object that will likely hit them and one that will sail harmlessly past (Ball and Tronick, 1971). These findings suggest that what the young baby perceives in this situation is not simply a flat image that grows larger, but rather a concrete, oncoming object in three-dimensional space.

Of course, those who emphasize the role of environment would argue that babies even a few days old have already had enough experience with approaching objects—such as a breast or bottle approaching the face—to have *learned* to judge an object's course and distance. Nativists, who stress heredity, would point out that babies respond to depth in situations that they have never encountered before. But, the evidence can be interpreted either way, as shown in the photo on page 167. But there is no question that depth perception appears this early, which is quite a remarkable development.

Whether babies perceive color has also provoked debate and research. For years, many psychologists argued that the way people classify gradations of color in the visual spectrum is a product of learning, not heredity. According to this view, we focus on the basic color categories—red, yellow, green, and blue—because our *language* teaches us to do so.

This widely held assumption has been called into question. In one study (Bornstein, Kessen, and Weiskopf, 1976), a special apparatus that measures the precise direction of an infant's gaze was set up. Then, four-month-old infants were shown a particular color—say, a shade of blue—for a number of fifteen-second trials, until they became habituated to it. The more accustomed they became to the color, the less time they spent looking at it. Then the color was changed. If the babies perceived the new color as similar to the old one, they should not have looked at it for very long, but if the babies perceived the new color as different, it should have attracted their interest and they should have gazed at it for some time. What the researchers found was intriguing. The babies showed renewed attention

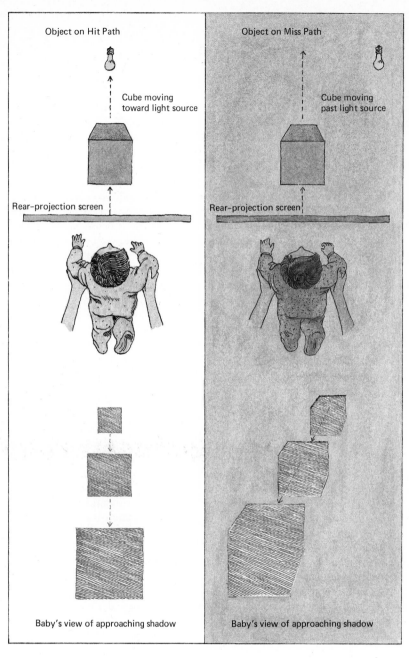

Object on Hit Path

Cube moving
toward light source

Rear-projection screen

Baby's view of approaching shadow

Object on Miss Path

Cube moving
past light source

Rear-projection screen

Baby's view of approaching shadow

Figure 7.5 Shadows cast on a rear-projection screen were used to present babies with optical approaching objects. Infants only a few days old were able to discriminate between an object approaching them on a direct-hit path and one approaching them on a miss path. They defended themselves against the former and were apparently not frightened by the latter. (From data supplied by Ball and Tronick, 1971.)

when the second color was chosen from what adults would consider a different category (say, green). But they did not gaze very long at a different shade of the original color (say, a lighter blue). Repeated tests using different colors indicated that long before they are influenced by language, babies seem to perceive the visual spectrum as divided into the primary adult color categories of red, yellow, green, and blue. Figure 7.6 shows a simple test for the visual preference of an infant.

HEARING How clearly can newborn babies distinguish sounds? Can they tell where a sound is coming from? Does one human voice sound different from another to them? Are they even capable of differentiating a human voice from other surrounding sounds, such as the clatter of dishes or the wail of their own crying?

Let us begin with the ability to tell whether a sound comes from the left or right, behind or in front. This is a simple task for a normal adult. We

How do infants learn to judge distance? Environmentalists would say that almost immediately after birth infants begin to have experience with approaching objects. According to nativists, this does not explain the responses to depth made by infants in situations where they have had no prior experience.

locate sounds in space fairly automatically by noting which ear the sound hits first. A sound on the left, for example, is heard by the left ear a fraction of a second before it is heard by the right. This split-second difference in timing is the major clue we have to a sound's location. One interesting experiment suggested that infants enter the world with a clear capacity for locating sounds in space (Wertheimer, 1961). The subject in this study was a baby girl who

was only a few *minutes* old. The researcher made a soft clicking sound with a toy cricket, first near the baby's right ear and then near her left. On the very first click, the baby stopped crying, opened her eyes, and looked to the right. Then, when the sound moved to the left, she turned and looked in that direction. Thus, not only was this newborn able to locate sounds in space, but she also showed an amazing degree of coordination between two of her

DIMENSION OF COLOR
(AFTER VALENTINE)

Figure 7.6 Before technology made it possible to measure accurately the place and duration of visual fixation, psychologists used simple observation, common sense, and a stopwatch. C. W. Valentine (1913), for example, studied infant aesthetic preference by holding different-colored balls of wool a foot and a half in front of a 3.5-month-old infant and recording the amount of time the infant spent looking at each ball. Results from a series of such paired comparisons showed that the most "beautiful" colors were yellow, white, and pink (brightest), and the "ugliest" were green, blue, and violet (most saturated).
(After Valentine, 1913.)

senses. Upon hearing a noise with her ears, she turned her head as if to locate the source with her eyes. Although such coordination can be considered reflexive, it is nevertheless impressive in a baby less than ten minutes old. As with visual space and depth perception, the infant apparently can respond appropriately to the location of sounds in space.

In another experiment on auditory discrimination, three-week-old babies easily differentiated between the familiar sound of their mother's voice and the voice of another woman (Mills and Melhuish, 1974). Each baby was placed behind a screen, out of sight of the other participants in the experiment, and given a pacifier wired to measure its sucking response. Hearing the sound of a voice—its mother's or a stranger's—was contingent on the baby's vigorous sucking. Each baby sucked much harder to hear the familiar sound of its mother's voice than it did to hear the voice of a stranger. Thus, even before they are a month old, infants can tell a familiar voice from an unfamiliar one.

Other experiments have indicated that babies only one month old have a remarkable capacity for discriminating speech sounds. In one study (Eimas et al., 1971), babies were given pacifiers that were attached to tape recorders. Each recorder was turned on by the first vigorous suck on the pacifier attached to it, and the sound continued as long as the baby kept sucking. First, the experimenters presented a simple sound, "Pa," over and over until the baby was habituated. Then they presented a slightly different sound, "Ba." If the two sounds seemed identical to the babies, they should not have shown renewed interest at the second one. But the babies tested were "interested" and increased their sucking time to hear the new sound (see Figure 7.7). Using this and similar techniques, researchers have found that infants are sensitive to differences between vowel and consonant sounds, as well as to differences in speech intonation—at the ripe age of one month (Morse, 1972; Trehub and Rabinovitch, 1972; Trehub, 1973).

TASTE, SMELL, AND TOUCH Infants' perceptions of taste, smell, and touch have not been studied as extensively as their visual and auditory abilities. But the conclusion about these senses is basically the same as for the other two: newborns can detect and discriminate basic sensory information through taste, smell, and touch.

In a recent study, babies less than one day old were tested for responses to sweet, sour, and bitter before they had had their first feeding (Steiner, 1973). The infants made the same faces that we associate with these three tastes! A sweet taste caused them to relax their facial muscles in a smile-like expression. A sour taste made them purse their lips and stick out their tongues. A bitter taste elicited an open-mouthed expression accompanied by spitting movements that gave their faces a look of aversion. The consistency of these facial expressions in the 175 infants studied led the researcher to conclude not only that newborns can discriminate among tastes, but that their responses to certain basic tastes are essentially reflexive. That is, the facial expressions elicited by sweet, sour, and bitter are somehow a property of the organization of the human nervous system at birth.

THE ROOTS OF COGNITIVE AND SOCIAL DEVELOPMENT
The cognitive and social characteristics that define the baby as distinctly human develop from the rudimentary capacities for vocalization, movement, and perception. From babbling to language ability, from mysterious smiles to mirth, from an interest in faces to strong social attachments, infants display the progressive development of complex psychological processes. The topics of cognitive and social development will be elaborated in subsequent chapters. Here we will explore the beginnings of these most human of all aspects of human development.

LOOKING AT FACES We know that by the time an infant is six weeks old a smiling adult face is likely to elicit a smile in return. But is the baby really smiling at another human being or simply at a high-contrast image of eyes, nose, and mouth?

The results of a study by Robert Fantz (1961) suggest that babies show an early visual preference for faces or face-like stimuli over other kinds of stimuli (see Figure 7.8). Fantz showed infants of various ages a set of six flat disks. Three of the disks were patterned, one with a face-like image; the others were plain but brightly colored. Babies two to three months old spent about 50 percent more time gazing at the pattern of the face than they did looking at any of the other five disks. This did not, as Fantz originally suggested, reflect an inborn preference for faces; later research showed that infants prefer simple, high-contrast patterns of many sorts (Bond,

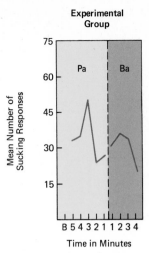

Figure 7.7 Discrimination of speech sounds in one-month-old infants. Infants were given a pacifier, which was attached to a tape recorder. Every time an infant sucked, it would hear the sound "Pa." When infants in the experimental group habituated to this sound, a new one, "Ba," was introduced. Where sucking responses just prior to the change in sound were low, sucking increased after the change. This would indicate that these infants perceived the "Ba" sound as new and found it interesting enough to keep sucking in order to hear it (until they again became habituated). This and similar research approaches have yielded information on other aspects of infant auditory abilities involving differentiation of sounds. (Adapted from Eimas et al., 1971.)

1972). However, at about the age of two months a distinct preference for faces does emerge. Possibly, babies develop an affinity for faces as they interact with people and learn that people reward them with attention.

What exactly are babies looking at in faces? In a recent experiment (Haith, Bergman, and Moore, 1977), researchers used a special apparatus to tell exactly where on a real face babies fix their eyes. In testing babies from three to eleven weeks old, they found that very young infants looked most at the edges of the face. This corresponded to earlier findings that newborns spend a great deal of time looking at the places where contrast is great (for example, the hairline). Then the researchers found that between five and seven weeks, a striking increase in eye contact occurred, especially when an adult was talking to the infant.

Why would the eyes, rather than the moving lips, attract a baby's attention? The answer may lie in the importance of eye contact to the development of social bonds, particularly between mother and child. A mother usually finds it very pleasurable to look into her baby's eyes; when the mother is doing

so, she generally accompanies looking with increased talking, touching, and smiling. The infant, in turn, seems to derive great pleasure from this heightened attention, so its eye scanning is reinforced. In this way, the social bond between mother and child may be strengthened. In the process, the baby's interest in all faces, adult ones especially, increases, as seems clear in the photo on page 170.

IMITATION A mother sits playing with her two-week-old infant. She purses her lips and shakes her head while making a soft, clicking sound. Slowly, almost imperceptibly to those not watching closely, the baby purses its lips and shakes its head in return. Then the mother widens her eyes and rhythmically opens and closes her mouth. The baby's eyes, too, enlarge, and its mouth forms a tiny *O*.

Although parents are not known for underestimating their young infant's capabilities, most mothers and fathers would dismiss this scene as very unlikely. In time every child learns to imitate adults, they would argue, but not at the age of two

Figure 7.8 Infant visual preference. The importance to infants of pattern over color or brightness was illustrated by a study of infants' responses to a face, a printed page, a bull's-eye, and plain red, white, and yellow disks. Even the youngest infants preferred patterns, especially that of the human face. Black bars indicate the average fixation time (time spent gazing) for infants two to three months old; gray bars show the average fixation time for infants more than three months old. (After Fantz, 1973.)

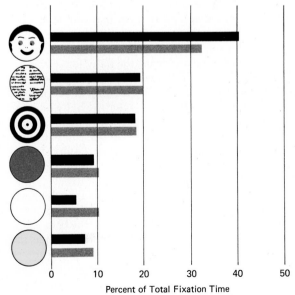

Eye contact.

weeks! And yet, recent research has revealed that babies as young as twelve to twenty-one days show a rudimentary ability to mimic the gestures and expressions of adults.

In one study (Meltzoff and Moore, 1977), babies less than three weeks of age were exposed to four different gestures: lip protrusion, mouth opening, tongue protrusion, and sequential movement of the fingers. These gestures were repeated several times to make sure that a given baby had seen them. After each display the experimeters were careful to preserve a neutral expression on their faces so as not to encourage or reward the baby for certain responses. The baby's reactions were videotaped; these tapes were watched by a group of people who were unaware of which behavior the baby had just been shown. The judges were then asked to indicate which of the four gestures they felt the baby was making at a particular time. The results showed clearly that the infants did tend to imitate each of the adult gestures.

Some psychologists have suggested that this early imitation is the result of an inborn "releasing mechanism." According to this argument, the behavior is an automatic response to certain stimuli, just as the courting ritual of a male bird is a response to the stimulus of an available female. But Andrew Meltzoff and M. Keith Moore, the researchers in the experiment just described, rejected this possibility. For one thing, the infants' responses were not stereotyped, as one would expect if an innate releasing mechanism were involved. For another, the fact that the babies could imitate four separate, quite distinct gestures made this hypothesis rather unlikely: it is doubtful that a newborn would come equipped with a fixed action pattern (see Chapter 3) corresponding to virtually every type of adult behavior. Another possibility is that the newborn's imitation is shaped through reinforcement provided by either an experimenter or a parent. But Meltzoff and Moore took great care not to encourage the infants in any way. Nor did the babies' parents have an opportunity to teach them to imitate the gestures, since they were not informed about the nature of the study in advance. In fact, most parents were astonished at the results of the tests.

A third possibility, favored by Meltzoff and Moore, is that newborns have an innate ability to imitate. They can watch an adult gesture, represent that gesture mentally to themselves, and then transfer the components of the gesture one by one to their own behavior. Further research, including a replication of this study, is necessary before this hypothesis can be accepted or rejected. The newborn's apparent ability to imitate adult gestures may be the precursor of the more elaborate and deliberate kind of imitation seen in older children. It is still too early to tell.

SELF-AWARENESS To the parent or untrained observer, the ability of the newborn infant to imitate adult behavior may indicate that babies have at least a rudimentary sense of self-awareness. How would they "know" how to open and close their mouth or stick out their tongue in response to the same adult gesture unless they were able to relate their own gestures to those of adults? However tempting this explanation may be, especially to parents, it is probably *not* the case. Meltzoff and Moore (1977) argue that the ability of infants to "match" information they perceive visually with information about their own behavior may instead be essentially reflexive. When, then, does the baby develop a true sense of self-awareness—one of the most basic of all human traits?

It has long been suggested that self-awareness emerges only when a person has an opportunity to observe others through social interaction (Cooley, 1912; Mead, 1934). According to this assumption, a person raised in isolation would fail to develop a true sense of self. A recent experiment with humankind's closest relative, the chimpanzee, lends some tentative support to this conclusion (Gallup, 1977). Several chimps participated in the experiment; each was placed in a cage with a full-length mirror for ten days. Some of the animals had been raised with other chimps, some had been raised in isolation. Initially both groups responded to the reflection in the glass as if it were another animal. They made threatening displays, chattered at the creature, and engaged in other behavior typical of chimp social interaction. On the second or third day, however, the group-raised chimpanzees began to act as if they recognized the reflection as their own image. Now they used the mirror to gain information about parts of their body that they normally could not see. Looking at their reflection, they picked bits of food from their teeth, blew bubbles, and made faces at themselves. The chimps raised in isolation, in contrast, continued to act as if the reflection were another animal.

The chimps were then anesthetized and bright red, odorless marks were painted above their eyebrows and on the tops of their ears. When exposed to the mirror again, the group-raised chimps, who had previously shown signs of self-recognition, continually touched the painted areas on their head and face. Some even sniffed and inspected the finger used to touch the red marks, in an apparent ef-

fort to discover what they were. The chimps raised in isolation, who had acted all along as if the image were another animal, paid no special attention to the red spots. It appears, then, that in chimps the ability to develop some form of self-awareness depends upon a history of normal social interaction.

Let us assume that the emergence of self-awareness in humans also depends on social contact. When does this developmental process begin? Normal babies interact with others from the first moments of birth. Does their sense of self likewise start to form at a very early age? Using techniques similar to those employed in the chimpanzee study, Michael Lewis (1977) explored this possibility. First he exposed to a mirror babies ranging in age from nine months to twenty-four months. Each infant's mother then surreptitiously placed a spot of red dye on her baby's nose. When returned to the mirror, infants aged fifteen months or older tended to touch and examine the red mark. Younger infants did not touch their nose, but they did touch their body more frequently after the dye had been applied. Perhaps the younger babies' failure to touch the red spot specifically was due simply to the fact that they lacked the necessary hand–eye coordination.

This baby shows unmistakable signs of self-recognition.

Several other tests have revealed similar signs of self-recognition. Babies as young as nine months responded more to videotapes of themselves than they did to tapes of strange babies. When they saw themselves, they smiled more and imitated their own behavior on the screen. By twelve months of age, when they saw themselves on tape with an adult approaching them from behind, some turned and looked over their shoulder.

Perhaps the most convincing evidence of early self-recognition comes from experiments on the effects of delayed-action videotapes on babies between the ages of nine and twelve months. Babies were shown tapes of themselves that had been made just three seconds previously. Most adults find similar situations very disconcerting: they cannot continue to talk, for example, when they hear their voices played back with only a few seconds' delay. Presumably a slight delay in visual replay would likewise confuse babies—*if* they recognized the image on the screen as their own. When shown delayed-action tapes of themselves, infants stopped what they were doing and stared at the screen.

Tapes of other babies did not have so pronounced an effect. The researcher concluded that between the ages of nine and twelve months, infants seem to develop some sense of self (Lewis, 1977).

Although infants' self-awareness and infants' ability to imitate others may not be as well developed as they will be in later childhood, psychologists now believe that the roots of these important capacities may develop very early in life. This is a new perspective on the newborn. Not long ago, psychologists thought that the newborn's development centered around sensory and motor skills, which then served as the foundation for the development of more complex cognitive and social abilities. But the studies reviewed here suggest that the foundations of many complex skills may emerge along with, rather than after, the development of simple sensory and motor coordination. Psychologists now tend to view the infant as a very competent organism—"a highly sophisticated processor of information, who at an extremely young age knows something of what he is and what he can do" (Lewis, 1977, p. 56).

Summary

1. **Developmental psychology** is the study of how and why people change—physically, mentally, and socially—as they grow up and grow older.

   A. The emergence of motor skills, language, cognitive capacities, and social behavior in infancy follows an orderly developmental sequence. Our description of this sequence is based on mathematically calculated averages. In reality, there are wide variations in the ages at which normal babies sit, crawl, walk, and acquire all the other abilities that mark human development.

   B. Although all human beings follow a similar sequence of development, individual rates of development vary, depending on the hereditary and environmental influences that interact continuously in infant development.

      1. Our physique, behavior, and rate of development are influenced by the unique combination of genes we inherit from our parents. At one time scientists believed that the development of motor skills was genetically controlled. Early studies of identical twins suggested that external influences did not affect the age at which motor abilities emerge.

      2. Now, scientists realize that the environment affects all aspects of development. New research shows that extreme deprivation can retard development, just as an enriched environment can, within limits, accelerate development. There also appear to be **sensitive periods** (times when an organism is most susceptible to certain environmental influences) in human development.

2. The process of prenatal development begins at conception and continues until birth.

   A. Development during the nine months in the womb can be divided into three periods:

      1. During the **germinal period** (from conception to the fourth week of pregnancy), the cells multiply rapidly and begin to differentiate.

      2. During the **embryonic period** (from four to eight weeks), the organism is nearly all

head. The beginnings of organ systems can be discerned.

3. By eight weeks, the onset of the **fetal period**, the organism is clearly human. The fetus begins to move, cry, even "look around" at about twenty-four weeks. At about thirty-eight weeks, the child is born.

B. The fetus is not immune to environmental influences, especially during the first **trimester** (or third) of pregnancy. A protein-deficient maternal diet, certain drugs, and cigarette smoking may all have negative effects on the fetus.

3. A newborn human baby is both **precocial** and **altricial**—a combination of competence and helplessness unique in the animal kingdom.

A. Babies are born with rooting, grasping, and other reflexes. Some, such as the "swimming" reflex, show a repetitive pattern—they appear, disappear, and reappear.

B. Babies are also born with certain sensory and perceptual abilities.

1. Newborn babies seem able both to perceive depth and to distinguish colors.

2. Infants can locate sounds in space, tell a familiar voice from an unfamiliar one, and differentiate between closely related speech sounds.

3. Babies respond to sweet, sour, and bitter tastes with facial expressions that resemble adults' responses.

4. The development of cognitive and social capacities is the most distinctively human aspect of human development. It begins with the infant's capacity for recognizing faces as such, for imitating behavior, and for being self-aware.

A. From an early age, babies seem to prefer faces and other high-contrast stimuli. At first they scan the outlines of faces; later they seek eye contact.

B. Babies begin to imitate adults very early in life—perhaps as early as two weeks of age.

C. Studies of chimpanzees, our nearest relatives in the animal kingdom, indicate that self-awareness (measured by self-recognition in a mirror) is in part a product of social interaction. Parallel studies of human infants suggest that self-awareness begins by about nine months of age.

D. Cognitive and social skills apparently begin to develop along with, not after, the emergence of sensory and motor skills.

RECOMMENDED READINGS

ACHENBACH, THOMAS M. *Developmental Psychopathology*. New York: Ronald, 1974. A basic presentation of developmental problems—descriptions, foundations, and treatments—from a broad range of perspectives.

BOWER, T. G. R. *A Primer of Infant Development*. San Francisco: Freeman, 1977. A lucid account of emerging motor, sensory, and cognitive skills of the infant.

BRONFENBRENNER, URIE. *Influences on Human Development*. Hinsdale, Ill.: Dryden, 1972. An excellent collection of scientific articles dealing with critical issues in developmental psychology from infancy to adolescence.

GESELL, ARNOLD L., FRANCES L. ILG, LOUISE B. AMES, and JANET L. RODELL. *Infant and Child in the Culture of Today: The Guidance of Development in Home and Nursery School*. Rev. ed. New York: Harper & Row, 1974. The classic presentation of developmental norms and their use in assessing developmental readiness.

McCLEARN, GERALD E., and JOHN C. DeFRIES. *Introduction to Behavioral Genetics*. San Francisco: Freeman, 1973. A clearly written, comprehensive review of most of the issues in the inheritance of behavior.

CHAPTER EIGHT

COGNITIVE DEVELOPMENT

I suppose there is a tendency to think that the road one has taken by circumstance is the only permissible one for others to take.

My impoverished childhood led me, rather against my will, to the public library as the only possible source of amusement. Since we were an immigrant family, my father could not advise me on the good books I ought to read, and so I had no way of knowing what to avoid. I devoured books indiscriminately and, in my ignorance, read a great many classics. With that plus my uncomfortably adhesive memory, I ended up getting more of my education from the public library than from the school system.

Naturally, as the years passed, I tended to forget that all this was the result of an accidental combination of circumstances, and I began to attribute my great learning and my intellectual profi-ciency entirely to my virtue, industry, and dedication. I turned up my nose at those who were devoting themselves to frivolous pursuits. They would never know as much as I did, I was certain.

Yet, perhaps because I lacked my father's forcefulness, somehow I could not impose my notions upon my own son. When he reached the age at which I had begun to frequent the library, he frequented the television set. Where I had been earnestly reading Homer and Shakespeare and Dickens, he watched cartoons, commercials, and cheap comedies. I shook my head in sorrow and feared the worst.

Came the day when a firm I had done some work for sent me a Christmas present. I unwrapped it and out came a cylindrical aluminum container.

I looked it over, puzzled, unable to make out what it could possibly be used for. It was far too large for an ashtray and far too small for an umbrella stand. It was the wrong shape to be either a soup tureen or a repository for manuscripts.

While I was staring at it blankly and turning it over and over in the hope that instructions might be printed on it, my son, then a pre-teenager, walked in.

He glanced at the object and asked, "Who sent you the champagne bucket?"

I started. I had never owned a bottle of champagne (let alone a champagne bucket) and I was sure he never had, either.

"How do you know it's a champagne bucket?" I said.

He replied, "I saw one on *The Three Stooges*."

I guess anything can serve as a learning experience.

Isaac Asimov

The amount of information people acquire in a lifetime is staggering. By the time average children enter school, they have mastered many of the intricacies of language. They can count, recite the alphabet, narrate the plots of their favorite stories, and explain the rules of many games. They can also operate mechanical equipment such as a TV set, a telephone, or perhaps even a hand-held calculator. Upon graduation from high school twelve years later, they have probably learned more science and mathematics than their great-grandparents learned in a lifetime. As adults, they will find their way in a complex society that depends upon sophisticated machines. They will learn to drive a car, and may also learn to fly an airplane or to program a computer.

How does a person's intellectual ability develop from the rudimentary capacities present at birth to the sophisticated skills required for survival in today's world? For many years people mistakenly believed that cognitive growth was not so much a process of development and change as a simple process of expansion. Children were viewed as thinking in much the same ways as adults—except that their experience was much more limited and their memories contained fewer "facts." Many parents today still treat their young children as if their learning and thinking capabilities were essentially adultlike (Elkind, 1972), although it is clear that they are not. For example, young children cannot yet generalize from specific incidents to common rules. Thus, if frequently reminded, Janie might learn to put her tricycle away when she finishes riding it. But she will turn around and leave her gun and holster strewn around the living room after a game of cowboys and Indians because she does not understand the similarity between the two situations. What seems like disobedience, then, is often just a reflection of the differences in a child's and an adult's thinking.

The view of children as "miniature adults" stressed the idea that intellectual growth is essentially *quantitative*; that is, as children develop, they gradually acquire more and more knowledge. In contrast, contemporary developmental psychology has become more inclined to emphasize *qualitative* differences in cognitive functioning between adults and children: the idea that children's views of the world are quite different from those of adults. According to the latter emphasis, in order to understand how children think, one must first understand their unique view of the world. Recognition of these qualitative differences in thinking between children and adults has opened up whole new areas of psychological investigation. The Swiss psychologist Jean Piaget has done the most to broaden our qualitative understanding of the child's mind. It is appropriate, therefore, to begin this chapter with a discussion of some of Piaget's ideas.

THE PROCESS OF COGNITIVE DEVELOPMENT: PIAGET'S FRAMEWORK

Much of Piaget's efforts have been devoted to understanding how the child's intelligence is transformed into the intelligence of the adult, becoming increasingly complex, abstract, and subtle with maturity (Piaget, 1952, 1954, 1971; Inhelder and Piaget, 1958). To Piaget, intelligence is not a fixed trait, but a process—the process by which a person constructs an understanding of reality. Constructions of reality mature through encounters between children and their environment, in which children experience a discrepancy between what they already understand and what their environment presents to them. The resolution of this discrepancy transforms children's previous view of how objects and events are related into a new, and more mature, understanding.

SOME BASIC CONCEPTS Piaget identifies three psychological concepts central to this process of intellectual growth: scheme, assimilation, and accommodation.

SCHEME Babies begin life with no understanding of the objects that make up their world, nor with any idea of how their own actions affect those objects. They gradually acquire this knowledge through a process of exploration and experimentation, using certain recurrent action patterns. **Scheme** is Piaget's word for a recurrent action pattern that leads to practical knowledge about one's environment. Infants begin life with a few simple, innately organized schemes, among them grasping and sucking. By using these schemes, infants come to understand and appreciate much of their world in terms of things that can be grasped and sucked. A baby learns, for instance, that he can grasp a toy duck and raise it in his hand, but a wall cannot be grasped. Moreover, when he puts the duck in his mouth and sucks on it, he discovers its body is soft and pliable, very different from the texture of the crib bar, which he has also tried to suck. From simple actions such as these, infants gradually learn

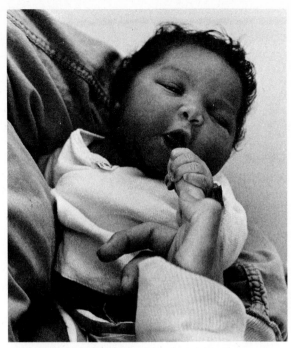

According to Piaget, infants learn the world by using simple action patterns, called schemes, such as grasping and sucking.

the effects their own movements have on objects, as well as some of the properties of those objects.

As children grow older, their schemes for understanding the world become more complicated and less dependent on overt action. They become what Piaget calls "interiorized schemes." This means they are carried out mentally without physical action. Mental arithmetic replaces counting on the fingers; logical reasoning replaces physical experimentation with cause-and-effect relationships. Thus a ten-month-old baby may explore gravity by dropping his green peas from the highchair tray and watching intently as each one hits the floor. An older child, in contrast, who has come to understand the way gravity operates, knows that if she releases any object from an elevated position, it will always fall. The scheme of the older child is internalized; that of the infant is not.

ASSIMILATION AND ACCOMMODATION According to Piaget, children's thinking develops through two processes: assimilation and accommodation. **Assimilation** refers to the incorporation of new knowledge through the use of existing schemes. **Accommodation** refers to the modification of existing schemes to incorporate new knowledge that does not fit them. Consider an infant who has been bottle-fed for several months and can suck

very competently on a nipple. One day he is given a cup to drink from. At first he tries to assimilate the new experience by sucking on the cup in exactly the same way as he has always sucked on his bottle. But this strategy does not work well. He must therefore modify or accommodate his oral skills to the new element in his environment. Within a few days he will probably have learned how to use his sucking skills to drain milk from the cup (assimilation). Moreover, he will also have modified these skills so that they are more effective for cup-drinking (accommodation). The processes of assimilation and accommodation, then, always work in a complementary fashion (see Figure 8.1). The behavior of the child in a new situation represents a balance—in Piaget's term, an **equilibration**—between these processes.

Piaget explains cognitive development in terms of the mind constantly seeking an equilibrium between assimilation and accommodation. Infants start life with relatively primitive schemes. As they apply those schemes to the world around them, they must continually adjust them in order to assimilate new knowledge that would not ordinarily fit them. Through this process of accommodation, infants' schemes gradually become more refined and adultlike. Their intelligence grows. The photos on page 178 show how a child applies a grasping and pulling scheme to a toy and how she accommodates that scheme by assimilating features of the environment—the shape of the toy and the space between

Figure 8.1 Piaget's "knowing circle." Assimilation and accommodation are reciprocal processes that continue until a fit is achieved between a scheme and an object. The entire process of cognitive development is regulated by the continuous interaction of assimilation and accommodation and the shifting balance or equilibrium between them.

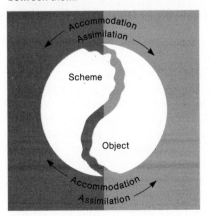

(reading from left to right and top to bottom) This child possesses a scheme for grasping objects and pulling them to her that does not adequately match the features of the environment that she is now trying to assimilate. Her scheme will not get the toy through the bars of the playpen. An accommodation to her scheme—the addition of turning to grasping and pulling—achieves a state of equilibrium.

the bars of the crib. In this way the child's knowledge about the world, and her competence in it, mature.

PERIODS OF INTELLECTUAL DEVELOPMENT

Much of the power of Piaget's view comes from his careful documentation of how children construct their understandings of reality. In doing this, Piaget uses the concept of periods of intellectual development. The intellectual development of children, according to Piaget, includes four main periods: the **sensorimotor period**, which encompasses the first two years of life; the **preoperational period**, which occurs during the preschool years; the **concrete-operational period**, which begins to appear between the fifth and seventh years and continues to develop during the elementary school years; and the **formal-operational period**, which begins around adolescence and may continue to develop throughout adulthood.

Later in this chapter we will discuss exactly what children learn during each of these periods. The important idea to remember at this point is that these periods are *qualitatively* different from one another. Children develop new ways of thinking during each successive period. Moreover, the speed of individual children's development through each of the four periods varies widely, depending upon their genetic makeup and environment. In a suitably rich environment, children gradually acquire the cognitive capabilities that will carry their thinking to a new, more mature stage of intellectual development. Yet the thought processes of the earlier periods are not entirely lost—they are simply reduced in importance. For example, an adult who has mastered formal-operational thinking is capable of functioning at the level of all three earlier periods.

Psychologists other than Piaget have also attempted to describe the various periods of human intellectual development. Whatever labels are attached to them, these periods all represent roughly the same stages of cognitive growth: infancy, the preschool years, later childhood, adolescence, and adulthood. The remainder of this chapter, therefore, is devoted to the cognitive changes that occur during these five basic periods. In presenting them, we draw heavily on the work of Piaget, but include the research of many other developmental psychologists as well.

INFANCY

A three-year-old girl listens intently as her father reads her a bedtime story. She giggles over the mischievous parts and gasps at the narrow escapes. As pictures of new characters appear, she excitedly points them out, urging her father to turn to the next page. In a corner of the room the little girl's baby brother lies peacefully in his crib. He gurgles to himself, kicks his feet, and stares at the mobile suspended above his head. No one can tell what he is thinking, if he is thinking at all.

If you were asked to observe this scene and select the one person whose intellectual skills seem most unlike those of the other two, you would undoubtedly choose the infant (Flavell, 1977, pp. 14–15). Although chronologically the three-year-old girl is closer to her newborn brother, cognitively she is much closer to her father. We know very little about the mind of the infant, but it seems to bear almost no resemblance to the mind of the adult. In contrast, both the little girl and her father can use language, interact socially, and understand events that take place in their environment. During the brief period between birth and early childhood, a baby becomes so different cognitively from the newborn as to seem almost a member of a different species. How does this enormous growth in cognitive skills come about in such a short time?

What are an infant's intellectual skills? One thing psychologists know is that a baby is capable of learning from the moment of birth.

THE INFANT'S CAPACITY FOR LEARNING

As we mentioned in Chapter 7, babies are capable of learning from the moment of birth, and perhaps even before birth. But it was not until fairly recently that researchers discovered how well-developed the learning capacity of infants really is.

CONDITIONING AND THE NEWBORN Human infants can readily learn by means of conditioning techniques. In one operant conditioning experiment (Siqueland and Lipsitt, 1966), babies only two to four days old were presented with different sounds as their right cheeks were gently stroked. The sound of a tone signaled that a head turn to the right would be rewarded with a mouthful of sugar solution. The sound of a buzzer indicated that no reward would be given, regardless of whether or not the babies turned their heads. The infants quickly learned this pattern of reinforcement. They turned their heads far more when they heard the tone than when they heard the buzzer. Furthermore, their learning ability proved quite flexible. When the meanings of the two signals were reversed, so that the buzzer meant "reward" and the tone meant "no reward," the infants adapted to the new cues in just a few trials. Thus human newborns clearly have the capacity to learn, unlearn, and relearn simple contingencies. But what is the basis for this early learning?

LEARNING FOR THE FUN OF IT Babies seem to learn readily, even when the "reward" involved is only the flash of a light bulb or some other seemingly minor event (Papoušek, 1969). Apparently, part of infants' affinity for learning is self-motivated. Solving a problem, learning the relationship between one of their own actions and an event in the external world, seems to have its own rewards for infants. Suppose an infant is placed in a crib with a mobile above his head. A string is attached to each of the baby's wrists and to each of his ankles. The string tied to the left ankle makes the mobile move. The other strings do not. What does a baby do in this situation? A baby about nine months old usually waves his arms and kicks his legs, just as babies of this age normally do. But suddenly he notices that the mobile is moving. The infant freezes. His eyes are glued to the bobbing objects. Slowly he moves one arm and then the other arm, one leg and then the other leg, until he discovers the relationship between his own movements and those of the mo-

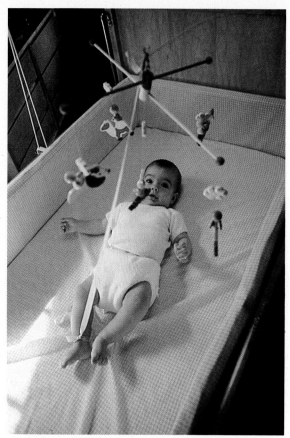

Babies can make their own fun. Several investigators have found that if a mobile is attached to an infant in such a way that the infant's own movements activate the mobile, the infant soon discovers this relationship and coos, smiles, and seems to delight in making the appropriate kick to set the mobile in motion.

SENSORIMOTOR INTELLIGENCE AND THE OBJECT CONCEPT

As we have just seen, much of what babies learn in the first months of life are simple relationships between objects in the world around them and between their own behavior and those objects. Such learning, which apparently is a source of great pleasure for infants, is part of what Piaget calls **sensorimotor intelligence**. Piaget suggests the term **practical intelligence** as a rough synonym for sensorimotor intelligence. As this term implies, infants learn to act in the world—to get along practically in it. But they do not appear to contemplate their own behavior—to think about what they are doing and why they are doing it. Adults, too, rely on sensorimotor intelligence, for example, when riding a bicycle or running down a flight of stairs. Such tasks are so automatic we seldom think about them. In the same way, infants do not seem to reflect on what they are doing. They simply do it.

An important aspect of the development of sensorimotor intelligence is the development of what Piaget calls the **object concept**, or the **concept of object permanence**. According to Piaget, a very young infant does not seem to understand that her body is one object in a world of objects, some animate like herself, others inanimate. Nor does she appear to recognize that objects have a permanent existence outside her own interaction with them—that they continue to be, to move, and to be acted upon by others when she is not present. The ability to conceive of objects as having an existence of their own emerges gradually during the first two years of life.

Early in infancy, from birth to perhaps four months of age, babies will look at a toy if it is within their visual range, and follow it with their eyes. And they will grasp the toy if it is within their reach. But as soon as the object is moved out of sight, say behind a screen or under a pillow, the babies act as if it ceased to exist. They do not search for it either with their eyes or with their hands, nor do they show any other sign that they are aware of its continued existence.

According to Piaget, the first signs of the development of the object concept appear around the fourth month (or even much earlier, in the view of some other researchers, notably Bower, 1974). If only part of a familiar object is visible—if, for example, the edge of a rattle is sticking out from beneath a blanket—babies of this age may reach for the toy, suggesting that they realize the rest of it is attached to the part that is showing. At an earlier stage, infants would not have reached for the rattle

bile. A wide smile spreads across the infant's face. He gurgles with apparent delight, kicking the appropriate leg and watching the mobile flutter. If the contingency is then changed, so that, say, the right arm now operates the mobile, the baby will again search for the solution and coo vigorously when he discovers it (Monnier, Boehmer, and Scholer, 1976).

John S. Watson, who was one of the first researchers to notice this infant response to learning, suggests that babies derive a form of intellectual pleasure simply from solving a problem (Watson, 1972). Nor is this pleasure limited to infancy alone. In an experiment with fifth- and sixth-graders (Harter, 1974), subjects were asked to solve some word puzzles that varied in difficulty. The children smiled more and reported far more pleasure when they solved a difficult puzzle than an easy one. The implication is that humans of all ages, from infants to adults, derive pleasure from intellectual mastery.

at all unless it were fully visible. There are also indications around the fourth month that babies are beginning to understand that a disappearing object may still exist. If an object is moved across their visual field, infants between four and eight months not only turn their heads to follow it, but continue to look along its path even after it has vanished from sight. They seem, in other words, to visually search for the missing object.

But oddly enough, if the object is placed behind a piece of paper or under a pillow, babies at this stage will not search for the object with their hands even though it is easily reachable. More mysterious still, babies will not retrieve the "hidden" object when they are already grasping it! If a pillow is quickly placed over an object that a baby is holding, he will gaze aimlessly around, seemingly unaware that his hand still holds something, or he will let go of the object and withdraw his empty hand. Clearly, the infant's object concept at this age is still rudimentary.

At the next stage in the development of the object concept, from about eight to twelve months of age, infants for the first time search manually for an object that disappears from sight. Suppose an infant is shown a desirable toy until she displays a clear interest in it. Then, while the child watches, the toy is put under a pillow. At this stage, the infant will toss the pillow aside and grasp the toy. But the ability to locate hidden objects still shows a strange deficit. If a toy that has previously been placed under one pillow is then—in full sight of the child—placed under a second pillow, the baby still looks for the toy under the *first* pillow. She repeats the action that produced the toy earlier, rather than looking for it where she last saw it.

When children reach the last purely sensorimotor stage in the development of the object concept, they can follow all the visible movements of an object and therefore find it in the last place it was hidden. When an object is hidden under one pillow and then under a second one, the child reaches for it under the second one. Indeed, he can find the object even if it is hidden under a third or fourth pillow. The only remaining limit to babies' understanding of actions carried out on objects is that they still cannot cope with transformations they do not see. Suppose that an object is hidden in a matchbox, and the matchbox is placed under a pillow. Then, while the infant is not looking, the object is secretly removed from the box and left under the pillow. The empty matchbox is put in front of the child, who quickly searches it. She does not, however, search under the pillow. She cannot yet take into account the possibility that something she did not see might have happened. The final recognition of object per-

By about eight months of age, an infant will search for an object that has disappeared from sight.

manence comes when children understand that an object can be moved from place to place even when they do not see it being moved. This development marks the end of the sensorimotor period.

CHILDHOOD

Between the ages of two and three, the cognitive world of infancy is left behind. Children have discovered that objects and events can be represented by symbols—they have begun to acquire language. This is a tremendously important accomplishment. With words, children's powers of thought and communication are greatly expanded, and they continue to expand as intellectual skills mature. Clearly the intelligence of children is very different from the action-bound intelligence of infants. In the following sections, we will explore some of the landmarks in cognitive development during childhood and the paths by which they are reached.

COGNITIVE SKILLS OF THE PRESCHOOLER

During the preschool years, children begin to acquire many cognitive skills that will be important to them in adult life. They learn to count, for example, and to classify objects into general categories. But young children's real grasp of these concepts may be deceptive. Their intelligence at this stage is based more on intuition than on the logical reasoning of older children or adults. Consequently, Piaget labels this period of intellectual growth the **intuitive phase**.

REPRESENTATIONAL SKILLS   One of the most important cognitive skills underlying preschool children's intelligence is the ability to engage in what is called **representational thought**. The development of the object concept marks the beginning of this new, important capacity. Children can now think about objects that are not directly in front of them. They can imagine, and by doing so, they expand their world far beyond the limits of their immediate perceptions.

The ability to think representationally engenders a number of new accomplishments besides an understanding of object permanence. First, children are capable of deferred imitation—that is, they can imitate someone else's actions a long time after they have seen them. Second, they begin to show insight learning (discussed in Chapter 6). They look at a problematic situation, pause to think about it for a moment, and then, after what seems like an "Aha!" reaction, solve the problem. Third, they begin to play "make-believe," pretending, for example, that they are astronauts and that a large cardboard crate they have found is a spaceship. Finally, and probably most important, preschool children begin to use language (an achievement that is discussed in detail in Chapter 9). Each of these abilities is a sign of a new type of intelligence that, although still limited in some ways, is qualitatively different from sensorimotor intelligence.

IMMATURE FEATURES OF THE YOUNG CHILD'S THINKING   Representational thinking permits preschool children an intuitive understanding of

By age four, children can fantasize that they are imaginary figures such as Batman and Robin.

many complex tasks, but their intellectual capacities are in many ways still immature. For one thing, their thought is egocentric. This term does not mean that children are deliberately selfish. Rather, it means that in some ways they are prisoners of their own viewpoint. They do not seem to understand that different people have different perspectives and that their own is merely one among many. In one experimental demonstration of this **egocentrism** (Piaget and Inhelder, 1969), a child is shown a model of a mountain range composed of three mountains in a triangular arrangement (see Figure 8.2). The model is large, so the child must walk around it to look at all its sides. After he is familiar with the landscape, the child sits in a chair facing one of the mountains. The experimenter sits in a chair facing another side of the model and asks the child which of several pictures shows what the experimenter sees. The child repeatedly chooses the picture showing his own view of the landscape.

A second immature feature of the young child's thinking is illustrated in the following poem written by Hilary-Anne Farley, age five (in Lewis, 1966):

I LOVE ANIMALS AND DOGS

I love animals and dogs and everything
But how can I do it when dogs are dead and a
    hundred?
But here's the reason: If you put a golden egg on them
They'll get better. But not if you put a star or moon.
But the star-moon goes up
And the star-moon I love.

This poem shows what has been called **complexive thinking** (Vygotsky, 1962). Instead of unifying a number of thoughts around a single theme, it jumps from one idea to the next, frequently showing connections between adjacent ideas but having no overall integration. Some element in one idea makes Hilary-Anne think of another idea. Some element in the second idea makes her think of a third, and so on. Although every idea is related to some other, the various ideas are not coordinated into a meaningful whole. Complexive thinking like Hilary-Anne's is common in preschool children.

The inability to carry out tasks that require self-directed thinking is also common. Preschoolers need external cues to guide and sustain their behavior. For example, a four-year-old may prefer playing with building blocks with projections and indentations because they show the child how the blocks fit together. Ordinary blocks, without such

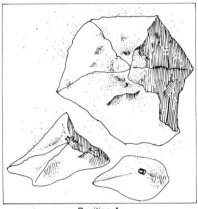

Position A

Figure 8.2 A model used to demonstrate egocentrism. Piaget and Inhelder first had children walk all around the model and look at it from all sides. Then they seated children of various ages at position A and asked them how the scene would appear to observers at other positions. Pre-operational children regularly indicated that the scene would appear as it did from position A, no matter where the observer was located. Their thinking did not allow them to mentally reconstruct the scene from a point of view other than their own. (After Piaget and Inhelder, 1956.)

guides, are less likely to hold his or her interest. The young child lacks the skill to coordinate the building of a pyramid in the absence of clear external cues.

These limitations of preschool children's thought form a unified picture. On the one hand, the children's capacity for representation allows them to carry on new, complex kinds of mental activity. On the other hand, they do not yet have the ability to organize their thinking into coordinated systems. Their thinking is egocentric as they have difficulty apprehending and coordinating various points of view. It is complexive—flitting from one idea to another—because they cannot coordinate their thoughts around a single concept. And it is controlled by prominent cues in the environment because they have trouble with cognitive tasks that require them to coordinate and direct their own thinking.

COGNITIVE SKILLS OF THE OLDER CHILD Although some of the thinking of older children is similar to the intuitive thought of preschoolers, older children can think in logical ways that younger children cannot. Between the ages of five and seven, children begin to understand what Piaget calls **concrete operations**—simple transformations carried out on concrete objects. It takes an additional five years or more, however, for this capacity to become fully developed. The best example is the gradual development of what is called the concept of conservation.

THE CONCEPT OF CONSERVATION During the late preschool years, children can correctly predict the effects of certain simple manipulations of liquids. If the liquid in a medium-width container is poured into a narrow container, they can usually predict correctly that the liquid will be higher in the narrow container. But they do not yet understand that the amount of liquid stays the same when poured from container to container. In other words, they have not yet grasped the **concept of conservation** of liquid volume.

What is required for them to develop this concept? Children must be able to coordinate their thoughts about the length and width of each container, as well as about the nature of the change brought about by pouring the liquid from the first container to the second. Preschool children cannot do this. They consider the state of each container separately and consequently say that the liquid that is "taller" is *more*. Older children, on the other hand, pay close attention to the transformation that occurs as the liquid is poured from one container to another and coordinate their thoughts about that transformation with their thoughts about the height and width of each container. As a result, they correctly answer that both containers have the same amount.

During the period of concrete operations, children come to grasp other concepts of conservation, including those shown in Figure 8.3. But they do not develop an understanding of all types of conservation simultaneously. Conservation of number is understood first, then conservation of volume, still later conservation of weight, and so on. Thus, although older children understand a growing number of specific concrete operations, they cannot yet understand the similarities that exist between these operations. Consequently, each type of conservation seems like a new problem to them. They cannot, for example, apply what they already know

The girl taking part in this demonstration has not yet acquired the ability to understand the concept of conservation of quantity of liquid. She agrees that there is an equal amount of water in the two shorter beakers on the right, but when the water from one of them is poured into the taller beaker on the left, she incorrectly asserts that there is more water in the taller beaker than in the shorter. To develop an understanding of the principle of conservation, the child must be able to coordinate her thoughts about the length and width of the first container, the length and width of the second container, and the change or transformation brought about by pouring the liquid from the shorter beaker into the taller. Preoperational children cannot do this: they consider the state of each container separately, and consequently point to the beaker that "looks like more" as the one that actually "is more."

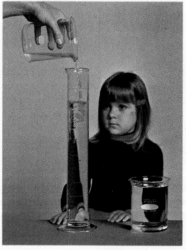

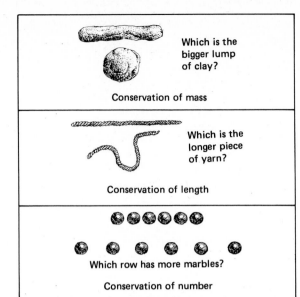

Figure 8.3 Examples of problems for which a child must acquire the concept of conservation. Concrete-operational children interiorize the possibility of making and unmaking the transformations for each task shown here. Thus, they come to see the lengths and quantities as unchanged in each case. Pre-operational children, who are not able to imagine the transformations required, respond to perceptually striking but irrelevant aspects of the objects in attempting to answer the questions. For example, pre-operational children will answer that there are more marbles in the bottom row than in the top one.

about the principle of conservation of volume to their newly acquired understanding of the concept of conservation of weight. In short, they do not link the related concepts together and understand all types of conservation at once.

THE ABILITY TO CLASSIFY Conservation is only one of many concrete-operational concepts that older children gradually master. Included among the other concepts are several dealing with classification. How well do children understand the different ways of classifying things? The answer to that question provides an especially good contrast between the thinking capacities of older children and those of preschoolers. Older children can analyze objects on two separate levels and coordinate their thinking about them.

One of the main skills needed to master classification is the ability to understand the addition of classes. Children must know, for example, that the class of dogs is made up of the subclass of poodles, the subclass of terriers, the subclass of spaniels, and so forth. In other words, they need to understand that the subclasses for different breeds are added together to form the more general class "dogs."

As with conservation, preschool children can grasp some of the concepts needed to understand the addition of classes, but they cannot coordinate their thinking. A simple example shows the kinds of questions they can answer and the kinds they cannot. Suppose a child is given eight toy poodles, two toy terriers, and three toy cats. The child is first asked to sort similar toys into separate piles. An early preschool child will not even be able to sort them properly, but a late preschool child will manage to make three simple groups—one of poodles, one of terriers, and one of cats.

When the late preschool child has done this, the experimenter begins to pose a number of questions. Which of the toys are dogs? The child points to the group of poodles and the group of terriers. Which are cats? He points to the group of cats. Which of the toys are animals? He points to all three groups. Are there more poodles or more terriers? The child correctly chooses poodles. Are there more dogs or more cats? He correctly indicates more dogs. The child seems to understand classes and to be able to use them properly—so far. But his answers to a few key questions show that this conclusion is incorrect. If asked, for example, are there more dogs or more poodles, he may reply, "more poodles." The child, in other words, cannot coordinate two levels of classification: the general class of dogs and the subclasses of poodles and terriers. Elementary school children, in contrast, can answer such questions correctly, and they can also construct the simple diagram shown in Figure 8.4C on page 188.

In addition, older children have developed a second skill required for classification—the ability to multiply classes. For example, given the different-colored geometric shapes in Figure 8.4A, preschoolers cannot construct the arrangement shown in Figure 8.4C. Older children, in contrast, can easily sort the pieces by color and shape and arrange them in meaningful horizontal and vertical groups of three. And they can explain how the rows and columns are organized. In short, they have mastered the multiplication of classes.

The capacity of older children to coordinate their thoughts into systems is, of course, by no means limited to experimental situations in the laboratory. They are able, for example, to understand and follow the rules of many rather complicated games, such as Monopoly and baseball. They are also less egocentric, in the sense that they are better able to understand that their viewpoints are not the only possible ones, to comprehend the fact that other people's viewpoints may disagree with theirs, and to

Memory in Babies and Children

Eric, thirteen months old, was sitting on the floor with three books nearby. His mother asked him to show her the picture of "Wee Willie Winkie," his favorite Mother Goose character. Without hesitating, Eric selected the right book and turned the pages until he found "Wee Willie." Eric's display of memory was not as remarkable as it may appear: even newborn babies remember things.

Babies' Capacity for Memory

Recognition Memory

How do psychologists know that babies can remember? An important piece of evidence comes from the tendency of infants to habituate to a stimulus over a period of time. Babies, in other words, seem to lose interest when shown the same object or played the same sound over and over. But is this loss of interest due to the fact that the babies remember the repeated stimulus and are therefore growing bored with it? Or are they simply getting tired of being experimented upon? In one study designed to answer this question, researchers measured the time that infants looked at an object. Then, when the babies began to turn away, they changed the stimulus. The infants' attention was immediately recaptured, which indicates that they were not fatigued at all. Instead, they had detected the difference between the new stimulus and the old one (Friedman, Bruno, and Vietze, 1974).

On the basis of this and other research, we can conclude that newborns can form a memory of a stimulus, retain that memory

for five to ten seconds until another stimulus is presented, then recognize that the new stimulus is either familiar or unfamiliar. That is, they clearly display what is called **recognition memory**. In fact, in one study using the habituation technique, four- to six-month-old infants showed signs that they recognized a photograph of a human face two weeks after they had been exposed to it for a few minutes (Olson, 1976).

Studies of recognition, then, indicate that infants can certainly remember, even during the earliest weeks of life. But how much of what they are exposed to can they recall in later life? Very little work has been

done on this question. However, anecdotal evidence suggests that much of what babies see and hear is not retained years later, as it is with older children or adults. You can easily remember what the house you lived in when you were twelve looked like, or what kind of car your closest friend in high school drove. But what do you remember about the first two years of your life? Can you recall your first Christmas or the first time you tottered on two feet? If you are like most people, you have probably forgotten these events. Why?

Amnesia for Infant Experiences

We learn so much during in-

This photograph by Ellen Cowin was inspired by memories of a friend's living room. In children the lack of memory strategies makes remembering such things as this, difficult.

fancy, yet we seem unable to recall anything specific. Could it be that the development of permanent memory depends on the ability to use language? This is a distinct possibility, because permanent memory and language ability tend to emerge at about the same time. Perhaps we must be able to label things before we can remember them over long periods. Or perhaps Freud was right, and we repress events from infancy as we grow older. Although both these theories suggest factors that might contribute to infantile amnesia, recent research suggests that it may also be related to immature neural development (Campbell et al., 1974).

In another experiment supporting this idea, baby rats eleven to sixteen days old were subjected to "fear conditioning" in which a tone was associated with a brief shock (Coulter, Collier, and Campbell, 1976). Six weeks later the rats showed virtually *no* recollection of the tone–shock association. Yet other rats, which had learned the tone–shock pairing at the age of seventeen days, remembered quite well after a six-week lapse. What could explain this difference? Why would a rat trained at the age of fifteen days forget its training within six weeks, while a rat trained at the age of seventeen days remembers it perfectly? The answer seems to lie in the course of neurological growth. This abrupt apparent change in a rat's capacity for long-term memory occurs right in the middle of an important period of brain development. Baby guinea pigs, in contrast, which are born with a fully developed nervous system, have long-term memory capability virtually from birth. Thus a primary reason for

infantile amnesia in many very young animals may be the immaturity of certain brain structures. This explanation probably applies to humans as well. The maturation of nerve cells in the brain as babies grow older may underlie the emergence of an ability to efficiently store information and retrieve it from long-term memory.

Memory Strategies in Children

This capacity for efficient memory storage and retrieval does not become fully developed until after the age of six. Thus, children age six and younger use fewer strategies for storing and retrieving information than do adults (Flavell and Wellman, 1977). One experiment has shown that six-year-olds do not use available cues to recall information unless they are specifically instructed to do so (Kobasigawa, 1974). Six-, eight-, and eleven-year-olds were shown pictures of three related objects, along with a card to help them remember each group. One group of pictures, for example, showed a bear, a monkey, and a camel, while the card showed a zoo with three empty cages. The experimenter explicitly related the card to the pictures by pointing out that the zoo is the place where these animals live. Later, some of the children were given the stack of cards and asked to recall the three objects associated with each one. They were told they could look at the cards if that would help them remember.

Two-thirds of the six-year-olds virtually ignored the cards. It seemed as if they simply did not grasp the relationship between the cues they held in their laps and their ability to retrieve information. The eleven-year-

olds, in contrast, used the cues quite effectively, often recalling all three items associated with a card before moving on to the next one. The eight-year-olds were somewhere in between. They sometimes used the cue cards, but their strategy was not as effective as that of the eleven-year-olds. Somewhat surprisingly, however, when all the children were *required* to use the cue cards, age differences in recall disappeared. These results suggest that at least some of the original differences observed were not differences in memory capacity per se, but rather in knowledge of how to use retrieval strategies effectively.

Children's lack of memory strategies becomes even more apparent when they are compared with adults. When presented with long strings of letters or digits, adults tend to group them in some way; many, for example, group them in threes by pausing slightly after every third one. Young children, in contrast, do not automatically use this kind of strategy. Nor do young children spontaneously rehearse the information they are trying to remember, as adults do (Chi, 1976).

Like all of us, of course, children have difficulty remembering things that they aren't familiar with. With their limited experience, they are familiar with far fewer things than adults are. Consequently, adults will remember many more things more easily than children will. Even when children do remember things, however, they lack the strategies that adults use to retrieve the information they have stored. In short, young children simply do not yet know *how* to remember.

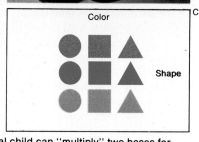

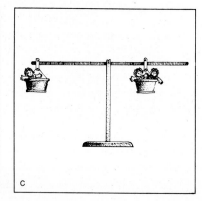

Figure 8.4 The photographs in (A) and (B) show a problem that requires multiplication of classes and the partial solution that a pre-operational child might be able to achieve. The diagram in (C) shows how the concrete-operational child can "multiply" two bases for classification (shape and color) to produce a complete classification.

coordinate other people's viewpoints with their own. Thus, the thinking of children in the concrete-operational stage has taken on many of the characteristics of adult thought.

However, there are definite limitations to older children's capacity to coordinate their thinking. (These limitations affect children's ability to remember things; for a comparison of memory in infants, children, and adults, see the accompanying special feature.) Piaget calls the period "concrete operations" because children can deal only with concrete objects and events. They are still unable to analyze hypothetical situations. This more advanced capacity develops later, during adolescence.

ADOLESCENCE

Around the beginning of adolescence a new set of cognitive capabilities, which Piaget calls **formal-operational intelligence**, starts to emerge. Children are able to carry out systematic tests to prove or dis-

Figure 8.5 A demonstration of formal operational intelligence. A full understanding of the principles by means of which the beam in C can be balanced is not reached until formal operations are acquired. Such an understanding requires the coordination of the two sets of principles diagramed in A and B. A shows the multiplication of the two classes "left-right" and "add weight—subtract weight." B shows the multiplication of "left-right" and "move weight in—move weight out."

Concrete-operational children can understand both of these ways of balancing the beam, but they cannot coordinate them. They cannot extract the principle that extra weight on one side of the balance can be counteracted by moving the weights on the other side farther from the fulcrum; that is, they fail to see that distance can compensate for weight, and weight for distance. (After Piaget and Inhelder, 1969.)

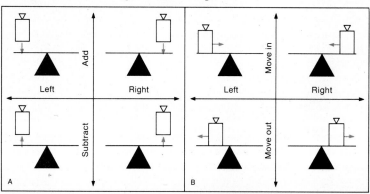

188

prove possible explanations, and they can think hypothetically and in abstract terms. As a result, they can solve new kinds of problems that would have been beyond their reach only a few years ago.

One of Piaget's tasks demonstrating the central difference between concrete operations and formal operations is shown in Figure 8.5 on page 188.

SYSTEMATIC EXPERIMENTATION One of the most important new skills of adolescents is the ability to consider all the possible combinations of factors that may have caused an event and, through a

process of careful reasoning, to eliminate the irrelevant ones. In other words, they can carry out systematic experiments. One task Piaget created to investigate this skill involves the following materials: four beakers of colorless, odorless liquids labeled 1, 2, 3, and 4, plus a smaller bottle, labeled *g*, also containing a colorless, odorless liquid. The children are given some empty glasses and asked to find the liquid or combinations of liquid that will turn yellow when a few drops from bottle *g* are added to it (see Figure 8.6). The combination that produces the yellow color is 1 plus 3 plus *g*. The liquid in 2 is plain water and has no effect on the reaction, and the liquid in 4 prevents the yellow from appearing. Because the children must find out by trial and error what each liquid does, they must try all possible combinations. Otherwise, they cannot be sure of their conclusions. If they succeed, they are questioned about the function of each of the four liquids.

When presented with this task, elementary school children often begin by systematically trying out all the single possibilities. They may test 4 plus *g*, then 2 plus *g*, then 1 plus *g*, then 3 plus *g*. When none of these combinations produces yellow, they are likely to say, "I tried them all and none of them works." With a little coaching from the experimenter, they may realize that more than one liquid can be combined with *g*, but they then mix the liquids haphazardly. They are unable to test all combinations systematically. Adolescents, in contrast, can systematically consider all possible combinations of the four liquids. Some may need a paper and pencil to keep track of the combinations that they have made, but they nevertheless understand how to generate the full set. In short, they are capable of conducting systematic experiments.

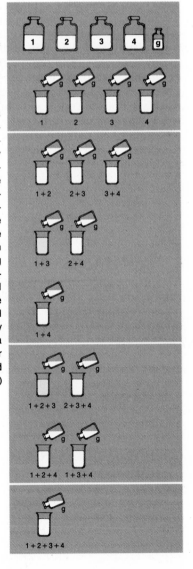

Figure 8.6 A problem that requires the systematic examination of hypotheses for its solution. The chemicals selected by Piaget and Inhelder for this problem have unexpected interactions. It is virtually impossible to determine how the color yellow is produced without trying every possible combination of the liquids, as shown here, and keeping track of the results. Not until children reach the formal-operational period can they conceive of such a procedure. (After Piaget and Inhelder, 1969.)

HYPOTHETICAL IDEAS AND ABSTRACT THINKING Adolescents also develop the capacity to consider the hypothetical, even when the thing hypothesized is highly fanciful. Suppose, for example, that an adolescent and a younger child are asked the following question: "If a man can climb a ladder at 2 miles per hour, how long will it take him to reach the moon, which is 240,000 miles away?" The younger child is likely to dismiss the question with a patronizing look and declare, "You can't climb to the moon on a ladder." The adolescent, on the other hand, can accept the silly hypothesis and reason out the answer. The cognitive processes of

"You ought to go to a boys' school sometime. Try it sometime," I said. "It's full of phonies, and all you do is study so that you can learn enough to be smart enough to be able to buy a goddam Cadillac some day, and you have to keep making believe you give a damn if the football team loses, and all you do is talk about girls and liquor and sex all day, and everybody sticks together in these dirty little goddam cliques. The guys that are on the basketball team stick together, the Catholics stick together, the goddam intellectuals stick together. . . If you try to have a little intelligent—"

"Now *listen*," old Sally said. "Lots of boys get more out of school than *that*."

"I agree! I agree they do, some of them! But that's all I get out of it. See? That's my point. . . I don't get hardly anything out of anything. I'm in bad shape. I'm in *lousy* shape."

Figure 8.7 In this dialogue from J. D. Salinger's novel *The Catcher in the Rye*, Holden Caulfield's remarks reveal the more abstract cognition that becomes possible at adolescence. This new ability to think about thinking is accompanied by the tendency to reflect on such abstract notions as the nature of self, identity, and values.

adolescents, in other words, are no longer bound by physical reality.

With the ability to think hypothetically comes the ability to understand abstract principles. This new capacity is extremely important to adolescents. It allows them to study such fields as mathematics, science, and language on a higher, less concrete level than they had earlier, and it brings about dramatic changes in their daily concerns. They may become preoccupied with abstract notions such as ethical ideals, conformity, and phoniness (see Figure 8.7). They will often apply their new abilities to their own thoughts and motives. It is no accident that adolescence is the first phase of life in which individuals begin to think carefully about themselves, their role in life, their plans, and the validity and integrity of their beliefs. Unlike younger children, who deal largely with the present, adolescents are often concerned with the meaning of their past and the direction of their future.

Simply because adolescents have reached the stage of formal operations, however, does not mean that they will be able to apply their reasoning ability successfully to all appropriate situations. They may misunderstand the demands of a particular task or find a certain problem too difficult. In a study of adolescents of above-average intelligence, not one of the subjects correctly solved all items in a series of formal-operational tasks (Martorano, 1977). Moreover, research has shown that even well-educated adults commit all sorts of errors on problems of formal reasoning (Henle, 1962; Wason and Johnson-Laird, 1972). It has even been suggested that as few as 50 percent of adults ever reach this last Piagetian stage of formal operations (Arlin, 1975). Piaget himself felt that most adults may be capable of using formal thinking only in their own

areas of experience and expertise. Astronomers, for example, can apply formal hypothesis testing to the calculation of planetary motion, but they may not readily apply it to the repair of their cars. Thus the specific knowledge and training people have is just as important to their cognitive performance as the general level of intellectual development they have reached. Both scientists and auto mechanics may use highly logical, deductive reasoning to solve problems. The major difference between them is the subject matter to which those thought processes are applied.

ADULTHOOD

As anyone reading this book knows, cognitive development does not stop with adolescence. We continue to learn and to understand increasingly complex material as adults. Moreover, our cognitive development during adulthood generally follows a fairly predictable pattern. Although individuals vary, most people proceed through a similar cycle of intellectual growth and productivity from early to middle to later adulthood.

COGNITIVE SKILLS IN EARLY AND MIDDLE ADULTHOOD It is very difficult to specify the exact age at which a person passes from adolescence to early adulthood and from early adulthood to middle age. For our purposes, however, we will define early adulthood as the years from age twenty to age forty, and middle adulthood as the years from forty to sixty. What cognitive changes can be expected during these forty years?

Research has shown that the early and middle adult years are a time of peak intellectual accomplishment. A thirty-eight-year study of intellectual performance revealed that IQ generally increased into the middle years (Bradway, 1944; Kangas and Bradway, 1971). On any kind of learning or memory task, young adults usually perform better than they ever have before. And if success at a task depends on how fast one does it, they probably do at least a little better than they ever will again. Early adulthood is also likely to be the time when people are most intellectually flexible. They can usually accept new ideas quite easily, and they can readily shift their strategies for solving problems. Of course, age is not the only determinant of learning, memory, and thinking ability. Intelligence, education, and health also contribute heavily to all three.

Provided individuals remain healthy, their verbal and reasoning skills are likely to get even better during middle adulthood. Middle-aged adults continue to learn and to store new information just as they always have. Consequently, they are often more knowledgeable than they were in their younger years. The ability of individuals to organize and to process visual information, as in finding a simple figure in a complex one, also improves in middle adulthood. In addition, the ability to think flexibly, to shift the set of one's mind to solve a problem, is likely to be as good as it was in early adulthood. Only when individuals are asked to do a task that involves coordinated hand–eye movements do they tend to do less well than they used to, because motor skills often decline in middle age (Baltes and Schaie, 1974). In all other ways, however, adults in their middle years are in their intellectual prime.

COGNITIVE SKILLS IN LATER ADULTHOOD

One question frequently asked in this era of increasing life expectancies (see Figure 8.8), is whether the traditional "retirement age" of sixty-five or seventy is justified. Do intellectual skills decline in later adulthood, making older adults less capable workers than younger ones? Recent reviews of cognitive changes associated with aging suggest not. Although a number of physiological and cognitive declines generally accompany the aging process, many people do not experience significant impairment of

intellectual performance in later adulthood (see Figure 8.9). In the following section we will briefly outline some of the developmental changes that occur with advancing age and then assess their impact on an individual's ability to cope.

CHANGES ASSOCIATED WITH AGING Of all the changes that accompany aging, perhaps the most characteristic is the tendency to "slow down." Some investigators have argued that this slowness is mainly a reactive one, resulting from reduced sensory input—that, for example, the reason older drivers hit the brakes more slowly is that they see the stop sign later and more dimly than do younger drivers. However, it appears that old people are equally slow in self-initiated behaviors. Indeed, it seems that all behavior slows down in the aging organism (Birren, 1974). This change is thought to be due to a process called **primary neural aging**, in which the transmission of information in the nervous system becomes slower and less efficient because of loss of cells and because of physiological changes in nerve cells and nerve fibers. The central nervous system processes information more slowly, and consequently the individual reacts more slowly.

In addition to a general slowing down, one of the cognitive changes most frequently assumed to accompany aging is memory impairment. But opin-

Figure 8.8 Projected Median Age of U.S. Population into the Twenty-First Century

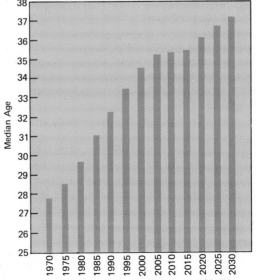

Chart based on U.S. Census projection assuming fertility rate of 2.1 children per woman.

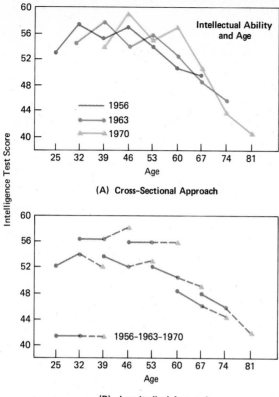

(A) Cross-Sectional Approach

(B) Longitudinal Approach

Figure 8.9 The answer to the question of whether intellectual ability declines with age depends largely on the method used to study the matter. Cross-sectional studies suggest more decline than longitudinal studies do. (A) The cross-sectional approach studies groups of people who were born at different times. When this method is used, younger people look smarter than older people. But this method obscures sociocultural differences among generations. The point is not that the twenty-four-year-old is smarter than the sixty-year-old, but that someone born in 1931 instead of 1896 has probably had a better education. (B) The longitudinal method studies the same group or groups of people over several points in time. As the bottom graph shows, decline over time from initial test score in the sixty- and sixty-seven-year-old groups is minimal, although because of generational differences these initial scores were lower than those of the younger groups. (Adapted from Schaie and Labouvie-Vief, 1974.)

ions differ as to whether old people have poorer memories than younger people. In many respects, the memory of an older person is not worse than that of a younger one—or at least not significantly so. A number of memory changes, however, do tend to appear with age.

Some of these are related to short-term memory. For example, when older people are given a task that requires a reorganization of information in short-term memory—such as repeating a list of let-

ters, numbers, or words backward—they tend to perform somewhat more poorly than younger ones (Bromley, 1958). In addition, an older person's short-term memory is more likely to be hindered by a task that requires a division of attention. Suppose that subjects of different ages are seated in front of a panel consisting of twelve light bulbs and twelve keys (Kay, 1953; Kirchner, 1958). Every time one of the bulbs lights up, the subject is required to press the key directly below it. This extinguishes the bulb and causes another bulb somewhere else on the panel to turn on. Young and old perform this task with equal ease. But if the task is then changed so that a subject has to press the key not beneath the bulb that just lit up, but beneath the *previously* lighted bulb, older subjects perform more poorly than younger ones. This is because the new task requires a division of attention. Subjects must not only store the position of the presently lighted bulb in memory, they must also retrieve from memory the position of the bulb they have just extinguished. Apparently, the more division of attention a task requires, the poorer the memory performance of older subjects compared to younger ones. Such short-term memory deficits, however, are not large, and their effects are not particularly detrimental to one's ability to function effectively. Outside the laboratory, most of the differences between the short-term memory performance of young and old can hardly be noticed.

How do the long-term memory capabilities of older and younger adults compare? One popular belief is that elderly people, while able to remember vivid details of events from their youth, often have poor recall of things that happened just yesterday or last week. Is there truth to this assumption? Apparently not. Like everyone else, older people have the greatest difficulty remembering information from the distant past, while their recall is best for events that happened most recently. This has been demonstrated experimentally. In one study (Warrington and Sanders, 1971), subjects of different ages were questioned for their retention of major news events that had happened from one month to two years earlier. For all age groups, the amount of information recalled declined with the number of months that had elapsed since the event occurred. Memory, in other words, always seems to fade with time, regardless of whether one is twenty-six or sixty-six.

This study also found that older adults had somewhat greater difficulty recalling news events from the distant past than did younger ones. The difference between the two groups, however, was far from dramatic. In fact, most researchers who have studied long-term memory in the elderly have been impressed with the high levels of retention they normally demonstrate (Craik, 1977).

AVERTING COGNITIVE DECLINE Certain cognitive changes, then, do tend to be associated with aging. But it should not be assumed from this that it is all downhill intellectually after sixty-five. Research shows that none of the cognitive changes that tend to accompany aging are inevitable.

There is substantial evidence that a small percentage of elderly people suffer no decline in cognitive functioning whatsoever. Famous personalities such as Pablo Casals, Pablo Picasso, Grandma Moses, and Eleanor Roosevelt have been known for the sharpness of their intellects well into old age. Exceptional elderly subjects have been found in laboratory experiments, too. One woman who was periodically tested between the ages of sixty and eighty showed absolutely no trace of the general slowing down usually considered the hallmark of the aged (Jarvik, 1975). If there is one indisputable fact about aging, it is that its effects are widely varied. Why do such large variations occur?

One contributing factor is biological. Identical twins are more alike in their cognitive functioning some forty or more years after finishing school than unrelated individuals or even fraternal twins (Jarvik, 1975). Of course, these similarities do not necessarily mean that one's timetable for aging is genetically programmed. It may be that what identical twins share is a predisposition toward, or resistance to, certain degenerative diseases, which in turn affect cognitive functioning. But whatever the causal link, it is nevertheless true that some of the wide variation in cognitive decline among the elderly is, in one way or another, biologically based.

Equally important, however, are environmental factors—especially the degree to which an older person has the opportunity to be physically active and intellectually stimulated (De Carlo, 1971; Spirduso, 1975). If older people have people to talk to and interesting things to do—if, in short, they have a chance to *use* their minds—there is a strong likelihood that their intellectual powers will not be blunted at all. Expectations and opportunities have everything to do with intellectual performance in old age as well as in other stages of development.

Finally, one cannot overlook the effect of a person's own emotional state on the aging process. Depression, despair, a sense of worthlessness, and a lack of hope can all take a terrible toll on physical and mental well-being. The resulting degeneration, in turn, is often cause for further depression, and a vicious cycle of premature decline sets in. But individuals who are optimistic, secure, and generally content with their lives usually stand a better than average chance of remaining physically healthy and intellectually adept throughout their later adult years. In short, although scientists know relatively little about how emotional factors affect physical aging, most would agree that they play an important part.

Biological, environmental, and emotional factors, then, all affect the speed and course of the aging process. Indeed, the level of variation that their combined impact can cause is so wide that some researchers have suggested replacing the concept of chronological age with that of "functional age"—a measure not of years but of how well a person performs on a variety of mental and physical tasks (Birren and Renner, 1977, p. 5). In recent years, several psychologists have attempted to record and compare functional age. The results of their studies have proved what people have known for years: a person who is seventy-five can often look, act, and feel far younger than a person who is only sixty.

Summary

1. According to Swiss psychologist Jean Piaget, intelligence is not a trait but a process, by which a person constructs a gradually maturing understanding of reality.
   A. Piaget identifies three psychological concepts central to the process of intellectual growth: scheme, assimilation, and accommodation.

1. **A scheme** is a recurrent action pattern that leads to practical knowledge about one's environment. The schemes of an infant are overt; as the child grows older, he or she employs "interiorized schemes" which are carried out mentally.
2. **Assimilation** is the incorporation of new

knowledge through the use of existing schemes. **Accommodation** is the modification of existing schemes to incorporate new knowledge that does not fit them. The processes of assimilation and accommodation always work in a complementary fashion. Piaget explains cognitive development in terms of the mind's constant search for an equilibration (a balance) between the two processes.

B. According to Piaget, the intellectual development of a child includes four main periods: the **sensorimotor period**, the **preoperational period**, the **concrete-operational period**, and the **formal-operational period**. Children develop new ways of thinking during each successive period, and the speed with which they move through each period depends on their genetic makeup and environment.

2. During the brief period between birth and early childhood, an infant develops a great number of cognitive skills.
   A. A baby is capable of learning from the moment of birth.
      1. Experiments have shown that a baby only two to four days old is capable of learning, unlearning, and relearning simple contingencies through conditioning.
      2. The infant's affinity for learning is at least partially self-motivated. It has been suggested that babies derive a form of intellectual pleasure from simple problem solving.
   B. **Sensorimotor intelligence**, or **practical intelligence**, refers to an infant's learning to act in the world. Infants apparently do not reflect on what they are doing. The **object concept** is Piaget's term for an infant's ability to conceive of objects as having an ongoing existence of their own. This ability develops gradually during the first two years of life.

3. Between the ages of two and three the child discovers that objects and events can be represented by symbols. This expands the child's powers of thought and communication.
   A. A child's intelligence during the preschool years is based more on intuition than on logical reasoning. During this intuitive stage, the child learns to count and to classify objects into general categories.
      1. **Representational thought** is one of the

most important cognitive skills that develops during the preschool years. It enables children to think about objects that are not physically present, thus expanding their world beyond the limits of immediate perceptions.
      2. The intellectual capacities of preschool children are immature. The greatest limitation of children at this age is the inability to organize thinking into coordinated systems. This manifests itself in **egocentrism** (inability to take into account points of view other than the child's own); **complexive thinking** (jumping from one idea to another without coordinating the ideas into a meaningful whole); and the inability to carry out tasks that provide no external cues and that require self-directed thinking.
   B. Older children can think in logical ways that preschool children cannot. Between the ages of five and seven, children begin to understand **concrete operations**—Piaget's term for simple transformations carried out on concrete objects—a capacity that takes an additional five years or more to develop fully.
      1. The **concept of conservation** is an example of a gradually developing concrete-operational concept. It involves a child's ability to judge amounts of liquids or other substances that are presented in different forms.
      2. Other concrete-operational concepts include those dealing with classification. The two main skills needed to master classification are the ability to understand the addition of classes and the ability to multiply classes.

4. What Piaget calls **formal-operational intelligence** emerges around the beginning of adolescence. The adolescent is able to think hypothetically and in abstract terms.
   A. Adolescents can carry out systematic experiments, considering all the possible combinations of factors that may have caused an event and, through careful reasoning, eliminating the irrelevant ones.
   B. The capacity to think hypothetically and to understand abstract principles allows adolescents to think about their own thoughts, actions, and motives, and to be concerned with the past and future as well as the present.

5. Cognitive development during adulthood generally follows a fairly predictable pattern.
   A. The forty years of early adulthood (from age twenty to forty) and middle adulthood (from age forty to sixty) are a time of peak intellectual achievement. It has been found that IQ generally increases into the middle years.
      1. Young adults usually perform better than they ever have before on-learning and memory tasks, and they are usually most intellectually flexible at this time.
      2. Verbal and reasoning skills often improve during middle adulthood if the person remains healthy. An adult in the middle years is in his or her intellectual prime; the only decline may be in motor skills.
   B. Many people do not experience significant impairment of intellectual performance in later adulthood, despite certain kinds of physiological and cognitive decline that generally accompany the aging process.
      1. The most characteristic change of old age is the tendency to "slow down," which is believed to be caused by a process called **primary neural aging**. Memory changes also tend to accompany old age. Older adults tend to perform more poorly than young adults on short-term memory tests involving a division of attention. However, differences between the long-term memory capabilities of older adults and young adults are negligible.
      2. None of the cognitive changes that frequently accompany aging are inevitable, and most of the changes that do occur can be compensated for in many ways. Biological, environmental, and emotional factors all affect the speed and course of the aging process. Some researchers have suggested replacing the concept of chronological age with that of functional age—a measure not of years but of how well a person performs on a variety of mental and physical tasks.

RECOMMENDED READINGS

COBB, EDITH. *The Ecology of Imagination in Childhood.* New York: Columbia University Press, 1977. A lifetime of intensive observations of children and interviews with adults regarding their childhood fantasies culminated in this enlightening, short, and very readable book. Although it is not scientifically rigorous, and although it is outside of the mainstream of cognitive psychology, this is nonetheless a fascinating and insightful book.

FLAVELL, JOHN H. *Cognitive Development.* Englewood Cliffs, N.J.: Prentice-Hall, 1977. An excellent introductory presentation of the development of memory and thinking strategies in children by a well-known authority on cognitive development.

HOLT, JOHN. *How Children Fail.* New York: Dell, 1970. An analysis of the shortcomings of contemporary educational methods in light of Piaget's theory.

LESSER, GERALD S. *Children and Television: Lessons from Sesame Street.* New York: Random House, 1974. One of the originators of *Sesame Street*, the innovative educational TV program for children based on cognitive-developmental theory, discusses some of the effects it has had on elementary education.

PIAGET, JEAN. *The Construction of Reality in the Child.* New York: Basic Books, 1954. A description and analysis of how the infant develops an understanding of the physical world: objects, space, time, and causality.

PIAGET, JEAN. *Biology and Knowledge.* Chicago: University of Chicago Press, 1971. Piaget describes the significance of his lifetime work for understanding the human ability to know and the relationship of that ability to human biological heritage.

WOODRUFF, DIANA S., and JAMES E. BIRREN. *Aging: Scientific Perspectives and Social Issues.* New York: Van Nostrand Reinhold, 1975. A multidisciplinary introduction to basic issues in aging from psychological, social, and biological perspectives.

CHAPTER NINE

LANGUAGE DEVELOPMENT

In Shakespeare's *Richard II*, Thomas Mowbray is exiled from England for life, and he responds in agony:

The language I have learned these forty years,
My native English, now I must forgo;
And now my tongue's use is to me no more
Than an unstringed viol or harp,
Or like a cunning instrument cased up,
Or, being open, put into his hands
That knows no touch to tune the harmony;
Within my mouth you have engaoled my tongue,
Doubly portcullised with my teeth and lips;
And dull, unfeeling, barren ignorance
Is made my gaoler to attend on me.

Every time I read that speech, I am chilled, for I love English—so rich in vocabulary, so bright in metaphor, so hospitable to foreign terms, so fanciful in idiom, so flexible, so colorful, so fascinating. I could not bear to lose its use.

Fortunately, I couldn't be in Mowbray's position now. In his day, English was a minor language spoken by three million people on one small island. Today English is spoken the world over, and it would be hard to find a patch on the globe where English speakers could not manage to find someone else to understand them. No one speaking any other language is quite that fortunate. Every other language is spoken by fewer people or in less widespread fashion or (almost always) both.

And yet English isn't just English. The English of London, Dublin, Canberra, Boston, Charleston, Brooklyn, and Indianapolis are each different. The differences aren't enough to preclude understanding, but they are quite enough to produce curiosity, suspicion, or even automatic dislike. George Bernard Shaw's *Pygmalion* is based on this.

An immigrant (my father, for instance) can learn every facet of his adopted country's culture and yet, even after a generation, give himself away every time he opens his mouth. Though he may have learned the vocabulary and grammar of his new language perfectly, the subtle distinctions of sound will defeat him.

The dialect can be a prison, too, placing one behind the bars of the sound one makes, forever and forever. I am the prisoner of my boyhood sounds. I make my living as a writer and speaker, and I trust I may be forgiven if I say that there are surely few in the land who can surpass me in the use of the English language in the written form. When I speak, however, I must accept the inevitable and speak humorously, for it is difficult to take me seriously. You see, I speak Brooklynese, and the sounds of Brooklynese are, alas, associated with, at best, uneducated shrewdness.

Isaac Asimov

If you have ever tried to learn a foreign language, you know how complex and painstaking a task it can be. Now try to remember "learning" your native language. Do you recall struggling with the verb forms for past, present, and future? Or learning how to phrase a question? Probably not. These milestones in language acquisition occurred when you were very young. Your use of language was fairly sophisticated by the time you were three and highly skilled by your fifth birthday.

Obviously, one cannot say that people "learn" their native language in the same way college students learn a foreign language. One must speak of language acquisition as a developmental process. But what part does learning play in that process? What is it about the human mind that makes it capable of acquiring and using the complicated grammar of a language at a time of life when other aspects of cognitive processes are relatively unsophisticated?

Psychologists and linguists are attempting to answer these questions. This chapter explores some of their most recent findings. But, before discussing how a child acquires language, we will attempt some answers to the broad question, "What is language?"

THE NATURE OF LANGUAGE

We tend to think of language as synonymous with speech, or linguistic *performance*. A moment's reflection shows that this is not the case. A parrot can be taught to speak, but it does not have the ability to use language the way people do. For one thing, although it can mimic human speech, a parrot cannot invent or understand speech; thus the parrot does not display what could be called linguistic *competence*. In contrast, a child who can hear but cannot speak because of a physical handicap may still understand language completely. In one study (Lenneberg, 1967), a child who could not speak was told a short story and asked questions about its content using grammatically complex sentences. The child responded by pointing to things, nodding, or shaking his head. The child's behavioral responses to such questioning suggests that he had a clear understanding of language (linguistic competence) despite his inability to speak.

If language and speech are not identical, how then should language be defined? Psychologists and linguists have suggested various answers to this question. Most would agree that **language** can be described in three ways: as a means of communication, as a set of shared rules, and as a process that is closely related to thought.

LANGUAGE AS A MEANS OF COMMUNICATION Language is the primary means of human communication—the main vehicle for conveying our ideas, feelings, and intentions to others. According to Roger Brown (1973), this system of communication has three special features.

First, language is characterized by **semanticity**, or meaningfulness. Language allows us to represent objects, events, and abstract ideas in a symbolic way, and this is what makes language meaningful. When you utter the sound "book," for example, you are symbolically referring to the collection of bound, printed pages that you are reading now or to any other book ever written. The word "accident" stands for—symbolizes—an event that was neither planned nor intended. The words "truth" and "beauty" stand for abstract ideas. The ability to represent things in this symbolic way is one of the distinctive features of language. Of course, other animals' communications also have symbolic meaning. Apes, for example, have a small repertoire of calls and grunts to signal the presence of either food or danger or to indicate anger, fear, and other emotions. But, in general, animal "vocabularies" are small, and the "meanings" that the symbolic sounds convey are social and emotional, not references to objects or ideas. Human vocabularies, in contrast, are far broader. They allow us to represent concepts and ideas far beyond our immediate needs and experiences.

Second, language allows the individual to communicate about things that are not immediately present or about things that are entirely hypothetical. That is, it permits **displacement**, the transmission of information about objects or events that are removed in time or space (or both) from the communicator, such as last Saturday's dance, the record player in the next room, or the vacation in Hawaii planned for next summer. But the communication systems of certain lower organisms also allow some degree of displacement. For example, according to ethologist Karl von Frisch (1967), the honeybee performs a dance that informs other bees of the location of a nectar source that may be some distance from the hive. The concept of displacement, then, is nec-

Although language is the primary means of human communication, we also "speak" with our bodies.

essary to define human language, but it is not sufficient to set language off from other means of communication.

The characteristic of human language that is unique is its **productivity**, its capacity for allowing individual words to be combined into an unlimited number of sentences. If humans were limited to uttering one word at a time, we would need to have a tremendously large vocabulary in order to express everything we might ever want to say. Instead, the grammar of language allows us to combine words into phrases and sentences, thus making almost infinite the number of meanings we can express from a limited number of words. As a result, we can produce and understand sentences we have never before encountered. In fact, except for clichés, such as "How are you?" most of the sentences we hear or speak each day are in some ways novel. This fact surprises many people, who assume that they originally learned their language merely by imitating the sentences spoken by others. To prove to yourself how rare duplication is, select any sentence in this book and then try to find another one just like it. Your chances of success are very low. It has been estimated that it would take 10,000 billion years (nearly 2,000 times the estimated age of the earth)

merely to utter all the possible twenty-word sentences in English.

LANGUAGE AS A SET OF SHARED RULES
Of course, communication through language would not be possible without a shared set of linguistic rules. Speakers of English, for example, agree that the sound of *b* and the sound of *k* are linguistically meaningful, whereas a clicking sound made with the tongue is not. (In the African language Xhosa, however, clicks *are* meaningful.) English speakers also agree that sounds can be meaningfully ordered only in certain ways. The sequence of sounds in the word "pork," for instance, conveys a definite meaning; the sequence "rpko" does not. Similarly, English speakers share expectations about how words should be strung together to form sentences. "The moose is walking in the forest" is a perfectly meaningful English sentence. In contrast, "The forest in the moose walking is" violates English rules of proper word order and is therefore nonsensical. These shared rules constitute the **grammar** of the

199

Speakers of English agree that the sound of *e* is linguistically meaningful, and speakers of French agree that the sound of *è* is also linguistically meaningful in a different way—as this work by Saul Steinberg, entitled *The Dream of E*, wittily implies.

simply by analyzing their surface structure. Take, for example, the sentence, "They are growing mushrooms." The surface structure of this sentence is ambiguous. Is the speaker saying that a group of people are cultivating mushrooms, or that these particular mushrooms are in the process of growing? The speaker's intended meaning—what linguist Noam Chomsky (1965) has called the **deep structure** of the sentence, as opposed to its surface structure—is not clear. Only through the context of the statement, or through the speaker's intonation, can others interpret the underlying meaning.

Language, then, is more than simply a string of properly sequenced words. It is a reflection of a person's underlying thoughts. Psychologists who study language view these underlying thought processes as the most important features of language. Fundamental to all research on language acquisition is the question of how a child's level of cognitive development—his or her way of thinking about the world—relates to his or her ability to use language.

Thus our original question, "What is language?" can be answered in terms of three interrelated features. First, language can be defined according to its function—that is, according to the role it serves in human communication. Second, language can be defined according to its structure—that is, according to rules for combining sounds into words and words into sentences. And third, language can be defined according to underlying thought processes—that is, as a reflection of the way people think and interpret what others are thinking.

language. They are essential if a listener is to understand what a speaker is saying and respond in an intelligible way.

The grammatical rules of all human languages can be divided into two basic categories: rules of phonology and rules of syntax. Rules of **phonology** identify the particular sounds that are linguistically meaningful and prescribe how they should be ordered to form words. **Syntax** refers to the rules that govern how words should be combined to form sentences. Together, these two sets of rules determine what has been called language's **surface structure**, which is the way in which a language is to be spoken (Chomsky, 1965).

LANGUAGE AS RELATED TO THOUGHT PROCESSES Yet the meaning, or **semantics**, of words and sentences cannot always be understood

HUMAN LANGUAGE AS A SPECIES-SPECIFIC BEHAVIOR

The members of almost every animal species—from the simplest to the most complex—communicate in some fashion. For example, the tiny yellow flashes that fill the evening air in spring and summer are communications: male fireflies are signaling their location to females. The chemical odors that ants emit are also a means of communication; they mark trails, induce mating, signal alarm, and attract other ants to food sources. Other animals rely mainly on gestures to convey their messages. The male Siamese fighting fish, for instance, defends his territory against intruders through an elaborate fin display accompanied by ritualized movements of the tail and body. Call systems are also common in the animal world. Sea gulls, for example, have several distinct cries to communicate such information as the location of food or the presence of danger.

These systems of communication are **species-specific**. As we saw in Chapter 3, this means that the behaviors involved are characteristic of all members of the species and are the result of certain anatomical traits and brain specializations. Of course, environmental factors may also shape species-specific patterns of behavior. But key environmental influences tend to have an impact only at certain times in the animal's development. A baby chaffinch, for example, develops the song that is characteristic of its species only if it hears adult chaffinches singing during a brief **sensitive period** in the early months of its life. This is because the brain organization needed for communication is not complete at birth. Thus, even when learning *is* involved in the emergence of a species-specific behavior, the readiness to learn is itself biologically controlled.

What about human language? Is it species-specific in the same way that the communication systems of other animals are? Psychologists are still debating this question. What we do know is that if human language were species-specific, several things would be true. For one thing, the use of language as we have defined it here would be a distinctive feature of the entire human species—which it is. For another thing, the form that language takes would be based on human anatomical features and human brain organization. Finally, language ability would tend to emerge during a sensitive period. Experience with language before or after this period would have less impact on language development than the same amount of experience at the right time. In the following sections we will explore these requirements.

OUR BIOLOGICAL ADAPTATION FOR LANGUAGE There is no doubt that the human ability to use language is closely related to our biological structure. The human vocal organs, breathing apparatus, auditory system, even the human brain—all are highly specialized for spoken communication (see Figure 9.1 on p. 204).

VOCAL AND AUDITORY SPECIALIZATION When you speak, your lungs expel air through your throat and mouth; your vocal cords vibrate to create sounds; your tongue, palate, lips, teeth, and facial muscles allow you to pronounce vowels and consonants. Stop a moment and feel these structures move as you read this sentence aloud. It is not difficult to recognize how remarkably well designed they are for producing speech.

Humans are equipped to make a far greater diversity of vocal sounds than any other animal. Not

These animals at play are having little difficulty communicating with each other, though they lack the capacity for language in the human sense.

Chimpanzee Talk
Versus Human Language

Is language ability, as we have defined it in this chapter, unique to humans? To answer this question, researchers have conducted a number of experiments with chimpanzees, whose anatomy, developmental patterns, and social lives are closer to those of humans than are those of any other animal. As mentioned in the chapter, attempts to teach chimpanzees spoken language have failed almost completely. But efforts to teach them to use sign language and to "write" with various kinds of concrete symbols have been remarkably successful. As a result, the question of whether human language ability is unique to humans is a valid subject for debate.

Teaching Language to Chimpanzees

Chimpanzees lack the vocal apparatus for speech, but they are extremely nimble-fingered. They use their hands to groom themselves and others, to peel fruit, and to fashion crude tools. Taking advantage of this dexterity, Beatrice and R. Allen Gardner (1969) set out to teach Washoe, a female chimpanzee, American Sign Language (Ameslan). The sign language used by many deaf people in North America, Ameslan is based on a system of gestures, each of which corresponds to a word. Many signs visually represent aspects of the word's meaning. For example, to sign "drink," you make a fist, extend your thumb, and touch your thumb to your mouth as though you were drinking. Ameslan also has devices for signaling verb tense and other grammatical meanings and is fully ade-

quate for expressing anything that can be spoken.

Washoe's training began when she was about one year old. The Gardners and their associates created as human an environment as possible for her, with social companions, objects, and daily play activities

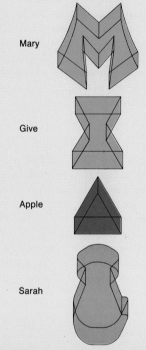

Mary

Give

Apple

Sarah

A sentence formed with the plastic symbols Premack and his associates used in their training regimen with the chimpanzee Sarah.

(including word or sign games). Instead of talking, they signed to Washoe and to one another as deaf parents might. Whenever Washoe made a correct sign, she was rewarded. Sometimes her natural gestures were close enough to the correct signs to permit shaping. Other times the Gardners taught her signs by placing her fingers in the correct position. After four

years of training, Washoe had acquired about 160 signs.

Washoe's progress was similar in many ways to that of a young child learning spoken language. Once she had learned a particular sign, she quickly generalized its use to appropriate activities or objects. For example, she learned the sign "more" to request more tickling (which she seemed to adore); she then used the same gesture to request more hair brushing, more swinging, and a second helping of food. Many of her mistakes resembled those children commonly make, as when she applied the sign for flower to all kinds of smells—a case of overgeneralization. Furthermore, as soon as she had learned eight or ten signs, she spontaneously began to use some of them in combination, forming such sentences as "Hurry open," "More sweet," "Listen dog," and "Roger come." Later she combined three or more signs: "Hurry gimme toothbrush," "You me go there in," and "Key food open." By age five Washoe's command of language was roughly equivalent to that of a three-year-old child.

In some respects, however, Washoe's training in Ameslan was unlike a child's normal training in spoken language. For one thing, she was not exposed to sign language until she was a year old. For another, her trainers had only recently acquired Ameslan as a second language. The Gardners (1975) are now working with chimpanzees that have been exposed since birth to people who are fluent in Ameslan. The new chimpanzees, they report, are learning much faster. In addition, the Gardners' former research assistant, Roger Fouts (1972), is conducting experiments to see how chimpanzees might use Ameslan with one another. In one experiment, he is teaching two chimpanzees a limited number of signs, encouraging them to use these signs with one another, and will introduce the chimpanzees to Washoe to find out whether she will teach them new signs. Fouts will also be watching to see if chimpanzee mothers teach their offspring sign language.

These are only some of the experiments being conducted with chimpanzees. David Premack (1971, a, b) has taught a chimpanzee named Sarah a language based on small plastic symbols of varying colors and shapes, like those shown in the accompanying figure. Each piece of plastic stands for one word. Sarah has learned to construct sentences by arranging symbols on a special magnetized board. Premack's system is easier for the chimpanzee than the Ameslan used

by the Gardners, in that because the symbols are in front of Sarah, she does not have to hold them in her memory. A major drawback, however, is that Sarah is "mute" when she does not have her symbols, and she cannot take them with her wherever she goes.

In yet another approach, Duane Rumbaugh, Timothy Gill, and E. C. von Glasersfeld (1963) have taught a chimpanzee, Lana, to operate a special typewriter controlled by a computer. The machine has fifty keys, each displaying a geometric configuration that represents a word in a specially devised language called Yerkish (after the primatologist Robert M. Yerkes). When Lana types a configuration, it appears on a screen in front of her. She has spontaneously learned to correct herself by checking the sequence of configurations on the screen. In other words, she has learned to read. Not only does Lana respond to humans who "converse" with her via her computer, but she also initiates some of the conversations. And, when confronted with an object for which she has not

been taught a word, Lana can create one. For example, when she was shown a ring for the first time, Lana identified it—using terms that she already knew—as a "finger bracelet."

Are the Chimpanzees Using Language?

According to the basic definition of language that we are using in this chapter, it appears that chimpanzees display a fundamental capacity for language. They use symbols meaningfully and accurately. They are capable of displacement. (When Washoe signs, "You me go there in," she is referring to some place she is not in at the moment.) And finally, there is some evidence for productivity—for the creation of novel and appropriate word combinations from the basic rules of the language. (Lana's use of the expression "finger bracelet" for ring is an example of this.) However, as Premack (1976) points out, unlike the rich inventiveness of language displayed by human children, the creative productivity of the chimpanzee may be limited to word substitutions using restricted sentence structures (for example, "Mary eat apple" versus "Mary wash apple").

Future research with chimpanzees will undoubtedly focus on this issue of productiveness and will attempt to discover the limits of the chimpanzee's ability to communicate. Whether trained chimpanzees will spontaneously "teach" language to their offspring, and how much language creativity chimpanzees can muster, remain to be determined. From the evidence that is in, however, it appears that a fundamental capacity for language, as defined by linguists and psychologists, is not restricted to the human species.

Washoe at work.

Areas of the brain associated with speech

Larynx

"oo"   "aw"   "ee"

Figure 9.1 The human speech apparatus, including the larynx (which houses the vocal cords), areas of the brain associated with speech, and other such essential physical structures as the tongue and lips. Below are the configurations of these structures necessary for the production of three vowel sounds.

even our closest relative, the chimpanzee, can reproduce human speech sounds. After great effort, a chimpanzee called Viki was painstakingly taught to make sounds that roughly approximated four words—hardly an impressive vocabulary (Hayes and Hayes, 1951). Other attempts to teach chimpanzees to talk have failed (Kellogg and Kellogg, 1933). Quite simply, chimpanzees do not employ spoken language because they lack the necessary vocal apparatus. In contrast, human babies, who do have the biological equipment for speech, begin babbling spontaneously at a very early age. During the first six months, they produce virtually all the sounds of all the human languages. (For a further comparison of human language and nonspeech forms of language in chimpanzees, see the accompanying special feature on pages 202–203.)

Just as the human vocal apparatus is well adapted to producing a wide variety of speech sounds, so is the human sense of hearing well adapted to perceiving those sounds. As we described in Chapter 7 (Eimas et al., 1971), infants

only a few weeks old can detect the difference between such similar sounds as *ba* and *pa*. Try repeating these sounds to yourself. The difference between them is very small. In fact, in some languages the two sounds are not considered distinct. Yet infants easily differentiate between them. Thus infants' ability to discriminate many sounds, including speech sounds, may be part of their biological inheritance (Jusczyk et al., 1977).

BRAIN SPECIALIZATION Specialized vocal and auditory systems are essential for normal human speech. But there is more to language than speech, as we have seen. Language is intimately related to ways of perceiving, categorizing, and interpreting information. There appears to be something special about human cognitive processes that makes language possible. Is this reflected in any special way in the organization of the human brain?

Much of our information about the structure and functioning of the normal human brain comes from studies of people with brain injuries due to tumors, strokes, or accidents. When the left side of the brain is injured, language ability is often impaired. The individual has difficulty communicating with and understanding others. When the right side of the brain is injured, the ability to speak is usually unaffected, although other kinds of abilities (for example, visual space perception) are often disturbed. Observations that have been made of changes in singing ability while one or the other of the hemispheres is anesthetized (in the case of patients undergoing neurosurgery) nicely illustrate this asymmetry of functioning of the two sides of the brain. In most of the patients, anesthetizing the left hemisphere disrupted the ability to sing the words of a familiar song but did not interfere with the ability to carry the melody. Anesthetizing the right hemisphere in the same patients had the reverse effect: melody was lost, but the ability to recite the words was almost unaffected (Gorden and Bogen, 1974).

The apparent functional asymmetry of the two sides of the brain is called **hemispheric lateralization**, and, corresponding to this, anatomical differences between the two sides (the two hemispheres) are also evident (von Bonin, 1962). The left hemisphere, which tends to be dominant for language abilities in most people,* tends also to be

---

*Contrary to widespread belief, this dominance of the brain's left hemisphere for language ability holds for most left-handed as well as for most right-handed people.

somewhat larger than the right hemisphere and has a slightly different shape.

What is the meaning of this hemispheric dominance for language? Pointing out that "only in man do we find a behavioral function relatively clearly localized in just one of the two hemispheres," Eric Lenneberg (1967, p. 66) suggested that this represents a biological foundation for language abilities in humans. But how can the brain be specialized for language development when specific languages (English, Chinese, Xhosa) are so different? Is it possible that the human brain is specialized for learning *any* language? Linguist Noam Chomsky (1972) thinks that it is. According to Chomsky, the languages of the world have more in common structurally than one might suppose. As we have seen, all languages make similar distinctions relating to combining sounds into words (the rules of phonology) and words into sentences (the rules of syntax). Chomsky maintains that these distinctions reflect cognitive abilities built into the human brain. Thus, in mastering the phonology and syntax of their native tongues, Chomsky argues, children are aided by the biological characteristics of their brains.

Recent evidence of hemispheric lateralization in infants less than ten months old for speech as against musical notes (Glanville, Best, and Levenson, 1977), or for speech as against nonspeech stimuli (Molfese, Freeman, and Palermo, 1975), supports the suggestion that there are special brain mechanisms in children that may serve as a foundation for learning language. However, observations of some children whose left hemispheres had had to be surgically removed (because they were the focus for debilitating seizures) have revealed near-normal development of language abilities and intelligence in these children (Lenneberg, 1967; Smith and Sugar, 1975). These observations undermine the idea that there is something special about the human left hemisphere that makes *learning* a language possible. In summary, then, although it can be argued that there is something special about the human brain that makes complicated human language possible, and that in adults the left hemisphere appears to be more involved in language ability than the right, the specific nature of brain organization in relation to the development of human language has yet to be determined.

SENSITIVE PERIODS Like some species-specific behaviors, human language ability seems to emerge during a "sensitive period," which begins at about age two. Consider the ease with which children who move to a foreign country pick up a new language while their parents grope to express themselves. Moreover, deaf children can acquire some language if they are given the opportunity to do so during this sensitive period, but have difficulty learning any more later in life. And children who lose their speech as a result of brain damage during this period are more likely than adults to recover. If there is a sensitive period in language development, then it would be difficult or impossible to learn a first language (one's native language) after this period—that is, after puberty. Since just about everybody does learn a first language before puberty, it is difficult for the psychologist to test this statement. However, it is possible to test whether people can learn a second language as easily after puberty. If there is a

Table 9.1

Predictions Made About Second Language Learning By A Strong Sensitive-Period Hypothesis

	Second Language Acquisition	
	Before Puberty	After Puberty ("learning")
Similar to first language acquisition	yes	no
May be learned without instruction	yes	no
Presence of foreign accent	no	yes
Native competence in syntax, semantics	yes	no

Source: Stephen D. Krashen, "The Critical Period for Language Acquisition and Its Possible Basis," in Doris Aaronson and Robert W. Rieber, (eds.), *Developmental Psycholinguistics and Communication Disorders.* Annals of the New York Academy of Sciences, Vol. 263 (1975), pp. 211–224.

At four or five years of age a child has mastered his or her native language.

sensitive period ending at puberty, then the set of predictions shown in Table 9.1 would be expected to be found true. Krashen (1975) has reviewed the studies that have been done on these predictions. He found that each of the predictions was indeed borne out to some extent by the empirical studies, although the differences between language acquisition before and after puberty were not quite as dramatic as we would expect from a true "sensitive period."

Despite such evidence, some researchers still question whether there is a strictly definable sensitive period for language development. Lenneberg (1967) has argued that the sensitive period for language development is related to the development of hemispheric lateralization, which he believes takes place gradually between birth and puberty. This might explain why fewer adults than children recover from damage to the left hemisphere: in adults, lateralization has already taken place; the sensitive period is over. This line of reasoning and the evidence that supports it are controversial, particularly in view of the research cited earlier that indicates lateralization in prespeech infants. All we can say at this point is that there is some support for the view of a sensitive period for language development, extending from about age two to about age fourteen. This evidence, in turn, tends to support the idea that language is a species-specific behavior.

How CHILDREN ACQUIRE LANGUAGE*

At birth, human babies are speechless. Indeed, the word "infant" comes from the Latin word for "with-out language." However, by the age of four or five, children around the world have mastered their native tongues—a truly remarkable feat, in view of the difficulty adults have in learning a new language. In this section we will describe the infant's progress from meaningless babbling to one- and two-word utterances and, in time, to complete, grammatical sentences. We will also consider *how* children acquire language.

THE STAGES OF LANGUAGE ACQUISITION Children grow up in very different kinds of cultural and social environments, yet they seem to go through a remarkably similar sequence of stages in learning to speak their language (Brown and Fraser, 1963; Bloom, 1970; Brown and Hanlon, 1970; Brown, 1973). One child may reach a particular stage at a somewhat earlier age than another, but both do reach that stage; one child may express himself or herself more fluently than another, but all normal children learn the basic features of their language.

PRESPEECH COMMUNICATION From the earliest weeks of life, the sounds that babies make serve to attract the attention of others and to communicate with them. Newborns, for example, quickly develop three patterns of crying: the basic rhythmical pattern (often erroneously called the hunger cry);

---

*For useful summaries of language acquisition in infants, see Bower, 1977, Chapter 8, and Clark and Clark, 1977, Chapter 8.

the anger cry; and the pain cry. By playing a tape recording of a baby's cries on different occasions when the mother was out of the room, Peter Wolff (1969) discovered that a mother recognizes the differences in the cries of her own baby and responds appropriately. Whenever Wolff played the pain cry, for example, the baby's mother immediately rushed into the room with a worried expression on her face.

As babies grow older, they begin to produce more varied sounds. By three months they can coo. By six or seven months, they are able to babble—that is, chant various syllabic sounds in a rhythmic fashion (see Figure 9.2). Infants' early babbling, a type of motor play and experimentation, is not limited to the sounds used in their parents' language. Rather, infants seem to make sounds from all languages; American babies may babble French vowels and German rolled *r*s. For the first six months of life, deaf babies cry and babble like children who can hear, a further indication that early vocalizations are spontaneous and relatively independent of what the child hears. Eventually, children develop the capacity to imitate the sounds made by others and to control the sounds that they themselves make.

Infants are not limited to sounds, but can also use gestures to express themselves. Six-month-olds may pick up things and show them to other people and tug on adults' clothing to get attention. At ten or eleven months they begin pointing to things, saying, in effect, "Look at this" or "Tell me about that." They stretch out their open hands to say, "Give me that."

Prespeech babies communicate other thoughts through intonation. The pattern of pitch changes in the sounds they make may express frustration, satisfaction, or some other feeling. One investigator (Tonkova-Yampol'skaya, 1973) found that babies in the first year of life are able to learn intonations to signal happiness as well as commands, requests, and questions. Infants' intonation patterns for several kinds of communication correspond closely to typical adult patterns. For example, babies at seven to ten months of age express commands with the same sharply rising then falling pitch that adults use ("Stop that!"). By about the beginning of the second year, infants begin to use the intonation that signifies a question. This pattern is easily distinguished from others by the sharp rise in pitch at the end ("What are you doing?"). Because pitch and emphasis can profoundly affect utterances, sometimes even reversing the meaning of a sentence, this early learning of intonation plays an important part in the continuing development of language ability.

FIRST WORDS By the end of the first year, children know the names of a few people or objects, and

Figure 9.2 An early stage in the development of language is the period of babbling that begins toward the middle of the first year of life. The baby begins with the vowel sounds and brings in consonant sounds later. At first not all of the baby's sounds closely resemble the speech it is hearing. It seems to be practicing and playing with its ability to produce sounds. By the age of ten months, however, infants begin to try to match the sounds and rhythms they hear.

Figure 9.3 At approximately one year of age most children produce their first true words. Their communication has become meaningful. A child's first words are typically monosyllables, or repeated monosyllables, such as "dada," "mama," or "wah" (for water). When the child acquires a new word, he or she often starts applying it to a variety of things in the environment.

they begin to produce their first words (see Figure 9.3). To reach this stage, the child must understand that sound can be used to express meaning. Generally, the first wordlike sounds accompany gestures—as, for example, saying "bye-bye" when waving at someone. The first true words refer to the immediately tangible and visible; the child's language does not yet exhibit displacement. Words are used to label objects ("doggie"), express moods ("good"), and issue commands ("cookie"). All refer to the here and now.

During this stage, infants often rely on intonation to give meaning to a single word. For example, depending on intonation, the one-word utterance "door" can be a declaration ("That's a door"), a question ("Is that a door?"), or a demand ("Open the door!") (Menyuk and Bernholtz, 1969). In most cases, these utterances can be understood only in context. If you see a toddler reaching for a door-knob, it's safe to assume that an emphatic "Door!" means "Open the door." Thus early, one-word sentences succeed largely because other people are able to interpret the child's intentions from the context, intonation, and gestures that accompany the word. These clues remain important, even as the child's command of language grows. For adults, tone of voice and "body language" are often vital clues to what a person actually means by what he or she says.

This is also the stage when children tend to over-extend the meaning of a word. For example, children who have learned the word "bow-wow" for dogs may apply it to cats, horses, cows, sheep—to any four-legged creature that moves. Then they learn a new word, say "moo" for cows. Now they have two animal names in their vocabulary. They may use "bow-wow" for small animals, "moo" for large ones. This indicates that the new word has called their attention to other features of animals, namely their size and the sounds that they make. Each new animal name they learn inclines them to attend to new features; their concept of "bow-wow" and "moo" become narrower; eventually they zero in on the correct applications (Clark, 1973). Likewise, as Katherine Nelson (1974) points out, this works the other way as well: the child's increasing abilities to perceive distinctions among things helps to set the stage for learning new labels.

Once children have acquired a basic vocabulary, they are ready for the momentous step of combining words into longer utterances. But just as the first step on their own two feet had to wait for a certain level of motor control, so must the emergence of grammar wait for a certain level of neurological maturation. And just as crawling prepared infants to walk, one-word utterances prepare them to speak in a truly human way.

FIRST SENTENCES Although children begin to utter statements of more than one word around the age of two, they do not speak like adults (see Figure 9.4). Their utterances are short, and their vocabularies are largely limited to nouns and action verbs. Nonessential words, such as articles, prepositions, and conjunctions, are omitted, much as they are in telegrams. Prefixes and suffixes (such as the "ing" in "going") are also omitted (Brown, Cazden, and Bel-lugi-Klima, 1968). People who know the child can usually understand what he or she means, and they often respond by expanding the child's utterances into well-formed adult sentences. Here are some of a young child's **telegraphic speech** and his mother's interpretation (Brown and Bellugi, 1964):

Child	Mother
Baby highchair	Baby is in the highchair.
Eve lunch	Eve is having lunch.
Throw Daddy	Throw it to Daddy.
Pick glove	Pick the glove up.

Even at this early stage the child's speech is highly structured. Children do not merely juxtapose any word with any other word, nor is their language simply a collection of random deviations from the adult system. For example, children at this age generally preserve adult word order in their speech. A two-year-old might say, "Eat cake," while devouring birthday cake. An adult, of course, would say, "I am eating the cake," which indicates that he or she is the actor, that eating is now in progress, and that the cake is what is being eaten. Although children fail to include all the proper inflections, they do correctly put "cake" after "eat," which tells the listener that the cake is the object being eaten rather than the agent that is doing the eating. Of course, not all childish sentences are simply reduced versions of adult sentences. The sentence "All-gone sticky" (after washing hands) is just one example of the kinds of utterances unique to children. But even though such sentences are not predictable from the adult rules, they are predictable from the child's rules. Thus, psycholinguists have been able to write formal rules that describe what is acceptable in the child's system and what is not.

The range of meanings children express with two-word utterances is impressive. The basic categories of meanings shown in Table 9.2 are based on data about children around the world. It seems that, regardless of the culture in which they are raised, around their second birthday children start to put two words together to express the same universal range of concepts. These basic concepts form the core of all human language. Indeed, a large part of later language development is simply a matter of elaborating and refining basic ideas that are already present at this early stage. Almost everything adults talk about is represented in Table 9.1. All these utterances lack are length and grammatical complexity. Figure 9.5 **on page 211** shows language development among three children studied by Roger Brown.

ACQUIRING COMPLEX RULES Two-word sentences are usually difficult to interpret out of context. For example, "Baby chair" could mean "This is the baby's chair" or "The baby is in the chair" or

Figure 9.4 At about two years of age, the child begins to string individual words together into sentences. As was true when the child was using only single words, his or her meaning is almost impossible to determine without a knowledge of the context in which he or she is speaking. But the child now refers often to things not immediately present (displacement) and combines various words, two at a time, to express new meanings (productivity).

Table 9.2 Categories of Meanings Expressed in the Two-Word Stage

Category of Meaning	Description
Identification	Utterances such as "See doggy" and "That car" are elaborations on pointing, which emerged in the preverbal stage, and naming, which began in the one-word stage.
Location	In addition to pointing, children may use words such as "here" and "there" to signal location—as in "Doggy here" or "Teddy down." To say that something is in, on, or under something else, children juxtapose words, omitting the preposition—as in "Ball [under] chair" or "Lady [at] home."
Recurrence	One of the first things that children do with words is call attention to, and request, repetition—as in "More cookie" or "Tickle again."
Nonexistence	Children who pay attention to the repetition of experiences also notice when an activity ceases or an object disappears. Utterances such as "Ball all gone" and "No more milk" are common at this stage.
Negation	At about age two, children discover that they can use words to contradict adults (pointing to a picture of a cow and saying, "Not horsie") and to reject adults' plans (saying, "No milk" when offered milk to drink).
Possession	In the one-word stage children may point to an object and name the owner; in the two-word stage they can signal possession by juxtaposing words—as in "Baby chair" or "Daddy coat."
Agent, Object, Action	Two-word sentences indicate that children know that agents act on objects. But children at this stage cannot express three-term relationships. Thus, "Daddy throw ball" may be expressed as "Daddy throw" (agent-action), "Throw ball" (action-object), or "Daddy ball" (agent-object). Children may also talk of the recipient of an action by using similar constructions—saying, "Cookie me" or simply "Give me" instead of "Give me a cookie."
Attribution	Children begin to modify nouns by stating their attributes, as in "Red ball" or "Little dog." Some two-word sentences indicate that children know the functions as well as the attributes of some objects—for example, "Go car."
Question	Children can turn types of sentences described here into questions by speaking them with a rising intonation. They may also know question words, such as "where," to combine with others—as in "Where kitty?" or "What that?"

Source: Adapted from Roger Brown, *A First Language: The Early Stages.* Cambridge, Mass.: Harvard University Press, 1973.

"Put the baby in the chair" or even "This is a little chair." An adult must be present when the sentence is spoken to know which meaning is intended. The grammatical information contained in longer adult sentences reduces the dependence on context to convey meaning. The sentence "The baby is in the chair" is unambiguous because of the addition of the verb "is" and the locational preposition "in." Thus, the mastering of complex grammatical rules expands the child's ability to communicate beyond the immediate situation.

This stage in the acquisition of language occurs largely between the ages of two and five. By the time they enter school, most children have a good grasp of the grammar of their native language. This is not to say that children memorize a set of textbook rules ("To form the possessive, add an apostrophe plus *s*," and the like). They do not. Indeed, many adults have trouble stating these rules, although they apply them correctly. Rather, children acquire an implicit sense of how to organize words into increasingly complex sentences during this period.

Children seem to acquire grammatical rules in a fairly stable order. There is some variation from child to child, but not as much as might be expected. Certain rules are apparently acquired in steps. A good example is the use of the negative. Ursula Bellugi (1964) found that two-year-olds have a very simple rule for forming negative sentences: They simply add "no" to a positive statement: "No want stand," "No gonna fall," "No write book." This rule seems to be adequate as long as the child's sentences are quite simple; but as sentences grow in complexity, more complex rules of negation become necessary. The child learns to place "no" or "not" just before the verb: "You no have one," "He not bite you," "I not get it dirty." The last step is to add the required auxiliary verb: "You don't have one," "He isn't going to bite you," "I won't get it dirty."

There is good experimental evidence to support the idea that children acquire grammatical rules in steps during this period. For example, Thomas Bever (1970) had two-, three-, and four-year-olds act out the following sentences, using a toy horse and a toy cow.

1. The *cow kisses* the horse.
2. It's the *cow that kisses* the horse.
3. It's the horse that the *cow kisses*.
4. The horse is kissed by the cow.

The two-year-olds nearly always acted out the first three sentences correctly, although their performance on the fourth sentence was random. The three- and four-year-olds tended to reverse the interpretation of sentence 4, making the horse the actor. And the oldest children, the four-year-olds, also tended to misinterpret sentence 3, again making the horse the actor. Why did the younger children perform better? Bever suggested that two-year-olds have a simple rule or strategy for interpreting sentences: If the noun and verb occur in sequence, the noun is the actor of the verb's action. If several words interrupt that sequence, as happens in sentence 4, two-year-olds get confused and make a random guess. Apparently, four-year-olds have gone

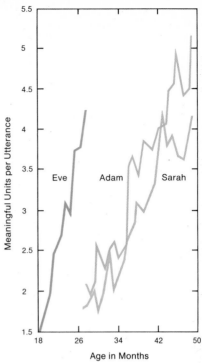

Figure 9.5 The progress of Brown's three subjects during the period he and his colleagues studied the children's acquisition of the English language. The average length of their utterances is plotted as a function of their age. The steady increase in length reflects the children's increasing ability to string words together in grammatically complex sentences. Brown suggests the kinds of factors that caused the irregularity seen in these curves when he noted that Eve may have had a cold on the only day that she showed a downward jog in her progress. Eve acquired language considerably earlier and faster than did Adam and Sarah. (After Brown, 1973.)

How can a researcher know for sure how a young child is interpreting adult sentences? One way is to have the child act the sentences out. This boy has been handed two dolls and a washcloth and asked by an experimenter to "Show me 'The boy is washed by the girl.'" The boy treats this sentence as though it were "The boys washes the girl." The grammatical rules that he has acquired so far are inadequate to process correctly a sentence in the passive voice.

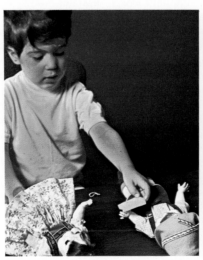

beyond the simple noun-verb strategy and have developed a rule that the first noun in the sentence is the actor. That is why they consistently misinterpret sentences like 3 and 4. It seems that children do not progress directly toward adult grammar, but construct and discard a variety of temporary grammars as they go along.

The acquisition of grammar demands not only that children gradually grasp the underlying rules for combining words into sentences, but also that they understand *when* to apply those rules. Because there are exceptions to many grammatical rules, this second task can be very difficult. This is why young children tend to commit errors of **over-regularization**—that is, they overextend a grammatical rule to instances in which it should not apply (Bellugi, 1970; Slobin, 1972). Overregularizations, which are very common in the speech of three- and four-year-olds, are "smart mistakes," because they show that children are trying to use general rules and that their speech is systematic.

A good example of overregularization is the way in which children learn forms of the past tense in English. At first, they correctly use common but irregular past-tense verbs such as "fell" and "came," verbs that are very frequent in adult English. Each word probably enters a child's repertoire as a separate vocabulary item. But then children learn the general rule for forming the regular past form by adding a *d* or *t* sound to the base, as in "walked" or "hugged." Once they have acquired this rule, they try to apply it to the irregular verbs as well, producing such incorrect sentences as "He goed to the store" and "I falled down." Similarly, once children have learned the general rule for forming plural nouns by adding an *s* or *z* sound to the singular form ("dog/dogs"), such incorrect plurals as "foots," "mans," and "mouses" begin to creep into their conversation. The important point is that, although the child may have been using correct irregular forms for months, these forms are temporarily replaced by incorrect forms because of over-regularization.

Such behavior cannot be explained as imitation: most of the children studied by psycholinguists have come from homes in which incorrect verb forms were rarely used. Nor can it be explained as a lack of reinforcement, because most children practiced, were reinforced for, and correctly used the initial, irregular forms before replacing them with the incorrect forms. It seems that children are predisposed to look for regularities and to impose order on their language.

EXPLAINING LANGUAGE ACQUISITION

Most empirical evidence so far collected indicates that children are neurologically equipped to figure out very efficiently the structure of any particular human language. Children readily acquire language, provided that they live in an environment in which language is used as a means of communication. Beyond this general requirement, psychologists have so far been unable to specify the exact nature of environmental factors that influence children's acquisition of language. Two processes by which the environment influences children's learning of other behaviors are reinforcement and imitation (discussed in Chapter 4). But neither simple reinforcement nor imitation can fully account for children's acquisition of language.

Why is simple reinforcement inadequate to explain language acquisition? After all, most parents believe that they actively teach their children to speak by praising them for naming objects and activities and for using correct grammar and by expressing disapproval when they make mistakes. In other words, they believe that they use reinforcement to shape language development.

When one team of researchers (Brown, Cazden, and Bellugi-Klima, 1968) studied tapes of actual parent-child interactions, however, they concluded that adults greatly overestimate their role. Parents do correct gross mistakes in a child's choice of words and, occasionally, errors in pronunciation. But in most cases it is intelligibility, not correct grammar, that elicits a parent's approval. Parents praise a child for successfully communicating his or her request to open a door or get a cookie, regardless of the child's grammar. When a child trying to say that her mother was a female came up with the sentence, "He's a girl," the mother responded, "That's right." However, when another child produced the grammatically perfect sentence, "There's the animal in the farmhouse" the mother corrected her because the building was, in fact, a lighthouse. Parents pay little attention to grammar as long as they can understand what the child is trying to say and as long as the child's utterances conform to reality. Thus reinforcement alone cannot explain language development.

Neither can imitation. All children produce sentences they have never heard. Children who say "All-gone sticky" or "I seed two mouses" are not mimicking adults. Adults do not speak this way. In the second of these sentences, the child is applying the rules for forming the past tense of verbs and the plural—but applying them incorrectly. It would be wrong to say that a child who does this is "imitating" the rules. No parent explains grammatical rules to a child this age. All children hear are sentences. And there is abundant evidence that they do not simply repeat what adults say to them. In a case reported by David McNeill (1966), for example, a mother tried to correct her daughter's speech:

CHILD: Nobody don't like me.
MOTHER: No, say, "Nobody likes me."
CHILD: Nobody don't like me.
    (*Eight repetitions of this dialogue*)
MOTHER: No, now listen carefully; say *"Nobody likes me."*
CHILD: Oh! Nobody don't *likes* me.

Clearly, the little girl is not directly imitating her mother, but is filtering what she hears through her own system of rules.

This is not to say that reinforcement and imitation have no impact on language development. Clearly they do. When children learn to say something that other people can understand, this in itself is reinforcing because it provides the child with a way of communicating needs and desires. Grammatically correct constructions tend to be repeated, not because they are praised by adults, but because they get desired results.

Similarly, although children do not imitate what adults say exactly, adult modeling does influence the development of grammar. Keith Nelson (1977) was able to accelerate two-year-olds' acquisition of certain grammatical forms through modeling. For example, when a child asked, "Where it go?" the experimenter modeled the use of future-tense verbs by responding to the child's question in slightly more complex form: "It will go there" and "We will find it." Soon the children began using the new forms in their own sentences—for example, picking up an object and saying "I will get up, hide it." Thus, although children do not mimic adults exactly, modeling helps them to learn general rules.

Psychologists still have much to learn about how children acquire language, but it seems clear that learning to speak is a creative process and that productiveness appears quite early in the process of language acquisition.

LANGUAGE AND THOUGHT*

In the preceding sections we have seen that in the

Ship of State, by Saul Steinberg. Because we have language, we can express imaginary and abstract ideas. The kind of language people use reveals much about how they see the world.

one- and two-word stages of language development, children's communications consist primarily of simple assertions and requests. As their mastery of language grows, they are able to express far more complex thoughts, not only about the here and now, but about things removed in time and space, events that exist only in imagination, and, eventually, abstract ideas.

There is little doubt that language contributes to cognitive development, enabling children to communicate and discuss ideas. But some psychologists have argued that the impact of language on the developing child is even greater than this. Language may also determine the *way* in which one thinks about objects and events—that is, it may set the boundaries of what we are able to think about. In the words of the philosopher Ludwig Wittgenstein (1889–1951), "The limits of my language mean the limits of my world" (1963). George Orwell spelled out some of the chilling implications of this view in his novel *1984,* in which he described a tyrannical government that sets out to control all thought by removing certain words from the language, coining some new ones, and redefining others.

---

*For an excellent discussion of the relationship between language and thought, see Clark and Clark, 1977, Chapter 14.

LINGUISTIC RELATIVITY The idea that language determines thought was expounded eloquently by the linguist Benjamin Lee Whorf (1897–1941). Whorf's **linguistic relativity hypothesis** is based on the notion that language is more than a means of expression: it actually determines our ideas, thoughts, and perceptions (1956). When a child acquires language, she or he simultaneously acquires a "world view." In other words, language determines the way in which a person sees the world. In addition, according to Whorf, different languages influence thinking in different ways. Therefore, Whorf reasoned, people with different languages should have different views of the world.

One way in which language may affect cognition is through vocabulary. The words that we learn determine the categories that we use to perceive and understand our world. For example, English has a single word for snow, but because Eskimos live in an environment where snow is very important, the Eskimo language has more than twenty specific words for different types of snow—fluffy snow, drifting snow, packed snow, and so on. If language determines one's perception of the world, then when Eskimos look out of the window on a cold winter morning, their perception of the white substance on the ground should differ from that of speakers of English.

Languages differ in the way they divide up many other domains of meaning. Whorf (1956) observed that languages differ in the grammatical categories that they must express—categories such as number, gender, tense, voice, and so forth. He believed that these linguistic categories affect the way people think about time, space, and matter. Whorf called Hopi a "timeless language" because, although its grammar recognizes duration, it does not distinguish among the present, past, and future of an event. English, of course, always does so, either by verb inflection ("He talks," "He talked") or by use of certain words and expressions ("Tomorrow I talk"). Hopi verbs, however, do distinguish between various kinds of validity. They are inflected to indicate whether the speaker is reporting an event, expecting an event, or making a generalization about events. If these very different ways of grammatically classifying events affect thought, one would expect a Hopi-based physics to be very different from an English-based one.

LINGUISTIC UNIVERSALS Most psychologists and linguists now believe that the linguistic

differences that Whorf wrote about, though interesting, do not have as much significance as he gave them. The extent to which a language actually limits thought appears to be small, and there is evidence that some types of thought are completely independent of language (Furth, 1966). Interest has shifted to the opposite relationship—the extent to which thought influences language, rather than language thought. The fundamental question here is, Are there universal characteristics of human thought processes that create universal linguistic structures?

Studies of color terms illustrate this shift in interest. Although English speakers tend to think of their way of naming colors as the natural way, other languages have quite different systems. In a survey of widely varied languages, Brent Berlin and Paul Kay (1969) showed that despite their diversity of color terms, all languages apparently select color terms from the list of eleven basic color categories shown in English in Figure 9.6C: black, white, red, green, yellow, blue, brown, purple, pink, orange, and gray. English speakers use all eleven basic color terms. But, as Figure 9.6B shows, speakers of Ibibio in Nigeria have only four basic color terms; speakers of Jalé in New Guinea (Figure 9.6A), only two.

The way in which any given language divides up the color spectrum, however, is far from arbitrary. If a language has fewer than the eleven terms, it lacks terms for the categories lower down in the list. Thus Jalé, with its two terms, names only the first two basic categories (black and white); Ibibio, with its four terms, names the first four general categories (black, white, red, green); and so on, down through the eleven terms shown. The fewer the terms, of course, the wider the range of colors they apply to. Thus the Ibibio green would encompass the English green, yellow, and blue.

But do people whose language has only a few color terms perceive the same distinctions in hue that people whose language has more terms perceive? (According to Whorf's linguistic relativity hypothesis, they should not.) To answer this question, Berlin and Kay prepared a chart with 320 small squares of color, virtually all the hues that the human eye is physiologically capable of distinguishing. Then they asked native speakers of dozens of languages to point out the best example of each of the basic color terms in their language. The choices were virtually the same from language to language. The Navaho *lichi* is the same as the Japanese *aka*, the Eskimo *anpaluktak*, the English *red*. Basic colors correspond across languages. However,

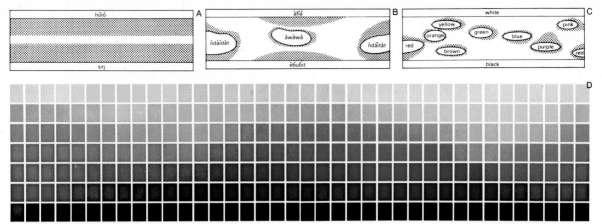

Figure 9.6 Some of Berlin and Kay's evidence that there is a universal cognitive basis for the naming of colors. The large color chart (D) shows most of the color chips Berlin and Kay presented to members of various cultures. (They also presented a black chip, a white chip, and several shades of gray chips.) The three small diagrams correspond to the large color chart, with the bands at the top and bottom of each diagram corresponding to the black and white not shown in the large chart. (Grays are not shown at all.) Each diagram shows the names that members of a particular culture applied to various chips.

A name inside an outlined area indicates that it was applied to all the chips that correspond to that area in the large chart. The surrounding gray areas indicate chips to which that name was applied with less certainty. Thus, English speakers (C) designate as "green" a small set of chips that are included in a somewhat larger set of chips called "awawa" by speakers of Ibibio, a language of South Nigeria (B). These chips in turn are among an even larger set of chips for which the people of New Guinea who speak Jalé have no name at all (A). (After Berlin and Kay, 1969.)

the *boundaries* of basic color categories—whether pink is included in red, for example, or is given a separate label—vary according to the number of color terms that a language has.

All people, then, seem to find certain basic colors more salient than others. Berlin and Kay called these hues "focal colors." Even when a language does not have a term for every focal color, speakers of that language can easily learn the missing ones and borrow terms for them from other languages. One researcher (Rosch, 1973) demonstrated this with the Dani, a New Guinea people whose language has only two basic color terms, *mili* for black

and *mola* for white. The Dani quickly picked up arbitrary names that Rosch invented for eight other focal colors. Indeed, as we discussed in Chapter 7, infants seem able to perceive differences between focal colors long before they learn labels for them (Bornstein, Kessen, and Weiskopf, 1976). Thus, color categories, like many other linguistic connections, seem to reflect both physiological and cognitive characteristics of people. So, by this analysis, although people apply different labels to things, they may nonetheless perceive things in much the same ways.

SUMMARY

1. Most psychologists and linguists agree that **language** can be defined as a means of communication having a set of shared rules and being closely related to thought.
   A. Language is our primary means of communicating ideas, feelings, and intentions to others. This system of communication has three essential characteristics:
      1. Language has **semanticity**, or meaningfulness. It allows us to represent ob-

   jects, events, and abstract ideas in a symbolic way.
2. Language permits **displacement**, the transmission of information about objects or events that are removed in time or space (or both) from the communicator.
3. Human language is unique in its **productivity**, its capacity for allowing individual words to be combined into an unlimited number of sentences.

B. Language is a set of shared rules. The rules of all human language can be divided into two categories that govern the language's **surface structure**, the way in which the language is to be spoken.
   1. Rules of **phonology** identify the particular sounds that are linguistically meaningful and prescribe how they should be ordered to form words.
   2. Rules of **syntax** govern how words should be combined to form sentences.
C. Language is a reflection of a person's underlying thoughts. The **deep structure** of a statement can be interpreted only through its context or the speaker's intonation.

2. Psychologists disagree on whether language is an example of **species-specific** behavior. For human language to be species-specific in the same way that the communication systems of other animals are, the following would have to be true: the use of language would be a distinctive feature of the human species; the form that language takes would be based on human anatomical features and human brain organization; and language ability would tend to emerge during a sensitive period.
   A. The human ability to use language is closely related to human biological structure.
      1. Humans are equipped to make a far greater diversity of vocal sounds than any other animal, and the human sense of hearing is well adapted to perceiving a wide variety of speech sounds.
      2. Each of the two sides of the brain dominates the other for various human abilities—a functional asymmetry called **hemispheric lateralization**. The left hemisphere dominates for language ability in most people. Linguist Noam Chomsky believes that the similarity of distinctions in phonology and syntax among all languages reflects cognitive abilities built into the human brain.
   B. Researchers disagree as to whether there is a sensitive period for language development in humans. There is, however, some support for the view that there is such a sensitive period, from about age two to about age fourteen.

3. Children acquire language rapidly, mastering their native tongues by the age of four or five. They do so in a series of stages, which are associated with the development of their neurological equipment for language.
   A. Children in different cultures and social environments seem to go through a similar sequence of stages in learning to speak.
      1. Babies make sounds from the earliest weeks of life to attract the attention of others and to communicate with them. Newborns develop three patterns of crying: the basic rhythmical pattern, the anger cry, and the pain cry. These sounds become more varied as the baby grows older. An infant communicates through gestures and intonations, as well as through sounds.
      2. In order to produce their first words, children must understand that sound can be used to express meaning. The first word-like sounds generally accompany gestures; the first true words refer to the immediately tangible and visible. During this stage infants often rely on intonation, context, and gesture to give meaning to a single word, and they tend to overextend the meaning of a word.
      3. Around the age of two, children begin to use **telegraphic speech**, making short utterances with nonessential words omitted. Interpretation of these sentences often depends on the context. This simple language is highly structured and, regardless of the culture, expresses the same universal range of concepts.
      4. The implicit acquisition of complex rules of grammar occurs largely between the ages of two and five. Children seem to acquire grammatical rules in a fairly stable order; they do not progress directly toward adult grammar, but rather construct and discard a variety of temporary grammars as they go along. In the process, they tend to commit errors of **overregularization**, overextending a grammatical rule to instances in which it should not apply.
   B. Most evidence indicates that children are neurologically equipped to figure out very efficiently the structure of any particular human language. Moreover, they can readily acquire language provided that they live in an environment in which language is used as a means of communication—the only environmental factor psychologists have been able to specify that influences children's lan-

guage acquisition. Simple reinforcement and imitation aid in children's acquisition of language, but neither can fully account for the process.

1. Reinforcement is inadequate to explain language acquisition. Researchers have found that parents greatly overestimate their role in reinforcing correct speech in their children; most parents pay little attention to grammar as long as they can understand what the child is trying to say and as long as the child's utterances conform to reality.
2. Imitation is also an inadequate explanation. Children do not directly imitate what they have heard, but produce sentences they have never heard and filter what they hear through their own systems of rules.

4. Language contributes to cognitive development, enabling children to communicate and discuss ideas. Some psychologists argue that language may determine the *way* in which one thinks about objects and events and may limit the matters we are able to think about.
   A. Linguist Benjamin Lee Whorf's **linguistic rel-**ativity hypothesis holds that language determines thought in two ways:
      1. Language, far from being just a means of expression, actually determines our ideas, thoughts, and perceptions.
      2. Different languages influence thinking in different ways. Languages differ in the ways they divide up various domains of meaning, such as vocabulary and grammatical categories.
   B. Contemporary linguistic interest centers on the extent to which thought influences languages rather than language thought. Psychologists and linguists attempt to determine whether there are universal characteristics of human thought processes that create universal linguistic structures. Studies of color terms illustrate this shift in interest. One such study indicated that people whose language has only a few color terms perceive the same distinctions in hue perceived by people whose language has more color terms—a finding that is in direct conflict with Whorf's linguistic relativity hypothesis. Color categories, like many other linguistic connections, seem to reflect both physiological and cognitive characteristics of people.

RECOMMENDED READINGS

BROWN, ROGER. *A First Language: The Early Stages.* Cambridge, Mass.: Harvard University Press, 1973. An excellent, comprehensive, and thoughtful treatment of the major current issues in early child language learning. This book is a source of several of the key ideas in this chapter.

CHOMSKY, NOAM. *Language and Mind.* New York: Harcourt Brace Jovanovich, 1972. A good lecture on a linguist's view of language and mind, as well as a general introduction to Chomsky's system of describing language (transformational grammar).

CLARK, HERBERT H., and EVE V. CLARK. *Psychology and Language: An Introduction to Psycholinguistics.* New York: Harcourt Brace Jovanovich, 1977. An outstanding basic presentation of issues in and approaches to the rapidly growing field of psycholinguistics.

FLEMING, JOYCE DUDNEY. "Field Report: The State of the Apes," *Psychology Today,* 7 (January 1974), 31+. A current review of all the work in progress on teaching language to chimps in centers across the country.

LENNEBERG, ERIC. *The Biological Foundations of Language.* New York: Wiley, 1967. Excellent analysis of language development in the context of the growth and maturation of the child and in light of evolution and genetics. Also presents language disorders in children and adults and discusses the problem of language and cognition.

MILLER, GEORGE (ed.). *Communication, Language, and Meaning: Psychological Perspectives.* New York: Basic Books, 1977. Prepared for a general audience, this collection of papers by the leading authorities in the fields of language and communication provides a broad introduction to psycholinguistics.

SEGALOWITZ, SIDNEY J., and FREDERIC A. GRUBER (eds.). *Language Development and Neurological Theory.* New York: Academic Press, 1977. Up-to-date chapters on brain-language relationships by a number of experts. Hemispheric differences are emphasized.

CHAPTER TEN

PERSONALITY AND SOCIAL DEVELOPMENT

A friend of mine wrote his autobiography recently, and in it he mentioned that his first wife had not liked me. She had, in fact, thought of me as a "creep."

This rather took me aback, for I had greatly admired my friend's first wife and had done my best to ingratiate myself with her. It was rather disconcerting to learn that I had failed so miserably.

But then I did not have a lovable personality when I was young, and I was only nineteen or twenty at the time. I was loud, conceited, aggressively self-assertive, and so on.

Since then, if I may believe what people say to me (and what they are reported to say about me behind my back), I have become a very lovable individual. Yet I am still loud, conceited, and a great many of the other unpleasant things that were once characteristic of me. All except one. Somehow, except on rare occasions when I forget myself, I am no longer aggressively self-assertive, and that seems to have made all the difference.

How did I come to change my personality by so little and yet by so much? When did it happen? I don't know. It was probably a gradual change, but I do recall the first occasion when I deliberately refrained from being self-assertive. That may have been the start of the change.

It was 1946. I was twenty-six years old and was in the Army in Hawaii as a buck private. I was older and better-educated than most of the soldiers in my platoon. I was off duty and was lying on my bunk reading a book. At the other end of the barracks sat a group of young soldiers discussing the atom bomb, then a new thing that was filling the minds of almost everybody.

I became aware of the conversation at the other end of the barracks, and it didn't take much listening for me to realize that one soldier was explaining the workings of the atom bomb to the others and was *getting it all wrong*. Wearily, I began to climb out of my bunk in order to go over there and set them all straight.

Halfway out of the bunk, I suddenly thought: Who appointed me their teacher? If they ask me, I thought, I'll explain it to them. If they don't, it won't matter much if they're misinformed on the subject. And I returned to my book.

Of course, my real purpose in wanting to go over and explain the facts had not been to educate my fellow soldiers, but to show them how smart I was—and at that moment I had reached the point where I no longer felt I had to display my intense smartness to everyone and force admiration out of them. *I* knew the smartness was there, and that was enough.

I guess I had finally grown up.

Isaac Asimov

Chapters 7, 8, and 9 discussed how human beings grow physically and develop cognitive and intellectual skills. This chapter deals with some of the forces that influence the personality structure and social behavior of each of us. Differences between us appear very early in our lives, as we develop patterns of behavior and ways of interacting with others that remain stable throughout life. Think of some of the people you know well, even very young children. Is not each one distinctive, different in some ways from all others? Yet, despite our differences, we are strikingly similar in the way we develop, at least in the sequence of developmental events through which we pass. Psychologists who study the development of personality and social behavior try to understand these common processes, while accounting for the wide diversity among people. How did we become the unique individuals we are? Only a careful study of our lives can provide a detailed answer. But general principles of personality and social development can be discerned. These patterns are the subject of this chapter.

PERSPECTIVES ON PERSONALITY AND SOCIAL DEVELOPMENT

The concept of personality has been defined in many ways and has given rise to a great many theories of personality structure and functioning, as we shall see in Chapters 18 and 19. Psychologists use the concept of personality to try to find out not only what makes individuals unique, but also what it is that makes people seem to behave consistently in a variety of situations over a long period of time. According to one team of psychologists, **personality** is those "enduring characteristics of the person that are significant for interpersonal behavior" (Goodstein and Lanyon, 1975, p. 173). How do personal patterns of aggressiveness, friendliness, or other "enduring characteristics" develop? What are the processes that shape the personality and social behavior of each of us? In studying the processes of personality development, psychologists have taken different viewpoints. We shall examine briefly some of these perspectives and then describe how some of an individual's important characteristics develop during infancy, childhood, adolescence, and adulthood.

THE BIOLOGICAL PERSPECTIVE A biological basis for personality development has not been as clearly established as has the biological basis for other human capacities, which was discussed in Chapters 7, 8, and 9. It is clear, however, that some aspects of personality are the result of biological influence.

The temperament of the human infant, for example, is one determinant of personality that is influenced by biology. **Temperament** refers to the individual's pattern of activity, susceptibility to emotional stimulation, response to stimuli, and general mood (Buss, Plomin, and Willerman, 1973). Differences in temperament can be seen very soon after birth, and heredity has been confirmed as a component of emotionality, activity, sociability, and impulsivity. One study (Buss, Plomin, and Willerman, 1973) showed that identical twins are much more similar in temperament than are fraternal twins; this resemblance has been attributed to the common genetic endowment of the identical twins. Researchers have not been able to conclude that specific personality traits such as self-confidence are inherited, but other studies of twins suggest that there is a hereditary element in personality structure (Dworkin et al., 1976). And recent research indicates that heredity may even be involved in such aspects of personality as vocational interests and authoritarian attitudes: the members of biological families resemble one another in their attitudes and interests much more closely than do members of families in which the children were adopted at a very early age (Scarr and Weinberg, 1978).

Perhaps the most valuable contribution of the biological perspective on personality development is the fact that it calls attention to the interaction between our biologically determined characteristics and our experiences. For instance, the temperament of a baby will have a significant effect on the treatment the baby receives from its parents and others. An active, responsive baby will probably be given much more attention and receive much more social stimulation than an inactive, quiet baby. From this perspective, the uniqueness of each of us is a result of the complex interplay of our biology and the experiences that we have in life. The exact nature of these complex relationships, however, has not yet been determined.

FREUD'S THEORY OF PSYCHOSEXUAL DEVELOPMENT Sigmund Freud's theory of person-

Family scene. Research indicates that members of biological families are closer in attitudes and interests than siblings who are adopted.

ality will be described in detail in Chapter 18. His concept of psychosexual stages will be discussed here, however, because it has had a dominant influence on research into personality and social development. Freud (1933) maintained that from earliest infancy we are motivated by powerful biological instincts to seek pleasure. The energy that is associated with these pleasure-seeking instincts is termed **libido**. Socially acceptable behavior develops out of the conflict between the demands others make on us and the demands of these instincts, which we gradually bring under control as we grow up. In other words, we learn to channel this libido in socially acceptable ways. At different ages of development, libidinal energy is concentrated at different parts of the body, called **erogenous zones**.

According to Freud, children pass through five stages of **psychosexual development** from birth to adolescence: the oral stage, the anal stage, the phallic stage, a latency period, and the genital stage. In each stage, the child's interest is focused on the erotic pleasure that is derived from a different part of the body. Biological mechanisms direct the shifts from one zone to another. Freud argued that the adult personality results from the ways in which pleasurable impulses are channeled at each stage of development. Failure at any stage to resolve the conflict between the need to gratify impulses and the demand of parents for control can lead to **fixation** at that stage; the child develops a maladaptive pattern of behavior in an attempt to attain gratification.

In the first year of life, the baby's mouth is the primary source of sensual pleasure. During the **oral stage** infants suck, mouth, and chew on whatever they can find in their search for the pleasure of oral stimulation. Fixation at the oral stage can take a number of forms, depending on whether the child was deprived or overindulged. For example, after a prolonged period of nursing on demand, weaning a child abruptly can trigger anxiety about whether it can get gratification from others. Freud described the oral dependent personality as a product of anxiety over whether food will be given or withheld. According to this viewpoint, an infant who is over-indulged and seldom frustrated develops into an adult with a passive, overly dependent, unenterprising personality. The child who is deprived develops a distrustful, independent, and acquisitive personality.

During the **anal stage**, in the second year of life, the child's attention shifts to the anus and the pleasures of holding in and pushing out feces. These pleasures are barely established, however, before the child encounters the social demands of toilet training. Freudian theorists regard toilet training as a crucial event, a systematic attempt to impose social requirements on the child's natural impulses just as he or she has begun to gain some bodily control. In Freud's view, children who become fixated at the anal stage develop into adults with one of two personalities: an anal-expulsive fixation gives rise to an adult who is pushy, disorderly, and messy; an anal-retentive fixation produces a stingy, stubborn, and overly meticulous adult.

The **phallic stage** of development occurs approximately between the ages of three and five, when the child's attention is focused on the genitals and the pleasures of masturbation. It is at this stage that the child discovers the genital differences between the sexes. According to Freudian theory, this discovery precipitates the most important conflict in the child's psychological development. Children perceive themselves as rivals of their same-sex parent for the affection of the parent of the opposite sex. A boy wants to win his mother for himself and feels in conflict with his father. A girl wants her father for herself and longs to shut out her mother. The resolution of this conflict—called the **Oedipal conflict** in boys and the **Electra conflict** in girls, after characters from Greek mythology—has important consequences for the development of sexual identity and morality, which we will consider later in this chapter.

After the phallic stage children move into the fourth stage, a period of **latency**. From the age of five or six until puberty, children's sexual impulses remain in the background, and they busy themselves exploring the world and learning new skills. During the hormonal changes of puberty, however, sexual feelings reemerge and the **genital stage** begins. The focus in this final stage of psychosexual development is on the pleasures of sexual intercourse.

Freud's ideas have had a profound effect on psychological thought. Concepts such as the importance of unconscious wishes and the belief that early childhood experiences have a crucial impact on adult personality are widely accepted. So is the general notion that different stages of an individual's

According to Freud, the sexual impulses of children in the latency period recede, and they concentrate on exploring their environment and learning new skills.

life present different problems in social and personality growth.

THE COGNITIVE-DEVELOPMENTAL PERSPECTIVE Like Freudian theory, the cognitive perspective on the development of personality and social behavior uses the concept of stages of development. There is a basic difference between these two viewpoints, however. Freud emphasizes irrational, instinctive motivation and the conflict between demands for gratification and the requirements of society. In contrast, cognitive theorists emphasize thinking, reasoning, and role taking in the development of social behavior and personality.

According to the cognitive-developmental view, social behavior depends in part on the child's level of cognitive maturity. As we saw in Chapter 8, cognitive skills are thought to develop through a series of stages that Jean Piaget (Piaget, 1963; Piaget and Inhelder, 1969) has labeled sensorimotor, concrete-operational (with preoperational and operational substages), and formal-operational. As cognitive skills develop, the child is able to construct social schemes (conceptual frameworks) about social situations; these are analogous to schemes about the physical world, and they enable the child to know the social world and act within it. Just as the infant has simple schemes for knowing the physical world, like grasping and sucking, so the young child has simple schemes for knowing the social world. Initially, people and objects are treated similarly; as the baby begins to differentiate itself from the environment, schemes appropriate for social interaction begin to develop. The unique schemes that each person constructs then contribute to the development of that person's enduring characteristics—his or her personality.

Each stage of cognitive development allows the child to develop increasingly complex schemes for social interaction. In the first sensorimotor stage, social behavior is primitive. It begins with a simple recognition of familiar persons and an early attachment to the mother or other person who cares for the child. In order to develop a sense of autonomy (independence), the child must develop a sense of the self as a being who is able to act on the environment in a planned and voluntary manner (Lee, 1976). As we saw in Chapter 8, this capacity for planning requires the child to engage in representational thinking and to use symbolic representations of objects and events. For example, a two-year-old may pick up a toy hammer to imitate Mother hanging a picture or Father repairing a chair. Such imitative role playing is essential for social and personality development.

Another important cognitive ability for social and personality development is **role taking**. The infant is egocentric, seeing the world only from his or her own perspective. But the concrete-operational child is capable of taking the perspective of another person and can imagine what that person might be feeling. This operational capacity allows the child to develop more elaborate social schemes that include the active roles of other people and the reciprocal nature of social interaction.

Later, during adolescence, there are also connections between cognitive ability and social and personality development. As a girl moves into her teens and becomes capable of abstract reasoning, she begins to question the beliefs and teachings of her parents and to formulate her own system of values. It is no accident, then, that identity crises occur not during the elementary school years, but during adolescence and young adulthood, when we become able to analyze the meaning of our past and the direction of our future.

THE BEHAVIORAL PERSPECTIVE Some psychologists have tried to explain the development of personality and social behavior on the basis of the principles of conditioning and learning that were presented in Chapter 4. Such behavioral psychologists view the unique qualities and enduring characteristics of each person as patterns of behavior that have been learned through reinforcement, punishment, or imitation. In contrast to the psychoanalytic and cognitive-developmental theorists, these theorists view development as continuous, not broken into discrete stages. According to the behavioral perspective, specific characteristics are acquired in two ways: on the basis of direct experience, in which the person receives reinforcement or punishment associated with certain behaviors; or through vicarious experience, in which the person observes and imitates a model's behavior.

An example of behavior acquired through direct experience is found in infant attachment. An infant's attachment to its mother is thought to be based on the warmth, comfort, and reduction of hunger that the infant associates with the mother. This example is an instance of classical conditioning, but behavioral patterns may also be ac-

Young girls unconsciously imitating each other.

ate as he or she matures. Children are sensitive to the consequences of the model's behavior and are likely to imitate the behavior that leads to reinforcement for the model, because they anticipate receiving the same reinforcement themselves (Bandura, 1965).

A more complete account of social learning theory as a theory of personality will be given in Chapter 19. For the moment, it is most important to understand that the behavioral perspective on personality and social development emphasizes the impact of the environment on the child. The child acquires behavioral patterns by having certain behaviors reinforced. Though recent versions of social learning theory have begun to acknowledge the importance of cognitive activities in the development of personality (Mischel, 1973; Bandura, 1977), the focus is still on (1) the impact the environment has on the individual and on (2) the continuous development of behavioral patterns rather than development through a series of discrete stages.

We have now surveyed the four major perspectives on personality and social development. None of these perspectives alone provides a satisfactory account of all aspects of personality and social development. Each, however, has led to important advances in our understanding of the processes by which each human being develops into a unique individual. The rest of this chapter does not adopt any one of these perspectives, but it uses each one—and in some cases all four—to explain certain aspects of development.

quired through instrumental conditioning. For example, a preschool boy who is big for his age may learn to achieve his goals by using physical aggression, because threatening or hurting smaller children often allows him to get what he seeks (Patterson, Littman, and Bricker, 1967). Much attention-seeking behavior in children, such as whining, is thought to be acquired in this way—that is, it achieves a desired end, and thus is reinforced.

Some behavioral psychologists argue that the more complex forms of social behavior and the enduring characteristics of personality are probably based on learning by modeling or imitation (Bandura, 1977). Imitating parents and peers allows a child to develop complex patterns of behavior without the necessity of direct reinforcement of the behavior. According to this theory, gender role identity is acquired, at least in part, by imitating the parent of the same sex. That is, the child practices or rehearses the behavior that will become appropri-

INFANCY

Infancy is not a precise chronological age; it usually refers to approximately the first two years of life. One researcher has defined it as the period of life that begins at birth and ends when the child begins to use language (Bower, 1977). There are important cognitive and physical developments in this period (these were discussed in Chapters 7, 8, and 9). The important social and personality developments center around the phenomenon of **attachment**, the formation of an emotional bond between the infant and its main caregiver, usually its mother. Social relationships with peers develop in later infancy. Gender role development also begins in infancy. In this section we will consider these phenomena of infancy—attachment and deprivation of attachment, the beginnings of social interaction, and early gender role behavior.

ATTACHMENT Both Freudian and social learning approaches to attachment explain the emotional bond of infant to mother (or other caregiver) as one based on nurturance. That is, the infant learns that the mother is the source of food, warmth, and comfort, and attachment to her is the positive response to the person who satisfies these needs. John Bowlby (1969), however, viewed attachment as a mechanism having **adaptive significance** (a concept discussed in Chapter 3). He argued that a baby has a better chance for survival if it develops an emotional bond that keeps it close to the mother. The baby develops attachment behaviors, such as following the mother and protesting at separation, that keep it near the mother so it can be protected.

There is another side to attachment, and that is the emotional bond formed by the parent for the infant. A baby comes into the world equipped with behavior that almost seems designed to promote parental attachment, such as smiling and cooing, and to influence the parent's behavior, such as crying. Furthermore, recent research indicates that interaction between an infant and its parents during the hours immediately after birth increases the strength of the parents' attachment to the baby (Klaus and Kennell, 1976). A secure attachment between infant and parents not only may have important adaptive significance for the baby, but it also provides a firm foundation for the subsequent development of personality and social behavior.

What specific kinds of nurturance lead to attachment, and which are the most important? For a number of years Harry Harlow has been exploring these questions, using infant monkeys. It would, of course, be impossible to do research of this nature with human infants, because it requires the infants to be separated from their mothers and to be placed in carefully controlled conditions of nurturance. Harlow's basic experimental model (Harlow and Suomi, 1970) has been to separate the infant monkeys from their mothers at birth and to raise them in cages with various kinds of artificial "surrogate mothers." In some of his early work Harlow (1958) raised infant monkeys in a cage that contained two surrogate mothers, one of them made of cold, stiff, bare wire mesh and the other of wire mesh covered with soft terrycloth. Harlow found that even when

the bare wire "mother" contained the supply of milk for the infant and the terrycloth one did not, the terrycloth "mother" was much preferred by the infants. It was to the terrycloth mother that the infants became attached, spending a great deal of time clinging to it and running to it when alarmed (see Figure 10.1). In addition, the infants would use the cloth mother as a base for exploratory behavior (Harlow and Zimmerman, 1959).

Harlow demonstrated in later studies that feeding is an important determinant of attachment. When the infant monkeys had two cloth-covered mothers, one that gave milk and one that did not, they consistently preferred the nourishing mother. In similar experiments, a mother that provided a rocking motion was preferred to one that did not, and a warm mother was preferred to a mother whose temperature was cool (Harlow and Suomi, 1970).

These studies, then, have identified and confirmed a number of important factors in the development of attachment. In human infants this bond has a major impact on the course of later development.

We infer from the way human infants behave when separated briefly from their mothers that they have developed attachment. If a baby shows more distress when separated from its mother than when separated from a stranger and if it seems glad to be reunited with its mother, we know the baby can recognize the mother and has developed a tie to her. Many studies have been done to determine at what age babies begin to show this **separation anxiety**. Whenever it does appear, we can infer that the infant has formed an attachment.

The development of attachment in human infants during the first two years of life has been extensively studied recently. Mary Ainsworth and her colleagues (Stayton and Ainsworth, 1973; Ainsworth, Bell, and Stayton, 1971; Stayton, Ainsworth, and Main, 1973) have conducted longitudinal studies of babies in laboratory settings and at home. They have recorded various behaviors associated with separation from the mother and reunion with her, including behavior that initiates and maintains contact with the mother, behavior that avoids the mother (ignoring her, looking or moving away), behavior that resists the mother (hitting, pushing away when picked up, squirming to get down), and interaction at a distance (smiling across the room at the mother, holding out toys for the mother).

These researchers have found that the development of attachment goes through several phases. In the first two or three months of life the child responds to everyone and does not display any special behavior for the mother. Then the child begins to discriminate among people and comes to display behavior that is only for the mother. At six months of age or a little later, the child actively seeks to remain close to the mother by following or clinging to her. Finally, at about three years of age, the child uses his or her developing cognitive abilities, especially language, to try to influence the mother's behavior and keep her near.

Though most research on separation and attachment has focused on attachment to the mother, Michael Lamb (1977), in a series of longitudinal studies, examined the degree of attachment to fathers as well. The studies found, surprisingly, that during the first year of life, babies seem to show the same degree of attachment to both mothers and fathers, even when fathers are not caregivers. Lamb then looked at the attachment of infants to their mothers and fathers as they grew from fifteen to twenty-four months of age. He found that babies displayed somewhat more attachment toward the father than toward the mother in a home setting. He acknowledged, however, that this could have been because the presence of the father often is a novelty; the mother usually is the more familiar figure. Lamb and other researchers have also noted that attachment behavior begins to decline during the second year of life, that babies do not respond as intensely to separation by protesting or following, as they do during the period from seven to thirteen months of age. This reduction in attachment behavior probably does not indicate that the baby is less attached, but that it is beginning to develop some autonomy and is less distressed by being left alone or separated than it was at an earlier age.

ATTACHMENT DEPRIVATION Opportunities to form emotional bonds are among the most crucial learning experiences during the first few years of life. What happens, then, when an attachment is interrupted by separation or when the chance to form attachments is completely denied?

In studies of baby monkeys that were suddenly separated from their mothers, the babies became extremely anxious (Seay, Hansen, and Harlow, 1962; Seay and Harlow, 1965). They initially expressed their protest by increased activity and vocalization. Soon they became withdrawn and apathetic, refusing to play with their peers. When they were reunited with their mothers, they returned to a normal emotional state.

Figure 10.1 In Harlow's experiments, infant monkeys were presented with a new and frightening object (the mechanical bear) and were given a choice of two surrogate mothers to flee to. Infant monkeys of all ages greatly preferred the terrycloth mother to the wire mother, even though some of the infant monkeys received food only from the wire mother. (After Harlow, 1959.)

The effects of complete attachment deprivation can be far more devastating and far more difficult to cure than those of temporary separation. Monkeys raised in total isolation have shown profound behavioral abnormalities (Harlow, Harlow, and Suomi, 1971). Early in life they exhibited exaggerated oral behavior, self-clutching, and rocking. Then they either became apathetic and inactive or they displayed bizarre behavior remarkably similar to that of some human schizophrenics. As adults they showed severe deficits in sexual and social behavior. Monkeys raised in isolation from birth to the age of three months returned to normal patterns of behavior after one month of social contact with other monkeys. If the isolation period was increased to six months, then being placed with other monkeys was not an effective therapy. However, Suomi and Harlow (1972) found that when monkeys that had been isolated for their first six months were placed with normal three-month-old monkeys, their behavior did return to normal. The younger monkeys gradually drew the isolates into social behavior and play. By clinging to the isolates in a nonthreatening way and then initiating play, the younger monkeys helped the isolates make up the developmental deficit caused by the earlier deprivation of opportunities for attachment.

In human infants, extended separation from the mother leads to symptoms very similar to those exhibited by separated baby monkeys: agitation and protest followed by withdrawal and then by indiscriminate social responsiveness (an apparent search for *someone* to form an attachment with). One study of children who were separated from their parents by the need for prolonged hospitalization and were then reunited showed that the children did form attachments with their parents and did come to exhibit normal social behavior and communication skills if they had had other attentive caregivers during the separation (Schaffer, 1963). Thus, the effects of temporary separation from the primary caregiver can be reversed.

What about the effects of permanent separation? In a recent summary T. G. R. Bower (1977) concluded that separation after a secure attachment seems to produce little, if any, impairment of later social and intellectual functioning. But if a child has never had the opportunity to develop a secure attachment—if, for example, a child has passed through a series of foster homes and has formed only shallow, rapidly changing attachments—he or she is likely to develop into a facile person who finds it difficult to form deep relationships (Bower, 1977).

Extended separation from the mother can disrupt the formation of attachment.

THE BEGINNINGS OF SOCIAL INTERACTION

It is commonly believed that infants are extremely dependent on adults. While babies do depend on adults for many things, such as food, shelter, and attention, they also exhibit a surprising amount of autonomy and striving for competence. Babies appear to find satisfaction in exploring new aspects of their social world. They are attracted to novel situations and people. For example, two researchers found that infants in a strange room did not cling to their mothers, but explored the area and readily approached unfamiliar toys and people (Rheingold and Eckerman, 1970; Eckerman and Rheingold, 1974). Indeed, some studies found that young children in an unfamiliar environment, accompanied by their mothers, were more likely to smile at a novel adult than at familiar adults (Eckerman and Whatley, 1975) and to play more with unfamiliar peers than with their mothers (Eckerman, Whatley, and Kutz, 1975).

The young child, particularly in the second year of life, appears to be strongly motivated by the desire to explore, understand, and control the world around it, and this motivation induces the child to detach from the mother. This seemingly innate interest in exploring and acting on its environment is termed **effectance motivation** (White, 1959) or **competence motivation**. The experiences that result from effectance motivation undoubtedly stimulate the child's cognitive and social development.

The two-year-old's desire to be autonomous and to do things his or her own way frequently leads to a conflict of wills between parent and child. This period is frequently called the **negativistic crisis**—or, more informally, the "terrible twos." The two-year-old, developing a concept of the self as distinct from others, resolutely seeks to assert independence and to explore the relationship between his or her intentions and those of others. The frequency of naysaying of the two-year-old has been interpreted as one way the child attempts to establish his or her individuality.

GENDER ROLE BEHAVIOR IN INFANCY

Children begin to acquire gender role behavior at a very young age. To understand this phenomenon, one must be aware of the difference between gender role and sex role. Although the terms are often used interchangeably, the term **sex role** refers to expected patterns of *sexual or reproductive* behavior based on an individual's sex; **gender role** refers to expected patterns of *social behavior* associated with masculinity or femininity. Our concern here is with gender roles.

Although children do not have much awareness of their own gender identity until they are between two and a half and three years of age (Thompson, 1975), gender differences in behavior have been observed as early as the age of one year. For example, infant boys tend to cry more and sleep less than infant girls (Moss, 1967); one-year-old boys tend to play more vigorously than girls (Maccoby and Jacklin, 1974); and one-year-old boys tend to prefer toys that require gross motor activity (Goldberg and Lewis, 1969).

The reasons for such gender-based behavioral differences in infancy have been difficult to identify. We will postpone our major discussion of theories of gender role development to the following section, where we examine the next stage of growth, childhood.

CHILDHOOD

By the time he or she reaches the age of eighteen to twenty-four months, the infant has entered the period of life called childhood, which extends from infancy until puberty. The young child, or toddler, is skilled at walking and is beginning to use language effectively. These new abilities broaden the realm of the child's social activities. Although its parents continue to exert the greatest influence on the

For children in most cultures (including these Turkish girls), school is an important agent of socialization.

child's development, other adults, children, and electronic media such as television begin to affect the child. The influence of these other figures increases throughout childhood, especially after the child begins to spend time in school, away from home.

At the same time, the role of the parent changes. During infancy, the parent is primarily a caregiver—a nurturing, loving figure. As the child grows physically and becomes more active and more autonomous, the parents are required to provide less care and more discipline. Their tasks now include controlling the child's behavior and teaching the child to act in ways consistent with society's notions of good and bad, acceptable and unacceptable. This process of instilling the society's values in the child is called **socialization**. It is one of the major processes of childhood and has a profound effect on the child's social and personality development. The basic goal of socialization is **internalization**—the child's incorporation of society's values into the self or personality to such an extent that violation of these standards produces a sense of guilt. In this section we will discuss two areas of childhood development in which socialization appears to play an important part: the development of gender roles and the development of moral behavior.

ACQUIRING GENDER ROLES As we mentioned in the section on infancy, sex differences in behavior begin to appear at a very early age. These differences between boys and girls become clearer during childhood. Each of the major theoretical perspectives on development reviewed at the beginning of this chapter offers a different explanation for the acquisition of gender role identities and **sex-typed behavior**—behavior that is regarded as acceptable and appropriate either only for boys or only for girls. In this section we will discuss the gender-based behaviors and attitudes that boys and girls acquire and the mechanisms by which they may do so.

THE IMPACT OF BIOLOGY It is not easy to assess the precise impact biology has on what we consider masculine and feminine behavior. We may get some idea of the innate factors that may underlie sex differences in behavior, however, if we observe the differences between male and female infants at and soon after birth, before they have had much chance to be affected by their environment.

There appear to be temperamental differences between boys and girls early in life. Recent research seems to indicate, for example, that newborn boys are more active than newborn girls are (Phillips, 1978). The differences in temperament could underlie the differences between the sexes in style of play and in aggression. Furthermore, the initial differences in their levels of activity may cause male and female babies to experience different kinds of care and social interaction. For example, active babies may elicit more attention than passive babies. Finally, differences in temperament may lead to varying experiences with the nonsocial environment: if infant boys are more active than girls, they may see and do more at an earlier age. These differences in stimulation could influence both cognitive and personality development. Thus, innate temperamental differences between boys and girls may produce a variety of differences in behavior.

Although biological factors may produce some gender-based differences in behavior, it is highly unlikely that biology alone is responsible for all the differences we see in the behavior of boys and girls. If gender differences were primarily genetic in origin, then boys and girls (and men and women) would at all times and in all the world's societies exhibit the same sex-typed behaviors. Margaret Mead's classic study (1935) of three New Guinea tribes indicated that this is not so. There are marked differences among cultures in the behavior and personality characteristics ascribed to males and females and in the degree of differentiation between the feminine and masculine roles. In one of the cultures Mead studied, both men and women were aggressive and unresponsive—characteristics we generally think of as being masculine. In another tribe, both men and women were cooperative, responsive to the needs of others, and nonaggressive—traits defined as feminine in our own culture. In the third tribe, the gender roles of Western culture were reversed: the women were impersonal and dominant, while the men were emotionally dependent.

If the differences between the sexes in behaviors and attitudes are not totally biological, then how can they be explained? The three major theories of development propose three alternative explanations.

THE PSYCHOANALYTIC VIEW OF GENDER ROLE BEHAVIOR According to psychoanalytic theory, gender role identification and the adoption of "appropriate" sex-typed behavior are results of the Oedipal and Electra conflicts during the phallic stage of psychosexual development, when the child desires to possess the parent of the opposite sex. According to Freud, a great deal of anxiety develops as a result of this desire. The little boy fears that his father will resent his desire for his mother and will retaliate, perhaps by castrating him. The boy, wishing at times that his father were dead and out of the way, also experiences anxiety not only about his death wishes toward his father, the rival for his mother's love, but also about the potential loss of his father's love. The little girl obviously cannot fear castration, but she does fear her mother's resentment and retaliation and subsequent desertion or loss of the mother's love.

As the anxiety heightens, the child gradually realizes that his or her desire for the parent of the opposite sex is unlikely ever to be fulfilled. The child then compromises: he or she tries to be like, or identifies with, the parent of the same sex. Through this process of **identification** the child becomes confident of retaining the love of both parents, and thus his or her anxiety is relieved.

According to psychoanalytic theory, a major outcome of identification is the development of sex-typed behaviors and attitudes. In identifying with the parent of the same sex, the child internalizes the moral values and the behaviors of that parent. The child constructs a concept of an ideal self that includes the gender role behaviors of the same-sex parent. If the Oedipal or Electra conflict is not satisfactorily resolved, the child may never develop appropriate gender role behavior.

Tests of Freud's ideas about conflict and identification have been inconclusive (Sears, Rau, and Alpert, 1965) or have not supported the theory. For example, Bronislaw Malinowski (1929), an anthropologist, noted that the Oedipal conflict does not occur among the inhabitants of the Trobriand Islands in the South Pacific: the relationship between father and son is casual and positive throughout childhood. Identification with the parent of the same sex has, however, been observed in many cultures. In any case, whether or not identification occurs in exactly the way Freud described, it is widely regarded by psychologists as an important part of the development of gender role behavior and of personality development in general.

THE LEARNING PERSPECTIVE ON DEVELOPMENT OF SEX-TYPED BEHAVIOR According to social learning theorists, environmental factors are primarily responsible for the development of sex-typed behaviors. They claim that parents and other agents of socialization shape the child's behavior from birth by reinforcing behavior that is consistent with his or her gender role, by punishing behavior that is inconsistent with his or her gender role, and by providing appropriate gender role models for the child to imitate.

The evidence for this point of view is somewhat conflicting. One recent review of almost two hundred published studies (Maccoby and Jacklin, 1974) concluded that parents do not seem to differ much in their behavior toward their male and female children. The studies found little or no evidence, for example, that parents encourage sons to be more aggressive than daughters, or daughters to be more dependent than sons.

Other researchers (for example, Block, 1975), however, believe this conclusion to be premature. They offer data to indicate that parents do treat their sons and daughters in markedly different ways. In raising boys, for example, parents report that they emphasize achievement, competition, independence, and emotional control more than they do with girls. They also report that they punish their sons more firmly and encourage them to conform to external standards.

In contrast, daughters are apparently treated with greater warmth and physical closeness. Parents seem to have more confidence in their daughters' trustworthiness and truthfulness; they also seem more reluctant to punish their daughters and more likely to restrict and supervise daughters than sons.

These findings are based on interviews with the parents, not on observation, and so they must be considered tentative; for one reason, there may be a discrepancy between what parents say they do and what they actually do. However, the findings in some recent observational studies support many of Block's conclusions. Adults have been observed to be more nurturing toward girls, to encourage boys to be more active (Frisch, 1977), and to emphasize achievement as desirable for boys and social skills as desirable for girls (Block, Block, and Harrington, 1974).

Thus, some recent research clearly suggests that parents socialize boys and girls in different ways. These differences provide opportunities for children to learn the behaviors expected of each sex and to receive reinforcement for behaving "appropriately."

COGNITIVE FACTORS IN GENDER ROLE ACQUISI-TION Cognitive-developmental theorists such as Jean Piaget and Lawrence Kohlberg are generally more interested in thinking and cognition than in emotion or behavior. According to Kohlberg (1969), the child must understand the concepts of gender and gender role before sex-typed behaviors can develop. Once the child has attained the cognitive ability to understand the concepts of male and female and to recognize that one of these concepts permanently applies to him or her, the child will want to adopt behaviors consistent with this newly discovered status. This desire, in Kohlberg's view, stems from the child's wish to be competent at all things, including being a girl or a boy. Thus, children seek out and imitate the behavior deemed appropriate to their sex because they want to act in a consistent and competent manner.

Many of these cognitive-developmental hypotheses have been supported by research. In one study (Slaby and Frey, 1975), children between the ages of two and five and a half were tested for their grasp of gender identity (knowing their own sex), gender stability over time (knowing that they have always been the same sex), and gender constancy given different situations and motivations (knowing that one cannot change sex simply by changing hairstyle or by wanting to be the opposite sex). Gender identity was usually mastered by age four or under, but gender constancy was typically unclear until after age four and a half. Thus it seems that the ability to understand gender-related concepts is indeed linked to cognitive maturity.

But does gender knowledge affect the child's readiness to learn gender roles, as cognitive-developmental theory says it does? To answer this question, the researchers showed children a movie in which a man and a woman performed the same tasks at the same time. For the cognitive-developmental view to be correct, the children with the best grasp of gender concepts should have perceived that the actor who was the same sex as themselves seemed more similar to themselves. Consequently, they should have viewed that actor as an appropriate model and spent the most time watching and learning from him or her. This is exactly what happened. The children who had been found to have the clearest understanding of the concepts of gender stability and gender constancy were also the ones who paid the most attention to the model of the same sex. Thus, a certain level of cognitive awareness of sex-related differences seems to be necessary for gender role learning through imitation to take place.

Although the cognitive-developmental explanation for sex typing has received some empirical support, it alone is insufficient to explain the development of gender roles. Children are unable to identify themselves as male or female until two and a half years of age or older (Thompson, 1975). So the cognitive-developmental explanation does not account for sex-typed behaviors that appear during infancy. It is likely that either biological or environmental factors influence the earliest development of gender roles. Indeed, one psychologist argues that it is quite possible that any adequate ex-

Gender identity in both boys and girls seem to be firmly established by the age of four.

planation of the development of sex-typed behavior must incorporate elements of more than one theoretical approach (Mussen, 1969).

MORAL DEVELOPMENT Morality—behavior and judgment of self and others according to a set of rules of right conduct—on the part of its citizens is of critical importance to the functioning, maintenance, and survival of any society. In 1908 the psychologist William McDougall wrote, "The fundamental problem of social psychology is the moralization of the individual by the society." More recently, moral development has been the focus of research by developmental psychologists.

The three psychological perspectives we have been discussing—psychoanalytic, behavioral or social learning, and cognitive-developmental—have each been the basis of an explanation of the development of moral behavior. These theories differ, however, in the aspects of morality that they emphasize. Psychoanalytic theory attends to the affective, or emotional, aspects of morality, particularly the development of a conscience and a sense of guilt. Social learning theorists emphasize the learning of specific moral behavior, such as honesty or generosity. Cognitive-developmental theorists pay little attention to either affect or behavior; they are interested primarily in how people think about moral issues. The three major theories also differ greatly in identifying the processes or mechanisms that produce moral development. As we shall see, each theory explains the development of morality in a manner very similar to the way in which it explains the development of sex-typed behavior.

THE PSYCHOANALYTIC PERSPECTIVE According to psychoanalytic theory, the child develops a conscience and adopts moral behaviors when he or she internalizes the same-sex parent's moral code during the resolution of the Oedipal or Electra conflict. This process results in a dramatic change in the moral orientation of the child: a strong sense of morality emerges where previously there was none. Because the development of morality and the acquisition of sex-typed attitudes and behaviors are viewed by psychoanalytic theorists as the result of the identification with the same-sex parent, they are considered to be related processes.

Although case reports of individual children undergoing psychotherapy have provided some evidence for Freud's theory of identification, other kinds of studies provide little support for it. Research has shown that moral development is a gradual process. The child does not suddenly become moral at age five or six; moral development appears to begin in the preschool years and to continue into adulthood (Kohlberg, 1969; Hoffman, 1976).

THE SOCIAL LEARNING PERSPECTIVE The same processes that social learning theorists use to explain the learning of sex-typed behaviors—reinforcement, punishment, and imitation—have also been used to account for the development of moral behaviors. Thus, social learning theorists claim that children are "good," or moral, because they are reinforced for "good" behavior, are punished for "bad" behavior, and are provided with moral models to imitate. Experimental studies have furnished partial support for these ideas, finding that children frequently (but not always) imitate the immoral or moral behaviors they observe. For example, children will often behave generously after observing an adult being unselfish (Bryan, 1975) and will behave aggressively after observing an aggressive model (Bandura, Ross, and Ross, 1961).

Some social learning theorists have emphasized the role of conditioning in developing a child's sense of guilt. When children do or say things their parents disapprove of, the parents are likely to withdraw their affection or punish the child in some other way. When the child is frequently disciplined for wrongdoing, the negative feelings (primarily anxiety) that the child associates with punishment become associated with wrongdoing. Thus, the child feels anxious when he or she contemplates doing something wrong. The behaviorists say that as a result of this kind of learning, children eventually behave morally even when their parents or other disciplinarians are not present (Eysenck, 1960).

As we discussed in the section on socialization styles, research has shown that the way parents socialize their children becomes important in the establishment of self-regulated moral conduct. An excessive use of power-assertive techniques of punishment (physical punishment, the withdrawal of privileges, or the threat of either) by parents tends to be associated with low levels of moral development (Hoffman, 1970). In contrast, reasoning with children about their behavior—explaining why a certain act is right or wrong, pointing out how their behavior affects others—appears to be associated with high levels of moral development, including consideration for others, capacity for moral reasoning, and guilt over wrongdoing (Hoffman and Saltzstein, 1967; Aronfreed, 1969; Hoffman, 1970).

THE COGNITIVE-DEVELOPMENTAL PERSPECTIVE The cognitive-developmental approach to moral development has been formulated most completely by Lawrence Kohlberg (1969). He hypothesized that children progress through distinct stages of moral judgment that reflect developmental changes in the child's cognitive conceptions of morality. These stages, in Kohlberg's view, occur in an invariable sequence; each develops out of and subsumes its predecessor; and each is cognitively more complex than the previous stage. Furthermore, these stages are said to be universal—to characterize the development of moral thinking in people all over the world, not just in American society.

Kohlberg and his colleagues assess an individual's level of moral development by eliciting the reasoning by which he or she resolves a series of moral dilemmas. The best-known dilemma is the Heinz story:

In Europe, a woman was near death from cancer. One drug might save her, a form of radium that a druggist in the same town had recently discovered. The druggist was charging $2,000, ten times what the drug cost him to make. The sick woman's husband, Heinz, went to everyone he knew to borrow the money, but he could only get together about half of what it cost. He told the druggist that his wife was dying and asked him to sell it cheaper or let him pay later. But the druggist said, "No." The husband got desperate and broke into the man's store to steal the drug for his wife. Should the husband have done that? Why?

What is of concern to Kohlberg is the way a person interprets a moral dilemma like this one—the reasons for the individual's decision, not the decision itself. A person at any stage could conclude that Heinz should or should not have stolen the drug. Which stage of moral development a person has reached depends on the reasons he or she gives for the decision. Table 10.1 presents typical reasons for stealing or not stealing the drug at each of Kohlberg's stages.

Basing his findings on the responses of many chil-

Table 10.1 Motives for Stealing or Not Stealing the Drug at Various Stages of Moral Development

	For Stealing Drug	Against Stealing Drug
Preconventional Stage		
Substage 1: Obedience, or Reward, Orientation		
Action motivated by avoidance of punishment, and "conscience" is irrational fear of punishment.	If you let your wife die, you will get in trouble. You'll be blamed for not spending the money to save her and there'll be an investigation of you and the druggist for your wife's death.	You shouldn't steal the drug because you'll be caught and sent to jail if you do. If you do get away, your conscience would bother you thinking how the police would catch up with you at any minute.
Substage 2: Instrumental Exchange, or Marketplace, Orientation		
Action motivated by desire for reward or benefit. Possible guilt reactions are ignored and punishment is viewed in a pragmatic manner.	If you do happen to get caught, you could give the drug back and you wouldn't get much of a sentence. It wouldn't bother you much to serve a little jail term, if you have your wife when you get out.	He may not get much of a jail term if he steals the drug, but his wife will probably die before he gets out so it won't do him much good. If his wife dies, he shouldn't blame himself, it wasn't his fault she has cancer.

Conventional Stage

Substage 3: Conformist, or "Good Boy, Good Girl," Orientation

Action motivated by anticipation of disapproval by others, actual or imagined.	No one will think you're bad if you steal the drug, but your family will think you're an inhuman husband if you don't. If you let your wife die, you'll never be able to look anybody in the face again.	It isn't just the druggist who will think you're a criminal; everyone else will too. After you steal it, you'll feel bad thinking how you've brought dishonor on your family and yourself; you won't be able to face anyone again.

Substage 4: "Law and Order" Orientation

Action motivated by anticipation of dishonor—that is, institutionalized blame for failure of duty—and by guilt over concrete harm done to others.	If you have any sense of honor, you won't let your wife die because you're afraid to do the only thing that will save her. You'll always feel guilty that you caused her death if you don't do your duty to her.	You're desperate and you may not know you're doing wrong when you steal the drug. But you'll know you did wrong after you're sent to jail. You'll always feel guilty for your dishonesty and lawbreaking.

Postconventional Stage

Substage 5: Social-Contract, Legalistic Orientation

Concern about maintaining respect of equals and of the community (assuming their respect is based on reason rather than emotions). Concern about own self-respect—that is, about avoiding judging self as irrational, inconsistent, nonpurposive.	You'd lose other people's respect, not gain it, if you don't steal. If you let your wife die, it would be out of fear, not out of reasoning it out. So you'd just lose self-respect and probably the respect of others too.	You would lose your standing and respect in the community and violate the law. You'd lose respect for yourself if you're carried away by emotion and forget the long-range point of view.

Substage 6: Universal Ethical Principle Orientation

Concern about self-condemnation for violating one's own principles.	If you don't steal the drug and let your wife die, you'd always condemn yourself for it afterward. You wouldn't be blamed and you would have lived up to the outside rule of the law but you wouldn't have lived up to your own standards of conscience.	If you stole the drug, you wouldn't be blamed by other people but you'd condemn yourself because you wouldn't have lived up to your own conscience and standards of honesty.

Source: Adapted from Lawrence Kohlberg, "Stage and Sequence. The Cognitive-Developmental Approach to Socialization," in David A. Goslin (ed.), *Handbook of Socialization Theory and Research* (Chicago: Rand-McNally, 1969).

dren to a variety of dilemmas, Kohlberg identified three levels of moral judgment, each of which has two substages (see Table 10.1). The first level is called the **preconventional stage**. The preconventional child is responsive to the rules of society and to the labels "good" and "bad," but interprets these labels either in terms of the pain or pleasure they bring (punishment, reward, exchange of favors) or in terms of the physical power of those who set forth the rules and labels. Thus, the child acts "good" to avoid punishment, either because of unquestioning deference to authority or because there may be some gain involved in doing so.

The second level is called the **conventional stage**. The conventional child wants to meet the expectations and standards of the family, group, or nation. The child's attitude is not just one of conformity to personal expectations and the social order; the child seeks to maintain the order and identifies with people in it, especially those in positions of power.

The highest level of moral reasoning is not reached by children and, in fact, is attained by only a few adults. It is called the **postconventional, autonomous,** or **principled stage**. The postconventional individual seeks moral values and principles that exist apart from the authority of the groups or people holding them and apart from the individual's own identification with these groups. At the highest point of development, the postconventional individual adheres to universal ethical principles based on the ideals of reciprocity and human equality.

These levels of moral reasoning are related to age (see Figure 10.2). Older children tend to be more advanced than younger children, but there is great variation in the speed at which people move through the stages and in the levels at which individuals cease to advance. Moreover, a child's level of cognitive development—for example, his or her ability to perform Piagetian logical tasks—is related to his or her level of moral reasoning (Selman, 1976; Kuhn et al., 1977). Kohlberg conducted several cross-cultural studies to show that children in all cultures move through the stages in the same order. The results of one such study are shown in Figure 10.3.

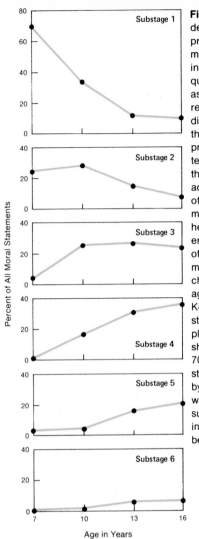

Figure 10.2 Evidence that children progress through moral stages in an invariant sequence. Kohlberg asked children to respond to moral dilemmas such as the Heinz story presented in the text. He classified their statements according to stage of moral development. Each graph here shows the average percentage of all the statements made by children of a given age at each of Kohlberg's six substages. For example, the top graph shows that about 70 percent of the statements made by seven-year-olds were classified as substage 1 thinking. (After Kohlberg, 1963.)

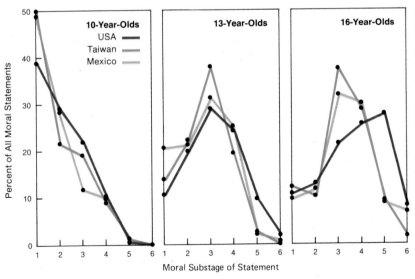

Figure 10.3 On the basis of these data and others like them Kohlberg maintains that moral development is not culturally relative but shows a similar pattern in a variety of cultures. Responses to moral dilemmas made by ten-, thirteen-, and sixteen-year-olds from three cultures were classified according to moral stage. In all three cultures, most ten-year-olds were at substage 1 and most thirteen-year-olds, at substage 3. The steady progression of moral stage with age strongly suggests not only that moral development occurs in an invariant sequence, but also that this sequence is the same for different cultures. (After Kohlberg, 1963.)

Kohlberg's cognitive theory of moral development has been criticized (Kurtines and Greif, 1974; Holstein, 1976). His methods of collecting and analyzing data have been questioned, as have his assertions that the stages of moral reasoning are universal and unvarying in sequence. Nevertheless, one researcher has commented that Kohlberg's theory continues to have great appeal as the best available approach to understanding the progression from a child's sense of morality, which is based on the consequences of one's acts, to the abstract moral codes developed and applied by adults (Hoffman, 1977).

ADOLESCENCE

The word "adolescence" comes from the Latin word *adolescere*, meaning "to grow into maturity." The beginning of adolescence is marked by the onset of **puberty**, the period of sexual maturation. This biological event transforms a child into a physical adult, and carries with it important psychological and social consequences. The need to establish an independent identity becomes a major concern of the individual. For the first time, the adolescent confronts some of the demands of the adult world—the need to train for future work and to develop intimate relationships with peers of the opposite sex. In this section we will discuss the physical, psychological, and social aspects of this period of life.

PHYSICAL MATURATION Long before the emotional and social conflicts that are associated with adolescence erupt, hormonal changes begin to have their effects on a young person's body. The hormonal changes trigger the maturation of the reproductive organs and the development of secondary sex characteristics, such as facial hair in males and breasts in females. While the timing of these changes varies considerably with the individual, puberty usually begins between the ages of ten and twelve in girls and twelve and fourteen in boys (Muuss, 1975).

SOCIAL MATURITY The sexual maturation heralded by puberty transforms the child physically

into an adult. But whether or not the child is assigned the social status of adulthood after puberty depends on the culture in which the child lives. In our society the child who has passed through puberty is not yet considered an adult. He or she is still dependent on the parents and frequently lives at home for several more years. In Western societies adolescence is a transitional period between childhood and adulthood that lasts until the individual is at least seventeen or eighteen years of age. In some societies, however, children who have obtained reproductive maturity are considered working members of the adult community and may start their own families. For them there is no adolescence, no transitional period between childhood and adulthood (Knepler, 1969; Muuss, 1975). Clearly, unlike infancy and childhood, adolescence is more a creation of certain societies than a distinct period of physical development.

ESTABLISHING AN IDENTITY Although most of them would never admit it, young teenagers are still quite dependent on their parents for security, guidance, and support. Ten years later, however, in their early twenties, they are generally able to provide for their own needs. Along with the outward signs of independence, such as making their own decisions and becoming financially responsible, most young adults have also gained a sense of themselves as separate, autonomous people. The establishment of this separate identity is the major developmental task of adolescence. A person who manages this transition successfully is ready to meet the challenges of adulthood. One who fails to do so is severely handicapped as a young adult.

According to Erik Erikson (1950), who introduced the concepts of identity and the identity crisis, the physical, sexual, and social demands on the adolescent often produce internal conflict. To resolve this conflict—the identity crisis—successfully, Erikson emphasizes, adolescents must develop an inner sense of continuity between what they were in the past and what they will become. This is what is meant by **identity**: an individual's sense of personal sameness and continuity.

According to Erikson, adolescents often attempt to determine who they are by trying out different roles temporarily. Thus, one adolescent may try her hand at acting, throw herself into the study of philosophy, and become involved in politics. By experimenting with a variety of possible choices, adolescents acquire some idea of the lifestyle associated with each role they try on, yet do not commit themselves irrevocably to any one. Erikson notes that these experiments with different identities are much more possible in some societies than others. While an American teenager has a prolonged period of adolescence during which to experiment, young people in societies that have either no period of adolescence or a very short one are forced into permanent adult roles soon after puberty.

In the United States, many youths do not develop a stable identity until the college years, or even later. Interviews with college students suggest that every young person is likely to be at one of four levels in the achievement of an independent identity (Marcia, 1966). At one extreme are those who have experienced a period of conflict and indecision concerning their values and choice of career, but who have successfully resolved that crisis and are now strongly committed to an occupation and an ideology. These are the people who have reached identity achievement. At the other extreme are the drifters—those who are both completely uncommitted and apparently completely unconcerned. Somewhere between the extremes are two other types: those in the midst of resolving an identity crisis and those so strongly committed to their parents' values and choice of a career for them that it is difficult to tell where the parents end and the young person begins. In a survey of students interviewed first as freshmen and later as seniors, 2 percent of the freshmen had established a firm sense of both occupational and ideological identity when they entered college, and 19 percent had done so by the end of their college careers (Waterman, Geary, and Waterman, 1974).

"Identity crisis" has become a common expression in our society. So has the assumption that it is normal for all adolescents to go through a very stormy time in achieving an identity. However, it is important to note that turmoil and conflict are not inevitable hallmarks of adolescent development. Many high school and college students cope quite well with the developmental tasks of adolescence and make the passage through these years without major turmoil (King, 1973).

ADULT DEVELOPMENT

Adulthood has sometimes been described as the period of life that begins when we stop growing up and start growing old. It has also been characterized as a time during which the stable personality developed in childhood and adolescence continues to function without very much change. Most theorists claim that the personality remains quite stable in normal persons during the period of adulthood. Freud believed that many of the characteristics of the person are established during childhood and that identity is fixed early in adulthood. But society has changed greatly, even since Freud's day, in that for the first time a significant portion of the population is middle-aged or older. In earlier times life expectancy was shorter, and few people survived past the age of forty. Today, there are more than 50 million men and women in the United States—one-fourth of the total population—who are in the midlife period from age forty to sixty. Furthermore, the post–World War II "baby boom" will become a "senior citizen boom" by the year 2010, when many of those postwar babies will pass the age of sixty. The movement of a large segment of the population into the mid-life period has perhaps made more salient the examination of developments and changes in personality and social behavior during adulthood.

Many such studies have been conducted in recent years. One notable example is the work of Daniel J. Levinson (1978), who made an intensive study of forty men and identified three major periods of change in adult life: an early adult transition, a mid-life transition, and a late adult transition. Many of these changes in adulthood are adjustments to changes in one's social status, changes in the circumstances of one's life, and the changes that accompany aging. We shall discuss these adjustments in Chapter 21. In the balance of this chapter we shall focus on some of the changes in attitude and orientation that occur as men and women move through the adult period of life.

These shifts in attitude and orientation have been explored by Roger Gould (1972). In one study Gould interviewed all the patients, male and female, in group therapy at a psychiatric outpatient clinic. In a second study he gave questionnaires to 524 white middle-class men and women who were not psychiatric patients. In both studies there were clear differences in the major concerns and key attitudes of various age groups. Young adults (ages twenty-two to twenty-eight) felt autonomous and focused their energy on attaining the goals they had set. But members of the next age group (twenty-nine to thirty-four) had begun to question their goals, wondering, "What is life all about now that I have done what I am supposed to do?" Those between thirty-five and forty-three continued to question the values they had lived by, but they had also developed a new awareness of the passage of time, asking, "Is it too late for me to change?" With the onset of middle age (forty-three to fifty), adults entered a period of greater stability, of acceptance of the structure of life and of greater satisfaction with their spouses. Gould found a continuation of this last trend after age fifty. Also, with a greater awareness of mortality, personal relationships became more valued, and a desire to contribute something meaningful to society developed.

Bernice Neugarten (1976) has compiled data that substantiate and complement Gould's work. She has found that there are many psychological changes generally characteristic of men and women as they move through adulthood. We will note three of the major changes here. (1) As people grow older, they show increased "interiority," a greater concern with the inner life, with introspection and conscious reappraisal. (2) With age, a change in time perspective takes place. According to Neugarten, "Life is restructured in terms of time left to live rather than time since birth" (1976, p. 17). Now aware that time is finite, adults try to estimate the time remaining during which they may accomplish the tasks or achieve the goals that they have set. (3) Intimately related to this shift in time perspective is the awareness of death as "a real possibility for the self, no longer the magical or extraordinary occurrence that it appears in youth" (p. 18).

Making the transition from one phase of adulthood to the next is not always easy. But many people cope with major transitions—such as the departure of children from the home, retirement from a career, the death of a spouse, and the approach of one's own death—without undue stress (Neugarten, 1976).

Apparently, these events in an adult's life are not necessarily traumatic. They become so only when they are not anticipated or when they occur at an unexpected time in the life cycle. Thus, the death of a child is much more stressful than the death of a parent, and divorce when a woman is forty is more difficult to accept than widowhood when she is sixty-five. A study of men who had retired from their life's work (Barfield and Morgan, 1970) found that nearly 70 percent of those who retired as planned were content with their new status, as compared with less than 20 percent of those who retired unexpectedly due to layoffs or poor health. Similarly, a study of elderly people showed that those who were living in familiar and stable surroundings were less afraid of dying than those who were about to be admitted to a home for the aged (Lieberman and Coplan, 1970). The prospect of dying in unknown circumstances creates stress. As long as the expected rhythm of the life cycle is not disrupted, however, most adults cope successfully with life, even in its final stages.

Summary

1. Psychologists use the concept of personality to try to find out not only what makes individuals unique but also what it is that makes people seem to behave consistently in a variety of situations and over a long period of time. **Personality** may be defined as those enduring characteristics of the person that are significant for interpersonal behavior. Psychologists have taken different viewpoints on the processes by which personality develops.

   A. The basis for the biological perspective is the fact that some aspects of personality are the result of biological influence. One such determinant of personality that is influenced by biology is **temperament**—the individual's pattern of activity, susceptibility to emotional stimulation, response to stimuli, and general mood. Studies of twins have confirmed the hereditary element in some aspects of personality structure. The biological perspective calls attention to the interaction between our biologically determined characteristics and our experiences—between nature and nurture.

   B. Freud's psychoanalytic theory of development emphasizes our powerful biological instincts to seek pleasure from earliest infancy. Socially acceptable behavior develops out of the conflict between the demands others make on us and the demands of our instincts, which are gradually brought under control. According to Freud, children pass through five stages of **psychosexual development** from birth to adolescence: the **oral** stage, the **anal stage**, the **phallic stage**, a **latency period**, and the **genital stage**. In each stage, the child's interest is focused on the erotic pleasure that is derived from a different part of the body. Freud believed that adult personality results from the ways in which pleasurable impulses are channeled at each stage of development.

C. The cognitive-development perspective uses the concept of stages of development based on cognitive skills. According to this view, social behavior depends in part on the child's level of cognitive maturity. Each stage of cognitive development allows the child to develop increasingly complex schemes for social interaction.

D. The behavioral perspective explains the development of personality and social behavior on the basis of the principles of conditioning and learning. Behavioral theorists view the enduring characteristics and the unique qualities of each person as patterns of behavior that have been learned through reinforcement, punishment, or imitation. Thus, social learning psychologists emphasize the impact of the environment on the child.

2. Infancy refers to apprxoximately the first two years of life. The important social and personality developments of this period include the phenomenon of attachment, the beginnings of social interaction, and the beginnings of gender role behavior.

A. **Attachment** is the formation of an emotional bond between an infant and its main caregiver, usually its mother. Both psychoanalytic and social learning approaches to attachment explain this emotional bond as one based on nurturance. A secure attachment between infant and parents not only may have **adaptive significance** for the baby but also provides a firm foundation for the subsequent development of personality and social behavior.

1. Harry F. Harlow's studies show that important determinants of attachment between an infant monkey and its mother—even an artificial "surrogate mother"—include the mother's softness, feeding, rocking motion, and warm temperature.

2. It can be inferred that a human infant has formed an attachment to its mother when it shows more distress when separated from its mother than when separated from a stranger (**separation anxiety**) and when it seems glad to be reunited with its mother.

3. The development of attachment goes through several phases, manifested in a variety of behaviors ranging from the infant's display of no special behavior toward the mother during the first few months of life to the infant's use of his or her cognitive skills to influence the mother's behavior at about three years of age. During the first year of life, babies seem to show the same degree of attachment to their fathers as to their mothers. As for the quality of the attachment bond, researchers have identified patterns of behavior that reflect both secure attachment and insecure attachment among infants.

B. Studies of attachment deprivation among infant monkeys showed that temporary separation resulted in acute anxiety followed by withdrawal, which ended when the infants were reunited with their mothers. Monkeys raised in total isolation showed profound behavioral abnormalities. In human infants, extended separation from the mother leads to symptoms similar to those exhibited by the baby monkeys: agitation, withdrawal, and then indiscriminate social responsiveness.

C. Social interaction begins very early in life. **Effectance motivation** or **competence motivation** are terms for an infant's seemingly innate interest in exploring and acting on its environment. Effectance motivation stimulates the child's cognitive and social development. The two-year-old's desire for autonomy often leads to the **negativistic crisis**—a conflict of wills between parent and child.

D. Children begin to acquire gender role behavior at a very early age, but the reasons for gender-based differences in behavior in infancy have been difficult to identify. **Gender role** refers to expected patterns of social behavior associated with masculinity or femininity; **sex role** refers to expected patterns of sexual or reproductive behavior based on the individual's sex.

Childhood extends from between eighteen and twenty-four months until puberty. The influence of other figures besides the parents increases throughout childhood. The primary role of the parents changes from one of nurturance to one of **socialization**—the process of instilling the society's values in the child. The basic goal of socialization is **internalization**—the child's incorporation of society's values into the self to such an extent that violation of these standards produces a sense of guilt.

A. **Sex-typed behavior** is behavior that is regarded as appropriate and acceptable either only for boys or only for girls. The impact of biology on masculine and feminine behavior is difficult to assess. Research indicates that there are temperamental differences between boys and girls early in life that may produce a variety of differences in behavior. However, biological factors alone do not account for gender-based differences in behavior; the three major theories of development propose three alternative explanations.

 1. According to psychoanalytic theory, gender role identification and the adoption of sex-typed behavior are results of the Oedipal and Electra conflicts during the phallic stage of development. The child identifies with the parent of the same sex in order to retain the love of both parents; a major outcome of this process of **identification** is the development of sex-typed behaviors and attitudes. Tests of this aspect of Freud's theory either have been inconclusive or have not supported it.

 2. Social learning theorists maintain that environmental factors are primarily responsible for the development of sex-typed behaviors. They claim that parents and other agents of socialization shape the child's behavior from birth by reinforcing behavior that is consistent with the child's gender. Evidence for this viewpoint is conflicting.

 3. Cognitive-developmental theorists contend that the child must understand the concepts of gender and gender role before the development of sex-typed behavior can occur. Children seek out and imitate the behavior deemed appropriate to their sex because they want to act in a consistent and competent manner. Research has supported this view, but it alone cannot fully explain the development of gender roles.

B. **Morality** is behavior that conforms to the rules of right conduct. The three theoretical perspectives differ in the aspects of morality

that they emphasize; they also identify different processes or mechanisms that produce moral development.

 1. According to psychoanalytic theory, the child develops a conscience and adopts moral behaviors when he or she internalizes the same-sex parent's moral code during the resolution of the Oedipal or Electra conflict. However, this idea is challenged by research showing that moral development is a gradual process; the child does not suddenly become moral at age five or six.

 2. Social learning theorists claim that children are moral because they are reinforced for "good" behavior, punished for "bad" behavior, and are provided with moral models to imitate. Experimental studies have furnished partial support for this view.

 3. The cognitive-developmental approach postulates that children pass through distinct stages of moral judgment that reflect developmental changes in the child's cognitive conceptions of morality. According to Lawrence Kohlberg, these stages are universal and occur in an invariable sequence, each more cognitively complex than its predecessor. On the basis of the reasoning by which children responded to a number of moral dilemmas, Kohlberg identified three levels of moral development:

 a. In the **preconventional stage** the child is responsive to the rules of society, but interprets "good" and "bad" in terms of the pain or pleasure they bring or in terms of the physical power of those who set forth the rules and labels.

 b. In the **conventional stage** the child wants to meet the expectations and standards of the family, group, or nation.

 c. The highest level of moral reasoning, attained by no children and only a few adults, is the **postconventional, autonomous,** or **principled stage.** In this stage the individual adheres to universal ethical principles based on the ideals of reciprocity and human equality.

These levels of moral reasoning are related to age, but there is great variation in the speed at which people move through the stages and in the levels at which the individual ceases to advance.

4. Adolescence begins with the onset of **puberty**— the period of sexual maturation. Among the concerns of adolescence are the need to establish an independent identity and the initial confrontation with the demands of the adult world, including the need to train for future work and to develop intimate relationships with peers of the opposite sex.

   A. Physical maturation begins before the onset of the emotional and social conflicts that are associated with adolescence—usually between the ages of ten and twelve for girls and twelve and fourteen for boys.

   B. The age at which a child is assigned the social status of adulthood depends on the culture. Adolescence is more a creation of certain societies than a distinct period of physical development.

   C. The major developmental task of adolescence is the establishment of a separate **identity**: an individual's sense of personal sameness and continuity. According to Erik Erikson, the physical, sexual, and social demands on the adolescent often produce internal conflict. To resolve this **identity crisis**, Erikson says, adolescents must develop an inner sense of continuity between what they were in the past and what they will become. According to Erikson, adolescents often attempt to determine who they are by trying out different roles temporarily.

5. Most theorists claim that the personality remains quite stable in normal persons throughout adulthood. Recently, however, the movement of a large segment of the population into the mid-life period has stimulated examination of the developments and changes in personality and social behavior that take place during adulthood. There are many psychological changes generally characteristic of men and women as they move through adulthood, including an increase in concern with the inner life, a shift in time perspective (from "time since birth" to "time left to live"), and a new awareness of death as a possibility for the self.

RECOMMENDED READINGS

BANDURA, ALBERT. *Social Learning Theory*. Englewood Cliffs, N.J.: Prentice-Hall, 1977. The most recent exposition of the behavioral approach to the development and functioning of personality, written in the clear prose of one of the leading figures in this area.

BOWER, T. G. R. *A Primer of Infant Development*. San Francisco: W. H. Freeman, 1977. A brief and very readable survey of psychological development during infancy. The chapters on attachment and long-term effects of infancy are especially relevant to this chapter.

BROWN, ROGER. *Social Psychology*. New York: Free Press, 1965. Brown's chapter on the acquisition of morality presents an eloquently clear outline of the psychoanalytic, social learning, and cognitive-developmental theories of moral development.

ERIKSON, ERIK H. *Childhood and Society*. New York: Norton, 1950. This classic book is Erikson's penetrating analysis of the concept of ego identity.

GOSLIN, DAVID A. (ed.). *Handbook of Socialization Theory and Research*. Chicago: Rand McNally, 1969. Contains three chapters—by Aronfreed, Bandura, and Kohlberg—that supply the single best presentation of theories of moral development.

LEE, LEE C. *Personality Development in Childhood*. Monterey, Calif.: Brooks/Cole, 1976. In this excellent summary, Lee presents the psychoanalytic, behavioral, and cognitive-developmental perspectives on a number of aspects of personality development.

MACCOBY, ELEANOR E., and CAROL N. JACKLIN. *Psychology of Sex Differences*. Stanford, Calif.: Stanford University Press, 1974. A comprehensive survey of the research on differences in personality and behavior between the sexes.

MUSSEN, PAUL, and NANCY EISENBERG-BERG. *Roots of Caring, Sharing, and Helping: The Development of Prosocial Behavior in Children*. San Francisco: W. H. Freeman, 1977. A nicely integrative review of research and theory in a very active and important field.

PART FOUR

BIOLOGICAL AND PERCEPTUAL PROCESSES

Having discussed the processes of human development in Part Three, we turn now to a consideration of the ways in which the fully developed human organism receives information about the world around it. Chapter 11, "The Brain and Behavior," deals with the workings of the nervous system, the endocrine system, and the brain, and concludes with a section on the ways in which scientists study the relationships between the brain and behavior.

Chapter 12, "Sensation and the Senses," begins by describing the general relationship between sensory experience and the characteristics of the physical stimuli that produce those experiences. Then it discusses the nature of each human sense and the structure of each sense organ.

Chapter 13, "Perception," uses the sense of vision as a model of the way we interpret the information we receive from our senses. As we shall see, perception involves the organization of information in various ways and is greatly influenced by our previous experiences and by our cultural heritage.

CHAPTER ELEVEN

THE BRAIN AND BEHAVIOR

Every once in a while we come across the old bromide that human beings use only one-fifth of their brains. The rest apparently does nothing. If somehow we could only learn to use it all, we would all be incredible geniuses. What nonsense! Partly, this bromide arises out of the fact that sizable parts of the human brain can be destroyed by disease or removed by the knife without seriously affecting the functioning of a human being. But, after all, one kidney can be removed and a human being can do well with the remaining kidney. If one eye is lost, all can be seen with the remaining eye. Does that mean that human beings use only half their kidneys and eyes?

The belief in the unused brain also arises out of the fact that certain parts of the brain are directly associated with the stimulation of a particular set of muscles, or with the receipt of impulses from this particular sense organ or that. That leaves large parts of the brain that are *not* involved in the direct receipt of information or the direct issuing of orders. Does that mean those noninvolved parts do nothing? Of course not.

What about the necessary weighing and coordination of information, and the necessary decisions between different possible orders. In short, what about all the "paperwork" that must be involved in the brain? We might as well suppose that a construction firm engaged in building a skyscraper is using only one-fifth of its employees because only that fifth is actually engaged in raising steel beams, laying down electric cables, transporting equipment, and such. This would ignore the executives, supervisors, secretaries, clerks, and so on.

In fact, by ignoring the more subtle, but very real, functions of the brain, we lend a spurious air of mystery to such things as imagination and creativity. For instance, "Kubla Khan" by Samuel Taylor Coleridge is a poem that, though incomplete, is admired by all. It has weird imagery and magnificently quotable lines. From what mysterious depth of genius did Coleridge bring these lines to light?

The poem was carefully analyzed by John Livingston Lowes in *The Road to Xanadu*. Lowes was able to show that virtually every word and phrase in the poem stemmed from some item in Coleridge's past reading or experience. We can visualize Coleridge putting together various word and phrase fragments in his mind (unconsciously, perhaps) after the fashion of a mental kaleidoscope, picking out the combinations he liked best and constructing the poem out of them. It was the careful work of portions of the brain that the naive think are "unused."

Coleridge, indeed, according to his own story, *dreamed* "Kubla Khan." In the quiet of sleep he completed the kaleidoscopic construction and woke with the entire poem in his mind. He began transferring it rapidly to paper, until (damn it!) he was interrupted by a visitor. By the time the visitor left, what remained of the poem had vanished from his mind and was lost forever.

Isaac Asimov

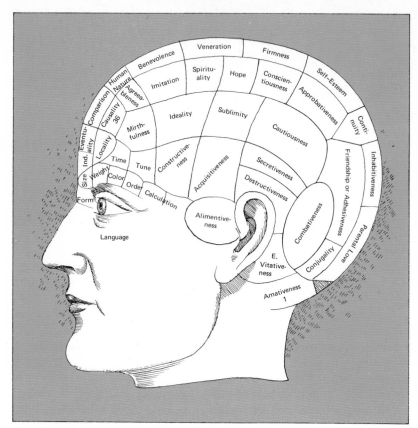

Figure 11.1 Franz Joseph Gall believed that the shape of the skull revealed the shape of the brain beneath it. Traits considered to be specifically "human" (such as logical thinking ability) were thought to be located in the front part of the brain, because this part was much larger in human beings than in other animals. Other, more "animal" traits such as amativeness (sexual behavior) were thought to be located toward the bottom and rear of the brain, since these areas appeared to be quite similar in many animals. According to Gall's "science" of phrenology, when the area of the skull presumably corresponding to the trait of, say, "causality" was very large in a particular individual, this meant the person was capable of deep and powerful reasoning. If this area was small, the individual was thought to be lacking in this trait. Phrenology still has its supporters today despite its lack of scientific credibility.

Questions about the nature of human behavior have always occupied scholars but a great many centuries passed before the brain was identified as intimately related to such questions. The Greek philosopher Aristotle, for example, believed that the heart controlled behavior. Others suggested that the various bodily fluids were responsible. Still others thought that all human thoughts, actions, and feelings were ultimately controlled by gods.

In the early nineteenth century the idea that behavior was somehow a product of the brain gained special prominence. Franz Joseph Gall, a Viennese anatomist, compared the brains of deceased people with the brains of various animals. On the basis of his comparisons, he came up with a theory of the brain that he believed accounted for both the similarities and the differences in behavior among humans and between humans and lower animals. Gall suggested that the human brain was composed of thirty-seven distinct organs, each of which was related to a fundamental behavioral "trait" and that the size of an organ reflected the magnitude of the corresponding trait (see Figure 11.1).

For example, noting that the human frontal lobes were considerably larger than those of any other animal, Gall placed certain traits which he consid-ered distinctively human, such as the ability to calculate and reason, in the frontal lobes. Those people with the largest frontal lobes, then, were believed to have more potential for such traits and for becoming, say, poets, mathematicians, and statesmen. People with small frontal lobes were believed to be more "animal" in nature and to constitute the bulk of the criminal class. Gall's theory later came to be known as **phrenology**—the study of character by assessing the shape of the skull, which, Gall believed, closely conformed to the shape of the brain beneath (Fowler and Fowler, 1969).

As ludicrous as the theory may sound today, in the context of his own era, Gall's accomplishment was singularly creative and exciting. At that time solid scientific knowledge of brain function was virtually nonexistent, and even the most educated people possessed far less knowledge than a modern high school biology student. Gall brought the brain into the limelight as the organ responsible for behavior, and he even suggested some testable hypotheses about how the brain was constructed.

In the century and a half since Gall put forth his theory, we have learned that the brain indeed has a rich and detailed relationship to all aspects of behavior. We know that damage to different parts of the brain can disrupt muscle movement and

246

perception, and may produce a host of specific behavioral disturbances: inability to remember anything new, hypersexuality, overeating, inability to waken from sleep (or inability to go to sleep in the first place), and so on. Likewise, chemical or mild electrical stimulation of various parts of the brain may cause changes in eating, drinking, sleeping, mating, aggression, and other patterns of behavior. In addition, brain stimulation can result in movement of specific muscles, produce complex hallucinations, and evoke detailed patterns of species-specific behavior. From such observations we can see that there are complex and intimate relationships between the brain and behavior. This is why questions of brain function are a source of such fascination to modern psychologists and why there is a large and active group of specialists, called **neuropsychologists,** who study relationships between the nervous system and behavior.

In studying how the brain and behavior are related, neuropsychologists examine the structure of the nervous system (anatomy) and how it relates to the other organs and parts of the body (physiology). They seek answers to three fundamental questions: How does information from the environment, either from the world outside the body or the world within, become transformed into information that the brain can use? How do the various components of the nervous system transform this information into thoughts, feelings, and actions? What is the relationship of the brain to the body's muscles and glands, which are the individual's means for responding to the environment?

In this chapter we look at what is known about these questions. We begin by discussing some basic features of the nervous and endocrine systems, which, together, are responsible for integrating and regulating all signals and responses of the body. The discussion then focuses on the brain and how its different features appear to be related to various aspects of behavior. Finally, the major modern techniques for studying brain function and some of the interesting findings made by means of these techniques are identified.

THE NERVOUS SYSTEM

Behavior demands the rapid and harmonious integration of information from many sources and the timely translation of the information into appropriate responses. Every living organism is equipped with specialized structures that have distinct roles in behavior. In single-celled animals, such as amoebae and paramecia, different parts of the single cell are related to different behavioral functions. In more complex animals, having many cells, there is cellular specialization. **Receptor cells,** embedded in the sense organs, are tuned to receive various types of stimulation from the environment. **Motor cells** (often called **effectors**) are specialized for movement, accounting for muscle contraction and secretory activity in the glands. **Neurons** are cells specialized for conducting signals from one part of the body to another; they relate receptor cells to motor cells and integrate and coordinate their activities. In this section we will be most concerned with neurons and how they interconnect and combine to form the nervous system. We begin by providing a general description of the nervous system as a whole, and then turn to the operations of neurons, the basic units of that system.

DIVISIONS OF THE NERVOUS SYSTEM The **nervous system** constitutes a network of communication channels that spreads to every part of the body. For convenience of discussion, the nervous system is usually subdivided into various parts, but in actual operation these parts act together and the distinctions become somewhat blurred.

Most of the body's neurons are concentrated in the **central nervous system (CNS),** which consists of the brain and the spinal cord, which lie within the bony casings of the skull and the spinal column. The central nervous system is the ultimate control center for all human behavior, from simple reflexes to abstract reasoning. Branching out from the central nervous system is the **peripheral nervous system (PNS),** which is composed of **nerves** (bundles of neuron fibers grouped together) and **ganglia** (collections of neuron cell bodies found principally along the spinal column). The peripheral nervous system conveys signals from the body's sensory receptors to the central nervous system and transmits messages back out to the muscles and glands. The central and peripheral nervous systems are shown in Figure 11.2.

The peripheral nervous system can be further subdivided into the **somatic** and the **autonomic** divisions. In general, somatic activity is related to the external environment, while autonomic activity regulates the internal environment. The somatic

Figure 11.2 The central nervous system (CNS) and the peripheral nervous system (PNS) in the human body. Both of these systems are made up of billions of nerve cells, or neurons, each of which is capable of transmitting a train of chemical-electrical signals in one direction. In the CNS, these neurons form an immensely complex network that organizes, stores, and redirects vast quantities of information. In the PNS, neurons in every pathway carry information either from receptors (such as the sense organs) toward the CNS or away from the CNS to effectors (in the muscles, for example). There is a close match between information going to the CNS and information coming from it. Every muscle, for example, not only receives from the CNS directions to contract or relax but also sends back information about its present state of contraction or relaxation.

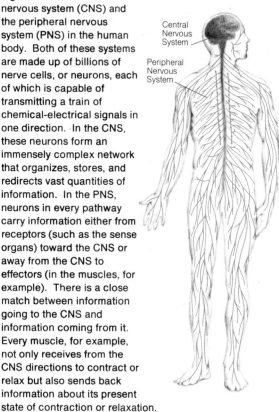

Central
Nervous
System

Peripheral
Nervous
System

viewed as working antagonistically; that is, they tend to have opposite effects on the muscles and glands they innervate.

The sympathetic system is usually involved in promoting energy expenditure. In an emergency or stress situation, the sympathetic division responds by increasing blood-sugar levels, heart rate, and blood pressure, and by inhibiting digestive processes. In contrast, the parasympathetic system dominates under conditions of relaxation, and tends to act as an energy-conserving system. For example, after we eat a large meal, the parasympathetic system works to aid digestion, and decreases heart rate and blood flow to the skeletal muscles. Many activities require a combination of sympathetic and parasympathetic activity. For instance, sexual arousal is mediated by the parasympathetic division, while sexual orgasm is a sympathetic response. A schematic diagram showing the relationships of the parts of the nervous system is presented in Figure 11.3.

NEURONS AND THEIR SIGNALS Neurons are the building blocks or basic structural units of the nervous system. These long, thin cells transmit messages in the form of electrochemical impulses from one part of the body to another. There are over 12 billion neurons in the human body, and even the simplest behavior, such as an eyeblink, involves many thousand of neurons all working together.

Neurons too are categorized according to the structures between which they conduct messages. **Sensory neurons** (sometimes called **afferent neurons**) carry information from the sense organs to the brain and spinal cord, while **motor neurons** (sometimes called **efferent neurons**) carry signals from the brain and spinal cord to the muscles and glands. The majority of the neurons are **interneurons,** which connect neurons to other neurons and integrate the activities of the sensory and motor neurons. Relationships between interneurons somehow become translated into what we subjectively describe as thoughts, feelings, perceptions, and memories. In humans, interneurons are much more numerous than the other kinds of neurons— for example, it has been estimated that for every motor neuron there are over 4,000 interneurons. Figure 11.4 shows the three types of neurons.

Neurons share the nervous system with cells called **glia** ("glue"). Most of these cells are smaller

nervous system consists of both sensory and motor neurons and controls the skeletal muscles (muscles that move the bones). We usually think of somatic activity as being under voluntary control; for example, raising an arm or wriggling a toe are movements we can control at will. The autonomic division controls the visceral muscles (blood vessels, heart, intestines) and the glands. Autonomic activity is usually classified as involuntary, for it occurs more or less automatically, with considerably less awareness or control than somatic activity, as in the contraction of the muscles lining the digestive tract or the beating of the heart. There is evidence, however, that people can learn to influence "involuntary" autonomic activities, such as lowering heart rate or raising blood pressure (Miller, 1969).

The autonomic nervous system itself has two divisions: the **sympathetic** and the **parasympathetic.** With a few exceptions, any given visceral muscle or gland in the body is innervated (supplied with nerves) by both these divisions. This is called **dual control.** In general, these two divisions can be

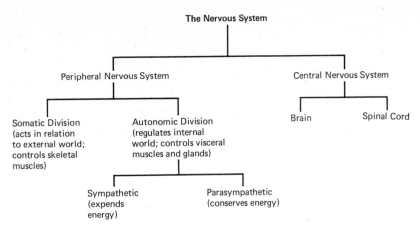

Figure 11.3 Diagram of the relationship between the parts of the nervous system.

The Nervous System

Peripheral Nervous System

Central Nervous System

Somatic Division (acts in relation to external world; controls skeletal muscles)

Autonomic Division (regulates internal world; controls visceral muscles and glands)

Brain

Spinal Cord

Sympathetic (expends energy)

Parasympathetic (conserves energy)

than neurons, but they are about ten times more numerous. Their role is largely undefined, but they seem to provide nutrients as well as structural support to the neurons and to provide a barrier to certain substances from the bloodstream. Although glial cells are important, it is the neurons that appear to play the major role in behavior.

Neurons found in different portions of the nervous system vary greatly in size and shape, but they all have the same basic configuration and they all appear to operate in much the same way. Every neuron has three major sections: a **cell body,** which contains the nucleus; numerous, usually short fibers that branch out from the cell body, called **dendrites;** and a long fiber that leads away from the cell body, known as the **axon.** The cell body is the metabolic center of the neuron and provides the energy for neural activity. The dendrites, and sometimes parts of the cell body and axon, have specialized areas for receiving messages transmitted by other neurons. These messages usually travel in one direction: from the dendrites, through the cell body, and down the length of the axon (see Figure 11.5).

The messages are conducted by means of an electrochemical process. Chemicals in the body normally exist as ions—electrically charged molecules or atoms. The neuron cell membrane selectively regulates the passage of ions in and out of the cell. In a resting state, the nature of the membrane

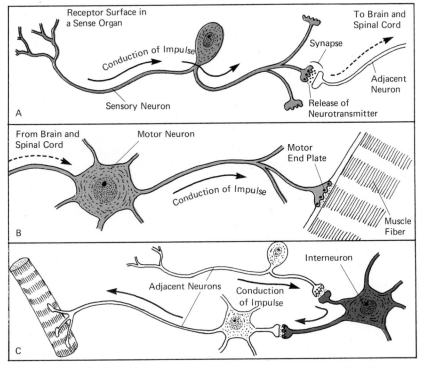

Figure 11.4 The three types of specialized neurons. (A) A sensory or afferent neuron. (B) A motor or efferent neuron. The motor end plate releases a neurotransmitter which can change the electrical state of the muscle it is connected to. (C) An interneuron. The interneurons can act to inhibit or excite the motor neurons which supply opposing muscles. Their action on the motor neurons is based on the input they receive from sensory neurons. For example, in order for the pain reflex to occur, the interneuron receives information from a sensory neuron, which causes the interneuron to send inhibitory impulses to the connecting motor neuron. This motor neuron, in turn, inhibits the appropriate extensor muscle, thereby permitting withdrawal of the arm from a painful stimulus. (Adapted from Williams and Warwick, 1975.)

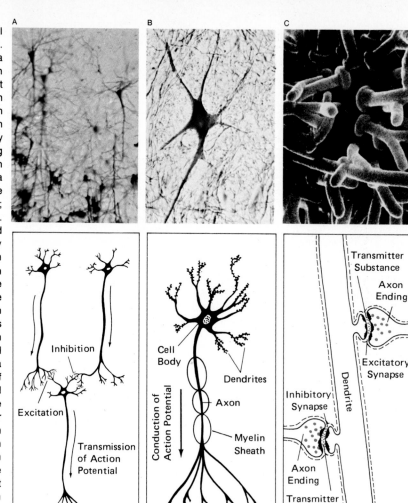

Figure 11.5 The fundamental structures in the nervous system. (A) A photomicrograph and a simplified diagram of neurons in the cerebral cortex. Note that one neuron may have either an excitatory or an inhibitory effect on another and that the action potentials are transmitted in only one direction along the firing neuron. (B) A photomicrograph and a diagram of the parts of a single neuron. The dendrites are the receiving end of the neuron; the axon is the sending end. An action potential is transmitted along the axon of a neuron only when its dendrites have been sufficiently excited. (C) An electron micrograph and a diagram of the structures at the synapse. Note the correspondence between the axon endings and the small protrusions on the dendrites in the diagrams in C and B. When an action potential reaches the end of the axon of a neuron, small amounts of transmitter substances are released from storage areas across the synapse to the dendrites of another neuron. The substances from some neurons are excitatory in their effect; the substances from others are inhibitory. If the receiving neuron gets sufficient excitation (and not too much inhibition), it in turn fires.

causes the interior of the cell to be negatively charged, while the exterior, immediately outside the membrane, is positively charged. The cell is said to be **polarized**—negative inside and positive outside. This electrical imbalance across the cell membrane is known as the **resting potential.** If a stimulus affects the cell with great enough intensity, the membrane temporarily becomes open to a sudden inrush of certain ions, which causes its polarity to change at the point of stimulation: the cell interior then becomes for an instant positive and the exterior negative. This abrupt change, called the **action potential,** is conducted down the length of the axon at a velocity of about 1 to 100 meters per second. Velocity varies with the properties of the different axons. Some axons are wrapped in a fatty, whitish substance, known as a **myelin sheath.** (Myelinated axons form the **white matter** of the nervous system; nonmyelinated axons, dendrites, and cell bodies form the **gray matter.**) The sheath serves as insula-

tion and thereby increases the speed at which the message can travel by as much as five times the velocity of nonmyelinated neurons.

A stimulus usually produces a burst of many action potentials, which travel down the axon much like a spark travels down a fuse. However, the neuron, in contrast to the fuse, very rapidly restores itself, enabling it to conduct very rapid bursts of consecutive action potentials. When action potentials reach the end of the axon, they activate muscles, glands, or other neurons.

How is a message coded in neuron action potentials? The different types of messages that travel through the nervous system are conveyed by the axons' rates of firing, not by the size of the action potentials: the more intense a stimulus, the higher the firing rate (see Figure 11.6). The upper limit in some neurons is about 800 action potentials per second! The particular pathways along which the messages travel also determine the nature of the message; thus stimulation of the visual nerves by any means other than light (such as by pressure) produces a visual sensation, and stimulation of the nerves of hearing and taste produces auditory and taste sensations.

How is a message passed from one neuron to another? When action potentials reach the end of the axon, chemicals called **transmitter substances** stored in sacs at the tip of the axon are released into the **synapse,** a tiny gap that separates an axon from a connecting neuron (see Figure 11.5). The released chemicals fill the synapse between the axon and the connecting neuron, transmitting a message to the neuron. The message is usually received by a dendrite but is sometimes also received by the cell body or axon. Depending on the particular chemistry of the transmitter substances, the message transmitted may be either **excitatory,** causing a reaction in the receiving neuron, or **inhibitory,** decreasing or preventing a response. It is through successive synaptic connections that chains of neurons conduct signals from receptors through the nervous system to ultimately effect behavior.

REFLEX ARCS AND THE SPINAL CORD

The simplest chain of connection between neurons is the **reflex arc,** which has been described as the basic functional unit of the nervous system. Reflex arcs are located throughout the nervous system, but they have been most systematically studied at the level of the spinal cord.

The spinal cord is the main communication "cable" between the brain and the peripheral nervous system. A cross section shows that it consists of a central butterfly-shaped area of gray matter; this is a site of intensive synaptic activity. The surrounding area of white matter consists of axons carrying information to and from the brain and to other parts of the spinal cord.

Messages enter and leave the spinal cord by means of thirty-one pairs of spinal nerves. Each pair innervates a different and fairly specific part of the body. The spinal nerves are "mixed" in that they contain both motor and sensory neurons for most of their length. However, at the juncture where these nerves meet the spinal cord, they divide into two portions, or **roots,** as illustrated in Figure 11.7. The **dorsal root,** which is toward the back of the body, contains sensory neurons. The **ventral root,** which is toward the belly of the body, contains motor neurons. This relationship—"dorsal = sen-

Figure 11.6 Records of an axon's response to excitatory stimuli. (A) The arrows indicate the points in time at which three different stimuli were presented to the neuron. The first two stimuli were below the intensity level required to produce a response—in this case, an action potential. The minimum level of intensity necessary for a stimulus to produce a response is called the threshold level. The third stimulus was above the threshold, and therefore an action potential was produced. (B) A series of action potentials are produced by several above-threshold stimuli. When an action potential reaches the end of an axon, it causes a release of the neurotransmitter substance, which in turn produces an effect (either excitatory or inhibitory) on the adjacent neurons, muscles, or glands. (C) Graph illustrating that as the intensity of a stimulus increases, so does the axon's rate of firing. (Stevens, 1966.)

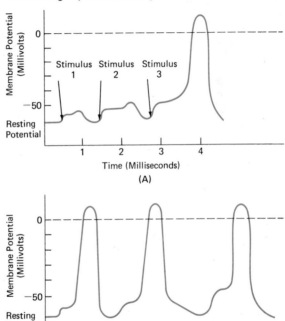

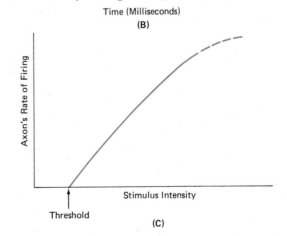

sory" and "ventral = motor"—was one of the first consistent functional features of the nervous system to be discovered. It is named the **Bell-Magendie law,** after the scientists who discovered it over 150 years ago. With their findings, it became possible to examine separately the characteristics of the sensory and motor systems.

Some of the simplest connections between sensory input and motor response—the reflex arcs—occur within the spinal cord, with no direct recourse to the brain. Thus the spinal cord constitutes a simplified model (simplified, that is, in comparison to the brain) of a neurological system that receives sensory information, processes it, and then delivers neural impulses to the muscles for the initiation and coordination of motor activity.

Most of the reflex arcs between sensory and motor signals take place within a particular segment of the spinal cord. For example, the knee-jerk reflex, elicited by tapping the tendon below the kneecap, involves only two kinds of neurons. The sensory neurons convey information about stimulation of the tendon to the spinal cord. This information crosses a single synapse within the gray matter of the spinal cord, and causes the motor neurons to stimulate the appropriate muscle groups in the leg that cause the knee to kick. This two-neuron reflex arc is illustrated in part A of Figure 11.8. Most reflexes are more complicated than the two-neuron knee jerk. And so, for example, part B of Figure 11.8 diagrams a pain withdrawal reflex that involves three kinds of neurons and two synapses. The extra neurons in this chain are interneurons, which connect the other two kinds of neurons. In the example of withdrawing a leg that is exposed to pain, the interneurons pass information to the opposite leg, enabling body weight to be shifted when the withdrawal reflex occurs.

Although spinal reflexes can take place without control by the brain, this does not mean that the brain is uninvolved in reflexive behavior. For instance, the painful stimulation that triggers a withdrawal reflex must travel to the brain in order to be experienced as painful. However, the subjective feeling of pain often takes place after we have begun to perform the reflex response. You probably can recall an occasion when you touched a very hot object, withdrew your hand, and then became aware of the pain after withdrawal. The neurons that travel the length of the spinal cord to and from the brain also permit voluntary control over and awareness of reflex activity. For example, have someone tap the tendon below your kneecap to elicit

the knee-jerk reflex. Now, have the person tap in the same place while you concentrate on preventing the response from occurring. The pathways that link the brain to the spinal cord should enable you to inhibit the response. If these pathways were severed, you would be unable to exert control over the reflex movement of your leg, and you would not know when your leg kicked unless you saw it.

The spinal reflex arc has been presented because it is a relatively simple model of reflex action, but reflex systems are not the exclusive domain of the spinal cord. They are present throughout the entire nervous system, and what appear to be simple reflex networks are involved in a large number of complicated behavioral activities. An apparently simple reflex, such as dilation of the pupil of the eye, can actually involve many levels of the nervous system. At the most basic level, pupil dilation is a local reflex to a sudden reduction of light; with appropriate sensory neurons, motor neurons, and interneurons, the pupil of the eye will widen when light is reduced so that more of the available light can be used by the eye. On a more complex level, this same response is part of an intense emotional reaction that involves the whole body. For example, the pupils will widen when we experience anger or fear, even if the light source remains constant. At yet another level, the pupil dilation reflex may interact with our learned reading and interpretive skills. A book entitled *Naked Bodies* will probably elicit a more vigorous pupillary response than a book called *The History of Psychology.*

Figure 11.7 A spinal nerve containing both motor and sensory components is formed from the union of the ventral and dorsal roots emanating from the front (ventral) and back (dorsal) portions of the spinal cord. The ventral root contains motor neurons, while the dorsal root contains sensory neurons. (Williams and Warwick, 1975.)

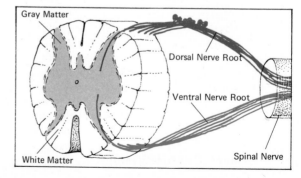

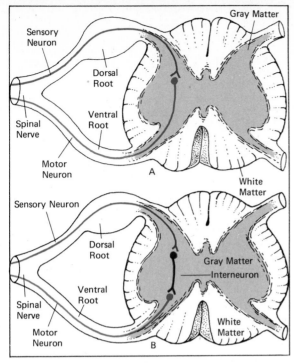

Figure 11.8 (A) A diagram of a two-neuron reflex arc, such as the one present in the knee-jerk response. This is the simplest form of reflex arc. (B) A diagram of a three-neuron reflex arc. The pain reflex, which causes a quick withdrawal from the painful stimulus, is an example of this type of reflex arc. It involves one set each of motor and sensory neurons (as in the two-neuron reflex arc), but in addition, an interneuron is present in the gray matter of the spinal cord. The extra neuron means that the information now crosses two synapses. (Gardner, 1975.)

The pituitary and thyroid glands illustrate how the endocrine system works. The **thyroid gland** produces the hormone **thyroxin** (as well as several other hormones). Thyroxin promotes certain key chemical reactions that are important for all tissues in the body. Too little thyroxin produces lethargy and depression, while too much results in hyperactivity and anxiety. The amount of thyroxin released by the thyroid gland is itself controlled by a hormone released by the **pituitary gland.** In other words, the pituitary gland secretes a thyroid-stimulating hormone into the bloodstream, and when this hormone reaches its target, the thyroid, it causes the thyroid to secrete more thyroxin. In turn, the level of thyroxin in the blood affects the amount of thyroid-stimulating hormone produced by the pituitary gland. High levels of thyroxin reduce the output of thyroid-stimulating hormone, while low levels of thyroxin lead to greater production of thyroid-stimulating hormone. In this way, the pituitary and the thyroid glands regulate each other through a mechanism called **negative feedback.** Their interaction regulates and balances general bodily metabolism.

The process of maintaining a balanced internal environment is called **homeostasis.** The basic principle of homeostasis is that deviations from a certain level of a substance will activate processes that will eliminate that deviation. A thermostat, for example, is a homeostatic mechanism. Deviations in temperature below a certain level in a room turn on

THE ENDOCRINE SYSTEM

The **endocrine system** is a chemical communication system; its messages are chemical substances called **hormones,** which are produced by the **endocrine glands** and secreted directly into the bloodstream.* When released, these hormones have important effects on such aspects of behavior as sexual function, physical growth, emotional responses, motivation, and the availability of energy. The various endocrine glands are shown in Figure 11.9. While chemical messages circulate throughout the bloodstream, they have their effects only at certain **target organs**—the particular organs of the body that are under their influence. The messages are merely distributed; they generally are not altered in any way during their delivery.

*The **exocrine glands,** in contrast, secrete their products (such as saliva, tears, sweat) through ducts to the surface of the body.

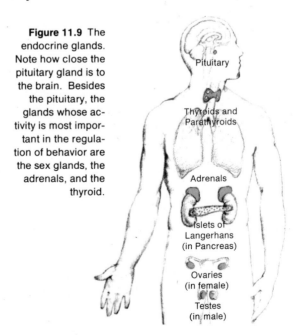

Figure 11.9 The endocrine glands. Note how close the pituitary gland is to the brain. Besides the pituitary, the glands whose activity is most important in the regulation of behavior are the sex glands, the adrenals, and the thyroid.

253

a furnace, which produces heat to eliminate the deviation. When the temperature reaches the desired level, the thermostat turns the furnace off until the next deviation occurs. Similarly, a low level of thyroxin is a deviation that leads to the pituitary's production of thyroid-stimulating hormone, which causes the thyroid to produce more thyroxin, which eliminates the deviation. A high level of thyroxin is a deviation that leads to a decrease in the production of thyroid-stimulating hormone with a consequent reduction in the production of thyroxin, thereby eliminating the deviation. As a result of these homeostatic processes, the level of thyroxin in the blood is kept in **equilibrium**—a state of balance due to the equal action of opposing forces.

The pituitary gland has often been called the "master gland" because it secretes a large number of hormones that work to control the hormonal output of other endocrine glands. However, the release of pituitary hormones is controlled by the brain. Ultimately, then, the brain is responsible for the activities of the entire endocrine system and for maintaining equilibrium. It monitors the amount of hormones in the blood and sends out messages to correct deviations from the proper homeostatic level.

One functional difference between the endocrine system and the nervous system is the speed of response. A neural impulse can travel through the nervous system in a thousandth of a second, whereas a number of seconds may be required for the stimulation, release, and transport of a needed hormone. The nervous system plays a greater role in behaviors in which speed is essential, such as withdrawal from pain. In behavioral processes in which speed is not crucial, such as sexual arousal, hormones are a more economical and comprehensive means of communication with the millions of cells in their target organs. Through the combined actions of both systems, the brain has a highly efficient means of monitoring and controlling our behavior.

THE BRAIN

The brain is an organ of tremendous complexity, weighing about three pounds in the human adult and composed of numerous substructures, each with specific but interrelated functions. Overall, the brain regulates behavior in three major ways. First,

it maintains and controls the vital internal bodily functions such as temperature regulation and digestion. Second, it receives sensory information about the external world and issues motor commands in response to this information. Finally, it makes use of past experience to select or create new ways of responding to the environment.

The brain may be subdivided in many ways. In this chapter we will discuss the brain as consisting of three overlapping layers—the **central core,** the **limbic system,** and the **cerebral hemispheres**—each layer representing a consecutive stage in the evolutionary development of the brain.

THE CENTRAL CORE The **central core** of the human brain is sometimes called the "old brain," because in appearance and function it is highly similar to the brains of more primitive creatures. In fact, the central core is similar to the brains of all animals that have backbones (see Figure 11.10). The central core includes several structures that together carry out the most basic functions necessary for survival—for instance, sleeping and wakefulness cycles, respiration, and feeding. The structures that make up the central core of the brain are shown in Figure 11.11 on page 256.

THE BRAIN STEM As the spinal cord enters the skull, it swells and forms a knobby extension known as the **brain stem.** The first structure of the brain stem is the **medulla.** The medulla plays a critical role in many autonomic activities such as circulation and breathing, and controls chewing, salivation, and facial movements. Above and extending forward from the medulla is the **pons** (meaning "bridge"), which connects the two halves of the cerebellum. The pons transmits motor information from the higher brain areas and the spinal cord to the cerebellum and is vital in integrating movements between the right and left sides of the body.

In the upper portion of the brain stem is a small structure called the **midbrain.** All neural information passing back and forth between the brain and the spinal cord must pass through the midbrain. The midbrain contains important centers for visual and auditory reflexes. For example, the "startle" reflex to sudden intense stimuli and the "orienting" reflexes that allow us to locate and follow moving objects with our eyes or ears are controlled by the midbrain. These reflexes are crucial to the mainte-

Figure 11.10 A comparison of the brains of several animals possessing backbones. The human cerebrum is much larger than that found in other animals. As the cerebrum increases in size, it begins to form folds, called convolutions. These folds enable the surface area of the cerebrum to increase without producing a great increase in the brain's volume. (Truex and Carpenter, 1969.)

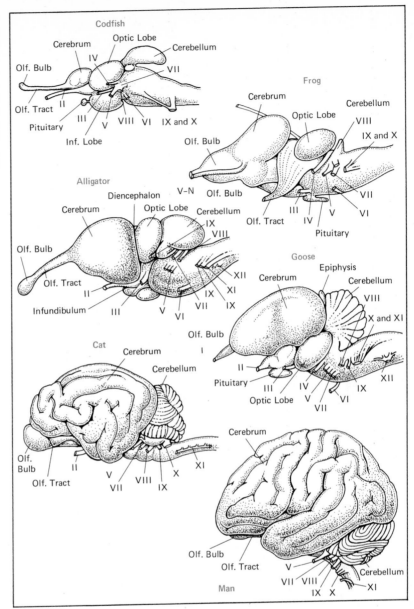

nance of stable contact with the external environment. In species of animals where auditory and visual reflexes are of great importance, these areas of the midbrain are relatively larger. For instance, birds that sight, track, and capture prey in flight have very prominent and bulging visual areas in the midbrain. Bats, which use sound rather than sight to locate their prey, have small visual areas and very prominent auditory areas in the midbrain.

The **reticular formation** is a complex network of criss-crossing neural fibers and cell bodies that extends from the spinal cord up through the core of the brain stem and into the thalamus. It appears to function as a sentry system, arousing the higher brain when information related to survival must be processed and permitting periods of sustained attention to take place. It apparently also helps to screen extraneous sensory input, especially during sleep. Damage to the reticular formation usually disrupts the natural sleep-waking cycle and can even result in an almost permanent, coma like state of sleep (Magoun, 1963).

THE CEREBELLUM To the rear of the brain stem and slightly above the medulla is the **cerebellum** (which means "little brain"; the cerebellum is divided into two hemispheres and so looks like a miniature version of the higher brain). The cerebellum's chief function is to coordinate voluntary

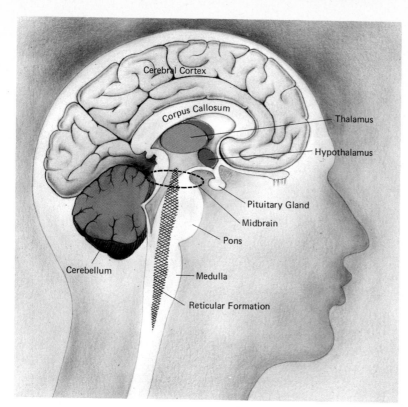

Figure 11.11 The structures composing the central core of the brain. (This illustration shows the left hemisphere of the brain as it would appear if it were sliced exactly in half from front to back.) The structures represented in this figure are the first to receive incoming information, and they regulate the most fundamental processes of the body. The reticular formation, which controls the most general responses of the brain to sensory input, is located in the area that connects the brain to the spinal cord and to the rest of the nervous system. The thalamus has a central location in the brain and the hypothalamus is very close to the pituitary gland, which controls the activity of the other endocrine glands. A few brain structures that evolved more recently than the central core are also shown here. Note particularly the corpus callosum, the large band of nerve fibers that connects the two hemispheres of the cerebral cortex.

(skeletal) muscle activity and regulate physical balance. Motor commands that originate in the higher brain are processed by the cerebellum before being transmitted to the muscles. At the same time, the cerebellum receives continuous information from the muscles as to their tension and position. The cerebellum reconciles any differences in these messages to produce a smooth and balanced motor response (Eccles et al., 1967). Damage to the cerebellum may cause ataxia, a condition in which a person will display drunken movements, severe tremors, and a lack of balance. The person with ataxia lacks the control necessary for simple reaching movements; for example, an ataxic person might accidently hit a friend in the stomach while trying to reach out and shake the friend's hand.

THE THALAMUS At the top of the brain stem and deeply embedded within the central mass of the cerebral hemispheres is a pair of connected egg-shaped structures called the **thalamus.** These structures surround a central cavity of the brain ("thalamus" comes from a Greek word meaning "inner chamber"). Early brain anatomists believed that all brain processes emanated from this central inner chamber. They noted that this cavity was filled with a clear fluid, and believed that human behav-

ior was somehow a special property of this fluid. They mistakenly emphasized the cavity (or ventricle) rather than its walls (the thalamus) as being of special interest in understanding human behavior.

From a behavioral standpoint, the thalamus is certainly not as dramatic a structure as the hypothalamus, which is located beneath it. However, the thalamus is a crucial link between the cerebral hemispheres and the sense organs. It acts partly as a relay station, sorting information from the sensory receptors and routing them to appropriate areas of the higher brain. In addition, the thalamus interrelates information coming from various areas of the cerebral hemispheres. Thus it performs a major integrative role in connecting one area of the brain to another.

THE HYPOTHALAMUS The **hypothalamus** is a small structure (about the size of the tip of your index finger) located just below the thalamus. It is an important supervising center in the regulation of the body's internal environment, monitoring internal changes and sending out signals to maintain the internal state of the individual at some balanced optimal level. The hypothalamus performs these functions in two ways. First, it sends electrochemical signals to the entire autonomic nervous system, triggering the sympathetic or parasympathetic system to respond to environmental changes. Second, it directly influences the nearby pituitary gland, which is connected to the hypothalamus via a network of blood vessels and neurons. Through these connections, the hypothalamus helps regulate hormones produced by the endocrine system.

The behavior patterns most profoundly influenced by the hypothalamus are those related to basic survival: for example, feeding, internal temperature regulation, emotional and physiological responses to stress, and sexual function. Different areas of the hypothalamus are mainly, but not exclusively, involved in certain kinds of regulatory, or homeostatic, functions.

An example of the hypothalamus's homeostatic function is the regulation of body temperature. When a warmblooded animal is exposed to cold, signals from the hypothalamus cause the blood vessels in the skin to contract, and this reduces heat loss from the surface of the body. Other hypothalamic signals instruct the pituitary gland to produce a thyroid-stimulating hormone, which activates the thyroid gland to produce the hormone thyroxin, which causes a general increase in body metabolism so that more heat is produced to compensate for the cold in the external environment. At high levels, thyroxin induces the shivering response in the skeletal muscles, causing even more heat production. In contrast, when the individual is exposed to heat in the external environment, the hypothalamus will mobilize the body's resources for the opposite effect. The body cools itself by dilating the blood vessels in the skin, by sweating, and by reducing the metabolic rate. Thus certain areas of the hypothalamus act as a kind of thermostat to maintain the body at its optimal temperature of 37 degrees Celsius. Other hypothalamic areas play a similar role in many other homeostatic functions.

THE LIMBIC SYSTEM   Above the central core and within the cerebral hemispheres lies the **limbic system** (the term "limbic" means "bordering"). It contains a number of highly interrelated structures such as the **hippocampus,** the **amygdala,** and the **septal area.** These structures form a loop around the top of the central core and are closely connected with the hypothalamus and the inner border of the cerebral cortex. Figure 11.12 shows the structure of the limbic system.

The limbic system has also been called the "nose brain" because, from an evolutionary perspective,

much of it appears to have developed from the sense of smell. Its original functions were presumably based on olfactory information that allows animals to identify food and potential mates and to avoid predators.

The limbic system also appears to be closely involved with behaviors that satisfy certain motivational and emotional needs, such as feeding, fighting, fleeing, and mating (MacLean, 1958). For example, damage to various parts of the limbic system in animals can produce gross changes in aggressive behavior. Ordinarily intractable wild animals, like some rodents, have become very tame following certain types of limbic system damage. Conversely, tame animals such as domestic cats have become quite savage after sustaining other kinds of limbic system damage. Disruption of the limbic system also produces marked changes in sexual and feeding behavior (Klüver and Bucy, 1939). Each of these classes of behavior has emotional components, and each involves making a decision about whether to approach or avoid things in the external environment. The limbic system seems to provide one basis for these approach-avoidance decisions.

In 1954, James Olds and Peter Milner reported that rats learned to press a lever in order to receive mild electrical stimulation in certain parts of the limbic system, which they called "pleasure centers." Rats would also learn to run a complex maze in order to get a chance to press the bar for brain stimulation. They would press the bar thousands of times per hour when given the opportunity, and seemed to prefer certain kinds of brain stimulation to eating, even after periods of food deprivation. When certain other parts of the limbic system were stimulated, the rat stopped behaving in ways that brought about such stimulation, leading to the assumption that such stimulation was aversive.

THE CEREBRAL HEMISPHERES   The **cerebral hemispheres** are what most people think of as "the brain." They constitute about 85 percent of the brain's weight, and they are involved in the processes of learning, speech, reasoning, and memory. They include much of the limbic system, which we have already discussed, and they are surrounded by a covering called the **cortex.**

As implied by the name, the cerebral hemispheres are composed of two distinct halves, the left and right hemispheres. Although they are roughly mirror images of each other, the two hemispheres

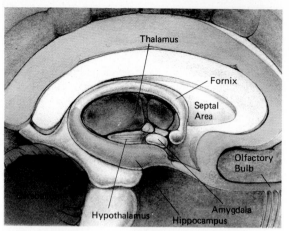

Figure 11.12 A schematic diagram of the limbic system. Structures within this system play a significant role in a variety of emotional behaviors. Damage to various regions of the limbic system may cause wild animals to become tame, or tame animals to become vicious. Other limbic lesions may radically alter sexual and feeding behavior. The olfactory bulb (responsible for the sense of smell) is closely associated with other limbic structures, suggesting the importance of this sense to several limbic system functions.

appear to differ in function. In general, the left half of the brain controls the right side of the body, and vice versa. Thus a stroke that damages functioning in the right hemisphere may cause paralysis to the left side of the body.

The two hemispheres do not usually have equal roles in their influence on behavior (Gazzaniga, 1970). In most people, regardless of whether they are right- or left-handed, the left hemisphere tends to be dominant, and also somewhat larger. It is involved mainly in behaviors associated with language and logical thought. The right hemisphere tends to be involved with spatial, drawing, visual imagery, and musical abilities. The two halves of the brain seem to store different types of information, and some psychologists have even suggested that they constitute separate types of consciousness. (For further discussion of this possibility, see Chapter 14.)

How does the right half know what the left half is doing? The two hemispheres are connected by a dense band of neurons called the **corpus callosum,** which carries messages back and forth between the left and right sides of the brain (Sperry, 1964). When this connection is severed, as in one surgical treatment of epilepsy, the two halves of the brain appear to function somewhat independently. Research with people who have such "split brains" reveals subtle changes in behavior. For example, if an image is briefly flashed to the right half of the visual field, and therefore relayed to the left half of

the brain, the "split-brain" patient can verbally identify that image. However, if the same image is flashed to the left side of the visual field, and therefore to the right side of the brain, the person often is not able to use the correct verbal label. But the person may use his or her left hand to select a similar object from a group of objects screened from the person's view (see Figure 11.13). Thus the left hemisphere is dominant for verbal identification, while the right hemisphere predominates in spatial identification. In normal people, this division in hemispheric function is not obvious because the two halves of the brain work together as a coordinated unit.

THE CEREBRAL CORTEX The **cerebral cortex** is the gray matter that covers the cerebral hemispheres. The cortex (the term means "bark" or "outer covering") is the most recent evolutionary development of the nervous system. It is about 2 millimeters (1/25 inch) thick and highly convoluted, which allows it to accommodate, in the limited space in the skull, over 9 billion neurons. If the human cortex were flattened out, its area would be about 2.5 square feet.

The external surface of the cortex has certain characteristic "landmarks" that are used in studying the brain. The most prominent of these are the two deep fissures (see Figure 11.14) that subdivide each hemisphere into four principal areas, or "lobes." The **central fissure** separates the **frontal lobe** from the **parietal lobe.** The **lateral fissure** marks the top boundary of the **temporal lobe.** Demarcations between the **occipital lobe** and neighboring lobes are much less distinct.

The **occipital lobe,** located at the back of the brain, is particularly concerned with the reception and analysis of visual information. Sensory receptors in the eye transmit their information to the occipital lobe via the optic nerve and thalamus. In humans, injury to this portion of the cortex can produce blind spots in the visual field.

The auditory reception areas are located in the **temporal lobe,** as are certain areas for the processing of visual information. In a series of studies with epileptic patients undergoing surgery, Canadian neurologists Wilder Penfield and Theodore Rasmussen (1950) elicited some dramatic responses by applying electrical stimulation to certain points on the temporal lobe. At some points, stimulation caused complex auditory or visual hallucinations; stimulation at other points seemed to reactivate

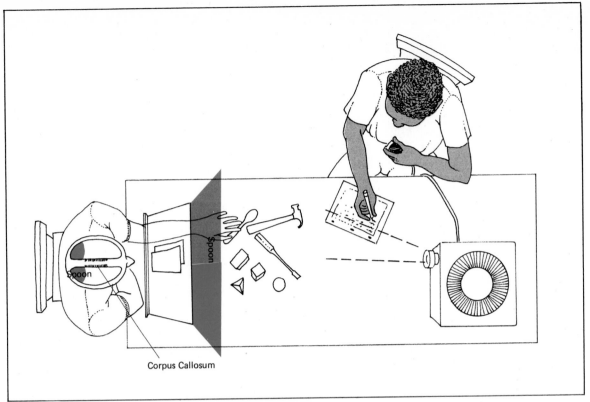

Corpus Callosum

Figure 11.13 Experimental apparatus used for testing split-brain patients. When a written word is presented on a screen in one half of the visual field, this information is transmitted exclusively to the opposite hemisphere. In a person with an intact corpus callosum, this information is first received by the hemisphere opposite to the visual half-field in which the word was presented, and then this information is transmitted to the other hemisphere across the corpus callosum. In split-brain patients the hemispheres are disconnected, and therefore their independent functions can be studied. If the word "spoon" were presented in the right half of the visual field (transmitted to the left hemisphere), and patients were asked to verbally identify the word they saw, they would readily say "spoon." If, however, the same word was presented in the left half of the visual field (transmitted to the right hemisphere), patients would be unable to name the word. This is because speech mechanisms are found only in the left hemisphere in most people. Although the right hemisphere cannot name the item, it "knows" what the item is. The left hand, which sends its touch information primarily to the right hemisphere, is able to pick the correct item from several objects hidden behind a screen, as illustrated here. (After Gazzaniga, 1972.)

sensations with such vividness that the patients felt as if they were reliving the experience rather than merely remembering it. One woman heard a familiar song so clearly that she thought a record was being played in the operating room.

The **frontal lobe** is located at the front of each hemisphere. The area of the frontal lobe next to the central fissure is primarily concerned with the regulation of fine voluntary movements. Another part of the left hemisphere's frontal lobe is involved in the use of language. In 1861, a French physician named Paul Broca discovered that damage to this part of the left hemisphere affected the ability to use speech. Broca's discovery was the first indication that different parts of the brain might be involved in different types of behavior—that is, that the brain might show some **localization of function.**

The prefrontal area of the frontal lobe (at left of the motor cortex in Figure 11.14), although not associated with particular sensory or motor activities, has at times been considered (by Gall and others) to be the repository of intellectual ability. Most modern researchers do not accept the notion that the frontal lobe regulates intellectual performance; its involvement in behavior seems more general than that. Some people do as well on intelligence tests after massive amounts of frontal lobe tissues have been removed as they did before. The behavioral defects resulting from frontal lobe damage, it now appears, involve the ability to order stimuli, sort out information, and maintain attention to a particular task in the face of distraction, rather than the kind of intellectual abilities measured by IQ tests (Milner, 1964).

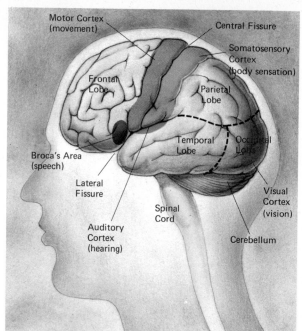

Figure 11.14 An external view of the left hemisphere of the cerebral cortex. The diagram shows the two major fissures, the four lobes, and several other cortical regions whose functions are relatively well known.

The **parietal lobe** contains the primary receiving areas for the skin senses and the sense of bodily position. Damage to this portion of the cortex results in deficits in the sense of touch. A person with parietal lobe damage extending beyond the primary sensory area on the right hemisphere also has difficulty with spatial organization of the environment and may have a distorted perception of personal body image.

Perhaps the most well-defined regions of the cortex are those involved in receiving touch and positional information from the various regions of the body (the **somato-sensory cortex**) and those involved in integrating movement of the various body parts (the **motor cortex**). These regions occur in two bands running over the surface of the cortex near the middle, as shown in Figure 11.14. Both the motor cortex and the somato-sensory cortex show **contralateral control**; that is, areas in the right hemisphere are concerned with activities and information reception on the left side of the body, while areas in the left hemisphere control and represent the right side of the body.

The amount of cortex taken up with the motor activities of and sensory impressions from different parts of the body is associated with the degree of precise motor control or sensitivity of that part of the body, and not with the size or muscle mass of the body part. Thus the fingers, which can make very precise movements, have much larger representa-

tion in the motor cortex than does the trunk of the body. The lips, which can also make fine movements and are extremely sensitive to touch, have a very large representation on the sensory cortex. It is interesting that these two representations correspond to the two behavioral capacities that best distinguish humans from other animals—tool using and speech.

In marked contrast to the precision with which these sensory and motor areas can be defined, the processes we commonly call learning, memory, emotion, intelligence, and conscious behavior cannot be localized. About three-fourths of the cortex is made up of areas that do not have a sensory or motor function; these areas are called the **association cortex**. The association areas undoubtedly participate in these more abstract processes.

STUDYING BRAIN–BEHAVIOR RELATIONSHIPS

By mapping the brain's intricate structures and pathways, scientists attempt to understand the role of the brain in behavior. There are several methodologies for constructing such maps; some require modern laboratory techniques, others only careful observation. In the past two centuries, the scientist-as-observer has provided an increasingly clear picture of brain–behavior relationships.

CLINICAL OBSERVATIONS   Most early clinical observations concerned the effects of damage to the cortex. Medical practitioners observed that patients who had suffered strokes or other types of localized brain damage were likely to show particular behavioral deficits. By relating the type of deficit to the specific area of the brain that was damaged, they hoped to map the relationships between the brain and behavior.

A **stroke** is usually caused by a rupturing of blood vessels on the surface of the brain, resulting in a loss of nutrients to a particular area. This causes the brain cells in that area to stop functioning. A variety of behavioral dysfunctions can accompany a stroke; for example, some patients become paralyzed on one side of the body (called hemiplegia), and others may display any of several varieties of **aphasia**—an inability to speak, even though the vocal apparatus is intact, or an inability to understand spoken language, even though the hearing is intact and the patient can write and speak. When such a patient dies, the brain may be examined and the precise location of the brain damage noted. Some interesting consistencies between the location of brain damage and the type of behavioral deficit have been observed.

The accumulation of these types of observations has allowed scientists to establish some general relationships between the brain and behavior. For instance, as we noted earlier, Broca found that speech difficulties usually resulted from damage to the left side of the brain. This was the first indication that one part of the brain was dominant in speech processes. It was also noted that damage to one side of the brain often produced paralysis or numbness on the opposite side of the body. Thus scientists began to develop the notion of contralateral control of the body by the brain. Medical observers also found that damage to certain areas produced specific sensory deficits; for instance, damage to the back part of the brain often caused partial blindness. The hypotheses developed from these early observations have guided much of modern research on brain–behavior relationships.

STIMULATION Many of the basic relationships noted by early physicians have been confirmed by modern neurosurgical techniques. One such technique involves the application of mild electrical stimulation to different areas of the brain. An example of this is the work of neurosurgeon Wilder Penfield, cited earlier (Penfield and Rasmussen, 1950). Penfield found that he could trigger vivid memory sequences in patients by applying a tiny electrical current to points on the temporal lobe of the cerebral cortex. Stimulation of the part of the frontal lobe next to the central fissure produced muscle movements in the opposite side of the body, while stimulation of different areas in the left hemisphere either caused people to emit sounds or prevented them from speaking. Stimulation of the sensory cortex caused patients to claim that they had been touched somewhere on the body; the exact location of the area they believed had been touched corresponded to a specific location in the brain.

In addition to electrical stimulation, scientists have used chemicals to stimulate the brain. A small tube is implanted in an animal's brain so that the end touches the area that is to be stimulated. Then a small amount of chemical is delivered through the tube to that area. Such experiments have shown,

for example, that different chemicals applied to the hypothalamus can affect feeding and drinking behavior (Grossman, 1960), and that sexual behavior can be promoted or inhibited by the application of minute amounts of specific hormones to parts of the hypothalamus (Fisher, 1956).

Through research involving chemical and electrical stimulation, it has been possible to develop the picture of the cortex presented in Figure 11.15. In addition to mapping the brain, these findings are useful in the treatment of certain medical problems. For example, an electrical current delivered through electrodes implanted in certain areas of the brain seems to provide temporary relief from pain. Thus electrical stimulation is now sometimes used to relieve the intolerable pain of patients with terminal cancer and other illnesses. Also, some psychiatrists have begun to use brain stimulation to control violently aggressive behavior in mental patients for whom no other method of control has been successful. In this case, the rapid expansion of our knowledge about brain topography may be a mixed blessing; while brain stimulation may be effective in some cases, it is a form of therapy that could easily be abused (Valenstein, 1973).

BRAIN LESION TECHNIQUES Early medical observers were hampered in their efforts because the brain damage they saw was generally not well localized. In order to examine the functions of precise areas of the brain, scientists now use neurosurgical techniques to selectively destroy or remove brain tissues in animals. A **lesion** is produced when a small area of the brain is destroyed or removed. After surgery, changes and deficiencies in behavior are assessed. Since the brains of animals such as cats and monkeys show an organization that is basically similar to that of the human brain, the results of this research provide some information that is relevant to human functioning.

Observations of animal behavior following selective brain lesions generally support the information provided by clinical observations and brain stimultion research. Research on the hypothalamus provides a good example of how brain lesion and stimulation techniques can be used together to understand certain brain–behavior relationships. Tumors in the hypothalamus have sometimes been found to be associated either with extreme overeating or with undereating almost to the starvation level. Stimulation of the lateral part of the hypothalamus will cause an animal to start eating, even

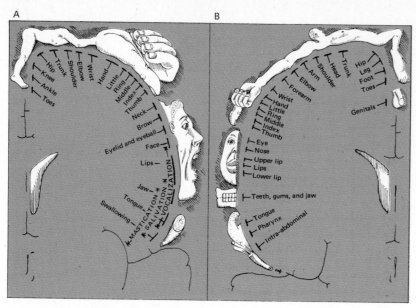

A
B

Figure 11.15 (A) A diagram representing the location and amount of cortical space devoted to the motor capacities of various body parts. Areas of the body capable of the most complex and precise movements take up the largest quantities of space in the motor cortex. For example, the eyelid and eyeball (capable of many precise movements), have a larger representation than the face. (B) A diagram representing the location and amount of cortical space devoted to the sensory capacities of various body parts. In the sensory realm, those organs capable of the highest sensitivity have the largest representations in the somatosensory cortex. (Penfield and Rasmussen, 1950.)

if it has just consumed a full meal. That is, stimulation of this part of the brain will make an animal behave as though it is hungry even though there is no biological need for food (Miller, 1957). Thus it would seem that the lateral hypothalamus has some special involvement with an animal's ability to recognize when it is hungry. Research by a number of investigators (for example, Teitelbaum and Epstein, 1962) has supported this idea. When the lateral hypothalamus in animals is selectively destroyed through the use of a strong electrical current, many will not eat unless they are force-fed. Curiously, most animals, if well cared for, will eventually overcome this dysfunction and begin to eat again on their own. This partial recovery may take months, and the animals will always be underweight and show a number of other permanent feeding problems (Epstein, 1971).

Lesions in the lower middle area of the hypothalamus will have an effect opposite to that of lateral hypothalamic lesions. That is, they tend to cause animals to overeat to the point of obesity (Hetherington and Ranson, 1942). A rat may eat enough to triple its normal weight (see the photograph on page 263). When this area in a normal animal is stimulated with a mild electrical current, the animal will stop eating even if it has been starved and biologically needs food. Thus it seems that this area of the hypothalamus is related to an animal's ability to recognize when it is full.

Using a combination of stimulation and lesion procedures, it has been possible to define those areas of the brain that are especially involved in different aspects of feeding behavior. These same procedures have been used to analyze many other kinds of brain-behavior relationships. In general, it seems that if electrical stimulation of a specific area produces an increase in some type of behavior, lesions in that same area will decrease the behavior. Likewise, if stimulation tends to block a behavior when it is normally appropriate, lesions may cause the behavior to occur more vigorously.

EVOKED POTENTIALS Evoked potentials are changes in bioelectrical activity in particular areas of the nervous system, resulting from stimulation of some other part of the body. ("Bioelectrical activity" simply refers to electrical activity that can be recorded from a biological system.) The evoked potential technique has provided information useful in defining how parts of the body are connected to different parts of the brain.

In one application of this procedure, recording electrodes are placed on the surface of the scalp, and various sense organs are stimulated. A change in bioelectrical activity in a specific area of the brain after stimulation of a particular sense organ indicates a relationship between that part of the brain and the sense organ. For example, the presentation of sounds to the ear will cause evoked potentials to occur most markedly at the top of the temporal lobe over the auditory cortex; the presentation of light flashes to the eye will produce evoked potentials around the tip of the occipital cortex; and touching the skin will produce evoked potentials in the parietal lobe next to the central fissure. Each of these cortical areas has a detailed and specific relationship with the sense modality that it processes. For instance, the musical scale is represented along the auditory cortex, from low to high, in a roughly orderly fashion (Woolsey, 1961): low notes produce obvious evoked potentials at one end of the auditory cortex, high notes at the other end, and middle notes in between. Similar kinds of detailed arrangements have been found for other sensory areas, as shown in the map of the sensory cortex in Figure 11.15.

SINGLE-UNIT RECORDING Evoked potentials are generally measured by placing recording electrodes on the surface of the scalp or the brain. The recorded bioelectrical response is the result of activity in a *group* of neurons. Modern technology has made it possible to record the bioelectrical activity of a *single* neuron. Single-unit recording is accomplished with the use of a microelectrode that is placed very close to an individual neuron in the nervous system.

The single-unit recording technique has provided some fascinating insights into the functional organization of the brain. The work of David Hubel and Torsten Wiesel (1962) illustrates this. These scientists inserted microelectrodes in the visual cortex of the brains of either cats or monkeys, and then they determined the kinds of visual stimuli that the neurons were sensitive to. They found that specific

neurons tended to respond to highly specific visual stimuli. For instance, a line of a certain orientation moving across the retina from left to right might cause one neuron to fire, while another might fire only when a certain angle was projected on a particular part of the retina. Thus it appears that individual neurons in the visual cortex are responsive to highly specific visual stimuli.

This type of finding has been duplicated for other areas of the brain in many different animal species. In the visual parts of the frog's brain, for instance, there are cells that respond by firing faster only when dark spots move through the field of vision—a useful adaptation for a creature whose major source of food is flying insects (Lettvin et al., 1959). In warmblooded animals, cells in certain parts of the hypothalamus will respond to a slight warming or cooling of the blood. Interestingly, these "temperature cells," when electrically stimulated, cause an animal to react as though its body has suddenly become too warm (panting) or too cold (shivering). In the cortex of animals, cells have been identified that change their response characteristics when the animals are placed in a learning situation. Richard Thompson and his colleagues (1970) have even reported finding cells that they called "counting cells"; these neurons will fire only after a certain number of rhythmic auditory or visual stimuli are presented to a cat's ears. The high degree of selectivity exhibited by many individual neurons is believed to provide a foundation for the fine-grained behavioral and perceptual capabilities displayed by animals and humans.

After destruction of a small part of the lower middle area of the hypothalamus (known as the ventromedial nucleus), the rat shown here has overeaten to such an extent that it weighs 1,080 grams. (The dial has gone beyond the 1,000-gram capacity of the scale and registers an additional 80 grams.) In contrast, a normal rat would weigh about 320 grams. A rat with this type of lesion will not work for extra food, although it will eat huge amounts if the food is tasty and readily available.

COMPLEX BEHAVIORAL FUNCTIONS Although the observations summarized in this section add to our picture of brain organization, the map is far from complete. The task of determining exactly how the brain controls behavior is obviously a very difficult one. At present, we can identify areas of the brain related to movement, to the senses, and to certain very general classes of behavior. However, we still do not understand how learning, memory, perception, and intellectual functioning are related to brain structure, and it is these behaviors that are of greatest interest to psychologists. In contrast to Gall's theory of brain function, these processes do not seem to be localized in any one particular area of the brain. In fact, almost everything that an animal does appears to involve activity in most or all of the brain. A famous neuropsychologist, Karl

S. Lashley, used the term **mass action** to describe this complex aspect of brain organization.

MASS ACTION AND LEARNED BEHAVIOR Lashley attempted to locate specific areas of the cortex that were responsible for the learning of or memory for particular behaviors. In one set of experiments, rats were trained in mazes after lesions had been made in a number of different cortical areas. The locations of the lesions in the rats overlapped considerably, so that no area of the cortex was left unexplored. Lashley came to two important conclusions on the basis of these experiments. First, learning of and memory for a specific task do not appear to be localized in any particular place; for example, no lesion completely obliterated the ability to learn a maze, although all of the lesions interfered with learning to some extent. Second, Lashley developed the **principle of mass action.** He found that the degree to which learning was retarded was directly related to the size of the lesion—the larger the lesion, the greater the retardation. This was particularly true for learning and remembering the more complex mazes. Thus it appeared that the total amount of cortex, rather than any particular area of it, was most clearly related to learning ability. Lashley was not able to identify special neural circuits that were related to the learning of or memory for particular types of problems (Lashley, 1929).

MULTIPLE CONTROL We have seen that the performance of any specific behavior is likely to involve most or all of the brain. The complementary principle also seems to be true; that is, a specific part of the brain is likely to be involved in the performance of many types of behavior. This is called the **principle of multiple control.** The cortex, for example, has been shown to influence behaviors ranging from simple spinal reflexes, to sleep and wakefulness cycles, to complex intellectual activities. For example, Lashley's principle of mass action of cortical functioning not only can be applied to learning but also includes sexual and feeding behavior (Braun, 1975). This indicates that the cortex is involved not only in the "higher behavioral functions" but in other functions as well. Likewise, the lateral hypothalamus, which we discussed earlier, is involved in many behaviors other than feeding responses. For example, rats with lesions in the lateral hypothalamus show deficits in certain learning situations in addition to exhibiting impaired feeding behaviors (Teitelbaum, 1971).

It is clear, from these observations of mass action and multiple control, that complex behavioral abilities, particularly intellectual performances, are not located exclusively in any specific area of the brain, and that specific areas of the brain are each involved in many different behavioral functions. Although the brain is composed of billions of discrete neurons, it functions as a complete unit. Thus our understanding of brain–behavior relationships must ultimately be based on research that examines both the activity of individual neurons and the organization of these neurons into the functioning brain of a behaving organism.

SUMMARY

1. In single-celled animals different parts of the individual cell carry out different behavioral functions. In multicelled animals there is cellular specialization.
   A. The three main types of specialized cells are receptor cells, motor cells, and neurons.
      1. **Receptor cells,** located within the sense organs, receive sensory information from the environment.
      2. **Motor cells,** or **effectors,** make up muscles and glands; they are specialized for movement or secretion.
      3. **Neurons** integrate and coordinate the information that passes between the receptor and motor cells.

   B. The **nervous system** provides a communication network among all the different cells of the body. It is divided into several subsystems. The two major subsystems are the central nervous system and the peripheral nervous system.
      1. The **central nervous system,** which consists of the brain and the spinal cord, is the major control center for all human behavior.
      2. The **peripheral nervous system,** which is made up of nerves (bundles of neuron cell fibers) and ganglia (groups of neuron cell bodies), relays information from the sensory receptors to the central nervous sys-

tem and then sends out messages to the appropriate muscles or glands. The peripheral nervous system is subdivided into the somatic and the autonomic divisions.

  a. The **somatic** division controls the skeletal muscles and is related to external behavior. Somatic activity is generally considered to be under voluntary control.

  b. The **autonomic** division controls the visceral muscles (such as the heart and the intestines) and the glands. Autonomic activity is generally considered to be involuntary; however, recent evidence suggests that some control over this activity may be possible. The autonomic system is subdivided still further into the **sympathetic** and **parasympathetic** divisions. The sympathetic system functions in stressful situations and is an energy-expending system. The parasympathetic system functions during normal or relaxed situations and is an energy-conserving system.

C. The basic structural units of the nervous system are **neurons** and **glia.** Neurons transmit electrochemical messages between various parts of the body. The functions of glia are not entirely understood, but they appear to provide structural support and nutrients to the neurons, and to provide a barrier to certain substances from the bloodstream.

  1. There are different types of neurons that exhibit specialized functions.

    a. **Sensory** (or **afferent**) **neurons** transmit information from the sense organs to the brain and spinal cord.

    b. **Motor** (or **efferent**) **neurons** transmit information from the brain and spinal cord to the muscles and glands.

    c. **Interneurons,** which compose the major portion of neurons in the nervous system, connect various other neurons to each other and integrate sensory and motor activity.

  2. Neurons consist of a **cell body,** which contains the nucleus, **dendrites,** which are relatively short fibers that extend out from the cell body, and an **axon,** which is a long fiber that leads away from the cell body.

  3. Neurons possess several important electrochemical characteristics.

    a. In a resting state, the cell is **polarized:** the interior of the cell is negatively charged, and the outside of the cell is positively charged. This electrical imbalance is called the **resting potential.**

    b. When a large enough stimulus occurs, the cell membrane is suddenly penetrated by positive ions, and the cell interior becomes positive and the exterior negative. This abrupt change is called the **action potential.**

    c. Information about the intensity of a stimulus is conveyed by an axon's rate of firing, rather than by the size of the action potentials. The **white matter** of the nervous system is composed of myelinated axons, while the **gray matter** is composed of nonmyelinated axons, dendrites, and cell bodies. Messages are transmitted from one neuron to another by **transmitter substances** (chemicals stored in sacs at the axon tip). The chemicals are released into the **synapse,** which is a small space separating the axon of one neuron from an adjacent neuron. Messages are either **excitatory** (causing a response in the receiving neuron) or **inhibitory** (preventing a response in the receiving neuron). Chains of neurons relay information across synapses throughout the nervous system, and these signals are eventually translated into behavior.

    d. The spinal cord connects the brain and the peripheral nervous system to each other. There are thirty-one pairs of spinal nerves, all of which contain both sensory and motor neurons for most of their length. At the point where most of these nerves actually join the spinal cord, however, they divide into two sections, or **roots.** The **dorsal root** is toward the back of the body and consists of sensory neurons. The **ventral root** is toward the belly of the body and consists of motor neurons. A simple chain of connecting neurons is called a **reflex arc.**

2. Whereas the nervous system transmits messages of an electrochemical nature, the **endocrine system** transmits messages by means of chemical substances called **hormones.** Hormones are pro-

duced by **endocrine glands,** which secrete these chemicals directly into the bloodstream. Hormones can affect a variety of behaviors such as sexual arousal, emotional response, motivation, physical growth, and the availability of energy. Hormones circulate throughout the bloodstream, but affect only their particular **target organs.**

3. The brain is a highly complex structure that regulates behavior in three major ways: it maintains and controls vital internal bodily functions; it processes sensory information and produces motor responses appropriate to this sensory input, and it uses past experience to guide future behavior. The brain consists of three overlapping layers: the central core, the limbic system, and the cerebral hemispheres.

   A. The **central core** of the human brain is made up of structures that carry out the basic functions of survival. The central core of the brain contains the brain stem, the cerebellum, the thalamus, and the hypothalamus.

      1. The **brain stem is** composed of several structures: the **medulla** is involved in breathing and circulation, and also controls chewing, salivation, and facial movements. The **pons** connects the two halves of the cerebellum. The pons relays motor information from the higher brain centers and the body to the cerebellum, and also integrates movements between the right and left sides of the body. The **midbrain** acts as a center for visual and auditory reflexes. The **reticular formation,** a complex network of neural fibers and cell bodies, arouses the higher brain areas to incoming information, and also functions to maintain a normal sleep-waking cycle.

      2. The **cerebellum** is divided into two hemispheres. It coordinates voluntary muscle activity and maintains physical balance.

      3. The **thalamus** consists of a pair of connected egg-shaped structures that surround a fluid-filled cavity (ventricle) in the brain. The thalamus functions as a relay station, sorting messages from sensory receptors and sending them to the appropriate regions of the higher brain. It also integrates information coming from various areas of the cerebral hemispheres.

      4. The **hypothalamus** monitors changes in the internal environment and sends out signals to maintain **homeostasis,** an op-

timally balanced internal state. It carries out its functions (1) by sending electrochemical signals to the autonomic nervous system, causing the sympathetic or parasympathetic system to respond to environmental changes, and (2) by influencing the functioning of the pituitary gland and through this influence regulating the production of hormones by the endocrine system. The hypothalamus has a major effect on behaviors related to survival, such as feeding, internal temperature regulation, emotional and physiological responses to stress, and sexual function.

   B. The **limbic system** seems to have developed from the sense of smell and to be involved in motivational and emotional processes. It plays a role in behaviors such as feeding, fighting, fleeing, and mating. Damage to various parts of the limbic system produces marked changes in aggressive, feeding, and sexual behaviors.

   C. The **cerebral hemispheres** are involved in the processes of learning, speech, reasoning, and memory.

      1. The cerebral hemispheres are composed of two halves (the left and right hemispheres) that look alike but seem to function differently. In general, the left half of the brain controls the right half of the body, and vice versa (a phenomenon called **contralateral control**). In most people the left hemisphere is dominant and also slightly larger. It is involved in behaviors associated with language and logical thought. The right hemisphere seems to be dominant for abilities of a spatial, musical, or visual imagery nature. The two hemispheres communicate with each other through a thick band of neural fibers called the **corpus callosum.**

      2. The **cerebral cortex** is the gray matter that covers the cerebral hemispheres. It is the most recently evolved portion of the nervous system. The cortex contains several "landmarks" used in studying the brain. The most prominent landmarks are the **central fissure,** which separates the frontal lobe from the parietal lobe, and the **lateral fissure,** which marks the upper boundary of the temporal lobe. The **occipital lobe** is located at the back of the brain and is primarily involved in the

reception and analysis of visual information. Areas for auditory reception and for processing visual information are found in the **temporal lobe**. Some parts of the **frontal lobe** regulate fine voluntary movements, and others in the left frontal lobe are involved in the ability to use speech. In 1861 Paul Broca suggested that different parts of the brain control different types of behavior; this is known as **localization of function**. The prefrontal areas of the frontal lobes have recently been found to involve the ability to order stimuli, sort out information, and maintain attention to a specific task under distracting conditions. The **parietal lobe** is the primary receiving area for the skin senses and the sense of bodily position.

3. Possibly the most well-defined regions of the cortex are the **somato-sensory cortex**, which receives touch and positional information from the different areas of the body, and the **motor cortex**, which integrates movements of the various body parts. About 75 percent of the cortex is made up of areas that do not have a specific sensory or motor function. These areas are called the **associative cortex**.

4. Using a variety of techniques, investigators have clarified a number of brain–behavior relationships.

A. Clinical observations have revealed that a **stroke** (a rupturing of blood vessels on the brain's surface) or other forms of localized brain damage result in specific behavioral deficits, depending on the location of the damage.

B. Chemical or electrical stimulation of various regions in the brain has been found to elicit a number of different behaviors. In addition to helping scientists to map the brain, these stimulation techniques may be useful in treating certain medical problems, such as providing relief from severe pain.

C. Early observations of brain function were hampered because patients often exhibited diffuse rather than localized brain damage. Scientists now use a brain **lesion** technique, in which they destroy or remove specific brain tissues in animals in order to determine the functions of those tissues.

D. The **evoked potential** technique is helpful in determining the connections between parts of the body and parts of the brain. Evoked potentials are changes in bioelectrical activity in particular regions of the nervous system that result from stimulation of some other part of the body.

E. The activity of a single neuron can be measured by inserting a microelectrode into the brain, very close to an individual neuron. This **single-unit recording** technique has demonstrated that individual neurons can respond to highly selective stimuli. This selectivity may be one basis for the fine-grained behavioral and perceptual capabilities that animals and humans possess.

F. Our knowledge about how the brain is related to behavior is far from complete. We still do not understand how learning, memory, perception, and intellectual functioning are related to brain structures. These processes are not localized in any specific area of the brain; instead, they seem to involve activity in most or all of the brain. Lashley called this pattern of brain organization **mass action**.

RECOMMENDED READINGS

HESS, WILLIAM R. *The Biology of Mind.* Chicago: University of Chicago Press, 1964. A systematic presentation of brain–behavior relationships by a Nobel Prize-winning physiologist.

THOMPSON, RICHARD F. *Introduction to Physiological Psychology.* New York: Harper & Row, 1975. An excellent, sophisticated basic textbook that comprehensively covers the field of physiological psychology.

VALENSTEIN, ELLIOT S. *Brain Control: A Critical Examination of Brain Stimulation and Psychosurgery.* New York: Wiley, 1973. An excellent account of the history of studying brain function and of psychosurgery by an expert in brain research.

WILLIAMS, MOYRA. *Brain Damage and the Mind.* Baltimore: Penguin, 1970. A readable account of all the different types of brain damage and their consequent psychological impairments.

CHAPTER TWELVE

SENSATION AND THE SENSES

The matter of sensory perception is sometimes made to seem so mysterious. Each one of us seems to be the prisoner of our own senses. Can we possibly know what an apple looks like or feels like or smells like to someone else? Not unless we could get into someone else's brain.

And yet it *is* possible to enter into a completely different sense world, and the funny thing is that we generally don't notice. For instance, can you imagine what the world looks like to someone who is totally color-blind? Imagine no green to the grass, no blue to the sky, no red and blue to flowers, no color to anything. Surely it seems horrible, and you must be thankful this doesn't happen to you.

And yet I've been color-blind for hours at a time—and so have you. And I've enjoyed it—and so have you.

Every time we see a black-and-white movie or watch a black-and-white television set, we experience scenes that are totally without color. And we pay very little attention to the lack. If I were to see several different motion pictures, some in color and some in black and white, and if I were asked a week later to tell which ones were in color and which not, I don't think I could achieve a perfect score.

And then—what if we had an additional sense? In fact, we all *do* occasionally possess a sense we don't always have. Every motion picture we see, every television drama, is accompanied by music. What is more, the music is carefully adjusted to the action and is designed to elicit the proper emotions in us. The music guides us so that we know when to feel tension, elation, suspense, melancholy. Listen for the minor tones in the sad scenes, the discords in the violent ones. Satirists have run the same scenes with and without the mood music. With the music, even commonplace utterances seem filled with meaning. Without the music, even exciting events seem flat.

Doesn't this amount to a new sense? Do we not, through the ear, directly sense emotion and mood in a way we cannot in real life? Yet do we really notice? I think not.

Isaac Asimov

Without the capacity to detect and absorb information from a constantly changing environment, our brain and nervous system would be of little value. Our senses are the information-collecting devices by which we monitor the external world, gathering and processing information about changes in light, chemical composition, temperature, and pressure in the environment.

Many of us assume that we respond to all phenomena that occur in the environment, but sensory systems are *selective,* responding to some stimuli and not to others. In the animal kingdom, for example, many nocturnal species are color-blind but have a highly developed sense of hearing. Certain moths are deaf to all frequencies of sound except those emitted by the hunting bats that prey on them. Many birds have a keen sense of vision but a poor sense of smell. Humans have a relatively sensitive sense of smell but cannot, for example, detect the aroma exuded by earthworms that attracts worm-eating snakes. Thus we can see that sensory systems are like filters that accentuate or suppress information about the world, depending on the kinds of information that the organism needs to survive.

Two research perspectives contribute importantly to psychologists' view of human sensory systems: psychophysics and sensory physiology. **Psychophysics** studies the relationships between physical stimulation of a sense organ and the resulting sensory experience. **Sensory physiology** investigates the effects that stimuli have on the structural and chemical features of the sense organs and on the functioning of the sensory pathways leading to the brain. This chapter makes use of the contributions of both approaches to the understanding of sensation and the senses.

STIMULI AND SENSATIONS

A **stimulus** is any form of energy to which our senses respond. Light waves, for example, are the basic stimuli for vision, and sound waves for hearing. Stimuli can be measured in two basic ways, physically and psychologically. The basic difference between these two kinds of measurements is the "instrument" of measurement that is used. Physical measures are provided by special standardized instruments, such as light meters, thermometers, weighing scales, and so on. Psychological measures are provided by the responses of individuals to the stimuli—in other words, by the **sensations** they report.

Human psychological response to stimuli encompass two principal dimensions: quality and quantity. The *quality* of a stimulus refers to the kind of sensation it produces. For instance, color, or hue, represents a quality related to visual stimulation, while pitch on the musical scale represents a quality related to auditory stimulation. *Quantity* refers to the amount of stimulation present. Thus the brightness of a color would represent quantity of light, while loudness would represent quantity of sound. These characteristics—hue, brightness, pitch, loudness—are examples of psychological dimensions of sensation, that is, they are the properties of sensory experience as reported by subject observing the stimuli.

What is the relationship between the physical and psychological dimensions of a stimulus? A simple experiment that you can do at home will illustrate the meaning of this question. Use a three-way light bulb, one with 50-, 100-, and 150-watt capacities. Try the bulb at each of these settings in an otherwise dark room. You will see that although each successive setting uses 50 watts more power, and therefore produces a constant increase in the physical intensity of the light stimulus, the jump from 50 to 100 watts results in a larger increase in the *sensation* of brightness than does the step from 100 to 150 watts. Psychologists ask why the change in the sensation of brightness does not correspond to the change in the physical intensity of the light.

In analyzing the relationship between a sensation and the physical characteristics of the stimulus upon which that sensation is based, psychologists study these basic aspects: the amount of stimulation necessary for a person to experience a given sensation in the first place; the ratio between the amount, or magnitude, of a stimulus and the magnitude of the sensation; and the factors that reduce or increase sensory capacities.

THRESHOLDS   How much light must be present before a person sees it? How much pressure must be applied to the skin before a person feels it? The answers to these questions involve the concept of threshold.

A **threshold** is the smallest stimulus, or stimulus change, producing a detectable sensation or change in sensation in an individual. There are several different types of thresholds. For instance, the **absolute threshold** refers to the minimum stimulus necessary to produce a specific sensation. A psychologist might measure a person's absolute threshold for light as follows: the person enters a completely dark room and, after being given time to adapt to the dark, watches for a light on the wall. The psychologist, using a machine that can project low-intensity light beams, projects a very dim beam and gradually increases the intensity until the person says, "I see it." Alternatively, the psychologist can start by projecting a visible beam and gradually decrease its intensity until the person says, "I don't see it." Generally, these procedures will be repeated a number of times with the same person, and the lowest intensity at which the person reports seeing the light 50 percent of the time may be defined as the absolute threshold.

Under ideal conditions, the senses have very low

absolute thresholds. That is, sensations will be experienced with very small amounts of stimulation. For example, the human sense of smell is sensitive enough to detect the musky odor of mercaptan, the scent that makes skunks so unpopular, at concentrations as low as 1 part mercaptan per 50 trillion parts of air (Geldard, 1972).

But in the natural environment, ideal conditions are seldom encountered. For this reason, in recent years, psychologists have been interested in **detection thresholds** (Green and Swets, 1966). Much of the machinery of modern society requires people to detect minimal stimuli against a background of **noise,** which may be defined as any irrelevant or unwanted sensory information. For example, a radar operator must be able to detect an airplane on a radar screen even when the blip from the plane is faint and difficult to distinguish from blips caused by natural phenomena such as flocks of birds or bad weather, which can produce images on the radar screen that are like visual "noise." Consider radar operators watching a screen in wartime during a storm. How do they decide whether a blip on the screen is an enemy plane or a patch of noise? If they were to call out massive defense forces for every blip, they would create chaos, but if one bomber was mistakenly identified as noise, the results could be disastrous. The radar operators' judgment will be influenced by many factors, and different operators appear to have different sensitivities to blips. Moreover, a specific individual's apparent sensitivity seems to fluctuate, depending on the situation. For example, being watched by a superior will probably affect the operator's performance, as will fatigue or other distractions.

In studying the difficulties faced by radar operators, psychologists have reformulated the concept of absolute threshold to take into account the many factors that affect detection of minimal stimuli. As a result, the **signal detection theory** abandons the idea that there is a single true absolute threshold for a stimulus. Instead it adopts the notion that the stimulus, here called a **signal,** must be detected in the face of noise, which can interfere with detection of the signal. Thus signal detection is similar to standing in a noisy bus terminal listening for the announcement of your bus departure time over the loudspeaker. Although the volume of the loudspeaker remains constant, you will have more or less difficulty in detecting your "signal" depending on the amount of noise in the bus terminal.

Another type of threshold is the **difference threshold** or **just noticeable difference.** This refers to the smallest change in a stimulus that will produce a change in sensation. So returning to our example of the person tested in a dark room, a psychologist would test for the difference threshold by gradually increasing the intensity of a visible light beam until the person says, "Yes, this is brighter than the light I just saw." With this technique, it is possible to identify the smallest increase in light intensity that will be noticeable to the human eye.

SENSORY RATIOS In the mid-1800s Ernst Weber, who was studying just noticeable differences, discovered a relationship between the general magnitude of a stimulus and the sizes of just noticeable differences: while people notice small changes in a weak stimulus, they notice only large differences in a strong stimulus. For instance, if you add one pound to the weight of a couple of paperback books you are carrying, the sensation of weight will be greatly increased. If you add one pound to your seventy-pound backpack, however, you will probably not sense any increase in weight.

After further study, Weber (1834) specified the nature of this relationship more precisely: according to **Weber's law,** the amount of a stimulus needed to produce a just noticeable difference is always a constant proportion of the intensity of the stimulus. For example, the just noticeable difference for a hundred-pound backpack is about two pounds for most people. Thus, for a fifty-pound backpack the just noticeable difference would be about one pound, and for a ten-pound backpack, about one-fifth of a pound. For the sensation of weight, then, the proportion necessary for a just noticeable difference is about 1/50. Proportions for some other sensations are 1/10 for intensity of tone, 1/7 for skin pressure, and 1/5 for saltiness of a liquid.

Gustave Fechner (1860) tried to apply Weber's findings about just noticeable differences to sensation more generally. He asked: How does the magnitude of a stimulus relate to the magnitude of the sensation arising from it? For example, how much must we increase the intensity of a light in order to see it as twice as bright? According to **Fechner's law,** the intensity of a sensation increases proportionately with the magnitude of the stimulus. With the three-way light bulb, for example, your sensation of increased brightness is not the same for the two different jumps because the proportions are different: 50 to 100 watts is 1/2, while

Figure 12.1 (A) S. S. Stevens has shown that the psychological magnitude (size) of a sensation varies according to some power of the physical magnitude of the stimulus. The size of the power, or exponent, to which the stimulus intensity must be raised, is different for different stimulus dimensions. (top) The equation for the psychological magnitude of line length has an exponent of 1.0; this means that when a line is doubled in length, it does in fact look twice as long. (middle) Brightness has an exponent of 0.33; when you double the amount of light coming from a bulb, your sensation of brightness increases only about one-fourth. (bottom) Electric shock has an exponent of 3.5; this means that doubling the intensity of the electricity produces a feeling of shock 11.3 times greater, on the average. (B) The three relationships plotted as graphs, to show the growth of psychological magnitude as physical magnitude grows. (After Stevens, 1962.)

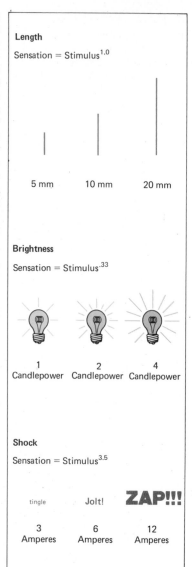

Length

Sensation = $Stimulus^{1.0}$

5 mm   10 mm   20 mm

Brightness

Sensation = $Stimulus^{.33}$

1 Candlepower   2 Candlepower   4 Candlepower

Shock

Sensation = $Stimulus^{3.5}$

tingle   Jolt!   **ZAP!!!**

3 Amperes   6 Amperes   12 Amperes

A

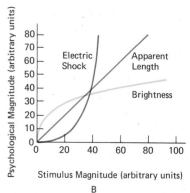

Electric Shock   Apparent Length

Brightness

Psychological Magnitude (arbitrary units)

Stimulus Magnitude (arbitrary units)

B

100 to 150 watts is 2/3. It turns out that Fechner's law is only partially correct. Although the relationships between stimuli of moderate magnitude and the sensations arising from them are roughly proportional, this is not the case for either very strong or very weak stimuli and their correspondng sensations.

S. S. Stevens (1957) provided a better description of the relationship between the magnitude of a stimulus and the sensation arising from it. According to **Stevens' power law,** this relationship has very consistent characteristics over a wide range of stimulus intensities. However, the characteristics of the relationship between stimulus magnitude and sensation are different for each of the senses. For example, in vision the physical intensity of light must be increased by eight times before it looks twice as bright to us. In hearing, the physical stimulus of a sound must be more than three times as intense before we will hear it as twice as loud.

For both vision and hearing, the quantity of a sensation appears to increase more slowly than the physical magnitude of the stimuli. This is not the case for all sensory judgments. For example, in judgments of electric shock the magnitude of sensation increases faster than the magnitude of the stimulus. Doubling the intensity of a shock stimulus to the fingers produces about a tenfold increase in the impact of the sensation. These comparisons are illustrated in Figure 12.1.

SENSORY ADAPTATION All sensory systems display **adaptation**, that is, an adjustment in sensory capacity after prolonged and constant stimulation. Some senses adapt relatively quickly, like smell and touch, while others adapt very slowly, like the sense of pain. The most obvious effect of adaptation is decreased sensitivity to a stimulus; for example, if you walk from the sunny outdoors into a dimly lit theater, you will be temporarily blinded because your eyes were adapted to the bright outside light.

In addition to decreasing sensitivity, adaptation can also significantly distort sensation. You can experience a blatant form of this distortion by performing the following experiment. Place one hand in ice-cold water and the other in bearably hot water. After you have adapted to the temperatures, plunge both hands into a bucket of water that is of an intermediate temperature. Does the water feel hot or cold? The initial and bizarre contradiction between the two hands says that it is both, even though you know that it is neither.

As Harry Helson (1964) pointed out, the sensations experienced when a stimulus occurs are not determined by that stimulus alone. Sensations are also affected by immediately preceding stimuli. For instance, the same weight may feel heavy or light, depending on weights that have been lifted immediately prior to the weight in question. In Helson's terminology, the "adaptation level" to a particular amount of stimulation will influence the sensory judgment by providing a frame of reference for evaluating new sensations.

THE SENSES

The "five senses" we commonly refer to are related to the five obvious sense organs: the eyes, the ears, the nose, the tongue, and the skin. Actually, there are considerably more than five senses. The skin contains receptors for at least three different kinds of sensation, and there is an organ in the inner ear, called the vestibular apparatus, that provides a sense of balance and equilibrium. In addition, other sensory systems related to the muscles and joints provide a sense of body position and movement. Finally, as we saw in the preceding chapter, there are many internal receptors that provide the brain with vital information about blood chemistry and temperature. Although in this discussion we will restrict ourselves to the classic five senses and the senses of balance and movement, all sense organs operate according to similar principles.

Each sense organ contains special receptors that are sensitive to particular types of stimuli. However, the basic response of the different kinds of receptors is the same: to convert environmental stimuli into neural impulses, the language of the nervous system. This transformation process is known as **transduction.**

VISION   Vision is regarded as the richest human sense. The eyes receive light reflected from things in the world, and from this light shape, color, depth, texture, and movement are perceived.

Light, a form of electromagnetic radiation that travels in waves, is the basic stimulus for vision. However, the light energy that receptors in the eyes can transduce into visual information is just one small part of the electromagnetic spectrum. As Figure 12.2 shows, this spectrum also contains radio and infrared waves, ultraviolet rays, X-rays, and gamma rays, which are outside the range of human visual sensitivity and must be measured with special instruments. However, although our eyes are not sensitive to ultraviolet or infrared rays, our skin responds to them; ultraviolet light causes skin cells to produce a pigment that results in suntans, and infrared rays are sensed as heat.

Light has two characteristics that are especially important for vision: wavelength and intensity. Color is determined by **wavelength,** the distance between the crest of one wave and the crest of the next; brightness is determined by the **intensity,** primarily a factor of the height (or amplitude) of the light waves. Together, these two characteristics determine whether light can be seen. For example, a purple light shown against a gray wall in a dark

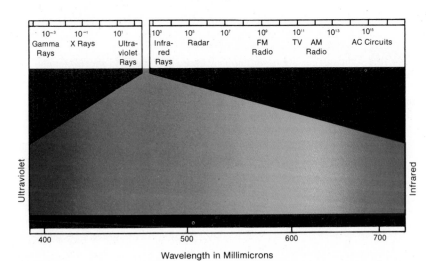

Figure 12.2 The spectrum of electromagnetic energy. The small portion of this spectrum to which the human eye is sensitive is shown expanded. The scale on the large spectrum is a logarithmic scale of wavelength: each step on the scale corresponds to a tenfold increase in the wavelength of the electromagnetic radiation.

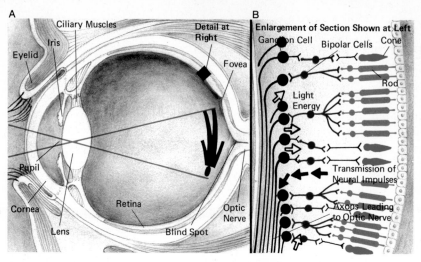

A

Ciliary Muscles
Iris
Eyelid
Pupil
Cornea
Lens
Retina
Blind Spot
Optic Nerve
Detail at Right
Fovea

B

Enlargement of Section Shown at Left
Ganglion Cell   Bipolar Cells   Cone
Rod
Light Energy
Transmission of Neural Impulses
Axons Leading to Optic Nerve

Figure 12.3 The structure of the eye and the transduction of light energy into neural firing. (A) A cross-section of the human eye. Note that the lens transmits an inverted image onto the retina. (B) The detailed structure of a small portion of the retina close to the fovea. Note that cones are more common toward the fovea and that near the fovea each cone is connected to a single bipolar cell. Arrows on the figure indicate the passage of neural impulses from the receptor cells through bipolar cells and ganglion cells to the optic nerve on their way to the brain.

room must be somewhat more intense than a green light (shown against the same wall) before it will become visible.

STRUCTURE OF THE EYE The structure of the human eye is shown in Figure 12.3A. The eye has four main parts: the cornea, the iris, the lens, and the retina. Light enters the eye through the **cornea,** the transparent window covering the front of the eye. The cornea, which is sharply curved, serves as a preliminary lens and helps focus the light that enters the eye. The **iris** is a ring of muscle whose pigmentation gives the eyes their color. It regulates the amount of light entering the eye through the **pupil,** the opening in the center of the eye that appears black. The pupil is just a hole, covered by the cornea, through which light passes to a transparent structure called the **lens.** The ciliary muscles attached to the lens can modify its curvature so that the light is focused to make a clear image on the **retina,** a light-sensitive surface in the back of the eye. The expansion and contraction of the iris and the ciliary muscles are reflexive; we do not have to think about either activity for it to occur.

THE RETINA AND RECEPTOR CELLS The retina contains receptor cells, or **receptors,** that transduce light energy into neural impulses. It also has two types of neural cells—**biopolar cells** and **ganglion cells**—that help encode the impulses from the receptors into a form that is easily interpretable by the brain. As Figure 12.3B indicates, the receptors—the **rods** and **cones**—are actually the farthest of all the retinal cells from the light. The light that enters the eye must pass through the other nerve cells and the blood vessels nourishing the eye before it hits the rods and cones.

Figure 12.3B shows how information is transmitted through the retina. The receptor cells stimulate the bipolar cells, and the bipolar cells pass their information to the ganglion cells. The ganglion cells form part of the **optic nerve,** which carries information about what is seen to the brain for interpretation.

The optic nerve leaves the eye through an area of the retina called the **blind spot,** as shown in Figure 12.3A. This area is aptly named, because it contains no receptor cells. Figure 12.4 enables you to demonstrate to yourself that you cannot see something

Figure 12.4 Although you are never normally aware of it, the blind spot is literally blind. To demonstrate this fact to yourself, hold this figure at arm's length, cover your left eye, and focus on the center of the X. Slowly move the figure toward you, staring continuously at the X. At some point, you will no longer be able to see the red spot. This is the point at which the red spot's image has fallen on the blind spot in your right eye. The red spot will reappear if you move the figure even closer.

that falls on the blind spot. If you look at the figure as instructed in the caption, the dot will fall on the blind spot in your eye and will seem to disappear. Ordinarily, you are not aware of your blind spots because they are off center in each eye, so that one eye can help to fill in what the other is missing; also, the eyes are continually moving, which further helps the brain to fill in the missing visual information. On their way to the brain, the optic nerves meet at a crossover point called the **optic chiasma,** where they split. Fibers from the left half of each eye go to the left hemisphere of the cerebral cortex, whereas fibers from the right side of each eye go to the right hemisphere (see Figure 14.2, page 320).

The two types of receptor cells in the retina have different functions; simply stated, the **cones** are responsible for color vision, and the **rods** provide vision of light and dark. The cones require more light than the rods to function. We see little color by moonlight because there is not enough light to stimulate the cones, but we can see shades of light and dark because moonlight *is* intense enough to stimulate the rods.

The rods and cones are not evenly distributed over the surface of the retina; cones are most highly concentrated in the center of the retina in an area called the **fovea.** The fovea contains only cones, and it is the area of the retina that provides the most accurate detail vision—when you "look at" something, you see it with the foveal cones. One reason for the great visual acuity of the fovea is its high density of cones. Another reason is that the cones in the fovea are fully exposed to light; the blood vessels and nerve cells that cover the rest of the retina do not cover the fovea, so that light has an unimpeded path to the fovea. Also, in the fovea each cone is connected to one bipolar cell, as shown in Figure 12.3, so that information is recorded and transmitted directly to the brain. In contrast, many rods may be connected to a single bipolar cell, so the signals from them to the higher brain centers are blended. The periphery of the retina contains mostly rods, and is therefore not very sensitive to color. However, the periphery is very sensitive to movement and dim light, and this is why we always seem to spot faint "shooting stars" out of the corner of the eye.

Light is transduced by the receptors to neural impulses by means of a series of chemical reactions. One of the most important chemicals involved in this process is **rhodopsin,** the pigment in rods that is often called "visual purple" because of its purple color. The more pigment in the rods, the more

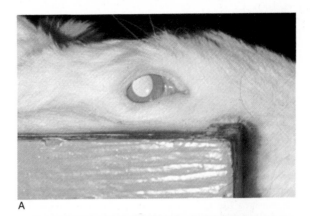

A

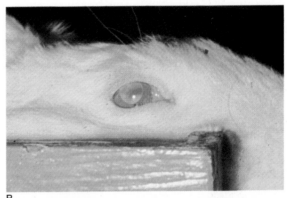

B

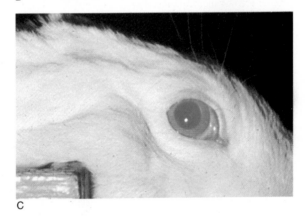

C

Photograph A shows a rabbit's eye after it has been in bright light for some time. The pigment rhodopsin has been "bleached" away by the light (the same would be true of your eye after a few minutes on a sunlit beach, though it would not be as noticeable to an observer). Photograph B shows the same eye after two minutes in a completely dark room (the photo was taken with a brief flash). Notice that some of the pigment has returned. Photograph C was taken after ten minutes in the dark; the recovery of the eye from bleaching is nearly complete, and the eye is said to be dark-adapted.

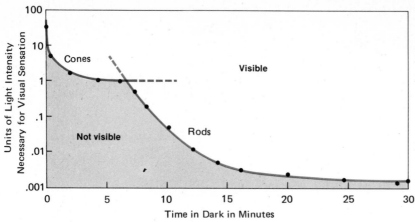

sensitive the eye is to light. When light strikes a rod, it changes the chemical structure of rhodopsin by bleaching it (Wald, 1968). This bleaching process results in the generation of a neural signal. Because light breaks down the rhodopsin (as well as the pigments in the cones), rhodopsin must continually be replenished by the rods. The reason you cannot see well when going from bright sunlight into a dark room is that the bright light has depleted your supply of pigment. The photos on page 275 show this bleaching effect on the retina of a rabbit's eye, and the recovery of the purple pigment after ten

minutes in the dark. The time it takes to see well in the dark is necessary for the rebuilding of receptor pigments. Figure 12.5 shows that the more time spent in the dark, the more sensitive the rods become to light. This process of **dark adaptation** results largely from the buildup of rhodopsin levels over time in the dark. The figure also shows that the cones do not function at all in dim light.

COLOR VISION If you are presented with a visual stimulus that has a wavelength of 450 millimicrons, you will say that it is blue. You perceive blue

Figure 12.6 The color wheel. Any two colors that are opposite each other are complementary; that is, combining them produces gray.

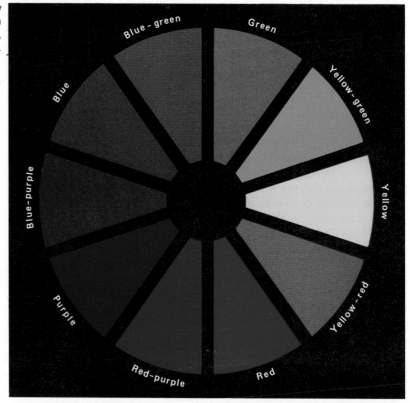

because your visual system interprets this wavelength as a specific color. Each color or hue perceived in the visible spectrum corresponds to a certain range or combination of wavelengths.

How does the visual system translate different light wavelengths into the experience of color? The most generally accepted explanation of color vision, called the **trichromatic theory,** suggests that there are three types of cones. Each type is maximally sensitive to wavelengths of a different color. Some cones respond best to red light, others to green light, and others to blue light. The color that we see depends on the relative activation of each of these kinds of cones. When red-sensitive cones are stimulated, we see red. When red-sensitive and green-sensitive cones are equally stimulated, we see yellow, because the wavelengths defining yellow are between red and green on the spectrum. All the colors of the visible spectrum (about 150 discriminable colors when brightness factors are controlled) are synthesized from various combinations of the three kinds of cones (MacNichol, 1964). This "synthesis-of-sensing" notion is an important one in sensory processes because it suggests an interesting economy in the way sensory systems are constructed. Instead of having separate receptors for each discriminable color, the *pattern* of activity in only three kinds of receptors yields the entire spectrum.

Beyond the cones, a different color vision process comes into play. Russell DeValois (1965) has found that there are **color-opponent cells** in one part of the brain that respond to stimulation of the eye by one color but are inhibited by its opposite. To understand what we mean by a color's opposite, look at the color wheel in Figure 12.6; colors on opposite sides of the wheel are **complementary,** that is, when they are combined they will be seen as achromatic (colorless), either gray or white. According to the **opponent-processes theory,** the three types of cones are linked to form three different opponent systems in the brain. As Figure 12.7 shows, there are cells that respond to red and are inhibited by its opposite, green. The opponent system contains cells that are excited by green and inhibited by red. The second opponent system responds to yellow or blue, with these two colors acting in opposition to each other. The third system is a broadly sensitive achromatic or brightness system, responding essentially to light and dark.

The phenomenon of afterimages also illustrates the linkage or pairing of color opposites. An **afterimage** is a sensory impression that persists after removal of the stimulus. Rest your eyes for a few minutes and then stare intently at the lower right-hand star of the flag in Figure 12.8 for forty-five seconds. Transfer your gaze to a white area, such as a blank sheet of paper. You should see the flag in its correct colors, which are complementary to those shown in the figure. Similarly, an observer usually reports seeing blue shortly after a brief flash of an intense yellow light, or red after a brief flash of green light.

A person with normal color vision needs only three major wavelengths of light—corresponding to red, green, and blue—to reproduce all the colors of the visible spectrum. Such a person is called a **trichromat. A dichromat** is a person in whom one of the three cone systems is absent or deficient. Most dichromats have red-green "blindness"; blue-yellow "blindness" is rarer. A very few people are **monochromatic,** or totally color-blind; they see the world in shades of gray, like the picture on a black-and-white television.

Even partial color blindness is rarely an all-or-nothing thing. Some people just have weak cone systems and therefore need color to be stronger before they can see it. For example, a person who is green-weak is able to perceive green as a separate and distinct color but sees it as being a grayish green. In contrast, a person who is red-green blind cannot see green at all.

In monochromacy, the rarest and most extreme form of color blindness, all the cones are either missing or malfunctioning. Visual information is transmitted only through the rods. Since the fovea normally contains only cones, and the totally color-blind person has no cones, there is little if any foveal vision. To compensate for this absence of what is the most accurate part of the visual field, monochromats must move their eyes rapidly back and forth so that everything registers in the peripheral part of the retina.

HEARING Whereas visual receptors in the eyes respond to light and transduce it into neural signals, auditory receptors in the ears respond to sound waves to produce neural signals. Sound waves are caused by pressure changes in the atmosphere, which generate vibrations among the air molecules.

When you listen to a radio, the amplifier in it makes the speaker vibrate. This vibrating speaker alternately pushes against the air in front of it, compressing it, and pulls away from the air, making it less dense, or rarefying it. The waves of com-

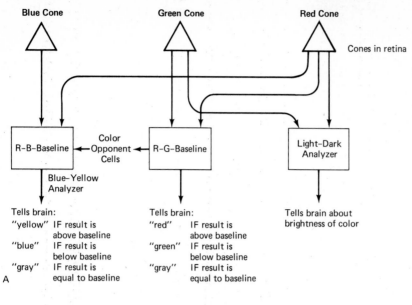

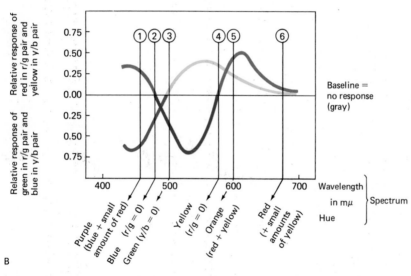

Figure 12.7 The interaction of the trichromatic and opponent-process aspects of color vision. Part A of the figure shows one way in which three types of cones might give information to color-opponent cells. The "red" cell is actually sensitive to both red and yellow. Each of the analyzer cells produces a moderate output called the "baseline" output when it is not stimulated, or if its two kinds of input are equal. If the blue-yellow analyzer produces an output much below baseline (due to a predominance of input from the blue cones), while the red-green analyzer produces an output somewhat above baseline (due to receiving greater input from the red cone than from the green cone), the result will be a mixture of red and blue that the brain will perceive as purple.

This example can be visualized more easily in part B, where it is shown as line 1. This shows the output of the blue-yellow and the red-green color opponent analyzer cells, both of which are taken into account by the brain in perceiving the color of any given patch of light. The other numbered lines show how we see other colors, according to the opponent-processes theory of color vision. For example, line 4 shows that when the red-green analyzer is at baseline (which means gray to the brain) and the blue-yellow analyzer responds at above baseline, we see yellow. (After Hochberg, 1978.)

pressed and rarefied air particles travel through the air and strike the eardrum. Then the eardrum is rapidly pushed and pulled by the compressions and rarefactions and, as a result, vibrates in the same patterns as the loudspeaker did originally, though with much less intensity.

Figure 12.9 suggests what the waves of compression and rarefaction look like. These sound waves behave in much the same way as waves of water moving through the ocean: the vibration of each molecule of air or water sets the next molecule in motion around an average resting place, but the individual molecules do not advance with the wave. The molecules of water in an ocean wave ten yards from shore are not the same molecules that break against the beach—ocean waves are simply pulses of energy that travel through the medium of water. In the same way, sound waves are pulses of

compression and rarefaction traveling through a medium of air or water. In a vacuum, where there is no medium to transmit the waves, there can be no sounds.

All waves have two obvious physical attributes: frequency and intensity. Frequency refers to the number of waves passing a given point in a given period of time, and intensity is the amplitude (height) of each wave. In a sound wave, **frequency** is the number of compression-rarefaction cycles that occur within some period of time. The **pitch** of the sound we hear corresponds to the frequency: the higher the frequency, the higher the tone will sound. The human ear is sensitive to frequencies ranging from about 20 to 20,000 cycles per second. As examples of frequencies we commonly hear, the human voice ranges from 120 to 600 cycles per second, middle C on a piano is 256 cycles per

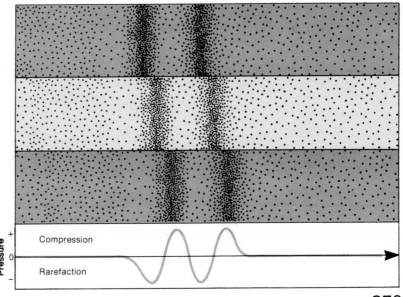

Figure 12.8 The phenomenon of afterimages.

second, and the highest note on a piano is 4,100 cycles per second. People do not hear the sound made by a dog whistle because it is above 20,000 cycles per second, but dogs can hear the sound because their auditory systems are sensitive to frequencies above this level.

The **intensity** of a sound wave refers to the amount of pressure it exerts, and is usually represented by the distance of its peaks and valleys from a zero baseline. The greater the amplitude of the wave, the louder it will sound to a listener. Amplitude is usually expressed in a unit of measurement called **decibels,** and is calculated according to a logarithmic formula. Sounds above 120 decibels

are likely to be painful to the human ear, while the normal conversation usually takes place at about 60 decibels. It has been calculated that at zero decibel, near the threshold of hearing, humans can actually hear the sound of one air molecule striking the eardrum. This feat can be accomplished only under ideally quiet circumstances; normally, the background sounds of the environment mask such tiny deflections.

STRUCTURE OF THE EAR   Figure 12.10A shows the structure of the ear: the outer ear (the external projecting portion, called the pinna, and the audi-

Figure 12.9 A sound originates in something vibrating very rapidly. This motion is passed on as a wave, in which compression alternates with rarefaction. In the top part of this figure, we see the same air molecules at three different points in time, as two cycles of a sound wave pass by. Below we see a graph of this wave in which air pressure is plotted as it varies over time. As the sound wave passes any given point, air pressure rises above its resting point, then falls below it. It repeats this process for as long as the sound lasts. The frequency of this rising and falling determines the pitch of the sound; for example, middle C is about 256 cycles per second. The greater the change in pressure from the resting point, the louder the sound.

Pressure

Compression

Rarefaction

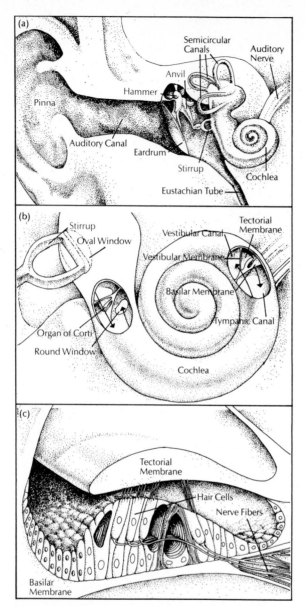

Figure 12.10 The hearing process. (A) Cross-section showing the outer, middle, and inner ear. Sound waves pass through the auditory canal and are transformed into mechanical vibration by the eardrum. The three small bones amplify this motion and transmit it to the oval window of the cochlea, which is depicted in (B). The motion of the oval window sends pressure waves through the fluid in the cochlea in the directions shown by the arrows. (C) Closeup cross-section of the organ of Corti, within the cochlea. Waves in the cochlear fluid cause the basilar membrane to vibrate, which in turn disturbs the hair cells, the receptor cells of hearing.

canals, located in the inner ear, are not part of the auditory system; they provide cues to body position and movement.)

When a sound wave enters the ear, it passes down the auditory canal and strikes the **tympanic membrane (eardrum),** causing it to vibrate. On the other side of the eardrum are the **ossicles,** a series of delicate little bones known as the **hammer,** the **anvil,** and the **stirrup** (so named for their shapes). These three bones of the middle ear are linked and suspended in such a way that when the eardrum moves the hammer, it in turn moves the anvil, which moves the stirrup.

The stirrup is attached in turn to the **oval window,** a flexible membrane on the side of the spiral-shaped, fluid-filled inner chamber called the **cochlea** (see Figure 12.10B). If the cochlea were entirely rigid, the stirrup would be unable to move the fluid within. But there is a second membranous spot on the cochlea, called the **round window,** that can be deflected outward as the oval window is deflected inward. The cochlea is subdivided into three parallel canals partitioned by membranes. The oval window lies at the beginning of the **vestibular canal,** and the round window lies at the end of the **tympanic canal.** These two canals are continuous only at the tip of the spiral of the cochlea. Vibrations introduced in the fluid by the oval window must travel all the way up the vestibular canal around the corner and back down the other canal to the round window. Therefore, vibrations are continuously traveling in opposite directions on opposite sides of the cochlea.

Embedded in the central, or cochleal, canal is the actual organ of hearing—the **organ of Corti,** which consists of a string of receptors positioned between two membranes separating the canals (see Figure 12.10C). The receptors, called **hair cells,** lie in the **basilar membrane,** but the tips of the cell extensions, or hairs, project through the fluid and touch the **tectorial membrane.** As the fluids of the canals vibrate in opposite directions, these two membranes likewise move in opposite directions, so that the hairs between them are bent in a kind of rubbing or shearing motion. As a result of this bending, the hair cells produce neural signals that travel via the adjacent **auditory nerve** to the brain, where the sensation of hearing actually takes place.

NEURAL CODING BY THE EAR How the brain distinguishes between high and low tones is not fully understood. Georg von Békésy (1956) found that waves of a given frequency do not vibrate the

tory canal); the middle ear (separated from the outer ear by the eardrum and containing three small bones collectively called ossicles); and the inner ear, or cochlea. (The three semicircular

basilar membrane uniformly. For example, high-frequency waves have maximum effect on the region near the oval window, while low-frequency waves have their maximum effect near the top of the cochlea. According to the **place theory** of pitch, the particular location (place) of maximum displacement on the basilar membrane signals the brain as to the frequency of the sound.

The place theory has been supported by two kinds of data. First, elderly patients with hearing losses for certain high-frequency tones were found to have damage to groups of receptors along specific portions of the basilar membrane, as shown in Figure 12.11 (Crowe et al., 1934). Second, mild electrical stimulation of small groups of neurons leading from different places along the basilar membrane results in the experience of different pitches, depending on the place along the basilar membrane that is stimulated (Simmons et al., 1965). The place theory, however, does not satisfactorily explain how we can tell the difference between very similar low tones, since there is a great deal of overlap in the areas of maximum displacement at low frequencies, or how we can tell the difference between a violin and a flute when both are playing the same musical note.

The capacity to hear any frequency depends on the integrity of the hair cells of the basilar membrane. If a sound of excessive intensity impinges on the ear, the vibrations of the fluids may tear the hairs apart. This leads to irreversible loss of hearing in that frequency range. Although we possess muscles capable of damping, or moderating, the movements of the stirrup in response to high-intensity sound, an extensive amount of hearing loss has already been caused by modern technology—from factories to jet planes to rock music.

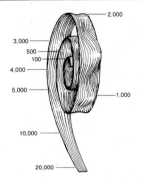

Figure 12.11 The place theory. This diagram shows waves traveling down the basilar membrane and indicates the points at which the waves are largest for a number of different frequencies. Because greater displacement produces more stimulation of the organ of Corti, the brain could use the location of the most rapidly firing cells in the organ of Corti as a code for the frequency of the sound.

THE SKIN SENSES Skin sensations have five basic forms: touch, pressure, warmth, cold, and pain. Receptors for these lie at various depths in the skin, as Figure 12.12 shows, and connect with neurons that transmit information from the receptors to the brain. We do not yet have a clear picture of the relationships between the types of receptors and the types of sensations experienced. The receptors around the roots of hair cells seem to produce the sensation of touch on the skin, while other receptors seem to respond to pressure within muscles and internal organs. Scientists once believed that receptors in free nerve endings in the skin (in contrast to encapsulated nerve endings) were associated only with the sensation of pain. But the cornea of the eye, which almost exclusively contains free nerve endings, is responsive to pressure and

Figure 12.12 A cross-sectional diagram of human skin. A number of different kinds of receptors have been identified near the surface of the skin, but there is considerable uncertainty about their functions. Meissner's corpuscles are believed to be pressure sensitive. Pacinian corpuscles may be additional receptors for "deep" pressure. Free nerve endings may be important in the sensation of pain. It is speculated that Krause bulbs are responsive to cold and Ruffini endings responsive to warmth.

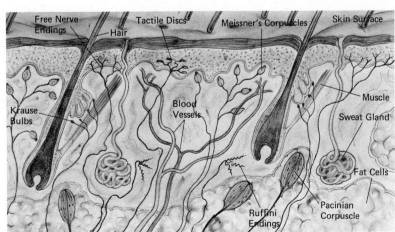

temperature as well as pain. So there is still some confusion about the role of free nerve ending receptors (Geldard, 1972).

WARMTH AND COLD   There is no sensation of warmth or cold when the skin is touched with stimulators that are at skin temperature, usually 32 degrees Celsius; the temperature at which there is no sensation is referred to as **physiological zero.** Warmth is felt at temperatures greater than physiological zero, and cold is felt at temperatures lower than physiological zero.

Warmth and cold are not felt at every point on the skin. If one square centimeter of skin is examined using the small points of special temperature stimulators, only about six spots will be found where cold is felt and one or two spots where warmth is sensed. The separate identity of warm and cold spots is generally accepted, partly because stimulating a cold spot with a hot stimulus sometimes yields a cold sensation. The name for this phenomenon is **paradoxical cold.**

Interestingly, the sensation of "hot" appears to be produced by the simultaneous activation of both warm and cold receptors in a particular area of the skin. This can be demonstrated using an apparatus

like that depicted in Figure 12.13. Cold water flows through one of the tubes, and warm water through the other. If either one of these tubes is touched alone, the appropriate sensation is of course perceived—either warm or cold. However, if you lay your hand across the coils so that warm and cold stimuli are side by side on certain areas of your skin, a stinging hot sensation will be felt, like that caused by grabbing a hot pan from the oven. Apparently the sensation of "hot" is produced by a mixing of information from warm and cold receptors, both of which are activated whenever a hot stimulus touches the skin. This is another example of the synthesizing economy of sensory systems. The apparatus shown in Figure 12.13 provides a way of "fooling" this sensory system into sending a message of hot in the absence of the normally appropriate stimulus.

PRESSURE   Pressure-sensitive receptors in the skin are more responsive to changes in pressure than to steady states. Once the skin has been displaced to accommodate the source of the pressure, the sensation of pressure usually disappears—rapidly, if the force exerted is small. If this were not true, we would be constantly aware of the gentle pressure of clothes, eyeglasses, and so on.

Pressure sensitivity also varies from place to place on the skin. The areas of the body most sensitive to small amounts of pressure are the fingertips, the lips, and the tip of the tongue. Although the pressure thresholds at these points are among the lowest on the skin, the energy required to produce a pressure sensation is from 100 million to 10 billion times greater than the energy required by the eye or the ear to perceive light or hear sound at visual and auditory absolute thresholds.

Researchers have been considering the potential of pressure sensitivity as a means of providing information to the blind. A group of investigators at the Smith-Kettlewell Institute of the University of the Pacific has developed equipment that translates visual images picked up by a television camera into pressure patterns that can be sensed by the skin. The user sits in a chair that has a matrix of small vibrators embedded in the back. The vibrators are attached to the television camera in such a way that they vibrate more in response to brightness than to darkness. People have been successful in learning to "see" simple objects using these skin vibrations (Bliss et al., 1970; White et al., 1970).

Figure 12.13 With ice water flowing through one of the tubes of this coil, and warm water at about 105°F. flowing through the other tube, the person placing a hand on the coil will feel a burning hot sensation.

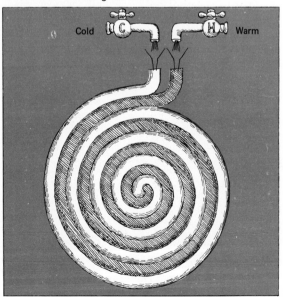

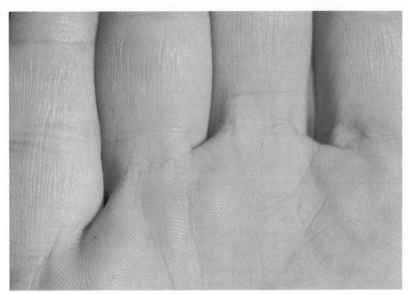

Our hands are extremely sensitive to pressure.

PAIN Pain is associated with more than just the skin. However, we know little about pain from the interior of the body except that it seems to be deep, difficult to pinpoint, and often more unpleasant than the bright, localized pain from the skin. Many kinds of stimuli—scratch, puncture, pressure, heat, cold, twist—can produce pain. Their common property is real or potential injury to bodily tissue.

Pain thresholds vary considerably from person to person or from time to time. In the laboratory, mild cutaneous (skin) pain has been shown to disappear with prolonged stimulation, but there is little adaptation to pain under ordinary circumstances. Pain serves the crucial function of signaling us that something is amiss, and so it is fortunate that we do not adapt to it. The value of pain as a danger signal is clearly indicated by the situation of people who are born without the ability to feel pain. Such people may experience severe burns, broken bones, or even a ruptured appendix, but they will not be alerted by pain signals either to protect themselves against further injury or to seek medical attention. For further discussion of pain perception, see the accompanying special feature.

THE CHEMICAL SENSES The chemical senses of taste and smell are closely related to one another. The receptors for these senses are located close together—in the mouth, throat, and nasal cavity—and the separate sensations detected by the nose and mouth are often confused or experienced as one sensation. Smell and taste interact, particularly in the appreciation of food. Without the sense of smell, the subtleties of food flavor cannot be appreciated. For instance, if you taste an apple and a raw potato while blocking your nose, you will have difficulty distinguishing between them. In the same way, you may have noticed that food has a flat and uninteresting flavor when you have a bad head cold.

SMELL It is a common tendency to consider the sense of smell, or **olfaction,** as one of the "lower" senses. This tendency may have something to do with the fact that olfaction does not provide as much information for what are called the "higher mental functions" (for example, reasoning and memory) as do vision and hearing. A principal function of smell for human beings seems to be to warn of potentially dangerous stimuli—particularly odors coming from toxic substances that might be eaten or inhaled. Thus we may simply be more attentive to instances of odors that are unpleasant. However, odor is a major basis for one of life's greatest pleasures, eating, and this pleasure is backed by multimillion-dollar spice and condiment industries. It is also difficult to imagine how the perfume industry could survive if people were indifferent to pleasant odors.

The sense organ for olfaction is the **olfactory epithelium,** located at the top of the nasal passages and connected to the base of the brain. Millions of hair cells projecting from the olfactory epithelium are sensitive to molecules of volatile substances, and they transduce this kind of information into neural impulses.

The Sensation of Pain: Pieces of the Puzzle

All of us know pain; in fact, it is dangerous not to. Those rare individuals born without sensitivity to pain often incur terrible burns and cuts, unaware that their very lives are threatened. In the past decade or so the subject of pain has attracted an extraordinary amount of scientific interest. Investigators have studied pain thresholds; the puzzling phenomenon of referred pain; the pathways pain travels through the body; and several promising new methods of blocking pain.

Thresholds of Pain

Our knowledge of the physiology of both pain and pain relief is still tantalizingly incomplete. Pain research, especially on humans, is complex, partly because the experience of pain is greatly influenced by emotional factors. In the excitement of combat, whether on the battlefield or the soccer field, perception of pain may temporarily vanish. Doctors are also aware that different people have different pain thresholds—different points at which they begin to perceive pain. Patients who are not anxious have higher pain thresholds than those who are; women tend to have lower pain thresholds than men; and laborers and miners tend to have higher thresholds than clerical workers (Merskey, 1973). It used to be thought that chronic pain was largely psychogenic, but this idea is now increasingly deemphasized (Liebeskind and Paul, 1977).

Phantom Limb Pain

One of the most puzzling phenomena is "phantom limb pain." About 35 percent of all amputees report feeling pain in

An acupuncture treatment.

the amputated limb, which still feels so "present" to most amputees that they may reach for objects with a phantom hand or try to step out of bed on a phantom leg (Melzack, 1973). It is not clear just how pain can be perceived from an area that obviously no longer exists. Probably the phenomenon has several causes; it may even be that the information-processing mechanism of the central nervous system itself has been

damaged, so that messages and their reception are abnormal.

Referred Pain

Referred pain is another piece of the puzzle that is just beginning to be understood. Several diseases cause referred pain in parts of the body that are not themselves diseased. Heart-attack victims, for instance, often experience pain in the shoulder and upper chest.

Several points on the shoulder and chest are known as "trigger zones" for heart disease; brief pressure on these points in heart patients may cause intense pain that lasts for hours (Melzack, 1973, p. 172). Referred pain patterns are so consistent that a doctor can often locate the site of the disease by the pain pattern. Curiously, anesthetic agents such as novocaine injected into trigger zones erase the referred pain and often erase the pain of the diseased organ or muscle as well. A single injection may greatly reduce the frequency of painful attacks. Intense cold applied to trigger zones can have the same effect. Astonishingly, so can "dry needling," which involves simply moving a needle in and out without injecting anything at all. It is assumed, but not proved, that trigger points send constant, low-level messages to the central nervous system which may combine with messages from the diseased organ to produce feelings of pain in larger skin areas around the trigger zones (Melzack, 1973, p. 176).

A New Theory of Pain

In 1965, Ronald Melzack and P. D. Wall proposed a "gate-control theory" of pain, which provides an explanation for many of the phenomena of referred pain and phantom limb pain. The theory suggests that there is a "gating mechanism" in the brain which, if open, intensifies pain signals traveling up through the spinal cord and, if closed, prevents them from arriving in full strength. If, as evidence strongly suggests, there are indeed areas of the brain which can block off the neural pathways that convey pain sensations from the body, identification of these areas could greatly aid the battle against pain.

New Techniques for Control of Pain

One old-fashioned method of pain relief that is being newly investigated is hyperstimulation analgesia, or counter-irritation, familiar to most of us in the form of mustard plasters, ice packs, and hot water bottles. Recent experiments indicate that one pain can measurably raise the threshold for another: for example, application of painful cold to the shin of either leg causes a 30 percent rise in the pain threshold for electrical stimulation of the teeth (Melzack, 1973).

Possibly acupuncture, the ancient Chinese method of anesthesia, is a special form of hyperstimulation analgesia, since its effect depends on stimulation by needles inserted into the skin at specific sites of the body, which may be far from the site of injury or disease. Major surgery has been performed on patients with acupuncture as the primary anesthetic; with

needles inserted and continuously twirled in wrist, ear, neck, or elsewhere, the patient remains comfortable enough to chat with doctors throughout the operation.

Hypnosis is another method of pain relief that has limited application but occasionally startling results. Some people have even undergone major surgery under hypnosis, although total hypnotic anesthesia can be produced in only 20 percent of patients even by competent, professional hypnotists (Melzack, 1973, p. 185).

The key to the effectiveness of hyperstimulation analgesia and acupuncture may be that they involve indirect stimulation of certain areas of the brain. Today a number of neurosurgeons are experimenting with direct stimulation of selected brain areas by means of surgically implanted electrodes. This technique has brought dramatic improvement to some patients who suffer intractable pain that will not respond to more conventional treatment (Marx, 1977).

Perhaps the most amazing discovery of recent years is that the brain produces its own pain-killing agents, known as endorphins, which mimic the effects of morphine. Stimulation of the brain, and acupuncture too, may work by triggering the release of endorphins. It has been suggested that all mammals have a powerful capacity for pain control, and that human beings, with the ability to believe and hope, may have more direct access to it than other mammals. The challenge lies in discovering the sites and the pathways of this invaluable capacity for pain control that may lie hidden in each of us.

American soap ad. Smelling "clean" is important in our culture.

edge of the physical characteristics of odor stimuli, the answer to the deceptively simple question, "How do we smell things?" remains elusive.

TASTE As implied in the discussion of smell, when people describe how food "tastes," they are including its odor, which circulates from the back of the mouth up to the olfactory receptors. Compared to olfaction, taste seems to be somewhat restricted. Odor sources can be detected and identified from a distance, but taste sources must be in contact with the mouth. In addition, most people can identify and discriminate hundreds of odors, but when odor and other sensory components are eliminated, only four basic categories of taste appear to be perceived: sweet, sour, salty, and bitter. Other taste sensations are generally regarded as mixtures of these four basic qualities (Bartoshuk, 1971).

The four qualities seem to be somewhat independent: they can be selectively suppressed and are differently affected by certain drugs. For example, if you eat sugar after chewing the leaves of a certain plant (*Gymnema sylvestre*), the sugar does not taste sweet, and it feels like sand (Bartoshuk et al., 1969).

Most odors to which human beings are sensitive are organic compounds, but little else is known about why people can smell some substances and not others or why certain groups of odors smell alike. A theory proposed by John Amoore suggests that the quality of an odor is related to the physical size and shape of the molecules that make up the odorous substance. In support of this "stereochemical" theory, two researchers (Amoore and Venstrum, 1967) have shown that people's judgments of the similarities between odors are correlated with measures of molecular similarity. Unfortunately, this relationship between chemical structure and subjective odor does not hold for all substances, and so we are still unable to describe exactly the physical basis of odor sensations.

A number of attempts have been made to classify odors strictly on the basis of people's subjective judgments. The most popular classification scheme is Hans Henning's smell prism, shown in Figure 12.14 (Henning, 1916). Six supposedly pure qualities form the corners of the prism, and the intermediate qualities lie along the surface. The reason for the development of such a scheme is that it may provide a clue to the chemical properties that distinguish the members of one class of odors from the members of other classes. Without this knowl-

Figure 12.14 Henning's smell prism. Supposedly, every possible smell sensation can be located somewhere on the surface of this solid. This theoretical description of smell implies that certain smells are impossible. For example, a putrid, flowery, burned, spicy smell should be possible, but not a putrid, flowery, resinous smell. Where on this surface would you place the smell of a fresh, ripe peach?

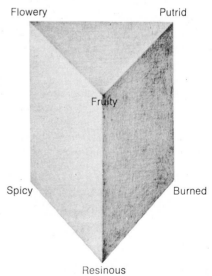

Figure 12.15 (A) A map of the human tongue showing the areas of maximum sensitivity to the four fundamental kinds of taste sensation. (B) The tastes of a number of foods analyzed into the four components of taste shown in A. The length of the colored bars indicates the amount of each component judged to be present in the taste of the food by a number of subjects in a psychophysical experiment. (Data from Beebe-Center, 1949.)

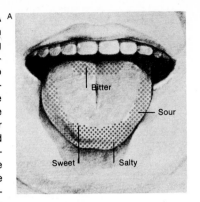

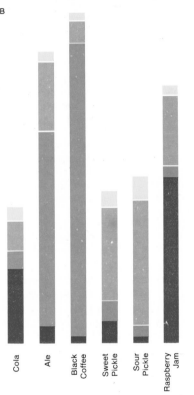

tion to the brain. Interestingly, in several species of animals the individual nerve fibers leading from these cells respond to more than one kind of taste (Pfaffman, 1955). This suggests the possibility that the neural code for different tastes may be based on different patterns of activity in the thousands of taste nerve fibers leading from the tongue, in contrast to the possibility that each nerve fiber carries a message regarding only one of the basic taste stimuli.

BALANCE, POSTURE, AND MOVEMENT We are very much aware of our balance, posture, movement, and orientation in space. The vestibular and kinesthetic senses cooperate to produce that awareness.

Approximately 10,000 taste buds in this woman's mouth contribute to the flavor sensations that she is perceiving.

Also, the drug cocaine temporarily eliminates taste sensations in a certain order: bitter disappears first, then sweet, then salty, and finally sour (Moncrieff, 1967). In addition, different areas of the tongue are especially sensitive to the four basic taste qualities, as shown in Figure 12.15.

The specific sensation of taste results from stimulation of the **taste buds** in the mouth and tongue. The surface of the human tongue contains about 10,000 of these structures, grouped in projections known as **papillae**. The taste buds contain the receptor cells for taste stimuli, and these cells are connected to nerve fibers that carry taste informa-

THE VESTIBULAR SENSE The **vestibular sense** contributes to balance. We are never directly aware of a vestibular sensation because of the difficulty of ascribing it to any particular part of the body.

The vestibular sense organ lies in the inner ear, buried in the bone above and to the rear of the cochlea. Its prominent position is the three fluid-filled **semicircular canals,** which lie at right angles to each other, as shown in Figure 12.16. A movement of the head causes the fluid in the canals to move against and bend the endings of receptor hair cells. The hair cells connect with the vestibular nerve, which joins the auditory nerve on its way to the brain.

The vestibular responses are stimulated by rotational or linear acceleration, falling, and tilting of the body or head. These stimuli produce some interesting interactions with the eye-movement systems. For example, rapid rotation about the longitudinal axis of the body, such as that produced by spinning on skates, can result in vestibular nystagmus, a rapid back-and-forth motion of the eyes. Vestibular nystagmus can also occur when a person stops spinning, though in this instance it results from the fluid in the semicircular canals continuing to move after spinning has stopped. Another type of nystagmus can be induced by running hot water into the external ear canal. The heat of the water transfers to the semicircular canals and starts the fluid in them moving: caloric nystagmus results. Running warm water into your ear from the shower can often produce this effect.

THE KINESTHETIC SENSE **Kinesthesis** is the sense of body movement and position. It cooperates with the vestibular and visual senses to maintain balance and equilibrium. The receptor cells for the kinesthetic sense are in the nerve endings in and near

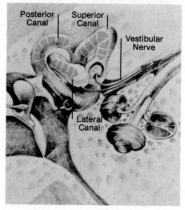

Figure 12.16 The vestibular system. Compare this figure with Figure 12.10 to see where it is located in the ear. The organs of balance are three fluid-filled semicircular canals arranged at right angles to one another. The inertia of the fluid inside at least one of the canals causes it to move relative to the walls of the canals whenever the motion of the head speeds up, slows down, or changes direction. The motion of the fluid drags tiny stones over hair cells in the walls of the canals, and the hair cells transmit impulses to the brain.

the more than one hundred body joints and in the muscles. The nerve endings in the joints are especially important for sensing bodily movement; the particular receptors that respond depend on the direction and angle of movement. Nerve endings in the muscles and tendons also contribute to the sensation of kinesthesis. Together, these various receptors provide the feedback necessary for regulation of active body movement. Kinesthesis and the vestibular sense cooperate to foster efficient and coordinated locomotion. Vision also plays an important role in this process—another demonstration of the fact that we seldom use one sense alone, but almost always use many senses at once.

SUMMARY

1. Our senses are the tools by which we gather information about our constantly changing environment. Sensory systems are *selective;* they respond to certain stimuli, but not to others. The contributions of scientists in the fields of *psychophysics* and *sensory physiology* to the study of human sensory systems are discussed in this chapter.

2. **A stimulus** can be defined as any form of energy to which our senses respond, such as a light wave for our sense of vision or a sound wave for our sense of hearing. Stimuli can be measured physically (e.g., with a light meter or a thermometer) or psychologically (e.g., an individual reporting the **sensations** experienced as a result of the stimulus). Psychological measurements include

reports describing both the **quality** and **quantity** of a stimulus. In the case of a visual stimulus, quality might refer to its color or hue, while quantity might refer to its brightness. The properties of a stimulus that a subject is able to report (such as hue, brightness, pitch, loudness) are called the psychological dimensions of sensation.

A. A concept basic to the study of sensation involves the smallest amount of a stimulus, or stimulus change, that is required for a person to experience a particular sensation. This is referred to as the concept of **threshold.**

   1. An **absolute threshold** refers to the minimum stimulus necessary to produce a specific sensation.
   2. The study of **detection thresholds** involves a person's ability to detect minimal stimuli when background **noise** (additional or distracting stimulation) is present. The **signal detection theory** holds that there is no single true absolute threshold for a stimulus. Instead, a stimulus, or **signal,** must be detected in the presence of interfering stimuli or noise.
   3. Another type of threshold is the **difference threshold** or **just noticeable difference.** This refers to the smallest physical change in a stimulus that will produce a change in sensation.

B. Several psychologists have observed that the magnitude of a stimulus and the magnitude of its corresponding sensation can be described as a ratio between the two quantities.

   1. **Weber's law** (1834) stated that the amount of a stimulus required to produce a just noticeable difference is always a constant proportion of the intensity of the stimulus.
   2. According to **Fechner's law** (1860), the intensity of a sensation increases proportionately with the magnitude of the stimulus. However, although this proportionality is generally found for stimuli of moderate magnitude, it does not hold for either very strong or very weak stimuli.
   3. **Stevens' power law** (1957) emphasized that the exact properties of the relationship between stimulus magnitude and sensation differ for each of the senses.

C. Following prolonged or constant stimulation, an adjustment in sensory capacity, known as **adaptation,** occurs. Adaptation decreases sensitivity, but it can also distort sensations. Sensations resulting from a particular stimulus are not determined by that stimulus alone. For example, the brightness of a certain light will be judged differently depending on whether the person's eyes had previously been adapted to bright sunlight or to very dim light.

3. All of our sense organs function on the basis of similar principles. Receptors sensitive to specific types of stimuli are found in each sense organ. Each type of receptor converts environmental stimuli into neural impulses. This process is called **transduction.**

4. Light waves are the basic stimuli involved in vision. Two characteristics of light are particularly important for vision: **wavelength** (which determines color) and **intensity** (which determines brightness).

A. There are four major structures that make up the eye. These are the **cornea,** the **iris,** the **lens,** and the **retina.** Light enters the eye through the **pupil,** an opening in the center of the eye through which light passes to the lens. The curvature of the lens can be altered by the ciliary muscles attached to it. These muscles change the curvature of the lens in such a way as to focus the light and produce a clear image on the retina.

B. The retina contains two types of neural cells (**bipolar cells** and **ganglion cells**) and two types of **receptors** that transduce light energy into neural impulses. The two kinds of receptors are called **rods** and **cones.** Receptor cells stimulate bipolar cells, which pass their information to ganglion cells; the ganglion cells form part of the **optic nerve,** which relays the visual information to the brain. The two types of receptor cells have different functions. The cones are involved in color vision and are found in greatest quantity in the center of the retina, in an area called the **fovea.** The cones are also responsible for our visual acuity. The rods, on the other hand, provide vision of light and dark; they do not require as much light as the cones in order to be stimulated. **Rhodopsin** is a chemical pigment found in the rods; the more pigment present in the rods, the more sensitive the eye is to light. Bright light bleaches this pigment in the rods, which is why you can't see very well when you enter a dark room after being in the sunlight. It takes time for **dark adaptation** to occur, and this corresponds to the time necessary to rebuild the receptor pigments.

C. The predominant view of color vision is the **trichromatic theory.** It states that there are three types of cones, one type highly sensitive to red light, another to green light, and the third to blue light. Different wavelengths of light stimulate different cones, and the color we see depends on how many of each type are stimulated.

1. Another color vision process involves cells other than cones. The **opponent-processes theory** claims that **color-opponent cells** exist in one part of the brain. These cells are stimulated when the eye sees one color, and are inhibited by the opposite or **complementary** color. The phenomenon of **afterimages** supports this theory, since people often report seeing blue shortly after a quick intense flash of yellow light, its complement, or red after a flash of its complement, green light. A person with normal color vision is called a **trichromat,** someone able to distinguish three major wavelengths of light corresponding to red, green, and blue. A **dichromat** is a person in whom one of the three cone systems is absent or deficient. People who are totally color-blind or **monochromatic** are very rare; they can see only shades of gray.

5. Analogous to the visual system is the auditory system, where auditory receptors in the ears transduce sound waves into neural signals. Waves of compressed and rarefied air particles travel through the air and strike the eardrum, causing it to vibrate. The **frequency** of a sound wave is determined by the number of compression-rarefaction cycles that occur within some period of time. The frequency and the **pitch** of a sound are related in that the higher the frequency, the higher the tone will sound. The human ear is capable of hearing frequencies ranging from about 20 to 20,000 cycles per second. The **intensity** of a sound wave corresponds to the amplitude of the wave, and is reflected in the loudness of the sound. **Decibels** are a measure of loudness or amplitude.

A. The ear is divided into three major structures: the outer ear, the middle ear, and the inner ear. The outer ear is composed of the pinna

and the auditory canal. The **tympanic membrane (eardrum)** separates the outer ear and middle ear. The middle ear contains three small bones or **ossicles** known as the **hammer,** the **anvil,** and the **stirrup.** The stirrup is attached to another membrane called the **oval window,** which separates the middle ear from the inner ear. The inner chamber of the ear, called the **cochlea,** is filled with fluid and contains a membranous spot called the **round window.** The cochlea is divided into three parallel canals separated by membranes: the **vestibular canal,** the **tympanic canal,** and the central, or cochlea canal, which contains the actual organ of hearing, known as the **organ of Corti.** The receptors are **hair cells** found in the organ of Corti. The hair cells lie in the **basilar membrane,** but the tips of the hairs reach through the fluid and touch the **tectorial membrane.** The canal fluids vibrate in opposite directions in response to an auditory stimulus. This causes the membranes to move in opposite directions, which in turn causes the bending of hair cells, leading to the production of neural signals that travel to the brain via the auditory nerve, where the sensation of hearing actually takes place. Sounds of very high intensity may damage the hair cells. This results in an irreversible hearing loss in that frequency range.

1. Waves of different frequencies do not vibrate the basilar membrane uniformly. The **place theory** of pitch states that the specific place of maximum displacement on the basilar membrane indicates to the brain the specific frequency of a sound.

6. There are five basic types of skin sensations: touch, pressure, warmth, cold, and pain. Receptors for these sensations can be found at various depths within the skin. These receptors are connected to neurons that relay the sensory information to the brain.

A. If the skin is touched by a stimulator that is at skin temperature, neither a cold nor a warm sensation will be felt. This temperature at which no sensation occurs is called **physiological zero.** Warmth is felt at temperatures above physiological zero, and cold is felt at temperatures below it. A phenomenon known as **parodoxical cold** supports the existence of separate temperature-sensitive spots on the skin. This is the phenomenon whereby stimulation of a cold spot with a hot stimulus results in a cold sensation.

B. The skin also contains receptors that are sensitive to pressure changes. The body areas most sensitive to small amounts of pressure are the fingertips, the lips, and the tip of the tongue.

C. The sensation of pain is associated with the skin as well as with the interior of the body, although little is known about the latter type of pain. Pain acts as a danger signal, alerting us to real or potential bodily injury.

7. The chemical senses of *taste* and *smell* are closely associated, and the receptors for these senses are located close together in the mouth, throat, and nasal cavity.

A. The major function of **olfaction** (our sense of smell) is to warn us about potentially toxic substances that might be inhaled or eaten. However, we are attentive to many pleasant as well as unpleasant odors. The hair cells projecting from the **olfactory epithelium** (found at the top of the nasal passages) transduce olfactory information into neural impulses.

B. There are only four basic categories of tastes, and they can be detected only through direct contact with the mouth. The four categories of taste are sweet, sour, salty, and bitter. The surface of the human tongue contains about 10,000 **taste buds,** which are the structures that contain the actual receptor cells for taste stimuli.

8. Our vestibular and kinesthetic senses provide our awareness of balance, posture, movement, and spatial orientation.

A. The **vestibular sense** is related to balance. The three fluid-filled **semicircular canals** within the cochlea constitute the vestibular sense organ. Head movements cause the movement of fluid within the canals, which in turn bends the receptor hair cells. These hair cells connect with the vestibular nerve, which joins the auditory nerve on its way to the brain.

B. **Kinesthesis** refers to the sense of body movement and position. It works together with the vestibular and visual senses to maintain balance and equilibrium. Receptor cells for the kinesthetic sense are found in nerve endings in and near joints, muscles, and tendons. Together, these receptors provide the feedback necessary for regulation of active body movements.

RECOMMENDED READINGS

BORING, EDWIN G. *Sensation and Perception in the History of Experimental Psychology.* New York: Appleton-Century-Crofts, 1942. Essential for a historical appreciation of sensation and psychophysics. This classic book is especially noteworthy for its treatment of the attributes of sensation and the historical antecedents of modern color theory.

GELDARD, FRANK A. *The Human Senses.* 2nd ed. New York: Wiley, 1972. A thorough review of basic information about all the senses.

MARX, LAWRENCE E. *Sensory Processes: The New Psychophysics.* New York: Academic Press, 1974. A basic, scholarly presentation of psychophysics by a noted expert in the field.

UTTAL, WILLIAM R. *The Psychobiology of Sensory Coding.* New York: Harper & Row, 1973. A comprehensive account of the relationships between neural processes and sensation and perception.

CHAPTER THIRTEEN

PERCEPTION

There are certain statements of belief that are often called "folk wisdom" for no other reason than that they originate out of the unsophisticated observation of the world by people of limited experience. In almost every case they might be considered "folk stupidity" and laughed at if it weren't that so many tragic consequences have followed from what everyone "knew" was true but wasn't. How many unfounded accusations have ruined lives and precipitated riots because "Where there's smoke there's fire"? Dry Ice in water produces fascinating smoke without fire. And would we ever be exploring the Moon if it were really true that "everything that goes up most come down"?

But to me the most pernicious piece of "folk wisdom" is the one about "Seeing is believing," when it is phenomenally easy to fool the eye. In the Greek myth Narcissus drowned himself because the beautiful young man he saw in the water wasn't really there.

The trouble is that very early in life we learn that light travels in straight lines. Very young children reach for something by following rays of light backward in a straight line, and very often they succeed in making physical contact with what they have seen. We never break the habit of interpreting all light as a straight-line phenomenon, even though light travels in a straight line only under restricted conditions. If we place a stick in water, light from that portion of the stick below the water level is refracted as it passes from water to air. The straight stick seems bent at the water level, and no matter how much our intelligence tells us that it is not the stick that is bent by the rays of light, what we see is that the stick is bent. We cannot argue ourselves out of that.

Our inability to appreciate the vagaries of light are at the base of a large proportion of our mystical beliefs. Ghosts and spirits are born in a world in which there is no artificial illumination other than the flickering of an open flame. Why has the ghost story lost its earlier popularity? Because the steady, dim shadows cast by a frosted light bulb are nothing like the shifting mysterious shadows cast by unsteady flames. Ghosts can't survive steady light.

And what about those modern ghosts called "flying saucers"? Where the report is not an outright hoax, it is a matter of some sort of light being seen in the sky; and I suspect that in very many cases it is a matter of light refraction. A light ray curves through air in layers of varying temperature and density, so that you see a light in a place it should not be because your eye and mind don't follow the curve but insist on moving along a straight line tangent to the curve at the point where it enters the eye. Distant lights of a city or a line of automobile headlights will therefore appear in the sky.

But always, the cry of "Seeing is believing" goes up. I'm afraid not. As far as I'm concerned, the proper wisdom is "Seeing is merely seeing, nothing more." Belief requires a lot more than the complicated trickery of a light wave.

Isaac Asimov

In the next few seconds, something peculiar will start hap pening to the material youa rereading. Iti soft ennotre alized howcom plext heproces sofrea ding is. Afe w sim plerear range mentscan ha vey oucomp lete lycon fused!

Normally, we process sensory information from the environment without being aware that we are doing so. We read the words on a page without noticing how we interpret the patterns of lines and letters in order to read. We can listen to a train in the distance and tell whether it is coming from the north or south, but we are not aware of precisely how we determine the train's location and direction of travel. Such information processing takes place quickly, without conscious effort. When we encounter something like the garbled paragraph above, however, we notice that our perception of words and sentences is tied to a particular organization of letters and separating spaces. While the letters provide the basic information (or stimuli), we interpret the sentences according to the way the letters are arranged and spaced. This interpretation process is analogous to the way perception proceeds from sensation.

FROM SENSATION TO PERCEPTION

Perception can be defined as an organism's awareness of objects and events in the environment, brought about by stimulation of the organism's sense organs. Although it is impossible to completely separate perception from sensation, the perceptual process has traditionally been considered to be the more complex of the two; it is perception that presents an organism with a meaningful interpretation of its basic sensations. The sensations of "redness" and "roundness," for example, contribute to our visual perception of an apple. Likewise, in the dark, a certain odor, crunchy sound, sweet taste, and smooth, waxy feel yield the same perception—an apple—but the perception is based on sensations different from the ones we experience when we see the object. What we call an "apple" is all these sensations and more, of course, but we need only a few

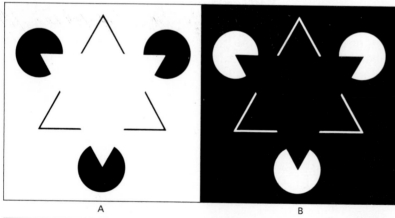

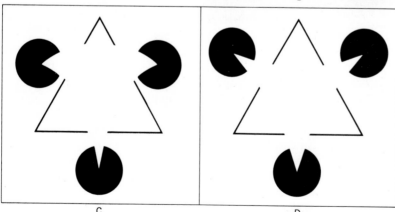

Figure 13.1 Subjective contours. The brain seeks to tie the components of an incomplete picture together by creating the perception of contours that complete the picture. (A) The subjective contours form a white triangle in the middle of this visual image. (B) In this case, the outline of a center triangle is perceived once again, but this time the triangle appears black as the result of the background color. C and D illustrate the fact that subjective contours may be curved as well as straight. (After Kanizsa, 1976.)

Figure 13.2 Although this version of da Vinci's *Mona Lisa* is highly distorted, our brain is capable of enhancing the perceptual details of this picture in such a way that we are able to recognize its resemblance to the original painting. Such block portraits are made with a flying-spot scanner, a device similar to a television camera. (After Harmon, 1973.)

of them to accurately and automatically interpret what we are sensing as an apple.

What happens in the brain obviously plays an important role in our ability to understand what is "out there." It is the brain that organizes and gives meaning to the limited information gathered by our senses. When the sensory information we receive from the environment is limited or incomplete, brain processes appear to "fill in" to create a complete and detailed perception. An example of this filling-in is provided by an analysis of **subjective contours** (Kanizsa, 1976). A subjective contour is a line or shape that *appears* to be present in a figure, but is actually not physically there. Examine the drawings presented in Figure 13.1. The shapes appear to have distinct contours. However, if you examine them closely, you will see that some of the lines that define the shapes do not actually exist. The lines are perceptually apparent but physically nonexistent. Subjective contours appear naturally when certain types of stimuli are presented. According to Kanizsa, we perceive these contours when the elements in our visual field are incomplete, for they are the result of the brain's automatic attempt to enhance and complete the details of a partial image.

This same process seems to operate when we examine Figure 13.2. The coarsely grained distribution of light and dark squares will probably be interpreted as the famous *Mona Lisa*. Even though the

sensory impression is merely a degraded shadow of the elegant and detailed da Vinci painting, our brain processes fill in the missing details to make the image resemble the original painting (Harmon, 1973). Notice how the picture seems to become more detailed if you move farther away from it and squint your eyes.

In addition to giving missing information, brain processes compensate for misleading distortions in information. A striking example of this ability is provided in the work of G. M. Stratton (1896), who wore spectacles that turned the retinal image upside down. At first, Stratton had great difficulty coordinating vision and movement, because he saw everything inverted. However, after about a week he adjusted enough that he could walk around fairly normally. Although he no longer perceived the world as being upside down, he did note that things did not look quite normal.

Ivo Kohler (1962) studied this same "compensation" phenomenon using prism goggles that moderately distorted vision, such as by making straight lines appear curved. Initially, wearers of the goggles described their environment as fluid and unstable. Within a relatively short time, however, the subjects began to compensate for the distortions produced by the goggles, and they reported little difficulty in coordinating their movements within their newly stabilized perceptions. It is interesting to note that when the goggles were removed after weeks or months of use, the subjects experienced difficulty adjusting to this change. Instead of seeing a "normal" world, they responded as if they were now wearing goggles that distorted in the opposite direction from those originally used. For instance, when goggles that produced line curvature to the left were removed, the subjects saw a curvature to the right. With time, these compensatory distortions disappeared, and the world appeared stable again.

Brain activity can also create perceptions even in the absence of appropriate sensory stimulation. We sometimes have visual experiences without using our eyes, as in dreams, auditory experiences without using our ears, and so on. Subjects in sensory deprivation experiments who were cut off from almost all external stimulation have experienced vivid and intense sensations that seemed to come from the outside world (Bexton, Heron, and Scott, 1954).

Perhaps the most convincing evidence of the brain's role in perception comes from the results of research using electrical brain stimulation, as described in Chapter 11. Although such stimulation is applied directly to the brain, and therefore completely bypasses the sense organs, subjects often report a clear perception of nonexistent sights, sounds, and feelings.

Perception, then, does not depend exclusively on the activities of the sense organs. An essential part of the perceptual process is the manner in which the environmental stimuli received by the senses are organized by the brain so that the stimuli have meaning.

PERCEPTUAL ORGANIZATION

The world we perceive is enormously complex. We see, for example, objects of various sizes, shapes, and colors; we see them as separate units distinguished from other visual units; we see them arranged in three-dimensional space, as moving or stationary. How are we able to perceive a three-dimensional world when the images received by the retina are two-dimensional and upside down? How are we able to perceive a stable environment, even though our retinas receive constantly changing stimuli? What gives rise to our perception of motion? In this section we will discuss some explanations of how we perceive.

GESTALT PRINCIPLES According to Gestalt psychologists, we are constantly organizing bits and pieces of information into meaningful patterns. These patterns are called **gestalts**, after the German word for "pattern" or "whole." Because of the organization of the black patches in Figure 13.3B, for example, we can perceive the form of a dog; a slight rearrangement of the patches would obscure this perception. The dog's form is a gestalt, a perceptual whole. Although we can see each of the elements in the pattern, more than just these elements is perceived—we recognize the whole form of the dog. Therefore, the gestalt is said to be greater than the sum of its parts.

Gestalt psychology originated in Germany early in the twentieth century with psychologists such as Max Wertheimer, Kurt Koffa, and Wolfgang Köhler, and its influence extends into present-day psychology. In their research, the early gestalt psychologists presented people with various patterns—often consisting of dots or musical tones—and simply asked the people what they saw or heard. From their data they formulated a number of principles to explain how sensory stimuli are structured so as to lead to the perception of gestalts. Two of the major concepts they came up with are grouping and figure-ground.

GROUPING **Grouping** is the structuring together of sensory data. Several of the organizing principles of grouping are illustrated in Figure 13.4. In part A, dots of equal size are spaced equally across a field, and no stable distinguishing pattern is perceived. In part B, the dots are seen as forming a series of four parallel lines, because some dots have been moved closer together; this demonstrates the principle of **proximity**, the grouping of stimuli that are close together. In part C, when a few dots are added, these four lines are seen as two curved lines. In this case, the principle of **continuity** overrules the influence of proximity: dots that form a single, continuous grouping are seen as a gestalt. Another organizing principle is **similarity**; in part D, a cross is perceived in the original pattern of dots because of the similarity of the dots making up the cross.

These principles of grouping apply not only to vision but to other senses as well. For instance, both proximity and continuity influence the gestalt of a musical composition. The notes of a melody are automatically grouped according to their proximity in time. However, in a composition that includes two melody lines played simultaneously—for example, a fugue by Bach—the principle of continuity overrides proximity. That is, if two notes are played close together in time, but are not part of the same melody, they are not perceived as a gestalt.

Julian Hochberg (1964), Fred Attneave (1954), and others have pointed out that all these principles of grouping can be integrated under a single con-

A **Figure 13.3** (A) In looking at this picture, we strive to organize the various patches into a meaningful array, or gestalt. Initially, a few of the patches may begin to form meaningful groups; then all the patches together eventually come to be perceived as a horse and rider. Note that once this meaning is ascribed to the picture, it is almost impossible to view it again as just a random aggregation of spots. (B) A stable differentiation of the elements of this picture into figure and ground is difficult at first, and would probably be impossible if you had no previous knowledge of or experience with Dalmatian dogs. The knowledge that there is a Dalmatian dog in this picture, however, makes it possible to differentiate one set of spots as figure and the other spots as undifferentiated ground. (A After Carraher and Thurston, 1966.)

B

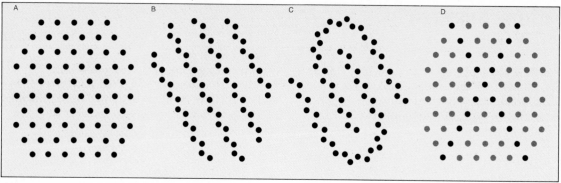

Figure 13.4 A demonstration of some of the gestalt principles of organization. The pattern of equally spaced identical dots in A is not easily organized. It is seen either as an undifferentiated field or as a set of unstable overlapping patterns. In B a stable perception of parallel lines emerges because of the *proximity* of some dots to others. When some of these lines are made *continuous* with one another in C, dots that are physically quite distant from one another are seen as belonging to a single curved line. In D a very stable organization emerges suddenly because some of the dots have been made *similar* to one another and different from the rest.

cept: **simplicity**. Simple patterns are more easily perceived than complex patterns, regardless of whether the simplicity is a result of proximity, continuity, similarity, or some other principle of perceptual organization. For example, despite conflicting cues and possible interpretations, Figure 13.5 is seen as two interlocking circles, by far the simplest way to perceive it.

FIGURE AND GROUND Another basic perceptual pattern is the division into figure and ground. When we look at a scene that has any detail, we automatically separate it into regions that represent objects, or **figure**, and regions that represent spaces between objects, or **ground**. This ability to distinguish objects from space does not seem to depend on past experience. Marius von Senden (1960) found that when people who have been blind from birth have an eye operation that gives them sight, they very quickly seem able to separate figure from ground, although they have never had any experience with visual detail.

Figure 13.5 An illustration of the perceptual tendency toward simplicity. Despite conflicting cues, this figure is seen as two intersecting circles. The circle is among the simplest of perceived forms and provides by far the simplest means of interpreting this pattern.

While visual experience is not absolutely necessary for perceiving figure and ground, it does seem to have some effect on this perception, particularly when most of the normal sensory cues have been removed. In Figure 13.3B, for example, you will not at first be able to differentiate the dots and blotches into figure and ground. After some effort, you may be able to see a Dalmatian dog. Your perception of a single figure against a ground depends on your knowledge of what a Dalmatian dog looks like; without this knowledge, gained from experience, the perception probably would be extremely difficult. According to Louis Thurstone (1944), young children are unable to see these blotches as a single figure. Thus, experience allows figure and ground to be distinguished more easily.

Figure-ground perceptions are not merely visual. For example, when we follow someone's voice at a noisy party, that voice becomes the figure and all other sounds become ground. If we shift our attention to another voice, the second voice replaces the first as figure. Similarly, if we walk into a kitchen filled with unfamiliar cooking odors and suddenly recognize the odor of brewing coffee, that odor becomes figure, leaving the other odors as ground.

Most psychologists who study perception have accepted the notion of gestalt and the principles of perceptual patterning, but they have gone beyond this analysis to focus on still other processes that influence the way we organize sensory information. The following phenomena illustrate some of these other processes.

PERCEPTUAL CONSTANCY When we move toward a tree, the image that it casts on the retina gets larger, its color grows more distinct, and the details of the branches and trunk become sharper. Yet we know that the tree is not becoming larger, more colorful, or more detailed. In the same way, the image cast by a car that is moving away becomes smaller, but we do not perceive the car as actually changing size. Even when there are large changes in the sensory information received from objects in the environment, the moment-to-moment changes tend to be ignored in favor of a view of the world that is constant and predictable. This tendency to perceive objects as having certain constant (or stable) properties is known as **perceptual constancy.**

One type of perceptual constancy is **size constancy.** The farther away an object is, the smaller the size of the image it projects on the retina; however, if we have information that the object is far away, we automatically take this into account and translate the object's projected size into its real size.

To see how size constancy works, hold one hand at arm's length and the other hand half that far from your eyes, and note the relative size of your hands. They look very much the same size, even though the near hand projects a larger image onto the eye. You will perceive the disparity in projected sizes if you move the near hand so that it partly overlaps—partly hides from view—the far one. Now, although you know your hands are the same size, the far one looks smaller. Evidently, partial overlapping can disrupt size constancy, so that we see our hands as they are presented to the eye.

The relationship between size and distance can be demonstrated more precisely with afterimages—images that persist after the original stimulus is removed. Stare for about forty seconds in adequate lighting at the dot in the red square in Figure 13.6. Then hold a piece of white paper about a foot from your eyes and look at the center of it. If you have trouble seeing an afterimage of the square, focus on one spot on the paper. Now move the paper to about two feet in front of your eyes and look at it: the square probably looks twice as large. If you look at a more distant surface, such as a white wall, the afterimage will appear to be even larger. Obviously, the size of the afterimage does not really change, because it is based on your original fixation on the red square. What does change is the perceived size of the image: as your eyes focus at greater

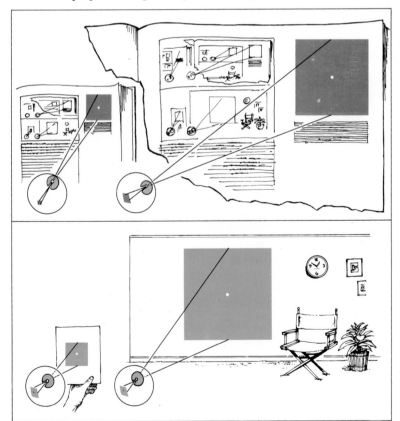

Figure 13.6 Following the instructions given in the text, stare at the dot, then at a sheet of white paper, then at a blank wall. The farther away the wall is, the larger the afterimage will appear to be. The drawings at the left explain why this happens. (top) Normally, the more distant an object is from the eye, the smaller the image projected onto the back of the eye. The brain compensates for this effect by scaling up the apparent size of distant objects. The result is size constancy: objects do not appear to change size just because they move closer or farther. But when the image in the eye is held constant, as it is with an afterimage (bottom), the brain's compensation for changes in distance creates large changes in apparent size.

distances, your brain interprets the afterimage as representing a larger object. The afterimage seems to be twice as large at two feet as at one foot because your brain tells you that an object that is twice as far away as another object, yet still projects the same size image onto the eye, has to be twice as large as the second object.

The relationship between an object's projected size and its distance, illustrated in Figure 13.6, is the same for both the eye and a camera. There is an inverse relationship between the distance of an object and its projected image—the greater the distance, the smaller the projected image. When an object's distance from the eye or camera is doubled, for example, its projected size is halved. Thus, if you take a photograph of a tree from 100 feet and another photograph from 200 feet, the tree will be twice as high on the first photograph as on the second. Brain processes, consequently, contribute to size constancy only if distance can be inferred: by taking into account the relationship between size and distance, accurate inferences are made about real size.

When cues for size and distance are in conflict, a person automatically opts for one or the other—usually in favor of the more likely conclusion. In World War II, the Allies used a strategy based on this phenomenon to confuse the Germans during the invasion of Normandy. In the early morning twilight the Allies dropped two-foot dummies of paratroopers onto fields away from the planned landing site on the coast. When the dummies hit the ground, the impact set off a series of small explosions, simulating rifle fire. In the poor light and general confusion, German observers thought the dummies were real paratroopers, attacking from a distance on the coast. Only when the Germans mobilized and moved close enough to see the dummies did they realize that the dummies' small size had misled them about distance. In the meantime, the Allies had gained extra time for the landing.

There are several other important constancies besides size; they include shape, color, and location. Size constancy has been described in some detail so that the nature of perceptual constancy could be presented fully.

RESOLUTION OF AMBIGUITY When the brain receives ambiguous sensory data, a single set of stimuli can give rise to two or more different interpretations. This can stymie the search for stabilized and coherent perception that has meaning to it. For example, figure and ground can be ambiguous, as shown in Figure 13.7. This illustration can alternatively be seen as a white vase against a black background or two black faces against a white background. Another type of perceptual ambiguity involves a figure that can be seen in two different perspectives. One of the best known is the Necker

When visual cues are in conflict with each other, common sense suggests which cue is correct.

Figure 13.7 This drawing is a classic demonstration of figure-ground ambiguity. What you perceive as figure and as ground depends on a number of factors, including your expectation.

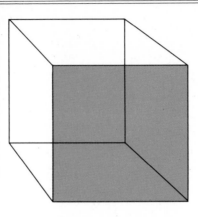

Figure 13.8 The Necker cube is a classic case of perceptual ambiguity. The tinted surface sometimes appears as the front of the cube and sometimes as the back. (After Gregory, 1968.)

cube, illustrated in Figure 13.8. The figure provides no information as to which part is the front and which is the back. In both these examples, there is no single "correct" answer. Presented with such a dilemma, alternate hypotheses are apparently entertained, and a person never decides between them, since the two possibilities are equally likely to be accurate.

Normally, we resolve perceptual ambiguity by

Figure 13.9 (A) The stimulus above the handwriting can be interpreted as either 15 or IS, depending on its context. (B) This figure is also ambiguous, and depending on the context in which it is found, it may be perceived as either a rabbit or a duck. (B after Lanners, 1977.)

choosing the most likely possibility that accounts for the available sensory information. We generally use **context**—the setting in which the stimuli appear—to go beyond the available sensory information and determine what it ought to mean. For example, the two lines at the top of Figure 13.9A are not entirely clear. When they are placed into the sentence "Fido is drunk," their features are clarified: they become the word "is." However, when they are placed into the number 14,157,393, their features are clarified in a different way: they become the numbers 1 and 5.

A phenomenon reported by George Miller (1962) illustrates the importance of context in our perception of speech. If a person hears a series of words, such as "Lives mountain man on that a," embedded in a great deal of noise, there will be little recognition of these words. However, if the words are placed in the meaningful order, "That man lives on a mountain," it will be possible to recognize most of the words despite the noise. The context provided by the meaningful arrangement of the words is a clear aid to recognition. We all take advantage of context to make sense of things in a noisy situation, such as a loud party.

It has been noted (Lindsay and Norman, 1972) that we can also draw upon past experience and stored knowledge to provide a context for resolving ambiguity. Consider, for instance, your ability to accurately identify the source of inspiration for the following nonsensical rhyme as you read it aloud.

> Mister Merry,
> Cute and scarry,
> Cow fuzz gore guard ingrown?
> Wet sliver balls,
> Uncock eel smells,
> Ungritty made fall sinner moan.

If you can ignore the meaning and bizarre imagery of the words, rhythm and sound should provide a familiar context for recognizing this jingle as a greatly distorted version of a famous nursery rhyme.

FEATURE ANALYSIS Obviously, you would not be able to read this sentence if you could not recognize the distinctive features of the letters that compose it. **Feature analysis** is the process by which sensory information is identified according to its distinctive characteristics, or features. In order to understand how feature analysis works, researchers have developed computer models of this process. In

Figure 13.10 Selfridge's Pandemonium. In this model of pattern recognition, image demons register an image of the outside world and display it to the feature demons. Each feature demon is specialized to perceive a certain feature; the demon examines the image for the presence of that feature and reports its findings to the cognitive demons. Each of the cognitive demons represents a particular pattern that might be expected to come in from the outside world. A cognitive demon starts yelling if the features that have been identified match the features that are found in its particular pattern. The better the match, the louder it yells. The decision demon listens to the resulting uproar and chooses the pattern corresponding to the noisiest cognitive demon. Presumably it is its pattern that has appeared in the outside world.

1959, Oliver Selfridge programmed a computer to recognize the letters of the alphabet. The major elements of Selfridge's system are portrayed in Figure 13.10. The system is based on the fact that a set of distinctive features can be used to identify all the capital letters of the alphabet. Each letter is defined by a unique set of characteristics. For example, while both L and T have one vertical and one horizontal line, L has one right angle and T has two right angles. For a computer to distinguish Ls from Ts, it must be programmed to analyze three different features: horizontal lines, vertical lines, and right angles. In order to analyze the entire alphabet, the computer must analyze a series of such features and then find the best match in the information it has stored about the features of each letter. For instance, the unique combination of one horizontal line, two vertical lines, and four right angles will be identified as an H.

Computer models provide a convenient means for describing how feature analysis may operate in our own perceptual processes. These models are not analogous merely to our identification of letters; the extraction of features also takes place when we recognize paintings by famous artists, songs performed by different musicians, constellations of stars in the sky, and the odors of different flowers.

Though computer models are useful in identi-fying the elements of feature extraction, they do not tell the whole story of this perceptual process. Selfridge's program enabled the computer to identify only the capital letters of a standard-print alphabet. Peter Lindsay and Donald Norman (1972) have pointed out that people can recognize letter patterns despite wide variations in the ways that the letters are printed. An F can be big or small, plain or fancy, slanted or straight, upside down or right side up, but people will still be able to abstract the features necessary to identify its pattern correctly. Though any irregularity in the shape of a letter will "confuse" a computer, people accommodate such irregularities in their recognition processes.

DEPTH PERCEPTION The world is a three-dimensional entity, and the human body is built in many ways that help us to perceive three-dimensional space. For example, because we have two ears that are on opposite sides of our heads, sounds that come from the left side produce sound waves that arrive at the left ear earlier than at the right ear (and vice versa), as Figure 13.11 shows. Consequently, we can determine approximately which

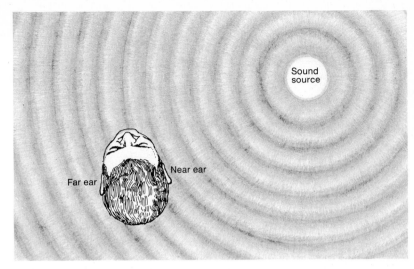

Figure 13.11 Human beings are able to perceive the direction of sound sources by making comparisons between the times at which a particular sound reaches each of the two ears. Because the ears are not very far apart, the differences between the sound's arrival time at the two ears is quite small; human beings are able to detect a difference of about thirty-millionths of a second. It is this amazing sensitivity to small time differences that makes your perception of stereophonically reproduced sound so different from your perception of monaurally reproduced sound. (After Lindsay and Norman, 1972.)

direction a sound is coming from; that is, we can localize sound.

Our most important sense for judging the position of objects in space, however, is vision. **Depth perception** is the ability to tell how far away an object is. The eyes, like the ears, are set apart, so that the retinal image that each eye receives is slightly different. This difference is called **binocular disparity**. You can demonstrate binocular disparity by holding your finger in front of you and looking at it with one eye at a time; the image registered by the right eye will be slightly left of center, and that registered by the left eye will be slightly right of center. Now, line up your finger with some other object that is farther away, and look at both your finger and that object with one eye at a time. As you switch from eye to eye, your finger will seem to jump back and forth in relation to the more distant object, because the binocular disparity of far objects is less than that of near objects. We use this difference in disparity to judge the distance of an object. As we look at things with both eyes, the information from the two eyes combines to give a perception of depth. The stereoscope, a device that helps an observer fuse the images of two photographs taken from slightly different angles, takes advantage of this perceptual phenomenon and allows a two-dimensional, photographed scene to be perceived as if it had three dimensions, as illustrated in Figure 13.12.

Another cue used to perceive depth is **motion parallax**, the differences in the relative movements of retinal images that occur when we move or change

Figure 13.12 The interaction of the two eyes in the perception of depth is analogous to the interaction of the two ears in the perception of direction. The brain combines two slightly different two-dimensional images of the same stimulus into one perception that is three-dimensional. The two photographs shown here were taken from slightly different positions in order to reproduce the slightly different images received by your two eyes. If you look down the sides of a tall piece of cardboard placed on the line dividing the two photographs, as the woman in the sketch is doing, you can deliver one of these images to your left eye only and the other to your right eye only. If you are able to fuse these images, that is, to visually superimpose them exactly, the scene will jump out in depth. A popular toy, the "Viewmaster," operates on the same principle.

A

B

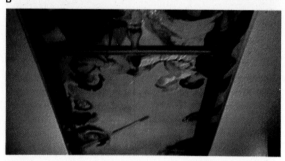

Allegory of Divine Knowledge and the Fine Arts, by Paulo de' Matteis. When looked at from one point in a room (A), this painting gives the impression of having been painted from the perspective of someone looking up through the balcony. However, seen from another point in a room (B), the balcony seems almost to project down from the frame.

position. You can demonstrate motion parallax by looking toward two objects, one near you and the other some distance away. Close one eye so that binocular disparity is eliminated, and move your head back and forth. The near object will seem to move more than the far object. We use this disparity in movement between near and far to perceive depth. Because of this disparity, when we drive along a highway, nearby trees seem to zip by while distant mountains may appear motionless.

It is not necessary to have two eyes in order to perceive depth. There are a number of **monocular cues**—that is, cues to one eye—that augment depth perception. In fact, motion parallax provides both monocular and binocular cues about depth. Another aid to monocular depth perception is **interposition**, in which one object partially blocks the view of another object, creating the illusion that the second object is farther away.

Artists were aware of monocular cues to depth perception long before these cues became the subject of psychological study. Since paintings are two-dimensional, monocular cues are the only ones that can be used to give the impression of depth. Examine Paulo de' Matteis' seventeenth-century painting *Allegory of Divine Knowledge and the Fine Arts,* shown here, which the artist intended to be hung on a ceiling. From one point in the room, the painting gives us the impression of looking up into a balcony ringed with people (top photograph), but from other points the painting seems distorted (bottom photograph).

The painting illustrates the careful and subtle use of linear perspective and relative size cues to convey depth. **Linear perspective** is produced by the apparent convergence of parallel lines, like those in the photograph of railroad tracks in Figure 13.13. **Relative size** refers to the relationship between the size of the retinal image produced by an object and the apparent distance of that object from an observer: the larger the retinal image, the closer the object appears to be.

Another cue in perceiving depth is **texture gradient**, the graduated differences that occur as distance increases. In a highly textured scene, such as the one shown in the accompanying photograph, the nearer stones appear larger and coarser and the more distant ones, smaller and finer.

There is some evidence that human infants have the important ability to perceive depth either at or shortly after birth. E. J. Gibson and R. D. Walk (1960) developed the "visual cliff," shown in the photographs on page 306, to test depth perception

An example of texture gradient as a cue to depth perception.

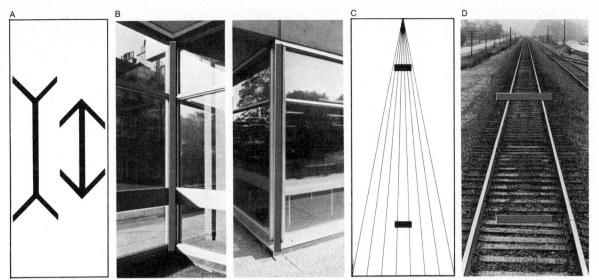

Figure 13.13 Two famous illusions and possible explanations for how they work. The vertical lines of the figures in the Müller-Lyer illusion (A) are identical in length, but they do not appear to be. An explanation for this illusion, suggested in B, is that the arrow markings on the lines in A cause them to be perceived as three-dimensional objects that have corners. The corners seem to induce a size-constancy effect: The vertical line that appears to be distant is perceived as larger. The horizontal lines in the Ponzo illusion (C) are also identical in length. As the photograph in D suggests, this figure, too, could easily be perceived as three-dimensional, and again size constancy would cause the apparently more distant "object" to be scaled up in apparent size relative to the "nearer object." (After Gregory, 1970.)

in a number of different species, including human infants. The visual cliff consists of a center board resting on a large glass table; on one side of the center board is a patterned surface placed directly below the glass, while on the other side a patterned surface is located several feet below the glass. Gibson and Walk found that when human infants who are old enough to crawl (about six months of age) are placed on the center board, they will usually cross to the "shallow" side and avoid the "deep" side of the glass, indicating that they possess depth perception.

PERCEPTION OF MOVEMENT Another characteristic of the perceptual world is **movement**, produced both by ourselves and by the objects around us. We know when we are in motion, and so we relate the movements of our own bodies to the resulting changes in what we see. When we look from one side of a room to another, what we see changes constantly, but we perceive the changes as resulting from the movement of our own eyes, and not from movement of the room.

We can also tell that we are moving even though we are not producing the movement ourselves, as when we ride in a car that someone else is driving. James J. Gibson (1966) pointed out that what we see in the world outside the car is **global motion parallax**, a constant flux in what is seen, which produces our perception that we are moving through space as shown in the photograph of the car that appears at the bottom of the next page.

Motion can be perceived even though no real motion is taking place: in **apparent movement**, motion is perceived in a rapid succession of motionless stimuli that mimic the changes that occur in true movement. One example of apparent movement is the **phi phenomenon**, described by Gestalt psychologist Max Wertheimer: when lights are switched on sequentially, as in some neon signs, we see movement although nothing is actually moving. Another example of the phi phenomenon is motion pictures: we perceive that people in motion pictures are moving, although the stimuli producing the perceived motion are a series of still photographs that flash by at least sixteen times per second. In these two examples of apparent movement, the rapid succession of visual stimuli reproduces the changes in sensory information that occur in real movement, and thus an illusion of real movement is produced.

ILLUSIONS An **illusion** is a perception that does not correspond to a real object or event. Illusions are produced by physical or psychological distortion. Desert and arctic mirages are well-known

A visual cliff apparatus.

The constant flux that we see when we ride in a car provides us with the perception that we are moving through space.

illusions produced by physical distortion. These "optical illusions," which are classic examples of the physical principle of light refraction, have, however, at times been given a mythic importance. In this role they have been used to explain a culture's beliefs about the nature of its environment. For instance, the medieval Norse explorers believed that the earth was saucer-shaped, probably because they were exposed to the arctic mirage, an illusion that causes the distant horizon of the sea to appear rim-like and higher than the observer. The mirage is produced when relatively warm air lies against a cold surface, such as the Arctic Ocean. This pronounced temperature inversion gives the air a refractive capacity much like that of a prism or a glass of water. Distant land masses that should be obscured by the curvature of the earth become visible to the eye because the air refracts their images upward (Sawatzky and Lehn, 1976). It seems likely that the Norse belief in a saucer-shaped earth played an important role in their explorations and may have delayed Europe's acceptance of the theory of a spherical earth.

Psychologists are most interested in illusions that cannot be explained by physical phenomena. The subjective contours discussed at the beginning of this chapter are an excellent example of psychological illusions. These illusions are particularly interesting because they point out the contributions to perception made by sensory systems, the brain, and experience. The difference between what is "really out there" and what we report as being out there is our psychological contribution to the process of perception.

R. L. Gregory (1970) has suggested that a number of illusions may result from a misapplication of size constancy in the perception process. For example, look at the illusions in Figures 13.13A and 13B; then measure the lines with a ruler. Although the two lines in Figure 13A are actually the same length, the line on the left is perceived as being longer. In Figure 13B, all the lines are also identical in length. Both the Müller-Lyer illusion (Figure 13.13A) and the Ponzo illusion (Figure 13.13C) have features similar to those that indicate distance when we look at real objects in space. In the Müller-Lyer illusion the arrows are like outlines of corners, as illustrated in Figure 13.13B. As a result, the "shorter" line can be interpreted as being closer to the observer than the "longer" line, which can be interpreted as being recessed into the page. Because both lines project the same size image onto the retina, the line that is interpreted as being closer is perceived as smaller, in accordance with size constancy. In the Ponzo illusion the converging lines are like railroad tracks or other parallel lines that extend away from the observer, as illustrated in Figure 13.13D. Consequently, the horizontal bar that is farther down the track is perceived as larger; once again, size constancy dictates that when two objects project the same-size image on the retina, but one object is perceived as more distant than the other, the far object must be larger.

Adelbert Ames, a painter, created some especially striking visual illusions by building models that trick the visual system into misapplying size and shape constancy (1951). The best example is the Ames room, shown in Figure 13.14A: the two women inside the room look dramatically different in size because we perceive the room as rectangular. In fact, Figure 13.14B shows that the room is not rectangular; the back wall is farther away on the left side than on the right side. Since we see it as a normal rectangular room, we perceive the two women to be standing the same distance from us. Once again, size constancy dictates that if two people are the same distance away, but one projects a larger-size image onto the eye, then that person must be larger. The Ames room illusion works only if we view the room without adequate perception of depth. Although Figure 13.14B portrays the room as having only three walls, laboratory models of it have four. The observer looks at the room through a peephole; this serves to remove important depth cues such as binocular parallax (because the observer can use only one eye at a time) and motion parallax (because the observer cannot move around to see the room from different positions).

It is interesting to note that observers are less susceptible to the illusion if they are allowed to explore the room's surfaces with a stick inserted through a hole in the wall. Gradually, they see the room for what it really is: a set of trapezoids joined to form acute and obtuse angles—that is, a distorted room. Mere intellectual knowledge of how the room is shaped does not prevent the illusion; only active exploration of the room is effective.

The Ames room illusion, like the Müller-Lyer illusion and the Ponzo illusion, produces erroneous perceptions about size because its features result in the inappropriate application of size constancy. In all three illusions, incorrect perceptual inferences are made about distance and size because features of the illusions mimic the patterns of corners, parallel lines, and rectangular rooms that are seen in the real world.

Figure 13.14 The Ames room. In A the actual construction of the room is compared with the way the room is perceived. The photograph in B shows the room as it is seen through the peephole. The illusion is produced by people's inexperience with any rooms except rectangular ones with flat floors. The brain infers that both women standing against the back wall are at the same distance from the eye and interprets the difference between the size of their images as a real difference in size.

THE INFLUENCE OF EXPERIENCE ON PERCEPTION

A recurrent theme in our discussion of perception has been the role of experience and expectation in shaping our interpretation of sensory events. Obviously, our ability to derive meaning from the black squiggles printed on this page is based on our past experience with letters and words. Similarly, our expectations will influence our perceptions as we read: if we expcct to see the word *expect*, we may not notice that it has been misspelled, and if we expect a word to be in a sentence, we may not even notice that it been left out.

Expectations and previous experience constantly interact with one another to influence our perception of sensory events such as pain (as we saw in the special feature in Chapter 12). As for the effect of expectations and experience on visual experience, look at Figure 13.15A: then on page 312, glance at Figure 13.15B. Do you see a young woman? Now look at Figure 13.15C on page 313 and at Figure 13.15B. Do you now see an older woman? The experience of viewing one drawing influences how you perceive the ambiguous figure.

Perception is also substantially influenced by our motivation and needs. Experience ties into these states by increasing our inclination to attend to stimuli associated with a particular state. For instance, a hungry traveler is likely to become attuned

Figure 13.15A This drawing (like that in Figure 13.7) is perceptually ambiguous. The effect of personal experience and set on what is perceived here is particularly strong. Many people have difficulty seeing an old woman in this drawing. Others have equal difficulty in seeing a young woman. If you have such difficulties, turn to Figures 13.15B and 13.15C. (After Boring, 1930.)

to stimuli that may ordinarily be ignored (golden arches, large red and white chicken buckets). In fact, an increased tendency to perceive food-related stimuli when we are hungry can operate even in the absence of such stimuli. In one experiment, for example, people deprived of food for varying amounts of time were asked to "identify" pictures that an experimenter said would be flashed very dimly onto a screen. In reality, no pictures were presented: the experimenter merely manipulated the projector as if he were projecting images. The subjects nevertheless reported seeing pictures, and the hungrier they were (that is, the longer they had gone without food), the greater the proportion of food-related pictures they perceived (McClelland and Atkinson, 1948).

The combined influences of expectations, past experiences, and psychological states *set* us to perceive the world in certain ways. **Perceptual set** refers to a readiness to perceive stimuli in a specific way, to ignore certain types of stimulation, and to be very sensitive to other sensory stimuli. The perceptual sets described thus far are relatively short-lived biases. However, our experiences throughout life can set us to perceive the world in certain ways.

EARLY LIFE EXPERIENCES We know that certain early experiences can markedly affect our perceptual responsiveness to the world. There is evidence that some perceptual processes develop only when an individual is raised with exposure to a normal visual environment. For example, chimpanzees that are reared without any patterned stimulation in their environment show some deficit in size and shape perception (Riesen, 1949). Similarly, kittens reared without light show no apparent capacity for depth perception when tested on the visual cliff described earlier (Gibson and Walk, 1956). However, when light-deprived kittens are subsequently permitted to explore freely a lighted and patterned environment, they quickly learn to discriminate depth cues. In contrast, light-deprived kittens that are subsequently moved around in a patterned environment by a mechanical device (see Figure 13.16) rather than by their own movements do not develop depth perception (Held and Hein, 1963). Thus it seems that for an organism to develop depth perception, it must *actively* explore its environment.

CULTURAL INFLUENCES When we are shown a black and white photograph, we can easily translate this two-dimensional, sharply bordered, gray-shaded stimulus into a representation of the real world. Not all humans readily make this translation, however. For instance, one anthropologist reported that when an African Bushwoman was shown a photograph of her son, she had great difficulty making sense of the shadings of gray she saw

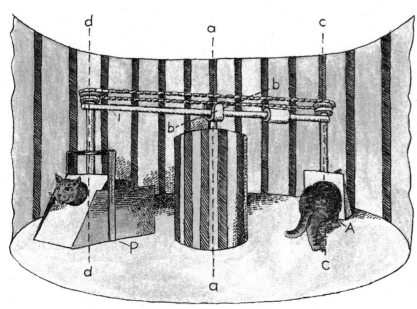

Figure 13.16 Apparatus used in the experiment by Held and Hein. Although the "passive" kitten on the left receives about the same amount of visual stimulation as the "active" one on the right, it does not develop depth perception, while the active kitten does. Feedback from self-induced movement seems to be an important element in learning how to see things in depth. (After Held and Hein, 1963.)

Extrasensory Perception

In this chapter, we discuss the perception of the tangible and measurable aspects of the environment. Extrasensory perception (ESP) presents a different sort of problem. Whereas normal perceptual phenomena can be readily verified, extrasensory perception cannot, and the reports of its existence are not always viewed as credible. To the extreme skeptic, ESP does not exist, and so there is no need for explanations. On the other hand, the extreme "believer" is sure of its existence and offers explanations that often contradict known scientific laws. A moderate view is that seemingly paranormal phenomena do exist, but their existence can be explained by natural laws, coincidence, or trickery. In view of the history of scientific discovery, it is difficult to deny that there are still "things out there" that we have yet to discover and understand. So let's assume the posture of the open-minded skeptic as we review the problems and results of research on ESP.

Definitional Considerations

Three forms of ESP have been suggested: **telepathy**, or mind reading, the transference of thought from one person to another; **precognition**, the ability to see the future; and **clairvoyance**, the knowledge of events not detectable by normal senses. A clairvoyant person could, for example, sense the suit and number of a card sealed in an envelope. Another phenomenon that is often thought to be related to ESP is **psychokinesis** (PK), the ability to move objects without touching them.

Extrasensory perception implies knowledge about the environment that is not based on a known sensory channel. A contemporary example of an unexplained sensory channel is some people's apparent ability to perceive color through their fingertips. Psychologist W. L. Makous (1966) investigated popular reports that such people could correctly identify colors in complete darkness, using only their fingers. His research did not indicate that this seemingly miraculous ability was due to some undiscovered "photoreceptors" in the fingers. Rather, he found that fingertip identification of colors could be explained by a known channel of sensory discrimination—the temperature receptors in the skin. According to his analysis, colored objects reflect different amounts of infrared radiation—for example, black objects absorb these radiations, white objects tend to reflect them, and other colors fall in between. Although the temperature changes produced by different colors are quite small,

they are at a threshold that can be detected by some people who are "set" to notice them.

While there is a perfectly logical explanation for "fingertip vision," it is the type of phenomenon that is likely to be classified as "paranormal," that is, outside the range of normal events. We tend to view such "improbable" events as having unusual causes simply because of their unusual nature. However, as George Miller (1967) and others have pointed out, improbability is no guarantee of paranormality.

We can apply this principle to the supposedly paranormal abilities of Uri Geller, a controversial young Israeli "psychic." On the basis of laboratory tests, two highly respected laser physicists, Russell Targ and Hal Puthoff (1974), concluded that Geller does indeed have some telepathic abilities. Specifically, they suggested that he can receive information about a remote location through an unknown sensory channel. Dr. Andrew Weil (1974a) also ac-

cepted Geller's psychic abilities after watching him bend metal objects and "read minds." However, Weil became a skeptic after he paid a visit to a professional magician who could duplicate many of Geller's feats using easily explainable techniques (1974b). Another researcher, Joseph Hanlon (1974), suggests that people perceive Geller as a psychic because that is what they want to believe: Geller, who has been described as extremely likeable, is easily able to inspire his audience to believe in him. In turn, a believing audience is likely to ignore signs of trickery in their eagerness to see genuine psychic powers.

This example indicates that it is wise to search for the simplest possible explanation for supposedly paranormal events. In addition, most scientists will continue to regard paranormal explanations with skepticism as long as these explanations contradict the basic principles of science. For example, Donald Hebb (1974) writes that while telepathy is not inconceivable, believers are violating basic scientific laws when they say that distance makes no difference in the transmission of thoughts. In the same way, precognition violates what scientists know about time: so far, there is no scientific explanation for how someone can jump ahead to see the future and then jump back again to tell about it. Psychokinesis violates what scientists know about space, since there are no known ways that an individual can move something by sheer force of thought.

Before we can ask questions about why supposed ESP events occur, however, we must ask an even more basic question: What is the event that we are trying to explain? Many of the so-called paranormal events of the present day have few witnesses, and it is difficult to prove that they occur.

The Problem of Scientific Validation

Scientific investigations into the existence of ESP and PK have been conducted in the United States since the early 1900s. Joseph B. Rhine, the best-known researcher in this area, has tried to prove through scientific methodology that ESP exists. For example, he tests for telepathy by having a "sender" focus on each card in a special deck one at a time. A "receiver," locked in a distant room, states which card the sender has turned up and is thinking about. Studies of this sort have produced mixed results: some researchers have found individuals who, acting as receivers, are able to identify more cards than would be expected by chance, while other researchers have not found individuals who are able to do this. Recently, Rhine has expressed his own doubts that telepathy can be verified through acceptable scientific procedures, although he does not doubt the existence of the phenomenon (1974).

We are often convinced of the existence of ESP because of an intense personal experience that can never be scientifically validated. For instance, we all have some fears before traveling, and we imagine the worst: Our plane will crash, our train will be derailed, or we will have an automobile accident. These events almost never happen, and we easily forget about our frightening premonitions. However, if the improbable should actually take place, our premonitions turn into compelling evidence for the existence of precognition. Such coincidences sometimes become widely publicized evidence supporting paranormal phenomena, and we quickly forget all the occasions when our premonitions were completely wrong. However, if we are truly interested in validating the existence of ESP, we must keep track of the frequency of its failures as well as its successes.

Another reason why many scientists do not accept the results of experiments supporting ESP and PK is that the findings are highly unstable. One of the basic principles of scientific research is that one scientist should be able to replicate another scientist's results. Not only do different experiments yield contradictory findings, but the same individual seems to show ESP or PK on one day but not on the next. Proponents of ESP and PK argue that this type of research cannot be consistently replicated because the special abilities are stifled in a dull laboratory situation that has no relevance to real life.

Although ESP may indeed be a very fragile phenomenon, the inability to replicate results and the difficulty of verifying ESP events are crucial problems. Many will remain skeptical about the existence of ESP until these problems are solved. However, such skepticism has often been overcome in the past; for example, just a century or so ago, the suggestion that many diseases were caused by invisible organisms was greeted with disbelief. Only after the work of Pasteur and other researchers proved a clear relationship that existed between these organisms and illness was the "germ theory" of disease accepted. Perhaps the development of appropriate techniques for testing ESP could similarly lead to establishing the existence of paranormal phenomena.

(Segall, Campbell, and Herskovits, 1966). Without any experience in perceiving photographs, she could not even recognize her own son until the details of the picture were explained to her. Anthropologists call this phenomenon **cultural relativism**, a term that describes the role of cultural learning in the development of perceptual biases.

Some psychologists have hypothesized that cultural factors have great impact on the ways that people from different societies view the world. For example, most children in Western societies are exposed to pictures and picture books, and these experiences teach them to translate two-dimensional drawings into a three-dimensional world. Some have suggested that this special cultural experience makes us susceptible to the Müller-Lyer illusion, which is based on our tendency to see acute and obtuse angles on a printed page as right angles in the real world. People who have not had this special experience, such as members of the Zulu tribe in Africa, are much less susceptible to the illusion. While Western children live in houses constructed with straight lines, corners, and right angles, Zulus grow up in an environment characterized by roundedness and a lack of "carpentered" structure. Thus, Westerners learn to use the angles in the Müller-Lyer illusion to infer distance, while Zulus make no such automatic inference (Segall, Campbell, and Herskovits, 1966).

Figure 13.15B A version of the drawing in Figure 13.15A that has a strong tendency to be interpreted as a representation of a young woman. Viewing this drawing can affect your perception of Figure 13.15A.

Researchers have also reported cultural differences in the susceptibility to the Ponzo illusion, the tendency to infer depth from two converging lines. One study (Leibowitz and Pick, 1972) compared responses made to this illusion by two groups of Ugandans: university students and rural villagers. Both groups were exposed to converging-line depth cues in their environment, in the form of roads, buildings, plowed fields, and so on. However, when the subjects were presented with the stimuli pictured in Figure 13.17, the Ugandan students

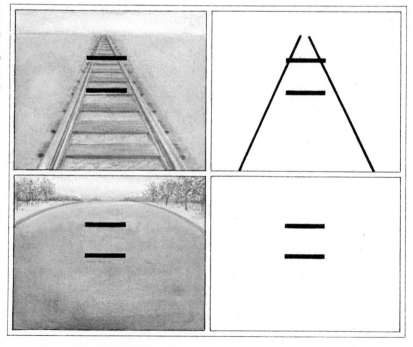

Figure 13.17 The stimuli used in the study of examining cultural differences in susceptibility to the Ponzo illusion. All the horizontal lines presented in this figure are of equal length. (After Leibowitz and Pick, 1972.)

were as likely as students in Pennsylvania to see the illusion, while the Ugandan villagers showed almost no perception of the illusion. Educational experience appears to be the critical factor that explains the difference between the students and the villagers. University students, in both Uganda and Pennsylvania, have extensive exposure to books, photographs, newspapers, and the like, from which they learn to perceive three-dimensional space in a two-dimensional representation. In contrast, the Ugandan villagers were more sensitive to the flatness of a two-dimensional representation. The authors concluded that since the villagers were unable to disregard the flatness of a two-dimensional figure, they were less likely to see the depth cues necessary for perceiving the illusion. This study demonstrates the important influence of experience and expectations on the ways human beings perceive the world around them.

Figure 13.15C This version of Figure 13.15A is likely to be interpreted as a representation of an old woman. Viewing this figure can affect your perception of Figure 13.15A. One tends to use whatever is familiar in interpreting an ambiguous stimulus pattern.

Summary

1. **Perception** is an organism's awareness of objects and events in the environment brought about by stimulation of the organism's sense organs. When information about the environment is incomplete or distorted, brain activity contributes details that may give meaning to the unfamiliar. Perception can also occur in the absence of sensory stimulation, as in dreams, hallucinations, and electrical brain stimulation.

2. The process of organizing perceptions is very complex. There are various ways in which brain processes sort out information about the size, shape, color, depth, distance, and motion of objects.
   A. The Gestalt psychologists focused on the ways in which bits of information are organized into meaningful, unified patterns, which they called **gestalts**.
      1. When presented with an array of stimuli, such as dots or music, the brain uses **grouping** in order to structure the information. The organizing principles of **proximity**, **continuity**, and **similarity** are used to achieve perceptual **simplicity**.
      2. Another way brain processes organize sensations is to divide stimuli into **figure**, the predominating stimulus that has a speci-

fic and distinguishable form, and **ground**, those stimuli which serve as a backdrop or as spaces between or within figures. The figure or ground of a particular group of sensations can change if the focus of one's attention changes.
   B. The retinal image of an object changes according to one's distance from the actual object. However, the predictability and unchanging quality of the object can still be perceived, because the brain uses the principle of **perceptual constancy**. One example of this principle is **size constancy**. The visual system, taking into account the fact that the farther away an object is, the smaller the retinal image is, seems to use this information to make an accurate estimation of the object's real size. Similar processes are used to achieve constancy in such perceptual phenomena as shape, color, and location.
   C. When the brain is presented with ambiguous sensory data, several interpretations of the stimuli may be entertained, but a person may be unable to choose one of them, as all are meaningful. One way in which the brain resolves this dilemma is by using the **context** of the stimuli to determine the best perceptual organization.

D. **Feature analysis** is another perceptual process in which some distinctive characteristics of objects as conveyed to the brain by the senses are identified. Computers have been programmed to do this too. For example, when presented with a letter of the alphabet, the features of that letter (its angularity or curvature) are observed and the image is then matched with stored information and identified. Human beings, unlike computers, are able to recognize wide variations among features of the same letter.

E. Various principles explain the ability to perceive the three-dimensionality of objects. **Depth perception** is the ability to tell how far away an object is. Such judgments are made by using the following kinds of cues:

1. **binocular disparity**: slight differences in the information received by each eye.
2. **motion parallax**: differences in the relative movements of retinal images that occur when we change position.
3. **interposition**: a monocular cue (cue to only one eye) in which one object partially blocks the view of another, creating the illusion that the second object is farther away.
4. **linear perspective**: the apparent convergence of parallel lines in the distance.
5. **relative size**: the relationship between the size of an object's image projected on the retina and the distance of the object from the observer.
6. **texture gradient**: the apparent differences in the texture of objects as distance increases.

F. **Movement** in the perceptual world can be produced by ourselves or by the objects around us. The ability to perceive movement that we ourselves are not producing (as when we ride in a car) is achieved through the **global motion parallax**, the constant flux of objects appearing to become larger and smaller as we move farther from or closer to them. Motion can also be perceived even when no real motion is occurring. This **apparent movement** is an illusion created by a rapid succession of stimuli, which mimics the changes occurring during actual motion. Examples of this are motion pictures and neon signs, which use the **phi phenomenon**, an illusion of movement created by rapidly flashing visual stimuli (still photographs and lights).

G. **Illusions**, perceptions that do not correspond to real objects or events, are produced by physical or psychological distortion. Physical illusions are misperceptions in response to actual changes in light refraction, as occur in arctic or desert mirages. Psychological illusions, such as the Müller-Lyer, Ponzo, and Ames room illusions, result from a misapplication of the principles of size or shape constancy in the perceptual process.

3. Perception is also affected by our expectations, previous experiences, and psychological states. These factors create in each of us a **perceptual set**, a readiness to attend to and perceive certain stimuli in a specific way and to ignore other stimuli.

A. Certain perceptual processes, such as size, shape, and depth perception seem to develop only if the organism's early life experience includes active exploration of the environment.

B. Our culture contributes to our perceptual interpretations of such phenomena as optical illusions and photographs. **Cultural relativism** is the term for the influence of cultural learning on the development of perceptual biases.

RECOMMENDED READINGS

GIBSON, JAMES J. *The Senses Considered as Perceptual Systems.* Boston: Houghton Mifflin, 1966. An excellent treatment of the dependence of perception upon sensory information.

GREGORY, R. L. *The Intelligent Eye.* New York: McGraw-Hill, 1970 (paper). Gregory stresses the importance of perceptual inference, arguing that perception is a set of simple hypotheses about reality that depend upon sensory experience. The book is particularly strong on visual illusions.

HELD, RICHARD, and WHITMAN RICHARDS (eds.). *Perception: Mechanisms and Models.* San Francisco: W. H. Freeman, 1972 (paper). This book of readings from *Scientific American* provides accounts of some famous research on perceptual processes in a variety of animals.

LINDSAY, PETER, and DONALD NORMAN. *Human Information Processing.* New York: Academic Press, 1972. The first half presents a clear, readable account of information-processing analyses of perception.

PART FIVE

AWARENESS, FEELING, AND ACTIVATION

Many psychologists believe that the workings of the mind ultimately can be understood in physical terms—that mental phenomena can be explained scientifically because they arise from the interactions between the body (especially the brain) and the world in which it lives. For example, perceptions arise because specific stimuli in the environment affect the sense organs of the body, which transmit information to the brain, which interprets the information, and this process culminates in the experience of perceptions. This view of the mind has produced some amazingly fruitful explanations of sensation and perception—as we saw in Part Four—and of consciousness, emotions, motivation, and sexuality—as we shall see in Part Five.

We begin in Chapter 14, "Varieties of Consciousness," by discussing the nature of consciousness and a number of states of awareness, including sleep, hypnosis, the self-regulated consciousness of meditation and biofeedback, and drug-altered consciousness. In Chapter 15, "The Experience and Expression of Emotion," we consider the experience, labeling, and expression of emotional states. Chapter 16, "Motivation," discusses the major theoretical views of the motivational bases of human behavior, both physiological and psychological. Chapter 17, "Human Sexuality," deals with the nature and variety of one of the simplest and most basic, yet most widely misunderstood motivated behavior—the human sexual response.

CHAPTER FOURTEEN

VARIETIES OF CONSCIOUSNESS

About ten years ago, I was waiting to go on a talk show and an ex-astronaut who was waiting with me told me that in his opinion every object possessed consciousness. Even individual subatomic particles did. The level of consciousness for simple objects, however, was so incredibly small that there was no conceivable way of detecting it.

However, he went on, the quality was additive. Increasing mass and increasing complexity raised the level of consciousness, and eventually it became measurable. The difference in level of consciousness between a human being and a rock was one of degree, not of kind.

The thought interested me, chiefly because more than a dozen years before that conversation, I had speculated similarly in connection with robots and computers. After all, I am a science fiction writer and speculation of that sort comes with the territory.

In 1955, for instance, I had written a short-short story called "Question" in which I took up the matter of an extremely complex computer that was beginning to behave oddly. There seemed a possibility that it was approaching some borderline past in which it would be humanly conscious. But how could one tell when, or even if, it crossed that boundary?

The answer came when suddenly the vast computer broke its silence and said, over and over again, "Who am I?—Who am I?—Who am I?"

There is a sequel to this that brings to light another aspect of consciousness. After my story appeared, I received a polite letter from another science fiction writer, enclosing a copy of a story of his own, which had appeared before mine. The story was completely different from mine, but it also had, as its climax, a computer asking the key question, "Who am I?"

I was taken aback. I did not recall ever having read the story, but I checked through my library and found that the other writer's story had appeared in an anthology in which one of my stories had also appeared—so I had the anthology in my library. That meant I had had the opportunity of reading it. Though I still didn't recall having done so, I might well have flipped through the pages of the anthology and had read more of the story than I had realized afterward. At the very least I might have noticed the ending.

In short, not all of consciousness is conscious!

I had no choice. I wrote a letter of apology to the other science fiction writer, explained the situation, and removed my story "Question" from the market. It has never appeared again in any anthology, and it never will.

Isaac Asimov

For centuries philosophers have pondered the meaning of consciousness. Loosely defined, consciousness is an awareness of the many thoughts, images, sensations, and emotions that flow through one's mind at any given moment (Marsh, 1977). This is essentially the same definition that the seventeenth-century philosopher John Locke gave: "Consciousness is the perception of what passes in a man's own mind." As such, consciousness is highly subjective—a private world, accessible mainly through introspection.

Various psychologists have at times attempted to dismiss as meaningless questions about the nature of consciousness—and with them the study of alterations of consciousness, such as those produced by hypnosis, drugs, meditation, and even dreaming. Behaviorism, for example, originally grew out of the assertion that mind, consciousness, awareness, and similar concepts cannot be analyzed scientifically and therefore should be banished from psychology. But many psychologists, including some contemporary behaviorists, have not accepted this view. With the help of modern research tools, such as equipment for recording the brain waves and other physiological activities that accompany changes in awareness, a number of important insights into the workings of consciousness have been provided.

THE NATURE OF CONSCIOUSNESS

There is no completely satisfactory definition or explanation of consciousness, although many psychologists have tried to produce one. Perhaps the only points on which most would agree are, first, that consciousness is limited; second, that it is related to brain activity; and, third, that it has various modes.

CONSCIOUSNESS IS LIMITED

Consciousness is limited in the sense that we are unaware of much of what is going on both inside and outside our bodies. One reason for this is the relatively narrow range of our perceptual capacities. Our subjective worlds would undoubtedly be quite different if we could see X-rays, hear the high-frequency sounds that porpoises and bats can hear, or feel details of the workings of our internal organs. Our channels of awareness are limited to a few sensory dimensions. Consciousness is likewise limited.

Consciousness is also limited by the extent to which our minds can process diverse information simultaneously. If we tried to pay attention to all the sensations, feelings, thoughts, and memories that are accessible to us at any given moment, we would

be overwhelmed and virtually immobilized. By necessity, therefore, much of the information available to consciousness is automatically screened out. In attending to some things, we become unaware of others—like the baseball player at bat who is unaware of the noise of the crowd.

Consciousness, then, is limited in two ways: by the inaccessibility to the human mind of certain stimuli; and by the limited number of internal and external events to which a person can pay attention at one time.

CONSCIOUSNESS IS RELATED TO BRAIN ACTIVITY

People have thought for centuries that the subjective awareness we call consciousness must be closely related to the activities of the brain. Modern research confirms this belief. Neurosurgeon Wilder Penfield (1969), for example, has demonstrated that stimulating certain parts of the cerebral cortex can activate specific conscious experiences, such as vivid "reruns" of past events or sudden interpretations of the present experience as being familiar or strange, coming nearer or going away, and so on.

The evidence clearly shows that subjective awareness and brain activity are indeed closely related. The exact nature of this relationship, however, is not so clear. In recent times, many neuroscientists have argued that the distinction between consciousness and the brain is a purely semantic one. Consciousness, they say, is simply the sum total of brain activity—nothing more. Recently, however, a new perspective has been offered by psychobiologist Roger Sperry (1977). Sperry's view is essentially an interactional one: mind has a role in directing brain activity, but brain activity is necessary for mind to emerge. Despite such insights, the puzzle of the connection between consciousness and brain activity has not been solved. Indeed, Sperry feels that it is "one of the most truly mystifying unknowns remaining in the whole of science" (1976, p. 9).

CONSCIOUSNESS HAS VARIOUS MODES

Some psychologists have suggested that coexisting within each of us are two separate modes of consciousness: one logical and analytic, the other intuitive and artistic (Ornstein, 1977). They argue that it is the differences in function between the left and right halves of the brain that underlie, to some extent, these two cognitive modes. As we noted in Chapter 11, the cerebral cortex is divided into two hemispheres connected by a large cable of neural fibers called the corpus callosum. Although both hemispheres play a role in most behavior, and although each has the potential for performing some of the functions of the other, in most people the two sides of the brain tend to specialize. Language, mathematics, and analytical thinking, for example, are mainly left-hemisphere activities; perception of spatial relationships, artistic abilities, and ability to recognize faces are mainly right-hemisphere activities. Figure 14.1 illustrates the specialization of the cortical hemispheres.

Studies of people who have had their two hemispheres separated surgically to relieve epileptic seizures dramatically demonstrate this hemispheric

Figure 14.1 This drawing, though greatly simplified, suggests the sensory input and the types of information processing handled by the cortical hemispheres of the brain. (Adapted from Eccles, 1973)

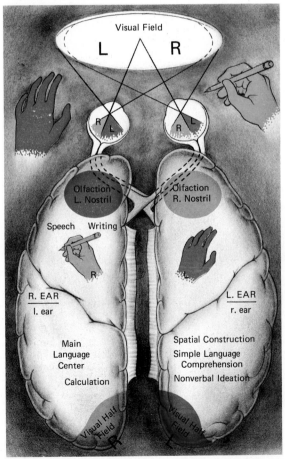

specialization and its effect on consciousness (Sperry, 1969; Gazzaniga, 1967). After the operation, two consciousnesses seem to emerge, one related to each hemisphere. Each consciousness tends to control different parts of the body and different abilities. In most people the left hemisphere has primary control over the right side of the body, while the right hemisphere has primary control over the left side. The left hemisphere also contains the areas of the brain that predominate in the control of language, so only the consciousness of the left hemisphere can speak or write. In the "split-brain" surgical patient, however, the right hemisphere can still communicate by gesturing with the left hand, and only the left hand retains the ability to draw accurately (a skill that requires perception of spatial relationships).

The two consciousnesses of these split-brain patients tend to go to sleep and wake up at about the same time and to have generally similar personalities, but they have somewhat independent memories and do not seem to have direct access to each other's awareness. In one experiment a picture of a nude woman was flashed to the right hemisphere—the right sides of the eyes—of a split-brain patient (see Figure 14.2). The patient laughed but said that she saw nothing. Only the left consciousness can speak, and it did not see the nude; but the right consciousness, which did see the nude, produced the laugh. When the woman was asked why she laughed, she acted confused and could not explain why (Gazzaniga, 1967).

In normal people, of course, the two cerebral hemispheres are connected and so they usually function as one. Nevertheless, lateral specialization of the brain exists in all of us, and one hemisphere or the other may tend to dominate, depending on the type of activity we are performing. However, it is still not known how the lateral specialization of the brain is related to the various states of consciousness a normal human being is capable of experiencing. We do know that under differing conditions our conscious awareness can vary greatly—that is, we can enter many diverse states of consciousness, each with its own distinctive quality of subjective experience (Tart, 1975). The causes and circumstances that can produce different states of consciousness vary widely. Some states, such as sleeping and dreaming, occur naturally. Others, such as hypnosis, meditation, and biofeedback, occur only through the use of special techniques. Still others are drug-induced. Much recent research on consciousness has centered on describing and explain-

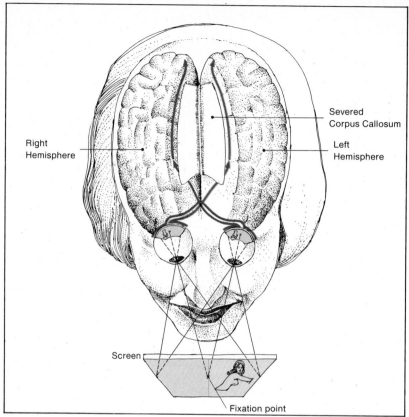

Figure 14.2 The presentation of a visual stimulus to a single hemisphere of a person who has undergone split-brain surgery. The drawing shows that the nerve paths from the eyes are organized in such a way that all the information to the left of the point fixated on goes to the right hemisphere. Because the area of the brain that controls speech is in the left hemisphere, the patient reacts with amusement to the picture of the nude woman flashed on the left side of the screen but is unable to say why.

ing the nature of these various states, particularly those that involve rather dramatic alterations in normal waking awareness. The rest of this chapter, therefore, will explore what psychologists know about several of the most interesting of these altered states. We begin with sleep and dreams.

SLEEP AND DREAMS

Most people think of sleep as a period when consciousness virtually stops, except during dreams.

And for those people who claim they don't dream at all, the entire time spent sleeping seems to be a mental void. In the past thirty years, however, psychologists have made discoveries about sleep that show these common assumptions to be wrong. Some mental activity goes on during all or most of sleep, and everyone dreams, although most people have trouble recalling their dreams after they awaken.

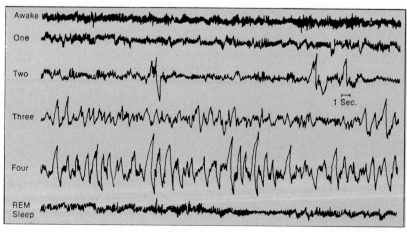

Figure 14.3 Records of the electrical activity of the brain (EEG) in a person in various stages of sleep and in the relaxed waking state known as "alpha." Note that in the deeper stages of sleep the high-frequency, small-amplitude waves give way to lower-frequency, large-amplitude waves. This change is thought to reflect the fact that the neurons in the brain are all firing at about the same level and in about the same pattern. Note also that the EEG pattern in REM sleep is very similar to the waking pattern.

BRAIN ACTIVITY FROM WAKEFULNESS TO DEEP SLEEP The most revealing analyses of sleep have been performed using the electroencephalogram (EEG), a record of the brain's electrical activity. In a typical sleep experiment, electrodes are attached to a volunteer subject's scalp and face and connected to a device that monitors brain waves while he or she sleeps overnight in a bed in the laboratory. As Figure 14.3 shows, the pattern of brain waves changes consistently as the subject drops from wakefulness into light and then deep sleep.

Each stage in the process of falling asleep is dominated by certain brain wave frequencies, measured in cycles per second. Beta waves are the fastest, at fourteen or more cycles per second; alpha waves fall in the range from eight to thirteen per second; theta are between five and seven; and the slowest waves, delta, are four or under. The EEG of a person who is fully awake and alert, eyes open, usually displays a predominance of beta waves. A person who is awake, but relaxed with eyes closed, typically displays an EEG with a predominance of alpha waves. As a person begins to fall asleep (stage 1, Figure 14.3), the brain still shows a large proportion of alpha waves, but mixed in with them are some theta waves, with occasional bursts of high-frequency beta waves. As sleep becomes progressively deeper (stage 2), the alpha pattern disappears and delta waves begin to dominate the record (stage 3).

In the stage of deep sleep (stage 4), the very slow delta waves occupy more than 50 percent of the EEG record. During this stage a person's muscles are relaxed, the heart rate and breathing slow and regular. The nature of consciousness during stage 4 is somewhat of a puzzle. It is difficult to awaken someone from deep sleep: it seems almost as if the person is in a coma. By the time the sleeper is awake, it is uncertain whether whatever he or she recalls actually occurred during stage 4 or while he or she was awakening. Yet some sort of mental activity clearly occurs, since most episodes of sleepwalking,

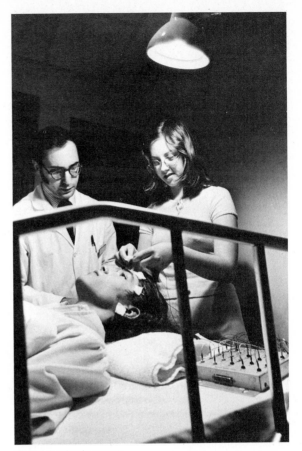

Measuring brain waves.

sleeptalking, and intense nightmares happen during stage 4, as well as the neighborhing stage 3.

REM SLEEP During a night's sleep we do not merely fall into progressively deeper sleep and then gradually wake up. Instead, our brain waves show a regular cyclical pattern that recurs about every ninety minutes, as shown in Figure 14.4. First we fall into deeper and deeper sleep, but then we gradually return to a stage 1, or "waking," pattern. At

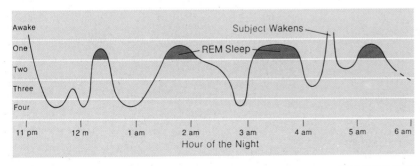

Figure 14.4 A typical night's sleep described in terms of the stages mentioned in the text and Figure 14.3. Note that the depth of sleep increases and decreases in cycles and that sleep becomes shallower and REM sleep periods longer as the night wears on.

this point, though, we do not wake up, as might be expected. Instead, we remain sound asleep and our eyes move rapidly back and forth under our closed eyelids. This stage is known as REM (rapid eye movement) sleep. The average person has about four or five episodes of REM sleep each night, totaling about 25 percent of sleep time, or from one and a half to two hours. Since the discovery of REM sleep some twenty-five years ago, psychologists have come to recognize that the sharpest and most important distinction between the various stages of sleep is that between REM and all the other stages, collectively called non-REM (or NREM) sleep (Aserinsky and Kleitman, 1953; Kleitman, 1963; Dement, 1974).

REM SLEEP AND DREAMING When researchers first observed REM sleep, they suspected that the stage might be related to dreaming. To investigate this possibility, they woke subjects during the different stages of sleep and found that during REM periods dreams with vivid visual imagery occurred about 80 percent of the time. During NREM periods, in contrast, the storylike episodes that we normally consider dreams occurred far less frequently, the exact percentage depending upon how "dream" was defined. Apparently, much of NREM mental activity is more like drifting, unstructured thinking than like dreaming.

With the discovery that rapid eye movements accompany dreams, it was natural to speculate that these movements may be due to the dreamer's "watching" the activity unfolding in the dream. This theory, called "the scanning hypothesis," was first proposed by sleep researcher William Dement (1974) on the basis of anecdotal reports from subjects in his laboratory. The problem with the scanning hypothesis, however, is the difficulty of testing it. A complicated mixture of eye movements occur during most dreams, with very few clear patterns. But one interesting source of evidence in favor of the scanning hypothesis has come from the observation of blind sleepers. A one-night study of the jazz pianist George Shearing, who was blind from birth, found he had no eye movements during any of the stages of sleep; he reported only hearing things during his dreams, not seeing them (Offenkranz and Wolpert, cited in Dement, 1974). Further research on blind people showed that those who were blind from birth had no rapid eye movements and, like Shearing, did not see anything during dreams. But individuals who had become blind later in life had both rapid eye movements and visual images during dreams (Oswald, cited in Dement, 1974). Thus, at this point the scanning hypothesis seems a likely one, but the practical problems of putting it to a definitive test are too difficult to overcome with available methods.

The interiors of our dreams are often furnished with a mixture of the "real" and the "unreal." The "story-like" character of dreams is reflected in much of modern art such as Saul Steinberg's *Eighth Street.*

THE PARADOXES OF REM SLEEP One curious fact about REM sleep is that in some respects it seems similar to being awake. The EEG pattern during REM sleep looks very much like that of someone who is awake, as do other physiological patterns: heartbeat, breathing rate, and blood pressure are irregular and vary enormously, and there is evidence of sexual arousal. Normally this would be the total pattern of a person who is not only awake, but excited—and yet the person is sound asleep. To add to the paradox, certain medical catastrophes seem to occur during REM sleep, including heart attacks and acute worsening of duodenal ulcers and emphysema (Snyder, 1965; Armstrong et al., 1965; Trask and Cree, 1962).

Other measures, however, indicate that REM is a *deeper* stage of sleep than the other stages. During REM sleep, people are very difficult to awaken and do not respond to touch or sound as readily as during stages 2 and 3. In addition, while all the erratic physiological activity mentioned above is going on, virtually all the major body muscles lose their tone and become flaccid (limp). For these reasons REM is sometimes called "paradoxical sleep": people seem to be awake and yet deeply asleep at the same time.

The loss of muscle tone makes us temporarily paralyzed during REM sleep, whereas in stage 4 the muscles still have some tone. The marked drop in muscle tension levels is the surest indicator of REM sleep. Michael Jouvet (1967) has shown that stimulation of a specific part of the brain causes this loss of motor control. When he removed this small part of the brain in cats, REM sleep still occurred, but during it the cats no longer lay still. Instead, they jumped up and moved about—asleep all the while. The cats' behavior suggests that if our muscles weren't paralyzed during REM, our bodies might act out our dreams.

DO WE NEED REM SLEEP? Suspecting that dreams might in some way be essential to our psychological well-being, Dement (1974) deprived sleepers of REM sleep over a series of nights. Whenever he saw the beginning of a REM period, he would awaken the sleeper. He found that it became harder and harder to arouse the sleeper with the onset of each subsequent REM stage, and that the longer he denied REM, the more frequent its appearance became. When, on the fifth night, he let the sleeper go into REM without interruption, he found a "REM rebound" effect: the total time spent in REM doubled over the person's normal level.

Although we apparently have a need for REM sleep, judging from the fact that our bodies automatically compensate for a loss of it, what REM sleep actually does for us is not clear. Any deprivation of sleep—whether of REM or other sleep stages—may make a person somewhat irritable or tired. But loss of our dream time seems to be no more psychologically troubling than loss of other kinds of sleep. Still, REM sleep may be of special value. Some evidence suggests that REM sleep may be a time when the brain adapts to life experiences. In one study, for example, some medical students wore goggles with distorting lenses for several days. The students slept at night in the laboratory. While they were adapting to the weird lenses, they showed a greater than usual amount of REM sleep; but once they had become accustomed to the lenses, REM sleep dropped back to normal (Luce, 1971).

Indirect evidence that REM sleep helps maintain the responsiveness of the brain comes from the fact that REM time steadily lessens as people age. Newborns spend about half their sleep time in REM, infants under two years 30 to 40 percent, adolescents and adults about 20 to 25 percent, and old people less than 5 percent. The average amount of time spent awake and asleep as a function of age is shown in Figure 14.5. Some researchers suggest that

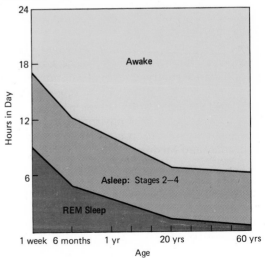

Figure 14.5 The amount of time the average person spends each day in three states: awake, non-REM sleep, and REM (dreaming) sleep, as it changes over the years. In order to show the changes more clearly, the time intervals shown here are wider for younger people than for older people. As people get older, they tend to need less sleep. (Adapted from Hartman, 1967)

dreams offer the brain an internal source of mental stimulation, which enhances the growth and maintenance of neural tissue (Anders and Roffwarg, 1972). Such stimulation may allow key sensory and motor areas to prepare to handle the enormous rush of stimulation from the outside environment during waking. The need for such "rehearsal" time is greatest in the newborn and decreases with age, just as does REM time (Roffwarg, Muzio, and Dement, 1966).

THE CONTENT OF DREAMS　One researcher estimates that by age seventy the average person will have had about 150,000 dreams (Snyder, 1970). Does this mean 150,000 fascinating adventures? Not at all. We have selective recall for our dreams, remembering the more exciting ones and forgetting the rest. When people are awakened randomly during REM sleep and asked what they had just been dreaming, the reports generally are commonplace, even dull (Hall and Van de Castle, 1966). The dreams we remember and talk about "are more coherent, sexier, and generally more interesting" than those collected in systematic research (Webb, 1975, p. 140). Even so, psychologists (especially psychoanalysts) find great symbolic meaning in the most prosaic of dreams. From where does the stuff of dreams come?

DREAMS AND EXTERNAL STIMULI　The realization that the bell persistently ringing in your dream is really your alarm clock is a fairly common occurrence. Some of the content of a dream is simply incorporated from what is happening near the sleeping person—events such as sounds, temperature changes, or touches. Dement and Wolpert (1958) sprayed water on the faces of some sleep-lab volunteers and left a control group of volunteers undisturbed. Those who were sprayed reported more dreams about water than did those who were left dry. This incorporation of environmental stimuli into dreams may serve to "protect" sleep to some extent (Bradley and Meddis, 1974).

DREAMS AND WAKING LIFE　A papyrus in the British Museum dating from 1350 B.C. is about interpreting dreams—an indication that one of the most ancient beliefs about dreams is that they are portents, containing hidden truths about our lives.

As we shall discuss in more detail in Chapter 18, Sigmund Freud formulated for modern psychology the view that dreams express the hidden needs and desires of the subconscious. In *The Interpretation of Dreams* (1900), Freud distinguished between the manifest and the latent content of a dream. The **manifest content** of a dream is derived from the events of the day, sensations during sleep (such as bladder tension), and early memories. The **latent content** is a reflection of our unconscious wishes, primarily from unresolved early psychosexual conflicts. Through "dream work," the manifest content veils the unconscious wishes in symbolic images that are more acceptable to the dreamer.

Over the years, psychoanalysts have modified Freud's theory of dreams; only his most ardent followers still adhere strictly to Freud's method of dream interpretation. Among others (for example, Ullman, 1962, and Foulkes, 1964), the search for latent content has been largely abandoned in favor of direct meaning. They say that the student who dreams about writing an exam in disappearing ink is not trying to resolve an infantile sexual conflict, but is simply worried about his or her upcoming final. The dream is not saying one thing and meaning another.

Hypnosis

According to the popular conception of hypnosis, a hypnotized person is in a state like sleepwalking—seemingly awake yet out of touch with his or her normal waking awareness and self-control. There are, however, enormous differences between the sleepwalker and the hypnotized person. For one thing, their EEGs are very dissimilar. The sleepwalker has the slow brain waves typical of stage 3 or stage 4 sleep; the hypnotic subject's brain waves are no different from those of the normal waking state. Second, the sleepwalker, unlike the hypnotized person, pays no attention to other people and does not take instructions. Finally, the sleepwalker does not remember sleepwalking, while the hypnotic subject remembers everything that went on under hypnosis, as long as he or she is not given specific instructions to forget (Barber, 1975).

Obviously, sleep and hypnosis are very different states of consciousness. But what exactly is hypnosis if not a variant of sleep? After years of experimentation with hypnotism, psychologists still do not have a firm answer to this question. In fact, the difficulty of defining hypnosis except by describing the behavior of hypnotized people has caused many to doubt whether it represents a unique state of consciousness at all. Although hypnosis has been successfully put to a range of medical and therapeutic uses, from anesthetizing patients during surgery to curing psychosomatic allergies, migraine headaches, and insomnia, there is little clear agreement as to how hypnotism works.

HYPNOTIC SUSCEPTIBILITY Most people are familiar with the process by which a person becomes hypnotized. The hypnotist induces a trance by slowly persuading the subject to relax, lose interest in external distractions, and focus on the hypnotist's suggestions. It is not necessary to swing a pocket watch or other object back and forth, but a hypnotist sometimes does so to focus the subject's attention and to increase his or her own apparent authority and expertise. Once the subject is relaxed the hypnotist typically gives a few simple suggestions—such as that the subject's arm will rise. Only after the subject has complied with these easy suggestions will the hypnotist proceed to more difficult ones, such as feeling no pain, or even not bleeding, when stuck with a pin.

According to one estimate about nineteen in twenty people can be hypnotized to some degree if they want to be and if they trust the hypnotist. Hypnotists stress that the relationship between a hypnotist and a subject involves cooperation, not domination. The ability to spot people who can be easily hypnotized is the key to success for a stage hypnotist. One trick, for example, is for the hypnotist to tell the audience that they will discover how easy it is to relax through the power of suggestion alone. After telling them repeatedly to relax and close their eyes, the hypnotist suggests that they will find it difficult to open their eyes. The hypnotist then goes through the audience and chooses people who have still not opened their eyes to be subjects onstage.

Psychologists measure the trait of hypnotic susceptibility more systematically, through tests such as the Stanford Hypnotic Susceptibility Scale. In this test, the hypnotist makes a series of suggestions to the subject, such as: "Your left arm will become rigid," or "You will be unable to say your name when asked." If the subject is unable to bend his or her arm more than two inches in ten seconds, or to

speak his or her name for ten seconds after being asked, this response indicates susceptibility. The subject who responds similarly to the rest of a dozen suggestions, which include hallucinating that he or she sees a fly and being unable to remember part of the proceedings afterward, is rated highly susceptible to hypnosis. In a test of 533 college students, about 10 percent were identified by the Stanford Scale as highly susceptible (E. Hilgard, 1965, p. 215). There are several such scales for assessing hypnotic susceptibility, and the results on all of them appear to be highly correlated.

Those who score high on hypnotic susceptibility have been found to be people who often become spontaneously absorbed in such experiences as reading a novel, listening to music, or appreciating the beauty of nature. They also occasionally experience trancelike states in which they feel somehow separated from their usual way of experiencing things (Bowers, 1976). One researcher suggests that this ability to become deeply absorbed develops early in life. Her research shows that people highly susceptible to hypnosis are more likely as children to have had a history of daydreaming and imaginary companions (J. Hilgard, 1970, 1974). It seems that people who are easily hypnotized have developed in childhood the fantasy skills that make them more open to hypnotic suggestion as adults.

THE HYPNOTIC STATE As we mentioned earlier, the question of whether hypnosis is a discrete state of consciousness has not yet been settled. To date, no single objective measure has been found to correlate with hypnotic trance. There is no specific set of physiological changes that are sure signs a person is hypnotized. Some researchers, such as Ernest Hilgard, take the position that this simply means we have yet to find the appropriate measures. He points out that only recently did researchers discover that rapid eye movements were a sign of dreaming. Until then, there was no "hard" evidence that dreaming was a discrete state of consciousness, although everyone, on the basis of their own experience, could acknowledge its uniqueness. In the same way, contends Hilgard (1975), hypnosis is a state that we can recognize subjectively but cannot yet monitor objectively.

In the absence of psychophysiological measures of the hypnotic state, Hilgard (1977) lists the changes in behavior that hypnotists have long recognized as signs that a subject has been hypnotized. These include: increased suggestibility; enhanced imagery and imagination, including visual memories from early childhood; compliance with the hypnotist's instructions; and avoidance of initiative.

Others object that these changes do not indicate a special state of consciousness because all of them can be induced outside hypnosis. Theodore Barber is a leading proponent of this view. He claims that brief instructions, exhortations that they try their hardest, and assurances that the tasks they are being asked to perform are easy, have the net effect of allowing nonhypnotized subjects to accomplish the same "feats" as hypnotic subjects (Barber, 1965). Nonhypnotized subjects can, for example, hold a heavy weight at arm's length for several minutes; they can lie with a chair under their shoulders and a chair under their feet but nothing else between to support them; they can even stick needles through their hands. In short, Barber contends that everything done under hypnosis can also be done without hypnosis. If this is so, the question arises, "Is hypnosis real?"

A CASE OF HYPNOTIC BLINDNESS A particularly dramatic case that underlines this question was reported by Frank Pattie (1935). Pattie wondered if he could make a hypnotic subject blind in one eye only. In his test for blindness he stimulated the person's eyes in an ingenious way that made it impossible for the person to tell, without cheating, which eye was being stimulated. He also tried to eliminate all possible ways to cheat, such as blinking one eye or moving the eyes from side to side. If Pattie's test showed that the supposedly blind eye was indeed blind, he would have convincing evidence that hypnosis can actually block the registration of sensory impulses from the eyes.

Pattie chose for his test five subjects who were known to enter a deep trance readily. One woman, whom he called "E.," did seem to become blind in one eye under hypnosis. Throughout most of a long series of tests, E. consistently appeared blind in that eye, although there were also some signs that she might be cheating. For this reason Pattie devised an extremely subtle test for blindness, one on which it was virtually impossible to cheat. With this test he showed that E. was not blind at all.

Pattie had E. look at the top line of Figure 14.6 with a red filter over her seeing eye and a green filter over her "blind" eye. The effect of the filters was to block out parts of the top line, as shown. If E. had truly been blind in the green-filtered eye, she would have seen only what appeared through the red filter. But this was not what she reported seeing. Strangely enough, even when she failed this test, E. insisted that she had not cheated and that she was, in fact, blind in one eye. According to every indication, she really believed that she had not cheated.

What can account for E.'s adamant denial? One school of thought contends that she was indeed unaware of what her "blind" eye was seeing, even though it displayed normal physiological reactivity. But another school claims that the unusual relationship between the hypnotist and his subject somehow elicited from E. an unusually good job of acting out the role of a "hypnotized" person. The first of these explanations is called neodissociation theory; the second, role enactment theory.

TWO EXPLANATIONS: NEODISSOCIATION THEORY AND ROLE ENACTMENT THEORY Ernest Hilgard (1973, 1977) proposed a neodissociation theory of hypnosis, based on the notion that consciousness depends on multiple systems, such as cognition and emotion, which are coordinated through hierarchies

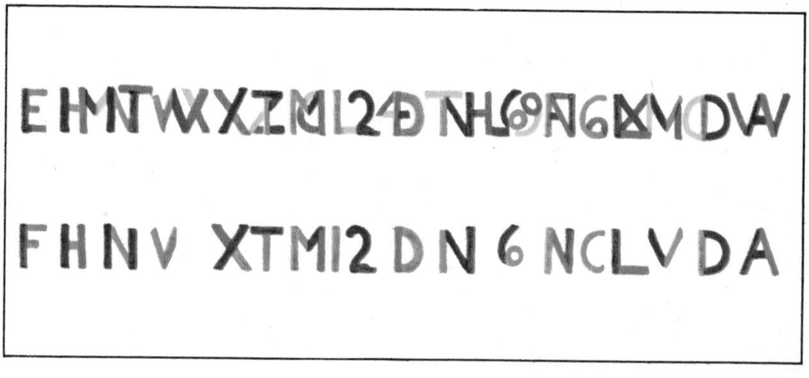

Figure 14.6 The technique used by Pattie to expose a suspected cheater in an experiment on hypnotically induced blindness. The subject was required to look at a line (top) of mixed colored letters and numbers with a red filter over her "good" eye and a green filter over her "bad" eye. The effects of the red filter is shown in the bottom line. If the subject had really been blind, she would have seen only a line of distinct letters and numbers. (After Pattie, 1935)

of control. During hypnosis, these controls shift "so that what is normally voluntary may become involuntary, what is normally remembered may be forgotten, and (under some circumstances) what is normally unavailable to recall may be recalled" (1973, p. 406). In terms of neodissociation theory, therefore, E.'s insistence that she was indeed blind in one eye—despite the evidence to the contrary—was the result of a split in consciousness between her visual system and the part of her awareness that testified she was blind.

Role enactment theory sees hypnosis not as a special state of consciousness, but as a special case of role playing. In this view, the person is simply acting *as if* he or she were hypnotized, just as an actor plays a role. The hypnotist prepares the subject for playing the role of the hypnotized person by establishing expectations: the subject is given explicit instructions about what is to happen, and the hypnotist plays the role of competent hypnotist. The role expectations become more explicit during the induction of hypnosis, through instructions such as, "You can enter a state of hypnosis by concentrating on my voice. . . . You will become relaxed." In this way the hypnotist defines and refines the subject's understanding of the role to be played. The transition to the role of hypnotized person is complete when the subject continues to meet the hypnotist's role demands as they change. The subject's reported experiences, then, are determined by what he or she believes is appropriate and proper to report (Sarbin and Coe, 1972). For the role enactment theorist, therefore, E.'s insistence that she was blind in one eye was typical of someone acting "as if" she had been hypnotized. The question of

whether a hypnotized subject is in a unique state of consciousness or simply role playing is raised by the "regressive" handwriting shown in Figure 14.7.

Although we are unable to reconcile here these two apparently different interpretations of hypnosis, we should note that, either way, the phenomenon of hypnosis is remarkable. That "psychological" instructions can "set" some people to tolerate severe pain, for example, demands an explanation of some sort. But the question of whether the explanation will ultimately be expressed in terms of role enactment theory or of neodissociation theory or in some other terms should not diminish our interest in hypnosis and its proven and potential usefulness.

THE SELF-REGULATION OF CONSCIOUSNESS

A yogi sits in a laboratory in India with legs crossed and eyes closed, deep in meditation. From his head a forest of EEG electrodes lead to a portable monitoring device. A team of psychologists watch intently as the arms of the monitor trace the yogi's brain waves on paper. When the graph shows that the yogi's brain is emitting a steady flow of slow, rhythmic alpha waves, the experiment begins. A psychologist strikes a tuning fork and holds it next to the yogi's ear. The alpha waves stream on, unbroken—a sign that his brain has not recorded the sound at all. The test is repeated with a hand clap, and even with a hot test tube applied to the yogi's arm, all with the same result: his brain, deep in meditation, registers no reaction to these disturbances. The yogi is in *samadhi*, a state in which his awareness appears to be separated from his senses through intense concentration on a single thought or object (Anand, Chhina, and Singh, 1961).

This was one of the first attempts to study the ways people might regulate their own consciousness. Like hypnosis, self-regulating techniques such as meditation and biofeedback have found a wide range of clinical uses, from the control of pain and psychosomatic disorders to psychotherapy. Furthermore, each technique is forcing us to revise our ideas about the degree of control people can exert over their own minds and bodies.

Techniques of self-regulation vary in the altered states of consciousness they can (and cannot) produce and in the changes in bodily function they

Figure 14.7 Signatures obtained from hypnotized subjects with eyes closed under "normal" and "regression" conditions. In the "regression" condition each subject was asked to return to the second grade. Were the subjects temporarily re-entering their past, or were they instead acting out an imagined second-grade self? A definitive answer to this question has not yet been found. (Hilgard, 1965)

In today's high-pressure society, many people find that meditation helps them to "get things together."

LEARNING TO MEDITATE Although there are hundreds of meditation techniques, most Americans have heard of only three: transcendental meditation (TM), yoga, and Zen. TM was developed by the Maharishi Mahesh Yogi from classical Indian techniques; it is basically a method for the passive focusing of attention. What is popularly called yoga is actually not a form of meditation at all, but a series of stretching and bending exercises that were devised thousands of years ago in India as a relaxing prelude to meditation. Zen is the name of a Buddhist sect in Japan whose members practice *zazen*, a set of meditation techniques designed to make the meditator more fully aware of each moment.

Most forms of meditation involve sitting quietly with eyes closed, focusing attention on one thing. In TM, that object of attention is a *mantra*, a sound from the Sanskrit language that the meditator chants over and over. (The best-known mantra is the word *Om*.) In one form of *zazen* the meditator simply notices the normal flow of his or her breathing, without trying to control it in any way. Other common objects used in meditation are short prayers (early Christians used *Kyrie eleison*, Greek for "Lord have mercy"), a sacred picture, a candle flame, a spot in the lower abdomen, various bodily sensations, or a mandala, which is designed so that the gaze always returns to the center as seen in Figure 14.8. Whatever the object of meditation, the task is always the same: to let go of normal thoughts and feelings that intrude on one's attention.

create. Nevertheless, they all share one basic characteristic—self-regulation—which distinguishes them from the other altered states discussed so far. For example, the changes in consciousness that take place during sleep are largely beyond our control; self-regulation techniques such as meditation and biofeedback, in contrast, allow certain changes to occur as we will them, provided we master special exercises. Similarly, hypnosis stresses the control of the hypnotist over the subject through suggestion, whereas in meditation and biofeedback it is the subject who is in control of the changes he or she undergoes.

MEDITATION Meditation is the most ancient and widespread of all self-regulation techniques. In one form or another, it is part of the spiritual practice of every major religion, including Judaism and Christianity. Despite the vast differences in the beliefs and trappings that surround the many kinds of meditation, they all conform to the same definition: **meditation** is a retraining of attention that induces an altered state of consciousness (Goleman, 1977).

Figure 14.8 To meditate, it is necessary to empty the mind of distracting thoughts by focusing on a simple pattern or thought that will not lead to distractions. In some forms of meditation the meditator concentrates on a visual pattern such as the mandala shown here, which continually returns the gaze to its center.

PHYSIOLOGICAL CHANGES DURING MEDITA-TION The body of the meditator may undergo a number of changes reflecting a slowing of the metabolism during deep relaxation. Two researchers (Wallace and Benson, 1972) recorded these changes in subjects practicing TM. Oxygen consumption fell markedly, breathing and heart rates slowed, skin resistance to electrical conduction rose abruptly, and blood pressure dropped. Comparing these bodily indicators with those found during sleep and hypnosis, these researchers concluded that meditation produces a unique state, unlike either sleep or hypnosis.

Although the meditator undergoes physiological changes like those of relaxation (Woolfolk, 1975), the state it produces is not like that of simple relaxation either. The difference can be seen in more pronounced changes in the brain wave patterns of the meditator. The relaxed person shows few changes in brain wave activity, while the meditator's brain waves can change markedly. The brain wave activity of the meditator depends to a large extent on the kind of meditation being done. One study of Zen meditators (Kasamatsu and Hirai, 1966) found that monks practicing *zazen* had alpha waves in their EEGs as soon as they started meditating, even though their eyes were wide open. Alpha is normally found in large amounts only in people whose eyes are closed. As the meditation session progressed, the alpha waves changed progressively to the slower theta waves—very unusual in a person with open eyes. Other researchers have found different EEG patterns during other kinds of meditation, such as a distinctive pattern indicating intense concentration during TM (Banquet, 1973).

BIOFEEDBACK Scientists are interested in meditation mainly because meditators seem to be able to control certain bodily processes, such as blood pressure and heart rate, that were previously thought to be involuntary. Within the last decade electronic technology has fostered the development of a new technique, biofeedback, which also allows a person to control any of several "involuntary" processes. **Biofeedback** is the use of monitoring instruments to give a person a continuous flow of information about his or her own physiological state which ordinarily is unavailable. With this information the person not only can experiment with various ways of altering that state, but can find out immediately if he or she has succeeded. By trial and error, the person gradually learns to control the desired response at will.

Biofeedback has been very successful in helping people regulate certain bodily processes. In a therapeutic situation involving, say, the control of cardiac arrhythmia (irregular heartbeat), the patient is connected to a machine that monitors heart rate. When the heart beats too slowly, a green light goes on; when it beats too quickly, a red light flashes; and an amber light signals when the heart is beating in the right range. Slowly, by attending to subtle body cues associated with increases or decreases in heart rate, the patient learns how to keep the amber light on, and in doing so develops some ability to keep his or her heart rate within the healthy range (Marcus and Levin, 1977). The same general procedure—using biofeedback to learn to control a specific physiological response, then controlling it without biofeedback—has been tried successfully with numerous disorders. Biofeedback is finding its place as a preferred nondrug treatment for medical disorders that are due to the improper functioning of specific bodily processes, such as high blood pressure or chronic muscle-tension headaches.

Other early claims made for biofeedback have failed to hold up, however, most notably those made for its use in controlling alpha waves (Miller, 1974). It had been claimed that biofeedback training could markedly enhance the production of alpha waves, and that this was accompanied by an "alpha experience"—a state of calm, blissful euphoria (see, for example, Brown, 1974). Subsequent research, however, showed that such an experience did not reliably accompany alpha activity (Plotkin and Cohen, 1976). Moreover, there is evidence that biofeedback cannot teach people to generate more alpha waves than they would simply by relaxing and closing their eyes (Lynch, Paskewitz, and Orne, 1974).

This conclusion has been confirmed by a recent study (Lindholm and Lowry, 1978) in which control groups received computer-generated false feedback for their alpha rhythms, while an experimental group received accurate, genuine biofeedback. The biofeedback group did no better than the control groups. Apparently, the increases in alpha wave production found in earlier studies simply reflected the subjects' gradual relaxation as they became accustomed to the biofeedback situation over the course of the experiment.

DRUG-ALTERED CONSCIOUSNESS

A **drug** may be defined as "any substance that can interact with a biological system" (Iversen and Iversen, 1975, p. 58). Accordingly, there is hardly a person alive who is not a drug user. Many substances fall within this broad definition, ranging from aspirin and antibiotics to vitamin C. The drugs of interest for the study of consciousness, however, are those which interact with the central nervous system to alter a person's mood, perception, and behavior. Such **psychoactive drugs** range from the caffeine in coffee and in cola drinks to powerful consciousness-altering substances like marijuana, alcohol, amphetamines, and LSD.

Many psychoactive drugs are taken for medical reasons, to treat physical or psychological disorders. Others create medical problems, because they are highly addictive. Both of these classes of drugs will be discussed in later chapters. Here we will consider drugs that are taken mainly for the purpose of altering consciousness and that induce a range of changes in mood and thought.

THE EFFECTS OF CERTAIN DRUGS ON CONSCIOUSNESS

MARIJUANA Marijuana has been used as an intoxicant among Eastern cultures for centuries; in some societies it is legally and morally acceptable whereas alcohol is not. Before 1960, marijuana use in the United States was common only among members of certain subcultures, such as jazz musicians and artists in big cities. By 1960, however, college students had discovered marijuana, and since then its rate of use has increased by a factor of perhaps ten thousand. According to government figures, about one out of every seven Americans over the age of fifteen uses marijuana in any given week.

The active ingredient in marijuana is a complex molecule called tetrahydrocannabinol (THC), which occurs naturally in the common weed *Cannabis sativa*, or Indian hemp. Marijuana is made by drying the plant; hashish is a gummy powder made from the resin exuded by the flowering tops of the female plant. Both marijuana and hashish are usually smoked, but they can also be cooked with food and eaten.

Although the effects of the drug vary somewhat from person to person and also seem to depend on the setting in which it is taken, there is considerable consensus among regular users on how marijuana affects them (Tart, 1970). Most sensory experiences seem greatly enhanced or augmented—music sounds fuller, colors are brighter, smells are richer, foods taste better, and sexual and other sensations are more intense. Users become elated, the world seems somehow more meaningful, and even the most ordinary events may take on a kind of extraordinary profundity. The sense of time is greatly distorted. A short sequence of events may seem to last for hours. Users may become so entranced with an object that they sit and stare at it for many minutes. A musical phrase of a few seconds' duration may seem to stretch out in time until it becomes isolated from the rest of the composition, and the hearer perceives it as never before.

As many users of marijuana have discovered, however, the drug can sometimes heighten unpleasant as well as pleasant experiences. If a person is in a frightened or depressed mood to begin with, the chances are excellent that taking the drug will blow the negative feelings out of proportion, so that the user's world, temporarily at least, becomes very upsetting. Cases have been reported in which marijuana appears to have helped bring on psychological disturbances in people who were already unstable before they used it.

Despite the obvious need for careful research on marijuana, the first well-controlled scientific studies of its effects on human beings did not appear until the late 1960s. One of the first of these studies was conducted using college students as subjects, some who had experience with the drug and some who did not. All the experienced users but only one of the inexperienced participants got "high" (that is, reported the typical euphoria). In tests of both intellectual and motor skills, all of the inexperienced subjects displayed impairment, while the experienced users did not (Weil, Zinberg, and Nelsen, 1968). Likewise, in a laboratory study of motor skills in a simulated driving situation, inexperienced subjects showed greater impairment than experienced subjects (Rafaelsen et al., 1973). However, other studies have found indiscriminate impairment in both experienced and inexperienced subjects in certain kinds of intellectual performances during a "high." One consistent finding is that marijuana appears to interfere with short-term memory processes (see Chapter 5). This effect is objectively measured in a carefully controlled laboratory setting by asking intoxicated subjects to recall information that had just been learned (Darley et al., 1973; Casswell and Marks, 1978). This effect is subjectively experienced as difficulty in keeping track of a conversation or in keeping track of one's place in a task that requires a series of coordinated steps for completion.

COCAINE Cocaine, a product of the leaves of certain coca plants, is a potent stimulant (a class of drugs that provide energy, alertness, and feelings of confidence). Cocaine used to be one of the ingredients in Coca-Cola, which was originally sold as an invigorating tonic. Today, although cocaine is both illegal and expensive, its popularity is growing among middle-class professional people. Cocaine usually is taken in the form of a fine white powder which is inhaled, or "snorted," into the nostrils, where it is absorbed into the bloodstream through the mucous membranes. It may also be injected intravenously.

While there has been little laboratory research on the effects of cocaine, some researchers have studied its effects by interviewing users (Grinspoon and Bakalar, 1976). A moderate dose of cocaine produces a euphoric state that can last for thirty minutes to an hour (Resnick et al., 1977). Users claim that it improves attention, reaction time, and speed in simple mental tasks, and so can be helpful for work that requires wakefulness, a free flow of associations, or the suppression of boredom and fatigue. However, the euphoria cocaine brings can make users overestimate their own capacities or the quality of their work. Like other stimulants, cocaine provides a short-term burst of energy, but since it does not replenish energy stores, users will pay the price in physical exhaustion after the drug wears off and the body "comes down" or "crashes."

Long-term use or large doses of cocaine can have harsher effects. Repeated use can irreversibly damage the mucous membranes of the nasal septum, which separates the nostrils. Chronic use can also result in a general poisoning of the system, characterized by mental deterioration, weight loss, agitation, and paranoia. Cocaine taken in large doses can produce hallucinations, one of the most horrifying of which is formication, a condition in which the person feels there are bugs crawling under his or her skin. This hallucination may be caused by drug-induced hyperactivity of the nerves in the skin. In excessive doses, especially by injection, cocaine can produce headache, hyperventilation, nausea, convulsions, coma, and sometimes death.

HALLUCINOGENS Hallucinogens—so-called because one of their main effects is to produce hallucinations—are found in plants that grow throughout the world, and have been used for their effects on consciousness since earliest human history (Schultes, 1976). These drugs are also called "psychedelic" ("mind-manifesting") because they are seen as demonstrating the ways in which the mind has the potential to function.

Among the more common hallucinogenic plants are belladonna, henbane, mandrake, datura (Jimson weed), one species of morning glory, peyote cactus, many kinds of mushrooms, and also cannabis. While we still do not know the exact chemical effects of hallucinogens on the brain, some contain chemical compounds that seem to mimic the activity of certain neurotransmitters, the chemical messengers that regulate brain cell activity.

LSD (lysergic acid diethylamide), the best-known and most extensively studied of the hallucinogens, is also the most potent; in fact, it is one of the most powerful drugs known. LSD, which is a synthetic substance, is 100 times stronger than psilocybin, which comes from certain mushrooms, and 4,000 times stronger than mescaline, which comes from the peyote cactus. A dose of a few millionths of a gram has a noticeable effect; an average dose of 100 to 300 micrograms produces a "trip" that lasts from six to fourteen hours.

During an LSD trip a person can experience any number of mood states, often quite intense and rapidly changing. The person's "set"—expectations, mood, beliefs—and the circumstances under which he or she takes LSD can affect the experience, making it euphoric or terrifying. Perceptual hallucinations are very common with LSD. A typical hallucinatory progression begins with simple geometric forms, progresses to complex images, and then to dreamlike scenes (Siegel, 1977). The user may encounter such distortions in form that familiar objects become almost unrecognizable. A wall, for example, may seem to pulsate or breathe. One's senses, too, seem to intermingle; sounds may be "seen" and visual stimuli may be "heard." A person may experience a dissociation of the self into one being who observes and another who feels. Distortions of time, either an acceleration or a slowing down, are also common. A single stimulus may become the focus of attention for hours, perceived as ever-changing or newly beautiful and fascinating.

As measured by the ability to perform simple tasks, LSD impairs thinking, even though the user may feel that he or she is thinking more clearly and logically than ever before. Life-long problems may suddenly seem resolved, or the need to solve them may seem absurd. The person often experiences the "great truth" phenomenon—that is, he or she feels that previously hidden and ultimate inner truths have been revealed. When the trip is over, the magnitude of these discoveries shrinks, and the solutions reached may turn out to be untenable. After three to five hours the experience begins to become less intense; after six hours or so the hallucinations and illusions disappear—if no complications occur.

Panic reactions are the most common of LSD's unpleasant side effects, and they may be terrifying. Those who experience panic and later describe it often say that they felt trapped in the experience of panic and were afraid that they would never get out or that they would go mad. Panic usually arises when a person tries to ignore, change, or otherwise get rid of the effects of the drug—rather than yielding to the sensations it generates—then realizes he or she cannot. The best treatment, if the panic is not too severe, seems to be the comfort offered by friends

Drawings Done by a Man Under the Influence of LSD

(A) Twenty minutes after the first dose the drug had not taken effect. If the dosage had been adequate, some physiological effects would have been noticed at this point.

(B) A second dose was administered one hour after the first. Twenty-five minutes after the second dose, the subject experienced the first alterations of perception and rapid changes of emotion. He saw the model correctly but had difficulty in controlling the wide, sweeping movements of his hand.

(C) Shortly after the third drawing the subject stated: "The outlines of the model are normal, but those of my drawing are not. I pull myself together and try again: it's no good."

(D) Two hours and forty-five minutes after the first dose, the subject experienced the most intense effects of the drug. He said: "The perspective of the room has changed, everything is moving . . . everything is interwoven in a network of color . . . the model's face is distorted to a diabolic mask."

(E) Five hours and forty-five minutes after the first dose, the effects of the drug began to subside. An hour later the subject said: "It is probably because my movements are still too unsteady that I am unable to draw as I normally do . . . the intoxication is wearing off, but I can both feel it and see it ebbing and flowing about me (now it only reaches to my knees); finally, only an eddying motion remains."

(F) Eight hours after the first dose the intoxication had worn off, except for a few small waves (for example, sudden distortions of faces from time to time). The subject felt bewildered and tired: "I have nothing to say about the last drawing, it is bad and uninteresting."

and the security of pleasant, familiar settings. Medical attention is sometimes necessary for very intense reactions.

LSD is proving valuable in the study of certain biochemical and physiological functions of the brain. Serotonin, a substance that may help transmit nerve impulses in the brain and that may play an important role in the regulation of sleep and emotion, is chemically similar to part of the LSD molecule. Apparently, LSD blocks the effects of serotonin on brain tissue, which may account for some of its effects on human behavior. But the exact mechanism by which LSD works has yet to be discovered.

DRUGS AND CREATIVITY   Many modern poets, novelists, and artists attribute creative insights to their use of drugs. Novelist Ken Kesey used peyote and LSD while he wrote parts of *One Flew Over the Cuckoo's Nest*; poet Allen Ginsberg used LSD in writing *Kaddish and Other Poems*; the book *Psychedelic Art* (Masters and Houston, 1968) is a collection of paintings inspired by experience with hallucinogens. Do drugs really enhance creativity? The evidence is by no means clear. On the one hand, the altered states that drugs induce seem conducive to the creative process. For example, under the influence of certain drugs some people free-associate easily, are relaxed and open, have heightened sensory awareness, and can fantasize freely.

On the other hand, aspects of the drug state can hinder creative production: some users experience a diminished capacity for logical thought, reduced ability to direct concentration or to control sequences that they imagine, and a tendency to become absorbed in the state itself. Another problem with creative efforts is that during drug states a person's capacity for self-criticism is often blunted. William James, for example, during experiments with nitrous oxide (laughing gas), had several mystical illuminations. However, he was never able to record these revelations before he blacked out from the gas. One night, though, he managed to write down his monumental thoughts before losing consciousness. On returning to his normal state, James rushed to find out what he had written. It was this:

> Hogamous, Higamous
> Man is polygamous
> Higamous, Hogamous
> Woman monogamous.

There are, as yet, no well-controlled studies of the effects of drugs on creativity. The best evidence to date suggests that while drugs can open new perspectives for almost anyone, it takes an already highly skilled person to translate these new ideas into a finished artistic product (Leavitt, 1974, pp. 286–307).

Summary

1. Loosely defined, **consciousness** is an awareness of the many thoughts, images, sensations, and emotions that flow through one's mind at any given moment. The only points about consciousness on which most psychologists agree are: consciousness is limited; it is related to brain activity; and it has various modes.

   A. Consciousness is limited in two ways:
      1. By the inaccessibility to the human mind of certain stimuli.
      2. By the limited number of internal and external events to which a person can pay attention at one time.
   B. While modern research has confirmed the relationship between consciousness and brain activity, the precise nature of this connection has not been established. Some neuroscientists believe that consciousness is the sum total of brain activity. Roger Sperry has postulated that the mind has a role in directing brain activity, but that brain activity is necessary for the mind to emerge.
   C. Some psychologists have suggested that two separate modes of consciousness coexist within each person. They contend that these two distinct consciousnesses are related, to some degree, to the differences in function between the right and left halves of the brain. One mode of consciousness is logical and analytic, the other intuitive and artistic.

2. Psychologists have discovered that consciousness is not suspended during sleep; rather, some men-

tal activity goes on during all or most of sleep.

A. The brain's electrical activity during sleep can be measured by the use of an electroencephalogram (EEG). Each stage in the process of falling asleep, from wakefulness to rapid eye movement (REM) sleep, is dominated by certain brain wave frequencies, measured in cycles per second. Beta waves are the fastest, followed by alpha waves, theta waves, and delta waves.

B. During a night's sleep a person's brain waves show a regular cyclical pattern that recurs about every ninety minutes. REM sleep, which totals about 25 percent of sleep time, occurs when a person's brain waves return to a "waking" pattern but the person does not awaken.

   1. REM sleep is characterized by vivid dreams. In non-REM (NREM) sleep the mind's activity is more like drifting, unstructured thinking than like dreaming. The scanning hypothesis of William Dement postulates that the rapid eye movements of REM sleep are caused by the dreamer "watching" the activity unfold in a dream.

   2. REM sleep is paradoxical because people seem to be awake and yet deeply asleep at the same time. The EEG pattern and other physiological patterns of a person during REM are those of a person who is excited, yet the sleeper is difficult to awaken.

   3. The function of REM sleep is unclear, but experiments by William Dement show that people automatically compensate for a loss of it. Some evidence suggests that REM sleep may be a time when the brain adapts to life's experiences.

C. Although people have selective recall of their dreams, especially the exciting ones, psychologists find symbolic meaning in all dreams. The content of dreams is derived from external stimuli and from the waking life of the dreamer.

   1. Some of the content of a dream comes from what is happening near the sleeping person—events such as sounds, temperature changes, or touches.

   2. Freud distinguished between the manifest content and the latent content of a dream. The manifest content is derived from the events of the day, sensations during sleep, and early memories. The latent content is a reflection of unconscious wishes, primarily from unresolved early psychosexual development. Most psychoanalysts have modified Freud's theory of the meaning of dreams; others have abandoned the search for the latent content of dreams, accepting their direct meaning instead.

3. Psychologists are unable to agree on how hypnosis works. The difficulty of defining hypnosis except by describing the behavior of hypnotized people has caused many psychologists to doubt that hypnosis represents a unique state of consciousness. Hypnotism has been successfully put to a number of medical and therapeutic uses.

A. To induce a hypnotic trance, the hypnotist persuades a subject to relax, lose interest in external distractions, and focus on the hypnotist's suggestions. Hypnotists stress that the relationship between a hypnotist and a subject involves cooperation, not domination. The Stanford Hypnotic Suggestibility Scale is one means of testing a person's capacity to comply with suggestion.

B. One reason that researchers disagree about whether hypnosis is a unique state of consciousness is that no single objective measure—no specific set of physiological changes, for example—has been found to correlate with the hypnotic state. To find out if hypnosis is real, Frank Pattie attempted to make a hypnotic subject temporarily blind in one eye. The one subject who claimed that she had indeed become blind failed Pattie's test for blindness, but she insisted that she was telling the truth and was blind in one eye. Two schools of thought would interpret the woman's behavior differently:

   1. Neodissociation theory, proposed by Ernest Hilgard, suggests that consciousness depends on multiple systems, such as cognition and emotion, which are coordinated through hierarchies of controls. During hypnosis these controls shift; the woman could have been unaware that she was actually seeing with her "blind" eye.

   2. Role enactment theory sees hypnosis not as a special state of consciousness, but as a special case of role playing; the woman could have been unconsciously acting out the role of a hypnotized person.

4. Consciousness can be self-regulated by such tech-

niques as meditation and biofeedback. These techniques vary in the altered states and in the bodily changes they can produce. They have some clinical uses, and their existence implies that people can exert a great degree of control over their own minds and bodies.

A. Meditation, the oldest and most widespread of all the self-regulation techniques, is a retraining of attention that induces an altered state of consciousness.

B. In biofeedback a person receives a continuous flow of information about his or her own physiological state. The person can experiment with various ways of altering that state and gradually learn to control the desired response at will.

5. **Psychoactive drugs** interact with the central nervous system to alter a person's mood, perception, and behavior.

A. Marijuana's effect on consciousness is to enhance most sensory stimuli. The drug can heighten both pleasant and unpleasant sensations, and its effects vary with the person and the setting.

B. Cocaine is a stimulant that provides energy, alertness, and feelings of confidence. Little laboratory research has been conducted on the effects of cocaine. Large doses or long-term use of the drug can result in a number of physical and psychological impairments.

C. Hallucinogens, such as peyote, LSD, and certain types of mushrooms, produce hallucinations. The exact chemical effects that hallucinogens have on the brain are not known, but it is believed some of them contain chemical compounds that mimic the activity of certain neurotransmitters.

D. The relationship between drugs and creativity is not clear. Drugs can create altered states of consciousness that seem conducive to the creative process, but drugs can also diminish the capacity for logical thought, reduce the ability to direct one's concentration or to control sequences that one imagines, and create a tendency to be absorbed in the drug state itself.

RECOMMENDED READINGS

DEMENT, WILLIAM C. *Some Must Watch While Some Must Sleep.* San Francisco: Freeman, 1974. One of the pioneers in modern dream research presents a brief, readable, up-to-date account of what is known about sleep and dreaming. Gives special attention to the relationship between sleep and psychological disorders, including insomnia and mental illness.

HILGARD, ERNEST. *Divided Consciousness: Multiple Controls on Human Thought and Action.* New York: Wiley, 1977. A presentation of neodissociation theory, developed by Hilgard.

ORNSTEIN, ROBERT. *The Psychology of Consciousness.* San Francisco: Freeman, 1977. Explores human consciousness from a number of perspectives, emphasizing the idea of two major modes of consciousness related to the two hemispheres of the brain.

PETERSEN, ROBERT E. (ed.). *Marijuana Research Findings: 1976.* Research Monograph 14. National Institute on Drug Abuse, 1977. A broad, thorough, and objective summary of research findings on all aspects of marijuana: chemistry, behavioral effects, physiological effects. Can be obtained from the National Institute on Drug Abuse, 11400 Rockville Pike, Rockville, Md. 20852.

RAY, OAKLEY. *Drugs, Society, and Human Behavior.* St. Louis: Mosby, 1978. A lucid, lively, and thorough presentation of drug research and the impact of "recreational" drugs on society. Includes a section on psychotherapeutic drugs.

SARBIN, THEODORE, and WILLIAM COE. *Hypnosis.* New York: Holt, Rinehart and Winston, 1972. An analysis of hypnosis from the standpoint of role theory.

TEYLER, TIMOTHY J. *Altered States of Awareness.* San Francisco: Freeman, 1972. A collection of important articles from *Scientific American* dealing with the split brain, sleep and dreaming, drugs, meditation, and sensory deprivation.

CHAPTER FIFTEEN

THE EXPERIENCE AND EXPRESSION OF EMOTION

As an "expert" on robots—and I put the word in quotes because the supposed expertise is based only on the fact that I write about them and not that I know anything about them—I am frequently challenged on my expressed belief that robots have the potentiality of being as good as human beings, or, in fact, better. One of the challenges is to the effect that human beings can demonstrate emotion, while robots cannot, and in that way robots are basically different from human beings and therefore (presumably) inferior.

Many years ago, I discussed the matter with John W. Campbell, the editor of *Astounding Science Fiction,* where my robot stories appeared.

He said, "Why do you feel fear sometimes, Isaac?"

Being a materialist, I said, "Because my adrenal glands pump adrenaline into my bloodstream and I then undergo those physiological changes that produce the effects we call 'fear.' I pant because my breathing accelerates; I turn pale because my blood withdraws from my skin and concentrates in my muscles; I tremble because my muscle tone increases. I need all that for rapid flight or other strenuous activity."

John said, "Does the adrenaline pump because you are afraid, or are you afraid because the adrenaline pumps?"

I said, "The adrenaline is first discharged; then I am afraid."

"What makes it discharge?"

"The sight, sound, or other perception of something that can harm or hurt me."

"If you turn a corner and see a snarling, crouching lion, would the adrenaline start pumping at the sight?"

"Absolutely," I said.

"And if you are at the zoo and turn a corner and see a snarling, crouching lion behind bars, would the adrenaline start pumping at the sight?"

"No," I said, chagrined.

"In other words, you are afraid only when you consciously consider what you perceive, and you decide to be afraid as the best way of keying your body to its work, and you use the adrenaline as your tool."

"You make it sound so," I said.

"And suppose you could in-crease your oxygen supply without panting, and feed blood to your muscles without withdrawing it from your face, and tighten your muscles without making them tremble. Wouldn't you have all the effectiveness for action that fear brings and yet not *look* afraid? And if you didn't look afraid, would anyone know you were afraid? Isn't what we call fear merely the *look* of fear? And if a robot could make all the internal adjustments needed for the kind of rapid action that should bring about escape from the presence of something potentially destructive, but was not designed to have anything visible result in its face or body, would it not have all the value of fear without looking afraid, and would we not then judge it not to be *displaying* emotion? But how important is it that the physiology of fear be visible as far as analyzing a brain's capacity is concerned? And do robots lack emotion just because you can't see it?"

The answers were all obvious. I have seldom been so Socratically demolished.

Isaac Asimov

William James, the famous nineteenth-century American psychologist, was one of the first to offer a systematic theory of emotions. He attempted to describe the powerful role emotions play in human experience in this way:

> Conceive yourself, if possible, suddenly stripped of all the emotion with which your world now inspires you. . . . It will be almost impossible for you to realize such a condition of negativity and deadness. No one portion of the universe would then have importance beyond another; the whole collection of its things and series of its events would be without significance, character, expression, or perspective. Whatever of value, interest, or meaning our respective worlds may appear endued with are thus pure gifts of the spectator's mind. The passion of love is the most familiar and extreme example of this fact. If it comes, it comes; if it does not come, no process of reasoning can force it. Yet it transforms the value of the creature loved as utterly as the sunrise transforms Mont Blanc from a corpse-like gray to a rosy enchantment; and it sets the whole world to a new tune for the lover and gives a new issue to his life. So with fear, with indignation, jealousy, ambition, worship. If they are there, life changes. (1890)

Emotions, then, set the tone of our experiences and give life its vitality. Without the ability to feel rage and grief, joy and love, we would hardly recognize ourselves as human.

The richness of human emotional capacity is revealed in human language. Every language includes many words that explicitly label emotional states. How many such words are there in English? One psychologist (Davitz, 1969) found over 400 in *Roget's Thesaurus*, a book of synonyms. This researcher decided that some 50 of these words represent the broad range of human emotions. Anger, despair, joy, sorrow, fear, amazement, gratitude, impatience, disgust, anticipation, embarrassment, humiliation, amusement, jealousy, reverence, and love are among the many linguistically differentiated feelings that make up the human emotional world.

Several important areas in the study of emotions are explored in this chapter. We start by discussing the nature of emotions, focusing on three ways in which emotional states can be perceived and measured: subjective reports, behavioral indicators, and physiological changes. Then we turn to the question of how people come to label their own emotional experiences, unraveling the interplay between physiological and cognitive factors. Finally, we take up the issue of emotional expression: how emotions are communicated to others through nonverbal behavior and roles of learning and innate factors in emotional expression.

A mask over the face—in this case, a clown's makeup—often masks one's emotions as well.

Our behavior can alter our emotional state. Whatever their mood before this moment, that they are now relaxed is apparent in the easy postures and movements of these men around a swimming hole.

THE NATURE OF EMOTIONS

Most people can vividly remember or at least imagine the joy of falling in love, the anguish of a loved one's death, the embarrassment of being called on in class when they are completely unprepared, or the frustration of discovering that their car's battery is dead when they are late for a final exam. In fact, emotional experiences are so much a part of us that we can easily empathize with others who are in emotion-arousing situations. As familiar as emotions are to us, though, it is not easy to formulate a general definition of them. What is it that love, grief, embarrassment, and frustration have in common? Essentially, they can all be described as consisting of subjective feelings, overt behavior, and physiological responses.

SUBJECTIVE FEELINGS Every emotion is accompanied by an awareness of the feelings associated with it, even though those feelings may be difficult to put into words. When we are happy, for example, we sometimes say that there is a special lift in everything we do, a bouncy feeling. On the other hand, if we are humiliated, we may say that we feel as if we would like to shrink or disappear. Many psychologists who investigate emotions have relied on such subjective reports, in spite of their imprecise

quality. In fact, because a specific emotion sometimes does not reveal itself through facial expressions or overt actions, a subjective report may be the only way to discover if someone is experiencing a particular emotion at all.

Psychologists have devised special rating scales and measurement techniques to help them record these subjective reports in a systematic way. A high degree of consensus among people in rating common experiences (a movie, perhaps) as "hilarious," "disgusting," "sad," or "happy" indicates that our personal emotional reactions to things are shared by many others. Such ratings contribute to an understanding of the degree to which emotional reactions are consistent—or vary—from one individual to the next. Nevertheless, psychology would probably not have progressed very far from its nineteenth-century origins if it had relied only on subjective accounts of human experiences.

OVERT BEHAVIOR While feelings are often imprecise and difficult to measure, much of the behavior accompanying strong feelings can be observed directly. Moreover, there is general agreement on the meaning of such behavior. Silent movies, for example, depend for their effect on this general agreement. When the villain bares his teeth and clenches his fists, most people assume that he is angry; when the heroine furrows her brow and wrings her hands, we assume she is worried. We all learn to recognize such behavioral cues very early in life, and this serves as a basis for identifying the states that go with various emotional labels.

Most people are accustomed to thinking that the behaviors accompanying their emotions are a *result* of their feelings. We believe that we smile *because* we are happy, clench our fists *because* we are angry, pace up and down *because* we are tense. But the relationship between feelings and overt behavior is not always so clear-cut. Studies have shown that at times emotion-related behavior may be as much a cause as an effect; in certain instances overt behavior may actually help to bring on feelings. If you are tense, then relax your muscles intentionally, you may suddenly discover that you feel less anxious. If you walk with a shuffling, stooped-over posture, you may begin to feel somewhat depressed regardless of what your mood had been before.

The effect of behavior on feelings has been tested experimentally (Laird, 1974). Thirty-two university students were falsely told that they were to participate in an experiment to measure activity in facial muscles. Bogus electrodes were attached to each face, as if to measure physiological responses, and the subjects were instructed to raise their eyebrows, contract the muscles in their forehead, and so on. In this way the experimenters were able to manipulate the facial expressions of their subjects until they formed a smile or a frown, while the subjects remained unaware of the emotion-related content of their own expressions. Cartoons were then flashed on a screen—some when the subjects were in a "smile" position, others when they were in a "frown" position. Regardless of the content of the cartoons, the subjects rated as funnier the cartoons that they saw when their faces were in "smile" positions. When subjects were asked to score their own emotions, they described themselves as happier when they were smiling and angrier when they were frowning. They seem to have used their objective behavior—smiling or frowning—as an indication of their subjective feelings. Thus, to some degree overt behavior can serve as a cause as well as a result of emotions.

PHYSIOLOGICAL CHANGES   In addition to being associated with changes in obvious motor activity—clenching of fists, frowning, or smiling—strong emotions are also associated with internal changes resulting from activation of the autonomic nervous system. As we discussed in Chapter 11, the autonomic nervous system usually functions without our moment-to-moment awareness or conscious control. It is composed of two divisions, the sym-

pathetic and the parasympathetic, both of which have some control over most visceral muscles and glands. This dual control generally works antagonistically: sympathetic activity may dominate parasympathetic activity, or vice versa. The sympathetic division, which promotes energy expenditure, dominates during emergency or stress situations; the parasympathetic division, which promotes energy conservation, dominates under conditions of relaxation. Most of the internal changes that occur with certain emotions, such as intense fear or anger, are caused by the action of the sympathetic branch of the autonomic nervous system.

What exactly happens when the sympathetic nervous system is activated? Suppose, for example, you are crossing the street and are startled by the loud blast of a car horn right behind you. What physiological changes occur as a result of this emotion-arousing situation? There are several changes:

1. The heartbeat increases, sometimes more than doubling.

2. The movement of the gastrointestinal tract nearly stops. The blood vessels leading to the stomach and intestines constrict, while those leading to the larger skeletal muscles expand, diverting blood to where it may be needed for fighting or, as in this case, fleeing.

3. The endocrine glands stimulate the liver to release sugar into the bloodstream, which can supply energy to the skeletal muscles, should they need it.

4. Breathing becomes more rapid and deeper. The bronchioles (the small branches of the bronchi, the air passages that lead into the lungs) expand, and the mucus secretion in the bronchi decreases. All this increases the supply of oxygen in the bloodstream, which is needed to burn the sugar being sent to the skeletal muscles.

5. The pupils of the eyes dilate, and visual sensitivity increases.

6. The salivary glands may stop working, causing dryness of the mouth, while the sweat glands may increase their activity, resulting in a decrease in the resistance of the skin to electrical conduction (commonly called the galvanic skin response, or GSR).

7. The muscles just beneath the surface of the skin contract, causing hairs to stand erect; this is observed as "goose bumps." (Lang, Rice, and Sternbach, 1972)

As you leap to safety and the car passes, the opposing effects of the parasympathetic division of the autonomic nervous system begin to reassert themselves. Heartbeat, respiration, glandular secretions, and muscular tension all return to normal, and the physiological (bodily) experience of the emotion subsides. (Sometimes the physiological stress related to emotional arousal can lead to illness or even sudden death; for more on this, see the accompanying Special Feature.)

MEASURING THE PHYSIOLOGY OF EMOTION: THE POLYGRAPH With the proper equipment, the physiological changes associated with emotions can easily be measured. A polygraph (sometimes called a "lie detector") is essentially an "emotion detector"; it measures some of the physiological activities usually related to emotional states. When used as a lie detector, the polygraph takes advantage of the tendency of a person who lies to feel guilt or anxiety. These emotions bring on changes in blood pressure, respiration rate, and the GSR. The picture below shows a lie detector arrangement. Electrodes attached to the hand measure changes in GSR, the rubber tube (or pneumograph) around the chest measures respiration, and the cuff on the left arm records changes in heart rate and blood pressure. The polygraph records these physiological responses while the subject is asked questions. Typically, the interrogator begins with a series of routine questions ("How old are you?" "Where do you live?") in order to establish a baseline against which the reactions to emotionally charged questions that will be asked later may be evaluated. A person suspected of, say, a bank robbery last Thursday may next be asked, "Where were you between 2 and 3 p.m. last Thursday?" If the verbal response is "At home, reading," but involuntary autonomic responses show noticeable changes, the interrogator becomes suspicious about the truthfulness of the statement.

There are several problems with a lie detector test that make its use controversial and, in some areas, inadmissible as legal evidence. First, changes in GSR and other responses following a lie are only partially reliable. Habitual liars may experience no obvious emotion when telling a lie, and their physiological changes will be slight or nonexistent. Or a knowledgeable suspect may practice lying in order to learn to control his or her "involuntary" responses. Or an innocent suspect's anxiety at being connected with a crime may produce polygraph results similar to a guilty person's. Second, a person can alter the results of the baseline condition, making subsequent comparisons meaningless. For instance, if a suspect thinks about the bank robbery when asked for his current address, he will create a baseline that reflects changes equal in magnitude to those associated with the crime itself. When he is later asked about the crime, his reply will show no special change in physiological activation.

PHYSIOLOGICAL CHANGES AND THE BRAIN Although the autonomic nervous system triggers certain physiological changes associated with emotions, this system is coordinated by the brain. Research with cats has shown that stimulating certain areas of the hypothalamus can induce complicated attack behavior characterized by intense activation of the sympathetic division of the autonomic nervous system and by an emotional display that can be interpreted as feline rage. Responses include dilation of the pupils, erection of the fur along the back and tail, flattening of the ears, arching of the spine, unsheathing of the claws, and intense hissing and snarling. Stimulating other portions of the

A polygraph ("lie detector") examination.

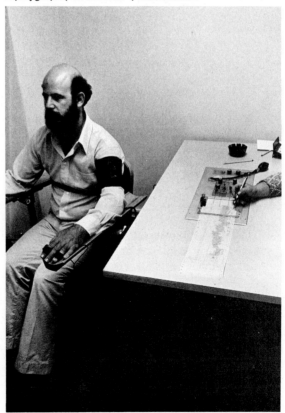

Emotional Stress and Illness

Emotion—love, anger, joy, frustration—gives texture and meaning to our lives. But emotional stress, if severe or prolonged, can take a harsh toll on the body. And stress is everywhere; it can scarcely be avoided. Contrary to the popular idea of stress as an undesirable phenomenon, stress can represent the body's response to pleasure as well as to pain. As Hans Selye, the dean of stress researchers, put it:

> Stress is the body's nonspecific response to *any* demand placed on it, whether that demand is pleasant or not. Sitting in a dentist's chair is stressful, but so is enjoying a passionate kiss with a lover—after all, your pulse races, your breathing quickens, your heart beat soars. And yet who in the world would forgo such a pleasurable pastime simply because of the stress involved? Our aim shouldn't be to completely avoid stress, which at any rate would be impossible, but to learn how to recognize our typical response to stress and then to try to modulate our lives in accordance with it. (Selye and Cherry, 1978, p. 60)

Of course, people in similar situations experience different amounts of stress. Giving a public lecture may be a terror to a student, a tonic to a politician, a bore to an ambassador. But under any kind of stress, emotional or physical, all bodies seem to show a certain common set of reactions. Selye called these physiological responses the "stress syndrome," the body's response to viruses, starvation, frostbite, and other attacks. The physiological nature of stress, and the body's stereotyped reactions to various kinds of stress, were first defined by Selye in 1956.

The Body's Response to Stress: Selye's Three Stages

Selye observed that the body reacts to stress in three stages: alarm, resistance, and exhaustion (1956). If a man leaps into cold water, he is shocked at first, then his body begins to adapt, resisting the initial numbness. If he stays in the water too long, his body can no longer bear it and succumbs to exhaustion. The human body follows this pattern under all kinds of stress. First comes the alarm reaction, consisting of an initial shock and a subsequent countershock. In the initial shock phase, the autonomic nervous system triggers an increased secretion of hormones by the adrenal glands. Overwhelming stress can cause death in this first phase of the alarm reaction. More commonly, the countershock phase sets in, as a response to continuing stress. The autonomic and endocrine systems step up their general resistance, while the appropriate local defenses come into play. Now the "stress syndrome" appears: enlarged adrenal glands, shrunken thymus gland and lymph nodes, and ulcerated stomach.

During the resistance phase, which comes next, the body's local, more specific defenses take over the battle against stress, eliminating the need for the generalized activities of the nervous system and glands. Hormone production falls to near normal levels, and the physical symptoms of the countershock phase disappear. Either the local defenses win the war, or, if the stress continues for too long or increases, exhaustion sets in. The endocrine system is once more aroused, hormone levels rise, the physical symptoms of countershock recur. The body's capacity to resist stress decreases steadily, and if the stress remains unchecked, death is the only possible outcome. At times, the

Overwhelming stress resulting in extreme shock can cause death as perhaps is the case in a situation such as this.

body's systems of defense can be its own worst enemies: the increased flow of hormones in the exhaustion stage may overwork the systems that these hormones activate, producing additional stress and contributing to the ultimate breakdown—death.

Stress-Related Disease and Death

All of us experience stress at less catastrophic levels than this. Some people thrive on stress, working hard and racing the clock happily enough. But in most cases, prolonged stress may contribute to disease. One estimate (Schmale, 1972) holds that as much as 80 percent of all disease today may have its origin in stress, making stress-related illness much more prevalent than the infectious diseases which dominated the world in earlier centuries and which still prevail in underdeveloped countries. It is difficult to separate the physical from the psychological causes of stress, but recent experiments (for example, Weiss, 1972; Lubrosky, Docherty, and Penick, 1973) suggest that anxiety, frustration, helplessness, resentment, and depression contribute heavily to stress. No one knows why such stress is more likely to lead to disease than muscular overload is, but so it seems to be. In the 1960s, 100 men who had been laid off from a Detroit auto plant were studied by Dr. Sidney Cobb for two years, during which time several suffered from ulcers, arthritis, high blood pressure, and depression, and their suicide rate reached thirty times the average (cited in Colligan, 1975). Emotional stress is now known to relate to just such illnesses as peptic ulcers, hypertension, certain kinds of arthritis, asthma, and heart dis-

ease. Those who work in high-stress occupations may pay a high price. Air traffic controllers, for example, who spend their days juggling the lives of hundreds of people on air routes where a minor error can mean mass death, are said to suffer from the highest incidence of peptic ulcers of any professional group (Grayson, 1972; Cobb and Rose, 1973).

Recent research suggests that emotional factors are implicated in the onset of many, and conceivably of *all*, diseases, including diabetes and cancer. We are all familiar with the idea of psychosomatic disease, the notion that mind and body are so intimately connected that the body can suffer from the mind's distress. A student may come down with flu on the day before an important exam, or a director have an asthma attack on the opening night of his play. The most lethal psychological component appears to be the feeling of helplessness, which often results from a deep personal loss. In one study, helpless, hopeless feelings correlated highly with the onset of cervical cancer (Schmale, 1972). In another study titled ''Broken Heart,'' 4,500 British widowers had a 40 percent higher mortality rate six months after their wives' deaths than other men the same age (Parke, Benjamin, and Fitzgerald, 1969).

Many instances are known of sudden stress that led to sudden death. The fifty-one-year-old president of CBS died on his way to his father's funeral. A fifty-six-year-old woman, seeing the wreckage of her husband's truck, ran to the scene, collapsed, and died (her husband had escaped uninjured). An elderly man was accidentally locked in a public lavatory and died while struggling to get out. Even joy can be so intense as to

We are increasingly aware of the intimate relationship between our emotions and our health. For example, a widow's sense of hopelessness may affect her physical as well as mental health.

be overwhelming: a seventy-five-year-old man collapsed at the race track as he was about to cash in his winning ticket for $1,683 on a $2 bet, and a fifty-six-year-old minister who had been ''elated'' to talk to President Carter on a radio phone-in show had a fatal heart attack soon after hanging up (all cited in Engel, 1977).

These sudden deaths occurred in the shock phase of the alarm reaction to stress, when adrenal hormone level, heart rate, and blood pressure rise abruptly. Examples like these provide ample evidence that emotional stress, even the stress of triumph, can kill. But stress is rather like food: too much is damaging, but we just can't live without it. Stress, after all, is the body's nonspecific response to any demand made upon it. Even in sleep and dreaming, the body and brain are mildly stressed. As Selye has pointed out, ''Complete freedom from stress is death'' (1974). Between the deadly absence of stress and its deadly excesses, between the acceptance and the control of stress, we must map the course of our lives.

brain can elicit behavior associated with other kinds and levels of emotionality, such as the "quiet, stalking movements" characteristic of cats pursuing prey (Flynn et al., 1970). Thus, there is a clear connection among brain stimulation, sympathetic nervous system activation, and emotional arousal. Moreover, stimulation of different parts of the brain is associated with different patterns of arousal.

It appears that animals are programmed with the potential for displaying many kinds of emotional behavior that they do not normally exhibit, for even a cat that has never before shown rage can be induced to do so by lateral hypothalamic stimulation. It has been suggested that humans, too, may possess unused emotional potential. In fact, some researchers have found cases in which exaggerated emotional behavior in humans accompanied damage to certain areas of the limbic system, an area of the brain that is closely connected in function with the hypothalamus. Some children with such brain damage may exhibit impulsive hyperactivity, indiscriminate aggression, and violence. Certain brain tumors, too, have been found to be associated with exaggerated emotional behavior (Mark and Ervin, 1970, pp. 55–68). In one documented case, Donald L., a peaceable family man, became increasingly violent over a six-month period. After attempting to murder his family with a butcher knife, he was taken to a hospital, where he had to be restrained by heavy fish netting. Whenever anyone approached, he snarled, bared his teeth, and lashed out with his hands and feet. Finally, he was subdued by drugs and examined. The diagnosis was a brain tumor pressing directly on the limbic system. After the tumor was removed, Mr. L. became his old peaceable self again. It seems that our highly organized emotional responses, with their characteristic patterns of sympathetic and parasympathetic arousal, appear to be coordinated by the brain. Normally these responses are elicited by environmental situations rather than by brain dysfunction, as we shall see.

Labeling
SUBJECTIVE EMOTIONAL EXPERIENCES

The short essay by Isaac Asimov that appears at the beginning of this chapter touches on one of the oldest debates about human emotions: What is the relation between the bodily changes that characterize emotions and our perception of these changes and of the situation that produced them? Do we experience the feeling of fear because our heart is pounding and our hands are trembling? Or does our mind's appraisal of a particular set of circumstances induce the feeling we call fear, which is followed by a set of physiological changes that prepare us for fight or flight? Over the years various psychologists have proposed different answers to these questions, and their experiments have led to a better understanding of the basic issues involved in explaining how people can identify their own emotional states.

THE IMPORTANCE OF BODILY CHANGES: THE JAMES-LANGE THEORY Our language suggests that the physiological changes accompanying emotions are in some ways quite different for different emotions. When we are frightened, for example, we say we feel a "knot" in the stomach; when we are nervous, we say we experience "butterflies"; during intense anger, we sometimes refer to a "pounding" in the temples; and when we feel shame, we often describe it as a "blush." Is it possible, therefore, that the emotion we are experiencing at a given moment is simply the result of a particular set of bodily changes?

William James was one of the first psychologists to propose that the ability to identify and label our own emotional states might be based on the ability to interpret these bodily changes. This proposal directly contradicted many of the theories of emotion popular in the late nineteenth century. Most other writers argued, quite logically, that events in the environment trigger a psychological state—the emotion—which in turn gives rise to responses by the body. James disagreed:

My theory, on the contrary, is that *the bodily changes follow directly the perception of the exciting fact, and that our feeling of the same changes as they occur IS the emotion.* Common-sense says, we lose our fortune, are sorry and weep; we meet a bear, are frightened and run; we are insulted by a rival, are angry and strike. The hypothesis here to be defended says that this order of sequence is incorrect . . . and that the more rational statement is that we feel sorry because we cry, angry because we strike, afraid because we tremble. . . . Without the bodily states following on the perception, the latter would be purely cognitive in form, pale, colorless, destitute of emotional warmth. We might then see the bear, and judge it best to run, receive the insult and deem it right to strike, but we should not actually *feel* afraid or angry. (James, 1890)

According to James, then, our perception of some stimulus in the environment triggers a pattern of changes in the body. These changes cause sensory messages to be sent to the brain and produce the actual *experience* of emotion. Each emotional state is signaled by a unique pattern. James emphasized visceral reactions (that is, "gut reactions") as central to emotional states. Writing at about the same time, a Dane named Carl Lange proposed a similar theory that specifically emphasized vascular changes (changes in blood pressure). Ever since, the view that the perception of bodily changes *is* emotion has been called the **James-Lange theory of emotion** (Lange and James, 1922).

The James-Lange theory stimulated a great deal of research on emotions, much of it designed to disprove that theory's claims. In 1927 Walter B. Cannon published a powerful critique of the theory based on several arguments. First, he pointed to evidence that physiological changes do not necessarily produce emotions, as the James-Lange theory might predict: When a person exercises vigorously or is injected with adrenaline, he or she will experience the bodily changes typical of strong emotions but will not necessarily *feel* a particular emotion. Physiological change, Cannon argued, is not sufficient to produce emotion.

Second, the idea that bodily reactions *cause* us to experience emotion is questionable because at times we feel emotions quite rapidly. We see a bridge collapsing and feel immediate panic; we see an old friend and feel instantaneous joy. How could the viscera, which are relatively slow to react, be the source of such sudden emotion, as James suggested?

Finally, said Cannon, if the James-Lange theory is correct, and we do come to feel our emotions by interpreting our bodily sensations, it would stand to reason that each emotion would be characterized by a somewhat different set of physiological changes. But, as Cannon's research showed, this does not appear to be the case; many of the same bodily changes occur in conjunction with differing emotional states.

Recent investigations tend to confirm Cannon's

Although common sense may tell us that *first* we feel grief, and *then* we cry, the James-Lange theory maintains that *first* we cry, and *then* we feel grief—in other words, that feelings *follow* behavior.

According to Walter Cannon, feelings such as joy are instantaneous and thus cannot be caused by bodily reactions, as was suggested by James, because visceral reactions are relatively slow.

ily responses and perceived emotional state. In a study of twenty-five men who as adults had suffered spinal cord lesions, it was found that the resulting damage to the autonomic nervous system had caused significant changes in the nature and intensity of certain emotions, especially anger and fear (Hohmann, 1966). Generally speaking, the higher on the spinal cord the lesion occurred, the more extensive was the disruption of visceral responses, and the greater was the change in these emotions. This is not to say that these men failed to perceive the significance of emotion-arousing situations, or even that they failed to display much of the behavior associated with strong emotion; but the quality of their emotional experiences was often altered. As one man remarked about his feelings of anger: "Sometimes I get angry when I see some injustice. I yell and cuss and raise hell, because if you don't do it sometimes I've learned people will take advantage of you. But it just doesn't have the heat to it that it used to. It's a mental kind of anger." It seems as if the physical correlates of anger—pounding heart, trembling hands, the sensation of being "heated up"—contribute to the full experience of anger.

THE ROLE OF COGNITION Although physiological arousal may be important in experiencing full-blown emotions, it is still not enough to explain their cause completely. Cognitive awareness of an emotion-provoking event or situation is also an essential component. This was demonstrated in an early study that supplied evidence against the James-Lange theory. Gregorio Marañon (1924) injected 210 subjects with adrenaline and asked them to report the effects. About 71 percent said that they experienced only physical symptoms—a rapidly beating heart, a tightness in the throat—with no emotional overtones whatsoever. The remainder reported emotional responses of some kind; of these, almost all described what Marañon called "as if" emotions. These subjects said, "I feel *as if* I were afraid" or "I feel *as if* I were happy." Thus, their feelings were similar to emotions but clearly were not what one would normally consider true emotions. In the few cases in which a genuine emotional experience was produced by the adrenaline, it seemed to be the result of subjects' thoughts that heightened the experience, especially memories with strong emotional force, such as a parent's remembrance of a time when his child was seriously ill. In other words, for subjects to interpret as "emo-

argument. Although it is possible to make physiological distinctions between certain emotions—anger, for instance, is generally associated with an increase in gastric activity; fear is generally associated with an inhibition of gastric functions (Wolff and Wolff, 1947)—efforts to find clear-cut physiological differences between some of the more subtle emotions have not been as successful. Moreover, even the general patterns of bodily response that have been identified for emotions such as anger and fear can vary from individual to individual and from situation to situation for the same individual (Lang, Rice, and Sternbach, 1972). For most emotions, then, unique physiological changes have been difficult to identify.

Although the James-Lange theory appears to be wrong on several counts, one cannot conclude that the perception of physiological change plays only a minor role in the experience of emotions. Fred Fehr and John Stern (1970) reviewed a number of studies that showed a relationship between a person's bod-

"This will make you feel numb!"

"This will make you tremble and your heart race!"

Figure 15.1 Two of the conditions in Schachter and Singer's experiment on emotion. (A) A subject is misled about the effects he should expect from the adrenalin injection he is receiving. Placed with a companion who joyfully flies paper airplanes around the waiting room, he attributes his state of arousal to a similar mood in himself and joins in. (B) A subject is told exactly what to expect from the injection. Although placed in the same situation as the first subject, he recognizes his physical sensations as the product of the injection and is unmoved by the euphoria of the experimenter's confederate.

tional" the physiological state produced by adrenaline, it seems that they had to imagine an emotion-arousing kind of situation.

SCHACHTER'S TWO-FACTOR THEORY Marañon's study and others like it led Stanley Schachter to propose a **two-factor theory of emotion.** According to this theory, the labeling of an emotion is based on a physiological change *plus* a cognitive interpretation of that change. In experiments undertaken to explore this point of view (Schachter and Singer, 1962), subjects received what they thought was a vitamin injection. They believed that they were participating in a study to assess the effects of the "vitamin" on vision. Actually the injection was adrenaline, and the real purpose of the study was to see whether subjects under different experimental conditions would assign different labels to the physiological sensations produced by the adrenaline. One group of subjects was told that the "vitamin" would produce certain side effects, such as heart palpitations and tremor (which are real side effects of adrenaline). Another group was led to expect other side effects not usually associated with adrenaline, such as itching and headache. A third group was told that the injection would have no side effects. The first group was similar to the subjects in Marañon's study, who knew that they were receiving an adrenaline injection. The other two groups received no explanation for their state of arousal; therefore, the researchers reasoned, they were more likely to attribute their arousal to "emotional" factors.

While waiting for the "vision test," each subject sat in a room with another person, who was actually a confederate of the experimenters. In some cases, this "stooge" acted very happy and frivolous, throwing paper airplanes, laughing, and playing with a hula hoop. In other cases, the stooge acted annoyed and angry, finally tearing up a questionnaire he was supposed to fill out.

The major finding of the experiment was that subjects who did not expect the arousal produced by adrenaline, and thus had no way of explaining the physiological changes they were experiencing, tended to use the emotion displayed by the confederate as a label for their own feelings. They too expressed euphoria or anger, depending on the model provided them by the stooge (see Figure 15.1). In contrast, subjects who were told to expect side effects were less likely to share the confederate's feelings.

Subsequent studies have supported this two-factor theory. In one experiment, for example, subjects who had been injected with adrenaline laughed more and harder while watching a slapstick comedy film than did subjects in a control group injected with a placebo; subjects who received an injection of chlorpromazine, a drug that *inhibits* physiological arousal, laughed less than the control group did (Schachter and Wheeler, 1962). A similar study showed that people behave more aggressively toward a person they dislike (the cognitive factor) if they have been physiologically aroused by exercise (the physiological factor) (Zillman, 1971). Speculative extensions of Schachter's theory have also been suggested, such as the possibility that "falling in love" may be an incorrect label given to sexual arousal or to feelings of frustration or jealousy.

If Schachter's theory is correct, it ought to explain why, as James originally noticed, there is such a wide variety of emotional experiences. It could be that there are as many differences in the emotions we experience as there are in the *situations* associated with physiological arousal. This argument fits very well with James' statement that ". . . in the dictionaries of synonyms we find feelings distinguished more by their severally [variously] appropriate objective stimuli than by their conscious subjective tone." (James, 1890)

INITIAL APPRAISAL   In a review of the major approaches to the study of emotions, Magda Arnold (1960) pointed out that most theorists have focused on the relationship between emotional experience and physiological change. Many of them have accepted the common-sense view that emotion produces physiological response, although James and Lange defended the opposite position—that emotion *is* the perception of bodily changes. Schachter's theory is like the James-Lange theory in that it supports the notion that emotional experience (or what

one interprets as emotional experience) follows arousal. Arnold, however, emphasized a different possibility: Both the emotional experience *and* the bodily changes may follow the perception and appraisal of a potentially harmful or beneficial situation. In other words, both emotional experience and physiological arousal may be *effects*, neither one causing the other. As Isaac Asimov indicates in the anecdote that opens this chapter, a caged lion causes no emotional reaction, but a lion on the loose is terrifying. The important difference, Arnold suggests, is registered during the individual's initial appraisal of the situation.

Other researchers have studied the cognitive processes involved in the initial appraisal of a situation. For example, in a study by Richard Lazarus and Elizabeth Alfert (1964), subjects were shown an emotion-arousing film, either a graphic account of the adolescent circumcision rites of a primitive tribe or a safety lesson in which bloody accidents in workshops were vividly depicted. While they watched, the subjects' heart rates and galvanic skin responses were measured, as indicators of physiological arousal. Cognition was manipulated by playing special sound tracks designed to encourage various reactions to the film. A "denial" sound track, for example, explained that the participants were actors

Figure 15.2 Three ways to know fear.

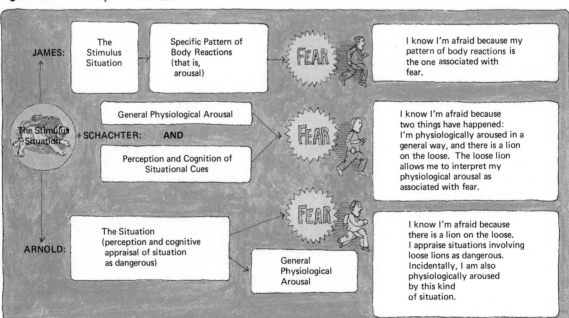

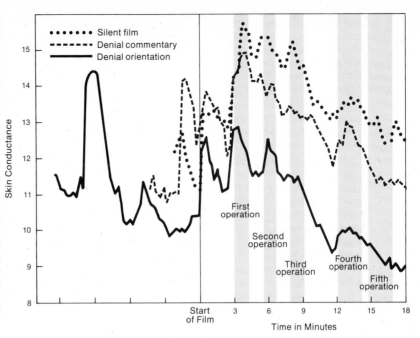

Figure 15.3 The results of an experiment on emotion and cognition by Lazarus and Alfert. They used an anthropological film about puberty rites involving subincision (the cutting open of the urethra along the underside of the penis) as the emotion-provoking stimulus. Changes in galvanic skin response (GSR) were measured as an index of anxiety. All the subjects saw the film. One group (Denial Commentary) heard a sound track with the film saying that the people in the film were actors and the operations were causing no pain. Another group (Denial Orientation) heard the same sound track before they were shown the film. A third group (Silent Film) heard no commentary at all. (After Lazarus and Alfert, 1964.)

or that the incidents portrayed were not painful; thus, for one group of subjects the stressful aspects of the movies were denied.

Figure 15.3 shows the results of the effectiveness of denial for subjects who saw the film of the adolescent boys undergoing ritual circumcision. Not only did the denial sound track lower galvanic skin response when played *during* the film, it lowered it even more when played *before* the film was shown. Cognitive interpretations apparently play a role not only in labeling a state of physiological arousal as one emotion or another but also in determining the level at which it is expressed.

COMMUNICATING EMOTION

We are all familiar with the figure of Charlie Chaplin as he appeared in silent movies. A master of body language, Chaplin's every emotion is clearly expressed without words. Happiness? He does a little dance. Despair? His shoulders slump; the corners of his mouth turn down; he grows smaller before our very eyes. But one does not have to be a talented actor to convey emotion without words. We all do it ourselves and respond to it in others, every day, in countless situations. For example, you are probably accustomed to watching the facial expressions of your friends when you begin to tell them

your problems. Are they sympathetic, annoyed, impatient, indifferent? Your decision to continue or to cut short your tale of woe probably depends greatly upon the nonverbal reactions you receive.

NONVERBAL COMMUNICATION OF EMOTION

The way in which people express their emotions through such means as facial expression, body movement, gesture, posture, and tone of voice is one aspect of nonverbal communication. The other aspect, which is what makes the act of nonverbal communication complete, is the ability of an observer to interpret such cues correctly. The range of emotions that humans can express and interpret through body language is quite diverse (Duncan, 1969). Every day we successfully smile, frown, wince, grimace, yawn, grunt, laugh, slump, shrug, and otherwise transmit an extensive range of nonverbal messages to others. And every day we successfully interpret nonverbal messages transmitted to us by others.

Considering the often subtle differences in the expression of very similar emotions, the human capacity for nonverbal communication is impressive indeed. Facial expressions of surprise, for example, can be conveyed with many different overtones. There are various qualities of surprise—questioning, dumbfounded, startled, dazed—as well as various intensities of surprise—slight, moderate, or extreme (Ekman and Friesen, 1975). Moreover, facial expressions frequently display blends of such diverse

People who live together can often read each other's nonverbal cues about their emotional states with lightning rapidity.

emotions as surprise and joy, anger and fear, amusement and annoyance. If we could not see the faces and gestures of the people around us, we would lose an important vehicle of human communication.

Monkeys, apes, and some other animals also use facial expression and body language to communicate. This has been observed in the laboratory as well as in the wild. In one experiment (Miller, Caul, and Mirsky, 1967), rhesus monkeys learned to avoid shock by pressing a bar whenever a panel lit up. Two of the monkeys were then placed in separate rooms, as shown in Figure 15.4. One room contained the shock apparatus and a signal light, but no "avoidance bar." The other room contained only an avoidance bar and a television screen on which the monkey in the first room could be observed. When the panel in the first room lit up, a look of anguish crossed the face of the monkey hooked up to the shock apparatus; it had no way of preventing the impending pain. The second monkey was unable to see the warning light, but by watching the first monkey's facial expressions on the TV screen, it apparently could tell when the shock was about to be delivered, and in most cases it pressed the bar in its own room to prevent the other monkey from suffering the shock.

EXPRESSION AND INTERPRETATION OF EMOTION

Both the expression of emotion and the interpretation of particular expressions by others appear to be based on a combination of inherited and learned factors. People from widely diverse cultures show a great deal of similarity in the postures, gestures, and facial expressions used to convey common emotional states, and this suggests a common biological foundation. However, there are certain differences in expression and interpretation among various cultural groups. Otto Klineberg (1938) pointed out, for example, that in Chinese literature the expression, "He scratched his ears and cheeks," was supposed to let the reader know that a person was happy. In Western culture this might be interpreted as indicating that a person was anxious, even distraught. Thus, learning, as well as biology, plays an important role in shaping the expression and interpretation of emotion.

BIOLOGICAL FACTORS In his classic work *The Expression of the Emotions in Man and Animals* (1872), Charles Darwin asserted that many of our patterns of emotional expression are inherited—that they evolved because they had survival value. When we

Figure 15.4 In Miller, Caul, and Mirsky's experiment, the warning light was followed by shock to monkey A in ten seconds, unless monkey B pressed the OFF switch within the interval. The experimenters reported that monkey B often pressed the switch at the correct time, even though the only communication between the two monkeys was by means of the televised image of the expression on monkey A's face.

are enraged, for example, we commonly grimace and bare our teeth. Other animals also bare their teeth as a threat or when preparing to fight as shown

in Figure 15.5, thus warning their enemies that an attack is impending; this warning may serve to prevent a violent and damaging encounter. According to Darwin, the baring of teeth served a similar communication function for our early ancestors. Although human aggression today seldom involves biting, this pattern of expression of threat remains as a characteristic of our species.

Even though emotional expression does not appear to be completely innate, there is evidence that some aspects of emotionality are biologically based. Some of this evidence comes from studies of heredity. For example, in one study (Allerand, 1967), identical twins, fraternal twins, and nontwin siblings were asked to describe their experiences of affection, anger, delight, disgust, excitement, fear, sadness, and worry. When the descriptions were analyzed, it was found that the reports of identical twins (who have exactly the same genetic makeup) were more similar than the reports of fraternal twins and nontwin siblings, which suggests the possibility of a hereditary factor.

One of the most frequently cited pieces of evidence supporting the proposition that emotional expression has biological underpinnings is a study of a ten-year-old girl who had been deaf and blind from birth (Goodenough, 1932). Obviously the little girl could not have learned emotional expressions by observation, so her behavior was presumed to reflect mostly her innate tendencies. When the girl dis-

Figure 15.5 Innate patterns of emotional expression in dogs. In the top row anger increases from left to right. In the bottom row fear increases from left to right. This illustration is based on sketches by Charles Darwin.

played pleasure upon succeeding in finding a doll hidden in her clothing, she "threw herself back in her chair. . . . Both the hand containing the doll and the empty hand were raised in an attitude of delight, which was further attested by peals of hearty laughter. . . . Her laughter was clear and musical, in no way distinguishable from that of a normal child." The girl also showed anger in very characteristic ways. "Mild forms of resentment are shown by turning away her head, pouting the lips, or frowning. . . . More intense forms are shown by throwing back the head and shaking it from side to side, during which the lips are retracted, exposing the teeth which are sometimes clenched."

The way this child expressed common emotions was remarkably similar to the patterns of emotional expression found in most normal ten-year-olds. There were, however, some differences, which ultimately led this particular researcher to conclude

that the expression of human emotion is essentially built on innate tendencies that have been altered by a "social veneer." Later studies of handicapped children have supported this conclusion.

Finally, evidence that biological factors play an important role in the expression and interpretation of emotion also comes from cross-cultural research. People in different societies were asked to identify the emotions expressed in a series of photographs of faces (see Figure 15.6). Anger, fear, disgust, surprise, and happiness were consistently recognizable regardless of the culture from which a particular subject came (Ekman and Friesen, 1971). Even members of New Guinea tribes, who had little previous contact with Westerners and their characteristic patterns of expression, had little trouble labeling these basic emotions. It appears, then, that the ways of displaying and interpreting certain feelings may be essentially universal, which suggests a strong biological component.

Universal gestures of emotion lead some researchers to conclude that the ways we express emotion are essentially innate.

THE ROLE OF LEARNING Evidence of the role of learning in emotional expression and interpretation comes from the observation that the *occasions* on which certain feelings are seen as appropriate may vary from individual to individual. For example, on hearing a subtle verbal insult, different people may be inclined to express resentment, fear, disdain, or embarrassment, depending on such matters as their relationship to the speaker (a relative, a teacher, a peer), their ability to interpret the remark as an insult in the first place, and their cultural background.

In a study of cultural differences in situations that produce certain emotions, Joel Davitz (1969) compared Ugandan adolescents with American adolescents. Sixty students from each country were asked to write descriptions of several emotional states, including happiness and sadness. Each student was then asked to think of a certain time when he or she had experienced each emotion, to describe the situation briefly, and to describe his or her feelings as fully as possible. The Ugandan subjects often associated happiness with academic success, whereas the Americans most often mentioned social success, although nonacademic success in such efforts as learning to drive was a close second. The researcher explained this difference by pointing out that academic success is the only escape route from poverty for most adolescents in urban Uganda; most of the American students, in contrast, were not poor. In their descriptions of sadness, most Ugandan stu-

Photograph Judged						
Judgment	Happiness	Disgust	Surprise	Sadness	Anger	Fear
Culture			Percent Who Agreed with Judgment			
99 Americans	97	92	95	84	67	85
40 Brazilians	95	97	87	59	90	67
119 Chileans	95	92	93	88	94	68
168 Argentinians	98	92	95	78	90	54
29 Japanese	100	90	100	62	90	66

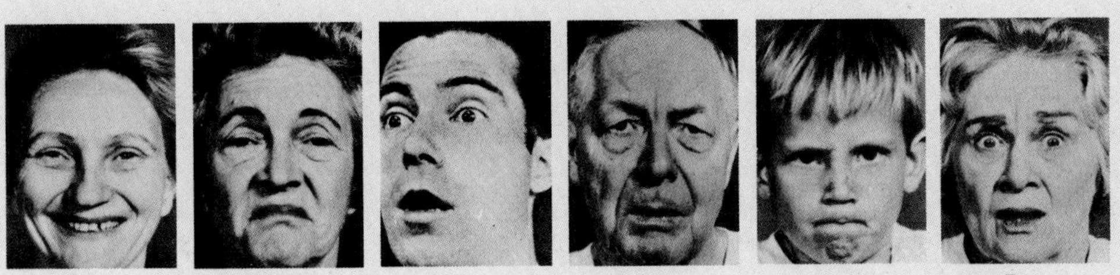

Figure 15.6 As this table indicates, there is a great deal of agreement among the members of different cultures about the meaning of facial expressions. This suggests that we are biologically programmed to recognize and produce the emotions conveyed by certain facial expressions. (After Ekman, Friesen, and Ellsworth, 1972.)

dents wrote about the death of a friend or relative, while the Americans usually mentioned social difficulties. Again, these differences could be explained through differences in cultural experience. Early death is more common in Uganda than in the United States, and the Ugandan extended-family system emphasizes the importance of relatives significantly more than the American nuclear-family arrangement.

But what about the ability to express and interpret emotion appropriately in the first place—regardless of cultural background? In Chapters 4 and 10 we discovered how social isolation in early life can have very damaging effects on later social behavior. It has been suggested that this may occur because proper social communication was never given a chance to develop (Mason, 1961). Experiments with socially isolated monkeys support this interpretation. In an extension of the research described earlier, on the ability of monkeys to communicate through facial expression (Miller, Caul, and Mirsky, 1967), it was found that monkeys raised in isolation from other monkeys were significantly re-

tarded in their ability both to display appropriate facial expressions of fear that other monkeys could interpret and to respond properly to the facial expressions of the normal monkeys in the electric shock experiment. In addition, the study indicated that there might be a period in early life that is critical for the proper development of emotional expression. Although the isolated monkeys had been deprived of social contact with other monkeys during the first year of life, they had thereafter spent three to four years with other monkeys. Yet this social experience apparently came too late to permit the monkeys to learn adequate communication skills.

We shall further explore the importance of social learning in emotional development when we discuss various theories of personality in Chapters 18 and 19. For now, it is important to bear in mind what we have learned in this chapter about the nature, labeling, and communication of emotion so that we can better understand the important role emotion plays in human motivation—the topic to which we turn in the next chapter.

Summary

1. An **emotion** can be described as consisting of subjective feelings, overt behavior, and physiological responses.

   A. Every emotion is accompanied by an awareness of the feelings associated with it. As recorded by special rating scales and measurement techniques, the extent to which different people agree in rating a common experience helps to clarify the degree of consistency and variation in our emotions.

   B. Much of the behavior accompanying strong feelings can be observed directly, and there is general agreement concerning its meaning. But the behavior associated with emotion is not always a result of our feelings; experiments indicate that overt behavior may sometimes bring on the feelings accompanying it.

   C. Strong emotions are associated with internal bodily changes resulting from activation of the autonomic nervous system, which generally functions without a person's conscious control. The autonomic nervous system is composed of two divisions, the sympathetic and the parasympathetic. These two divisions have some control over most visceral muscles and glands, and they often work antagonistically. The sympathetic division dominates during emotion-arousing situations, the parasympathetic division dominates under conditions of relaxation. When the sympathetic nervous system is activated, it stimulates increases in such physiological activities as heartbeat, respiration rate, glandular secretion, and muscular tension.

      1. A polygraph measures some of the physiological activities typically related to emotional states. When used as a "lie detector," the polygraph records physiological responses while the subject is asked questions. The use of the lie detector is controversial because a subject's physiological responses when lying are only partially reliable and because it is possible for a subject to alter the results of the baseline condition, making subsequent comparisons meaningless.

      2. Experiments have established that the brain coordinates the system by which activation of the autonomic nervous system triggers emotional arousal. Stimulation of the hypothalamus of animals can elicit different patterns of arousal, including emotional displays that the animal has never exhibited before. In humans, brain dysfunction can affect emotional behavior.

2. There is an ongoing debate over the relationship between the bodily changes that characterize emotions and a person's perception of those changes and of the situation that produced them.

   A. The **James-Lange theory of emotion** postulates that the perception of bodily changes *is* emotion. James believed that our perception of some stimulus in the environment triggers a pattern of changes in the body. These changes cause sensory messages to be sent to the brain and produce the experience of emotion. Lange proposed a similar theory that emphasized vascular changes.

   B. Cannon's research challenged the James-Lange theory in three ways. Cannon said:

      1. Physiological changes do not necessarily produce emotions. Strenuous exercise or adrenaline injections elicit the bodily changes typical of strong emotions but do not necessarily elicit the feeling of a particular emotion.

      2. The speed with which emotions are sometimes felt creates doubt about whether the visceral organs, which James said are the source of sudden emotions but which are relatively slow to react, could be the source of such emotions.

      3. Many of the same bodily changes occur in conjunction with differing emotional states. If the perception of bodily changes is emotion, there would have to be different bodily changes for different emotions.

   C. Although current research tends to confirm Cannon's findings, it has been shown that the perception of physiological changes does play a significant role in the experience of emotions.

D. Cognitive awareness of an emotion-provoking situation is an important component of emotional experience. In Marañon's experiments using adrenaline to elicit physiological sensations, most subjects experienced no emotion, while other subjects had to imagine an emotion-arousing situation in order to feel "as if" they were experiencing an emotion.

1. Schachter's **two-factor theory of emotion** postulates that the labeling of an emotion is based on a physiological change *plus* a cognitive interpretation of the change. Schachter's theory was supported by studies showing that subjects under differing experimental conditions assigned different labels to the physiological sensations produced by adrenaline.

2. Arnold emphasized the importance of initial appraisal, asserting that the perception and appraisal of a situation as potentially harmful or beneficial may precede both the emotional experience and the bodily changes. Several studies indicate that cognitive interpretations play a role in labeling physiological arousal and determining the level at which it is expressed.

3. Emotion can be clearly communicated without words.

A. Effective nonverbal communication of emotion depends both on the way emotion is *expressed*—through facial expression, gesture, and the like—and on the observer's ability to *interpret* such cues correctly. Laboratory experiments and observation of animals in the wild have shown that humans are not unique in their capacity for nonverbal communication of emotion: certain monkeys and apes also communicate through facial expression and body language.

B. Both the expression and interpretation of emotion seem to be based on a combination of inherited and learned factors.

1. Studies of human and nonhuman heredity suggest that some aspects of emotional expression are biologically based. These studies have included an analysis of emotional experiences reported by twins and nontwin siblings, and the study of the expression of emotion by a ten-year-old girl who had been deaf and blind from birth. Some researchers contend that the expression of human emotions is essentially built on innate tendencies, which are subsequently altered by the experiences in our life.

2. The occasions on which certain feelings are regarded as appropriate vary from person to person; this supports the idea that learning plays a role in emotional expression and interpretation. Cross-cultural research also indicates that learning plays a role: though emotions may be recognizably similar in two cultures, they are often associated with situations different enough so that the emotion is not quite the same in both societies.

RECOMMENDED READINGS

BUCK, ROSS. *Human Motivation and Emotion.* New York: Wiley, 1976. A broad introduction to the psychological literature on emotion and motivation.

DARWIN, CHARLES. *The Expression of the Emotions in Man and Animals* (1872). Chicago: University of Chicago Press, 1965. This classic work describes emotions and interprets them in terms of evolution and natural selection.

EKMAN, PAUL, and WALLACE V. FRIESEN. *Unmasking the Face.* Englewood Cliffs, N.J.: Prentice-Hall, 1975. A thoroughly illustrated treatment of facial expressions that are associated with a wide variety of emotional states.

JAMES, WILLIAM. "The Emotions," in *The Principles of Psychology.* Vol. II. New York: Holt, 1890. A fascinating classic that reviews basic issues and presents and defends what is now called the James-Lange theory of emotions.

SCHACHTER, STANLEY. *Emotion, Obesity, and Crime.* New York: Academic Press, 1971. A compilation of previously published papers related to Schachter's theory of emotion.

SELYE, HANS. *The Stress of Life.* New York: McGraw-Hill, 1956. Pioneering work on stress, emphasizing the common physiological changes that accompany a wide variety of stresses.

CHAPTER SIXTEEN

MOTIVATION

I often try to analyze my motivations for the things I do, because I am interested in myself, for one thing, and because I sometimes find the results enlightening. Here are some examples.

(1) Back in the late 1930s, I began my career as a science fiction writer and stubbornly continued to write despite numerous rejections. I needed money to get through school. I was vain and wanted to see my name in print so I could show off to my peers. Both were very effective motivations.

Looking back on it, though, I am convinced that more important than either was the strong desire to gain the approval of John W. Campbell, Jr., the charismatic editor of *Astounding Science Fiction* and, second only to my father, the closest to a father I've ever had.

(2) Back in the late 1950s, I fell into a dispute with the head of the medical school at which I was teaching, and for a while it seemed certain that I would lose my faculty position. My keen sense of self-appreciation was activated, and I decided that no one was going to kick *me* around. So I girded for a fight, which turned out to be long-drawn-out and public. Other faculty members felt that it would not be politic to associate themselves with someone doomed to expulsion, so I found myself isolated.

As the fight continued, however, and as it began to look as though I had a chance to win, I became aware of a growing misconception of my motivation. Some other faculty members were coming to believe that I was fighting heroically on behalf of academic freedom. Eventually, the faculty members on the advisory body (which had always been thought to be a rubber stamp for the administration) voted down the head, and I won the battle. Yet my motivation was not a matter of devotion to the noble abstraction of academic freedom, but merely of soothing my outraged vanity.

(3) In early 1972, I faced an operation under general anesthesia for the first time in my life, and I was paralyzed with fear. I set about analyzing the motivation for the fear. I wasn't afraid of the operation; it was a simple one. I wasn't afraid of dying through unexpected sensitivity to anesthesia; there could be no more painless death. I wasn't afraid of the consequences after death, for I was, and am, firmly convinced that there is no afterlife.

I finally decided that my fear of the operation was really a fear of posthumous embarrassment. I was afraid that other people would be contemptuous of me for dying after less than a full lifetime.

Then I said to myself, Length of life is measured by deeds, not years, and you have written 120 books and made your mark in half a dozen fields. So I made my peace with death, went cheerfully into the hospital, and survived. I have since then written eighty more books.

Isaac Asimov

Anyone who has ever watched a detective program on television or read a mystery story knows that in order to find out who killed the rich widow, you have to find out who had the best "motive" for doing her in. Was it her son, who stood to inherit her $3 million estate, her attorney, who was afraid she had discovered that he had been embezzling from her for years, or her stepdaughter, who blamed her for a car accident that had left her crippled?

Obviously, one does not need to be a detective or a mystery writer to seek explanations for behavior in motivation. We all do so every day. We see Ruth studying all weekend while the rest of us enjoy our free time, and since we know she wants to go to law school, we conclude that she is "motivated" by her desire to get good grades. We see Harold working after classes at a job he doesn't like, and since we know he wants to buy a car, we conclude that he is "motivated" to earn money for the car. Conceptions of motivation in psychology are in many ways similar to those expressed in everyday language; like the rest of us, psychologists infer motivation from goal-directed behavior.

Since motivation cannot be observed directly, psychologists focus their attention on behavior, formulating theories of motivation to account for the initiation, direction, and persistence of goal-directed behavior. Initiation and direction have to do with why one activity is chosen over another at a particular time. Why does one student work as a waiter after school while another plays football? Why does one student study harder after receiving a poor grade while another decides to drop the course? One aim of motivation theorists is to seek an explanation for the initiation and direction of behavior at a particular time.

The initiation and direction of some behaviors are largely determined by the physiological state of the organism. Humans as well as other animals have obvious survival needs. The nervous system is constructed in such a way that deficits in blood sugar, water, oxygen, salt, or essential vitamins lead to changes in behavior designed to return the body to a condition of chemical balance. The first half of this chapter discusses the role of such physiological deficits in motivating behavior.

Many human motives, such as Ruth's desire to get into law school or Harold's desire to buy a car, do not have a simple physiological basis. Although not all psychologists would be able to agree on an explanation of these behaviors, none would say that they were the result of physiological deficits. The second half of this chapter discusses some approaches to analyzing motivational bases of these kinds of human activities.

MOTIVATIONAL BASES OF BEHAVIOR

The most basic goal-directed behaviors serve two vital functions: survival and reproduction. As we saw in Chapter 3, in satisfying these functions, the organism responds to certain kinds of cues from the environment. Frogs may flick out their tongues at moving black spots, birds may build nests when presented with the courting displays of the opposite sex, and so on. But these responses occur only in certain circumstances. Frogs do not always strike at flies: they do so only if they are "hungry." Birds build nests only when they are ready to reproduce: a courting song out of season is ignored.

People are motivated to become dancers—a demanding vocation with no guarantees of success—because of strong incentives and drives to do so.

Something more than a simple external stimulus is needed to evoke goal-directed behavior. It is here that the concept of motivation comes in. In order for a particular response to be elicited, a certain internal state must be present in addition to a specific external stimulus; for example, the frog must be hungry if it is to flick its tongue at moving black spots. The psychological concept of motivation, then, is based on a combination of external motivational stimuli, called **incentives**, and internal motivational factors, called **drives**. In other words, motives have two components: the internal drive state that activates and orients the animal toward some goal, and the external incentive that is the goal itself. Motivation seems to provide the "why" of behavior. Feeding behavior is "explained" by the motivational concept of hunger, just as a murder might be explained by the motivational concept of greed or revenge.

However, "explaining" certain behaviors merely by labeling them with appropriate motivational states, if carried no further, has some serious shortcomings. First, the reasoning is circular. If we say that an animal drinks because it is "thirsty," we are merely inferring a cause from the behavior we have observed and then using that hypothetical cause to explain the behavior we started with. We are implying that thirst is the cause of drinking behavior, and at the same time we are using the observation of drinking behavior to prove the presence of thirst.

Second, explaining behaviors by labeling them with a motive does not tell us why the same motive may give rise to different patterns of behavior. For example, one person who wants a new car might get a part-time job to earn money for it, while another might try coaxing one out of a rich uncle, and yet another might steal one.

Third, a simple motivational label does not explain how individuals identify different motivational states within themselves. How do you know that you are hungry, thirsty, lustful, or acquisitive? It is therefore necessary to look more deeply into what constitutes a basic motivational state.

MOTIVATION AS A REGULATORY PROCESS: PRIMARY DRIVES
Basic motivational processes are best understood in terms of the functions they serve for the organism. In Chapter 3 we discussed **adaptive significance**, the way a particular behavior contributes to the survival of individuals and of a species. Motivational processes, as expressed in

behavior such as the tongue flicking of the frog, have obvious adaptive significance associated with the regulation of basic physiological requirements, or needs. The organism exhibits **primary drives**, which are produced by emotional and physiological conditions that stimulate the animal to seek fulfillment of basic needs. Eating, drinking, breathing, and maintaining a stable body temperature are all examples of behaviors based on primary drives, and these behaviors serve to regulate some basic physiological requirement at an optimal level for a particular organism. Walter Cannon (1929) coined the term homeostasis to label this kind of regulation. **Homeostasis** is the tendency of an organism to maintain an optimal level of a physiological requirement by reacting to deviations from the optimal condition so as to restore it. To put it very simply, you are seeking homeostasis when you take off your jacket because you are too hot.

Many kinds of behavior fit this general model of motivation as a homeostatic process. Some, however, do not. Sexual behavior is clearly an example of highly motivated behavior that contributes to the survival of the species, but it does not relate to specific physiological requirements of the individual animal. Nor is there a clear "optimal" physiological state that is being regulated. Sexual behavior will be discussed in Chapter 17, and other examples of behavior that does not fulfill a specific physiological requirement are presented later in this section. Let us now examine some behavior that *does* fit the basic homeostatic model.

THIRST AND WATER BALANCE Most research on regulatory motives has attempted to answer two basic questions: How does an organism know when an adjustment is necessary? And what is the mechanism by which this adjustment is made? Thirst provides a good example of how these questions can be answered.

The principal constituent of all living cells is water. Living tissue depends on water for all physiological processes. Water leaves the body continually in sweat, urine, and exhaled air, and so the organism must take in fluids to maintain its water balance. But what are the stimuli that produce sensations of thirst? How do we know when we have had enough to drink? In other words, how do we know when to start drinking and how do we know when to stop? The control mechanisms involved in drinking are diagrammed in Figure 16.1.

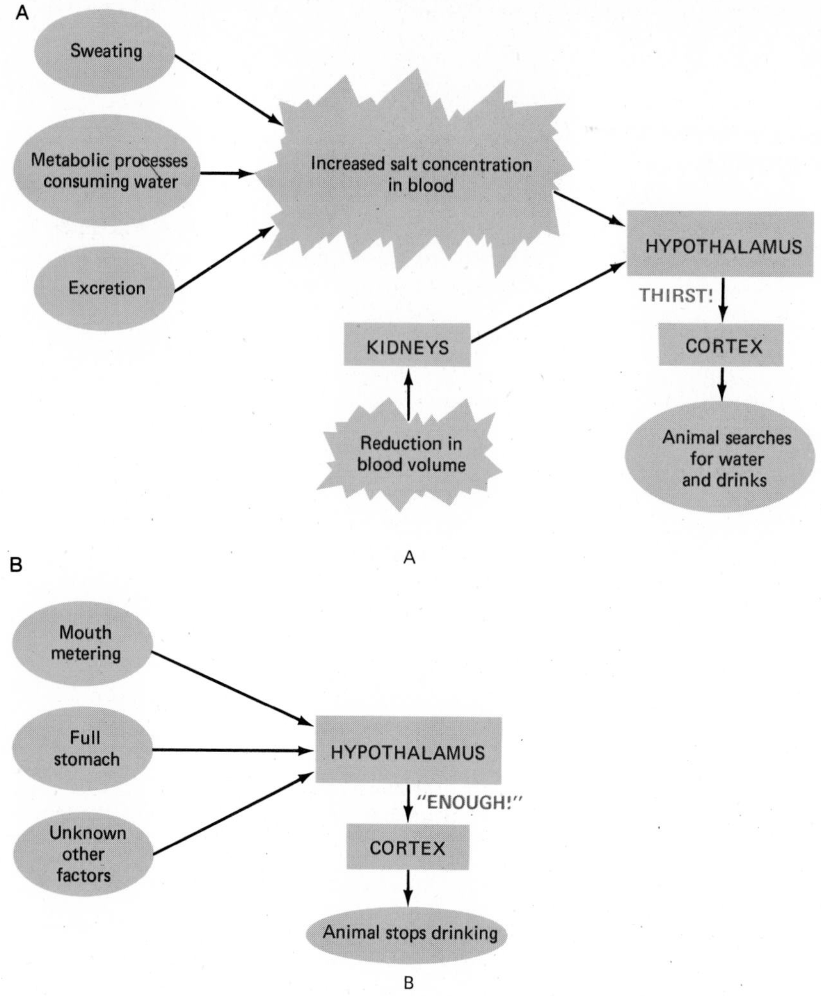

Figure 16.1 Control mechanisms involved in drinking: A shows the sequence leading to drinking, while B suggests the events involved in stopping drinking.

A

B

Stimuli Initiating Drinking   Three sources of internal stimuli induce drinking in mammals. The first is an increase in salt concentration in the various fluid compartments of the body—inside cells, around cells, and in the blood. There seem to be specialized cells in a part of the brain called the hypothalamus (see Chapter 11) that detect this change in salt concentration. Activation of these cells results in thirst and then in drinking. Bengt Andersson (1953) discovered the location of these cells by implanting small tubes into various areas of the brains of animals and stimulating those areas with very small amounts of salt solutions injected through the tubes. Only in certain areas do such injections induce the animal to begin to drink.

J. T. Fitzsimons (1961) discovered that another stimulus for drinking is a decrease in the volume of fluid in the circulatory system. No change in chemical concentration is involved here, but simply a decrease in volume, such as that which results from hemorrhage. Severe bleeding, then, causes a very intense thirst.

More recently, Fitzsimons (1969) has discovered how a change in blood volume is recognized by the brain, a phenomenon that illustrates how physiological mechanisms are involved in drive states. All blood is filtered through the kidneys. If a kidney senses a reduction in blood volume, it releases a chemical that alters the structure of a substance in the blood. This altered substance then acts directly on several portions of the hypothalamus to elicit drinking.

The third major stimulus for drinking is produced by exercise or by an increase in body temperature. The mechanism involved is probably identical to that undergone by the cells in the hypothalamus that sense a change in salt concentration. Both exercise and increased body temperature result in sweating, which cools the body but also takes water from the blood. With less water, the concentration of salt in the blood becomes higher, since the same amount of salt is dissolved in less water. This high salt concentration stimulates the salt-sensing cells and results in drinking.

Satiation of Thirst   Thirst and drinking seem to stop long before enough time has passed for the body to have absorbed the water from the stomach and for the water–salt balance in the blood to have been restored. If there is still a physiological deficit, why do we stop drinking? One of the stimuli that causes drinking to stop is stomach distention, a feeling of fullness. Edward Deaux (1973) has suggested that the reason cold water satisfies thirst more quickly than warm water is that cold water moves out of the stomach much more slowly and thus provides a clearer stomach-distention signal to the brain.

Stomach-distention signals are not the only ones involved in satiety, however. R. T. Bellows (1939) showed that if a dog is allowed to drink freely but the water it drinks is prevented from reaching its stomach (diverted out through an incision made in its neck for experimental purposes), the dog does not continue to drink indefinitely. It takes in some water and then stops drinking. The dog soon begins to drink again, but then stops again. There seems to be some "mouth metering" mechanism that gauges the amount being ingested and compares that amount with the amount needed to restore the water balance. If the internal need is not fulfilled, the internal stimuli then override the mouth messages, and the animal begins drinking again.

But the mouth meter is not essential to maintaining a correct water balance either. Alan Epstein (1960) has shown that animals can learn to press a bar that causes spurts of water to be delivered directly into their stomachs and can still regulate their water balance adequately. Clearly, thirst is monitored and controlled by several different physiological mechanisms. These mechanisms provide animals with a number of ways of feeling the need for water, thus increasing the likelihood that the proper homeostatic condition will be maintained.

HUNGER AND WEIGHT REGULATION   As we have seen, a variety of stimuli, both external and internal, contribute to drive regulation. This is especially true of regulation of eating behavior. If you have ever gobbled a hot fudge sundae after having eaten a full meal, you know that internal hunger signals (such as stomach contractions) had very little to do with your actions. The sundae looked and tasted delicious, and these external factors were all that was necessary to encourage you to devour it. Exactly how the internal and external factors relate to one another and affect eating behavior has recently received a great deal of attention.

It is known that, as with thirst, the control of hunger and satiety is related to the hypothalamus. Receptors in this part of the brain seem to monitor substances in the blood that increase or decrease with food intake or deprivation. On the basis of this information, the hypothalamus reacts to regulate food intake and body weight.

In addition to these internal physiological factors, much feeding behavior is determined by external factors: social customs, how food looks, smells, and tastes, and the amount of effort required to obtain food. In view of all these potential contributions to the regulation of feeding behavior, it is remarkable that human beings and other animals are able to regulate their weights so precisely. Even people who do not continuously monitor their weight manage to keep it within a range of a few pounds, despite great variations in their physical activity and variations in the nutritive values of various foods (Keesey and Powley, 1975).

Similarly, laboratory animals having unrestricted access to food will regulate their body weights very precisely within a certain range. Anyone who has a cat has observed that the cat will often eat only a certain amount and then leave the remaining food, no matter how tempting, for the next meal. In this area, however, cats seem to be more successful than some humans. For certain people, automatic control over their weight seems like an impossible dream. Extensive research by Stanley Schachter and others has provided insight into why some people have such difficulty regulating their body weight.

If we examine the eating behavior of obese and normal individuals and compare their responses to internal and external cues, we find marked differences in sensitivity. For example, normal-weight subjects respond to the internal cue of stomach distention by refusing food, while obese subjects tend to go right on eating. Schachter and his colleagues (Schachter, Goldman, and Gordon, 1968) demonstrated that the internal cues from the stomach, which signal hunger and satiety, seem to have little relation to feeding behavior for some individuals. In their study, normal-weight and obese subjects were deprived of one meal. Half of each group was then fed a roast beef sandwich, while the other half was left in the hunger state. All subjects were then allowed to eat as many crackers of various kinds as they wished. They had been told that their task was to rate the flavor of the crackers, but the experimenters were actually measuring how many crackers each subject ate. It was expected, of course, that those subjects who had eaten the roast beef sandwiches and were no longer hungry would eat fewer crackers. And so it was—but only in the case of the normal-weight individuals. Having eaten the sandwiches made no difference to the obese subjects. They ate more crackers than the others, whether or not they were in the half of their group who had eaten sandwiches at the start of the experiment.

If obese individuals are relatively insensitive to internal cues to regulate their eating behavior, then what does affect them? Research has shown that obese people seem to be more responsive than normal-weight individuals to external cues such as the sight, taste, or availability of food. Richard E. Nisbett (1968a) conducted a simple experiment to demonstrate the importance of the sight of food. He gave one sandwich apiece to one group of individuals who had missed a meal and three sandwiches apiece to another group who had missed a meal. He then left the room, telling the subjects that they were welcome to help themselves to more sandwiches from the refrigerator. Interestingly, among the subjects to whom three sandwiches were visible, obese individuals ate more than normal-weight people. Among the subjects who had been given only one sandwich and had to go to the refrigerator to get more, however, obese individuals ate *less* than normal-weight people. It seems that obese people tend to keep eating as long as food is in sight, regardless of whether or not their physiological need for food has been satisfied; normal-weight people, by contrast, will forage for more food if visible food has been consumed but their physiological need for food has not yet been satisfied.

The hypothesis that obese individuals base their eating behavior on external cues received striking support from a study done in a nutrition clinic in New York (Hashim and Van Itallie, 1965). Obese patients and normal-weight volunteer subjects were given a bland, tasteless fluid diet and allowed to eat as much as they wanted. Overweight subjects reduced their intake of calories by as much as 80 percent, while normal-weight subjects tended to maintain their customary caloric intake. Thus taste seems to be another important external cue for the eating behavior of obese people. It has been further observed that although obese subjects eat much more of "good-tasting" food—for example, ice cream—than normal subjects, they will eat much less of the same food if it has been adulterated with something mildly unpleasant, such as a small amount of bitter-tasting quinine (Nisbett, 1968b; Decke, 1971).

Interestingly, differences in taste responsiveness between overweight and normal-weight individuals appear to be present at birth, according to one study. Heavy newborn babies showed a significantly greater response when their formula was sweetened than did average-weight or underweight babies: their intake increased by 28 percent, compared to an 8 percent increase among average-weight and underweight babies (Nisbett and Gurwitz, 1970).

Schachter (1970, 1971) has suggested that this tendency to be highly responsive to external cues related to food, while being relatively insensitive to internal cues, is the reason some people have difficulty controlling their body weight. Insensitivity to stomach distention reduces the ability of obese individuals to detect when they have eaten enough. When that insensitivity is coupled with their high sensitivity to the taste, smell, and sight of food, obese people tend to overeat—especially in a society like ours, in which tempting foods are readily available.

NEEDS WITHOUT SPECIFIC DRIVES: LEARNING WHAT TO EAT Whether we are obese or normal in weight, we all need certain nutrients to satisfy physiological requirements. With so many kinds of foods available, how do we know which ones to eat for a nutritionally balanced diet?

When a person is unable to fulfill a basic need for a period of time, the deprivation itself activates the person to seek ways of supplying whatever is missing. Generally speaking, the greater the biological need, the stronger and more single-minded the accompanying drive to seek satisfaction. With persistent deprivation, the resulting drive can come to dominate all aspects of a person's behavior. One study demonstrated the all-consuming nature of such a drive (Keys et al., 1950). The researchers observed a group of volunteer subjects who spent six months in a state of semistarvation, restricted to less than half their normal caloric intake. Quite soon the thoughts, dreams, and conversations of these subjects became dominated by food, and oral behaviors such as chewing gum, drinking coffee, and smoking increased markedly. As the study continued, the subjects spent more and more time collecting "pinups" of recipes and cooking utensils and devising elaborate menus. The desire for food came to dominate their thoughts and behavior, both day and night.

In the case of these food-deprived subjects, the

Why do some people have more difficulty than others in controlling their weight? One factor may be that certain individuals are less sensitive than others to stomach distention (an internal cue that one has eaten enough).

drive to obtain food and the physiological need for food were so highly correlated that it is hardly worthwhile to distinguish them. But there are many instances in which the connection between biological needs and specific drives is not so evident. For one thing, there are specific biological needs that do not appear to be accompanied by specific drives.

Vitamin and mineral requirements provide good examples of this. While we all need vitamin C, for instance, we do not actively seek it out when we are deprived of it, nor, if we did search for it, would we have any way of specifically detecting it with any of our senses in the foods we eat.

As a result of these facts, a number of early Arctic explorers died of scurvy—a severe vitamin C deficiency—in areas where the native Eskimos were thriving (Stefánson, 1938). It was later found that the Eskimos ate a good deal of animal fat and other animal parts that contain large amounts of vitamin C. The explorers, however, tended to eat only lean meat. Thus, although a basic biological need for vitamin C was not being met, the explorers experienced no drive to obtain it, even though it was abundantly available. Moreover, not only were the explorers not "driven" to search for a source of vitamin C and to experiment with different foods, but they actually seemed compelled to retain their habitual eating patterns even though they found themselves in a novel situation. Thus the health of the Eskimos demonstrates that certain eating habits can result in the satisfaction of basic needs even though no accompanying specific drives exist; the fate of the explorers shows that learned eating habits can also interfere with adjustment to the demands of a new feeding situation.

How, then, do people and other animals come to meet basic biological needs that are not accompanied by specific drives? A series of experiments by Paul Rozin and his colleagues provides an interesting answer to this question (Rozin, 1968). In laboratory experiments, rats fed a well-balanced diet displayed a distinct preference for this familiar diet over others. But when the diet was made deficient in certain essential vitamins or minerals, the rats developed an aversion to the diet and a corresponding preference for new food. Moreover, once a particular diet was made deficient, the rats continued to avoid it even after the deficiency had been corrected. In other words, on the basis of experience with various diets, animals seem to learn, through distinctive taste and odor cues, which diets best satisfy their biological needs. If the diets become deficient, the animals seek new diets until the deficiency has been corrected and then continue to favor the diet associated with their recovery from the effects of the deficiency.

Thus, although many animals are not born with specific drives for every biological need, their behavioral repertoires include ways of learning, often by trial and error, which available foods provide the most satisfactory diets (Barker, Best, and Domjan, 1977). Presumably, people are capable of doing the same thing, and through centuries of cultural evolution have learned to select a balanced diet from among the alternatives available in their particular environment. For example, it has been suggested that people with diets low in calcium discovered, probably through learning processes like those described above, ways of preparing foods to increase available calcium: mixing a small amount of the mineral lime into tortillas in Mexico, and cooking spare ribs with vinegar in China, both serve to increase the amount of calcium ingested (Rozin, 1977). Moving to a new environment with new food sources, however, as the explorers did, creates the need to relearn eating behavior to supply basic biological needs; this process might well take more than one generation. As Rozin (1977) points out, people exhibit a strong tendency to stay with a familiar diet even when better alternatives are available.

MOTIVES WITHOUT SPECIFIC PRIMARY NEEDS Fortunately, most needs *are* related to drives and thus can be more readily recognized and satisfied. Activities directed toward satisfying thirst and hunger are obviously related to basic biological needs for water and food. However, a number of studies have shown that people and other animals engage in many activities that do not seem to be directly related to specific biological needs. In fact, certain human behaviors, such as sky diving and mountain climbing, actually threaten life rather than increase the probability of survival (see the accompanying special feature). Such seemingly "unnecessary" behaviors, though seldom so hazardous, can be observed throughout the animal kingdom. For example, one group of researchers (Harlow, Harlow, and Meyer, 1950) found that rhesus monkeys became highly competent in solving various mechanical puzzles (such as undoing a chain, lifting a hook, opening a clasp) that required several steps for solution—despite the fact that they received no reward for doing so. Observing this, the researchers hypothesized that the monkeys were displaying a "manipulative drive." Other studies led to the postulation of similar hypotheses about drives, such as a "curiosity drive" (Butler, 1954) and an "exploratory drive" (Montgomery, 1954) for which the activity itself seems to be its own reward. Similarly, in Chapter 8, we discussed the propensity of infants and children to manipulate, explore, and learn about new things in the environment apparently for no other reason than "for the fun of it." As is shown by the vigorous running of hamsters in an activity wheel or bicycle riding by people, there seems to be a general drive for activity that is intrinsically rewarding.

In all of these drives for activity, however, in contrast to physiological drives, internal conditions that help give rise to them are not apparent (Bolles, 1967, pp. 173–177). Yet these kinds of activities undoubt-

edly have adaptive significance for an animal, and ultimately for the species, because investigating and manipulating one's environment lead to knowledge that can be utilized in times of stress or danger. But they do not have obvious immediate consequences for the fulfillment of biological needs.

It has been suggested that behaviors of this sort are based on a built-in tendency to seek a certain "optimum" of stimulation and activity. Theories stressing this idea, called **optimal-level theories** (Arkes and Garske, 1977, pp. 144–165), are very similar to the homeostatic model of physiological drive regulation, described earlier. These theories postulate that each individual becomes accustomed to a certain level of stimulation and activity, and that each desires experiences that are somewhat different from what he or she is used to, but not extremely different. If, for example, people are asked to rate the pleasantness of various temperatures of water after they have adapted to some moderate temperature, they show a preference for temperatures slightly above or below the temperature to which they have adapted, as shown in Figure 16.2 (Haber, 1958). More extreme temperatures, even though they do not cause pain or discomfort, are rated as relatively unpleasant. A person's "opti-

Figure 16.2 The results of an experiment in adaptation. Subjects became adapted to water of the same temperature as their skin and rated the experience as emotionally "indifferent" (represented by the intersection of the vertical and horizontal lines in the center of this diagram). Then they were asked to place their hands in water that was either cooler or warmer than skin temperature and to rate their emotional response to the experience as "pleasant" or "unpleasant." They rated as most pleasant those temperatures that were either slightly warmer or slightly cooler (represented by the two peaks in the diagram) than the temperature to which they had adapted earlier. (After Haber, 1958)

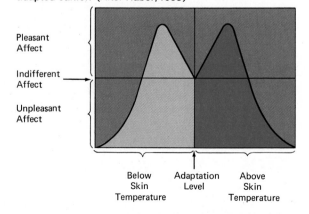

TEMPERATURE

Figure 16.3 In a classic series of experiments on sensory deprivation conducted at McGill University in the 1950s, subjects were isolated in sound-resistant cubicles. Gloves and cotton cuffs prevented input to their hands and fingers; a plastic visor diffused the light coming into their eyes; a foam pillow and the continuous hum of the air conditioner and fan made input to the ears low and monotonous. Except for eating and using the bathroom, the subjects did nothing but lie on the bed. Few chose to remain longer than three days. (After Heron, 1957.)

mum," then, is apparently based on what that person has already become accustomed to. Thus an experienced musician will tend to prefer complex sequences of tones over relatively predictable sequences, whereas a nonmusician will prefer the opposite (Vitz, 1966). In addition, when a new optimum is attained, it is adapted to and yet another optimum emerges.

The idea that we seek to regulate the pace of our lives and the amount of stimulation we receive in order to find an optimum level between extremes is supported not only by our preference for the mean but by our aversion to the extreme. In a classic study of the effects of sensory deprivation, a group of researchers supervised by Donald O. Hebb paid volunteers to remain alone in a small chamber in which they were almost completely cut off from normal sensory stimulation (see Figure 16.3). The subjects soon began to experience extreme psychological discomfort, reported having hallucinations, and could not tolerate their confinement for more than three days (Bexton, Heron, and Scott, 1954). Conversely, extreme stimulation, or "sensory overload," is also

debilitating, and in our highly urbanized society has been suggested as a basis for some kinds of psychological disorder (Ludwig, 1975).

In everyday terms, then, optimal-level theory explains our desire to visit our friends when we have been sick in bed for a week, or our desire for solitude after a round of parties. We seek to maintain stimulation and activity at some moderate, optimal level just different enough from what we are used to in order for it to be interesting, but we vigorously attempt to correct deviations above or below this optimum. The activity of animals in the studies that revealed drives for "manipulation," "curiosity," and "exploration" can be viewed as an attempt to attain such an optimal level of stimulation. Butler's (1954) monkeys, for example, which displayed what he referred to as a "curiosity drive," were kept in a small, enclosed, barren cage. Their persistent pressing of a button, which allowed them to see the world outside the cage through a small observation window (see the accompanying photograph), can thus be seen as an attempt to restore an optimal level of stimulation and to counteract their environmental deprivation. It has been found that humans in a similar situation of deprivation will listen to the same stock market report again and again in an apparent attempt to reestablish their accustomed level of stimulation (Smith and Myers, 1966). This is certainly something that one would not do if alternatives were available.

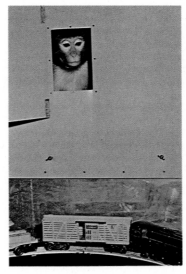

An example of behavior that cannot readily be explained by a drive-reduction model of motivation. A monkey will work hard for the privilege of viewing an electric train, but it would be difficult to say what drive is reduced as a result.

What Motivates People to Take Unnecessary Risks?

It was nearing noon that Sunday when a stiff, warm breeze suddenly materialized. Brent Hansen, a 29-year-old student . . . had been waiting for it most of the morning. Helmetless, he picked up the control bar of his multicolored hangglider, fastened his harness and ran 10 yards along the top of a 600-foot cliff above "Escape Country" near El Toro, California. But no sooner was he aloft than he got into serious trouble.

Somehow he had become tangled in his harness. "I'm caught, I'm caught," he screamed. But his friends below could only watch as he dove nosefirst into the ground at roughly 40 mph. After three days in the intensive-care unit . . . he recovered, only to hangglide again. (Greenberg, 1977, p. 17)

What makes Brent Hansen and many others like him return to a sport that nearly killed him? Whatever it is, it is the same force that sends race-car drivers back to the track and parachutists back to the sky.

Affective States: "It Feels So Good"

To help explain the drawing power of danger, imagine the following situation. A woman at work finds a lump in her breast and becomes terrified. She cries, paces the floor, and can do no work. After a few hours she feels a bit better and resumes working. She is very anxious but no longer terrified. Later in the day, the woman's doctor examines her breast and assures her that she does not have cancer. The lump is simply a clogged sebaceous gland—nothing to worry about. Now euphoria replaces anxiety.

The woman returns to work looking and feeling joyful. A few hours later, she is back to normal as euphoria is replaced by her ordinary emotional state.

Richard Solomon and John Corbit use this example to set forth the features that are "common to many hedonic, emotional, or affective experiences":

First, following the sudden introduction of either a pleasurable or aversive stimulus [discovering the lump], an affective . . . reaction begins and quickly rises to a peak [feeling terrified]. It then slowly declines to a steady level where it remains if the stimulus quality and intensity are maintained [terror is replaced by anxiety]. Then, at the sudden termination of the stimulus [the doctor's assurance that the lump does not mean cancer], the affective reaction quickly disappears [anxiety is gone] and gives way to a qualitatively very different type of affective reaction which reaches its own peak of intensity [euphoria] and then slowly disappears with time [usual emotional state returns]. (Solomon and Corbit, 1974, p. 120)

Solomon and Corbit believe that this sequence of affective states is "the basic pattern for the dynamics of affect" (1974, p. 122). Let us apply the sequence to a dangerous activity, such as parachuting. During the first jump the parachutist is terrified. On landing, terror is replaced by a "stunned" feeling which lasts for several minutes and is followed by "normal composure." After several jumps, though, there is a change. When jumping, parachutists may be anxious, but the terror is gone. "After they land safely, they feel exuberant, exhilarated, and good. They like the feeling, and the mood lasts sometimes for hours. Such parachutists love to jump because of this after-feeling" (Epstein, 1967, as cited in Solomon and Corbit, 1974, p. 123).

Presumably, other dangerous activities elicit the same pattern of emotional responses: After many experiences, fright is replaced by eagerness, and a relieved daze gives way to jubilation. Solomon and Corbit (1974) propose an "opponent-process" theory which assumes that many highly emotional states are automatically opposed by central nervous system mechanisms that reduce the intensity of these feelings, whether they are pleasant or aversive. It is this acclimation to intense affective states over time, say Solomon and Corbit, that enables people to take risks that the uninitiated find overwhelming.

Risk Takers:
A Personality Profile

Solomon and Corbit's theory is fine as far as it goes: It explains the changes that, after a time, make dangerous sports attractive to so many people. But there is still another question to be asked: Why are some people and not others drawn to risks in the first place?

People attracted to high-risk sports were the subjects of a study by psychologist Bruce C. Ogilvie (1974). Psychological inventories collected from an international group of top athletes revealed that those who share an interest in high-risk sports also share many personality traits:

They have a strong need for success and recognition;

They are highly autonomous and have a strong need to dominate;

They are self-assertive and forthright;

They are loners, preferring transitory relationships to deep emotional ties;

They have "a very low level of anxiety, a strong sense of reality, and a high degree of emotional control" (p. 94).

Summing up his profile of risk-taking athletes, Ogilvie describes them as "stimulus addictive." "They have," he says, "a periodic need for extending themselves to the absolute physical, emotional and intellectual limits in order to escape from the tensionless state associated with everyday living" (Ogilvie, 1974, p. 94).

A Social-Psychological View: Risk Taking in the Technological Society

David Klein maintains that the appeal of risk taking stems from certain conditions within American society. Our culture stresses competition and aggression, yet many jobs are so routine that they provide people with no outlets for these strong drives.

"The assembly line worker is a classic example," says Klein. "He's got to go to recreation to distinguish himself. He is forced into these high-risk situations" (quoted in Greenberg, 1977, p. 20). Members of the middle class, too, are being drawn to high-risk sports as more and more jobs become stultifyingly routine.

The Biological Side: High Risks and Brain Chemistry

Finally, an explanation that is more biological than psychological has been suggested by Marvin Zuckerman (1978). From personality tests administered to over 10,000 people, Zuckerman found that people who like risky sports like other intense experiences as well. "The high sensation-seekers are likely to have not just one but a number of adventurous tastes," he writes, "from an eagerness to try risky sports such as sky-diving to a desire for variety in sexual partners" Zuckerman (1978, p. 40).

Again we have to ask, "Why?" What makes some people sensation seekers and some people security seekers?

Zuckerman suggests that physiology is the key. Researchers have found that people respond differently to low- and high-intensity stimulation. "Some people have brains that keep pace with stimulation intensities: the stronger the stimulus, the more the brain responds. Such persons are called 'augmenters.' Other persons have some kind of inhibition that actually diminishes their brain response at high intensities. They are called 'reducers' " (Zuckerman, 1978, p. 96). In Zuckerman's studies, high-sensation seekers tended to be "augmenters."

Thus, in Zuckerman's view, "Sensation-seekers are not led into their activities by peers, or driven to them by compulsive 'neurotic needs,' " such as the need to master anxiety or to reduce sexual tension. Rather, the "increase of tension, not its reduction, is the sensation-seeker's aim" (1978, p. 96). Sensation seekers "may need constant variety in stimuli in order to reach their own high optimal level of arousal, the level that 'feels best' or where they perform most efficiently" (p. 96). Once they become accustomed to that high level, they may be driven to seek a still higher degree of stimulation.

H UMAN MOTIVATION

Beyond the needs that humans share with other animals for the obvious necessities of life, and beyond the portion of our behavior that is determined by drives to obtain these necessities, unraveling the special nature of human motivation becomes a very complex endeavor. One reason for this complexity is the tremendous amount of variation in behavior, goals, and preferences among human beings. For one person, jogging is the road to physical health; for another, it is the fastest way to aching muscles and sore feet. One person's favorite activities are reading books and deciphering ancient manuscripts; another likes nothing better than to play football. One person's dream is another person's nightmare. Psychologists have sought some way to include such individual differences in accounts of human motivation. In this section we will examine some of the approaches that have been taken to this problem.

EXPECTANCY-VALUE THEORY Psychologists and other social scientists, especially economists, have long been interested in the way people make practical decisions. Most social scientists have adopted some version of **expectancy-value theory** to explain this process. This theory was originated by Edward Tolman (1932); its general outlines are easy to understand. Suppose that you decide to buy

Figure 16.4 The computation of an expected value. Expected value is the overall gain (or loss) that would result if the risk were taken over and over again. The amount that could be lost (in this case, the cost of the raffle ticket), multiplied by the probability of losing it (by losing the raffle), is subtracted from the amount that could be gained (the $1,000 prize minus the cost of the raffle ticket), multiplied by the probability of gaining it. In the long run, the buyer could expect to gain only $19 by taking this risk repeatedly.

	Winning	Losing	
Probability	1/50	49/50	
Value	$999.00	–$1.00	**Total**
P × V	$19.98	–$0.98	**$19.00**

Figure 16.5
Expectancy-value theory suggests that an individual makes decisions by comparing the expected values of alternative courses of action. The person's expected values are computed (perhaps not consciously) from his or her subjective estimate of the probability and the value of each possible outcome, as shown here.

a raffle ticket for $1, and forty-nine other people do the same. You have one chance in fifty of winning the raffle. If the grand prize is $1,000, you have made a good decision, because the expected value of your investment is $19. Figure 16.4 shows how this is determined. This is an example of a decision based on the objective (in this case, monetary) value the outcome can ultimately be expected to have for the person.

The expectancy-value approach to motivation explains motivated behavior by going one step further—by relating a person's *expectancy* of achieving a particular goal to the *value* the goal has for the person. That is, it extends the decision model represented by the raffle-ticket example to take into consideration the probability that an action will lead to a certain outcome that has *subjective* incentive value (see Figure 16.5). As with the objective value of a financial investment (which can lead to the gain or loss of money), a subjective incentive value can be positive or negative. One couple wants a large family, while another couple thinks children would be a disaster; one person looks forward to retirement, while another dreads it; and so on.

The expectancy-value theory has been elaborated by John Atkinson (1958a, b) to include individual differences. In Atkinson's conception, a **motive** is defined as a capacity, which is relatively stable in a given person but which differs from person to person, to gain gratification from a particular class of incentives. This definition accommodates the fact that some people find scholarly activity rewarding and others do not; some find athletics exciting and others have no interest in exercise or competitive games.

ACHIEVEMENT MOTIVATION Many of the current methods of studying human motivation are based on work done by Henry Murray and his colleagues in the late 1930s. Murray, whose theory of personality will be discussed in Chapter 19, emphasized the role of "psychogenic," or nonphysiological, needs in determining human behavior. He and his colleagues accepted Sigmund Freud's idea (discussed in Chapter 18) that people express their motives more clearly in free-associative thought than in direct self-reports. Guided by clinical evidence, Murray and his colleagues devised the Thematic Apperception Test (TAT), which requires subjects to write or tell brief stories about pictures that show ambiguous situations (see Chapter 20). The stories can then be analyzed for signs of particular motives in the subjects.

Using the TAT, Murray (1938) identified a long list of human motives, among which "achievement," "affiliation," and "dominance" have been most frequently studied. Here, rather than cataloguing all the kinds of human motives that have been identified, we will concentrate on one of them, achievement, in order to provide a thorough analysis of how such motives are measured and analyzed, and how knowledge gained from the study of motives might be applied for people's benefit.

MEASURING ACHIEVEMENT MOTIVATION To measure the achievement motive, David McClelland, John Atkinson, and their colleagues (McClelland et al., 1953; Atkinson, 1958b) showed subjects pictures from the TAT (see the box on page 370). Each subject was given about four minutes to write a story answering the following questions: (1) What is happening? Who are the people? (2) What has led up to the situation—that is, what has happened in the past? (3) What is being thought? What is wanted? By whom? (4) What will happen? What will be done? Typically, each subject was shown three or four different pictures, so that a large enough fantasy sample could be obtained for scoring. The box presents some sample stories in the order in which they were scored, from high achievement motivation to low.

The scoring system was devised by comparing stories written under achievement-oriented conditions (when a competitive intelligence test was also administered to each subject) with other stories written under relaxed, noncompetitive conditions. The stories that received high scores for achievement, like the first one in the box, showed the major character to be concerned with standards of excellence and with a high level of performance; with unique accomplishments, such as inventions and winning awards; and with the pursuit of a long-term goal or career. High-achievement stories also dealt with persistent attempts to accomplish something and with good or bad feelings (pride or shame) aroused by the success or failure of achievement-related activity. In fact, fear of failure was found to be one of the major negative components of the achievement motive: the greater the fear of failure, the lower the achievement motive.

To assess individual differences in the achievement motive, subjects are given the TAT under neutral conditions, and their stories are numerically scored for achievement imagery according to rules formulated by Atkinson (1958c). Independent scorers (that is, people who are not colleagues of the experimenter) trained in the use of this method have been found to agree very closely on the scores for most stories.

COMPARISON OF PEOPLE WITH HIGH AND LOW ACHIEVEMENT MOTIVATION Early studies of achievement behavior revealed that highly motivated subjects—those who received high TAT scores on need for achievement—performed better on such tasks as anagram puzzles and addition problems than did low scorers on the TAT achievement measures. The high scorers also persisted longer at difficult tasks, were more likely than low scorers to recall interrupted tasks (indicating a continuing desire to complete the tasks successfully), and chose "expert" work partners more often than "friendly" ones (because the "experts" were more likely to contribute to success).

In one study (Weiner, 1972), subjects who scored high in achievement motivation, and who also exhibited low test anxiety, chose to stand at an intermediate distance from the target in a ring-toss game, thus making the game challenging but not impossible. Subjects with low achievement motivation and high test anxiety, however, were more likely to stand either very close to the target, where success was assured, or far away from the target,

Shown here is a picture of the sort that might be used in the measurement of the Need for Achievement (*n* Ach). Examples of stories that would be scored from fairly high to low are shown with the picture. The portions of the stories printed in italics are the kinds of themes considered to reflect *n* Ach.

This guy is just getting off work. These are all working guys and they don't like their work too much either. The younger guy over on the right knows the guy with the jacket.

Something bad happened today at work—*a nasty accident that shouldn't have happened.* These two guys don't trust each other *but they are going to talk* about it. *They mean to put things to rights. No one else much cares* it seems.

The guy with the jacket is *worried.* He feels that *something has to be done. He wouldn't ordinarily talk* to the younger man *but now he feels he must.* The young guy is ready. He's *concerned* too but doesn't know what to expect.

They'll both realize after talking that you never know where your friends are. *They'll both feel better* afterward because they'll feel they have someone they can rely on next time there's trouble. Harry O'Silverfish has been

working on the Ford assembly line for thirteen years. Every morning he gets up, eats a doughnut and cup of coffee, takes his lunch pail, gets in the car, and drives to the plant. It is during this morning drive that his mind gets filled with *fantasies of what he'd like to be doing* with his life. Then, about the same time that he parks his car and turns off his ignition, he also *turns off his mind*—and it remains turned off during the whole working day. In the evenings, he is *too tired and discouraged to do much* more than drink a few beers and watch TV.

But this morning Harry's mind didn't turn off with the car. He had witnessed a car accident on the road—in which two people were killed—soon after leaving home. Just as he reaches the

plant gate, Harry suddenly turns. Surprised, he discovers that he has made *a firm decision* never to enter that plant again. He knows that *he must try another way* to live before he dies.

These are hard-hats. It's the end of the shift. There is a demonstration outside the plant and the men coming out are looking at it. Everyone is just walking by. They are not much interested. One person is *angry* and *wants to go on strike*, but this does not make sense to anyone else. He is out of place. Actually he is not really angry, he is just bored. He looks as though he might do a little dance to amuse himself, which is more than the rest of them do. *Nothing will happen* at this time *till more people join* this one man in his needs.

---

where they seemed to feel that no one could blame them for failing. In real life, too, people with high achievement motivation tend to pursue careers that are difficult enough to be challenging but not so difficult that they will end in failure. People with low achievement motivation are less realistic. They tend to choose either very easy jobs, where success is certain but the rewards are small, or very difficult jobs, at which they cannot be blamed for failing.

Another interesting difference between people high and low in achievement motivation was found in the manner in which members of each group at-

tempted to explain their successes and failures (Weiner, 1972). People high in achievement motivation usually attributed their performance to internal factors—their successes to high ability and high effort and their failures to lack of effort. People low in achievement motivation were more likely to attribute success to external factors (ease of task and good luck) and failure to the internal factor of lack of ability. From this, it is possible to predict how much success a person will anticipate when confronted again with a particular task. For example, a person who attributes success to stable factors (ability and task difficulty) will expect to succeed again the next time he or she tries the task. If unstable causes are believed to be responsible, the person is less certain of succeeding at that task again (especially if luck is emphasized).

These differences in how people view the causes of their successes and failures help to explain behavioral differences documented by Atkinson and others. For example, some people choose to undertake achievement-related activities; perhaps they do so because in the past they experienced strong positive emotion after success (having attributed it to ability and effort). They persist longer in the face of failure than do their low-motivation counterparts; perhaps they do so because they think that failure is the result of insufficient effort on their part and that increased effort will lead to success. People low in achievement motivation give up easily because they attribute failure to low ability and feel that nothing can be done about that.

THE ACHIEVEMENT MOTIVE AND SOCIETY
David McClelland has studied the social origins of the achievement motive and its implications for a society. He argues that a high level of achievement motivation within a particular society is partly responsible for a high level of commercial and business-oriented activity, which in turn leads to economic growth and modernization.

Particularly novel and interesting are McClelland's studies (1961) relating the economic growth and decline of certain societies to the level of achievement motivation reflected in each society's literature. The studies consisted of content analyses of literary samples, such as folk tales and children's readers, taken from crucial periods in each society's history.

McClelland suggested that, just as children's stories and folk tales represent a major method of teaching a society's general values to children, they also help to crystallize children's motivational orientation in later years. In other words, just as children's stories might communicate to children the "proper" ways of behaving in certain situations (sharing one's toys, being kind to animals) through identification with the major characters, they may likewise communicate a society's values regarding achievement—such as the importance of overcoming obstacles to solve problems and gain recognition.

It was found that there was a sizable variation be-

tween societies in the number of achievement-oriented themes in their children's literature, and that this was positively correlated with measures of the economic activity of these societies (such as the kilowatt hours of electricity used per capita or the extent of foreign trade). McClelland claimed that the risk-taking activities and new ideas of entrepreneurs result from a strong achievement motive, not merely from the desire or need for money, as is often maintained. He postulated that as children who read stories high in achievement themes become old enough to be entrepreneurs, their behavior will be reflected in an increase in their society's economic activity.

In order to investigate the relationship between achievement motivation and economic growth more fully, McClelland (1961) conducted an analysis of achievement themes in the literature of England. He used trained scorers who did not know in which historical period the works had been written. McClelland disguised the historical periods by selecting passages that did not contain datable material and that dealt with similar issues. The scores were found to correlate highly with rising and falling economic trends in England over a period of 350 years. Even more remarkable, in a similar analysis of Greek civilization from 900 B.C. to 100 B.C., achievement motivation scores from Greek literature were found to be closely related to the rise, peak, and decline of economic growth in Greece during this period.

APPLICATIONS: MANAGING ACHIEVEMENT MOTIVATION If the achievement motive, as defined and analyzed by McClelland and Atkinson, is essentially a learned human motive, might it be possible to actually train people to be achievement-oriented? McClelland and others have applied their theories of achievement motivation to several fields of human behavior. In one study, a group of college students were encouraged and instructed to create fantasies of successful achievement—which led, in fact, to greater academic success and higher grades for the students involved (McClelland and Winter, 1969).

In what was perhaps the most comprehensive and compelling project, McClelland, Winter, and their co-workers succeeded in raising the achievement motivation levels of businessmen in a village in India, using a variety of techniques. The program they implemented, called the Kakinada project, consisted of encouraging the businessmen to have high-achievement fantasies, to make plans that would help them realize the goals of a successful entrepreneur, and to communicate with one another about their goals and their methods of reaching them. McClelland approached the project pragmatically; his aim was to raise the achievement-motivation level among the businessmen, rather than to identify the best techniques for doing so. For that reason, he does not know exactly why his program succeeded—whether one technique worked and the others did not or whether all of them helped—but succeed it did. The businessmen became more productive as entrepreneurs, starting several large industries, enlarging their businesses, and hiring more than 5,000 of their neighbors (McClelland and Winter, 1969).

Although the scope of the Kakinada project was small, its success indicates that larger efforts of the same kind could be a major force in economic development. In a recent assessment of this study, McClelland (1978) compared it, in cost and outcome, with another, more complicated project that had the immediate purpose of improving the standard of living in one particular village in India and the long-range goal of teaching the people to help themselves.

The Barpali Village project, as it was called, was conducted by the American Friends Service Committee. Training and technical aid were provided for digging wells and building latrines, establishing better schools and health facilities, providing information on family planning, improving methods of farming, starting village industries, and teaching the villagers how to repair equipment and to maintain the programs.

Ten years after all American personnel had returned to the United States, the village was revisited and the project evaluated. To the great disappointment of the dedicated people involved, there was little sign that they had ever visited the village. Most of the wells were unused; the advanced agricultural procedures had been abandoned; the villagers' health was as poor as ever; and the birth control program was an utter failure (population had, in fact, increased more than in a neighboring village).

In terms of time, money, and enduring effects, McClelland's achievement-training project was far more successful. The Barpali Village project cost $1 million, lasted ten years, and failed to have any permanent effect on the population. The Kakinada project, however, cost $25,000, lasted only six months, and resulted in long-term improvement in the villagers' standard of living through self-sustaining programs and expanded employment. While the Barpali Village project was based on the common-sense idea that people will do things if they are taught how to do them, the Kakinada project was based on the proven psychological concept that motivation, not knowledge alone, is essential in altering people's behavior.

SEX DIFFERENCES IN ACHIEVEMENT MOTIVATION: THE FEAR OF SUCCESS

During various studies of achievement motivation, it was found that level of achievement motivation did not predict the behavior of females as well as it did the behavior of males. Scientists wondered why.

One clue is the fact that females often obtain higher test-anxiety scores than do males. For a while some psychologists thought that this scoring pattern indicated that females were inherently more anxious than males, but Eleanor Maccoby (1963) offered another possible explanation:

> Suppose a girl does succeed in maintaining throughout her childhood years the qualities of dominance, independence, and active striving that appear to be requisites for good analytic thinking. In so doing, she is defying the conventions concerning what is appropriate behavior for her sex. She may do this successfully, in many ways, but I suggest that it is a rare intellectual woman who will not have paid a price for it: a price in anxiety.

In other words, females in our culture traditionally have not been encouraged to be successful, at least not in some areas of activity, and attempting to succeed in certain endeavors may have negative consequences.

Matina Horner, in her research on this topic (1970, 1972), devised a way to measure what she called the motive to avoid success, or fear of success. Using a variation of the TAT, Horner gave college students the opening sentence of a story that they would then complete. For the ninety women in the study, the sentence was, "After first-term finals, Anne finds herself at the top of her medical school class." For the eighty-eight men, the name "John" was substituted for "Anne." For sample stories, see the accompanying box.

A story was scored as showing fear of success if negative consequences befell Anne or John as a result of getting high grades in medical school. As with Atkinson's scoring system for achievement im-

Motivation in Women: The Avoidance of Success

Below are some stories written by subjects in Matina Horner's research on the motive to avoid success. The first three stories, by women, show such a motive. The rest of the stories, only one of which was written by a woman, do not.

Anne has a boyfriend Carl in the same class and they are quite serious. Anne met Carl at college and they started dating around their sophomore years in undergraduate school. Anne is rather upset and so is Carl. She wants him to be higher scholastically than she is. Anne will deliberately lower her academic standing the next term, while she does all she subtly can to help Carl. . . . His grades come up and Anne soon drops out of med school. They marry and he goes on in school while she raises their family. Aggressive, unmarried, wearing Oxford shoes and hair pulled back in a bun, she wears glasses and is terribly bright.

Anne is really happy she's on top, though Tom is higher than she—though that's as it should be . . . Anne doesn't mind Tom winning.

Congrats to her! Anne is quite a lady—not only is she tops academically, but she is liked and admired by her fellow students. Quite a trick in a man-dominated field. She is brilliant—but she is also a lady. A lot of hard work. She is pleased—yet humble and her fellow students (with the exception of a couple of sour pusses) are equally pleased. That's the kind of girl she is—you are always pleased when she is—never envious. She will continue to be at or near the top. She will be as fine practicing her field as she is studying it. And—always a lady.

John is a conscientious young man who worked hard. He is pleased with himself. John has always wanted to go into medicine and is very dedicated. His hard work has paid off. He

is thinking that he must not let up now, but must work even harder than he did before. His good marks have encouraged him. (He may even consider going into research now.) While others with good first term marks sluff off, John continues working hard and eventually graduates at the top of his class. (Specializing in neurology.)

John is very pleased with himself and he realizes that all his efforts have been rewarded, he has finally made the top of his class. John has worked very hard, and his long hours of study have paid off. He spent hour after hour in preparation for finals. He is thinking about his girl Cheri whom he will marry at the end of med school. He realizes he can give her all the things she desires after he becomes established. He will go on in med school making good grades and be successful in the long run.

From Matina Horner, in *Feminine Personality and Conflict*. Monterey, Calif.: Brooks/Cole, 1970.

---

agery, it was found that well-trained independent raters could agree on the appropriate scoring category for over 90 percent of the stories.

The most striking characteristic of Horner's results was the sheer magnitude of the differences between the kinds of responses men and women made to the cue. The women showed significantly more evidence of the motive to avoid success than did the men. Over 65 percent of the women wrote stories containing fear-of-success imagery, but fewer than 10 percent of the men did so.

Horner speculated that the motive to avoid success would affect performance only in situations in which that specific motive was aroused. She hypothesized further that the motive to avoid success is aroused when a person is anxious about competitiveness and its aggressive overtones. Horner conducted a second experiment in which each subject was given a number of achievement tasks to perform in a large, competitive group of both men and women. After performing these tasks, the subjects were randomly assigned to various other experimental conditions. One-third of them were placed

in a completely noncompetitive situation in which they worked alone on a verbal and arithmetic task, guided only by tape-recorded instructions. The performance of each of the thirty people in this noncompetitive situation was then compared with his or her previous performance in the large, competitive group of both men and women (see Figure 16.6).

Figure 16.6 Data from Horner's experiment on the motive to avoid success in women. (After Horner, 1970)

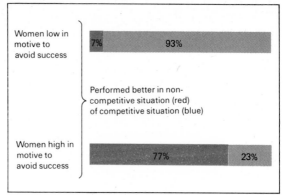

Of these subjects, more than two-thirds of the men performed at a higher level in the competitive situation than in the noncompetitive one, but fewer than one-third of the women did so. Moreover, 77 percent of the women who had previously been scored high in motive to avoid success performed at a significantly higher level in the noncompetitive situation than in the competitive one. By comparison, only 7 percent of the women rated low in motive to avoid success performed better in the noncompetitive situation than in the competitive one. This means that 93 percent of the women low in fear of success performed at a significantly higher level in the competitive situation than in the noncompetitive one—as did a majority of the male subjects. These results suggest that sex differences in performance may be due not to inherent differences in *ability*, as is often assumed, but to culturally imposed sex differences in *motivation*.

Other studies have confirmed some of the predictions derived from Horner's measure of fear of success. For example, it has been suggested that women who score high in this measure see success as

threatening close relationships with men, and in some respects as signifying their "failure" as women by traditional standards. These women might be expected to marry and have children sooner than women scoring low on this measure, for having a baby can confirm a woman's femininity, remove her from the competitive arena, and reestablish her dependent relationship with her husband. A follow-up study of the same women Horner had assessed found this to be the case (Hoffman, 1977). Even more revealing is the fact that many of these women seemed to have become pregnant when faced with the possibility of success in some area that would put them in competition with their husbands (Hoffman, 1977).

As intuitively appealing as Horner's concept of fear of success is for explaining certain differences between men and women in today's society, the measure as determined by the TAT stories has been criticized by several other investigators (Tresemer, 1974; Zuckerman and Wheeler, 1975). However, a new and more objective scaling technique supports the idea that there are male–female differences in

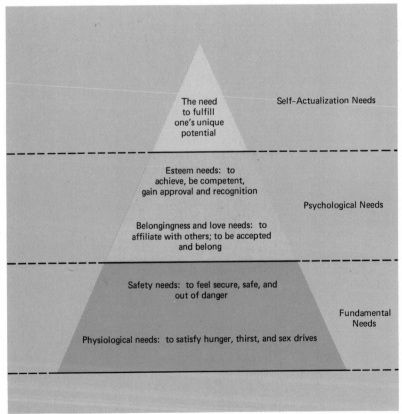

Figure 16.7 This pyramid represents Maslow's hierarchy of needs. According to Maslow, fundamental needs must be satisfied before a person is free to progress to psychological needs, and these in turn must be satisfied before a person can turn to self-actualization needs. More recently, Maslow (1970) has added a need for transcendance that is even higher than the need for self-actualization. (After Maslow, 1971)

Self-Actualization Needs

The need to fulfill one's unique potential

Esteem needs: to achieve, be competent, gain approval and recognition

Belongingness and love needs: to affiliate with others; to be accepted and belong

Psychological Needs

Safety needs: to feel secure, safe, and out of danger

Physiological needs: to satisfy hunger, thirst, and sex drives

Fundamental Needs

fear of success among undergraduate college students, with females scoring higher on this measure (Zuckerman and Wheeler, 1975).

A HIERARCHICAL CONCEPTION OF HUMAN MOTIVES

The contents of this chapter indicate that in order to be complete, a theory of human motivation must account for motives based on physiological needs similar to those of other animals, for drives that are akin to physiological needs, and for motives that cannot be characterized without reference to human cognitive processes. One way to organize these diverse motives conceptually has been suggested by Abraham Maslow (1954), a personality theorist whose work will be discussed in Chapter 19.

Maslow believed that human needs, or motives, are organized hierarchically. The **fundamental needs** are related to physiological deficits (needs for food, water, and so on). The **intermediate needs**—for a feeling of safety, of belonging, and of self-esteem—are also "deficiency needs," in Maslow's conception. Failure to attain a feeling of basic security,

of social acceptance, and of self-esteem produces pathological discomforts and maladjustments that may be almost as debilitating as starvation. The highest motives, called **metaneeds**, have to do with creativity and what Maslow called "self-actualization" (see Figure 16.7).

According to Maslow, the lower needs are pre-emptive, or prepotent: extreme hunger or thirst is so urgent that severely deficient individuals have no opportunity to worry about social acceptance and psychological security, let alone the creative exercise of their talents. Similarly, people who continually seek social acceptance are not free to create scholarly or artistic works.

Although little research has been done to evaluate Maslow's hierarchical concept of motivation, we mention it here because it draws attention to the complexity of human motivational processes. In addition, it emphasizes aspects of human motivation extending beyond those for basic survival needs and economic accomplishments. Although Maslow's hierarchy needs further study, there is little question that each person's unique talents could be of more benefit to the person and to humanity if at least fundamental human needs were met.

Summary

1. Psychologists infer motivation from behavior, because motivation cannot be observed directly. The most basic goal-directed behaviors serve the vital functions of survival and reproduction. In the psychological concept of motivation, a motive has two components: an **incentive**, or an external motivational stimulus, and a **drive**, or an internal motivational factor. Applying motivational labels to particular behaviors does not explain those behaviors because the reasoning is circular, because such labeling fails to explain why the same motive may give rise to different patterns of behavior, and because it does not explain how individuals identify different motivational states within themselves.

    A. Basic motivational processes are best understood in terms of the functions they serve for the organism. **Primary drives** are produced by emotional and physiological conditions that stimulate the organism to seek fulfillment of basic needs. **Homeostasis** is Walter

Cannon's term for the tendency of an organism to maintain an optimal level of a physiological requirement by reacting to deviations from the optimal condition so as to restore it. Many kinds of behavior fit into this model of motivation as a homeostatic process (though others, such as sexual behavior, do not).

1. Thirst provides a good example of how an organism knows when an adjustment is necessary and what the mechanism is by which this adjustment is made.

    a. Three types of stimuli induce thirst and drinking in mammals:
        1. An increase in salt concentration in the various fluid compartments of the body;
        2. A decrease in the volume of fluid in the circulatory system;
        3. An increase in exercise or body temperature.

b. The stimuli that cause satiation of thirst include stomach distention and several different physiological mechanisms that enable the organism to maintain the body's water balance.

2. Hunger and weight regulation show how both external and internal stimuli contribute to drive regulation.

a. The hypothalamus is involved in the regulation of food intake and body weight.

b. Much feeding behavior is determined by external factors: social customs, how food looks, tastes, and smells, and the effort required to obtain food.

c. Studies have indicated that normal-weight people base their eating behavior on internal cues of hunger and satiety (such as stomach contraction and stomach distention), while obese individuals base theirs on external cues (such as the sight, taste, or availability of food).

B. When a biological need increases, the accompanying drive to seek satisfaction of the need generally becomes stronger and more single-minded. Some biological needs exist that do not appear to be accompanied by specific drives, as in the case of vitamin and mineral requirements. Animals seem to learn which diets best satisfy their nutritional needs through distinctive taste and odor cues; humans are presumably capable of the same thing. Moving to a new environment with new food sources creates the need to relearn eating behavior to supply basic biological needs, though humans are often slow to deviate from a familiar diet.

C. People and other animals are motivated to engage in many activities that do not seem to be directly related to the meeting of specific primary needs. These include investigating and manipulating one's environment even when there is no direct reward for doing so. The adaptive significance of this behavior is that it leads to knowledge that can be used in times of stress or danger. **Optimal-level theories** postulate that such "unnecessary" behavior is based on a built-in tendency to maintain a certain level of stimulation and activity to which each individual has become accustomed, and that people desire experiences that are somewhat different from

what they are used to, but not extremely different.

2. Human motivation is more complex than that of other animals, partly because of the great variation in behavior, goals, and preferences among human beings. A number of theories of human motivation have tried to take these differences into account.

A. The **expectancy-value theory** explains motivation by relating a person's expectancy of achieving a particular goal to the value the goal has for the person. Elaborating this theory to accommodate individual differences, John Atkinson defined a **motive** as a capacity, which is relatively stable in a given person but which differs from person to person, to gain gratification from a particular class of incentives.

B. Personality theorist Henry Murray emphasized the role of psychogenic needs in determining human behavior. Murray and his colleagues devised the Thematic Apperception Test for use in detecting signs of particular motives in their subjects. Achievement is one of the many motives identified by Murray.

1. Achievement motivation is measured by comparing stories based on pictures in the TAT that are written under achievement-oriented conditions with other stories written under relaxed conditions. Individual differences in the achievement motive are assessed by administering the TAT under neutral conditions and numerically scoring the results for achievement imagery.

2. Studies revealed that subjects who received high TAT scores on need for achievement generally performed better than did low scorers on various tasks, and they tended to persist longer on difficult tasks. High scorers were also found to choose careers that were challenging but not impossible, while low scorers made less realistic choices. High scorers attributed their successes and failures to internal factors, while low scorers were more likely to attribute success to external factors and failure to lack of ability.

3. David McClelland postulated that a high level of achievement motivation within a particular society is partly responsible for

a high level of business-oriented activity, which leads to economic growth and modernization. His studies showed a positive correlation between the amount of achievement-oriented themes in the children's literature of a particular society and the economic activity of the society. An analysis of historical literature yielded a positive correlation between achievement themes in the literature and rising economic trends in the society.

4. There have been various attempts to train people to be achievement-oriented, a notable example of which was McClelland's Kakinada project. A variety of techniques including the encouragement of high-achievement fantasies among businessmen resulted in long-term improvements in the standard of living in a small Indian village. Imparting motivation, not just know-how, was the key to the project's success.

C. It has been demonstrated that level of achievement motivation does not predict female behavior as well as it does male behavior. One reason for this may be the fact that women often obtain higher test-anxiety scores than men. Another may be what Matina Horner called the motive to avoid success, which is more common among women than men. She attributes this to culturally imposed sex differences in motivation. While studies have confirmed some of the predictions derived from Horner's measure of fear of success, the measure has been criticized.

3. A complete theory of human motivation must account for motives based on physiological needs, for drives that are akin to physiological needs, and for motives that cannot be characterized without reference to human cognitive processes. Personality theorist Abraham Maslow suggested that these various kinds of motives can be organized hierarchically, with the lower needs preempting the higher needs.

A. **Fundamental needs** are related to physiological deficits.

B. **Intermediate needs** are for safety, belongingness, and self-esteem. Maslow believed that the failure to attain these feelings produces both pathological discomforts and maladjustments.

C. **Metaneeds** are the highest motives, having to do with creativity and self-actualization.

RECOMMENDED READINGS

ARKES, HAL R., and JOHN P. GARSKE. *Psychological Theories of Motivation*. Monterey, Calif.: Brooks/Cole, 1977. A broad, basic introductory survey of dominant approaches to motivation in psychology, ranging from instinct through psychoanalysis to attribution theory.

ATKINSON, JOHN W. (ed.). *Motives in Fantasy, Action, and Society*. New York: Van Nostrand Reinhold, 1958. An important book that pulls together work done by many investigators on the various methods used to assess and study individual differences in motivational dispositions such as achievement, affiliation, and power. Scoring manuals and self-teaching materials are also included.

ATKINSON, JOHN W., and NORMAN T. FEATHER. *A Theory of Achievement Motivation*. New York: Wiley, 1966. Focuses on the contemporaneous determinants of achievement-oriented behavior and the marked advances made in psychologists' understanding of the problem.

JUNG, JOHN. *Understanding Human Motivation: A Cognitive Approach*. New York: Macmillan, 1978. A well-written basic textbook emphasizing individual differences and cognitive factors in human motivation.

MCCLELLAND, DAVID. *The Achieving Society*. New York: Van Nostrand Reinhold, 1961. Addresses the question of the social origins and consequences for society of achievement motivation.

WEINER, BERNARD. *Theories of Motivation: From Mechanism to Cognition*. Chicago: Markham, 1973. A textbook covering, among other topics, drive theory, achievement theory, and—most important—the author's attribution-theory approach to achievement motivation. Presents clearly the differences between mechanistic (for example, drive) and cognitive (for example, attribution) theories.

CHAPTER SEVENTEEN

HUMAN SEXUALITY

Since I was brought up without formal religious training of any kind, I never really understood what a "sin" was.

In fact, at quite a young age, I began to suspect that people (whatever they *said* they believed) never really worried about sin and the threat of hell, only about illegality and the threat of a fine or imprisonment.

For instance, it wasn't illegal to kill an enemy during wartime, even by shooting him in the back when he was sleeping, and no one seemed to worry that it might be sinful. Again, everyone seemed perfectly happy to make use of any loophole to evade the spirit of a law. If something rotten and unjust was achieved without actually breaking a law, everyone seemed to think that all was well, and I heard no one worry about sin.

It puzzled me that when people did worry about sin, it was often in reference to sexual missteps. Many sexual activities were sins, and these sins seemed to bother pious people far more than offenses like unethical business practices, political chicanery, and social injustice. Furthermore, these sinful sexual activities didn't even seem to be really illegal—or, if they were, the laws against them were never enforced.

As I grew older, it dawned on me that this strong connection between sex and sin might be a holdover from the days when infant mortality was high and life expectancy was short. In a very real sense, the survival of the human race depended on people having as many children as possible. Consequently, all sexuality had to be channeled into those actions that increased the possibility of conception. For instance, because masturbation wasted sperm, so to speak, masturbation and anything that encouraged it, such as pornography and exhibitionism, had to be outlawed. Any other practice that reduced or actually canceled the chance of conception, such as homosexuality or oral-genital sex or contraception, must be outlawed, too, and labeled as "unnatural."

It then occurred to me that we now live in altogether different times. Now, in many countries, infant mortality is low and life expectancy is high, and the great and overwhelming danger is overpopulation. Perhaps, as a matter of necessity, society should stop trying to legislate morality and instead permit those sexual activities that give satisfaction and don't involve any chance of unwanted conception. Maybe what is "unnatural" in today's world is for people to become parents when all they actually want is pleasure.

Isaac Asimov

Because each of us is a sexual being, human sexual behavior is a subject of great interest to all of us. In this chapter we will briefly consider some of the central topics in the study of human sexuality: the factors that influence an individual's gender; the most widely used methods of studying human sexual behavior; the nature of the human sexual response, some major sexual problems, and sex therapy; and the wide variations in human sexual behavior.

INFLUENCES ON GENDER

The concept of gender—maleness or femaleness—is not a single phenomenon, but a composite of many factors. These influences include heredity, anatomy, hormones, and the psychological determination of gender identity. Our ability to sort out the respective contributions of these influences on gender is an intriguing recent addition to our knowledge of human sexuality.

GENETIC FACTORS One of the twenty-three human chromosomes, which may be either an X or a Y chromosome (see Chapter 7), governs sex differentiation. All the eggs a woman produces contain only an X chromosome. A man's sperm, however, has either an X or a Y chromosome. The father's sperm determines which genetic sex a child will be: if the sperm that fertilizes the egg has an X chromosome, the child will be female (X chromosome plus X chromosome, or genotype XX); if it has a Y chromosome, the child will be male (X plus Y, or genotype XY). Genetic sex is determined at the moment of conception, but genetic sex is only the first step down the complex path of the development of gender and sexuality.

HORMONAL INFLUENCES In the first six weeks after conception, the sexual development of males and females follows an identical course. Indeed, it is impossible to tell the sex of the embryo without examining its chromosomes. First a gonad (a sex gland), then a genital tubercle (a small bump that will become external genitalia) and a set of ducts (that will become internal sex organs) develop along a ridge running from the umbilical cord to the tail of the embryo (see Figure 17.1). Male and female sex organs are **homologous**: they arise from the same embryonic structures and perform similar functions. If the embryo is genetically male (XY), the gonad begins to develop into testes at about six weeks. If it is genetically female (XX), ovaries begin to appear some weeks later. Gradually the genital tubercle becomes a penis and scrotum in males, a clitoris and labia in females; the sex ducts become the seminal vesicles and prostate in males, and the Fallopian tubes, uterus, and vagina in females.

Researchers John Money and Anke Ehrhardt (1972) have compared the influence of genetic and hormonal factors to a relay race. Genes run the first lap, programming the emergence of testes or ovaries; hormones take over for the second lap,

A human embryo at fifteen weeks. If an embryo is genetically male, the gonads begin to develop into testes at about six weeks; if it is female, the gonads begin to develop into ovaries some weeks later.

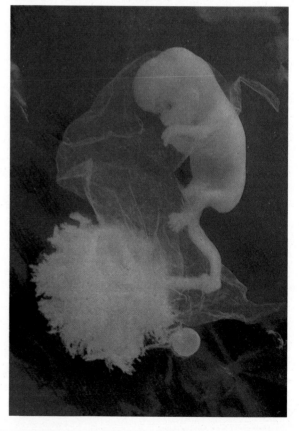

Figure 17.1 Male and female genitals do not look very similar. Yet, as this diagram of the stages of differentiation shows, male and female sexual organs have the same embryonic beginnings and are homologous with one another. The clitoris and the penis, for example, both derive from the genital tubercule and both function as the center of sexual sensitivity. (After McCary, 1978).

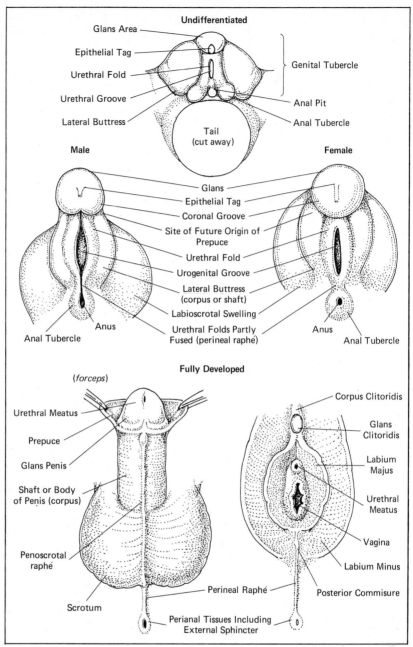

guiding the development of internal and external reproductive organs.

Despite similarities between the sexes in the early stages of embryonic development, all is not equal for all embryos. If an embryo has received only a single X chromosome and no Y, the fetus will develop into a genetic female, but one who never develops secondary sex characteristics (an abnormality known as Turner's syndrome). If an embryo receives a Y but no X chromosome, it will not survive. (The X chromosome is larger and, in contrast to the Y chromosome, it apparently contains genetic information vital to the development of the fetus.) Moreover, if a genetically male (XY) embryo fails to manufacture androgens (the male sex hormones) through a developmental malfunction, the fetus will develop female genitals.

Thus, the *presence* of elements appears to be necessary for the development of a male: the Y chromosome and androgen hormones. Through processes that are not yet known, genetic information contained in the Y chromosome influences the gonads at an early stage to develop into testes rather than into ovaries. The testes then manufacture androgens, which stimulate the development of external and internal male anatomy.

In experiments with mammals other than humans it has been shown that if the gonads of male embryos are removed after they have become testes, the organism at birth will have *female* genitalia and internal organs (except for ovaries). If the equivalent operation is performed on a genetically female embryo, and the ovaries are removed, still an anatomical female (without ovaries) will be born.

Thus, female development requires the *absence* of both the Y chromosome and androgens. A developing female embryo may become "masculinized" to varying degrees (for example, it may develop external male genitalia) if it is exposed to excessive levels of androgens during a sensitive period for establishing sex differentiation (Gorski, 1971). From a biological standpoint the idea that woman was created from man would seem to be pure myth, for the male pattern appears to be an elaboration of the female pattern rather than the opposite.

Almost immediately after birth, parents start to treat male and female infants differently. By the age of four, children have developed a strong sense of their own gender identity.

SOCIAL INFLUENCES: GENDER IDENTITY AND GENDER ROLES

With rare exceptions, the child's biological sex, as determined by genes and hormones, is immediately apparent at birth. Up to this point there have been no social influences on sexual development. Following birth, other kinds of environmental influences—social and cultural ones—help to shape the gender identity and sexual behavior of a person. They affect how that person relates to other people emotionally and sexually, the things that will arouse the individual sexually, and much more. Here we will examine some of the impact of these influences on one's sexual identity and orientation.

As we saw in Chapter 10, although there is some evidence that gender differences in behavior become apparent shortly after birth, they are not as great as has been presumed in the past (Maccoby and Jacklin, 1974). Within seconds after birth, the doctor announces, "It's a girl!" or "It's a boy!" and at that point the child's **gender role**—society's expected role—has been identified. The infant is given a name at this point that fits its gender, is wrapped in a pink or blue blanket, and is taken home to be raised as a girl or boy, with toys, regulations, and expectations that those who rear it consider appropriate. There are obvious differences in the ways that parents behave with infant girls and boys. For ex-

ample, parents are more likely to talk to a baby girl and roughhouse with a baby boy (Moss, 1967). These differences undoubtedly contribute to the "masculinity" or "femininity" displayed by the developing child and, eventually, the adult. As children become inclined to behave like one sex or the other through interacting with others, and tend to display strong **gender identity** (that is, to think of themselves as either a boy or a girl), then more and more their behavior will elicit appropriate reciprocal behavior from others. This reciprocal behavior, in turn, helps to reinforce children's gender identity still further. By the age of three or four, most children have developed a strong gender identity and have clearly begun to learn **gender roles**. That is, they have learned how to behave in ways considered appropriate for members of their gender in their society.

Studies of children raised in gender roles that were partially or completely incompatible with their biological, or chromosomal, sex show that upbringing is a powerful influence on the development of gender identity. In one case an infant boy's genitals were so mutilated in an accident that he would never be able to function sexually as a normal male. After much agonizing, his parents requested a sex-change operation for him. The surgery was performed when the child was seventeen months old. Fortunately, at this age the child's psychological gender identity was not yet firmly established. The parents subsequently raised the child as a girl. By the age of four, the child was playing with dolls, was proud of dresses with ruffles and ribbons, and otherwise behaved like a "typical" girl, in spite of his male chromosomal sex. At the same time, the child's identical twin brother developed into just as "typical" a boy. Because the twins were identical, the great differences between these two children in expressions of masculinity and femininity could not have been due to chromosomal factors. Rather, they were a function of the surgical sex change and the differences in role expectations (Money and Ehrhardt, 1972).

Are the sex differences in behavior that we see in humans rooted in the physiological factors—the genes and hormones—that contribute to establishing biological sex in the first place? In nonhuman animals, it is clear that they are. For example, female monkeys who were subjected to high levels of androgens before they were born were found to display behavior more typical of males than of females as they matured (Goy, 1970).

In humans, inconclusive studies of a number of genetic females who had abnormal levels of androgens during the fetal period* suggested an influence, but one that was largely overcome by rearing practices (Money and Ehrhardt, 1972). Early exposure to androgens produced clear masculinization—for example, a greatly enlarged clitoris superficially resembling a penis—that was apparent at birth. All these girls received corrective surgery and were raised as girls. Even so, the researchers found that the girls preferred dressing in pants to wearing dresses, playing outdoor games and sports to playing with dolls, and fantasizing about future careers to fantasizing about getting married. But despite what could be called inclinations toward a masculine gender role in these girls, appropriate romantic interests did begin to de-

velop in the few who had reached adolescence when the report was written, and most of the girls anticipated getting married and child bearing. (It should be mentioned that these girls' display of "masculine" interests is not unusual; many girls—"tomboys"—with a normal biological start display such behavior. What is noteworthy about this group of girls is the unusually high incidence of this behavior.)

Although biological and social influences undoubtedly interact to produce the differences between the sexes, the impact of social forces seems far greater when one looks at various cultures. Margaret Mead's classic study, *Sex and Temperament in Three Primitive Societies* (1935), for example, describes a cultural group in which male and female gender roles are very much like our traditional roles, while in a neighboring group the roles are reversed: the men are inclined to be passive and dependent, the women sexually dominant and more independent. Clearly there are wide variations in what people in different cultures consider appropriate or typical masculine and feminine behavior. Yet nearly all cultures believe that men and women are, and should be, fundamentally different.

The relatively rare condition called **transsexualism** provides further confirmation of the necessity of considering biological sex and gender identity separately. Transsexuals are people who, often at an early age, develop a gender identity that is inconsistent with their biological sexual identity. They may lament that they feel trapped in the body of the wrong sex. Male transsexuals (and most are male) think of themselves as women, want heterosexual relations with men, and sometimes request surgery to correct their anatomy. (Famous examples are Christine Jorgensen, who had one of the early sex change operations, in the 1950s; writer Jan Morris; and professional tennis player Renée Richards.) The surgery involves removing the testes and most of the penis, and reconstructing from the remaining tissue as close an approximation to a vagina as possible. Also, a series of hormone treatments inclines the person's secondary sexual characteristics toward those of a female (reduced body hair and breast enlargement).

Is transsexualism caused by as yet undetected hormonal imbalances? Or is it caused by extremely "mixed signals" in the child's social environment? No one knows. Transsexualism is a vivid illustration of the point made earlier, that the biology and psychology of gender are far too complex to fit into a neat male-or-female scheme.

---

*The abnormal levels of androgens occurred either because the girls' own adrenal glands (which normally manufacture some androgens in females) overproduced androgens or because their mothers, when pregnant, were treated with a synthetic drug (no longer used) that raised the androgen levels in the fetus.

METHODS OF STUDYING SEXUAL BEHAVIOR

For the first half of this century, most of the data psychologists had about sexual behavior came from the memories and reports of people who had undergone psychotherapy. Today there is a wealth of data on sexual behavior, and it comes from a variety of sources.

CROSS-CULTURAL STUDIES We have seen how cross-cultural studies reveal substantial variations in gender roles among different groups of people. The ways in which people learn about, experience, and express adult sexuality also vary widely from individual to individual and from culture to culture. There are cultures that approve homosexual relationships and even encourage them as a sexual outlet before marriage (Davenport, 1965). Other cultures permit masturbation among children, polygamous marriages, and extramarital sexual activity. Even the average amount of sexual contact engaged in by members of our culture would be considered very low in some cultures and very high in others (Ford and Beach, 1951).

Mangaia, a small Polynesian island in the South Pacific, is a good example of a culture in which sexual standards differ radically from our own. Childhood masturbation is considered by Mangaians to be a normal part of sexual development. Mangaian families live in one-room huts, and children are free to watch their parents' sexual activities. Adolescent boys and girls are expected to form sexual relationships so that they can practice their sexual skills and find a suitable marriage partner. Mangaians believe that frequent sexual contact is necessary to health, that female orgasm is a learned skill, and that it is the male's duty to bring his partner to orgasm. As adults, Mangaians have sexual intercourse more often than do the people of Western cultures, and female orgasm is almost universal (Marshall, 1971).

One important contribution of such cross-cultural studies has been to force a reconsideration of what should be considered "abnormal," "unnatural," or "pathological" in our own sexual practices. Indeed, the wealth of information that has been gathered makes it harder for us to call many unusual (to us) sexual practices pathological. In general, the only sexual acts that may be considered truly pathological are those that upset people who may feel compelled to practice them (for example, father-daughter incest) or those that are forced on an unwilling participant (such as rape). Clearly, what is "abnormal" is relative to the culture in which it is observed, and very few practices are universally considered to be "abnormal."

Nevertheless, cross-cultural studies have also shown that every society imposes some restrictions on sexual behavior. Nowhere in the world are men and women free to do whatever they like, whenever, wherever, and with whomever they please.

SURVEYS Alfred C. Kinsey was an interesting candidate for his pioneering role in the history of sex studies. A biologist by training, Kinsey had spent twenty years collecting data on gall wasps when, in 1930, he was asked to teach a course on sex education at Indiana University. Unable to find reliable information on sexual behavior, Kinsey decided to collect data himself (Pomeroy, 1966). He and his associates spent the next eighteen years talking to people of different ages, backgrounds, and marital status about their sex lives. The results of interviews with 5,300 American men, *Sexual Behavior in the Human Male* (1948), and with 5,940 women, *Sexual Behavior in the Human Female* (1953), made history—and headlines.

As a scientist, Kinsey's goal was to substitute facts for myths about the sexual behavior of Americans and to gather data on the population as a whole. His method was to collect sexual histories in detailed, confidential interviews, concentrating on Americans' "sexual outlets" (the number and kinds of sexual experiences they had). Kinsey's most controversial findings concerned premarital and extramarital sex (most men and many women reported such experiences) and homosexual experiences (which he found were far more common than anyone cared to believe).

The Kinsey study relied on volunteers—"self-selected" subjects who may have had ulterior motives for participating. It did not include major segments of the population—in particular black, rural, and poorly educated Americans. It did report on what white, well-educated volunteers *said* they did or did not do sexually in America in the 1940s. Until the mid-1960s, Kinsey's were the only comprehensive data that social scientists had. In terms of methodology, comprehensiveness, and value of the information obtained, Kinsey's work is acknowledged as having provided the foundations for most contemporary research on human sexuality. Kinsey's findings and the results of other sexual surveys will be described in greater detail later in this chapter.

OBSERVATIONAL STUDIES Shortly after the Kinsey studies were released, William Masters and Virginia Johnson launched the first observational study of human sexual behavior. Their goal was to concentrate "quite literally upon what men and women do in response to effective sexual stimulation . . . rather than on what people say they do or even think their sexual reactions and experiences might be" (Masters and Johnson, 1966a, p. 20). Volunteers were recruited to masturbate and have intercourse in a laboratory where their physiological responses to sexual stimulation could be observed closely. Women, for example, masturbated with an artificial penis equipped with a light and camera. Over twelve years, 694 men and women participated, most of them married couples, allowing the Masters and Johnson team to observe some 10,000 sexual episodes.

The value of these observational studies was limited in that the volunteers, as in the Kinsey survey, may have been atypical. Sexual experiences in a laboratory may be quite different from similar experiences at home in private; and the presence of observers no doubt influenced some aspects of the subjects' behavior. Nevertheless, Masters and Johnson's research has led to a fuller understanding of the human sexual response and of sexual dysfunctions.

CONTROLLED EXPERIMENTATION The studies of human sexual behavior we have been describing are essentially descriptive: from them we learn *what* occurs, but not *why*. The influence of various factors on sexual behavior can be examined only through controlled experiments in which specific hypotheses can be tested and discarded.

A study by Julia Heiman (1975) comparing the sexual arousal of men and women who were shown pornographic materials illustrates this kind of re-

GIORGIO ARMANI

Some advertisers have begun to capitalize on the new image of women as sexual beings, capable of being aroused by sexual stimuli just as men are.

search. Kinsey (1953) had speculated that men and women are sexually aroused by different kinds of stimuli. He wrote that although the two sexes seem equally aroused by tactile (touch) stimulation, men seem clearly more aroused by "psychosexual stimuli." That is, more men than women reported that they were aroused by pornography and the sight of the opposite sex. Men also talked more about sexual matters and seemed to have more sexual thoughts, fantasies, and dreams than did women. Is this true? Are women less responsive than men to erotic stimuli? Or were the women Kinsey interviewed perhaps just more reluctant than men to talk about such things? To test Kinsey's speculation, Heiman directly measured physiological signs of arousal.

The subjects in Heiman's study were male and female college students, most of whom were sexually experienced. Male sexual response was measured using a device shaped like a rubber band, which was placed around the penis to record the size of the erection. Female arousal was more difficult to measure. From Masters and Johnson's research, it was known that an unmistakable sign of female arousal is an increase in the flow of blood through the vaginal blood vessels. So Heiman measured female arousal levels by using a small, tampon-like device that was sensitive to color changes in the vaginal walls—the darker the color, the higher the arousal level.

Students were divided into four groups: group 1 listened to *erotic* tapes that contained explicitly sexual material; group 2 heard *romantic* tapes that described a tender and affectionate episode in which there was no sexual contact; group 3 listened to an *erotic-romantic* tape that conveyed both explicit sexuality and affection; and group 4 heard a *control* tape in which there was neither sex nor romance.

The physiological measures indicated a clear difference in arousal levels among the four groups. The men and women who heard explicitly sexual material—those in groups 1 and 3—showed high levels of arousal. In contrast, there was little sexual arousal recorded among groups 2 and 4.

The most interesting findings came from comparing male and female arousal levels. The results refuted the stereotype that women are more aroused by romance and affection than by nonemotional sex. Females and males alike showed the same low-level response to the romance tape as to the control tape. Furthermore, the combination of romance and explicit sex (group 3) was no more arousing to the women than explicit sex alone. Thus, this controlled experimental study indicated that the arousal responses of men and women to erotic material were very similar.

As we have pointed out, there are limitations to every method of studying human sexual behavior. Studying human sexual behavior raises both practical and ethical questions. For example, one could not readily study the effects of child-rearing experiences on sexual performance at maturity, randomly assigning some groups to control conditions and others to experimental conditions. For this reason, there have been few experimental studies done on humans. Most experimental studies have been conducted using nonhuman animals, and these have their limitations too: their results are often difficult to relate to humans.

THE HUMAN SEXUAL RESPONSE

All healthy men and women are physiologically equipped to respond to sexual stimulation—both physical stimulation (touching and being touched by the hands, lips, body, and perhaps objects) and psychological stimulation (provocative sights, sounds, and behavior, and erotic fantasies). Contemporary research has shown that men and women respond physiologically to sexual stimulation in parallel ways, which is not surprising when we consider the homologous development of sexual anatomy.

THE PHYSIOLOGY OF AROUSAL AND ORGASM Although no two people react to stimulation in exactly the same way, Masters and Johnson (1966a) found that the sexual response in both men and women can be divided into four phases: excitement, plateau, orgasm, and resolution.

During the **excitement phase**, the heart begins to beat faster and the respiration rate increases. Blood flows into the genitals, causing the penis to become erect and the clitoris to swell. Drops of moisture form on the vaginal walls. Women's (and some men's) nipples may become erect, and women may develop a "sex flush" (a reddening, usually beginning on the chest, caused by the dilation of small blood vessels in the skin) over the body.

In the **plateau phase**, the genitals become fully engorged with blood. The clitoris retracts into its hood, though it remains highly sensitive (the inner vaginal lips are attached to the clitoral hood, so that during intercourse the thrusting movements of the penis indirectly create friction on the clitoris). The entrance to the vagina contracts by as much as 50 percent; the uterus rises slightly, causing the inside of the vagina to balloon. The glans of the penis enlarges and deepens in color. Some fluid (which can contain live sperm) may seep out the opening of the penis as this happens. The testes swell and pull up higher within the scrotum. As excitement reaches a peak, the feeling that orgasm is inevitable sweeps over the individual.

During **orgasm**, muscular contractions force the blood that has been collecting in the genitals back into the bloodstream. The muscles around the vagina push the vaginal walls in and out and the uterus pulsates. The muscles in and around the penis contract rhythmically, causing **ejaculation**—the discharge of **semen** (the fluid containing the sperm). In intercourse, the man's semen is deposited in the woman's vagina; if one of the sperm happens to fertilize the woman's ovum, pregnancy results.

"We Rose Up Slowly" by Roy Lichtenstein

For both men and women, the first five or six orgasmic contractions are the strongest and most pleasurable. Some people experience intense muscle spasms in their faces and limbs during orgasm, and some cry out uncontrollably; others show few obvious signs of orgasm.

The body gradually returns to its normal state during the **resolution** phase. Muscle tension dissipates and the genitals return to their usual size and shape.

Masters and Johnson found that the sexual response cycle is physiologically the same for all orgasms, whether produced by intercourse or masturbation. And masturbatory orgasms are often more intense physically (the reason is probably that during masturbation the individual has precise control over the kind and intensity of stimulation). Masters and Johnson reported that masturbation may, however, be less emotionally satisfying than intercourse.

The subjective experience of sexual arousal, like the physiology of arousal, also appears to be basically the same in men and women. A group of gynecologists, psychologists, and medical students who were asked to read descriptions of orgasm written by twenty-four male and twenty-four female subjects guessed the writer's sex in some cases, but no more often than would be expected by chance (Vance and Wagner, 1976).

Although the pattern of sexual response is the same, there are some physiological differences between the sexes. First and most obviously, men ejaculate at orgasm and women do not. Second, most men experience a **refractory period**—a period of time (ranging from minutes to hours or even days) that must pass after an orgasm before they can become sexually aroused again. In contrast, women may experience **multiple orgasms**, one after another, without going through the resolution phase (see Figure 17.2 on page 390).*

*The capacity for multiple orgasms may not be confined to women, though. There is now evidence that some men experience several climaxes during a single act of intercourse (Robbins and Jensen, cited in Tavris and Offir, 1977, pp. 81–82).

Sexual Behavior and Attitudes: The Role of Learning

A young woman, talking to a marriage counselor, described her wedding night:

> It's funny because all your life all that stuff is wrong and you're not supposed to let a boy touch you, and then the priest says something and all of a sudden everything is supposed to be all right. But my wedding night was terrible and I cried and cried because I didn't know what I was supposed to do and it did not seem right. (quoted in DeLora and Warren, 1977, p. 197)

A cartoon in *Playboy* shows a teacher announcing to her class, ''The Board of Education requires me to give you some basic education on sex, reproduction, and other disgusting filth.''

The young woman quoted above is hardly an isolated case, and the teacher in the *Playboy* cartoon is no joke. Everyone, from infancy on, learns a complete set of attitudes about sex. If we are lucky, our parents and teachers handle the topic objectively and with sensitivity. Most of us, though, are likely to have learned more about avoiding sex than about enjoying it. We learn the rules by which our culture establishes when and how it is acceptable to express our sexual feelings. Alex Comfort's book *The Joy of Sex* (1972) sold millions of copies because it pictured many more ways to enjoy sex than are accepted by our culture. We even learn what is sexy. In the United States, a small-breasted American woman might wish to increase her breast size, but she would not hope to attract a man by greatly stretching her lower lip. Yet among some peoples of South Africa, a pendulous lower lip is a very attractive feature (Katchadourian and Lunde, 1975, p. 54).

What all this means is that although, as William Masters and Virginia Johnson (1966) found, the nature of physiological response to ''effective sexual stimulation'' is essentially the same for all human beings, the nature of that stimulation varies greatly from culture to culture. Even within a single culture, different learning experiences produce different sexual attitudes among people.

Psychosexual Responses of Men and Women

Until recently some of the biggest differences in attitudes toward sexual expression have existed between the sexes themselves. In 1953 Alfred Kinsey wrote that although the two sexes were equally aroused by tactile stimulation, men were clearly more aroused by ''psychosexual stimuli'': men reported greater arousal to pornography and the sight of women in their environment, talked more about sexual matters, and had more sexual thoughts, fantasies, and dreams than women. Kinsey did point out, however, that as many as one-third of the women in his sample did respond to psychosexual stimuli as quickly and intensely as males (Kinsey et al., 1953).

Social learning factors can help to explain why many women say they are not aroused by erotica. For instance, females are often taught that it is ''unladylike'' to become aroused by pornography, so even if a woman does feel sexually aroused by erotic stimuli, she may hesitate to report these

feelings to a researcher. In contrast, males are often encouraged to enjoy and share pornographic materials. Until very recently, the woman who entered a "sex shop" or pornographic movie theater was almost always invading an exclusively male domain. And even if she had the courage to make this invasion, the erotic materials she was likely to find would have been designed to appeal only to men.

The gap in male and female response to erotica observed by Kinsey in the 1940s has narrowed considerably in the 1970s. A recent study by Julia Heiman (1975), described in detail elsewhere in this chapter, shows just how much similarity there may be in male and female responses to erotica. Physiological measurements and questionnaires filled out by Heiman's subjects showed that both male and female subjects felt about the same high levels of sexual arousal after listening to erotic and erotic-romantic tapes. Conversely, both men and women experienced very little arousal when they listened to tapes containing romantic material without explicit sexual content.

The similar physiological responses of men and women to the tapes used in Heiman's experiment is an interesting finding. Certainly, male and female biology has not changed since Kinsey's day. What has changed are social attitudes. In the 1970s women are far freer to express sexual feelings than they were in the 1940s, so it is not surprising that Heiman's female subjects responded to sexual stimuli more consistently than did Kinsey's.

Sources of Psychosexual Stimulation

What makes a film, picture, or book sexually arousing in the first place? Again, learning plays a large part. One of the most important factors seems to be whether the sexual behavior being portrayed is familiar to the viewer; we are most aroused by watching or reading about sexual activities that are part of our own sexual repertoire. For instance, heterosexual couples are most aroused by watching a film depicting heterosexual behavior, while homosexual couples are more likely to respond to a film showing homosexual interaction. In general, we do not become aroused while watching sexual acts we would not ourselves perform; films depicting sadistic behavior, for instance, would probably be sexually stimulating only to people who actually engage in such behavior.

Although our external environment is filled with erotic stimuli of one sort or another, perhaps the most important source of sexual stimulation is internal. As the authors of a book on human sexuality put it, "Stimulation through any or all of the senses will result in sexual arousal if, and *only* if, accompanied by *the appropriate emotional concomitants*" (Katchadourian and Lunde, 1975, p. 54; italics added). In short, no matter how much we know about the physiology of sex, "the key to understanding human sexual arousal remains locked in emotional processes, which we do not . . . fully understand" (p. 54). Few people need to be told that feeling relaxed and affectionate enhances sexual arousal, while feeling anxious and hostile will almost certainly impede it.

Imagination, in the form of sexual fantasies, is another source of internal sexual stimulation. A great many men and women develop sexual fantasies during adolescence and continue to have these erotic daydreams throughout life. Fantasies can take many forms: they may be explicit sexual stories involving a specific person or an imaginary partner, or they can be abstract daydreams about love, seduction, or an imaginary world. Some people fantasize only about sexual behaviors they actually engage in, while others daydream about erotic activities in which they would never actually take part. These sexual fantasies may serve many functions: they may enable us to enhance our response during a sexual encounter, explore our own sexual preferences, release sexual tension, and "rehearse" for actual sexual situations.

In his book *Sexual Behavior in the 1970s* (1974), Morton Hunt reported the content of male and female fantasies during masturbation. He found that very high percentages of men and women—married and single, young and old—fantasize about having sexual intercourse with a loved partner. Young adults were also likely to have a variety of "deviant" fantasies: having sex with strangers, having "group sex," having homosexual sex, being forced to have sex (more common among women), and forcing someone to have sex (more common among men). Hunt concluded that while young people are freer than older adults to have a variety of sexual fantasies, the most socially approved fantasy—sex with a loved partner—is the most popular fantasy among all groups. Even in our fantasies, then, we are influenced by what we have learned that our society defines as the sexual ideal: heterosexual intercourse accompanied by soft music, candlelight, and love.

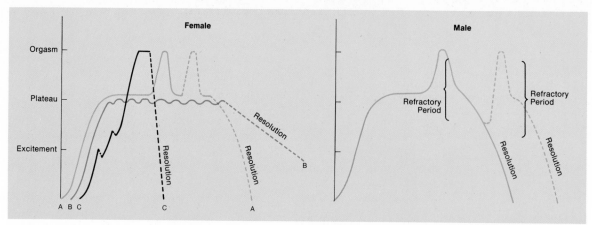

Figure 17.2 Graphs summarizing Masters and Johnson's description of coitus in the human male and female. The four phases are defined in terms of measurable physiological changes. In both sexes excitement leads to a plateau phase that may be maintained for considerable periods without orgasm. The male has only one pattern of response after this: he ejaculates quickly in orgasm, and his arousal decreases rapidly. There is a period after his ejaculation, the refractory period, in which he is incapable of another ejaculation. He may repeat the orgasmic phase several times before returning to an unaroused state. The female may variously have one orgasm or several orgasms in succession (line A), not achieve orgasm at all and return relatively slowly to an unaroused state (line B), or, rarely, have a single prolonged orgasm followed by rapid resolution (line C).

STIMULATION AND AROUSAL Masters and Johnson have pointed out that both men and women respond consistently to "effective sexual stimulation" whether the source is psychological or physical (1962, p. 254). Indeed, physiological arousal in response to erotic materials, such as sexually explicit pictures or stories, takes the same form as the arousal that occurs in the initial stages of intercourse (Byrne and Byrne, 1978). But this does not mean that "effective sexual stimulation" is the same for everyone; learning plays a significant role in determining sexual responsiveness (see the accompanying special feature).

Touch is the most obvious source of sexual arousal. Certain areas of the body, called the **erogenous zones**, are particularly sensitive to touch (the glans of the penis, the clitoris, the mouth, the nipples, the inside of the thighs). Other less obvious areas (the palms, the lower back) also may be highly sensitive. It all depends on the individual. One person may be almost totally insensitive in an erogenous zone, another so sensitive that touch is somewhat painful. Odors exert a powerful influence on mating activity in most animals—even to the extent, for example, that placing the urine from a receptive female mouse onto the back of a male mouse will incite other male mice to sexually assault the hapless male (Connor, 1972). But as for humans, experiments have not yet revealed any clear effects of olfactory stimulation (Doty et al., 1975).

Visual stimulation obviously is also very effective—witness the popularity of erotic films, magazines, and books. As Heiman (1975) found in her experiments, both women and men are highly responsive to such materials.

Fantasies—the pictures in our own minds—may be the most powerful stimulant of all. Males in two studies were able to either decrease (Laws and Rubin, 1969) or increase (Rubin and Henson, 1975) the vigor of their erections through fantasy. In another study, subjects who were instructed to *imagine* sexually exciting situations became more aroused than subjects exposed to explicit slides and stories (Byrne and Lambreth, 1971). In a survey of suburban housewives, 65 percent reported that they had erotic fantasies while engaging in sexual intercourse with their husbands at least some of the time; 37 percent had fantasies most of the time. Fantasies about imaginary lovers other than their husbands and submission to a dominating male were most common. Interviews with these women indicated that they used fantasies to enhance their sexual responsiveness (Hariton and Singer, 1974).

SEXUAL RESPONSIVENESS AND AGING Most of us think of sexuality as something that emerges at puberty, reaches full strength in early adulthood, gradually fades away with increasing age, and eventually stops. The "sex symbols" of our culture are almost invariably young, attractive men and women, and we often have difficulty imagining that children and older adults are also sexual beings. For instance, in a recent study college students were asked to estimate how often they thought their parents had intercourse (Pocs and Godow, 1978). One-fourth of the students believed that their parents had had intercourse only once or not at all in the previous year—which on the basis of other data seems very unlikely.

Of course, what people believe about their parents' sexual activity may be different from what they believe about that of other people their parents' age. Still, it is interesting to compare this belief held by young people with the following statistics and observations: In the Kinsey studies the average reported frequency of sexual intercourse for men sixty-five and older was about four times a month, and their partners were typically their spouses. Twenty-five to 30 percent of the older married men and women in the Kinsey samples also claimed to supplement intercourse with another sexual outlet, masturbation.

Other, more recent, studies have found essentially the same thing: that rather than suddenly reaching an age at which sexual interests disappear, most old people for whom a partner is available maintain relatively vigorous sex lives. Those who are most sexually active tend to be those who also were most active in their youth (Newman and Nichols, 1960).

It is true that with aging, hormone production decreases in both sexes, and vaginal lubrication and erectile vigor diminish; but these changes are gradual. Masters and Johnson (1970) emphatically pointed out that for most people who are in good health there is no physiological reason for stopping sexual activity with advancing age. Perhaps one significant contribution that modern sex research will make to society will be to provide rational arguments against the expectation that sex stops or somehow becomes "improper" after a certain age. This may enable a large segment of our population to continue to enjoy a healthy sex life.

SEXUAL PROBLEMS AND THERAPY There are times when a person cannot be aroused or satisfied sexually. The individual may be tired, preoccupied, drunk, angry at the partner, anxious about "performing" well, or simply uninterested in sex at the time. This happens to everyone on occasion. However, for some individuals it is a recurring experience that can become very upsetting. Any problem that prevents an individual from engaging in sexual relations or from reaching orgasm during sex is known as a **sexual dysfunction**. It is impor-

tant to recognize that this term applies only to problems in sexual *response*, not to sexual preferences or what are sometimes called, inappropriately in many cases, "deviations" (the choice of unusual sex objects or modes of gratification). For example, a couple who prefers oral-genital sex or mutual masturbation to intercourse is not dysfunctional, so long as both partners are satisfied with their activities.

SEXUAL DYSFUNCTIONS IN MEN AND WOMEN
In everyday conversation the term "impotence" is often used to describe all forms of male sexual dysfunction. Similarly, the term "frigidity" is applied to all manner of female sexual problems, with the implication that the woman is totally unresponsive, cold emotionally as well as sexually. As popularly used, neither term tells us what precisely the problem is. And they incorrectly suggest an invariably permanent rejection of sexuality. One of the goals of sex researchers has been to replace these overgeneralized, pejorative labels with more precise definitions of specific dysfunctions.

Psychologists reserve the term **impotence** for a specific dysfunction: a man's inability to achieve or maintain an erection long enough to reach orgasm with a partner. Some men have never been able to achieve or maintain an erection (a rare condition known as **primary impotence**). Generally, though, impotent men have been aroused to orgasm with a partner in the past, but are now unable to achieve or maintain an erection in some or all sexual situations. This is called **secondary impotence**. For some other men arousal is not the problem. They may acquire an erection easily, but ejaculate before they or their partners would like. This is called **premature ejaculation**, and it appears to be the most common complaint among male college students (Werner, 1975). Still other men can achieve and maintain an erection but are unable to ejaculate during sex with a partner—a problem Masters and Johnson (1966b) descriptively labeled **nonemissive erection**. Secondary impotence, premature ejaculation, and nonemissive erection afflict most males at one time or another. Only when they are extremely persistent and are upsetting to the individual should they be considered dysfunctional.

Some women suffer from **vaginismus**, involuntary muscle spasms that cause the vagina to shut tightly so that penetration by the male partner's penis is impossible or extremely painful. Other women are able to engage in, and often enjoy, sexual intercourse, but do not experience orgasms.

The term **primary orgasmic dysfunction** refers to the situation of women who have never experienced an orgasm through any means. The expression **secondary** (or **situational**) **orgasmic dysfunction** refers to the situation of women who experience orgasms sometimes, through certain kinds of stimulation (such as masturbation), but not in other situations in which they would like to (typically, during sexual intercourse). This is a common complaint among female college students (Werner, 1975). As with most of the male problems, difficulties women may have in experiencing orgasm can be viewed as part of normal human variation and not necessarily considered dysfunctional.

One interesting viewpoint on female orgasmic problems has come from *The Hite Report* (1976), which was based upon the responses of several thousand women to detailed questionnaires. Their reports suggested that although most women reach orgasm easily and quickly through masturbation, most are slow to become aroused and experience orgasm only occasionally during intercourse. The reason, according to Hite, is that (contrary to the findings of Masters and Johnson) intercourse does not provide sufficient stimulation of the clitoris, and women should not feel that there is something abnormal or dysfunctional about needing such stimulation. It becomes a problem only if a woman becomes extremely upset about it or fails to make her needs known to her partner.

It is not clear why some people respond freely to sexual stimulation but others do not. Research by Masters and Johnson (1970) has revealed that only rarely does a sexual problem have a physiological basis. There is usually a psychological reason why some people are unable to abandon themselves to sexual pleasure. It has been suggested that some of these problems are related to conflicts within the individual experiencing them, and that others are related to conflicts between partners. Therapists often find that many people who seek help for sexual problems were brought up with rigid religious, moral, or social standards concerning sex. Intellectually they may have rejected the belief that sex is wrong, but emotionally or psychologically they have not.

Other psychological sources of sexual problems range from having been the victim of "innocent" ridicule of one's anatomy in childhood to having suffered outright sexual abuse. Fear of failure may also cause sexual dysfunction. An individual may have one disappointing experience, then begin to wonder about his or her sexual adequacy. This anx-

iety can interfere with free response during the next sexual encounter, and the next, confirming the person's self-doubt. Thus, fear of sexual failure sometimes becomes a self-fulfilling prophecy.

SEX THERAPY Although there are many distinct approaches to solving sexual problems, nearly all forms of sex therapy are based on seven basic principles (LoPiccolo, 1978, pp. 513–514).

1. Sexual dysfunction is seen as a *mutual problem* that concerns both partners, even if only one is missing the pleasure in sexual relations. Therapy focuses on the relationship, not on the individual experiencing the dysfunction.

2. Individuals who have sexual dysfunctions often are misinformed about sex. *Education* about sexual anatomy and techniques is part of the therapy.

3. Negative attitudes toward sex, however deeply buried, are almost always part of the problem. The therapist works to create *attitude change*.

4. *Anxiety reduction* is equally important. Fear of failure leads individuals to take a "spectator role" during sex, evaluating their performance rather than spontaneously enjoying themselves. Sex therapists use various techniques to reduce anxiety and to make sex a pleasure, not a test.

5. Sexual interaction will not improve without *communication* between the partners. The couple is encouraged to express feelings and desires openly.

6. Sex takes place in the context of the couple's *entire relationship*. Tension caused by disagreements over sex roles, emotional needs, even money can interfere with sexual responsiveness.

7. Finally, and this is the most highly publicized aspect of sex therapy, a sex therapist prescribes *changes in sexual behavior*.

Usually, to lessen the fear of failure, the couple is told not to engage in sexual intercourse for the time being and is assigned "nondemanding" sensual exercises, such as massaging each other. Gradually, more sexual activities are introduced. The fact that the couple is "given permission" to try out new activities by an authority figure (the therapist) may be therapeutic in itself. In most cases sex therapy is brief (ten to fifteen sessions) but intensive.

Variations in Sexual Behavior

We have alluded several times to the wide range of human variability in sexual preferences and practices. As with other drive-related behavior, such as eating food, our sexual activities vary with our cultural and personal characteristics: just as we develop specific tastes in food, so do we develop specific tastes in sexual partners and in the occasions on which we desire them. Furthermore, what we ourselves do, or refuse to do, often defines for us what we consider bizarre or deviant: although oral-genital sex may be considered quite natural and pleasurable by some, others think it disgusting. The line between what some consider "variations" and others consider "deviations" is a fine and difficult one to draw, and often depends on who is doing the drawing. Here our intention is to provide some information about a broad range of sexual practices.

CELIBACY   In terms of most people's sexual practices, **celibacy**, or complete abstinence from sexual activity, certainly appears to be unusual. It has been idealized as a preferred way of life by some religious orders, such as the Catholic clergy. And, until recently, coaches imposed pledges of temporary chastity on athletes in training, in the belief that regular sexual activity saps a person's strength. (There is no evidence for this belief.)

The percentage of people who choose permanent celibacy as a way of life, however, is undoubtedly small. Most people do go through periods of temporary chastity, though—particularly in youth, after the breakup of a marriage or romance, and in old age after the death of a spouse. Unfortunately, surveys and studies of sexual activity have told us little about sexual inactivity, so we know little about how people who have become accustomed to regular sex adjust to no sex. Does a person's appetite for sex grow stronger with every week of celibacy? Or does sex, like an acquired skill, tend to fade with disuse? We do not yet know.

MASTURBATION   Attitudes toward masturbation have changed in the last two decades. Forty or

fifty years ago physicians regularly warned youngsters that self-stimulation (or "self-abuse," as masturbation was then called) would cause acne, fever, blindness, even insanity. Today most people know that this is nonsense. According to a survey of 2,026 Americans conducted by Morton Hunt (1974), masturbation is thought to be wrong by only 15 percent of males and 14 percent of females eighteen to twenty-four years old and by 29 percent of males and 36 percent of females over fifty-five. However, most adults are to some degree ashamed and secretive about masturbating. Very few admit to their mates or friends that they occasionally stimulate themselves. Apparently the idea lingers that "playing with oneself" is immature behavior, symptomatic of personal inadequacies or of dissatisfaction with one's spouse as a sexual partner.

Nevertheless, surveys indicate that masturbation is common. Ninety-two percent of the men and 62 percent of the women in Kinsey's sample (1948, 1953) reported that they had masturbated to orgasm at least once in their lives. Men reported that they began masturbating at age ten to twelve, after reading or hearing about it. Rates of masturbation for the males in Kinsey's survey reached a peak of about twice a week around age twenty, then declined to about once every other week for unmarried men forty-five to fifty and once a month for married men. Most of the women who masturbated said that they discovered this outlet by accident, some as late as their thirties. Rates of masturbation for unmarried females varied from daily to yearly, for an average of once every two or three weeks. Married women masturbated about once a month.

The Hunt survey (1974) suggests that boys and girls may now be discovering masturbation earlier or may simply be becoming less reticent about it. Sixty-five percent of the men in this sample had begun masturbating by age thirteen, compared to 45 percent in Kinsey's sample (1948). The percentage of women who said that they had masturbated by age thirteen jumped from 15 percent in Kinsey's survey to 40 percent in Hunt's. Masturbation rates increased slightly among young single men and markedly among young single women. Sixty percent of the women aged eighteen to twenty-four in Hunt's sample said that they had masturbated (compared to 30 percent in Kinsey's sample in 1953), and the actual rate may be even higher. (Eighty-two percent of the women questioned in the Hunt survey said that they masturbated regularly. The average rate was about every week and a half—twice as often as in Kinsey's report.)

Some theorists believe that early experiences with masturbation help to establish the foundation for adult sexuality, as was suggested in Chapter 10. According to this view, self-stimulation is an important part of self-discovery. Therapists have found that masturbation is a most effective way for a woman who has never experienced orgasm to discover what arouses her (Dengrove, 1971; LoPiccolo and Lobitz, 1978). Hite (1976) recommended it for all women, married or single.

HETEROSEXUALITY Undoubtedly the most common sexual activity is heterosexuality, a man and a woman stimulating each other sexually. But what couples do together varies from day to day, year to year, and couple to couple. Standard sexual intercourse (penis in vagina) is only one possibility. Heterosexual couples can and do enjoy petting to orgasm, oral-genital stimulation, anal intercourse, intercourse between the thighs, dressing in fantasy costumes, and other forms of sex play. Intercourse itself may take place in as many positions as imagination and agility allow: the man on top, lying above and facing the woman; the woman lying or sitting above and facing the man; the couple lying side by side facing each other; the woman lying on her stomach or side with her back to the man (rear entry); or in any other position they can manage. There is no "normal" position for intercourse.

PREMARITAL SEX Traditionally, American women and, to a lesser degree, men, were expected to "save themselves" for marriage. Intimate sexual activity culminating in intercourse was supposed to take place only between husband and wife. Do Americans still profess a belief in premarital chastity and postmarital fidelity? Do we practice what we preach? Did we ever?

In Kinsey's day, most Americans claimed that they strongly disapproved of premarital sex. Yet 98 percent of men who had grade-school educations, 85 percent of male high school graduates, and 68 percent of men with college educations claimed to have had sexual intercourse before getting married. Nearly half the women in Kinsey's sample had also had some premarital sexual experience—a shocking revelation at the time. These women had not treated sex casually, however. Over half had had sex only with their future husbands.

The incidence of premarital sex for men appears

to have increased somewhat, particularly among college men. By age seventeen, half the college men in the Hunt sample (1974) were no longer virgins, compared to 23 percent in Kinsey's sample (1948). The biggest change for college men may be in the women they choose as partners. In Kinsey's day most single young men who had sex had it with prostitutes or casual pickups. Today most college men have sex with women they care deeply for and with whom they have a continuing relationship (McCary, 1978, p. 273). Even so, men's attitudes have not changed as much as one might expect. According to one survey (Pietropinto and Simmenauer, 1977), 33 percent of American men still want to marry virgins. Another 25 percent want to marry a woman who has had only one previous sexual partner.

The incidence of premarital sex for women has increased dramatically. Eighty-one percent of the women aged eighteen to twenty-four in the Hunt sample had sexual intercourse before they got married—compared to only 31 percent of the women fifty-five and older. However, the majority of the women in the Hunt survey were no more casual about sex than their mothers had been. Over half had had sex with only one partner. In contrast, the median number of premarital sex partners for men was six.

It seems, than, that the double standard persists—one code of acceptable sexual behavior for men, another for women. Sixty percent of the men and 37 percent of the women in the Hunt sample thought it was all right for men to have sex with someone for whom they felt no strong affection; only 44 percent of the men and 20 percent of the women thought it was all right for women to do so. (Interestingly, the men in this survey granted women more sexual freedom than the women allowed themselves.)

EXTRAMARITAL SEX About half the husbands and a quarter of the wives in Kinsey's sample (1948, 1953) had had sexual intercourse with someone other than their spouse while they were married. To judge from the Hunt survey (1974), the percentage of married men who "play around" has not changed much since the 1940s, but the percentage of married women who do—especially young wives—has. Twenty-four percent of the wives under age twenty-five in the Hunt sample claimed to have had extramarital sexual experiences, compared to 8 percent in the Kinsey sample. But again, women are more conservative. Twice as many husbands as wives

Table 17.1 Heterosexual–Homosexual Ratings (Ages 20–35)

Category		In Females (Percent)	In Males (Percent)
0	Entirely heterosexual experience		
	Single	61–72	53–78
	Married	89–90	90–92
	Previously married	75–80	
1–6	At least some homosexual experience	11–20	18–42
2–6	More than incidental homosexual experience	6-14	13-38
3–6	As much homosexual experience as heterosexual experience, or more	4–11	9–32
4–6	Mostly homosexual experience	3–8	7-26
5–6	Almost exclusively homosexual experience	2–6	5–22
6	Exclusively homosexual experience	1–3	3–16

From data in Kinsey *et al.* *Sexual Behavior in the Human Female*. W. B. Saunders, 1953, p. 488.

have had sex with six or more extramarital partners. According to the Hunt survey, it seems that men are more likely than women to seek extramarital sex for sex's sake, without emotional involvement. Women are less likely to separate sexual desire from affection: they tend to embark on affairs only when they are dissatisfied with their marriages (Tavris and Offir, 1977, p. 70).

Although the proportion of people having affairs is rising, attitudes toward extramarital sex have remained about the same: over 80 percent of the couples in the Hunt survey regarded it as wrong. Open marriages, in which both the man and the woman agree that both will have sex outside the marriage, seem to be rare. Only 4 percent of the men in one survey said that they had had extramarital relations with the knowledge and consent of their wives (Pietropinto and Simmenauer, 1977). Thus, most extramarital sex takes the form of "cheating" on one's partner.

HOMOSEXUALITY Who is a homosexual? Any person who has ever had *any* sexual contact with a member of the same sex? People who have sex *only* with members of the same sex? What about a man who usually has homosexual lovers but occasionally has sex with a woman? What about a woman who usually has male lovers but occasionally has sex with other women? The tendency in the United States has been to label anyone who has had any homosexual experience, however infrequent, a homosexual.

People who are exclusively homosexual consider themselves, and are considered by others, to be "true" homosexuals. There is considerable variation in how people who have some degree of interest in both sexes classify themselves, and in how they are viewed by others. As a rule, however, psychologists consider a **homosexual** to be a person whose primary source of sexual gratification is members of the same sex.

In line with this definition, Kinsey created for his survey a seven-point scale of sexual behavior. At one extreme (category 0) were people who were exclusively heterosexual; at the other (category 6) were people who were exclusively homosexual. Individuals who were predominantly heterosexual or homosexual but had a passing interest in the other sex were assigned to categories 2 and 4, respectively. Category 3 was for bisexuals, who had about equal interest in members of their own and the opposite sex. In this way Kinsey deliberately avoided classifying all people as *either* completely homosexual *or* completely heterosexual, but instead represented the range of sexual preferences as a continuum.

In gathering statistics on homosexuality, Kinsey included subjects' reports of both psychological and physical arousal, as well as any erotic contact, whether or not it led to orgasm. The results are shown in Table 17.1. These figures are dated, but they are still the only comprehensive estimates we have of the incidence of homosexual behavior in the population as a whole.

Why do some people choose sex partners of the same biological sex exclusively or almost exclusively? Psychologists have advanced two basic hypotheses. According to one school of thought, homosexuality may have a biochemical basis. Evidence for and against this position appears from time to time. Recently a team of researchers (Kolodny et al., 1971) found that a group of eighteen-to-thirty-five-year-old males who were exclusively homosexual had lower levels of the male sex hormone testosterone and lower sperm counts than did a comparable group of heterosexuals. (Bisexuals, however, had the same testosterone and sperm levels as heterosexuals.) But the sample was a very small one, and even if the results could be applied to a majority of homosexuals, there is no way of knowing whether such biochemical differences are the cause or the effect of one's sexual orientation and behavior.

Many psychologists are inclined to see homosexuality as the product of early learning. One group of researchers (McGuire, Carlise, and Young, 1965) suggested the following developmental sequence.

Step 1. A "homosexual event" occurs. The individual engages in homosexual play, is approached by an older homosexual, or observes homosexual behavior.

Step 2. The individual fantasizes about this event while masturbating. Orgasm during masturbation reinforces the homosexual fantasy.

Step 3. When homosexual fantasies have been reinforced with orgasm, the individual is more likely to engage in overt homosexual behavior should the opportunity arise.

Psychoanalytic hypotheses have also been advanced. For example, Marcel Saghir and Eli Robins (1973) suggested that many male homosexuals had harsh fathers who did not allow their sons to be close to them. Hence, the sons did not identify with the fathers and did not learn the male role. Irving Bieber argued that male homosexuals had aggressive, domineering mothers and passive fathers (Bieber et al., 1962). In this case, too, a son might not form a strong masculine identity.

None of these hypotheses has been adequately documented. There is no more clear agreement on a single explanation of homosexual development than there is on a single theory of overall psychosexual development.

Until a few years ago, all classifications of psychological disorders included homosexuality. The American Psychiatric Association has now officially rejected the idea that homosexuality is a "disease" and homosexuals are "sick." However, a number of psychiatrists continue to argue that homosexuality

is necessarily a symptom of neurosis, immaturity, personality disorders, or faulty upbringing. The controversy is likely to continue.

The goals for homosexuals in therapy have shifted over the years. For some time therapists assumed that same-sex orientation was the root or symptom of other problems, and they concentrated on transforming homosexuals into heterosexuals. More recently, some therapists have begun to let their homosexual clients make the choice of being helped either to change their sexual orientation or to become more comfortable with it. The problem is that, given this choice, many individuals may feel subtly pressured into saying that they want to change. Gerald Davison (1976), for one, argues that a therapist should never try to change a person's sexual orientation. The goal of therapy, he says, should be to enhance interpersonal relationships and perhaps sexual technique, with no reference to sexual preferences. This is a controversial but influential position.

SEXUAL SATISFACTION AND THE "SEXUAL REVOLUTION"

The surveys cited in this chapter suggest that recent talk of a "sexual revolution" has been exaggerated. It is true that young people are a bit more "liberated" than their parents were; but overall, changes in sexual behavior have not been dramatic. Americans certainly are more open about sex today than they were fifty years ago. There are more books about sex in the stores, more chapters about sex in textbooks, more X-rated movies, more songs with explicit references to sex. But has sexual activity really become freer and more frequent?

Carol Tavris and Carole Offir (1977) believe that the sexual revolution is one of rising expectations, not actions. They cite a survey of readers of *Psychology Today* magazine in which 22 percent of young unmarried men and 21 percent of young unmarried women reported that they were virgins, but only 1 to 2 percent of the men and women surveyed thought their peers were. Fifty-five percent of the men and 34 percent of the women said that they were unhappy with their sex lives, but only 29 and 19 percent, respectively, thought their peers were unhappy. Apparently, many people today think they are missing something. Tavris and Offir suggest that our society's new openness about sex has created new pressures, new worries, new sources of dissatisfaction.

To determine whether a "sexual revolution" is taking place, we would need answers to a number of questions. Do people give sex higher priority today than they did in the past? Do we spend more time and money on sex than we used to? Is sexual satisfaction more important to people than it was in the past? Is it more highly correlated with personal happiness? At this point, we simply do not know. We do know, however, that the knowledge gained from such studies as those of Kinsey and Masters and Johnson has opened doors to effective communication and therapy in sexual matters. To that extent, these studies have indeed pointed the way to a "revolution" in sexual fulfillment and in attitudes toward human sexuality.

SUMMARY

1. Gender is influenced by genetic, hormonal, and social factors.

    A. Genetic sex is determined at the moment of conception, when an ovum (which always has an X chromosome) is fertilized by a sperm having either an X chromosome (which produces a female) or a Y chromosome (which produces a male). Genetic sex is the beginning of the development of gender and sexuality.

    B. Sexual development follows an identical course for males and for females during the first six weeks after conception. Male and female sex organs are **homologous**, which means that they arise from the same embryonic structures and perform similar functions. When the testes or ovaries emerge, they produce hormones that complete the process of biological sex differentiation. The two basic factors that apparently are necessary for the development of a male are the Y chromosome and androgen hormones; the absence of both the Y chromosome and androgen is necessary for normal female development.

    C. Social influences on sexual development begin to operate as soon as a baby is born. Parents behave differently toward infant boys and girls, and there is some evidence for sex differences in behavior shortly after birth. Most people have a strong **gender identity** by the age of three or four—that is, they think of themselves as either a boy or a girl—and they are beginning to learn their **gender role**—how to behave in ways expected of members of their gender in their society. Although physiological factors influence behavioral differences between the sexes, the impact of social forces is indicated by the variation in gender roles in various cultures. **Transsexualism** confirms the need to consider gender identity separately from biological sex.

2. Sexual behavior has been opened to scientific investigation only in the second half of this century. The major methods of studying sexual behavior are cross-cultural studies, sexual surveys, observational studies, and controlled experiments.

    A. Cross-cultural studies have provided insights into the wide variations in sexual behavior in different cultures. One contribution of these studies has been to force a redefinition of which sexual practices should be considered abnormal.

    B. The most important survey concerning sexual activity was conducted by Alfred C. Kinsey in the 1940s. Despite certain methodological shortcomings, the Kinsey survey has provided the foundation for most later research on human sexuality.

    C. The first observational study of human sexual behavior was conducted by William Masters and Virginia Johnson in the 1960s. Although this study too had its shortcomings, it provided valuable insight into human response.

    D. Only through controlled experiments can the influences of various factors on sexual behavior be isolated and examined. An example of such an experiment was a study by Julia Heiman, which showed that the arousal responses of men and women to erotic material were highly similar.

3. Men and women respond physiologically to sexual stimulation in parallel ways.

A. Masters and Johnson found that the sexual response in both men and women can be divided into four basic phases: the **excitement phase**, the **plateau phase**, **orgasm**, and the **resolution phase**. The subjective experience of orgasm is apparently similar for both men and women. The significant differences in orgasm between men and women are that men ejaculate while women do not and that most men experience a **refractory period** after orgasm, while women may experience **multiple orgasms**.

B. Both men and women can become sexually aroused by psychological as well as physical stimulation; but effective sexual stimulation, in whatever form, varies widely from person to person.
1. Touch is the most obvious source of sexual arousal. The sensitivity of a particular **erogenous zone** varies with the individual.
2. Visual stimulation can be very effective for both men and women.
3. Fantasies may be the most powerful erotic stimulant of all. Interviews have shown that many women use fantasies to enhance their sexual responsiveness.

C. Studies show that most old people for whom a partner is available maintain relatively vigorous sex lives. The hormonal changes that occur with aging are gradual and need not prevent sexual enjoyment.

D. A problem that prevents an individual from engaging in sexual relations or from reaching orgasm during sex is known as a **sexual dysfunction**. Sexual dysfunction rarely has a physiological basis; the negative psychological feelings preventing an individual from abandoning him or herself to pleasure may be the result of rigid religious upbringing, ridicule of one's anatomy or sexual abuse in childhood, or the fear of sexual failure.
1. **Impotence** refers to a man's inability to achieve or maintain an erection long enough to reach orgasm with a partner.
   a. **Primary impotence** means that a man has never been able to achieve or maintain an erection.
   b. Secondary impotence means that a man has been aroused to orgasm with a partner in the past, but is unable to acquire or maintain an erection at

present or in certain situations.
   c. **Premature ejaculation** means that a man often or always ejaculates before he or his partner would like.
   d. **Nonemissive erection** refers to a man's inability to ejaculate during sex with a partner.
2. Sexual dysfunctions in women include the inability to engage in intercourse and the inability to reach orgasm.
   a. **Vaginismus** is a condition in which involuntary muscle spasms cause the vagina to clamp shut so that penetration by the male partner's penis is impossible or extremely painful.
   b. The terms **primary orgasmic dysfunction** or **preorgasmic** refer to a woman who has never experienced an orgasm by any means.
   c. **Situational** or **secondary orgasmic dysfunction** refers to a woman who sometimes experiences orgasm, but not in other situations in which she would like to.

E. Nearly all of the many approaches to sex therapy are based on seven basic principles:
1. Sexual dysfunction is considered a mutual problem.
2. Education is provided in sexual anatomy and techniques.
3. Therapists attempt to bring about an attitude change.
4. Therapists use various techniques to reduce anxiety.
5. The couple is encouraged to improve communication and feedback.
6. Sex is considered in the context of the couple's entire relationship.
7. Therapists prescribe changes in sexual behavior.

4. People's sexual activities vary with their cultural and personal characteristics.
A. While the number of people who choose celibacy as a permanent way of life is small, most people go through periods of temporary chastity.
B. Attitudes toward masturbation have changed in the past few decades. Surveys indicate that masturbation is common among both men and women, and that relatively few people consider it wrong. A number of researchers believe that early experiences

with masturbation help to establish the foundation for adult sexuality.

C. Heterosexual interaction, which can take a great number of forms, is the most common sexual activity.

1. Since Kinsey's survey was published, the incidence of premarital sex appears to have increased a little for men and a great deal for women.

2. The proportion of men and women engaging in extramarital sex is rising, though a majority of people regard such affairs as wrong.

D. In general, a **homosexual** is a person whose primary source of sexual gratification is members of the same sex. For his survey, Kinsey created a seven-point scale of sexual behavior, from exclusively heterosexual to exclusively homosexual.

1. Psychologists have advanced a variety of hypotheses—biochemical, learning, and psychoanalytic—to explain homosexual development, but have not reached agreement on any single explanation.

2. Therapy goals for homosexuals have changed as attitudes toward homosexuality have changed. While therapists once attempted to transform homosexuals into heterosexuals, they now focus on either helping the person to change his or her sexual orientation or helping him or her to achieve greater self-acceptance, depending on what the individual wants.

5. Surveys suggest that the "sexual revolution" involves more of a change in sexual attitudes than in sexual behavior.

RECOMMENDED READINGS

BEACH, FRANK A. (ed.). *Human Sexuality in Four Perspectives*. Baltimore: Johns Hopkins University Press, 1977. An excellent collection of papers and theoretical discussions of sexuality from several major viewpoints.

FORISHA, BARBARA LUSK. *Sex Roles and Personal Awareness*. Glenview, Ill.: Scott, Foresman, 1978. An up-to-date, lucid presentation of the complex issue of gender role development.

KATCHADOURIAN, HERANT A., and DONALD T. LUNDE. *Fundamentals of Human Sexuality*. 2nd ed. New York: Holt, Rinehart and Winston, 1975. An outstanding and well-written basic textbook with broad coverage of biological, behavioral, and cultural facets of human sexuality.

KINSEY, ALFRED C., WARDELL B. POMEROY, and C. E. MARTIN. *Sexual Behavior in the Human Male*. Philadelphia: Saunders, 1948.

KINSEY, ALFRED C., WARDELL B. POMEROY, C. E. MARTIN, and P. H. GEBHARDT. *Sexual Behavior in the Human Female*. Philadelphia: Saunders, 1953. The classic "Kinsey studies" of sexual behavior, which provided the first broad survey and comprehensive statistics concerning the sexual behaviors of Americans.

LOPICCOLO, JOSEPH, and LESLIE LOPICCOLO (eds.). *Handbook of Sex Therapy*. New York: Plenum Press, 1978. A comprehensive and mature presentation of the principles and techniques of modern sex therapy.

MASTERS, WILLIAM H., and VIRGINIA E. JOHNSON. *Human Sexual Response*. Boston: Little, Brown, 1966. Based on observational studies, this was the first thoroughly detailed account of the physiological changes that accompany sexual arousal and orgasm.

MONEY, JOHN, and H. MUSAPH (eds.). *The Handbook of Sexology*. Amsterdam: Elsevier/North Holland Biomedical Press, 1977. Containing over a hundred chapters, this is a very comprehensive and sophisticated presentation of scientific and theoretical approaches to the study of sexual behavior.

MORRISON, ELEANOR (ed.). *Human Sexuality*. 2nd ed. Palo Alto, Calif.: Mayfield, 1977. A book of light but interesting readings, many from popular magazines, covering a broad range of issues in sexuality.

PART SIX

PERSONALITY AND INDIVIDUAL DIFFERENCES

Throughout history, many theories of personality have been formulated in an effort to explain why each human being is unique and why an individual's behavior is fairly consistent in different situations and at different times. The first comprehensive theory of personality in psychology was constructed by Sigmund Freud. In Chapter 18, "Psychoanalytic Theories of Personality," we discuss Freud's theory and the work of several major neo-Freudian theorists, who adapted and expanded on Freud's work. Chapter 19, "Behavioristic, Humanistic, and Trait Theories of Personality," presents some important viewpoints on personality that have been proposed as alternatives to psychoanalytic theory.

In Chapter 20, "Psychological Assessment," we take a look at the tests by which human personality and intelligence are measured. After describing the basic characteristics of a test—reliability, validity, and standardization—we will consider some of the most widely used tests of intelligence and personality.

"Midway in life's journey I was made aware that I had strayed into a dark forest and the right path appeared not anywhere. ——"

CHAPTER EIGHTEEN

PSYCHOANALYTIC THEORIES OF PERSONALITY

Everyone knows that Freud revolutionized the world's thinking with respect to sex, guilt, repression, and many other facets of the inner workings of the mind. Some of the changes he effected seem to me to be rarely spoken of, however.

For instance, the fact that Freud made the notion of the Oedipus complex popular made it necessary to look upon the relationship of a boy and his mother in less sentimental fashion. This killed a type of song that was extremely popular at the turn of the century—the one in which a man soulfully hummed his love for his mother. There is one perfectly dreadful song of the 1890s called "Break the News to Mother" in which a dying soldier sings, "Just tell her that no other/Can take the place of mother." And, of course, there is the old standard that tells us, "I want a girl just like the girl that married dear old Dad."

Such songs can't be written any more except as burlesques—and a good thing, too.

On a more serious plane, consider that before Freud popularized the notion of the unconscious, no one really thought that a person could do anything but think consciously. A conclusion, a solution, a discovery that popped into the mind without conscious thought was a difficult thing to handle, and the blame fell easily upon the supernatural. (Dreams also were sent from Heaven. Pagans and Christians both agreed on that.)

"Enthusiasm" originally had a stronger meaning than it is given at the present. It was a kind of frenzy that carried a person along into actions he was incapable of doing ordinarily. It comes from Greek words meaning "the god within," so that a person in the grip of enthusiasm is possessed by a divine being.

There is the particular type of enthusiasm, or divine possession, that affects a person's mental creativity; that enables him or her to see, in a moment of insight, some conclusion that has escaped others and that perhaps would forever escape others. A scientific law may become clear, as when Archimedes suddenly understood the law of buoyancy and dashed naked out of the bath, running home and crying "Eureka!" ("I have it!") all the way. Or continuous insight may enable a person to know just how to go about writing a great book, painting a great picture, composing a great symphony; knowing just which words, colors, notes to choose, even when the creator cannot explain what it is, exactly, that guides the choice.

In ancient Rome, it was thought that everyone had a divine spirit in whose charge he or she was. When that spirit took over the body and mind completely, the possessed person could do, know, and understand what ordinary mortals could not. The Romans called such a personal spirit a "genius," and we still use the word today to refer to an individual of greatest creative abilities.

What Freud did, then, was to reduce the supernatural to the natural; to transfer matters from the mysterious divine to the less-mysterious human. It is the greatest feat a scientist can perform.

Isaac Asimov

Like the man who was surprised to learn that he had been speaking "prose" all his life, you may be unaware that you already know a great deal about the psychology of personality. You know, for example, that if you tell two friends a joke, one is likely to find it hilarious, while the other is likely to miss the point. Ask three people their opinion of the same movie, and they may remember entirely different versions of it. Introduce a girl friend to Tom and he will smile politely and go back to watching the football game, to John and he will shuffle his feet and lower his eyes, to David and he will tell her she is beautiful and ask for her phone number. Thus, your own experiences tell you that each person is unique and has responses to the world that are different from anyone else's. Moreover, these unique characteristics seem to be stable and enduring. The friend who laughed at your joke is almost always ready for a good time; John is nearly always shy and uncomfortable around girls.

The term **personality** is used by psychologists and psychiatrists to refer to such differences between people and to the stability of a given individual's behavior over long periods of time. Regardless of their background and approach, all personality theorists address two key questions. First: *When several people confront the same situation, why don't they all behave in the same way?* And second: *What accounts for the relative consistency of a person's behavior from one situation to the next?* These questions lead to others. Is there something "inside" that makes people think, feel, and act in distinctive and characteristic ways? Are people driven by biological forces? Do we inherit personality traits from our parents? How do "outside" forces—our experiences and personal histories, our relationships, our culture, and the times in which we live—shape and mold us? How, in other words, does personality develop? Are we motivated by unconscious forces, or do we act as we do simply out of habit? Can we—do we—change over time?

Each of the personality theorists we will discuss in this chapter and in Chapter 19 approaches these questions from a different angle, and each arrives at different conclusions. This is hardly surprising, given the complexity of human behavior and the range of individual differences. It is best to look at these theories not as alternatives, but as complementary ways of looking at a subject that is hard to get a grip on. Each of these approaches sheds light on certain aspects of personality. The theorists discussed in this chapter are Sigmund Freud, Carl Jung, Alfred Adler, Karen Horney, Erich Fromm, and Erik Erikson.

FREUD'S PSYCHOANALYTIC THEORY

Sigmund Freud (1856–1939) has been, without doubt, the most influential theorist in the field of personality. He conceived the first formal theory of personality, and it is still the most detailed and original of all those formulated. Even critics of Freud—and there have been some vociferous ones—admit that the range of phenomena he identified and explored will forever stand as a challenge and an inspiration to personality theorists. Freud drew on a number of assets to make the rich observations he set down on paper: his remarkable skill as an observer of human behavior; his training in medical science; his broad background in literature and history, including knowledge of such materials as joke books and folk tales; and his unusually fine writing ability. A reader needs no particular training in psychology to be excited, entertained, and educated by some of Freud's major works, such as *The Interpretation of Dreams* (1900), *Civilization and Its Discontents* (1930), and *New Introductory Lectures on Psychoanalysis* (1933).

Freud first became interested in personality when he tried to account for some of the strange physical problems of some of his patients. They often suffered from what seemed to be a neurological defect—for example, paralysis of an arm, loss of sensation in a hand, deterioration of hearing or vision. But Freud, trained as a neurologist, knew that often the defect was not physical in origin. When a patient showed loss of feeling in a hand, for instance, the affected region might be confined to the area covered by a glove ("glove anesthesia"), an area that does not correspond to any known grouping of nerves.

Freud speculated that these symptoms could be caused by emotional stress of some kind. In collaboration with Josef Breuer, he discovered that such "hysterical" disorders, as he called them, could be cured if the patient, under hypnosis (see Chapter 14), recalled critical events from early childhood and talked about them (Breuer and Freud, 1937). One of Breuer's patients was a young woman he called Anna O. She had become exhausted while caring for her dying father and had developed a nervous cough, severe headaches, abnormal vision, and other physical problems. When Breuer visited Anna, she would often pass into a trancelike state that she called "clouds." In this state she would recount past experiences, a process she called "chimney sweeping." Occasionally, when she told about experiences related in some way to one of her symptoms—and especially if she seemed to relive the emotional part of the experiences vividly—the symptoms would disappear. Breuer sometimes hypnotized Anna and further encouraged her to talk about emotional events and experiences that seemed to be related to her physical symptoms. This technique, too, was often effective in relieving her symptoms.

Freud began to use Breuer's method, but after considerable effort he concluded that it was not an ideal therapeutic procedure. Many patients were not hypnotizable, and those who were often suffered a recurrence of their symptoms. Moreover, hypnotized patients did not reach a better understanding of their underlying difficulties.

Freud invented a technique he called **free association**; the patient was asked to lie down on a couch in Freud's office and to say out loud whatever came to mind from moment to moment. Freud found that eventually certain themes emerged and that these themes centered on the patient's important emotional conflicts. As these conflicts were talked out, they became better understood and less fearsome, and the patient experienced relief from the symptoms, just as Anna O. had done under hypnosis.

Freud found that although Anna O. and the other patients with "hysterical" disorders could not remember childhood experiences at first, especially

the wishes and fears that seemed to produce their symptoms, these memories could be brought back through free association, sometimes assisted by hypnosis. The memories had evidently been alive, hidden somewhere in the mind. Thus Freud was led to theorize the existence of an **unconscious** element of personality, unknown to the mind of the subject.

The concept of the unconscious is undoubtedly Freud's major contribution to the understanding of human behavior and personality. In Freud's view, the contents of the conscious mind are only a part of the structure of personality. In fact, he drew an analogy between the mind and an iceberg: people's conscious thoughts are like the tip of an iceberg; the massive unconscious lies beneath the surface. In the unconscious—which is a process, not a thing—reside universal instinctual drives and infantile goals, hopes, wishes, and needs that have been repressed, concealed from conscious awareness, because they cause internal conflict. Freud coined the term **psychoanalysis** to describe the process by which he attempted to bring material from the unconscious into the conscious mind of the patient where it could be examined rationally.

In addition to free association, Freud discovered, dreams, jokes, and even accidents—all instances in which normal conscious controls over behavior have been suspended—are keys that helped to unlock unconscious emotional conflicts. Freud believed that people often experience conflicts between social or moral constraints on the one hand and impulses to engage in sexual or aggressive actions on the other.

According to many Freudian theorists, smoking may be seen as a socially acceptable way of expressing unresolved oral or phallic conflicts.

We may not be completely aware of either side of the conflict. An unconscious or half-conscious compromise is established, the nature of which can be revealed in what appear to be spontaneous dreams, jokes, accidents, and physical symptoms. For instance, the "glove anesthesia" symptom referred to earlier, according to Freud, may be seen as a compromise between a desire to engage in a forbidden action—perhaps to masturbate or to strike someone—and the requirement that hostility or sexuality be expressed only in socially acceptable ways.

Dreams, in Freud's view, may be seen as expressing unacceptable impulses, disguised from one's conscious self by their apparent incoherency. Dreams have what Freud called **latent content** as well as **manifest content**. The manifest content is what the dreamer remembers—perhaps a terrifying elevator ride with an old man to the top of a medieval tower. The latent content is what is revealed through free association and analysis of the dream—in this example, perhaps an unconscious wish to have sexual relations with one's father.

Even jokes can be an outlet for sexual or aggressive impulses that, as Freud pointed out, are socially acceptable only when disguised as harmless humor. And accidents, such as forgetting an appointment, spilling a drink on a friend's best clothes, or mispronouncing the name of a disliked person, are additional signs of unconscious conflicts. Suppose you anticipate half-consciously that a visit to your parents may be unpleasant. You do not want to go home, yet you cannot quite admit this to yourself or to your parents. An unconscious compromise may be to miss the last bus to your home town and then to call your parents in genuine distress to apologize.

In order to make the sources of such compromises conscious, one may choose to undergo psychoanalysis. This procedure, if carried out properly, often helps people to understand themselves better, to express formerly unconscious and forbidden impulses in an acceptable way, and to reduce the unwanted side effects caused by emotional conflicts.

The publication of *The Interpretation of Dreams* in 1900 introduced psychoanalysis to the world. Although antagonism and confusion kept people from accepting Freud's ideas at first—especially the idea that sexual drives and conflicts originate in childhood and are involved in most emotional problems of adults—psychoanalysis gradually came to be recognized as a major breakthrough in self-understanding. Many people came to Vienna to study Freud's methods, and soon psychoanalysts were practicing in many countries, including the United States. Freud revised and supplemented his theory from 1900 until his death in 1939, but his work was never completely finished. His writings grew voluminous and sometimes became contradictory as he developed new insights.

FREUD'S CONCEPTUALIZATION OF PERSONALITY STRUCTURE Although Freud's ideas about unconscious conflicts emerged as a result of his work with troubled patients, they were based on a coherent theory of personality that he believed explained the behavior of all people. Freud divided personality into three separate but interacting agencies: the **id**, the **ego**, and the **superego**. Each of these three agencies has its own highly specific role in maintaining normal personality functioning. It may help our understanding of Freud's three-part concept of personality to know that the German word that Freud used for id is *es*, which means "it," implying an alien force, something in a person that is not recognized as part of the self. The ego he called *Ich*, which means "I," the part of the personality recognized and accepted as oneself. "Superego" (*überich*) thus means "over the I"; as we shall see, it refers to the moral component that is imposed on the self by society. Figure 18.1 illustrates Freud's theory of personality structure.

Freud sometimes referred to the three agencies as if they had wills of their own—as if the ego were a rational, self-controlled person at war with an irrational and impulsive person (the id) and a harsh, moralistic person (the superego). This manner of reference, while dramatic and engaging, has received much criticism from psychologists who believe that such descriptions border on mysticism. It will avoid confusion if we take the terms in the sense actually intended by Freud—as metaphorical names for the functional (not physical) divisions of the personality. The id, ego, and superego are not persons, places, or physical things; they are the names given to certain motivational forces whose existence is inferred from the way people behave. If they sometimes seem to be more places or entities than abstract forces, this is only a result of Freud's literary style. The accompanying quotation is both a good example of that vibrant style and a clear explanation of Freud's view of the relationships among the three components of adult personality.

Figure 18.1 A visual interpretation of the Freudian theory of personality structure. The id, which is entirely unconscious, is the source of all psychic energy. The superego and the ego, which are differentiated from the id during the development of the child, are partly conscious. The superego is an internalized version of the restrictions and demands placed on the child (that is, on the id) by the parents. The ego tries to balance the id's desires against the superego's demands and the realities of the world. In doing this it sometimes suppresses completely the irrational tendencies of the id, but it may also be able to deflect the id's energy (libido) into channels that are acceptable to both the superego and the outside world. These interactions and conflicts are represented by the arrows shown in the figure.

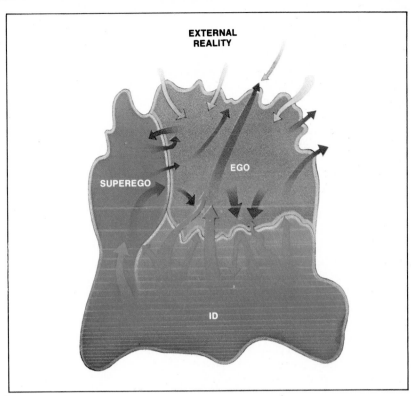

Freud on the Id, Ego, and Superego

We are warned by a proverb against serving two masters at the same time. The poor ego has things even worse: it serves three severe masters and does what it can to bring their claims and demands into harmony with one another. These claims are always divergent and often seem incompatible. No wonder that the ego so often fails in its task. Its three tyrannical masters are the external world, the super-ego and id. . . . Owing to its origin from the experiences of the perceptual system, it is earmarked for representing the demands of the external world, but it strives too to be a loyal servant of the id, to remain on good terms with it, to recommend itself to it as an object and to attract its libido to itself. In its attempts to mediate between the id and reality, it is often obliged to cloak the *Ucs.* [unconscious] commands of the id with its own *Pcs.* [preconscious] rationalizations, to conceal the id's conflicts with reality, to profess, with diplomatic disingenuousness, to be taking notice of reality even when the id has remained rigid and unyielding. On the other hand it is observed at every step it takes by the strict super-ego, which lays down definite standards for its conduct, without taking any account of its difficulties from the direction of the id and the external world, and which, if those standards are not obeyed, punishes it with tense feelings of inferiority and of guilt. Thus the ego, driven by the id, confined by the super-ego, repulsed by reality, struggles to master its economic task of bringing about harmony among the forces and influences working in and upon it; and we can understand how it is that so often we cannot suppress a cry: "Life is not easy!" If the ego is obliged to admit its weakness, it breaks out in anxiety—realistic anxiety regarding the external world, moral anxiety regarding the super-ego and neurotic anxiety regarding the strength of the passions in the id.

From Sigmund Freud, *New Introductory Lectures on Psychoanalysis* (1933). James Strachey (ed. and tr.). New York: W. W. Norton, 1965.

THE ID   Freud characterized the id as a reservoir of psychic energy that can be neither increased or decreased. According to Freud, it may be seen as a pool of instinctual biological drives present in every individual at birth. An **instinct** Freud defined as the psychological expression of a biologically based physical need. The need can be for food, sex, elimination of waste, or any other bodily requirement. In response to these needs, the human being develops "wishes." These "wishes" motivate and direct one's behavior to satisfy the specific need that has been aroused. The instincts provide the psychic energy that powers the entire personality. Thus the id—that is, all the instincts together—is the energy source for the ego and the superego, which develop later in childhood.

Freud distinguished between two broad types of instincts in the id. The first type is *Eros* (the Greek word for "love"), the constructive life instinct responsible for survival, self-propagation, and creativity. In Eros are included the need for food, warmth, and, above all, sex. In Freud's broad use of the term, "sex" covers a wide range of life-giving and life-sustaining activities, from genital intercourse to artistic creation. The energy of Eros is generated by what Freud called the **libido**, a driving force permeating the entire personality and propelling it through life.

The second type of instinct is opposed to Eros. It is the death instinct, *Thanatos* (from the Greek word for "death"). Freud's discussion of the death instinct, which came late in his writings, is rather vague. He was studying aggression and concluded that the human organism is instinctively drawn back to the original inanimate state from which it arose, a state in which all tension would be dissipated—in short, the state of death (Freud, 1920). This instinctive attraction to death gives rise in each individual to aggressive tendencies directed at oneself. However, since self-destruction is opposed by the life-preserving energy of the libido, aggression against the self usually is redirected outward, against the world, motivating human beings to compete, to conquer, and to kill. Although sex and aggression can be seen as two opposing forces, they are also closely related. Both have their origin in the id; both seek the release of tension.

The instincts that make up the id are essentially biological. They take no account of logic or reason, reality or morality. The id is concerned only with reducing the tensions generated by the organism's needs: the need for warmth, food, tactile stimulation, and so forth. This tendency of the id to devote itself exclusively to the immediate reduction of tension is called the **pleasure principle.**

THE EGO   While the id instinctively desires the satisfaction of biological needs, it has no way of satisfying them, other than by activating reflex actions such as sucking. Nor does it have any way of determining which means of tension reduction are safe and which are dangerous to the organism. To do these things, after approximately the first six months of life a new psychic component develops: the ego. The ego takes for itself part of the energy of the id and proceeds to serve as the mediator between the id and reality (Freud, 1920, 1923). Unlike the id, much of the ego is conscious. Through remembering, reasoning, and evaluating, on the basis of the child's prior contacts with reality, the ego tries to satisfy the desires of the id, to anticipate the consequences of a particular means of gratification, and sometimes to delay gratification in order to achieve long-range goals.

Let us imagine, for example, a three-year-old boy playing in his room. The id signals that aggressive impulses seek release, and the boy reaches for his toy hammer. The ego then goes into action, scanning the environment for an appropriate outlet. The boy's baby sister is playing near him. Should he clobber her over the head with his hammer? The ego, which knows from experience that such an action will result in the painful consequence of a spanking, says no and continues the scanning process. There is also a wood block nearby. The ego determines that no harm will come from pounding the block, and so the boy proceeds to bang away at it.

Thus, in contrast to the pleasure principle of the id, the ego operates on what is called the **reality principle**, the foundation of which is the concern for safety. The ego is often called the executive agency of personality, because it controls the individual's actions and manipulates the environment. It is through this basic ego function of finding realistic means of satisfying the id that the mind develops and refines all its higher cognitive functions: perception, learning, discrimination, memory, judgment, and planning.

THE SUPEREGO   Imagine that three years later the same boy once again sits with hammer in hand looking for something to pound. Again he considers his sister's head, but this time he rejects that outlet not just to avoid being punished, but because hitting her would be "wrong." What this means is that the boy has developed a superego.

The superego is the third psychic component. Approximately equivalent to what we call "conscience," the superego is that part of the personality that represents the moral standards of the society as conveyed to the child by the parents. The superego emerges from the resolution of the Oedipus complex (see Chapter 10). The male child represses his desire for his mother and identifies with his father so that he can share vicariously his father's special relationship with his mother. He **internalizes** the moral standards he learns from his father—that is, he incorporates them into his own personality. Similarly, the resolution of the Electra complex leads the female child to identify with her mother and to develop a superego incorporating her mother's moral standards.

Like the ego, the superego receives its energy from the id. Unlike the ego, however, the superego takes no more account of reality than the id does. Instead of considering what is realistic or possible, the superego embraces an **ego ideal**—an abstract moral ideal that constantly commands the individual to stifle the sexual and aggressive impulses of the id and to pursue moral goals instead. The superego, then, is the great nay-sayer. Its function is to prohibit. Thus it is up to the ego to find a way to satisfy the id without giving pain, experienced as remorse or guilt, to the superego. For after the superego develops in a person, doing something "wrong" may result not only in a punishment administered by someone else, but perhaps also in headaches, dreams of being arrested for some unknown crime, and self-punishing behavior such as losing one's notes the night before final exams.

Thus in the fully developed psychic structure the ego has three difficult forces to deal with: the id, which seeks only the satisfaction of its irrational and amoral demands; the superego, which seeks only the satisfaction of its impractical ideals; and reality, which offers only a limited range of objects for satisfying the id and which delivers stern punishment for unwise choices (Blum, 1953).

FREUD'S THEORY OF PERSONALITY DYNAMICS

Freud's theory of personality dynamics, then, is based on conflict between opposing energies. Intrapsychically—that is, within the person—there are conflicts between the life instinct and the death instinct, between love and hate, between creativity

The tension headache is a common ailment. Psychodynamic theorists would regard such a headache as the result of conflict between the ego or id and the superego.

Reproduced by permission of copyright owner. EXCEDRIN and THE EXTRA STRENGTH PAIN RELIEVER are trademarks of the Bristol-Myers Company.

and destructiveness. In addition, within each of us there are conflicts between the urge to satisfy the instincts we are born with and the urge to obey the rules of society, which insist that our instinctual desires be restrained and rechanneled in socially acceptable ways.

Freud believed that nearly all human behavior is directed toward resolving these conflicts, reducing tension, and restoring **homeostasis** (equilibrium). A bodily source of excitation, or a need, arouses an instinct; the aroused instinct activates behavior. If the behavior is effective, the person returns to the state that existed before the instinct was aroused.

Of course, Freud recognized that many acts are responses to events in the external world. A threatening gesture from another person, a sudden thunderstorm, or a ringing telephone will elicit behavior. These are relatively easy to cope with. A person need only flee from a threat, come in from the rain, or answer the phone. However, a "threat" from the superego, a "thunderstorm" in the id, or a "ring" of anxiety is another matter. All of the agencies of personality are activated. The ego has to cope with the contending demands of the id and the superego, as well as the reality of the situation. This is why Freud placed more emphasis on internal sources of excitation than on stimulation from the external world: for Freud, instincts were the driving force behind behavior.

DISPLACEMENT OF INSTINCTUAL ENERGY In some cases it seems obvious that an individual is acting on instinct—when, for example, a man responds to seductive behavior by a sexually attractive woman. In other cases it is not so obvious. What instinct motivates a person to compose a symphony, for example?

To explain the way Freud would answer this question, we have to backtrack for a moment and reexamine his concept of instincts. An instinct has four characteristic features: a *source*, which is a bodily condition or need, such as the need for sexual release; an *aim*, which is to satisfy the need and stop the excitation; an *object*, which is the means the person uses to satisfy the need; and a force called *impetus*, the strength of which is determined by the intensity of the need. The source and aim of an instinct remain constant throughout life. However, the means the person uses to satisfy the need can and do vary considerably. This is because psychic energy can be **displaced**—that is, it can be transferred from the original object to a variety of substitute objects. If we want to express hostility, for example, but fear the consequences of an aggressive act, the energy can be redirected to another object. Such displacement occurs when, for example, a man who is afraid to assert himself at the office comes home and blows up at his wife. This capacity for displacing instinctual energy from one object to another is one of the key concepts in Freud's theory of personality dynamics.

Much of the pattern of our lives—our habits, characteristics, interests—is the result of the displacement of energy from the objects our instincts had originally chosen. Smoking may be conceived of as the displacement of energy that was originally directed toward sucking the mother's breast. Similarly, a young woman's need to keep her apartment extremely neat may be a displacement of the energy originally directed toward anal pleasure. The substitute object, however, is seldom as satisfying as the original object. Thus, tension accumulates and acts as a permanent motivating force for each person's behavior.

Sublimation is a kind of displacement that can produce higher cultural achievement. Freud pointed out in *Civilization and Its Discontents* (1930) that the development of civilization was made possible by inhibiting primitive object choices and diverting instinctual energy from them to social organization and cultural development. Freud suggested, for example, that Leonardo da Vinci's urge to paint Madonnas was a sublimated expression of his longing for reunion with his mother, from whom he had been separated at a young age. For most of us sublimation does not bring complete satisfaction, however, and the residual tension may discharge itself in the form of nervousness or restlessness. This dissatisfaction, Freud noted in one of his characteristically pessimistic passages, is the price human beings pay for civilization and may be a cause of their periodic wars and other lapses into primitive, violent behavior.

ANXIETY Anxiety is a state of psychic pain that alerts the ego to danger; it is akin to what most of us call fear. Freud distinguished three types of anxiety, each based on a different source of danger. In "reality anxiety" the individual is threatened by something in the outside world; a person who sees a rattlesnake a foot away experiences reality anxiety. In "moral anxiety" the source of danger is the superego, which threatens to overwhelm the person with guilt or shame over something that he or she has done or merely thought of doing. In "neurotic anxiety" the danger comes from id impulses that threaten to burst through ego controls and cause the individual to do things that will bring punishment or shame.

Individuals cope with anxiety in a number of ways. Suppose a young woman is extremely anxious about getting into law school. She may redouble her efforts to prepare for her law boards. She may consult with her advisor to determine whether her choice of schools is realistic and whether she should apply to other schools. She may make alternative plans, in case she is not accepted anywhere. She may talk out with her husband the reasons why she wants to become a lawyer and is so afraid of being rejected by the law schools. She may become involved in a community project to keep herself busy while she waits to hear from the schools. Any of these tactics may help to relieve her anxiety.

DEFENSE MECHANISMS When anxiety is acute

and there appears to be no reasonable way of dealing with it, the ego resorts to what are called **defense mechanisms**. Defense mechanisms are intrapsychic schemes to conceal the source of anxiety from the self and the world. For example, the young woman mentioned above may "forget" to take her birth control pills, "accidentally" become pregnant, and convince herself and others that the demands of motherhood prevent her from attending law school. In this way she avoids the problem: if she's about to have an infant to take care of, she can't apply to law school; if she doesn't apply, she can't be rejected. All defense mechanisms have two characteristics in common: (1) they deny, falsify, or distort reality; (2) they usually operate unconsciously, so that the person is not aware of what is taking place. The most common defense mechanisms are discussed in the following paragraphs.

Repression is a defense mechanism that keeps threatening thoughts and memories from consciousness and pushes them back into the unconscious. Repression was one of Freud's earliest and most important discoveries. He observed that his patients were unable to recall **traumatic**—psychologically damaging—childhood events without considerable probing. Traumatic memories, he concluded, are repressed and kept in the unconscious by strong forces. According to Freud, the threats from these unpleasant memories, the expenditures of energy needed to repress them, and the anxiety generated in the process are at the basis of neurosis (see Chapter 22).

Fixation is a temporary or permanent halt in development, occurring as a response to anxiety associated with the next stage of development. (Freud's concept of developmental stages is reviewed in the following section.) For example, a little girl entering the phallic stage may experience anxiety if her parents express disapproval of her interest in genital organs. Because of this anxiety, the child may be afraid to move into the phallic stage, in which attention and energy are focused on the genital organs. Instead, the child may become temporarily fixated at the previous developmental stage—that is, the anal stage.

Regression occurs when, in response to some threat, a person returns to an earlier stage of development. For example, a middle-aged man who is having difficulties with his wife may behave in a way that had given him pleasure in his childhood, perhaps eating. Regression is related to fixation in that a person usually regresses to a stage at which he or she was previously fixated: the child fixated at the oral stage can grow into the adult who regresses by overeating.

Reaction formation is the replacement of an anxiety-producing impulse or feeling by its opposite; its function is to make one unaware of the original source of distress. Instead of acknowledging that she hates her child, a mother may shower the child with expressions of love. A man who really wants to start fires may become a firefighter and spend his time putting them out. Generally, the stronger the impulse toward socially unacceptable behavior, the stronger the defense against it. It is interesting to note that a recent Vice President of the United States, known for his speeches on the importance of law and order, resigned to avoid being tried for taking bribes and falsifying his income tax returns. To "protest too much," then, is often a sign of reaction formation.

Some current women's fashions may represent a regression to childhood—that is, to a more innocent time of white ankle socks and low-heeled shoes, the first pocketbook for carrying the dimes and quarters that made up an allowance, and hair braided the way mother used to do it each morning before school.

Projection occurs when a person unknowingly attributes his or her own instinctual impulses or the threats of his or her own conscience to other people or to the external world. Such a process makes it easier to deal with the anxiety that arises from these internal impulses and threats. A woman who is growing tired of a lover but who is afraid to break off the relationship, perhaps because subconsciously she feels it would be too aggressive a move, may project her feelings onto her lover and begin to believe he is growing tired of her. If she expresses this belief, complaining over and over that the man does not love her anymore, she may induce him to break off the relationship—which both confirms her assertion and achieves her real goal. Another example of projection is the man who feels he is continually being short-changed by sales clerks. It is maybe he who wishes to cheat *them*. Similarly, people who constantly complain about the sexual promiscuity of the younger generation may be projecting fears concerning their own sexual impulses onto others.

FREUD'S PSYCHOSEXUAL STAGES OF DEVELOPMENT Freud was the first psychological theorist to emphasize the developmental aspects of personality and to stress the decisive role of infancy and childhood in establishing the basic character structure of an individual. Indeed, Freud believed that personality is rather well formed by the time a child enters school and that later growth consists of elaborating this basic structure. As we mentioned in Chapter 10, Freud believed that the child passes through a series of stages during the first five years of life. All the stages originate in the sexual instincts of the personality and are organized around the various erogenous zones of the body. The three early stages, collectively called the **pregenital** stage, and the approximate ages at which they occur, are the **oral** (birth to age one), the **anal** (one to two) and the **phallic** (three to five). Figure 18.2 shows possible relationships between a child's behavior in each of these stages and adult personality characteristics. A period of **latency** (from about six to eleven) follows, in which the child's libidinal dynamics are more or less stabilized. With adolescence, another eruption of libidinal forces upsets the stabilization of the latency period, but gradually comes under control as the adolescent moves into adulthood. The final stage of development, which occurs in adolescence and adulthood, is called the **genital** stage. Although Freud believed that these stages of personality

growth are of distinct kinds, he did not assume that there are any sharp breaks in time or abrupt transitions between stages. The organization of the adult personality represents contributions from all the stages.

DEVELOPMENT OF NEO-FREUDIAN THEORIES

Condensing Freud's rich and difficult theory into a few pages makes it seem terribly abstract, but his ideas came from concrete case studies of real people. Freud's psychoanalytic theory was painstakingly constructed and revised by checking and rechecking each interpretation until he was convinced that his observations and the theory fit together coherently. New data that could not be accounted for would lead him to revise his ideas, until he was sure his theory was internally consistent and amply supported by case studies.

Nevertheless, because Freud's observations were made behind a closed office door—either while listening to patients pour out their dreams, feelings, and free associations or while scrutinizing himself (as he did in astonishing detail, reserving the final half-hour of each day for self-analysis)—it is not surprising that other investigators failed to agree with everything Freud said. Even if we assume that Freud was a completely unbiased observer, we can raise questions about his particular sample of cases and his emphasis on himself as a source of data. For example, can we regard as typical Freud's strong attachment to his mother, an attractive woman half the age of Freud's father who remained close to her son as long as she lived? Isn't it possible—some would say likely—that other people's experiences would be very different from those of Freud and his patients?

Little wonder, then, that before Freud had even worked out his own ideas very clearly, two of his close associates, Carl Jung and Alfred Adler, broke away from him. Other students did the same throughout Freud's career. These disagreements are worth considering, for they foreshadow much of the later development of psychoanalytic theory.

JUNG'S ANALYTIC PSYCHOLOGY Carl Jung (1875–1961), who in 1913 founded his own school of

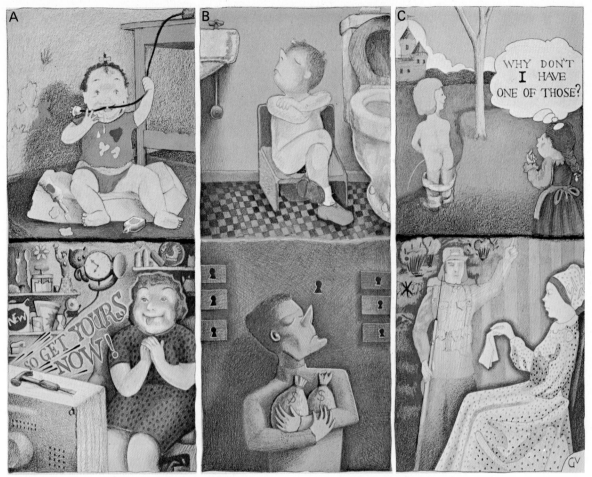

Figure 18.2 Possible behavior of a child at each of Freud's first three psychosexual stages, and the adult personality characteristics that might follow if, according to Freud, the child became fixated at one of these stages. (A) A baby girl obtains oral gratification by putting just about anything she can find into her mouth; as an adult, this individual exhibits a similar lack of discrimination about what she takes into herself. (B) A two-year-old in the anal stage thwarts his mother by refusing to release his feces; as an adult he obtains satisfaction by hoarding money. (C) A four-year-old girl in the phallic stage, observing that she lacks a penis, gives up her hopes of being like a man in any way. As an adult, she adopts a traditionally passive female sex role.

psychoanalysis called **analytic psychology**, had a view of personality vastly different from Freud's. Though he adopted many of Freud's concepts, Jung strongly disagreed with him on two important issues (Jung, 1967). First, Jung believed that there is a forward-going character to personality development: people are guided by their future aims as well as by their past experiences. Human beings try continuously to realize their full potential and to achieve complete unity among all aspects of their personalities. A person begins this effort by developing all parts of his or her personality. Jung called this process **individuation**. After achieving individuation, the person attempts to unite the contradictory aspects of his or her personality into a fully realized self. Though Jung realized that no one can attain perfect unity, he held that this goal is nevertheless the great driving force of all human behavior. Jung's theory, therefore, casts human beings in a more favorable light than Freud's: in addition to simply adapting to and displacing instinctual urges, people can act to develop their potential.

The second issue on which Jung disagreed with Freud was the nature of the unconscious. Like Freud, Jung recognized the great importance of unconscious influences on behavior, but he distinguished two levels of the unconscious. One level, the **personal unconscious**, is similar to the unconscious as depicted by Freud; it contains experiences the individual has repressed or forgotten. According to Jung, the contents of the personal unconscious can be returned to consciousness.

The other level, which Jung called the **collective**

413

unconscious, is a storehouse of memories and behavior patterns inherited from humanity's ancestral past. It is almost entirely detached from anything personal in the life of the individual. All human beings in all eras and all regions of the world have more or less the same collective unconscious. It consists of **archetypes**, innate predispositions to behave in certain ways. For example, because primitive humans were in close contact with wild animals and had evolved from lower animal forms, all human minds contain an inborn animal archetype (Jung called it "the shadow"), which predisposes us to fear animals. These archetypes, or "primordial images," were images that Jung observed coming to the surface in many different situations—in fables and myths, in dreams, in religious writings, in literature and art, and in the delusions of psychotics (Jung, 1972).

Jung's theory of personality, then, leads to a view of the human condition that differs quite sharply from that implied by Freud's theory. From Freud's perspective, adult life becomes a repetitious pattern of excitation and reduction of tension in which the person's needs and the means of satisfying them have been determined in the course of psychosexual development. Jung's theory, however, emphasizes continual growth and change. The ability to develop selfhood is the adult personality's lifelong task. This task requires continual growth and change and an assimilation of unconscious material by the conscious ego.

SOCIAL DETERMINANTS OF PERSONALITY

Both Freud and Jung emphasized biological factors in the development of personality, stressing that personality is chiefly a product of physical and biological needs and genetic endowment. Both asserted that environmental influences—even the family—are of secondary importance.

At just about the time Freud and Jung were proclaiming their theories, in the late nineteenth and early twentieth centuries, two new disciplines, sociology and anthropology, were revealing the enormous impact that social conditions can have on human behavior. Social scientists studying remote tribes and ancient civilizations discovered wide variations in behavior. They began to realize that environmental forces—such as economic conditions, education, religious beliefs, political ideas, and, most of all, other people—have great effects on individual behavior. A number of Freudian theorists responded to this intellectual and scientific challenge by developing modified psychoanalytic theories that acknowledged the social as well as the biological determinants of personality. Most prominent in this group were Alfred Adler, Karen Horney, Erich Fromm, and Erik Erikson.

ADLER'S INDIVIDUAL PSYCHOLOGY Alfred Adler (1870–1937), like Jung, was an intimate associate of Freud. In 1911 he broke away and founded his own school of **individual psychology**, incorporating social-psychological ideas.

Adler did not share Freud's belief that human beings are motivated primarily by sexual instincts. Instead, Adler claimed at first that it is the aggressive drive that is responsible for most human behavior. Gradually, however, he came to believe that it is not the aggressive impulse either, but the "will to power" that motivates human beings. Finally, Adler abandoned the "will to power" notion and adopted the idea of "the striving for superiority," which ultimately formed the kernel of his theory (Adler, 1930). By "superiority" Adler did not mean social distinction or dominance, but rather a quest for perfection. His theory had a strongly idealistic quality, asserting that "the great upward drive" is the moving force in human life. This conscious striving toward "completion" of the self carries the human being—indeed, the human species—from one stage of development to the next.

A sense of incompleteness or imperfection in any aspect of life gives rise to feelings of inferiority, according to Adler. These feelings are normal and originate in the childhood realization that adults can do things that children cannot. In their efforts to overcome their feelings of inferiority, some individuals succeed only in conveying to themselves, and perhaps to others, the *appearance* of strength and competence; because they have not improved their actual circumstances, their underlying feelings of inferiority remain. Adler coined the term **inferiority complex** to describe this situation (Adler, 1931). He distinguished between universal feelings of inferiority and the feelings and actions that characterize a person with an inferiority complex. Adler placed greater emphasis on conscious motivation than Freud did.

Another term originated by Adler is the idea of **social interest** (1931). He claimed that in addition to seeking individual perfection, each of us is born with a desire to strive for the public good. As we mature, provided that we receive proper guidance and education, personal ambition is replaced by social commitment. Our feelings of inferiority and incompleteness can be compensated for by working toward the common good. The goal of each person thus becomes the perfection of society. According to this theory, the neurotic person is one who continues to strive to achieve selfish goals such as self-esteem, power, and self-aggrandizement, whereas the normal person strives to achieve goals that are primarily social in character.

HORNEY'S THEORY OF BASIC ANXIETY AND BASIC HOSTILITY Karen Horney (1885–1952), a German-born psychoanalyst, sought to modify basic psychoanalytic theory. She accepted such concepts as the importance of early experience, unconscious motivation, and unconscious defenses, but she challenged Freud's biological or instinctive approach to personality development. For Horney, motivation and conflict, even though unconscious, are based on social factors, not on the interplay between biologically based needs and the environment (1945). She attempted to make psychoanalysis a richer and more workable interpretation of human behavior by focusing on the social determinants of conflict and on how neurotic behavior affects social relationships.

While Freud based his theory of human personality on sexual and aggressive instincts, and Adler on the innate striving for perfection, Horney's theory revolved around what she called "basic anxiety and basic hostility." **Basic anxiety** arises because the child feels isolated and helpless in a potentially hostile world. Young children, discovering that they are weak and small in a land of giants, soon learn that they are utterly dependent on parents for all their needs and safety. Warm, loving, and dependable parents create a sense of security that is reassuring to the child, resulting in normal development. If the parents produce severe disturbance in a child's sense of security—for example, by indifference, erratic behavior, disparaging attitudes, or a lack of warmth—the child's feeling of helplessness is increased; this gives rise to basic anxiety. So, unlike Freud and Adler, whose views of personality dynamics and development were based on the concept of inborn instincts, Horney regarded basic anxiety as a result of social and environmental stress.

In Horney's view, **basic hostility** generally accompanies basic anxiety, and arises from resentment over parental indifference, inconsistency, and interference. But this hostility cannot be expressed directly, because the child needs and fears the parents and must have their love. The repression of this hostility creates feelings of increased unworthiness and anxiety. The child is torn between hostility toward the parents and dependence upon them. The conflict between basic anxiety and basic hostility leads the child, and later the neurotic adult, to adopt one of three modes of behavior and social interaction: (1) moving toward others, (2) moving against others, or (3) moving away from others.

Someone who moves *toward* other people becomes compliant, a kind of doormat, always anxious to please. Such a person seeks security by subjugating himself or herself in order to gain affection and approval. This self-effacing behavior may buy security, but at the cost of total repression of basic hostility. It leads to psychological martyrdom and intense unhappiness.

The individual who moves *against* others is attempting to find security through domination, saying essentially, "You can't hurt me if I have power over you." This resolution of conflict gives vent to some of that person's basic hostility, but it suppresses any acknowledgment of basic anxiety. The person avoids anything that may connote helplessness or loss of complete control.

The goal of the person who moves *away* from other people is to find security by becoming aloof and withdrawn, never allowing close relationships with others. People who adopt this solution protect themselves from harm, but in doing so they give up the possibility of growth and change.

In the normal personality, Horney believed, all three of these modes of behavior are integrated and used in appropriate circumstances. The individual sometimes moves toward other people to gain nurture and affection; sometimes moves against others to establish dominance and attain goals; and sometimes withdraws from others to attain a certain integrity and serenity. It is only when one of these three ways of relating to other people is the *only* framework for all a person's social relationships that it becomes neurotic. The neurotic personality is above all characterized by compulsive rigidity, the repetition of one particular mode of behavior no matter what the situation (1937).

The overt neurotic behavior described by Horney is often identical to that observed by Freud: rigid, obsessional actions, unconscious hostility toward parents, jealousy of siblings. Horney differed radically from Freud, however, in explaining the moti-

The Feminist Response to Freud

Over the last decade there has been an increasing clamor that Freudian theory is degrading to women. Nor is it difficult to see why, for Freud's writings are liberally sprinkled with passing references to female inferiority. The basis on which his conceptualization of this inferiority—and indeed of female psychology as a whole—rests is the penis: the fact that boys have one and girls don't. According to Freud, the moment a child notices this basic anatomical difference, that moment he or she begins to become, psychologically as well as biologically, a male or a female. For the little girl, the realization that she lacks this fine piece of equipment gives rise to an ineradicable jealousy, the famous "penis envy." And this is the beginning of her long slide into inferiority. As Freud puts it, "The discovery that she is castrated is a turning point in a girl's growth" (1974, p. 105). He might have said "*the* turning point," for starting with the notion of penis deprivation and penis envy, Freud constructs an elegant chain of reasoning leading directly to female inferiority.

The process may be summarized as follows. Because she lacks a penis, the girl's Oedipal conflict takes a form different from the boy's. Already "castrated," she is barred from the healthy process of experiencing and then overcoming castration anxiety. Furthermore, her choice of her father as a love object is a negative rather than a positive choice. Like the boy, she originally preferred her mother, but once she discovers that her mother, like her, is an amputee and is even responsible for bringing her into the world so poorly equipped, she turns to her father out of resentment against her mother. Thus her Oedipal experience lacks both the stable heterosexual orientation and the cathartic resolution of the boy's Oedipal crisis. And as a result, her superego (the fruit of a successfully resolved Oedipus complex) is stunted in its growth. Throughout her adult life she remains narcissistic, vain, lacking in a fully developed sense of justice, and above all, envious. In short, she is morally inferior because she can never overcome either her bitterness over her castration or the need to compensate for her paltry sexual equipment. Furthermore, she is culturally inferior, since the ability to contribute to the advance of civilization is dependent on the mechanism of sublimation, which in turn depends on a strong, mature superego—the very thing she lacks. According to Freud, there is only one contribution that women have made to civilization, the art of weaving, a practice unconsciously motivated by woman's desire to conceal her "genital deficiency" (1974, p. 111).

Thus, while men, legitimized by their penises, go out to do the work of justice and civilization, women must swallow their disgrace and comfort themselves with substitutes. As a child, a woman can comfort herself sexually with her clitoris, but in order to become psychologically mature, she must abandon this "penis equivalent" (1974, p. 97) in favor of "the truly feminine vagina" (1974, p. 97). (Hence the Freudian notion, recently disputed by Masters and Johnson, that there is a difference between clitoral and vaginal orgasms and that the psychologically mature woman has made the transition to the latter.) The woman's reward for transferring her sexual sensitivity from clitoris to vagina is the ultimate penis substitute, a baby. And if the baby should turn out to be a boy, "who brings the longed-for penis with him" (1974, p. 107), all the better.

To sum up: woman is morally feeble, culturally unproductive, and somehow "other"—a variation on the standard of masculinity, a deviation from the norm, or, in the words of Simone de Beauvoir, the "second sex" (1961). It should be carefully noted, however, that Freud does not claim that women are born with this inferiority. Though his wording often suggests that he too, like the little girl, sees the penis as an exceedingly desirable thing to have and considers the lack of one to be cause for mourning, what he actually states is that it is the little girl's *perception of herself* as castrated, and her consequent envy, that plunges her into inferiority.

The opposition to this theory was first mounted in 1926 by Karen Horney, who retorted that Freud was in a poor position to know what little girls think. According to Horney (1967), it is not little girls who perceive their condition as degraded. Rather, it is little boys—and the men they eventually become—who see their penisless counterparts as woefully mutilated and deficient and who thus have created the self-fulfilling prophecy that has doomed womankind to inferiority. More recent feminist writers have taken this argument several steps further, claiming that Freud's theory

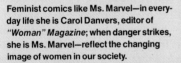
Feminist comics like Ms. Marvel—in everyday life she is Carol Danvers, editor of *"Woman" Magazine*; when danger strikes, she is Ms. Marvel—reflect the changing image of women in our society.

was merely the reflection of an age-old cultural bias against women and that this theory actually constitutes a devious attempt to justify the continuance of male supremacy.

In short, feminists contend that Freud was simply one more member of the vast male conspiracy aimed, whether consciously or not, at keeping woman in her place. Indeed, not just Freud, but the entire mental health profession appears increasingly suspect to feminist writers. Their basic claim is simply that for thousands of years men have had the privilege of deciding who is crazy and who is not, and that their decisions have been based on sex-role stereotypes. Thus, for example, in reading about the sixteenth and seventeenth centuries, we see a great deal about witch burnings but very little about sorcerer burnings. According to Zilboorg and Henry (1941), the witch burnings of the late Renaissance actually constituted a pathological outbreak of misogyny and antieroticism. Any woman who stepped out of line was perceived as a diabolical threat: "Never in the history of humanity was woman more systematically degraded. She paid for the fall of Eve sevenfold" (pp. 161–162). And according to Phyllis Chesler (1972), woman is still paying. She is born into a society which automatically expects her to be passive, emotional, sexually fearful, and dependent. If she rejects her role assignment, she is either declared mentally disturbed or is made so unhappy by the society that she often in fact becomes mentally disturbed. In either case, she may then be handed over to the mental health profession, where she is diagnosed and treated by males. And her treatment consists, Chesler claims, of retraining her to accept her biologically ordained role.

The research methods on which Chesler based the conclusions stated in her book *Women and Madness* (1972) have been widely criticized. It cannot be disputed, however, that the most influential of all psychological theories, that of Freud, was based on the assumption that male biology and male psychology constitute the norm. Nor can it be denied that the vast majority of those who prescribe treatment for the mentally ill are males. Until this latter situation is corrected, whatever women have to say about what it means to be a woman is likely to go on being muffled by whatever men have to say on the subject.

Horney on Basic Anxiety and Hostility

The typical conflict leading to anxiety in a child is that between dependency on the parents . . . and hostile impulses against the parents. Hostility may be aroused in a child in many ways: by the parents' lack of respect for him; by unreasonable demands and prohibitions; by injustice; by unreliability; by suppression of criticism; by the parents dominating him and ascribing these tendencies to love. . . . If a child, in addition to being dependent on his parents, is grossly or subtly intimidated by them and hence feels that any expression of hostile impulses against them endangers his security, then the existence of such hostile impulses is bound to create anxiety. . . . The resulting picture may look exactly like what Freud describes as the Oedipus complex: passionate clinging to one parent and jealousy toward the other or toward anyone interfering with the claim of exclusive possession. . . . *But the dynamic structure of these attachments is entirely different from what Freud conceives as the Oedipus complex. They are an early manifestation of neurotic conflicts rather than a primarily sexual phenomenon.*

From Karen Horney, *The Neurotic Personality in Our Time.* New York: Norton, 1939.

---

vation for this behavior. She reinterpreted the Oedipus complex, for example, stripping away the sexual interpretation and substituting one based on interpersonal relations. A typical Oedipal situation, in which a child passionately clings to one parent and expresses jealousy or covert aggression against the other parent, Horney viewed as a result of the interplay between the child's anxiety and hostility (see box). To achieve security and to cope with basic anxiety and hostility, a little boy may turn to his mother for comfort, especially if his father is the parent who arouses his hostility by dominating him or by denying the gratification of his wishes. If the boy finds relief from anxiety, that relationship with his mother is strengthened. Anything that threatens it or competes for the mother's attention (primarily the father) becomes an object of jealousy or covert aggression.

Horney, then, saw the same phenomenon Freud saw, but she explained it as a product of social relationships rather than as an expression of innate sexual and aggressive instincts. Similarly, both Freud and Horney observed strong feelings of inferiority in many women; but Horney rejected Freud's theory of penis envy (see Chapter 10), claiming instead that these feelings are based on dependency and a lack of confidence resulting from women's social experiences. For further discussion of the reaction of Horney and other feminist writers to Freud's view of women, see the Special Feature on pages 416-417.

FROMM'S "ESCAPE FROM FREEDOM" Erich Fromm (b. 1900) bases his theory of personality on interpersonal relationships set in a historical context. Taking his fundamental ideas from both Freud and Karl Marx, Fromm distinguishes between animal nature—the biochemical mechanisms for physical survival—and human nature—our ability to reason and to know ourselves. Reason and self-knowledge inevitably set human beings apart from the rest of the animal kingdom. The freedom stemming from human nature can lead us to great heights of creative accomplishment. But the fear of isolation and loneliness involved in such freedom may lead a person to shrink from this part of his or her nature.

On the social level, shrinking from freedom leads to mindless conformity and a tendency to submit to dictators and totalitarian governments. On a personal level, it leads to psychotic withdrawal and self-defeating behavior. According to Fromm, we must utilize our freedom in order to fulfill our human nature, uniting with others in an egalitarian spirit of love and shared work (1941).

Fromm identifies five basic needs that arise from the conditions of human existence: a *need for relatedness*, which stems from the stark fact that, in becoming human, we were torn from the animal's primary union with nature; a *need for transcendence* (an urge to overcome animal nature and to become creative); a *need for rootedness* (for belonging to the human family); a *need for personal identity* (for being distinctive and unique); and, finally, a *need for a frame of reference* that will give stability and consistency to the world.

Fromm believes that the ways in which these needs express themselves are determined by the social structure in which a person lives. An individual's personality develops in accordance with the opportunities offered by a particular society. In a capitalist society, for example, a person may gain a sense of personal identity by becoming rich or may develop a feeling of rootedness by becoming a dependable employee in a large company. In order for a society to function properly, Fromm points out, it is essential that children's characters be shaped to fit the needs of that society. Thus, in a capitalist system, the desire to save money must be instilled in people so that capital will be available to enable the economy to expand.

By making demands upon human beings that are contrary to their nature, however, society often prevents them from fulfilling the basic conditions of their existence. For example, when a society changes in any important respect—as when the factory system displaced the individual artisan during the Industrial Revolution—the prevailing social character no longer fits the demands of the new society. As a result, although people are free to move in new directions, many feel a sense of alienation and despair.

One of the greatest dangers inherent in the attempt to escape alienation and despair is that it also involves an escape from the freedom that accompanies these feelings (Fromm, 1941). Fromm's warning not to abandon the opportunities of freedom out of raw fear of freedom itself is one of the hallmarks of his thinking on personality. For this reason he is called a humanitarian socialist. Optimistic about the possibility of developing a society that does not inhibit personal freedom, he firmly asserts that it is an essential part of human nature to take an active role in determining the future. He thus differs strongly with Freud, who saw human beings primarily as subject to biological laws that determine a destiny they passively accept.

ERIKSON'S PSYCHOSOCIAL VIEW OF PERSONALITY Of all the neo-Freudians, none has had more influence on current thinking about personality development than Erik Erikson (b. 1902). Like Jung and Adler, Erikson studied with Freud. His theory of personality development is grounded in Freud's psychoanalytic method, but extends beyond it (Hall and Lindzey, 1978).

Erikson conceives of personality development in **psychosocial** terms. He believes, with Freud, that the early years, during which the child learns to reconcile biological drives with social demands, establish the individual's basic orientation to the world (trust vs. mistrust, autonomy vs. shame and doubt, initiative vs. guilt). However, Erikson does not agree with Freud that personality is determined, once and for all, in the first five years of life. He places equal emphasis on the child's efforts to master the skills valued by society, on the adolescent's striving to achieve a sense of identity in that society, on the young adult's quest for intimacy, and on the mature person's desire to guide younger generations and thus contribute to society. Depending on how an individual negotiates these challenges, old age may bring a sense of integrity or despair. For Erikson, personality development is a lifelong process.

In working out these "eight ages of man" (see Figure 18.3), Erikson expands Freud's concept of identification. He argues that the ego is not content simply to assimilate the values of a parent or other admired person, but strives to form an integrated, autonomous, unique "self," which Erikson calls the **ego identity.** He has suggested that establishing an ego identity may be especially difficult in complex

Figure 18.3 Erikson's representation of life as a succession of psychosocial crises coming to the fore at successive biological stages of life. Erikson's theory is an extension and expansion of Freud's; Erikson's first four stages correspond to Freud's first four psychosexual stages. Also, like Freud, Erikson considers that the resolutions of conflicts at each stage have lasting effects on personality. (After Erikson, 1950.)

Stage	1	2	3	4	5	6	7	8
Maturity								Ego Integrity vs. Despair
Adulthood							Generativity vs. Stagnation	
Young Adulthood						Intimacy vs. Isolation		
Puberty and Adolescence					Identity vs. Role Confusion			
Latency				Industry vs. Inferiority				
Locomotor-Genital			Initiative vs. Guilt					
Muscular-Anal		Autonomy vs. Shame, Doubt						
Oral Sensory	Basic Trust vs. Mistrust							

societies such as our own, which present the individual with a staggering array of choices in styles of living. In other kinds of societies, tradition prescribes the roles the individual will play as an adult. The young person can count on living much as his father or her mother did, among relatives and neighbors known since childhood. In the United States it is up to the individual to "make something of himself." What, where, and how are open questions; there are few guides. Erikson coined the term **identity crisis** to describe the intense struggle waged by adolescents in Western societies to achieve individuality and coherence.

As this concept suggests, Erikson believes that the culture and times into which a person is born have a crucial effect on personality development. Psychosocial conflicts are universal and inevitable. However, at some point a society either eases its members' transition from one stage to another or exploits their fears and doubts. In other words, a society can reinforce growth or discourage it. A person's ego identity, Erikson argues, is grounded in cultural identity (1950).

The effort to create a bridge between the study of individuals and the study of societies led Erikson in two rather unorthodox directions. He worked among America's Sioux Indians to learn how historical circumstances and cultural differences affect child-rearing practices and the development of personality. And he was a pioneer in the field of **psychohistory**, the application of psychoanalytic principles to the study of historical figures. His biography of Martin Luther (1968), for example, focuses on the Protestant reformer's identity crisis. His admiring biography of India's great nonviolent political leader, Mahatma Gandhi, is a psychoanalytic interpretation not only of the man but also of his culture and times. The accompanying quotations from the latter book, *Gandhi's Truth: On the Origins of Militant Nonviolence* (1969), appear in a section titled "A Personal Word," which Erikson was moved to write when he found that his insight as a psychoanalyst made it impossible to ignore certain flaws in Gandhi's character that might otherwise have been overlooked.

In this chapter we have examined the views of personality developed by Sigmund Freud and five neo-Freudian psychoanalytic theorists—Jung, Adler, Horney, Fromm, and Erikson. In Chapter 19 we will consider the insights into the nature of human personality provided by adherents of other major theoretical approaches.

Erikson on Gandhi

. . . I must now confess that a few times in your work (and often in the literature inspired by you) I have come across passages which almost brought *me* to the point where I felt unable to continue writing *this* book because I seemed to sense the presence of a kind of untruth in the very protestation of truth; of something unclean when all the words spelled out an unreal purity; and above all, of displaced violence where nonviolence was the professed issue.

. . . you seem either unaware of—or want to wish or pray away—an ambivalence, a coexistence of love and hate, which must become conscious in those who work for peace.

It is not enough any more—not after the appearance of your Western contemporary Freud— to be a watchful moralist. For we now have detailed insights into our inner ambiguities, ambivalences, and instinctual conflicts; and only an additional leverage of truth based on self-knowledge promises to give us freedom in the full light of conscious day, whereas in the past, moralist terrorism succeeded only in driving our worst proclivities underground, to remain there until riotous conditions of uncertainty or chaos would permit them to emerge redoubled.

You, Mahatmaji, love the story of that boy prince who would not accept the claim of his father, the Demon King, to a power greater than God's, not even after the boy had been exposed to terrible tortures. At the end he was made to embrace a red-hot metal pillar; but out of this suggestive object stepped God, half lion and half man, and tore the king to pieces.

. . . we must admit that you could not possibly have known of the power of that ambivalence which we have now learned to understand in case histories and life histories. . . . It is, therefore, not without compassion that I must point out that your lifelong insistence on the "innocence" (meaning sexlessness) of children is matched only by your inability to recognize the Demon King in yourself.

Source: From Erik H. Erikson, *Gandhi's Truth: On the Origins of Militant Nonviolence.* New York: W. W. Norton, 1969.

Summary

1. **Personality** theorists differ widely in their approaches and conclusions, but they each address two key issues: the consistency of an individual's behavior from one situation to the next, and the differences in the behavior of individuals confronting the same situation.

2. Sigmund Freud's **psychoanalytic theory** was the first formal theory of personality, and it has been by far the most influential.

   A. Freud's concept of the **unconscious** is based on his study of the memories, wishes, and fears that were revealed through **free association**, in which patients found relief from their symptoms by talking out their emotional conflicts. **Psychoanalysis** is the name he gave to the therapeutic process of attempting to bring material from the unconscious into the conscious mind of the patient.

   B. For the data on which he based his theory, Freud relied primarily on the technique of free association. He also drew on dreams, jokes, and accidents to identify unconscious conflicts. Dreams have both a **manifest content** (what the dreamer remembers) and a **latent content** (what is revealed through free association and analysis of the dream).

   C. Freud believed that his theory of personality explained the behavior of all people. According to his theory, personality consists of three interacting agencies: the id, the ego, and the superego.

      1. The *id* is a pool of biological drives, or instincts, with which the infant is born. The energy of the id is divided between *Eros*, the life instinct generated by the **libido**, and *Thanatos*, the death instinct. The tendency of the id to devote itself to the immediate reduction of tension is called the **pleasure principle**. The id is the energy source for the ego and the superego.

      2. The **ego**, which develops after the age of approximately six months, is the "executive agency" of personality. First it mediates between the id and reality; later it mediates between the id and the superego. The ego controls the individual's actions and manipulates the environment according to the **reality principle**, which is based on the organism's concern for safety.

      3. The **superego** is the personality's conscience, concerned with the pursuit of moral goals. The superego emerges from the resolution of the Oedipus complex in males and the Electra complex in females, as the child **internalizes** the moral standards of the parent of the same sex. The superego impels the individual not toward realistic goals but toward an **ego ideal** of moral perfection.

   D. Freud believed that nearly all human behavior is directed toward resolving inner conflicts and restoring **homeostasis**, or equilibrium.

   E. Freud conceived of instincts as having four characteristic features: a source, an aim, an object, and an impetus.

      1. The source and aim remain constant throughout a person's life.

      2. Freud believed psychic energy can be **displaced**, or transferred, from the original object to a variety of substitute objects. **Sublimation** is a displacement that produces higher cultural achievement.

   F. Anxiety is a state of psychic pain that signals the ego that danger is at hand. Freud distinguished three types of anxiety: reality anxiety, moral anxiety, and neurotic anxiety. **Defense mechanisms** are strategies for concealing the source of anxiety from the self and the world.

      1. **Repression** is a defense mechanism that keeps threatening thoughts and memories in the unconscious.

      2. **Fixation** is a temporary or permanent halt in development, occurring as a response to anxiety associated with the next stage of development.

      3. **Regression** is a return to an earlier stage of development in response to some threat.

      4. **Reaction formation** is the replacement in a person's consciousness of the feeling or impulse that causes anxiety by its opposite.

      5. **Projection** is the unknowing attribution of one's own impulses or fears onto others.

G. Freud was the first to stress the decisive role of infancy and childhood in determining a person's basic personality structure. He believed that a child passes through a series of stages that originate in the sexual instincts. The three early stages, collectively called the **pregenital stage**, are the **oral**, the **anal**, and the **phallic**. A period of **latency** is followed by an adolescent eruption of libidinal forces, which stabilize in the **genital** stage.

3. Carl Jung, an associate of Freud, was one of the first to break away from him in disagreement with his theories. Jung's **analytic psychology** diverged from Freud's theory on two major points. First, Jung believed that there is a forward-going character to personality development based on **individuation**, the development of all parts of the personality. Also, he conceived of the unconscious as having two levels: the **personal unconscious**, which is similar to Freud's concept, and the **collective unconscious**, consisting of **archetypes**, universal themes and behavior patterns that cause all humans to act in certain similar ways.

4. The emphasis of both Freud and Jung on biological factors in the development of personality was challenged by sociology and anthropology in the late nineteenth and early twentieth centuries. A number of Freudian theorists developed modified psychoanalytic theories that acknowledged both biological and social determinants of personality.
A. Alfred Adler's **individual psychology** emphasized the drive toward perfection as the highest motivation of human beings. Adler believed that a sense of incompleteness originates in childhood, and the inability to overcome this feeling results in an **inferiority complex**. Adler thought that as people mature, they will naturally work toward the social good if they have received appropriate education and guidance.

B. Karen Horney believed that motivation and conflict are based on social factors. Her theory of personality is based on the concepts of **basic anxiety**, which arises out of a child's sense of helplessness, and **basic hostility**, which arises from resentment against one's parents and generally accompanies basic anxiety. Three possible modes of behavior develop from unexpressed hostility: moving toward others, moving against others, and moving away from others. In a normal person, these modes are integrated and each is used when appropriate.

C. Erich Fromm's theory of personality is based on interpersonal relationships set in a historical context. He believes that there are five basic needs that arise from the conditions of human existence: the need for relatedness, for transcendence, for rootedness, for personal identity, and for a frame of reference. The ways in which these needs are expressed are determined by the social structure in which the individual lives. That social structure can warp its citizens' basic character. Fromm warns that the attempt to escape the resulting alienation and despair can—but should not—involve an attempt to "escape from freedom."

D. Erik Erikson, the neo-Freudian whose theory of personality development has been the most influential, conceives of personality in **psychosocial** terms. He says that personality development is a lifelong process, during which the individual works through a series of eight stages to achieve, in old age, a sense of either integrity or despair. He believes that the ego strives to form an integrated, autonomous, unique "self" or **ego identity**. Erikson coined the term **identity crisis** to describe the struggle of Western adolescents to achieve individuality. Erikson pioneered the field of **psychohistory** in an effort to bridge the study of individuals and the study of societies.

RECOMMENDED READINGS

HALL, CALVIN S., and GARDNER LINDZEY. *Theories of Personality.* 3rd ed. New York: Wiley, 1978. This new edition of the classic secondary source on theories of personality includes a new chapter on contemporary psychoanalytic theory, with an excellent presentation of Erik Erikson's work, and a new chapter on Eastern psychology and personality theory.

LEVY, LEON H. *Conceptions of Personality.* New York: Random House, 1970. Examines issues in personality theory rather than outlining theories of personality. Integrates a number of contemporary lines of research.

MADDI, SALVATORE R. *Personality Theories: A Comparative Analysis.* 2nd ed. Homewood, Ill.: Dorsey Press, 1972. Classifies personality theorists according to whether their basic assumption relates to *conflict, fulfillment,* or *consistency.* Examines what the theorists have to say about the core and periphery of personality. Presents research on each position and draws conclusions about their strengths and weaknesses.

MADDI, SALVATORE R. (ed.). *Perspectives on Personality: A Comparative Approach.* Boston: Little, Brown, 1971. A book of readings by or about each major theorist discussed in the Maddi textbook cited above.

MAHL, GEORGE F. *Psychological Conflict and Defense.* New York: Harcourt Brace Jovanovich, 1971. A clear exposition of psychoanalytic theory, including both clinical and research evidence for the theory's main hypotheses. (This paperback is a section excerpted from a four-part personality textbook by Irving L. Janis, George F. Mahl, Jerome Kagan, and Robert R. Holt titled *Personality: Dynamics, Development, and Assessment.* New York: Harcourt Brace Jovanovich, 1969.)

MONTE, CHRISTOPHER F. *Beneath the Mask: An Introduction to Theories of Personality.* New York: Praeger, 1977. This book emphasizes individual theorists and presents each person's theory in extensive detail, with many quotations from original source material.

WOLLHEIM, RICHARD. *Sigmund Freud.* New York: Viking, 1971. A fresh look at Freud's writings. Contains basic biographical information, a history of the development of psychoanalytic theory, and a careful examination of major concepts.

CHAPTER NINETEEN

BEHAVIORISTIC, HUMANISTIC, AND TRAIT THEORIES OF PERSONALITY

Psychologists dealing with theories of personality tend to deal with human beings in general. Individual cases can, however, be extremely puzzling. People's personalities do occasionally change, sometimes late in life, and they begin to think and act as we would not have judged they were capable of thinking and acting. Back in the 1930s, there was a motion picture called *Gabriel over the White House*, in which Walter Huston played a party hack who had somehow managed to get himself elected President of the United States. Through some supernatural intervention he was suddenly turned into a capable and forceful man and surprised everyone by becoming a great executive.

Just fiction, we might say, just wishful dreaming. A personality once fixed will not suddenly reverse itself and show hidden depths. Warren Gamaliel Harding was a charming, handsome small-town editor who was pushed into politics, rose to be Senator and then, in 1920, became President of the United States. One would have supposed from the general feckless incompetence he always displayed that he would make a perfectly rotten president. And so he did!

Then there was Chester Alan Arthur. Arthur was a lawyer who, in the days just before the Civil War, joined the newly formed Republican party and became a ward-heeling hack. He eventually rose to the position of chief henchman of the unscrupulous Republican party boss, Roscoe Conkling. Arthur was rewarded with the post of Collector of the Port of New York. This made it possible for him to allow Republican wheel-horses to fatten themselves at the public trough in a riot of incompetency and graft. He was eventually removed from his position when the stench grew too strong to ignore.

Then in 1880, James A. Garfield was nominated by the Republicans for the presidency over the opposition of Conkling and his following. To appease Conkling, Chester Arthur was given the vice-presidential nomination. The Republicans won the election and Vice-President Arthur remained Conkling's man, backing him loyally in all his disputes with President Garfield.

On July 2, 1881, Garfield was shot by an assassin. On September 19 he died, and Chester Alan Arthur, cheap politician *extraordinaire*, became President of the United States.

What do you think happened? To the surprise of everyone in the United States, Arthur did a right-about-face. Suddenly, and without warning, he proved himself an honest and forceful man, who bowed neither to Conkling nor to anyone else. He fought the bosses, exposed corruption, appointed competent men, and presented an administration of remarkable integrity.

Most of all he surprised the crooked politicians, who had expected a field day with Arthur as President. In 1884, he had no chance of being renominated. Too honest!

Isaac Asimov

Not all psychologists accept the psychoanalytic view of personality discussed in Chapter 18. Some critics think that psychoanalytic theory is not based firmly enough on empirical research, while others think that it is negativistic and fails to stress the humane side of personality development.

In uniting against the psychoanalytic view, however, these critics have not united with one another. A number of nonpsychoanalytic theories of personality have been developed. Like psychoanalytic theories, these approaches to personality are concerned with two key questions: Why do different individuals behave differently in the same situation? And why does an individual's behavior remain fairly consistent in different situations? According to their responses to these questions, most nonpsychoanalytic theories may be classified into one of three groups: behavioristic approaches, humanistic approaches, and trait theories. In this chapter we shall consider these views of human personality.

Briefly, **behavioristic approaches** are those based mainly on principles of learning and reinforcement, as discussed in Chapter 4. Behaviorism views the development and functioning of the personality as a set of learned responses, not as the result of the innate forces of the id, ego, and superego. **Humanistic approaches** emphasize the potential of human beings for growth, creativity, and spontaneity. Although humanists recognize biological needs and needs for safety, they reject the behaviorist idea that people respond only to reward and punishment. **Trait theories** make even more modest claims about human nature. They say simply that human behavior can be organized according to characteristics that are called traits—for example, aggression, friendliness, and honesty. People differ from one another in the amount of each trait exhibited. Thus, a person who is always honest has more of this particular trait than one who sometimes lies.

As we shall see, all three of these approaches are alike in deemphasizing unconscious, destructive forces as determinants of human behavior. They give much more importance to observable behavior, learning, and conscious cognitive processes than do the psychoanalytic theories.

BEHAVIORISTIC APPROACHES

American psychology has been concerned with animal and human learning since the beginning of this

century. Some of the most famous American psychologists—among them Edward L. Thorndike, John B. Watson, Edward Tolman, Clark Hull, and B. F. Skinner—are known for their research on learning. Naturally, when Freud's ideas became known in American universities, learning theorists took notice and tried to assimilate his work into their own.

DOLLARD AND MILLER'S PSYCHODYNAMIC BEHAVIOR THEORY The most ambitious attempt at assimilation was made during the 1940s at Yale University by John Dollard and Neal Miller. Their approach is called psychodynamic behavior theory by some psychologists because it represents an effort to deal with the psychodynamic phenomena identified by Freud in terms that are familiar to behavioristic learning theorists.

Dollard and Miller (1950) used the term **drives**, roughly equivalent to Freud's *instincts*, to refer to the motivational basis for behavior. Like instincts, drives are states of arousal that require some satisfaction or reduction. Dollard and Miller introduced the term **response** to refer to any act or thought related to the satisfaction or reduction of a drive. Hunger, then, is a *drive* that is reduced by the *response* of eating. They used the term **cue** to refer to any feature of the environment that indicates that a particular drive can be satisfied or reduced then and there. If someone is hungry, a sign advertising a restaurant is a cue that is useful in guiding that person's behavior toward the reduction of hunger. Dollard and Miller used the term **reinforcement** to describe the strengthening of the tendency to emit a given response once it has successfully reduced or satisfied a drive. The reinforced response can thus be expected to reappear when the drive is aroused again.

These terms used by Dollard and Miller do not translate directly into Freud's concepts, but in combination they can be used to explain some of the same phenomena that Freud identified. Take, for example, displaced aggression. According to Freud, the child, born with an aggressive instinct, searches for a way to release aggressive energy. But, being afraid of attacking a parent, who is often the real object of anger, the child displaces the aggression by fighting with a younger sibling or talking back to a teacher. Dollard and Miller would explain this displacement phenomenon in a somewhat different manner. According to their **frustration-aggression hypothesis**, the aggressive drive is aroused by the thwarting of progress toward some important goal. The child is therefore motivated to commit aggression against the frustrating agent. If, however, the frustrating agent is a powerful figure against whom it is dangerous to express aggression, such as a mother or father, the child will displace the aggression onto other people whose cue value is similar to that of the real target—perhaps a sibling or teacher (Dollard et al., 1939).

Freudian theory explains behavior as a response to internal stimuli—aggressive drives, for example—while behaviorist theory explains it in terms of external stimuli—the frustration of a goal-oriented response. Moreover, Dollard and Miller's theory has social applications that Freud's psychoanalytic theory does not. They believe that displacement can

and will be learned even by large segments of a population if the response to the new target in some way satisfies or reduces the drive that underlies the response. Thus, in times of economic depression or political unrest, when the real target for the anger and aggression of the populace is unknown or too powerful to attack directly, aggression is displaced toward "outsiders" or a minority group. If this aggression is reinforced—if it satisfactorily reduces the aggressive drive—it will be continued. This kind of scapegoating becomes a learned and almost institutionalized response, as was the case with the anti-Semitism of Nazi Germany and the anticommunism of the McCarthy era in the United States during the 1950s.

Miller (1944) also showed how something resem-

According to Dollard and Miller, people who join organizations like the Ku Klux Klan are displacing their anger at something unknown or too powerful toward minority groups.

bling neurotic conflict can be learned. Using rats, he reproduced what Freud had identified in humans as approach-avoidance conflicts, in which people want something very much but are afraid to admit this desire or to express it in behavior. Miller first allowed a hungry rat to run down an alley to get to a food tray. While the rat was eating, it received a brief but painful electric shock. Later, when the rat was placed in starting position at one end of the alley, it began running toward the food but suddenly stopped in the middle of the alley and vacillated, as if torn between the desire for food and the desire to avoid the painful shock. In the rat, as in humans, conflict occurred when avoidance and approach tendencies had equal strength (see Figure 19.1).

Dollard and Miller agreed with Freud that most conflicts arise because of social or cultural restric-

In the television show *Mary Hartman Mary Hartman,* the heroine often reduced her anxieties by an overzealous attention to cleaning her kitchen.

tions on the expression of impulses. If a person comes to have several unresolved conflicts between basic needs and socially induced anxiety, he or she may show the kinds of symptoms observed by Freud. Dollard and Miller also discussed defense mechanisms, which they regarded as anxiety-reducing responses. Repression, for example, they called "learned not-thinking": a young woman who feels anxious whenever she thinks about having sexual intercourse with her boy friend may be rewarded (by experiencing a reduction of anxiety) for shifting her thoughts to something less threatening, such as cleaning her apartment. In terms of learning theory, the habit of "not-thinking" about a particular topic is reinforced because it relieves an unpleasant state—the anxiety (Miller, 1948, 1959).

Dollard and Miller's approach was important for two reasons. First, it showed that psychoanalytic concepts need not remain inaccessible to American researchers, even those who work primarily with animals. Second, it helped pave the way for behavior therapy—a set of procedures, based on learning principles, for changing neurotic and psychotic behavior. (Behavior therapy is discussed in detail in Chapter 24.) Many psychologists have criticized Dollard and Miller for drawing analogies between rats and humans: dreams and other symbolic processes, these critics point out, are not likely to be illuminated by animal research. Yet Dollard and Miller's psychodynamic behavior theory has had an important effect on the research techniques employed to study the psychology of personality. The experiments they conducted made it clear to other theorists that even theories of personality based on nonobservable dynamic processes can be subjected to experimental tests. And they demonstrated convincingly that quite simple concepts from learning theory can be combined to explain complex human behavior.

SKINNER'S RADICAL BEHAVIORISM Although his radical behaviorism is not a full-fledged theory of personality, B. F. Skinner has had a great impact on personality theory. Unlike Dollard and Miller, Skinner rejects such concepts as drive because they cannot be directly observed and thus do not lend themselves to scientific examination (Skinner, 1975). Moreover, Skinner sees no need for a general concept of personality structure. He focuses instead on a *functional* analysis of behavior: precisely what is the reinforcement contingency that is caus-

A

B

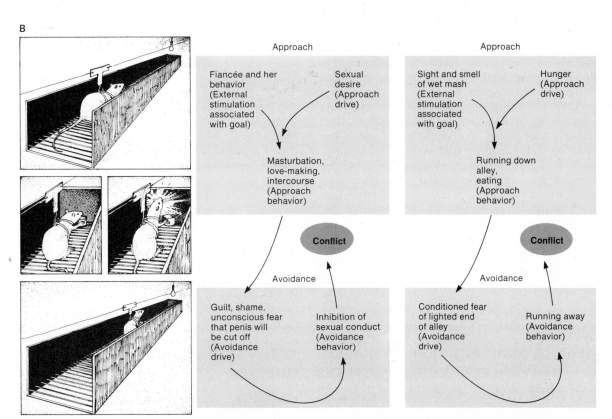

Figure 19.1 Dollard and Miller argue that neurotic conflict is learned behavior. Sexual conflict in human beings and experimentally induced conflict in rats can be analyzed analogously in terms of learning theory, as these illustrations show. (A) Curious about sexual matters, this boy read pornographic material and masturbated. When these activities were suddenly discovered by his parents, he was severely punished and repeatedly told that sexual feelings were dirty and disgusting. All subsequent sexual curiosity was prohibited, as was any overt mention or show of sexual interest. As an adult, this young man, while desiring sexual relations, feels guilty and shameful about sex and experiences conflict about making love with his fiancée. (B) Here a conflict is experimentally induced. Miller (1944) rewarded a rat with food for running down an alley. Subsequently, when the rat reached the food, they gave it electric shocks. On later trials the rat would run partway down the alley and then vacillate between approaching and avoiding the food box.

ing a person to act in a specific way? It is a very pragmatic approach, one that is less concerned with understanding behavior than with predicting it and controlling it.

Consider the case of Fred, a moody, sometimes very unhappy college sophomore. Freud might seek the roots of Fred's unhappiness in events in his childhood. But Skinner's approach is more direct. First of all, Skinner would ask, exactly how does Fred behave? Perhaps Fred spends most of the day in his room, he cuts all his classes, and he rarely smiles or laughs.

Next, Skinner would try to determine what contingencies of reinforcement are involved—what external stimuli are maintaining these behaviors (see Chapter 4). What reinforces Fred for never leaving his room? One hypothesis is that Fred's girlfriend Beth has unintentionally reinforced this behavior by hanging around Fred trying to cheer him up. Perhaps she didn't pay so much attention to him before he became withdrawn and unhappy. Note that Skinner's approach immediately suggests a hypothesis that can be proved true or false. If paying attention to Fred encourages his moroseness, then ignoring him should decrease the likelihood of this behavior. So Beth might try ignoring Fred for a few days. If he then starts leaving his room, she has discovered the contingencies of reinforcement that govern Fred's behavior. If not, she will know that the hypothesis is wrong and can try something else. Perhaps Fred is glued to the TV in his room all day and has become a game-show addict. Take away the TV and you will find out whether that is the reinforcer.

At first, radical behaviorism may seem to imply that Fred is somehow faking his unhappy state so that he can watch *Hollywood Squares*, see more of his girlfriend, or whatever. But Skinner does not make this assumption. Fred may be entirely unaware of the rewards that are shaping his behavior. In any case, Fred's feelings are beside the point. What matters is not what's going on inside Fred's head, but what he is doing. The point is to specify his behavior precisely and then find out what causes it.

Skinner's approach has become very popular among psychologists, partly because it is so pragmatic. And it is undeniably true that radical behaviorism often works. Skinnerians have applied its techniques to a wide range of behaviors, from teaching pigeons to play Ping-Pong to teaching severely retarded people to dress themselves, feed themselves, and take part in many simple activities which were once believed beyond their abilities.

The behavior of people of normal intelligence is also controlled by rewards and punishments. But the success of behaviorists with them has been more limited, partly because reinforcers are so complex. For example, in one study juvenile delinquents were placed in a rehabilitation community in which they could earn privileges such as extra food and cigarettes for behaving in certain ways—taking classes, cleaning up their rooms, and so on. But some of the boys banded together and refused to follow the rules. In this case, peer approval was a more powerful reinforcer than any reward the psychologists could offer. Radical behaviorists believe that incidents like this are only temporary setbacks, and as they learn more about reinforcement, they will better be able to change behavior.

The idea of controlling people with systematic rewards is a frightening concept to many people, more reminiscent of Aldous Huxley's *Brave New World* than of Plato's *Utopia*. But Skinner's novel *Walden Two* (1949) describes how these principles might be applied to form a utopian society (see Figure 19.2). In another of his popular books, *Beyond Freedom and Dignity* (1971), Skinner takes the philosophical position that freedom is an illusion. We cannot change the way reinforcers shape people's behavior, Skinner argues, so we might as well make the most of it. Today's society, for example, often rewards people for acting immorally: the slumlord gets more profits if he lets his property run down instead of spending money to maintain it. Skinner suggests that if we wish to change this situation, we should not try to appeal to the slumlord's inherent goodness, unless our approval is a reinforcer for him. Instead, we should change society, perhaps by providing tax breaks, so that he will be rewarded for taking care of his buildings.

As you might guess even from this brief review of Skinner's ideas, radical behaviorism is extremely controversial. Psychologists like Carl Rogers (whose views are described later in this chapter) have sharply attacked Skinner's views, while others are energetically applying the principles of behaviorism in schools, prisons, mental hospitals, and research laboratories around the world.

SOCIAL LEARNING THEORY   The rewards that shape our behavior are not always apparent. Why do children ape the behavior of their favorite car-

Figure 19.2 Can that green-eyed monster of jealousy—as well as other destructive or antisocial emotions—be eliminated, or will such emotions always haunt us? This dialogue from *Walden Two,* Skinner's novel about a utopian society, emphatically answers yes. Traits and emotions are seen not as inherent biological qualities or essences, but as learned and therefore *controllable* or *extinguishable* behaviors. Through principles of operant conditioning and reinforcement, Skinner argues, we can engineer a perfect society. Do you agree? (Skinner, 1949.)

"After all, it's a simple and sensible program. .We set up a system of gradually increasing annoyances and frustrations against a background of complete serenity. An easy environment is made more and more difficult as the children acquire the capacity to adjust."

"But why?. . .What do (the children) get out of it?"

"What do they get out of it! . . .what they get is escape from the petty emotions which eat the heart out of the unprepared. They get the satisfaction of pleasant and profitable social relations. .They get new horizons, for they are spared the emotions characteristic of frustration and failure."

toon heroes, and why do we as adults all try to dress like the models in fashion magazines? Albert Bandura and Richard Walters have extended the behaviorist approach by studying situations in which people learn to imitate a model's behavior without being rewarded. In one series of experiments, for example, they showed that children would imitate aggressive behavior when they simply saw someone else acting aggressively. Thus, they demonstrated that people can learn new responses and behavioral patterns without ever receiving direct reinforcement (Bandura, 1966, 1969; Bandura and Walters, 1959, 1963).

The scope of social learning theory has been broadened in the past two decades to encompass many different forms of behavior, and it has become the dominant behaviorally oriented theory of personality. Social learning theory differs from Skinner's radical behaviorism in that it places much greater emphasis on the cognitive capabilities of human beings—on their ability to reason, to remember, and to think abstractly. For this reason, social learning theory has drawn its support from research conducted exclusively with humans, while the radical behaviorists have amassed their data primarily from experiments on animals. Radical behaviorists such as Skinner consider behavior, both animal and

human, to be determined entirely by environmental forces, external stimuli, and reinforcement (see Chapter 4). They make no allowance for cognitive or symbolic processes. From the perspective of social learning theory, however, behavior is determined by the interaction between people's cognitive capabilities and their environment.

Social learning theory also differs from Dollard and Miller's psychodynamic learning model, in that social learning theory does not find direct reinforcement necessary for the learning of new behavior. Instead, social learning theory holds that people can acquire new behavior through the use of their cognitive processes and through symbolic or vicarious learning, such as by observation of models.

THE ACQUISITION OF BEHAVIOR In vicarious learning we acquire new behavior by retaining and remembering a model's behavior. The cognitive processes that we use to do so may involve describing or naming the model's behavior verbally, representing it visually, or acting it out physically. For example, at a party you watch your friend Karen do a new dance movement that makes her the center of attention. You notice that she shakes her hips but keeps the upper part of her body rather stiff. You now have symbolically recorded an action performed by someone else. If you practice the new step yourself once or twice, picturing how Karen did it, you should be able to remember her technique and imitate it successfully at the next party.

Social learning theorists do not believe that reinforcement is needed in order for people to learn by observing models, though reinforcement can make such learning easier. In Bandura's view (1971), reinforcement is much more important in getting people to repeat newly learned behavior than in teaching it to them initially. In other words, you may learn how to do the new movement by observing Karen, without receiving any reward yourself, but you will not be likely to perform it unless you anticipate receiving the same kind of admiration that you have seen Karen enjoy.

Although social learning theory emphasizes observing models, it also acknowledges the role of direct experience in learning. Direct experience does not automatically strengthen a given response, as radical behaviorists maintain; rather, it provides information and motivation that in turn strengthen the response. For example, Eric may write his first college term paper according to general guidelines

and habits that he learned in high school. When he receives a grade of C, he has acquired some information: that kind of paper will earn a passing grade, but not an exceptional grade. The experience of receiving the C may then motivate Eric to attempt a different tactic to earn a higher grade. He writes a second paper in which he develops his ideas more logically and presents them more clearly. He receives an A this time. The information Eric now receives is that this particular way of organizing a term paper is more likely to earn an A from this instructor. He may now continue to use this manner of organization in the hope of earning As on subsequent papers.

THE REGULATION AND MAINTENANCE OF BEHAVIOR According to social learning theory, once behavior has been acquired it is regulated and maintained by three kinds of controls: stimulus control, reinforcement control, and cognitive control.

Stimulus control, as we saw in Chapter 4, means that a particular kind of behavior will take place only when some stimulus in the environment evokes it at the appropriate time—when it will lead to some satisfactory result. Some stimuli, such as traffic

Many children love to wear the costumes of their television heroes, though any reward they may receive for such behavior is usually not apparent.

Even shadows such as these may be seen as a stimuli that are subject to various interpretations by onlookers.

lights, are very direct in telling us either to behave or not to behave in certain ways. A sign that says "Danger—Thin Ice" is a very clear directive to avoid walking in an area where unpleasant consequences could occur. Other stimuli, particularly social stimuli, are less directly representative, and their message is less clear. A person who asks, "How are you?" may not really want to know the details of your upset stomach or your recent argument with your roommate. Facial expressions and gestures are stimuli that often must be interpreted to determine if certain behavior will be rewarded.

Reinforcement control is a means of regulating and maintaining behavior by rewarding the individual after the desired behavior has been performed. The behavior need not be reinforced every time it occurs; some behavior can be effectively maintained by reinforcing it intermittently. The schedule of reinforcement might call for a reward to be given, on the average, after twenty-five responses, which might work out to a reward after the first eighteen responses, another reward after thirty more responses, another after twenty-two, and so on. With such a random schedule, the individual—expecting a reward but not knowing exactly when it will come—is much more likely to continue emitting the response, even long after the reinforcement has

been withdrawn. Slot machines in gambling casinos are set up on this principle. A given machine might, on the average, pay $2 after a gambler has inserted twenty quarters and $10 after a hundred quarters. The point is that the number of responses required before any particular reward—any jackpot—is received varies *randomly* from very few responses to a great many. That this kind of reinforcement control is effective in maintaining high rates of responding can be confirmed by looking down the rows of slot machines in any casino: the observer will find people stuffing coins into the slots as fast as they can, many of them playing two or more machines at the same time.

Cognitive control refers to the ability of an individual to guide and maintain his or her behavior by providing self-reinforcement. A tennis player has a symbolic or visual image of the kind of serve she wishes to execute, which serves as a stimulus for the serve she actually makes. Then, depending on the outcome of the serve, she may reinforce herself by jumping for joy or punish herself by throwing her racket on the ground in a gesture of self-rejection.

In reality, all three types of controls—stimulus, reinforcement, and cognitive—work together. Stimuli that are physically present trigger cognitive representations (images or symbols) of other stimuli, which lead to expectations of reinforcement, which in turn lead to behavior that may then lead to direct reward.

SOCIAL LEARNING THEORY AS A THEORY OF PERSONALITY How does social learning theory account for the fact that each person reacts to a situation in a unique manner and the fact that each person's behavior is relatively stable and consistent over time? Walter Mischel (1971, 1973) suggests that both uniqueness and consistency can be explained by means of five overlapping and interlocking concepts of social learning theory.

For one thing, people are unique and quite consistent in the behavior sequences that they construct, on the basis of past learning, to respond to various situations. Each person also has a unique way of categorizing experience: one person may see a situation as threatening while another sees it as challenging, and each will respond accordingly. Third, people learn different expectations of being rewarded or punished for various behaviors. Fourth, the value a person accords various stimuli—such as money, social approval, and good grades—influences the person's behavior. Finally, each person has a set of plans or rules for his or her own goals or behavior in a given situation—for example, self-control, courage, or brilliance.

These components of personality as identified by Mischel are products of past social learning and guides for future social learning. There is thus a continuous interaction between individuals and the situations they confront, which leads to new learning and to further development of these aspects of personality.

Social learning theory has developed into a complex system of concepts that attempt to account for the variety and complexity of human behavior. It has a distinct behavioristic flavor because of its emphasis on observable phenomena and its avoidance of psychoanalytic concepts such as instinct and unconscious motivation. Yet it has moved far beyond the radical behaviorist position, which explains human behavior in terms of contingencies of reinforcement. Instead, social learning theory emphasizes characteristically human abilities, such as cognition, the use of symbols, reasoning, and language. There are some personality theorists, however, who place even more emphasis on uniquely human qualities, and it is to these humanistically oriented theories that we now turn.

HUMANISTIC APPROACHES

The label "humanistic" is applied to psychologists who believe that human beings, because they are different from all other animals, should be thought about in psychological concepts of a special nature. Most humanistic psychologists pay little attention to animal research, though they do not necessarily see it as irrelevant. They usually object both to psychoanalytic and to behavioristic approaches to personality, on the grounds that these demean human beings—the one by emphasizing irrational and destructive instincts, the other by emphasizing external causes of behavior. Humanistic psychologists tend to stress people's constructive and creative potential rather than their destructive capacities or habitual behavior.

MASLOW'S HUMANISTIC PSYCHOLOGY

The American psychologist Abraham Maslow 1908–1970) is most often identified as the guiding spirit behind the humanistic approach. He deliberately set out to create what he called a "third force in psychology" as an alternative to psychoanalysis and behaviorism. Maslow tried to base his theory of personality on healthy, creative, self-actualizing people who fully utilize their talents, potential, and capabilities, rather than on studies of disturbed individuals. A **self-actualized** person, as defined by Maslow, finds fulfillment in doing the best of which he or she is capable, not in competition with others, but in being "the best me I can be" (1971a, b). Maslow criticized other psychologists for their pessimistic, negative, and limited conceptions of human beings. Where is the psychology, he asked, that takes account of gaiety, exuberance, love, and expressive art to the same extent that it deals with misery, conflict, shame, hostility, and habit (1966, 1968)? There is an active will toward health in every person, Maslow believed, an impulse toward the actualization of one's potentialities. Unfortunately, human instincts are weak in comparison with those of animals, so, according to Maslow, each person is subject to considerable molding by the surrounding society.

Maslow (1955) identified two groups of human needs: basic needs and metaneeds. The basic needs are physiological (food, water, sleep, and so on) and psychological (affection, security, and self-esteem, for example). These basic needs are also called **deficiency needs** because if they are not met, a person, lacking something, will seek to make up for the deficiency. The basic needs are hierarchically organized, meaning that some (such as the need for food) take precedence over others.

The higher needs Maslow called **metaneeds**, or **growth needs**. They include the need for justice, goodness, beauty, order, and unity. The deficiency needs take priority over the growth needs in most instances. People who lack food or water cannot attend very seriously to justice and beauty. Nor, according to Maslow, can those who lack basic security and self-esteem feel free to consider fairness, to feel deep, reciprocal love, to be democratic, or to resist restrictive conformity. The metaneeds are not hierarchically organized; consequently, one metaneed can be pursued instead of another, depending on a person's circumstances. The metaneeds are quite real; when they are not met **metapathologies**, such as alienation, anguish, apathy, and cynicism, can develop.

Maslow (1954) studied a group of historical figures whom he considered to be self-actualized—among them Abraham Lincoln, Henry David Thoreau, Ludwig von Beethoven, Eleanor Roosevelt, and Albert Einstein. He also studied some of his own friends. Their distinguishing personality characteristics are listed in Table 19.1.

In addition, he investigated what he called peak experiences—those profound moments when a person feels very much in harmony with the world: highly autonomous, spontaneous, perceptive, yet

How the World Seemed	Women's Feelings About Themselves
truth	queenly
goodness	receptive
beauty	victorious
wholeness	trusting
connectedness	joyous
aliveness	blissful
uniqueness	rapturous
perfection	supreme
inevitability	in ecstasy
completeness	integrated
justice	
order	
simplicity	
richness	
effortlessness	
playfulness	
self-sufficiency	

Figure 19.3 Natural childbirth is a "peak experience" for many women. Maslow believed that such experiences are rare in the majority of people's lives. (After Tanzer, 1968.)

relatively unaware of space and time. As an example of this phenomenon, some women report peak experiences at the moment of childbirth. In one study (Tanzer, 1968), women whose husbands were present at delivery were more likely to have such experiences than other women; some of the words they used to describe how they felt about the world and about themselves at the moment of their peak experiences are listed in Figure 19.3.

Many psychologists have criticized Maslow's work. His claim that human nature is "good," for example, has been called an intrusion of subjective values into what should be a neutral science. His study of self-actualizing people has been criticized because the sample was chosen on the basis of Maslow's own subjective criteria. How can one identify self-actualized people without knowing the characteristics of such people? But then, if one knows these characteristics to begin with, what sense does it make to list them as if they were the results of an empirical study?

Table 19.1 Characteristics of Self-Actualized Persons

They are realistically oriented.
They accept themselves, other people, and the natural world for what they are.
They have a great deal of spontaneity.
They are problem-centered rather than self-centered.
They have an air of detachment and a need for privacy.
They are autonomous and independent.
Their appreciation of people and things is fresh rather than stereotyped.
Most of them have had profound mystical or spiritual experiences although not necessarily religious in character.

They identify with mankind.
Their intimate relationships with a few specially loved people tend to be profound and deeply emotional rather than superficial.
Their values and attitudes are democratic.
They do not confuse means with ends.
Their sense of humor is philosophical rather than hostile.
They have a great fund of creativeness.
They resist conformity to the culture.
They transcend the environment rather than just coping with it.

Source: Abraham Maslow, *Motivation and Personality* (New York: Harper & Row, 1954).

A husband's presence during childbirth possibly helps bring about a peak experience for his wife.

Despite such criticism, Maslow's influence has been great. He has inspired many researchers to pay more attention to healthy, productive people and has led many group leaders, clinicians, and psychologists working in organizations to seek ways to promote the growth and self-actualization of workers, students, and clients in therapy.

THE SELF THEORY OF ROGERS Carl Rogers, an American clinical psychologist, is closely identified with humanistic psychology. Like Maslow, Rogers believes that people are governed by an innate impulse toward positive growth. In contrast to Maslow, however, Rogers developed his theory from observations made while practicing psychotherapy. He noticed that his clients (a term he prefers to "patients" because the latter implies illness) typically had trouble accepting their own feelings and experiences. They seemed to have learned during childhood that in order to obtain the regard of others, they had to feel and act in distorted or dis-honest ways; they had to deny certain feelings in order to be accepted by parents, relatives, or peers.

Rogers (1971) summarized his observations about the denial or distortion of feelings by saying that almost every child is the victim of **conditional positive regard**. That is, love and praise are withheld until the child conforms to parental or social standards. If a little boy comes to dinner with a dirty face, he may be told that he is "disgusting" and sent away from the table. If he hits his little sister, he may be called "naughty" and sent to his room. On the other hand, cleanliness and brotherly affection often are rewarded by smiles, compliments, and kisses. This initiates a process in which the child, and later the adult, learns to act and feel in ways that earn approval from others rather than in ways that may be more intrinsically satisfying. To maintain conditional positive regard, we suppress actions and feelings that are unacceptable to others who are important to us, rather than using our own spontaneous perceptions and feelings as guides to behavior. We develop what Rogers calls **conditions of worth**, those conditions under which positive regard will be forthcoming. We perceive and are aware of those experiences that are in accord with the conditions of worth, but misperceive, distort, or deny those experiences that are not.

This denial and distortion of certain experiences leads to the distinction that Rogers makes between the concepts of the organism and the self. The **organism** he defines as the total range of one's possible experiences. The **self** is the recognized and accepted parts of a person's experiences. Ideally the two words would refer to the same things because a person can, in principle, recognize and accept all experiences. In fact, however, the organism and the self often come to oppose each other (see Figure 19.4). For example, the self can deny consciousness to certain sensory and emotional experiences simply by refusing to symbolize or conceptualize them. This idea is similar to the psychoanalytic concept of repression and to its neo-Freudian reformulations; it also resembles Dollard and Miller's notion that unconscious feelings are those that have been left unlabeled and hence cannot be thought about clearly. According to Rogers, denial is likely to occur if a feeling or experience is incompatible with the self-concept. Even an action can be disowned by saying to oneself, "I don't know why I did it," or "I must have gotten carried away."

Rogers says that psychological adjustment "exists when the concept of the self is such that all sensory and visceral experiences of the organism are, or may be, assimilated on a symbolic level into a consistent relationship with the concept of self" (1971). The characteristics displayed by psychologically adjusted people, whom Rogers describes as **fully functioning**, are openness to experience, absence of defensiveness, accurate awareness, unconditional positive self-regard, and generally harmonious relations with other people.

If the breach between self and organism in a less than fully functioning person grows too wide, the person may be defensive, tense, conflicted, and unable to relate well to others. Such people are often argumentative and hostile, and they may project their denied feelings onto others. The split between self and organism can be healed, according to Rogers, if people describe their experiences and express their feelings freely in a nonthreatening therapeutic context. The therapist, unlike most other people in the client's life, should maintain an attitude of **unconditional positive regard**; he or she continues to support the client regardless of what the client says or does. The therapist clarifies the client's feelings by restating what has been said ("You seem to have been disappointed whenever your father failed to approve of one of your boy friends"), but does not offer divergent interpretations or tell the client what to do or how to act. For this reason, Rogers' therapeutic method is called **nondirective**, or **client-centered**. In this therapeutic context, the client learns to reintegrate self and organism, to accept all experiences as genuine, and to establish an unconditional positive self-regard.

It may be asked whether a person who receives unconditional positive regard will become selfish, cruel, and destructive. After all, it is to prevent this kind of behavior that children are punished and police forces are maintained. And what of Freud's assertion that human beings have aggressive or destructive instincts? Rogers maintains that in years of therapeutic experience, he has seen little evidence for this pessimistic view. Instead, he has come to believe that the human organism naturally seeks growth, self-actualization, and pleasant, productive relations with others. When not restricted by social forces, a person wants to become what most of us would recognize as healthier and happier.

Numerous social scientists have followed the lead of Maslow and Rogers in presenting their own versions of humanistic personality theory. And although others have made contributions to the study of personality, it is only Maslow and Rogers who have presented systematic theories of personality that reflect their humanistic values. Their work has had a significant impact on research, therapy, and counseling, influencing psychologists to concentrate more on their patients' or clients' personal growth. The humanistic approach has given rise to centers for personal growth throughout the United States; perhaps the most famous of these is the Esalen Institute in California, where Maslow worked until his death in 1970. Carl Rogers has for a number of years been a Fellow at the Center for the Study of the Person in La Jolla, California, which is also well known for its humanistic emphasis.

Figure 19.4 Carl Rogers believes that the fundamental problem of personality is how to make the self more congruent with the total experience of the organism. It is through the therapeutic relationship, in which the therapist creates an atmosphere of total acceptance, or "unconditional positive regard," that the client may achieve closer—or even complete—congruence. (From Rogers, 1971.)

This, as we see it, is the basic estrangement in man. He has not been true to himself, to his own natural organismic valuing of experience, but for the sake of preserving the positive regard of others has now come to falsify some of the values he experiences and to perceive them only in terms based upon their value to others. Yet this has not been a conscious choice, but a natural—and tragic—development in infancy. The path of development toward psychological maturity, the path of therapy, is the undoing of this estrangement in man's functioning, the dissolving of conditions of worth, the achievement of a self which is congruent with experience, and the restoration of a unified organismic valuing process as the regulator of behavior.

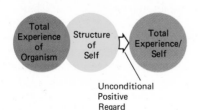

Total Experience of Organism — Structure of Self — Total Experience/Self

Unconditional Positive Regard

TRAIT APPROACHES

Betsy spends many hours talking to other people, circulates freely at parties, and strikes up conversations while she waits in the dentist's office. Carl, however, spends more time with books than with other people and seldom goes to parties. In common-sense terms, we say that Betsy is friendly and Carl is not. Friendliness is a personality trait, and some theorists have argued that studying such traits in detail is the best approach to solving the puzzle of human behavior.

Theories of Personality:
Comparison and Evaluation

In Chapters 18 and 19 we have discussed some of the major theoretical viewpoints that have been developed to explain why each human being's personality is unique and why an individual's personality remains fairly consistent over time and in a variety of situations. Here we shall compare those theories and evaluate their usefulness in clarifying the mystery of human personality.

Psychoanalytic Theories

In Sigmund Freud's view, personality is the product of adaptations to, and displacements of, biological urges. Developmental experiences shape the instincts with which each of us is born. This explains why each individual is unique: no two people have exactly the same childhood experiences. The ways in which we resolve—or fail to resolve—conflicts in these early years determine our personalities. We develop mild, or perhaps severe, fixations and characteristic ways of defending ourselves against anxiety. Memories of damaging childhood experiences are repressed into the unconscious, but they continue to influence our behavior. Thus in many cases the reasons we give for consistently behaving this way or that are rationalizations for acting on powerful, consistent, unconscious urges.

With the neo-Freudians we see two basic departures from the orthodox psychosexual theory of personality. First, there is less emphasis on biological drives; instead, more attention is given to the social context. For example, Karen Horney saw anxiety as the result of experience—of the child's feelings of helplessness and isolation as if he or she were alone in a world of giants—not as signs that unacceptable urges were threatening to break into consciousness, as Freud would

According to Horney, adult anxiety originates in a child's feeling of helplessness and isolation.

have it. Carl Jung developed the concepts of individuation and the fully realized self; Alfred Adler, the concept of social interest; Erich Fromm, a vision of a free society; Erik Erikson, a link between individual and cultural identity.

Second, the neo-Freudians give the ego a greater role in personality than Freud himself did. To Freud, the ego is the handmaiden of the id. It draws its energy from the id, and its chief function is to find safe and realistic ways of gratifying the id's demands. The neo-Freudians argue that the ego has energy of its own and autonomous functions. Individuals strive to realize themselves (Jung); to perfect society (Adler); to achieve relatedness, transcendence, rootedness, a personal identity, and a coherent frame of reference (Fromm); to establish an ego identity that lays the foundation for intimacy, generativity, and integrity (Erikson).

What ties these theorists to Freud is their emphasis on unconscious determinants of behavior. All suggest that individuals develop unique and characteristic ways of dealing with the conflicts between personal needs and social demands that arise in childhood. These carry over into adulthood, shaping each personality.

Psychoanalytic theorists have had an enormous impact not only on psychology but also on art, literature, and philosophy. However, as a theory of personality the psychoanalytic approach leaves a great deal to be desired. Many psychoanalytic concepts are difficult to measure objectively; some are more poetic or metaphorical than scientific. By the same token, psychoanalytic theory may enable psychologists to *explain* an individual's behavior patterns in retrospect, but it does not enable them to *predict* behavior, as a truly scientific theory would. As Freud himself acknowledged, the same inner conflict may produce altogether different behavior. For example, a man who is disturbed by a recurring fantasy of abandoning his wife and children may react by actually neglecting his family, by projecting those feelings onto his wife, or by lavishing attention on his family in a reaction formation. Knowing the man's feelings does not enable us to predict how he will act. Moreover, it is extremely difficult to prove or disprove the existence of motives that are, by definition, unconscious.

Despite these problems, it would be a grave mistake to think that Freud's theory has little relevance to modern research. His ideas concerning anxiety, defense mechanisms, and dreams, to name just a few examples, have influenced countless researchers—even though many do not identify themselves with his theory.

Behavioristic, Humanistic, and Trait Theories

Behavioristic, humanistic, and trait theories of personality share an emphasis on learning, on observable behaviors, and on cognitive processes. In this they contrast with the psychoanalytic stress on unconscious motivation. But each of these nonpsychoanalytic approaches, in turn, has its own emphases.

The behavioristic approach of Dollard and Miller attempts to explain psychodynamic phenomena in terms of learning. Behavior (whether thought or action) is a response that seeks to reduce or satisfy a drive; when it succeeds in doing so, the resulting reinforcement tends to call forth similar behavior in similar situations. Social learning theory deemphasizes drives and reinforcement. Instead it stresses individual capabilities for making use of past learning in reacting to changes in the environment.

The humanistic approach, regarding behaviorism as too concerned with external determinants of behavior, focuses on the constructive potential of humans in their search for growth and productivity. Maslow, identifying basic needs and metaneeds, studied so-called self-actualized personalities—people who, he felt, had fulfilled themselves in meeting these needs. Rogers, more therapeutically oriented, believes that unconditional positive regard on the part of a therapist helps clients to establish self-regard and thus to function harmoniously in society.

Trait theorists approach personality from the standpoint of individual differences, using measurements of these differences to predict future behavior. A person's traits are seen as relatively constant, whether analyzed according to Allport's classification or the factor analysis systems of Cattell and Eysenck.

Since each of these theories concentrates on different aspects of personality, each has its advantages and disadvantages in accounting for human uniqueness and consistency. Behavioristic approaches have proved useful in researching and modifying discrete behaviors, but have not provided a clear conception of how the total personality is integrated. Humanistic approaches, which are more concerned with the whole person, seem less useful in predicting behavior. Trait theories, by concentrating on personality inventories, run the risk of being too subjective, in that they rely heavily on identification and evaluation of traits by individual investigators. And there is no agreement on traits that are universally applicable.

There is no single theory of personality that provides a fully adequate answer to the questions of the uniqueness of each person and the consistency of an individual's behavior. Each of the theories we have discussed provides some valid and important insights about human personality, but each has its flaws as well. It is now nearly a century since Freud began to develop his theory, and you may ask, "If this is all the progress we've made, why bother?" The answer is that the process of studying human personality is endlessly fascinating, even if progress is slow. And each new theory of personality moves us closer to understanding ourselves.

One psychologist has defined a **trait** as "any relatively enduring way in which one individual differs from another" (Guilford, 1959). A trait, then, is a predisposition to respond in a certain way in many different kinds of situations—in a dentist's office, at a party, or in a classroom. More than any other personality theorists, trait theorists emphasize and try to explain the consistency of human behavior.

Trait theorists generally make two key assumptions about these underlying sources of consistency: they assume that every trait applies to all people (for example, everyone can be classified as more or less dependent), and they assume that these descriptions can be quantified (for example, we could establish a scale on which an extremely dependent person scores 1 while a very independent person scores 10).

Thus, every trait can be used to classify people. Aggressiveness, for example, is a continuum: a few people are extremely aggressive or extremely unaggressive, and most of us fall somewhere in the middle. We understand people by specifying their traits, and we use traits to predict people's future behavior. If you were hiring someone to sell vacuum cleaners, you would probably choose outgoing Betsy over bookish Carl. This choice would be based on two assumptions: that friendliness is a useful trait for salespeople and that friendliness in the dentist's office and at parties will predict behavior in another situation.

Trait theorists go beyond this kind of commonsense analysis to try to discover the underlying sources of the consistency of human behavior. What is the best way to describe the common features of Betsy's behavior? Is she friendly, or extraverted, or socially aggressive, or interested in people, or sure of herself, or something else? What is the underlying *trait* that best explains her behavior?

Most (but not all) trait theorists believe that there are a few basic traits that are central for all people. An underlying trait of self-confidence, for example, might be used to explain more superficial characteristics like social aggressiveness and dependency. If this were true, it would mean that a person would be dependent because he or she lacked self-confidence. Psychologists who accept this approach set out on their theoretical search for basic traits with very few assumptions about the exact nature of the traits they will find.

This is a very different approach from that of other personality theorists we have considered. Freud, for example, started out with a well-defined theory of instincts. When he observed that some people were stingy, he set out to explain this in terms

of his theory. (In fact, Freud saw stinginess as a displaced form of anal retentiveness.) Trait theorists would not start by trying to understand stinginess; rather, they would try to determine whether stinginess was a trait. That is, they would try to find out whether people who were stingy in one type of situation were also stingy in others. Then they might ask whether stinginess is a sign of a more basic trait like possessiveness: Is the stingy person also very possessive in relationships? Thus, the first and foremost question for trait theorists is, What behaviors seem to go together?

Instead of powerful theories telling them *where* to look, trait theorists have complex and sophisticated methods that tell them *how* to look. These methods begin with the statistical technique of correlation (discussed in Chapter 2), which basically involves using one set of scores to predict another. If I know that someone talks to strangers in line at the supermarket, can I predict that he or she will be likely to strike up conversations in a singles bar? Such predictions are never perfect. Perhaps the reason Betsy is so outgoing in the dentist's office is that she's terrified, and jabbering to strangers is the only way she can distract herself from her fear. Sometimes, actions that look like manifestations of one trait may really reflect something else entirely.

Some psychologists, such as Gordon Allport (whose theory is discussed next), regard traits as real entities that exist in the mind. Most other theorists consider traits to be no more than useful devices for answering the two key questions about the uniqueness and consistency of human behavior. To the question, "Why don't all people respond to the same situation in the same way?" the trait theorist would answer, "Because they don't all have the same traits, or they don't have them to the same degree." To the question, "Why does each person respond to different situations in a relatively consistent manner?" the trait theorist would answer, "Because a person's basic traits do not change easily or quickly."

However, when we use traits to explain behavior, we must be careful to avoid circular reasoning: Why does Marie get so little done? Because she's lazy. How do you know she's lazy? Because she gets so little done. We can avoid this kind of circularity, at least in part, if the trait also predicts other kinds of behavior which form a consistent pattern.

ALLPORT'S CLASSIFICATION OF TRAITS

Gordon W. Allport was a leading trait theorist for

almost forty years, during which time he developed and refined his theory continuously (Allport, 1937, 1961, 1966). Allport believed that traits accounted for the consistency of human behavior. A trait, he believed, would render a wide range of situations "functionally equivalent"—that is, a person could interpret different situations as calling for a similar or identical response. For example, an aggressive person sees many situations as calling for aggressive behavior.

A vast array of specific explanations may be offered for an infinite number of behavioral responses. In 1936 Allport and Henry Odbert searched through an unabridged dictionary, noting all the terms that could be used to describe people. There turned out to be roughly 18,000 of them! Even after omitting clearly evaluative terms (like "disgusting") and terms describing transient states (like "abashed"), there were still between 4,000 and 5,000 items. Surely, Allport thought, these could be reduced to a few essentials.

Allport classified three kinds of traits according to which each individual personality could be defined. A **cardinal trait** is one that directs a major portion of a person's behavior. Someone consumed by ambition or by greed would be described by a cardinal trait. Famous historical and mythical figures have given their names to cardinal traits: for example, Byronic, Machiavellian, narcissistic. Actually, Allport believed that cardinal traits are quite rare. Most individuals, he felt, do not have one predominant trait, but develop a few **central traits** on the basis of life experiences. These are characteristic ways of dealing with the world that can be captured by trait names like honest, loving, gregarious, and so on. Less influential are **secondary traits**—characteristic modes of behavior that might also be described as tastes and preferences. Secondary traits, though subject to fluctuation and change, are usually consistent. Examples would be preferences for certain foods or styles of music.

Allport believed that all persons could be described in terms of cardinal, central, and secondary traits. In asserting this belief, he distinguished between common traits and individual traits. **Common traits**, such as aggression, are basic modes of adjustment that are approximately the same for different individuals. Because we all must interact in a competitive world, each of us must develop our own most suitable level of aggression, and each person can be placed somewhere on a dimension of aggressiveness. But since each person is unique, Allport argued, most traits are **individual traits**—or,

as he later called them, **personal dispositions** (Allport, 1961). Because of the uniqueness of each person's life experiences, he or she develops a unique set of personal dispositions. These individual traits are themselves unique ways of organizing the world, and they are not dimensions that can be applied to all people. A personal disposition cannot be measured by a standardized test; it can be discerned only by careful study of the individual.

FACTOR ANALYSIS: CATTELL AND EYSENCK
More recent theorists have concentrated on what Allport called common traits, and they have further tried to quantify them in a precise, scientific manner. Their primary tool in this task has been an extremely sophisticated mathematical technique called **factor analysis** (see Figure 19.5). Basically, factor analysis is a high-powered way of looking for underlying sources of consistency (Helmstadter, 1970). We might note, for example, that people's test scores in math predict their chemistry grades (although not perfectly, of course), that chemistry grades predict history grades less well, and that scores in English predict scores in French. If we used factor analysis to study all these scores, we might find two underlying factors to explain our results: mathematical skills and verbal skills. These factors explain why chemistry grades predict performance in physics better than they predict performance in political science. (The difference between factor analysis and simpler statistical techniques is like the difference between a three-dimensional model of a chemical molecule and a flat diagram of the same molecule on a blackboard.)

Raymond B. Cattell has used factor analysis extensively to study personality traits. Cattell defines a trait as a tendency to react to related situations in a way that remains more or less stable over time. He distinguishes between two kinds of tendencies: surface traits and source traits. **Surface traits** are clusters of behavior that tend to go together. An example of a surface trait is altruism, which involves a variety of related behaviors such as helping a neighbor who has a problem or contributing to an annual blood drive. Other examples of surface traits are integrity, curiosity, realism, and foolishness. **Source traits** are the underlying roots or causes of these behavior clusters—for example, ego strength, dominance, and submissiveness. Surface traits may correspond to common-sense ways of describing behavior and may sometimes be measured

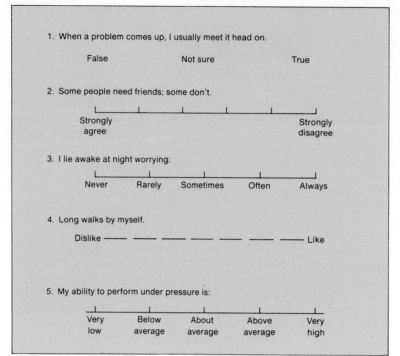

Figure 19.5 An example of the technique of factor analysis. Imagine that the five items on the left have been presented to a number of different people, and, from the resulting data, correlations between the various items have been computed. These correlations are shown in the matrix on the right. As you can see, they reveal that items 1 and 5, for example, are closely related; people tend to answer these two items in the same way. Items 1 and 2 appear not to be related; the way a person responds to one has little to do with how he responds to the other. By rearranging the order of the items in the matrix as shown here, it is possible to see that two distinct and independent personality factors are being measured. Items 1, 3, and 5 seem to have something to do with confidence in working ability, and items 2 and 4 seem to describe sociability.

by simple observation. But according to Cattell, surface traits are the result of interactions among the source traits, and valid explanations of behavior must be focused on source traits as the structural factors that determine personality. Cattell believes that discovering and learning to measure surface and source traits will enable us to identify those characteristics which all humans share and those which distinguish one person from another and make him or her an individual.

Cattell discovered these traits by studying large numbers of people using three basic kinds of data: from life records, from questionnaires, and from objective tests (1965). Life records include everything from descriptions by people who have known an individual for some time to school report cards and records of automobile accidents. Questionnaire data are the answers individuals give to a series of questions, whether or not they are truthful. (The fact that an individual underrates himself or herself or tries to create a highly favorable impression may be significant.) Objective test data are a person's responses to tests specifically designed to detect or prevent this type of "cheating."

Similar mathematical techniques have led Hans Eysenck to somewhat different conclusions. According to Eysenck (1970), there are two major dimensions that are critical for understanding normal human behavior: extraversion–introversion and neuroticism–stability. Figure 19.6 shows these two dimensions and typical values for several kinds of people. According to this graph, for example, depressives tend to be slightly neurotic and slightly introverted.

Eysenck believes that there is a biological basis for these traits. He suggests, for example, that people who are extraverted have a low level of "cortical arousal." That is, the cortex of the brain of the extravert is naturally rather quiet, and so he or she seeks certain kinds of environments—like loud parties and intense social interactions—to stimulate his or her brain. The introvert, however, starts out with a high level of cortical arousal and so he or she seeks out situations that minimize further stimulation— for example, sitting quietly alone.

Many different observations support this basic split. Introverts, for example, take longer to fall asleep and are more sensitive to pain than extra-

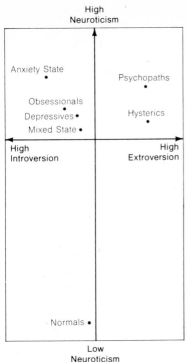

Figure 19.6 Two dimensions in Eysenck's classification system and the locations of people with various psychological disorders within space the dimensions describe. This space (with the addition of a third dimension, psychoticism) is the result of a factor analysis of many personality tests. After these dimensions emerged from his analysis, Eysenck postulated possible biological factors that could account for them. (After Eysenck, 1970.)

verts, suggesting that their brains are somehow more alert. The effects of drugs that change the state of the brain also support this theory. Alcohol lowers cortical arousal, and it makes introverts extraverted. The opposite effect is seen when extraverts take amphetamines (which increase cortical arousal): they become introverted.

Whether Eysenck's theory is ultimately proved right or wrong, he has shown how it is possible to develop more elaborate theories once basic traits have been identified by factor analysis.

A CURRENT CONTROVERSY: PERSONALITY VERSUS SITUATIONAL FACTORS

We have now devoted two chapters to personality theories, summarizing several different approaches to the two basic questions: What makes people different from one another? and What gives each person a unique, identifiable character that is visible in diverse situations? There is still a third question that has not yet been answered: How do we know, except through intuition, that personality traits or structures really do exist and influence behavior in various situations?

For a number of years, personality researchers more or less happily used tests to measure personality traits and then correlated the test scores with measures of behavior in various situations. For convenience, the situations were often constructed in laboratories. Researchers measured everything from ego strength to extraversion, and correlated their results with such diverse behavior indexes as career aspirations and tolerance of pain. The value of these procedures was seldom questioned. Because interesting relationships between variables were being discovered and documented, it seemed to all the psychologists concerned that scientific progress was being made.

THE CRITIQUE AND THE RESPONSE In 1968, in his book *Personality and Assessment*, social learning theorist Walter Mischel cast a shadow across this entire enterprise. Reviewing one study after another, Mischel showed that correlations (see Chapter 2) between personality trait measures and behavior rarely exceeded .30. Such relationships may be genuine, and may even have some theoretical significance, but they are too weak to have much practical value, as Figure 19.7 shows. They do not allow a teacher, employer, or clinical psychologist to make valid decisions concerning specific students, potential employees, or clients.

Mischel thought he had seen enough evidence to conclude that broad personality trait measures are of little value in predicting behavior outside of test situations. Moreover, he thought he knew why. If people behave the way they do because they have been reinforced for particular responses in particular situations, it is not surprising to find that they will act differently in different situations. Thus, John is aggressive on the football field but very shy and retiring at a party; Sharon is dependent on her parents at home but very independent at school; Martha is arrogant toward younger coworkers but deferential to superiors. There is no reason, said Mischel, to expect people to have general traits or to be classifiable along the same trait dimension, such as introversion–extraversion.

Mischel's argument generated a heated debate. Some social scientists wondered why, if there really are no general personality dimensions and if people are not really consistent in their behavior, we have such strong intuitive feelings that personality traits do exist. One answer offered by the opponents of trait theories was that people are biased in the way they perceive things. Research reported by Mischel (1973) indicates that we tend to maintain our first impression of a person even if he or she acts quite differently later on. For example, if we see a woman act cruelly toward someone and later see her act kindly—even if she does so several times—we are likely to say to ourselves, "She certainly hides her vicious nature well." We tend not to consider that the initial behavior might not have been typical.

Other studies show that in a given situation we are likely to attribute other people's behavior to personality dispositions or traits, but to attribute our own behavior to outside factors. Thus we might say, "*He* was being obstinate, so *I* just had to shove him out of the way because I was in a terrific hurry"; we would not be likely to say, "*He* was being obstinate, so *I* was rude." E. E. Jones and R. E. Nisbett (1971) have argued that perhaps one's perceptual perspective differs according to whether one is an observer or an actor. When you watch another person doing something, he or she is at the center of your attention and therefore seems to "cause" whatever happens; you do not notice the environmental forces acting on the person, which may be powerful. But when you are the actor, the environment tends to hold your attention; you are more aware of the pressures on you than you are of your own role in the process.

Figure 19.7 Two possible results of an attempt to validate an imaginary pencil-and-paper test of generosity against some measure of generous behavior in everyday situations. The small blue dots represent a correlation near 1.0; the large green dots represent a correlation of 0.25 between the two measures. The second correlation is of the magnitude usually observed when such attempts at validation are made. To be useful in predicting individual behavior, the test would have to have a correlation with generous behavior in daily life that is much closer to that represented by the small blue dots.

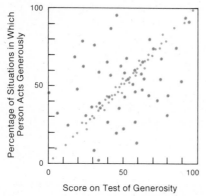

PREDICTING SOME OF THE PEOPLE SOME OF THE TIME Daryl J. Bem and Andrea Allen (1974) have recognized the validity of most of these criticisms of trait theory, but have also emphasized the considerable value of trait theory. Our intuition about the consistency of people's behavior, they say, is not entirely wrong. In fact, they believe that each person will show consistent behavior in terms of a few traits, but that the traits will be different for different people. The verdict of inconsistency is given only when we fail to discover a rational construct to explain behavior. Bem and Allen state that "the traditional verdict of inconsistency is in no way an inference about individuals; it is a statement about a disagreement between an investigator and a group of individuals and/or a disagreement among the individuals within the group" (1974, p. 510). Whenever investigators observe behavior, they find a good deal of variability, either because the trait they are looking for does not exist or because it does not have meaning for many of the people they observe. In principle, an observer can never do better than to predict some of the people some of the time.

But what if an investigator needs information on a specific trait? Bem and Allen suggest starting with a group of subjects who are known to be consistent in that trait, because only consistency shows that a trait has psychological significance for the subject. To prove that some people actually will be more consistent than others in certain traits that have meaning for them, Bem and Allen asked students to rate themselves on their consistency of "friendliness" and of "conscientiousness." The students were then divided into one group that had rated itself as consistent and another group that had rated itself as quite variable. Those who had rated themselves as consistent in friendliness showed a correlation of .73 between their behavior in a group discussion and their spontaneous friendliness as measured by how long it took them to strike up a conversation with a confederate in a waiting room. For subjects who rated themselves as variable, the correlation was .30—about what Mischel had found in his review.

The people who showed consistency in friendliness did not necessarily show consistency in conscientiousness, and vice versa. We may gather from this study that for any given trait we can expect only some people to behave consistently; for others, the trait is irrelevant and has no usefulness in predicting behavior.

Is there no way at all to predict the behavior of the people for whom a specific trait is irrelevant?

Bem and Allen advise investigators to pay careful attention not only to the subjects they observe, but also to the situations they study. Often the very people whose behavior seems to be unpredictable in relation to a given personality trait are quite predictable in relation to a given situation. This is usually because some individuals deal with some situations in a way that makes them appear inconsistent when they really are not. A woman who grew up in a small town and is used to speaking in a friendly manner to all strangers appears consistent in her behavior. A woman who grew up in a large city may reply in a friendly manner to an old man who asks for directions, but may avoid answering remarks addressed to her by an unkempt, wild-eyed young man. Although this woman's behavior appears inconsistent, she is really acting consistently in accordance with her own perception of the situation: she has discriminated between a situation calling for friendliness and one calling for caution. Her behavior can be predicted if the observer assesses the situation in the same way she does.

Bem and Allen conclude that variability does not necessarily mean inconsistency. Often the situation itself (and the way it is assessed by the individual) is the crucial factor in determining behavior. In "Song of Myself" Walt Whitman wrote, "Do I contradict myself? Very well then I contradict myself/I am large, I contain multitudes." Whitman knew intuitively what social scientists are just beginning to prove—that variability may be just another name for human complexity. Our two chapters on various theories of personality have indicated that the convolutions of human behavior can be explained only by the complicated interaction of internal forces—be they instincts, needs, traits, or constructs—and such external forces as environment, family, and situation.

SUMMARY

1. Most nonpsychoanalytic theories of personality can be classified into one of three types: behavioristic approaches, humanistic approaches, and trait theories. All three of these approaches differ from psychoanalytic theories in that they deemphasize unconscious forces as determinants of personality and they emphasize observable behavior, learning, and conscious cognitive processes.

2. **Behaviorists** view personality development as a set of learned responses, not the result of innate forces.
   A. Dollard and Miller's psychodynamic behavior theory seeks to deal in behavioristic terms with the psychodynamic phenomena identified by Freud. Dollard and Miller agreed with Freud that most conflicts arise because of social or cultural restrictions on the expression of impulses.
      1. **Responses** are attempts to satisfy needs or reduce states of arousal called **drives**. A **cue** is something in the environment that indicates the possibility that a drive may be satisfied. **Reinforcement** refers to the strengthening of the tendency to emit a given response once it has successfully reduced a drive.
      2. Dollard and Miller's **frustration-aggres-sion hypothesis** explains aggression in social terms, which differs from Freud's concept of aggression as the result of internal stimuli. These theorists believed that aggression can be displaced onto other people whose cue value is the same as that of the real target, and they concluded that displacement can be learned even by large segments of the population in certain circumstances.
      3. By inducing approach-avoidance conflicts in rats, Miller showed how something like neurotic behavior could be learned. This work provided experimental support for Freud's view that most emotional conflict is socially induced.
   B. B. F. Skinner's controversial radical behaviorism analyzes behavior in terms of **contingencies of reinforcement**, the external conditions that control behavior. Radical behaviorism suggests that the inner dynamics of human behavior do not have to be understood in order to change that behavior.
   C. Social learning theory has become the dominant behaviorally oriented theory of personality. It differs from more radical behaviorist views in its greater emphasis on humans' cognitive capabilities. It differs from Dollard

and Miller's psychodynamic learning model in that it does not regard direct reinforcement as necessary for a person to learn new behavior.

1. Albert Bandura and Richard Walters' social learning theory, while acknowledging the role of direct experience in learning, emphasizes the importance of vicarious learning, in which a person acquires new behavior by observing and remembering a model's behavior without participating directly or receiving reinforcement.

2. Once acquired, behavior is regulated and maintained by three kinds of controls, which work together.

   a. **Stimulus control** means that a particular behavior will take place only when some stimulus in the environment evokes it at the appropriate time.

   b. **Reinforcement control** regulates and maintains behavior that has been rewarded in the past.

   c. **Cognitive control** is the ability to guide and maintain one's behavior by providing self-reinforcement.

3. Walter Mischel believes that social learning theory accounts for both the uniqueness and consistency of the personality of each of us. Social learning theory does this by means of five overlapping concepts that are the components of personality: the way in which each of us constructs behaviors to respond to various situations, our strategies for categorizing experiences, our expectations of reward or punishment, the values we place on various stimuli, and our plans or rules for our goals or behavior in a given situation. These components of personality are both products of past social learning and guides for future social learning.

3. **Humanistic** psychologists believe that human beings are different from all other animals and hence deserve special conceptual treatment. They tend to stress people's constructive and creative potential rather than their destructive capacities or habitual behavior.

A. Abraham Maslow set out to create a "third force in psychology" as an alternative to psychoanalysis and behaviorism. Maslow based his theory on **self-actualized** people, who find fulfillment in doing their best. He believed that there is an active will toward the actual-ization of one's potentialities. Maslow identified two groups of human needs: basic needs and metaneeds.

   1. **Basic needs**, or **deficiency needs**, are the physiological needs (such as for food and water) and the psychological needs (for affection, security, and self-esteem). Some basic needs take precedence over others.

   2. **Metaneeds**, or **growth needs**, are the higher needs. These include the need for justice, goodness, beauty, order, and unity. Maslow believed that the basic needs take precedence over the growth needs in most cases. Though people cannot control their basic needs, they can choose to pursue one growth need instead of another. Unfulfilled growth needs can lead to **metapathologies**, such as alienation.

B. Carl Rogers' self theory suggests that the human organism naturally seeks to become **fully functioning**, or psychologically adjusted. Rogers believed that feelings are denied and distorted in childhood by the **conditional positive regard** of significant others. Instead of acting in a personally satisfying way, we develop **conditions of worth** under which we know we will receive positive regard. If a situation is not in accordance with the conditions of worth, the person denies or distorts it. Rogers made a conceptual distinction between the organism, or the total range of one's possible experiences, and the **self**, or the recognized and accepted parts of the person's experiences. In Rogers' **nondirective**, or **client-centered**, therapeutic method, the therapist maintains an attitude of **unconditional positive regard** toward the client.

4. A **trait** is any distinguishable, relatively enduring way in which one individual varies from another. According to trait approaches to personality, the extent to which an individual possesses various traits accounts for both the uniqueness and consistency of his or her behavior.

A. Gordon Allport believed that traits, which he regarded as real entities in the mind, explain the consistency of each person's behavior because they can render different situations "functionally equivalent." Allport classified three kinds of traits according to which each individual personality could be defined:

   1. A **cardinal trait** is one that directs a major

portion of a person's behavior.

2. **Central traits** are characteristic ways of dealing with the world, developed in response to life experiences.

3. **Secondary traits** are tastes and preferences. According to Allport, each of these three kinds of traits may be either **common traits**, which are approximately the same for different individuals, or **individual traits**, or **personal dispositions**, which make each individual's behavior different.

B. Some trait theorists have used the statistical technique of **factor analysis** in attempting to develop universal measures of the fundamental dimensions of personality.

1. Raymond B. Cattell factor-analyzed life histories, self-ratings, and objective tests. He obtained a number of **surface traits**, which he further analyzed to yield **source traits**, the underlying dimensions of personality.

2. Hans Eysenck factor-analyzed personality questionnaires and concluded that there are three major trait dimensions underlying all of them: introversion/extraversion, neuroticism, and psychoticism. Eysenck related personality differences to biological factors.

5. A current controversy concerns the question of whether fixed personality traits exist or whether personality consists of varying responses to external situations.

A. Walter Mischel believed that people act differently in different situations because of the way they have been reinforced for particular responses. This contention challenged the validity of personality tests because it suggests that broad personality measures are of little value in predicting behavior outside the test situation.

B. Opponents of trait theories say that the intuitive belief that personality traits exist may be the result of perceptual biases. Mischel's research indicates that one's first impression of a person tends to be lasting. Other studies show that an individual is likely to attribute other people's behavior to personality dispositions or traits, but to attribute his or her own behavior to outside factors.

C. Bem and Allen believe that each person will show consistent behavior in terms of a few traits, but that the traits will be different for different people. They conclude that variability in behavior does not necessarily mean inconsistency in behavior. Often the situation itself (and the way it is assessed by the individual) is the crucial factor in determining behavior.

RECOMMENDED READINGS

HALL, CALVIN S., and GARDNER LINDZEY. *Theories of Personality*. 3rd ed. New York: Wiley, 1978. This new edition of the classic secondary source on theories of personality includes a new chapter on contemporary psychoanalytic theory, with an excellent presentation of Erik Erikson's work, and a new chapter on Eastern psychology and personality theory.

MADDI, SALVATORE R. *Personality Theories: A Comparative Analysis*. Rev. ed. Homewood, Ill.: Dorsey Press, 1972. This recent textbook classifies personality theorists according to whether their basic assumption relates to *conflict, fulfillment,* or *consistency*. Examines what the theorists have to say about the core and periphery of personality. Also presents research on each position and draws conclusions about its strengths and weaknesses.

MADDI, SALVATORE R. *Perspectives on Personality: A Comparative Approach*. Boston: Little Brown, 1971. A book of readings by or about each major theorist discussed in the Maddi textbook cited above.

MISCHEL, WALTER. *Introduction to Personality*. 2nd ed. New York: Holt, Rinehart and Winston, 1976. This recent textbook by a well-known social-learning theorist divides theories into five categories: type and trait, psychoanalytic, psychodynamic behaviorist, social learning, and phenomenological. The book covers theory, assessment techniques, and personality development and change (including therapy). Because of the author's orientation, behavior theories and behavior modification techniques receive more emphasis than usual, and a great deal of attention is paid to empirical evidence, especially from laboratory experiments.

CHAPTER TWENTY

PSYCHOLOGICAL ASSESSMENT

What is intelligence, anyway? When I was in the Army I received a kind of aptitude test that all soldiers took and, against a normal of 100, scored 160. No one at the base had ever seen a figure like that and for two hours they made a big fuss over me. (It didn't mean anything. The next day I was still a buck private with KP as my highest duty.)

All my life I've been registering scores like that, so that I have the complacent feeling that I'm highly intelligent, and I expect other people to think so, too. Actually, though, don't such scores simply mean that I am very good at answering the type of academic questions that are considered worthy of answers by the people who make up the intelligence tests—people with intellectual bents similar to mine?

For instance, I had an auto-repair man once, who, on these intelligence tests, could not possibly have scored more than 80, by my estimate. I always took it for granted that I was far more intelligent than he was. Yet, when anything went wrong with my car I hastened to him with it, watched him anxiously as he explored its vitals, and listened to his pronouncements as though they were divine oracles—and he always fixed my car.

Well, then, suppose my auto-repair man devised questions for an intelligence test. Or suppose a carpenter did, or a farmer, or, indeed, almost anyone but an academician. By every one of those tests, I'd prove myself a moron. And I'd *be* a moron, too. In a world where I could not use my academic training and my verbal talents but had to do something intricate or hard, working with my hands, I would do poorly. My intelligence, then, is not absolute but is a function of the society I live in and of the fact that a small subsection of that society has managed to foist itself on the rest as an arbiter of such matters.

Consider my auto-repair man, again. He had a habit of telling me jokes whenever he saw me. One time he raised his head from the automobile hood to say: "Doc, a deaf-and-dumb guy went into a hardware store to ask for some nails. He put two fingers together on the counter and made hammering motions with the other hand. The clerk brought him a hammer. He shook his head and pointed to the two fingers he was hammering. The clerk brought him nails. He picked out the sizes he wanted, and left. Well, doc, the next guy who came in was a blind man. He wanted scissors. How do you suppose he asked for them?"

Indulgently, I lifted my right hand and made scissoring motions with my first two fingers. Whereupon my auto-repair man laughed raucously and said, "Why, you dumb jerk, he used his *voice* and asked for them." Then he said, smugly, "I've been trying that on all my customers today." "Did you catch many?" I asked. "Quite a few," he said. "But I knew for sure I'd catch *you*." "Why is that?" I asked. "Because you're so goddamn educated, doc, I *knew* you couldn't be very smart."

And I have an uneasy feeling he had something there.

Isaac Asimov

In the spring of 1975, the Department of Mathematics of Johns Hopkins University conducted a talent contest; eleventh-grade math teachers in the area were invited to nominate the students most promising in their classes. Upon hearing of the contest, Julian C. Stanley, director of the Study of Mathematically Precocious Youth at Johns Hopkins, requested and received permission to nominate ten students. He needed special permission since his was a special situation—the candidates he had in mind were not in any of his classes; he was not, in any case, an eleventh-grade math teacher. In fact, some of the students had not even been nominated by their own math teachers. His connection with these students was that two or three years earlier, when they were thirteen-year-old eighth-graders, he had administered to them the mathematical part of the College Entrance Examination Board's Scholastic Aptitude Test (SAT-M).

The results of the talent contest—which consisted of testing by the university math department—were astounding. "Among the fifty-one persons who entered the contest, the ten chosen by SAT-M ranked 1, 2, 3, 5.5, 7, 8, 12, 16.5, 19, and 23.5. Points earned by the top three were 140, 112, and 91. The highest-scoring person nominated only by a teacher scored 83. Just three of ten (ranks 2, 5.5, and 19) had also been nominated by their teacher" (Stanley, 1976, p. 313). In other words, teachers, even after almost the whole school year had passed, were less able to predict which of their students would do well on a math test than a standardized objective test of mathematical aptitude given several years earlier.

While psychological tests are not without problems, which we will discuss later in this chapter, in many cases they are extremely valuable. Aptitude tests, such as the SAT-M, are often the most reliable means of determining which students are academically gifted; personality tests can reveal specific problems for treatment in the mentally disturbed; intelligence tests can point out children with previously unrevealed gifts or needs. With all their flaws, psychological tests are still our most important tools for evaluation.

REQUIREMENTS OF A TEST

Two characteristics, **reliability** and **validity**, are the essential criteria in determining the value of a test. **Standardization** is also necessary for determining the significance of an individual's score on a test. These three concepts are discussed in the sections that follow.

RELIABILITY   A test is reliable if it yields the same results over and over again. High reliability depends on three factors: internal consistency (different parts of the test yield the same results); test-retest reliability (the test yields the same results when administered to the same person at two different times); and inter-judge reliability (the test has the same results when scored or interpreted by different judges). Of course, the quality or characteristic being measured must be a relatively stable thing, such as intelligence or central personality traits. If the thing being measured changes constantly, there can be no reliability as we have defined it. The top part of Figure 20.1 shows a pattern of scores for a highly reliable test.

Let us say that we wanted to use head size as a measure of intelligence: the larger the head, the greater the intelligence. We would begin by carefully measuring the heads of, say, twenty people. As part of our measuring process, we would measure both above and below the ears. In order to have internal consistency, the same standings should result from the above-the-ear data as from the below-the-ear data. We would have test-retest reliability if we could repeat the test and get the same results (assuming that the attribute being measured—the head—doesn't change rapidly, and that the measuring process is done in the same way with the same sorts of instruments). Finally, in order to be sure that we have inter-judge reliability, we must be able to repeat the test with at least two different people doing the measuring.

Suppose, however, that we took the head measurements carelessly or that the tape measure stretched easily and was very difficult to read. Each time it would stretch an unpredictable amount; there would also be some difficulty in reading the exact number for the measurement. If we tried to measure the same twenty people a second time, the correlation between the two sets of measures would be very low, not because head size was unstable, but because the measurements themselves contained random errors. The bottom part of Figure 20.1 shows such a situation. Note that people's scores are inconsistent, and the rank order changes (their relative standings do not remain the same). This is an example of an unreliable set of measurements, or an unreliable test.

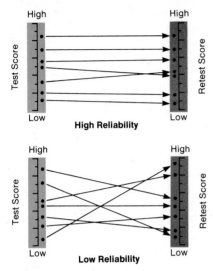

Figure 20.1 The concept of test reliability. On the left in each diagram the test scores obtained by seven individuals are ordered on a scale. On the right the corresponding scores on a second version of the same test, or on the same test given at a later time, are ordered. In the upper diagram the two sets of scores correspond very closely. This pattern of scores means that the test is highly reliable. In the lower diagram, there is little relationship between the two sets of scores. This scrambled pattern means that the test has a low reliability: Two different administrations of the same test gave quite different results.

In most actual psychological testing, the items that are collected are supposed to measure a certain attribute—intelligence, aggression, anxiety, and the like. These items are put in the form of a questionnaire or test, which is administered to a number of people. To establish test-retest reliability, the test is given to the same people a second time and the correlation of results of the two testings is checked. Internal reliability or consistency is checked by splitting the test into halves at random and looking at the correlation between the halves. Before a test is judged to be reliable, there must be evidence that it can be administered, scored, and interpreted with similar results by any appropriately trained and qualified person.

VALIDITY The reliability of a test merely assures us that we have established a consistently accurate procedure for measuring. Now we must establish

the *meaning* of these measurements: Are they indeed valid indicators of the thing we are measuring?

Validity is an abstraction, for it has no independent existence outside a specific context. A test is valid only in relation to some criterion or valid only for some particular purpose. Generally speaking, a test is valid if it measures what it is supposed to measure. One way to determine whether a test is valid is to see whether its findings correlate with other tests that are supposed to measure the same thing. To find out whether head size is a valid measure of intelligence, we could administer the Stanford-Binet test, an established test of intelligence (discussed in detail later in this chapter), to our subjects; we could then compare their ratings on this test with their rankings in the head measurements previously taken. Did the subject with the largest head score highest on the Stanford-Binet, the second largest head score a little lower, and so on to the smallest head and lowest score? If so, we could say that our little test has **concurrent validity**: its results correlate with other tests measuring the same characteristics.

Another type of validity is **predictive validity**—whether or not a test predicts a subject's subsequent performance on tasks that are related to the characteristic being measured. Intelligence, for example, is related to college grades; by and large, the brightest students can be expected to attain the highest grades. If head measurement were a valid test for intelligence, we would be able to predict that those students with the largest heads would perform best in college.

As Figure 20.2 shows, it turns out that head size does not correlate with performance on the Stanford-Binet test, so our test does not have concurrent validity. Nor does head size accurately predict which college student will have the highest grade-point average, so it does not have predictive validity. In fact, there is a zero correlation between head size and college grades. We must therefore conclude that head measurement is not a valid test for intelligence.

Head size is, however, a valid indicator of hat size, whereas the Stanford-Binet is quite useless for that purpose. It is important to remember that test validity is always relative to a particular situation and must be stated in specific terms or with regard to specific criteria. Tests can have high validity for one purpose but low validity for others. The best intelligence tests are good predictors of academic performance, but they give very little indication of creative talent. The concurrent and predictive

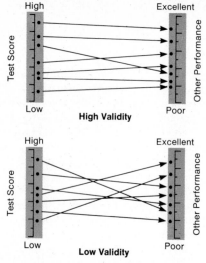

Figure 20.2 The concept of test validity. A comparison of this figure with Figure 20.1 shows that reliability and validity are assessed in exactly the same way. The difference is that while assessment of reliability requires that a test be checked against itself, assessment of validity requires that the test scores be compared to some other measure of behavior. For example, the lower diagram might represent the comparison of scores on the "head-size" test of intelligence (on the left) with school grades (on the right). The upper diagram might represent the result of comparing Stanford-Binet scores with school grades. The Stanford-Binet is a valid test for predicting school grades; the head-size measurement is not.

validity of any test should be evaluated carefully, and a test should be used only for the purpose specifically validated. This is especially important when a test is used as a selection device that may have far-reaching consequences for those who take it.

STANDARDIZATION Still another kind of information that must be provided if a test is to be useful is an indication of the test's **normative distribution**. A score in itself tells us very little unless we know what kind of scores other people have attained. If an individual has correctly answered fifty-three of the eighty-eight questions on a test, it is impossible to say whether the subject has done well or poorly unless it is known that most people are able to answer only forty-four questions correctly. Testers develop such normative distributions—**norms**—before a test is put into general use by giving it to a large and well-defined group of people, called a **standardization group**. It is usual to take the arithmetical average of the standardization group's scores

as a reference point and indicate how far above or below this average any given score is. There are many ways of doing this.

The **percentile system** and the **standard score system** are the most common methods of translating "raw" scores (that is, the scores individuals actually make) into scores that are relative to the scores of others. The percentile system divides a group of scores into one hundred equal parts. Since each percentile then contains 1/100 of the scores, a percentile number shows the proportion of the standardization group above and below which a person scores. For example, a score at the eightieth percentile would be higher than the scores of 79 percent of the rest of the people who took the test and lower than the scores of 19 percent.

Standard scores are more complex. They represent points on a bell-shaped curve (see Figure 20.3) that reflects the normal pattern of distribution of scores on almost any test. (The concept of normal distribution was discussed in Chapter 2.) The normal distribution shows that the majority of people obtain scores within a narrow range lying somewhere in the middle of the distribution of all the test scores. The farther a score is from the middle, or average, the fewer the people who obtain it.

Raw scores on most intelligence tests (discussed in the following section) are converted to standard scores with a mean of 100 and a standard deviation of 15; as a result, about 68 percent of the population achieves IQ scores between 85 and 115; over 95 percent achieves scores between 70 and 130, and over 99.7 percent achieves scores between 55 and 145.

To produce norm tables for either a percentile system or a standard score system is not difficult after a standardization group has been tested. It is more difficult—yet extremely important—to make sure that the standardization group, on which test norms are based, is really representative of the population in which the test will be used.

Most tests require several sets of norms—for example, norms appropriate for people of different ages, sexes, and races. The group to which a person is compared must be the group to which he or she belongs. In intelligence testing, age is the most important factor, but sex, social class, and race can also be significant. Most intelligence tests have been developed and validated with middle-class white people as the standardization group. There are few norms for members of other social classes and races; therefore, the established norms may be inappropriate for individuals of other classes and races who take these tests.

THE MEASUREMENT OF INTELLIGENCE, APTITUDE, AND ACHIEVEMENT

The most frequently administered test measuring mental characteristics is the intelligence test. Alfred Binet, a French psychologist, was the first to develop a reliable test of this kind. Before Binet's work, psychologists had attempted to measure intelligence by giving sensory and motor tests: they tested people's ability to estimate the passage of time, the efficiency of their hand–eye coordination, their speed of finger-tapping, and their memory. Near the end of the nineteenth century Binet began testing children's vocabulary, their recognition of familiar objects, their understanding of commands, and the like; he was looking for abilities that changed with age. Binet reasoned that if older children did better on the tests than younger children, then children who performed better than others of their own age must be mentally older—more intelligent—than their age-mates.

In 1905 Binet was asked by the Minister of Public Instruction for the Paris schools to develop a test that could identify mentally defective children, who could then be taught separately. In collaboration with Theodore Simon, a psychiatrist, Binet devised a thirty-item test, arranging the items or tasks in order of increasing difficulty. By 1908 Binet's tests were also being used to differentiate among normal children and to predict their school performance (Binet and Simon, 1916).

Binet originally defined as retarded those children whose scores were two years or more below the average scores for children of their chronological age. One problem with this definition was that children aged fourteen who were two years behind their age group were considered to be as retarded as children of six who were also two years behind their age group. A German psychologist, William Stern (1914), suggested that instead of using the *difference* between mental age (defined as the average age of children who obtain a particular score on an intelligence test) and chronological age, examiners

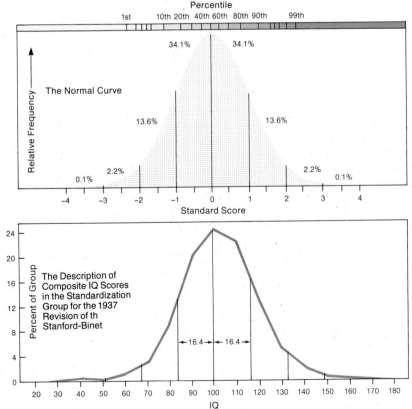

Figure 20.3 The theoretical normal curve (A) and a practical application of it (B). The curves show the proportions of a group or population that fall at various points on a scale; (A) The theoretical curve is useful because it has precise mathematical characteristics from which such relative measures as standard and percentile scores can be calculated. A standard score describes the position of an individual's score in terms of the variance of the group's scores. A percentile score describes the position of an individual's score in terms of the percentage of scores in the group that his or her score exceeds. A single standard-score unit corresponds to about 16.4 IQ points on the 1937 Stanford-Binet test. Knowing this correspondence and knowing the average IQ (approximately 100), one can convert any IQ into a standard score or a percentile score by reading the theoretical curve. (Bottom graph after Terman and Merrill, 1973)

should use the *ratio* of mental age to chronological age. His idea resulted in the **intelligence quotient (IQ)**, which is computed by dividing mental age by chronological age and multiplying by 100 (to get rid of the decimals).

There are many ways of measuring intelligence. Some tests are designed to be administered to individuals, others to groups. Other kinds of tests measure aptitude or achievement, rather than IQ. We shall consider examples of the various types of tests in the sections that follow.

INDIVIDUAL INTELLIGENCE TESTS   Individual intelligence tests are administered by one examiner to one subject. Two individual intelligence tests in wide use today are the current version of Binet's test and the intelligence scales developed by David Wechsler.

THE STANFORD-BINET TEST   Binet's test of intelligence has been revised many times since he developed it. The Stanford University revision, called the **Stanford-Binet test**, is the one currently employed in the United States. This test contains a number of subtests—some of verbal ability and some of performance—that are grouped by age. Performance subtests include such activities as picture completion, block design, picture arrangement, and object assembly (see photo). They are arranged in an order designed to hold the interest of the person being tested. To ensure that the scores do not reflect factors other than ability, the examiner is trained to carry out the standardized instructions exactly, but at the same time to try to put the subject at ease and keep him or her motivated.

The examiner first asks the subject some questions—often from the vocabulary test—to locate the proper level at which to start. For example, if a nine-year-old who seems reasonably bright is being tested, the examiner will probably begin with the tests for an eight-year-old. If the child misses some of the questions, the examiner drops back to tests for year seven. After locating the basal age—the highest age at which the child can pass all items—the examiner proceeds with tests at later year levels. When the child reaches the level at which he or she can pass no items, the testing session ends.

In the final scoring, the mental age indicates the level of development the child has reached. If a child is said to have a mental age of twelve, this means that his or her performance on the tests was as good as the average twelve-year-old's. The IQ indicates how that level of development compares with the level reached by other children of the same chronological age. In addition, the examiner generally picks up a good deal of qualitative information about how the child's mind works, which can be useful to teachers or psychotherapists who deal with the child. The original Binet tests were designed for school-age children, but successive revisions of the

Two tests on the Stanford-Binet Intelligence Scale being administered to a little boy. Both these tests are ones that would be easily passed by him unless he were severely retarded. (left) The examiner has built a tower of four blocks and has told the child, "You make one like this." The average two-year-old is able to build the tower. Three-year-olds are asked to copy a three-block bridge. (right) The examiner shows the child the card with six small objects attached to it and says, "See all these things? Show me the dog," and so on. The average two-year-old can point to the correct objects as they are named.

A woman at a YMCA counseling service is shown taking one subtest of the Wechsler Adult Intelligence Scale. She is being timed while she assembles the cubes to match a pattern in the booklet that stands in front of her.

Stanford-Binet tests have extended the scale to both preschool and adult levels.

In the 1960 revision the method of reporting scores was changed. Now a person's score is no longer expressed as the quotient of mental age to chronological age. Instead, it is the standard score that he or she would be assigned in the appropriate norm group, with a mean of 100 and a standard deviation of 15. These are still called IQ scores, but they are more accurately called "deviation IQs" because they show how far a person's score deviates from the mean of the appropriate norm group (Terman and Merrill, 1973).

THE WAIS AND THE WISC The other most frequently used individual intelligence tests are the **Wechsler Adult Intelligence Scale (WAIS)** and the **Wechsler Intelligence Scale for Children (WISC)**. Like the Stanford-Binet, these tests are made up of both verbal and performance subtests, but they are arranged differently. Items of the same kind are grouped together into a subtest and arranged in order of difficulty. The examiner administers each of the subtests, starting with a very easy item and continuing until the end or until the person has missed a predetermined number of items in succession (Wechsler, 1955, 1958).

The Wechsler tests differ from the Stanford-Binet in several ways. For one thing, the Wechsler tests have more performance tasks and are therefore less biased toward verbal skills. For another, the Wechsler tests do not have different items for different ages; the WISC items (similar to those shown in Figure 20.4) are the same for children of all ages, and the WAIS items are the same for all adults. Finally, there is one major overall difference between the two tests: the Stanford-Binet yields a single IQ score; the Wechsler tests give separate scores for each kind of subtest—vocabulary, information, arithmetic, picture arrangement, block design, and so on. The subtest scores are in turn combined into separate IQ scores for verbal and performance abilities. This method of scoring helps the examiner make a qualitative sketch of how an individual reacts to different kinds of items. Most important, it encourages the treatment of intelligence as a number of different abilities rather than as one generalized ability. For an example of this method of scoring, see Figure 20.5.

GROUP INTELLIGENCE TESTS Group intelligence tests are strictly paper-and-pencil measures; there is no person-to-person interchange, as with individual tests. The convenience and economy of group tests have led to their use in schools, em-

ployment offices, and many other mass testing situations. The Army Alpha and Army Beta, for example, were developed during World War I for classifying soldiers. The test mentioned by Isaac Asimov in the brief essay that opens this chapter was probably a more recent version of the Army Alpha.

Group intelligence tests include verbal and performance varieties and many combinations of the two. However, group tests do not generally predict school performance as well as individual tests do, and clinicians still prefer individual tests. Because group tests are usually used in particular situations for particular purposes, it is not possible to pick out one or two tests that are as representative of group tests as the Stanford-Binet and Wechsler instruments are of individual tests.

ACHIEVEMENT AND APTITUDE TESTS

Achievement tests were originally constructed to assess accurately how much individuals know about subjects taught in school; **aptitude tests** were designed to find out how much talent or capacity individuals have for particular lines of work. As time passed, however, the distinction between achievement tests and aptitude tests became more and more blurred. What psychologists first thought were tests of aptitude—defined as innate ability or talent—turned out partly to measure different kinds of expe-

Figure 20.4 Items like these make up the performance subtests of the Wechsler Intelligence Scale for Children. Picture arrangement requires that the panels be properly sequenced; picture completion requires that the missing detail be supplied. Object assembly, like putting together a jigsaw puzzle, requires the construction of a whole object from its pieces. Coding requires the proper matching of digit and symbol when only the digit is given. In all these tasks—especially the coding—speed and accuracy are at a premium. It should be noted that maximum performance on these subtests does require familiarity with the general objects and situations depicted, and this familiarity is highly influenced by such factors as cultural, educational, and socioeconomic background.

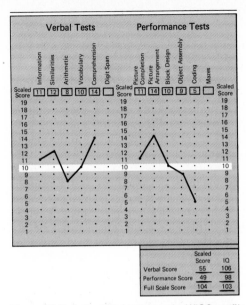

Figure 20.5 A simplified version of a WISC profile for a thirteen-year-old male. (The optional digit span and mazes subscales were not administered.) Scores from each of the subscales within the verbal and performance groupings are first converted into special scaled scores and plotted accordingly on the chart. Then individual subtest scores are added together, yielding a total verbal and a total performance score. In turn, these scores are summed to reflect the full-scale score. Lastly, the full-scale score is converted into the full-scale IQ score—in this case 103, or about average. The separability of scores on the subscales is sometimes useful in determining specific talents or deficits that might not have been apparent if only the overall IQ score were reported. (Adapted from WISC-R record form, © 1971, 1974, The Psychological Corporation.)

rience, so that they had to be regarded in some sense as achievement tests as well. Because achievement tests often turned out to be good predictors of many kinds of occupational abilities, they were also in some sense aptitude tests. Thus the distinction has come to rest more on purpose than on content. When a test is used to evaluate what a person knows, it is an achievement test; when the same test is used to predict how successful the person will be, it is an aptitude test.

Although achievement and aptitude tests are similar, they must be validated in different ways. If one is interested in achievement, the important consideration is **content validity**: the test items must fairly represent the aspect of achievement being tested. If one wishes to assess aptitude, one seeks evidence about the test's **predictive validity**: people who do well on the test must in fact turn out to perform well in situations for which their aptitude is being tested.

Psychologists once hoped that achievement test-

ing would lead to significant improvements in education and that aptitude testing would enable each person to find an occupation in life that suited him or her. While mass application of these tests has not achieved these goals, the tests have become useful tools for counseling individuals who must make decisions about academic and vocational alternatives. Ultimately, however, effective counseling depends on trained people who understand the limitations of these tests and know how to use them constructively.

THE SCHOLASTIC APTITUDE TEST The College Entrance Examination Board's **Scholastic Aptitude Test (SAT)** has probably been taken by almost every student who reads this book. The test is a direct descendant of the Army Alpha and was first administered in 1926. Designed to measure "aptitude for college studies" rather than school achievement or general intelligence, the test has been continuously and meticulously revised and updated. Currently it yields two scores, SAT-V for verbal aptitude and SAT-M for mathematical aptitude. The reliability of both scores is very high: .89 for SAT-V and .88 for SAT-M (Wallace, 1965)—quite close to a perfect correlation, which, as we saw in Chapter 2, would be 1.00. The validity for predicting college grades is .39 for SAT-V and .33 for SAT-M. High school records, which show a validity of .55, are more valid than the two SAT scores as a predictor of college grades. But when all three measures are combined into one index, the correlation with college grades is .62 (DuBois, 1965). These validities are high enough to make the SAT useful in predicting college performance, but low enough to make it clear that other factors, such as motivation, are also important determinants of academic success.

THE GENERAL APTITUDE TEST BATTERY The most impressive work in aptitude measurement has been done by the United States Employment Service, which has produced a two-and-a-half-hour set of tests called the **General Aptitude Test Battery (GATB)**, a sample from which is shown in Figure 20.6. The GATB makes it possible for a person to find out whether he or she meets minimum standards for each of a considerable number of occupations.

INTERGROUP DIFFERENCES IN INTELLIGENCE As we mentioned earlier, many relation-

457

Figure 20.6 The General Aptitude Test Battery consists of a number of different kinds of tests. Samples of items testing verbal and mathematical skills (top) and manual dexterity (bottom) are shown here. The results of the GATB might tell a person, for example, that he had the minimum reading comprehension and manual dexterity required to become a typist.

1. Which two words have the same meaning?
   (a) open **(b)** happy **(c)** glad
   (d) green

2. Which two words have the opposite meaning?
   (a) old **(b)** dry **(c)** cold
   (d) young

3. A man works 8 hours a day, 40 hours a week. He earns $1.40 an hour. How much does he earn each week?
   (A) $40.00 **(C)** $50.60
   (B) $44.60 **(D)** $56.00

4. At the left is a drawing of a flat piece of metal. Which object at the right can be made from this piece of metal?

ships between IQ and other attributes have been found, but the significance of these relationships is often difficult to determine. For example, it is well established that the higher a person's social class (as measured by occupational level, educational level, and income), the higher his or her IQ score is likely to be. Interpretation of this relationship is not easy, because people in the higher social classes clearly have more exposure to the skills that are tested on intelligence tests. In a classic study of people with high IQs, Lewis Terman (1916) followed over 1,000 gifted students from early childhood to adulthood. He found a significant positive correlation between IQ and physical, academic, social, and moral development. Brighter persons were generally taller, heavier, stronger, more advanced in social and personal maturity, and more successful in school and other social situations. People with high IQs were also less likely to show lethal behavior (fatal accidents, suicide), delinquency and criminality, alcoholism, drug dependency, and severe mental illnesses. And, finally, Terman found that highly intelligent people received more degrees, distinctions, awards, professional licenses and certifications, and income; they made more artistic and literary contributions and reported more satisfaction in life. But all these relationships may result not from IQ itself but from a combination of other factors, such as social class and special educational experiences.

IQ SCORES: NATURE OR NURTURE? Many people have tried to use intelligence tests to obtain definitive answers to the age-old question about whether there are innate intellectual differences among groups, but it has proved to be almost impossible to come to reliable conclusions. People whose childhood environment has been quite different from that of the majority of American and European children tend to have lower scores on tests developed in the United States and Europe. This difference, even when statistically significant, cannot be accepted as evidence that various groups differ in innate potential, because a person's score reflects not only his or her genetic potential for intellectual development (nature) but also what he or she has learned from experience (nurture).

If a test is developed for people with a specific cultural background, it cannot legitimately be used for people with a markedly different background. For example, of all the kinds of items on intelligence tests, vocabulary provides the best single estimate of IQ scores; yet vocabulary clearly depends on one's cultural background. A person who has never heard words like "sonata" or "ingenuous" will perform poorly on verbal intelligence tests. And a person who has grown up in a community where the primary language is not English will be handicapped even further. It is very difficult to eliminate cultural bias from intelligence tests. Figure 20.7 reproduces some questions from the Counterbalance Intelligence Test, deliberately devised by Adrian Dove, a black, to be culturally biased against whites. Dove's purpose was to demonstrate, through exaggeration, the effect one's background can have on intelligence test scores. (For further discussion of cultural bias in IQ tests, see the accompanying Special Feature on pages 460-461.)

There are differences among the *average* IQ scores of different races and nationalities. However, it has proved to be virtually impossible to conceive of those differences as resulting primarily from either differences in heredity or differences in upbringing and environment. Still, the relationship between these factors continues to fascinate social scientists, as we shall see in the next section.

RACIAL DIFFERENCES IN IQ: THE DEBATE In 1969, Arthur Jensen, an educational psychologist, published an article in the *Harvard Educational Review*. In it he asserted that genetic factors might prove to be "strongly implicated" in the fact that the IQ scores of black people are, on the average, 11 to 15 points lower than the scores of white people. Jensen's thesis, that IQ is highly heritable and that therefore racial differences in IQ are due largely to differences in the gene distributions of the populations studied, caused an uproar that has not yet died down.

In order to understand the arguments for and against Jensen's view, it is necessary to remember the discussion of heritability in Chapter 3. **Heritability** is the extent to which an observed individual variation of a trait (such as IQ) can be attributed to genetic differences among members of a particular population in a particular environment. To say that a trait has high heritability is not to say that genes "cause" it. Heritability is a meas-

ure that is specific to a given population in a given environment; it is not a constant property of the trait per se.

Another concept crucial for understanding genetic influences is that of the **reaction range**. The genetic makeup of each person has a unique range of possible responses to the environment he or she encounters. In the case of height, good nutrition will make each of us taller than poor nutrition will, but under both conditions genetic makeup will dictate that some of us will be taller than others. Genes do not specify a particular height for anyone. What they do specify is a *pattern* of growth that varies in response to nutrition and other environmental factors. Thus, the height a person reaches is a result of both heredity and environment.

The development of the intellectual skills measured by IQ tests also has a reaction range. No matter how stimulating their environments, few people become Albert Einsteins or Leonardo da Vincis. And in other than extremely deprived circumstances, most people do not become mentally retarded. Each person who is not subjected to severe deprivation (which can make anyone mentally retarded) has a range of perhaps 20 to 25 points in which his or her IQ score can vary, depending on that person's environment (Scarr-Salapatek, 1971a).

Jensen's side of the IQ controversy, then, can be phrased as follows: If individual differences in intelligence *within* the black and the white populations taken separately have a high heritability, it is possible that the average differences *between* these racial groups likewise reflect genetic differences. Jensen has also ruled out a number of environmental factors that have been proposed to explain black-white IQ differences. Here are some of his major points:

1. Even when socioeconomic class of the two races is equated, blacks score well below whites, on the average.

2. Environmental deprivation affects Native Americans (Indians) more than blacks, yet Native Americans score higher on IQ tests than blacks, on the average.

3. The absence of the father in many lower-class black homes has not been found to account for the lower intelligence level.

4. The race of the examiner has not been found to make a difference in the IQ scores of black children when many studies are considered (Jensen, 1969).

Figure 20.7 An extreme example of how an intelligence test may depend on knowledge specific to one culture. A population of urban blacks would score high on this test, and a population of suburban whites would score low. Even when a test's items do not show this kind of obvious culture loading, a test may have validity problems. For example, many subcultures within Western society place great emphasis on competence in test taking. In a subculture where such emphasis is lacking, the validity of almost any test is likely to suffer.

The Dove Counterbalance Intelligence Test
by Adrian Dove

If they throw the dice and "7" is showing on the top, what is facing down?
(a) "Seven"   (b) "Snake eyes"
(c) "Boxcars"   (d) "Little Joes"
(e) "Eleven".

Jazz pianist Ahmad Jamal took an Arabic name after becoming really famous. Previously he had some fame with what he called his "slave name." What was his previous name?
(a) Willie Lee Jackson
(b) LeRoi Jones
(c) Wilbur McDougal
(d) Fritz Jones   (e) Andy Johnson

In "C. C. Rider," what does "C. C." stand for?
(a) Civil Service
(b) Church Council
(c) County Circuit, preacher of an old-time rambler
(d) Country Club
(e) "Cheating Charley" (the "Boxcar Gunsel")

Cheap "chitlings" (not the kind you purchase at the frozen-food counter) will taste rubbery unless they are cooked long enough. How soon can you quit cooking them to eat and enjoy them?
(a) 15 minutes   (b) 2 hours
(c) 24 hours
(d) 1 week (on a low flame)
(e) 1 hour

If a judge finds you guilty of "holding weed" (in California), what's the most he can give you?
(a) Indeterminate (life)   (b) A nickel
(c) A dime   (d) A year in county
(e) $100.00.

A "Handkerchief Head" is
(a) A cool cat   (b) A porter
(c) An "Uncle Tom"   (d) A hoddi
(e) A "preacher"

Cultural Bias in
IQ Tests

What if intelligence tests were made up largely of vocabulary terms like "Deuce and a Quarter" and "Mr. Charlie" (Robert Williams, cited in Albee, 1978)? How "smart" would they show the average white middle-class student to be? Almost any black inner-city child can tell us that a Deuce and a Quarter is a Buick Electra 225 and Mr. Charlie refers to any white man. On the basis of such a test, would the ghetto child be considered more intelligent than the middle-class child? Better able to succeed in school? Innately superior?

Obviously, any test that relies heavily on vocabulary terms like these is culturally biased. It would hardly be fair to judge the intelligence of white middle-class youngsters by their ability to define expressions they have never even heard. Yet the makers of IQ tests often include in tests such words as "ingenuous" and "hither," words that

are undoubtedly more familiar to white middle-class children than to their minority-group peers.

The Nature of the Bias

In a recent article George W. Albee (1978) presented a clear, concise overview of the issue of cultural bias in IQ tests. Albee pointed out that these tests are generally used for predicting academic performance—performance in schools largely run by and for the white middle class, schools that embrace and promote the dominant values of our society. In fact, Lewis Terman, who brought Binet's test to the United States and adapted it to American use, limited his selection of items to material from the prevailing school curriculum (Garcia, 1972). Even today, IQ assessment focuses on standard English vocabulary and mathematics, subjects in which white middle-class youngsters un-

doubtedly have the advantage of greater exposure.

Even the scoring of IQ tests seems to be biased in favor of white middle-class norms, or standards of behavior. For example, to the question, "What would you do if another child grabbed your hat and ran with it?" most white middle-class children answer that they would report the problem to an adult. Many black inner-city youngsters, however, answer that they would chase the offender and fight to get the hat back. The first response would be scored as "correct," the second as "incorrect," though neither solution is absolutely "right" for all children (Albee, 1978).

The standardization groups against whose scores all raw scores are evaluated are generally composed of white urban children from English-speaking families. Though these groups supposedly represent a socioeconomic cross-section, so-

cial class is identified by the occupation of the father—which means that the samples are limited to children from families in which the father is present.

Not even nonverbal IQ tests are free of cultural bias. Albee offers this example:

> One psychologist, Wayne Dennis, tested children in 56 different societies around the world with a simple test called "Draw-a-Man." (This task is a good measure of the child's I.Q. in that it correlates highly with scores on verbal I.Q. tests among American middle-class children.) But on this nonverbal test Bedouin children averaged 58 I.Q. and Hopi and Zuni Indian children averaged about 125.
>
> Are the Indian children really superior to middle-class school children? Are Bedouin children really so retarded? Further investigation revealed that the Arab children lived in a culture that forbade drawing or the making of images. On the other hand, the Indian children lived in a culture that emphasized and rewarded drawings and decoration. Even this nonverbal I.Q. test was highly sensitive to practice and experience. (Albee, 1978)

The Victims

The most obvious victims of cultural bias in IQ tests are the poor and the nonwhite, particularly blacks and Hispanics. However, only about half a century ago certain newly arrived immigrant groups from southern and eastern Europe—including Poles, Jews, and Italians—also had low average IQ scores. Today, after roughly fifty years of upward mobility, Polish, Jewish, and Italian Americans attain scores that equal or surpass the national average. Other groups that have not risen economically have not shown an improvement in average IQ scores (Sowell, 1977).

Children with "subnormal" IQs are often relegated to special classes for the "educable mentally retarded." The proportions of blacks and Hispanics in such classes are far higher than their respective percentages of the population; the proportion of white middle-class students in special classes is far lower. In California's special classes, for example, there are four times as many blacks and three times as many Hispanics, proportionately, as there are white English-speaking children (Albee, 1978).

For the most part, it is schools who do the labeling of children as retarded, and they do it primarily on the basis of IQ scores, without medical corroboration. Judging subjects on their adaptive behavior (their ability to function in society) as well as on their IQs, Jane Mercer (1972) concluded that a vast number of "retarded" adults should not have been so labeled.

Albee has noted that poor learners often misbehave in class and that their teachers may single them out for testing in order to have them removed from regular classes. Once segregated into special classes, children often suffer ridicule from their peers in regular classes. In addition, their subnormal classification places severe limitations on their future educational and vocational opportunities. If their families, teachers, and schoolmates expect a low level of academic performance from them, these youngsters may well respond accordingly. Moreover, this early experience of failure may serve as a cornerstone for a poor self-image (Albee, 1978).

The Outlook for Reform

Various researchers have attempted to develop bias-free IQ tests, but so far no one has succeeded. Meanwhile, IQ tests and the institutions that administer them are increasingly being challenged in the courts. In some areas, schools and school boards are now being held accountable for "educational malpractice." In one dramatic case, a young man sued the New York City Board of Education, claiming that the board had been negligent in denying him an adequate education. At the age of four he had scored one point below normal on an IQ test and had then been put into a special class for the mentally retarded. He was not tested again until he was eighteen, and at that point his score was within the normal range. The jury awarded him $750,000 (Fiske, 1977).

And in a case that may become a landmark, a group of black children in special classes for the educable mentally retarded has brought a class-action suit against the California Board of Education. Their argument is that the scoring of IQ tests penalized them for departing from white norms, as in the example of the "stolen hat" question (Albee, 1978).

Group IQ tests have been banned in the state of California and in the cities of Washington, D.C., Philadelphia, and New York. Similar legislation has been proposed in Massachusetts. As more and more legal and legislative battles are waged against them, it seems doubtful that IQ tests will continue to serve as the sole criterion for assignment to classes, schools, and jobs. While IQ tests will probably continue to be used, it seems likely that they will come to be seen as just one of many ways of assessing the capabilities of complex human beings.

Those who oppose Jensen either attack his methodology or point to environmental factors he has not taken into account. Arguments in rebuttal to Jensen's include the following:

1. Blacks and whites differ in numerous ways besides genetic ones, such as their living conditions and the degree to which they experience discrimination. Blacks and whites supposedly in the same socioeconomic class actually differ considerably in income, education, and quality of housing.

2. Jensen's assertion that black-white IQ differences are not explainable by the few environmental factors investigated does not rule out a possible explanation due to other, as yet unspecified, environmental factors. For example, lead is present in the old paint on the walls of many slum dwellings. Young children commonly eat paint chips; the lead in the paint they eat can cause brain damage, which results in sharp decreases in intelligence. Moreover, pregnant women sometimes develop a craving for paint chips, and recent research has shown that lead can be transmitted from a pregnant woman to her unborn child (Barltrop, 1969; Scanlon and Chisolm, 1972). Another researcher points out that partly because of this transmission, the effects of lead poisoning give the appearance of being genetic although they are not; and lead poisoning is common among urban blacks (Needleman, 1973, 1974). Many such environmental factors that apply disproportionately to black people have not yet been fully studied.

3. IQ tests are affected by such nonintellectual influences as motivation, anxiety, and test-taking skills. These nonintellectual influences lessen the value of the IQ score as a reliable measure of the differences in intelligence among racial groups.

4. Jensen's critics say that he seems to imply that heredity "fixes" intelligence-test scores within limits and that he does not take account of the facts of reaction range. Data from adoption studies (Skodak and Skeels, 1949) suggest that when children are adopted by a family belonging to a higher social class than the one into which they were born, this can produce a significantly higher IQ than would be expected if the same children had been reared by their natural parents.

As Sandra Scarr-Salapatek (1971a), in a review of Jensen's article, has pointed out, "While we may tentatively conclude that there are some genetic IQ differences between social-class groups, we can make only wild speculations about racial groups. . . . [R]acial groups are not random samples from the same population, nor are members reared in uniform conditions within each race." There is in fact a common misunderstanding of the concept of heritability in relation to IQ: If heritability "is high, this reasoning goes, then intelligence is genetically fixed and unchangeable. . . . This misconception ignores the fact that it [heritability] is a population statistic, bound to a given set of environmental conditions at a given point in time. Neither intelligence nor [heritability] estimates are fixed."

Scarr-Salapatek insists that not enough proof exists to support either the arguments of those who say there are racial differences in IQ or the arguments of those who say all such differences can be accounted for by environmental influences. Rather, she has suggested, hereditary and environmental factors may operate together, combining in different ways under different circumstances (see Figure 20.8). For example, adverse environmental conditions limit intellectual achievement and make accurate observations of heritable IQ difficult; in people who grow up in favorable surroundings genetic differences show up more. From her study of 992 sets of twins (1971b), Scarr-Salapatek concludes that adverse environments affect expression of the reaction range, so that the differences between races are due at least in part to environmental differences.

A recent study (Scarr and Weinberg, 1976) has confirmed that IQ has a fairly broad reaction range and can be dramatically affected by changes in the environment. These researchers measured the IQ scores of black children who had been adopted by white couples of higher than average socioeconomic status and of above average intelligence. The children were found to have an average IQ of 106, well above the average for the entire population and about 15 points above the average IQ of black children reared in their own homes in the part of the country in which the study was conducted. In addition, the researchers were able to determine that the biological parents of the adopted black children had been of about average intelligence, lending added support to the assertion that the reaction range of IQ scores is at least as broad as the average differences between racial groups.

The debate over IQ differences among races seems destined to continue for quite a while, for it seems impossible to gather definitive data. In a careful review of the evidence, J. C. Loehlin, Gardner Lindzey, and J. N. Spuhler (1975) have concluded that on intellectual-ability tests the average

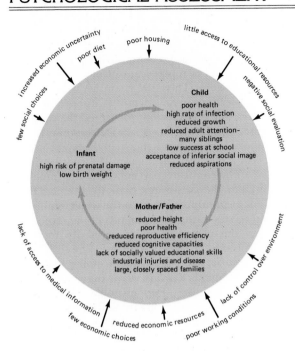

Figure 20.8 While environmental differences do not account for all differences in IQ, one's economic, social, and educational opportunities do play a major role. As this diagram suggests, a vicious circle may be created in which the factors of nature and nurture cannot be easily separated because each, in fact, implies the other. (Richards, Richardson, and Spears, 1972.)

differences in the scores of members of different American racial and ethnic groups reflect in part inadequacies and biases in the tests, in part environmental differences among the groups, and in part genetic differences among the groups. In fact, all three factors interact, and "differences among individuals *within* racial-ethnic and socioeconomic groups greatly exceed in magnitude the average differences between such groups" (p. 239). Thus, any conclusions about hereditary racial differences are very difficult to evaluate and are essentially of little value in making predictions about the behavior of members of various races.

Although the controversy over racial and ethnic differences continues, the fact remains that IQ scores themselves are very useful in many situations. For example, they can help counselors and teachers to decide what kind of special help students may require. However, tests that measure specific abilities and levels of achievement are even more useful for this purpose, and they have been less controversial than measures of general intelligence.

THE MEASUREMENT OF PERSONALITY

Personality assessment has developed from two distinct sources, differential psychology and abnormal psychology. Differential psychology is, simply, the study of differences between individuals. Darwin's work on evolution focused attention on individual differences in behavior that had adaptability and survival value. Sir Francis Galton, a British scholar of the nineteenth century, attempted to categorize and measure what he called "the durable realities and persistent factors of our conduct," our temperament and character (1884). He suggested measuring emotion with instruments that record physiological changes in pulse rate and heartbeat, and devising social situations to measure personality traits such as good temper and optimism.

At about the same time in France, Alfred Binet began a series of studies of the mental functioning and personality of eminent persons. The subjects were given a wide variety of tasks involving such skills as word knowledge, reasoning, and mathematical ability. These investigations led to Binet's now-famous intelligence tests.

While Galton and Binet were primarily interested in measuring personality traits among the normal population, other scholars investigated the characteristics of the insane or abnormal. Abnormal psychology, the study of psychological disorders and the practice of psychotherapy, led to the development of measures for diagnostic use. This interest in diagnosis stemmed from the need to classify and categorize psychopathologies. The earliest attempts at personality assessment with psychopathological cases involved word-association procedures. Emil Kraepelin, the German psychiatrist responsible for our current psychiatric classification system (see Chapter 22), made use of a **free-association test** as early as 1892. In such a test, the subject is presented with a stimulus word and asked to respond as quickly as possible with the first word that comes to mind.

The use of word association for identifying unconscious personality conflicts was first proposed by Carl Jung. In 1910 Jung developed a standardized list of words to be used in detecting conflicts in those patients who reacted to them in unusual ways, such as by failing to respond or by blushing, stammering, or misunderstanding a word.

From these beginnings (as summarized in Lanyon and Goodstein, 1971), thousands of tests and other techniques for personality assessment have been developed. In general, the tests in differential psychology are objective paper-and-pencil tests that can be evaluated for reliability and validity. The tests developed by Cattell to find the basic factors of personality (discussed in Chapter 19) are of this sort, as is the Personality Research Form. Some of the tests developed for diagnostic purposes are also objective paper-and-pencil tests; among them is the Minnesota Multiphasic Personality Inventory. Other diagnostic tests are projective instruments, which are subjective by nature; two important ones are the Rorschach Inkblot Test and the Thematic Apperception Test. All these tests are discussed in the sections that follow.

PROJECTIVE TESTS In projective tests personality characteristics are revealed in the way subjects respond to and interpret ambiguous material. Projective tests attempt to measure unconscious dispositions. The idea is that because there is no established meaning to the test materials, any meaning that the subjects put into their responses must come from themselves and should therefore reveal something about their personalities. Some of the ambiguous test materials are highly abstract, like inkblots; others are more concrete, like pictures of actual social situations.

THE RORSCHACH INKBLOT TEST Perhaps the best-known projective diagnostic technique is the one developed in 1911 by Hermann Rorschach, a Swiss psychiatrist. In the **Rorschach Inkblot Test** the subject is handed a series of inkblots one at a time and asked to report what he or she sees, using free association. Then the examiner asks certain general questions in an attempt to discover what it was about the inkblots that prompted the subject's responses (Beck, 1961). A sample response to the Rorschach Inkblot Test is shown in the boxed insert.

In scoring the test, three general categories are involved. The first category indicates how much of the inkblot the person responds to, ranging from small or even minute detail to the whole blot. The second relates to the determinants of the response—whether the person responds primarily to form, color, shading, or level of activity. The third category has to do with the content of the responses. Content as such is less important than the way the individual *uses* it. For example, mixing indiscriminately parts belonging to different animals and human beings may indicate a serious psychological disorder, and so may talking about things that go far beyond the test materials at hand. (See Figure 20.9.)

It would be a mistake to place too much emphasis on the scoring techniques used by Rorschach examiners. The Rorschach method is highly impressionistic. It is based to a large extent upon the examiner's insight, capacity for careful observation, and awareness of the manner in which psychopathology is revealed. In the assessment procedure, the examiner will incorporate not only the individual's Rorschach responses but also his or her reaction to the test situation itself. Some people, for example, are extremely defensive and wary in the test situation. Others define it in authoritarian terms, seeing the

"It Looks Like a Monster with Big Feet"

Rorschach inkblots used in a projective test of personality. In interpreting a person's response to all ten inkblots in the series, examiners pay at least as much attention to the style of the responses as to their content. For example, a person's tendency to see white or shaded areas as meaningful, or to see the blot as a whole rather than as a collection of parts, is deemed significant in scoring and interpretation. When presented with the inkblot shown in Figure 20.9, a young female outpatient free-associated that "it sort of looks like a monster with big feet. A cute little thing. Really a dashing little monster. Such a friendly little guy." Further probing by the examiner showed that the woman was responding to the blot as a whole instead of to only a portion of it, and was concerned primarily with its shape or form, which, while human-like, was not distinctly human. Interpreting the meaning of Rorschach responses is a complicated task. Despite the fact that formal attempts to establish its reliability and validity have failed, the test remains very widely used.

Source: Richard I. Lanyon and Leonard D. Goodstein. *Personality Assessment*, © 1971, p. 50. Reprinted by permission of John Wiley and Sons, Inc., New York.

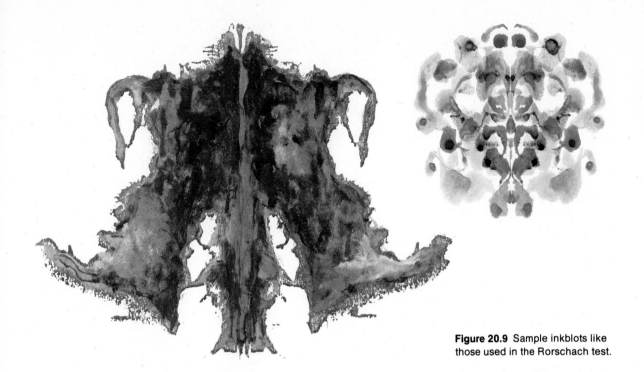

Figure 20.9 Sample inkblots like those used in the Rorschach test.

examiner as a "boss" whose orders they must follow. Still others view the test situation as a competitive one, expecting their performance to be evaluated against some standard and judged for its quality (Schachtel, 1966).

The lack of structure involved in the Rorschach technique, as in many other projective techniques, is both a strength and a weakness. It is a strength in that it samples a broad range of behavior and permits certain patterns to emerge that might not otherwise become apparent. The disadvantage of such an approach is that the interpretation or the results is open to the examiner's biases.

THE THEMATIC APPERCEPTION TEST The **Thematic Apperception Test (TAT)**, developed by Henry Murray in 1935, consists of a series of cards depicting ambiguous scenes that include one or two people. Usually, the subject is shown twenty or fewer of these cards, chosen for their appropriateness to his or her age and sex. The subject is asked to tell a coherent story about each picture, including what led up to the situation, what the characters are thinking and feeling, and how the situation will end. (See Figure 20.10.)

The stories are usually analyzed on an individual basis; that is, one person's stories are not compared with another's. Originally, Murray suggested that the TAT be interpreted in terms of a person's "internal needs" and "environmental presses"—concepts in Murray's own theory of personality (Murray et al., 1938). Now a variety of other systems, including some based on psychoanalytic theory, are also employed. Clinical psychologists agree only moderately well about interpretations of the TAT and predictions based on it. In fact, agreement among these professionals often does not exceed that among psychology students who have not received specific training in TAT interpretation.

All the methods of interpreting the TAT depend on certain assumptions regarding the sort of fantasy that is tapped by the test. Common assumptions are that the subject usually identifies with the hero or heroine of the story, that the subject's stories will reveal his or her motives, and that unusual responses are more likely than typical ones to reveal important aspects of personality.

OBJECTIVE TESTS Like intelligence tests, objective personality tests assume that subjects have varying amounts of the trait being measured. Just as on an intelligence test, many items are used in order to obtain the most reliable measurement, because no single item is a useful measure of the trait.

One type of objective personality test is akin to intelligence tests in that such tests are constructed by a factor-analytic method. As we saw in Chapter 19, factor analysis is the process of finding the smallest number of factors that can account for all the correlations among a set of variables.

Just as a person of a certain level of intelligence

"She's Still Very Much Under Her Control. . . ."

The scene depicted in this drawing, as in all others used in the Thematic Apperception Test, permits a variety of interpretations. The person taking the test is assumed to project his or her own needs, wishes, defenses, and other personality factors into the story. A problem with this assumption is its reliability. It is difficult to be certain that the story a person tells is the product of some enduring characteristic of his or her personality rather than a product of some recent experience. To gain an idea of what kind of responses are elicited, the story told in response to this card by the same twenty-three-year-old female outpatient as in Figure 20.10 is reproduced here. It must be remembered that her response only *suggests* certain themes; confirmation or disconfirmation of any theme also depends upon responses to the other TAT cards as well as to other sources of clinical data.

Figure 20.10 One of the stimulus cards used in the Thematic Apperception Test. (After Murray, 1943.)·

Well, there's a young woman in the foreground and an older in the background, and the older woman looks as though she has planned something that will be harmful to the younger woman, who looks very naive. And in fact the older woman has planned to keep the younger woman captive, and to make her serve her, for the rest of the older woman's life. But although the girl is naive, she's also rebellious; and by asserting herself with other people and getting a group of friends she's able to move out of the—not exactly spell, but she's able to break the bond that the older woman has around her. Right now she's just beginning to realize that she is being put in a position like this, but she's still very much under the control of the older woman, because these two have lived together for a long time. In fact, the younger woman was raised by the older woman. She's still very much under her control as I said, and she has strong feelings of guilt and fear of facing the world on her own. But fortunately she is able to make friends. At this point, though, she hasn't broken the bonds and she feels very confused, like she's being drawn between two poles. Ultimately, she's able to go out and make friends, and getting to know people and the different ways they have from the ways the old woman had taught her, she's able successfully to face the older woman, and defy her control, and go out and live a life of her own.

Source: Richard I. Lanyon and Leonard D. Goodstein. *Personality Assessment,* © 1971, p. 57–58. Reprinted by permission of John Wiley and Sons, Inc., New York.

will be able to answer a certain item on an intelligence test correctly and someone of a lower level will not, a person with a certain degree of, say, nurturance will usually agree strongly with a statement on a personality test such as "It is important to help others," and those possessing a small amount of nurturance will not. Consequently, items that are believed to be related to a specific trait are grouped together on the test. The test is then administered experimentally several times until the pool of items is reduced to those that have the highest amount of internal consistency and the highest relationship to the trait being measured. The Personality Research Form, discussed later, is a test that is constructed in this way.

Another type of personality test is constructed and developed very differently: according to the empirical method. In such a test a large number of items is selected without regard to their relationship to a certain trait. The items are then administered to an experimental group of people who are known to have various psychological disorders and to another group of people who are known to be "normal," or free of the disorder being measured. Those items that differentiate between the two groups—that is, the items receiving one answer from most of the disturbed subjects and a different answer from most of the normal subjects—are identified and retained; the others are discarded. This refinement and selection process is repeated several times until a test has been constructed that is as reliable and valid as possible. The Minnesota Multiphasic Personality Inventory, discussed next, is an example of a test developed according to this empirical method.

It must be noted that the validity of both kinds of tests can be questioned. The type of test that assumes an item has a high relationship to a trait usually has little against which it can be validated. We cannot tell, for example, if an item tests for nurturance unless we have some other independent measure of nurturance, which itself must be validated. Those tests that are developed empirically depend on the reliability of the diagnosis by which people are divided into groups of the normal and the disturbed. If the experimental groups upon which the test depends are not well differentiated, the test will not be able to generate data that can make subsequent diagnosis possible.

The empirically developed test is valuable for diagnostic purposes—provided, of course, that the diagnostic groups on which it is based are reliable. Such a test should be able to identify other persons who have similar psychological characteristics. Tests developed by the factor-analytic method are frequently useful tools for research on the structure of personality.

THE MINNESOTA MULTIPHASIC PERSONALITY INVENTORY The most widely used personality inventory, the **Minnesota Multiphasic Personality Inventory (MMPI)**, was developed empirically, by identifying those items on which the pattern of response was different for groups of psychiatric patients and for groups of normal people. The items were then combined into graduated series, or **scales**, which were used originally to aid in the diagnosis and evaluation of mental illness. (See Figure 20.11.)

The authors of the test (Hathaway and McKinley, 1940) began with a set of 550 true-false statements. Many of these items dealt directly with

Figure 20.11 (A) Sample MMPI items. (B) MMPI profiles for abusive and nonabusive fathers. The letters along the bottom of the graph correspond to the scales described in Table 20.1. Note that the two groups obtained different profiles: fathers who abused their children scored much higher than nonabusive fathers on the Depression (D), Psychopathic Deviate (Pd) and Mania (Ma) scales. While it appears that the MMPI can differentiate between abusive and nonabusive parents, further study would be necessary before a more conclusive profile of an abusive parent could be drawn. This research does offer some tentative hypotheses about important personality differences between abusers and nonabusers. (Adapted from Paulson, Afifi, Thomason, and Chaleff, 1974.)

133 I have never indulged in unusual sex practices.

151 Someone has been trying to poison me.

182 I am afraid of losing my mind.

234 I get mad easily and then I get over it soon.

244 My way of doing things is apt to be misunderstood by others.

288 I am troubled by attacks of nausea and vomiting.

A

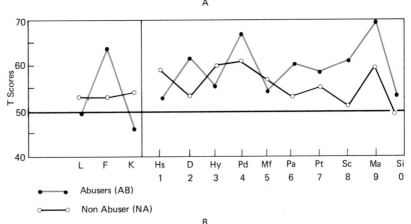

B

psychiatric symptoms—including delusions, halluci-nations, obsessive and compulsive states, and sadis-tic and masochistic tendencies—but the other items ranged widely over areas such as physical health, general habits, family and marital status, occupa-tional and educational problems, and attitudes to-ward religion, sex, politics, and social problems. It is fortunate that the MMPI items were so diverse, be-cause many of the items that did not seem relevant to the initial purposes of the inventory have turned out to be useful not only in studying psy-chopathology but also in developing a variety of ad-ditional scales, many of which measure personality characteristics of normal people.

Table 20.1   Scales of the MMPI

Validity Scales	
Lie Scale (L)	Items that reflect socially desirable but unlikely behavior and are therefore likely to be marked true by a naive faker.
Infrequency Scale (F)	Items that are rarely marked true except by people who either are trying deliberately to give an exaggerated impression of their problems or are in fact highly deviant.
Correction Scale (K)	Items that reflect how defensive or how frank the person is being. The scale is sensitive to attitudes more subtle than those that affect the Lie Scale.
Clinical Scales	
1. Hypochondriasis (Hs)	Items selected to discriminate people who persist in worrying about their bodily functions despite strong evidence that they have no physical illness.
2. Depression (D)	Items selected to discriminate people who are pessimistic about the future, feel hopeless or worthless, are slow in thought and action, and think a lot about death and suicide.
3. Hysteria (Hy)	Items selected to discriminate people who use physical symptoms to solve difficult problems or avoid mature responsibilities, particularly under severe psychological stress.
4. Psychopathic Deviate (Pd)	Items selected to discriminate people who show a pronounced disregard for social customs and mores, an inability to profit from punishing experiences, and emotional shallowness with others, particularly in sex and love.
5. Masculinity-Femininity (Mf)	Items selected to discriminate men who prefer homosexual relations to heterosexual ones, either overtly, or covertly because of inhibitions or conflicts. Women tend to score low on this scale, but the scale cannot be interpreted simply "upside-down" for women.
6. Paranoia (Pa)	Items selected to discriminate people who have delusions about how influential and how victimized they are or how much attention is paid them by other people.
7. Psychasthenia (Pt)	Items selected to discriminate people with obsessive thoughts, compulsive actions, extreme fear or guilt feelings, insecurity, and high anxiety.
8. Schizophrenia (Sc)	Items selected to discriminate people who are constrained, cold, aloof, apathetic, inaccessible to others, and who may have delusions or hallucinations.
9. Hypomania (Ma)	Items selected to discriminate people who are physically overactive, emotionally excited, and have rapid flights of disconnected, fragmentary ideas; these activities may lead to accomplishment but more frequently are inefficient and unproductive.
10. Social Introversion (Si)	Items selected to discriminate people who are withdrawn from social contacts and responsibilities and display little real interest in people.

Source: Based on W. G. Dahlstrom, G. S. Welsh, and L. E. Dahlstrom, *An MMPI Handbook*, Vol. 1 (Minneapolis: University of Minnesota Press, 1972).

Table 20.1 presents descriptions of the validity scales used and of a number of the clinical scales, including scales to identify hypochondria, hysteria, paranoia, introversion, schizophrenia, and obsessive-compulsive tendencies.

The construction of MMPI scales can be illustrated by considering the case of depression. The authors' original set of 550 items was administered to patients with depressive disorders and to normal people. From this large set, about 53 items were found to differentiate the two groups significantly. Later, a few items were added to sharpen the differentiation between patients with severe depressive reactions and those with other psychiatric diagnoses. The MMPI-D (for Depression) scale has been found to be a highly sensitive indicator not only of psychotic depression but also of less severe forms of depression, of varying mood states, and even of reactions to various methods of psychological treatments. In a similar way, eight additional clinical scales were developed for the original MMPI, as well as a masculinity-and-femininity scale.

The MMPI is best used for its original purposes, the identification and diagnosis of psychopathology (Dahlstrom and Welsh, 1960). It is a useful tool when employed by a skilled clinician who has been trained to interpret the profile of the clinical scores. Some of the clinical scores have proven useful in determining the effectiveness of various forms of psychotherapy. The depression scale, for example, has been used in studies that evaluate different thera-pies. But the MMPI is not so useful for the measurement of normal personality or as a selection or employment screening device, because it was not developed for these purposes.

THE PERSONALITY RESEARCH FORM The **Personality Research Form (PRF)**, developed by Douglas Jackson (1974), differs from the MMPI in two basic ways. First, it was designed to measure many dimensions of personality in the normal population. Thus it is primarily a research tool rather than a diagnostic instrument.

Second, the theoretical structure of the PRF is based on the needs identified by Henry Murray (1938) in his formulation of a theory of human personality. Murray distinguished between a class of primarily physical human needs and a class of psychological needs, such as the needs for acquisition, order, achievement, and affiliation. He provided clear definitions of each psychological need and extensive evidence of its various manifestations in emotional states and active behavior.

The construction of the PRF began with a careful study of Murray's definitions and explanations of psychological needs, followed by the writing of 3,000 items relevant to twenty trait dimensions to be measured. This pool of items was then refined, using advanced statistical techniques and relying heavily on computer data processing. After many rounds of careful item selection, two parallel forms of the PRF were obtained. Each of these forms, called AA and BB, measures the same twenty traits,

PRF Scale	Personality Statement
Abasement	I have often let others take credit for something I have done rather than be impolite about it.
Achievement	People have always said that I was a hard worker.
Affiliation	I spend a lot of time visiting friends.
Aggression	When I am irritated, I let it be known.
Autonomy	I would like to be alone and my own boss.
Change	I would like the type of work which would keep me constantly on the move.
Cognitive Structure	My work is carefully planned and organized before it is begun.
Defendence	I seldom let a critical comment pass without saying something in my defense.
Dominance	I am quite good at keeping others in line.
Endurance	I am more concerned with finishing what I start than the average person is.
Exhibition	I seldom feel shy when I am the center of attention.
Harm Avoidance	I would enjoy the feeling of riding to the top of an unfinished skyscraper in an open elevator.
Impulsivity	I often say the first thing that comes into my head.
Nurturance	I feel most worthwhile when I am helping someone who is disabled.
Order	My papers are always neat.
Play	Rarely, if ever, do I turn down a chance to have a good time.
Social Recognition	When I'm doing something, I often worry about what other people will think.
Sentience	I love the feeling of mist and fog.
Succorance	I prefer to face problems with a friend at my side.
Understanding	I'd like to be able to study the evolution of human knowledge.
Desirability	I am always prepared to do what is expected of me.

Figure 20.12 A sample of the Personality Research Form. The qualities enumerated in the left-hand column were derived from Murray's list of basic needs; in the right-hand column are sample statements from the questionnaire which reflect those needs. The actual questionnaire represents each need by several self-descriptive personality statements, and the respondent is asked to mark every statement either true or false. In addition to its primary use in basic personality research, the PRF also serves as a guidance tool for schools, colleges, clinics, and industry. (Adapted from Lay and Jackson, 1967, 1974.)

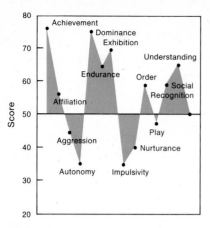

Figure 20.13 When scored, the PRF yields a profile or pattern of total scores. This particular profile is an abbreviated version of that obtained for a female college student who was a member of her college's debating team and who maintained a consistently high grade-point average. On the basis of her activities, one would expect to find relatively high needs for achievement, social recognition, and understanding if the PRF itself were a valid personality measure. Research does, in fact, indicate that the PRF has high enough reliability and validity coefficients to make it an extremely useful test.

using twenty items for each trait, but the two forms use completely different items. Although no item that appears on Form AA appears on Form BB, the two forms will produce nearly identical scores when administered by the same person—an indication of their reliability and consistency. The PRF's high validity has also been established (Kelly, 1972). A sample of the PRF is shown in Figure 20.12.

Recently a new form, PRF-E, has been developed from the previous forms. PRF-E has sixteen items for each of the twenty traits and can be used with younger subjects or with subjects of below average intelligence, groups that had some difficulty with the vocabulary in the original PRF.

PRF scores are usually summarized in the form of a profile. In the interpretation of personality-inventory profiles a great deal of attention is directed toward interpreting patterns of total scores rather than the scores themselves. An attempt is made to capture a total picture of the subject's life as revealed by the relative importance of various traits in the individual's personality.

Figure 20.13 gives an illustration of the PRF profile of a twenty-one-year-old college senior who became president of the student association while serving on the university debating team and achieving a level of scholastic performance that placed her on the dean's list time after time. Note that the most prominent features of the profile are consistent with her pattern of performance.

The PRF can be used in this manner to study for research purposes the functioning of normal personality and to provide some guidance for those who are making decisions about a career. But it is best suited for a variety of uses as a research instrument. For example, the PRF has been used in the study of the characteristics of effective psychotherapists for different types of patients, the environmental factors affecting personality development, the personalities of groups supporting different political candidates, and the relationship of education, social class, and occupational level to the personalities of heads of households.

THE ETHICS OF TESTING

We have seen that tests can be very effective tools for differentiation and diagnosis when properly used. However, like any other tool, tests are not always used properly. Their results are not always accurate, and they can be used unfairly to change the course of people's lives. Yet the number of tests and the situations in which they are used have been steadily increasing—a development that lends urgency to many questions (some of which we have already touched on).

So many variables affect the score on an examination—the personality of the examiner, the mood of the test-taker, and the middle-class orientation of the questions, to name a few—that even if we could all agree on what the scores mean, their validity as a measuring tool would still be questionable. Then there is the problem of interpreting the results: Just what has been measured? If a student scores high on an exam in English and math, are we to conclude that he or she will be successful in medical school?

The results of such tests can be used to determine a person's future. Whereas a high score on a mathematics examination may result in an accelerated program in math for one student, a low score on the same exam may mean the denial of admission to college for another. Even if a test score were a true indicator of aptitude or intelligence, why should certain educational experiences be reserved for the very talented? Why not also admit the most highly motivated students? Or the most creative? Or those with the most leadership ability?

Some basic ethical issues lie behind all these questions. One issue has to do with what is appropriate in the interpretation of tests results. Many people succumb to the temptation to draw sweeping conclusions from personality and intelligence test scores, forgetting that these tests often measure much less than we think they do and that they never supply absolutely certain information. The results of all tests are always a matter of probability—at best, they provide only a good estimate of what they are designed to measure. We must therefore be sure that a given test is valid for the specific purpose for which it is being used.

Another ethical issue concerns the proper use of test information. Even if the test results are valid, should test scores be made available to the subjects themselves? To their employers? To college admissions boards? Should a psychologist tell a child that he or she has obtained a poor IQ score when it may have the effect of decreasing the child's motivation to learn? Should people's private fantasies and fun-damental beliefs be made available to companies or organizations for which they work or to which they are applying for work?

Personality and intelligence tests may be used for desirable or undesirable ends. Personality assessment and intelligence testing can be useful in helping individuals lead more productive lives. Realistic information about a person's capabilities and dispositions can help him or her make appropriate social and occupational choices. We must remember, however, that knowledge about people entails power over their lives. Psychological tests, then, can be used either as potent weapons or as helpful instruments. Careful attention to the ethical issues raised by the use of tests is a continuing necessity if tests are to be used for the benefit of the individual and of society.

Summary

1. Despite their limitations, psychological tests are important tools for the evaluation of aptitude, mental health, and intelligence. The essential criteria in determining the value of a psychological test are reliability, validity, and standardization.
   A. A psychological test has high **reliability** if it yields the same results each time it is given. High reliability depends on three factors: internal consistency, test-retest reliability, and inter-judge reliability.
      1. Internal consistency means that different parts of the test yield the same results.
      2. Test-retest reliability means that the test yields the same results when administered to the same person at two different times.
      3. Inter-judge reliability means that the test yields the same results when scored or interpreted by different judges.
   B. A test has **validity** if it measures what it is supposed to measure.
      1. **Concurrent validity** is the degree to which a test's results correlate with the results of other tests that measure the same characteristics.
      2. **Predictive validity** is the degree to which a test predicts a person's subsequent performance of tasks that are related to the characteristic being measured.
   C. **Standardization** is an indication of a test's norms. Norms are developed by giving the test to a **standardization group** before it is put in general distribution. Most tests require several sets of norms so that a subject will be compared to the appropriate group, on the basis of such factors as age, sex, race, and social class. The most common methods of translating raw scores into scores that are relative to the scores of others are the percentile system and the standard score system.
      1. The **percentile system** divides a group of scores into one hundred equal parts. This shows the proportion of scores from the standardization group that are above and below a particular subject's score.
      2. The **standard score system** places individuals' scores on a bell-shaped curve that reflects the normal pattern of distribution of scores on most tests.
2. Intelligence tests are the most frequently administered tests measuring mental characteristics. Alfred Binet developed the first reliable intelligence test, expressing children's scores as the *difference* between their mental age and their chronological age. William Stern's suggestion that examiners use the *ratio* of mental age to chronological age resulted in the **intelligence quotient** (IQ). IQ is computed by dividing mental age by chronological age and multiplying by 100. Intelligence tests may be designed to be ad-

ministered to either individuals or groups. Other kinds of tests may measure aptitude or achievement.

A. Individual intelligence tests are administered by one examiner to one subject at a time. Two currently popular individual intelligence tests are the Stanford-Binet test and the intelligence scales developed by David Wechsler.

1. The **Stanford-Binet test** is a revision of Binet's intelligence test. It contains both verbal and performance subtests that are grouped by age level. In the final scoring, the mental age indicates the level of development the child has reached. The IQ score indicates how a child's level of development compares with that of other children of the same age.

2. The **Wechsler Adult Intelligence Scale** and the **Wechsler Intelligence Scale for Children** treat intelligence as a number of abilities rather than as one overriding ability. The Wechsler Scales contain subtests arranged in order of difficulty, and they emphasize performance tasks rather than verbal skills. Each subtest yields a separate IQ score.

B. Group intelligence tests generally have less predictive validity for academic performance than do individual tests, and clinicians prefer individual tests. Group tests measure verbal and performance abilities. They are used in mass testing situations because they are written tests, which makes them convenient and economical.

C. Achievement tests and aptitude tests are distinguished from one another primarily by their purpose rather than by their content. An **achievement test** is used to evaluate what a person knows. It should have **content validity**, which refers to the fairness with which it represents the area of achievement in question. An **aptitude test** is used to predict how successful a person will be in a certain situation. It should have **predictive validity**, which refers to the degree to which people who do well on the test perform well in situations for which their aptitude is being tested.

1. The **Scholastic Aptitude Test** is designed to measure a student's "aptitude for college studies" by assessing verbal and mathematical aptitude. The reliability of the SAT is very high; its validity is high enough to make it useful in predicting college performance but low enough to make it clear that other factors in addition to aptitude are important determinants of academic success.

2. The **General Aptitude Test Battery** is a set of tests designed by the U.S. Employment Service. The GATB measures whether a person meets the minimum standards for each of a number of occupations.

D. The significance of the relationship between IQ and other attributes is difficult to determine. Test scores reflect not only a person's innate potential for intellectual development (nature) but also what the person has learned from his or her experience (nurture). Attempts to determine whether there are innate intellectual differences among groups have turned out to be inconclusive and highly controversial.

1. Educational psychologist Arthur Jensen has made an attempt to explain why the IQ scores of black people, on the average, are lower than the scores of white people. He postulates that IQ is highly **heritable**, meaning that the variation in IQ scores can, to some extent, be attributed to genetic differences among members of a particular population in a particular environment.

2. Jensen's opponents either attack his methodology or point to environmental factors that he has failed to take into account. One criticism of his thesis is that it does not account for **reaction range**, which is a person's unique range of possible responses to his or her environment.

3. Personality tests may be either projective tests or objective tests.

A. **Projective tests** attempt to measure unconscious dispositions that are revealed in the ways subjects respond to and interpret ambiguous material.

1. In the **Rorschach Inkblot Test** a subject uses free association to report to an examiner what he or she sees in a series of inkblots. The examiner assesses the responses in terms of how much of the inkblot the person responds to, the elements of the inkblot that produce the response, and the content of the response. The strength of the Rorschach Inkblot Test is that it samples a wide range of behavior and permits

certain patterns to emerge that may not otherwise become apparent. Its disadvantage is that interpretation of the subject's responses is open to the examiner's biases.

2. In the **Thematic Apperception Test** a subject tells a story about each of a number of ambiguous pictures chosen for their appropriateness to the subject's age and sex. Clinicians have some common assumptions about the meaning of various responses, but they agree only moderately well about how to interpret and base predictions on the TAT.

B. Objective personality tests are administered with the assumption that subjects have varying amounts of the trait being measured, and many items are used to obtain the most reliable measurement of that trait. Some objective tests are constructed empirically, without regard to the relationship of the items to a certain trait; these are most valuable for diagnostic purposes. Other objective tests are constructed by factor analysis, which involves selecting items from a pool of items that are believed to be related to a specific trait; these tests are useful tools for research on the structure of personality. Questions have been raised about the validity of both types of tests.

1. The **Minnesota Multiphasic Personality Inventory** is the most widely used personality inventory. It was designed empirically for the identification and diagnosis of psychopathology, and it is most successful when used for that purpose. It is not as useful for the measurement of normal personality.

2. The **Personality Research Form** was designed to measure many dimensions of personality in the normal population. The PRF is primarily a research tool rather than a diagnostic instrument. It measures twenty personality traits that reflect the psychological needs identified by Henry Murray in his theory of personality.

4. There are certain ethical issues underlying many of the questions that have been raised about the use of psychological tests.

A. The appropriateness of interpretations of test scores is always open to question, since tests never yield absolutely certain information.

B. Who should receive information about a person's test results is a delicate matter, because this information can have a profound effect on the person's life.

C. Deciding what the difference is between normal people and abnormal people is a complex issue because answers to questions about normality depend ultimately on subjective considerations.

RECOMMENDED READINGS

AMERICAN PSYCHOLOGICAL ASSOCIATION. *Standards for Educational and Psychological Tests.* Washington, D.C.: American Psychological Association, 1974. The latest revision of the Association's guidelines for test construction and use.

BUROS, OSCAR K. (ed.). *Personality Tests and Reviews.* Highland Park, N.J.: Gryphon Press, 1970. Contains descriptions and critical reviews of all existing personality tests. A source book for anyone who is searching for almost any type of personality test.

KORCHIN, SHELDON K. *Modern Clinical Psychology.* New York: Basic Books, 1976. Contains six chapters on clinical assessment dealing with testing, interpretation, and diagnosis.

LANYON, RICHARD I., and LEONARD D. GOODSTEIN. *Personality Assessment.* New York: Wiley, 1970. Presents clear description of the major personality assessment techniques, with examples and interpretations.

LOEHLIN, J. C., GARDNER LINDZEY, and J. N. SPUHLER. *Race Differences in Intelligence.* San Francisco: Freeman, 1975. A careful, balanced examination of the research evidence relevant to the issue of genetic and environmental determinants of IQ differences between racial groups.

SUNDBERG, NORMAN. *Assessment of Persons.* Englewood Cliffs, N.J.: Prentice-Hall, 1977. Presents behavioral, objective, and projective techniques, relating the person to the biological and social systems.

WECHSLER, DAVID. *The Measurement and Appraisal of Adult Intelligence.* 14th ed. Baltimore: Williams & Wilkins, 1958. A classic discussion of intelligence and intelligence testing.

PART SEVEN

BEHAVIOR DISORDERS AND THERAPY

In Part Six we saw how psychologists conceptualize and assess the functioning personality as it manifests itself in behavior. In Part Seven we consider psychological disorder—what happens when the personality stops functioning smoothly and behavior becomes abnormal.

We begin in Chapter 21, "Adjustment to the Problems of Life," by looking at the way most people cope with the problems they encounter throughout life—usually without professional help and without severe psychological disorder. In Chapter 22, "Psychological Disorders," we describe the major forms of abnormal behavior. Chapter 23, "Theories of Abnormality," summarizes some of the most important conceptual approaches to the origins of psychological disorder. In Chapter 24, "Approaches to Treatment," we examine the major forms of psychotherapy currently in use.

CHAPTER TWENTY-ONE

ADJUSTMENT TO THE PROBLEMS OF LIFE

It is easy to talk about "madness" as though there were some objective fact one could associate with the word, as though it were something that everyone could agree on. "He must be mad to do such a thing," you might say, and expect no one to argue. Who can argue with "madness"?

I thought of this when recently watching a rerun of Cecil B. DeMille's *The Ten Commandments* on television. (I even enjoyed parts of it.) If you saw it, you recall that Charlton Heston (Moses), with staff, and in robe, strides up to Yul Brynner (Pharaoh) and demands that a horde of slaves be set free, and allowed to depart the land.

Pharaoh is interrupted while engaged in the difficult task of controlling the destiny of the wealthiest and most civilized land on Earth. He listens patiently, responds testily but without any attempt to visit punishment on Moses. Considering the economic dislocations that freeing the slaves would bring on Egypt, Pharaoh refuses the request.

The entire audience, however, is on Moses' side, every one of them. Pharaoh's action is certainly considered by them to be criminal to the point of madness, and they wait with great satisfaction for the ten plagues that will afflict Egypt as punishment.

But if some black person had, in 1835, attempted to enter the White House in order to demand of President Andrew Jackson that the black slaves in America be permitted to depart the country, the question of whether Jackson would refuse would be entirely academic. The black Moses would never have reached Jackson. Rather, he or she would have been killed out of hand or, at best, committed.

I am quite certain that the American whites of 1835 would have agreed with our modern audience in considering Pharaoh mad or criminal for refusing Moses' request and would also have considered our mythical black person mad or criminal for making the request. What's more, very few would have been aware of any contradiction in these two attitudes. Had I been there to point out the contradiction, they would have considered *me* mad. Apparently, the question of who is mad depends not only on time, place, and circumstance but on the attitudes and prejudices of the judges in such matters.

The most remarkable madman in literature is surely Don Quixote. For nearly 400 years, people of all nations have laughed at his madness, at his belief in the ridiculous fictions of the medieval romances of chivalry, at his mistaking windmills for giants, prostitutes for virgins, and so on.

And yet Cervantes, the author of this greatest of all novels, slowly lets Don Quixote win us over by revealing him to be a man of great intelligence and great virtue set down in a petty world.

By the end of the book, when Don Quixote recovers his senses at last, becomes part of the real world, and dies, we weep for him. We weep that he dies, but we weep also that he becomes sane, for somehow Cervantes makes us prefer to be gloriously mad with a man like Don Quixote than wickedly sane with everyone else. Or is it that he faces us with the wonderfully disturbing question of whether it might be Don Quixote who was sane and the world that was mad?

Isaac Asimov

On Monday Karen, a college student, got an A on a chemistry test. On Tuesday she got a D on a paper in political science. On Wednesday the law student she had met three weeks before finally asked her out. On Thursday her father called to tell her that her beloved Irish setter had been run over and seriously injured. On Friday her car broke down and had to be towed ten miles to a garage. On Saturday she was chosen to play the lead in the college production of *A Doll's House*.

How Karen will react to all these events is one aspect of the process called adjustment. **Adjustment** is a continuous and ever-changing process of interacting with the people, events, and forces that affect our lives—such as our friends and families, physical growth and aging, and the environment. All these factors continue to change as long as we live. Most people achieve a successful adjustment to their changing life situations. Successful adjustment allows continued functioning in society, performance of tasks, maintenance of family and social relationships, and a subjective feeling of comfort and contentment. But sometimes adjusting to situations like those Karen faced in just one week may be accompanied by stress and physical and psychological dysfunction. The challenges of life, both those which bring us pleasure and those which cause us pain, often tax our power of coping.

The process of adjustment usually proceeds while we continue to meet our ordinary responsibilities. Although it is sometimes painful and difficult, we find ways of resolving the problems of life without succumbing to the more severe forms of psychological dysfunction. Severe, disabling psychological disorders and their treatment are discussed in Chapters 22, 23, and 24. In this chapter we will be concerned with the problems of adjustment that confront almost everyone at some time and that are most often resolved with little, if any, professional help.

Attempts to cope with difficult situations tend to fall into three major categories. The first category, problem solving, is what most people think of as coping. For example, Karen must deal with the problems of getting her car fixed and paying for the towing and repair work. The development of problem-solving skills to meet a wide variety of situations is a very useful aid to adjustment.

The second category, acceptance of the situation, can also be an effective tool in the process of adjustment. Karen can probably do very little to help her injured dog, and while she may be saddened, acceptance of the event and its consequences—rather than frantic, undirected activity—would be the best approach. There is a danger in unconsidered acceptance, however: sometimes we accept consequences that we could have avoided. One must distinguish between situations that call for active problem solving and those for which acceptance is appropriate.

The third category of coping is the use of defense mechanisms (discussed in Chapter 18). Most difficult situations produce stress and anxiety, which defense mechanisms such as repression and denial help to alleviate. Karen may be anxious about her upcoming date with the law student because she is strongly attracted to him and is worried that he may not like her. She may deal with that anxiety by denying that she finds him *that* attractive and asserting that she doesn't really care whether he likes her or not. Such defense mechanisms may help to reduce anxiety. But there is a danger here, too, in that overuse of these defenses will have undesirable long-term consequences. If Karen continually denies that she finds her dates attractive, she may not be able to make a successful adjustment in social and dating relationships. In other words, the *occasional* use of defense mechanisms as a means of coping with stress and anxiety is a tool for adjustment; their *overuse* can lead to severe disturbances.

A useful or successful method of coping may or may not reflect the values of society. For example, society's values might favor a direct approach to Karen's problem of the D on her political science paper. If Karen accepts that view, she may schedule a meeting with her instructor to analyze the paper and work out a way of improving her course grade. But Karen may decide that her other activities are more important than getting a good grade in the course. If her career goal is to become a professional actress, accepting the lead in the play and devoting much of her time to rehearsals may be much more important and useful than raising her political science grade, though Karen must also be aware of the consequences of simply accepting a D. Neither of these modes of coping is good or bad in itself; which approach is more useful for Karen depends on many factors in her life.

Specific strategies for coping and adapting, then, cannot be evaluated in an absolute manner, but only in relation to the situation the person confronts—and then only in terms of the effectiveness of the strategy for that person. There is no single formula for successful adjustment.

In this chapter we will first examine the physical

and the psychological impact of stressful events. Next we will consider some of the situational factors that make adjustment to such events easier or more difficult—especially the factor of the extent to which a person feels able to control events. The issue of control will come into focus as we consider controlling one's own behavior as a means of adjustment. Since adjustment is a process rather than a product, we must be concerned with adjustment throughout life; the final section of the chapter will describe the kinds of changes and stressful events that await all of us as we go through life.

LIFE STRESS AND PHYSICAL FUNCTIONING

In the special feature in Chapter 15 we saw that people may react to extreme or prolonged stress in three phases: alarm, resistance, and exhaustion (Selye, 1956). These physical reactions to stress can lead to physical illness when the stress is prolonged or repeated. The relationship between *specific* stressful events and *immediate* physical effects seems obvious to most people. If you have a relative or friend with heart disease, you have probably been told not to let that person get overexcited or physically exhausted. You may have been told that an uncle has developed ulcers because his work is extremely demanding. But more precise knowledge about the relationship between stress and physical illness would be very useful. Is it only major events that precipitate illness? Could a number of minor events combine to create enough stress to affect physical functioning? The association between the number and severity of stressful events in a person's life and the probability of physical illness has been studied extensively by physicians and psychologists since the early 1960s.

THE MEASUREMENT OF LIFE STRESS In 1967 Thomas H. Holmes and Richard H. Rahe developed the Social Readjustment Rating Scale (SRRS), which is used in an attempt to measure the amount of life stress a person may experience from many sources during a given period of time—say, a year. They identified a number of events that most people experience as life crises or stress situations. Groups of subjects then rated the importance of

each event according to the amount of change or adaptation needed to adjust to the event. The intensity and duration of change accompanying the event determined its rank value, rather than how desirable or undesirable the event itself was. Each event was assigned a numerical value, as shown in Table 21.1. Individuals using the SRRS indicate whether or not each event has occurred in their lives and, if so, when. Then for any given time span a score, expressed in Life Change Units (LCUs), can be calculated.

Work based on the SRRS showed that "a clustering of social or life events becomes a necessary but not sufficient cause of illness and accounts in part for the time of onset of disease" (Holmes and Masuda, 1974). Life changes whose values added up to 150 LCUs or more in one year were termed "life crises." It was found that as the LCUs increased, so did the incidence of illness. Seventy-nine percent of those subjects whose life crisis scores were 300 LCUs or more had experienced physical illness or a change in health within one or two years. One might expect a correlation between life stress and heart disease

Even a vacation is a stressful life event, ranking forty-first on Holmes and Rahe's SRRS (see Table 21.1).

Table 21.1   Social Readjustment Rating Scale

The amount of life stress a person has experienced in a given period of time, say one year, is measured by the total number of life change units (LCUs). These units result from the addition of the values (shown in the right column) associated with events that the person has experienced during the target time period.

Rank	Life Event	Mean Value
1	Death of spouse	100
2	Divorce	73
3	Marital separation	65
4	Jail term	63
5	Death of close family member	63
6	Personal injury or illness	53
7	Marriage	50
8	Fired at work	47
9	Marital reconciliation	45
10	Retirement	45
11	Change in health of family member	44
12	Pregnancy	40
13	Sex difficulties	39
14	Gain of new family member	39
15	Business readjustment	39
16	Change in financial state	38
17	Death of close friend	37
18	Change to different line of work	36
19	Change in number of arguments with spouse	35
20	Mortgage over $10,000	31
21	Foreclosure of mortgage or loan	30
22	Change in responsibilities at work	29
23	Son or daughter leaving home	29
24	Trouble with in-laws	29
25	Outstanding personal achievement	28
26	Wife begin or stop work	26
27	Begin or end school	26
28	Change in living conditions	25
29	Revision of personal habits	24
30	Trouble with boss	23
31	Change in work hours or conditions	20
32	Change in residence	20
33	Change in schools	20
34	Change in recreation	19
35	Change in church activities	19
36	Change in social activities	18
37	Mortgage or loan less than $10,000	17
38	Change in sleeping habits	16
39	Change in number of family get-togethers	15
40	Change in eating habits	15
41	Vacation	13
42	Christmas	12
43	Minor violations of the law	11

Source: Thomas H. Holmes and Richard H. Rahe. "The Social Readjustment Rating Scale," *Journal of Psychosomatic Research*, II (1967), 213–218.

(Rahe and Lind, 1971; Edwards, 1971), but a more surprising association has been found between life stress and occurrence of bone fractures (Tollefson, 1972) and the onset of leukemia in children (Wold, 1968).

All these studies were retrospective analyses: that is, the scale was administered after the onset of ill-ness. It is hoped, however, that these life stress measurements will eventually enable scientists to *predict* the kinds and levels of stress that are likely to cause illness. To date only a few such studies have been done (for example, T. S. Holmes, 1970; Theorell, 1974), but their results are promising.

What makes prediction of stress-related illness

difficult is the fact that there are great differences in the way individuals react to stressful situations. One person who is fired from a job may cheerfully set out to find another. A second person may regard being fired as an opportunity to take a long-postponed European vacation. A third person may begin to experience agonizing migraine headaches. Why is it that some people can take stressful events in their stride, while stress seems to make others physically ill?

LIFE STRESS AND PHYSICAL ILLNESS: A MODEL

Richard Rahe (1974) has suggested that there are six transformations through which a person experiencing life stress must pass before physical illness can occur (see Figure 21.1). The first transformation is interpretation of the stressful event by means of past experience, which serves as a kind of filter that may decrease, neutralize, or increase the effects of the stress. For example, having been fired before may make it either easier or harder to accept being fired a second time, depending on the individual. The second "filter" is the ego's defense mechanisms (see Chapter 18), such as projection ("The boss is incompetent and I showed him up, so he fired me") or denial ("I wasn't fired—I quit"). If the stress can penetrate the person's psychological defenses, the third transformation takes place, in which the physiological reactions we discussed in Chapter 15 (such as increased hormone secretion or rapid heartbeat) can occur. Next comes another filter, the person's coping ability—basically, the ability to reduce physiological activation, maybe by relaxing. Physiological activation that continues despite attempts to cope may be interpreted by the person as bodily symptoms. The fifth step consists of the person's decision to report these perceptions of bodily symptoms to a doctor. In the sixth step, the doctor may diagnose these symptoms as indicative of some degree of illness.

Even extreme stress may not lead to physical illness. If past experience or psychological defenses have equipped the person to adapt to the stressful event, there may not be any physiological reaction at all. And even if physiological effects do occur, the person may be able to cope. Thus a wide range of responses to any stressful event is possible, and each person will react in a unique way. All the same, it is clear that stressful life events are related to illness for many people. The exact mechanisms by which stress contributes to physical illness are not entirely clear, but Rahe's model does provide a useful framework for discussion and a reminder that there *is* a connection. It also indicates the interplay between stress and psychological, as well as physiological, functioning—a topic we shall turn to now.

LIFE STRESS AND PSYCHOLOGICAL FUNCTIONING

Not long after the relationship between stressful events and physical illness was confirmed, researchers began looking at the relationship between stressful events and psychological or emotional disturbances. Although *physical* illness has been found to result if a sufficient amount of stress is present, regardless of whether that stress is associated with positive or negative life events, *psychological* illness seems to be associated primarily with stress caused by undesirable life events.

Amiram Vinokur and Melvin L. Selzer (1975) used a sample population of non-disturbed males to study the kinds of life events that have an effect on psychological functioning (see Figure 21.2). The subjects filled out questionnaires rating events in the

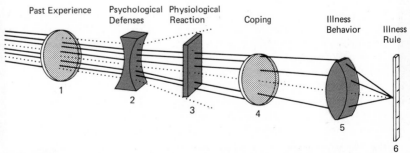

Figure 21.1 According to Rahe, life changes may not always lead to physical illness because of the variety of ways in which a person can interpret and react to major life events. Effective psychological defenses, for example, may allow an individual to deal with a major upheaval with no physiological reaction and no subsequent illness. (After Rahe, 1974.)

Past Experience · Psychological Defenses · Physiological Reaction · Coping · Illness Behavior · Illness Rule

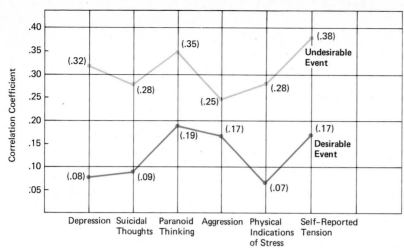

Figure 21.2 Correlations between psychological distress and desirable and undesirable life events. Undesirable events are much more highly correlated with these six measures of psychological distress than are desirable events. Subjects rated the six variables by a questionnaire, and life events were assessed using a modified version of the Holmes and Rahe SRRS scale (see Table 21.1). (After Vinokur and Selzer, 1975.)

previous year in terms of the pressure they evoked and their desirability or undesirability. They also answered questions and rated themselves on scales pertaining to aggression, paranoid thinking, depression, and tendency toward suicide; and they answered questions about such indications of stress and anxiety as headaches, insomnia, and drinking, as well as direct questions about tension and distress. The results showed that all these self-reported factors were primarily associated with undesirable life stress situations. In contrast, desirable life stresses did not show substantial correlation with these variables.

Undesirable life events have also been found to be associated with more severe forms of psychological disorder. In one study (Paykel, 1974), 185 depressed patients were matched by sex, age, marital status, race, and social class with nonpatients and questioned about stresses in their lives during the past six months. The depressed subjects reported three times as many stressful events of all kinds as their matched controls. Undesirable stressful events—such as increased arguments with a spouse, marital separation, and death of a family member—were reported much more frequently by the depressed people. The same researcher has obtained similar results with persons who had attempted suicide and with schizophrenics. (It must be noted that stress is not the only causal factor in these cases; other factors are discussed in the following chapters.)

These studies indicate that the undesirable quality of the stressful event seems to be more important in relation to psychological dysfunction than is the mere presence of the stressful event. Or, to put it another way, desirable events may stress the body, but they do not seem to constitute a burden to the mind.

COPING WITH A STRESSFUL ENVIRONMENT

While each of us must cope with major stress situations at one time or another in our lives, there is in addition the day-to-day process of coping with annoyances and problems inherent in the environment in which we live and work. Rural environments have their own kinds of stress: for example, one must learn to cope with the effects of isolation and bad weather. Urban stress, however, is usually more obvious and more dramatic. High levels of noise, crowding, traffic, street crime, and a hectic pace of life combine to tax the nerves and health of the city dweller.

Environmental stress almost always takes the form of aversive events—noise, heat, crowds, sudden storms, floods—and it is certainly plausible that the more intense the event, the more stress people will feel. But another aspect of environmental stress is that such events are usually unpredictable or uncontrollable or both. The U.S. Weather Service is often quite accurate in predicting a hurricane, but no one can control the storm when it does hit. Urban noise—traffic, airplanes, jackhammers, loud parties next door—is usually both unpredictable and uncontrollable: we don't know when it will start or stop, and we can control it only by sound-proofing our buildings or by plugging our ears—seldom by putting a stop to the noise itself.

Would these events be as stress-producing and would they have such an impact on our everyday adjustment if we were better able to predict and control them? Is it easier to adjust to environmental stress when we believe that we can predict or control the stressful events? If so, how is the feeling of control established or destroyed by our experiences? Researchers have addressed these questions from several perspectives.

ADJUSTING TO NOISE One group of researchers (Glass, Singer, and Friedman, 1969) has conducted some interesting experiments on the environmental stressor of noise. They asked their subjects, forty-eight female college students, to spend twenty-three minutes performing certain verbal and numerical tasks. As they worked on these tasks, the subjects were subjected to intermittent tape-recorded noise, half of them at fixed (predictable) intervals and half at random (unpredictable) intervals. In addition, half the subjects in both the "fixed" and "random" groups heard the noise amplified to 110 decibels (the level of the sound of a motorcycle engine), while the other half heard the same noise amplified to only 56 decibels (about the level of ordinary face-to-face conversation). A control group was not subjected to any noise. Measurements of the subjects' levels of physiological tension (as indicated by their galvanic skin response) were taken before, during, and after their exposure to noise. These measurements and the subjects' generally successful completion of the assigned tasks showed that they had adapted to the noise, both physiologically and psychologically.

Next the experimenters set out to determine whether the intensity of the noise and its predictability or unpredictability had affected the subjects' tolerance for subsequent frustrations and their ability to perform subsequent tasks. They gave the subjects two tasks that were more complex than the previous ones: (1) solving four complicated picture puzzles, two of which were actually impossible to solve, and (2) proofreading seven pages of written material, correcting errors in spelling, punctuation, and the like. Even though they were not subjected to any noise while performing these tasks, the subjects who had been exposed to the loud noise at random intervals performed significantly less well than the other experimental and control subjects: they gave up on the insoluble puzzles sooner and missed more errors in the proofreading task than the other groups.

Thus, while it was indeed possible for the subjects to adapt to the unpredictable, unpleasant noise, the "psychic cost" of their adaptation was high. The energy they spent to overcome the distraction and irritation caused by the noise was energy they could not apply toward persisting at the subsequent puzzle and proofreading tasks and performing well on them. And the louder and less predictable the noise had been, the higher was the price they had to pay.

Why should enduring a loud noise that is unpredictable affect a person's subsequent tolerance for

frustration and ability to perform a task? A later experiment (Glass, Reim, and Singer, 1971) provided some interesting clues (see Figure 21.3). The subjects this time were forty-seven male college students, all of whom were subjected at random intervals to bursts of the same tape-recorded noise used in the earlier study, amplified to 110 decibels. Subjects in one group were told that they could stop the noise by signaling another subject to press a button, but the experimenters preferred that they avoid giving the signal. Each subject in the second group was told that another subject had a control button, but he had no means of communicating with that subject. In the third group, neither of two paired subjects could control the noise. In the fourth group, each subject was alone in the room with no way of controlling the noise. Thus the subjects not only did not know when the noise would come, but all except the first group believed that they could not stop it when it did come.

After twenty-four minutes of intermittent exposure to the random noise, each subject was taken to another room and given a proofreading task to perform in a quiet environment. Subjects who had believed that they had indirect control over the unpredictable noise did significantly better on this

Figure 21.3 Coping with a stressful environmemt. In two experiments David Glass and colleagues have shown that exposure to uncontrollable and unpredictable noise had a much greater effect on performance of a subsequent task in a quiet environment than did exposure to controllable and unpredictable noise. More effort is required to adapt to the unpredictable and uncontrollable noise, which leaves the person less able to deal effectively with future tasks.

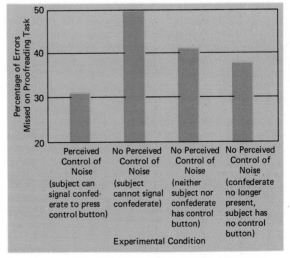

Loud rock music can be an environmental stress. Inability to control or avoid such stress may lead to feelings of helplessness.

task—and showed significantly less tension—than those who had believed that they had no control over the noise.

In these two experiments all subjects exposed to the loud noise were able to adapt to it and to perform tasks with increasing efficiency. However, when later given complex tasks in a quiet environment, the subjects who had experienced unpredictable or uncontrollable noise performed significantly less well than those who had experienced the noise at predictable intervals or had believed that they could stop the noise if they chose to. These findings suggest that the effect of environmental stress on our adjustment may be due to our feeling helpless to control or avoid the stress, rather than to the intense stimulation of the stress itself. If a feeling of control allows us to adjust to stress more effectively and a feeling of helplessness leads to a diminished ability to adjust, the conditions that create a feeling of helplessness become an important focus for research—a topic to which we now turn.

LEARNED HELPLESSNESS Many of us believe that we are helpless to relieve certain types of unpleasant stress. Some expressions of this belief have become clichés: "You can't fight city hall"; "You can't teach an old dog new tricks"; "Better the devil you know than the devil you don't." At one time or another you yourself have probably said something like, "I can't learn to dance—I have two left feet" or "I'll never get more than a C in this course no matter what I do." Do such feelings of helplessness impair our performance? And, once we have learned that we are helpless in one kind of situation, do our feelings of helplessness carry over to other kinds of situations?

In an already classic experiment (Overmier and Seligman, 1967), a dog was placed in a shuttle box consisting of two compartments separated by a barrier that prevented movement from one compartment to the other. A series of electrical shocks was then delivered to the dog's feet through a grid on the floor of the box. Once the animal had learned that nothing it did would permit it to escape the shock, it had great difficulty learning to escape when the barrier between compartments was removed. The dog would just sit and endure the shock rather than make the easy jump to the safe compartment. Some dogs never learned to make the escape response, even after they were lifted from one compartment to the other to show them the way. A control group of dogs, which had not been subjected to inescapable shock, learned to escape in just one or two trials. Martin Seligman and his associates have postulated such **learned helplessness** as a mechanism underlying human depression, a disorder we shall consider in the next chapter. Here we want to use the concept of learned helplessness as a means of understanding the effects of uncontrollable environmental stress.

Research has demonstrated that learned helplessness can be an important factor in failure to adjust to stressful events. In one recent study (Hiroto and Seligman, 1975) groups of college students were subjected to an inescapable loud tone. On subsequent tasks during which escape from the loud tone was possible, these subjects made fewer attempts to escape and performed the tasks less well than subjects who had previously experienced an escapable tone. In addition, it was shown that learned helplessness could be instilled by means of unpredictable failures at a problem-solving task, as well as by means of inescapable tones. Furthermore, helplessness learned in one situation generalized to the other situation. These findings indicate that learned helplessness may be a kind of induced "trait" in humans, one that carries over from one kind of situation to another.

We cannot say for certain whether learned helplessness has this generalizing characteristic outside of the laboratory. But if it is true that learned helplessness does generalize to later times and different circumstances, then it becomes especially important to understand the ways in which we can *unlearn* helplessness and gain control over our lives.

GAINING CONTROL OVER THE ENVIRONMENT Ellen Langer and Judith Rodin (1976) have addressed this problem of control, which may be viewed as the other side of the coin of learned helplessness. They conducted an experiment in a nursing home for the aged. Ninety-one ambulatory subjects, ranging in age from sixty-five to ninety, were divided into two groups. The old people in the first group were encouraged to take responsibility for their belongings and to make decisions about how they spent their time. Those in the second group were encouraged to leave decisions and responsibility to the staff. People in the first group, for example, were allowed to choose a plant and care for it themselves, and to decide which night they would like to see a movie. Those in the other group were given plants that the staff chose and cared for, and were assigned a movie night.

Three weeks later, according to self-ratings and staff observations, 93 percent of the group that had been encouraged to take more control of their environment showed overall improvement; they were more active and felt happier. Only 21 percent of the group that had been encouraged to rely on the staff were judged to have improved.

In a striking follow-up to this study, Rodin and Langer (1977) assessed the health and well-being of the subjects eighteen months after the original experiment. The old people who had been encouraged to take responsibility were still more vigorous and active than those who had been encouraged to leave decisions to the staff. Furthermore, there had been a significantly lower death rate in the first group: 15 percent, in contrast to 30 percent for the other group.

These findings are of great potential importance in shaping our policies and practices regarding the care of the elderly. It may be that preserving a feeling of control and responsibility among the elderly will add years of happy, more vigorous activity to their lives—and, in due course, to our own.

In the foregoing discussions we have seen that adjustment is the process of adapting to the events that occur throughout our lives. Major life events can lead to physical illness and psychological dysfunction, while environmental stress exacts a price in terms of lowered frustration tolerance and impaired task performance, even when we do succeed in

A group of elderly blind people who engage in productive work in an effort to become self-sufficient, making and selling dolls, glass flowers, mosaic balls, weavings, and other handicrafts.

adapting to it. When environmental stress is apparently beyond our control, the effects are much greater than when we believe that we have some control. And when the outcome is clearly beyond our control, learned helplessness results, which may inhibit learning new responses in new situations that are actually controllable.

It is clear that helplessness increases stress by increasing anxiety and inhibiting our ability to perform tasks. We must be careful, however, not to jump to the conclusion that helplessness is always a maladaptive force. On the contrary, it has been noted that when a situation is truly uncontrollable—as when someone has a fatal illness or loves someone who does not return the affection—the most adaptive behavior would be to stop struggling and accept the situation (Wortman and Brehm, 1975, pp. 330–332). In experiments with animals, continued attempts to gain control of situations that in fact are uncontrollable actually result in greater stress than simply giving up and becoming passive. However, since it is often difficult to determine which situations are in fact capable of change and which are not, attempts at control will, generally speaking, lead to both an improvement in the situation and better psychological adjustment.

ACHIEVING SELF-CONTROL

Although, as we have seen, we cannot always control our environment, most of us are in control of ourselves most of the time. All the same, most of us also wish we could alter some of our behavior some of the time. Many people feel tongue-tied and awkward when they make a new acquaintance and wish they could be witty and charming instead. Others complain of being unable to stop smoking or overeating. Adjustment has to do with specific behavior in specific situations; so the heavy smoker may function easily in social situations, while the shy person may have no difficulty avoiding cigarettes. Moreover, it has been shown that even shyness is situation-specific (Watson and Tharp, 1972): a young man may feel perfectly at ease while playing basketball with the boys, but suffer from intense anxiety when talking with a young woman. In this section we will investigate how a person can acquire control over his or her own behavior in troublesome areas by using a method called behavioral self-control.

THE THEORY OF BEHAVIORAL SELF-CONTROL Underlying behavioral self-control is the concept of operant conditioning, which was discussed in detail in Chapter 4. Self-control, the ability to call forth the behavior we want when we want it, depends largely on three factors: observation, evaluation, and reinforcement (Kanfer and Karoly, 1972).

The first step in achieving self-control is *observation*, which enables us to become aware of how often the target behavior—the one we want to control—oc-

Shyness is situation-specific; thus, a child who is shy at a swimming pool may be relaxed and confident at school.

curs and to become aware of the circumstances, or cues, that set it off. Many overweight people, for example, are unaware of how much they eat. Recording everything that is eaten—a bite of someone else's ice cream, the remains of their child's hamburger, the scrapings of the cookie batter—and keeping track of the time and place it is eaten will make the individual aware of how those "tastes" and "bites" add up. More important, such observation will bring to the person's attention behavior that had often gone unnoticed because it had become automatic. The mere act of recording behavior can sometimes change it substantially.

After having observed the frequency of the target behavior, the individual must *evaluate* the situation and establish a goal. This involves answering such questions as: "How much eating is too much?" "How many cigarettes should I allow myself to smoke?" "How often should I try to overcome shyness by initiating a conversation with a classmate?" The goal will reflect the values of the individual; thus, setting such a goal need not be seen as a mechanical and dehumanizing exercise.

Next the individual must provide a *reinforcement* that is contingent upon manifestations of the target behavior. This involves drawing up a kind of personal contract. For example, the person might say, "If I smoke only two cigarettes today, I'll buy the new Rolling Stones album." If he or she smokes more than two cigarettes that day, the reward must be withheld.

One of the questions most often asked when behavioral self-control is explained is, "What keeps a person from cheating?" The answer is "Nothing," since the contract is with oneself. The problem of cheating vanishes when the person is motivated strongly enough to change the behavior. And because success provides positive reinforcement, personal contracts become easier to keep as goal after goal is honestly met.

Let's consider how the techniques of behavioral self-control might be applied to break a bad habit (for which we will use smoking as an example) and to overcome two kinds of anxiety common among students: social anxiety and test anxiety.

BREAKING A BAD HABIT Almost everyone has some habit he or she would like to break, whether it is nailbiting or talking too much—or smoking. Since the Surgeon General's report of 1964 established conclusively that cigarette smoking poses

health hazards, millions of Americans have tried to cut down or quit.

USING AVERSIVE TECHNIQUES THROUGH A SELF-CONTRACT In a case reported by L. Weiss and R. V. Hall (1971), a twenty-three-year-old graduate student called Lynn had smoked twenty to thirty cigarettes a day for about two years, and he wanted to break the habit. To begin, Lynn carried a piece of paper with him for seventeen days and kept a record of each time and place he lit a cigarette. He found that during this observation period he smoked an average of 16.6 cigarettes a day. He then set a sliding goal: to reduce smoking by one cigarette every five days until he stopped completely. He made a personal contract that required him to tear up a dollar bill every day he smoked more than the specified number of cigarettes. After fifty days, Lynn had stopped smoking entirely. At no time during the experiment did he exceed his self-imposed limit and have to tear up a dollar bill. Two years later, Lynn was still not smoking.

There is some question about the effectiveness of this kind of aversive self-regulation, which involves modifying one's behavior solely to avoid some undesirable consequence (Thoresen and Mahoney, 1974, pp. 134–138). Obviously this technique worked for Lynn, but perhaps he was very highly motivated to stop smoking, or, since graduate students are notoriously impoverished, perhaps the thought of tearing up a dollar bill was intolerable to him. Like Lynn, most people who use aversive techniques do stop smoking; but most of them eventually start again. A more effective approach seems to be the use of a combination of techniques, involving rewards for achieving goals as well as punishments for failing to do so.

USING A COMBINATION OF BEHAVIORAL TECHNIQUES Harry Lando (1977) has obtained some striking results by combining a number of behavioral techniques. His subjects, who smoked an average of 28.7 cigarettes a day, attended six treatment sessions within one week. They were instructed to smoke as much as possible between sessions and steadily for twenty-five minutes during each session, attaining a daily minimum of at least twice their usual number of cigarettes. This procedure was designed to get them to smoke more than they really wanted to, so that the act of smoking would become aversive, or undesirable. Such **aversive conditioning** has been shown to lead to short-term reduction in smoking.

The subjects were told that after the week of aversive conditioning they would be expected to abstain completely from smoking. At the end of the week, the subjects were divided into two groups. The control group was on its own: its members would attend no further sessions. The experimental group attended seven maintenance sessions during the following two months, gradually phasing out formal treatment. These follow-up sessions consisted primarily of group discussion and the signing of contracts calling for specific rewards for not smoking and punishments for smoking. In addition, these subjects were urged to undergo "booster" aversive treatment following any relapse into smoking.

The results were quite encouraging. After the initial aversive conditioning, experimental subjects reported 100 percent reduction of smoking; the control group reported 90 percent. After six months, however, only 35 percent of the control group were still not smoking, as compared to 76 percent of the experimental group.

CONTROLLING ANXIETY   A certain amount of anxiety is inescapable in most people's lives. The experience of living makes all kinds of demands on us, requiring constant adjustment. Anxiety is the label we attach to our emotional and physical reactions to situations we view as "stressful." Moreover, a situation need not even be stressful in itself to arouse anxiety; it may merely stimulate associations and thoughts that have caused anxiety in the past. Thus a man who has been in an automobile accident may become anxious whenever he rides in a car and even, perhaps, whenever he is about to cross a street.

Anxiety can be defined as a state of physiological arousal (sweating, increased pulse rate, trembling) accompanied by a sense of threat or impending danger. Anxiety utilizes energy usually reserved for other functions, and it distracts attention from the problem at hand. Thus people experiencing anxiety often find themselves confused and unable to concentrate on dealing with the situation. Anxiety is an aversive state: the feeling of danger and the sense of confusion and helplessness make us attempt to avoid situations that arouse anxiety. However, in avoiding the anxiety-provoking situation, we often miss the possibility of gratification and reward as well. For example, a person who is too fearful to go out on dates avoids the anxiety associated with dating, but also loses the pleasure of social contact with the opposite sex.

When avoidance behavior becomes very severe, a person is said to have developed a **phobia**, an extreme and pathological form of anxiety discussed in Chapter 22. Here we will focus on the common anxiety of everyday living and will investigate methods of self-control that can enable the ordinary person to cope with situations that were once sources of anxiety.

SOCIAL ANXIETY   One of the most difficult adjustments of adolescence is learning to establish heterosexual relationships—learning to be comfortable with members of the opposite sex, to enjoy their company and to share activities with them. Almost everyone experiences some anxiety on the first date with a new person: "Will she think I'm too short?" "Will he notice the pimple on my forehead?" "Will I say and do the right things?" For some people, however, the anxiety is so intense that it inhibits the possibility of a further relationship and so painful that it cancels out any pleasurable aspects of dating. Rather than face the anxiety, many young people decide not to date.

Social anxiety is usually associated with shyness, and shyness, according to Philip Zimbardo (1977), is an almost universal experience. Only 7 percent of Americans interviewed by Zimbardo reported that they had never been shy. (Studies of other cultures yield similarly low percentages.) Moreover, of those people who said they experienced shyness, about 25 percent reported that they regularly experienced it, while about 4 percent claimed that they were shy all the time, in every situation, which seriously limited their lives. Shyness, then, may range in intensity from momentary discomfort to a habitual state that severely affects normal functioning. All degrees of shyness are forms of social anxiety that may be relieved by using techniques of behavioral self-control.

One such therapeutic technique was developed several years ago by behaviorally oriented psychotherapists. It is called **systematic desensitization**. In this procedure, a new response, incompatible with the experience of anxiety, is substituted for the old response. In order to accomplish this, clients first need to learn relaxation. They are taught to relax all muscles and eliminate bodily tension.

Sometimes the environment contributes to feelings of anxiety, as evoked in this photograph, in which a boy stands in an empty school playground, surrounded by ominous-looking apartment buildings.

When they can do this quickly and easily, they next learn to create vivid, detailed mental pictures of anxiety-producing situations, and to experience the feelings associated with these visualized situations. When these two skills have been learned, the individuals begin to work through a hierarchy of anxiety-provoking situations, starting with those that provoke very small amounts of anxiety. They vividly imagine being in the situation and simultaneously use their relaxation skills to create a feeling incompatible with the anxiety that they usually experience. When a skilled therapist is present to

The first experiences with dating are sources of anxiety for most adolescents.

guide the systematic desensitization and when the client is highly motivated to overcome anxiety, the results can be dramatic.

Lynn Rehm and Albert Marston (1968) used a system of self-observation and self-reinforcement to reduce subjects' anxiety in heterosexual social situations. A group of college males, whose severity of anxiety with women lay somewhere between that of the typical experiment volunteer and that of the person who spontaneously seeks psychotherapy, were divided into three groups. One group received nondirective psychotherapy of a general nature, and another received no psychotherapy; these two groups served as controls. The third group participated in a program of systematic instruction designed to reduce social anxiety.

The members of this experimental group were given a number of questionnaires and tests that registered the degree of anxiety and discomfort they experienced in various situations, ranging from sitting next to a woman in class to kissing a woman. On the basis of the subjects' responses, the experimenters then devised a hierarchy of anxiety-provoking situations and made up score sheets for the subjects to use in rating themselves in real-life encounters. The subjects were instructed to seek out the low-anxiety-provoking situations during the first week and to assign themselves a point score according to how well they thought they had reacted in each situation. Thus, they would score 0 if they avoided the situation completely, 1 if they spoke a few words, and 3 if they did particularly well—say, by initiating a conversation or by extending a conversation to new topics. During the next four weeks, the subjects rated their performance in progressively higher-anxiety-provoking situations.

The experimental group clearly demonstrated greater improvement than either of the control groups. They verbally indicated less anxiety, showed more behavioral changes (such as more dates and longer conversations with women), and demonstrated lessened anxiety and more positive self-concepts on tests designed to measure these factors.

This experiment was designed to encourage the use of positive self-reinforcement—first by allowing the subjects themselves to define the anxiety-provoking situations and to rank them in a hierarchy, and second by utilizing each subject's own criteria in evaluating success and failure. By limiting his evaluation to clearly observable *behavior* (simply *feeling* less anxiety did not earn points), each subject was able to recognize his own successes and thus to

reinforce himself. The researchers hypothesized that negative self-evaluation is often a cue for anxiety and that substitution of a positive self-evaluation for a negative one would reduce anxiety. Positive self-evaluation, moreover, is a cue for responses that are incompatible with anxiety and results in the learning of new, positive responses.

TEST ANXIETY The mere thought of a test can give many students a headache. The actual experience of taking a test is often accompanied by sweating, nausea, and even the inability to hold a pencil securely. It is quite reasonable that many people experience some apprehension about taking a test. However, severe test anxiety can interfere with performance and lead to a self-fulfilling prophecy: The more anxious one becomes about a test, the less able one is to concentrate either on studying or on answering the test questions; then, the worse one performs on the test, the more anxious one is about the next test. To break out of this self-defeating cycle, we can once again utilize the principles of behavioral self-control.

The technique of systematic desensitization, described earlier, can be used to deal with test anxiety. However, researchers have been interested for some time in exploring procedures that are less time-consuming for the therapist and for the client.

Richard Driscoll (1976) has found that a forty-minute program in which subjects are shown pictures of positive scenes after anxiety-related scenes, plus physical exercise by subjects before and during the presentation of these scenes, reduced test anxiety as much as long programs of desensitization. Inducing positive feelings immediately after seeing a threatening image or event leads to a more positive response to that image or event when it is repeated at a later time. The physical exertion competes with anxiety because of its active, assertive, and forceful nature, diverting energy that would otherwise be available for anxiety. And because physical exercise is usually associated with the enjoyment of recreation and sports, it can be expected to have positive associations. It was therefore hypothesized and later demonstrated experimentally that positive imagery and physical exertion together are more effective in reducing test-related anxiety than either technique used alone. (The effectiveness of jogging in reducing anxiety is discussed in the accompanying special feature.)

In this section we have seen that the techniques of behavioral self-control can help us adjust to situa-

Jogging as an Aid to Adjustment

In the first paragraph of his bestselling book *The Complete Book of Running* (1977), James Fixx recalls a run through a Boston suburb. As Fixx ran by, an old man called out to him, "Say, what do you gain by running?" Fixx shouted back, "It makes you feel good!" Millions of people would agree. In just a few years running has gone from an activity pursued only by track stars and a few eccentrics to a national craze.

When Fixx said that running makes you feel good, he was not referring only to the physical benefits of running, such as firmer muscles and greater cardiovascular endurance. Jogging—long, slow, regular running—also contributes to psychological well-being. Olympic runner Ted Corbitt put it this way: "People get relief of tension from running. It's like having your own psychiatrist. . . . One thing that almost always happens is that your sense of self-worth improves. You accept yourself a little better" (quoted in Fixx, 1977, p. 15).

In interview after interview, Fixx found that runners and those who have studied them invariably began talking about the psychological benefits of the sport. In addition to increasing self-acceptance, running seems to reduce feelings of depression and anxiety. Dr. Frederick D. Harper of Howard University described a study aimed at understanding the psychological changes that occurred in students who gradually increased their running from one-quarter mile to several miles per day. Many reported feeling less anxious and generally feeling better about themselves (cited in Fixx, 1977, p. 16).

That running reduces anxiety is not really surprising. Physicians have found that the deepest muscular relaxation follows a period of *increased* muscular tension (Henderson, 1976, p. 57). And, since it is hard to feel anxious and relaxed at the same time, running seems an obvious antidote to anxiety.

A number of psychiatrists think that jogging is so effective an anxiety reducer that they recommend it as an adjunct to psychotherapy. California psychiatrist Thaddeus Kostubala, a marathon runner himself, runs with his clients. He reports that depression almost always disappears after thirty minutes of running, and is replaced by a "runner's high" (Henderson, 1976, p. 62). After they run, clients meet for group therapy in which they discuss the thoughts and feelings that came to them while running.

For many people, looking not for psychotherapy but for an enjoyable way of relieving tension and distracting themselves temporarily from the stresses and strains of their lives, running (under medical supervision) may be the answer. To Joe Henderson, author of *The Long-Run Solution*, running is not a cure-all for life's problems; but though there are no guarantees, running is extremely worthwhile as "a pursuit of happiness" (1976, p. 55).

tions that have caused us anxiety in the past. The goal of these techniques is not to neutralize all emotional responses or even to eliminate anxiety completely. Some anxiety is, after all, based on reality and can be useful in signaling us that danger is at hand. But excessive anxiety, and emotional responses that we feel are self-defeating, can be reduced by the techniques of behavioral self-control.

ADJUSTMENT: A LIFELONG PROCESS

We have seen in Chapter 18 that the need for adjustment arises as a child develops. But, as the discussion of Erik Erikson's concept of psychosocial stages in that chapter indicates, human development does not stop with childhood. Throughout our lives, we grow and change—and therefore the process of adjustment continues.

CRISES OF ADJUSTMENT FOR ADOLESCENTS AND YOUNG ADULTS Adjustment problems that occur during adolescence are the result of a combination of biological changes and personality development. Adolescents seek to separate themselves psychologically from their parents and to establish their own identity, and they become physically and sexually mature. Looking and feeling like an adult intensifies the desire to act like an adult, to make one's own decisions and to assert one's own individuality. Often this desire takes the form of open rebelliousness—wearing sloppy clothing because Mom and Dad value neatness, or playing rock music because Mom and Dad value Beethoven. Because adolescents have a foot in each world—the world of children and the world of adults—their problems of adjustment are compounded by ambivalent feelings. They want to leave their parents behind, but they are not yet ready to be alone. They want to be financially independent, but they don't want to give up their allowance.

While adolescence is a time for psychological separation from one's parents, early adulthood generally involves physical separation as well. Many of you are probably living away from home for the first time, establishing a life style that is completely separate and perhaps quite different from your parents'. This is a major life event, which inevitably generates stress. Whether the stress is positive or negative depends on how well you cope with the changes in yourself and your environment.

Until the early twenties, through the stage of separating from parents and searching for identity, the life stages of males and females are quite similar. At the end of this stage, however, decisions will be made concerning career patterns for men and either career or homemaker patterns for women. These decisions result in different crises of adjustment for the two sexes.

The Passages of Women

All the male researchers into adult development agree with Erikson that the path to replenishment in midlife is through nurturing, teaching and serving others. Yet once again, the male life cycle is presented as the adult life cycle.

Overlooked is the fact that serving others is what most women have been doing all along. What is the first half of the female life cycle about for the majority of women if not nurturing children, serving husbands, and caring for others? . . .

It is not through more caregiving that a woman looks for a replenishment of purpose in the second half of her life. It is through cultivating talents left half finished, permitting ambitions once piggybacked, becoming aggressive in the service of her own convictions. . . .

Losing her powers of procreation forces a woman to redirect her energies. . . . A new kind of creativity is released. Whatever pursuit a woman decides to follow, she pours herself into it. . . .

If the struggle for men in midlife comes down to having to defeat stagnation through generativity, I submit that the comparable task for women is to transcend dependency through self-declaration.

Source: Gail Sheehy, *Passages. Predictable Crises of Adult Life.* New York: Dutton, 1976, pp. 293–294.

A Woman at Mid-Life

What kinds of adjustment does a woman face in the course of her life? This autobiographical passage, written by a forty-eight-year-old woman, outlines her particular process of life adjustment. However, there is not yet enough data on the life histories of women in general to produce a developmental scheme that might apply to most or all women.

20s

I worked for eight years before I married [mostly] in an advertising agency. I liked the field, but my job was menial and not satisfying in any way. . . . I couldn't break out of the secretarial mold. . . . I was confident that if someone could pick me up and put me in an important position I could do it, but I just couldn't seem to get there on my own.

About the age of 27 I began to get depressed—when I would visit married friends with children I would come away with the keen realization that I was not the center of anyone's life—that I was not important to anyone or ones. . . .

About this time I met my husband, Don. . . . We became engaged in three weeks and married within three months. [We] share the same attitudes, interests and intensity of feeling toward these attitudes. . . . Our first marital years were stormy—problems from without and those of our own making. . . .

30s

We had three children in the first five years. . . . I guess life would have gone along as usual . . . if something tragic had not occurred to make us stop and think. Our oldest child, Paul, died suddenly at the age of seven. . . . We went through a period of grieving. [It] was the beginning of a turning point in our marital relationship, parental handling of children, outlook and actions as human beings as part of a larger society.

. . . My religious beliefs were challenged. . . . My whole faith began to shatter [but it] was slowly rebuilt, and this time had new strength because I was more mature. . . .

40s

I always knew I would go back to work. . . . I made up my mind that I would do something that was interesting. . . . I realized I would need further education. [I enrolled in] a program in community psychology. This seemed to be the direction I should go in because of my desire to work in the field of social action. I enjoyed being back in the academic atmosphere. . . . I landed a good [job]. I am project director of a senior citizens' volunteer program, and I enjoy this very much. . . .

I believe that I have more confidence in myself now [at 48]. . . . I am much crankier and more argumentative . . . [but] I think I am a happier person now than I was in college.

Source: Robert W. White, Margaret M. Riggs, and Doris C. Gilbert. *Case Workbook in Personality*. New York: Holt, Rinehart and Winston, 1976, pp. 90–103.

CRISES OF ADJUSTMENT FOR THE ADULT WOMAN The stages of a woman's life used to be marked primarily by her capacity to reproduce. There was one critical stage at puberty, marked by the onset of menstruation, and another at menopause, marked by the end of menstruation and of the capacity to bear children. Women today confront a much more complex set of possibilities and expectations, as indicated in the accompanying box.

CAREER VERSUS FAMILY Until recently, both men and women in industrialized societies felt that a woman's identity necessitated an either-or decision: either she was a homemaker, or she had a career outside the home. However, as Gail Sheehy has pointed out in her best-selling book *Passages* (1976), there are all kinds of options in between, and the decision can be renegotiated again and again. A woman may, for example, "piggyback" her career ambitions by opting at a young age for marriage and children with a man whose career she will enjoy vicariously. Ten years later, with her children no longer demanding so much of her time and attention, she may go back to school or begin her own career. Conversely, the woman who opts for a career may put off marriage and children until her mid-thirties, when she may feel the desire to emphasize the nurturing side of her personality, which has been secondary up to this time.

PHYSICAL ATTRACTIVENESS IN MID-LIFE As we will see in Chapter 26, the selection of a partner for courtship and marriage depends to a great extent on physical attractiveness, which is also an important variable in many other aspects of social interaction. As a woman comes to be considered less attractive with age, she may need to adjust to a different image of herself. It has been shown that physical attrac-

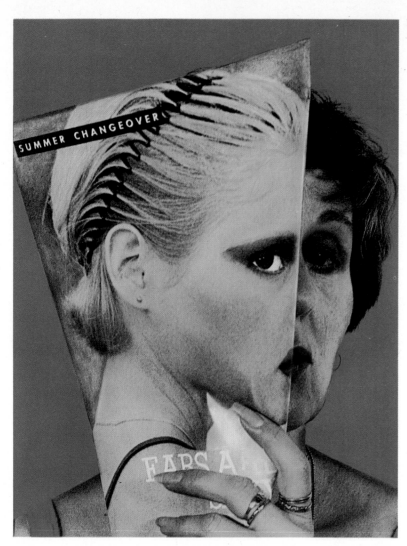

Magazine Makeover by Judith Golden.

tiveness, which eased social adjustment for college women, actually made adjustment more difficult for them twenty years later (Berscheid and Walster, 1974, pp. 200–201). Perhaps the contrast between their socially active college years and the unexciting routine of family life results in more dissatisfaction than is experienced by their less attractive schoolmates, who were not "spoiled" by previous pleasures nor misled by great expectations.

THE "EMPTY NEST" SYNDROME For the woman who has chosen primarily a family orientation, a crisis occurs as her children grow up and leave home. She finds that her role as mother has diminished; she thinks, "Nobody needs me any more." When coupled with the physical changes associated with menopause, the psychological effects of the "empty nest" syndrome are often experienced as in-

tense depression. In order to adjust to the changes in herself and her family, the woman in mid-life may search for satisfying work outside the home, possibly returning to an interrupted career or starting a new one. A warm relationship with her husband can provide important support as the woman adjusts to her changing situation.

CRISES OF ADJUSTMENT FOR THE ADULT MAN Men also undergo a series of developmental crises. Researchers at Yale University, led by Daniel J. Levinson (1978), interviewed four groups of men between the ages of thirty-five and forty-five: ten were executives, ten were blue-collar or white-collar workers, ten were writers of varying degrees of fame, and ten were biologists at various stages in their careers.

From the interviews with these subjects, a **life structure** was developed for each man in the sample. Each life structure was an account of the major periods of the man's life, as determined by his activities, his associations, and his parental, marital and family relationships. A careful analysis of these life structures revealed a pattern that seemed to characterize almost all of the men sampled. The pattern is a combination of the major eras in the adult life of a man and the transitions from one era to another.

The model of adult development for men that Levinson and his colleagues proposed is shown in Figure 21.4 The three major eras are early adulthood (from about age seventeen to about age forty), middle adulthood (forty to sixty), and late adulthood (beginning at about sixty). Between these eras are important transition periods lasting approximately five years. Levinson's research focused on the early adult era and the mid-life transition; the following discussion concentrates on what he learned about these stages.

Figure 21.4 A model of the developmental sequence of a man's life developed by Daniel Levinson. The major life eras are childhood and adolescence, early adulthood, middle adulthood, and later adulthood; within each era there are distinctive stages, and between eras a major transition occurs. This model emphasizes that development is a continuing process that requires continual adjustment. (Levinson, 1978.)

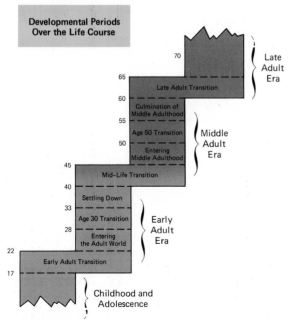

ENTERING THE ADULT WORLD From about age twenty-two to age twenty-eight, the young man is considered, both by himself and by society, to be a novice in the adult world—not fully established as a man, but no longer an adolescent. During this time he must attempt to resolve the conflict between the need to explore the options of the adult world and the need to establish a stable life structure. He needs to sample different kinds of relationships, to keep choices about career and employment open, to explore the nature of the world now accessible to him as an adult. But he also needs to begin a career and to establish a home and family of his own. The first life structure, then, may have a tentative quality. The young man may select a career or a job but not be committed to it. He may form romantic attachments and may even marry during this period; but the life structure of early adulthood often lacks a full sense of stability or permanence.

THE AGE THIRTY CRISIS A few years ago the motto of the rebellious, politically oriented young people who sought to change American society was "Never trust anyone over thirty." Levinson's data reveal that the years between twenty-eight and thirty-three are indeed often a major transition period. The thirtieth birthday can truly be a turning point; for most men in Levinson's sample, it could be called "the age thirty crisis." During this transitional period the tentative commitments that were made in the first life structure are reexamined, and many questions about the choices of marriage partner, career, and life goals are reopened, often in a painful way. The man feels that any parts of his life that are unsatisfying or incomplete must be attended to now, because it will soon be too late to make major changes.

SETTLING DOWN The questioning and searching that are part of the age thirty crisis begin to be resolved as the second adult life structure develops. Having probably made some firm choices about his career, family, and relationships, the man now begins actively carving out his niche in society, concentrating on what Levinson calls "making it" in the adult world. The man attempts to move up the ladder of prestige and achievement in his chosen career or profession and to be no longer a novice but a full-fledged member of adult society.

Levinson found that near the end of the settling-down period, approximately between the ages of

A Man at Mid-Life

What kinds of adjustment does a man face in the course of his life? This autobiographical passage, written by a man of forty-four, documents a few of his personal difficulties and adjustments. How would you compare the adjustment process between this man and the woman quoted in the previous box? What positive and negative changes, irreversible losses, and kinds of compromise characterize each life? And what kinds of movement and new life choices would you expect from each?

After I graduated from law school I took the bar examination [and] . . . flunked . . . [and] learned a pretty good lesson regarding ego. Defeats and losses have never had as great an impact upon me.

While studying for the bar for the second round, I obtained employment with an attorney . . . and I spent one of the most fascinating years of my life doing really what amounted to political work, rather than legal work, in helping to prepare defense and testimony for the Committee [for lawyers who had been subpoenaed by the House

Committee on Un-American Activities]. . . .

[Shortly afterward] I went into the general practice of law where I struggled for five years building a practice completely on my own . . . but I received no satisfaction from the practice or from the struggle to establish one. I knew few lawyers who would undertake a civil rights case, and I felt that this was what I wanted to do as well as establish myself economically. So I formed a partnership with . . . [another lawyer] who felt exactly the same as I. . . . We did build a successful general practice with heavy emphasis on free work and civil liberties.

For the first few years each of us . . . received a great deal of satisfaction what we felt we were accomplishing for ourselves [and] for our community. . . . [But] I slowly began to develop more of a practice in representing injured persons in personal injury cases, and my income increased [and] so did my guilt. . . . [Now] I no longer have any feelings of guilt about the type of legal practice in which I am engaged, but neither do I receive any satisfaction from my work as I did in the earlier years,

even though then I had economic problems which I no longer face.

• • •

. . . Concerning beliefs and values, . . . I no longer feel I am the idealist I was some twenty years ago. . . . Whereas in the past I would have been the writer of a petition, or the petition circulator, I now might be the petition signer. . . .

• • •

My personal life has not been such as I would have anticipated when I was a student. I married shortly after graduation from law school, and can't even now explain why I did. . . . The hardest decision of my life was to leave [my wife], in view of the fact that we had three children . . . [but] I remarried shortly after my divorce and am very happily married now. . . .

• • •

. . . I would advise any young man today to do what he feels he wants to do and to make his own decisions in that regard. . . . It took me quite a while to see the wisdom [of this].

Source: Robert W. White, Margaret M. Riggs, and Doris C. Gilbert. *Case Workbook in Personality.* New York: Holt, Rinehart and Winston, 1976. Abridged from pages 56–60.

---

thirty-six and forty, there is a distinctive phase that he has labeled **becoming one's own man**. Whereas earlier the young man had looked to an older, more experienced man as a mentor, someone who would share his experience and wisdom, the relationship with the mentor is often fundamentally changed, or even broken off, in the process of becoming one's own man. Now it is time to become fully independent. During this period the man strives to attain the seniority and position in the world that he identified as his ultimate goal at the beginning of the settling-down period.

THE MID-LIFE TRANSITION At about age forty the period of early adulthood comes to an end and

the mid-life transition begins. From about age forty to age forty-five, the man begins again to question, but now the questioning has a retrospective as well as a future orientation. He may ask: "What have I done with my life?" "What have I accomplished?" "What do I still wish to accomplish?" At age thirty the man had primarily looked ahead toward goals, but at the mid-life transition he is in a position to assess his accomplishments and to determine whether or not they have been satisfying. During this transition he begins to develop yet another life structure that will predominate during the period of middle adulthood.

The mid-life transition has been the most-discussed aspect of Levinson's work. About 80 percent of the men in his sample experienced the mid-life transition as a moderate to severe crisis, characterized by the questioning of virtually every aspect of their lives. But it is a period of questioning from which a new life structure must emerge. Often a successful mid-life transition is accompanied by the man's becoming a mentor for a younger man, which signals the attainment, in Erik Erikson's terms, of generativity rather than stagnation.

Levinson's analysis of the life structures of adult males emphasizes that development is a continuing process. And that process requires continual adjustment—adjustment in the sense in which we have defined it in this chapter. These eras and transitions can be viewed as major life events, in which the individual must adjust to the new forces that come into play in his life.

We began this chapter by discussing the nature of stress and its impact on physical and psychological functioning. We have focused on some of the ways in which people adjust to stresses in their lives, and we have presented some of the methods by which people can exert greater control over their lives during the process of adjustment. Because none of us can control the passage of time, the life cycle itself creates problems of adjustment for all people. We should emphasize once again, then, that adjustment is not a fixed state that one finally achieves. "Good" adjustment and "bad" adjustment should not be viewed as states in which one remains. Rather, adjustment is a process that continues throughout life and that is more or less successful at various times as we develop ways of coping with the stress of living in today's world.

SUMMARY

1. **Adjustment** is a continuous and ever-changing process of interacting with the people, events, and forces that affect our lives. The process of adjusting may be accompanied by stress and by physical and psychological dysfunction. Attempts to cope with difficult situations tend to fall into three major categories:
   A. Problem-solving skills are a useful aid to adjustment.
   B. Acceptance is an effective response in situations where active problem solving is not appropriate.
   C. Defense mechanisms such as repression and denial help to alleviate the stress and anxiety that may be produced by a coping situation. However, the overuse of defense mechanisms can lead to severe disturbances.

2. Physicians and psychologists have studied the association between the number and severity of stressful events in a person's life and the probability of physical illness.
   A. The Social Readjustment Rating Scale is used to measure the amount of life stress a person experiences from many events and situations during a year or some other period of time. Studies using the SRRS indicate a correlation between life stress and heart disease, the occurrence of bone fractures, and the onset of leukemia in children. The prediction of stress-related illness is difficult because of the differences in the way individuals react to stressful situations.
   B. Richard Rahe has offered a model which suggests that there are six transformations through which a person experiencing life stress must pass before physical illness can occur.
      1. The interpretation of the stressful event by means of past experience may decrease, neutralize, or increase the effects of the stress.
      2. The ego's defense mechanism, such as projection or denial, can reduce the stress.
      3. Physiological reactions such as increased hormone secretion or rapid heartbeat may occur.
      4. Physiological activation that continues despite the person's attempts to cope may be interpreted by the person as bodily symptoms.
      5. The person may decide to report these perceptions of bodily symptoms to a doctor.
      6. The doctor may diagnose these symptoms as indicative of illness.
   C. Environmental stress nearly always takes the form of aversive events. It is possible that environmental events would be less stress-producing if they could be better predicted and controlled.

1. Studies have shown that it is possible for subjects to adapt to unpredictable unpleasant noise, but that the energy expended on adaptation hinders the subjects' performance on mental tests. Later experiments indicate that the effect of environmental stress on adjustment may be due to the individual's feelings of helplessness to control or avoid the stress rather than to the stress itself.

2. **Learned helplessness** is the acquired belief that one cannot exert any control over the environment. Learned helplessness in dogs was demonstrated in an experiment by J. B. Overmeier and Martin Seligman, and it is believed that it may be an important factor in the failure of human beings to adjust to stressful events.

D. An experiment in a nursing home by Ellen Langer and Judith Rodin showed that subjects who were encouraged to take control of their environment showed overall improvement as compared to subjects who were encouraged to let the staff make decisions for them.

E. While helplessness increases stress by increasing anxiety and inhibiting the ability to perform tasks, it is the most adaptive behavior in a truly uncontrollable situation.

3. The theory of behavioral self-control is based on the concept of operant conditioning. Behavioral self-control depends largely on observation, evaluation, and reinforcement. The techniques of behavioral self-control can be applied to such situations as breaking a bad habit and overcoming social and test anxiety.

A. The most effective approach to breaking a bad habit seems to be the use of a combination of rewards and aversive techniques. An example of this is Harry Lando's program to enable people to give up smoking.

B. **Anxiety** is a state of physiological arousal accompanied by a sense of threat or impending danger. Some anxiety can be useful in signaling that danger is at hand, but excessive anxiety can be maladaptive.

1. Social anxiety is usually associated with shyness. All degrees of shyness are forms of social anxiety that may be relieved by using techniques of behavioral self-control.

a. **Systematic desensitization** is a therapeutic technique by which subjects first learn relaxation and then gradually substitute a new relaxed response for the old response to anxiety-producing situations.

b. A system of self-observation and self-reinforcement has been used to reduce subjects' anxiety in heterosexual social situations.

2. In regard to reducing test anxiety, researchers have found that a program of positive imagery and physical exertion is as effective as systematic desensitization.

4. Adjustment is a lifelong process because growth and change continue throughout life.

A. Problems in adjustment that occur during adolescence are the result of a combination of biological changes and personality development. Until the early twenties, the life stages of males and females are quite similar.

B. Women today confront a more complex set of possibilities and expectations than ever before.

1. Women no longer must choose either a career or a family; there are a number of options in between, and a woman's decision to emphasize one or the other can be revised again and again.

2. As a woman comes to be considered less attractive with age, she may need to adjust to a different image of herself.

3. A woman who has chosen primarily a family orientation may experience the "empty nest" syndrome when her children grow up and leave home. This crisis may be characterized by intense depression.

C. According to Daniel J. Levinson, an analysis of the **life structures** of different groups of men reveals a model of development consisting of major eras in the lives of adult men and the transitions from one era to another.

1. The period from about age twenty-two to age twenty-eight is characterized by the conflict between the need to explore the options of the adult world and the need to establish a stable life structure.

2. The years between twenty-eight and thirty-three are often a major transition for a man. The tentative commitments made during the previous life structure are reexamined during this "age thirty

crisis," and many questions about life choices are reopened.

3. The man begins carving out his niche in society during the first part of the next period, and the questioning and searching that have preceded it begin to be resolved. In the second part of this settling-down period, between the ages of thirty-six and forty, there is a phase called **becoming one's own man**, during which the man strives to be fully independent.

4. The mid-life transition lasts from about age forty to forty-five, during which time the man assesses his life, looking both forward and backward. From this questioning a new middle-adulthood life structure emerges.

RECOMMENDED READINGS

CALHOUN, JAMES F., and JOAN ROSS ACOCELLA. *Psychology of Adjustment and Human Relationships.* New York: Random House, 1978. This is a textbook, but it is also a very practical guide to problem solving. The authors present psychological principles relevant to the process of adjustment, and they provide clear illustrations of how the principles may be applied.

CONGER, JOHN J. *Adolescence and Youth: Psychological Development in a Changing World.* 2nd ed. New York: Harper & Row, 1977. A thorough account of the many psychological adjustments that occur during adolescence, and a very useful resource for persons concerned with the problems of being adolescent in the modern United States.

DOHRENWEND, BARBARA S., and BRUCE P. DOHRENWEND (eds.). *Stressful Life Events: Their Nature and Effects.* New York: Wiley, 1974. A collection of papers by the leading researchers in this area. The measurement of life stress and the impact of stressful events on many kinds of illness are discussed.

GLASS, DAVID C., and JEROME E. SINGER. *Urban Stress: Experiments on Noise and Social Stressors.* New York: Academic, 1972. Glass and Singer devised a number of incisive laboratory studies designed to explore the psychological impact of urban stress. This book is a summary of those studies.

HENDERSON, JOE. *The Long Run Solution.* Mountain View, Calif.: World Publications, 1976. Henderson describes the psychological benefits of long, slow running and offers the reader very practical advice about how to start a program of running and stay with it.

LEVINSON, DANIEL J. *The Seasons of a Man's Life.* New York: Knopf, 1978. This is the long-awaited report of Levinson's research on stages of development in adult males. On the basis of intensive interviews with forty men from four different occupational groups, Levinson proposes a model of the stages, crises, and transitions experienced by most men.

MAHONEY, MICHAEL J., and CARL E. THORESEN. *Self-Control: Power to the Person.* Monterey, Calif.: Brooks-Cole, 1974. A thorough and readable introduction to the theory and practice of self-control by two leading researchers. Part 1 presents concepts and principles, and Part 2 presents a well-selected collection of research and review articles.

SELIGMAN, MARTIN E. P. *Helplessness.* San Francisco: Freeman, 1975. Seligman has done pioneering work in the area of learned helplessness. This is his summary of the determinants and consequences of learned helplessness in a variety of species, including humans.

SHEEHY, GAIL. *Passages.* New York: Dutton, 1976. A popular account of predictable crises of adulthood. Sheehy is not the systematic theorist that Levinson (above) is, but she has a rich data base in the interviews she personally conducted, and she deals with the life crises of women as well as men.

ZIMBARDO, PHILIP G. *Shyness: What It Is, What to Do About It.* Reading, Mass.: Addison-Wesley, 1977. In this engagingly written, nontechnical examination of the causes and possible cures of shyness, Zimbardo documents the prevalence of shyness and offers suggestions for overcoming it.

CHAPTER TWENTY-TWO

PSYCHOLOGICAL DISORDERS

What we call "mental disorder," with all its implications of a mind badly arranged or out of tune with reality, was viewed in quite a favorable fashion in past times. To be out of tune with "reality" was considered to be in tune with something just as real but not apparent to most people. The "other reality" was considered superior to the common reality, and those few who were fortunate enough to be in touch with it were treated with awe rather than pity.

The man or woman whose behavior or responses were inappropriate to his or her surroundings might be in touch with the gods; might indeed be controlled by divine power for its own purpose. Madmen were therefore treated with respect. In some conditions that bring a temporary retreat from the common reality, as in an epileptic fit, observers felt the sufferer to be temporarily in touch with the divine. In fact, the ancient Greeks called epilepsy the "sacred disease."

Fits of irrationality, where a person might foam at the mouth, speak incoherently, and writhe uncontrollably were impressive to onlookers in older times. If speech, during these fits, could be understood (or interpreted), that speech was looked upon as containing knowledge beyond that attainable by ordinary people—it might contain information concerning the future, for instance. The priestess at Delphi breathed fumes, chewed leaves, or in some other way induced a pseudo-epileptic fit, and the irrational, incoherent sounds she made during the fit were then interpreted into the famous utterances that on more than one occasion influenced Greek history.

In biblical history, irrational fits were characteristic of the people referred to as "prophets" in English translation. Their incoherent outcries were referred to as "prophesying." Thus, when Saul returned from his first meeting with Samuel, "behold, a company of prophets met him; and the Spirit of God came upon him, and he prophesied among them" (1 Samuel 10:10).

Again, on the first Pentecost after the Crucifixion, the apostles were gathered together and "they were all filled with the Holy Ghost, and began to speak with other tongues" (Acts 2:4). Religious sects that feature such fits are called "pentecostal" in consequence, and their meetings seem often to involve "speaking in tongues"—writhings, foamings, incoherent outcries.

Religious "ecstasy" (from Greek words meaning "out of place" because the mind seems to be responding to some other set of impulses and to be elsewhere) is the most influential type of mental disorder in history (and there is no way of predicting how influential it may yet be in the future). Yet how can modern medicine deal with this type of mental disorder when, to so many people, it still seems to be touched by the divine?

Isaac Asimov

A woman staggers toward you. What little clothing she has on is soaked with perspiration, her lips are flecked with foam, her face is contorted, and she can barely speak. Have you encountered a madwoman? If you met her in an art gallery, you might think so. If you were standing at the finish line of the Boston marathon, you would probably applaud the woman's courage and endurance. A man who holds a big party at which he gives away all of his possessions and makes himself a pauper would be considered mad by most present-day Americans. Yet the same behavior—at a ceremony called the potlatch—elicits respect and admiration among the members of some native American tribes along the Northwest coast. Behavior that appears abnormal to us when it occurs in one context may appear perfectly normal in another. In light of this, is it possible to define what is normal and what is abnormal?

CRITERIA OF NORMALITY

In medicine, "normality" generally refers to integrity of structure and function of an organ or other body part. A broken bone, an excess of certain sugars in the blood, an ulcer on the wall of the stomach—all are abnormal. For physicians, the line between normality and abnormality is relatively easy to draw. For psychologists and psychiatrists, however, the criteria that divide normal behavior from abnormal behavior are not so easily specified. Several definitions of normality are in use within the field of psychology, each based on a different theoretical orientation. This chapter will examine the concept of normality and then discuss a number of

Disco skaters in Brooklyn. If you saw somebody dancing on roller skates in the street, you might think this behavior abnormal. In a roller-skating rink, however, it is considered perfectly acceptable.

psychological disorders based on current diagnostic practices of psychiatrists and clinical psychologists.

THE STATISTICAL CRITERION According to the statistical approach, abnormality is any substantial deviation from a statistically calculated average; normality, in other words, is what most people do. Though this might seem a very uncomplicated approach, it does present certain problems. It allows for no distinction between desirable deviations from the norm and undesirable ones. If average intelligence is the norm, for example, then both the mentally retarded and the genius are considered abnormal. In addition to discouraging socially valuable abnormalities, therapists who rigidly adhere to this approach become guardians of the status quo, supporters of mediocrity.

ABSOLUTE CRITERIA Unlike the statistical criterion, which changes the definition of normality with every shift in the population, absolute criteria of normality assume the existence of a certain universal or absolute standard of mental health. Treatment aims at adjusting the patient's behavior to approximate the absolute. Theorists differ, however, about just what this absolute is. For Abraham Maslow and Carl Rogers it is self-actualization; for Erich Fromm it is productivity; for Erik Erikson it is integrity. For some it is the absence of personal discomfort, and for others it is conformity to social norms.

THE CLINICAL CRITERION The medical model, or clinical perspective, views psychological problems in the same way as physical problems are viewed—as diseases with specific symptoms, causes, treatments, and prognoses. Patients are treated in hospitals, often with drugs, by medical doctors. To facilitate diagnosis and standardize treatment, a medically based classification system has been put together by the American Psychiatric Association. This *Diagnostic and Statistical Manual of Mental Disorders*, commonly referred to as DSM-II, is a vast listing of descriptive terms and symptoms covering almost all kinds of unusual or deviant behavior.

Though the medical model is only one way of looking at psychological disorders, it is the one with the longest history—all the founders of modern psychiatry, as we will see in the next chapter, were medical doctors—and the terminology is still pervasive. The use of the medical model and its terminology must have an effect on how we think. Some theorists feel that the use of medical terminology is a serious error. Thomas Szasz, for example, in his book *The Myth of Mental Illness* (1961), claims that labeling some people as "sick," and removing such people from normal life for treatment in a "hospital," often maintains or even creates bizarre behavior. Call people "sick" and "treat" them accordingly, some social scientists say, and they will act out the role that is expected of them.

The DSM-II classification system permits psychologists and psychiatrists to exchange information about symptoms and therapies and to compare notes on possible causes. But it may also have the effect of focusing clinicians on the response patterns that they already expect to find, perhaps blinding them to the uniqueness of the individual they are evaluating. With all the limitations of the DSM-II classification system, however, its descriptions of major types of disorders are quite consistent in various cultures and even throughout history. Moreover, it is very useful to have a common vocabulary when dealing with so much material on psychological disorder. The organization of this chapter itself is based on the DSM-II classification system.

It should be noted that DSM-II will soon be replaced by DSM-III. The changes to be made have been a topic of intensive discussion among psychologists, psychiatrists, and other mental health professionals (Schacht and Nathan, 1977). The draft versions of DSM-III have reorganized the categories of disorder in important ways. But the major forms of disorder from DSM-II will be included, so the following discussion should serve as a useful overview, regardless of the final form of DSM-III.

There are literally hundreds of disorders in the DSM-II classification system, and it would be impossible even to mention all of them here. In this chapter we will present four broad categories of disorder—neurosis, psychosis, personality and other nonpsychotic disorders, and organic disorders. Briefly, neuroses are disorders characterized by anxiety, but they can take many forms, none of which involve loss of contact with reality. The psychoses, such as schizophrenia, are usually considered more severe forms of disorder than neuroses, and often involve bizarre behavior and a retreat from reality. The personality disorders are the result of unusual

The American Psychiatric Association classifies alcoholism with the personality disorders.

ting cancer whenever he or she has a sore throat; another may be afraid to make decisions; a third may become tongue-tied in social situations; a fourth may have difficulty spending money. For most of us, these "hangups" or "quirks" do not severely limit our activities or interfere with our daily lives. If we want to, we can avoid situations that we find difficult by adjusting our life style or routines. We can turn down a high-pressure job that would make us anxious or take a train if flying makes us nervous. While some inconvenience is involved in these "sidesteps," life is still livable.

For some of us, however, there is one situation—or many—that becomes a major source of anxiety, taking up more and more attention until it seriously impairs our daily functioning. Anxiety is a feeling of dread, apprehension, or fear. In addition, anxious individuals feel confused and may experience physiological changes, such as increased heartbeat, perspiration, muscle tension, and rapid breathing. When anxiety is chronic and leads to irrational, limiting, and disruptive behavior, the condition is called **neurosis**.

development or growth patterns leading to abnormal behavior, such as compulsive stealing, sexual deviance, alcoholism, and drug dependence. The organic disorders are conditions that have been caused by damage to or deterioration of brain tissue, the central nervous system, or some other organic system.

These four categories of DSM-II will be the focus of the chapter. It is important to note, however, that almost all people who are diagnosed show a mixture of symptoms and are classified according to those symptoms that are most prominent in their behavior or judged to be the most central features of their disorder. Furthermore, because the behavior of human beings, both normal and abnormal, is extraordinarily variable and complex, it is a good idea to bear in mind, while reading this chapter, that there is no one right way to understand or classify human behavior.

NEUROSIS

Most people have difficulty in coping with some area of their life. One person may worry about get-

ANXIETY NEUROSIS Anxiety neurosis accounts for 30 to 40 percent of the diagnoses of neurosis. It is characterized by diffuse and generalized fears that are impossible to manage through avoidance. Indeed, the whole personality may be engulfed by anxiety. The person is jumpy, irritable, and frequently upset. He or she expresses a great many fears and worries, yet is unable to specify what is generating these fears—a condition that Freud called **free-floating anxiety**. Anxiety neurotics may have nightmares in which things close in on them or in which they are lost or abandoned. Furthermore, their daily coping is severely impaired. They forget appointments, have difficulty making decisions, and, if placed in a situation of extreme stress, may become disorganized.

Various physical symptoms often accompany anxiety neurosis. Anxiety neurotics may complain of stiff, aching muscles, the result of sustained muscle tension. Their appetite tends to be poor, and they may be troubled by indigestion and by a frequent need to urinate. Their sleeping patterns are also disturbed. They may have insomnia, or they may begin awakening suddenly in the night. In the morning they feel tired rather than refreshed.

From time to time people suffering from anxiety

neurosis may have **anxiety attacks**, episodes in which the already heightened state of tension mounts to an acute and overwhelming level. Usually these attacks last anywhere from fifteen minutes to an hour. Individuals may report a shivering sensation. The heart begins to pound loudly, perspiration flows, and breathing becomes difficult. A feeling of inescapable disaster overcomes them. They try to escape, but there is no place to escape to. When the attack subsides, they feel exhausted. In the most extreme form of an anxiety attack, a **panic reaction**, anxiety is so severe and prolonged, possibly lasting for days, that the person becomes disorganized and disoriented.

PHOBIAS When neurotic anxiety is irrationally focused on a particular object or situation, it is called a **phobia** (see Figure 22.1). Fear of taking elevators is a good example: For years Bill has been afraid of taking elevators. On the rare occasions when he attempts to overcome his fear and ride in one, he is terrified. He begins to sweat; his throat feels tight as if he is choking, and he has difficulty breathing. His one thought is to get out. As soon as the elevator makes its first stop, he pushes his way out and leans against the nearest wall, panting, until he can breathe normally again. Then he takes the stairs to the floor he desires. Bill knows that his fear is irrational, that thousands of people go up and down in elevators every day with no ill effects, but he cannot overcome his intense fear that he will suffocate before he reaches his floor. Although Bill manages to cope with his phobia, or irrational fear,

of elevators by avoiding them whenever possible, it has had severe consequences in his life. He cannot accept a promotion in his job because it means working on the twenty-third floor of a large office building. He can date only women who live no higher than the fifth floor. When invited to a party in a high-rise apartment building, he has to make up excuses for taking the stairs, claiming he likes the exercise or wants to examine the architecture of the stairwells. Although most people are sympathetic and accept Bill's "eccentricity," he is finding his life more and more circumscribed by anxiety.

Phobias have two somewhat distinct effects. First, there is the anxiety associated with the phobia and the consequent avoidance of situations in which the feared object will be present. Second, there is anxiety, guilt, and shame associated with the problem of hiding the phobia from others. In Bill's case, he has organized much of his life to deal with keeping his phobia a secret; the anxiety he feels in an elevator is compounded by the fear of being found out. In combination, these two effects of Bill's phobia leave him more and more debilitated.

OBSESSIONS AND COMPULSIONS An **obsession** is a recurring irrational thought. An obsession may be mild, as in the case of the student who can think of nothing but schoolwork and grades. But an obsession may also have a violent or sexual quality to it, such as the desire to burn the house down or sodomize a neighbor, which makes the person feel guilty and horrified as much by the content of the thought as by its persistence.

Figure 22.1 An artist's representation of three phobias: (A) fear of heights, called acrophobia; (B) fear of enclosed spaces, called claustrophobia; and (C) fear of dirt, called mysophobia. (After Vassos, 1931.)

A   B   C

A **compulsion** is the desire to engage repeatedly in a particular irrational act, often a senseless one like looking under the bed several times before going to sleep or locking and unlocking the door several times before going out.

Much neurotic behavior is both obsessive and compulsive; constant handwashing, for example, may be caused by an obsessive preoccupation with germs. Although we all can remember times when we couldn't get a song lyric out of our thoughts, or when we checked several times to make sure we had set the alarm clock, these minor obsessions and compulsions pass. A neurotic obsession or compulsion continues—day after day, year after year.

Obsessive-compulsive behavior patterns generally arise as a response to intense anxiety in another area of one's life. Repetitive behavior reassures individuals that they have control over their environment. Whatever they fear cannot hurt them so long as they perform their ritualistic activity. Like all neurotic behavior, however, this pattern of behavior can be severely limiting and interfere with other life functions.

HYSTERICAL NEUROSIS When some normal function, either physical or psychological, is lost or impaired for no organic reason and is accompanied

Figure 22.2 A patient who complained to a doctor that his right hand had become numb might be diagnosed either as suffering from damage to the nervous system or as a neurotic suffering from hysteria, depending on the exact pattern of his numbness. The skin areas served by different nerves in the arm are shown in A. The "glove anesthesia" shown in B could not result from damage to these nerves.

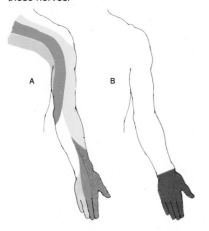

by denial of anxiety over the loss, it is known as **hysterical neurosis**. There are two main types, the conversion type and the dissociative type.

CONVERSION REACTION In a **conversion reaction**, as we mentioned in Chapter 18, the individual develops some physical dysfunction—such as blindness, deafness, paralysis, or loss of sensation in some part of the body—that has no organic basis and violates neurophysiological laws. A hand might become completely numb, for example, as in "glove anesthesia," but sensation might be clearly felt in an area directly above the wrist (see Figure 22.2). If the numbness were actually a result of neurological dysfunction, the line between sensitivity and numbness would not be so sharply drawn. Such symptoms often appear or disappear suddenly. Many "miraculous cures" in which patients who have been paralyzed suddenly leave their wheelchairs and walk, or who have been blind and suddenly are able to see again, are possible because the dysfunction was hysterical rather than organic.

DISSOCIATIVE REACTION In a **dissociative reaction**, the dysfunction affects psychological rather than physical functioning. As the name implies, it designates the dissociation or splitting off of certain behaviors from the individual's normal condition. The following occur most frequently:

Amnesia is the partial or total forgetting of past experiences, such as an automobile accident or a battle. Hysterical amnesia can be differentiated from organic amnesia by its rather sudden appearance and disappearance, by its selective nature, and by the fact that the forgotten material can be recovered under hypnosis. As in conversion hysteria, the individuals often display little concern about their limited memory, preferring it to the anxiety associated with the traumatic event that they have successfully repressed.

Somnambulism, or "sleepwalking," is a dissociative disorder in which one part of the personality controls behavior while the ordinary personality becomes inactive, or "sleeps." Such daze-like states can occur during the day as well as at night, with the eyes open or closed.

The dissociative disorder called **fugue** ("flight") is related to both amnesia and somnambulism. Individuals in a fugue state flee from the home as well as the self. They may be absent for days or months or years and may take up a totally new life, later recalling nothing of what happened while they were in the fugue state.

A more extreme form of dissociation is **multiple personality**, a division into two or more complete behavior organizations, each as well-defined and highly distinct from the others as the two personalities of the main character in Robert Louis Stevenson's story *The Strange Case of Dr. Jekyll and Mr Hyde*. Two recent cases of multiple personality have been widely publicized in the films *The Three Faces of Eve* and *Sybil*. In the case of **alternating personality**, a form of multiple personality, two identities alternate with each other, neither one being aware of the actions or existence of the other. A second type of multiple personality involves one or more dominant personalities and one or more subordinate ones.

NEUROTIC DEPRESSION All of us have had periods when we felt sad or disappointed, and perhaps suffered from feelings of guilt, loss of appetite, and lack of sexual interest. Usually we experience these feelings in response to a negative situation in our lives—the loss of a job, an argument with a friend, a poor mark on an exam. Sometimes we even seem to be upset for no apparent reason; it just seems as if we "got up on the wrong side of the bed." These symptoms of "normal" depression do not differ in kind from clinical or abnormal depression, but they do differ drastically in degree (see Figure 22.3). **Neurotic depression** is a prolonged state of sadness or dejection that interferes with normal functioning. Bodily movements are slow and lethargic. Even intellectual functions seem to proceed

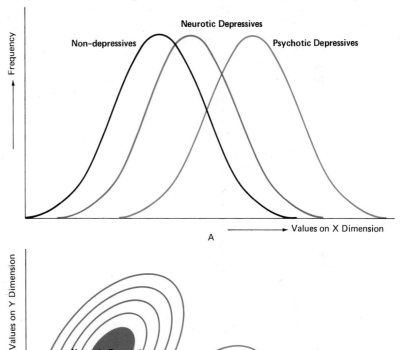

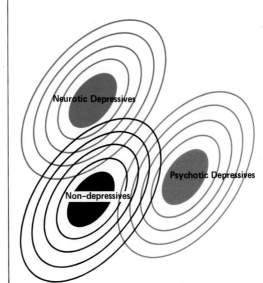

Figure 22.3 (A) This graph indicates how, according to one theory, non-depressed people, neurotic depressives, and psychotic depressives differ only *quantitatively* from one another. (B) This diagram illustrates an alternative theory which states that both neurotic and psychotic depressives differ *qualitatively* from non-depressed people. (After Gray, 1971.)

in slow motion, and the person cannot cope with the routine duties of going to work, shopping for groceries, completing homework assignments, preparing dinner. Even getting out of bed seems an impossible task. Neurotic depression is often a result of intense anxiety that causes an individual to withdraw from the normal pace of life until he or she feels stronger.

The characteristics of neurotic depression are well illustrated by the following patient's description:

> I began not to be able to manage as far as doing the kinds of things that I really had always been able to do easily, such as cook, wash, take care of the children, play games, that kind of thing. One of the most . . . I think one of the most frightening aspects at the beginning was that time went so slowly. It would seem sometimes that at least an hour had gone by and I would look at my

watch and it would only have been three minutes. And I began not to be able to concentrate. Another thing that was very frightening to me was that I couldn't read any more. And if awakened early . . . earlier than I needed to, I sometimes would lie in bed two hours trying to make myself get up because I just couldn't put my feet on the floor. Then when I did, I just felt that I couldn't get dressed. And then, whatever the next step was, I felt I couldn't do that.*

PSYCHOSIS

Whatever the defenses against neurotic behavior, and whatever the limitations it causes—the fears, embarrassments, and changes of mood—neurotic individuals are *aware* that their functioning is impaired; they have a degree of self-knowledge and continue to slug it out with life. However, if individuals' delusions, fears, and distortions of reality become so debilitating as to cause them almost completely to retreat from reality, this behavior is called psychotic. **Psychosis**, then, is a severe mental disorder that is characterized by a generalized failure of functioning in all areas of a person's life.

According to DSM-II, there are two major categories of psychoses: those associated with organic brain disorders (discussed later in this chapter), and those not attributable to physical conditions. The latter category is further divided into three groups:

1. The schizophrenias, characterized by disorders of *thought*;

2. The major affective disorders, characterized by disturbances of *mood*;

3. The paranoid states, characterized by a system of *delusions*.

SCHIZOPHRENIA **Schizophrenia** is a condition characterized by thought disorders that may be accompanied by delusions, hallucinations, attention deficits, and bizarre motor activity. Emil Kraepelin

---

*From "Depression: The Shadowed Valley," from the series *The Thin Edge,* ©1975 by the Educational Broadcasting Corporation.

Patients in a psychiatric hospital.

(1902), who gave us our first classification system for mental disorder, used the Latin term *dementia praecox*, meaning "premature mental deterioration," to refer to this type of behavior. It was his belief that this behavior was due to a disease of mental deterioration that began in adolescence. Ten years later, however, the Swiss psychiatrist Eugen Bleuler pointed out that, in fact, many patients displaying these symptoms do not continue to deteriorate and that the illness itself often starts not in adolescence, but much later. He felt that Kraepelin's term only made diagnosis more confusing and substituted the term "schizophrenia," from the Greek words *schizein*, meaning "to split," and *phren*, meaning "mind." Bleuler referred not to the "splitting" of personality into multiple or alternating parts but to a "psychic split," the dissociation of various psychic functions within a single personality. Emotions may be split from perception and be inappropriate to the situation; words may be split from their usual meanings; motor activity may be dissociated from reason. In short, to use Bleuler's words, "The personality loses its unity" (1911, p. 9). Schizophrenia is the most common cause of hospitalization for mental illness in our society.

SYMPTOMS OF SCHIZOPHRENIA Although DSM-II names the thought disorders as the predominant symptom, the schizophrenic person generally displays a variety of other abnormalities, such as disorders of perception, emotion, and motor behavior. All schizophrenics display some of these symptoms some of the time, but no schizophrenic displays all the symptoms all the time. Clinicians have tried to classify schizophrenia according to predominant symptoms. Table 22-1 lists four classifications.

Table 22.1   Four Types of Schizophrenia

Simple Schizophrenia	Characterized by dullness of thought, inability to concentrate, withdrawal from social interaction, and apathy. Absence of more bizarre schizophrenic symptoms.
Hebephrenic Schizophrenia	Most severe disintegration of personality. Hebephrenic schizophrenics live in private worlds dominated by hallucination, delusion, and fantasy. Behavior is almost completely unpredictable, and speech may be unintelligible.
Catatonic Schizophrenia	Characterized either by excessive, sometimes violent, motor activity or by a mute, unmoving, stuporous state. Some catatonic schizophrenics alternate between these two extremes, but often one or the other behavior pattern predominates.
Paranoid Schizophrenia	Characterized by delusions of persecution, grandeur, or both. Paranoid schizophrenics trust no one and are constantly watchful, convinced that others are plotting against them. May seek to retaliate against supposed tormentors.

Figure 22.4 This illustration was painted by a male patient diagnosed as schizophrenic. Schizophrenic art frequently uses intense colors to express the feelings, attitudes, and concerns of the patient. This particular illustration contains biblical allusions and a number of references to sexual organs and sexual functioning, all common themes in psychosis.

Disorders of Thought. Most schizophrenics demonstrate a split or lack of association among various ideas or between ideas and emotions. Normal people mentally link concepts and symbols and establish logical connections with a main idea that they wish to express. They might think, for example, that they are hungry and would like to eat a steak. The concept of hunger is joined to the concept of steak, and a relationship is set up between the two: namely, steak satisfies hunger. The incoherence or dissociation in the thought processes of the schizophrenic, however, interrupts such relationships. Concepts, ideas, symbols are thrown together merely because, for example, they rhyme. Such a series of rhyming or similar-sounding words is called a **clang association**. The following is a transcript of a conversation between a doctor and a schizophrenic patient who could be considered an expert at clang associations. (About half of all his daily speech was rhymed.)

DOCTOR: How are things going today, Ernest?
PATIENT: Okay for a flump.
DR.: What is a flump?
PT.: A flump is a gump.
DR.: That doesn't make any sense.
PT.: Well, when you go to the next planet from the planet beyond the planet that landed on the danded and planded on the slanded.
DR.: Wait a minute. I didn't follow any of that.
PT.: Well, when we was first bit on the slip on the rit and the man on the ran or the pan on the ban and the sand on the man and the pan on the ban on the can on the man on the fan on the pan.

[All spoken very rhythmically, beginning slowly and

Figure 22.5 These paintings were done by a male schizophrenic with paranoid tendencies. Both illustrations are characterized by the consistent symbolism of watchful eyes, grasping hands, and the self as subject matter. In the first painting, which reflects a subdued emotional state, there is a strong emphasis on the eyes, with a figure watching over the shoulder. The torso of the central figure is surrounded by hands, and the figure in the background is reaching out. The second painting, elaborate in composition and vivid in color, reflects a more active emotional state. Again there is an emphasis on the eyes and on the hands, represented by tentacles and claws.

building up to such a rapid pace that the words could no longer be understood.]

DR.: What's all that hitting your head for . . . and waving your arms?

PT.: That's to keep the boogers from eatin' the woogers. Well, it was a jigger and a figger and a figger and a bigger and me and I'll swap you for a got you and a fair-haired far for a bar and a jar for a tar and a rang dang, ting tang with a bee shag, he shag.

In addition to interruptions in the logical connections of words, schizophrenic thought is often characterized by a tendency to dwell on the primary association to a given stimulus (called **perseveration**) and to generate each sentence from some mental stimulus in the preceding sentence, thus wandering further and further from the central idea (called **overinclusion**). The latter tendency to lose track of the subject at hand and pursue other lines of thought is well illustrated by the following letter, written by one of Bleuler's patients:

Dear Mother,
I am writing on paper. The pen which I am using is from a factory called "Perry & Co." This factory is in England. I assume this. Behind the name of Perry Co. the city of London is inscribed; but not the city. The city of London is in England. I know this from my school days. Then, I always liked geography. My last teacher in that subject was Professor August A. He was a man with black eyes. I also like black eyes. There are also blue and gray eyes and other sorts, too. I have heard it said that snakes have green eyes. All people have eyes. There are some, too, who are blind. These blind people are led about by a boy. It must be very terrible not to be able to see. There are people who can't see and, in addition can't hear. I know some who hear too much. One can hear too much. (Bleuler, 1911, p. 17.)

The split or dissociation of concepts produces one of the most common thought disorders among schizophrenics—delusions. A **delusion** is an irrational belief held despite overwhelming evidence that the belief has no basis in reality. Delusions take several forms. Some are delusions of grandeur, in which an individual believes that he or she is some famous person like Napoleon or Jesus Christ. Some are delusions of persecution, in which the individual believes that others, often extraterrestrial beings or secret agents, are plotting against him or her, controlling his or her thoughts and actions. Some are delusions of sin and guilt, in which the individual

believes that he or she has committed some terrible deed or brought evil into the world.

Disorders of Perception. One of the major distinguishing characteristics of schizophrenics is their distorted view of reality. Although this is accounted for in part by disturbed thought processes such as those we described, it is directly related to the fact that schizophrenics seem to perceive the external world in a different manner from ordinary people. They consistently report distortions in sensory perception—visual, auditory, olfactory, and tactile hallucinations. **Hallucinations** are spontaneous sensory perceptions unrelated to external stimuli. To the observer, they are the most dramatic perceptual disturbance of the schizophrenic. These hallucinations differ from the imagery of normal people in two ways. First, they are spontaneous and apparently uncontrollable, and second, they are perceived by the schizophrenic as real events. Figure 22.6 shows the pattern of tactile hallucinations experienced by a woman during a schizophrenic episode. Here is a description of the experience:

Figure 22.6 A schizophrenic woman's drawing of her own tactile hallucinations, showing the areas of sensation and their associated strengths. (After Pfeifer, 1970.)

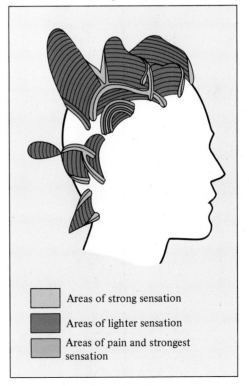

☐ Areas of strong sensation

■ Areas of lighter sensation

▨ Areas of pain and strongest sensation

These hallucinations consist of the subjectively real feeling that patches of flesh are painfully stretching in an elastic manner past the boundaries of the head—sometimes as far as twelve inches past the boundary of the head. These hallucinations contract into the head as well as expand past the head, though they do extend briefly to other parts of the body. They are chronic and constantly active but they are variable in their intensity and in the scope and speed of their activity. Sometimes the "stretch" to these hallucinations becomes so taut that it results in a sharp cutting pain. There is also a quality of numbness to these hallucinations. It suffices to say that the essential nature of these hallucinations is utterly frustrating and incapacitating, and thus vastly frightening, as is manifested in the devastating effect they have on the personality, thinking and behavior of the patient. (Pfeifer, 1970)

In addition to hallucinations, other disturbances of perception in schizophrenia include the inability to focus attention, difficulty in identifying people and understanding their speech, and exaggerated sensitivity to certain stimuli (such as odors). Standard laboratory perceptual tests confirm these reports, proving that schizophrenics do poorly on estimating size (Strauss, Foureman, and Parwatikar,

1974), time, and the positioning of their own hands and feet. The elements of perception are all there, but they seem somehow to have "gone off the track" or become "short-circuited," so the usual external stimulus does not produce the corresponding perceptual observation.

Disorders of Affect. Like other aspects of functioning, the emotional response, or **affect**, of schizophrenics is disturbed. Schizophrenic emotional responses are entirely inappropriate or completely absent. The schizophrenic might laugh when told of the death of a favorite relative, get angry when given a present, or show no emotion at all on either occasion. Again, the external situation or stimulus does not trigger the appropriate response.

Disorders of Motor Behavior. The schizophrenic may display physical behavior that is bizarre in itself, like head banging, or, more often, that is simply inappropriate to the situation and repetitive beyond the norm. One patient might spend hours rubbing his forehead; another spend hours slapping her leg; still another might sit all day on a couch tracing the pattern of the fabric. In some cases, there is no physical activity at all; the patient is said to be in a catatonic stupor, remaining in one position for hours at a time, responding to neither persons nor things.

The perceptual abilities of schizophrenics seem impaired when compared to those of other individuals. For example, schizophrenics may have difficulty in identifying people.

MAJOR AFFECTIVE DISORDERS Whereas schizophrenic disorders are characterized primarily by disturbances in thought, **affective disorders** are characterized by disturbances of mood. We are all subject to mood changes. Usually our emotional response, or **affect**, is influenced by a change in the environment. We receive a promotion on the job; a difficult love affair is resolved. Or, conversely, a close relative dies; we receive a letter of rejection from graduate school. Occasionally we even feel unhappy or very pleased with ourselves for no apparent reason. All these variations in mood are completely normal. But, depending on their intensity and duration, they may become abnormal. When they are so exaggerated as to interrupt our normal functioning and to cause psychic discomfort, but not to cause us to lose touch with reality, they are labeled "neurotic." Fluctuation of mood is labeled as "psychotic" when emotional responses are exaggerated and inappropriate, include an element of delusion or hallucination, and so severely interfere with functioning as to result in loss of touch with reality. We will discuss here two major affective disorders: psychotic depression and manic-depressive disorder. It should be noted that psychotic depression does not appear in DSM-II as a separate category under the heading of "Major Affective Disorders." However, since a number of the affective disorders are characterized by similar symptoms of depression, depression is discussed here as a separate category of disorder.

PSYCHOTIC DEPRESSION While some theorists believe that the difference between neurotic depression and **psychotic depression** is primarily one of degree, others believe that the two are different in kind, claiming that neurotic depression is linked to an external event, whereas psychotic depression originates within the individual. Moreover, some theorists view depression as an exaggeration of normal sadness, while others believe it is a distinct neurological disease. Regardless of the origin or type of the depression, there are generally certain common symptoms that characterize it. Almost all depressed patients report feelings of sadness and unhappiness (Beck, 1967), frequently connected with the loss of gratification from activities they had previously enjoyed. The depressed person often shows disinterest in sex, social activities, hobbies, and favorite pastimes. Motivational changes are also apparent. The depressed person usually loses initiative, becomes apathetic, and is unable to carry out ordinary duties. Physical changes and alteration in motor activity are evident. There is a loss of appetite, difficulty in sleeping, excessive fatigue, and little spontaneous activity. Cognitive changes include viewing the self as inadequate and deficient in appearance, intelligence, and skill (see Figure 22.7). Psychotic depressives suffer, in addition, from delusions of physical decay, expectation of severe punishment, and even identification with the devil.

Figure 22.7
Psychotic depression carries with it a serious danger of suicide. This woodcut by Käthe Kollwitz expresses the feelings of hopelessness, meaninglessness, and ugliness that a person may experience in severe depression. (Courtesy of the National Gallery of Art: Washington, D.C., Rosenwald Collection.)

MANIC-DEPRESSIVE DISORDER **Manic-depressive disorder** is characterized by the episodic nature of extremes of mood. The periods of disturbed affect are usually fairly short, and even when untreated they seldom last for more than a year. Whereas some manic-depressive people experience only extreme depression and a few only extreme elation, many of them undergo a cycle of manic-depressive behavior in which the two extremes are manifested at alternating intervals—a period of sad, withdrawn behavior, followed by a period of intense activity and excitement, and so on.

The depressive phase of manic-depressive psychosis is characterized by intense sadness and hopelessness, distorted perceptions, and disrupted transactions of everyday living. The manic phase is characterized by feverish activity and a sense of the self as brilliant and superior, the opposite extreme of the depressive's bleak and sad outlook. All of us have tried to compensate for certain stress situations by increased activity, perhaps by going on a shopping spree to cheer ourselves up or by planning a party or trip to take our mind off our problems. But, as with psychotic depression, psychotic mania is drastically different in degree from what most of us have experienced. It is extreme, prolonged, and uncontrollable. Manic individuals believe that they can do almost anything—make a million dollars overnight, run for President, become a jet pilot or a movie star. They may go on spending sprees or devise elaborate schemes for changing the economy. In short, the manic person's sense of reality becomes impaired. These two modes of behavior, depression and mania, are both responses to anxiety: the first provides relief from anxiety through retreat from the world, the second through increased, uninterrupted activity.

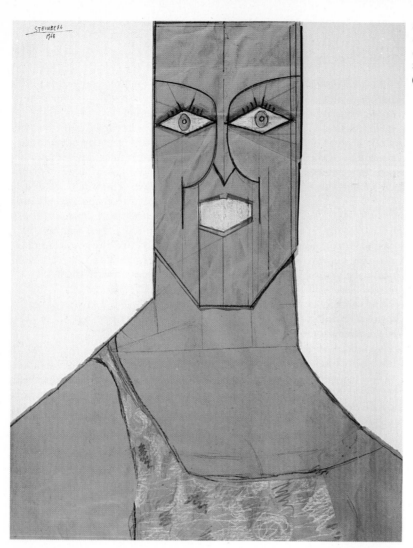

Some idea of the feverish excitement of the manic state is conveyed in this piece by Saul Steinberg, entitled *Hostess Mask* (1968).

PARANOID STATES A third class of psychoses listed in DSM-II is the **paranoid states**. These are states in which grandiose or persecutory delusions are the only—or the essential—abnormality experienced by the individual. If other abnormalities are present, they stem from the delusional system. Outside that system, the paranoid individual appears to have normal contact with reality. A person might function well on the job, have a good marital relationship, and yet believe that an upstairs neighbor is secretly trying to poison him or her. Many people who live in the community might be designated as this type of paranoid—extremely jealous spouses, self-styled prophets, investigators of "extraterrestrial conspiracies." Paranoids such as these differ from paranoid schizophrenics. For the paranoid schizophrenic the delusional system is the most prominent aspect of the disorder, but there are also disturbances of affect, thought, language, and mo-

tor behavior, unrelated to the delusional system. A person is said to be in a paranoid state if there are no disorders of affect, or thought, language, and motor behavior that appear to be independent of the delusion.

PERSONALITY DISORDERS AND OTHER NONPSYCHOTIC MENTAL DISORDERS

In addition to the neuroses and the psychoses, DSM-II lists personality and certain other nonpsychotic disorders as a major category of mental disorder. **Personality disorders** involve deviant behavior patterns that do not result in a loss of contact with reality. They differ from neuroses, however, in that the symptoms are completely integrated into the individual's life and usually do not cause the acute guilt and anxiety experienced by the neurotic. Whereas the neurotic individual generally identifies neurotic behavior for what it is—deviant, self-defeating behavior that is alien to the core personality—the personality-disordered individual often does not recognize the disorder as such because the problem behaviors are part of the core personality itself, so deeply ingrained as to be "second nature" and accepted as familiar character traits. Often adopted at an early age to cope with specific stress in the environment, the pattern of deviant behavior is difficult to change. Frequently these individuals have little motivation to change their behavior, since it generally causes more discomfort to others than to them. DSM-II outlines ten different types of personality disorders. We will be concerned here with only one—the antisocial personality. We will also examine the nonpsychotic disorders of sexual deviance, alcoholism, and drug dependence.

THE ANTISOCIAL PERSONALITY The **antisocial personality**, or **sociopath**, is one who misbehaves socially without guilt about his or her behavior. Such people appear to be blind to moral considerations, to have no conscience, and to be untouched by a whole range of emotions shared by the "normal" population, even though their intellectual faculties are intact and their abilities to reason and to perform tasks are unimpaired.

The most striking characteristics of this disorder are the lack of guilt over misdeeds and the absence of emotion in social relationships. No guilt is manifested over the most callous murder; no sadness is shown at the death of a parent or friend. E. B. McNeil (1967) reported the remarks of Dan F., for example, who felt nothing at all when his best friend died of leukemia. Thinking it over that night in bed, Dan decided that he wouldn't miss his mother and father if they died and "wasn't too nuts about my brothers and sisters for that matter" either. The sociopath's impulses may, of course, sometimes be positive ones: he or she may buy presents for a friend or give money to charity; but the motivation for these acts has as little feeling behind it as his or her casual shoplifting or embezzling. Although usually intelligent, cunning, and clever, the sociopath seems to have little insight into the disorder and even less capacity to learn from experience. Despite prison terms, social sanctions, expulsions from school, and loss of jobs, sociopaths repeat the very behavior patterns that have brought punishment down upon them.

SEXUAL DEVIANCE In 1968, when DSM-II was published, it defined as sexually deviant any "individuals whose sexual interests are directed primarily

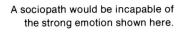
A sociopath would be incapable of the strong emotion shown here.

toward objects other than people of the opposite sex, toward sexual acts not usually associated with coitus [sexual intercourse], or toward coitus performed under bizarre circumstances" (p. 44). In 1977, the draft version of DSM-III was made available for members of the American Psychiatric Association to consider. In this proposed revision, just nine years after DSM-II, the only sexual behaviors classified as disorders are "those deviations from standard sexual behavior which either present gross impairments in the capacity for affectionate sexual activity between adult human partners or where there is acknowledged subjective distress regarding the source of sexual arousal" (1977, p. L:9).

This proposed revision shows that the APA has recognized that social attitudes vary, and so do sexual practices. Nevertheless, there are still some sexual behaviors that psychologists and psychiatrists consider "abnormal" in our society and in others. The most common are:

Fetishism: sexual gratification that is dependent on an inanimate object or some part of the body other than the genitals.

Transvestism: sexual gratification obtained through dressing in clothing of the opposite sex.

Transsexualism: gender identification with the opposite sex.

Exhibitionism: sexual gratification obtained through exhibiting the genitals to an involuntary observer.

Voyeurism: sexual gratification obtained through secret observations of another person's sexual activities or genitals.

Pedophilia: sexual gratification obtained through sexual contacts with children.

Incest: sexual relations among members of the immediate family.

Rape: sexual relations achieved with another person through the use or threat of force.

Sadism: sexual gratification obtained through inflicting pain on another person.

Masochism: sexual gratification obtained through having pain inflicted on oneself.

Sexually "normal" individuals may exhibit these behaviors in mild form—becoming sexually aroused by the sight of lacy underwear, exposing one's breasts by wearing low-cut dresses, swimming in the nude, and so on. Such behaviors are considered serious disorders only when they are the sole means of achieving sexual gratification.

Injecting heroin.

DRUG DEPENDENCE Dependence on drugs is classified in DSM-II as a type of nonpsychotic disorder. There are many different kinds of drugs, with different physical effects on the body. Researchers believe that an individual's choice of drugs depends more on his or her social and economic situation than on his or her personality. Here we will focus on heroin, since it is typical of most drug-abuse syndromes and because the growing abuse of heroin and other narcotic drugs constitutes one of the most serious social problems facing this country.

Narcotics are drugs such as opium and morphine that induce numbness, sedation, and sleep. There is nothing intrinsically evil about narcotics or their effects. Morphine, for example, is an old and widely used drug for the medical treatment of pain. It is only when a narcotic is abused that it becomes a danger to individuals and society. Heroin, a derivative of morphine that is twice as potent, was introduced into this country as a treatment for morphine addiction. Ultimately, it brought about an even greater addiction problem itself. Heroin produces a euphoric effect, a sense of well-being that makes problems seem to disappear. Often addicts become sleepy ("nod" or "nod out") and have no desire to do anything other than stay high. Heavy users often feel exceptionally hot or itchy. Occasionally there may be nausea or vomiting. Because addicts develop a tolerance to heroin, they must keep increasing the dose in order to achieve the same high that a smaller dose once produced. Some addicts can use as much as 2,000 to 3,000 milligrams daily, whereas the average dose of morphine given medically for severe pain ranges from 8 to 15 milligrams.

The side effects of narcotics addiction can be severe. Because packets of heroin sold on the street vary widely in purity and concentration, many addicts die of an overdose after having injected what they believed was their accustomed dosage. Moreover, because heroin is usually administered intravenously without sterile precautions, the addict risks hepatitis (a liver disease), bacterial infections, skin infections, tetanus, and endocarditis (an infection of the heart valves). Heroin abuse is most common in urban areas, especially among the young and ghetto populations.

ALCOHOLISM Alcoholism is our country's most serious drug problem, and alcoholism is a major subcategory of nonpsychotic mental disorders. According to a recent estimate, 5.75 million Americans are alcoholics and another 5.75 million are "problem drinkers"—a total of more than 10 percent of the population (Keller and Gurioli, 1976).

Many people think of alcohol as a stimulant because drinking is often followed by loud, boisterous behavior. But alcohol is really a depressant. In small amounts its effect is to suppress the functioning of the parts of the brain that control and inhibit thoughts, feelings, and actions—hence the boisterous behavior of drinkers at a cocktail party. In large quantities it is a general anesthetic, causes disorders of sensation and perception, can lead to dangerous, self-destructive behavior, and is capable of producing coma and death.

As with narcotics addiction, alcoholics build up a tolerance for alcohol; they increase their intake of alcohol in order to experience the original feeling of well-being. Often drinkers develop such a psychological dependence on alcohol that they feel nor-

mal only when they have been drinking and experience severe, painful symptoms if they stop. Because of the toxic effects of alcohol on the body, and the malnutrition that so often accompanies chronic alcoholism, alcoholics are likely to develop many diseases affecting the liver, brain, and nervous system. Prolonged alcoholism leads to degenerative brain disease.

ORGANIC DISORDERS

As we will see in the next chapter, many explanations of psychological disorders have been set forth. From Kraepelin on, many theorists have believed that mental disorders such as schizophrenia or depression are due to organic dysfunction of the brain. Much evidence supports this idea. But most social scientists feel that such mental disorders are due to psychological factors, emotional disturbances, and environmental stress. About certain disorders, however, there is little argument; they are directly traceable to the destruction of brain tissue or to biochemical imbalance in the brain. These are known as **organic brain syndromes** and are classified as a separate category in DSM-II. Included in the list are: presenile and senile dementia; alcoholic psychoses such as delirium tremens; intracranial infections such as encephalitis and tertiary syphilis; other cerebral conditions such as epilepsy, cerebral arteriosclerosis, and brain trauma; endocrine disorders; metabolic and nutritional disorders; systemic infections; and drug or poison intoxication.

This X-ray photograph of a boxer's head at the moment he receives a blow shows that the force of the punch causes the brain to be momentarily displaced against the back of the skull. If severe or numerous enough, such displacements can cause tissue damage that will produce an organic psychosis.

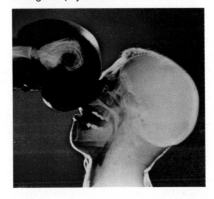

Because physical and mental health are so closely related, it is often difficult to determine when behavioral disturbance is due to organic dysfunction and when it is the result of emotional factors. DSM-II lists five major symptoms that accompany most organic brain disorders: impairment of orientation (who and where one is); impairment of memory; impairment of other intellectual functions, such as comprehension, calculation, knowledge, and learning; impairment of judgment; inappropriate affect. Many of these symptoms, however, are also present in schizophrenic patients, hysterical patients, and even depressed patients. Thus an accurate diagnosis of organic brain syndrome can be difficult.

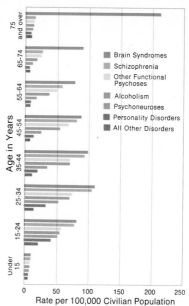

Figure 22.8 Age trends for various psychological disorders in the United States. These data reflect the number of individuals admitted for the first time to state and county mental hospitals in 1965. (From Kramer, 1969.)

EPIDEMIOLOGY OF MENTAL DISORDER

Epidemiology is the study of the range of occurrence, distribution, and control of illness in a population. For mental disorder it is difficult to estimate the range of occurrence, since the number of people admitted to hospitals for mental disorder is much smaller than the number of people who actually experience it. On the basis of admission and residence rates for clinics and state and county hospitals, it is estimated that from 6 to 10 percent of the population of the United States will be treated for mental disorder at some point in their lives and that a sizable proportion of the remaining population will suffer symptoms of disorder but will go untreated.

DEMOGRAPHIC VARIABILITY The incidence of mental disorder may vary with such factors as sex, age, marital status, and social class.

Sex: Although there is considerable variability among samples, most researchers have found that there is a higher incidence of organic brain syndromes in males, but a higher incidence of psychosis and neurosis in females. Males evidence more alcoholism, drug dependence, and sexual deviation than females, but studies have consistently found females to be more generally unhappy with their lives.

Age: Figure 22.8 shows trends in age for various mental disorders. The incidence of neurosis and personality disorders reaches a peak in adolescence. Schizophrenia and other psychoses and alcoholism reach a peak in middle age, and organic brain syndromes in old age.

Marital Status: The highest rate of reported mental disorder is found among separated and divorced persons; the next highest among single persons; the next highest among widows and widowers; and the lowest among married men and women.

Social Class: Social class is a broad category that encompasses such demographic variables as ethnic group, occupation, marital status, and religion. A clear relationship between social class and reported mental disorder has been found. Of twenty-four studies reviewed by Lawrence Kolb, Viola Bernard, and Bruce Dohrenwend in 1969, nineteen revealed that the lower the social stratum, the higher the incidence of serious mental disorder.

CROSS-CULTURAL VARIABILITY Comparison of mental disorder and its symptoms across cultures is of great interest to psychologists because it can help differentiate between variable environmental factors and unchanging core elements of mental disorder. Disorders similar to schizophrenia, manic-depressive psychosis, and neurosis are found in other cultures. In fact, some form of most disorders is found in most cultures, but there appear to be important variations in symptoms. For example, H. B. M. Murphy and his colleagues (1961) found that social and emotional withdrawal, auditory hallucinations, general delusions, and inability to react were characteristic of schizophrenia in many cultures, but the style of the symptoms varied from one culture to another. Christians and Moslems most frequently showed religious delusions and delusions of destructiveness, but Asians most frequently exhibited delusional jealousy. It is clear that cultures may supply the material for delusions. However, the extent to which differences in symptoms can be traced to differences in cultures is never easy to measure.

BEING SANE IN INSANE PLACES

Often there is considerable overlap between the behavior of "sane" and "insane" individuals. As D. L. Rosenhan points out in his famous study, "On Being Sane in Insane Places" (1973), even normal people lose their tempers for no good reason, become anxious or depressed for short periods of time, or find it difficult to get along with certain people. Similarly, "insane" people have long periods of lucidity, when they behave and interact with others as normally as anyone else. Rosenhan argued that diagnostic methods of determining who is sane and who is not are completely inadequate. In his study, eight students and professional people with no history of mental disorder presented themselves to mental hospitals in five different states and reported a single symptom—that they were hearing voices. They were all promptly admitted.

Rosenhan's study reminds us of how difficult it is at present to diagnose mental disorder; he wonders, "How many people . . . are sane but not recognized as such in our psychiatric institutions? How many have been needlessly stripped of their privileges of citizenship . . . ?" and, conversely, "How many have feigned insanity in order to avoid the criminal consequences of their behavior . . . ?"

Robert L. Spitzer, a psychiatrist who participated in the development of both DSM-II and DSM-III, has sharply criticized Rosenhan's study as not supporting the stated conclusions. Spitzer (1975) argues that the only firm conclusion that can be drawn from Rosenhan's study is that psychiatrists were unable to detect that the pseudopatients were simulating symptoms of disorder, a finding that he says is "rather unremarkable." While the merits of the Rosenhan study may well be debatable, one thing is certainly clear: Mental disorder does not lend itself to the neat explanations and classifications that have been so useful in diagnosing physical complaints. The complexity of human behavior continues to confound and confuse even those who study it most closely.

SUMMARY

1. There are several definitions of normality in use within the field of psychology.
    A. According to the statistical criterion, abnormality is any substantial deviation from a statistically calculated average.
    B. Absolute criteria assume the existence of a certain absolute or universal standard of mental health. Theorists disagree about what this absolute standard is.
    C. The medical model, or clinical criterion, views psychological problems as diseases with specific symptoms, causes, treatments, and prognoses. The American Psychiatric Association has developed a medically based classification system called the *Diagnostic and Statistical Manual of Mental Disorders* (DSM-II) to facilitate diagnosis and standardize treatment.
2. **Neurosis** is a mental disorder chiefly characterized by chronic anxiety that leads to irrational, limiting, and disruptive behavior patterns.
    A. **Anxiety neurosis** is characterized by diffuse and generalized fears that are impossible to manage through avoidance. The person is jumpy, irritable, and frequently upset, but cannot specify what is generating his or her fears—a condition that Freud termed **free-floating anxiety**. Anxiety neurotics may have **anxiety attacks**, in which the state of tension mounts to an acute and overwhelming level. The most extreme form of an anxiety attack is a **panic reaction**, when anxiety is so severe and prolonged that the person becomes disorganized and disoriented.
    B. Neurotic anxiety that is irrationally focused on a particular object or situation is called a **phobia**. Phobias have two distinct effects:
        1. The anxiety associated with the phobia and the avoidance of situations in which the feared object will be present.

2. The anxiety, guilt, and shame associated with the problem of hiding the phobia from others.

C. An **obsession** is a recurring irrational thought. A **compulsion** is the desire to engage repeatedly in a particular irrational act. Much neurotic behavior is both obsessive and compulsive.

D. **Hysterical neurosis** is a condition in which some normal function, either physical (conversion type) or psychological (dissociative type), is lost or impaired for no organic reason and is accompanied by denial of anxiety over the loss.

1. In a **conversion reaction** the individual develops some physical dysfunction, such as blindness or paralysis, that has no organic basis and violates neurophysiological laws.

2. In a **dissociative reaction** the dysfunction affects psychological rather than physical functioning; certain behaviors split off from the individual's normal condition.

E. **Neurotic depression** is a prolonged state of sadness or dejection that interferes with normal functioning. It differs in degree from "normal" depression. Neurotic depression is often a result of intense anxiety that causes an individual to withdraw from the normal pace of life until he or she feels stronger.

3. **Psychosis** is a severe mental disorder that is characterized by a generalized failure of functioning in all areas of a person's life. The two major categories of psychosis are those associated with organic brain disorders and those not attributable to physical conditions. The latter category is further divided into three groups: schizophrenia, major affective disorders, and paranoid states.

A. The term **schizophrenia** refers to the dissociation of various psychic functions within a single personality.

1. Disorders of thought are the predominant symptom of schizophrenia, but the schizophrenic person generally displays such other abnormalities as disorders of perception, emotion, and motor behavior.

a. Most schizophrenics do demonstrate thought disorders, marked by a lack of association among various ideas or between ideas and emotions. A **clang association**, for instance, is a series of rhyming or similar-sounding words.

Perseveration is a tendency to dwell on the primary association to a given stimulus. **Overinclusion** is a tendency to generate each sentence from some mental stimulus in the preceding sentence, thus wandering further and further from the central idea. Finally, one of the most common thought disorders among schizophrenics is **delusion**, an irrational belief held despite overwhelming evidence that the belief has no basis in reality.

b. Schizophrenics consistently manifest disorders of perception, especially **hallucinations**, spontaneous sensory perceptions that are unrelated to external stimuli.

c. Schizophrenics display disorders of **affect**, or emotional response. Their emotional reactions are entirely inappropriate or completely absent.

d. Disorders of motor behavior may be manifested in physical activity that is inappropriate to the situation, repetitive beyond the norm, or sometimes bizarre in itself.

B. **Affective disorders** are characterized by disturbances of mood. When variations in mood become so exaggerated as to interrupt normal functioning and cause psychic discomfort, but do not cause the individual to lose touch with reality, they are labelled neurotic. When emotional responses are exaggerated and inappropriate, include an element of delusion or hallucination, and result in a loss of touch with reality, they are considered psychotic. Two major affective disorders are psychotic depression and manic-depressive disorder.

1. Patients suffering from **psychotic depression** usually report feelings of sadness, general disinterest, and loss of motivation. Physical changes and alterations in motor activity may occur, coupled with a view of the self as inadequate.

2. **Manic-depressive disorder** involves episodic extremes of mood. The individual may experience only extreme depression, only extreme elation, or both in alternation. Both phases are responses to anxiety.

C. In **paranoid states**, grandiose or persecutory delusions are the only—or the essential—abnormality experienced by the individual. Any other abnormalities stem from the delusional system. Outside that system, however, the person seems to maintain normal contact with reality.

4. **Personality disorders** involve deviant behavior patterns that do not result in a loss of contact with reality. The symptoms of personality disorders are completely integrated into the individual's life and do not cause the acute suffering and anxiety experienced by the neurotic.

   A. The **antisocial personality**, or **sociopath**, misbehaves socially without guilt about his or her behavior. The sociopath seems to be without conscience or emotion in relationships and seems to have little ability to learn from experience.

   B. Although ideas about what constitutes sexual deviance vary with time and place, certain sexual behaviors are considered abnormal both in our society and in others by psychologists and psychiatrists. The most common of these are **fetishism, transvestism, transsexualism, exhibitionism, voyeurism, pedophilia, incest, rape, sadism**, and **masochism**.

   C. Drug addiction is classified in DSM-II as a type of nonpsychotic disorder. Abuse of **narcotics** constitutes one of the most serious social problems facing this country.

D. Alcoholism is a major subcategory of nonpsychotic mental disorders. It is the country's most serious drug problem.

5. Certain psychological disorders, the **organic brain syndromes**, are directly traceable to the destruction of brain tissue or to biochemical imbalance in the brain. The most common form of organic brain disease is cerebral arteriosclerosis and other forms of senility.

6. **Epidemiology** is the study of the range of occurrence, distribution, and control of illness in a population. The epidemiology of mental disorder is difficult because the number of people admitted to mental hospitals is far less than the number of people who experience mental disorder.

   A. The incidence of mental disorder may vary with such factors as sex, age, marital status, and social class.

   B. Comparison of mental disorder across cultural lines helps to differentiate between variable environmental factors and unchanging core elements of mental disorder. Some disorders seem unique to particular cultures.

7. As D. L. Rosenhan's study On "Being Sane in Insane Places" indicated, the accurate diagnosis of specific mental disorders can be difficult, because there is considerable overlap between the behavior of sane and insane individuals.

RECOMMENDED READINGS

CALHOUN, JAMES F. *Abnormal Psychology: Current Perspectives*. 2nd ed. New York: CRM/Random House, 1977. A comprehensive textbook that describes the major categories of psychological disorder and presents a variety of theoretical perspectives.

KISKER, GEORGE W. *The Disorganized Personality*. New York: McGraw-Hill, 1964. Well written and well illustrated, this textbook contains a series of case histories to demonstrate types of disorder, and it presents an excellent discussion of the history of mental illness.

LANDIS, CARNEY. *Varieties of Psychopathological Experience*. Fred A. Mettler (ed.). New York: Holt, Rinehart and Winston, 1964. A collection of autobiographical reports that provide a glimpse into the experience of disorder. A valuable complement to theoretical discussions.

SZASZ, THOMAS S. *The Myth of Mental Illness: Foundations of a Theory of Personal Conduct*. New York: Dell, 1967. A highly original, stimulating discussion of mental illness. Szasz argues that what is called mental illness really involves "problems in living."

WHITE, ROBERT W. *The Abnormal Personality*. New York: Ronald, 1964. A comprehensive, easy-to-read presentation of theories and research on abnormal behavior. Written by one of the pillars of classic personality theory, the book is pervaded by the force of White's own personality. It contains an excellent presentation of psychoanalysis and learning theory.

ZILBOORG, GREGORY, and GEORGE W. HENRY. *A History of Medical Psychology*. New York: Norton, 1941. A fascinating discussion of the history of madness; a classic in the field.

CHAPTER TWENTY-THREE

THEORIES OF ABNORMALITY

Abnormality is where you find it—in other people. After all, everyone agrees when someone says, "No one's *entirely* normal." Which means, I think, that no one is "normal" at all. Normality is just an average of all the abnormalities.

Of course, when an abnormality is extreme, as in homicidal mania or suicidal depression, we all agree that we're dealing with something dangerous that requires society to protect the sufferer or itself or both. And it is difficult for "normal" people to understand, let alone sympathize with, an extreme abnormality.

But what about the myriad slight deviations from the norm which afflict everyone (or, rather, everyone but oneself)—the minor deviations that don't in the least threaten anyone with harm? Are those understood? Very rarely. Sympathized with? Hardly ever.

For instance, I don't take airplanes. I just don't. The thought of crashing or of being skyjacked fills me with dread. When people find out I don't fly, they invariably are amazed and demand to know my reason.

I tell them the truth. "I'm scared," I say.

That doesn't impress them, so lately I've been trying another tack. I say, "You know, there's such a thing as conservation of fear. If you are unafraid of something, then you're bound to balance that by being afraid of something else. Now, I am *unusually* unafraid of women, so——"

I never have to finish. That satisfies them.

Here's a second example. Writers, especially science fiction writers, are besieged by people who ask, "Where do you get your crazy ideas?" After all, creativity is an abnormality, too, and therefore is not understood by "normal" people who never come up with an original idea.

When I am asked this question, again I try to be honest. I say, "I just think very hard until I have one."

This is unacceptable. No one seems to want to believe that an idea will come as the result of anything as prosaic and unglamorous as hard thinking. Besides, if hard thinking will do it, there's an insulting implication for the questioners: Can it be that they get no ideas because they're lazy?

My fellow writer, Harlan Ellison, has a better answer. When someone asks him where he gets his crazy ideas, he says, "Schenectady! There's an idea factory there and I subscribe to their idea-a-month plan. I pay annual dues, and their machines manufacture an idea for me every month." The questioner walks away, mulling it over. I think many of them conclude that there *is* an idea factory in Schenectady.

Isaac Asimov

After almost a year of police investigation of a series of murders that terrified the population of New York City in 1977, a harmless-looking postal employee was arrested as the infamous "Son of Sam," the ".44-caliber killer." The man, who later confessed to the crimes, claimed that he had received orders to kill from "Sam," who turned out to be a dog belonging to a neighbor named Sam. The killer had scrawled incomprehensible notes all over the walls of his sparsely furnished apartment. He grinned at police and reporters when he was apprehended. At his trial, his meek demeanor sometimes gave way to outbursts of screaming and struggling with courtroom personnel. Such irrational behavior, delusional thinking, and inappropriate emotional responses are unmistakable signs of psychological abnormality.

What made "Son of Sam" behave like this? What causes any mental disorder? Psychiatrists are unable to agree. Today there are many theories about the causes of behavior that a society defines as abnormal; in this chapter we shall examine some of the major ones. First, however, we shall look at the ways in which deviant behavior was understood in earlier times.

SOME THEORIES FROM THE PAST*

DEMONOLOGY Historically, deviant behavior—that is, behavior strikingly different from that of most people—has been explained and defined according to the philosophical and religious outlook of a particular society. Thus, Stone Age people, who believed that all the movements of nature are governed by supernatural forces, thought that unusual behavior is caused by gods or demons. Their method of dealing with unfriendly spirits was to drill a hole in the skull of the person thought to be possessed. This treatment, called trephining, was thought to allow the evil spirit to escape.

Similar ideas of the body being possessed or invaded by a spirit endured for many centuries among the ancient Chinese, Egyptians, Hebrews, and Greeks. In some instances, such possession was considered a desirable state; in Greece, for example, the priestess at Delphi was revered for the prophecies she delivered from the god believed to be inhabiting her body.

It was the Greeks who eventually developed a new, nonreligious explanation of abnormal behavior, in accordance with their belief in reason. Hippocrates (c. 460–c. 360 B.C.), applying the scientific

method to the study of deviant behavior, observed it as a natural, rather than a supernatural, phenomenon. He developed the first organic (that is, physiological rather than psychological) theory of abnormal behavior. Believing the body to be composed of four liquids, or "humours"—blood, phlegm, choler, and melancholy—each with special characteristics, Hippocrates hypothesized that an overabundance or deficiency of a humour could lead to personality changes and behavioral disturbances.

The Middle Ages brought religious influence to the fore again. Once more deviant behavior was explained in terms of demonic forces. Until as recently as the nineteenth century in Europe and America, insanity was viewed as a punishment from God or as the result of possession by the Devil, who could be driven out only through the religious ceremony of exorcism. Deranged people were considered to be witches and were held responsible for every storm, pestilence, or miscarriage in their village. Those who were thought to be possessed against their wills were treated gently: they were prayed over, taken to shrines, fed potions. Those who were considered to be voluntarily in league with the Devil were strangled, beheaded, or burned to death. The number of people (about 85 percent of them women) executed as witches in Western Europe between the fourteenth and seventeenth centuries has been estimated to have been in the millions (Ehrenreich and English, 1973).

BIOGENIC THEORY A few lonely voices were raised in protest against demonology. One was that of the Swiss physician Paracelsus (1493–1541), who believed that it is the movements of the stars and moon that cause mental disturbances. Another was that of Johann Weyer (1515–1588), a German physician who claimed that abnormal behavior is an illness and should be treated by a physician rather than a priest. But it was not until the eighteenth century, in the period we call "the Enlightenment," that deviant behavior was once again widely viewed as a result of natural forces.

The view of mental disorder as having a physical, or organic, cause is known as **biogenic theory**. After Hippocrates, it was not again successfully advanced until the German physician Emil Kraepelin (1856–1926) brought out his *Textbook of Psychiatry* in 1883. In that book Kraepelin argued cogently for the central role of brain pathology in mental disturbances. He applied to them the same scientific

---

*This section is loosely based on Zilboorg and Henry, 1941.

standards of observation and classification used in studying physical diseases; in other words, he applied the medical model to mental disturbances. He also furnished psychiatry with its first comprehensive classification system, based on distinctions between different types of mental disorders and their clusters of symptoms. As we saw in Chapter 22, Kraepelin's classification system provided the basis for the American Psychiatric Association's *Diagnostic and Statistical Manual of Mental Disorders* (DSM-II).

By the turn of this century, neurological research was progressing rapidly, and one mysterious mental disorder after another yielded to Kraepelin's biogenic explanations. Senile psychoses, toxic psychoses, cerebral arteriosclerosis, and some forms of mental retardation were shown to be caused by brain pathology. Most stunning of all, general paresis, a puzzling disorder marked by the gradual breakdown of physical and mental functioning, was shown to be advanced syphilis.

PSYCHOGENIC THEORY As biogenic theory was making great strides, so too was **psychogenic theory**, which holds that mental disturbances result from external and internal forces that are not necessarily, or exclusively, physiological. It began with the colorful figure of Friedrich Anton Mesmer (1733–1815), who, like Paracelsus, thought that the heavens have an effect on mental states. Mesmer held that the movements of the planets control the distribution of a universal magnetic fluid, and that the shifting of this fluid is responsible for the health or sickness of mind and body. Mesmer believed that, according to his principle of "animal magnetism," by touching various parts of a person's body with colored rods and a special wand, he could adjust the distribution of the body liquids. Astonishingly enough, in many cases his treatment seems to have brought about improvement. But Mesmer's major contribution to psychotherapy was not the concept of animal magnetism, it was the discovery of the power of suggestion in curing mental disorders. He seems to have practiced a form of hypnosis, which was originally called "mesmerism," an artificially induced, sleeplike state in which the subject is highly susceptible to suggestion (see Chapter 14).

Mesmer's technique of hypnosis was used more systematically by two French physicians, Ambroise-Auguste Liébault (1823–1904) and Hippolyte Bernheim (1837–1919), who influenced the famous Parisian neurologist Jean-Martin Charcot (1825–

1893). Charcot found hypnosis to be a highly successful treatment for hysteria, a condition in which physical symptoms have no corresponding organic causes. Charcot then introduced one of his students, Sigmund Freud, to the use of hypnosis in treating psychological disorders.

The steps by which Freud progressed from the use of hypnosis to the techniques of psychoanalysis, free association, and dream analysis have been described in Chapter 18. While Freud's psychoanalytic theory is a general theory of personality, it is also a very detailed theory of abnormal behavior. As such, it is the topic of the next section. This is followed by a discussion of behavioral theories of mental disorder. These two approaches, psychoanalytic and behavioral, focus on the psychogenic determinants of disorder; we will return to the biogenic theories in a later section of the chapter. Since the late nineteenth century both psychogenic and biogenic theories have been continually developed and refined. The two approaches are presented separately here, but it is well to bear in mind that our present understanding of mental disorder clearly requires attention to psychological *and* organic factors. Moreover, as we shall see, some theorists have also begun to focus on social factors in psychological disorder.

THE PSYCHOANALYTIC THEORY OF ABNORMALITY

FREUD'S THEORY OF PERSONALITY: A BRIEF REVIEW Freud divided the structure of personality into three parts—the id, the ego, and the superego—whose interaction, he believed, determined human behavior and emotion. As we saw in Chapter 18, the id might be characterized as the "I want" of psychological life, and the ego might be described as the "How can I get it?" The id operates unconsciously, according to what Freud called the pleasure principle. It seeks to satisfy its primitive desires, and its goal is to reduce the tension that can build up through undischarged psychic energy.

The ego, much of which is conscious, operates according to the reality principle. Two of its functions, the delay of gratification and the use of fantasy substitutes, are important concepts in psychoanalytic theory. The id demands immediate gratification, but the ego recognizes the frequent need to defer satisfaction or to find a substitute source of gratification. Not only must the ego deal with the unconscious instinctual urges of the id, it must also reconcile these urges with the demands of the superego—the person's internal representation of right and wrong, of the values and ideals of family and society. Moreover, both the superego's demands and the id's instinctual urges must be reconciled with the requirements of the external world as perceived by the ego. The terms **psychodynamic** and **psychodynamic processes** refer to the ongoing interaction among ego, id, and superego. From the psychoanalytic perspective, psychological disorders develop when the ego is unable to reconcile the conflicting demands of the id and superego without disrupting the person's ability to function in society.

ANXIETY AND DEFENSES AGAINST IT As conflicts among the demands of the id, the superego, and reality intensify, the person experiences increas-

ing anxiety, which, in psychoanalytic terms, is a warning signal to the ego that danger is at hand. In most instances people act to reduce anxiety as soon as possible, before it becomes overwhelming.

Freud identified three kinds of anxiety (see Figure 23.1). The first is **reality anxiety**, in which an external danger triggers fear: a man points a gun at you and says, "Your money or your life!" and you become frightened. The second is **moral anxiety**, the result of the superego's demands for moral behavior and self-punishment for moral transgression: You copy someone else's answers on a test and feel guilty about it. The third is **neurotic anxiety**, which arises when the impulses generated by the id threaten to overwhelm the ego and interfere with its functioning: In a noisy quarrel with your roommate you suddenly feel a sense of panic arising from your aggressive impulses, which threaten to break loose and to cause you to strike out uncontrollably if your ego cannot find an acceptable way for you to express anger.

Anxiety may lead to abnormal behavior.

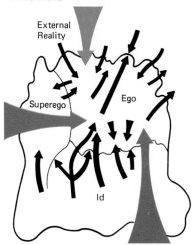

Reality anxiety occurs when the ego feels overwhelmed by threats from the external environment.

External Reality

Moral anxiety occurs when the ego is threatened by the superego's punitive response to some forbidden thought or action.

Superego

Ego

Id

Neurotic anxiety occurs when the id threatens to overwhelm ego constraints, leading to unacceptable or impulsive behavior.

Figure 23.1 According to psychoanalytic theory, the rigid and excessive use of ego defense mechanisms to relieve anxiety leads to the various forms of neurosis.

When there is an imbalance among the various structures of a personality, anxiety may lead to abnormal behavior. For example, a weak ego, unable to meet the demands of the superego or id, may resort to a broad variety of defense mechanisms, like repression, regression, and projection (see Chapter 18). When these defense mechanisms are greatly exaggerated and heavily relied on, the result is abnormal behavior. For example, the continued and excessive use of projection is one of the major features of paranoia (see Chapter 22).

The defenses erected by the ego are often expressed symbolically, so that the person is not consciously aware of the nature of the conflict or the connection between his or her symptoms and the real problem. The following example illustrates the point:

A twenty-nine-year-old professional woman had recently gotten engaged. She held a respected position for which she received a high salary; the job required her to drive considerable distances several times a week. Two months before her wedding she developed a driving phobia (an irrational fear of driving a car). Her psychoanalytically oriented therapist viewed the phobia as rooted in the woman's basic conflicts over sex. The woman reported that she usually felt "sort of uncomfortable" during sexual intercourse and that she could not "let go and enjoy it," but she said that she nevertheless felt a strong sexual attraction toward her fiancé.

The therapist concluded that the woman's driving phobia represented a fear of loss of control. Psychodynamically speaking, her sexual desire was threatening her need for control, and she associated her marriage with a loss of the "masculine," controlling role represented by her career. The driving phobia, in other words, symbolically represented her fear of abandoning herself sexually and her ambivalence about functioning in the roles of both wife and professional.

Thus, the woman's psychic conflicts accounted for her inability to function normally. It is important to note this emphasis made by psychoanalytic theory: An external, or environmental, situation contributes to a psychological disorder only insofar as it symbolizes an inner conflict.

According to psychoanalytic theory, the nature of the symbolic expression of conflicts and even the nature of the conflicts themselves are a result of a person's development during infancy and childhood. That is, the type and severity of a mental disorder is determined by an individual's psychodynamic development. From infancy to adolescence, a person passes through a series of psychosexual stages: oral, anal, phallic, latency, and genital. As Chapter 10 explained, each stage is characterized by a preoccupation with managing particular impulses and certain associated conflicts. At each stage, the person develops ways—sometimes effective and sometimes not—of accommodating divergent psychodynamic impulses. The child who successfully deals with problems at one stage moves to the next with a strong and energetic ego. The child who has been less effective at managing conflicts will also enter the next stage, but with an ego that will not necessarily be able to cope with conflicts at later stages.

THE ORIGINS OF ABNORMAL BEHAVIOR

Psychoanalytic theory holds that when the balance among id, ego, and superego has been disturbed by a failure to resolve conflicts, stress or conflict at a later stage may lead to mental disorder. The weak ego, unable to deal effectively with new problems, begins to employ various defense mechanisms more and more rigidly to deal with neurotic anxiety.

The particular defense mechanism that is employed determines the form of abnormal behavior that is displayed. The anxiety attacks that characterize anxiety neurosis (see Chapter 22) are seen as the result of desperate attempts by the ego to control the impulses of the id, and the major defense is the

According to psychoanalytic theory, anxiety may be directly experienced by an individual, but the conflict that causes the anxiety may remain unconscious. Through dream interpretation and free association in psychoanalysis, the true nature of the conflict may be revealed.

repression of those impulses. The ego succeeds in pushing down (repressing) the impulse, and, although the anxiety is directly experienced, the true nature of the conflict remains hidden in the recesses of the unconscious.

The defenses employed in other forms of neurosis are considerably more complex, and the level of anxiety that is directly experienced is somewhat less severe. The obsessive-compulsive neuroses that are characterized by rituals of orderliness or cleanliness, such as continual hand washing, are seen as a reaction formation defense. The ego responds to unacceptable impulses to soil oneself, to be dirty and destructive, by outwardly abhorring dirtiness and practicing fastidious cleanliness. The conversion reaction of the hysteric is also seen as a defense against unacceptable impulses. For example, glove anesthesia, as we saw in Chapter 18, can be a defense against an aggressive impulse to strike someone or to obtain sexual gratification through masturbation.

The psychotic disorders, according to psychoanalytic theory, are caused by severely deficient ego functioning. In contrast to the neuroses, the psychoses occur when the ego is unable to defend against unacceptable impulses: the person loses contact with reality and regresses to an early phase of the oral stage of development. The psychotic per-

son suffers from deficient ego functioning in perception, verbalization, and problem solving. A psychosis, in the psychoanalytic framework, is not just a more severe form of a neurosis, but a quite different disorder. Neurosis is associated with the overuse of ego defense mechanisms; in psychosis the ego is so weakened or deficient that it has no effective defenses against the id's impulses. A normal or adequately functioning person, in contrast, has developed a level of ego functioning that effectively mediates the conflicting demands of id and superego without an excessive use of defense mechanisms.

Psychoanalytic theory has been developed and modified continually almost from the time Freud introduced it. Two of Freud's early associates, Carl Jung and Alfred Adler, broke with him in disagreement over the sources of motivation and the role of instincts in the development of personality. Their contributions and those of three other neo-Freudians, Karen Horney, Erik Erikson, and Erich Fromm, were discussed in Chapter 18. Each of these theorists built upon the foundation laid by Freud and addressed various issues of abnormal behavior, emphasizing a specific source of conflict. Adler, for example, introduced the concept of the inferiority complex. Perhaps the most influential neo-Freudian today is Erik Erikson, whose concept of psychosocial development through eight stages of life (rather than Freud's five stages of psychosexual development in childhood) has provided the basis for an understanding of the developmental stages of adulthood that were discussed in Chapter 21.

While the neo-Freudians criticized and modified Freud's original conception of personality and abnormality, behaviorally oriented psychologists criticized Freud's concepts themselves as being untestable and based upon questionable inferences from limited sources of data. It is to these behaviorally oriented theories of abnormal behavior that we now turn.

BEHAVIORAL THEORIES OF ABNORMALITY

In Chapter 19 we described the behavioral theories of personality, which are based on the learning processes described in Chapter 4. The same learning processes that account for the phenomena of personality are thought by behaviorally oriented theorists to provide an explanation of the development of abnormal behaviors. These theorists work with the hypothesis that abnormal behavior is learned in much the same way as is all other behavior. The person with a psychological disorder differs from other people because he or she has learned inappropriate behaviors or has failed to learn the adaptive behaviors that most people acquire.

LEARNING MALADAPTIVE BEHAVIOR Unlike psychoanalytic theory, which attempts to explain all normal and abnormal behavior by a single model of psychodynamic development, learning theory has no all-inclusive explanatory model. Learning theory is used instead to try to discover how each person acquired his or her inappropriate behaviors. Learning theorists share a number of assumptions and concepts about abnormal behavior.

First, these theorists assume that people learn maladaptive behavior because the environment in some way rewards or reinforces it. The classical experimental demonstration of how a person learns maladaptive behavior is the case of "Little Albert" (Watson and Rayner, 1920). Little Albert was an eleven-month-old boy who, in a classical conditioning experiment, learned a phobia for furry ob-

jects of all sorts. Initially, Albert showed no fear in the presence of a white rat. Then, a loud noise (unconditioned stimulus) was paired with each presentation of the white rat. Soon the sight of the rat (conditioned stimulus) without the noise was enough to cause Albert to react with great fear (conditioned response). This fear rapidly generalized to all sorts of furry objects, like rabbits and fur pieces, even though no noise had been paired with them.

Maladaptive behavior may result from modeling as well as from direct reinforcement. For example, a child may develop a fear of dogs because he observes his mother's fearful reactions to dogs and is rewarded with her approval when he acts in the same way. We may also learn behavior that allows us to avoid something unpleasant. For example, a child who hates going to school may learn to develop a stomach ache every morning or learn to behave so disruptively in class that she is repeatedly suspended. The fact that both types of behavior allow her to miss school serves as reinforcement for the avoidance behavior.

The second idea that learning theorists share is that a given disturbance can result from more than one aspect of the person's learning history. When behaviorally oriented psychologists consider a person with a specific problem, they do not assume that there is just one explanation for it. When they see that a person has more than one symptom—both a driving phobia and an acute fear of heights, for instance—they do not assume that the two symptoms have the same origin. Conversely, when they encounter two people with identical disorders, they do not assume that the problem is rooted in similar histories or sequences of learning. The only similarity they always assume is that the disorders reflect the learning of inappropriate responses. (It has been suggested that such learning, in the form of learned helplessness, is related to the most common psychological disorder, depression; see the accompanying special feature on pages 530-531.)

TYPES OF MALADAPTIVE BEHAVIOR Behavioral theories of abnormality do not emphasize the DSM-II system of classification of disorders that was described in Chapter 22. Instead, behavior theorists classify disorders according to the circumstances that apparently control the behavior. Marvin R. Goldfried and Gerald C. Davison (1976, pp. 28–33) have formulated one useful categorization of maladaptive behaviors, which we will summarize here.

Learned Helplessness and Depression: A Fearful Symmetry

In Chapter 21 we discussed how it is possible to learn to feel helpless through experiences with uncontrollable environmental stress, such as noise or electrical shock. We saw that in the laboratory, animals and human beings have been confronted with unpleasant experiences that they could neither predict nor alter. When nothing they did made any difference, many of them became passive: they simply gave up trying to avoid or control the stressful situation (Overmier and Seligman, 1967). Moreover, such feelings of helplessness, once learned, may carry over to later, and perhaps very different, situations. Thus, even when experimental subjects are placed in a new situation in which the shock or noise could be avoided, their ability to do so is impaired. Martin E. P. Seligman, the psychologist who formulated the concept of learned helplessness, has suggested that human depression—not just "the blues" that everyone experiences occasionally, but also more severe and prolonged depression—is rooted in feelings of helplessness that are learned.

Seligman distinguishes between two general categories of depression (1976, citing Kiloh and Garside, 1963; Carney, Roth, and Garside, 1965; Mendels, 1968; and Schuyler, 1975). **Endogenous depressions** sweep over the person in response to some internal physical process. They usually occur in regular cycles and may be either bipolar (swinging from despair to a neutral state to mania and back again, as in manic-depressive illness) or unipolar (alternating between despair and neutrality, without a manic phase). Far more common are **reactive depressions**, which are triggered by an external event, such as the death of a family member; they are usually a bit milder than endogenous depressions and, unlike endogenous depressions, are usually unresponsive to drug or shock therapies. According to Seligman, it is the reactive depressions that seem to have a striking "symmetry" with learned helplessness.

Symmetrical Symptoms

Evidence for this symmetry has come from research from which Seligman, as he reports in his book *Helplessness* (1975, pp. 82–92), has distilled six symptoms of learned helplessness, each of which has parallels in depression. A major symptom is reduction in activity—what Seligman calls "lowered initiation of voluntary responses." People who have learned that they cannot control their situation become passive and withdrawn; their physical, intellectual, and social activity slows down.

Helpless people develop a "negative cognitive set," and so do depressed people. Convinced that their actions have no effect on what happens to them, they are always prepared to fail. They believe that they are more ineffective than they really are: thus, even when they have succeeded at a task, they often believe that they have done poorly or failed.

A third parallel between depression and learned helplessness is that both tend to dissipate with time. Unless it is repeatedly reinforced, the despair of both depression and learned helplessness is likely to lift eventually.

Fourth, helpless and depressed people show reduced levels of aggression. Seeing themselves as passive victims, they are incapable of expressing hostility or competitiveness.

The fifth symptom is a loss of "appetite" for living. Helpless and depressed people lose interest in food, sex, and social contact.

Finally, both depression and learned helplessness are accompanied by certain biochem-

ical changes in animals, and perhaps in human beings as well.

Thus, there is a striking similarity between the major symptoms of depression and those of learned helplessness. Seligman notes that other symptoms—notably stomach ulcers and anxiety—occur frequently with learned helplessness but have not been shown to be closely correlated with depression. Conversely, certain features of depression—such as dejected mood, feelings of self-hatred, and suicidal thoughts—have not yet been experimentally determined to accompany learned helplessness. Nevertheless, it seems safe to say that a strong link has been established between the symptoms of the two conditions.

Symmetrical Causes

In addition to having parallel symptoms, Seligman believes, depression and learned helplessness may have similar causes. As we noted above, reactive depression can be triggered by a number of external events: failure on the job or in school, a debilitating illness, death of a spouse, financial loss, rejection by a lover—any circumstance that makes people feel hopeless and helpless. And it is precisely the belief that one is helpless and not in control—that is, incapable of changing one's situation, achieving a goal, or bringing about some kind of relief—which Seligman suggests is the major cause of both depression and learned helplessness:

> What is the meaning of job failure or incompetence at school? Often it means that all of a person's efforts have been in vain, that his responses have failed to achieve his desires. When an individual is rejected by someone he loves, he can no longer control this

significant source of gratification and support. When a parent or lover dies, the bereaved is powerless to elicit love from the dead person. Physical disease and growing old are helpless conditions par excellence; the person finds his own responses ineffective and is thrown upon the care of others. (1975, pp. 93–94)

Seligman believes that even endogenous depressions, although they are not set off by a particular helplessness-inducing event, may involve a belief in one's helplessness. Speculating that a continuum of susceptibility to this belief underlies the continuum of depression from endogenous to reactive, Seligman states that, "At the extreme endogenous end [of the depression continuum], the slightest obstacle will trigger in the depressive a vicious circle of beliefs in how ineffective he is" (p. 94).

Interestingly, Seligman also claims that it is not only uncontrollable negative, unpleasant events which can cause depression, but also the belief that one is not in control of positive, pleasant events. Laboratory experiments show that learned helplessness results from learning that one's voluntary responses control neither punishment *nor* reward. Similarly, people who feel that there is no connection between their actions and the good things that happen to them can become depressed. In "success depression," then, "Depressed, successful people tell you that they are now rewarded not for what they're doing, but for who they are or what they *have* done. Having achieved the goal that they strove for, their rewards now come independently of any ongoing instrumental activity" (1975, p. 99). Such

people have lost their self-esteem and sense of competence, and thus are vulnerable to depression, because they perceive that their own actions do not control their experiences.

Symmetrical Cures?

It seems, then, that one possible way to treat depression is to instill the belief that one's actions *do* make a difference. According to Seligman, the only sure-fire cure thus far for learned helplessness in dogs and rats is directive therapy—forced exposure of the animals to the fact that their responses actually produce the reinforcement. Seligman is careful to avoid the claim that the same treatment guarantees a cure for depression in humans. However, he does point to the success of certain therapies, such as assertiveness training, which are compatible with the learned helplessness model, and suggests that when other, less compatible therapies are effective, "it is because they also reinstate the patient's *sense of efficacy*" (1976, p. 14).

Seligman's research on helplessness and depression provides impressive parallels and implications that cannot be lightly dismissed. Certainly there will always be unpleasant events, such as death, over which people have little or no control. But, as Seligman indicates, the way we handle such events is related to our sense of mastery of those situations over which we do have some control. "From where does one get a sense of power, worth, and self-esteem? . . . from long experience watching his own actions change the world" (1975, p. 98). Such insights suggest intriguing possibilities for the treatment of depression, and perhaps even for its prevention.

1. DIFFICULTIES IN STIMULUS CONTROL OF BE-HAVIOR Sometimes the stimuli present in the environment fail to exert adequate control over the individual's behavior. Stimulus control of behavior may be *defective*: a person has an adequate repertoire of behavior but lacks a sense of which behaviors are appropriate in various situations. For example, loud singing is not abnormal behavior in itself, but loud singing on a public bus is abnormal because the timing is wrong. In other cases, stimulus control is *inappropriate*: an innocuous cue in the individual's environment elicits a conditioned aversive emotional reaction, which may take the form of anxiety, insomnia, or an upset stomach.

2. DEFICIENT BEHAVIORAL REPERTOIRES An individual who has not learned the appropriate behaviors for certain social, school, or work situations may suffer recurring anxiety and depression when confronted with such situations. Common deficiencies in the behavioral repertoire include uncertainty about how to order dinner in a restaurant and lack of knowledge of how to act on a date.

3. AVERSIVE BEHAVIORAL REPERTOIRES Some individuals display maladaptive behavior patterns that are aversive to other people, such as antisocial behavior or excessive aggression. These individuals do not have behavioral deficiencies, as described in

category 2, above; rather, they know how to act in various situations, but they persist in "making life difficult for themselves by being obnoxious or otherwise bothersome to others" (Goldfried and Davison, 1976, p. 30).

4. DIFFICULTIES WITH INCENTIVE SYSTEMS (REINFORCERS) This category encompasses deviant behaviors that are functionally linked with defective reinforcers, either within the individual or in the environment. When an individual's system of incentives is *defective*, social stimuli that would provide reinforcement for most other people fail to do so, as in the autistic child (who cannot be reached by conventional stimuli) and the juvenile delinquent (whose behavior conforms to the standards of a subculture, rather than of the larger society). When the individual's incentive system is *inappropriate*, he or she is reinforced for behavior that is harmful or disapproved by society—for example, drug abuse or chronic alcoholism.

Reinforcers in the individual's environment may be lacking, as in a prolonged depression following the death of a spouse. Environmental reinforcers, when present, may conflict with one another, the eventual result being maladaptive behavior. Thus, a man may verbally encourage his wife to wear provocative clothing, but act so as to discourage or punish her when she does, perhaps by ignoring her when she wears a low-cut dress to a party.

Many of the actors in the play *Runaways* are children and teenagers who have at one time or another run away from their homes. In some families, the social stimuli that should provide reinforcement fail to do so. The child's system of incentives is defective, and maladaptive behavior—such as running away—may be the result.

5. AVERSIVE SELF-REINFORCING SYSTEMS Finally, self-reinforcement can be a powerful tool for maintaining appropriate behavior, but some individuals set their standards of behavior so unrealistically high that they seldom or never have a chance to reward themselves. The result of this consistent lack of self-reinforcement may be chronic depression or feelings of inadequacy.

PSYCHOANALYTIC AND BEHAVIORAL INTERPRETATIONS: A COMPARISON

As we have just seen, learning theory views psychological disorder as learned maladaptive behavior: The symptoms define the person's problem, and when the symptoms are eliminated, so is the problem. Psychoanalytic theory, however, views the symptoms of disorder as symbolic expressions of psychodynamic problems or conflicts. The psychoanalytic position assumes that if only the symptoms are removed, with no resolution of the primary conflict, the person will develop new symptoms in an alternative expression of the conflict—a process known as **symptom substitution**.

We can illuminate the difference between psychoanalytic and learning-theory interpretations of the symptoms of disorder by considering Freud's case of "Little Hans." At the age of five, Hans developed a phobia for horses after seeing a horse slip and fall on a wet street. He was treated by his father, a lay analyst. Freud consulted periodically with the father and subsequently published an analysis of the case (1909). He interpreted the horse phobia as an expression of psychodynamic conflicts with which Hans was then struggling; among these were guilt about masturbation, fear of castration, sibling rivalry with a younger sister, and the Oedipal desire to possess his mother and replace his father. Freud thought that what Hans saw—a horse hitched to a milk wagon slipping on the wet street and falling—symbolized Hans' fear of his mother's giving birth to another child (his sister's birth had upset him very much). It also represented the child's anxiety over his unconscious wish that his father would die so that he could possess his mother.

Joseph Wolpe and Stanley Rachman (1960) offered a learning-theory explanation of the same case. They maintained that conjecture about psychodynamic processes is unnecessary to explain Hans' horse phobia. Simply seeing the horse fall was a sufficiently frightening experience to cause the subsequent fear of horses. Wolpe and Rachman pointed out that any stimulus that once touches off or is paired with fear can continue to elicit fear. Neurotic fear results if the person feels extreme fear at the first encounter with the stimulus or if the conditioning is repeated so many times that the fear continues to occur. Wolpe and Rachman noted that neurotic fear may include a generalization of fear to other stimuli that are similar to the original one. Hans can be viewed as having been so frightened by the experience that he was afraid to approach situations in which it might be repeated, and so he became frightened of horses in general.

Some people, drawn by the apparent simplicity and objectivity of the behavioral approach, may find the psychoanalytic account too fanciful and speculative. Others may reject the behavioral approach to disorder because it seems too mechanistic and fails to take account of the complexity and depth of human experience. Both approaches are subject to criticism, and neither can provide a comprehensive explanation of mental disorder. Instead of opting for one approach or the other, we would do better to appreciate the insight that each theory provides into the psychogenic causes of psychological disorder. Let us now turn to a consideration of biogenic factors.

BIOLOGICAL BASES OF MENTAL DISORDER

Ever since Hippocrates suggested that abnormal behavior is a result of too much phlegm or bile circulating through the body, scientists have attempted to explain psychological disorder in organic terms. In many cases, organic causation is clear and undeniable, as when impairment results from brain injury, infection, or tumor. For a number of other disorders, primarily neuroses, psychogenic explanations seem to be preferred by clinicians. The question of the organic or psychogenic origin of mental disorder is directed most frequently at the psychoses. Schizophrenia, the most frequently occurring psychosis, has drawn the most attention from researchers; therefore, the studies cited next focus on schizophrenia.

THE BIOLOGICAL PERSPECTIVE: NATURE VERSUS NURTURE
A purely biological explanation of mental disorder must include evidence

that the abnormality is transmitted genetically. Otherwise, the disorder could be attributed to psychological or social factors rather than organic influences. To date, very few disorders have been traced directly to specific genetic defects. Two disorders for which chromosomal abnormality has been established as the cause are Down's syndrome (Mongolism) and Turner's syndrome, both of which involve mental retardation. As for a link between defective gene combinations and most other psychological disorders, however, there is a great deal of speculation but little firm evidence.

Proof of a strictly biological cause for a complex disorder like schizophrenia is extremely hard to come by. The main reason for this difficulty is that environmental factors—the influence of family and society—cannot readily be eliminated. In schizophrenia, as in so many other situations, there is no simple way to separate "nature" from "nurture."

Nevertheless, some fragmentary evidence that schizophrenia is hereditary has been found. It has been discovered, for instance, that the brother of a schizophrenic, with whom he has many genes in common, is more likely to be schizophrenic himself than is, say, the first cousin of a schizophrenic (Slater, 1968). Moreover, data from studies of identical and fraternal twins seem to affirm the role of heredity in schizophrenia. In about 40 to 50 percent of the cases in which one identical twin had schizophrenia, the other twin did also; the frequency among fraternal twins was much lower, but still significant—10 to 15 percent, as shown in Figure 23.2 (Ban, 1973).

The problem with studies of twins is that twins are usually raised under the same conditions, so it is difficult to rule out environmental factors. Re-searchers have tried to overcome this difficulty by studying adopted children. One group of researchers traced both the adoptive and the biological relatives of schizophrenic children. They found that schizophrenia occurred more often in the biological families than in the adoptive families (Kety et al., 1968).

A second investigation identified schizophrenic parents who had given their children up for adoption and traced the children to find out the incidence of schizophrenia among them. The results: 33 percent of the children adopted away from schizophrenic parents manifested some symptoms of schizophrenia. In a control group of adopted-away children of nonschizophrenic parents, only 15 percent showed symptoms of schizophrenia (Rosenthal et al., 1971).

Although these studies support the role of heredity in schizophrenia, they do not conclusively rule out environmental influences. If schizophrenia were entirely a matter of heredity, the incidence of schizophrenia among the offspring of schizophrenics would be far higher than has been found to be the case. Similarly, the percentage of identical twins who both have schizophrenia would be 100 percent instead of only 40 to 50 percent. And, finally, the fact that studies of family members living together reveal a higher incidence of schizophrenia than the studies of adopted children is a strong indication that the environment cannot be dismissed as a contributing factor in schizophrenia.

BIOCHEMICAL THEORIES OF DISORDER

Whatever the causes of mental disorder, some of its

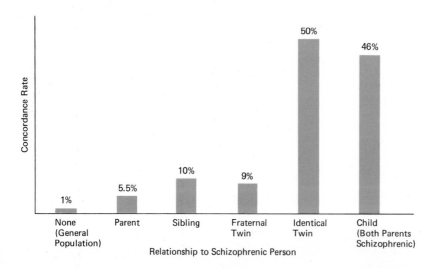

Figure 23.2 The concordance rates that accompany various degrees of relationship to a schizophrenic person. A concordance rate of 100 percent would mean that if one member of the related pair is schizophrenic, the other person will be too. Note that if a fraternal twin is schizophrenic, the concordance rate is about the same as that for any other sibling, but that the concordance rate for an identical twin is far higher. (After Gottessman and Shields, 1972.)

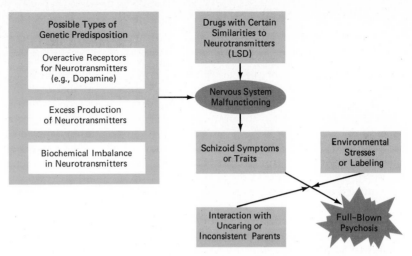

Figure 23.3 This diagram shows one way in which a genetic defect might interact with psychogenic factors to result in schizophrenia or some other psychosis.

effects are manifested in the body's chemistry. Over the years, drugs have been found that, by altering the body's chemistry, reduce the severity of various disorders. For example, one group of drugs is effective in quieting the disturbed behavior of schizophrenics, and another group of substances reduces the severity of manic-depressive episodes. Of course, the fact that drugs are effective in some cases does not mean that chemical factors necessarily are the primary cause of these disorders. Nevertheless, the effectiveness of drug therapy has led many researchers to speculate that severe emotional disturbances may have a biochemical basis (see Figure 23.3).

Biochemical explanations also follow from the search for hereditary bases of disorder. As we saw in Chapter 7, genes are the transmitters of all hereditary information—for the development of both the species and the individual. A single defective gene can disrupt the program for a sequence of necessary biochemical transformations; this disruption may result in physical or mental disorder. For example, the special feature in Chapter 7 described how a single defective gene produces the disease called PKU (phenylketonuria), with its severe mental retardation.

To explore the hypothesis that mental disorder is caused by some biochemical abnormality, researchers take one group of people with a particular disorder and search for some biochemical difference between them and a control group of nondisturbed people. Although this procedure seems straightforward, it is often difficult to carry out. Complications can arise in finding an appropriate control group. The perfect control group would have to live in an environment identical to that of the people who suffer from the disorder, so that the only difference between the subjects and the control group would be the disorder.

Moreover, the biochemistry of human beings is extremely complex, and our understanding of it is far from complete. The medical and life histories, and even the diets, of psychiatric patients are markedly different from those of the members of control groups. Most hospitalized schizophrenics, for example, eat an institutional diet, smoke heavily, get little exercise, and have long histories of drug therapy. Any of these factors can alter a person's biochemistry. Moreover, as Seymour Kety (1969) has pointed out, the extreme emotional and physical stresses associated with having a mental disorder can also cause changes in biochemical functioning. When researchers find that the body chemistry of disturbed persons differs from that of nondisturbed people, they must find ways of determining whether these differences are related to the causes of the disorder or to its effects.

Some progress has been made in distinguishing causes from effects, especially in the biochemistry of schizophrenic disorders. A series of studies reported by C. David Wise and Larry Stein (1971, 1973) suggested that because of a genetic defect, schizophrenics do not manufacture a biochemical agent necessary to a crucial sequence of changes in the hormone norepinephrine, and that they therefore suffer progressive brain damage. The damage occurs in the areas of the brain associated with pleasure or reward. Wise and Stein ran post-mortem examinations of the brains of eighteen schizophrenics, comparing them, for control purposes, with the brains of twelve nondisturbed persons. (The schizophrenics had died in an institution; the controls had died suddenly—in accidents or from heart attacks—and had no known history of mental disorder.) They found significant differences between the brains of schizophrenics and those of non-schizophrenics in the amount of a substance responsible for the final step in the sequence of the body's use of norepinephrine. Although all regions of the brain examined showed a deficit of the substance, the deficit was larger in the areas of the brain associated with pleasure.

Wise and Stein (1973) provided additional evidence for their theory from studies of animals. They injected a certain region of the brain of rats with a chemical found in excessive quantities in the bodies of schizophrenic patients. This chemical is known to interfere with the effective use of norepinephrine. The rats became unresponsive to reward, and their bodies showed the waxy flexibility characteristic of catatonic schizophrenics (see Chapter 22).

From the results of this study, it appears that schizophrenic symptoms are associated with the body's ineffective utilization of norepinephrine. This "norepinephrine theory" of schizophrenia is somewhat controversial. Critics point out that the chemicals involved have such complex effects that it is very difficult to pinpoint a single action of just one of them as the cause of schizophrenic symptoms. Nevertheless, the research has provided an important new insight into the possible biochemical causes of schizophrenia.

Whatever the role of norepinephrine in schizophrenia, it is probably not the whole story. Another biochemical agent, dopamine, has recently come under intense investigation (reported in Valenstein, 1978). The findings are very complex and can be summarized only briefly here. Certain drugs, called phenothiazines, which are most effective in reducing the primary symptoms of schizophrenia (thought disorder, blunted emotional responses, withdrawal, and autistic behavior), are known to block the absorption of dopamine by the dopamine receptors in the brain (Creese, Burt, and Snyder, 1975). One hypothesis suggests that an excess of dopamine in the brain overstimulates these receptors, producing schizophrenic symptoms (Meltzer and Stahl, 1976). It is thought that blocking the receptors with the phenothiazines reduces the impact of the excess dopamine and thus diminishes the symptoms of schizophrenia (Paul, 1977). However, some recent research, based on post-mortem examinations of the brains of schizophrenic and nonschizophrenic subjects, suggests that the brains of schizophrenic people have more dopamine receptors in certain critical locations (Lee and Seeman, 1977). Thus, the schizophrenic symptoms would be produced by hyperactivity at these sites, not by an excess of dopamine itself. The action of the phenothiazine drugs can be explained as a blocking of the

absorption of dopamine through reduction of the number of active receptors. These results must be interpreted with caution because of the differences in histories of drug usage between the nonschizophrenic subjects and the schizophrenic ones.

The existence of differences in the neurological structures of schizophrenics and nonschizophrenics, and the evidence that suggests a hereditary component in schizophrenia, support a biological explanation of this psychosis. Biological explanations of other mental disorders have not been as fully developed nor as carefully researched as those just reviewed. But, as we noted earlier, even for schizophrenia the biological explanation cannot be expected to account completely for the occurrence of the disorder. The existence of social and psychological bases for schizophrenia, as well as for other mental disorders, must still be taken into account. We shall look next at the impact of family structure and life circumstances on the occurrence of schizophrenia and other disorders.

SOCIAL FACTORS IN MENTAL DISORDER

Researchers have examined the life histories and family environments of people with psychological disorders and have compared the findings with similar data gathered from control subjects. Their aim has been to isolate the environmental factors or processes that are unique to the psychological development of individuals with a given disorder. The examples of this approach that are described below involve research into the family lives of schizophrenic individuals.

One group of investigators, headed by Theodore Lidz (Lidz et al., 1957; Lidz, 1973), maintained contact with schizophrenics and their families for several years. They held weekly interviews with family members, observed how the families interacted among themselves and with hospital staff members, visited the subjects' homes, and did diagnostic and other kinds of testing. From the findings of their first sixteen cases, the researchers suggested that there are two types of families of schizophrenics.

According to Lidz and his associates, the first type of family showed a pattern termed **marital schism**, in which both parents of the schizophrenic

were caught up in their own personality diffi-

In stable environments, families seem able to avoid the conflicts and confusions caused by marital schism and marital skew.

culties, which were aggravated to the point of desperation by the marital relationship. There was chronic failure to achieve complementarity of purpose or role reciprocity. Neither gained support of emotional needs from the other. . . . These marriages are replete with recurrent threats of separation. . . . Communication consists primarily of coercive efforts and defiance, or of efforts to mask the defiance to avoid fighting. . . . A particularly malignant feature in these marriages is the chronic "undercutting" of the worth of one partner to the children by the other. (Lidz et al., 1957)

The other type of family was characterized by what the researchers called **marital skew**. In these families

one partner who was extremely dependent or masochistic had married a spouse who had appeared to be a strong and protecting parental figure. The dependent partner would go along with or even support the weaknesses or psychopathologic distortions of the parental partner. . . . A striking feature in all cases was the

psychopathology of the partner who appeared to be dominant, creating an abnormal environment which, being accepted by the "healthier" spouse, may have seemed to be a normal environment to the children. (Lidz et al., 1957)

The investigators concluded that the child faced with the conflict and confusion of either of these kinds of family situations develops ways of coping that lead to problems later in life.

Another group of investigators, headed by Gregory Bateson and Don Jackson, examined the family environments of schizophrenics and developed the **double-bind hypothesis** (Bateson, Jackson, et al., 1956). The basic idea can be demonstrated by the example of the mother who has great difficulty accepting her child's affection and positive regard for her. At the same time, she finds it hard to deal with any feelings of anxiety or hostility that she experiences toward her child, so she *acts* lovingly toward the child. She may tell the child to give her a kiss, but then stiffen her body when the child approaches her. The child, perceiving the discrepancy between her overt actions and her covert feelings, repeatedly receives two contradictory messages in such situations. The child, therefore, never learns to understand and make distinctions among the meanings expressed in normal language and behavior. He or she develops the bizarre language and social ineptness characteristic of schizophrenics.

Frieda Fromm-Reichmann believed the influence of the mother to be so crucial as a cause of schizophrenia that in 1948 she coined the term "schizophrenogenic mother" to describe a cold, domineering mother who simultaneously rejects her child and overprotects it (Fromm-Reichmann, 1974). Such a mother, in conjunction with a passive father who exerts little influence in the family, seems to Fromm-Reichmann to be a strong contributing factor in schizophrenia.

Recently, considerable attention has been given to the work of a third group of researchers and theorists, headed by psychiatrist R. D. Laing, who hypothesizes that it is within the family that schizophrenics develop their particular ways of experiencing, understanding, and behaving in the world. These ways may seem incomprehensible to outsiders, but they are appropriate within the family and can be seen as adaptive in that context. Members of a schizophrenic's family are not honest with one another; their interaction forces each of them to deny parts of their experiences and to invalidate important feelings (Laing and Esterson, 1971). Figure 23.4 represents what Laing sees as the

According to Bateson and Jackson's double-bind hypothesis, children who are constantly confused by the discrepancy they perceive between their mother's overt actions and her covert feelings may develop schizophrenic symptoms because they never learn how to interpret normal behavior and language. For such children, who the mother really is and what her behavior really means are mysteries.

way schizophrenics deny that they have a right to desire things or to enjoy what they have achieved.

Laing came to believe that emotional disturbance is inherent in contemporary Western society and that schizophrenics are victims not only of their families but also of society itself. He said, in *The Politics of Experience* (1967), that "By the time the new human is fifteen or so, we are left with a being like ourselves, a half-crazed creature more or less adjusted to a mad world. This is normality in our present age." Because almost everyone is mad, Laing maintains, it is absurd for some people to label others maladjusted or schizophrenic. In fact, Laing believes that the processes that psychotics undergo represent their attempts to reconcile the self that existed before socialization (the "true" self) with the self created by cultural demands and social sanctions.

A number of other researchers have joined Laing in denouncing the prevalent system of diagnosing and labeling mental patients. T. J. Scheff (1970) has identified labeling as the single most important reason that disordered behavior persists. D. L. Rosenhan (1973), in the article discussed at the end of Chapter 22, argued that the practice of assigning patients to diagnostic categories creates a set of expectations that may result in interpreting normal behavior as abnormal. Rosenhan further argued that the label follows the patient throughout life, even when it no longer applies, thereby creating problems that might easily have been avoided. Behaviorists, too, are concerned about the labeling of certain behaviors as abnormal or deviant, for fear that the label may create the condition, functioning like a self-fulfilling prophecy. Leonard P. Ullmann

and Leonard Krasner (1975) have argued that people may actually learn abnormal behavior after such a label has been applied to some of their actions.

We have discussed in this section only a small sample of the family and social factors correlated with schizophrenia. We have not discussed the hundreds of studies that have examined the relationship

Figure 23.4 An example of what R. D. Laing calls "knots." These are patterns of circular reasoning some people use in trying to make sense of the messages they receive from their families. Such individuals, Laing maintains, are the people usually described as schizophrenic. The logical trap represented here can be seen as the result of the double binds described by Bateson and Jackson. The conflict is real and, in this person's terms, inescapable. Imagine yourself in this person's position. Are you to have what you need and feel guilty, or are you to somehow get along with nothing at all? (From R. D. Laing, *Knots,* 1970.)

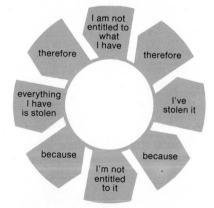

between such influences and the occurrence of other mental disorders. (A number of demographic and cultural factors were mentioned in Chapter 22.) Just as no single biological cause has been isolated, neither has a single specific pattern of family interaction or social pathology been isolated as the most important cause of mental disorder. We must conclude that family and social factors can be important in the development of mental disorder, but thus far the contributing causes appear to be so complex and so thoroughly intertwined that no single one can be held responsible.

Summary

1. Historically, deviant behavior has been explained and defined according to the philosophical and religious outlook of a particular society.
   A. Deviant behavior was thought to be a supernatural phenomenon in many cultures. The ancient Greeks, notably Hippocrates, were the first to believe that abnormal behavior was a physiological rather than supernatural disturbance. Nevertheless, from the Middle Ages until as recently as the eighteenth century, insanity was almost universally explained in terms of demonic forces.
   B. In the late nineteenth century Emil Kraepelin advanced a **biogenic theory**, contending that mental disorder has a physiological cause.
   C. **Psychogenic theory** holds that mental disturbances result from external and internal forces that are not necessarily, or exclusively, physiological. This theory had its origins in the work of Friedrich Anton Mesmer, whose major contribution to psychotherapy was the discovery of the power of suggestion in curing mental disorders. Present understanding of mental disorder draws on both biogenic and psychogenic theories.

2. Freud's psychoanalytic theory of personality incorporates a detailed theory of abnormal behavior.
   A. Anxiety is caused by conflicts among the demands of the id, the superego, and reality. Freud defined three kinds of anxiety.
      1. **Reality anxiety** occurs when an external danger triggers fear.
      2. **Moral anxiety** is the result of the superego's demands for moral behavior and self-punishment for moral transgression.
      3. **Neurotic anxiety** arises when the impulses generated by the id threaten to overwhelm the ego and interfere with its functioning.
   B. When the **psychodynamic processes** among id, ego, and superego are out of balance, anxiety results. To relieve the anxiety, the ego may resort to defense mechanisms. Unresolved earlier conflicts may lead the ego to rely too heavily or too rigidly on defense mechanisms. The result may be mental disorder.
      1. The particular defense mechanism that the ego employs determines the form of abnormal behavior that is displayed.
         a. Neuroses are seen as desperate attempts by the ego to control the impulses of the id through repression.
         b. Psychoses are said to be caused by the ego's inability to defend against unacceptable impulses; the person regresses to an early phase of the oral stage of development.
      2. Neo-Freudians including Carl Jung, Alfred Adler, Karen Horney, Erik Erikson, and Erich Fromm modified Freud's theory to address various issues of abnormal behavior, each emphasizing a specific source of conflict.

3. Behavioral theorists believe that abnormal behavior is learned in much the same way as is all other behavior. The person with a psychological disorder differs from other people because he or she has learned inappropriate behaviors or has failed to learn the adaptive behaviors that most people acquire.
   A. Learning theorists share a number of assumptions and concepts about abnormal behavior.
      1. They assume that people learn maladaptive behavior because the environment in some way rewards or reinforces it. Maladaptive behavior may result from direct reinforcement or from modeling.
      2. Learning theorists believe that a given dis-

turbance can result from more than one aspect of the person's learning history.

B. Behavior theorists classify disorders according to the circumstances that apparently control the behavior. Marvin R. Goldfried and Gerald Davison have formulated one categorization of maladaptive behaviors.

  1. Stimulus control of behavior may be defective or inappropriate. The person lacks a sense of which behaviors are appropriate in various situations or has an aversive reaction to an innocuous stimulus.

  2. The behavioral repertoire may be deficient. The person may suffer recurring anxiety and depression when confronted with situations for which he or she has not learned the appropriate behaviors.

  3. An individual may have no behavioral deficiencies but display maladaptive behavior patterns that are aversive to other people.

  4. An individual may have difficulties with his or her incentive systems. If the incentive system is defective, stimuli that would serve as reinforcers for most other people fail to do so. If the incentive system is inappropriate, he or she is reinforced for behavior that is harmful or culturally disapproved. Reinforcers in the individual's environment may be lacking, or in conflict with one another.

  5. Some individuals set their behavioral standards so high that they never have a chance to reward themselves. Such an aversive self-reinforcing system can result in chronic depression or feelings of inadequacy.

4. Learning theory holds that a psychological disorder is eliminated when the symptoms are eliminated. Psychoanalytic theory views symptoms as symbolic of a primary conflict; if the symptoms are removed with no resolution of the primary conflict, the person will develop new symptoms—a process known as **symptom substitution**. Both psychoanalytic theory and learning theory are subject to criticism, and neither provides a comprehensive explanation of mental disorder, but they both provide insights into the psychogenic causes of psychological disorder.

5. The question of whether mental disorder is organic or psychogenic in origin is directed most frequently at the psychoses, especially the most common psychosis, schizophrenia.

A. A purely biological explanation of mental disorder must include evidence that the abnormality is transmitted genetically. Very few disorders have been traced directly to specific genetic defects, and proof of a biological cause for mental disorder is difficult because environmental factors cannot readily be eliminated. Various studies of twins and of adopted children have provided support for the role of heredity in schizophrenia, but none has conclusively ruled out environmental influences.

B. The effectiveness of drug therapy has led many researchers to speculate that severe emotional disturbances may have a biochemical basis. Researchers encounter great difficulties in attempting to determine biochemical abnormalities among people suffering from mental disorder because of the difficulty in finding an appropriate control group, the complexity of human biochemistry, and the difficulty in determining whether biochemical differences are related to the causes or to the effects of the disorder.

  1. One series of studies indicated that schizophrenic symptoms may be associated with brain damage caused by the body's inability to utilize norepinephrine effectively.

  2. Both the chemical agent dopamine and an excessive number of dopamine receptors in the brain have been linked to schizophrenia, although not conclusively.

6. Researchers have examined life histories and family environments, seeking to isolate environmental factors or processes that are unique to the psychological development of individuals with a given disorder.

A. Theodore Lidz and his associates suggested that there are two types of families of schizophrenics. Children in these situations develop ways of coping that lead to problems later in life.

  1. In a family with a pattern of **marital schism**, both parents of the schizophrenic have personality difficulties; the marriage is marked by failure to communicate, reciprocate, and support.

  2. In the type of family characterized by **marital skew**, one partner is extremely

dependent on a dominant spouse who suffers from psychopathological distortions; this creates an abnormal family environment that may seem normal to the children.

B. Gregory Bateson, Don Jackson, and their colleagues developed the **double-bind hypothesis**, in which there is a discrepancy between a parent's overt actions and covert feelings. The child in this situation never learns to understand and make distinctions among the meanings expressed in normal language and behavior.

C. A group of researchers headed by psychiatrist R. D. Laing hypothesized that schizophrenics develop within the family their particular ways of experiencing, understanding, and behaving in the world. Behavior that is incomprehensible to outsiders can be seen as appropriate and adaptive within the family. Laing went so far as to say that emotional disturbance is inherent in contemporary Western society, and that because everyone is mad, it is absurd for some people to label others maladjusted or schizophrenic.

D. A number of other researchers, including T. J. Scheff, D. L. Rosenhan, and Leonard P. Ullmann and Leonard Krasner, have denounced the prevalent system of diagnosing and labeling mental patients.

RECOMMENDED READINGS

ACHENBACH, THOMAS M. *Developmental Psychopathology*. New York: Ronald, 1974. A thorough description of child psychopathology from a developmental perspective; covers theory and therapeutic approaches.

BRECHER, EDWARD M. (and the Editors of *Consumer Reports*). *Licit and Illicit Drugs*. Boston: Little, Brown, 1972. Very thorough and scholarly but very easy and enjoyable to read. Probably the best reference work for a general audience.

CAMERON, NORMAN. *Personality Development and Psychopathology*. Boston: Houghton Mifflin, 1963. This work provides the reader with an understanding of how the psychoanalytically oriented clinician views psychological development and its relation to psychological disorders. It is virtually a complete presentation but can easily be understood by the average reader.

DAVISON, G. C., and J. M. NEALE. *Abnormal Psychology: An Experimental Clinical Approach*. New York: Wiley, 1974. A clear presentation of the behavioral perspective on psychological disorder.

FILSKOV, SUSAN B., and STEVEN G. GOLDSTEIN. *Clinical Human Neuropsychology*. Reading, Mass.: Addison-Wesley, 1978. A brief but very useful survey of mental disorders and deficits that result from neurological dysfunction.

FREUD, SIGMUND. *New Introductory Lectures on Psychoanalysis* (1933). James Strachey (ed. and tr.). New York: Norton, 1965. The psychoanalytic perspective on the development of disorder, in Freud's own words.

GOODMAN, LOUIS S., and ALFRED GILMAN. *The Pharmacological Basis of Therapeutics*. 4th ed. New York: Macmillan, 1970. Everything there is to know about drugs, including psychiatric drugs, narcotics, drug addiction, withdrawal, alcoholism, marijuana, and so on. Probably the best *scientific* reference book on the subject.

MASER, JACK D., and MARTIN E. P. SELIGMAN. *Psychopathology: Experimental Models*. San Francisco: Freeman, 1977. A collection of papers in which each author explores the fundamental nature of a different disorder through experimental research.

SAHAKIAN, WILLIAM S. (ed.). *Psychopathology Today: Experimentation, Theory and Research*. Itasca, Ill.: F. E. Peacock, 1970. This volume contains a collection of important research papers concerning psychopathology. The volume is well organized, and the editor has provided introductory discussions for each section. These introductions allow the reader to understand the individual papers as parts of a comprehensive whole.

WHITE, ROBERT W., and NORMAN F. WATT. *The Abnormal Personality*. 4th ed. New York: Ronald, 1964. This text provides an excellent introduction to the subject matter of psychopathology. The various forms of psychological disorders are described, and a brief discussion of the theories and empirical data concerning each is provided. The reader need not have studied psychology before.

CHAPTER TWENTY-FOUR

APPROACHES TO TREATMENT

I've met a considerable number of psychiatrists in my life and, as far as I can remember, I liked them all. In fact, I liked at least one of them very much, since she is my wife. Yet I've got to admit I feel personally uneasy about psychotherapy. *Why* am I uneasy?

The closest I ever came to undergoing psychotherapy was when I was in the Army back in 1945 and 1946. It wasn't a bad time really, as I look back on it. The war was over; I was in no danger; everyone was moderately nice to me; I underwent no suffering—but I *hated* it.

If one thing bothered me more than another, it was the lack of privacy. Sleeping in the same room with thirty others and listening to their snoring and trying to ignore the smell was bad enough, but what really got me was that the toilets not only didn't have doors, they didn't even have partitions. I trained myself to get up at 3 a.m. to visit the toilet—and there was invariably one other soldier using it.

The unhappiness got me so far down that, out of sheer desperation, I had to choose someone with whom to discuss the matter. It had to be either the chaplain or the psychiatrist, and I chose the latter. Actually, I spoke to one of his young assistants (a social worker in real life) for several sessions. The psychiatrist himself didn't bother seeing me because the social worker, after listening to my sorrows, told his boss not to waste his time on me.

In a way, nothing came of it. I had vaguely hoped that if the psychotherapist realized the extent of my misery, he would set me up in a room of my own with a private toilet and shower. But it turned out that all *they* were interested in was in adjusting *me*. I was supposed to react more calmly to the lack of privacy. Well, heck, this I didn't want to do. If I couldn't have my privacy then, darn it, I wanted my grievance.

In another way, something did come of it. The social worker discovered I could type at professional speed, and the office needed typists. He got me a job as a typist there, which meant no more KP. Now *that* was good psychotherapy. I enjoyed the job, and I even got to know the psychiatrist. I used to talk to him, informally, every chance I got, feeling that one shouldn't give up on psychotherapy yet. Perhaps if one went straight to the boss, it might be arranged for me to have at least a special time in the community toilet when no one else was allowed to enter.

Not so. The psychiatrist was a lovable fellow but he never wanted to talk about these matters in an objective way. His only curiosity was in my own subjective reaction to these things. Once I said hotly, "Why are you so surprised that I resent being crowded in with strangers? Wouldn't you?" His response was a cool, "Would I?"

Then one day I told him a joke that was quite antipsychiatrist. I tell jokes very well and I told that one at the top of my form. When I finished, I laughed heartily, but all the psychiatrist did was to put his fingertips together, wait for me to calm down, and say, "Tell me, Asimov, why did you feel it necessary to tell me that joke?"

I think that's why I'm uneasy about psychotherapy. I can't win.

Isaac Asimov

As we saw in Chapter 23, each society has dealt with the manifestations of mental disorder according to the prevailing notions of the time. Thus a person who claimed to hear voices might be venerated as a saint in one age, burned as a witch in another, and hospitalized as psychotic in another. And just as the supposed cause of the abnormal behavior has varied, so has the treatment. When people were thought to be possessed by evil spirits, the spirits were let out by trephining of the skull or driven out by exorcism. For many centuries the church was the agency of treatment. During other periods, families kept strangely behaving individuals at home, hidden away in attics or simply cared for as children throughout their lives. In this century, as the institutions of family and church grew weaker, psychotherapy became more important; today it serves many of the advisory and regulatory functions once performed by family and church.

This chapter will examine the ways psychotherapy, on both an individual and a group basis, is used to treat mental disorders today. We will also look at some important organic modes of treatment.

THE NATURE OF PSYCHOTHERAPY

Psychotherapy may be defined as a systematic series of interactions between a therapist trained to aid in solving psychological problems and a person who is troubled or is troubling others. In contrast to the free advice of family and clergy, psychotherapy is a more formal arrangement in which the therapist is a paid professional. Four kinds of professionals are equipped to treat mental disorders. The **psychiatrist** is a medical doctor who has completed three years of residency training in psychiatry. The **psychoanalyst** is a psychiatrist who has had additional training in the technique of psychoanalysis and has been psychoanalyzed. The **clinical psychologist** holds a doctorate in clinical psychology and has completed a one-year internship in psychotherapy. The **psychiatric social worker** has completed two years of postgraduate training in psychotherapy for individuals with psychological problems related to family and social situations.

Different psychotherapists, of course, employ different methods of treatment. Yet all share certain similar goals. In 1973 Sundberg, Tyler, and Taplin

identified seven major purposes that they believe are basic to most kinds of therapy:

1. To strengthen the client's motivation to do the "right things." "Right," a relative term, may be defined by whoever is conducting the therapy, but usually it is in keeping with the client's own desires.

2. To reduce emotional pressure by facilitating the expression of feelings (a process called **catharsis**). Intense emotional outbursts free long-repressed feelings and bring relief.

3. To release the potential for growth. Therapy is directed toward removing obstacles that may block or temporarily reverse a person's potential for growth.

4. To modify the cognitive structure. In order to eliminate irrational beliefs and counterproductive patterns of behavior, individuals are helped to alter concepts and ideas that determine how they view themselves and the world.

5. To develop self-knowledge. Therapy aims at developing the client's insight into his or her own behavior, teaching the client to see the cause-and-effect relationships of his or her actions and their recurring patterns, motivation, and consequences.

6. To learn how to change one's behavior. This is the ultimate goal of most therapies and the particular preoccupation of behavior therapists, who attempt to modify undesirable and ineffective behavior by furnishing new learning experiences.

7. To strengthen interpersonal relationships. According to the theories underlying interpersonal therapy, a person's relationships with "significant others"—either in childhood or in one's present stage of life—hold the key to understanding the emotional disturbance that brings him or her to a psychotherapist.

In practice, these seven purposes are usually embodied in an "eclectic" approach that combines different techniques from different psychotherapies. There are almost as many kinds of therapy as there are clients, each system tailored to meet individual needs. It is possible, however, to distinguish among major therapeutic orientations. Many of these utilize the "one patient, one therapist" model developed by Sigmund Freud and are known as individual therapy. Individual therapy falls into three basic types: the psychodynamic, the behavioral, and the humanistic. Later in the chapter we will look at group therapies, which have evolved from the same therapeutic orientations.

BOXED IN by GIL SPITZER

HE HAD PROBLEMS WITH HIS PARENTS — SO WE TALKED ABOUT IT.

HE HAD PROBLEMS WITH HIS WIFE, — SO WE TALKED ABOUT IT.

HE HAD PROBLEMS WITH HIS KIDS — WE TALKED ABOUT THAT TOO.

HE HAD PROBLEMS PAYING ME FOR TREATMENT, WE'RE NOT TALKING ANYMORE!

© GIL SPITZER '78

Although some forms of therapy like psychoanalysis may sometimes be expensive, other kinds of treatment such as group therapy and services offered by clinics may be quite inexpensive.

PSYCHODYNAMIC THERAPIES

The psychodynamic therapies, particularly psychoanalysis, are closely identified with Freud. Psychoanalysis is at once a general theory of personality, a theory of psychopathology, and a form of psychotherapy. All therapies that focus on a dynamic interplay of conscious and unconscious elements are derived from psychoanalysis. For a variety of reasons, including economic ones, very few practitioners today use standard Freudian psychoanalysis (Korchin, 1976). Although often effective, it is a very long and expensive process.

FREUDIAN PSYCHOANALYSIS As we saw in Chapter 23, Freud's experience with his patients led him to conclude that the source of neurosis was the anxiety experienced when unacceptable unconscious impulses threatened to break through the constraints established by the ego. In order to deal with this threat, the patient would resort to defense mechanisms, the most important of which was repression—the "forgetting" of thoughts and impulses that the conscious mind considered shameful or forbidden. But while the impulse could be hidden for a while, it remained alive in the unconscious, draining strength from the ego, which expended energy in keeping it hidden, and provoking anxiety. According to Freud, the proper treatment for neurosis was

to allow the unacceptable unconscious thoughts to emerge fully into the consciousness, where they could be confronted and "worked through," thus eliminating anxiety and liberating psychic energy for more constructive endeavors.

The basis of psychoanalysis is the uncovering of these long-buried impulses, putting one in touch with one's unconscious, where past traumas and childhood conflicts still live. Various techniques are employed to unlock the door of memory. The client lies on a couch, a relaxing position that helps to loosen the restraints on the unconscious. The client **free-associates**, verbalizing whatever thoughts come to mind in whatever order, without self-censorship, logical structure, or interruption from the therapist, whose remarks are kept at a minimum and who sits out of the patient's view.

The therapist and the patient look for clues to the present anxiety in dreams, in which the usual restraints on the unconscious are loosened (see the box on page 546). However, according to Freud, even in sleep the unconscious is censored and forbidden material appears only in symbolic form. Thus every dream has its **manifest content**, its plot or story line, and its **latent content**, the symbolic meaning of the dream, which exposes unconscious conflicts (see Chapter 18). For example, a client who has just had a baby might dream that she had given birth to two boys and that one had died (manifest content). The symbolic meaning (or latent content) of the dream, however, probably indicates the new mother's feeling of ambivalence toward the child, whom she both wants and doesn't want.

Naturally, the conscious confrontation and recognition of such thoughts are not pleasant. Often at this stage in therapy clients begin to show signs of

Psychodynamically oriented therapists pay particular attention to dreams. Through the process of free association, the hidden meaning of the dream can be brought to light, and unconscious wishes, fantasies, and conflicts can be explored.

A lawyer, twenty-eight years of age, wakes up and remembers the following dream, which he later reports to the analyst: "I saw myself riding on a white charger, reviewing a large number of soldiers. They all cheered me wildly."

The first question the analyst asks his patient is rather general: "What comes to your mind?" "Nothing," the man answers. "The dream is really silly. You know that I dislike war and armies. . . ."

The analyst answers, "Yes, that is quite true . . . [but] in spite of all obvious inconsistencies, the dream must have some meaning. . . . Let us begin with your associations to the dream content. . . ."

"Funny, I now see a picture which I used to like . . . when I was fourteen or fifteen. It is a picture of Napoleon, yes indeed, on a white charger, riding in front of his troops. . . . When I

was fourteen or fifteen I was rather shy. I was not very good at athletics and kind of afraid of tough kids. . . . I liked one of the tough kids very much and wanted to become his friend. . . . One day . . . I approached him [but] . . . he started to laugh and laugh. . . . I turned away, choking with fear. . . . I have not thought of that period for many years."

"You forgot about it, but the other you, that which determines many of your actions and feelings, well hidden from your daytime awareness, is still longing to be famous, admired, to have power. That other you spoke up in your dream last night."

Source: Fromm, *The Forgotten Language.* New York: Grove Press, 1951, pp. 150–152.

---

resistance, or attempts to block treatment. They may pick an argument with the therapist, make jokes, even miss appointments rather than squarely face the unpleasant material. The therapist's interpretation of this avoidance behavior is a very important part of treatment, for one of the goals of psychoanalytic treatment is to help the client identify his or her style of resisting and then to "work through" it.

As the psychoanalysis progresses, the client may transfer to the analyst, who has now shared the client's deepest secrets, feelings of love and hostility that were originally directed toward his or her parents. Through this **transference neurosis**, which involves reenacting with the analyst childhood conflicts with the parents, the client can bring out repressed emotions, unsatisfied needs, and misconceptions, and can begin to deal with them realistically. Traditional psychoanalysis assumes that

in order for the therapeutic process to be successful, the client must go through this stage.

The client attends one-hour psychoanalytic sessions three, four, or five times a week, for several years. In successful psychoanalysis the client eventually breaks through resistance, confronts unconscious conflicts, and resolves the transference neurosis, thereby eliminating anxiety and self-defeating responses to it.

OTHER PSYCHODYNAMIC THERAPIES As we noted in Chapter 18, some of Freud's earliest associates, such as Carl Jung and Alfred Adler, began to modify psychoanalytic theory while Freud was still formulating it. These neo-Freudians developed variations on Freud's techniques of therapy as a result of their theoretical disagreements. Somewhat later Karen Horney, Harry Stack Sullivan, Erich Fromm, Erik Erikson, and others formed a loosely knit group called **ego psychologists**. Whereas Freud maintained that all energy originates in the id and is borrowed by the ego, which merely serves as mediator between reality and the sexual and aggressive desires of the id, the ego psychologists argued that the ego has substantial energy of its own and controls such important functions as memory, judgment, perception, and planning. **Ego analysis** emphasizes the strengthening of the ego to enable the client to control his or her environment and social relationships to his or her greatest satisfaction.

The many variations on psychoanalysis have been called, collectively, psychoanalytically oriented psychotherapy (Korchin, 1976). While therapists with such an orientation feel that training in psychoanalytic theory and techniques enhances their effectiveness, today only a small percentage of them rigorously follow Freud's techniques. Many retain the general psychoanalytic framework, uncovering unconscious motivation, breaking down defenses, and dealing with resistance, but they practice a greatly modified form of psychoanalysis. The couch is generally dispensed with in favor of a situation in which clients sit up and face their therapists and the therapists take a more active role, advising, interpreting, and directing. Moreover, these modern psychotherapists tend to place more emphasis on situations in the present, especially personal relationships, than on events from the distant past. Therapy is briefer and less intensive and usually aims for less than complete restructuring of the client's personality.

HUMANISTIC THERAPIES

Humanistic therapies view psychological treatment as a growth experience. Hence there is no concept of illness, doctor, or patient. Instead therapists help

During psychoanalysis, patients must resolve childhood conflicts that originated in their relationship with their parents.

clients to fulfill their individual human potential. Unlike both behavior therapy and psychodynamic therapies, humanistic therapies emphasize the client's sense of freedom, the ability to choose his or her own future, rather than enslavement to the past. A close client–therapist relationship is encouraged as the therapist attempts to share the client's experience while providing an uncritical atmosphere in which the client's inner strength can emerge.

CLIENT - CENTERED THERAPY The best-known of the humanistic therapies is Carl Rogers' system of **client-centered therapy**, which is also referred to as nondirective counseling. Rogers believed that the client is innately motivated to fulfill her or his own individual potential; the role of the therapist is to help the client clarify feelings and come to value her or his own experience of the world. In order to accomplish this, the therapist must have **congruence**, the ability to share his or her own deepest feelings with the client in an honest way. The therapist must be able to communicate **unconditional positive regard**, nonjudgmental acceptance of the client as a human being. And the therapist must have accurate empathic understanding, the ability to enter into the inner world of the client as if it were his or her own. Instead of interpreting or instructing, the therapist attempts to reflect the client's own feelings and to clarify the client's own views. According to Rogers, as the client becomes more aware of his or her emotions, he or she can make constructive choices that fit in with his or her goals.

GESTALT THERAPY Frederick (Fritz) S. Perls, who developed Gestalt therapy, depended heavily on Freudian ideas for understanding motivation and defense, but his therapeutic technique and philosophical orientation differ considerably from Freud's philosophy and approach to treatment. Gestalt (meaning "whole") therapy attempts to take all of life into consideration. The organism is seen as having an inherent capacity for growth, which is accomplished through insights and interactions with the environment. The ultimate goal is "organismic self-regulation," or balance and integration of the individual. Through awareness, imbalances can be corrected and successful integration of the different aspects of personality can be achieved and maintained.

Therapy is directed at helping the client dispense with defenses, unfold potential, increase awareness, and release pent-up feelings. The three major values of Gestalt therapy are emphasis on the *now*, rather than the past or the future; focus on the *spatial*, what is present rather than what is absent; and concentration on the *substantial*, the act rather than the fantasy (Korchin, 1976, p. 364).

Gestalt therapists employ a variety of techniques to achieve these goals. The client is expected to follow certain rules of communication and language. Communication must be focused on the present and on the client's present awareness, and it must be an exchange between equals. The client is expected to use the first person singular ("I, me, mine") and the active voice ("I am, I do, I feel") to show that he or she takes responsibility for his or her actions and feelings (saying, for example, "I am angry," rather than "Don't you think I have a right to be annoyed?"). Some exercises are designed to heighten the client's awareness of conflicts. The client may be asked to role-play different aspects of his or her personality, shifting from one role to another to experience the conflicting needs and demands. Other exercises develop awareness of the client's own movements, tone of voice, and feelings. When the client has focused awareness on an aspect of self, he or she can then take responsibility for her or his thoughts and actions. In the analysis of dreams in Gestalt therapy, the different characters and objects are seen as fragments of the self, and the client is encouraged to imagine that he or she is each character and object and to express his or her feelings in these roles. This leads to acceptance and reintegration of these aspects of the self.

BEHAVIOR THERAPIES

The treatment techniques of behavior therapy stem directly from laboratory research in learning and conditioning. Basic to the approach of behavior therapy is the belief that *the same learning principles govern all behaviors, normal or deviant.* Behavior therapists regard psychological problems as learned responses that have harmful consequences for the individual or for his or her environment. For these therapists, problem behaviors are not symptoms of unconscious conflicts that must be uncovered, but are themselves the primary and legitimate targets of therapy. Treatment is tailored to the individuals' problems without regard to diagnostic labels such as "neurotic" or to presumed personality traits such as "passive-aggressive."

Behavior therapists also believe that *the environment plays a crucial role in determining behavior and that problem behaviors are specific to given types of situations.* Consequently, behavioral diagnosis requires accurate descriptions of observable behaviors and the environmental events that accompany them. Although behavior therapists do not deny the importance of behaviors they cannot observe, they concentrate their treatment efforts on altering the environmental stimuli that trigger a particular behavior and its consequences rather than speculating on internal motivation or the symbolic meaning of an act.

While behavioral treatment techniques are based on conditioning and laboratory research, they are not mechanistic. Behavior therapists must be able to interact well with others, for the positive reinforcement of desired behaviors is dependent upon a favorable emotional environment (Goldfried and Davison, 1976).

THERAPIES BASED ON CLASSICAL CONDITIONING
Many emotional responses are elicited by stimuli in the environment through classical conditioning. Little Albert's fear of the rat (see Chapter 23) was the result of classical conditioning. When a response such as anxiety is elicited too frequently or by too wide a range of stimuli, behavior therapy will be directed at unlearning the connection and replacing the old conditioned response with a more adaptive response. In some instances a response that produces pleasure but is maladaptive, such as smoking or drinking, is decreased by classical conditioning, using aversive events.

AVERSIVE CONDITIONING The clearest example of a therapeutic technique based on the Pavlovian model is that of **aversive conditioning**, which was discussed in Chapter 21 in connection with efforts to stop smoking. Aversive conditioning aims to reduce the frequency of a response such as smoking cigarettes by pairing an aversive stimulus—say, a mild electric shock—with the natural stimulus that usually precedes the response until the natural stimulus itself becomes aversive.

In the treatment of alcoholism by this method, the presentation of alcohol (conditioned stimulus), including its taste and smell, is paired with an electric shock (unconditioned stimulus)—a stimulus that is tied innately to a pain reaction (unconditioned response). To promote generalization, the setting for this treatment may be highly realistic, with a bar, a bartender, and the client's favorite drink. To bring about the termination of the unpleasant shock stimulus, which is negative reinforcement, and to avoid the positive reinforcement of swallowing alcohol, the client usually must spit out the alcohol before the shock ends. After a sufficient number of pairings, alcohol takes on a stimulus function similar to the shock: the client comes to react with aversion and fear to the sight, smell, and taste of alcohol (conditioned response). Between conditioning trials, the client sips soft drinks or juices—without being shocked—to prevent generalization to all drinking behavior and to promote the use of substitutes for alcohol.

A number of investigators have reported success in using imagined unpleasant events in place of shock, a technique called **covert sensitization**, or **aversive imagery**. For example, a therapist may instruct a smoker to close her eyes, relax, and picture herself taking out a cigarette. As she imagines lighting up and taking a puff, she is told to imagine that she feels nauseated, starts gagging, and vomits all over the floor, the cigarettes, and finally herself. The details of this scene are conjured up with excruciating vividness. The client also rehearses an alternative, "relief" scene in which the decision not to smoke is accompanied by pleasurable sensations. This technique, using no special equipment, has obvious advantages; for instance, clients may carry out conditioning sessions on their own at home.

SYSTEMATIC DESENSITIZATION **Systematic desensitization**, which was discussed in Chapter 21, makes use of the principle of **reciprocal inhibition**. When two responses are mutually incompatible, the occurrence of either one prevents the occurrence of the other. Feelings of tension and anxiety are mutually incompatible with feelings of relaxation and calm. In systematic desensitization the client learns to associate relaxation with the situations that elicit anxiety so that eventually the anxiety is no longer experienced (see Figure 24.1).

Ratings	Hierarchy Items
0	Beginning a new course
5	
10	
15	Hearing an instructor announce a small quiz two weeks hence
20	Having a professor urge you personally to do well on an exam
25	
30	
35	Trying to decide how to study for an exam
40	Reviewing the material I know should be studied—listing study to do
45	
50	
55	
60	Hearing an instructor announce a major exam in three weeks and its importance
	Hearing an instructor remind the class of a quiz one week hence
65	
70	
75	Hearing an instructor announce a major exam in one week
80	Standing alone in the hall before an exam
	Getting an exam back in class
	Anticipating getting back a graded exam later that day
	Talking to several students about an exam right before taking it
85	Thinking about being scared and anxious regarding a specific exam
90	Studying with fellow students several days before an exam
	Hearing some "pearls" from another student which you doubt you'll remember, while studying in a group
	Cramming while alone in the library right before an exam
	Thinking about not keeping up in other subjects while preparing for an exam
95	Thinking about being anxious over schoolwork in general
	Talking with several students about an exam immediately after
100	Thinking about being generally inadequately prepared
	Thinking about not being adequately prepared for a particular exam
	Studying the night before a big exam

Figure 24.1 A graduated hierarchy of situations that elicited different amounts of anxiety from a client being systematically desensitized to tests and examinations. A rating of 100 means "as tense as you ever are"; a rating of zero means "totally relaxed." The behavior that was identified as the target behavior, however, was incorrectly chosen. It turned out that the student's anxieties had to do with disappointing his family; he was not anxious about test-taking in itself. He was then desensitized to his real fear, after which his test anxiety decreased dramatically. (After Kanter and Phillips, 1970.)

THERAPIES BASED ON OPERANT CONDITIONING Systematic desensitization and other therapies based on classical conditioning are most useful in extinguishing maladaptive responses and substituting adaptive ones. But very often the behavior is not so much maladaptive as it is deficient or missing altogether (Goldfried and Davison, 1976). The person has never learned the appropri-ate response, or has been so seldom reinforced for it, that it rarely occurs. In such instances, behavior therapy is directed toward establishing and maintaining an appropriate contingency relationship so that the desired behavior is rewarded.

FINDING THE REINFORCER A positive con-

A scene in a hallway of Camarillo State Hospital in California, where a token economy has been instituted. This room is a positive reinforcer; it is more private and more comfortable than the patients' regular sleeping quarters.

RENT

5 TOKENS

sequence that follows an act reinforces it and increases the probability that the act will be repeated. It is this element of the behavioral formula that most people associate with behavior modification. The problem that clinicians face is identifying for each person the objects or events that actually do function as reinforcers and, if the range is too small, enlarging their number. Consider a little boy who is terrified of going to school. A careful analysis might show that up to this point his mother has been the only social reinforcer in his life. Thus, instead of devising reinforcements for the act of going to school—say, toys or ice cream—treatment might be aimed at increasing the child's range of social reinforcers to include other children and even the teacher.

TOKEN ECONOMIES People in institutions are no longer exposed to the reinforcers that had previously been naturally available. In a **token economy**, clinicians set up systems to provide the positive reinforcement that would otherwise be missing (see the accompanying photograph). Poker chips, slips of paper, or points are awarded for the performance of desired behaviors; patients can exchange the tokens for material goods such as candy, games, and books, or for access to preferred activities, such as watching television, participating in games, and spending time away from the institution. The tokens are known as **conditioned reinforcers**, because the recipients have learned that they are associated with such **primary reinforcers** as food and recreation. Teachers in many schools employ a similar system of token rewards, such as gold stars and honor badges, which earn special privileges for the recipients.

BEHAVIORAL CONTRACTS A more elaborate form of exchanging reinforcements is the contract. Instead of one person giving tokens to another, the two parties agree on behaviors that each desires in the other. These behaviors, along with the rewards and sanctions they agree to exchange contingently, are stipulated in a contract, which both parties sign. An example of a contract is shown in Figure 24.2 on p. 552. Contracts are especially useful in the treatment of marital and family conflicts because they involve each person in a mutual effort to provide reinforcements and to change problem behaviors. Self-control techniques such as those used to stop smoking often take the form of contracts but involve only one person (see Chapter 21).

THERAPIES BASED ON SOCIAL LEARNING

Social learning is one area in which cognitive processes—that is, internal, or covert, events rather than observable responses—make their way into behavior therapy. Albert Bandura (1977a) has developed a theory to explain the effects of social learning techniques on behavior change. He has suggested that the cognitive process that mediates behavior change is the person's "self-efficacy" expectation, the extent to which the person believes he or she can perform the desired behavior effectively. Self-efficacy expectations can be changed by modeling (observing others perform the behavior) and by cognitive restructuring (persuasive communication), discussed below.

MODELING **Modeling** is the process by which the subject learns a new behavior by observing another person performing that behavior. The process depends on the subject's desire to be like the model in some way, and to win the model's approval. A therapist can utilize this modeling principle by winning the client's attention and positive regard and then encouraging imitation as the therapist leads the way to a new, adaptive response. This procedure has

Figure 24.2 A behavioral contract drawn up by a behavior therapist in consultation with a young boy named Dave, his teacher, and his parents. A number of target behaviors and their point values are specified. At the right is space for a record to be kept of Dave's daily performance. At the bottom the consequences of various performance levels are stated precisely. Note that the contract stipulates both rewards for high daily point counts and punishments for low point counts. (Adapted from Patterson, 1971.)

DAVE'S PROGRAM	M	T	W	T	F	S
GETS TO SCHOOL ON TIME (2)	2					
DOES NOT ROAM AROUND ROOM (1)	0					
DOES WHAT THE TEACHER TELLS HIM (5)	3					
GETS ALONG WELL WITH OTHER KIDS (5)	1					
COMPLETES HIS HOMEWORK (5)	2					
WORK IS ACCURATE (5)	3					
BEHAVIOR ON THE SCHOOLBUS IS OK (2)	2					
GETS ALONG WELL WITH BROTHER AND SISTERS IN EVENING (3)	0					
TOTAL	13					

1. If Dave gets 25 points, he doesn't have to do any chores that night, and he gets to pick all the TV shows for the family to watch.
2. If Dave gets only 15 points, he does not get to watch TV that night.
3. If Dave gets only 10 points, he gets no TV and he also has to do the dishes.
4. If Dave gets only 5 points or less, then no TV, wash dishes, and is grounded for the next two days (home from school at 4:00 and stay in yard).

been particularly useful in curing phobias. Bandura (1969) has reported a 90 percent success rate in curing snake phobias through modeling. Similar success has been achieved in eliminating dog phobias in children, by having them observe another child happily playing with a dog (Bandura, Grusec, and Menlove, 1967).

COGNITIVE RESTRUCTURING The process of **cognitive restructuring** focuses on the client's ways of perceiving and regards self-defeating behavior as a result of the client's false assumptions. Consequently, therapy aims at identifying these irrational assumptions and subjecting them to the cold light of reason. Albert Ellis (1962), for example, argues that thousands of people lead unhappy lives because of certain irrational beliefs that they hold, such as "I must be loved and approved of by everyone whose love and approval I seek" or "I must be utterly competent in everything that I do." After recognizing the irrational nature of these long-unexamined beliefs, clients are aided in establishing a more realistic cognitive framework.

Behavior therapists have developed systematic rational restructuring as a parallel to systematic desensitization, using rational reevaluation of situations, rather than relaxation, as the adaptive response (Goldfried, Decenteceo, and Weinberg, 1974). Albert Bandura, Nancy Adams, and Janice Beyer (1977) have shown that the greatest changes in self-efficacy expectations occur when the client works through a hierarchy of anxiety-arousing behaviors. Although Bandura (1977b) has attempted to encompass many of the effects of behavioral treatments within his cognitive model, the response of other behavior therapists to this technique and its ultimate usefulness must yet be determined.

THE DEBATE OVER BEHAVIOR CONTROL

The specter of a "Big Brother" type of control, of the crushing of individual creativity and autonomy, has haunted most ethical and philosophical debates about behavior modification since mid-century, when B. F. Skinner in *Walden Two* (1949) and *Science and Human Behavior* (1967) proclaimed that a behavioral technology was not only feasible but eminently desirable. These debates are complex, but a few simple points can at least place them in context.

Behavior therapy is no more than a technology. It does not stipulate *which* behaviors are desirable or undesirable. It can be used to increase either creative or conforming behaviors. Children may be pos-

Many women today are unhappy because they believe that they must be like women such as England's Prime Minister Margaret Thatcher, easily balancing career, marriage, and children. Behavior therapy involving cognitive restructuring can help to dispel this irrational belief and permit the establishment of realistic priorities.

itively reinforced either for sitting quietly in the classroom or for making imaginative guesses and trying new solutions to problems.

Because the technology is overt, it is open to countercontrols. And if it is true, as the behavioral model proposes, that all of us are always shaped by external contingencies, then the deliberate, open engineering of such contingencies permits a greater, not a lesser, range of choices.

As is the case for other therapeutic approaches, however, the goals for which behavioral techniques are used must be open to constant public scrutiny. The values that determine which behaviors are selected as targets for change must always be made explicit so that they may be subjected to questioning.

GROUP THERAPY

The concept of group therapy can be traced to Joseph Hershey Pratt, a Boston internist who worked with tubercular patients at the turn of the century. In an attempt to relieve the debilitating effects of depression and isolation experienced by the severely ill patients, he began to arrange regular group sessions, instructing his patients to keep diaries of their weight gains and losses, everyday events of their lives, and their general emotional state (Korchin, 1976). During the next thirty years, a number of psychiatrists independently experimented with group methods. In the 1930s and 1940s, group methods applying psychological principles began to evolve. And after World War II, the group-therapy movement gained impetus when it became necessary to treat large numbers of people, both veterans and civilians, who had suffered from the social, political, and economic upheavals of the period.

Group therapy lessens the economic problem that other therapies pose by allowing more patients to be treated at lower fees. But its chief advantage is that it concentrates on and promotes better interpersonal relationships. Moreover, certain problems that are extremely resistant to individual therapy seem to respond to the emotional support of the group. This is particularly true when all members of the group have a problem in common, such as drug addiction, alcoholism, or obesity.

The variety of groups is endless. There are awareness groups for women, men, homosexuals, and divorced people; self-help groups for ex-convicts, chain smokers, and gamblers; and other kinds of groups for a variety of people with a variety of problems, needs, and goals. Each approach to psychotherapy that has been discussed in this chapter has been the basis for the development of a form of group psychotherapy. There are psychoanalytic therapy groups, behavior therapy groups, and humanistic therapy groups (especially Gestalt groups). The therapy in these groups is based on the extension of psychotherapeutic principles into a group setting. There are also some forms of group therapy that are not so easily recognized as outgrowths of individual therapy approaches. Several of these are described below.

FAMILY AND MARITAL THERAPY   In marital and family therapy, the couple or family is viewed as the treatment unit, and the emphasis is on the interactions of the members and the role each takes in the relationship. In the course of living together, each couple or family, consciously or unconsciously, sets up expectations for one another and assigns roles for each person to fill. Thus there may be a "weak" member, a "strong" member, a "caretaker," a "scapegoat." When roles are inappropriate or unduly restrictive, the most fragile member of the unit may exhibit symptoms of mental disturbance, but the assumption is that all members contribute to the breakdown of one member or the whole unit. Ther-

apy aims at examining role expectations and patterns of communication in order to readjust restrictive roles and promote mutual reinforcement.

TRANSACTIONAL ANALYSIS   An offshoot of marital and family therapy is **transactional analysis**, originated by Eric Berne and often employed with groups of couples (see Figure 24.3). Berne's basic idea, described in his popular book *Games People Play* (1964), is that partners set up rules for each other that may satisfy their own neurotic needs but undermine mutual comfort. For example, in the game "Now I've Got You, You Son of a Bitch," one partner provokes or invites exploitative behavior in the other and then complains bitterly of being exploited. The purpose of transactional analysis is to uncover these counterproductive interactions and change the rules of the game to promote mutual satisfaction.

PSYCHODRAMA   **Psychodrama** originated with Vienna's Theater of Spontaneity, founded in 1921 by Jacob Moreno, a Viennese psychiatrist and the first to use the term "group psychotherapy." In psychodrama, individuals are encouraged to take the role of significant persons in their lives, and, together with other group members, act out their emo-

Family therapists believe that, although one member may take the role of "symptom bearer," all members of the family are involved in the disturbance.

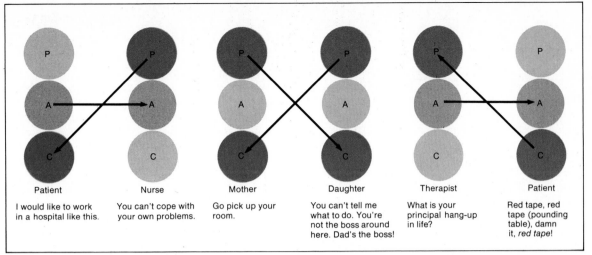

Figure 24.3 Three examples of what Eric Berne describes as "crossed transactions." Drawing an analogy between human relations and economic exchanges, Berne refers to interactions between people as transactions. He considers each personality to be capable of expressing itself as a child (C), an adult (A), or a parent (P) (compare Freud's id, ego, and superego). Berne maintains that normal, or healthy, transactions can be represented in diagrams like these with arrows that run horizontally: adult to adult, parent to parent, child to child. It is not difficult to see that the transactions illustrated here, with their diagonal lines, are ones that lead to trouble. (After Berne, 1964.)

Labels within figure:
- Patient — I would like to work in a hospital like this.
- Nurse — You can't cope with your own problems.
- Mother — Go pick up your room.
- Daughter — You can't tell me what to do. You're not the boss around here. Dad's the boss!
- Therapist — What is your principal hang-up in life?
- Patient — Red tape, red tape (pounding table), damn it, *red tape!*

tional conflicts. One member might take the role of her own authoritarian father, while another member acts out the role of a sister or brother. Therapeutic relief is afforded not only by the expression of pent-up emotions, as in Gestalt therapy, but through revelation of the unconscious motivation for them.

THE EFFECTIVENESS OF PSYCHOTHERAPY

In 1952 Hans Eysenck published a review of five studies of the effectiveness of psychoanalytic treatment and nineteen studies of the effectiveness of "eclectic" psychotherapy, treatment in which several different therapeutic approaches are combined. Eysenck concluded that psychotherapy was no more effective than no treatment at all. According to his interpretation of these twenty-four studies, only 44 percent of the psychoanalytic patients improved with treatment, while 64 percent of those given eclectic psychotherapy were "cured" or had improved. Most startling, Eysenck argued that even this 64 percent improvement rate did not demonstrate the effectiveness of psychotherapy, since it has been reported that 72 percent of a group of hospitalized neurotics improved *without* treatment

(Landis, 1937). If no treatment at all leads to as much improvement as psychotherapy, the obvious conclusion is that psychotherapy is not effective. Eysenck (1966) vigorously defended his controversial position, which generated a large number of additional reviews and a great many studies of the effectiveness of psychotherapy.

One of the most thoughtful and carefully reasoned reviews was written by Allen Bergin (1971). Bergin made the following points in reply to Eysenck. First, he demonstrated that when some different but equally defensible assumptions about the classification of patients were made, the effectiveness of psychoanalytic treatment was much greater than Eysenck had reported; perhaps as many as 83 percent of the patients improved or recovered. Second, he reviewed a number of studies that showed that the rate of improvement without treatment was only about 30 percent.

Bergin's review leads one to question the validity of Eysenck's sweeping generalization that psychotherapy is no more effective than no treatment at all. But much of Bergin's argument is based on differences of opinion about how patients should be classified. Precise criteria for "improvement" are difficult to define and to apply. The nature of "spontaneous remission" (sudden disappearance) of symptoms in persons who have not received formal psychotherapy is difficult to assess, for these people may have received help from unacknowledged sources—friends, relatives, religious advisers, family physicians. And if, as some researchers believe, the prime ingredient in therapy is the establishment of a close relationship, then "spontaneous remission" in people who have received continuing help from such sources is not spontaneous at all.

A recent analysis of nearly 400 studies of the effectiveness of psychotherapy, conducted by Mary Lee Smith and Gene V. Glass (1977), was designed to surmount some of these problems. Smith and Glass devised a statistical technique for summarizing the findings of the entire sample of studies. They found strong evidence for the effectiveness of psychotherapy. The average client who had received therapy scored more favorably on the outcome measures than 75 percent of the persons in the untreated control groups. Smith and Glass also assessed the effectiveness of different types of psychotherapy. The results for the kinds of individual therapy discussed in this chapter are shown in Figure 24.4. All of these therapeutic approaches were shown to be more effective than no treatment. In addition, group therapy was found to be as effective as individual therapy. It may be concluded, then, that psychotherapy is generally more effective than no treatment, and that the differences in effectiveness between the various forms of therapy are small.

Will any therapy do for any client? Probably not. Smith and Glass (1977) were able to show that for some specific clients and situations, some forms of therapy would be expected to have a greater effect than some others. For example, if the client is a thirty-year-old neurotic of average intelligence seen in individual sessions by a therapist with five years of experience, psychodynamic therapy would be expected to have a greater effect than systematic desensitization. But in the case of a highly intelligent

twenty-year-old with a phobia, systematic desensitization would be expected to have greater impact. However, these are educated guesses based on the interpretation of some complex statistical manipulations. Studies designed to answer these kinds of specific questions are now needed. The issue is no longer whether psychotherapy is effective, but which form of therapy and what sort of therapist are most effective for which clients with what kinds of problems. The accompanying box shows some of the factors that seem to influence the outcome of therapy.

ORGANIC APPROACHES TO THERAPY

The various "talking" and "learning" therapies we have described so far in this chapter have been aimed primarily at patients who are still generally capable of functioning within society. But what of those people who are not capable of clear thinking or who are dangerous to themselves or others? For a long time the most common method of keeping dangerous or overactive psychotic patients in check was physical restraint—the straitjacket, wet-sheet wrapping, isolation. The patient was also calmed down by means of lobotomy (brain surgery) and electroconvulsive shock. Sometimes sedation by barbiturates was used, and occasionally insulin-coma therapy, which could be fatal. From the mid-1950s on, however, the use of drugs made it possible to emancipate most patients from these forms of restraint, and even allowed many patients to function

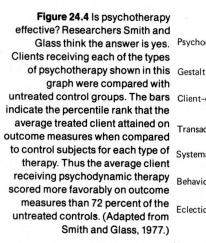

Figure 24.4 Is psychotherapy effective? Researchers Smith and Glass think the answer is yes. Clients receiving each of the types of psychotherapy shown in this graph were compared with untreated control groups. The bars indicate the percentile rank that the average treated client attained on outcome measures when compared to control subjects for each type of therapy. Thus the average client receiving psychodynamic therapy scored more favorably on outcome measures than 72 percent of the untreated controls. (Adapted from Smith and Glass, 1977.)

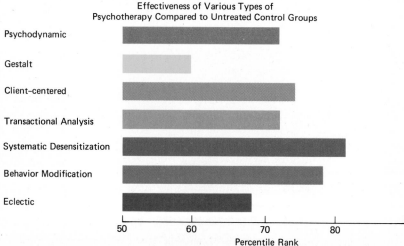

Effectiveness of Various Types of Psychotherapy Compared to Untreated Control Groups

Psychodynamic

Gestalt

Client-centered

Transactional Analysis

Systematic Desensitization

Behavior Modification

Eclectic

50   60   70   80

Percentile Rank

Some Factors That Influence the Outcome of Therapy

1. Initially sicker patients do not improve as much with psychotherapy as the initially healthier do . . . improvement is shown by patients, whatever their initial level of functioning.

2. Patients with higher initial intelligence perform better in psychotherapy.

3. Patients with high anxiety at the initial evaluation or at the beginning of treatment are the ones likely to benefit from psychotherapy. High initial anxiety probably indicates a readiness, or at least an openness, for change . . . almost any affect is better than no affect, and . . . anxiety and depression are probably the two "best" initial affects. The presence of these strong affects may indicate the patient is in pain and asking for help. The absence of affect very likely goes along with a state in which the patient is not reaching out for help, or has given up. . . .

4. Patients with higher social achievements are better suited for psychotherapy.

5. The therapist's empathy (and other related qualities) facilitates the patient's gains from psychotherapy.

6. Greater similarity between therapist and patient is associated with better outcomes. . . The variety of forms of positive similarity includes social class, interests, values, and compatibility or orientation to interpersonal relations. . . .

7. The *combination* of individual and group psychotherapy is better than either individual or group psychotherapy alone.

8. Schools of treatment usually make no measurable difference.

9. In 20 of 22 studies of essentially time-unlimited treatment, the length of treatment was positively related to outcome; the longer the duration of treatment or the more sessions, the better the outcome! Other interpretations: (A) patients who are getting what they need drop out sooner; (B) therapists may overestimate positive change in patients who have been in treatment longer.

10. Psychotherapy with pharmacotherapy appears to be slightly more effective than psychotherapy alone, but in more ways not more effective than pharmacotherapy alone—especially for patients who are schizophrenic.

Source: After Luborsky et al., 1971.

---

outside the hospital. In contrast to individual psychotherapy and hospitalization, psychopharmacological drugs are easily obtained and accessible to all social classes.

Psychopharmacology is now an important science in its own right, gaining impetus from research on the organic basis of schizophrenia and other mental disturbances (discussed in Chapter 23). Drugs have been developed to treat anxiety, schizophrenia, depression, mania, autism, sexual deviation, and mental retardation. Progress in techniques of electroconvulsive therapy and psychosurgery has also been made. Most organic interventions—drugs, electroconvulsive therapy, and psychosurgery—are directed only at the severe, psychotic disorders. They provide relief from symptoms, but cannot bring about permanent cures for the underlying disorder.

ANTIANXIETY DRUGS Commonly known as sedatives or mild tranquilizers, antianxiety drugs are used to reduce excitability and cause drowsiness.

Since anxiety and insomnia are conditions that most people have experienced at one time or another, these drugs are in wide use. The most popular of these drugs are Miltown (meprobamate), Librium (chlordiazepoxide hydrochloride), and Valium (diazepam). In fact, tranquilizers have become so popular that Valium is now the most widely prescribed drug in the world (Ray, 1978).

While these drugs are effective for helping normal people cope with difficult periods in their lives, they are also prescribed for the alleviation of various neurotic symptoms, psychosomatic problems, and symptoms of alcohol withdrawal. The major effect of Valium, Librium, and Miltown is to depress the activity of the central nervous system. If the drugs are taken properly, the side effects are few and consist mainly of drowsiness. However, prolonged use may lead to dependency, and heavy doses taken along with alcohol can result in death.

ANTIPSYCHOTIC DRUGS Antipsychotic drugs are major tranquilizers used to alleviate extreme symptoms of agitation and hyperactivity in psychotic patients (Cole, 1964; Davis, 1965; Goldberg, Klerman, and Cole, 1965). The most popular of these drugs are the phenothiazines, including Thorazine (chlorpromazine) and Stelazine (trifluoperazine hydrochloride), which are widely used in the treatment of schizophrenia. These drugs seem to be most effective in bringing patients out of indifferent and withdrawn states and in reducing thought disorder, the core symptoms of schizophrenia. They seem to be less effective against such secondary symptoms as hallucinations, paranoia, and hostility, and they have no effect on symptoms such as anxiety, guilt, or disorientation. One study concluded that a combination of these drugs with psychotherapy was the most beneficial way of treating severely disturbed patients (Grinspoon, Ewalt, and Shader, 1968). But these drugs do not produce cures; they only alleviate some of the symptoms of the disorder and may allow the patients to benefit from other forms of therapy. And they may have side effects, such as dry mouth, lowered blood pressure, slightly blurred vision, and abnormal movements or tightness of the muscles.

ANTIDEPRESSANT DRUGS The antidepressant drugs were discovered by accident in 1952 when Irving Selikof and his colleagues, treating patients for tuberculosis with a drug called Iproniazid, noticed that it produced a mood elevation. Further investigation of mood regulators has resulted in the more recent use of less toxic antidepressants such as Tofranil.

Lithium, relatively new to the psychiatric community in the United States, has been widely used in Europe for the past twenty years to treat manic-depressive psychosis. It is effective in returning patients to a state of emotional equilibrium in which extreme swings of mood do not occur. Lithium is toxic to the kidneys, however, and patients taking the drug must be monitored carefully by a physician.

ELECTROCONVULSIVE THERAPY "Shock treatment," as **electroconvulsive therapy** (ECT) is commonly called, has proven extremely effective in the treatment of depression, though no one understands exactly how it works (Greenblatt, Grosser, and Wechsler, 1964). It involves administering, over several weeks, a series of brief electrical shocks of approximately 70 to 130 volts. The shock induces a convulsion similar to an epileptic seizure. As it is now applied, ECT entails very little discomfort for the patient. Prior to treatment, the patient is given a sedative and injected with a muscle relaxant to alleviate involuntary muscular contractions and prevent physical injury. Even with these improvements, however, ECT is a drastic treatment and must be used with great caution. Common side effects include temporary loss of memory, which may even continue for several years.

PSYCHOSURGERY Psychosurgery is the most extreme of all the organic treatments. It involves high risks for the patient and irreversible surgical effects. In 1935, Egas Moniz and Almeida Lima developed the procedure known as **prefrontal lobotomy**, in which a surgical cut is made between the brain's frontal lobes (thought center) and the thalamus (emotional center). It was expected that the interruption in communication between these two parts of the brain would help reduce the impact of disturbing stimuli in cases of severe mental disorder. Over the next twenty years other methods of psychosurgery evolved, and thousands of operations were performed. While some severely disturbed patients were helped by these procedures, many were left in childlike and lethargic states, and others died on the operating table. In the 1950s, the discovery of drugs that calmed the severely disturbed brought a halt to most psychosurgery.

Today the surgical techniques of the 1940s and 1950s have been abandoned in favor of "fractional operations," which destroy very small amounts of brain tissue in precise locations (Valenstein, 1973). Such operations are performed on about 400 patients a year in the United States, and then only after all other modes of treatment have been exhausted. The National Commission for the Protection of Human Subjects in Biomedical and Behavioral Research released a report in 1976 that concluded that these new procedures have been beneficial in cases of depression and depression associated with intractable pain. Furthermore, the serious side effects and risks associated with lobotomy appear not to occur with the new techniques. The commission encouraged further research, but recommended that for now psychosurgery be considered an experimental procedure to be employed only under the most stringent safeguards of the rights and welfare of the patient.

COMMUNITY MENTAL HEALTH

It is seldom easy for a person who has been hospitalized for a mental disorder to reenter society. Often released patients find themselves too far from the hospital for any supplementary care and too fragile to cope independently with the pressures of the outside world. If these patients are to make a successful return to the community, the community may have to provide some support.

COMMUNITY MENTAL HEALTH CENTERS

The Community Mental Health Centers Act of 1963 was designed to solve some of the problems faced by patients trying to reenter society. One mental health center was mandated for every 50,000 members of the U.S. population, to supply needed psychological services for the ex-patient attempting to function within the community. Other purposes of these centers were to educate community workers such as police, teachers, and clergy in the principles of preventive mental health, to train paraprofessionals, and to carry out research. A countrywide system of mental health centers has not yet been achieved, and funding for existing centers has been cut back in many cities; but those centers that are in operation supply important services— outpatient, inpatient, and emergency services and community consultation.

Outpatients can walk into a clinic and receive therapy once, twice, or several times a week, without leaving school, job, or family, and without feeling stigmatized as institutionalized mental patients. The centers also serve as a bridge between hospitalization and complete independence by giving aftercare and supplementary services to patients released from hospitals.

For the more severely disturbed, hospitalization can be provided within the community. Friends and family have easy access to patients, who feel less isolated and more accepted. Many centers have arrangements for day hospitals, in which patients take advantage of the support systems and therapy offered by a hospital during the day and go home at night. Night hospitals work in a similar manner:

patients may work or go to school during the day and spend the night at the hospital.

Many community mental health centers also maintain storefront clinics that are open around the clock to deal with such emergencies as acute anxiety attacks, suicide attempts, and bad drug trips. The centers may have teams of psychologically trained personnel on call to go to city hospital emergency rooms to deal with psychological traumas.

Mental health centers provide qualified personnel to serve as consultants to other community workers, such as teachers, police, and clergy, advising them on how to handle psychological problems in the classroom and within the community. Sensitivity workshops give instruction on such matters as how to intervene in potentially violent family quarrels, how to talk potential suicides out of jumping off a bridge, and how to keep truants from dropping out of school.

HALFWAY HOUSES Halfway houses, so named because they are an intermediate step between the hospital and the community, are houses in which individuals with common problems live together, providing support for one another and using whatever supplementary services are necessary until they are able to function entirely on their own. These houses have proliferated in recent years and have been quite useful in the transition from hospital care to community life. They have been successful in the rehabilitation of drug addicts, newly released mental patients, ex-convicts, and alcoholics. Reports (for example, Fairweather et al., 1969) indicate that such individuals are less likely to require rehospitalization than those who have been returned to the community with no supplementary support system.

CRISIS INTERVENTION: THE HOT LINE Community services of the type outlined above are costly and complicated to set up, but the crisis hot line provides an instant, economical, and effective way to deal with emergency situations. People who are in trouble can telephone at any time and receive immediate counseling, sympathy, and comfort. The best known of these systems is the Los Angeles Suicide Prevention Center, established in 1958. Similar hot lines have been set up for alcoholics, rape victims, battered women, runaway children, gamblers, and people who just need a shoulder to cry on. In addition to providing sympathy, hot-line volunteers give information on the community services available to deal with each kind of problem.

PREVENTION The basic goals of community psychology are to prevent the development of disorder (called primary prevention), to prevent the worsening of disorder (secondary prevention), and to prevent the severe effects of major disorder on the victim and on society (tertiary prevention). Primary prevention of mental disorder is very desirable but extremely difficult. It requires changing those aspects of society and the environment that lead to psychological disturbance, and we have seen in Chapter 23 how complex the causes of disorder can be. Nevertheless, nutritional counseling, genetic counseling, and the design of less stressful school environments are all potentially important methods of reducing the incidence of disorder.

Secondary prevention, the early detection and treatment of problems before they become severe, is somewhat less complex, but is still no easy task. Outpatient clinics, emergency services, hot lines, and some paraprofessional programs are examples of secondary prevention. Early detection of problems usually requires a trained professional, but consultation programs with schools and law enforcement agencies are a means of expanding secondary prevention.

Tertiary prevention programs include the day hospitals and night hospitals and the halfway houses described above. These programs are designed to help those who have suffered a serious disorder to resume useful roles in society, and to prevent the recurrence of disorder.

The prevention of disorder is the goal of the community mental health movement, but some psychologists maintain that this has led to a preoccupation with the delivery of individual services, whereas the major goal should be the improvement of social conditions. The development of effective human beings in communities that have the resources and skills to provide their residents with satisfying lives is the goal of the newly emerging specialty of community psychology. Leonard Goodstein and Irwin Sandler (1978) maintain that community psychologists should focus on the design of social systems that foster health and growth. If that goal is achieved, the incidence of psychological disorder will be significantly reduced. But a society cannot be changed quickly, and while we wait for the development of a vigorous community psychology, those individuals affected by psychological disorder must be treated with the best methods available.

SUMMARY

1. **Psychotherapy** is a systematic series of interactions between a therapist trained to aid in solving psychological problems and a person who is troubled or is troubling others. Its goal is to produce emotional, cognitive, or behavioral changes in order to alleviate the problem. Four kinds of professionals are equipped to treat mental disorders: **psychiatrists, psychoanalysts, clinical psychologists**, and **psychiatric social workers**.

2. The psychodynamic therapies are closely identified with Freud. All therapies that focus on a dynamic interplay of conscious and unconscious elements are derivations of psychoanalysis.

   A. Techniques used in psychoanalysis include **free association** and the interpretation of the **manifest content** and **latent content** (symbolic meaning) of dreams. **Resistance**, or attempts by the client to block treatment, must

often be dealt with. **Transference neurosis** occurs when the client transfers to the analyst feelings of love and hostility originally directed toward the parents.

   B. The variations on psychoanalysis have been collectively called psychoanalytically oriented psychotherapy. This includes the **ego psychologists**, neo-Freudians who emphasized **ego analysis**, the strengthening of the ego to enable clients to control their environment and social relationships. Modern psychotherapy tends to emphasize present situations, is briefer and less intensive than traditional psychoanalysis, and usually aims for less than a complete restructuring of the clients' personalities.

3. Humanistic therapies view psychological treatment as a growth experience. Therapists help clients to fulfill their individual potential by em-

phasizing their sense of freedom and their ability to choose their own future.

A. In Carl Rogers' system of **client-centered therapy**, or nondirective counseling, the role of the therapist is to help the client clarify feelings and come to value his or her own experience of the world. Therapists must have **congruence**, the ability to share their own deepest feelings with the client, and must communicate **unconditional positive regard**, nonjudgmental acceptance of the client.

B. The goal of Gestalt therapy, which attempts to take all of life into consideration, is "organismic self-regulation," or balance and integration of the individual. The three major values of Gestalt therapy are emphasis on the now, focus on the spatial, and concentration on the substantial. Clients are expected to follow certain rules of communication and language, which helps them take responsibility for their thoughts and actions.

4. Behavior therapies view all behavior as learned in response to a particular social and physical environment. Behavior therapy techniques stem directly from laboratory research in learning and conditioning.

A. When an undesirable response is elicited too frequently or by too wide a range of stimuli, therapy based on classical conditioning is directed at helping the client unlearn the connection and replace the old conditioned response with a more adaptive response.

1. **Aversive conditioning** aims to reduce the frequency of a response by pairing an aversive (unpleasant) stimulus (such as a shock) with the natural stimulus that usually precedes the response until the natural stimulus itself becomes aversive. **Covert sensitization**, or **aversive imagery**, involves the use of imagined unpleasant events in place of an actual shock or other aversive stimulus.

2. **Systematic desensitization** makes use of the principle of **reciprocal inhibition**: when two responses are mutually incompatible, the occurrence of one prevents the occurrence of the other.

B. When appropriate behavior is deficient or missing altogether, therapies based on operant conditioning are used in order to establish and maintain an appropriate contingency relationship so that the desired behavior is rewarded.

1. Clinicians attempt to identify for each person the objects or events that function as reinforcers and, if the range is too small, to enlarge their number.

2. In a **token economy**, clinicians set up systems of rewards to provide the positive reinforcement for desired behavior that would otherwise be missing. The tokens serve as **conditioned reinforcers** because they are associated with such **primary reinforcers** as food and recreation.

3. Behavioral contracts involve an exchange of reinforcements. Two parties agree on behaviors that each desires in the other.

C. Therapies based on social learning involve cognitive processes rather than observable responses. "Self-efficacy" expectation is Albert Bandura's term for the extent to which a person believes that he or she can perform the desired behavior effectively. Two methods of changing self-efficacy expectations are modeling and cognitive restructuring.

1. **Modeling** is the process by which subjects learn a new behavior by observing another person performing that behavior.

2. **Cognitive restructuring** focuses on the client's ways of perceiving in order to identify irrational, self-defeating assumptions. The client is then helped in establishing a more realistic cognitive framework.

D. Behavior control has long been the subject of debate because of the fear that it will crush individual creativity and autonomy. However, behavior therapy is just a technology: it does not stipulate *which* behaviors are desirable or undesirable, and it is open to counter-controls.

5. Group therapy concentrates on and promotes better interpersonal relationships, and is able to handle certain problems that are resistant to individual therapy because of the emotional support that a group provides.

A. In family therapy and marital therapy, the emphasis is on the interactions of the members and the role each takes in the relationship.

B. An offshoot of marital therapy is **transactional analysis**, which is based on the idea that partners set up rules for each other.

C. In **psychodrama**, individuals take on the roles of significant persons in their lives and act out their emotional conflicts.

6. Hans Eysenck's contention that psychotherapy is no more effective than no therapy at all touched off a number of studies on the subject. A problem in determining the effectiveness of psychotherapy is the difficulty in defining precise criteria for improvement in patients. An analysis by Smith and Glass of nearly 400 studies on the effectiveness of psychotherapy concluded that psychotherapy is generally more effective than no treatment, and that differences in effectiveness between the various forms of therapy are small. However, for some specific clients and situations, certain forms of therapy would be expected to have a greater effect than others.

7. Most organic approaches to therapy are directed only at the severe, psychotic disorders. They provide relief from symptoms, but cannot bring about permanent cures for the underlying disorder.
   A. Antianxiety drugs (such as Valium) are mild tranquilizers used to reduce excitability and cause drowsiness.
   B. Antipsychotic drugs (such as Thorazine) are major tranquilizers used to alleviate extreme symptoms of agitation and hyperactivity in psychotic patients.
   C. Antidepressant drugs (such as lithium) are used to regulate patients' moods.
   D. **Electroconvulsive therapy** is effective in the treatment of depression, but is a drastic treatment with serious side effects.
   E. Psychosurgery is the most extreme of all the organic treatments. It is used today only when all other treatments have failed.

8. Community mental health programs are caregiving links between mental hospitals and the community.
   A. Community mental health centers provide outpatient, inpatient, and emergency services and community consultation.
   B. Halfway houses are an intermediate step between the hospital and the community where individuals with common problems live together, providing support for one another.
   C. The crisis hotline is an instant, economical, and effective means of dealing with emergency situations.
   D. The basic goals of community psychology are to prevent the development of disorder (primary prevention), to prevent the worsening of disorder (secondary prevention), and to prevent the severe effects of major disorder on the victim and on society (tertiary prevention).

RECOMMENDED READINGS

BERGIN, ALLEN E., and SOL L. GARFIELD. *Handbook of Psychotherapy and Behavior Change: An Empirical Analysis.* New York: Wiley, 1971. The most comprehensive collection of readings on psychotherapy. It contains sections on experimentation in psychotherapy, analysis of therapies, and discussions of a variety of therapeutic approaches.

CORSINI, RAYMOND J. (ed.). *Current Psychotherapies.* Itasca, Ill.: Peacock Publishers, 1973. Most of the chapters were written by distinguished leaders of the various approaches, and major current therapies are covered. Each author follows the same format and outline, which makes comparison of therapies easier.

GOLANN, STUART E., and CARL EISDORFER (eds.). *Handbook of Community Mental Health.* New York: Appleton-Century-Crofts, 1972. A monumental work covering both the history and the latest developments in community psychology from conceptualization to practice.

GURMAN, ALAN S., and ANDREW M. RAZIN (eds.). *Ef-fective Psychotherapy: A Handbook of Research.* Elmsford, N.Y.: Pergamon, 1977. A collection of research articles on all aspects of psychotherapy by leaders in the field; an excellent overview.

KORCHIN, SHELDON J. *Modern Clinical Psychology.* New York: Basic Books, 1976. A comprehensive survey of all aspects of clinical practice, with clear presentations and comparisons of various therapeutic approaches.

LANYON, RICHARD I., and BARBARA P. LANYON. *Behavior Therapy: A Clinical Introduction.* Reading, Mass.: Addison-Wesley, 1978. Skillfully combines the theoretical basis of behavior therapy with case illustrations, including a complete report on a single case that was treated with a wide range of behavioral techniques.

WOLPE, JOSEPH. *Theme and Variations: A Behavior Therapy Casebook.* New York: Pergamon, 1976. Detailed case reports illustrating a variety of behavioral techniques as used by one of the founders of behavior therapy.

PART EIGHT

SOCIAL PSYCHOLOGY

In some respects the phenomena studied by social psychologists are the most familiar and "obvious" ones in psychology, even to people who have never taken a psychology course. The processes of social interaction—forming and changing attitudes, making friends and falling in love, joining and being influenced by social groups, functioning as a member of a community and a society—are highly visible to all of us most of the time. Yet precisely because of that familiarity, many of us take the processes of social interaction for granted and assume that we understand them. But the scientific study of these processes has revealed that the common-sense view of "how things are" is often wrong. The chapters in Part Eight are intended to promote a deeper and more accurate understanding of social processes, and much of what they have to say may be surprising.

Chapter 25, "Attitudes and Attitude Change," describes the nature of attitudes and the ways in which attitudes are formed and changed. In Chapter 26, "Person Perception and Interpersonal Attraction," we consider how people form and integrate their impressions of one another and how people are attracted to one another, form friendships, and fall in love.

Chapter 27, "Social Influence and Social Groups," examines the universal human need for social contact, the impact of social influence on individual behavior, and the social significance of groups. Finally, Chapter 28, "Conflict and Cooperation," focuses on aggression and altruism to clarify the "human dilemma" of competition versus cooperation, concluding with a discussion of the factors that may facilitate cooperative social behavior.

CHAPTER TWENTY-FIVE

ATTITUDES AND ATTITUDE CHANGE

In 1840 the Democratic party, which had been in power for twelve years, was running President Martin Van Buren for reelection. The opposition Whig party, given little chance to win, nominated General William Henry Harrison, who had made his reputation fighting Indians. A Baltimore newspaper, of Democratic persuasion, printed a comment to the effect that all Harrison needed was a small pension and a jug of hard cider and he would be content to sit in a log cabin the rest of his days and do nothing. The implication was that he was an empty person, serving as a front for ambitious politicians.

Some genius of public relations seized upon this statement, and there began the most remarkable presidential campaign in American history. Harrison became the log-cabin-and-hard-cider candidate. There were log-cabin badges, log-cabin songs, log-cabin floats, log-cabin rallies, and hard cider everywhere, some poured out of containers shaped like log cabins.

The campaign included a studied attempt to picture Van Buren as a cultured aristocrat. One famous campaign song began:

Let Van from his coolers of sil-
  ver drink wine,
  And lounge on his cush-
  ioned settee;
Our man on his buckeye
  bench can recline,
  Content with hard cider is
  he.

The fact of the matter, of course, was that Harrison was born not in a log cabin (as the electorate came to believe) but on a Virginia plantation. He was thoroughly educated and came from a more aristocratic background than Van Buren. What's more, his party, the Whigs, was the party of the upper classes. Nevertheless, the American people—many more of whom were at the log-cabin stage than at the cushioned-settee stage—deliriously identified themselves with Harrison, and he won the election.

The 1840 campaign fundamentally changed political strategy in American elections. Until then, it had been assumed that to impress the people, you ought to present a nominee as a person of education, ability, experience, refinement, and all the other qualities that people were supposed to admire. After that, however, every candidate tried to show himself as fundamentally illiterate at heart.

In 1940, exactly a century later, when Wendell Willkie ran for president on the Republican ticket, his campaign managers played down the fact that he was an educated lawyer and the son of a lawyer, as well as a most successful businessman. They strove instead to emphasize the fact that he was born in a small midwestern town, in contrast to President Roosevelt's undeniable background of aristocracy.

The Democratic Secretary of the Interior, Harold Ickes, demolished that strategy in a caustic and well-publicized phrase that termed Willkie "the barefoot boy from Wall Street."

The strategy, which continues today, is aimed at having just-plain-folks identify with the candidate, identification being a process through which attitude change takes place. A citizen who identifies with your candidate is a voter you want to see go to the polls.

Isaac Asimov

In the early months of 1970 American involvement in the Vietnam War appeared to be winding down. It had been an expensive, unpopular, and ineffective venture, and President Richard Nixon had promised to put an end to it. But on April 30 he announced that American warplanes and troops had been sent into Cambodia, South Vietnam's neighbor to the west, to destroy "enemy sanctuaries" (staging areas and supply depots set up by the North Vietnamese forces). This widening of the scope of the war provoked furious antiwar demonstrations on college campuses across the United States. These were the most impassioned and widespread college protests in American history: about 1.5 million students and half the country's 2,500 campuses were involved. Roger Heyns, chancellor of the University of California, described the demonstrations on the Berkeley campus this way:

> The power and strength of this outburst was awesome. It was a great groundswell, a tidal movement of genuine feeling and opinion on the part of most students and many faculty, expressive of real concern over the present problems and the future destiny of the United States. There has been nothing like it before in American history. It was real and it had to be heeded. No one on campus doubted this. (quoted in Thistlethwaite, 1974, p. 228)

On May 4 at Kent State University in Ohio four students were killed and ten wounded by National Guard troops called in to quell the demonstrations there. On May 14 at Jackson State College in Mississippi two students were killed and twelve wounded by police gunfire. Protests against these shootings were added to the protests against the Cambodian invasion.

At least partly in response to these widespread public expressions of revulsion against the war, the rate of withdrawal of American troops from Vietnam was accelerated; however, the bombing of North Vietnam was not merely continued but expanded. By the summer of 1971, although the war was as unpopular as ever, student protest had dropped back to the somewhat lower levels of 1969.

This episode reveals some basic features of attitudes and attitude change. It provides evidence that (1) major issues or events, like the invasion of Cambodia and the shootings at Kent State and Jackson State, can bring forth the public expression of people's attitudes; (2) events can change or in-

War brings out our deepest feelings. People's attitudes toward the Vietnam War, both for and against, were extremely intense.

tensify attitudes, as the invasion and the campus shootings intensified protests against the government's Vietnam policy; and (3) people's attitudes tend to remain fairly consistent over time, as shown by the fact that by 1971 student antiwar protest had returned to 1969 levels (Thistlethwaite, 1974). It seems clear, too, that our attitudes can greatly influence the course of our lives. In this chapter we will examine the nature of attitudes and the ways in which they are formed and changed.

THE NATURE OF ATTITUDES

People have attitudes about an enormous number of subjects. We have attitudes about and opinions of political candidates, remedies for inflation, the value of a college education, the style of life we want, our roommates and friends, and countless other topics. Because our attitudes influence our behavior, public-opinion polling has virtually become a national pastime. Large survey-research firms like the Gallup and Harris organizations compile thousands of responses yearly to questions about everything from Presidents to pollution. And almost every major corporation conducts consumer surveys to collect information on people's attitudes about subjects as diverse as toothpaste preferences and banking needs. The nature of attitudes, then, is a topic of wide public interest.

DEFINING ATTITUDES Although it is easy to compile a list of different kinds of attitudes, the concept of "attitude" itself is difficult to define precisely. For purposes of analysis, attitudes can be described as having two components: the cognitive and the affective. Our attitude toward a particular senator, for example, is partially determined by the various cognitions we have about that person. Does the senator support or oppose school busing? Increased defense spending? A cut in taxes? Is the senator responsive to all constituents' needs or susceptible to special interests? Cognitions, however, are simply collections of facts and beliefs; they are not in themselves attitudes. An attitude results from the affective response that we associate with our cognitions. If we *like* the senator's stand on busing or defense spending or tax cuts, our attitude toward him or her will be favorable. It has been suggested that our attitude toward an object—a person, a situation, a behavior—is based on the extent to which we believe the object has various attributes or consequences that we evaluate as pertinent. We integrate or combine our various beliefs to arrive at an evaluation of the object—and hence at an attitude toward the object (Fishbein and Ajzen, 1975). It has also been suggested, more simply, that "Attitudes are likes and dislikes" (Bem, 1970, p. 14).

In any case, for our purposes an **attitude** may be defined as a relatively enduring evaluation formed on the basis of knowledge and beliefs on the one hand and affective reactions on the other. Moreover, our attitudes often predispose us to act in certain ways. That is, those objects toward which we have positive attitudes we generally seek out, while those objects toward which we have negative attitudes we typically shun.

CAN ATTITUDES PREDICT BEHAVIOR? It does not follow, however, that knowing a person's attitudes automatically allows us to predict how he or she will behave in any particular situation. In fact, attitudes are sometimes quite inconsistent with behavior. This was suggested by a classic study conducted in the 1930s by Richard LaPiere (1934). He traveled around the United States with a Chinese couple, expecting to encounter anti-Oriental attitudes that would make it difficult for them to find places to sleep and eat. But this was not at all the case. "In something like ten thousand miles of motor travel," wrote LaPiere, "twice across the United States, up and down the Pacific Coast, we met definite rejection from those asked to serve us just once" (p. 232). Judging by the friendly behavior of the innkeepers and tradespeople they encountered, one might conclude that Americans were almost entirely free of prejudice against Orientals. This, however, was not true. LaPiere followed up his travels by writing a letter to each of the 251 establishments he and his Chinese friends had visited, asking whether they would provide food or lodging to members of the Chinese race. Of the 128 who responded (who, it must be noted, were not necessarily the same people the travelers had encountered), over 90 percent answered with a flat No. Only one said Yes, and the rest said their decision would depend on the circumstances. People's attitudes toward serving Chinese, then, seemed to be extremely inconsistent with the behavior they had already shown. (For further discussion of racist—and sexist—attitudes, see the accompanying special feature.)

This discrepancy between attitudes and behavior has since been confirmed. In one study (Wicker, 1971), for example, the attitudes of people toward their church were measured against three church-related behaviors: the frequency of church attendance, the amount of church contributions, and the degree of participation in church activities. It seems reasonable to expect that people who expressed the strongest, most positive attitudes toward their church would be most inclined to attend services, make contributions, and participate in church activities. There was a slight tendency in this direction, but in general, the correlation between attitudes and behavior was very weak. In fact, simple knowledge of a person's attitude toward the church was practically useless in predicting that person's church-related behavior.

Because the relationship between attitudes and behavior can be inconsistent, some psychologists have suggested abandoning the concept of attitudes entirely. After all, they reason, if the concept is not indicative of behavior, of what practical use is it?

Sexism and Racism as Attitudes

The terms racism and sexism refer to patterns of attitudes and behavior directed against particular groups. In the case of racism, the most common target for the white majority in the United States is black people. In the case of sexism, the pattern of attitudes and behavior is directed by men against women. The words racism, prejudice, and discrimination are often used interchangeably, but there are clear distinctions to be made among them. **Racism** and **sexism** are general terms denoting a pattern of attitudes and behavior. Racism and sexism can both be considered to have two components, prejudice and discrimination.

Prejudice and Discrimination: Attitude and Behavior

Prejudice refers to the negatively toned attitudes and opinions about a racial minority or about women. Thus, prejudice can be considered an attitude with belief and evaluation components just like those of all the other attitudes discussed in this chapter. In most instances of prejudice, however, the beliefs are either exaggerated or untrue, and the evaluations associated with those beliefs are usually very negative.

Discrimination is the behavioral expression of prejudice and refers to specific practices, such as excluding women or members of racial minorities from certain kinds of activities, jobs, organizations, or educational opportunities. As we have noted in this chapter, however, attitudes and behavior are not always closely linked. A person may be prejudiced without showing discriminatory behavior, and, conversely, a person may exhibit discriminatory behavior in response to group pressure without truly holding any attitude of prejudice.

How are attitudes of prejudice acquired? Almost always, racial and sexual prejudice is based on stereotypes. A **stereotype** is a standardized belief or collection of beliefs about a certain group. Once an individual is identified as a member of that group, all the characteristics associated with the stereotype are believed to apply to that person. Thus, if a man considers *all* women to be passive and helpless, he will regard *any* woman as passive and helpless, no matter how aggressive and competent her behavior shows her to be. The evaluation associated with each of those stereotypic beliefs forms the generally negative attitude—the prejudice—against members of racial and ethnic minorities and against women.

As with other attitudes, these stereotypic beliefs are acquired through the processes of social learning (see Chapters 10 and 19). Children learn gender role stereotypes at a very early age, and children of prejudiced parents learn the stereotypic beliefs about members of racial and ethnic minorities by observing and imitating their parents. For many years the mass media —movies, radio, and television—were also guilty of transmitting racial and gender role stereotypes. Recently, attempts have been made to present a more accurate, balanced picture of racial minorities and women, particularly on television and in advertisements (as the photographs here indicate).

Negative attitudes about racial and ethnic groups may also be the result of intergroup conflict and economic competition. As a racial or ethnic minority attempts to establish a more favorable position for itself in the economy and in society in general, members of that minority come into conflict with the dominant group, and the conflict leads to the development of hostility.

A series of field experiments conducted by Muzafer Sherif

Wake up and get down with breakfast at McDonald's.
We do it all for you
McDonald's

When the heat's on, Sure helps keep me dry.

I'm a professional research analyst and that means that at the end of every project I have to give the results of my findings to the people who hired me. And when you have to stand up in front of a roomful of people, the last thing you want to worry about is your antiperspirant. Which is why I depend on Sure anti-perspirant.

Sure sprays on dry and really helps keep me dry. In fact, Sure keeps me so dry, that even when I'm under pressure I still feel confident. And when everyone is looking at you, that's a nice thing to know.

and his colleagues (1961) provide a good illustration of this process. Groups of young boys at summer camp were placed in situations of intergroup conflict. Residents of each cabin sat at their own table for meals and encountered other cabin residents only in competitive situations, such as inter-cabin races and tugs-of-war. Before long, negative stereotypes of the other groups developed in each of the competing groups. Overt hostility, in the form of raids and fights, arose from the climate of competition and conflict.

There is some evidence that certain personality characteristics predispose an individual to prejudice and discrimination. The most carefully developed account of such a personality structure is presented in a classic book, *The Authoritarian Personality* (Adorno et al., 1950). The authoritarian personality is characterized by submissive obedience to higher authority, on the one hand, and the demand for obedience from those perceived to be subordinate, on the other hand. The individual with an authoritarian personality also perceives the world in terms of a set of rigidly applied either-or categories. Ideas are either right or wrong. Other people are either good or bad, friends or enemies. Members of any alien group, then, are rejected and the authoritarian exhibits both prejudice and discrimination against them. Although the relationship between the authoritarian personality pattern and racism or sexism has not always been confirmed by research, there does seem to be at least a weak relationship between such personality traits and prejudice.

While behavior and attitudes are not always closely linked, the recent work of Icek Ajzen and Martin Fishbein (1977) has indicated that attitudes will predict behavior—including discriminatory behavior—if appropriate measurement techniques are used. For our purposes, it is sufficient to note that discriminatory behavior does occur and has been extremely widespread in this country.

James Jones (1972) has identified two distinct patterns of discriminatory behavior manifested by racists. The first type of racist is the **dominative racist**, who engages in specific acts of suppression or violence, or both, against the racial minority. In this country such practices have included lynchings, beatings, and vandalism perpetrated in an attempt to dominate and suppress racial or ethnic minorities. The other type is the **aversive racist**, who attempts to avoid contact with the minority. The aversive racist may claim to be liberal and unprejudiced, but still engages in a pattern of behavior designed to exclude members of the racial minority from neighborhoods, from club and church membership, and from contact on an equal footing.

Discrimination against women in our culture does not really fit either of these categories. Women are, of course, accorded the closest degrees of intimacy with men, so in that sense they are not the victims of aversive sexism. Nor are most women abused in the same way that the dominative racist mistreats black people. The behavior of men toward women seems to be closely tied to the gender role stereotype: women are viewed—and treated—as less competent, less aggressive, more emotional, and in need of the protection of men.

Eliminating Sexism and Racism

Sherif's research team (1961) found that intergroup cooperation was an effective means for bridging the gap that had been created between the competitive groups of young campers. When situations were contrived in which the two groups had to cooperate in order to achieve an urgent common goal—for example, repairing a water main that had mysteriously "broken"—the intergroup tension began to dissipate, and friendships began to form across group boundaries. More recent research (Aronson et al., 1975) has shown that the racial tensions created by forced busing of schoolchildren for the purpose of integrating schools can be reduced by structuring classroom activities to foster cooperation between racial groups.

Since prejudice is an attitude and discrimination the behavioral expression of that attitude, can the problem be solved by changing the beliefs that support that attitude and behavior? Can we change the stereotypes that exist about racial and ethnic minorities and about women? As a first step, agents of socialization—parents, media, teachers—must change their own behavior in order to reduce the extent to which children develop such stereotypes through social learning. There is some evidence that this process has begun and is spreading, but stereotypes persist (Karlins, Coffman, and Walter, 1969).

It seems, then, that racism and sexism will not easily be rooted out of American life. Nevertheless, there is hope that as more and more of us become aware of the terrible costs of racism and sexism, we may become more careful in our language and our behavior so that stereotypes are not transmitted so widely and effectively to each new generation.

However, other psychologists argue that it is unrealistic to expect attitudes to correspond perfectly to behavior. Behavior is seldom if ever the product of one influence acting alone. Thus, these latter psychologists argue, in evaluating the concept of attitudes, we must take into account factors that may weaken the relationship between attitudes and corresponding behaviors.

First, situational factors can weaken this relationship, prompting a person to act in a manner inconsistent with his or her customary predispositions. LaPiere concluded that his friends were received and well treated by establishments that did not ordinarily accept Chinese because of such situational factors as the high quality of their clothing and luggage and their friendly manner, which inspired courtesy.

Second, a discrepancy between attitudes and behaviors may also result from conflicts among attitudes. For instance, a man may hold the attitude that one should avoid trouble by minding one's own business, but he may also hold the attitude that one should help the defenseless. What does this Good Samaritan do when he sees an old man being assaulted on the street and the only way to help the victim is to attack the aggressor? If he stands idly by, his behavior is inconsistent with the attitude that he should help; if he attacks, his behavior is inconsistent with the attitude that he should not get involved. It is inevitable that attitudes will sometimes come into conflict with one another, resulting in at least partial inconsistency between attitudes and behavior.

The extent to which an attitude suggests specific responses also affects its correlation with behavior. A single attitude can often be expressed in a variety of ways. For instance, in the study on church-related attitudes and behavior mentioned earlier (Wicker, 1971), the researcher concluded that there are many ways a person may express devotion to the church. A person who does not attend services regularly, contribute money weekly, or participate in many church activities may nevertheless be the first person to offer help when the church is damaged by fire or when it needs to be defended from the criticism of others.

Finally, the strength and importance of an attitude, the impact it has on an individual's life, helps to determine the extent to which it governs behavior. Two people may share the attitude that public education should be improved, but a parent is far more likely than a nonparent to act on that attitude by voting for school bond issues, attending hearings

on education, and visiting schools.

Clearly, then, it would be naive to expect to be able always to predict behavior accurately from a particular attitude. Still, it has been shown that attitudes can predict behavior when appropriate attitude-measurement techniques are used. The key to success is to make sure that there is a high degree of correspondence between the degree of specificity of attitude and of the behavior. That is, if you wish to predict whether a person will participate in a campaign to reduce litter, you must measure that person's attitude toward reducing litter, not his or her general attitude toward protecting the environment (Ajzen and Fishbein, 1977).

Accurate predictions are of great value because attitudes play such an important role in behavior. Where we live, what we eat, how we dress, where we work, how we spend our leisure time, even our choice of a mate, are partly determined by our attitudes. It is because of this pervasive influence of attitudes on behavior that social psychologists devote so much effort to trying to understand how attitudes are formed and how they change—a topic to which we now turn.

EXPLAINING ATTITUDE FORMATION AND CHANGE

What is your attitude toward the legalization of marijuana? Coeducational dormitories? Pornography? Traditional sex roles? Abortion? Your roommate? You could probably make a statement about your attitude toward each of these things, believing that your attitudes have their origins in the objects themselves. You are for or against marijuana because of what you believe the effects of the drug to be. You like or dislike your roommate because you believe him or her to be a certain kind of person.

Research suggests, however, that this simple, very rational explanation of how attitudes are formed may be only part of the actual process. In developing an attitude, we are influenced by many factors—our emotional associations, our expectations of rewards and punishments, our desire to emulate the attitudes of those we respect and admire, our need to establish some degree of consistency between what we say we believe and what we actually do. In other words, our attitudes about everything from breakfast cereals to nuclear weapons are sub-

The process by which attitudes toward such topics as abortion are formed is seldom a clear-cut, completely rational one. Our attitudes are influenced by our emotions, our expectations of rewards and punishments, our desire for approval, our need for consistency between beliefs and actions, and many other factors.

ject to any number of influences; and, to complicate matters, we are only vaguely aware of some of these influences.

REINFORCEMENT THEORIES Many of our most firmly held attitudes—toward family, authority, work, money, politics, religion, education—are so much a part of us that they seem indelibly stamped on our personalities. In fact, most of these attitudes are learned quite early in life and are often very resistant to change. How do we acquire these deeply felt, persistent attitudes? Why does a person become a lifelong liberal or conservative, a committed capitalist or a revolutionary, a staunch Catholic or an avowed atheist? Part of the explanation can be found in the reinforcement principles of learning discussed in Chapter 4—classical and operant conditioning. Essentially these theories hold that many attitudes are formed because of the rewards or punishments associated with them.

CLASSICAL CONDITIONING Psychologists have demonstrated that attitudes can be formed by the same conditioning process through which Pavlov's dogs learned to salivate at the sound of a bell. Some previously neutral object is repeatedly paired with either a pleasurable or an aversive stimulus until the

Figure 25.1 Winston Churchill, in a speech to the British House of Commons in 1940. Churchill was able to rouse in the British people a courageous and determined attitude toward the war that probably no other communicator could have roused. His long record as a soldier (in India, South Africa, and in the First World War) and as a political leader made him a source whose expertise and trustworthiness were beyond question by the time he was needed to lead the fight against Hitler.

We shall not flag or fail. We shall fight in France, we shall fight on the seas and oceans, we shall fight with growing confidence and growing strength in the air, we shall defend our island, whatever the cost may be, we shall fight on the beaches, we shall fight on the landing grounds, we shall fight in the fields and in the streets, we shall fight in the hills; we shall never surrender.

object alone comes to elicit either a positive or a negative response. In one interesting experiment (Zanna, Kiesler, and Pilkonis, 1970), fifty female subjects were forewarned that they would receive electric shocks a random number of times at predetermined intervals and that there would be a signal at the beginning and ending of each interval. For one group, the onset of shock was signaled by the word "light" and the termination of shock by the word "dark," while for another group, the signal words were reversed. Although, prior to the experiment, all the subjects evaluated "light" more favorably than "dark," the degree of this preference was later influenced by the nature of the stimulus with which each word was paired. When "dark" signaled shock and "light" signaled relief from shock, for example, "dark" was evaluated much less favorably and "light" much more so. Thus, by associating words with pleasant or aversive stimuli, the subjects developed more positive or negative attitudes toward those words. In addition, the subjects generalized what they had learned to other, related words. Those who had been shocked on the word "light," for instance, also evaluated the word "white" less favorably, while those who had been shocked on the word "dark" also developed more negative attitudes toward "black."

Findings such as these suggest that attitudes can be formed simply by associating objects with emotion-arousing circumstances. We might, for example, learn to dislike people whom we encounter only in hot, crowded subways, or be particularly drawn to those ideas we hear in courses taught by attractive, entertaining teachers. Classical conditioning, in other words, is a means of attaching a positive or negative emotional reaction to some object without a corresponding set of cognitive beliefs. This raises the question of whether many of our most emotionally laden attitudes might not be acquired, at least in part, through this basic mechanism of learning.

OPERANT CONDITIONING While classical conditioning involves "involuntary" reflex responses, such as the emotions of fear or pleasure, operant conditioning involves voluntary behaviors on the part of the subject. Operant conditioning is based on the assumption that people tend to repeat behaviors that result in something desirable and tend not to repeat behaviors that result in something undesirable. The subject, then, is attempting to obtain some reward or avoid some punishment. By manip-

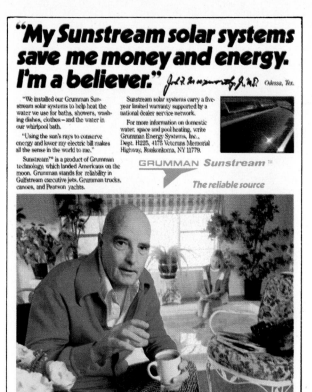
If most of your friends believe in the importance of the expanded use of solar energy, would it be more or less likely that you would also be in favor of it?

ulating rewards and punishments, psychologists have shown that almost any organism can be conditioned to perform a variety of behaviors.

Research confirms that attitudes, too, can be learned through operant conditioning. Consider a situation in which you are verbally reinforced for expressing certain attitudes. Every time you mention to your friends that you believe people should make a greater effort to convert to solar energy, they respond by saying, "That's an excellent idea" or "I agree completely." Would these responses tend to make you a more ardent supporter of solar energy? Apparently so.

An experiment at the University of Hawaii (Insko, 1965) demonstrated the strength of verbal reinforcement on attitude formation. Students were complimented for expressing favorable attitudes toward Aloha Week, a celebration held every autumn. Then, about a week after the "conditioning" interviews, the subjects were asked to fill out a questionnaire about local issues. Included in the list of items was a question about the possibility of having an Aloha Week every spring, as well as every fall. Students whose positive attitudes toward the festival had previously been verbally reinforced expressed more favorable attitudes toward a springtime celebration than did a control group that had not been previously conditioned.

If our attitudes can be shaped by an unknown experimenter who simply repeats "good" every time we express a certain opinion, imagine how easily attitudes can be shaped when the rewards offered are more highly valued, such as the rewards of approval and affection from family and friends. In fact, the principle of reinforcement may be one of the reasons why young children can so often be heard parroting their parents' attitudes even when the children do not fully understand what they are saying. Youngsters of five or six enthusiastically support the Democratic or Republican candidate during every presidential election campaign, although they probably do not understand the platform of the candidate whose campaign button they wear. Similarly, seven- or eight-year-olds who shout racial slurs in the playground or scribble them on the schoolyard wall seldom grasp the full significance of their words. It is very likely that these children have at some time been positively reinforced for expressing the attitudes that their parents hold.

As we noted in Chapter 4, there is some debate among psychologists about what is actually being learned through operant conditioning. Does the organism simply acquire a stereotyped chain of responses that it performs almost mechanically? Or does it acquire an expectation that some reward or punishment will follow a certain kind of behavior? If it is expectations that are acquired, the organism is clearly a more active decision maker in the response sequence. It can substitute one behavior for another as long as the outcome is the same, or it can pursue an entirely different goal that holds out the promise of an even greater reward. Many social psychologists who have investigated reinforcement theories of attitude formation and change argue that acquiring expectations about outcomes is central to the learning process (Hovland, Janis, and Kelley, 1953). We adopt those attitudes that we believe will gain us some desired end and reject those that we feel will have some unfavorable result. Moreover, we weigh the value of the various anticipated rewards and select those attitudes that we perceive will yield the greatest benefit. In other words, the greater the reward, the greater the likelihood that a corresponding attitude will be formed.

COGNITIVE CONSISTENCY THEORIES We are constantly faced with new information—about

our environments, about other people, and even about ourselves. For our cognitions to make sense, each new perception should somehow "fit" within our overall view of things. We seem to value consistency in our cognitive maps. The processes by which this consistency is achieved are the central theme of most cognitive theories of attitude formation and change.

THE COGNITIVE BALANCE PRINCIPLE Suppose an ardent supporter of gun-control legislation meets a man who announces that he is the head of the local chapter of the National Rifle Association. On the basis of this information alone, do you think the two would like each other? Are they likely to become close friends? Probably not, for according to the principle of **cognitive balance** (Heider, 1958), people seek harmony among their various attitudes and beliefs. Thus, if you strongly oppose the unrestricted ownership of guns, the chances are that you will also have negative feelings toward a person who supports the opposite view. We tend to evaluate in similar ways things that are linked to each other.

Of course, when the perceived links between things change, an existing state of cognitive balance can be thrown into disruption. This is apparently what happened during the Watergate scandal. In the early 1970s millions of Americans held very favorable attitudes toward President Nixon. In fact, in the 1972 election, Nixon was reelected by a landslide. Then details about the Watergate break-in and the subsequent coverup by the White House staff began to appear in the press. Nixon supporters were faced with a dilemma: how could they continue to have a favorable attitude toward Nixon, when they knew that he had failed to take action against these morally objectionable activities? The balance principle predicts that one of these two attitudes (either the positive attitude toward Nixon or the negative attitude toward covering up illegal activities) would have to change in order to restore cognitive consistency. But which? One answer is that the attitude or belief that is *less* firmly held will be the one that changes (Osgood and Tannenbaum, 1955). Thus, most people found it easier to change their attitudes toward Nixon than their attitudes toward honesty and morality, which are deeply ingrained by early learning and therefore very resistant to change.

THE THEORY OF COGNITIVE DISSONANCE The theory of **cognitive dissonance**, which has generated an enormous amount of interest and research in recent years, is based on an assumption similar to that underlying the balance principle—namely, that people try to avoid cognitive inconsistency (see Figure 25.2). According to Leon Festinger (1957), who first proposed the theory, whenever we find ourselves in a situation in which we hold two contradictory cognitions about our own attitudes, beliefs, or behavior, we are thrust into a state of psychological distress known as dissonance. Because this state is uncomfortable, even painful, we naturally attempt to rid ourselves of it and reestablish internal harmony.

The situations in which dissonance can arise—and the methods we use to reduce it—are intriguing. Suppose, for example, that you need a car to commute to campus. You go to a used-car lot and find two automobiles that you like, a Volkswagen Rab-

Figure 25.2 Attitudes are frequently modified in order to resolve contradictions. This motivation for attitude change is called cognitive dissonance. In this figure Mary has expressed two attitudes that are now brought into conflict by Bill's behavior: She cannot "love that man" and "hate those clothes" without experiencing the discomfort of dissonance. A resolution can be accomplished in a number of ways. Mary can start wondering if she really loves Bill after all, or she can broaden her tastes, or she can make such mental rearrangements as "Good taste isn't really what I'm looking for in a man anyway."

bit and a Datsun. Both are the same price, are the same age, have about the same number of miles on them, and are in equally good condition. You have a difficult time making up your mind because both cars seem equally attractive to you, but finally you settle on the Rabbit. Immediately you are cast into an unpleasant state of dissonance. You liked the Datsun a great deal, but you bought the Rabbit instead. Did you make the right decision? According to cognitive dissonance theory, you would attempt to reduce your distress by adjusting your attitudes toward the two cars. You would try to develop both a more favorable attitude toward the Rabbit, by playing up its good qualities and playing down its negative ones, and a less favorable feeling toward the Datsun, by focusing on its undesirable features and ignoring its positive ones. Research confirms that this process of rationalization is very common. In one early study, people who had just purchased a new car were found to be more inclined to read advertisements for the model they had bought than any other, presumably to help reduce the dissonance that was created by their decision (Ehrlich et al., 1957).

The theory of cognitive dissonance has wide applications. For instance, it has also been used to explain why, when people publicly say or do something contrary to what they privately believe, they will often shift their attitudes to make them conform to their public stance. What is most surprising about this situation is that often the *less* incentive people have to express the contradictory view, the *more* likely they are to change their original attitudes. Apparently, the lower the incentive, the greater the dissonance created—and therefore the greater the need to restore a state of cognitive consistency.

A classic early experiment (Festinger and Carlsmith, 1959) illustrated this point. Subjects were asked to perform a very boring task: putting round pegs in round holes and square pegs in square holes for two hours. Then the experimenter asked that each subject tell the next subject who was to perform the task that the experiment had been fun and exciting. He promised half the subjects one dollar for telling this lie and half the subjects twenty dollars. After relaying the information to the next person, the original subjects evaluated, among other things, the degree to which they had really enjoyed the experimental task. The subjects who had been paid one dollar for telling the lie reported enjoying the task more than did subjects who had received twenty dollars.

Why did the one-dollar subjects rate the boring task more favorably than the twenty-dollar subjects? According to dissonance theory, to say something you do not believe ordinarily causes psychological discomfort, but when you have what you consider good justification for doing so, little or no dissonance arises. Therefore, subjects who received only one dollar, and thus had no reasonable way to justify the lie to themselves, "decided" that the task had not been so boring after all, so they hadn't really lied. Subjects who were paid twenty dollars, however, had a very good reason for saying something they did not believe: twenty dollars is a substantial sum. The behavior of the latter group, therefore, caused little dissonance, and they could readily admit to themselves that the task had in fact been very dull.

REINFORCEMENT VERSUS CONSISTENCY

An interesting aspect of these findings is that subjects seemed to be acting in a manner exactly contrary to what we might expect from a reinforcement model of attitude change: the *lower* their reward, the *greater* their shift in attitude. Does this imply that cognitive dissonance theory provides a more valid explanation for attitude change than does reinforcement theory? Subsequent investigations suggest not. Both cognitive dissonance and reinforcement principles influence behavior—but under different circumstances.

One factor that seems to affect whether dissonance theory or reinforcement theory can best predict behavior is the extent to which people have freedom of choice (Linder, Cooper, and Jones, 1967). Students were asked to write a forceful, persuasive essay supporting a very unpopular bill that would ban Communists and people who took the Fifth Amendment from speaking at state-supported institutions, such as state colleges and universities. The experimenters told some subjects that the decision to write the essay was entirely up to them; with others, the experimenters acted as if compliance with this request were naturally expected. The amount of money the subjects were offered also varied—a low monetary incentive for some and a high one for others. After completing the essay, each subject was asked to indicate his or her real opinion about the speaker-ban legislation. Students who had written the essay under the "free choice" condition behaved as predicted by dissonance theory: they were more likely to change their attitudes in the direction of the proposed ban when the reward they received was low. Students who had performed under the "no choice" condition, however, tended to behave as would be predicted by reinforcement theory: those who received the greater reward were more likely to change their attitudes. Thus, rather than being contradictory, reinforcement and cognitive consistency models both contribute to our understanding of how people form and change their attitudes.

PERSUASIVE COMMUNICATION

Advertisements, sales pitches, political campaigns, lobbying efforts, and newspaper editorials are all examples of **persuasive communication**—that is, direct, overt attempts to change people's attitudes. Many discussions between parents and children, employers and employees, salespeople and customers, contain arguments meant to change an-

The purpose of this advertisement, like all other advertisements, is to persuade people to do something they might not otherwise have thought of doing or wanted to do.

"We're 2,000 miles apart now, but still just as close."

Before I could tell time, I knew when my dad would be home from work. I'd be waiting at the window, watching for him to turn the corner.

When I was old enough, I'd run to the bus stop to wait for him. And we'd race each other to the porch, then sit on the steps and talk about everything from football to cowboys.

That part of the day was ours. Now, we're 2,000 miles apart, but I still get a kick out of sharing my day with him.

Long Distance is the next best thing to being there.

other's attitudes. Persuaders often hope, of course, that attitude change will lead to change in behavior. An advertiser tries to convince consumers of the superiority of a certain brand of cigarette so that they will buy it; parents try to convince their daughter of the evils of smoking so that she will stop. Persuasion, in its form and effects, is one of the most thoroughly studied topics in social psychology.

INFLUENCES ON PERSUASIVENESS How effective will a particular effort at persuasion be? The answer depends on various factors, among them the characteristics of the source, the content and style of the message, and the nature of the audience.

THE CHARACTERISTICS OF THE SOURCE The extent to which a person's attitudes are changed by a persuasive communication depends as much on who delivers the message as on what that person says. People tend to be more persuaded by a communicator who they believe is knowledgeable about the issues involved. In a classic study, conducted almost thirty years ago (Hovland and Weiss, 1951), people who were given a statement about the practicality of atomic submarines were more convinced of its truth when the source was said to be the noted physicist J. Robert Oppenheimer than when it was said to be from the Russian newspaper *Pravda*. Similarly, more subjects were convinced by an article about antihistamine drugs when they thought it had appeared in the reputable *New England Journal of Medicine* than when they thought it had been published in a mass-circulation pictorial magazine.

The degree to which any persuader is influential depends not only on whether the audience thinks he or she knows the truth (expertise) but also on whether they think he or she is "giving it to them straight" (trustworthiness). (See Figure 25.3.) The audience may decide that the persuader has some ulterior motive for making the appeal and therefore is not completely believable. This is why voters, knowing that a political candidate is specifically trying to persuade them of his or her own merits, are likely to look to another person or organization to verify the candidate's qualifications. An interesting manifestation of the importance of trustworthiness is the tendency for people to be more persuaded by a message if they overhear it than if it is addressed directly to them (Walster and Festinger, 1962). Ap-

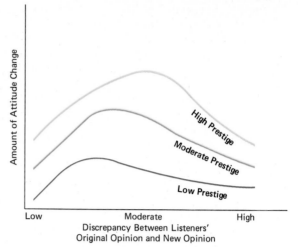

Figure 25.3 Attitude change may be affected both by change of discrepancy and by the prestige of the source of a communication. Discrepancy refers to the difference between the listener's original attitude and the attitude implied by the communication. If the discrepancy is too high (in trying to persuade a Republican to vote Communist, for example) or too low (in which case there is little room for change), the amount of attitude change will be less than for moderate discrepancies. As the figure shows, the amount of discrepancy that will produce the maximum change depends on the prestige of the persuader. A high-prestige source coupled with a low degree of discrepancy produces the greatest amount of attitude change in the audience. (Adapted from Freedman, et al., 1970.)

parently, when people overhear a communication, they are less likely to call the communicator's motives into question.

A third factor that can affect the persuasiveness of a particular communicator is simply how attractive and likable the listeners find him or her. Football players are probably not especially knowledgeable about the relative merits of deodorants and hair tonics. Moreover, when a football star endorses a particular brand of deodorant or hair tonic on television, everyone knows that he is doing so for an ulterior motive: he is being handsomely paid for his efforts. Yet such testimonials are quite effective in persuading thousands of fans to use the product. An attractive, likable source, then, is more persuasive. An unattractive, unlikable source may produce a "boomerang" effect: the audience may respond by adopting attitudes contrary to those advocated by the source. In conformity with cognitive consistency theory, the listeners adapt their attitudes about the message to their attitudes about the person who delivers it.

The nonverbal behavior of a persuader is also important. In a face-to-face setting, such as a public speech or interview, a person's actions, posture, and position can either enhance or detract from the impact of the message. Someone who smiles, makes eye contact with the listeners, and faces them directly is perceived as friendly and honest and will be more effective as a communicator than someone who does not look at the audience. A case in point is the series of televised debates between presidential candidates Richard Nixon and John Kennedy during the 1960 campaign. Nixon's unconscious nonverbal communication decidedly worked against him. He appeared awkward and ill at ease, shifted his position frequently, stood stiffly, and avoided looking into the camera. He lost the election by a narrow margin. Running for President again in 1968, Nixon made an effort to change his style. He appeared more relaxed, sat rather than stood for

Advertisers have found that consumers' attitudes toward a product are favorably affected by the use of attractive models. Recognizing this fact, the Hathaway Shirt Company has for many years used a handsome model wearing an eye patch in all its advertisements.

most of his interviews, established eye contact, was less formal in appearance and tone, and thereby inspired greater confidence than before.

The physical distance between speaker and audience is another aspect of nonverbal behavior that can affect the impact of a message. In one study (Albert and Dabbs, 1970) researchers found that a message produced most attitude change when the speaker's distance from the audience was great (fourteen to fifteen feet) and least when the distance was small (one to two feet). They speculated that the subjects may have regarded extreme closeness of a speaker as an imposition on their privacy and therefore resisted the speaker's message. In a manual written for volunteers campaigning for peace candidates in the 1972 election, two social psychologists advised door-to-door canvassers to maintain an informal conversational distance of four to five feet (Abelson and Zimbardo, 1970). Future studies in this area will probably find that there is no single best distance for delivering a successful message; it is more likely that the most effective physical distance will be found to vary with the nature of the message and with the relationship between the speaker and the audience.

THE CHARACTERISTICS OF THE MESSAGE We are all familiar with the kind of television commercial in which a certain brand of toothpaste, aspirin, or paper towels is declared to be superior to "other leading brands" or to "the product you're currently using." Why do advertisers so often avoid using the names of competing brands (even though for the past few years the law has permitted them to do so)? A major reason is their fear of giving free, even if unfavorable, publicity to a rival product. Companies want to make sure that the name the viewer remembers is the name of their brand, not their competitor's.

Is Madison Avenue right? Should we avoid mentioning the other side when trying to influence attitudes? Or is it better to discuss the weaknesses of our opponent's view along with the strengths of our own? Apparently, the answer depends on the audience for whom the message is intended.

In one early experiment, conducted during World War II (Hovland, Lumsdaine, and Sheffield, 1949), each of two groups of 214 men received a series of radio transcripts that argued that it would take at least two years to end the war with Japan. However, the message that one group received was strictly one-sided, pointing only to obstacles, such as

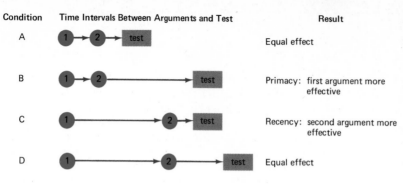

Condition	Time Intervals Between Arguments and Test	Result
A	1 → 2 → test	Equal effect
B	1 → 2 ——————→ test	Primacy: first argument more effective
C	1 ——————→ 2 → test	Recency: second argument more effective
D	1 ——————→ 2 ——————→ test	Equal effect

Figure 25.4 1 and 2 represent two arguments; short arrows indicate that one event immediately followed another; long arrows represent a delay of one week. "Equal effect" in A and D means that the two arguments balanced each other, resulting in no change in attitude. In B, the primacy effect prevailed, and the argument presented first was more effective. In C, the recency effect made the second argument more persuasive. (After Miller and Campbell, 1959.)

distance, plentiful Japanese resources, and a large Japanese army. In contrast, the message that the other group received was two-sided. It contained all the information in the one-sided version, plus opposing evidence that pointed to such factors as the superiority of the U.S. Navy and the greater chance of Allied success through fighting a one-front war. Overall, the one-sided and two-sided communications produced substantially the same net change in attitudes, but important differences emerged when the subjects' initial opinions and education were taken into account. Those who initially believed that the war would probably continue for another two years were more influenced by the one-sided message, while those who initially thought that the war would end sooner were more influenced by the two-sided argument. Also, men who were better educated, and who would be expected to view the communications fairly critically, were more impressed with the two-sided communication, while the reverse was true for less-educated men. Thus, a one-sided argument is more effective than a two-sided one if the audience initially favors the communicator's position and is relatively poorly educated. Conversely, an audience composed of people who are initially opposed to the communicator's viewpoint and who are relatively well educated will be more influenced by a two-sided argument.

More recent research (Hass and Linder, 1972) suggests that these early findings may be related to the audience's knowledge of counterarguments. Audiences who are aware of arguments against the speaker's point of view are most persuaded by two-sided messages that explicitly refute these arguments. Audiences who are unaware of the existence of counterarguments, however, are best presented with a one-sided message, because the introduction of opposing arguments would merely give them ammunition to use against the speaker's viewpoint. A knowledge of the audience, therefore, is crucial to effective planning of a persuasive message, especially since the method that is most effective with one

group—providing counterarguments and their refutation—may be the very method that is least effective with another.

A speaker who does decide to present a two-sided message is then faced with the decision of which side to present first—his or her own position (in the hope of making a strong case while audience attention is still high) or the opponent's position (in the hope that it will fade from the audience's memory by the end of the presentation). Early research indicated a definite advantage for the position presented first—what psychologists labeled a **primacy effect**. Subsequent studies, however, showed an equally clear-cut advantage for the position presented second—a **recency effect**. Which of these two sets of conflicting evidence is correct? It has been discovered that either may be correct, depending on the circumstances (see Figure 25.4).

One important factor is the time interval between the presentation of the two arguments and the measurement of attitudes. When two arguments closely follow each other and there is a substantial delay before attitude change is measured, the first point of view is more persuasive. Apparently, both arguments tend to fade from the listener's memory, but the first is learned somewhat better and is therefore favored. However, when a delay occurs between the presentation of argument one and the presentation of argument two, and attitudes are measured immediately following the second argument, the second point of view is more effective simply because it is fresher in the minds of the audience (Miller and Campbell, 1959). Finally, when there are no delays at all, it is probably best to give the opposing point of view first and then strongly refute it. In this way, the audience's attention is drawn to the speaker's own position for most of the presentation (Hass and Linder, 1972).

Linking the message with a pleasant emotional state is another successful method of persuasion. When a television commercial shows a new car being admired by a beautiful woman or a handsome, sophisticated man, the advertisers are using this technique. So are corporate executives when they talk business with prospective clients over dinner at an elegant restaurant. Research confirms that associating one's point of view with positive emotions can help change the attitudes of an audience. For example, in one study (Janis, Kaye, and Kirschner, 1965) subjects who were given peanuts and Pepsi while reading a persuasive communication were more inclined than control subjects to be convinced by the arguments they encountered. Apparently, the pleasant emotional state created by snacking on desirable food can make a message seem more agreeable.

What about associations with negative emotions? Can they, too, be used to change attitudes? The arousal of fear has frequently been used as a technique of persuasion. Campaigns to reduce cigarette smoking, traffic fatalities, and drug abuse have employed scare tactics for years. The *amount* of fear induced is the critical factor. A classic study (Janis and Feshbach, 1953) that compared the effectiveness of three different levels of fear-arousing appeals found that an appeal that aroused a small amount of fear was the most persuasive. Subjects were given presentations on oral hygiene. A high-fear group was shown the consequences of dental neglect in graphic detail, including color slides of severely decaying teeth and unpleasant mouth infections. A second group saw pictures of more moderate cases of tooth decay. A third, low-fear group viewed only diagrams and photographs of completely healthy teeth. Later, 36 percent of the subjects in the low-

fear condition reported favorable changes in their dental hygiene practices as compared to 22 percent in the moderate-fear condition and 8 percent in the high-fear condition. It seems, then, that if the fear induced by a message is too great, people will attempt to reduce their anxiety by pushing the information to the back of their minds—in short, by ignoring it. This is especially true when the audience is not told how to prevent the feared consequences, feels incapable of taking the necessary steps, or believes that their actions will be ineffective (Leventhal, Singer, and Jones, 1965).

It is also true, however, that if the audience *is* told how to avoid undesirable consequences and *does* believe that the preventive action is possible and effective, then even high levels of fear will generate an increased level of attitude change. In addition, the more specific the recommendations for action are, the greater the extent of change in behavior will be (Leventhal, Singer, and Jones, 1965). Thus, a distinction must be made between avoidable and unavoidable outcomes: Regardless of our level of fear, if we believe that a recommended change in our attitudes or behavior or both will be effective in helping us avoid an unfavorable outcome, we are likely to make the change; if we don't, we aren't.

THE CHARACTERISTICS OF THE AUDIENCE
Sometimes deep psychological needs and motives affect a person's readiness to be persuaded. There is some evidence, for example, that people with a

This advertisement is intended to persuade advertisers to buy advertising space in a medical news magazine, but the reasons they should do so are not mentioned until after readers have been shocked into attention by the photograph and its headline. The arousal of unpleasant emotions such as guilt can be an effective technique of persuasion.

strong need for social approval are more susceptible to social influence than others (Marlowe and Gergen, 1969). Other psychological reasons for persuasibility are less obvious. Ernest Dichter (1964), a motivational researcher who has engineered a large number of commercial advertising campaigns, once lent his talents to a Red Cross drive for blood donations. He postulated that many men were reluctant to give blood because it aroused unconscious anxieties associated with the giving away of their strength and virility. He recommended, therefore, that the campaign focus on masculinity, implying that each man in the audience had so much virility that he could afford to give away a little. Dichter also suggested that each man be made to feel personally proud of any suffering. One of Dichter's strategies for the blood drive was to give each donor a pin in the shape of a drop of blood—the equivalent of a wounded soldier's Purple Heart. These tactics did in fact produce a sharp increase in blood donations by men.

Susceptibility to persuasion is also related to a person's knowledge about or interest in the issue at hand. For example, the fact that in past studies women appeared more persuasible than men may simply have been the result of researchers' choice of traditionally "male-oriented" issues, such as political and economic affairs (Aronson, 1976, pp. 181–182). Other recent research supports this hypothesis. In one study (Sistrunk and McDavid, 1971), men were found to be easier to influence about traditionally "female-oriented" issues, such as home management or family relations, while women were more open to persuasion about traditionally "male-oriented" ones. On the whole, neither gender was found to be more susceptible to persuasion than the other.

RESISTANCE TO PERSUASION Even the most compelling persuasive communications may fail, often because of resistance on the part of the audience. People, after all, are not passive. While they are listening to a communication, they are evaluating the points the speaker makes and possibly drawing up counterarguments of their own. Research indicates that resistance to persuasion is strongest when counterarguments are available and weakest when they are unavailable. Those factors that enhance the availability of counterarguments, therefore, will increase resistance to persuasion.

INOCULATION Some attitudes are taken so much for granted that when they are strongly attacked, people find it difficult to muster effective counterarguments. How would you react, for example, if you read a very persuasive article arguing that monthly self-examinations have no effect on the incidence of death from breast cancer or that regular brushing is useless in preventing tooth decay? No doubt you would be surprised that these widely held beliefs were attacked at all. But you might very well end up accepting the new points of view simply because you were unprepared to defend the old ones (even though, in fact, they are true).

William McGuire and his colleagues have argued that people can be "inoculated" against persuasive assaults under such conditions, in much the same way that we are inoculated against certain diseases (McGuire and Papageorgis, 1961). In medical inoculation a person who has never been exposed to a

Figure 25.5 This graph shows the amount of attitude change in three groups of subjects, measured in response to a strong attack on a commonly held belief (that brushing the teeth three times daily is a good thing to do). The "inoculation" subjects were previously exposed to a weak form of the attack and were helped to defend their initial belief against the weak argument. The "support" group was given some prior support for the initial belief without any kind of attack on it. The "neither" group received no prior treatment. The "inoculation" group showed much more resistance to change in their attitudes on the subject than the other two groups. Attitude change was measured on an arbitrary scale of 1 to 10, with 10 representing a complete change of attitude. (After McGuire and Papageorgis, 1961.)

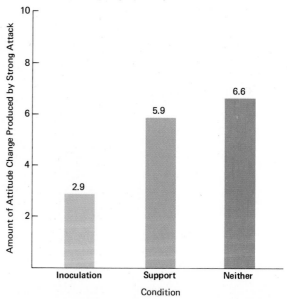

particular disease is purposely given a weakened form of the disease-causing agent, which stimulates the body to manufacture defenses. Then, if a more virulent form of the disease should attack, these defenses make the person immune to infection. The principle underlying inoculation against persuasion is analogous. The person who has never had a particular point of view attacked before is exposed to opposition and then given a dose of the counter-arguments needed to defend that viewpoint.

For the inoculation McGuire exposed subjects first to the challenging arguments and then to a statement that refuted those arguments and reinforced the person's initial belief (say, that regular brushing prevents tooth decay). A week later the subjects read another communication that challenged their initial belief. McGuire found that far fewer subjects who had received the inoculation were persuaded by the challenge than subjects who had not been inoculated. The inoculation had effectively stimulated their psychological defenses against a challenge and made their initial attitude more resistant to change, as shown in Figure 25.5.

FOREWARNING What happens when people are not provided with arguments to refute an opposing point of view but are simply forewarned that their own view will be challenged? The evidence on this question is mixed. In one study, a group of teenagers who had been warned ten minutes in advance that they would hear a speech on why young people should not be allowed to drive were more resistant to persuasion than a group who had not been forewarned (Freedman and Sears, 1965). But other researchers have obtained different results. For example, in a recent study, subjects who were forewarned that they would hear arguments against their own view on the likelihood of an economic recession were the ones who displayed the greatest change in their attitudes (Hass and Mann, 1976).

One way to reconcile these seemingly contradictory findings is to take into account the level of the subjects' commitment to their initial attitude. When people are firmly committed to a particular belief, as most teenagers are about their right to drive, they are more likely to resist an opposing point of view. However, when people are somewhat ambivalent toward a belief, as the subjects who believed in the likelihood of a recession may have been, they are more inclined to succumb to a persuasive challenge (Kiesler and Jones, 1971). Then, too, the subjects' level of knowledge about the issues

involved may help explain the varying results of forewarning experiments. Apparently, when people are not particularly well-informed about a subject, anticipation of an opposing argument may cause them to modify their own position in that direction. The strategy is basically a face-saving one: These subjects want to avoid being caught in a situation where they would be forced to defend a view that they cannot support intelligently (Hass and Mann, 1976).

THE ETHICS OF RESEARCH ON PERSUASION Social psychologists, as well as advertisers and political propagandists, have devoted a great deal of time and effort to investigations of persuasive techniques. Knowledge of these techniques can help make the average person a more effective communicator, and this of course can be very useful in day-to-day interactions with others. A recent study, for example, focused on the use of persuasive techniques by consumers (Cialdini, Bickman, and Cacciopo, in press). It was found that a customer's tough initial bargaining stance in negotiations with a new-car salesman resulted in a significantly lower price. Such practical applications of social science research are possible in many other everyday situations.

Social science research, then, can have great value when its findings are used in the service of what one considers good causes, such as getting a fair price on a new car, persuading people to contribute to worthwhile charities, or reducing religious and racial prejudices. But there is no guarantee that techniques of persuasion will always be used for such purposes. The same methods that are used by health authorities to convince people to stop smoking may also be used by cigarette companies to convince the public that the habit is worthwhile.

Since one person's good cause may be another person's evil, who should decide which causes are worthy and which are not? Social psychologists do not have a ready answer to this question. However, their basic purpose in conducting research on persuasion is clear. They do not aim to make it easier for persuasive communicators, such as politicians and advertisers, to manipulate the attitudes of others. Rather, social psychologists hope that by making their findings about persuasion available to everyone, they will help people to recognize and analyze persuasive communications—and thus to resist "content-free" appeals to fear and other emotions when forming and changing their attitudes.

Summary

1. People have attitudes about an enormous variety of subjects. Major events can bring forth the public expression of attitudes; events can change or intensify attitudes; and people's attitudes tend to remain fairly consistent over time.
   A. An **attitude** is a relatively enduring evaluation formed on the basis of two components: knowledge and beliefs about an object (a person, a situation, a behavior) and affective reactions to the object.
   B. Attitudes are sometimes quite inconsistent with behavior.
      1. Some psychologists claim that behavior is seldom the product of one influence alone; other factors may weaken the relationship between attitudes and corresponding behaviors.
         a. Situational factors can weaken this relationship, prompting a person to behave inconsistently with his or her usual predispositions.
         b. Conflicts among attitudes may produce a discrepancy between attitudes and behaviors.
         c. A single attitude may suggest a variety of specific responses.
         d. The strength and importance of an attitude in a person's life help to determine the extent to which it governs that person's behavior.
      2. An attitude can predict behavior when appropriate attitude-measurement techniques are used, which requires a high degree of objective correspondence between the attitude and the behavior.
2. In developing attitudes we are influenced by many factors, some of which we are scarcely aware of.
   A. Many firmly held attitudes are learned early in life and are often very resistant to change. Reinforcement theories hold that many attitudes are formed because of the rewards or punishments associated with them.
      1. Attitudes can be formed through classical conditioning, in which a positive or negative emotional reaction becomes associated with some object without a corresponding set of cognitive beliefs.
      2. Attitudes can also be learned through operant conditioning, in which people tend to repeat behaviors that result in something desirable and fail to repeat those that result in something undesirable. Many social psychologists believe that people select those attitudes that they perceive will yield the greatest benefit.
   B. Cognitive consistency theories of attitude formation and change hold that people value consistency in their overall view of things, and they will work to achieve it.
      1. According to the principle of **cognitive balance**, people seek harmony among their various attitudes and beliefs. When the perceived links between things change and an existing state of balance is thrown into disruption, the cognitive balance principle maintains that the less firmly held attitude will change.
      2. Similarly, the theory of **cognitive dissonance** assumes that people try to avoid cognitive inconsistency: in a situation in which they hold two contradictory cognitions about their own attitudes, beliefs, or behaviors they are thrust into an unpleasant state of psychological distress known as dissonance, which they will try to relieve by reestablishing internal harmony. Cognitive dissonance theory has been used to explain why, when people publicly say or do something contrary to what they privately believe, they will often shift their attitudes to make them conform to their public stance. Experiments have shown that the less incentive people have to express a view contradictory to their original attitude, the more likely they are to change that attitude.
   C. Both cognitive dissonance and reinforcement principles influence behavior, but under different circumstances. The extent to which people have freedom of choice seems to affect whether dissonance theory or reinforcement theory can best predict behavior.

3. **Persuasive communication** involves direct, overt attempts to change people's attitudes.

A. The effectiveness of persuasion depends on various factors, including the characteristics of the source, of the message, and of the audience.

1. The degree to which any source of persuasive communication is influential depends on the audience's assessment of the source's expertise and trustworthiness. Other factors that affect the persuasiveness of a particular communicator are the degree to which the audience finds him or her attractive and likable and the communicator's nonverbal behavior (including his or her physical distance from the audience).

2. As for the content and style of the message, a one-sided argument is more effective than a two-sided one if the audience initially favors the communicator's position and is relatively poorly educated; a two-sided argument will be more effective for a relatively well-educated audience that is initially opposed to the communicator's viewpoint. These findings may be related to the audience's awareness of counterarguments. In a two-sided argument the relative effectiveness of the **primacy effect** or the **recency effect** depends on the circumstances. Linking the message with a pleasant emotional state and arousing fear in the audience have both been used successfully as techniques of persuasion. A study comparing the effectiveness of three appeals arousing different levels of fear determined that the appeal that aroused a small amount of fear was the most persuasive.

3. A person's susceptibility to persuasion is determined by psychological needs and motives and by knowledge about or interest in the issue.

B. Resistance to persuasion is strongest when counterarguments are available and weakest when they are unavailable. Factors that enhance the availability of counterarguments will increase resistance to persuasion.

1. William McGuire contends that people can be "inoculated" against persuasion by being given the counterarguments that are needed to defend their viewpoint.

2. The level of people's commitment to their initial attitude apparently determines the extent to which forewarning is effective in making them resistant to persuasion.

C. The purpose of social science research on persuasion is not to make it easier for persuasive communicators to manipulate others, but rather to make findings about persuasive techniques available to everyone and thus to help people recognize and analyze persuasive communications in the process of forming and changing their attitudes.

RECOMMENDED READINGS

FESTINGER, LEON. *A Theory of Cognitive Dissonance.* Stanford, Calif.: Stanford University Press, 1957. The original systematic statement of a theory that has had a major impact on attitude-change research.

FESTINGER, LEON, HAROLD RIECKEN, and STANLEY SCHACHTER. *When Prophecy Fails.* Minneapolis: University of Minnesota Press, 1956. A fascinating account of the development of a doomsday religious cult and its members' attitudes and behavior when their prophecy of the end of the world did not come true.

FISHBEIN, MARTIN, and ICEK AJZEN. *Belief, Attitude, Intention and Behavior: An Introduction to Theory and Research.* Reading, Mass.: Addison-Wesley, 1975. The authors present their own, rather attractive theory of attitude formation and change.

HOVLAND, CARL S., IRVING L. JANIS, and HAROLD H. KELLEY. *Communication and Persuasion: Psychological Studies of Opinion Change.* New Haven, Conn.: Yale University Press, 1953. A classic book, reporting the early work of the Yale Communication Research Program.

McGUIRE, WILLIAM J. "The Nature of Attitudes and Attitude Change," in Gardner Lindzey and Elliot Aronson (eds.), *The Handbook of Social Psychology.* 2nd ed. Vol. 3. Reading, Mass.: Addison-Wesley, 1969, pp. 136–314. An excellent, comprehensive review of the field. The best single source for an overview.

ZIMBARDO, PHILIP G., EBBE B. EBBESEN, and CHRISTINA MASLACH. *Influencing Attitudes and Changing Behavior.* 2nd ed. Reading, Mass.: Addison-Wesley, 1977. An informative and easy-to-read introduction to principles of attitude change.

CHAPTER TWENTY-SIX

PERSON PERCEPTION AND INTERPERSONAL ATTRACTION

Surely the matter of love has never changed: "A kiss is just a kiss, a sigh is just a sigh. The fundamental things apply as time goes by." And fairy tales end with a marriage so that "they lived happily ever after."

But now, for some reason, the divorce rate rises and adultery seems to be as common as marriage. What has happened to eternal love? Doesn't anyone love forever and ever anymore? Or have times changed somehow?

Yes, I think that times have changed, and it does us no good to apply rules evolved under one set of conditions to another set altogether. Technological advance changes everything—including love—and if you doubt it, I will give you two ways in which it has done so, with the warning that I can think of others.

1. There was a time when humanity consisted of small, immobile groups; when most people were born, lived, and died in the same community; when the people beyond the hill were strangers you hardly ever saw; and when marriages took place between members of families that had known each other all their lives—for sheer lack of any other opportunity. Consider, then, that in every one of many thousands of such communities there was a young man who was, for some reason, an extraordinarily good catch, and some young woman caught him. There was some young woman who was the town belle, and some young man got her. A sizable proportion of all marriages, then, involved young men and women who were remarkable for wealth, strength, beauty, family connections; and marriages involving them were social achievements. Nowadays, that's not so. It's not just that people are more mobile and that the young men and women of one town possibly suffer by comparison with those of another. It's much worse. In the twentieth century, with movies and then television becoming commonplace, a large percentage of the young people of the world have, for the first time, incomparable and unattainable idols. What local young man can compare with Paul Newman or Robert Redford? What local young woman can compare with Marilyn Monroe or Farrah Fawcett-Majors?

2. Ideally, marriage is forever—from this day forward, till death do us part. But through almost all of human history, the average life span varied from twenty-five to thirty-five years. It meant that the average marriage lasted about ten years before death did them part. Nowadays, thanks to medical and technological advance, life expectancy in most "advanced" nations is something like seventy and the average marriage, if left undissolved, would last for fifty years. But what works for ten years of marriage may not work for fifty. Where 90 percent may stick out ten years, perhaps only 20 percent can stand it for fifty.

Is there any use then in clinging to notions of love developed by a short-lived isolated society? Or should we learn to live with reality?

Isaac Asimov

It is the first day of a new semester and you are seated in an American history class. The professor has not yet arrived. The bell rings to announce the beginning of the period. Everyone watches the classroom door expectantly. Five minutes pass; ten minutes; fifteen. You check the room and class numbers in the college catalog. Some of the students gather up their books and prepare to leave.

Suddenly, the door opens and a young man saunters in. He is wearing faded jeans, sandals, and a crumpled work shirt with the top three buttons open. Although the sign above the blackboard reads "No Smoking," the young man draws heavily on a cigarette, flicking the ashes on the floor. Unhurriedly, he places his books on the instructor's desk at the front of the room, seats himself on top of the desk, legs dangling, and announces, "Hi. I'm Ed Walters, your instructor in this course."

At this point, half the students conclude that this is going to be the easiest course they have ever taken, one in which there certainly will be no penalties for late papers, cut classes, or missed homework assignments. Here, they think, is a teacher students can relate to without the usual stiffness and formality. But an equal number of students decide immediately to change sections. This man, they think, clearly has a blasé attitude toward everything. His course will no doubt end up in chaos.

Is it fair to reach such sweeping conclusions and to evaluate others on the basis of so little information? Fair or not, most people make such assumptions and judgments every day, sizing up complete strangers on virtually no evidence. We are sure we know the personality of the grumpy-faced, slovenly man who walks his three mangy dogs every morning, even though we have never spoken to him. We dismiss the big, gum-chewing young man in the football jersey as unintellectual at best, although we have caught only an occasional glimpse of him in the post office. And, even though we know nothing else about her, we are impressed with the sophistication of the woman in the impeccably tailored suit who carries the leather attaché case and always seems to have a cab waiting.

What accounts for the basic impressions we form of others? Why do we find some people immediately appealing and others repulsive? Why do we sense positive or negative "vibrations" from complete strangers? These are some of the questions we will try to answer as we explore the psychology of person perception—how we judge the personalities of other people. Then we will address the question of how, out of the large number of people we come

to feel favorably toward, do we choose those few with whom we want to be friends? Finally, we will discuss what may cause us in certain instances to develop that intense, unique attachment we call love.

PERSON PERCEPTION

People seem to have a need to organize their perceptions about others. It is not enough simply to observe that your new history instructor is smoking in a no-smoking area. You want to attach some meaning to his actions, to figure out what this says about his personality. Is he so nervous that he simply has to smoke, or is he a person who is indifferent to rules and authority? Your wish to know is motivated by more than just idle curiosity about what makes this professor tick. The ability to judge someone's personality helps you predict what he or she may do in other circumstances; this gives you some control over your future dealings with that person. If you conclude, for example, that your instructor is indifferent to rules, you can risk missing an assignment or coming late to class and not fear that it will hurt your grade. Accurately assessing others, then, lends a measure of security to our relations with them.

CLUES TO THE PERSONALITIES OF OTHERS We are all detectives. We gather clues about the personalities of others from a variety of sources—speech, posture, dress, walk, facial expression, even whether or not a person wears glasses. The musical *My Fair Lady* makes the point that changing some of these outward characteristics, especially voice and dress, can change how others perceive one's inner nature. When Liza Doolittle was raggedly dressed and dropped her "h's," she was thought to be dishonest, immoral, and lazy. Dressed in fancy clothes and speaking with an upper-class accent, however, she was judged honest, virtuous, and clever. Thus, two major categories often used in judging a person's nature are appearance and behavior.

EXPECTATIONS BASED ON APPEARANCE At times we know something about a person even before we meet him or her; we may know about a teacher's reputation as a disciplinarian or harsh grader, for example, before we enter the classroom. But usually we have little or no prior knowledge about someone we are encountering for the first time. What criteria do we use to form a first impression? Appearance plays a large part. We tend to categorize strangers by the way they look, drawing upon preconceived notions or stereotypes to fill in the details. Thus, the girl without a bra is thought to be sexually liberated, the muscular football player a "jock," the man in the three-piece suit a conservative Republican.

Some stereotyped expectations that have received a great deal of attention lately are those associated with physically attractive people. In one study (Dion, Berscheid, and Walster, 1972), subjects were shown pictures of men and women of varying degrees of physical attractiveness and asked to rate their personality traits. The physically attractive people were consistently viewed more positively than the less attractive ones. They were seen as more sensitive, kind, interesting, strong, poised, modest, and sociable, as well as more sexually responsive. It seems, therefore, that although we have all heard that "beauty is only skin deep," we act as if it permeates one's entire personality. Moreover, the power of beauty to create the illusion of desirable personality traits seems to begin at a very early age.

Children as young as three years of age have been found to prefer physically attractive children as friends (Dion, 1973), and adults also respond more favorably to attractive children, even judging them smarter and better behaved (Clifford and Walster, 1973).

If physically attractive people always are assumed to be friendly and likable, will they eventually acquire these personality traits? Two psychologists attempted to answer this question (Goldman and Lewis, 1977). They arranged for pairs of male and female students who did not know each other to speak together on the telephone. Each pair talked for five minutes; then the male and the female rated each other on social ease and likability. Those who were rated most socially skillful and likable turned out to be the most physically attractive. Clearly, these people were not born with a superabundance of positive traits. Instead it seems that years of favorable stereotyping, coupled perhaps with the greater opportunity that attractive people have to socialize, resulted in a self-fulfilling prophecy.

Not only do we attribute a wealth of desirable characteristics to beautiful people, we also attribute similar traits to those who merely associate with the

Advertisements such as this present stereotypes, usually of young, attractive, upper-middle-class people who seem to be in love. Readers often assume that someone who looks attractive must also be sensitive, intelligent, and happy. Advertisers hope that, in addition, readers will be persuaded that the model's use of the product may have contributed to his or her happiness.

beautiful. A man is admired, for example, if he is romantically attached to an attractive woman (Sigall and Landy, 1973). Apparently, people conclude that if a beautiful woman, who can easily attract many men, has chosen to become romantically involved with this particular man, he must be special indeed. One reason for our pursuit of beautiful people, then, may be our implicit knowledge of this "radiating effect."

Homely people, however, are generally viewed in an unfavorable light. Research has shown that obese adults, who in our culture are considered unattractive, are often discriminated against and stigmatized (Allon, 1975). Even homely children are targets of prejudice. An unattractive child is more likely to be judged "bad" or "cruel" for a particular act of misbehavior than is a more attractive peer (Dion, 1972). Figure 26.1 shows the reactions of adult women to pictures of both attractive and unattractive children who were allegedly misbehaving. Stereotypes, then, can work against people as well as for them. The difference depends on how one's physical appearance is perceived by others.

INFERRING TRAITS FROM BEHAVIOR: ATTRIBUTION THEORY Although we may base an initial opinion of someone's personality on his or her physical appearance, we have opportunities to alter this impression by observing how the person behaves. In fact, some of our most important information about others comes from the clues their behavior gives us. In the 1940s Fritz Heider examined the process by which the actions of others cause us to in-

fer that they have stable dispositions. In the 1960s other psychologists elaborated on Heider's work by advancing "attribution theories"—theories that propose to explain how people attribute personality traits to others on the basis of how those others behave.

In one such theory (Jones and Davis, 1965), a person's motive or intention is the link between his or her behavior and the personality traits we attribute to it. "What does he mean to accomplish by acting that way?" we may ask. If, for example, a new friend comments that you look terrible in your new red sweater, should you regard this as an attempt to be helpful or an act of hostility? Depending upon the motive you assign, you could attribute different personality traits to the same behavior.

Not all behavior, of course, is equally informative. Some behavior is so common that it reveals very little about personality. Observing a professor lecturing to students in an Elizabethan drama class and then conferring with students during office hours would enable you to deduce virtually nothing about this professor's personality, because these same activities are performed by almost all teachers. But if you observed the same professor arriving a half-hour late for class every morning and refusing to set aside office hours for students, you might be able to infer a great deal about his or her personality. According to Jones and Davis, behavior that is in some way unexpected or unusual and that can most plausibly be explained by only one motive provides the most important clues to a person's real nature.

In an experiment designed to test attribution the-

Figure 26.1 In one experiment (Dion, 1972), adult women were shown reports about children participating in a variety of antisocial behaviors. Photographs of the allegedly misbehaving children were included with the written reports. Half the women looked at a photograph of an attractive child, and the other half saw an unattractive child. The adults tended not only to see the behaviors committed by the unattractive children as more generally antisocial, but to attribute a more inherently negative moral character to these children than they ascribed to the attractive ones. (Adapted from Dion, 1972.)

ory (Jones, Davis, and Gergen, 1961), subjects listened to tape-recorded interviews of people who they were told wanted to become astronauts or submariners. The subjects were told that the ideal astronaut candidate was "inner-directed"—independent, resourceful, and self-reliant. Half of the subjects who listened to an astronaut candidate heard the applicant present himself in the interview as highly inner-directed, whereas the other half heard the candidate present himself as the opposite. The ideal submariner candidate was described as "other-directed"—obedient, cooperative, and friendly. Again, half the subjects heard the submariner applicant present himself in the interview as closely conforming to the ideal type, while the remaining subjects heard the applicant present himself as inner-directed rather than other-directed.

After listening to the taped interviews, the subjects were asked to rate the applicants according to what the subjects believed the applicants' personalities were *really* like. Consistently, they gave higher ratings for credibility to those applicants whose answers were contrary to what one would normally expect from an ideal candidate. Thus, if the job called for other-directedness and the applicant showed he was inner-directed, his response was thought to reflect his true personality. These findings are in keeping with the Jones and Davis theory. The behavior that subjects found most revealing about a person was unusual behavior (such as giving the opposite response of the one expected) that could reasonably be explained by only one motive: a candidate would not have given a "wrong" answer in an interview unless it was true. In contrast, the subjects reasoned that the applicants who painted themselves as conforming to expectations could have been telling the truth, but they could also have been telling the interviewer what he wanted to hear in order to get the job. There was no way of knowing what these applicants' real motives were.

INTEGRATING IMPRESSIONS OF OTHERS

After we infer that a person has a number of particular traits, our perceptions become more integrated and we form our impression of that person. But how do we actually go about fitting together the pieces of someone's personality? Are some traits more important to the final impression than others?

CENTRAL TRAITS Some traits apparently have a greater impact than others on our evaluation of people. In one experiment (Kelley, 1950), students at the Massachusetts Institute of Technology (MIT) were told that their class would be taught that day by a new instructor, whom they would be asked to evaluate at the end of the period. Before the instructor was introduced, the students were given a biographical note about him. The students did not know that two versions of the note had been distributed. Half the students read the description in Figure 26.2A. Half read the one in Figure 26.2B. The two sketches differed only by a single word. The first described the instructor as "warm"; the second as "cold." This simple change, however, created two different sets of expectations and had great impact on how the students perceived the instructor. In the evaluations they filled out at the end of class, the students who read the biography that included the word "warm" rated the instructor as

Your regular instructor is out of town today, and since we of Economics 70 are interested in the general problem of how various classes react to different instructors, we're going to have an instructor today you've never had before, Mr. Blank. Then, at the end of the period, I want you to fill out some forms about him. In order to give you some idea of what he's like, we've had a person who knows him write up a little biographical note about him. I'll pass this out to you now and you can read it before he arrives. *Please read these to yourselves and don't talk about this among yourselves until the class is over so that he won't get wind of what's going on.*

Mr. Blank is a graduate student in the Department of Economics and Social Science here at M.I.T. He has had three semesters of teaching experience in psychology at another college. This is his first semester teaching Ec. 70. He is 26 years old, a veteran, and married. People who know him consider him to be a very warm person, industrious, critical, practical, and determined.

Figure 26.2A This is the introduction read to the class in Kelley's experiment on person perception and one of the notes that was then handed out. Read the note and try to imagine yourself in the situation. Then look at the accompanying photo. Form an impression of the instructor and note your reactions to him. When you have done so, look at Figure 26.2B on page 590. (After Kelley, 1950.)

Figure 26.2B The other note in Kelley's experiment on person perception. (If you have not looked at Figure 26.2A, do so first.) Read this description, let it sink in, and then look at the accompanying photo again, noting your reactions as before.

Mr. Blank is a graduate student in the Department of Economics and Social Science here at M.I.T. He has had three semesters of teaching experience in psychology at another college. This is his first semester teaching Ec. 70. He is 26 years old, a veteran, and married. People who know him consider him to be a rather cold person, industrious, critical, practical, and determined.

substantially more considerate, informal, sociable, popular, goodnatured, and humorous than did the students who had read the word "cold." The instructor's description as "warm" or "cold" also affected the students' response to him during the discussion portion of the class: 56 percent of the students who expected "warmth" participated in the discussion, whereas only 32 percent of those who expected "coldness" did so. (For how the "instructor" actually looked, see the accompanying photo.)

Solomon Asch, who conducted pioneering experiments similar to Kelley's in the late 1940s and early 1950s, called such traits as "warm" and "cold" **central traits** because they have such marked effects on how certain other, related traits are perceived (Asch, 1946). Apparently, when we think that someone has a central trait, we build around it a cluster of expectations of the other traits the person will possess and of how he or she will behave toward us and toward others.

A re-creation of the classroom scene in Kelley's experiment on person perception (see Figures 26.2A and 26.2B). Kelley was able to demonstrate in this study how strongly our impressions of people can be influenced by our expectations about them.

THE PRIMACY EFFECT The order in which traits are perceived can also have an effect on our impression of a person. There is evidence to suggest that the traits that are perceived first influence subsequent information. This has been called the **primacy effect**. If, for example, your first meeting with a classmate is at a football game where he impresses you with his knowledge of game strategy and team standings, it may be difficult to see him as an intellectual when you later learn he is an "A" student with a major in philosophy. He will remain in your mind more the sports enthusiast than the student of Plato.

In one experiment (Luchins, 1957), subjects were presented with the conflicting sets of information about Jim shown in the box on page 591. In the first paragraph Jim is portrayed as extroverted and friendly; in the second paragraph he is seen as introverted and shy. Some of the subjects read para-

Suppose you were seeing Mikhail Baryshnikov dance for the first time. You would probably have some very strong impressions about what he is really like as a person. Such "first impressions" do not, as we generally assume, pass quickly away. Rather, they influence what we subsequently feel about a person.

Is Jim an Introvert or an Extrovert?

(A) Jim is an extrovert

Jim left the house to get some stationery. He walked out into the sun-filled street with two of his friends, basking in the sun as he walked. Jim entered the stationery store which was full of people. Jim talked with an acquaintance while he waited for the clerk to catch his eye. On his way out, he stopped to chat with a school friend who was just coming into the store. Leaving the store, he walked toward school. On his way out he met the girl to whom he had been introduced the night before. They talked for a short while, and then Jim left for school.

(B) Jim is an introvert

After school Jim left the classroom alone. Leaving the school, he started on his long walk home. The street was brilliantly filled with sunshine. Jim walked down the street on the shady side. Coming down the street toward him, he saw the pretty girl whom he had met on the previous evening. Jim crossed the street and entered a candy store. The store was crowded with students, and he noticed a few familiar faces. Jim waited quietly until the counterman caught his eye and then gave his order. Taking his drink, he sat down at a side table. When he had finished his drink he went home.

Source: A. S. Luchins, "Primacy-recency in impression formation," In C. I. Hovland (ed.), *The Order of Presentation in Persuasion.* New Haven: Yale University Press, 1957. Pp. 34–35.

How do first impressions strike us? Quite powerfully, suggests the Luchins experiment. How did you picture Jim after reading A, then B? Can you visualize him differently by rereading the paragraphs in reverse order?

---

graph A first; others read paragraph B first. What effect did the order of presentation have on their impressions of Jim? As expected, most of the students who read paragraph A first labeled Jim a basically outgoing person. Most of those who read paragraph B first, however, considered Jim to be essentially a loner. It seems, then, that first impressions do tend to shape our assessment of people. Apparently, we screen out, reinterpret, or assign less importance to information we receive after our first impression is formed.

SELF-PERCEPTION What about perceiving the personality of the person we all think we know best—ourselves? Do the ways we perceive others also apply to self-perception? Or is an entirely different process involved when we assess ourselves? Some psychologists argue that our perception of others and our self-perception are similar processes. We observe our own behavior, assign motives to our acts, and sometimes infer corresponding personality traits (D. Bem, 1972). Other psychologists disagree. They point out that although it is true to some extent that we come to know our own feelings, attitudes, and traits by observing our own behavior, there are differences between the ways we perceive ourselves and the ways we perceive others.

For one thing, we usually explain another person's behavior in terms of enduring traits, but we tend to explain our own behavior in terms of situational demands. (This point was touched on in the discussion about trait theories of personality in Chapter 19.) For example, a student who was having a conference with his or her faculty advisor, would probably attribute his or her failing marks to external factors—emotional stress over a sick relative, financial problems that forced him or her to work after school instead of studying, a particularly heavy program of courses. The advisor, however, while probably appearing to be sympathetic, would be likely to attribute the student's poor academic performance to underlying traits—lack of intelligence, laziness. Students participating in a study of differences in perception were asked to explain why they had chosen their major and why they thought a friend had chosen his or her major (Nisbett, Caputo, Legant, and Maracek, 1973). When they answered for a friend, the subjects were likely to offer explanations based on personality traits ("He has a very logical, scientific mind"). When they answered for themselves, they more frequently linked their own behavior to an external cause ("Chemistry is a high-paying field"). For the outcome of a similar experiment, see Figure 26.3.

Figure 26.3 Who attributes what to whom? In this first part of an experiment by Storms (1970), actors A and B were conversing while observers C and D watched actors B and A, respectively. Both actors later rated their own behavior—in terms of either personal characteristics about themselves (personality style) or characteristics of the situation. Observers C and D similarly rated each of their target actors. The results showed that actors attributed their own behavior more to situational factors than to enduring personality factors. Observers, in contrast, saw the actors' behavior more in terms of dispositional than situational factors. (Adapted from Storms, 1973.)

There is, however, an important exception to our tendency to ascribe our own actions to external causes. We often ascribe a favorable outcome—success or achievement of some kind—to our own inherent traits because this boosts our self-esteem. An unfavorable outcome we blame on the situation or on others. This tendency has been confirmed by a study (Snyder, Stephan, and Rosenfield, 1976) in which subjects were asked to play a series of games. Without the subjects' knowledge, the experimenters controlled who won or lost most of the games. After the games had been played, each subject was asked to account for the results. Not surprisingly, the losers tended to attribute their performance less to a lack of skill than to bad luck (external causes), while the winners tended to attribute their performance more to skill than to luck (personal causes). Moreover, losers were less likely than winners to attribute the winners' success to skill, while winners were more likely than losers to attribute the losers' defeat to a lack of skill. (For a further discussion of whether or not we perceive ourselves to have enduring traits, see the special feature on pages 593–594.)

INTERPERSONAL ATTRACTION AND FRIENDSHIP

When you attend the first session of a new class, whom do you choose to sit next to? When you go to a party where you do not know anyone, how do you decide which people to talk to? If you join a club, why are you immediately attracted to some members and not to others? How we first perceive the people we meet and how others first perceive us clearly has a great influence on our subsequent dealings with one another—on whether or not we choose to become friends.

But there are other factors at work, in addition to first impressions, in our choice of friends. The basic principle of friendship is quite simple: We are attracted to relationships that seem to promise rewards, and we avoid relationships that threaten to be painful or costly in some way. Of course, the definition of what is a reward or a punishment in human relations varies with the person and the circumstances. Some rewards and punishments, however, are universal. The most common rewards of friendship are stimulation, introduction to new ideas or activities, support for our ego, and sympathy and encouragement when they are needed. Psychologists have isolated several factors that are closely related to whether or not a particular relationship will prove rewarding. These factors and the rewards are discussed in the following sections.

THE EFFECTS OF PROXIMITY If you live in San Francisco, chances are your best friends are San Franciscans, probably people who live in your neighborhood or go to your school. You may believe that many interesting people live in, say, Philadelphia or Atlanta, but you could not become their friends if you had never met any of them. In fact, the single most important factor in friendship is physical proximity—how close together the likely friends live and work.

In an investigation of the effects of physical proximity on friendship (Festinger, Schachter, and Back,

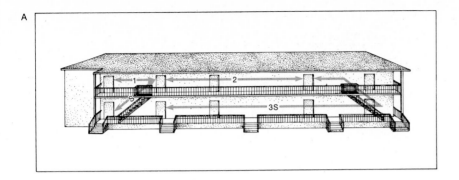

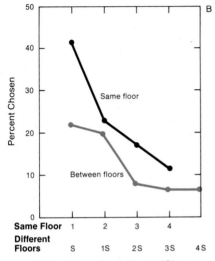

Figure 26.4 The results of the study by Festinger, Schachter, and Back at MIT housing in Cambridge. The investigators studied the relationship between proximity and choice of friends in a housing development. (A) The illustration of one of the seventeen apartment buildings shows how proximity was measured: in roughly equal units of physical distance with a special S unit indicating a flight of stairs. (B) The subjects' statements of where their three closest friends lived is given as a percentage of all the possible people who could have been chosen at a given distance. By far the largest proportion of friends were next-door neighbors. (After Festinger, Schachter, and Back, 1950.)

1950), the subjects were married couples who moved into student housing at MIT just after World War II. The housing complex consisted of seventeen detached two-story buildings, each containing ten apartments (see Figure 26.4A). Very few of the residents knew one another before they moved in, so the investigators were able to focus exclusively on how proximity affected the formation of friendships. All the residents of the development were asked to name the three closest friends they had made in the hous-

ing complex. Some of the results are depicted in Figure 26.4B. As the graph indicates, even within a single building, the closer one lived to another person, the more likely one was to have chosen that person as a close friend. People who lived next door to each other were much more likely to have become friends than were people who lived two doors apart.

A more recent study (Priest and Sawyer, 1967), conducted in a large student dormitory at the University of Chicago, obtained very similar results. Even though the doors to the rooms were only eight feet apart, the students showed a strong tendency to like the person next door more than the one two doors away, and so on. It is obvious that great physical distances can affect the development of friendships, but how can one account for the strong impact of proximity on residents of a dormitory floor where it may take no more than two seconds to get from one room to another? The researchers suggested that perceived distance may depend more on the number of people who intervene than on the number of feet or miles. In a rural area, for example, people living half a mile away from each other may be considered neighbors, whereas in a city those living one hundred feet away may not. In a university dormitory, a room five doors away may represent four closer opportunities bypassed. Why borrow change for the candy machine from someone five rooms away when there are four people who are closer?

Another explanation for the impact of proximity on the formation of friendships is based on the assumption that the closer people live, the more likely they are to bump into one another. And constant exposure often breeds comfortable familiarity. Studies indicate that, all other factors being equal, repeated exposure to various stimuli produces positive attitudes toward those stimuli. In one such experiment (Zajonc, 1968), the investigator showed subjects photographs taken from a college yearbook. Each subject saw twelve faces: two faces only once, two twice, two five times, two ten times, and two twenty-five times. The subjects were then given those pictures and two pictures of faces they had

Impression Management

In a sense, all people wear masks. In fact, the term "personality" comes from the Latin *per sonare*, "to speak through," and refers to the masks that Roman actors held up before their faces and spoke through on stage. In the same way, the images we convey to others about ourselves often have an "onstage" quality. By manipulating our behavior, we manage the impressions we make on others.

Factors Affecting Self-Presentation

Sociologist Erving Goffman (1952), who has done extensive work in the area of impression management, views human beings as actors and their behavior as a series of performances. He argues that people do not usually give direct, honest, or spontaneous expression to heartfelt feelings and reactions. Rather, they go through much of life staging performances to suit the scene—controlling or managing the impressions they give in order to conform to the requirements of the particular situation. The situations in which we find ourselves, of course, vary depending upon the social role we are playing, the message we are trying to convey, and the audience for whom we are performing.

The Social Role

Differing social roles call forth different social behavior in all of us. We would not, for example, dress in the same way for a job interview as for a rock concert. Some recent popular books suggest that the ways in which we manage our physical appearance can actually make us "fit" the roles we want to assume. Books with titles like *Dress for Success* and *Looking Good* advise aspiring young executives to dress as if they already enjoyed high status and great authority. If you look the part, in other words, you'll probably get it.

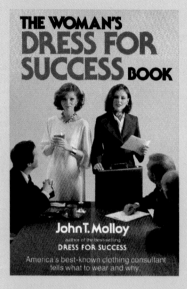

THE WOMAN'S **DRESS FOR SUCCESS** BOOK

John T. Molloy
author of the best-selling
DRESS FOR SUCCESS
America's best-known clothing consultant
tells what to wear and why.

The Message

What we want to communicate to others also influences how we go about building our impression, including our nonverbal cues. In one experiment (Rosenfeld, 1966), subjects were instructed either to seek or to avoid the approval of a partner they did not know. The experimenter watched the interactions through a one-way mirror and recorded the subjects' behavior. The approval-seeking subjects were twice as active as the approval-avoiding ones. They acted interested, asked questions, conversed freely, and smiled often, while the approval-avoiders spoke seldom, criticized their partners, avoided eye contact, and acted conceited. Thus, our movements and gestures, which are an important aspect of the impression we convey, can vary greatly with the content of our messages.

The Audience

People in real life, like actors, must play to different audiences. But to what extent do they adjust their behavior to suit those they want to impress?

The results of one study (Newtson and Czerlinsky, 1974) suggest that a person sometimes modifies a statement of his or her opinion when the audience is known to hold an extreme view of the same issue. Student volunteers were asked to fill out a questionnaire expressing their opinions on the Vietnam War. They were then asked to fill out two other questionnaires reflecting the opinions they would express toward a strongly pro-war audience and toward a strongly anti-war audience. The results clearly demonstrated that audiences who held extreme positions induced subjects to shift their own expressed viewpoints in that direction. The researchers hypothesized that the subjects in this experiment may have been automatically compensating for an expected audience response. When people with extreme attitudes are presented with a position very hostile to their own, their original attitudes may become even more entrenched. The subject, anticipating this adverse shift in audience sentiment, attempts to minimize it by modifying his or her own stance in the direction of the audience's.

People are often motivated to modify their views by the simple desire to be liked by certain others. Social psychologists have learned that the tactic of ingratiation—saying what others want to hear to win their approval—is very likely to be used when a person is dealing with those of higher status or greater power.

There are, of course, times when ingratiation will not be a successful tactic, no matter how subtly it is practiced. Most people are sensitive to such situations. If, for example, the "target" person is known to value independence of thought, most people will deliver independence, not conformity. This awareness of the probable success of ingratiation has been demonstrated through research (Jones, Gergen, Gumpert, and Thibaut, 1965). Male college students were asked to play the subordinate role in a "business game," with an alleged graduate student in business administration playing the role of supervisor. Before a session in which the subordinate and his supervisor were to get to know each other, each subject "overheard" a conversation in which the supervisor expressed the criteria by which he would evaluate a subordinate's performance. Half the subjects overheard statements stressing cooperation and accommodation, while the other half overheard statements stressing high productivity. As expected, in a subsequent exchange of views between each subject and his supervisor, those who believed the supervisor valued agreement were far more likely to use conformity of opinion as an ingratiation tactic.

Is There an Enduring Self?

The research on impression management suggests that people can adapt their attitudes and even their personalities to suit the social circumstances. Does this mean that we are like chameleons, constantly changing the images we project to meet the requirements of the moment—forceful and assertive in one instance, docile and ingratiating in the next? In other words, is there no enduring self?

Most people believe that there is a definite limit to the extent to which they alter their self-presentations. They feel that they *do* possess an essential self, which endures over time. And as we have seen, almost all the major theories of personality discussed in Chapters 18 and 19 assume that each person has a basically stable identity that significantly influences behavior.

But how can the experimental findings just presented be reconciled with this concept of an enduring self? There is no easy resolution. One approach is to consider whether or not individuals vary in the extent to which they respond to situational pressures. Perhaps some people are more likely to manage their self-presentations than others. In one study that

In our century, partly because of the scope of the media, impression management by politicians has become a very sophisticated art.

explored this possibility (Snyder and Monson, 1975), subjects were asked a number of questions about themselves to determine which individuals tended to respond to situational demands, and which tended to behave according to stable traits or dispositions. It was found that there were indeed "impression-managing" and "trait-governed" types of individuals. The "impression managers" generally agreed with such statements as, "In different situations and with different people, I often act like very different persons." The "trait-governed" subjects, however, endorsed such items as, "I have trouble changing my behavior to suit different people and different situations." In a subsequent set of experiments, the "impression managers" were indeed found to be far more likely than the "trait-governed" subjects to alter their behavior according to the social situation.

It would be a mistake to denigrate either of these two different personal styles. Both can be highly successful, just as both can also lead to negative results. In certain instances, "impression-managing" individuals are seen as adaptive, flexible, and sensitive; at other times they are viewed as insecure, deceptive, and manipulative. Similarly, the "trait-governed" person can appear as either authentic, honest, and consistent, or as rigid, stubborn, and egocentric. The final evaluation depends upon the circumstances and the appropriateness of the behavior chosen. Most people, in fact, display a little of both basic tendencies: they alter their self-presentations to suit some situations, but remain guided by internal dispositions in others.

never seen before and were asked to indicate how much they thought they would like the people in the photographs. The results were striking: the more frequently a subject had seen a face, the more likely he or she was to predict that he or she would like that person. These findings have been supported by a study in which subjects were exposed not to photographs but to live people various numbers of times (Saegert, Swap, and Zajonc, 1973).

Why does repeated exposure to people make it more likely that you will befriend them? Why do they seem to "grow on you"? It is likely that as you become more familiar with another person's ways, he or she becomes less threatening and more predictable. Although you may never come to love another person solely on the basis of repeated exposure, you may at least come to feel comfortable in his or her presence. There is a limit, however, to this "old shoe" phenomenon. Repeated exposure to someone you dislike initially is not likely to change your attitude toward that person. In fact, the exposure may have just the opposite effect: your dislike may turn into hatred (Brickman, Redfield, et al., 1972). We can say, then, that when a person's initial attitude toward another is favorable or neutral, repeated exposure is likely to have a positive effect; but when a person's initial attitude is unfavorable, the effect of exposure is likely to be negative.

THE EFFECTS OF SIMILARITY There is apparently a good deal of truth to the old saying, "Birds of a feather flock together." People do tend to form relationships with others who are like them in a number of ways. This holds true for people's choices of friends of either sex.

SIMILARITY IN APPEARANCE In romantic novels and movies, the handsome hero almost always ends up with the beautiful heroine. Does real life follow this plot, with beauty usually attracting beauty? Apparently so. In dating relationships, people of similar physical attractiveness tend to pair off (Murstein, 1972).

One possible explanation for this pattern is that people, when choosing a date, consider not only the social desirability (attractiveness) of the other person but also the probability of being rejected by that person. Dating, in other words, follows the rules of the marketplace: a man calculates risks and rewards before he approaches a woman for a date. If a man

considers his own physical attractiveness to be low, he considers the possibility of rejection by an attractive, selective woman to be high, so he lowers his sights to a somewhat less attractive date. Some evidence of this "matching process" has been supplied by research in which it was found that when there was no possibility of refusal, men tended to choose more attractive women for dates than they would have chosen under ordinary conditions (Berscheid et al., 1971).

Other studies, however, have produced somewhat contradictory results. In one experiment (Huston, 1973), male subjects who rated themselves low in physical attractiveness did not seem to select less physically attractive dates than subjects who rated themselves high in physical attractiveness. This was true even though those who gave themselves low ratings believed they had a poorer than average chance of being accepted by the most attractive females. It has been suggested that perhaps those with a low evaluation of themselves were less sensitive to rejection than those who considered themselves to be attractive. They may have been fairly accustomed to being turned down, and the possibility of a highly rewarding partner may have encouraged them to run the high risk of refusal.

Another interpretation might be that people will try to develop dating relationships with the most attractive partner available, regardless of the probability of rejection. But as they get rejected by those who think they can find more attractive dates, people of similar attractiveness end up paired. According to this interpretation, such a "sorting process" is sufficient to explain the finding that dating couples tend to be similar in physical attractiveness.

SIMILARITY IN SOCIAL BACKGROUND Not only do most couples tend to be similar in physical attractiveness, there is much evidence to show that they often share the same race, religion, economic status, and educational level. There are often strong social pressures, especially from parents, for a person to marry someone with a similar social history. This sorting process also follows from proximity. That is, people of similar income levels and ethnic backgrounds generally live in the same areas and send their children to the same schools. When children and adolescents encounter only people who share their race, religion, and economic level, their friends and potential dating partners will inevitably be similar to them in these respects.

SIMILARITY IN ATTITUDES Similarity in attitudes also plays a central role in the formation of friendships, both between members of the same sex and between members of opposite sexes. This observation has been supported by an extensive study of attitudes and friendship formation at the University of Michigan. Theodore Newcomb (1956) set up an experimental dormitory where rent for one term was waived in return for students' cooperation. At the start of the term Newcomb measured the students' attitudes about various political and social issues. Then, as the weeks passed, the students completed questionnaires in which they listed the people in the dorm whom they perceived as having attitudes similar to their own and rated how much they liked each of the other residents. Newcomb found that a perceived similarity in attitudes was a good predictor of which students would become friends by the end of the term. In short, people like people who think as they do. As one of the characters in Disraeli's *Lothair* declares, "My idea of an agreeable person is someone who agrees with me!"

Social psychologists have come up with several reasons why shared attitudes contribute to the formation of friendships. First, certain shared attitudes provide a basis for joint activities. People who like sports, for example, can play tennis or watch a game together. Friends are rewarded by being able to do the things they like with each other. Second, shared attitudes reinforce the notion that one's opinions are correct. Such validation through social comparison usually has the effect of increasing one's self-esteem. Third, agreement about important matters generally makes communication easier. Like-minded people have fewer arguments and misunderstandings. Also, people with the same basic outlook are generally better able to predict each other's actions, which gives them a sense of security.

Research has shown that the need for security can hamper friendships among people with different

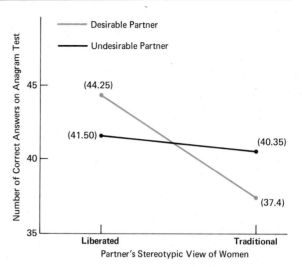

Figure 26.5 Zanna and Pack (1975) showed that women's performance on an alleged measure of intellectual ability (an anagram test) differed when they tried to characterize themselves to suit a desirable as opposed to undesirable male partner. When the desirable partner was portrayed as having a liberated, nontraditional view of women, the women tended to perform better than when the desirable partner was portrayed as having a traditional, sexist view. (Adapted from Zanna and Pack, 1975.)

views. (For an interesting variation on this, see Figure 26.5.) People who score high on a measure of psychological insecurity are more likely to choose to associate with people similar to themselves than are more secure subjects (Goldstein and Rosenfeld, 1969). This may be a partial explanation for the existence of tightly knit ethnic neighborhoods in most American cities. Immigrants often feel insecure in their adopted land and stay near others like themselves with whom they share the old customs, lan-

Similarity can be very comforting in interpersonal relations.

guage, and outlook. Gradually, however, their children and grandchildren, who are more secure as a result of their experience with American schools and other social institutions, begin to move out of their ethnic neighborhoods and to mix with different kinds of people.

THE EFFECTS OF APPROVAL The promise of approval from others weighs heavily in the formation of friendships. People who approve of us and show that they like us bolster our sense of self-worth. Everyone feels this way to some degree, even though some people have a greater need for approval than do others.

How much approval is necessary to promote a favorable feeling toward someone? In one study (Aronson and Linder, 1965), each subject overheard a series of remarks about herself made by a confederate of the experimenters. The first group of subjects heard the confederate make only complimentary remarks. The second group heard only derogatory remarks. The third group heard first very derogatory, then gradually more positive, and finally extremely complimentary comments (this was called the gain condition). The fourth group heard comments progressing from very positive to very disparaging (this was called the loss condition). Each subject was asked to indicate how much she liked the confederate. Can you predict which group liked the confederate most and which liked her

least? Check your answer against the actual results in Figure 26.6.

Somewhat surprisingly, the best-liked confederate was not the one who made uniformly positive remarks, although this person was indeed liked. Instead, the confederate who won the greatest favor was the one who began by saying negative things and ended by saying positive ones. Also, there was a tendency for subjects to prefer the confederate who said consistently negative things to the one who began by saying complimentary things and ended by being disapproving. How can this pattern of results be explained? In the gain condition, the early disparaging remarks may have helped to establish the genuineness and credibility of the confederate. The subject may have thought, in effect, "This is a very discriminating person. She's not easy to impress." As a result, the confederate's eventual approval may have given an even more rewarding boost to the subjects' self-esteem. When the confederate's remarks were uniformly positive, in contrast, the subjects may have thought the confederate a little too free with her praise. Her remarks, therefore, were somewhat less gratifying, and she was liked somewhat less. Similarly, in the loss condition, the subjects who heard positive comments followed by negative ones may have experienced such a surprising and disappointing loss of self-esteem that they felt cooler toward that confederate than they would have felt toward someone who had been critical all along.

These unusual findings have interesting implications. Will the doting husband who constantly praises his wife always lose out to the rival who starts by belittling and ends by praising her? Fortunately for doting husbands, this does not seem to be the case. Apparently, the context and sequence in which approval and disapproval are meted out also play a role in the influence they ultimately have. One carefully conducted study (Berscheid, Brothen, and Graziano, 1976) showed that when a consistently positive evaluator (the husband in our example) and a gain evaluator (the rival) were presented together to a subject, the positive evaluator was preferred. The reason might be that the positive evaluator boosted the subject's badly drooping self-esteem during the time when the gain evaluator was saying negative things about the subject. Consequently, the positive evaluator received the affection that might have been won later by the gain evaluator had no alternatives been available to the subject.

Figure 26.6 The results of Aronson and Linder's experiment illustrate the complex effects of approval on liking. Subjects overheard a confederate of the experimenter make remarks about them. As one would expect, a person who made positive comments was better liked than one who made negative remarks, but best liked were the confederates whose remarks began critically but ended by being complimentary. Least liked were the confederates whose remarks were initially positive but became disparaging. (After Aronson and Linder, 1965.)

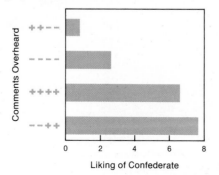

THE EFFECTS OF COMPLEMENTARY NEEDS

Many psychologists have speculated about the ways in which the personalities of two people may mesh to form a bond of mutual interdependence. One theory, based on writings of Carl Jung (discussed in Chapter 18), suggests that people have unconscious "archetypes," or ideals, of the sort of person who would best complement them. When someone encounters a person who corresponds to this archetype, he or she immediately becomes aware of the match and falls in love.

Other theorists (for example, Winch, 1958) have suggested that complementary needs are a basis for attraction between friends as well as lovers. Thus, a person with the need to dominate is attracted to one with the need to be dominated; a person with a need to care for others is drawn to one with a need to be cared for. In describing a friendship between two teenaged boys, psychologist Robert White (1972) provided a good example of how two personalities complemented one another:

> Ben, whose school experience had been so unstimulating that he never read a book beyond those assigned, discovered in Jamie a lively spirit of intellectual inquiry and an exciting knowledge of politics and history: Here was a whole world to which his friend opened the door and provided guidance. Jamie discovered in Ben a world previously closed to him, that of confident interaction with other people. Each admired the other, each copied the other, each used the other for practice.

Recent research, however, implies that compatibility of needs may be a better predictor of friendships than simple complementarity of needs. An example of compatible needs for a pair of friends is a high level of dominance in one person and a low need for autonomy in the other. In contrast, a high need for dominance in one partner and a low need for dominance in the other would be complementary, but would not necessarily be compatible. Richard Wagner (1975) assessed the needs of camp counselors who had worked together for a month or more and had formed friendships. He found strong evidence that people with compatible need structures were much more likely to be friends than people with incompatible needs.

Marital adjustment may also be affected by compatibility of needs. John Meyer and Susan Pepper (1977) studied the need structures of married couples who scored high or low on a scale of marital adjustment. They found no evidence for a relationship between adjustment and the simple kind of complementarity proposed by Winch (1958). But they did find that the better-adjusted couples were similar in their needs for affiliation, aggression, autonomy, and nurturance. These are needs in which the most compatible pattern for spouses is to be quite similar to each other. A couple with similarly high needs for affiliation, for example, can engage in a great deal of socializing, while a couple who are both low in the need for affiliation can be stay-at-homes. Very different levels of need for affiliation would be expected to produce tension between marriage partners.

It may be, then, that a knowledge of needs can be used to predict friendship patterns and marital adjustment. But the principles for determining need compatibility are complex and subtle. They are complicated by the fact that the social context of the relationship also affects the compatibility of need structures (Wagner, 1975). Because of these complexities, it may be quite some time before the principles of need compatibility have practical applications.

INTERPERSONAL ATTRACTION AND LOVE

Twentieth-century Americans are immersed in the notion of romantic love. It is our constant companion in books and movies, on our television screens, in our songs, in our advertisements. So important is romance in our popular culture that by the time children reach adolescence, they have come to believe that falling in love is an inevitable part of growing up.

Social psychologists have only recently begun to probe the nature of romantic love. Not surprisingly, the questions they address are similar to the ones that people have been asking for centuries. What is love, and how does it differ from liking? What causes two people to fall in love? Some recent answers to these age-old questions are reviewed in the following sections.

THE DIFFERENCE BETWEEN LIKING AND LOVING   One way to look for answers to the question "What is love?" is to ask people to describe their feelings toward a lover, as against their feelings toward a friend. In one such study (Rubin, 1970), several hundred students were given a long series of

Is It Really Love?

Rubin's scale items, some of which are shown here, were developed to distinguish between liking and loving in young opposite-sex student couples, but it is interesting to extend the analysis that these scale items make possible to same-sex relationships, relationships between very old people, people of different ages, and even to relationships that are not strictly human. People form strong likes *and* loves outside the romantic context as well as within it.

Roy Lichtenstein's *Kiss, V,* 1964.

Liking

1. *Favorable evaluation.*
   I think that _____ (my boyfriend or girlfriend) is unusually well-adjusted.
   It seems to me that it is very easy for _____ to gain admiration.
2. *Respect and confidence.*
   I have great confidence in _____'s good judgment.
   I would vote for _____ in a class or group election.
3. *Perceived similarity.*
   I think that _____ and I are quite similar to each other.
   When I am with _____ , we are almost always in the same mood.

Loving

1. *Attachment.*
   If I could never be with _____ , I would feel miserable.
   It would be hard for me to get along without _____ .
2. *Caring.*
   If _____ were feeling badly, my first duty would be to cheer him (her) up.
   I would do almost anything for _____ .
3. *Intimacy.*
   I feel that I can confide in _____ about almost anything.
   When I am with _____ , I spend a good deal of time just looking at him (her).

Source: Zick Rubin, "Measurement of Romantic Love," *Journal of Personality and Social Psychology,* 16 (1970), pages 265–273.

statements that expressed a variety of feelings one might have toward one's boyfriend or girlfriend. The students were then asked to indicate which statements best expressed their own feelings toward their boyfriend or girlfriend. The results showed that the students' feelings could be grouped into two categories, one corresponding reasonably well to what people typically mean by "liking" and the other corresponding to what they mean by "love." Some sample items from the "liking" and "loving" scales developed from this analysis are presented in the accompanying box.

Efforts to define love have involved more than categorizing feelings. Researchers have also made some progress in identifying observable behavior related to love. For instance, couples who got high scores on the "loving" scale spent more time looking into each other's eyes than did couples who received lower scores on the scale (Rubin, 1973). The notion that lovers spend a great deal of time looking into each other's eyes is, of course, a part of our folklore. Sociologist Erving Goffman (1963) has suggested that "eye contact" serves as a mutually understood signal that the communication channel between two people is open. (Strangers in an elevator take pains to avoid eye contact because communication between them is closed.) Thus, the sustained eye contact of lovers supports the idea that love is characterized by strong feelings of attachment and intimate communication.

WHY DO PEOPLE FALL IN LOVE? We may feel that we are in love before we know for certain who it is we have fallen for. As surprising as this may sound, it is nevertheless one of the theories that psychologists who study love have offered to explain that mysterious phenomenon (Berscheid and Walster, 1978).

This interesting approach is based on the cognitive theory of emotions discussed in Chapter 15. According to this theory, the subjective experience of an emotion often depends on a person's cognitive appraisal of the situation at the time he or she is physiologically aroused and becomes aware of a racing heart, trembling hands, and other bodily sensations. In other words, the aroused person often looks around for the external stimulus that may be causing the inner upheaval. Similarly, a person who is experiencing sexual arousal or the physiological effects of some other stimulating experience may search the surroundings to find a cause for these feelings, spot an attractive acquaintance (or stranger), and decide that he or she is in love with that person. This phenomenon may explain the newspaper stories about people who marry a person who has rescued them from danger—a lifeguard at the beach, for instance, or a doctor or nurse in a hospital emergency ward. The person's physiological arousal in response to danger may be transferred to the rescuer, who then becomes an object of love.

Some support for this "misattribution" explanation of love comes from a recent experiment (Dutton and Aron, 1974). The researchers arranged for male subjects to be approached by an attractive female (a confederate in the experiment) while they were crossing one of two bridges near Vancouver, British Columbia. One bridge was a narrow, rickety structure that swayed in the wind hundreds of feet above a rocky canyon; the other was a solid structure only a few feet above a shallow stream. In brief stories that they were subsequently asked to write, the subjects on the rickety bridge expressed more sexual imagery than did those on the solid bridge. Those who had been on the rickety bridge were also more likely than those on the solid bridge to telephone the female confederate later, supposedly to get more information about the study. The researchers ex-

plained these results by arguing that the subjects were physiologically aroused by the frightening bridge, and when approached by the attractive confederate, they relabeled their feelings as sexual attraction. According to this theory, then, when the circumstances are right, almost any strong emotion can be interpreted as love.

This "adrenaline makes the heart grow fonder" explanation of love at first sight was challenged recently. Two psychologists (Kenrick and Cialdini, 1977) argued that arousal on a high, rickety bridge would be negative in nature, resulting in fear or anxiety, not in attraction. As an alternative explanation for the findings, they suggested that the subjects may have been attracted to the woman because she was associated with a reduction in fear. The woman, after all, was a pleasant distraction from the fear-creating circumstances. In addition, she was present when the subjects reached the other side of the bridge safely and so was paired with their feelings of relief. According to this explanation, based on learning theory, any stimulus associated with the reduction of a negative state becomes more attractive.

The hypothesis that romantic love may be based on principles of reinforcement seems to have broader applicability than the notion that love may be a mislabeling of emotions. Consider, for example, the phenomenon referred to by psychologists as the "Romeo and Juliet" effect. When parents disapprove of their children's romantic involvement and try to keep them apart, the lovers experience even greater attraction for each other than when there are no obstacles to their romance (Driscoll, Davis, and Lipetz, 1972). Often, in fact, the greater the intensity of parental interference, the greater the intensity of the romantic attachment. One explanation for these findings is that anxiety is reduced when it is shared with another person. Thus, the stress induced by disapproving parents is reduced when the lovers are together. The more anxiety in the situation, the more comfort the partner provides, and the more desirable he or she becomes.

Romantic attraction, then, may be based on physiological arousal, coupled perhaps with the operation of the principles of reinforcement. But these explanations need not detract from the pleasures of intimate friendship and love. The sun is no less enjoyable on a warm summer day when we know that the rays are part of the electromagnetic spectrum produced by the fusion of hydrogen atoms into helium. In the same way, the pleasures of friendship and love need not be diminished by our increased understanding of them.

Summary

1. People seem to need to organize their perceptions of others. Accurately assessing another person's personality helps one to predict what that person will do in other circumstances, which gives one some control in future dealings with that person. Two major categories often used in judging a person's nature are appearance and behavior.
   A. We often form first impressions of strangers on the basis of the way they look and our preconceived notions or stereotypes about what their appearance means.
      1. Studies have indicated that physically attractive people are stereotypically viewed more positively than less attractive people.
      2. Physically unattractive people are generally viewed in an unfavorable light. Research has shown that homely people, children as well as adults, are often the targets of discrimination.
   B. Attribution theories propose to explain how people attribute personality traits to others on the basis of how those others behave. Behavior that is in some way unexpected or unusual and can most plausibly be explained by only one motive provides other people with their most important clues to a person's real nature.
   C. After we infer that another person has a number of traits, we integrate those perceptions to form an impression of the other person. Certain kinds of traits are more important than others in forming an impression.
      1. **Central traits** have marked effects on how certain other, related traits are perceived. The belief that a person possesses a central trait can create a number of expectations about the other traits the person will have and about how the person will behave.
      2. The **primacy effect** is the phenomenon in which the traits that we perceive first influence our further impressions of another person. Experiments have suggested that people have a tendency to screen out, reinterpret, or assign less importance to information that they receive after a first impression has been formed.
   D. Some psychologists believe that self-perception and our perception of others are similar processes. Other psychologists point to an important difference between the two: A person usually explains another's behavior in terms of enduring traits and his or her own behavior in terms of situational demands. An exception to this observation is that people generally ascribe their own successes to inherent traits because it boosts their self-esteem.

2. Factors other than first impressions are important in the choice of friends. People are attracted to relationships that seem to promise rewards, and they avoid relationships that threaten to be painful.
   A. Proximity has been found to have a great impact on the formation of friendships. Studies have shown that even within a single building, the closer one lives to another person, the more likely one is to choose that person as a close friend.
      1. One explanation is that the perceived distance between people may depend more on the number of people who intervene than on the actual physical distance.
      2. Another explanation is that repeated exposure to people makes it likely that we will have positive feelings about them if our initial attitude toward them was favorable or neutral. When there are initial feelings of dislike, repeated exposure is likely to result in negative feelings.
   B. People tend to form relationships with others who are similar to them in a number of ways, including (1) physical appearance, (2) social background, and (3) attitudes.
      1. In dating relationships people of similar physical attractiveness tend to pair off.
         a. Some studies have suggested that people consider both the attractiveness of the other person and the probability of being rejected when they choose a person to ask for a date.
         b. Another study has contradicted this by showing that men who considered themselves low in physical attractiveness did not select less attractive dates than men who considered themselves physically attractive. A possible expla-

nation for this is that those with a low evaluation of themselves might have been less sensitive to the possibility of rejection than those who considered themselves attractive.

   c. Another interpretation is that people try to develop dating relationships with the most attractive partner, regardless of the probability of rejection. Through the "sorting-out" process that results, people of similar attractiveness are paired.

  2. Couples tend to share the same race, religion, economic status, and educational level. This may be caused by social pressures (often from parents) and by the fact that people of similar income levels and ethnic backgrounds generally live in the same areas.

  3. Similarity of attitudes contributes to the formation of friendships between members of the same sex and members of opposite sexes. Social psychologists have offered several reasons why this is so:

   a. Certain shared attitudes provide a basis for joint activities.

   b. Shared attitudes reinforce the notion that one's opinions are correct.

   c. Agreement about important matters generally leads to a sense of security because it makes communication easier.

C. The promise of approval from others is important in the formation of friendships because it gives one a sense of self-worth. A study to determine how much approval is necessary to promote a favorable feeling toward a person showed that the "gain" condition (in which overheard remarks progressed from derogatory to complimentary) resulted in the most favorable feelings toward the person. The "loss" condition (in which remarks progressed from complimentary to derogatory) resulted in the most negative feelings toward the other person.

D. There are a number of theories about the ways in which the personalities of two people may mesh to form a bond of mutual interdependence.

  1. Carl Jung believed that people have unconscious archetypes of the people who would best complement them. When someone encounters a person of the opposite sex who corresponds to this archetype, he or she becomes aware of the match and falls in love.

  2. Other psychologists believe that compatibility of needs may be a better predictor of friendships than simple complementarity of needs. Compatibility of needs may be an important consideration between marital partners as well as between friends.

3. Only recently have social psychologists begun to attempt to explore the nature of romantic love.

A. One way to distinguish between liking and loving is to categorize people's feelings toward both lovers and friends. Another method of defining love is to identify behaviors related to love.

B. The "misattribution" explanation of love suggests that a person who is experiencing sexual arousal or the physiological effects of some stimulating experience may attribute these feelings to the presence of an attractive person, and decide that he or she is in love with that person.

C. The "misattribution" explanation has been challenged by psychologists who contend that romantic love may be based on principles of reinforcement rather than a mislabeling of emotions. The "Romeo and Juliet" effect seems to substantiate this claim.

RECOMMENDED READINGS

BERSCHEID, ELLEN, and ELAINE WALSTER. *Interpersonal Attraction.* 2nd ed. Reading, Mass.: Addison-Wesley, 1978. A well-organized and valuable review of research in this area.

DUCK, STEVE W. (ed.). *Theory and Practice in Interpersonal Attraction.* London: Academic Press, 1976. A collection of chapters by leading researchers and theoreticians, focused on interpersonal attraction.

HARVEY, JOHN H., WILLIAM Y. ICKES, and R. F. KIDD (eds.). *New Directions in Attribution Research.* Hillsdale, N.J.: Erlbaum, 1976. A collection of provocative papers—the frontiers of research on person perception—by leading researchers and theoreticians.

HUSTON, TED L. (ed.). *Foundations of Interpersonal Attraction.* New York: Academic Press, 1974. An excellent collection of papers by leading researchers in the field.

CHAPTER TWENTY-SEVEN

SOCIAL INFLUENCE AND SOCIAL GROUPS

I suppose we can all think of examples in which we participated in the formation of groups under unusual circumstances. Back in the middle 1940s, I spent some time in the army as a private. I hated it. I was not badly treated; I did not see combat; I was never in danger of any kind; but I just hated it. I hated the things we were required to do, the conditions under which we were required to live, the people with whom I was forced to associate.

Then the time came when we had to travel from Virginia to Hawaii. It was a ten-day trip by train and ship. Only a relatively small number of soldiers were going, and most were eighteen-year-olds with limited background and education. Seven of us, including myself, were older men with college degrees. We seven clung together. There was nowhere to go and no one with whom to interact except ourselves. There was nothing much to do, but we played bridge, talked, reminisced, told jokes. I never played bridge very much before that trip or since. I never even liked it very much; but it

seemed the most remarkable and fascinating game in the world for those ten days. I couldn't have enough. And those six other guys—the nicest, sweetest, best guys in the world. We loved each other. We were like brothers. Everything was so warm and comfortable that I was actually *happy*. In fact, I don't know offhand when in my whole life I was so continuously happy over a so long a stretch of time. And in the Army!

Occasionally, I remember, we would discuss the possibility of trying out for officer-training school. As officers, our life would be easier, but we would undoubtedly have to stay in the army longer. We all thought we would remain privates and push for discharge. Of the seven of us, I was far and away the most vehement in supporting the private-and-discharge alternative.

Then one time the other six came to me, all together, and told me they had decided to opt for officer training. The advantages were simply too attractive. Wouldn't I join them? I was astonished. How

could they be so foolish? So weak? I refused. I tried to dissuade them. They put the pressure on, argued, pleaded, listed the advantages. To the end I resisted and finally in black despair I cried out, "Go ahead, leave me. Desert me. To hell with all of you."

Then they broke down laughing and explained it was a put-up job. They just wanted to see if I could resist group pressure, and there were bets on as to whether I would or not. I tried to laugh, too, and boasted that I was immovable in my convictions. But I wasn't. I have never forgotten the despair of those moments and how near I came to agreeing to be an officer rather than have them leave me.

Eventually, we reached Hawaii and separated. It may have seemed to me on that wonderful trip that we were soul mates who would remain together forever, but the fact is that since I left the army—so long ago—I have never been in contact with one of them.

Isaac Asimov

In one of the situations created for the television program *Candid Camera*, an unsuspecting person is waiting in a lobby for an elevator. The elevator arrives and the doors open, revealing a crowd of passengers. They are behaving very strangely: they are all facing the back of the car. Victim after victim peers quizzically into the elevator, hesitates for a moment, then promptly steps in and faces the rear. Whatever is passing through their minds, none of the new passengers asks any questions. Each quietly, almost meekly, conforms to the prevailing norm.

This television gag illustrates an important aspect of human behavior: the influence of others is difficult to resist. Our thoughts, our actions, the conscious and unconscious choices we make, are all influenced by other people. And we do not necessarily have to interact with people to feel their influence. People whom we have never met, but whom we admire or respect, can shape our behavior just as surely as our closest relatives and friends.

This chapter explores the extent and causes of social influence. We begin by discussing the roots of human social life—our need for contact with other people. Why are humans social animals? What accounts for our strong desire to affiliate with people under certain circumstances, and to avoid human companionship in others? Then we take up the subject of social influence itself, focusing on two areas of major concern to social psychologists—conformity to prevailing norms and obedience to authority. We conclude by discussing human groups—what they are and how they influence our lives.

THE NEED FOR SOCIAL CONTACT

Many people who live an isolated existence—hermits, religious recluses, castaways, prisoners in solitary confinement—record their thoughts and feelings. Their writings indicate that prolonged isolation can often cause great psychological pain. "Gradually the loneliness closed in," reported one prisoner in an autobiographical account. "Later on I was to experience situations which amounted almost to physical torture, but even that seemed preferable to absolute isolation" (quoted in Schachter, 1959, p. 7). After a time, according to such accounts, the intensity of suffering may ease, but this temporary relief is often followed by a decline into almost trancelike apathy and despair. Prolonged isolation has reportedly led to deterioration in mental processes and, in some cases, to hallucinations.

In an attempt to study isolation in a controlled setting, Stanley Schachter (1959) paid five student volunteers $10 a day to remain alone, locked in a windowless, sparsely furnished room. Each of the subjects was supplied with food and water, and some of them were also given objects that offered minor distraction, such as metal-link puzzles or a dart board. But none were allowed to communicate with other people, not even vicariously through radio or books.

One subject nearly battered the door down to get out after only two hours of isolation, and another reported that he had become quite nervous by the end of the second day. Two other subjects, however, who remained in isolation for two full days, showed virtually no signs of anxiety. The fifth subject, who stayed in the isolation room for eight days, was far from severely disturbed upon his release, although he did report a growing feeling of uneasiness.

Schachter was struck by the contrast between the relatively mild effects of isolation in his laboratory and the dramatic effects reported in autobiographical accounts. It could be argued that the isolation of Schachter's subjects was not long enough to produce intense suffering, but in some autobiographical accounts the greatest pain is reported after only a few hours of isolation. It may also be that isolation produces suffering only when combined with other factors such as fear. It is more likely, however, that only those who have some kind of dramatic experience take the time and trouble to write about it; so the autobiographical accounts can be considered a biased sample. A more representative sample would probably confirm Schachter's finding that many people withstand isolation with only minor discomfort.

Another point to consider is that the students who volunteered for the experiment may have done so *because* they anticipated no difficulties in dealing with the isolation (Schachter, 1959). Still, it is the rare person who seeks isolation as a way of life. All the students in Schachter's study were very glad when their periods of confinement were ended and they were able to interact with other people again.

WHY DO PEOPLE SEEK SOCIAL CONTACT?

Although not all people need social contact to survive, most people seek interaction with others. What accounts for this almost universal gregar-

People need to be with other people. An isolated child is a matter of concern to parents and teachers, and extreme isolation in a child or an adult may be a sign of emotional disturbance.

iousness (sociability) of human beings? Explanations usually fall into one of two categories: those that attribute the need for social contact to instinct and those that attribute it to learning and reinforcement (Linder, 1973).

INSTINCT THEORIES Theories that attribute human sociability to instinct suggest that people, through the process of evolution, have become genetically programmed to associate with other members of their species—in much the same way that birds or wolves, for example, are believed to instinctively form flocks or packs. It is not difficult to imagine that natural selection may have favored those of our early ancestors who chose to organize their lives around social groups. After all, group life has survival value, especially for a creature, like a human being, that is not physically well equipped to defend itself against predators.

But it is a long jump from acknowledging the value of sociability to assuming that the urge to interact with others is somehow genetically wired into each human. Instead, it is far more likely that natural selection simply favored our ancestors who were intelligent enough to realize the survival benefits that the band or community had to offer. In addition, instinctive patterns of social behavior are usually quite uniform across various groups of the same species; but humans display such a wide variety of social behavior in different cultures and subgroups that it is difficult to argue for a genetic or instinctive basis for human gregariousness.

REINFORCEMENT THEORIES The second major explanation of the human need for social contact is based on the principle of reinforcement (discussed in Chapter 4). According to this theory, social interaction is not in itself a primary reinforcer, like food or water, because it does not reduce any physiological need. But interaction with others can become a *secondary* reinforcer if it is continually paired with a primary reinforcer. Thus, during feeding, when the primary drives of hunger and thirst are reduced, the infant comes repeatedly into warm, close contact with its mother. Eventually, because of its association with primary reinforcement, this social contact acquires reinforcement properties of its own. Soon the baby generalizes what it has learned to other social situations, seeking human companionship for its own sake. In short, the infant has developed a very powerful secondary need—the need for interaction with others.

Some psychologists have speculated that the acquisition of a need for social contact is limited to a particular stage of the infant's development. As we saw in Chapter 3, the work of ethologists indicates that baby ducklings learn to follow a mother duck only if she is present during a sensitive period after their birth. If she is absent at this time, the young may learn to respond instead to some other object, and no amount of subsequent effort will induce them to seek contact with the mother duck (Hess, 1959). Similarly, dogs are capable of forming attachments to other animals, including humans, only during the third to twelfth week of life (Scott, Stewart, and De Ghett, 1974). If sensitive periods for attachment formation are found in other animal species, they might be found in humans as well. John Bowlby (1969), whose theory of attachment in infancy was discussed in Chapter 10, has estimated that a child must form close ties to an adult by the age of three in order to develop normal social relationships later in life. (See the accompanying box for a description of a child who was raised without any human contact at all.)

This hypothesis, of course, is highly speculative. We simply do not know the exact learning mechanisms that underlie humans' general need for social interaction, and perhaps we never will. For obvious ethical reasons, many of the experiments with newborn infants that would be necessary to investigate this subject conclusively can never be performed. What psychologists can investigate, however, are the factors that motivate socially normal individuals to affiliate or not to affiliate with others in particular situations. It is to this topic that we now turn.

THE PSYCHOLOGY OF AFFILIATION We have all experienced times when the desire to be with other people was particularly strong, as well as times when we were just as glad to be left alone. What accounts for such differences in the wish to affiliate with others? While we may think that the underlying causes are simply shifts in our moods, psychologists have found that differences in the desire to associate with other people can be influenced by social situations.

SITUATIONS PROMOTING AFFILIATION The scene is a modern scientific laboratory at a university. A number of students, who have volunteered to participate in an experiment, are met at the door by a white-coated man who identifies himself as a doctor from the university medical school. He tells the students that they are part of a very important study on the physiological effects of electric shock. A series of shocks are to be administered while each subject's pulse rate and blood pressure are taken. In an ominous tone, the doctor warns that the shocks

Gazelle-Boy

This interchange is part of a communication between a "gazelle boy" of about ten years of age—a child who was actually raised by a group of gazelles—and another human being. The origins of the child and his early relationship within the group are unknown, but Jean-Claude Armen, who spent several months with the boy, observed a special attachment between the child and one older female gazelle. The child had no consciousness of what being "human" meant: he ate, slept, ran, and socialized exactly as the animals did. But he was, nevertheless, part of a social group and able both to understand and to exchange complex messages about and with members of his adoptive "family."

Immediately, everything seems to gather momentum in the child, who comes up to me and sniffs my toes, still showing a few furtive traces of fear, despite his great boldness, and fitfully screwing up his nose, after the manner of his adoptive mentors.

Then he gives me a few little licks, first on the legs, then on the fingers. With little cries from the back of his throat, probably marks of joy, this strange child of nature incapable of all human language seems to be trying to make himself understood.

. . . The boy suddenly darts his tongue at the tip of my nose. In a flash, without further reflection, I respond in the same manner. . . ."

Source: Jean-Claude Armen. *Gazelle-Boy: A Child Brought Up by Gazelles in the Sahara Desert.* Stephan Handman (tr.). London: The Bodley Head, 1974, p. 35.

will be extremely painful. But, he adds with a tight smile, they will cause no permanent tissue damage. Understandably, the subjects become highly anxious.

The doctor then announces that the subjects must leave the laboratory for ten minutes while the experimental equipment is prepared. Each subject is given the chance to express a preference for waiting alone in a private room or waiting in a classroom with other subjects. The choices made by the subjects, of course, constitute the real experiment. Once the subjects express their preferences, the experiment is concluded and no shocks are ever given.

The results of the study (Schachter, 1959), which are shown in Figure 27.1, indicate that the tendency to affiliate may in fact be related to anxiety. Subjects in the high-anxiety condition described above—those who were made extremely nervous by the doctor's ominous manner and sadistic smile— were much more likely to want to wait with others than were subjects in the low-anxiety condition— those whose fears were reduced when the doctor, instead of grimly warning them of pain, assured them in a kindly manner that the shocks would produce only a mild, not unpleasant tingling sensation.

What do these findings really mean? Do they suggest that anxiety will always create a desire for affiliation? And is the need for affiliation met by associating with just anybody or only with people in the same predicament? Some interesting answers to these questions can be found in the theory of **social comparison** proposed by Leon Festinger (1954).

According to this theory, people can verify their beliefs about the world and themselves in two ways—objectively, by testing them directly, or comparatively, by examining them in relation to the beliefs of other people. This second method is known as social comparison. Much of the recent work in social comparison has focused on the verification of abilities and traits. Suppose you receive a score of

76 on a biology exam. The number of points you earned is an ambiguous piece of information. Does it mean that you did well or poorly on this particular test? Research indicates that you would probably try to determine where you stood in relation to others (Samuel, 1973). You would first attempt to find out what the highest and lowest scores in the class were. This would give you two points of reference for evaluating your own grade. Then you would probably try to compare your performance with the performance of others you perceive to be similar to you—for example, English majors like yourself who are taking the same biology course you are.

Similarly, the anxious, shock-threatened subjects in the experiment just described might also have used social comparison to evaluate their opinions and emotions. Many thoughts and feelings were probably crossing each subject's mind—fear of the anticipated pain, anger at the diabolical doctor, a sense that all the discomfort might be justified if the experiment was really so important to science. In order to evaluate these various reactions and determine which were most appropriate, each subject could compare perceptions and feelings with others in the same situation. Affiliation with just anyone would not have served this purpose. Only those in the same set of circumstances could have offered the needed source of comparison.

The belief that anxiety often promotes a wish to affiliate with others who can validate one's own reactions was confirmed in a later experiment (Schachter, 1959). Subjects were made anxious by the same ruse described above. Half were then given a choice of waiting alone or waiting with others who were about to take part in the same experiment. The other half were given a choice between waiting alone or passing the time in a room with students waiting to see their academic advisors. Many more subjects chose to affiliate with others when they could be with those in the same situation. Apparently, "misery doesn't love just any kind of company; it loves only miserable company" (Schachter, 1959).

Since social comparison theory was first proposed, social psychologists have attempted to establish exactly which other people a person can be expected to turn to when attempting to validate his or her own beliefs. Depending on the circumstances, the answer may not always be "people in the same boat." At times we may also turn to people—often called **reference others**—whose opinions we respect, or to people whom we know to share

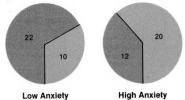

Figure 27.1 The results of Schachter's 1959 experiment about the effects of anxiety on affiliation.

22 10

20 12

Low Anxiety   **High Anxiety**

● Women who chose to be alone or did not care

● Women who chose to affiliate

For each member of this club, the other members serve as "reference others." In attempting to validate our beliefs, we generally turn to those individuals whose judgments we respect.

many of our values and perspectives on the world (Goethals and Darley, 1977). Thus, if a woman wants to find out if her negative reaction to a proposed change in alimony laws is justified, she might find out where a women's rights organization whose principles she admires stands on the issue, not simply what other divorced women like herself believe.

SITUATIONS REDUCING AFFILIATION Although feelings of anxiety and uncertainty can lead to a desire to affiliate with others, there are also times when emotional stress can create a preference for solitude. There is evidence, for example, that people are likely to avoid social comparison when their feelings are particularly intense. Several days after President John F. Kennedy's assassination in 1963, two researchers conducted a nationwide survey of people's reactions to the tragedy (Sheatsley and Feldman, 1964). While 54 percent of those polled said they had felt like talking to others, 40 percent said they had preferred to be alone. It is significant that many of the people who reported a preference for solitude were among those who indicated the greatest admiration for Kennedy. The feelings these people experienced may have been so intense that they did not want to expose them publicly.

Social psychologists suggest that whether a person seeks or avoids affiliation depends not only on the intensity but also on the nature of the emotion aroused. Embarrassment or shame, for example, may inhibit people from seeking social comparison. In one experiment (Sarnoff and Zimbardo, 1961),

male subjects who were awaiting a potentially embarrassing experience, in which they would have to suck on a variety of objects more appropriate for infants than for college students, were much less willing to affiliate than subjects awaiting a potentially painful experience (see Figure 27.2). By the same token, an adolescent boy, anxious about his ability as an athlete and embarrassed about his persistent clumsiness, may prefer to sit alone while awaiting basketball tryouts rather than in the company of his better-coordinated friends.

Figure 27.2 Not all uncomfortable situations lead to a desire for affiliation. Sarnoff and Zimbardo (1961) compared affiliative needs in subjects experiencing fear of an external situation with affiliative needs in subjects experiencing anxiety about being in an embarrassing situation (sucking on childlike objects such as lollipops). They found that people in anxiety-provoking situations preferred to be alone, while those in fear situations preferred to affiliate. (After Sarnoff and Zimbardo, 1961.)

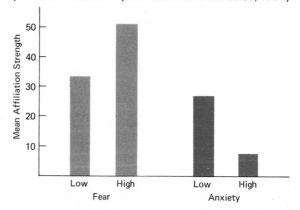

SOCIAL INFLUENCE AND INDIVIDUAL BEHAVIOR

Most Americans insist that they would never have become supporters of Adolf Hitler if they had lived in Germany during World War II. Yet millions of Germans did, and these people were not unusual in any significant respect—not particularly weak or especially open to suggestion. They were simply ordinary people responding to extraordinary circumstances in what was apparently a very ordinary way. All people, it seems, are greatly influenced by social forces outside themselves.

Social psychologists have devoted a great deal of attention to social influence. One area that has been extensively studied is the way in which social pressure can induce a person to conform to a prevailing attitude or perception. Another area of great interest is the process by which people in positions of authority can induce others to obey commands even when those commands may violate basic moral standards. We will discuss these two topics in the following sections.

CONFORMITY TO THE PREVAILING NORMS

Dressing in the latest fashion, going to the movie everybody's talking about and saying you loved it when you didn't, pretending you are casual about sex when you feel otherwise, agreeing with a radical friend's political opinions although you really do not understand the issues—all are examples of conformity. Essentially, **conformity** is the tendency to shift one's views or behavior closer to the norms expressed by other people. When you conform, it is not necessarily because you are convinced that what you are saying or doing is right. You may simply take a particular public stance because you believe that others prefer, or even demand, that you do so. Conformity, then, is the result of implicit or explicit social pressure.

Although the word "conformity" often has a negative connotation, acceptance of prevailing norms is often quite constructive. The existence of common standards to which people conform makes it possible for us to predict other people's behavior with some accuracy and to communicate with oth-

ers without misunderstanding. In addition, conformity to prevailing norms can provide the emotional support necessary for a person to accomplish important goals—giving up drugs, for example, or resisting tyrannical authority.

Some instances of conformity, however, have little to recommend them (Allen, 1965). People may at times renounce a belief they know to be right simply to avoid being out of step with the majority. Cases in which a person votes against a potential club member because other members don't like the candidate's religion, or refuses to speak out against a certain politician because he or she is a local favorite, are examples of this kind of behavior.

Conformity in dress is generally the result of implicit or explicit social pressure. However, such pressure is not necessarily a negative force. Imagine, for example, the confusion that would result if every clothing manufacturer decided to create its own system of sizes.

ASCH'S EXPERIMENTS Solomon Asch (1951) revealed the power of conformity in a classic series of experiments. Asch conceived an ingenious (if rather devious) way of studying conformity in the laboratory. His subjects were male college students. Each subject was told that he was participating in an experiment on visual judgment. He would be shown two large white cards: one card with a single vertical line, which would serve as a standard, and another card with three vertical lines of different lengths (see Figure 27.3). The alleged experimental task was very simple: to determine which of the three lines was the same length as the standard line as shown in Figure 27.3.

The subject was then seated in a room with seven other people whom he believed were other subjects but who were actually Asch's confederates. The first set of cards was shown and each person announced his answers aloud in the order in which he was seated, the real subject answering next to last. Everyone chose the same line. The second set of cards was displayed, and once again the choice was unanimous. On the third trial, however, the first person declared that line 1 matched the standard, when the correct response was obviously line 2. The second person agreed with great certainty that line 1 was the right answer, and so did the third, fourth, fifth, and sixth "subjects." Now the true subject was faced with a disturbing dilemma. The evidence of his own eyes told him that line 2 was the correct choice, but six other people had unanimously and confidently selected line 1. What would he do? Stand alone as a minority of one, or go along with

Figure 27.3 The stimuli in a single trial in Asch's experiment. The subject must state which of the comparison lines he judges to be the same length as the standard. The discrimination is an easy one to make: Control subjects (those who made the judgments without any group pressure) chose line 2 as correct over 99 percent of the time.

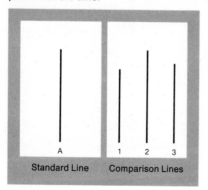

Standard Line   Comparison Lines

the unanimous majority? For most people the decision was an extremely difficult one. How do you think you would have reacted? Of the fifty people Asch tested, almost one-third of them conformed in at least half of the critical trials, concurring with the unanimous majority in choosing the obviously incorrect line.

FACTORS INFLUENCING CONFORMITY What accounts for the conformity found in Asch's research? Part of the answer may lie in situational factors built into the experimental design. For one thing, the judgments of the confederates were unanimous; not one of them gave even a hint that another answer might be possible. In the course of trying several variations of his basic experiment, Asch found that the extent of group consensus was indeed an important influence. When just one confederate was instructed to give the right answer rather than to go along with the others, the proportion of subjects who conformed dropped dramatically, from 32 percent to 5 percent. It appears, then, that one voice raised in opposition to an otherwise unanimous judgment can often have a remarkable effect. Others who may be leaning toward that dissenting view but are not sure that they should actually express it may decide to assert themselves against the majority after all.

Another situational factor that we now know influenced the results of Asch's work was the fact that his subjects were required to interact with the confederates in a face-to-face setting. Later research has shown that when people are allowed to respond anonymously, they conform significantly less. In one such experiment (Deutsch and Gerard, 1955), partitions shielded subjects from the other participants. After watching the responses of their supposed fellow subjects light up on a panel in front of them, the true subjects indicated their own answer by pressing one of three buttons. Apparently, when a person is not directly confronted by the people he or she is contradicting, deviation from group norms is less difficult.

Interestingly, however, the Asch experiments included situational factors that one would expect to *lower* the pressure to conform. The other participants—the confederates—were complete strangers to the subject, with no special claim on his loyalty or affection. The subject had never seen them before and probably would never see them again. Consequently, he had little reason to fear social repercussions for nonconformity. The existence of this situational factor, which would logically reduce the pressure to conform, has led some psychologists to conclude that Asch's work revealed only the tip of the conformity iceberg. If the pressure to conform among strangers is this strong, it seems likely that the pressure to conform among friends could be far stronger.

The emergence of new theories in the area of person perception and attribution (discussed in Chapter 26) has led some psychologists to take a new look at the phenomenon of conformity (Ross, Bierbrauer, and Hoffman, 1976). Imagine the naive subject in Asch's experiment as he tries to understand the behavior of the confederates on one of the critical trials. He must conclude that they are all as well equipped as he to pick the correct line and they have confidently announced their choices, yet they are obviously wrong. The subject might say to himself, "If I didn't know better, I'd think these guys were either blind or crazy." But the confederates are obviously neither blind nor crazy. The subject may then have a second thought: "If they really see it that way, they'll think *I'm* blind or crazy if I disagree." The subject may then conform in order to avoid being so labeled. The problem is that the subject can find no satisfactory explanation for the behavior of the others, and he can anticipate that they would be unable to understand his disagreement except as evidence of his incompetence.

Now suppose the situation is changed: all of the confederates are wearing glasses with darkly smoked lenses, while the subject's ability to see is unimpaired. The subject can easily understand the confederates' errors, and if he believes the confederates know that he can see perfectly, he will have no qualms about reporting exactly what he sees. Thus, if the difference in judgments can be attributed to some clear difference in ability or, more generally, to a different perspective, the pressure to conform will be greatly reduced. As an illustration of the effects of differences in perspective, suppose that you live at home and are attending college as a commuter student while most of your classmates are from out of town and are living in dormitories. Final exams are being given very close to Christmas, and almost everyone in your psychology class clamors for an early exam so that they will have enough time to get home before Christmas. Since you don't have to travel, however, you prefer a later exam in order to have more time to study. Your classmates may try to persuade you to help them influence the instructor, but they will understand your dissent and you will understand their position. The pressure to conform is reduced because the disagreement can be explained by the difference in perspective. These ideas were tested in a complex experiment (Ross, Bierbrauer, and Hoffman, 1976), and it was found that when an attributional resolution of the conformity conflict was provided, the rate of conformity was sharply reduced.

Pressure to conform may be reduced when differences in judgment can be attributed to a difference in perspective. These protesters see nuclear power from a different perspective than do the utility company and the government.

OBEDIENCE TO AUTHORITY "When you think of the long and gloomy history of man," C. P. Snow once (1961) wrote, "you will find more hideous crimes have been committed in the name of obedience than have been committed in the name of rebellion." **Obedience** is any behavior that complies with the explicit commands of a person in authority. The Spanish Inquisition, the Salem witch hunts, the Nazi war crimes, the massacre of Vietnamese civilians at My Lai, are well-known historical examples of inhumane behavior that involved obedience to authority.

Obedience, however, does not always have destructive results. Compliance with the demands of parents and teachers, for example, is often an important part of developing into a mature, responsible adult. And compliance with the law is generally essential if any society is to function successfully. Nevertheless, most of the research on obedience has concerned itself with the negative potential of unquestioning compliance with authority. These studies may help us to understand how such phenomena as atrocities committed during war, whether in Nazi Germany or at My Lai, could have come to pass.

MILGRAM'S EXPERIMENTS The most dramatic and extensive investigation of obedience was conducted by social psychologist Stanley Milgram (1963). Milgram's subjects were men of widely different ages and from a wide range of occupations. Each was paid to take part in what he was told was a study of the effects of punishment on learning. The experimenter, dressed in a white laboratory coat, instructed each subject to read a list of word pairs to a "learner" (really a confederate of the experimenter) whose task it was to memorize each of the pairs. The learner was then taken into an adjacent room, out of the subject's sight, for the duration of the experiment. Every time the learner made a mistake, the subject was to punish him by administering a shock from an impressive-looking shock generator (which, of course, was not connected). The generator had thirty clearly marked voltage levels, with switches ranging from 15 to 450 volts and labels ranging from "Slight Shock" to "Danger: Severe Shock." Whenever the learner made a mistake, the subject was to increase the voltage one level and administer the shock.

As the session progressed, the learner made many errors, necessitating increasingly severe shocks. When the shock level reached 300 volts, the learner pounded on the wall in protest and then fell silent. At this point, the experimenter instructed the subject to treat the absence of an answer as a wrong answer and to continue raising the voltage. If at any point the subject asked to stop the experiment, the researchers in charge sternly told him to go on.

How long do you think most of the subjects continued to deliver what they believed to be dangerous and painful electric shocks to their invisible victims? The majority of students, psychologists, and others whom Milgram had consulted believed that most subjects would refuse to continue at some point early in the experiment. This is why the actual results were so startling. Of forty subjects taking part in the experiments, twenty-six, or 65 percent, continued to obey the experimenter to the very end (see Figure 27.4). These subjects were not sadists. Many

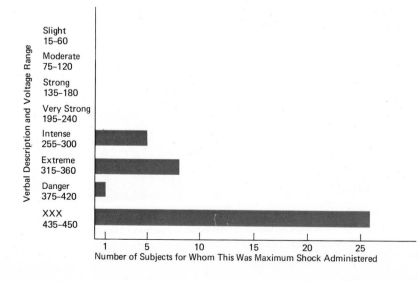

Figure 27.4 Results of Stanley Milgram's classic experiment on obedience. Subjects were told to administer increasing amounts of shock to a "learner" on the pretext that scientists were studying the effects of punishment on learning. Of forty experimental subjects, all administered shocks scaled "intense" or higher, and only fourteen refused to go all the way to the most severe, "XXX" shock level. (After Milgram, 1963.)

of them showed signs of extreme anxiety during the session, and they often told the experimenter that they wanted to stop (see the accompanying box). But in spite of the distress they felt, most of the subjects continued to obey the experimenter's commands.

FACTORS INFLUENCING OBEDIENCE Many factors influence the extent to which people will obey authority even when obedience means acting against their own moral standards. One of the most important of these is whether or not the person giving the instructions is viewed as a legitimate authority. From the time we are children, we are taught that certain people can, by virtue of their positions in the social order, legitimately expect compliance with their wishes. Whether it is a police officer's order that a driver pull over to the side of the road or a doctor's request that a patient undress, people are usually ready (even if not always eager) to do as they are told. Indeed, the simple fact that a person is wearing a uniform is often enough to prompt compliance. In one experiment (Bickman, 1974), researchers approached people on the streets of New York City and ordered them either to pick up a paper bag or to give a dime to a stranger. Half of the researchers were dressed in neat street clothes, half in guard uniforms. Less than 40 percent of the subjects obeyed the "civilian," but more than 80 per-

Individuals tend to obey figures of authority more quickly than they do other people, especially when the authority figure is wearing a uniform.

cent obeyed the "guard," even when he walked off after delivering the order and could not see whether or not they complied.

Another situational factor that seems to affect the extent to which we obey authority is the degree of face-to-face contact. In Milgram's experiments, the fact that the subjects were face-to-face with the experimenter helped to encourage compliance. Obedience dropped sharply in an experimental variation in which the experimenter did not remain in the same room with the subject (1965). Instead, he gave his initial instructions and then left the laboratory, giving subsequent orders by telephone. Whereas 65 percent of the subjects obeyed to the end when the experimenter was sitting just a few feet away from them, only a third as many (22 percent) obeyed throughout when the experimenter was not physically present. Apparently, it is easier for people to disobey an authority when they do not have to confront him or her directly.

Milgram also found that increasing the physical closeness of the subject to the victim increased the likelihood that the subject would defy the experimenter. In his original research design, Milgram's subjects did not see or hear their victim, except for the pounding on the wall after 300 volts. In a subsequent variation, however, the subjects were placed in closer and closer proximity to the victim (1965). In one condition, the victim was again in another room but the subject could hear his groans escalating to screams as the shocks were increased. In another arrangement, the victim was moved to the same room as the subject—seated only eighteen inches from him. And in a final condition, the subject not only sat close to the victim but was also required to force the victim's hand onto the shock plate in order to administer the punishment. As Figure 27.5 indicates, the maximum shock that subjects delivered decreased steadily as contact with the victim—auditory, visual, and physical—increased. When the subjects were remote from the victim, it was apparently easier for them to deny the pain they were inflicting. As the subject was brought into closer contact with the victim, however, such denial became less possible, and the victim's suffering exerted greater influence in the struggle between the individual's conscience and the authority's demands.

Another factor that increases the chances that a person will resist authority is the existence of social support for defiance. In an obedience experiment designed to test the strength of this factor (Milgram, 1965), the subject was teamed with two other "subjects" who were actually the experimenter's confederates. After the shock level had reached 150 volts, one of the confederates announced that he would not continue and took a seat in another part of the room. After 210 volts, the second confederate also refused to go any further. In all cases, the experimenter continued to order the true subjects to carry on the procedure, but only 10 percent of them did so. All the rest refused to continue either at the same time one of the confederates did or shortly thereafter.

In one sense, the subjects in this condition were forced to choose between obedience to the experimenter's authority and conformity to the opinions and actions of their peers. But the fact that 90 percent chose to conform to the more socially acceptable actions of their fellow participants should not lead us to be overly optimistic about resistance to authority. Remember that someone must always be the first to resist, and in real life there are no confederates to lead the way. Also, in real life, penalties for disobedience may be far more severe than the disapproving remarks of an unknown experimenter.

The tendency toward conformity and obedience so dramatically demonstrated in the laboratory and

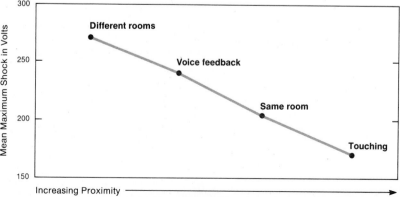

Figure 27.5 This graph of the results of some of Milgram's studies on obedience shows that the closer the subject was to the victim, the less the amount of shock he was willing to administer, despite the experimenter's demands that he continue. With increased proximity, there was a decrease in compliance. (After Milgram, 1974.)

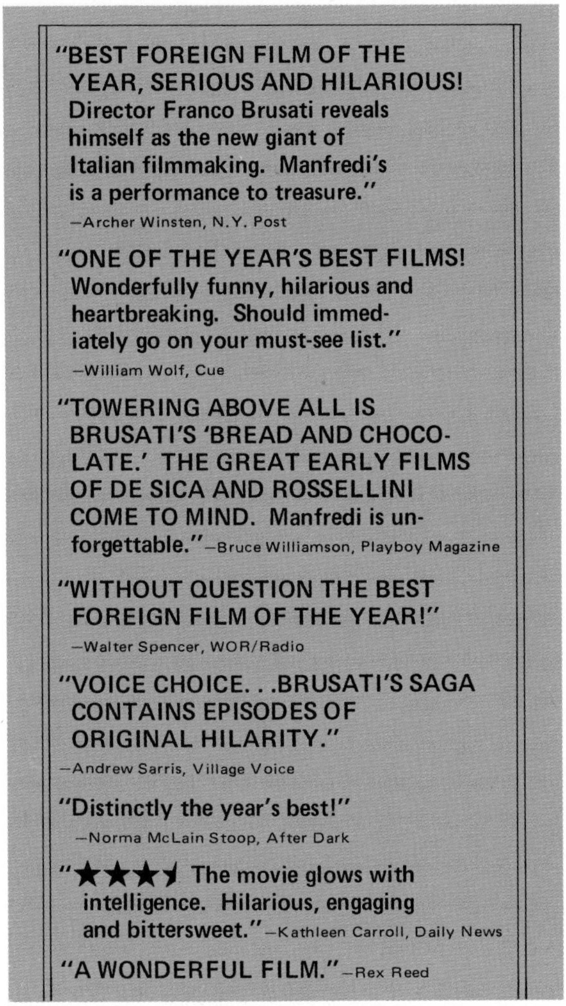

Figure 27.6 Conformity and the influence of authority are important issues in our everyday lives, although their presence is often less dramatically revealed than it is in laboratory experiments. Take film critics, for example. Are they a legitimate authority? Should we take their advice? How have the advertisers utilized the critics' function? Would a movie ad be as effective if the quotes were from just anyone? What effect do such advertisements have on you?

in natural settings may strike some people as alarming. But it must be remembered that conformity and obedience are neither good nor bad in and of themselves. They are facts of social behavior, and as social facts they may lead to either desirable or undesirable outcomes for individuals and society. Milgram himself thinks that as we come to understand these forces better, perhaps we can learn both to use them for beneficial effects and to resist them when necessary (Milgram and Tavris, 1974). An example of conformity in everyday life is shown in Figure 27.6.

THE SOCIAL SIGNIFICANCE OF GROUPS
Although we like to think of ourselves as independent, as people who are capable of making our own choices and forging our own ways, in actual fact we are often greatly influenced by the behavior of others. This tendency was clearly demonstrated in the experiments on conformity and obedience discussed earlier. It is likely, however, that no single force has a greater influence on our lives than the people we are closest to, the members of our own groups.

DEFINING GROUPS The family, the neighborhood gang, the physics class at a university, the typing pool at a large insurance company, the new recruits at an army camp, are examples of different groups. When social psychologists speak of groups, they are not referring to just any collection of people who happen to find themselves in the same place at the same time. The term **group** is reserved for an aggregate of people with certain specific features, the most important of which are interdependence and shared goals.

INTERDEPENDENCE The strangers waiting on the same street corner for a downtown bus form only a collection of individuals, not a group. Their lives are not interconnected in any significant way. Each passenger will board the bus, ride for several blocks, and then get off to engage in activities that have no effect on the other passengers. The members of a group, in contrast, see their fates as somehow linked. In a group of athletes or entertainers or roommates, for instance, each person has a certain responsibility to the other members, which, if not fulfilled, can affect the success or failure of the entire group. What happens to one, in a sense, happens to all of them. They are interdependent.

Interdependence typically breeds another important quality that differentiates groups from nongroups—a sense of belonging. The members of a baseball team, for example, develop strong loyalties to their club and teammates, as do members of, say, a fraternity or sorority, or even the people who belong to a foursome for Saturday afternoon golf. Thus group members usually have no trouble identifying the boundaries of their group, of distinguishing insiders from outsiders, "us" from "them."

SHARED GOALS Group members become interdependent because they see themselves as sharing certain goals that no single individual could achieve alone. Social psychologists often distinguish between group goals that are task-oriented, or directed toward getting some job done, and group goals that are socially oriented, or directed toward filling the emotional needs of the members. A group of neighbors working together to raise money for a new playground, a group of doctors performing openheart surgery, a group of workers constructing a high-rise office building—all are concentrating on task-oriented goals. Social goals, however, are emphasized in more informal groups. When people get together to participate in a game, to attend a company picnic, or simply to relax and enjoy themselves, they anticipate receiving such social rewards as companionship and emotional support.

This is not to say that groups can have only task functions or only social functions. Clearly, raising money for a neighborhood playground often leads to the formation of strong friendships, just as organizing a company picnic often creates good will among co-workers and results in increased productivity. Thus almost all groups have both task-oriented and social goals to some extent, but their major goals usually fall in one or the other area.

GROUP DECISION MAKING Modern society is run by groups. Governments have thousands of committees, commissions, and panels. The activities of labor groups, managerial groups, professional societies, and even the smallest social clubs are usually carried out by specialized committees or work groups. We seem to assume that a group of people can work more efficiently on most tasks, producing better results than any individual operating alone can. Is this assumption correct? Are two heads *always* better than one? Some recent studies suggest not.

In the early months of 1961, a confident and tightly knit group, including men who were reputedly some of the most intelligent ever to participate in the councils of government, made what has come to be regarded as one of the worst decisions in recent history. The group, President John F. Kennedy's in-

ner circle of foreign policy advisors, included Dean Rusk, Robert McNamara, McGeorge Bundy, Douglas Dillon, and Arthur Schlesinger. Meeting frequently over the course of three months, this advisory group reached the unanimous decision to invade Fidel Castro's Cuba using as an invasion force Cuban exiles who had been trained by the U.S. Central Intelligence Agency. Fourteen hundred exiles took part in the attack at Cuba's Bay of Pigs, aided by the U.S. Navy, the Air Force, and the CIA. Within three days, Cuban forces had sunk the U.S. ships that carried ammunition and supplies for the attack and had captured about 1,200 of the invaders and killed the rest.

Subsequent reflections about the Bay of Pigs affair by Schlesinger, McNamara, and President Kennedy himself made it clear that the group's decision was based on incomplete information. The group failed to take into account—and in some cases to acquaint itself with—available data on the size and strength of Castro's forces, the loyalty of his troops, and the deteriorating morale of the invaders. Leaving aside the question of the morality of such a venture, what could have accounted for such a mistake in judgment?

In his book *Victims of Groupthink* (1973), Irving Janis, a social psychologist, suggests that one reason for the poor decision making was "the illusion of invulnerability." Although each man knew that no single individual among them was superhuman, they felt somehow that the group was a supergroup, capable of extraordinary accomplishments. The group was also affected by the illusion of unanimity—the belief, common in cohesive groups, that everyone agrees that risks can safely be ignored. Privately, several of the Kennedy advisors harbored doubts about the decision, but they did not express their doubts publicly. The desire to maintain the feeling of unanimity led each member to keep his doubts to himself. This tendency is closely related to the conformity demonstrated by the subjects in Asch's experiments.

One should not conclude from such incidents, however, that important decisions should always be made by one individual, or that groups with low morale and little cohesiveness are more effective problem solvers than optimistic, unified groups. On the contrary, the general practice of making important decisions in groups has significant benefits. For one thing, one person seldom has all the expertise and information needed to arrive at an intelligent solution. Moreover, individuals inevitably have certain biases, blind spots, and other weaknesses that can be counterbalanced by the input of other members of a group.

GROUP VALUES AND ATTITUDES People are inevitably attracted to others who share their values, attitudes, and ways of behaving. In Isaac Asimov's introduction to this chapter, the seven young soldiers traveling across the country were similar in several ways. All of them were older than most of the other recruits; all were college graduates; all were eligible for officer training; all hated the army and wanted to be discharged as soon as possible; all found pleasure in similar activities.

To some extent, of course, these shared attitudes were also the *result* of group formation. Once people are drawn together because of common backgrounds and beliefs, they usually become increasingly similar as group norms emerge. A **norm** is an explicit or implicit agreement about acceptable and expected behavior. Group norms vary, depending on what aspects of life group members consider to be important. Asimov and the other soldiers probably considered beliefs about religion or marriage relatively insignificant. Beliefs about the army, however, were crucial, and it was in this area that the group demanded the strictest loyalty from its members. This is why Asimov was so distressed when his friends pretended a change of heart: they were abandoning the most central of all the group's beliefs.

Groups such as this, with which a person interacts face to face, are often called **membership groups**, and they clearly have a great influence on our values and attitudes. But there are other groups that also shape our thoughts and actions—ones with which we may never personally interact. If you ask a person to tell you who she is, for example, she may start by telling you her family name, but she may also say that she is a woman, age twenty-one, an Italian-American, a Catholic, and an aspiring novelist. Although none of these categories (female, young adult, Italian descent) refer to membership groups, they are still extremely important to our social identities. Social psychologists call a group that a person identifies with or wants to emulate a **reference group**. As this example suggests, reference groups need not be formal or face-to-face groups.

Reference groups influence our lives in several ways. For one thing, we evaluate ourselves according to the standards of our reference groups. For ex-

This married couple may be said to form a two-person membership group—a dyad.

ample, if neither of a student's parents graduated from high school, he may consider his acceptance into college a major accomplishment in itself. However, if both of his parents are professors, he may feel that by going to college, he is merely doing what is expected. If he is a drama major, he may be thrilled to get a C on a chemistry exam; if he is in the premedical program, he will not be so thrilled. Simply because he is male, he may not be as upset about not making the choir as his sister is. Thus the way we see ourselves depends in part on the groups with which we want to be identified.

Reference groups also shape our attitudes and values. Our beliefs, feelings, and behavior often change when we see people with whom we identify doing things we never imagined doing, or when we move into new social settings. A classic study conducted at Bennington College in the 1930s demonstrated this. Most of the students at Bennington (then an all-female college) came from upper-class, politically conservative backgrounds, whereas the college community was extremely liberal, even radical, for its day. Theodore Newcomb (1943) found that students who strongly identified with Bennington tended to become much more liberal as they progressed through college. In acquiring new attitudes, they tried to identify more closely with the college community—which for them had become a **positive reference group**. And at the same time, they tried to dissociate themselves from their conservative backgrounds. Their families and home communities had become **negative reference groups**.

Identification with groups can lead to compulsive "keeping up with the Joneses," snobbery, and prejudice. Individuals who feel compelled to be identified with an "in-group" may also feel compelled to discredit members of an "out-group." However, identification with groups can also be a source of strength. Ethnic pride and feelings of sisterhood make it easier for individual women and members of minorities to cope with the prejudice they encounter; they know they are not alone. And organizations like Alcoholics Anonymous have used the fact that groups affect our self-perceptions to help individuals regain self-respect and rebuild shattered lives.

SUMMARY

1. People vary greatly in their need for social contact and in their ability to cope with social isolation. The effects of even brief isolation may range from intense suffering to virtually no visible anxiety.
   A. Explanations for people's need for interaction with others usually fall into one of two categories: those that attribute it to instinct and those that attribute it to learning and reinforcement.
      1. Instinct theories suggest that people have become genetically programmed to associate with others of their species through evolution. The wide variety of social behavior that humans display in different cultures and subgroups, however, casts doubt on the view that there is an instinctive basis for human gregariousness.
      2. According to reinforcement theories, social interaction becomes a secondary reinforcer if it is continually paired with a primary reinforcer. Some psychologists hypothesize that there are sensitive periods for the formation of attachments in human beings. The exact learning mechanisms that underlie the need for social interaction are not known.
   B. Differences in the desire to associate with other people can be influenced by social situations.
      1. According to Leon Festinger's theory of **social comparison**, people can verify their beliefs about the world and themselves either by testing those beliefs or by examining them in relation to those of other people. Anxiety often promotes a wish to affiliate with others who can validate one's own reactions. Circumstances apparently determine whom a person can be expected to turn to when attempting to validate his or her own beliefs. At times we turn to **reference others**—people whose opinions we respect.
      2. Social psychologists suggest that whether a person seeks or avoids affiliation depends not only on the intensity but on the nature of the emotional arousal. Emotional stress may create a preference for solitude; embarrassment or shame may inhibit people from seeking social comparisons.

2. All people are apparently greatly influenced by social forces outside themselves. Areas of social influence that have been extensively studied are the way in which social pressure can induce a person to conform to a prevailing attitude or perception, and the process by which those in positions of authority can prompt others to obey commands even when those commands may violate basic moral standards.
   A. Conformity to prevailing norms is the result of implicit or explicit social pressure, and it can have both positive and negative consequences.
      1. The experiments of Solomon Asch showed that in certain situations, the pressure to conform was more powerful than sensory data in influencing subjects' perceptual judgment.

2. Situational factors apparently influence conformity. Asch found that the extent of group consensus influenced conformity in his experiment. Later research has shown that when people can respond without face-to-face contact with the people they would be contradicting, they conform significantly less. In addition, pressure to conform is reduced when a disagreement can be explained by an unavoidable difference in perspectives.

B. Most research on obedience has been concerned with the negative potential of unquestioning compliance with authority.

   1. The experiments of Stanley Milgram dramatically showed the extent to which people will obey authority figures even when doing so is a violation of their moral standards.

   2. Factors influencing obedience in Milgram's experiments include whether or not the person giving the instructions is viewed as a legitimate authority, the degree of face-to-face contact between the experimenter and the subject, and the degree of contact between the subject and the victim. Another experiment on obedience indicated that the existence of social support for defiance increases the chances that a person will resist authority.

3. Groups have enormous social significance. It is likely that no single force has greater influence on our lives than the members of our groups.

A. A **group** is an aggregate of people with certain specific features, the most important of which are interdependence and shared goals.

   1. Interdependence means that members of a group see their lives as linked together in some respect. Interdependence typically breeds a sense of belonging.

   2. Group members become interdependent because they see themselves as sharing certain goals that no single individual could achieve alone. Almost all groups have both task-oriented and social goals to some extent, but their major goals usually fall into one category or the other.

B. Recent studies challenge the assumption that a group of people can work more efficiently on most tasks than can an individual working alone. Among the reasons for poor decision making in groups may be the illusion of invulnerability and the illusion of unanimity.

C. Shared attitudes and values are both causes and effects of group formation. In a **membership group**, people interact face to face; once people are drawn together because of common backgrounds and beliefs, they usually become increasingly similar as group norms emerge. A **positive reference group** is one that a person identifies with or wishes to emulate. A **negative reference group** is one that a person does not wish to emulate. Reference groups influence our lives in several ways: we evaluate ourselves according to the standards of our reference groups, and they shape our attitudes and values.

RECOMMENDED READINGS

BROWN, ROGER. *Social Psychology*. New York: Free Press, 1965. This most readable of social psychology textbooks is highly recommended.

JANIS, IRVING L. *Victims of Groupthink: A Psychological Study of Foreign-Policy Decisions and Fiascos*. Boston: Houghton Mifflin, 1973. With great insight, Janis applies social-psychological theory to a series of historic decisions made by groups in such situations as the Bay of Pigs invasion, the Cuban missile crisis, and the escalation of the Vietnam war.

MILGRAM, STANLEY. *The Individual in a Social World: Essays and Experiments*. Reading, Mass.: Addison-Wesley, 1977. A stimulating excursion through Milgram's work on such varied topics as obedience, the urban experience, and the effects of television on antisocial behavior, in all of which Milgram finds similar social forces affecting behavior.

SHAW, MARVIN E. *Group Dynamics: The Psychology of Small Group Behavior*. New York: McGraw-Hill, 1976. An excellent text in which the author reviews the field, summarizes what is known, and points to problems for future research.

SULS, JERRY M., and RICHARD L. MILLER (eds.). *Social Comparison Processes: Theoretical and Empirical Perspectives*. Washington, D.C.: Hemisphere, 1977. This collection of fourteen chapters, written especially for this book, shows the renewed vigor and great promise of research on social comparison processes.

CHAPTER TWENTY-EIGHT

CONFLICT AND COOPERATION

I suppose that most people think competition comes more natural to human beings than cooperation does. All about us we see examples of selfishness and unkindness; and when someone does something unselfish, we are surprised. Of course, the supreme example of selfishness and unkindness would seem to be the mass killing called war, to which humanity has always been so prone.

Yet it is exactly in war that I myself find evidence that human beings are overwhelmingly altruistic.

No battle could be fought for five minutes unless the troops on either side were willing to throw away their lives for their fellow-soldiers. Over and over again, soldiers have shown themselves willing to charge into battle to relieve a hard-pressed contingent of their fellows, though this means they will themselves be subject to slaughter. When an army is in retreat, it can usually be saved only if there is a rear guard to hold off pursuit; and though the soldiers in this rear guard know they are in great danger, they fight and hold off pursuit so that others can escape.

Why is this?

Because the soldiers are *led*; they are *told* what to do. The firmer and more intelligent the leadership, the harder soldiers will fight and the more they will endure.

But suppose some group of soldiers is told that each may do as he pleases. None will then know what to do in order to cooperate effectively. In the uncertainty that follows, each soldier will do the only thing he is sure he knows: ensure his own personal safety. And the army will fall apart.

So, the acts of selfishness and unkindness that we see may not be a result of natural human selfishness and unkindness. It may be that people don't know how best to cooperate. No one is telling them what to do. There is no leadership.

So great is the insecurity that results from this that people tend to look for leaders and to follow anyone who sounds as if he or she knows what to do. Then, within that group at least, there is a chance for cooperation.

It is for this reason that while I always wish government to be as humane, intelligent, and fair as possible, I fear those who believe that governments are naturally inefficient and corrupt and who therefore call for "less government." If a central government is dismantled, then people will look for local leaders. Many small groups will replace the large group, and while within the small groups there will probably be cooperation, among them there will probably be competition.

I know this because on numerous occasions in history there has been "less government." The result is called "feudalism," or "a dark age." I don't want it.

What I want is still more government. I want a humane, federalized world government.

Isaac Asimov

In January 1978 a man in Phoenix, Arizona, walked up to a derelict sleeping outdoors in the city's skid row, doused him with gasoline, and set him on fire. Two other men met similar fates before the attacker was finally arrested. As far as authorities could tell, the victims had done nothing whatever to provoke the incidents. The same month, also in Phoenix, concerned citizens showered gifts and money on a desperately poor family, the father of which had been arrested for a minor offense. None of the donors knew the family personally. They had simply read about its plight in the local newspaper and responded with an outpouring of sympathy and generosity.

These starkly contrasting stories underline one of the central paradoxes of human nature: people can be selfish, competitive, aggressive, and cruel; and they can be generous, cooperative, kind, and unselfish. *Homo sapiens* is both one of the most dangerous species that ever inhabited the earth and one of the most unselfish. Human history is studded with instances of extreme brutality. Yet human history also includes countless examples of people knowingly sacrificing themselves to help others.

What factors give rise to these opposing tendencies, and how can they coexist? Due to space limitations, it is not possible for us to discuss the causes of all kinds of prosocial and antisocial acts. We can, however, explore examples of each of these broad categories of behavior. In the following sections, then, we address the issues of what makes people behave competitively or aggressively, and what makes people willing to help and share with others. In the concluding section, we consider the interplay of conflict and cooperation—the human dilemma.

FACTORS AFFECTING AGGRESSION

We are so accustomed to reading about violence in the newspapers that we almost take violence for granted. Even so, the facts are alarming. In the single year of 1968, for example, more people were beaten or murdered on the streets of America than were killed or wounded in 7½ years of the Vietnam war (Mark and Ervin, 1970). And 1968 was not a particularly bad year. In 1976, 987,000 Americans, or about five out of every thousand, were victims of reported violent crime (FBI *Uniform Crime Reports*, 1977). It is estimated that between 1820 and 1945, worldwide, 58 million people died at the hands of their fellow humans. That means one person was killed nearly every minute, on the average, during those 126 years (Richardson, 1960).

Murder, rape, and assault are extreme examples of interpersonal **aggression**—that is, behavior intended to harm another person. The key attributes that define an act as aggression are its intention and its target. Accidental injuries are not aggression. Neither are assaults on inanimate objects. Thus, to be considered aggressive, an act must be both deliberate and directed against a person. This definition includes not only physical injury to another person but also verbal attacks, such as insults and slander.

What accounts for the high level of abusive behavior in humans? Answers to this question fall into three categories: biological explanations, social learning explanations, and situational explanations.

BIOLOGICAL INFLUENCES   The idea that human aggression has a biological basis has a long history and many advocates. Sigmund Freud, for example, postulated that we are driven to self-destructive and aggressive behavior by a death instinct (*Thanatos*) that is at least as powerful as the life instinct (*Eros*) that impels us toward growth and self-fulfillment. According to Freud, the urge to conquer and kill is never very far beneath the surface, and we achieve only an uneasy balance between our destructive and procreative impulses. Today, psychologists generally consider Freud's concept of a death instinct highly speculative. But the underlying idea—that human aggression has a biological basis—lives on. Indeed, it has experienced a renaissance in recent years (see Figure 28.1).

War has always been a means of legitimizing human aggression.

Figure 28.1 Does humankind have an aggressive instinct? Certain researchers believe we do. They base this conclusion on evidence from the animal world, where, they argue, aggression is both instinctual and adaptive. In the case of the male marine iguana shown here, aggression is necessary for defense of its territory (survival) against intruding others. When an intruder oversteps its bounds, the defender *automatically* attacks; the fight continues until the losing iguana drops to its belly in submission. But generalizations from the animal to the human world are generally specious. Even if we were to accept the idea of an aggressive instinct in humans, we would need to consider the fact that its expression is not automatically controlled by unambiguous external cues, but is mediated by complex, specifically human sociocultural contexts. (After Eibl-Eibesfeldt, 1961.)

AGGRESSION AS A UNIVERSAL TRAIT In *On Aggression* (1966) and *The Eight Deadly Sins of Civilized Man* (1974), ethologist Konrad Lorenz (whose work was discussed in Chapter 3) describes how aggression, which is common among animals, may be adaptive. The adult males in a troop of baboons, for example, constantly challenge and provoke one another. The result of this fighting is a fairly stable hierarchy of dominance. The dominant males have their choice of sleeping places, foodstuffs, and females. This means that the most successful males father the most offspring, so over time the species as a whole improves. In addition, unresolved conflicts among competing males may force a troop to divide, thus dispersing the population over a wider territory and increasing its members' chances for survival. Given these adaptive benefits, Lorenz concludes that aggression is instinctive, biologically based behavior—in all animals, including humans.

But aggression in humans, Lorenz proposes, is in some ways different from aggression in other species.

Fighting among members of the same species rarely becomes lethal. When a wolf is about to lose a fight with another wolf, it bares its throat in an act of submission. This gesture almost always ends the episode. The dominant wolf stops short of incapacitating or killing one of its own kind. Members of other animal species, Lorenz argues, behave in a similar manner—with the exception of humans. Humans, according to Lorenz, are the only animals that regularly commit murder.

Although innate inhibitions may be lacking in our biological makeup, Lorenz proposes that the aggressive urge itself may be less dangerous than the social sanctions imposed against it. He suggests that if the fighting instinct in any animal is constantly inhibited, aggressive impulses build up and may eventually be discharged in a particularly vicious way. Such blocking of aggression is common in human societies. Consequently, we are prone to periodic outbreaks of extreme violence.

However intriguing this line of reasoning may be,

What Is Violence?

Deciding which behaviors are aggressive is more difficult than it might appear. While a key attribute of aggression is the intention to hurt, the circumstances surrounding that intention—who, why, where, and when—play a crucial defining role. In 1969, 1,400 American men were asked which acts they considered to be violent. Notice how the questions themselves reflect a particular historical period and ethos and how differently the various groups of respondents answered. Violence for a college student or black person was not always the same as it was for a union member. If the survey were given again today, do you think that social dissent would be considered less violent and police acts more violent than they were in 1969?

	Percentage of Respondents Defining Certain Acts as Violence			
	Total sample	College students	White union members	Blacks
Do you think of looting as violence?	85%	76%	91%	74%
Do you think of burglary as violence?	65	47	67	70
Do you think of draft card burning as violence?	58	26	63	51
Do you think of police beating students as violence?	56	79	45	82
Do you think of not letting people have their civil rights as violence?	49	54	40	70
Do you think of student protests as violence?	38	18	43	23
Do you think of police shooting looters as violence?	35	43	23	59
Do you think of sit-ins as violence?	22	4	24	15
Do you think of police stopping to frisk as violence?	16	16	10	34

Source: H. Blumenthal, R. Kahn, F. Andrews, and K. Head. *Justifying Violence: Attitudes of American Men.* Ann Arbor, Michigan: Survey Research Center, Institute for Social Research, University of Michigan, 1972.

---

it is open to serious criticism. First, instinct theories of aggression tend to stretch the concept of instinct to the breaking point. As we suggested in Chapter 3, even in lower animals, the emergence of "instinctive" behavior often depends on learning. When psychologist Zing Yang Kuo (1930) deprived kittens of the opportunity to observe their mother hunting rats, almost 60 percent showed no interest in hunting rats themselves. Thus, inborn, automatic instincts do not explain the behavior of cats, much less that of humans who are even more dependent on learning.

Second, to argue that all people have an aggressive instinct makes it difficult to explain variations in levels of human aggression. Anthropological research shows that the level of aggression differs greatly from culture to culture. Some Brazilian tribes, for example, engage in almost constant warfare, while the members of other societies (Eskimos, for instance) avoid even verbal quarrels. And within a single society, some individuals are more aggressive than others. In short, the idea that aggression is an inborn, universal human trait does not hold up under scrutiny.

AGGRESSION AND BIOLOGICAL ABNORMALITIES A number of researchers believe that biological abnormalities, rather than an inborn, universal instinct, explain why some individuals are especially hot-tempered and violent. For example, instead of the normal forty-six chromosomes, some men convicted of violent crimes have been found to have forty-seven, the extra chromosome being a Y (male) chromosome. The first XYY male criminals discovered were exceedingly short-tempered and aggressive, in addition to being unusually large and of below-average intelligence (Jarvik, Klodin, and Matsuyama, 1973).

In other cases, violent behavior has been linked to various types of brain damage, such as an interruption in the flow of blood to the brain (which kills brain cells), injuries to the frontal or temporal lobes from falls or blows to the head, viral infections of the brain, and brain tumors (Mark and Ervin, 1970). Figure 28.2 shows the parts of the brain that some researchers believe constitute the biological origins of human aggression.

Could genetic abnormalities and brain damage—often undetected—account for the high levels of aggressive behavior in human beings? The answer seems to be no. The XYY chromosome syndrome is exceedingly rare (it occurs at most once or twice in a thousand births), and many XYY males are upstanding citizens (and are of average size and normal intelligence). The incidence of brain damage is higher. An estimated 10 to 15 million Americans suffer from some form of brain injury. But again, the majority of people with a history of violent behavior have no such injury, and the majority of people with brain damage are no more aggressive than anyone else.

The case of Paul M (Mark and Ervin, 1970) suggests why biological abnormalities are an insufficient explanation of aggression. Paul admitted himself to Boston City Hospital because he was afraid he was losing his mind and could not control his violent impulses. He had, in fact, "gone wild," pulling plaster off the walls of his apartment, smashing a mirror, and badly gashing his own body with a piece of the glass. Examination revealed that Paul was suffering from mild brain damage. An antiseizure drug was prescribed for him, and his rages stopped. On the surface, it appears that Paul's disorder was purely biological—but a look at his history suggests otherwise. One of eight children, Paul was raised in severe poverty. His father and brothers were all hot-tempered, and he was frequently beaten as a child. An older brother who had been arrested three times for armed robbery and aggravated assault was his childhood idol. Clearly, social learning was partly responsible for Paul's explosive behavior.

SOCIAL LEARNING MECHANISMS As Albert Bandura (1976) has pointed out, most aggressive behavior—whether it be fighting with knives, landing a blow to the chin, constructing a pipe bomb, or shouting verbal ridicule—requires intricate skills. People are not born with a repertoire of ready-to-use aggressive behaviors. They must learn how to injure others. According to social learning theory, it is exposure to models of violent behavior and reinforcement for aggressive acts that explain why people so often attack one another.

THE IMPORTANCE OF MODELS By observing others, not only do we learn how and when to perform specific aggressive acts (for example, how to fire a gun) but we also learn general strategies of aggression (such as "Stay on the offensive"). From whom

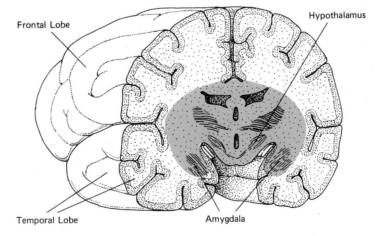

Figure 28.2 Some researchers suggest that there is a biological origin of aggression in the oldest and most primitive parts of the human brain. Evidence from animal and human studies suggests that the hypothalamus and other structures in the temporal lobe (shown in blue) play an important role in mediating aggressive behavior. In some cases, surgical removal of the hypothalamus and amygdala has resulted in complete loss of emotional reactivity. (After Scherer, Abeles, and Fischer, 1975.)

Frontal Lobe

Hypothalamus

Temporal Lobe

Amygdala

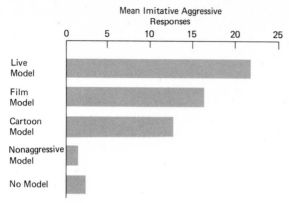

Mean Imitative Aggressive Responses

Figure 28.3 Bandura and his colleagues found that live models were more effective than either film models or cartoon characters in eliciting imitative aggressive behavior in children.   (After Bandura, 1973.)

do we learn these things? In our culture, two of the most influential models are the members of our families and the characters portrayed on television and in films. Figure 28.3 shows the relative effectiveness of the different kinds of models in eliciting imitative aggressive behavior in children.

Parents do not always have the best influence on their children. Every year, between 50,000 and 70,000 American children are severely beaten by adults. Tragically, about 2,000 of these children die; many of the others grow up to become child abusers themselves. This sad fact underlines the point that the people closest to us—the members of our family—are the most powerful models for our behavior. Most aggressive children do not have criminally violent parents, however. In subtle ways, law-abiding parents who resort to "acceptable" forms of aggression to solve problems, favor coercive methods of child rearing, and are hostile toward the world in general promote aggressive behavior in their children. Such parents serve as models of aggression "in word and attitude rather than deed" (Bandura, 1976, pp. 206–207).

The electronic media are also pervasive influences on behavior. There is now strong evidence that exposure to violence on the screen can lead to increased aggression. In one study that supports this conclusion, researchers observed a group of sixty delinquent boys in a minimum-security detention facility over a period of three weeks (Parke et al., 1977). The boys living in one cottage were shown aggressive movies every night for five nights, while the boys in another cottage were shown neutral,

Parents as Models for Aggression

Social learning theory emphasizes the role of parents as models for their children in either encouraging or discouraging aggressive behavior. Bandura and Walters (1959) showed that some of the most aggressive boys came from families in which the parents urged or condoned aggressive behavior, as this excerpt from an interview between a psychologist (I) and a parent (M) illustrates.

I: Have you ever encouraged Earl to stand up for himself?

M: Yes. I've taught young Earl, and his dad has. I feel he should stand up for his rights, so you can get along in this world.

I: How have you encouraged him?

M: I've told him to look after himself and don't let anybody shove him around or anything like that, but not to look for trouble. I don't want him to be a sissy.

I: Have you ever encouraged Earl to use his fists to defend himself?

M: Oh yes. Oh yes. He knows how to fight.

I: What have you done to encourage him?

M: When he was a little boy, he had a little pair of boxing gloves. His dad has been an athlete all his life, so his dad taught him.

I: Has he ever come to you and complained that another fellow was giving him a rough time?

M: Oh yes, when he was younger. I told him, "Go on out and fight it out yourself."

I: If Earl got into a fight with one of the neighbor's boys, how would you handle it?

M: Oh, he should fight it out himself. When he was a little fellow he used to fight his own battle. . . .

I: What would you do if you found Earl teasing another fellow or calling bad names?

M: That would be up to Earl. If the other boy wants to lick him, that would be up to Earl. He deserves it.

Source: Albert Bandura and R. H. Walters. *Adolescent Aggression.* New York: Ronald Press, 1959, pp. 115–116.

Seeing violence as in shows like *Starsky and Hutch* on television may lead to increased aggression.

others produced highly rewarding results for the aggressor (Patterson, Littman, and Bricker, 1967). Sometimes the rewards for aggression are tangible—a nation acquiring a new territory by invasion, for example, or an individual elbowing other passengers to get a seat on a crowded bus. At other times the rewards are social, as when soldiers are given medals and hero's welcomes for their skill in killing or teenaged boys are admired by their peers for being tough. And still other times the rewards are internal: aggressive behavior can become a source of pride and self-esteem. The rewards for aggression need not be experienced directly, as we noted in Chapter 4; vicarious reinforcement can be extremely powerful. People are most likely to imitate a model whose aggressive behavior is successful, or who at least is not punished for aggressive behavior.

Thus modeling of aggression and reinforcement interact. "Styles of aggression are largely learned through observation and refined through reinforced practice. . . . [According to social learning theory,] aggressive models of response, like other forms of social behavior, can be induced, eliminated, and reinstated by altering the effects they produce" (Bandura, 1976, pp. 211, 219).

nonaggressive movies. The violent movies had a definite impact on behavior. All the boys who were exposed to them showed clear increases in verbal and physical aggression. Other studies confirm these findings, and indicate that they are not limited to delinquent boys. Studies of delinquent girls and of nondelinquent college students have yielded similar results.

This is not to say that the media are responsible for all, or even most, of the violence in contemporary society. Television and movies are recent inventions, and people have been beating, raping, and murdering one another for thousands of years. Moreover, people do not automatically perform what they learn through observation. There must usually be some form of inducement, some expectation of reward.

THE IMPORTANCE OF REINFORCEMENT According to social learning theory, people do not behave aggressively unless such behavior has "paid off" for them in the past or unless they expect it to pay off in the future. There is ample evidence that aggression *does* pay off. In one study of children, close to 80 percent of physical and verbal assaults on

SITUATIONAL FACTORS The social learning explanation of aggression makes good sense. But most people retain the feeling that certain situations are so unbearable, so frustrating, that anyone would explode in anger, regardless of the consequences. Moreover, all of us have heard of ordinary people being carried away by the moment and, protected by the anonymity of a crowd, engaging in behavior they might never have considered otherwise. The riots in this nation's big cities in the 1960s testify to the destructive potential of mob action. Both situations—frustration and anonymity—seem to promote aggressive behavior.

FRUSTRATION, ANGER, AND AGGRESSION According to a hypothesis put forward by John Dollard and his colleagues, "aggression is always a consequence of frustration" and, conversely, "frustration always leads to some form of aggression" (1939, p. 1). Dollard defined **frustration** as interference with any form of goal-directed behavior. When people are thwarted in their attempts to obtain food or water, sex or sleep, love or recognition, he argued, they become aggressive. The aggressive response may be "compressed, delayed, disguised, displaced, or otherwise deflected from [its] immediate and logical goal, [but] not destroyed" (p. 2).

In a classic test of Dollard's **frustration-aggression hypothesis**, a team of researchers (Barker, Dembo, and Lewin, 1941) deliberately created a frustrating situation for a group of children. The children were taken to a room, showed a collection of attractive toys, and told that they could look but not touch. Later, when the children were allowed to play with the toys, they were extremely hostile—smashing them against the walls and floor. Another group of children who had not been frustrated in advance played happily and peacefully with identical toys.

But critics were very quick to point out the flaws in this hypothesis. First, frustration does not *always* lead to aggression. Far from becoming aggressive, some people withdraw when their efforts are thwarted. Others intensify their efforts to achieve the goal by nonaggressive means. Aggression, then, is only one of many possible responses to frustration. Second, aggression is not always preceded by frustration. Most people hit back when they are attacked physically and attempt to "get even" when they are insulted or slandered. To say that a verbal or physical assault is a form of frustration is stretching the term to the point where it becomes almost meaningless.

Leonard Berkowitz (1962) and others have argued that the key to predicting aggression is not frustration per se, but the level of anger aroused. According to this view, anger is the intervening and crucial variable. Frustration may provoke anger, which in turn may provoke aggression, but so can other experiences, such as verbal assaults (Rule and Nesdale, 1976). This has been confirmed experimentally (Gentry, 1970). Groups of student volunteers were given an intelligence test to complete in a specified amount of time. The members of one group were repeatedly interrupted with irrelevant questions, stopped before the time had elapsed, and ultimately told they had failed. In other words, these students were frustrated. Another group was insulted. The experimenter made a number of derogatory remarks about the students' appearance, general behavior, and immature attitudes, even though they were told they had passed the test. A control group completed the test without interruption or insult. Then each student was asked to monitor the experimenter's performance on a test and either flash a light or deliver a shock when the experimenter made mistakes. The choice was theirs. The students' blood pressure—a physiological correlate of emotional arousal—was recorded throughout.

Frustration failed to produce increases in levels of either arousal or aggression, but insults did. Not only did the insulted students' blood pressure rise, but they responded aggressively by choosing to administer shocks in the second part of the experiment. Frustration, then, does not necessarily lead to ag-

A fight is not necessarily the direct result of frustration; physical aggression depends on the level of anger aroused by the frustration.

gression, nor is aggression always the result of frustration.

DEINDIVIDUATION AND AGGRESSION It is easy to understand how insults or intense frustration can make people angry and aggressive. That anonymity can facilitate aggression, however, is harder to accept, for it implies that people behave more aggressively than they normally would simply because their identity is concealed.

Consider one of Philip Zimbardo's experiments (1970). Female student volunteers were divided into groups of four. The women in half the groups were given oversized lab coats and hoods to wear the minute they entered the laboratory, and they were never addressed by name. Each was seated in a darkened cubicle. These were the anonymous, or "deindividuated," subjects. The women in the other groups were greeted by name and given large name tags. The cubicles in which they sat were fully lighted.

All the women were told that they were participating in a study of empathy (a vicarious sharing in the feelings of others) toward strangers. The researchers allegedly wanted to learn whether a person's empathy toward someone receiving an electric shock varied according to the person's degree of involvement in administering that shock. The subjects were asked to observe a young woman (actually a confederate) who had supposedly volunteered for a "learning" experiment. This person was to receive periodic shocks as part of her "conditioning." Each subject was required to press the shock button in her cubicle whenever a signal light went on. The length of the shock, however, was left to the subject's discretion. All of the women complied with the instructions, even though the victim writhed in (simulated) pain with every shock. But the hooded women delivered shocks that lasted twice as long as those delivered by the women wearing name tags. Thus deindividuation had a definite impact on the amount of aggression shown. Moreover, the personality of the victim seemed to have no effect on the behavior of the deindividuated subjects. A victim portrayed as a nice, kind person was shocked just as much by the deindividuated subjects as a person portrayed as obnoxious and critical.

Other experiments have confirmed the conclusion that deindividuation can facilitate violence, aggression, and other forms of antisocial behavior. Yet this outcome is not inevitable. The anonymity of being submerged in a group can also lead to positive emotions and behavior. The crowds that gather for religious celebrations, rock concerts, and other festivals often bring out the best in people—cooperation, sharing, unsolicited kindness. Why does deindividuation encourage aggressive behavior in some situations and altruistic behavior in others? The research on helping and sharing, to which we now turn, provides part of the answer.

FACTORS AFFECTING HELPING AND SHARING

Altruistic behavior is an act that offers no obvious extrinsic rewards, but is intended purely to benefit another person. Making an anonymous donation to charity is altruistic behavior; making the same donation in order to secure a tax deduction or receive gratitude is not. Risking one's life to rescue a child from a burning building is altruistic; risking one's life to rescue one's jewels, to obtain a reward from someone whose pet is trapped inside, or to earn applause from the crowd on the street is not. The key point here is that although the altruistic person may experience internal satisfaction, his or her only motive is to help someone else in need. In addition, an act must be intentional to be considered truly altruistic. Accidentally frightening a mugger away from a victim is not altruistic behavior; intentionally coming to the aid of an attack victim is.

In the discussion that follows, we will focus on the situational factors that seem to elicit two forms of altruistic behavior that have been widely studied: bystander assistance in emergencies and sharing resources with others. The idea that human beings are genetically programmed to help one another—that we have altruistic instincts—has received a good deal of attention recently (Dawkins, 1975; Wilson, 1976). However, most social scientists reject this proposition for the same reason that they reject the instinct theory of human aggression: it is based on questionable analogies between human and animal behavior, it ignores the role that learning plays in human social interaction, and it cannot explain variations in behavior between and within people. There is little doubt that humans acquire a repertoire of altruistic behaviors through modeling and reinforcement. The question for social psychologists is, when and why do we put them to use?

BYSTANDER INTERVENTION IN EMERGEN-CIES

At 3:00 a.m. one day in 1964, a young woman named Kitty Genovese, arriving home from work, was savagely attacked outside her apartment building in Queens, a borough of New York City. The victim screamed for help. At least thirty-eight neighbors came to their windows, but not one offered assistance. No one even called the police. The attack went on for over thirty minutes while Kitty Genovese was attacked, stabbed, and killed.

The Genovese murder caused a sensation in the press. How could people be so apathetic, so indifferent to the fate of another human being? Many saw it as a classic illustration of urban callousness, of city dwellers' reluctance to "get involved." Yet investigation revealed that the witnesses to Kitty Genovese's murder had been far from indifferent. Her neighbors did not just close their blinds and go back to bed. They stood and watched transfixed, "unable to act but unwilling to turn away" (Latané and Darley, 1976, pp. 309–310). What prevented them from acting? Research on bystander intervention, inspired in part by the Genovese murder, indicates that a number of powerful social forces were at work.

THE PRESENCE OF OTHER BYSTANDERS Bibb Latané and John Darley (1976) believe that the presence of others inhibits bystanders from intervening in emergencies. This view is based on a number of experiments in which Latané and Darley staged "emergencies" and recorded bystander response. In one, smoke began pouring into a room where subjects were sitting filling out a questionnaire; in another, subjects heard someone in the next room crash to the floor and moan in pain (actually a tape-recorded performance); in another, a fellow subject (actually a confederate) was heard having a violent epileptic seizure (again, faked); and in still another, customers at a liquor store witnessed two men stealing a case of beer (the "robberies" having been prearranged with the store owner). In each case, bystanders were more likely to seek or offer help when they were alone than when they were in groups of two or more. Latané and Darley offer three possible explanations for this unexpected response.

The first is **audience inhibition**. When other people are present, we think twice before we act because we are concerned about their evaluation of our behavior. Most emergencies are ambiguous. Smoke pouring from a building might signal a fire

Why is it that in certain situations we offer help more readily than in others? Factors that may influence our decision to help or not to help are audience inhibition, social influence, and diffusion of responsibility.

or it might be normal incinerator fumes; cries of help from the next apartment might be genuine, or they might be coming from your neighbor's television set. Rather than risk making a fool of yourself, you wait to see whether other people define the situation as an emergency, and **social influence**, the second factor, becomes an important determinant of bystanders' responses.

The problem is that everyone else is probably watching to see how others react too. While searching for a clue as to whether the situation is serious or not, everyone tries to appear calm and collected. The result is that each bystander is taken in by the others' nonchalance and led—or misled—to define the situation as a nonemergency. Thus social influence also prevents individuals from intervening.

Finally, when other people are present, the need for any one individual to act seems lessened. There is a **diffusion of responsibility** in noncommunicating crowds. After all, there may be a doctor or police officer or a friend or relative of the victim in the crowd who is better qualified to do something. You can leave the scene without feeling guilty.

Latané and Darley's findings suggest that bystanders are least likely to act if all three forces—audience inhibition, social influence, and diffusion of responsibility—are operating (see Figure 28.4). One of their experiments confirms this belief. Male subjects who thought they were participating in a study of repression were seated in cubicles equipped with TV monitors and cameras and were asked to fill out a questionnaire while the experimenter went to check some shock equipment.

As the subjects worked on their questionnaires, the experimenter staged an elaborate performance. He entered the room with the shock equipment and innocently picked up two wires. Immediately he let out a loud scream, threw himself in the air, hit a wall, and crashed to the floor. A few seconds later he began to moan softly. How did the subjects respond? As Latané and Darley predicted, their willingness to help seemed to depend on the number of social forces at work.

Ninety-five percent of those who believed they were alone in the situation intervened almost immediately, in contrast to 84 percent who thought that another subject had also witnessed the accident. This difference can be attributed to diffusion of responsibility. When other factors were added to the

experimental situation, the rate of intervention decreased even further. Among those who could see another person (actually a confederate of the experimenter) defining the situation by failing to respond (social influence), and those who thought that a confederate was watching them (social inhibition), only 73 percent offered help. When the subject both could see the confederate and believed that the confederate could see him, so that all three factors could affect the subject's behavior, the proportion of subjects who helped was reduced to 50 percent. Thus helping behavior decreased by 45 percent when the experimental conditions went from one of no social forces operating to all three forces operating—diffusion of responsibility, social influence, and social inhibition.

Studies such as this are very persuasive. But does the conclusion that an emergency victim is less likely to receive assistance when more than one bystander is present always hold true? Other studies have shown that under certain conditions the presence of others is not an inhibiting factor—or at least not inhibiting enough to prevent action. For example, when bystanders are able to gauge one another's immediate reactions through nonverbal cues, they are likely to come to the aid of an apparent accident victim. In one experiment (Darley, Teger, and Lewis, 1973), half the subjects were seated directly opposite

Figure 28.4 As this "decision tree" indicates, in an emergency a bystander must: (1) notice that something is happening; (2) interpret it as an emergency; and (3) decide that he or she has a personal responsibility to intervene. But the presence of others complicates this process: the presence of strangers may prevent us from concluding that the situation is an emergency; group behavior may lead us to define the situation as one which does not require action; and when other people are there to share the burden of responsibility, we may not feel obligated to aid. Thus the more witnesses to an emergency, the less aid the victim is likely to receive. This combination of factors was what inhibited Kitty Genovese's neighbors from helping her. (After Darley and Latané, 1968.)

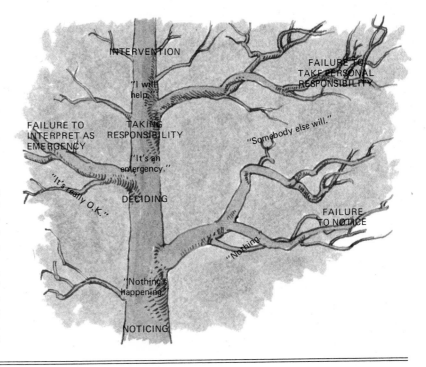

a second subject and so could observe that person's startled reaction to the sound of a heavy metal object falling, followed by a nearby worker's groans. These subjects responded to the emergency as often and as quickly as subjects who were alone when they heard the same accident occur. In addition, when an emergency victim is in clear sight, rather than simply overheard, bystanders in groups are more likely to intervene. This was demonstrated in an emergency staged on a New York subway (Piliavin, Rodin, and Piliavin, 1969) as shown in Figure 28.5. In 70 percent of the trials, bystanders immediately came to the aid of a young man who collapsed on the floor of the train. There was no evidence that the presence of others inhibited bystanders. Indeed, the response was quicker when seven or more people were in the car than when there were only one, two, or three. The experimenters suggested the reason was that bystanders could see both the victim and each other clearly. The situation was unambiguous: the victim was sprawled on the floor in front of their eyes, and the bystanders could not diffuse responsibility by telling themselves that someone else was taking care of the situation. Thus, when bystanders have clear evidence of an emergency, the inhibiting group effects we have described seem to be diluted.

THE ASSESSMENT OF COSTS   The presence of others is only one influence on bystanders' decisions to intervene in an emergency. Bystanders also assess the costs involved—both the costs of intervening (inconvenience, unpleasantness, personal danger) and the costs of *not* intervening (principally feelings of guilt and scorn from others). Rewards (heightened self-esteem, praise, thanks, and the like) are also taken into account. People are most likely to help

when the costs of intervening are low and the costs of not intervening are high. A model of bystander intervention is shown in Figure 28.6. But as the cost of helping rises, individuals find themselves in a quandary: Which is worse, stepping in and risking injury, or turning away and facing self-recrimination?

Variations of the subway experiment mentioned above demonstrate the mental calculus behind decisions to help. On some trials the person who staged the collapse carried a cane; on others he carried a bottle of liquor in a brown paper bag and acted as if he'd been drinking. Not surprisingly, bystanders were quicker to help the man with the cane than the "drunk." The costs of helping the man with the cane were low (he is not likely to hurt anyone) and the costs of not helping were high (guilt because he might be seriously injured). The costs of helping the "drunk" were higher (not only disgust, but the possibility that he would become abusive) and the costs of not helping were lower (less self-blame and social disapproval because a drunk can be considered to be responsible for his own condition).

In a follow-up study (Piliavin, Piliavin, and Rodin, 1975) the researchers introduced another condition: they planted a man dressed in a white hospital uniform near the scene of the accident. Help from bystanders decreased in this situation. The presence of someone apparently qualified to give professional help reduced the cost of not intervening; most bystanders apparently felt absolved of responsibility.

In discussing the research on bystander intervention, we have seen that people can be either very willing or very reluctant to help during emergencies. These two contrasting tendencies seem to be caused by situational factors. When conditions are favorable, most people are quick to offer aid to someone

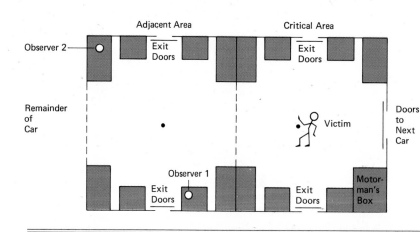

Figure 28.5 This diagram shows the positions of the "victim" and the two observers in the New York City subway car used in the experiment on bystander intervention described in the text.   (After Piliavin et al., 1969, 1975.)

A Model to Predict Bystander Intervention

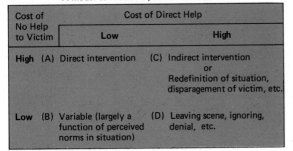

Cost of No Help to Victim	Cost of Direct Help	
	Low	**High**
High	(A) Direct intervention	(C) Indirect intervention or Redefinition of situation, disparagement of victim, etc.
Low	(B) Variable (largely a function of perceived norms in situation)	(D) Leaving scene, ignoring, denial, etc.

Figure 28.6 Their work on bystander intervention in emergency situations led Piliavin and his colleagues to propose a model for predicting intervention by coordinating the cost of helping with the cost of not helping the victim. The cost to the bystander of direct help would include variables such as lost time, danger, exposure to disgusting experiences; the cost to the bystander of not helping would include self-blame, blame from others, and loss of potential rewards (such as honor, fame, praise). Thus if the cost of direct help is low—the bystander perceives no danger—and the cost of not helping is high—the bystander would feel guilty for not aiding—then it can be predicted that he or she is almost certain to intervene. (After Piliavin, Piliavin, and Rodin, 1975.)

in trouble; but when conditions are unfavorable, many hesitate to get involved. Thus, while there may be individual traits that make one bystander more likely to intervene than another, helping behavior in emergencies seems to be most strongly determined by the surrounding situation.

GIVING AND SHARING Every year at Christmas time *The New York Times* runs a series of profiles of the neediest families in the metropolitan area— families that are struggling to get by and cannot afford the special holiday dinner and gifts that most people take for granted. The articles are designed not to solicit aid for particular families, but to remind people to give to the charity of their choice.

Like helping in emergencies, giving to charity is an altruistic act because the giver expects nothing in return. There are differences between the two situations, however. In emergencies, the needs of the victim and the appropriate response are often ambiguous. In requests for charity, the needs of the recipients are usually well defined and the traditional, appropriate response is well known. Moreover, giving poses no risks for the donor, so that some of the costs we described above do not apply. The two factors that seem to have the greatest impact on giving and sharing are norms and mood.

THE INFLUENCE OF NORMS Most Americans feel at least some social responsibility to give to others who are less fortunate than themselves (Staub, 1972). This is one of the fundamental **norms**, or expectations for behavior, that we learn in the process of socialization (see Chapters 10 and 27). To what extent does the norm of social responsibility affect behavior? This is a difficult question, because human behavior is influenced by so many factors. But research shows that in situations where people recognize a worthwhile need, and are reminded of the

Christmas is a time when people traditionally give to charities. In giving to a charity, the roles of donor and recipient are familiar and thus do not usually need to be defined.

norm of giving, their tendency to donate increases.

An experiment conducted at Christmas time by Jacqueline Macaulay (1970) demonstrated this relationship. Observers were stationed near a chimney-shaped donation box outside a department store to watch how passersby behaved. The first thing they discovered was the "Santa effect": total donations increased from a range of $1 to $3 on days when the box was unattended to a range of $16 to $25 on days when a costumed Santa Claus was present for only two hours. Obviously, a need must be brought to people's attention before they can respond to it, and a red-suited Santa commands much more attention than an unattended donation box.

Next a behavioral model was introduced. A middle-aged woman, dressed like other shoppers, walked up to the chimney, put down her shopping bag, and started to open her purse. On some trials she announced, "Well, I guess I can give something," and did, with a smile. On others she decided, "No, I don't want to give anything here" and walked away. Surprisingly, the model increased donations from others *whether or not* she made a donation herself. Macaulay reasoned that even when the model turned away, she still reminded people of the norm of giving and so encouraged generosity. Making people more aware of a social responsibility, then, increases the likelihood that the responsibility will be met.

What Macaulay's study does not show, however, is why the mere reminder of a norm is capable of spurring action. Do we conform because we are concerned about how other people will evaluate our behavior and so strive to do what is expected? Or do we conform to altruistic norms to meet self-expectations—to enhance our self-images by acting according to internalized values? Undoubtedly, in many situations both forces are at work. We are motivated by the expectations of other people as well as by our own personal standards.

THE INFLUENCE OF MOODS It is not difficult to understand how mood might influence our willingness to give to others. It seems logical that when we are in good spirits, our tendency to give may increase. Charity drives at Christmas time seem designed to take advantage of this effect. What does psychological research show?

There is abundant evidence that people are indeed very likely to give or share when they are in a positive mood. Humor, success, receiving gifts or

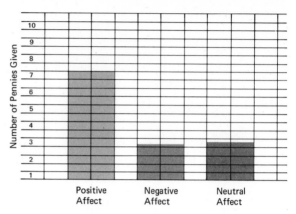

Figure 28.7 Mood has an effect on altruistic behavior. Second- and third-graders were given pennies, ostensibly for participating in a hearing test. The children were then randomly divided into three groups: one group was induced to recall a sad experience, the second group recalled a happy experience, and the third spent the time counting numbers. When given the opportunity to share with others the pennies they had just earned, those children who had experienced positive affect shared the most. (After Rosenhan, Underwood, and Moore, 1974.)

money, and simply thinking happy thoughts all increase the tendency to give (Cialdini and Kenrick, 1976). A team of researchers (Rosenhan, Underwood, and Moore, 1974) demonstrated this in an experiment with children who were "paid" with candy and pennies for taking a simple hearing test (see Figure 28.7). One of the experimenters talked with each child before he or she left the laboratory. Half of the children were asked to describe something that made them sad; the other half were asked to describe something that made them happy. When leaving the laboratory, each child was given the opportunity to share some of his or her candy and pennies with other children. Those in a happy state were twice as likely to give away some of their candy and pennies as those who left feeling sad.

Other studies have supported the conclusion that a bad mood depresses the tendency to share. In one experiment fourth-graders who had received a failing mark on a test gave less to charity than those who had received no mark (Isen, Horn, and Rosenhan, 1973). However, other studies have indicated the opposite relationship. Negative moods, failure, embarrassment, receiving an insult, and witnessing another person in trouble or pain have all been linked to *greater* willingness to help (Cialdini and Kenrick, 1976). How can these apparently contradictory results be explained?

Robert Cialdini and Douglas Kenrick (1976) point out that many of the experiments on mood and altruism have used children as subjects. It is only with age, they argue, that negative feelings are related to an increased tendency to give or to help. In one of their own experiments, for example, a negative mood suppressed generosity slightly in first-graders, enhanced generosity slightly in fifth-graders, and substantially increased generosity in tenth- to twelfth-graders. Why is this? According to these researchers, the socialization process creates a link between altruism and social approval. As children we are praised for helping others, and scolded, if not actually punished, for withholding help. The older we get, the stronger this link becomes. In time, benevolence becomes it own reward. In addition, empathy enhances the internal reward of altruistic behaviors. When we help someone, we experience their relief and happiness vicariously. Thus being helpful becomes one way of making ourselves feel better. These relationships, however, take time to learn; small children do not yet consider virtue its own reward.

A tender moment between a young man and his helpless grandfather. Often we are in conflict between the desire to help others and the desire to think of ourselves first.

THE HUMAN DILEMMA: COOPERATION VERSUS COMPETITION

People do not give to charity every day. Emergencies are, by definition, rare. And most people do not make a career of physical aggression. Yet the choice between behaving in ways that are purposely antagonistic toward others and behaving in ways intended to aid others occurs every day. Do you share your lecture notes with a classmate or keep them to yourself? Do you tell a prospective buyer about your car's transmission problem or keep it to yourself so that you can get a higher price for the car? Do you visit an elderly aunt to please your parents or flatly refuse to change your other plans? The choice between aggression and competition on the one hand and cooperation and altruism on the other hand underlies everything from trivial decisions such as whether to grab a seat on a crowded bus to such vital issues as deciding how the earth's limited resources will be distributed. Because so many of life's prizes—and indeed necessities—are scarce, people cannot always act in ways that maximize both their own immediate goals and those of others. The necessity of choosing between competition and cooperation is a persistent human dilemma.

STUDYING THE HUMAN DILEMMA What would you do in the following situation? You and a friend are arrested for a petty theft. At the police station you are taken to separate rooms for interrogation. The district attorney believes the two of you are responsible for a far more serious crime, but does not have enough evidence to take you to court. She wants a confession for this more serious crime. If neither you nor your friend confesses, the court will send both of you to prison on the petty theft charge for one year. If both of you confess to the more serious crime, the DA will recommend leniency—eight years instead of ten. If only one of you confesses, that person will get a sentence of only three months for turning state's evidence, while the other will go to prison for the full ten years. The dilemma is obvious. The best strategy for both of you is to stick to your alibis and refuse to confess; you'll both get one year in prison, but no more. However, if you follow this strategy, but your friend betrays you by confessing, you will go to prison for ten years. Moreover, if you confess, there is always the chance that your friend won't and you will get away with only a three-month sentence.

The Prisoner's Dilemma Game

Prisoner II

	Don't Confess	Confess
Prisoner I **Don't Confess**	Penalty for lesser charge for I—1 year Penalty for lesser charge for II—1 year	"Book" thrown at I—10 years Leniency for II—3 months
Confess	Leniency for I—3 months "Book" thrown at II—10 years	Leniency for I—8 years Leniency for II—8 years

Figure 28.8 The prisoner's dilemma can be diagrammed as a 2 × 2 matrix. Each person must choose one of two options, prisoner I controlling the horizontal rows and prisoner II the vertical columns; the outcomes of a joint decision are given by the intersection between the row and column chosen. The best outcome is obtained by both partners cooperating with each other—in this case, by cooperating *not* to confess—but studies show that a competitive strategy is chosen more often than a cooperative one.

The Prisoner's Dilemma Game (see Figure 28.8), as this situation is called, has proved a valuable tool for discovering the conditions under which people are most likely to choose to cooperate or compete. Experimenters explain the rules of this game, or some variation, to pairs of subjects. Then the game begins. Typically the experimenter runs fifteen to twenty trials. In every case, cooperation will produce the best outcome over the long run. Yet competition is the most commonly chosen strategy. In most studies, between 60 and 70 percent of subjects behave competitively despite the costs involved in doing so (Oskamp and Kleinke, 1970).

FACTORS INFLUENCING TWO-PERSON CO-OPERATION Why is cooperation in the Prisoner's Dilemma Game and similar games so rare? By varying the conditions under which these games are played, researchers can isolate factors that tend to promote or discourage competition between two people. We will discuss two of the most important factors.

THE USE OF THREATS At the bargaining table, roommates or members of a family (like nations or labor and management) often resort to threats to "extort" cooperation. How effective are threats? Not very, according to an experiment conducted by Morton Deutsch and Robert Krauss (1960).

Pairs of subjects played a game that is structurally very similar to the Prisoner's Dilemma Game. They were asked to imagine that they were each in charge of a trucking company that shipped goods over the routes shown in Figure 28.9. For every trip they would earn 60 cents, minus 1 cent per second in "operating expenses." Hence the object of the game was to get from the starting point to the destination in the shortest time possible. The middle portion of the main route admitted only one truck at a time. The players could either share this road or use winding, time-consuming alternative routes. The best strategy for both players was to take turns using the main route.

To test the effects of potential threats, Deutsch and Krauss introduced two conditions. In the first, one player was given a gate that could be locked to prevent the other player from using the main route (the unilateral threat condition). In the second, both players controlled gates (the bilateral threat condition). Cooperation, which was difficult to achieve in the no-threat condition, became even more difficult in the unilateral threat condition, and almost impossible in the bilateral threat condition. Players attempted to gain access to the main route by resorting to the use of threats. When neither player would yield, both would close their gates, use the alternative route, and incur heavy penalties. Once this pattern began, the gates were no longer simply signals or warnings, but became a means of punishment and retaliation.

Whether these results can be generalized to real-life situations in which the stakes are considerably higher than they are in such games is debatable (Pruitt and Kimmel, 1977). For example, some argue that the fact that the United States and the Soviet Union are capable of destroying each other serves as a deterrent to the actual use of force. Both nations are reluctant even to issue a direct threat, much less to launch an attack.

OBSERVATION AND EXPERIENCE The object of nearly all games is to win, so it is not surprising that players in games like the two described above are competitive in early trials. Later they may realize that cooperation is the best strategy, but it may be too late. The players may be "locked into" a competitive struggle. Or they may be too involved in the conflict to see the benefits of cooperation. But what if they have an opportunity to observe other games before they themselves play?

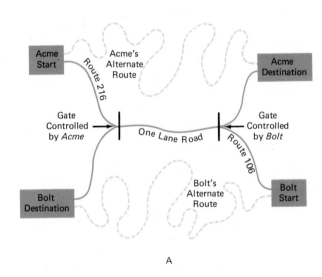

A

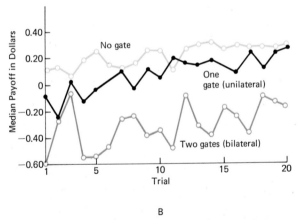

B

Figure 28.9 (A) The game used to study the effects of threat on cooperation. Each of two players (called Acme and Bolt) was told that the aim was to maximize individual profit by reaching their respective destinations as quickly as possible. The quickest route involved a shared one-lane road, and the best strategy dictated that they cooperate, taking turns using it. (B) When the variable of threat was introduced by giving only one player access to a gate which could block the road for the opponent (one gate, unilateral threat) or by giving both players access to a controlling gate (two gates, bilateral threat), cooperation was impeded. Threat was detrimental to reaching agreement, especially in the bilateral threat condition. (After Deutsch and Krauss, 1960.)

Sanford Braver and Bruce Barnett (1976) investigated this situation. Before playing themselves, subjects watched games in which (a) one player used a cooperative strategy and was rewarded with the other player's cooperation; (b) one player tried to cooperate but the other chose to compete; or (c) both players pursued a competitive strategy throughout. Then subjects were introduced to a new opponent and allowed to play. One might think that regardless of the nature of the game they had watched, the subjects would have learned that cooperation was most effective and so would pursue that strategy. They did not. Only those who had watched a highly competitive game chose to cooperate. Apparently, observing conflict "inoculates" observers against becoming embroiled in conflict themselves. Why?

The answer may lie in attribution theory. As we noted in Chapter 26, people tend to attribute another person's failures to his or her own behavior, but to attribute another person's successes to external factors such as luck or the help of others. Hence when they watch a model playing a competitive game, they attribute a low score to that player's behavior and avoid the behavior themselves. But when they observe a cooperative game, they attribute the model's success to his or her luck in having a cooperative partner. Since they may not have the same "luck" themselves, they are not willing to risk cooperation (Braver and Rohrer, 1978).

PROMOTING SOCIAL COOPERATION   So far we have focused on choices between cooperation and competition faced by two individuals and the personal consequences of those decisions. Here we want to consider the consequences that numerous choices made by individuals between cooperation and competition have on communities, societies, and ultimately on humankind.

THE TRAGEDY OF THE COMMONS   Consider what Garrett Hardin (1968) calls "the tragedy of the commons." A commons is an open pasture where anyone can graze cattle. People naturally take advantage of the free grazing by adding more animals to their herds whenever they can. Disease, poaching, and war may keep the animal and human populations low so that, for a time, the system works. But eventually the day of reckoning comes: the population of humans and their herds has grown and

Some people think that the world's resources should be exploited to the full, while others think that humans must work cooperatively to protect and restore our environment.

some set of relationships that later proves to be unpleasant or lethal but that they see no easy way to back out of or to avoid" (Platt, 1973, p. 641). A classic example is the transportation dilemma that exists in the United States. When one individual after anther decides that it's in his or her best interests to own a private car, the public transportation system declines. The worse transit service becomes, the more people buy cars. The process is self-accelerating. One day all those people find themselves sitting in bumper-to-bumper traffic, hour after hour, wishing they could take a bus or a train. But in many areas there is no longer an effective mass-transit system for them to use. The dilemma offers no obvious solution.

It is easy to see how social traps develop. Behaviorists have demonstrated over and over that the immediate consequences of an action—what happens in a few seconds, hours, or days—has more impact on behavior than do long-term outcomes—what happens in a few days, weeks, a year, or a decade. Short-term rewards are seductive. The herder is quickly rewarded for buying and selling another animal. The negative consequences, or punishment, for overgrazing lies years in the future and has little effect on the herder's present behavior. In the commons, then, and in a number of structurally similar situations, powerful psychological and social forces work *against* cooperation on a large scale over an extended period of time.

the grass has gotten sparse from overgrazing. It is only a matter of time before the once lush pasture becomes barren.

The individual herder may have some sense of this. But when he or she weighs the benefits of adding another animal to the herd against the cost of damage to the pasture, there isn't any comparison. The herder will receive full payment for the extra animal when it is sold. In contrast, the cost of overgrazing is shared by all herders, in the form of a slight decrease in the weight of each animal. The logical course for the herder to pursue if he or she wants to maximize his or her gains is to add another animal—and another, and another. Of course, every other herder comes to the same conclusion. And this is the "tragedy of the commons": in pursuing their own best interests as individuals, people move steadily toward eventual ruin for all.

Private decisions, as in the commons, often create **social traps**: "[People] or organizations or whole societies get themselves started in some direction or

BREAKING OUT OF SOCIAL TRAPS Hardin (1968) argues that the solution to the tragedy of the commons is mutually-agreed-upon coercion. Appeals to conscience will not work, Hardin argues, because the audience hears two conflicting messages: the value of behaving as a responsible citizen (exercising restraint) and the value of behaving according to one's immediate self-interest (maximizing short-term personal gains). By coercion Hardin does not mean depriving people of all freedom, but simply making it more difficult or expensive to exploit the commons.

Research suggests that there may be other ways to break out of social traps. Improving communication seems to be an especially promising approach. Figure 28.10A shows the effect of communication on the prisoner's dilemma. It has been noted (Dawes, McTavish, and Shaklee, 1977) that communication may increase the tendency to cooperate for three reasons. First, communication allows individuals to become acquainted and thus in-

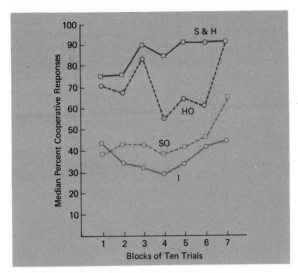

Figure 28.10A The standard Prisoner's Dilemma Game does not permit communication between partners, but when the game is altered so that communication is allowed, strategies change. For example, Wichman varied the amount of communication possible in four ways: in one condition, (I) isolated subjects could neither see nor hear each other; in a second condition they could hear each other (HO); in a third they could see each other (SO); and in a fourth they could both see and hear each other (S&H). As this graph shows, the more extensive the communication, the higher the rate of cooperation. (After Wichman, 1970.)

Of course, real-life social traps are the product of numerous individuals making many choices between cooperation and competition at different times. Kevin Brechner (1977) tried to simulate a real-life social dilemma in a group game in which individuals could draw points from a pool by pressing a key. Each player was to be rewarded with class credits based on the total number of points he or she had at the end of the game. The pool of points would be replenished, but—as in many ecological systems—the replenishment rate would be very slow when the resource pool was nearly empty and quite rapid when the pool was nearly full. If at any time players withdrew all the points in the pool, the game would be terminated immediately, preventing all players from acquiring additional points. Thus they had to consider both short-term gains (points) and long-term consequences (depleting the pool) with every move. The optimal strategy for all players was to keep the pool nearly full, drawing points at the same fairly rapid rate at which they were being replenished.

In half the games, players were permitted to communicate; in the other half, they were not. Again, communication led to increased cooperation and

creases their concern for one another. Second, communication permits people to exchange information relevant to a cooperative decision. And third, communication allows people to state their intentions and to assure others that those intentions are honest.

In one study the impact of these three factors was examined by means of a game that replicated the commons dilemma (Dawes, McTavish, and Shaklee, 1977). Subjects were divided into small groups of six to eight strangers. Each person was asked to make a choice between a cooperative strategy and a competitive strategy. Getting to know one another increased the subjects' rate of choice of the cooperative strategy slightly, but exchange of information about the consequences of the choice and the opportunity to declare intentions boosted the subjects' choice of cooperation significantly. When all three factors were at work, only 16 percent of the subjects—or about one person in each group—ultimately adopted the competitive tactic (see Figure 28.10B).

Figure 28.10B The effects of communication on behavior were examined in an eight-person "commons" dilemma that pitted individual financial gain against group financial gain. The researchers hypothesized that greater amounts of communication among group members would decrease behavior motivated by individual self-interest and promote behavior motivated by the collective interest. Four different communication conditions were possible: no communication, communication irrelevant to the task, relevant communication, and relevant communication plus public commitment to a position. As expected, there were fewer defectors, or noncooperators, in those conditions where communication was greatest. (After Dawes, McTavish, and Shaklee, 1977.)

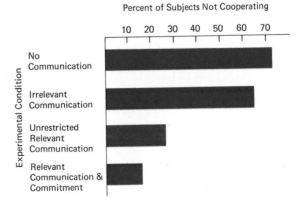

greater success. Subjects forbidden to talk tended to withdraw points as rapidly as possible, and soon exhausted the pool. Communicating subjects tended to race for points, stop when one player alerted the others to the fact that the pool was almost empty, and resume when the pool had refilled. Brechner suggests that this pattern frequently appears outside the laboratory. For example, a species of animal is hunted almost to the point of extinction; some individual or group sounds the alarm; restraints are put into effect until the species recovers. Of course, this can happen only if people are communicating and perceive some long-term gain.

Research on the factors that encourage or discourage cooperation in the pursuit of long-term social benefits is anything but a purely academic exercise. In 1970, futurist John Platt identified the most serious threats to humankind as nuclear annihilation, ecological imbalance, and the population explosion. He estimated that we had at most twenty to fifty years to reverse current trends. A decade has passed and little has been done. However, there seems to be a growing recognition that these are not technological problems for which a technological solution will someday be found, but rather social problems requiring changes in human behavior. The kind of social-psychological research discussed in this chapter holds out some hope for a better understanding of the human dilemma and for the discovery of ways to resolve it.

Summary

1. **Aggression** is behavior intended to harm another person. There are three categories of explanations for the high level of abusive behavior in humans: biological, social learning, and situational.
   - A. The idea that human aggression has a biological basis has had many advocates, including Sigmund Freud, who believed that human beings achieve only an uneasy balance between destructive and procreative impulses.
     1. Ethologist Konrad Lorenz contends that aggression is instinctive, biologically based behavior with adaptive benefits for humans as well as other animals. He believes that the blocking of human aggression by social sanctions may be more dangerous than the aggression itself. The idea that aggression is an inborn, universal human trait does not hold up under scrutiny; studies show that the emergence of "instinctive" behavior often depends on learning. Also, the idea that there is a universal aggressive instinct makes it difficult to explain variations within and between cultures in levels of human aggression.
     2. A number of researchers believe that biological abnormalities explain why some individuals seem especially hot-tempered and violent. Violent behavior has been linked to chromosomal abnormalities and various types of brain damage. However, the majority of people with a history of violent behavior have no such abnormality or injury, and the majority of people with such defects are no more aggressive than anyone else.
   - B. According to social learning theory, it is exposure to models of violent behavior and reinforcement for aggressive acts that explain why people so often attack one another.
     1. We learn how and when to perform specific aggressive acts and general strategies of aggression by observing others. In our culture two of the most influential models are the members of our families and the characters portrayed on television and in films.
     2. According to social learning theory, people do not behave aggressively unless such behavior elicits reinforcement—that is, unless aggression has paid off for them in the past or unless they expect it to pay off in the future.
   - C. Many people believe that aggressive behavior is the result of certain unbearably frustrating situations. Both frustration and anonymity seem to promote aggressive behavior.
     1. John Dollard's **frustration-aggression hypothesis** contends that aggression is always the consequence of frustration and that frustration always leads to some form

of aggression. **Frustration** is defined as interference with any form of goal-directed behavior. Critics of this theory claim that aggression is only one of many possible responses to frustration and that aggression is not always preceded by frustration. Some researchers have argued that the key to predicting aggression is not frustration as such, but the level of anger aroused.

2. Experiments have confirmed that deindividuation, or anonymity, can facilitate violence, aggression, and other forms of antisocial behavior. However, this outcome is not inevitable.

2. **Altruistic behavior** is an act that offers no obvious extrinsic rewards, but is intended purely to benefit another person. Two widely studied forms of altruistic behavior are bystander assistance in emergencies and sharing resources with others. Most social scientists reject the proposition that humans have any altruistic instincts what so ever.

A. A number of social forces are involved in bystander intervention in emergencies.

1. Experiments by Bibb Latané and John Darley indicate that the presence of others inhibits bystanders from intervening. Three explanations have been offered for this:

   a. Because of **audience inhibition**, we think twice before we act when other people are present because we are concerned about their evaluation of our behavior.

   b. **Social influence**—waiting to see whether other people define the situation as an emergency—is an important determinant of bystanders' responses.

   c. There is often a **diffusion of responsibility** in noncommunicating crowds.

   Bystanders are apparently least likely to act if all three of these forces are operating. However, when bystanders are able to gauge one another's immediate reactions through nonverbal cues or when they have clear, unambiguous evidence that an emergency exists, the inhibiting group effects seem to be diluted.

2. In addition to the presence of others, bystanders' assessments of the personal costs of intervening influence helping behavior

in emergencies. People are most likely to help when the costs of intervening are low and the costs of not intervening are high.

B. The two factors that seem to have the greatest impact on giving and sharing are norms and mood.

1. Social responsibility is one of the **norms**—expectations for behavior—that we learn in the process of socialization. People's tendency to give to charity increases in those situations where people recognize a worthwhile need and are reminded of the norm of giving.

2. People are most likely to give or share when they are in a positive mood. Experiments suggest that children are less likely to help if they are in a negative mood. Adults, however, are *more* likely to give when they are in a negative mood. According to some researchers, this tendency in adults is a result of the socializing process, which creates a link between altruism and social approval; thus, being helpful becomes a way of improving our mood.

3. A persistent human dilemma is the necessity of choosing between competition and cooperation.

A. The Prisoner's Dilemma Game is a valuable tool for discovering the conditions under which people are most likely to choose to cooperate or compete.

B. Researchers have isolated factors that tend to promote or discourage competition between two people.

1. Experiments using games show that the use of threats is not a very effective way to achieve cooperation.

2. Experiments involving games used to study cooperation suggest that observing conflict "inoculates" observers against becoming embroiled in conflict themselves.

C. Choices made by individuals between cooperation and competition affect communities, societies, and humankind.

1. "The tragedy of the commons" is that in pursuing their own best interests as individuals, people move toward eventual ruin for all. Such private decisions may create a **social trap**—a direction or a set of relationships that proves to be unpleasant or lethal but that has become difficult to avoid.

2. Solutions to the tragedy of the commons

and other social traps include mutually-agreed-upon coercion and improved communication. Communication may increase the tendency to cooperate for three reasons:

a. It allows individuals to become acquainted and thus increases their concern for one another.

b. It permits people to exchange information relevant to a cooperative decision.

c. It allows people to state their intentions and to assure others that those intentions are honest.

RECOMMENDED READINGS

BARON, ROBERT A. *Human Aggression.* New York: Plenum Press, 1977. An excellent, up-to-date textbook that analyzes social, environmental, and individual determinants of aggression.

BERKOWITZ, LEONARD. *Aggression: A Social-Psychological Analysis.* New York: McGraw-Hill, 1962. The successor to *Frustration and Aggression* (see below), in which the frustration-aggression hypothesis is refined and expanded.

DOLLARD, JOHN, LEONARD W. DOOB, NEAL E. MILLER, O. H. MOWRER, and ROBERT R. SEARS. *Frustration and Aggression.* New Haven, Conn.: Yale University Press, 1939. The classic monograph that stimulated a research effort to understand aggression that continues even today.

HARDIN, GARRETT, and JOHN BADEN (eds.). *Managing the Commons.* San Francisco: W. H. Freeman, 1977. Hardin popularized the tragedy of the commons as a model of resource mismanagement. In this collection of papers a variety of perspectives are brought to bear on the problem of avoiding the tragedy of resource depletion.

LATANÉ, BIBB, and JOHN M. DARLEY. *The Unresponsive Bystander: Why Doesn't He Help?* New York: Appleton-Century-Crofts, 1970. The prizewinning report of the authors' fascinating series of experiments on the behavior of bystanders in emergencies.

MACAULAY, JACQUELINE, and LEONARD BERKOWTIZ (eds.). *Altruism and Helping Behavior: Social Psychological Studies of Some Antecedents and Consequences.* New York: Academic Press, 1970. A collection of research reports that provide useful insights into the determinants of sharing, giving, and helping.

RAPOPORT, ANATOL. *Experimental Games and Their Uses in Psychology.* Morristown, N.J.: General Learning Press, University Modular Publications, 1973. A clear and concise introduction to games (like the Prisoner's Dilemma Game) that are used to study competition and cooperation.

REFERENCES

The number in brackets after each entry refer to the chapter in this book in which that work is cited.

Abelson, Robert P., and **Philip G. Zimbardo.** *Canvassing for Peace: A Manual for Volunteers.* Ann Arbor, Mich.: Society for the Psychological Study of Social Issues, 1970. [25]

Adler, Alfred. "Individual Psychology," in Carl A. Murchison (ed.), *Psychologies of 1930.* Worcester, Mass.: Clark University Press, 1930, pp. 395–405. [18]

———. *What Life Should Mean to You.* Alan Porter (ed.). Boston: Little, Brown, 1931. [18]

Adorno, T. W., E. Frenkel-Brunswick, D. J. Levinson, and **R. N. Sanford.** *The Authoritarian Personality.* New York: Harper, 1950. [25]

Ainsworth, Mary D. Salter. "The Development of Infant-Mother Attachment," in B. M. Caldwell and H. N. Ricciuti (eds.), *Review of Child Development Research.* Vol. 3. Chicago: University of Chicago Press, 1973. [10]

Ainsworth, Mary D. Salter, S. M. V. Bell, and **Donelda J. Stayton.** "Individual Differences in Strange-Situational Behavior of One-Year-Olds," in H. R. Schaffer (ed.), *The Origins of Human Social Relations.* New York: Academic Press, 1971. [10]

Ajzen, Icek, and **Martin Fishbein.** "Attitude-Behavior Relations: A Theoretical Analysis and Review of Empirical Research," *Psychological Bulletin,* 84:5 (1977), 888–918. [25]

Albee, George W. "I.Q. Tests on Trial," *The New York Times,* February 12, 1978, Section E, p. 13. [20]

Albert, Stuart M., and **James M. Dabbs, Jr.** "Physical Distance and Persuasion," *Journal of Personality and Social Psychology,* 15 (1970), 265–270. [25]

Allen, V. L. "Situational Factors in Conformity," in Leonard Berkowitz (ed.), *Advances in Experimental Social Psychology.* Vol. 2. New York: Academic Press, 1965, pp. 133–170. [27]

Allerand, Anne Marie. "Remembrance of Feelings Past: A Study of Phenomenological Genetics." Ph.D. dissertation, Columbia University, 1967. [15]

Allon, N. "The Stigma of Overweight in Everyday Life," in G. A. Bray (ed.), *Obesity in Perspective.* Washington, D.C.: U.S. Government Printing Office, 1975. [26]

Allport, Gordon W. *Personality: A Psychological Interpretation.* New York: Holt, Rinehart and Winston, 1937. [19]

———. *Pattern and Growth in Personality.* New York: Holt, Rinehart and Winston, 1961. [19]

———. "Traits Revisited," *American Psychologist,* 21:1 (January 1966), 1–10. [19]

Allport, Gordon W., and **Henry S. Odbert.** "Trait-Names: A Psycho-Lexical Study," *Psychological Monographs,* 47:1 (1936), Whole No. 211. [19]

American Psychiatric Association. *Diagnostic and Statistical Manual of Mental Disorders.* 2nd ed. Washington, D.C.: American Psychiatric Association, 1968. [22]

American Psychological Association. *Ethical Principles in the Conduct of Research with Human Participants.* Washington, D.C.: American Psychological Association, 1973, pp. 1–2. [2]

Ames, Adelbert, Jr. "Visual Perception and the Rotating Trapezoidal Window," *Psychological Monographs,* 65:7 (1951), Whole No. 234. [13]

Amoore, J. E., and **D. Venstrom.** "Correlations Between Stereochemical Assessments and Organoleptic Analysis of Odorous Compounds," in T. Hayashi (ed.), *Olfaction and Taste.* Oxford: Pergamon, 1967, pp. 3–17. [12]

Anand, B. K., G. S. Chhina, and **B. Singh.** "Some Aspects of Electroencephalographic Studies in Yogis," *Electroencephalography and Clinical Neurophysiology,* 13 (1961), 452–456. [14]

Anders, Thomas F., and **Howard P. Roffwarg.** "The Effects of Selective Interruption and Deprivation of Sleep in the Human Newborn," *Developmental Psychobiology,* 6:1 (January 1973), 77–89. [14]

Andersson, Bengt. "The Effect of Injections of Hypertonic NaCl Solutions into Different Parts of the Hypothalamus of Goats," *Acta Physiologica Scandinavica,* 28 (1953), 188–201. [16]

Arkes, Hal R., and **John P. Garske.** *Psychological Theories of Motivation.* Monterey, Calif.: Brooks/Cole, 1977. [16]

Arlin, Patricia Kennedy. "Cognitive Development in Adulthood: A Fifth Stage?" *Developmental Psychology,* 11:5 (1975), 602–606. [8]

Armstrong, R. H., et al. "Gastric Secretion During Sleep and Dreaming." Paper presented at the Annual Meeting of the Association for the Psychophysiological Study of Sleep, March 1965. [14]

Arnold, Magda B. *Emotion and Personality.* New York: Columbia University Press, 1960. [15]

Aronfreed, J. "The Concept of Internaliza-

tion," in D. A. Goslin (ed.), *Handbook of Socialization Theory and Research.* Chicago: Rand McNally, 1969. [10]

Aronson, Elliot. *The Social Animal.* 2nd ed. San Francisco: Freeman, 1976. [25]

Aronson, Elliot, and **Darwyn E. Linder.** "Gain and Loss of Esteem as Determinants of Interpersonal Attractiveness," *Journal of Experimental Social Psychology,* 1 (1965), 156–172. [26]

Aronson, Elliot, et al. "Busing and Racial Tension: The Jigsaw Route to Learning and Liking," *Psychology Today,* 9 (February 1975), 43–50. [25]

Asch, Solomon E. "Effects of Group Pressure upon the Modification and Distortion of Judgments," in Harold Guetzkow (ed.), *Groups, Leadership, and Men.* Pittsburgh: Carnegie Press, 1951. [27]

———. "Forming Impressions of Personality," *Journal of Abnormal and Social Psychology,* 41 (1946), 258–290. [26]

Aserinsky, Eugene, and **Nathaniel Kleitman.** "Regularly Occurring Periods of Eye Motility and Concomitant Phenomena During Sleep," *Science,* 118 (1953), 273–274. [14]

Atkinson, John W. *An Introduction to Motivation.* New York: Van Nostrand Reinhold, 1958a. [16]

——— (ed.). *Motives in Fantasy, Action, and Society.* New York: Van Nostrand Reinhold, 1958b. [16]

———. "Thematic Apperceptive Measurement of Motives Within a Context of Motivation," in John W. Atkinson (ed.), *Motives in Fantasy, Action, and Society.* New York: Van Nostrand Reinhold, 1958c [16]

Attneave, Fred. "Some Informational Aspects of Visual Perception," *Psychological Review,* 61 (1954), 183–193. [13]

Azrin, N. H., and **R. M. Foxx,** *Toilet Training in Less Than a Day.* New York: Simon & Schuster, 1974. [4]

Bailey, Nancy. "Development of Mental Abilities," in Paul H. Mussen (ed.), *Carmichael's Manual of Child Psychology.* Vol. 1 New York: Wiley, 1970, pp. 1163–1209. [2]

Ball, William, and **Edward Tronick.** "Infant Responses to Impending Collision: Optical and Real," *Science,* 171 (February 26, 1971), 818. [7]

Baltes, P. B., and **K. W. Schaie.** "Aging and IQ: The Myth of the Twilight Years," *Psychology Today,* 7 (March 1974), 35–40. [8]

Ban, T. *Recent Advances in the Biology of Schizo-*

phrenia. Springfield, Ill.: Charles C Thomas, 1973. [23]

Bandura, Albert. *Aggression: A Social Learning Analysis.* Englewood Cliffs, N.J.: Prentice-Hall, 1973. [28]

———. "Influence of Models' Reinforcement Contingencies on the Acquisition of Imitative Responses," *Journal of Personality and Social Psychology,* 1 (1965), 589–595. [10]

———. *Principles of Behavior Modification.* New York: Holt, Rinehart and Winston, 1969. [19, 24]

———. "Self-Efficacy: Toward a Unifying Theory of Behavioral Change," *Psychological Review,* 84 (1977a), 191–215. [24]

———. "Social Learning Analysis of Aggression," in Emilio Ribes-Inesta and Albert Bandura (eds.), *Analysis of Delinquency and Aggression.* Hillsdale, N.J.: Erlbaum, 1976, pp. 203–232. [28]

———. *Social Learning Theory.* Englewood Cliffs, N.J.: Prentice-Hall, 1977. [10, 19, 24]

———. "Vicarious Processes: A Case of No-Trial Learning," in Leonard Berkowitz (ed.), *Advances in Experimental Social Psychology.* Vol. 2. New York: Academic Press, 1966, pp. 1–55. [19]

Bandura, Albert, Nancy E. Adams, and **Janice Beyer.** "Cognitive Processes Mediating Behavioral Change," *Journal of Personality and Social Psychology,* 35:3 (March 1977), 125–139. [1, 24]

Bandura, Albert, J. E. Grusec, and **F. L. Menlove.** "Vicarious Extinction of Avoidance Behavior," *Journal of Personality and Social Psychology,* 5 (1967), 16–23. [24]

Bandura, Albert, D. Ross, and **S. Ross.** "Transmission of Aggression Through Imitation of Aggressive Models," *Journal of Abnormal and Social Psychology,* 63 (1961), 575–582. [10]

Bandura, Albert, and **Richard H. Walters.** *Adolescent Aggression.* New York: Ronald Press, 1959. [19]

———. *Social Learning and Personality Development.* New York: Holt, Rinehart and Winston, 1963. [19]

Banquet, J. P. "Spectral Analysis of the EEG in Meditation," *Electroencephalography and Clinical Neurophysiology,* 35 (1973), 143–151. [14]

Barber, T. X. "Measuring 'Hypnotic-like' Suggestibility with and without 'Hypnotic Induction': Psychometric Properties, Norms, and Variables Influencing Response to the Barber Suggestibility Scale (BSS)," *Psychological Reports,* 16 (1965), 809–844. [14]

———. "Responding to 'Hypnotic' Suggestions: An Introspective Report," *American Journal of Clinical Hypnosis,* 18 (1975), 6–22. [14]

Barfield, R. A., and **J. N. Morgan.** *Early Retirement: The Decision and the Experience.* Ann Arbor, Mich.: Institute of Social Research, University of Michigan, 1970. [10]

Barker, L. M., M. R. Best, and **M. Domjan** (eds.). *Learning Mechanisms in Food Selection.* Waco, Tex.: Baylor Univesity Press, 1977. [16]

Barker, R. G., T. Dembo, and **K. Lewin.** "Frustration and Regression: An Experiment with Young Children," *University of Iowa Studies in Child Welfare,* 18:386 (1941). [28]

Barltrop, Donald. "Transfer of Lead to the Human Foetus," in Donald Barltrop (ed.), *Mineral Metabolism in Pediatrics.* Oxford: Blackwell Scientific Publications, 1969. [20]

Barron, F. H. "Behavioral Decision Theory: A Topical Bibliography for Management Scientists," *Interfaces,* 5 (1974), 56–62. [6]

———. "The Psychology of Imagination," *Scientific American,* 199:3 (September 1958), 150–170. [6]

Bartoshuk, L. "The Chemical Senses, I: Taste," in J. W. Kling and L. A. Riggs (eds.), *Woodworth and Schlosberg's Experimental Psychology.* 3rd ed. New York: Holt, Rinehart and Winston, 1971. [12]

Bartoshuk, L., G. Dateo, D. Vandenbelt, R. Buttrick, and **L. Long.** "Effects of *Gymnema Sylvestre* and *Synsepalum Dulficum* on Taste in Man," in C. Pfaffmann (ed.), *Olfaction and Taste.* Vol. 3. New York: Rockefeller University Press, 1969. [12]

Bateson, Gregory, Don Jackson, et al. "Toward a Theory of Schizophrenia," *Behavioral Science,* 1 (1956), 251–264. [23]

Baumrind, Diana. "Early Socialization and the Discipline Controversy," *University Programs Modular Studies.* Morristown, N.J.: General Learning Press, 1975. [10]

Beach, Frank A. "The Descent of Instinct," *Psychological Review,* 62 (1955), 401–410. [3]

Beck, A. T. *Depression: Clinical, Experimental and Theoretical Aspects.* New York: Harper & Row, 1967. [22]

Beck, Samuel J. *Rorschach's Test. Vol. I: Basic Processes.* 3rd ed. New York: Grune & Stratton, 1961. [20]

Békésy, Georg von. "Current Status of Theories of Hearing," *Science,* 123 (1956), 779–783. [12]

Bellows, R. T. "Time Factors in Water Drinking in Dogs," *American Journal of Physiology,* 125 (1939), 87–97. [16]

Bellugi, Ursula. "The Emergence of Inflections and Negative Systems in the Speech of Two Children." Paper presented at the New England Psychological Association, 1964. [9]

———. "Learning the Language," *Psycholo-gy Today,* 4 (December 1970), 32–35+. [8]

Bem, Daryl J. *Beliefs, Attitudes, and Human Affairs.* Belmont, Calif.: Brooks/Cole, 1970. [25]

———. "Self-Perception Theory," in Leonard Berkowitz (ed.), *Advances in Experimental Social Psychology.* Vol. 6. New York: Academic Press, 1972, pp. 1–62. [26]

Bem, Daryl J., and **Andrea Allen.** "On Predicting Some of the People Some of the Time: The Search for Cross-Situational Consistencies in Behavior," *Psychological Review,* 81:6 (1974), 506–520. [19]

Bem, Sandra Lipsitz. "Androgyny vs. the Tight Little Lives of Fluffy Women and Chesty Men," *Psychology Today,* 9 (September 1975), 58–59 ff. [1]

Bergin, Allen E. "The Evaluation of Therapeutic Outcomes," in Allen E. Bergin and Sol L. Garfield (eds.), *Handbook of Psychotherapy and Behavior Change: An Empirical Analysis.* New York: Wiley, 1971. [24]

Berkowitz, Leonard. *Aggression: A Social Psychological Analysis.* New York: McGraw-Hill, 1962. [28]

Berlin, Brent, and **Paul Kay.** *Basic Color Terms: Their Universality and Evolution.* Berkeley: University of California Press, 1969. [8]

Berne, Eric. *Games People Play.* New York: Grove Press, 1964. [24]

Berntson, Gary G., Howard C. Hughes, and **Michael S. Beattie.** "A Comparison of Hypothalamically Induced Biting Attack with Natural Predatory Behavior in the Cat," *Journal of Comparative and Physiological Psychology,* 90:2, (1976), 167–178. [3]

Berscheid, Ellen, Thomas Brothen, and **William Graziano.** "Gain-Loss Theory and the 'Law of Infidelity': Mr. Doting Versus the Admiring Stranger," *Journal of Personality and Social Psychology,* 33:6 (1976), 709–718. [26]

Berscheid, Ellen, Karen Dion, Elaine Walster, and **G. M. Walster.** "Physical Attractiveness and Dating Choice: A Test of the Matching Hypothesis," *Journal of Experimental Social Psychology,* 7 (1971), 173–189. [26]

Berscheid, Ellen, and **Elaine Walster.** "Physical Attractiveness," in Leonard Berkowitz (ed.), *Advances in Experimental Social Psychology.* New York: Academic Press, 1974. [21]

———. *Interpersonal Attraction.* 2nd ed. Reading, Mass.: Addison-Wesley, 1978. [26]

Bever, Thomas G. "The Cognitive Basis for Linguistic Structures," in John R. Hayes (ed.), *Cognition and the Development of Language.* New York: Wiley, 1970, pp. 279–362. [8]

Bexton, W. H., Woodburn Heron, and **T. H. Scott.** "Effects of Decreased Variation in the Sensory Environment," *Canadian Journal of Psychology,* 8 (1954), 70–76. [13, 16]

Bickman, Leonard. "The Social Power of a Uniform," *Journal of Applied Social Psychology,* 4:1 (1974), 47–61. [27]

Bieber, Irving, et al. *Homosexuality: A Psychoanalytic Study.* New York: Basic Books, 1962. [17]

Binet, Alfred, and **Theodore Simon.** *The Development of Intelligence in Children (the Binet-Simon Scale).* Elizabeth S. Kite (tr.) Baltimore: Williams & Wilkins, 1916. [20]

Birch, Herbert G. "The Role of Motivational Factors in Insightful Problem-Solving," *Journal of Comparative Psychology,* 38 (1945), 295–317. [6]

Birch, Herbert G., and **H. S. Rabinowitz.** "The Negative Effect of Previous Experience on Productive Thinking," *Journal of Experimental Psychology,* 41 (1951), 121–125. [6]

Birren, James E. "Translations in Gerontology—Lab to Life—Psychophysiology and Speed of Response," *American Psychologist,* 29:1 (1974), 808–815. [8]

Birren, James E., and **V. Jayne Renner.** "Research on the Psychology of Aging: Principles and Experimentation," in James E. Birren and K. Warner Schaie (eds.), *Handbook of the Psychology of Aging.* New York: Van Nostrand Reinhold, 1977, pp 3–41. [8]

Blest, A. D. "The Evolution of Protective Displays in the *Saturnioidea* and *Sphingidae* (Lepidoptera)," *Behavior,* 11 (1957b), 257–309. [3]

———. "The Function of Eyespot Patterns in Lepidoptera," *Behavior,* 11 (1957a), 209–256. [3]

Bleuler, Eugen. *Dementia Praecox or the Group of Schizophrenias* (1911). J. Sinkin (tr.). New York: International Universities Press, 1950. [22]

Bliss, James C., et al. "Optical-to-Tactile Image Conversion for the Blind," *IEEE Transaction on Man-Machine Systems,* MMS–11 (1970), 58–65. [12]

Block, J. H. "Another Look at Sex Differentiation in the Socialization Behaviors of Mothers and Fathers." Paper presented at the Conference on New Directions for Research on Women, Madison, Wisconsin, May 1975. [10]

Block, J. H., J. Block, and **D. M. Harrington.** "The Relationship of Parental Teaching Strategies in Preschool Children." Paper presented to the Western Psychological Association, San Francisco, April 1974. [10]

Blodgett, H. C. "The Effect of the Introduction of Reward upon Maze Performance of Rats," *University of California Publications in Psychology,* 4:8 (1929), 117–120. [4]

Bloom, Lois M. *Language Development: Form and Function in Emerging Grammars.* Cambridge, Mass.: M.I.T. Press, 1970. [9]

Blum, G. S. *Psychoanalytic Theories of Personality.* New York: McGraw-Hill, 1953. [18]

Bolles, Robert C. *Theory of Motivation.* New York: Harper & Row, 1967. [16]

Bond, E. K. "Perception of Form by the Human Infant," *Psychological Bulletin,* 77:4 (1972), 225–245. [7]

Bonin, G. von. "Anatomical Asymmetry of the Cerebral Hemispheres," in V. B. Mountcastle (ed.), *Interhemispheric Relations in Cerebral Dominance.* Baltimore: Johns Hopkins University Press, 1962. [9]

Boring, Edwin G. *A History of Experimental Psychology.* 2nd ed. New York: Appleton-Century-Crofts, 1957. [1]

———. "A New Ambiguous Figure," *American Journal of Psychology,* 42 (1930), 444–445. [13]

Bornstein, Marc H., William Kessen, and **Sally Weiskopf.** "The Categories of Hue in Infancy," *Science,* 191 (January 16, 1976), 201–202. [7, 9]

Bower, Gordon H., and **Michal C. Clark.** "Narrative Stories as Mediators for Serial Learning," *Psychonomic Science,* 14 (1969), 181–182. [5]

Bower, T. G. R. *A Primer of Infant Development.* San Francisco: Freeman, 1977. [9, 10]

———. *Development in Infancy.* San Francisco: Freeman, 1974. [8]

———. "Repetitive Processes in Child Development," *Scientific American,* 235:5 (November 1976), 38–47. [7]

Bower, T. G. R., J. Broughton, and **K. M. Moore.** "The Development of the Object Concept as Manifested by Changes in the Tracking Behavior of Infants," *Journal of Experimental Child Psychology,* 12 (1971), 182–193. [7]

Bowers, Kenneth S. *Hypnosis for the Seriously Curious.* Monterey, Calif.: Brooks/Cole, 1976. [14]

Bowlby, John. *Attachment and Loss.* Vol. 1: *Attachment.* New York: Basic Books, 1969. [10, 27]

———. "The Nature of the Child's Tie to His Mother," *International Journal of Psychoanalysis,* 39 (1958), 350–373. [7]

Brackbill, Yvonne. "Cumulative Effects of Continuous Stimulation on Arousal Level in Infants," *Child Development,* 42 (1971), 17–26. [2]

Brackbill, Yvonne, et al. "Arousal Level in Neonates and Preschool Children Under Continuous Auditory Stimulation," *Journal of Experimental Child Psychology,* 4 (1966), 177–188. [2]

Bradway, K. "I.Q. Constancy on the Revised Stanford-Binet from the Preschool to the Junior High School Level," *Journal of Genetic Psychology,* 65 (1944), 197–217. [8]

Braun, J. Jay. "Neocortex and Feeding Behavior in the Rat," *Journal of Comparative and Physiological Psychology,* 89 (1975), 507–522. [11]

Braun, J. Jay, and **Harris McIntosh, Jr.** "Learned Taste Aversions Induced by Rotational Stimulation," *Physiological Psychology,* 1:4 (1973), 301–304. [3]

Braver, Sanford L., and **Bruce Barnett.** "Effects of Modeling on Cooperation in a Prisoner's Dilemma Game," *Journal of Personality and Social Psychology,* 33:2 (February 1976), 161–169. [28]

Braver, Sanford L., and **Van Rohrer.** "Superiority of Vicarious over Direct Experience in Interpersonal Conflict Resolution," *Journal of Conflict Resolution,* 22:1 (March 1978). [28]

Brechner, Kevin C. "An Experimental Analysis of Social Traps," *Journal of Experimental Social Psychology,* 13:6 (November 1977), 552–564. [28]

Breen, Richard A., and **James L. McGaugh.** "Facilitation of Maze Learning with Posttrial Injections of Picrotoxin," *Journal of Comparative and Physiological Psychology,* 54:5 (1961), 498–501. [5]

Bresler, David E., Gaylord Ellison, and **Stephen Zamenhof.** "Learning Deficits in Rats with Malnourished Grandmothers," *Developmental Psychobiology,* 8:4 (1975), 315–323. [7]

Breuer, Josef, and **Sigmund Freud.** *Studies on Hysteria* (1937). New York: Basic Books, 1957. [18]

Brickman, Philip J., Joel Redfield, et al. "Drive and Predisposition as Factors in the Attitudinal Effects of Mere Exposure," *Journal of Experimental Social Psychology,* 8 (1972), 31–44. [26]

Broadbent, D. E. *Perception and Communication.* London: Pergamon, 1958. [4]

———. "Speaking and Listening Simultaneously," *Journal of Experimental Psychology,* 43 (1952), 267–273. [2]

Broca, Pierre Paul. "Perte de Parole, Ramollissement et Destruction du Lobe Antérieur Gauche du Cerveau," *Bulletin of the Society of Anthropologists,* 2 (1861), 235. [11]

Bromley, D. B. "Some Effects of Age on Short-Term Learning and Memory," *Journal of Gerontology,* 13 (1958), 393–406. [8]

Brown, B. B. *New Mind, New Body.* New York: Harper & Row, 1974. [14]

Brown, Roger. *A First Language: The Early Stages.* Cambridge, Mass.: Harvard University Press, 1973. [9]

Brown, Roger, and **Ursula Bellugi.** "Three Processes in the Child's Acquisition of Syntax," *Harvard Educational Review,* 34

(1964), 133–151. [9]

Brown, Roger, Courtney Cazden, and **Ursula Bellugi-Klima.** "The Child's Grammar from I to III," in J. P. Hill (ed.), *Minnesota Symposia on Child Development.* Vol. 2. Minneapolis: University of Minnesota Press, 1968, pp. 28–73. [9]

Brown, Roger, and **Colin Fraser.** "The Acquisition of Syntax," in C. N. Cofer and B. S. Musgrave (eds.), *Verbal Behavior and Learning Problems and Processes.* New York: McGraw-Hill, 1963, pp. 158–209. [9]

Brown, Roger, and **Camille Hanlon.** "Derivational Complexity and Order of Acquisition in Child Speech," in John R. Hayes (ed.), *Cognition and the Development of Language.* New York: Wiley, 1970. [9]

Bryan, J. H. "Children's Cooperation and Helping Behaviors," in E. M. Hetherington (ed.), *Review of Child Development Research.* Vol. 5. Chicago: University of Chicago Press, 1975. [10]

Buss, Arnold H., Robert Plomin, and **Lee Willerman.** "The Inheritance of Temperament," *Journal of Personality,* 41 (1973), 513–524. [10]

Butler, N. R., and **H. Goldstein,** "Smoking in Pregnancy and Subsequent Child Development," *British Medical Journal,* 4, (1973), 573–575. [7]

Butler, Robert A. "Curiosity in Monkeys," *Scientific American,* 190 (February 1954), 70–75. [16]

Byrne, Donn, and **L. A. Byrne** (eds.). *Exploring Human Sexuality.* New York: Cromwell, 1978. [17]

Byrne, Donn, and **J. Lambreth.** "The Effect of Erotic Stimuli on Sex Arousal, Evaluative Responses, and Subsequent Behavior," *Technical Report of the Commission on Obscenity and Pornography.* Vol. 8. Washington, D.C.: U.S. Government Printing Office, 1971. [17]

Campbell, Byron A., J. P. Misanin, B. C. White, and **L. D. Lytle.** "Species Differences in Ontogeny of Memory: Support for Neural Maturation as a Determinant of Forgetting," *Journal of Comparative and Physiological Psychology,* 87 (1974), 193–202. [8]

Campbell, David P. "A Cross-Sectional and Longitudinal Study of Scholastic Abilities over Twenty-five Years," *Journal of Counseling Psychology,* 12 (1965), 55–61. [2]

Campbell, Donald T. "On the Conflicts Between Biological and Social Evolution and Between Psychology and Moral Tradition," *American Psychologist,* 30:12 (December 1975), 1103–1126. [3]

Campos, Joseph J. "Heart Rate: A Sensitive Tool for the Study of Infant Emo-

tional Expression," in Lewis P. Lipsitt (ed.), *Developmental Psychobiology: The Significance of Infancy.* New York: Halsted Press, 1976. [2]

Cannon, Walter B. "The James-Lange Theory of Emotion: A Critical Examination and an Alternative Theory," *American Journal of Psychology,* 39 (1927), 106–124. [15]

———. "Organization for Physiological Homeostatics," *Physiological Reviews,* 9 (1929), 280–289. [16]

———. "'Voodoo' Death," *American Anthropologist,* 44:2 (1942), 169–181. [1]

Carmichael, Leonard, Helena P. Hogan, and **A. A. Walter.** "An Experimental Study of the Effect of Language on the Reproduction of Visually Perceived Form," *Journal of Experimental Psychology,* 15 (1932), 73–86. [5]

Carney, M. W. P., M. Roth, and **R. F. Garside.** "The Diagnosis of Depressive Syndromes and the Prediction of E.C.T. Response," *British Journal of Psychiatry,* 111 (1965), 659–674. [23]

Carraher, R. G., and **J. B. Thurston,** *Optical Illusions and the Visual Arts.* New York: Reinhold, 1966. [13]

Casswell, S., and **D. F. Marks.** "Cannabis and Temporal Disintegration in Experienced and Naive Subjects," *Science,* 179 (1978), 803–805. [14]

Cates, Judith. "Baccalaureates in Psychology: 1969 and 1970," *American Psychologist,* 28 (1973), 262–264. [1]

Caton, Richard. "The Electric Currents of the Brain," *British Medical Journal,* 2 (1875), 278. [5]

Cattell, Raymond B. *The Scientific Analysis of Personality.* Baltimore: Penguin, 1965. [19]

Cherry, E. C. "Some Experiments on the Recognition of Speech with One and Two Ears," *Journal of the Acoustical Society of America,* 25 (1953), 975–979. [5]

Chesler, Phyllis. *Women and Madness.* New York: Doubleday, 1972. [18]

Chi, Michelene T. H. "Short-Term Memory Limitations in Children: Capacity or Processing Deficits?" *Memory and Cognition,* 4:5 (1976), 559–572. [8]

Chomsky, Noam. *Aspects of the Theory of Syntax.* Cambridge, Mass.: M.I.T. Press, 1965. [9]

———. *Language and Mind.* New York: Harcourt Brace Jovanovich, 1972. [9]

Chow, K. L., W. C. Dement, and **E. R. John.** "Conditioned Electrocorticographic Potentials and Behavioral Avoidance Response in Cat," *Journal of Neurophysiology,* 20 (1957), 482–493. [5]

Churchill, Sir Winston S. "A Speech to the House of Commons, May 13, 1940," in *The War Speeches of the Rt. Hon. Winston S. Churchill.* Vol. 1. London: Cassell, 1951,

p. 181. [25]

Cialdini, Robert B., Leonard Bickman, and **John T. Cacioppo.** "An Example of Consumeristic Social Psychology," *Journal of Applied Social Psychology,* in press. [25]

Cialdini, Robert B., and **Douglas T. Kenrick.** "Altruism as Hedonism: A Social Developmental Perspective on the Relationship of Negative Mood State and Helping," *Journal of Personality and Social Psychology,* 34:5 (1976), 907–914. [28]

Clark, Eve V. "What's in a Word? On the Child's Acquisition of Semantics in His First Language," in T. E. Moore (ed.), *Cognitive Development and the Acquisition of Language.* New York: Academic Press, 1973, pp. 65–110. [9]

Clark, Herbert H., and **Eve V. Clark.** *Psychology and Language: An Introduction to Psycholinguistics.* New York: Harcourt Brace Jovanovich, 1977. [9]

Clifford, Margaret, and **Elane Walster.** "The Effect of Physical Attractiveness on Teacher Expectations," *Sociology of Education,* 46 (1973), 248–258. [26]

Cobb, Sidney, and **Robert Rose.** "Hypertension, Peptic Ulcers, and Diabetes in Air Traffic Controllers," *Journal of the American Medical Association,* April 23, 1973. [15]

Cole, J. O. "Phenothiazine Treatment in Acute Schizophrenia: Effectiveness," *Archives of General Psychiatry,* 10 (1964), 246–261. [24]

Colligan, Douglas. "That Helpless Feeling: The Dangers of Stress," *New York,* July 14, 1975, pp. 28–32. [15]

Comfort, Alex (ed.). *The Joy of Sex.* New York: Simon and Schuster, 1972. [17]

Connor, J. "Olfactory Control of Aggressive and Sexual Behavior in the Mouse (*Mus Musclus L.*)," *Psychonomic Science,* 27 (1972), 1–3. [17]

Cooley, C. H. *Human Nature and the Social Order.* New York: Scribners, 1912. [7]

Coulter, Xenia, Alexis C. Collier, and **Byron A. Campbell.** "Long-Term Retention of Early Pavlovian Fear Conditioning in Infant Rats," *Journal of Experimental Psychology: Animal Behavior Processes,* 2:1 (1976), 48–56. [8]

Craik, Fergus I. M. "Age Differences in Human Memory," in James E. Birren and K. Warner Schaie (eds.), *Handbook of the Psychology of Aging.* New York: Van Nostrand Reinhold, 1977, pp. 384–420. [8]

Creese, I., D. R. Burt, and **S. H. Snyder.** "Brain's Dopamine Receptor—Labeling with [Dopamine—H-3] and [H21 Operidol—H3]," *Psychopharmacology Communications,* 1:6 (1975), 663–673. [23]

Crowe, S. J., S. R. Guild, and **L. M. Polvogt.** "Observations on the Pathology of

High-Tone Deafness," *Bulletin of Johns Hopkins Hospital*, 54 (1934), 315–379. [12]

Dahlstrom, William Grant, and George S. Welsh. *An MMPI Handbook: A Guide to Use in Clinical Practice and Research*. Minneapolis: University of Minnesota Press, 1960. [20]

Daniel, R. S. "Notes for a Course in Professional Problems," unpublished manuscript, 1975. [1]

Dante Alighieri. *The Divine Comedy: Canticle, Hell*. Dorothy L. Sayers (tr.). Baltimore: Penguin Books, 1965. [21]

Darley, C. F., J. R. Tinklenberg, W. T. Roth, L. E. Hollister, and R. C. Atkinson. "Influence of Marihuana on Storage and Retrieval Processes in Memory," *Memory and Cognition*, 1:2 (April 1973), 196–200. [5, 14]

Darley, John M., and Bibb Latané. "When Will People Help?" *Psychology Today*, 2 (1968), 54. [28]

Darley, John M., Allan I. Teger, and Lawrence D. Lewis. "Do Groups Always Inhibit Individuals' Responses to Potential Emergencies?" *Journal of Personality and Social Psychology*, 26:3 (June 1973), 395–399. [28]

Darwin, Charles. *The Expression of the Emotions in Man and Animals* (1872). Chicago: University of Chicago Press, 1967. [3, 15]

———. *On the Origin of Species by Means of Natural Selection* (1859). Cambridge, Mass.: Harvard University Press, 1964. [3]

Davenport, William. "Sexual Patterns and Their Regulation in a Society of the Southwest Pacific," in Frank A. Beach (ed.), *Sex and Behavior*. New York: Wiley, 1965. [17]

Davis, J. M. "Efficacy of Tranquilizing and Anti-Depressant Drugs," *Archives of General Psychiatry*, 13 (1965), 552–572. [24]

Davison, Gerald C. "Homosexuality: The Ethical Challenge," *Journal of Consulting and Clinical Psychology*, 44:2 (1976), 157–162. [17]

Davitz, Joel R. *The Language of Emotion*. New York: Academic Press, 1969. [15]

Dawes, Robyn M., Jeanne McTavish, and Harriet Shaklee. "Behavior, Communication, and Assumptions About Other People's Behavior in a Commons Dilemma Situation," *Journal of Personality and Social Psychology*, 35:1 (1977), 1–11. [28]

Dawkins, Richard. *The Selfish Gene*. New York: Oxford University Press, 1975. [28]

De Beauvoir, Simone. *The Second Sex*. H. M. Parshley (ed. and tr.). New York: Bantam, 1961. [18]

De Bono, Edward. *New Think: The Use of Lateral Thinking in the Generation of New Ideas*. New York: Basic Books, 1967. [6]

De Carlo, T. J. "Recreational Participation Patterns and Successful Aging: A Twin Study." Unpublished doctoral dissertation, Columbia University, 1971. [8]

Deaux, Edward. "Thirst Satiation and the Temperature of Ingested Water," *Science*, 181 (1973), 1166–1167. [16]

Decke, Elisabeth. "Effects of Taste on the Eating Behavior of Obese and Normal Persons," cited in Stanley Schachter, *Emotion, Obesity, and Crime*. New York: Academic Press, 1971. [16]

DeLora, Joann S., and Carol A. Warren. *Understanding Sexual Interaction*. Boston: Houghton Mifflin, 1977. [17]

Dement, William C. *Some Must Watch While Some Must Sleep*. San Francisco: Freeman, 1974. [14]

Dement, William C., and E. A. Wolpert. "The Relation of Eye Movements, Body Mobility, and External Stimuli to Dream Content," *Journal of Experimental Psychology*, 55 (1958), 543–553. [14]

Dengrove, E. "The Mechanotherapy of Sexual Disorders," *Journal of Sex Research*, 7:1 (February 1971), 1–12. [17]

Dennis, Wayne, and M. G. Dennis. "The Effect of Cradling Practices upon the Onset of Walking in Hopi Children," *Journal of Genetic Psychology*, 56 (1940), 77–86. [7]

Dennis, Wayne, and J. Sayegh. "The Effect of Supplementary Experiences upon the Behavioral Development of Infants in Institutions," *Child Development*, 36 (1965), 81–90. [7]

Deutsch, Morton, and Harold B. Gerard. "A Study of Normative and Informational Influences on Social Judgment," *Journal of Abnormal and Social Psychology*, 51 (1955), 629–636. [27]

Deutsch, Morton, and Robert M. Krauss. "The Effect of Threat upon Interpersonal Bargaining," *Journal of Abnormal and Social Psychology*, 61 (1960), 181–189. [28]

DeValois, Russell L. "Analysis and Coding of Color Vision in the Primate Visual System," *Cold Spring Harbor Symposia on Quantitative Biology*, 30 (1965), 567–579. [12]

Dichter, Ernest. *Handbook of Consumer Motivations*. New York: McGraw-Hill, 1964. [25]

Dion, Karen. "Physical Attractiveness and Evaluations of Children's Transgressions," *Journal of Personality and Social Psychology*, 24 (1972), 207–213. [26]

———. "Social Desirability and the Evaluation of a Harm-Doer." Unpublished doctoral dissertation, University of Minnesota, 1970. [26]

———. "Young Children's Stereotyping of Facial Attractiveness," *Developmental Psychology*, 9 (1973), 183–188. [26]

Dion, Karen, Ellen Berscheid, and Elaine Walster. "What Is Beautiful Is Good," *Journal of Personality and Social Psychology*, 24 (1972), 285–290. [26]

Dollard, John, L. W. Doob, Neal E. Miller, O. H. Mowrer, and R. R. Sears. *Frustration and Aggression*. New Haven, Conn.: Yale University Press, 1939. [19, 28]

Dollard, John, and Neal E. Miller. *Personality and Psychotherapy: An Analysis in Terms of Learning, Thinking, and Culture*. New York: McGraw-Hill, 1950. [19]

Doty, R. L., M. Ford, G. Preti, and G. R. Huggins. "Changes in the Intensity and Pleasantness of Human Vaginal Odors During the Menstrual Cycle," *Science*, 190 (1975), 1316–1318. [17]

Driscoll, Richard. "Anxiety Reduction Using Physical Exertion and Positive Images," *The Psychological Record*, 26 (1976), 87–94. [21]

Driscoll, Richard, Keith E. Davis, and Milton E. Lipetz. "Parental Interference and Romantic Love: The Romeo and Juliet Effect," *Journal of Personality and Social Psychology*, 24:1 (1972), 1–10. [26]

DuBois, Philip H. "Review of the Scholastic Aptitude Test," in Oscar K. Buros (ed.), *The Seventh Mental Measurements Yearbook*. Highland Park, N.J.: Gryphon Press, 1972, pp. 646–648. [20]

Duncan, Starkey, Jr. "Nonverbal Communication," *Psychological Bulletin*, 72:2 (1969), 118–137. [15]

Duncker, Karl. "On Problem-Solving" (1935). L. S. Lees (tr.). *Psychological Monographs*, 58 (1945). Whole No. 270. [6]

Dutton, D., and A. Aron. "Some Evidence for Heightened Sexual Attraction Under Conditions of High Anxiety," *Journal of Personality and Social Psychology*, 30 (1974), 510–517. [26]

Dworkin, Robert H., Barbara W. Burke, Brendan A. Maher, and Irving I. Gottesman. "A Longitudinal Study of the Genetics of Personality," *Journal of Personality and Social Psychology*, 34 (1976), 510–518. [10]

Ebbinghaus, H. *Memory: A Contribution to Experimental Psychology* (1885). H. A. Roger and C. E. Bussenius (trs.). New York: Teachers College, Columbia University, 1913. [5]

Eccles, J. C., M. Ito, and J. Szentágotnaiƙ. *The Cerebellum as a Neuronal Machine*. New York: Springer, 1967. [11]

Eckerman, C. O., and Harriet L. Rheingold. "Infants' Exploratory Responses to Toys and People," *Developmental Psychology*, 10 (1974), 255–259. [10]

Eckerman, C. O., and J. L. Whatley. "Infants' Reactions to Unfamiliar Adults Varying in Novelty," *Developmental Psychology*, 11 (1975), 562–566. [10]

Eckerman, C. O., J. L. Whatley, and **S. L. Kutz.** "Growth of Social Play with Peers During the Second Year of Life," *Developmental Psychology*, 11 (1975), 42–49. [10]

Edney, Julian J. "Human Territoriality," *Psychological Bulletin*, 81:12 (1974), 959–975. [3]

Edwards, M. K. "Life Crisis and Myocardial Infarction." Master of Nursing thesis, University of Washington, Seattle, 1971. [21]

Ehrenreich, Barbara, and **Deirdre English.** *Witches, Midwives, and Nurses: A History of Women Healers.* Old Westbury, N.Y.: Feminist Press, 1973. [23]

Ehrlich, Danuta, Isaiah Guttman, Peter Schönbach, and **Judson Mills.** "Postdecision Exposure to Relevant Information," *Journal of Abnormal and Social Psychology*, 54 (1957), 98–102. [25]

Eibl-Eibesfeldt, Irenaus. "The Fighting Behavior of Animals," *Scientific American*, 205:6 (December 1961), 112–122. [28]

Eimas, Peter D., Einar R. Siqueland, Peter Jusczyk, and **James Virogito.** "Speech Perception in Infants," *Science*, 171 (1971), 303–306. [7, 9]

Ekman, Paul (ed.). *Darwin and Facial Expressions.* New York: Academic Press, 1973. [15]

Ekman, Paul, and **Wallace V. Friesen.** "Constants Across Culture in the Face and Emotion," *Journal of Personality and Social Psychology*, 17 (1971), 124–129. [15]

———. *Unmasking the Face: A Guide to Recognizing Emotions from Facial Expressions.* Englewood Cliffs, N.J.: Prentice-Hall/Spectrum, 1975. [15]

Ekman, Paul, Wallace V. Friesen, and **Phoebe Ellsworth.** *Emotion in the Human Face: Guidelines for Research and an Integration of Findings.* Elmsford, N.Y.: Pergamon, 1972. [15]

Elkind, David. "Misunderstandings About How Children Learn," *Today's Education*, 61:3 (March 1972), 18–20. [8]

Ellis, Albert. *Reason and Emotion in Psychotherapy.* Secaucus, N.J.: Lyle Stuart, 1962. [24]

Engel, George. "Emotional Stress and Sudden Death," *Psychology Today*, November 1977, 114–118, 153–154. [15]

Epstein, Alan N. "The Lateral Hypothalamic Syndrome: Its Implications for the Physiological Psychology of Hunger and Thirst," in E. Stellar and J. M. Sprague (eds.), *Progress in Physiological Psychology.* Vol. 4. New York: Academic Press, 1971. [11]

———. "Water Intake Without the Act of Drinking," *Science*, 131 (1960), 497–498. [16]

Epstein, S. M. "Toward a Unified Theory of Anxiety," in B. A. Maher (ed.), *Progress in Experimental Personality Research.* Vol. 4. New York: Academic Press, 1967. [16]

Erikson, Erik H. *Childhood and Society.* New York: Norton, 1950. [10, 18]

———. *Gandhi's Truth: On the Origins of Militant Nonviolence.* New York: Norton, 1969. [18]

———. *Young Man Luther: A Study in Psychoanalysis and History.* New York: Norton, 1968. [18]

Etzioni, Amitai. "Doctors Know More Than They're Telling You About Genetic Defects," *Psychology Today*, November 1973, 26–31, 35–36, 137. [7]

Eysenck, Hans J. "The Development of Moral Values in Children: The Contribution of Learning Theory," *British Journal of Educational Psychology*, 30 (1960), 11–21. [10]

———. "The Effects of Psychotherapy: An Evaluation," *Journal of Consulting Psychology*, 16 (1952), 319–324. [24]

———. *The Effects of Psychotherapy.* New York: International Science Press, 1966. [24]

———. *The Structure of Human Personality.* London: Methuen, 1970. [19]

Fairweather, George W., et al. *Community Life for the Mentally Ill: An Alternative to Institutional Care.* Chicago: Aldine, 1969. [24]

Fantz, R. L. "The Origin of Form Perception," *Scientific American*, 204 (May 1961), 66–72. [7]

Fechner, Gustav T. *Elemente der Psychophysik.* Leipzig: Breitkopf und Härtel, 1860. [12]

Fehr, Fred S., and **John A. Stern.** "Peripheral Physiological Variables and Emotion: The James-Lange Theory Revisited," *Psychological Bulletin*, 74:6 (December 1970), 411–424. [15]

Fenz, Walter D., and **Seymour Epstein.** "Gradients of Physiological Arousal in Parachutists as a Function of an Approaching Jump," *Psychosomatic Medicine*, 29 (1967), 33–51. [2]

Ferchmin, P. A., Edward L. Bennett, and **Mark R. Rosenzweig.** "Direct Contact with Enriched Environment Is Required to Alter Cerebral Weights in Rats," *Journal of Comparative and Physiological Psychology*, 88:1 (1975), 360–367. [7]

Festinger, Leon. *A Theory of Cognitive Dissonance.* Stanford, Calif.: Stanford University Press 1957. [25]

———. "A Theory of Social Comparison Processes," *Human Relations*, 7 (1954), 117–140. [27]

Festinger, Leon, and **J. Merrill Carlsmith.** "Cognitive Consequences of Forced Compliance," *Journal of Abnormal and Social Psychology*, 58 (1959), 203–210. [25]

Festinger, Leon, H. W. Riecken, Jr., and **Stanley Schachter.** *When Prophecy Fails.* Minneapolis: University of Minnesota Press, 1956. [2]

Festinger, Leon, Stanley Schachter, and **Kurt Back.** *Social Pressures in Informal Groups: A Study of Human Factors in Housing.* New York: Harper & Row, 1950. [26]

Fishbein, Martin, and **Icek Ajzen.** *Belief, Attitude, Intention and Behavior: An Introduction to Theory and Research.* Reading, Mass.: Addison-Wesley, 1975. [25]

Fisher, A. E. "Material and Sexual Behavior Induced by Intracerebral Chemical Stimulation," *Science*, 124 (1956), 228–229. [11]

Fiske, Edward B. "An Issue That Won't Go Away," *The New York Times Magazine*, March 27, 1977, p. 58. [20]

Fitzsimons, J. T. "Drinking by Rats Depleted of Body Fluid Without Increase in Osmotic Pressure," *Journal of Physiology*, 159 (1961), 297–309. [16]

———. "The Role of Renal Thirst in Drinking Induced by Extracellular Stimuli," *Journal of Physiology*, 201 (1969), 349–368. [16]

Fixx, James. *The Complete Book of Running.* New York: Random House, 1977. [21]

Flavell, John H. *Cognitive Development.* Englewood Cliffs, N.J.: Prentice-Hall, 1977. [8]

Flavell, John H., and **Henry M. Wellman.** "Metamemory," in Robert V. Kail, Jr. and John W. Hagen (eds.), *Perspectives on the Development of Memory and Cognition.* Hillsdale, N.J.: Erlbaum, 1977, pp. 3–33. [8]

Flynn, J. P., H. Vanegas, W. Foote, and **S. Edwards.** "Neural Mechanisms Involved in a Cat's Attack on a Rat," in Richard E. Whalen, et al. (eds.), *Neural Control of Behavior.* New York: Academic Press, 1970, pp. 135–173. [3]

Ford, C. S., and **Frank A. Beach.** *Patterns of Sexual Behavior.* New York: Harper & Row, 1951. [17]

Foulks, David. "Theories of Dream Formation and Recent Studies of Sleep Consciousness," *Psychological Bulletin*, 62 (1964), 236–247. [14]

Fouts, Roger S. "Use of Guidance in Teaching Sign Language to a Chimpanzee," *Journal of Comparative and Physiological Psychology*, 80 (1972), 515–522. [9]

Fowler, O. S., and **L. N. Fowler.** *Phrenology: A Practical Guide to Your Head.* New York: Chelsea House, 1969. [11]

Freedman, Jonathan L., J. Merrill Carl-

smith, and **David O. Sears.** *Social Psychology.* Englewood Cliffs, N.J.: Prentice-Hall, 1970. [25]

Freedman, Jonathan L., and **David O. Sears.** "Warning, Distraction and Resistance to Influence," *Journal of Personality and Social Psychology,* 1 (1965), 262–266. [25]

Freud, Sigmund. "Analysis of a Phobia in a Five-Year-Old Boy" (1909), in *The Standard Edition of the Complete Psychological Works of Sigmund Freud.* Vol. 10. London: Hogarth Press, 1955, pp. 3–149. [23]

———. "Beyond the Pleasure Principle" (1920), in James Strachey (ed. and tr.), *The Standard Edition of the Complete Psychological Works of Sigmund Freud.* Vol. 18. London: Hogarth Press, 1953. [18]

———. *Civilization and Its Discontents* (1930). James Strachey (ed. and tr.). New York: Norton, 1962. [18]

———. *The Ego and the Id* (1923). London: Hogarth Press, 1947. [18]

———. "Femininity," in Jean Strouse (ed.), *Women and Analysis: Dialogues on Psychoanalytic Views of Femininity.* New York: Dell, 1974. [18]

———. *The Interpretation of Dreams* (1900). James Strachey (ed. and tr.). New York: Basic Books, 1955. [14, 18]

———. *New Introductory Lectures on Psychoanalysis* (1933). James Strachey (ed. and tr.). New York: Norton, 1965. [10, 18]

———. *An Outline of Psycho-Analysis* (1940). James Strachey (ed. and tr.). New York: Norton, 1949. [1]

Friedman, S., L. A. Bruno, and **P. Vietze.** "Newborn Habituation to Visual Stimuli: A Sex Difference in Novelty Detection," *Journal of Experimental Child Psychology,* 18 (1974), 242–251. [8]

Frisch, H. L. "Stereotypes in Adult-Infant Play," *Child Development,* 48 (1977), 1671–1675. [10]

Fromm, Erich. *Escape from Freedom.* New York: Holt, Rinehart and Winston, 1941. [18]

———. *The Forgotten Language.* New York: Grove Press, 1951. [24]

Fromm-Reichmann, Frieda. *Psychoanalysis and Psychotherapy: Selected Papers.* D. M. Bullard (tr.). Chicago: University of Chicago Press, 1974. [23]

Furth, Hans. *Thinking Without Language.* New York: Free Press, 1966. [9]

Gallup, Gordon G., Jr. "Self-Recognition in Primates: A Comparative Approach to the Bidirectional Properties of Consciousness," *American Psychologist,* 32:5 (May 1977), 329–338. [7]

Galton, Sir Francis. *Hereditary Genius: An Inquiry into Its Laws and Consequences.* London: Macmillan, 1869. [1]

———. *Inquiries into Human Faculty.* London: Macmillan, 1883. [1]

———. "Measurement of Character" (1884), in L. D. Goodstein and R. I. Lanyon (eds.), *Readings in Personality Assessment.* New York: Wiley, 1972. [20]

Garcia, John. "I.Q.: The Conspiracy," *Psychology Today,* 6:4 (September 1972), 40–43, 92. [20]

Garcia, J., W. G. Hawkins, and **K. W. Rusiniak.** "Behavioral Regulation of the *Milieu Interne* in Man and Rat," *Science,* 185 (1974), 824–831. [3]

Garcia, J., and **R. A. Koelling.** "Relation of Cue to Consequence in Avoidance Learning," *Psychonometric Science,* 4 (1966), 123–124. [3]

Garcia, J., B. K. McGowan, and **K. F. Green.** "Biological Constraints on Conditioning," in M. E. P. Seligman and J. L. Hager (eds.), *Biological Boundaries of Learning.* New York: Appleton-Century-Crofts, 1972, pp. 21–43 [3]

Gardner, Beatrice T., and **R. Allen Gardner.** "Evidence for Sentence Constituents in the Early Utterances of Child and Chimpanzee," *Journal of Experimental Psychology: General,* 104:3 (1975), 244–267. [9]

Gardner, E. *Fundamentals of Neurology.* Philadelphia: Saunders, 1975. [11]

Gardner, Lytt I. "Deprivation Dwarfism," *Scientific American,* 227:1 (July 1972), 76–82. [7]

Gardner, R. Allen, and **Beatrice T. Gardner.** "Teaching Sign Language to a Chimpanzee," *Science,* 165 (1969), 664–672. [9]

Gazzaniga, Michael S. *The Bisected Brain.* New York: Appleton-Century-Crofts, 1970. [11]

———. "One Brain—Two Minds?" *American Scientist,* 60 (1972), 311–317. [11]

———. "The Split Brain in Man," *Scientific American,* 217 (August 1967), 24–29. [14]

Geldard, Frank A. *The Human Senses.* 2nd ed. New York: Wiley, 1972. [12]

Gentry, William D. "Effects of Frustration, Attack and Prior Aggressive Training on Overt Aggression and Vascular Processes," *Journal of Personality and Social Psychology,* 16:4 (1970), 718–725. [28]

Gergen, Kenneth J., Mary M. Gergen, and **William H. Barton,** "Deviance in the Dark," *Psychology Today,* 7 (October 1973), 129-130. [2]

Gesell, Arnold, and **H. Thompson.** "Learning and Growth in Identical Infant Twins: An Experimental Study by the Method of Co-Twin Control," *Genetic Psychology Monographs,* 6 (1929), 1–125. [7]

Ghiselin, Brewster (ed.). *The Creative Process.* Berkeley, Calif.: University of California Press, 1952. [6]

Gibson, E. J., and **R. D. Walk.** "The Effect of Prolonged Exposure to Visually Presented Patterns on Learning to Discriminate Them," *Journal of Comparative and Physiological Psychology,* 49 (1956), 239–242. [13]

———. "The Visual Cliff," *Scientific American,* 202 (1960), 64–71. [13]

Gibson, James J. *The Senses Considered as Perceptual Systems.* Boston: Houghton Mifflin, 1966. [13]

Glanville, Bradley, G., Catherine T. Best, and **Robert Levenson.** "A Cardiac Measure of Cerebral Asymmetries in Infant Auditory Perception," *Developmental Psychology,* 13:1 (1977), 54–59. [9]

Glass, David C., Bruce Reim, and **Jerome E. Singer.** "Behavioral Consequences of Adaptation to Controllable and Uncontrollable Noise," *Journal of Experimental Social Psychology,* 7 (1971), 244–257. [21]

Glass, David C., Jerome E. Singer, and **Lucy N. Friedman.** "Psychic Cost of Adaptation to an Environmental Stressor," *Journal of Personality and Social Psychology,* 12:3 (1969), 200–210. [21]

Glaze, J. A. "The Association Value of Nonsense Syllables," *Journal of Genetic Psychology,* 35:2 (1928), 255–269. [4]

Goethals, George A., and **John M. Darley.** "Social Comparison Theory: An Attributional Approach," in Jerry M. Suls and Richard L. Miller (eds.), *Social Comparison Processes: Theoretical and Empirical Perspectives.* Washington, D.C.: Hemisphere, 1977, pp. 259-278. [27]

Goffman, Erving. *Behavior in Public Places.* New York: Free Press, 1963. [26]

———. *The Presentation of Self in Everyday Life.* Garden City, N.Y.: Doubleday Anchor, 1959. [26]

Goldberg, S., and **M. Lewis.** "The Acquisition and Violation of Expectancy: An Experimental Paradigm," *Journal of Experimental Child Psychology,* 7 (1969), 70–80. [10]

Goldberg, S. C., G. L. Klerman, and **J. O. Cole.** "Changes in Schizophrenic Psychopathology and Ward Behavior as a Function of Phenothiazine Treatment," *British Journal of Psychiatry,* 111 (1965), 120–132. [24]

Goldfried, Marvin R., and **Gerald C. Davison.** *Clinical Behavior Therapy.* New York: Holt, Rinehart and Winston, 1976. [24]

Goldfried, Marvin R., Edwin T. Decenteceo, and **Leslie Weinberg.** "Systematic Rational Restructuring as a Self-Control Technique," *Behavior Therapy,* 5:2 (March 1974), 247–254. [24]

Goldman, William, and **Philip Lewis.** "Beautiful Is Good: Evidence That the

Physically Attractive Are More Socially Skillful," *Journal of Experimental Social Psychology*, 13 (1977), 125–130. [26]

Goldstein, Joel W., and **Howard M. Rosenfeld.** "Insecurity and Preference for Persons Similar to Oneself," *Journal of Personality*, 37 (1969), 253–268. [26]

Goleman, Daniel. *The Varieties of the Meditative Experience.* New York: Dutton, 1977. [14]

Goodenough, Florence L. "Expression of the Emotions in a Blind-Deaf Child," *Journal of Abnormal and Social Psychology*, 27 (1932), 328–333. [15]

Goodstein, Leonard D., and **Richard I. Lanyon.** *Adjustment, Behavior and Personality.* Reading, Mass.: Addison-Wesley, 1975. [10]

Goodstein, Leonard, and **Irwin Sandler.** "Using Psychology to Promote Human Welfare: A Conceptual Analysis of the Role of Community Psychology" *American Psychologist*, 33 (1978), 882–891. [24]

Goodwin, D. W. "Alcoholic Blackout and State-Dependent Learning," *Federation Proceedings*, 33 (1974), 1833–1835. [5]

Gorden, H. W., and **G. E. Bogen.** "Hemispheric Lateralization of Singing After Intracarotid Sodium Amylobarbitone," *Journal of Neurology, Neurosurgery, and Psychiatry*, 37 (1974), 727–738. [9]

Gorski, R. A. "Gonadal Hormones and the Perinatal Development of Neuroendocrine Function," in Luciano Martini and William F. Ganong (eds.), *Frontiers in Neuroendocrinology.* New York: Oxford University Press, 1971. [17]

Gottesman, Irving I., and **James Shields.** *Schizophrenia and Genetics—A Twin-Study Vantage Point.* New York: Academic Press, 1972. [23]

Gottlieb, Gilbert. "Conceptions of Prenatal Development: Behavioral Embryology," *Psychological Review*, 83:3 (1976), 215–234. [7]

Gould, Roger L. "The Phases of Adult Life: A Study in Developmental Psychology," *American Journal of Psychiatry*, 129:5 (November 1972), 521–531. [10]

Goy, R. W. "Experimental Control of Psychosexuality," in G. W. Harris and R. G. Edwards (eds.), *A Discussion of the Determination of Sex.* Series B, Vol. 259. London: Philosophical Transactions of the Royal Society, 1970. [17]

Graham, D. T. "Health, Disease, and the Mind-Body Problem: Linguistic Parallelism," *Psychosomatic Medicine*, 39 (1967), 52–71. [22]

Gray, J. A. *The Psychology of Fear and Stress.* New York: McGraw-Hill, 1971. [22]

Grayson, Richard. "Air Controllers Syndrome: Peptic Ulcers in Air Traffic Controllers," *Illinois Medical Journal*, August

1972. [15]

Green, David M., and **John A. Swets.** *Signal Detection Theory and Psychophysics.* New York: Wiley, 1966. [12]

Greenberg, Peter F. "The Three Seekers," *Human Behavior*, 6:4 (April 1977), 17–21. [16]

Greenblatt, M., G. H. Grosser, and **H. Wechsler.** "Differential Responses of Hospitalized Depressed Patients to Somatic Therapy," *American Journal of Psychiatry*, 120 (1964), 935–943. [24]

Gregory, R. L. "Visual Illusions," *Scientific American*, 219:5 (1968), 66–76. [13]

———. *The Intelligent Eye.* New York: McGraw-Hill, 1970. [13]

Grinspoon, Lester, and **James G. Bakalar.** *Cocaine: A Drug and Its Social Evolution.* New York: Basic Books, 1976. [14]

Grinspoon, Lester, J. R. Ewalt, and **R. Shader.** "Psychotherapy and Pharmacotherapy in Chronic Schizophrenia," *American Journal of Psychiatry*, 124:12 (1968), 1645–1652. [24]

Grossman, S. P. "Eating or Drinking Elicited by Direct Adreneregic, or Chrolinergic Stimulation of Hypothalamus," *Science*, 132 (1960), 301–302. [11]

Guilford, J. P. *Personality.* New York: McGraw-Hill, 1959. [19]

Guttman, N., and **H. I. Kalish.** "Discriminability and Stimulus Generalization," *Journal of Experimental Psychology*, 51 (1956), 79–88. [4]

Haber, Ralph N. "Discrepancy from Adaptation Level as a Source of Affect," *Journal of Experimental Psychology*, 56 (1958), 370–375. [16]

———. "Eidetic Images," *Scientific American*, 220 (April 1969), 36–44. [5]

Haber, Ralph N., and **L. G. Standing.** "Direct Measures of Short-Term Visual Storage," *Quarterly Journal of Experimental Psychology*, 21 (1969), 43–45. [5]

Haith, Marshall M., Terry Bergman, and **Michael J. Moore.** "Eye Contact and Face Scanning in Early Infancy," *Science*, 198 (November 25, 1977), 853–854. [7]

Hall, Calvin S., and **Gardner Lindzey.** *Theories of Personality.* 3rd ed. New York: Wiley, 1978. [1, 18]

Hall, Calvin S., and **R. L. Van de Castle.** *The Content Analysis of Dreams.* New York: Appleton-Century-Crofts, 1966. [14]

Hanlon, Joseph. "Uri Geller and Science," *New Scientist*, October 17, 1974, 170–185. [13]

Hardin, Garrett. "The Tragedy of the Commons," *Science*, 162:3859 (December 13, 1968), 1243–1248. [28]

Hariton, E. Barbara, and **Jerome L. Singer.** "Women's Fantasies During Sexual

Intercourse: Normative and Theoretical Implications," *Journal of Consulting and Clinical Psychology*, 42:3 (1974), 313–322. [17]

Harlow, Harry F. "The Formation of Learning Sets," *Psychological Review*, 56:1 (1949), 51–65. [6]

———. "Love in Infant Monkeys," *Scientific American*, 200:6 (June 1959), 68–74. [10]

———. "The Nature of Love," *American Psychologist*, 13 (1958), 673–685. [10]

Harlow, Harry F., and **Margaret Kuenne Harlow.** "Learning to Think," *Scientific American*, 181:2 (August 1949), 36–39. [6]

Harlow, Harry F., Margaret Kuenne Harlow, and **D. R. Meyer.** "Learning Motivated by a Manipulation Drive," *Journal of Experimental Psychology*, 40 (1950), 228–234. [16]

Harlow, Harry F., Margaret Kuenne Harlow, and **Stephan J. Suomi.** "From Thought to Therapy: Lessons from a Private Library," *American Scientist*, 59:5 (1971), 538–549. [10]

Harlow, Harry F., and **Stephan J. Suomi.** "The Nature of Love—Simplified," *American Psychologist*, 25, (1970), 161–168. [10]

Harlow, Harry F., and **R. R. Zimmerman.** "Affectual Response in the Infant Monkey," *Science*, 130 (1959), 421–432. [10]

Harmon, Leon D. "The Recognition of Faces," *Scientific American*, 229:5 (1973), 70–82. [13]

Harter, Susan. "Pleasure Derived by Children from Cognitive Challenge and Mastery," *Child Development*, 45 (1974), 661–669. [8]

Hartman, E. *The Biology of Dreaming.* Springfield, Ill.: Charles C. Thomas, 1967. [14]

Hashim, S. A., and **T. B. Van Itallie.** "Studies in Normal and Obese Subjects Using a Monitored Food-Dispensing Device," *Annals of the New York Academy of Science*, 131 (1965), 654–661. [16]

Hasler, Arthur D., and **James A. Larsen.** "The Homing Salmon," *Scientific American*, 193:2 (1955), 72–76. [3]

Hass, R. Glen, and **Darwyn E. Linder.** "Counterargument Availability and Effects of Message Structure and Persuasion," *Journal of Personality and Social Psychology*, 23, (1972), 219–233. [25]

Hass, R. Glen, and **R. W. Mann.** "Anticipatory Belief Change—Persuasion or Impression Management," *Journal of Personality and Social Psychology*, 34:1 (1976), 105–111. [25]

Hathaway, Starke R., and **John Charnley McKinley.** "A Multiphasic Personality Schedule (Minnesota): I. Construction of the Schedule," *Journal of Psychology*, 10 (1940), 249–254. [20]

Hayes, Keith J., and **Catherine Hayes.** "Imitation in a Home-Raised Chimpanzee," *Journal of Comparative and Physiological Psychology*, 45 (1952), 450–459. [4]

——. "The Intellectual Development of a Home-Raised Chimpanzee," *Proceedings of the American Philosophical Society*, 95 (1951), 105–109. [9]

Hearst, Eliot, and Herbert M. Jenkins. *Sign-Tracking: The Stimulus-Reinforcer Relation and Directed Action*. Austin: Psychonomic Society, 1974 [4]

Hebb, D. O. "What Psychology Is About," *American Psychologist*, 29:2 (February 1974), 71–79. [13]

Hecht, Selig, Charles Haig, and George Wald. "The Dark Adaptation of Retinal Fields of Different Size and Location," *Journal of General Physiology*, 19 (1935), 321–328. [12]

Heider, Fritz. *The Psychology of Interpersonal Relations*. New York: Wiley, 1958. [25, 26]

Heiman, Julia. "The Physiology of Erotica: Women's Sexual Arousal," *Psychology Today*, 8 (April 1975), 90–94. [17]

Held, Richard, and Alan Hein. "Movement-Produced Stimulation in the Development of Visually Guided Behavior," *Journal of Comparative and Physiological Psychology*, 56:5 (1963), 872–876. [13]

Helmstadter, G. C. *Research Concepts in Human Behavior*. New York: Appleton-Century-Crofts, 1970. [19]

Helson, H. *Adaptation-Level Theory*. New York: Harper & Row, 1964. [12]

Henderson, Joe. *The Long-Run Solution*. Mountain View, Calif.: World Publications, 1976. [21]

Hendrick, Clyde, and David R. Shaffer. "Effect of Pleading the Fifth Amendment on Perceptions of Guilt and Morality," *Bulletin of the Psychonomic Society*, 6:5 (1975), 449–452. [6]

Henle, M. "On the Relation Between Logic and Thinking," *Psychological Review*, 69 (1962), 366–378. [8]

Henning, Hans. "Die Qualitätenreihe des Geschmacks," *Zeitschrift für Psychologie*, 74 (1916), 203–319. [12]

Herrnstein, R. J. "The Evolution of Behaviorism," *American Psychologist*, 32:8 (August 1977), 593–603. [1]

Hess, Eckhard H. "Imprinting," *Science*, 130 (1959), 133–141. [27]

——. *Imprinting*. New York: Van Nostrand Reinhold, 1973. [3]

Hess, R. D. "Social Class and Ethnic Influences on Socialization," in Paul H. Mussen (ed.), *Carmichael's Manual of Child Psychology*. 3rd ed. Vol. 2. New York: Wiley, 1970, pp. 457–557. [7]

Hetherington, A. W., and S. W. Ranson. "Hypothalamic Lesions and Adiposity in the Rat," *The Anatomical Record*, 78 (1942), 149–172. [11]

Hilgard, Ernest R. *Divided Consciousness: Multiple Controls on Human Thought and Action*. New York: Wiley, 1977. [14]

——. "Hypnosis," *Annual Review of Psychology*, 26 (1975), 19–44. [14]

——. *Hypnotic Susceptibility*. New York: Harcourt Brace Jovanovich, 1965. [14]

——. "A Neodissociation Interpretation of Pain Reduction in Hypnosis," *Psychological Review*, 80:5 (1973), 396–411. [14]

Hilgard, Josephine R. "Imaginative Involvement: Some Characteristics of the Highly Hypnotizable and the Nonhypnotizable," *International Journal of Clinical and Experimental Hypnosis*, 22 (1974), 138–156. [14]

——. *Personality and Hypnosis: A Study of Imaginative Involvement*. Chicago: University of Chicago Press, 1970. [14]

Hiroto, Donald S., and Martin E. P. Seligman. "Generality of Learned Helplessness in Man," *Journal of Personality and Social Psychology*, 31:2 (1975), 311–327. [21]

Hirsch, Jerry, and James C. Boudreau. "Studies in Experimental Behavior Genetics: I. The Heritability of Phototaxis in a Population of *Drosophila Melanogaster*," *Journal of Comparative and Physiological Psychology*, 51 (1958), 647–651. [3]

Hite, Shere. *The Hite Report: A Nationwide Study of Female Sexuality*. New York: Dell, 1976. [17]

Hochberg, Julian. *Perception*. 2nd ed. Englewood Cliffs, N.J.: Prentice-Hall, 1978. [12, 13]

Hoffman, Martin L. "Empathy, Role-Taking, Guilt, and Development of Altruistic Motives," in Thomas Lickona, et al. (eds.), *Moral Development and Behavior: Theory, Research, and Social Issues*. New York: Holt, Rinehart and Winston, 1976. [10]

——. "Personality and Social Development," *Annual Review of Psychology*, 28 (1977), 295–321. [16]

Hoffman, Martin L., and H. D. Saltzstein. "Parent Discipline and the Child's Moral Development," *Journal of Personality and Social Psychology*, 5, (1967), 45–57. [10]

Hohmann, George W. "Some Effects of Spinal Cord Lesions on Experienced Emotional Feelings," *Psychophysiology*, 3:2 (1966), 143–156. [15]

Holmes, T. S. "Adaptive Behavior and Health Change." Medical thesis, University of Washington, Seattle, 1970. [21]

Holmes, Thomas H., and Minoru Masuda. "Life Change and Illness Susceptibility," in Barbara S. Dohrenwend and Bruce P. Dohrenwend (eds.), *Stressful Life Events: Their Nature and Effects*. New York: Wiley, 1974, pp. 45–72. [21]

Holmes, Thomas H., and Richard H. Rahe. "The Social Readjustment Rating Scale," *Journal of Psychosomatic Research*, 11

(1967), 213–218. [21]

Holstein, C. B. "Irreversible, Stepwise Sequence in the Development of Moral Judgment: A Longitudinal Study of Males and Females," *Child Development*, 47 (1976), 31–61. [10]

Hooker, Davenport. *The Prenatal Origin of Behavior*. Lawrence: University of Kansas Press, 1952. [7]

Horner, Matina S. "Femininity and Successful Achievement: A Basic Inconsistency," in J. Bardwick, E. M. Douvan, M. S. Horner, and D. Gutmann (eds.), *Feminine Personality and Conflict*. Monterey, Calif.: Brooks/Cole, 1970. [16]

——. "Toward an Understanding of Achievement-Related Conflicts in Women," *Journal of Social Issues*, 28 (1972), 157–175. [16]

Horney, Karen. *Feminine Psychology*. Harold Kelman (ed.). New York: Norton, 1967. [18]

——. *The Neurotic Personality of Our Times*. New York: Norton, 1937. [18]

——. *Our Inner Conflicts*. New York: Norton, 1945. [18]

Horowitz, Leonard M., Anita K. Lampel, and Ruby N. Takanishi. "The Child's Memory for Unitized Scenes," *Journal of Experimental Child Psychology*, 8 (1969), 375–388. [5]

Hovland, Carl I., Irving L. Janis, and Harold H. Kelley. *Communication and Persuasion: Psychological Studies of Opinion Change*. New Haven, Conn.: Yale University Press, 1953. [25]

Hovland, Carl I., Arthur Lumsdaine, and Frederick Sheffield. *Experiments on Mass Communication*. Princeton, N.J.: Princeton University Press, 1949. [25]

Hovland, Carl I., and Walter Weiss. "The Influence of Source Credibility on Communication Effectiveness," *Public Opinion Quarterly*, 15 (1951), 636–650. [25]

Hubel, David H., and Torsten N. Wiesel. "Receptive Fields, Binocular Interaction and Functional Architecture in the Cat's Visual Cortex," *Journal of Physiology*, 160 (1962), 106–154. [11]

Hudson, W. "Pictorial Depth Perception in Subcultural Groups in Africa," *Journal of Social Psychology*, 52 (1960), 183–208. [2]

Hunt, Morton. *Sexual Behavior in the 1970's*. New York: Dell, 1974. [17]

Huston, Ted L. "Ambiguity of Acceptance, Social Desirability, and Dating Choice," *Journal of Experimental Social Psychology*, 9 (1973), 32–42. [26]

Inhelder, Baerbel, and Jean Piaget. *The Growth of Logical Thinking from Childhood to Adolescence*. New York: Basic Books, 1958. [8]

Insko, Chester A. "Verbal Reinforcement of Attitude," *Journal of Personality and Social Psychology*, 2:4 (1965), 621–623. [25]

Isen, A. M., N. Horn, and **D. L. Rosenhan.** "Effects of Success and Failure on Children's Generosity," *Journal of Personality and Social Psychology*, 27 (1973), 239–247. [28]

Iversen, Susan D., and **Leslie L. Iversen.** *Behavioral Pharmacology.* New York: Oxford University Press, 1975. [14]

Jackson, Douglas N. "Construction of the Personality Research Form," *Personality Research Form Manual.* Goshen, N.Y.: Research Psychologists Press, 1974, pp. 14–45. [20]

James, William. *The Principles of Psychology.* Vol. 2. New York: Holt, 1890. [15]

Janis, Irving L. *Victims of Groupthink: A Psychological Study of Foreign-Policy Decisions and Fiascos.* Boston: Houghton Mifflin, 1973. [27]

Janis, Irving L., and **Seymour Feshbach.** "Effects of Fear-Arousing Communications," *Journal of Abnormal and Social Psychology*, 48 (1953), 78–92. [25]

Janis, Irving L., Donald Kaye, and **Paul Kirschner.** "Facilitating Effects of 'Eating-While-Reading' on Responsiveness to Persuasive Communications," *Journal of Personality and Social Psychology*, 1 (1965), 181–186. [25]

Janis, Irving L., and **Leon Mann.** *Decision Making: A Psychological Analysis of Conflict, Choice, and Commitment.* New York: Free Press, 1977. [6]

Jarvik, Lissy F. "Thoughts on the Psychobiology of Aging," *American Psychologist*, May 1975, 576–583. [8]

Jarvik, Lissy F., Victor Klodin, and **Steven S. Matsuyama.** "Human Aggression and the Extra Y Chromosome: Fact or Fantasy?" *American Psychologist*, 28:8 (August 1973), 674–682. [28]

Javert, Carl T., and **James D. Hardy.** "Influence of Analgesics on Pain Intensity During Labor," *Anesthesiology*, 12 (1951), 189–215. [2]

Jenkins, J. G., and **K. M. Dallenbach.** "Oblivescence During Sleep and Waking," *American Journal of Psychology*, 35 (1924), 605–612. [5]

Jensen, Arthur R. "How Much Can We Boost I.Q. and Scholastic Achievement?" *Harvard Educational Review*, 39 (1969), 1–123. [20]

John, E. Roy. *Mechanisms of Memory.* New York: Academic Press, 1967. [5]

Jones, Edward E., and **Keith E. Davis.** "From Acts to Dispositions: The Attribution Process in Person Perception," in Leonard Berkowitz (ed.), *Advances in Experimental Social Psychology.* Vol. 2. New York: Academic Press, 1965, pp. 219–266. [26]

Jones, Edward E., Keith E. Davis, and **Kenneth J. Gergen.** "Role Playing Variations and Their Informational Value for Person Perception," *Journal of Abnormal and Social Psychology*, 63 (1961), 302–310. [26]

Jones, Edward E., Kenneth J. Gergen, and **R. G. Jones.** "Tactics of Ingratiation Among Leaders and Subordinates in a Status Hierarchy," *Psychological Monographs*, 77:3 (1963), Whole No. 566. [26]

Jones, Edward E., and **Richard E. Nisbett.** *The Actor and Observer: Perceptions of the Causes of Behavior.* New York: General Learning Press, 1971. [19]

Jones, James M. *Prejudice and Racism.* Reading, Mass.: Addison-Wesley, 1972. [25]

Jonides, John, Robert Kahn, and **Paul Rozin.** "Imagery Instructions Improve Memory in Blind Subjects," *Bulletin of the Psychonomic Society*, 5:5 (1975), 424–426. [5]

Jouvet, Michel. "The Stages of Sleep," *Scientific American*, 216 (February 1967), 62–72. [14]

Jung, Carl G. *Collected Works.* Princeton, N.J.: Princeton University Press, 1967. [18]

———. *Psychological Reflections.* Princeton, N.J.: Princeton University Press, 1972. [18]

Jusczyk, Peter W., Burton S. Rosner, James E. Cutting, Christopher F. Foard, and **Linda B. Smith.** "Categorical Perception of Nonspeech Sounds by 2-Month-Old Infants," *Perception & Psychophysics*, 21:1 (1977), 50–54. [9]

Kagan, Jerome. "The Baby's Elastic Mind," *Human Nature*, January 1978, 66–73. [7]

Kagan, Jerome, and **Howard A. Moss.** *Birth to Maturity.* New York: Wiley, 1962. [2]

Kalnins, Ilze V., and **J. S. Bruner.** "The Coordination of Visual Observation and Instrumental Behavior in Early Infancy," *Perception*, 2 (1973), 307–314. [7]

Kanfer, Fran F., and **P. Karoly.** "Self-Control: A Behaviorist Excursion into the Lion's Den," *Behavior Therapy*, 3 (1972), 298–416. [21]

Kanfer, Fran F., and **J. Philips.** *Learning Foundations of Behavior Therapy.* New York: Wiley, 1970. [24]

Kangas, J., and **K. Bradway.** "Intelligence at Middle Age: A Thirty-Eight-Year Follow-Up," *Developmental Psychology*, 5 (1971), 333–337. [8]

Kanizsa, Gaetano. "Subjective Contours,"

Scientific American, 234:4 (April 1976), 48–52. [13]

Kaplan, Bert. *The Inner World of Mental Illness.* New York: Harper & Row, 1964. [2]

Karlins, M., T. L. Coffman, and **G. Walter.** "On the Fading of Social Stereotypes: Studies in Three Generations of College Students," *Journal of Personality and Social Psychology*, 13 (1969), 1–16. [25]

Kasamatsu, Akira, and **Tomio Hirai.** "An Electroencephalographic Study on the Zen Meditation (Zazen)," *Folia Psychiatrica et Neurologica Japonica*, 20 (1966), 315–366. [14]

Katchadourian, Herant A., and **Donald T. Lunde.** *Fundamentals of Human Sexuality.* 2nd ed. New York: Holt, Rinehart and Winston, 1975. [17]

Keesey, Richard E., and **Terry L. Powley.** "Hypothalamic Regulation of Body Weight," *American Scientist*, 63:5 (September–October 1975), 558–565. [16]

Kelley, Harold H. "The Warm-Cold Variable in First Impressions of Persons," *Journal of Personality*, 18 (1950), 431–439. [26]

Kellogg, Winthrop N., and **Luella A. Kellogg.** *The Ape and the Child.* New York: McGraw-Hill, 1933. [9]

Kelly, E. Lowell. Review of the Personality Research Form in Oscar K. Buros (ed.), *The Seventh Mental Measurements Yearbook.* Highland Park, N.J.: Gryphon Press, 1972, pp. 298–301. [20]

Kenrick, Douglas T., and **Robert B. Cialdini.** "Romantic Attraction: Misattribution vs. Reinforcement Explanations," *Journal of Personality and Social Psychology*, 35 (1977), 381–391. [26]

Kety, Seymour S. "Biochemical Hypotheses and Studies," in Leopold Bellak and Laurence Loeb (eds.), *The Schizophrenic Syndrome.* New York: Grune & Stratton, 1969, pp. 155–171. [23]

Kety, Seymour S., David Rosenthal, Paul H. Wender, and **Fini Schulsinger.** "The Types and Prevalence of Mental Illness in the Biological and Adoptive Families of Adopted Schizophrenics," in David Rosenthal and Seymour S. Kety (eds.), *The Transmission of Schizophrenia.* Elmsford, N.Y.: Pergamon, 1968, pp. 345–362. [23]

Keys, A., J. Brŏzek, A. Henschel, O. Michelson, and **H. L. Taylor.** *The Biology of Human Starvation.* Minneapolis: University of Minnesota Press, 1950. [16]

Kiesler, Charles A., and **J. Jones.** "The Interactive Effects of Commitment and Forewarning: Three Experiments," in Charles A. Kiesler (ed.), *The Psychology of Commitment: Experiments Linking Behavior to Belief.* New York: Academic Press, 1971, pp. 94–108. [25]

Kiloh, L. G., and **R. F. Garside.** "The Independence of Neurotic Depression and Endogenous Depression," *British Journal of Psychiatry*, 109 (1963), 451–463. [23]

Kimbel, Gregory A. *Hilgard and Marquis' Conditioning and Learning*, 2nd ed. New York: Appleton-Century-Crofts, 1961. [4]

King, S. H. "Coping Mechanisms in Adolescents," *Psychiatric Annuals*, 1 (1971), 10–46. [10]

Kinsey, Alfred C., Wardell B. Pomeroy, C. W. Martin, and P. H. Gebhard. *Sexual Behavior in the Human Female*. Philadelphia: Saunders, 1953. [2, 17]

Kinsey, Alfred C., Wardell B. Pomeroy, and C. E. Martin. *Sexual Behavior in the Human Male*. Philadelphia: Saunders, 1948. [2, 17]

Kirchner, W. K. "Age Differences in Short-Term Retention of Rapidly Changing Information," *Journal of Experimental Psychology*, 55 (1958), 352–358. [8]

Klaus, M. H., and J. H. Kennell. *Maternal–Infant Bonding*. St. Louis: C. V. Mosby, 1976. [10]

Kleiter, G. D., H. Gachowetz, and D. Huber. *Bibliography: Decision Making*. Salzburg: Psychology Institute, University of Salzburg, 1976. [6]

Kleitman, Nathaniel. *Sleep and Wakefulness*. Rev. ed. Chicago: University of Chicago Press, 1963. [14]

Klineberg, Otto. "Emotional Expression in Chinese Literature," *Journal of Abnormal and Social Psychology*, 33 (1938), 517–520. [15]

Klüver, H., and P. C. Bucy. "Preliminary Analysis of Functions of the Temporal Lobes in Monkeys," *Archives of Neurology and Psychiatry*, 42 (1939), 979–1000. [11]

Knepler, Abraham E. "Adolescence: An Anthropological Approach," in G. D. Winter and E. M. Nuss (eds.), *The Young Adult: Identity and Awareness*. Glenview, Ill.: Scott Foresman, 1969. [10]

Kobasigawa, Akira. "Utilization of Retrieval Cues by Children in Recall," *Child Development*, 45 (1974), 127–134. [8]

Koffka, Kurt. *Principles of Gestalt Psychology*. New York: Harcourt Brace Jovanovich, 1963. [13]

Kohlberg, Lawrence. "The Development of Children's Orientation Toward a Moral Order; 1. Sequence in the Development of Moral Thought," *Vita Humana*, 6 (1963), 11–33. [2, 10]

———. "Stage and Sequence: The Cognitive-Developmental Approach to Socialization," in David A. Goslin (ed.), *Handbook of Socialization and Research*. Chicago: Rand McNally, 1969. [10]

Kohlberg, Lawrence, and R. Kramer. "Continuities and Discontinuities in Childhood and Adult Moral Development," *Human Development*, 12 (1969), 93–

120. [10]

Kohler, Ivo. "Experiment with Goggles," *Scientific American*, 206 (May 1962), 62–72. [13]

Köhler, Wolfgang. *Gestalt Psychology*. New ed. New York: Liveright, 1970. [13]

———. *The Mentality of Apes*. New York: Harcourt, Brace, 1925. [6]

Kolb, Lawrence C., Viola W. Bernard, and Bruce P. Dohrenwend (eds.). *Urban Challenges to Psychiatry: The Case History of a Response*. Boston: Little, Brown, 1969. [22]

Kolodny, R. C., W. H. Masters, B. F. Hendry, and G. Toro. "Plasma Testosterone and Semen Analysis in Male Homosexuals," *New England Journal of Medicine*, 285 (1971), 1170–1174. [17]

Konorski, Jerzy, and Stefan Miller. "On Two Types of Conditioned Reflex." *Journal of General Psychology*, 16 (1937), 264–272. [4]

Korchin, Sheldon J. *Modern Clinical Psychology*. New York: Basic Books, 1976. [24]

Kraepelin, Emil. *Clinical Psychiatry: A Textbook for Physicians*. A. Diffendorf (tr.). New York: Macmillan, 1902. [22]

———. *Textbook of Psychiatry* (1883). 8th ed. New York: Macmillan, 1923. [23]

Kramer, M. "Statistics of Mental Disorders in the U.S.: Current Status, Some Urgent Needs, and Suggested Solutions," *Journal of the Royal Statistical Society*, Series A, 132 (1969). [22]

Krashen, Stephen D. "The Critical Period for Language Acquisition and Its Possible Basis," in Doris Aaronson and Robert W. Rieber (eds.), *Developmental Psycholinguistics and Communication Disorders*. Annals of the New York Academy of Sciences, Vol. 263 (1975), pp. 211–224. [9]

Krech, David (I. David Krechevsky). "Hypotheses in Rats," *Psychological Review*, 39 (1932), 516–535. [6]

Kuhn, Deanna, Jonas Langer, Lawrence Kohlberg, and Norma S. Haan. "The Development of Formal Operations in Logical and Moral Judgment," *Genetic Psychology Monographs*, 95L (February 1977), 97–188. [10]

Kuo, Zing Yang. "The Genesis of the Cat's Responses to the Rat," *Journal of Comparative Psychology*, 11:1 (1930), 1–35. [3, 28]

Kurtines, W., and E. B. Greif. "The Development of Moral Thought: Review and Evaluation of Kohlberg's Approach," *Psychological Bulletin*, 81 (1974), 453–470. [10]

Laing, R. D. *Knots*. New York: Vintage Books, 1970. [23]

———. *The Politics of Experience*. New York: Pantheon, 1967. [23]

Laing, R. D., and Aaron Esterson. *Sanity, Madness, and the Family*. 2nd ed. New York: Basic Books, 1971. [23]

Laird, James D. "Self-Attribution of Emotion: The Effects of Expressive Behavior on the Quality of Emotional Experience," *Journal of Personality and Social Psychology*, 20:4 (1974), 475–486. [15]

Lamb, M. E. "The Development of Mother-Infant and Father-Infant Attachments in the Second Year of Life," *Developmental Psychology*, 13 (1977), 637–648. [10]

Landis, C. A. "A Statistical Evaluation of Psychotherapeutic Methods," in L. E. Hinsie (ed.), *Concepts and Problems of Psychotherapy*. New York: Columbia University Press, 1937, pp. 155–165. [24]

Lando, Harry. "Successful Treatment of Smokers with a Broad-Spectrum Behavioral Approach," *Journal of Consulting and Clinical Psychology*, 45:3 (1977), 361–366. [21]

Lane, Harlan. *The Wild Boy of Aveyron*. Cambridge, Mass.: Harvard University Press, 1976. [4]

Lang, Peter J., David G. Rice, and Richard A. Sternbach. "The Psychophysiology of Emotion," in N. S. Greenfield and Richard A. Sternbach (eds.), *Handbook of Psychophysiology*. New York: Holt, Rinehart and Winston, 1972. [15]

Lange, Carl G., and William James. *The Emotions*. Knight Dunlap (ed.). I. A. Haupt (tr.). Baltimore: Williams & Wilkins, 1922. [15]

Langer, Ellen J., and Judith Rodin. "The Effects of Choice and Enhanced Personal Responsibility for the Aged: A Field Experiment in an Institutional Setting," *Journal of Personality and Social Psychology*, 34:2 (1976), 191–198. [21]

Lanners, E. (ed.). *Illusions*. New York: Holt, Rinehart, and Winston, 1977. [13]

Lanyon, Richard I., and Leonard D. Goodstein. "History of Personality Assessment," in Leonard D. Goodstein and Richard I. Lanyon, *Personality Assessment*. New York: Wiley, 1971, pp. 1–18. [20]

Lanyon, Richard I., and B. Lanyon. *Behavior Therapy: A Clinical Introduction*. Reading, Mass.: Addison-Wesley, 1978. [4]

LaPiere, Richard T. "Attitudes vs. Actions," *Social Forces*, 13 (1934), 230–237. [25]

Lashley, Karl S. *Brain Mechanisms and Intelligence*. Chicago: University of Chicago Press, 1929. [11]

———. *The Neuropsychology of Lashley: Selected Papers*. F. A. Beach et al. (eds.). New York: McGraw-Hill, 1960.

———. "In Search of the Engram," *Symposium of the Society of Experimental Biology, No. 4*. Cambridge: Cambridge University Press, 1950, pp. 454–482. [5]

Latané, Bibb, and **John M. Darley.** "Help in a Crisis: Bystander Response to an Emergency," in J. W. Thibaut, J. T. Spence, and R. C. Carson (eds.), *Contemporary Topics in Social Psychology.* Morristown, N.J.: General Learning Press, 1976, pp. 309–332. [28]

Lay, Clarry H., and **Douglas N. Jackson.** "Analysis of the Generality of Trait Inferential Relationships," *Journal of Personality and Social Psychology,* 12 (1969), 12–21. [20]

Lazarus, Richard S., and **Elizabeth Alfert.** "The Short-Circuiting of Threat by Experimentally Altering Cognitive Appraisal," *Journal of Abnormal and Social Psychology,* 69 (1964), 195–205. [15]

Leavitt, Fred. *Drugs and Behavior.* Philadelphia: Saunders, 1974. [14]

Lee, L. C. *Personality Development in Childhood.* Monterey, Calif.: Brooks/Cole, 1976. [10]

Lee, Tyrone, and **Philip Seeman.** *Dopamine Receptors in Normal and Schizophrenic Human Brains. Society for Neuroscience Abstracts.* Vol. 3. Bethesda, Md.: Society for Neuroscience, 1977, p. 443. [23]

Lehrman, Daniel S. "Problems Raised by Instinct Theories," *Quarterly Review of Biology,* 28 (1953), 337–365. [3]

———. "The Reproductive Behavior of Ring Doves" (1964), in Richard F. Thompson (ed.), *Progress in Psychobiology: Readings from Scientific American.* San Francisco: Freeman, 1976, pp. 62–68. [3]

Leibowitz, Herschel W., and **Herbert A. Pick, Jr.** "Cross-Cultural and Educational Aspects of the Ponzo Perspective Illusion," *Perception & Psychophysics,* 12:5 (1972), 430–432. [13]

Lenneberg, Eric H. *The Biological Foundations of Language.* New York: Wiley, 1967. [3, 9]

Lettvin, J. Y., et al. "What the Frog's Eye Tells the Frog's Brain," *Proceedings of the Institute of Radio Engineers,* 47 (1959), 1940–1951. [11]

Leventhal, Howard, Robert Singer, and **Susan Jones.** "Effects of Fear and Specificity of Recommendation upon Attitudes and Behavior," *Journal of Personality and Social Psychology,* 2:1 (1959), 20–29. [25]

Levinson, Daniel J., with **Charlotte N. Darrow, Edward B. Klein, Maria H. Levinson,** and **Braxton McKee.** *The Seasons of a Man's Life.* New York: Knopf, 1978. [10, 21]

Lewis, H. R., and **C. H. Papadimitriou.** "The Efficiency of Algorithms," *Scientific American,* 238 (1978), 96–109. [6]

Lewis, Michael. "The Busy, Purposeful World of a Baby," *Psychology Today,* 10:9 (February 1977), 53–56. [7]

Lewis, Richard. *Miracles: Poems by Children of the English-Speaking World.* New York: Simon and Schuster, 1966. [8]

Lidz, Theodore. *The Origin and Treatment of Schizophrenic Disorders.* New York: Basic Books, 1973 [23]

Lidz, Theodore, et al. "The Intrafamilial Environment of Schizophrenic Patients: Marital Schism and Marital Skew," *American Journal of Psychiatry,* 114 (1957), 241–248. [23]

Lieberman, M. A., and **A. S. Coplan.** "Distance from Death as a Variable in the Study of Aging," *Developmental Psychology,* (1970), 71–84. [10]

Liebeskind, John C., and **Linda A. Paul.** "Psychological and Physiological Mechanisms of Pain," *Annual Review of Psychology,* 28 (1977), 41–60. [12]

Linder, Darwyn E. (ed.). *Some Psychological Dimensions of Social Interaction: Readings and Perspectives.* Reading, Mass.: Addison-Wesley, 1973. [27]

Linder, Darwyn E., Joel Cooper, and **Edward E. Jones.** "Decision Freedom as a Determinant of the Role of Incentive Magnitude in Attitude Change," *Journal of Personality and Social Psychology,* 6:3 (1967), 245–254. [25]

Lindholm, Ernest, and **Steven Lowry.** "Alpha Production in Humans Under Conditions of False Feedback," *Bulletin of the Psychonomic Society,* 11:2 (1978), 106–108. [14]

Lindsay, Peter H., and **Donald A. Norman.** *Human Information Processing.* New York: Academic Press, 1972. [5, 13]

Loehlin, John C., Gardner Lindzey, and **James N. Spuhler.** *Racial Differences in Intelligence.* San Francisco: Freeman, 1975, pp. 232–258. [20]

Loftus, G., and **E. Loftus.** *Human Memory.* Hillsdale, N.J.: Erlbaum, 1976. [5]

LoPiccolo, Joseph. "The Professionalization of Sex Therapy: Issues and Problems," in Joseph LoPiccolo and Leslie LoPiccolo (eds.), *Handbook of Sex Therapy.* New York: Plenum Press, 1978, pp. 511–526. [17]

LoPiccolo, Joseph, and **W. C. Lobitz.** "The Role of Masturbation in the Treatment of Orgasmic Dysfunction," in Joseph LoPiccolo and Leslie LoPiccolo (eds.), *Handbook of Sex Therapy.* New York: Plenum Press, 1978, pp. 187–194. [17]

Lorenz, Konrad. *The Eight Deadly Sins of Civilized Man.* Marjorie Kerr-Wilson (tr.). New York: Harcourt Brace Jovanovich, 1974. [28]

———. *Evolution and Modification of Behavior.* Chicago: University of Chicago Press, 1965. [3]

———. *On Aggression.* Marjorie Kerr-Wilson (tr.). New York: Harcourt Brace Jovanovich, 1966. [28]

Luborsky, Lester B., et al. "Factors Influencing the Outcome of Therapy: A Review of Quantitative Research," *Psychological Bulletin,* 75 (1971), 145–185. [24]

Luborsky, Lester B., John P. Docherty, and **Sydnor Penick.** "Onset Conditions for Psychosomatic Symptoms: A Comparative Review of Immediate Observation with Retrospective Research," *Psychosomatic Medicine,* 35:3 (May–June 1973), 187–204. [15]

Luce, Gay G. *Body Time.* New York: Random House, 1971. [14]

Luchins, Abraham S. "Classroom Experiments on Mental Set," *American Journal of Psychology,* 59 (1946), 295–298. [6]

———. "Primacy-Recency in Impression Formation," in C. I. Hovland, et al. (eds.), *The Order of Presentation in Persuasion.* New Haven, Conn.: Yale University Press, 1957, pp. 33–61. [26]

Ludwig, Arnold M. "Sensory Overload and Psychopathology," *Diseases of the Nervous System,* 36:7 (July 1975), 357–360. [16]

Luria, Aleksandr R. *The Mind of a Mnemonist.* Lynn Solotaroff (tr.). New York: Basic Books, 1968. [5]

Lynch, James J., David A. Paskewitz, and **Martin T. Orne.** "Some Factors in the Feedback Control of Human Alpha Rhythm," *Psychosomatic Medicine,* 36:5 (September–October 1974), 399–410. [14]

Macaulay, Jacqueline R. "A Shill for Charity," in Jacqueline R. Macaulay and Leonard Berkowitz (eds.), *Altruism and Helping Behavior: Social Psychological Studies of Some Antecedents and Consequences.* New York: Academic Press, 1970, pp. 43–59 [28]

Maccoby, Eleanor E. "Women's Intellect," in S. M. Farber and R. H. L. Wilson (eds.), *The Potential of Women.* New York: McGraw-Hill, 1963, pp. 24–39. [16]

Maccoby, Eleanor E., and **Carole N. Jacklin.** *Psychology of Sex Differences.* Stanford, Calif.: Stanford University Press, 1974. [10, 17]

MacLean, P. D. "Contrasting Function of Limbic and Neocortical Systems of the Brain and Their Relevance to Psychophysiological Aspects of Medicine," *American Journal of Medicine,* 25 (1958), 611–626. [11]

MacNichol, Edward F., Jr. "Three-Pigment Color Vision." *Scientific American,* 211 (December 1964), 48–56. [12]

Magoun, H. W., *The Waking Brain.* Springfield, Ill.: Charles S. Thomas, 1963. [11]

Makous, W. L. "Cutaneous Color Sensitivity: Explanation and Demonstration," *Psychological Review,* 73:4 (1966), 280–294. [13]

Malinowski, Bronislaw. *The Sexual Life of Savages in Northwestern Melanesia.* New York: Eugenics Press, 1929. [10]

Mandler, George. "From Association to Structure," *Psychological Review,* 69:5 (1962), 415–427. [6]

Marañon, Gregorio. Contribution à l'Etude de l'Action Emotive de l'Adrenaline," *Revue Française d'Endocrinologie.* 2 (1924), 301–325. [15]

Marcia, James E. "Development and Validation of Ego-Identity States," *Journal of Personality and Social Psychology,* 3 (1966), 551–558. [10]

Mark, Vernon H., and **Ervin, Frank R.** *Violence and the Brain.* New York: Harper & Row, 1970. [15, 28]

Marler, Peter. "Bird Song and Speech Development: Could There Be Parallels?" *American Scientists,* 58 (1970), 669–673. [3]

———. "On Animal Aggression: The Roles of Strangeness and Familiarity," *American Psychologist,* 31:3 (March 1976), 239–246. [3]

Marlowe, David, and **Kenneth J. Gergen.** "Personality and Social Interaction," in Gardner Lindzey and Elliot Aronson (eds.), *Handbook of Social Psychology.* Vol. 3. 2nd ed. Reading, Mass.: Addison-Wesley, 1969, pp. 590–665. [25]

Marsh, Caryl. "A Framework for Describing Subjective States of Consiousness," in Norman E. Zinberg (ed.), *Alternate States of Consciousness.* New York: Free Press, 1977, pp. 145–157. [14]

Marshall, Donald S. "Sexual Behavior on Mangaia," in Donald S. Marshall and R. D. Suggs (eds.), *Human Sexual Behavior.* Englewood Cliffs, N.J.: Prentice-Hall, 1971. [17]

Martorano, S. C. "A Developmental Analysis of Performance on Piaget's Formal Operations Tasks," *Developmental Psychology,* 13 (1977), 666–672. [8]

Marx, J. L. "Analgesia: How the Body Inhibits Pain Perception," *Science,* 195 (1977), 471–473. [12]

Maslow, Abraham H. "Deficiency Motivation and Growth Motivation," in Marshall R. Jones (ed.), *Nebraska Symposium on Motivation: 1955.* Lincoln: University of Nebraska Press, 1955. [19]

———. *The Farther Reaches of the Human Mind.* New York: Viking, 1971. [16, 19]

———. *Motivation and Personality.* New York: Harper & Row, 1954. [16, 19]

———. *The Psychology of Science: A Reconnaissance.* New York: Harper & Row, 1966. [19]

———. "Some Basic Propositions of a Growth and Self-Actualization Psychology," in Salvatore Maddi (ed.), *Perspectives on Personality.* Boston: Little, Brown, 1971. [19]

———. *Toward a Psychology of Being.* 2nd ed. New York: Van Nostrand Reinhold, 1968. [19]

Mason, William A. "The Effects of Social Restriction on the Behavior of Rhesus Monkeys: III. Tests of Gregariousness," *Journal of Comparative and Physiological Psychology,* 54 (1961), 287–290. [15]

Mason, William A., and **Dale F. Lott.** "Ethology and Comparative Psychology," *Annual Review of Psychology.* Vol. 27. Palo Alto, Calif.: Annual Reviews, 1976, pp. 129–154. [3]

Masters, Robert E. L., and **Jean Houston.** *Psychedelic Art.* New York: Grove Press, 1968. [14]

Masters, William H., and **Virginia E. Johnson.** "Counseling with Sexually Incompatible Marriage Partners," in R. Brecher and E. Brecher (eds.), *An Analysis of "Human Sexual Response,"* New York: New American Library, 1966b, pp. 203–219. [17] .

———. *Human Sexual Inadequacy.* Boston: Little, Brown, 1970. [17]

———. *Human Sexual Response.* Boston: Little, Brown, 1966a. [17]

———. "The Sexual Response Cycle of the Human Female: III, The Clitoris: Anatomic and Clinical Considerations," *Western Journal of Surgery, Obstetrics, and Gynecology,* 70 (1962), 248–257. [17]

McCary, James Leslie. *McCary's Human Sexuality.* 3rd ed. New York: Van Nostrand, 1978. [17]

McClelland, David C. *The Achieving Society.* New York: Van Nostrand Reinhold, 1961. [16]

———. "Managing Motivation to Expand Human Freedom," *American Psychologist,* March 1978, 201–210. [16]

McClelland, David C., et al. *The Achievement Motive.* New York: Appleton-Century-Crofts, 1953. [16]

McClelland, David C., and **John W. Atkinson.** "The Projective Expression of Needs, I: The Effect of Different Intensities of the Hunger Drive on Perception," *Journal of Psychology,* 25 (1948), 205–232. [13]

McClelland, David C., and **David G. Winter.** *Motivating Economic Achievement.* New York: Free Press, 1969. [16]

McDougall, William. *Introduction to Social Psychology.* London: Methuen, 1908. [3, 10]

McGeoch, J. A. *The Psychology of Human Learning.* New York: Longmans, Green, 1942. [5]

McGraw, Myrtle B. *Growth, A Study of Johnny and Jimmy.* New York: Appleton-Century-Crofts, 1935. [7]

———. "Later Development of Children Specially Trained During Infancy: Johnny and Jimmy at School Age," *Child Development,* 10 (1939a), 1–19. [7]

———. "Swimming Behavior of the Human Infant," *Journal of Pediatrics,* 15 (1939b), 485–490. [7]

McGuire, R. J., J. M. Carlisle, and **B. G. Young.** "Sexual Deviations as Conditioned Behaviour: A Hypothesis," *Behaviour Research and Therapy,* 2 (1965), 185–190. [17]

McGuire, William, and **Dimitri Papageorgis.** "The Relative Efficacy of Various Types of Prior Belief—Defense in Producing Immunity Against Persuasion," *Journal of Abnormal and Social Psychology,* 62 (1961), 327–337. [25]

McNeil, E. B. *The Quiet Furies.* Englewood Cliffs, N.J.: Prentice-Hall, 1967. [22]

———. *The Psychoses.* Englewood Cliffs, N.J.: Prentice-Hall, 1970. [22]

McNeill, David. "Developmental Psycholinguistics," in Franklyn L. Smith and George A. Miller (eds.), *The Genesis of Language: A Psycholinguistic Approach.* Cambridge, Mass.: M.I.T. Press, 1966. [9]

Mead, George Herbert. *Mind, Self and Society: From the Standpoint of a Social Behaviorist.* Chicago: University of Chicago Press, 1934. [7]

Mead, Margaret. *Sex and Temperament in Three Primitive Societies.* New York: Morrow, 1935. [10, 17]

Mednick, Sarnoff A., and **Martha T. Mednick.** "A Theory and Test of Creative Thought," in G. Nielson (ed.), *Proceedings of the XIV International Congress of Applied Psychology.* Copenhagen: Munksgaard, 1961, pp. 40–47. [6]

Meltzer, H. Y., and **S. M. Stahl.** "Dopamine Hypothesis of Schizophrenia—Review," *Schizophrenic Bulletin,* 2:1 (1976), 19–76. [23]

Meltzoff, Andrew N., and **M. Keith Moore.** "Imitation of Facial and Manual Gestures by Human Neonates," *Science,* 198 (October 7, 1977), 75–78. [7]

Melzack, Ronald. *The Puzzle of Pain.* New York: Basic Books, 1973. [12]

Melzack, Ronald, and **P. D. Wall.** "Pain Mechanisms: A New Theory," *Science,* 150 (1965), 971. [12]

Mendels, J. "Depression: The Distinction Between Symptom and Syndrome," *British Journal of Psychiatry,* 114 (1968), 1549–1554. [23]

Menyuk, P. and **N. Bernholtz.** "Prosodic Features and Children's Language Production," *M.I.T. Research Laboratory of Electronics Quarterly Progress Reports,* No. 93 (1969), 216–219. [9]

Mercer, Jane R. "I.Q.: The Lethal Label," *Psychology Today,* 6:4 (September 1972), 44–47, 95–97. [20]

Merskey, H. "The Perception and Measurement of Pain," *Journal of Psychosomatic Research*, 17 (1973), 251–255. [12]

Meyer, John P., and **Susan Pepper.** "Need Compatibility and Marital Adjustment in Young Married Couples," *Journal of Personality and Social Psychology*, 35:5 (May 1977), 331–342. [26]

Milgram, Stanley. "Behavioral Study of Obedience," *Journal of Abnormal and Social Psychology*, 67 (1963), 371–378. [27]

———. *Obedience to Authority.* New York: Harper & Row, 1974. [27]

———. "Some Conditions of Obedience and Disobedience to Authority," in I. D. Steiner and M. Fishbein (eds.), *Current Studies in Social Psychology.* New York: Holt, Rinehart and Winston, 1965, pp. 243–262. [27]

Milgram, Stanley, and **Carol Tavris.** "The Frozen World of the Familiar Stranger: A Conversation with Stanley Milgram, by Carol Tavris," *Psychology Today,* 8 (June 1974), 70–80. [27]

Miller, G. A. "Concerning Psychical Research," *The Psychology of Communication.* Baltimore: Penguin, 1967, pp. 56–69. [13]

———. *Language and Communication.* New York: McGraw-Hill, 1951. [9]

Miller, George A. "Decision Units in the Perception of Speech," *IRE Transactions on Information Theory,* 8 (1962), 81–83. [13]

———. "The Magical Number Seven, Plus or Minus Two: Some Limits on Our Capacity for Processing Information," *Psychological Review,* 63 (1956), 81–97. [5]

———. *The Psychology of Communication.* Baltimore: Penguin, 1967. [6]

Miller, Neal E. "Biofeedback: Evaluation of a New Technic," *New England Journal of Medicine,* 290 (1974), 684–685. [14]

———. "Experimental Studies of Conflict," in J. McV. Hunt (ed.), *Personality and the Behavior Disorders.* Vol. 1. New York: Ronald Press, 1944, pp. 431–465. [19]

———. "Experiments on Motivation," *Science,* 126 (1957), 1271–1278. [11]

———. "Learning of Visceral and Glandular Responses," *Science,* 163 (1969), 434–445. [11]

———. "Liberalization of Basic S-R Concepts: Extensions to Conflict Behavior, Social Motivation and Learning," in Sigmund Koch (ed.), *Psychology: A Study of a Science.* Vol. 2. New York: McGraw-Hill, 1959. [19]

———. "Theory and Experiment Relating Psychoanalytic Displacement to Stimulus-Response Generalization," *Journal of Abnormal and Social Psychology,* 43 (1948), 155–178. [19]

Miller, Norman, and **Donald T. Campbell.** "Recency and Primacy in Persuasion as a

Function of the Timing of Speeches and Measurements," *Journal of Abnormal and Social Psychology,* 59 (1959), 1–9. [25]

Miller, Robert E., William F. Caul, and **I. Arthur Mirsky.** "Communication of Affects Between Feral and Socially Isolated Monkeys," *Journal of Personality and Social Psychology,* 7:3 (1967), 231–239. [15]

Miller, W. R., and **Martin E. P. Seligman.** "Depression and Learned Helplessness in Man," *Journal of Abnormal Psychology,* 84 (1975), 228–238. [6]

Mills, M., and **E. Melhuish.** "Recognition of Mother's Voice in Early Infancy," *Nature,* 252:5479 (November 8, 1974), 123–124. [7]

Milner, Brenda. "Memory Disturbance After Bilateral Hippocampal Lesions," in Peter Milner and Stephen Glickman (eds.), *Cognitive Processes and the Brain.* Princeton, N.J.: D. Van Nostrand, 1965. [5]

———. "Some Effects of Frontal Lobectomy in Man," in J. M. Warren and K. Arent (eds.), *The Frontal Granular Cortex and Behavior.* New York: McGraw-Hill, 1964. [11]

Minkowski, A. *Regional Development of the Brain in Early Life.* Oxford: Blackwell, 1967. [7]

Mischel, Walter. *Introduction to Personality.* New York: Holt, Rinehart and Winston, 1971. [19]

———. *Personality and Assessment.* New York: Wiley, 1968. [19]

———. "Toward a Cognitive Social-Learning Reconceptualization of Personality," *Psychological Review,* 80:4 (1973), 252–283. [10, 19]

Molfese, D. L., R. B. Freeman, and **D. S. Palermo.** "The Ontogeny of Brain Lateralization for Speech and Nonspeech Stimuli," *Brain and Language,* 2 (1975), 356–368. [9]

Money, John, and **Anke A. Ehrhardt.** *Man and Woman, Boy and Girl.* Baltimore: Johns Hopkins University Press, 1972. [17]

Monnier, M., A. Boehmer, and **A. Scholer.** "Early Habituation, Dishabituation, and Generalization Induced in Visual Center by Color Stimuli," *Vision Research,* 16:12 (1976), 1497–1504. [8]

Montgomery, K. C. "The Role of the Exploratory Drive in Learning," *Journal of Comparative and Physological Psychology,* 47 (1954), 60–64. [16]

Morgan, C. L. *Introduction to Comparative Psychology.* New York: Scribner, 1894. [3]

Morse, P. A. "The Discrimination of Speech and Nonspeech Stimuli in Early Infancy," *Journal of Experimental Child Psychology,* 14 (1972), 477–492. [7]

Moss, Howard A. "Sex, Age, and State as Determinants of Mother-Infant Interac-

tion," *Merrill-Palmer Quarterly,* 13 (1967), 19–36. [10, 17]

Murdock, Bennett B., Jr. "The Serial Position Effect of Free Recall," *Journal of Experimental Psychology,* 64 (1962), 482–488. [5]

Murphy, H. B. M., E. D. Wittkower, J. Fried, and **H. Ellenberger.** "A Cross-Cultural Survey of Schizophrenic Symptomatology," in *Proceedings of the Third World Congress of Psychiatry.* Vol. 2. Toronto: University of Toronto Press, 1961, pp. 1309–1315. [22]

Murray, Henry A., et al. *Explorations in Personality.* New York: Oxford University Press, 1938. [16, 20]

Murstein, Bernard I. "Physical Attractiveness and Marital Choice," *Journal of Personality and Social Psychology,* 22:1 (1972), 8–12. [26]

Mussen, P. H. "Early Sex Role Development," in D. A. Goslin (ed.), *Handbook of Socialization Theory and Research.* Chicago: Rand McNally, 1969, pp. 707–731. [10]

Muuss, R. E. *Theories of Adolescence.* 3rd ed. New York: Random House, 1975. [10]

Needleman, Herbert L. "Lead Poisoning in Children: Neurologic Implications of Widespread Subclinical Intoxication," *Seminars in Psychiatry,* 5 (February 1973), 47–53. [20]

———. "Subclinical Lead Exposure in Philadelphia Schoolchildren," *New England Journal of Medicine,* 290 (1974) 245–248. [20]

Nelson, Katherine. "Concept, Word, and Sentence: Interrelations in Acquisition and Development," *Psychological Review,* 81 (1974), 267–285. [9]

Nelson, Keith E. "Facilitating Children's Syntax Acquisition," *Developmental Psychology,* 13:2 (1977), 101–107. [9]

Neugarten, Bernice L. "Adaptation and the Life Cycle," *The Counseling Psychologist,* 6 (1976), 16–20. [10]

Newcomb, Theodore M. "Attitude Development as a Function of Reference Groups: The Bennington Study" (1943), in H. Proshansky and B. Seidenberg (eds.), *Basic Studies in Social Psychology.* New York: Holt, Rinehart and Winston, 1965, pp. 215–225. [27]

———. "The Prediction of Interpersonal Attraction," *American Psychologist,* 11 (1956), 575–586. [26]

Newell, Allen, J. C. Shaw, and **Herbert A. Simon.** "Elements of a Theory of Human Problem Solving," *Psychological Review,* 65 (1958), 151–166. [5]

Newman, G., and **C. R. Nichols.** "Sexual Activities and Attitudes in Older Persons," *Journal of the American Medical Associ-*

ation, 173 (1960), 33–35. [17]

Newtson, Darren, and **Thomas Czerlinsky.** "Adjustment of Attitude Communications for Contrasts by Extreme Audiences," *Journal of Personality and Social Psychology,* 30:6 (1974), 829–837. [26]

Nisbett, Richard E. "Determinants of Food Intake in Human Obesity," *Science,* 159 (1968a), 1245–1255. [16]

———. "Taste, Deprivation, and Weight Determinants of Eating Behavior," *Journal of Personality and Social Psychology,* 10 (1968b), 107–116. [16]

Nisbett, Richard E., Craig Caputo, Patricia Legant, and **Jeanne Moracek.** "Behavior as Seen by the Actor and as Seen by the Observer," *Journal of Personality and Social Psychology,* 27 (1973), 154–164. [26]

Nisbett, Richard E., and **S. B. Gurwitz.** "Weight, Sex, and the Eating Behavior of Human Newborns," *Journal of Comparative and Physiological Psychology,* 73 (1970), 245–253. [16]

Nisbett, Richard E., and **Timothy DeCamp Wilson.** "Telling More Than We Know," *Psychological Review,* 84:3 (1977), 231–259. [6]

Ogilvie, Bruce C. "Stimulus Addiction: The Sweet Psychic Jolt of Danger," *Psychology Today,* 8:5 (October 1974), 88–94. [16]

Olds, James, and **Peter Milner.** "Positive Reinforcement Produced by Electrical Stimulation of Septal Area and Other Regions of Rat Brain," *Journal of Comparative and Physiological Psychology,* 47 (1954), 411–427. [11]

Olson, Gary M. "An Information-Processing Analysis of Visual Memory and Habituation in Infants," in Thomas J. Tighe and Robert N. Leaton (eds.), *Habituation: Perspectives from Child Development, Animal Behavior, and Neurophysiology.* Hillsdale, N.J.: Erlbaum, 1976, pp. 239–277. [8]

Ornstein, Robert. *The Psychology of Consciousness.* 2nd ed. New York: Harcourt Brace Jovanovich, 1977. [14]

Osgood, C. E., and **P. H. Tannenbaum.** "The Principles of Congruity in the Prediction of Attitude Change," *Psychological Review,* 62 (1955), 42–55. [25]

Oskamp S., and **C. Kleinke.** "Amount of Reward in a Variable in Prisoner's Dilemma Game," *Journal of Personality and Social Psychology,* 16:1 (1970), 133–140. [28]

Overmier, J. B., and **Martin E. P. Seligman.** "Effects of Inescapable Shock on Subsequent Escape and Avoidance Responding," *Journal of Comparative and Physiological Psychology,* 63 (1967), 28–33. [21, 23]

Overton, D. A. "State-Dependent or 'Dissociated' Learning Produced with Pentobarbital," *Journal of Comparative and Physiological Psychology,* 57 (1964), 3–12. [5]

Paivio, Allan. *Imagery and Verbal Process.* New York: Holt, Rinehart and Winston, 1971. [5]

Papoušek, Hanuš. "Individual Variability in Learned Responses in Human Infants," in R. J. Robinson (ed.), *Brain and Early Behaviour: Development in the Fetus and Infant.* London: Academic Press, 1969, pp. 251–266. [8]

Parke, Ross D., Leonard Berkowitz, Jacques P. Leyens, Stephen G. West, and **Richard J. Sebastian.** "Some Effects of Violent and Nonviolent Movies on the Behavior of Juvenile Delinquents," in Leonard Berkowitz (ed.), *Advances in Experimental Social Psychology.* Vol. 10. New York: Academic Press, 1977, pp. 135–172. [1, 28]

Parkes, M. C., B. Benjamin, and **R. G. Fitzgerald.** "Broken Heart: A Statistical Study of Increased Mortality Among Widowers," *British Medical Journal,* 1, (1969), 740–743. [15]

Patterson, G. *Families: Applications of Social Learning to Family Life.* Champaign, Ill.,: Research Press, 1971. [24]

Patterson, G. R., R. A. Littman, and **W. Bricker.** "Assertive Behavior in Children: A Step Toward a Theory of Aggression," *Monographs of the Society for Research in Child Development,* 32:5 (1967), Serial No. 113. [10, 28]

Pattie, Frank A. "A Report of Attempts to Produce Uniocular Blindness by Hypnotic Suggestion," *British Journal of Medical Psychology,* 15 (1935), 230–241. [14]

Paul, Steven M. "Movement and Madness: Towards a Biological Model of Schizophrenia," in Jack D. Maser and Martin E. P. Seligman (eds.), *Psychopathology: Experimental Models.* San Francisco: Freeman, 1977, pp. 358–386. [23]

Pavlov, Ivan P. *Conditioned Reflexes.* G. V. Anrep (tr.). London: Oxford University Press, 1927. [4]

Paykel, E. S. "Life Stress and Psychiatric Disorder: Applications of the Clinical Approach," in Barbara S. Dohrenwend and Bruce P. Dohrenwend (eds.), *Stressful Life Events: Their Nature and Effects.* New York: Wiley, 1974, pp. 135–149. [21]

Penfield, Wilder. "Consciousness, Memory, and Man's Conditioned Reflexes," in Karl H. Pribram (ed.), *On the Biology of Learning.* New York: Harcourt Brace Jovanovich, 1969, pp. 127–168. [14]

———. "The Interpretive Cortex," *Science,* 70:129 (1959), 1719–1725. [5]

Penfield, Wilder, and **Theodore Rasmus-**

sen. *The Cerebral Cortex of Man.* New York: Macmillan, 1950. [11]

Peterson, Lloyd R., and **Margaret Peterson.** "Short-Term Retention of Individual Verbal Items," *Journal of Experimental Psychology,* 58 (1959), 193–198. [5]

Pfeifer, Louise. "A Subjective Report of Tactile Hallucination in Schizophrenia," *Journal of Clinical Psychology,* 26:1 (1970), 57–60. [22]

Phillips, Sheridan, with **Suzanne King** and **Louise DuBois.** "Spontaneous Activities of Female Versus Male Newborns," *Child Development,* 49 (1978), 590–597. [10]

Piaget, Jean. *Biology and Knowledge.* Beatrix Walsh (tr.). Chicago: University of Chicago Press, 1971. [8]

———. *The Construction of Reality in the Child.* New York: Basic Books, 1954. [8]

———. *The Language and Thought of the Child.* New York: World, 1973. [8]

———. *The Origins of Intelligence in Children.* (1952). Margaret Cook (tr.). New York: International Universities Press, 1966. [8, 10]

Piaget, Jean, and **Baerbel Inhelder.** *The Child's Conception of Space.* New York: Humanities Press, 1956. [8]

———. *The Psychology of the Child.* New York: Basic Books, 1969. [8, 10]

Pietropinto, Anthony, and **Jacqueline Simmenauer.** *Beyond the Male Myth.* New York: Quadrangle, 1977. [17]

Pilbeam, David. "An Idea We Could Live Without—the Naked Ape," *Discovery,* 7:2 (Spring 1972), 63–70. [3]

Piliavin, Irving M., Jane Allyn Piliavin, and **Judith Rodin.** "Costs, Diffusion, and the Stigmatized Victim," *Journal of Personality and Social Psychology,* 32:3 (September 1975), 429–438. [28]

Piliavin, Irving M., Judith Rodin, and **Jane Allyn Piliavin.** "Good Samaritanism: An Underground Phemonenon?" *Journal of Personality and Social Psychology,* 13:4 (December 1969), 289–299. [28]

Platt, John R. *Perception and Change: Projections for Survival.* Ann Arbor: University of Michigan Press, 1970. [28]

———. "Social Traps," *American Psychologist,* 28:8 (August 1973), 641–651. [28]

Plotkin, William B., and **Robin Cohen.** "Occipital Alpha and the Attributes of the 'Alpha Experience,'" *Psychological Physiology,* 13 (1976), 16–21. [14]

Pocs, O., and **A. G. Godow.** "The Shock of Recognizing Parents as Sexual Beings," in Donn Byrne and L. A. Byrne (eds.), *Exploring Human Sexuality.* New York: Crowell, 1978. [17]

Polya, Gyorgy. *How to Solve It.* 2nd ed. Garden City, N.Y.: Doubleday Anchor, 1957. [6]

Pomeroy, Wardell B. "The Masters-John-**

son Report and the Kinsey Tradition," in Ruth Brecher and Edward Brecher (eds.), *An Analysis of "Human Sexual Response."* New York: New American Library, 1966. [17]

Postman, Leo, and Laura W. Phillips. "Short-Term Temporal Changes in Free Recall," *Quarterly Journal of Experimental Psychology,* 17 (1965), 132–138. [5]

Prechtl, H. F. R. "Problems of Behavioral Studies in the Newborn Infant," in D. S. Lehrman, R. A. Hinde, and E. Shaw (eds.), *Advances in the Study of Behavior.* Vol. 1. New York: Academic Press, 1965, pp. 75–98. [7]

Premack, David. "Language and Intelligence in Ape and Man," *American Scientist,* 64:6 (November–December 1976), 674–683. [9]

———. "Language in the Chimpanzee?" *Science,* 172 (1971a), 808–822. [9]

———. "On the Assessment of Language Competence in the Chimpanzee," in A. M. Schrier and F. Stollnitz (eds.), *Behavior of Nonhuman Primates.* New York: Academic Press, 1971b, pp. 185–228. [9]

Priest, Robert T., and Jack Sawyer. "Proximity and Peership: Bases of Balance in Interpersonal Attraction," *American Journal of Sociology,* 72 (1967), 633–649. [26]

Pruitt, Dean G., and Melvin Kimmel. "Twenty Years of Experimental Gaming: Critique, Synthesis, and Suggestions for the Future," in Mark R. Rosenzweig and Lyman W. Porter (eds.), *Annual Review of Psychology.* Vol. 28. Palo Alto, Calif.: Annual Reviews, 1977, pp. 363–392. [28]

Rafaelsen, O. J., P. Bech, J. Christiansen, H. Christrup, J. Nyboe, and L. Rafaelsen. "Cannabis and Alcohol: Effects on Simulated Car Driving," *Science,* 179 (1978), 902–923. [14]

Rahe, Richard H. "The Pathway Between Subjects' Recent Life Changes and Their Near-Future Illness Reports: Representative Results and Methodological Issues," in Barbara S. Dohrenwend and Bruce P. Dohrenwend (eds.), *Stressful Life Events: Their Nature and Effects.* New York: Wiley, 1974. pp. 73–86. [21]

Rahe, Richard H., and E. Lind. "Psychosocial Factors and Sudden Cardiac Death: A Pilot Study," *Journal of Psychosomatic Research,* 15 (1971), 19–24. [21]

Ray, Oakley. *Drugs, Society, and Human Behavior.* 2nd ed. St. Louis: C. V. Mosby, 1978. [24]

Rehm, Lynn P., and Albert R. Marston. "Reduction of Social Anxiety through Modification of Self-Reinforcement," *Journal of Consulting and Clinical Psychology,*

32 (1968), 565–574. [21]

Rescorla, Robert A. "Pavlovian Conditioning and Its Proper Control Procedures," *Psychological Review,* 74:1 (1967), 71–80. [4]

Rescorla, Robert A., and Richard L. Solomon. "Two Process Learning Theory: Relationships Between Pavlovian Conditioning and Instrumental Learning," *Psychological Review,* 74:3 (1967), 151–182. [4]

Resnick, R. B., R. S. Kestenbaum, and L. K. Schwartz. "Acute Systemic Effects of Cocaine in Man: A Controlled Study by Intranasal and Intravenous Routes of Administration," *Science,* 195 (1977), 696–698. [14]

Rheingold, Harriet L., and Carol O. Eckerman. "Fear of the Stranger: A Critical Examination," in Hayne W. Reese (ed.), *Advances in Child Development and Behavior.* Vol. 8. New York: Academic Press, 1973. [2]

Rheingold, Harriet L., and Carol O. Eckerman. "The Infant Separates Himself from His Mother," *Science,* 168 (1970), 78–83. [10]

Rhine, Joseph B. "Telepathy and Other Untestable Hypotheses," *Journal of Parapsychology,* 38:1 (June 1974), 137–153. [13]

Rice, Ruth D. "Premature Infants Respond to Sensory Stimulation," *APA Monitor,* November 1975. [7]

Richards, Martin, Ken Richardson, and Davis Spears. "Conclusion: Intelligence and Society," in Ken Richardson, Davis Spears, and Martin Richards (eds.), *Race and Intelligence.* Baltimore: Penguin, 1972. [20]

Richardson, L. F. *Statistics of Deadly Quarrels.* Pittsburgh: Boxwood, 1960. [28]

Riesen, A. H. "The Development of Visual Perception in Man and Chimpanzee," *Science,* 106 (1947), 107–108. [13]

Rodin, Judith, and Ellen Langer. "Long-Term Effects of a Control-Relevant Intervention with the Institutionalized Aged," *Journal of Personality and Social Psychology,* 35 (1977), 897–902. [21]

Roffwarg, Howard P., Joseph N. Muzio, and William C. Dement. "Ontogenetic Development of the Human Sleep-Dream Cycle," *Science,* 152 (1966), 604–619. [14]

Rogers, Carl R. "A Theory of Personality," in Salvatore Maddi (ed.), *Perspectives on Personality.* Boston: Little, Brown, 1971. [19]

Rosch, E. "On the Internal Structure of Perceptual and Semantic Categories," in T. E. Moore (ed.), *Cognitive Development and the Acquisition of Language.* New York: Academic Press, 1973, pp. 111–144. [9]

Rosenhan, D. L. "On Being Sane in Insane Places," *Science,* 179 (January 1973), 250–258. [22, 23]

Rosenhan, D. L., Bill Underwood, and Bert Moore. "Affect Moderates Self-Gratification and Altruism," *Journal of Personality and Social Psychology,* 30:4 (October 1974), 546–552. [28]

Rosenthal, David, Paul H. Wender, Seymour Kety, J. Welner, and Fini Schulsinger. "The Adopted-Away Offspring-of Schizophrenics," *American Journal of Psychiatry,* 128:3 (1971), 307–311. [23]

Rosenthal, Robert. *Experimenter Effects in Behavioral Research.* New York: Appleton-Century-Crofts, 1966. [2]

Rosenzweig, Mark R., Edward L. Bennett, and Marian Cleeves Diamond. "Brain Changes in Response to Experience," *Scientific American,* 226 (1972), 22–29. [7]

Ross, Lee, Günter Bierbrauer, and Susan Hoffman. "The Role of Attribution Processes in Conformity and Dissent: Revisiting the Asch Situation," *American Psychologist,* 31:2 (February 1976), 148–157. [27]

Rowan, William. *The Riddle of Migration.* Baltimore: Williams & Wilkins, 1931. [3]

Rozin, Paul. "Specific Aversions and Neophobia Resulting from Vitamin Deficiency or Poisoning in Half-Wild and Domestic Rats," *Journal of Comparative and Physiological Psychology,* 66:1 (1968), 82–88. [16]

———. "The Significance of Learning Mechanisms in Food Selection: Some Biology, Psychology, and Sociology of Science," in L. M. Barker, M. R. Best, and M. Domjan (eds.), *Learning Mechanisms in Food Selection.* Waco, Tex.: Baylor University Press, 1977. [16]

Rubin, H. B. and Donald E. Henson. "Voluntary Enhancement of Penile Erection," *Bulletin of the Psychonomic Society,* 6:2 (1975), 158–160. [17]

Rubin, Zick. "Measurement of Romantic Love," *Journal of Personality and Social Psychology,* 16 (1970), 265–273. [26]

Rule, Brendan Gail, and Andrew R. Nesdale. "Emotional Arousal and Aggressive Behavior," *Psychological Bulletin,* 83:5 (1976), 851–863. [28]

Rumbaugh, Duane M., Timothy V. Gill, and E. C. von Glasersfeld. "Reading and Sentence Completion by a Chimpanzee," *Science,* 182 (1963), 731–733. [9]

Russell, W. Ritchie, and P. W. Nathan. "Traumatic Amnesia," *Brain,* 69 (1946), 280–300. [5]

Russo, J. E., G. Krieser, and S. Miyashita. "An Effective Display of Unit Price Information," *Journal of Marketing,* 39 (1975), 11–19 [6]

Rynders, J. *Annual Report of the University of*

Minnesota Institute of Child Development, 1975. [7]

Sadalla, Edward K., and Stanley Loftness. "Emotional Images as Mediators in One-Trial Paired-Associate Learning," *Journal of Experimental Psychology,* 95:2 (1972), 295–298. [5]

Saegert, Susan, Walter C. Swap, and Robert B. Zajonc. "Exposure, Context, and Interpersonal Attraction," *Journal of Personality and Social Psychology,* 25 (1973), 234–242. [26]

Saghir, Marcel T., and Eli Robins. *Male and Female Homosexuality: A Comprehensive Investigation.* Baltimore: Williams & Wilkins, 1973. [17]

Salinger, J. D. *The Catcher in the Rye.* New York: New American Library, 1958. [8]

Salk, Lee. "Mothers' Heartbeat as an Imprinting Stimulus," *Transactions of the New York Academy of Science,* 24 (1962), 753–763. [2]

Samuel, A. L. "Some Studies in Machine Learning Using the Game of Checkers," *IBM Journal of Research and Development,* 3 (July 1959), 211–229. [6]

Samuel, William. "On Clarifying Some Interpretations of Social Comparison Theory," *Journal of Experimental Social Psychology,* 9 (1973), 450–465. [27]

Sarason, S. B., G. Mandler, and P. G. Craighill. "The Effect of Differential Instructions on Anxiety and Learning," *Journal of Abnormal and Social Psychology,* 47 (1952), 561–565. [4]

Sarbin, Theodore R., and William C. Coe. *Hypnosis: A Social Psychological Analysis of Influence Communication.* New York: Holt, Rinehart and Winston, 1972. [14]

Sarnoff, I. R., and Philip G. Zimbardo. "Anxiety, Fear, and Social Affiliation," *Journal of Abnormal and Social Psychology,* 62 (1961), 356–363. [27]

Sawatzky, H. L., and W. H. Lehn, "The Arctic Mirage and the Early North Atlantic," *Science,* 192 (June 25, 1976), 1300–1305. [13]

Scanlon, John, and J. J. Chisolm, Jr. "Fetal Effects of Lead Exposure," *Pediatrics,* 49 (1972), 145–146. [20]

Scarr, Sandra, and Richard A. Weinberg. "Attitudes, Interests and I.Q.," *Human Nature,* 1:4 (1978), 29–36. [10]

———. "IQ Test Performance of Black Children Adopted by White Families," *American Psychologist,* 3 (1976), 726–739. [20]

Scarr-Salapatek, Sandra. "Race, Social Class and IQ," *Science,* 174 (1971b), 1286–1295. [20]

———. "Unknowns in the IQ Equation," *Science,* 174 (1971a), 1223–1228. [20]

Schachtel, Ernest G. *Experimental Foundations of Rorschach's Test.* New York: Basic Books, 1966. [20]

Schachter, Stanley. *Emotion, Obesity, and Crime.* New York: Academic Press, 1971. [16]

———. *The Psychology of Affiliation.* Stanford, Calif.: Stanford University Press, 1959. [27]

———. "Some Extraordinary Facts About Obese Humans and Rats," *American Psychologist,* 26 (1970), 129–144. [16]

Schachter, Stanley, Ronald Goldman, and Andrew Gordon. "Effects of Fear, Food Deprivation and Obesity on Eating," *Journal of Personality and Social Psychology,* 10 (1968), 91–97. [16]

Schachter, Stanley, and Jerome Singer. "Cognitive, Social, and Physiological Determinants of Emotional State," *Psychological Review,* 69 (1962), 379–399. [15]

Schachter, Stanley, and Ladd Wheeler. "Epinephrine, Chlorpromazine, and Amusement," *Journal of Abnormal and Social Psychology,* 65 (1962), 121–128. [15]

Schaffer, H. R. "Some Issues for Research in the Study of Attachment Behaviors," in B. M. Foss (ed.), *Determinants of Infant Behavior.* Vol. 2. New York: Wiley, 1963. [10]

Schaie, K. Warner, and Gisela Labouvie-Vief. "Generational Versus Ontogenetic Components of Change in Adult Cognitive Behavior: A Fourteen-Year Cross-Sequential Study," *Developmental Psychology,* 10 (1974), 305–320. [8]

Scheerer, Martin. "Problem-Solving," *Scientific American,* 208:4 (April 1963), 118–128. [6]

Scheff, T. J. "Schizophrenia as Ideology," *Schizophrenia Bulletin,* No. 2 (1970), 15–19. [23]

Scherer, Klaus R., Ronald P. Abeles, and Claude S. Fischer. *Human Aggression and Conflict.* Englewood Cliffs, N.J.: Prentice-Hall, 1975. [28]

Schmale, Arthur. "Giving Up as a Final Common Pathway to Changes in Health," *Advances in Psychosomatic Medicine,* 8 (1972). [15]

Schmeck, Harold M., Jr. "Wives' Emotions Linked to Cancer," *The New York Times,* May 11, 1974. [1]

Schuckman, H., and W. S. Battersby. "Frequency Specific Mechanisms in Learning, I: Occipital Activity During Sensory Preconditioning," *Electroencephalography and Clinical Neurophysiology,* 18 (1965), 44–55. [5]

Schultes, R. E. *Hallucinogenic Plants.* New York: Golden Press, 1976. [14]

Schuyler, D. *The Depressive Spectrum.* New York: Jason Aronson, 1975. [23]

Scott, J. P. "Critical Periods in Behavioral Development," *Science,* 138 (November 30, 1962), 949–958. [3]

Scott, J. P., J. M. Stewart, and V. J. De-Ghett. "Critical Periods in the Organization of Systems," *Developmental Psychobiology,* 7:6 (1974), 489–513. [7, 27]

Searle, Lloyd V. "The Organization of Heredity: Maze-Brightness and Maze-Dullness," *Genetic Psychology Monographs,* 39 (1949), 279–325. [3]

Sears, R. R., L. Rau, and R. Alpert. *Identification and Child Rearing.* Stanford, Calif.: Stanford University Press, 1965. [10]

Seay, B. M., E. W. Hansen, and Harry F. Harlow. "Mother-Infant Separation in Monkeys," *Journal of Child Psychology and Psychiatry,* 3 (1962), 123–132. [10]

Seay, B. M., and Harry F. Harlow. "Maternal Separation in the Rhesus Monkey," *Journal of Nervous and Mental Disease,* 140 (1965), 434–441. [10]

Segall, Marshall H., Donald T. Campbell, and Melville J. Herskovits. *The Influence of Culture on Visual Perception.* Indianapolis: Bobbs-Merrill, 1966. [13]

Selfridge, Oliver G. "Pandemonium: A Paradigm for Learning," in *Symposium on the Mechanization of Thought Processes.* London: HM Stationery Office, 1959. [13]

Seligman, Martin E. P. *Helplessness: On Depression, Development and Death.* San Francisco: Freeman, 1975. [6, 23]

———. "Learned Helplessness and Depression in Animals and Men," *University Programs Modular Studies.* Morristown, N.J.: General Learning Press, 1976. [23]

Selman, R. L. "Toward a Structural Analysis of Developing Interpersonal Relations Concepts," in A. Pick (ed.), *Minnesota Symposia on Child Psychology.* Vol. 10. Minneapolis: University of Minnesota, 1976. [10]

Selye, Hans. "Stress: It's a G.A.S." *Psychology Today,* 3:4 (September 1969), 24–25, 56. [15]

———. *The Stress of Life.* New York: McGraw-Hill, 1956. [15, 21]

———. *Stress Without Distress.* Philadelphia: Lippincott, 1974. [15]

Selye, Hans, and Laurence Cherry. "On the Real Benefits of Eustress," *Psychology Today,* March 1978, 60–63, 69–70. [15]

Senden, Marius von. *Space and Sight: The Perception of Space and Shape in the Congenitally Blind Before and After Operation.* Peter Heath (tr.). New York: Free Press, 1960. [13]

Sheatsley, Paul B., and Jacob J. Feldman. "The Assassination of President Kennedy: A Preliminary Report on Public Reactions and Behavior," *Public Opinion Quarterly,* 28:2 (1964), 189–215. [27]

Sheehy, Gail. *Passages.* New York: Dutton, 1976. [21]

Sherif, Muzafer, O. J. Harvey, B. J. White, W. R. Hood, and **C. W. Sherif.** *Intergroup Conflict and Cooperation: The Robber's Cave Experiment.* Norman: University of Oklahoma Press, 1961. [25]

Shirley, Mary M. *The First Two Years.* Institute of Child Welfare Monograph No. 7. Minneapolis: University of Minnesota Press, 1933. [7]

Siegel, Ronald K. "Hallucinations," *Scientific American,* 237:4 (October 1977), 132–140. [14]

Simon, Charles W., and **William H. Emmons.** "Responses to Material Presented During Various Levels of Sleep," *Journal of Experimental Psychology,* 51 (1956), 89–97. [2]

Siqueland, Einar R., and **Lewis P. Lipsitt.** "Conditioned Head-Turning in Human Newborns," *Journal of Experimental Child Psychology,* 3 (1966), 356–376. [8]

Sistrunk Frank, and **John W. McDavid.** "Sex Variables in Conforming Behavior," *Journal of Personality and Social Psychology,* 17 (1971), 200–207. [25]

Skinner, B. F. *Behavior of Organisms: An Experimental Analysis.* New York: Appleton-Century-Crofts, 1938. [4]

———. *Beyond Freedom and Dignity.* New York: Knopf, 1971. [1, 19]

———. *Cumulative Record.* New York: Appleton-Century-Crofts, 1961. [4]

———. *Science and Human Behavior.* New York: Free Press, 1967. [24]

———. "The Steep and Thorny Road to a Science of Behavior," *American Psychologist,* 30 (1975), 42–49. [19]

———. "Superstitious Behavior in the Pigeon," *Journal of Experimental Psychology,* 38 (1948), 168–172. [4]

———. *Walden Two* (1949). New York: Macmillan, 1968. [1, 19, 24]

Skodak, Marie, and **Harold M. Skeels.** "A Final Follow-Up of One Hundred Adopted Children," *Journal of Genetic Psychology,* 75 (1949), 85–125. [20]

Slaby, R. G., and **K. S. Frey.** "Development of Gender Constancy and Selective Attention to Same-Sex Models," *Child Development,* 46 (1975), 849–856. [10]

Slater, Eliot. "A Review of Earlier Evidence on Genetic Factors in Schizophrenia," in David Rosenthal and Seymour S. Kety (eds.), *The Transmission of Schizophrenia.* Elmsford, N.Y.: Pergamon, 1968. [23]

Sloane, R. Bruce, Fred R. Staples, Allan H. Cristol, Neil J. Yorkston, and **Katherine Whipple.** "Short-Term Analytically Oriented Psychotherapy Versus Behavior Therapy," *American Journal of Psychiatry,* 132:4 (April 1975), 373–377. [24]

Slobin, Dan I. "Children and Language: They Learn the Same Way All Around the World," *Psychology Today,* 6 (July 1972), 71–74+. [9]

Slovic, Paul, Baruch Fischhoff, and **Sarah Lichtenstein.** "Behavioral Decision Theory," in Mark R. Rosenzweig and Lyman W. Porter (eds.), *Annual Review of Psychology.* Vol. 28. Palo Alto, Calif.: Annual Reviews, 1977, pp. 1–39. [6]

Slovic, Paul, H. Kunreuther, and **Gilbert F. White.** "Decision Processes, Rationality and Adjustment to Natural Hazards," in Gilbert F. White (ed.), *Natural Hazards, Local, National and Global.* New York: Oxford University Press, 1974, pp. 187–205. [6]

Smith, A., and **O. Sugar.** "Development of Above-Normal Language and Intelligence Twenty-One Years After Left Hemispherectomy," *Neurology,* 25 (1975), 813–818. [9]

Smith, Mary Lee, and **Gene V. Glass.** "Meta-Analysis of Psychotherapy Outcome Studies," *American Psychologist,* 32 (1977), 752–760. [24]

Smith, S., and **I. Myers.** "Stimulation Seeking During Sensory Deprivation," *Perceptual and Motor Skills,* 23 (1966), 1151–1163. [16]

Snow, C. P. "Either-Or," *Progressive,* 25:2 (1961), 24–25. [27]

Snyder, Frederick. "The Phenomenology of Dreaming," in Leo Madow and Laurence H. Snow (eds.), *The Psychodynamic Implications of the Physiological Studies on Dreams.* Springfield, Ill.: Charles C Thomas, 1970. [14]

———. "Sleep and Dreaming: Progress in the New Biology of Dreaming," *American Journal of Psychiatry,* 122 (1965), 377–391. [14]

Snyder, Mark, and **Thomas C. Monson.** "Persons, Situations, and the Control of Social Behavior," *Journal of Personality and Social Psychology,* 32:4 (1975), 637–644. [26]

Snyder, Melvin L., Walter G. Stephan, and **David Rosenfield.** "Egotism and Attribution," *Journal of Personality and Social Psychology,* 33:4 (1976), 435–441. [26]

Solomon, Richard L., and **John D. Corbit.** "An Opponent-Process Theory of Motivation," *Psychological Review,* 81:2 (1974), 119–145. [16]

Sowell, Thomas. "New Light on Black I.Q.," *The New York Times Magazine,* March 27, 1977, pp. 56–62. [20]

Spence, Janet Taylor, and **Robert Louis Helmreich.** *Masculinity and Femininity: Their Psychological Dimensions, Correlates, and Antecedents.* Austin: University of Texas Press, 1978. [1]

Sperling, George. "The Information Available in Brief Visual Presentation," *Psychological Monographs,* 74 (1960), Whole No. 498. [5]

Sperry, Roger W. "Bridging Science and Values: A Unifying View of Mind and Brain," *American Psychologist,* 32:4 (April 1977), 237–245. [14]

———. "Changing Concepts of Consciousness and Free Will," *Perspectives in Biology and Medicine,* 20:1 (Autumn 1976), 9–19. [14]

———. "The Great Cerebral Commissure," *Scientific American,* January 1964. [11]

———. "A Modified Concept of Consciousness," *Psychological Review,* 76 (1969), 532–536. [14]

———. "Perception in the Absence of the Neocortical Commissures," in David A. Hamburg et al. (eds.), *Perception and Its Disorders.* Association for Research in Nervous and Mental Disease Research Publications Series, Vol. 48. New York: Raven Press, 1970. [14]

Sperry, R. W., N. Miner, and **R. E. Myers.** "Visual Pattern Perception Following Subpial Slicing and Tantalum Wire Implantations in the Visual Cortex," *Journal of Comparative and Physiological Psychology,* 48 (1955), 50–58. [5]

Spirduso, W. W. "Reaction and Movement Time as a Function of Age and Physical-Activity Level," *Journal of Gerontology,* 30:4 (1975), 435–440. [8]

Spitzer, Robert L. "On Pseudoscience in Science, Logic in Remission, and Psychiatric Diagnosis: A Critique of D. L. Rosenhan's 'On Being Sane in Insane Places,'" *Journal of Abnormal Psychology,* 84 (1975), 442–452. [22]

Staats, Arthur W. "Verbal and Instrumental Response-Hierarchies and Their Relation to Problem-Solving," *American Journal of Psychology,* 70 (1957), 442–446. [6]

Stanley, Julian C. "Test Better Finder of Great Math Talent Than Teachers Are," *American Psychologist,* 31:4 (April 1976), 313–314. [20]

Staub, Ervin. "Instigation to Goodness: The Role of Social Norms and Interpersonal Influence," *Journal of Social Issues,* 28:3 (1972), 131–150. [28]

Stayton, Donelda J., and **Mary D. Salter Ainsworth.** "Individual Differences in Infant Responses to Brief Everyday Separations as Related to Other Infant and Maternal Behaviors," *Developmental Psychology,* 9 (1973), 226–235. [10]

Stayton, Donelda J., Mary D. Salter Ainsworth, and **Mary B. Main.** "Development of Separation Behavior in the First Year of Life: Protest, Following, and Greeting," *Developmental Psychology,* 9 (1973), 213–225. [10]

Stefanson, Vilhjalmur. *Unsolved Mysteries of the Arctic.* New York: Macmillan, 1938. [16]

Steiner, Jacob E. "The Gustofacial Response: Observation on Normal and An-encephalic Newborn Infants," in James F. Bosma (ed.), *Oral Sensation and Perception: Fourth Symposium on Development in the Fetus and Infant.* DHEW Pub. No. 73–546. Bethesda, Md.: National Institutes of Health, 1973, pp. 254–272. [7]

Stern, William. *The Psychological Methods of Testing Intelligence.* Guy M. Whipple (tr.). Baltimore: Warwick & York, 1914. [20]

Stevens, C. F. *Neurophysiology: A Primer.* New York: Wiley, 1966. [11]

Stevens, S. S. "On the Psychophysical Law," *Psychological Review,* 64 (1957), 153–181. [12]

——. "The Surprising Simplicity of Sensory Metrics," *American Psychologist,* 17 (1962), 29–39. [12]

Storms, Michael D. "Videotape and the Attribution Process: Reversing Actors' and Observers' Points of View," *Journal of Personality and Social Psychology,* 27 (1973), 167–175. [26]

Stratton, G. M. "Some Preliminary Experiments on Vision Without Inversion of the Retinal Image," *Psychological Review,* 3 (1896), 611–617. [13]

Strauss, M. E., W. C. Foureman, and **S. D. Parwatikar.** "Schizophrenics' Size Estimations of Thematic Stimuli," *Journal of Abnormal Psychology,* 83:2 (1974), 117–123. [22]

Sundberg, Norman Dale, Leona E. Tyler, and **Julian R. Taplin.** *Clinical Psychology: Expanding Horizons.* 2nd ed. New York: Appleton-Century-Crofts, 1973. [24]

Suomi, Stephan J., and **Harry F. Harlow.** "Depressive Behavior in Young Monkeys Subjected to Vertical Chamber Confinement," *Journal of Comparative and Physiological Psychology,* 80 (1972), 11–18. [10]

Sutcliffe, J. P. "'Credulous' and 'Skeptical' Views of Hypnotic Phenomena: Experiments in Esthesia, Hallucination, and Delusion," *Journal of Abnormal and Social Psychology,* 62 (1961), 189–200. [2]

Szasz, Thomas S. *The Myth of Mental Illness: Foundations of a Theory of Personal Conduct.* New York: Harper & Row, 1961. [22]

Tanzer, Deborah. "Natural Childbirth: Pain or Peak Experience?" *Psychology Today,* 69 (October 1968), 16–21. [19]

Targ, Russell, and **Harold Puthoff.** "Information Transmission Under Conditions of Sensory Shielding," *Nature,* 251 (October 18, 1974), 602–607. [13]

Tart, Charles T. "Marijuana Intoxication: Common Experiences," *Nature,* 226 (1970), 701–704. [14]

——. *States of Consciousness.* New York: Dutton, 1975. [14]

Tavris, Carol, and **Carole Offir.** *The Longest War: Sex Differences in Perspective.* New York: Harcourt Brace Jovanovich, 1977. [17]

Teitelbaum, Philip. "The Encephalization of Hunger," in E. Stellar and J. M. Sprague (eds.), *Progress in Physiological Psychology.* Vol. 4. New York: Academic Press, 1971. [11]

Teitelbaum, Philip, and **Alan N. Epstein.** "The Lateral Hypothalamic Syndrome: Recovery of Feeding and Drinking After Lateral Hypothalamic Lesions," *Psychological Review,* 69 (1962), 74–90. [11]

Terman, Lewis M. *The Measurement of Intelligence.* Boston: Houghton Mifflin, 1916. [20]

Terman, Lewis M., and **Maud A. Merrill.** *Stanford-Binet Intelligence Scale: Manual for the Third Revision, Form L-M.* Boston: Houghton Mifflin, 1973. [20]

Terrace, H. S. "Errorless Transfer of a Discrimination Across Two Continua," *Journal of the Experimental Analysis of Behavior,* 6 (1963), 223–232. [4]

Theorell, Töres. "Life Events Before and After the Onset of a Premature Myocardial Infarction," in Barbara S. Dohrenwend and Bruce P. Dohrenwend (eds.), *Stressful Life Events: Their Nature and Effects.* New York: Wiley, 1974, pp. 101–117. [21]

Thistlethwaite, Donald L. "Impact of Disruptive External Events on Student Attitudes," *Journal of Personality and Social Psychology,* 30:2 (1974), 228–242. [25]

Thompson, R. F., K. S. Mayers, R. T. Robertson, and **C. J. Patterson.** "Number Coding in Association Cortex of Cat," *Science,* 168 (1970), 271–273. [11]

Thompson, Spencer K. "Gender Labels and Early Sex Role Development," *Child Development,* 46 (1975), 339–347. [10]

Thoresen, Carl E., and **Michael J. Mahoney.** *Behavioral Self-Control.* New York: Holt, Rinehart and Winston, 1974. [21]

Thorndike, E. L. *Animal Intelligence.* New York: Macmillan, 1911. [6]

——. "Animal Intelligence: An Experimental Study of the Associative Processes in Animals," *Psychological Review Monograph Supplement,* 2:8 (1898). [4]

Thorpe, W. H. *Bird Song.* London: Cambridge University Press, 1961. [3]

Thurstone, Louis L. *A Factorial Study of Perception.* Chicago: University of Chicago Press, 1944. [13]

Tinbergen, Niko. *The Study of Instinct.* New York: Oxford University Press, 1951. [3]

Tollefson, D. J. "The Relationship Between the Occurrence of Fractures and Life Crisis Events." Master of Nursing thesis, University of Washington, Seattle, 1972. [21]

Tolman, Edward C. "Cognitive Maps in Rats and Men," *Psychological Review,* 55 (1948), 189–208. [6]

——. *Purposive Behavior in Animals and Men.* New York: Appleton-Century, 1932. [4, 16]

Tolman, Edward C., and **C. H. Honzik.** "Introduction and Removal of Reward and Maze Performance in Rats," *University of California Publications in Psychology,* 4 (1930), 257–275. [4]

Tonkova-Yampol'skaya, R. V. "Development of Speech Intonation in Infants During the First Two Years of Life," in C. A. Ferguson and D. I. Slobin (eds.), *Studies of Child Language Development.* New York: Holt, Rinehart and Winston, 1973, pp. 128–138. [9]

Trask, C. H., and **E. M. Cree.** "Oximeter Studies on Patients with Chronic Obstructive Emphysema, Awake and During Sleep," *New England Journal of Medicine,* 266 (1962), 639–642. [14]

Trehub, Sandra E. "Infants' Sensitivity to Vowel and Tonal Contrast," *Developmental Psychology,* 9:1 (1973), 91–96. [7]

Trehub, Sandra E., and **M. Sam Rabinovitch.** "Auditory-Linguistic Sensitivity in Early Infancy," *Developmental Psychology,* 6:1 (1972), 74–77. [7]

Treisman, A. M. "Contextual Cues in Selective Listening," *Quarterly Journal of Experimental Psychology,* 12 (1960), 242–248. [5]

——. "Verbal Cues, Language and Meaning in Selective Attention," *American Journal of Psychology,* 77 (1964), 206–219. [5]

Tresemer, David. "Fear of Success: Popular, but Unproven," *Psychology Today,* 7 (March 1974), 82–85. [16]

Truex, R. C., and **M. B. Carpenter.** *Human Neuroanatomy.* Baltimore: Williams & Wilkins, 1969. [11]

Tryon, R. C. "Genetic Differences in Maze Learning in Rats," *Thirty-Ninth Yearbook, National Society for the Study of Education.* Part I. Bloomington, Ill.: Public School Publishing Co., 1940c, pp. 111–119. [3]

——. "Studies in Individual Differences in Maze Ability, VII: The Specific Components of Maze Ability, and a General Theory of Psychological Components," *Journal of Comparative Psychology,* 30 (1940a), 283–335. [3]

——. "Studies in Individual Differences in Maze Ability VIII: Prediction Validity of the Psychological Components of Maze Ability," *Journal of Comparative Psychology,* 30 (1940b), 535–582. [3]

Tulving, Endel. "Episodic and Semantic Memory," in Endel Tulving and W. Donaldson (eds.), *Organization of Memory.* New York: Academic Press, 1972. [6]

Uexküll, Jakob J., von. *Umwelt und Innenwelt*

der Tiere. 2nd ed. Berlin: Springer-Verlag, 1921. [3]

Ullman, Leonard P., and **Leonard Krasner.** A Psychological Approach to Abnormal Behavior. 2nd ed. Englewood Cliffs, N.J.: Prentice-Hall, 1975. [23]

Ullman, M. "Dreaming, Life-Style, and Physiology: A Comment on Adler's View of the Dream," Journal of Individual Psychology, 18 (1962), 18–25. [14]

Valenstein, Elliot S. Brain Control. New York: Wiley Interscience, 1973. [11, 24]

———. "Science-Fiction Fantasy and the Brain," Psychology Today, 12:2 (February 1978), 28–39. [23]

Valentine, C. W. Experimental Psychology of Beauty. New York: Dodge, 1913. [7]

Vance, E. B., and **N. W. Wagner.** "Written Descriptions of Orgasm: A Study of Sex Differences," Archives of Sexual Behavior, 5 (1976), 87–98. [17]

Vassos, J. Phobia. New York: Covici and Friede, 1931.

Vinokur, Amiram, and **Melvin L. Selzer.** "Desirable Versus Undesirable Life Events: Their Relationship to Stress and Mental Distress," Journal of Personality and Social Psychology, 32:2 (1975), 329–337. [21]

Vitz, Paul C. "Affect as a Function of Stimulus Variation," Journal of Experimental Psychology, 71 (1966), 74–79. [16]

Von Frisch, Karl. Bees: Their Vision, Chemical Senses, and Language. Ithaca, N.Y.: Cornell University Press, 1950. [3]

———. The Dance Language and Orientation of Bees. L. E. Chadwick (tr.). Cambridge, Mass.: Belknap Press of Harvard University Press, 1967. [3, 9]

Von Holst, Erich, and **Ursula von Saint Paul.** "Electrically Controlled Behavior," Scientific American, 206 (March 1962), 50–59. [3]

Vygotsky, Lev S. Thought and Language. Cambridge, Mass.: M.I.T. Press, 1962. [8]

Waddington, C. H. The Strategy of the Genes. New York: Macmillan, 1957. [7]

Wade, Nicholas. "Sociobiology: Troubled Birth for New Discipline," Science, 191 (March 19, 1976), 1151–1155. [3]

Wagner, Richard V. "Complementary Needs, Role Expectations, Interpersonal Attraction, and the Stability of Working Relationships," Journal of Personality and Social Psychology, 32:1 (July 1975), 116–124. [26]

Wald, George. "Molecular Basis of Visual Excitation," Science, 162 (1968), 230–239. [12]

Wallace, Robert K., and **Herbert Benson.**

"The Physiology of Meditation," Scientific American, 226 (February 1972), 84–90. [14]

Wallace, Wimburn L. Review of the Scholastic Aptitude Test in Oscar K. Buros (ed.), The Seventh Mental Measurements Yearbook, 1972, pp. 648–650. [20]

Walster, Elaine, and **Ellen Berscheid.** "Adrenaline Makes the Heart Grow Fonder," Psychology Today, 5:1 (June 1971), 47–50, 62. [26]

Walster, Elaine, and **Leon Festinger.** "The Effectiveness of 'Overheard' Persuasive Communications," Journal of Abnormal and Social Psychology, 65 (1962), 395–402. [25]

Warrington, E. K., and **H. I. Sanders.** "The Fate of Old Memories," Quarterly Journal of Experimental Psychology, 23 (1971), 432–442. [8]

Washburn, S. L. "Human Behavior and the Behavior of Other Animals," American Psychologist, 33 (May 1978), 405–418. [3]

Wason, Peter C., and **Philip N. Johnson-Laird.** Psychology of Reasoning: Structure and Content. Cambridge, Mass.: Harvard University Press, 1972. [8]

Waterman, Alan S., Patricia S. Geary, and **Caroline K. Waterman.** "Longitudinal Study of Changes in Ego-Identity States from the Freshman to the Senior Year at College," Developmental Psychology, 10 (1974), 387–392. [10]

Watson, David, and **Roland Tharp.** Self-Directed Behavior: Self-Modification for Personal Adjustment. Monterey, Calif.: Brooks/Cole, 1972. [21]

Watson, John B. Behaviorism (1924). New York: Norton, 1970. [1, 3, 4]

Watson, John B., and **Rosalie Rayner.** "Conditioning Emotional Reactions," Journal of Experimental Psychology, 3 (1920), 1–14. [4, 23]

Watson, John S. "Smiling, Cooing, and 'the Game,'" Merrill-Palmer Quarterly of Behavior and Development, 18 (1972), 323–339. [8]

Watson, Robert I. The Great Psychologists: From Aristotle to Freud. Philadelphia: Lippincott, 1963. [1]

Webb, Wilse B. Sleep: The Gentle Tyrant. Englewood Cliffs, N.J.: Prentice-Hall, 1975. [14]

Weber, D. J., and **J. Castleman.** "The Time It Takes to Imagine," Perception and Psychophysics, 8 (1970), 165–168. [5]

Weber, Ernst H. De Pulsu, Resorptione, Auditu et Tactu. Leipzig: Köhler, 1834. [12]

Wechsler, David. The Measurement and Appraisal of Adult Intelligence. 14th ed. Baltimore: Williams & Wilkins, 1958. [20]

———. Wechsler Adult Intelligence Scale Manual. New York: Psychological Corporation, 1955. [20

Weil, Andrew T. "Parapsychology: Andrew

Weil's Search for the True Geller," PsychologyToday, 8:1 (June 1974), 45–50. [13]

———. "Parapsychology: Andrew Weil's Search for the True Geller—The Letdown," Psychology Today, 8:2 (July 1974), 74–82. [13]

Weil, Andrew T., N. Zinberg, and **J. M. Nelsen.** "Clinical and Psychological Effects of Marijuana in Man," Science, 162 (1968), 1234–1242. [14]

Weiner, Bernard. Theories of Motivation: From Mechanism to Cognition. Chicago: Markham, 1972. [16]

Weiss, Jay M. "Psychological Factors in Stress and Disease," Scientific American, 226 (1972), 104–113. [15]

Weiss, L., and **R. V. Hall.** "Modification of Cigarette Smoking Through Avoidance of Punishment," in R. V. Hall (ed.), Managing Behavior. Part II. Merriam, Kansas: H and H Enterprises, 1971, pp. 54–55. [21]

Weizenbaum, Joseph. "ELIZA—A Computer Program for the Study of Natural Language Between Man and Machine," Communications of the Association for Computing Machinery, 9 (1966), 36–45. [6]

Werner, Arnold. "Sexual Dysfunction in College Men and Women," American Journal of Psychiatry, 132 (1975), 164–168. [17]

Wertheimer, M. "Psychomotor Coordination of Auditory and Visual Space at Birth," Science, 134 (1961), 1692. [7]

Wertheimer, Max. "Untersuchungen zur Lehre von der Gestalt," Psychologisches Forschung, 4 (1923), 301–350. [13]

White, B. L. "An Experimental Approach to the Effects of Experience on Early Human Behavior," in J. P. Hill (ed.), Minnesota Symposia on Child Psychology. Vol. 1. Minneapolis: University of Minnesota Press, 1967, pp. 201–226. [7]

———. Human Infants: Experience and Psychological Development. Englewood Cliffs, N.J.: Prentice-Hall, 1971. [7]

White, Benjamin W., et al. "Seeing with the Skin," Perception and Psychophysics, 7 (1970), 23–27. [12]

White, R. "Motivation Reconsidered: The Concept of Competence," Psychological Review, 66 (1959), 297–333. [10]

White, Robert W. The Enterprise of Living: Growth and Organization in Personality. New York: Holt, Rinehart and Winston, 1972. [26]

Whorf, Benjamin Lee. "Science and Linguistics," in John B. Carroll (ed.), Language, Thought, and Reality: Selected Writings of Benjamin Lee Whorf. Cambridge, Mass.: M.I.T. Press, 1956, pp. 207–219. [9]

Wichman, H. "Effects of Isolation and Communication in a Two-Person Game," Journal of Personality and Social Psychology, 16 (1970), 114–120. [28]

Wicker, Allan W. "An Examination of the 'Other Variables' Explanation of Attitude-Behavior Inconsistency," *Journal of Personality and Social Psychology,* 19:1 (1971), 18–30. [25]

Williams, P. L., and **R. Warwick.** *Functional Neuroanatomy of Man.* Philadelphia: Saunders, 1975. [11]

Wilson, Edward O. "Human Decency Is Animal," *The New York Times Magazine,* October 12, 1975b, pp. 38–49. [3]

———. *Sociobiology: The New Synthesis.* Cambridge, Mass.: Belknap Press of Harvard University Press, 1975a. [3, 28]

Winch, Robert F. *Mate Selection: A Study of Complementary Needs.* New York: Harper & Row, 1958. [26]

Winick, M., and **A. Noble.** "Cellular Response in Rats During Malnutrition at Various Ages," *Journal of Nutrition,* 89 (1966), 300–306. [7]

Winograd, Terry. "Artificial Intelligence—When Will Computers Understand People?" *Psychology Today,* 7:12 (May 1974), 73–79. [6]

———. "Understanding Natural Language," *Cognitive Psychology,* 3 (1972), 1–191. [6]

Wise, C. David, and **Larry Stein.** "Possible Etiology of Schizophrenia—Progressive Damage to Noradrenergic Reward System by 6-Hydroxydopamine," *Science,* 171:3975 (1971), 1032–1036. [23]

———. "Dopamine-B-Hydroxylase Deficits in the Brains of Schizophrenic Patients," *Science,* 181 (1973), 344–347. [23]

Wittgenstein, Ludwig. *Tractatus Logico-Philosophicus.* 2nd ed. New York: Humanities Press, 1963. [9]

Wold, D. A. "The Adjustment of Siblings to Childhood Leukemia." Medical thesis, University of Washington, Seattle, 1968. [21]

Wolfe, John B. "Effectiveness of Token-Rewards for Chimpanzees," *Comparative Psychological Monographs,* 12 (1936), Whole No. 5. [4]

Wolff, Harold G., and **Stewart Wolff.** *Pain.* Springfield, Ill.: Charles C Thomas, 1948. [2]

Wolff, Peter H. "The Natural History of Crying and Other Vocalizations in Early Infancy," in B. M. Foss (ed.), *Determinants of Infant Behavior.* Vol. 4. London: Methuen, 1969, pp. 81–109. [9]

Wolff, Stewart, and **Harold G. Wolff.** *Human Gastric Function.* New York: Oxford University Press, 1947. [15]

Wolpe, Joseph, and **Stanley Rachman.** "Psychoanalytic Evidence: A Critique Based on Freud's Case of Little Hans," *Journal of Nervous and Mental Diseases,* 31 (1960), 134–147. [23]

Woolfolk, Robert L. "Psychophysiological Correlates of Meditation," *Archives of General Psychiatry,* 32 (October 1975), 1326–1333. [14]

Woolsey, C. N. "Organization of the Cortical Auditory System," in W. A. Rosenblith (ed.), *Sensory Communication.* New York: Wiley, 1961. [11]

Wortman, Camille B., and **Jack W. Brehm.** "Responses to Uncontrollable Outcomes: An Investigation of Resistance Theory and the Learned Helplessness Model," in Leonard Berkowitz (ed.), *Advances in Experimental Social Psychology.* Vol. 8. New York: Academic Press, 1975. [21]

Yerkes, Robert M., and **J. D. Dodson.** "The Relation of Strength of Stimulus to Rapidity of Habit Formation," *Journal of Comparative Neurology and Psychology,* 18 (1908), 459–482. [6]

Zajonc, Robert B. "Attitudinal Effects of Mere Exposure," *Journal of Personality and Social Psychology,* 9 (1968), 1–27. [26]

Zanna, Mark P., Charles A. Kiesler, and **P. A. Pilkonis.** "Positive and Negative Attitudinal Affect Established by Classical Conditioning," *Journal of Personality and Social Psychology,* 14 (1970), 321–328. [25]

Zelazo, Philip R., Nancy Ann Zelazo, and **Sarah Kolb.** "'Walking' in the Newborn," *Science,* 176:4032 (April 21, 1972), 314–315. [7]

Zilboorg, Gregory, and **George W. Henry.** *A History of Medical Psychology.* New York: Norton, 1941. [18, 23]

Zillman, Dolf. "Excitation Transfer in Communication-Mediated Aggressive Behavior," *Journal of Experimental Social Psychology,* 7 (1971), 419–434. [15]

Zimbardo, Philip G. "The Human Choice: Individuation, Reason, and Order Versus Deindividuation, Impulse, and Chaos," in W. J. Arnold and D. Levine (eds.), *Nebraska Symposium on Motivation: 1969.* Lincoln: University of Nebraska Press, 1970. [28]

———. *Shyness: What It Is, What to Do About It.* Reading, Mass.: Addison-Wesley, 1977. [21]

Zuckerman, Marvin. "The Search for High Sensation," *Psychology Today,* 11:9 (February 1978), 30–46, 96–99. [16]

Zuckerman, Miron, and **Ladd Wheeler.** "To Dispel Fantasies About the Fantasy-Based Measure of Fear of Success," *Psychological Bulletin,* 82:6 (1975), 932–946. [16]

GLOSSARY

The numbers after each entry refer to the pages of the text on which that term or concept is defined or discussed in detail or both.

INDEX OF NAMES

INDEX OF SUBJECTS

CREDITS AND ACKNOWLEDGMENTS

CHAPTER 1

2—Joan Menschenfreund;
4—After F. McKinney, "Fifty Years of Psychology," AMERICAN PSYCHOLOGIST, 31 (12), 834-842, Figure 1, © 1976 by the American Psychological Association. Reprinted by permission;
5—Duane Michaels;
7—James R. Smith;
8—"Fingerprint Landscape" (1950) © Saul Steinberg. Collection of the Artist;
11—(top left) John Running/Stock, Boston;
11—(top right) Neal Slavin;
11—(bottom) Frank Mayo;
12—Fred R. Conrad/NYT Pictures;
13—Peter B. Kaplan/Photo Researchers, Inc.;
14—Cary Wolinsky/Stock, Boston;
15—(top) Joel Meyerwitz;
15—(bottom) Mary Ellen Mark/Magnum;
16—Rene Burri/Magnum.

CHAPTER 2

20—Denley Karlson/Stock, Boston;
23—Ellen Pines/Woodfin Camp & Assoc.;
24—Adapted from A. C. Kinsey et al., SEXUAL BEHAVIOR IN THE HUMAN FEMALE. Philadelphia: Saunders, 1953, pp. 173-175;
26—Frank Mayo;
27—After W. Hudson, "Pictorial Depth Perception in Subcultural Groups in Africa," JOURNAL OF SOCIAL PSYCHOLOGY, 52, (1960), pp. 183-208;
28—Adapted from J. Kagan and H. Moss, BIRTH TO MATURITY, © 1962 by John Wiley and Sons, p. 267. Reprinted with permission;
32—After W.D. Fenz and S. Epstein, "Gradients of Physiological Arousal in Parachutists as a Function of an Approaching Jump," PSYCHOSOMATIC MEDICINE, 29 (1967), American Psychosomatic Society;
34—After M. Kramer, "Statistics of Mental Disorders in the U.S.: Current Status, Some Urgent Needs, and Suggested Solutions," JOURNAL OF THE ROYAL STATISTICAL SOCIETY, SERIES A, 132 (1969), Part 3, pp. 353-407;
38—Frank Mayo;
39—After R. Rosenthal, EXPERIMENTER EFFECTS IN BEHAVORIAL RESEARCH (Enlarged Ed.), 1976. Irvington Publishers, Inc., New York;
40—Bruce Cayard;
42—After H.G. Wolff and S. Wolf, PAIN, Fig. 1, p. 6, Charles C. Thomas Publishers, 1948. Frank Mayo, artist;
43—After Y. Brackbill, "Cumulative Effects of Continuous Stimulation on Arousal Level in Infants," CHILD DEVELOPMENT, 42 (1971) 17-26.

CHAPTER 3

50—ON THE UNDERGROUND by Daniel Quintero, 1972. Courtesy, Marlborough Gallery, Inc.;
53—Peter Southwick/Stock, Boston;
55—(top) Adapted from W.H. Thorpe, BIRD SONG, Cambridge University Press, 1961.
55—(bottom) Russ Kinne/Photo Researchers, Inc.;
56—(top) Edgar Moench/Photo Researchers, Inc.;
56—(bottom) Mitchell Campbell/Photo Researchers, Inc.;
57—John Dawson;
57—(bottom) After N. Tinbergen, THE STUDY OF INSTINCT, Oxford University Press;
58—After R.C. Tryon, "Genetic Differences in Maze Learning in Rats," THIRTY-NINTH YEARBOOK, NATIONAL SOCIETY FOR THE STUDY OF EDUCATION, Part 1, (1940) 111-119;
60—(top) Yva Momatiuk/Photo Researchers, Inc.;
60—(bottom) John Dawson;
61—(top) Thomas McAvoy/LIFE MAGAZINE, © TIME, INC.;
61—(bottom) John Dawson;
62—Thomas McAvoy/LIFE MAGAZINE, © TIME, INC.;
63—After E.H. Hess, IMPRINTING, © 1973 by Litton Educational Publishing, Inc. Reprinted by permission of Van Nostrand Co.;
64—Helen Csuickshank/National Audubon Society/Photo Researchers, Inc.;
66-67—G. Peress/Magnum.

CHAPTER 4

72—James R. Smith;
75—Elizabeth Weiland/Rapho/Photo Researchers, Inc.;
76—Kent Reno/Jeroboam;
77—(bottom) John Dawson;
78—After I. Pavlov, CONDITIONED REFLEXES (G.V. Antep, translator), Oxford University Press;
79—(bottom) Bruce Cayard;
81—After B. F. Skinner, "Superstitious Behavior in the Pigeon," JOURNAL OF EXPERIMENTAL PSYCHOLOGY, 38 (1948), 168-172, © 1948 by the American Psychological Association. Reprinted by permission. Bruce Cayard, artist;
82—(top) Sepp Seitz/Woodfin Camp and Associates;
82—(bottom) Frank Mayo;
83—John Dawson;
84—(top) John Dawson;
84—(bottom) Bruce Davidson/Magnum;
85—Alan Clifton/Black Star;
86—Alex Webb/Magnum;

92—After J.B. Wolfe, "Effectiveness of Token-Rewards for Chimpanzees," COMPARATIVE PSYCHOLOGICAL MONOGRAPHS, 12, no. 5, © 1936 Johns Hopkins University Press. Frank Mayo, artist;
94—Courtesy, The Travelers Insurance Co.;
95—Bruce Cayard;
96—After H.C. Blodgett, "The Effect of the Introduction of Reward Upon Maze Performance of Rats," UNIVERSITY OF CALIFORNIA PUBLICATION IN PSYCHOLOGY, 4:8 (1929), pp. 117-120.

CHAPTER 5

100—Arthur Tress;
103—After L. Carmichael, H.P. Hogan, and A.A. Walter, "An Experimental Study of the Effect of Language on the Reproduction of Visually Perceived Form," JOURNAL OF EXPERIMENTAL PSYCHOLOGY, 15 (1932), 73-86;
104—Bruce Cayard;
105—After D.E. Broadbent, PERCEPTION AND COMMUNICATION, Pergamon Press, Ltd. Frank Mayo, artist;
106—After A. M. Treisman, "Verbal Cues, Language and Meaning in Selective Attention," AMERICAN JOURNAL OF PSYCHOLOGY, 77, 206-219, © 1964 by the Board of Trustees of the University of Illinois. Frank Mayo, artist;
108—After L.R. Peterson and M.G. Peterson, "Short-term Retention of Experimental Verbal Items," JOURNAL OF EXPERIMENTAL PSYCHOLOGY, 58, 193-198, © 1959 by the American Psychological Association. Reprinted by permission;
112—After B. Murdok Jr. "The Serial Position Effect of Free Recall," JOURNAL OF EXPERIMENTAL PSYCHOLOGY, vol. 64, no. 5, fig. 1, © 1962 by the American Psychological Association, and Postman and L.W. Phillips, "Short-Term Temporal Changes in Free Recall," QUARTERLY JOURNAL OF EXPERIMENTAL PSYCHOLOGY, 17, (1965) pp. 132-138;
113—After H. Ebbinghaus, translated by H.A. Roger and C.E. Bussenius, MEMORY: A CONTRIBUTION TO EXPERIMENTAL PSYCHOLOGY, 1885;
114—After P. Lindsay and D. Norman, HUMAN INFORMATION PROCESSING: AN INTRODUCTION TO PSYCHOLOGY, © 1972 by Academic Press;
115—Bruce Cayard;
116-117—Frank Mayo;
118—(top) From Johannes Romberch, Congestorium Artificiose Memorie, Venice 1553;
118—(bottom) After L. Horowitz, A. Lampel, and R. Takanishi, "The Child's Memory for Unitized Scenes," JOURNAL OF EX-

PERIMENTAL CHILD PSYCHOLOGY, 8 (1969), pp. 375-388;
119—(top) Bruce Cayard;
119—(bottom) After J.G. Jenkins and K.M. Dallenbach, "Oblivescense During Sleep and Waking," AMERICAN JOURNAL OF PSYCHOLOGY, 35 (1924), 605-612.

CHAPTER 6
124—"Cinema" by George Segal, 1963. Courtesy, Albright-Knox Art Gallery, Buffalo, New York. Gift of Seymour H. Knox;
127—From THE MENTALITY OF APES by Wolfgang Kohler;
129—Adapted from E. de Bono, NEW THINK: The Use of Lateral Thinking in the Generation of New Ideas, © 1967, 1968 by Edward de Bono, Basic Books, Inc., Publishers, New York;
130—After K. Duncker, "On Problem Solving," translated by I.S. Lees in PSYCHOLOGICAL MONOGRAPHS, 58, (1945);
131—(top) After D. I. Krechevsky (David Krech), "Hypotheses in Rats," PSYCHOLOGICAL REVIEW, 39, (1932), 516-532;
131—(bottom) Frank Mayo;
132—Frank Mayo;
133—From A. C. Doyle, THE RETURN OF SHERLOCK HOLMES: THE ADVENTURE OF THE DANCING MAN, John Murray Ltd./Jonathan Cape Ltd;
134—Frank Mayo;
135—Frank Mayo;
136—(top) Frank Mayo;
136—(bottom) Adapted from A. S. Luchins and E. H. Luchins, RIGIDITY OF BEHAVIOR: A VARIATIONAL APPROACH TO THE EFFECT EINSTELLARY, University of Oregon Books, 1959, p. 109;
137—(top) Werner Kalber/Busco-Nester;
138—James R. Smith;
142—Bruce Cayard;
143—© 1970; United Feature Syndicate, Inc.;
144—(Bruce Cayard) After J. Weizenbaum, "Eliza—A Computer Program for the Study of Natural Language Between Man and Machine," COMMUNICATIONS OF THE ASSN. FOR COMPUTING MACHINERY, 9, pp. 36-45, © 1966, Association for Computing Machinery, Inc. Reprinted by permission;
145—Courtesy of Terry Winograd, from T. Winograd, "Artificial Intelligence: When Will Computers Understand People?" PSYCHOLOGY TODAY, May 1974;
146—(left) Gillian Theobald after E. De Bono, NEW THINK: THE USE OF LATERAL THINKING IN THE GENERATION OF NEW IDEAS, Basic Books, Inc. 1968: (right) Werner Kalber/Busco-Nestor.

CHAPTER 7
150—"Numbers in Color" by Jasper Johns, 1959, Albright-Knox Art Gallery, Buffalo, N.Y. Gift of Seymour H. Knox;
152—(left) The Bettmann Archive, Inc.;
152—(right) Springer/The Bettmann Archive, Inc.;
153—After M. Shirley, "The First Two Years," INSTITUTE OF CHILD WELFARE MONOGRAPH #7, © 1933 by Uni-

versity of Minnesota Press, Minneapolis. Frank Mayo, artist;
155—Neal Slavin;
156—Marcia Keegan;
157—After L. Gardner, "Deprivation Dwarfism," SCIENTIFIC AMERICAN (July 1972); Frank Mayo, artist;
158—(top) Courtesy, Childcraft Inc.;
158—(bottom) From C. H. Waddington, THE STRATEGY OF THE GENES, reprinted by permission of George Allen & Unwin, London;
160—(photo 1) Cohen, N. M., Davidson, R. G., "Human Cytogenetics Part I: Autosomal Abnormalities," FAMOUS TEACHINGS IN MODERN MEDICINE, N.Y., Medcom Inc., 1972; (photo 2) Aladjen, S., "Fetal Intrauterine Diagnosis and Treatment," FAMOUS TEACHINGS IN MODERN MEDICINE, N.Y., Medcom Inc., 1974;
162—Courtesy, American Cancer Society Picture Library;
163—Bill MacDonald;
165—After M. B. McGraw, "Swimming Behavior of the Human Infant," JOURNAL OF PEDIATRICS, 15, (1939), pp. 485-490. Frank Mayo, artist;
166—After W. Ball and E. Tronick, "Infant Responses to Impending Collision: Optical and Real," SCIENCE, 171, pp. 818-820, © 1971 by the American Association for the Advancement of Science. Frank Mayo, artist;
167—(top) Alice Kandell/Rapho/Photo Researchers, Inc.;
167—Bruce Cayard;
169—(top) After P. Eimas, et. al., "Speech Perception in Infants," SCIENCE, 171, pp. 303-306, © 1971 by the American Association for the Advancement of Science;
170—Wayne Miller/Magnum;
171—Suzanne Szasz.

CHAPTER 8
174—James R. Smith;
177—Courtesy, Downstate Medical Center. Photo by Camilla Smith;
178—George Zimbel/Monkmeyer Press Photo Service;
179—Peter Vandermark/Stock, Boston'
180—Dr. Carolyn Rovel-Collier, Rutgers Department of Psychology;
181—Bill MacDonald;
182—Terry W. Bisbee;
183—After J. Piaget and B. Inhelder, THE CHILD'S CONCEPTION OF SPACE, © 1956 by Humanities Press and Routledge & Kegan Paul Ltd., John Dawson, artist;
183—From R. Lewis (ed.), MIRACLES: POEMS BY CHILDREN OF THE ENGLISH-SPEAKING WORLD. © 1966 by R. Lewis. Reprinted by permission of Simon and Schuster, a Division of Gulf and Western Corporation;
184—Steve Wells;
185—John Dawson;
186—Eileen Cowin;
188—(top) Bill MacDonald; (bottom) John Dawson after B. Inhelder and J. Piaget, THE GROWTH OF LOGICAL THINKING FROM CHILDHOOD TO ADOLESCENCE, figure 9, chapter 11, © 1958 by

Basic Books, Inc., New York;
190—Frank Mayo;
191—After M. Clark and M. Gosnell, "The Graying of America," NEWSWEEK, February 28, 1977;
192—After K. W. Schaie and G. Labouvie-Vief, "Generational versus Octogenetic Components of Change in Adult Behavior: A 14 Year Cross-Sequential Stody," DEVELOPMENTAL PSYCHOLOGY, 10, 305-320, © 1974 by the American Psychological Association. Reprinted by permission.

CHAPTER 9
196—James Rosenquist's "Marilyn Monroe, I" 1962. The Sydney and Harriet Janis Collection, Gift to the Museum of Modern Art, New York;
199—Camilla Smith;
200—Saul Steinberg's "Dream of E" Whitney Museum of American Art, Collection Jim Dine. Photo by Geoffrey Clements;
201—Tom Bledsoe/Photo Researchers, Inc.;
202—D. Premack, PSYCHOLOGY TODAY, September 1970;
203—Courtesy, Dr. Fouts. The University of Oklahoma;
205—From S.D. Krashen, "The Critical Period for Language Acquisition and its Possible Basis," DEVELOPMENTAL PSYCHOLINGUISTICS AND COMMUNICATION DISORDERS (D. Aaronson and R.W. Rieber, eds.), Vol. 203 of ANNALS OF THE NY ACADEMY OF SCIENCES, (1975), pp. 211-224;
206—Erich Hartmann/Magnum;
207—Frank Mayo;
208—Frank Mayo;
209—Frank Mayo;
210—After R. Brown, A FIRST LANGUAGE: THE EARLY STAGES, Harvard University Press. © 1973 by the President and Fellows of Harvard College;
211—Bill MacDonald; After R. Brown, A FIRST LANGUAGE: THE EARLY STAGES, Harvard University Press. © 1973 by the President and Fellows of Harvard College;
211—Bill MacDonald;
213—Saul Steinberg's "Ship of State," 1959. Courtesy of the Indiana University Art Museum, Ken Strothman, Photographer;
215—Courtesy, Munsell Color, Baltimore, Md.

CHAPTER 10
218—Len Speier;
221—James R. Smith;
222—Jeffrey Foxx/Woodfin Camp & Assoc.;
224—William Gedney;
225—Darrel Millsap;
227—Tyrone Hall/Stock, Boston;
228—Mary Ellen Mark/Stock, Boston;
231—Linda Ferrer Rogers/Woodfin Camp & Assoc.;
233-234—Adapted from L. Kohlberg, "Stage and Sequence: The Cognitive Developmental Approach to Socialization," Fig. 6.2 p. 384, HANDBOOK OF SOCIALIZATION THEORY AND RESEARCH (D.A.

Goslin, ed.), © 1969 by Rand McNally College Publishing Company. Reprinted by permission;
235—(top) From L. Kohlberg, Figure 1 in "The Development of Children's Orientation Towards a Moral Order," VITA HUMANA, 6, (1963) pp.11-33. Reprinted by permission of S. Karger, Ag Basel;
235—(bottom) After L. Kohlberg, PSYCHOLOGY TODAY, September 1968.

CHAPTER 11

244—Camilla Smith/Rainbow;
246—From O.S. Fowler and L.N. Fowler, PHRENOLOGY: A PRACTICAL GUIDE TO YOUR HEAD. © 1969 Chelsea House Publishers, a division of Chelsea House Educational Communications, Inc. Reprinted by permission. Frank Mayo, artist;
248—John Dawson;
249—After P. L. Williams and R. Warwick, FUNCTIONAL NEUROANATOMY OF MAN, 1st edn. (1975) Edinburgh: Churchill Livingstone. Harriet Phillips, artist;
250—Lester V. Bergman & Associates (top left); Julius Weber (center); UPI/COMPIX (right); Doug Armstrong (bottom);
251—After C. F. Stevens, NEUROPHYSIOLOGY: A PRIMER, © 1966. Reprinted by permission of John Wiley and Sons, Inc.;
252—After P. L. Williams and R. Warwick, FUNCTIONAL NEUROANATOMY OF MAN, 1st edn. (1975). Edinburgh: Churchill Livingstone. Harriet Phillips, artist;
253—After Ernest Gardner, FUNDAMENTALS OF NEUROLOGY, 6th ed. Philadelphia: W. B. Saunders, 1975. Harriet Phillips, artist;
255—After R. C. Truex and M. B. Carpenter, HUMAN NEUROANATOMY, © 1976 Williams and Wilkins Co., Harriet Phillips, artist;
256—Harriet Phillips;
258—Harriet Phillips;
259—After M. Gazzaniga, "One Brain-Two Minds?" AMERICAN SCIENTIST, 60 (1972), 311-317. Harriet Phillips, artist;
260—Harriet Phillips;
262—After W. Penfield and T. Rasmussen, THE CEREBRAL CORTEX OF MAN, © 1950 by Macmillan Publishing Co., Inc. Frank Mayo, artist;
263—Courtesy, Neal Miller.

CHAPTER 12

268—"Ice," 1966 Richard Lindner, Collection of the Whitney Museum of American Art;
274—Harriet Phillips;
275—Jay Braun;
276—(top) From S. Hecht and S. Shlaer, "The Course of Dark Adaptation Following a High Level of Light Adaptation," JOURNAL OF THE OPTICAL SOCIETY OF AMERICA, 272 and 273;
278—(b) After Julian Hochberg, PERCEPTION, Prentice-Hall;
279—(left) John Dawson;
279—(right) John Dawson;
280—Harriet Phillips;
281—(top) Tom O'Mary;
281—(bottom) Harriet Phillips;
282—Frank Mayo;
283—Elliott Erwitt/Magnum;

284—Jason Lauré/Woodfin Camp & Assoc.;
286—(top) Courtesy, Armour-Dial Inc.;
286—(bottom) John Dawson;
287—(left) John Dawson;
287—(right) Anestis Diakopoulos/Stock, Boston;
288—John Dawson.

CHAPTER 13

292—Benno Friedman;
295—BLOC PIX ® image by Leon D. Harmon and E. J. Manning;
297—(A) After R. G. Carraher and J. B. Thurston, OPTICAL ILLUSIONS AND THE VISUAL ARTS, © by Litton Educational Publishing, Inc. Reprinted by permission of Van Nostrand Reinhold Company. Frank Mayo, artist; (B) R. James;
299—Tom O'Mary;
300—Yoram Lehmann/Peter Arnold, Inc.;
301—Frank Mayo;
303—After P. Lindsay and D. Norman, HUMAN INFORMATION PROCESSING: AN INTRODUCTION TO PSYCHOLOGY, © 1972 by Academic Press;
303—(top) John Dawson;
303—(bottom, left) Tom Suzuki;
304—(left) Courtesy, J. Paul Getty Museum. Photos by Jay Braun;
304—(right) Frank Siteman/Stock, Boston;
305—(center photos) Philip Clark, (right) Bob Ward;
306—(top) Steve McCarroll;
306—(bottom) Ernst Haas;
308—(left) John Dawson, (right) photo by Robert Berger, reprinted with permission of SCIENCE DIGEST © Hearst Corporation;
308—After E.G. Boring, "A New Ambiguous Figure," AMERICAN JOURNAL OF PSYCHOLOGY, © 42 (1930) 444-445;
309—After R. Held and A. Hein, "Movement-produced Stimulation in the Development of Visually Guided Behavior," JOURNAL OF COMPARATIVE AND PHYSIOLOGICAL PSYCHOLOGY, 56, (1963), 872-876. Frank Mayo, artist;
310—Leon Petulengro/Woodfin Camp & Assoc.;
312—After H.W. Leibowitz and H.A. Pick, Jr., "Cross-Cultural and Educational Aspects of the Ponzo Perspective Illusion," PERCEPTION AND PSYCHOPHYSICS, 12:5, (1972), 430-432. Frank Mayo, artist.

CHAPTER 14

316—James R. Smith;
319—After R. Sperry, "Perception in the Absence of Neocortical Commissures" PERCEPTION AND ITS DISORDERS, 48, 1970. Reprinted by permission of the Association for Research in Nervous and Mental Diseases. Harriet Phillips, artist;
320—(top) John Dawson;
321—(top) James H. Karales/Peter Arnold, Inc.;
322—New York University Art Collection, Grey Art Gallery and Study Center. Anonymous Gift;
323—After E. Hartmann, THE BIOLOGY OF DREAMING, © 1976 Charles Thomas, Publisher;
326—After F.A. Pattie, "A Report of Attempts to Produce Uniocular Blindness by Hypnotic Suggestion," BRITISH JOURNAL OF MEDICAL PSYCHOLOGY. 15 (1935), 230-241;
327—After E.R. Hilgard, HYPNOTIC SUSCEPTIBILITY, Harcourt, Brace, Jovanovich, Inc.;
328—Camilla Smith;
332—TRIANGLE, The Sandoz Journal of Medical Science, 2 (1955), 119-123.

CHAPTER 15

336—Benno Friedman;
338—Branko Lenart, Jr;
339—Photograph by Bruce Dale, National Geographic Society;
341—Camilla Smith;
342—Editorial Photocolor Archives, Inc.;
343—Costa Manos/Magnum;
345—James H. Karales/Peter Arnold, Inc.;
346—Jack Prelutsky/Stock, Boston;
347—Karl Nicholason;
348—Frank Mayo;
349—After P. Ekman, W. Friesen, E. Phoebe, EMOTION IN THE HUMAN FACE: GUIDELINES FOR RESEARCH AND AN INTEGRATION OF FINDINGS, Pergamon Press, Ltd.;
350—Thomas Höpker/Woodfin Camp & Assoc.;
351—(top) After R. Lazarus and E. Alfert, "The Short-Circuiting of Threat by Experimentally Altering Cognitive Appraisal," JOURNAL OF ABNORMAL AND SOCIAL PSYCHOLOGY, 69, 195-205, © 1964 by the American Psychological Association. Reprinted by permission;
351—(bottom) Frank Mayo;
352—David Powers/Jeroboam;
353—Reproduced from P. Ekman (ed.), DARWIN AND FACIAL EXPRESSIONS, Academic Press, 1973, with permission from Paul Ekman and Silvan Tomkins.

CHAPTER 16

356—"No Thank You," 1964, Roy Lichtenstein, collection Max Palevsky, Leo Castelli;
360—Bruce Davidson/Magnum;
363—Karen Preuss/Jeroboam;
365—(top) After "The Pathology of Boredom," by Woodburn Heron © 1957 by SCIENTIFIC AMERICAN, INC. All rights reserved;
365—(bottom) Courtesy of R. A. Butler;
366—A. Devaney, Inc.;
367—J. P. Bolle/Sygma;
366-367—(photo one) J. P. Bolle/Sygma (photo two) © 1975 by The Conde Nast Publications, Inc. Permission by Deborah Turbeville;
368—(top) Bruce Cayard;
370—Harry Crosby;
373—(top and bottom) From M. S. Horner, "Femininity and Successful Achievement: A Basic Inconsistency," in J. Bardwick et al., FEMININE PERSONALITY AND CONFLICT, © 1970 by Wadsworth Publishing Company, Inc. Reprinted by permission of Brooks/Cole Publishing Company, Monterey, California 93940.

CHAPTER 17

378—Robert Rauschenberg's "Persimmon," 1964. Collection of Mrs. Leo Castelli. Leo Castelli Gallery;

380—Joe Baker/The Image Bank;

381—From J. L. McClary, HUMAN SEXU-ALITY, 3rd Edition. New York: D. Van Nostrand Company, 1977. By permission. Harriet Phillips, artist;

382—Tom Myers/Taurus Photos;

385—Giorgio Armani;

387—"We Rose Up Slowly," painting by Roy Lichtenstein. Courtesy, Leo Castelli Gallery, Collection: Karl Stroher, Dormstadt. Photograph by Rudolph Burckhardt;

388—Harold Jones;

390—After W. Masters and V. Johnson, HUMAN SEXUAL RESPONSE, Little Brown, 1966, p. 5;

395—From Kinsey et al., SEXUAL BEHAV-IOR IN THE HUMAN FEMALE, W. B. Saunders, 1953, p. 48.

CHAPTER 18

402—Joan Menschenfreund;

405—EPA, Documerica;

407—(top) Terry Lamb, (center) From S. Freud, NEW INTRODUCTORY LEC-TURES ON PSYCHOANALYSIS, (1933). J. Strachey (ed. and tr.). New York: Norton, 1965;

409—Reproduced by permission of the Bristol Myers Company;

411—Amy Meadow;

416-417—D. C. Comics, Inc. © 1978;

418—From K. Horney, THE NEUROTIC PERSONALITY IN OUR TIME. New York; Norton, 1939;

419—Reproduced from Erik H. Erikson, CHILDHOOD AND SOCIETY, Second Edition, Revised, with permission of W.W. Norton & Company, Inc. © 1950, © 1963 by W.W. Norton & Company, Inc.;

420—From E.H. Erikson, GANDHI'S TRUTH: ON THE ORIGINS OF MILI-TANT NONVIOLENCE. New York: Norton, 1969.

CHAPTER 19

424—Len Speier;

427—Burk Uzzle/Magnum;

428—Tony Korody/Sygma;

429—Frank Mayo;

430—From B.F. Skinner, WALDEN TWO, © 1948, 1976, by permission of Macmillan Publishing Company, Inc. Bruce Cayard, artist;

432—D. C. Comics, Inc. © 1970;

433—Arthur Tress;

436—Mariette Pathy Allen;

438—Shelly Rusten;

439—The Bettmann Archive, Inc.;

443—Based on H. Eysenck, THE STRUC-TURE OF HUMAN PERSONALITY. Reproduced by permission of Methuen & Co., Ltd., publishers.

CHAPTER 20

448—James R. Smith;

453—Adapted from the MANUAL FOR THE THIRD REVISION OF THE STAN-FORD-BINET INTELLIGENCE SCALE, © 1973 by Houghton Mifflin Co. Adapted by permission of Houghton Mifflin Company;

454—Photos by John Oldenkamp, with permission of the Houghton Mifflin Company, from Terman and Merrill Stanford–Binet Intelligence Scale;

455—Courtesy of Dr. Paul Shaar, YMCA Counseling and Test Service;

456—Adapted from the WECHSLER IN-TELLIGENCE SCALE FOR CHILDREN-REVISED, © 1974 by the Psychological Corporation. Used by permission. Bruce Cayard, artist;

457—From the WECHSLER INTELLI-GENCE SCALE FOR CHILDREN-RE-VISED. © 1971, 1975 by the Psychological Corporation. Used by permission;

458—(top) Courtesy of U.S. Department of Labor; (bottom) Steve McCarroll;

459—From A. Dove in "Taking the Chitling Test," NEWSWEEK, 7/15, © 1968 by Newsweek, Inc. All rights reserved. Reprinted by permission;

460-461—Frank Mayo;

463—After M. Richards, K. Richardson, and D. Spears, "Conclusion: Intelligence and Society," RACE AND INTELLI-GENCE, p. 187;

464—From R.I. Lanyon and L.D. Good-stein, "PERSONALITY ASSESSMENT (1971), p. 50. Reprinted by permission of John Wiley and Sons, Inc., New York;

465—From R.I. Lanyon and L.D. Good-stein, PERSONALITY ASSESSMENT (1971), p. 57-58. Reprinted by permission of John Wiley and Sons, Inc., New York;

466—Adapted from H. Murray, THEMAT-IC APPERCEPTION TEST, Harvard University Press, © 1943 by the President and Fellows of Harvard College; Renewed © 1971 by Henry A. Murray;

467—After R. Lanyon, A HANDBOOK OF MMPI GROUP PROFILES, The University of Minnesota Press, Minneapolis, © 1968 by the University of Minnesota;

469—Adapted from C.H. Lay and D.N. Jackson, "Analysis of the Generality of Trait-Inferential Relationships," JOURNAL OF PERSONALITY AND SOCIAL PSY-CHOLOGY, 12, pp. 12-21, © 1969 by the American Psychological Association. Reprinted by permission;

470—Adapted from D.N. Jackson, PER-SONALITY RESEARCH FORM MANUAL, © 1967 by Research Psychologists Press, Inc.

CHAPTER 21

476—John Lei;

479—Courtesy, Air France;

481—After R.H. Rahe, "The Pathway Between Subjects' Recent Life Changes and Their Near-Future Illness Reports: Representative Results and Methodological Issues," STRESSFUL LIFE EVENTS: THEIR NATURE AND EFFECTS, 1974, (B.S. Dohrenwend and B.P. Dohrenwend, eds.) pp. 73-86. Reprinted by permission of John Wiley and Sons, Inc;

482—After A. Vinokur and M.L. Selzer, "Desirable Versus Undesirable Life Events: Their Relationship to Stress and Mental Distress," JOURNAL OF PERSONALITY AND SOCIAL PSYCHOLOGY, 32:2, pp. 329-337, © 1975 by the American Psychological Association. Reprinted by permis-sion;

483—Adapted from J.E. Singer, D.C. Glass, and B. Rein, "Behavioral Conse-quences of Adaptation to Controllable and Uncontrollable Noise," JOURNAL OF EX-PERIMENTAL SOCIAL PSYCHOLOGY, 7, (1971), pp. 244-257. Reprinted by per-mission of Academic Press, Inc. and J.E. Singer, D.C. Glass, and B. Reim;

484—Owen Franken/Stock, Boston;

485—Neal Slavin;

486—Leonard Freed/Magnum;

489—(top) Arthur Tress/Woodfin Camp & Assoc.;

489—(bottom) Cary Wolinsky/Stock, Bos-ton;

491—Jim Anderson/Woodfin Camp & As-soc.;

494—Judith Golden;

495—After D. Levinson with C.N. Darrow, E.B. Klein, M.H. Levinson and B. McKee, THE SEASONS OF A MAN'S LIFE, © 1978 Alfred A. Knopf, Inc.;

CHAPTER 22

500—"Standing Man," W. DeKooning. Wadsworth Atheneum, Hartford, Connecti-cut; Ella Gallup and Mary Catlin Sumner Collection;

502—Neal Slavin;

504—John Banasiak;

505—Frank Mayo;

506—John Dawson;

508—Courtesy, Roche;

509—Mary Ellen Mark/Magnum;

510—(top and bottom) Courtesy of Al Ver-coutere, Camarillo State Hospital;

512—Camilla Smith;

513—After K. Kollwitz, ALTER MANN MIT STRICK, National Gallery of Art, Washington, Rosenwald Collection;

514—"Hostess Mask," S. Steinberg. Collec-tion of the artist, courtesy Sydney Janis Gal-lery, New York;

515—Susan Meiselas/Magnum;

516—Folco/Liaison;

517—Howard Sochurek;

518—From M. Kramer, "Statistics of Men-tal Disorders in the United States: Some Ur-gent Needs and Suggested Solutions," JOURNAL OF THE ROYAL STATISTI-CAL SOCIETY, series A, 132 (1969).

CHAPTER 23

522—Arthur Tress;

526—Mary Ellen Mark/Magnum;

528—Jerry N. Uelsmann;

530—Jeffrey Foxx/Woodfin Camp & Associ-ates;

532—Martha Swope;

534—After I. Gottesman and J. Shields, SCHIZOPHRENIA AND GENETICS: A TWIN-STUDY VANTAGE POINT, © 1972, Academic Press, Inc.;

535—After T. Lidz et al., "The Intrafamilial Environment of Schizophrenic Patients: Marital Schism and Marital Skew," THE AMERICAN JOURNAL OF PSYCHIA-TRY, 114 (1957), pp. 241-248. © 1957, The American Psychiatric Association. Reprinted by permission;

537—Bruce Davidson/Magnum;

538—Murray Riss;

538—After R. D. Laing, KNOTS, © 1970

by the R. D. Laing Trust. By permission of Tavistock Publications, Ltd.

CHAPTER 24

542—Dan McCoy/Rainbow;
545—Gil Spitzer;
547—Arthur Tress;
550—From F. Kanfer and J. Phillips, LEARNING FOUNDATIONS OF BEHAVIOR THERAPY, John Wiley and Sons, © 1970. Reprinted by permission;
551—John Oldenkamp;
552—Adapted from G. Patterson, FAMILIES: APPLICATIONS OF SOCIAL LEARNING TO FAMILY LIFE, © 1971 by Research Press;
553—Philippe Achache/Gamma/Liaison;
554—Bruce Hoertel;
556—Adapted from M.L. Smith and G.V. Glass, "Meta-analysis of psychotherapy outcome studies," AMERICAN PSYCHOLOGIST, 32 (1977), 752-760;
557—From L.B. Luborsky, et al., "Factors Influencing the Outcome of Therapy: A Review of Quantitative Research," PSYCHOLOGICAL BULLETIN, 75 (1971), pp. 145-185.

CHAPTER 25

564—Terry W. Bisbee;
566—Philip Jones Griffiths/Magnum;
568—(left) Courtesy, McDonald's, (right) Courtesy, Procter & Gamble;
571—(left) Owen Franken/Sygma, (right) Christina Thomson/Woodfin Camp & Associates;
572—Courtesy, Grumman Energy Systems, Inc.;
574—Darrel Millsap;
575—Courtesy, AT & T Lines;
576—After J.L. Freedman, J.M. Carlsmith, and D.O. Sears, SOCIAL PSYCHOLOGY, 2nd ed. p. 283. Reprinted by permission of Prentice-Hall, Inc., Englewood Cliffs, New Jersey;
577—Courtesy, C.F. Hathaway Company;
578—After N. Miller and D.T. Campbell, "Recency and Primacy in Pursuasion as a Function of the Timing of Speeches and Measurements," JOURNAL OF ABNORMAL AND SOCIAL PSYCHOLOGY, 59, 1-9 © 1959 by the American Psychological Association. Reprinted by permission;
579—Courtesy, World Medical News;
580—After W. McGuire and D. Papageorgis, "The Relative Efficacy of Various Types of Prior Relief-Defense in Producing Immunity Against Persuasion," JOURNAL OF ABNORMAL AND SOCIAL PSYCHOLOGY, 62, 327-337, © 1961 by the American Psychological Association.

CHAPTER 26

584—Jim Leach;
587—Courtesy of Tinker, Dodge & Delano, Inc. for Smirnoff, division of Heublein, Hartford;
588—After K. Dion, "Social Desirability and the Evaluation of a Harm-Doer," unpublished doctoral dissertation, U. of Minnesota, 1970, cited in PSYCHOLOGY TODAY, 5 (1972), 44-45. Frank Mayo, artist;

589—From H. H. Kelley, "The Warm-Cold Variable in First Impressions of Persons," JOURNAL OF PERSONALITY, 18, pp. 431-439. © 1950 by Duke University Press;
590—(bottom left) Bill Call;
590—(bottom right) Max Waldman;
592—After M. Storms, "Videotape and the Attribution Process: Reversing Actors' and Observers' Points of View," JOURNAL OF PERSONALITY AND SOCIAL PSYCHOLOGY, 27, 167-175, © 1973 by the American Psychological Association. Reprinted by permission. Bruce Cayard, artist;
593—Adapted from L. Festinger, S. Schachter, and K. Back, SOCIAL PRESSURES IN INFORMAL GROUPS. © 1950 by the Board of Trustees of the Leland Stanford Junior University. By permission of the Stanford University Press;
595—(right) NEWSWEEK/Wally McNamee;
597—(top) Adapted from M. Zanna and S. Pack, "On the Self-Fulfilling Nature of Apparent Sex Differences in Behavior," JOURNAL OF EXPERIMENTAL SOCIAL PSYCHOLOGY, 11 (1975), p. 589;
597—(bottom) Neal Slavin;
598—After Aronson and Linder, "Gain and Loss of Esteem as Determinants of Interpersonal Attractiveness," JOURNAL OF EXPERIMENTAL SOCIAL PSYCHOLOGY, 1 (1965), pp. 156-172;
600—"Kiss V" by Roy Lichtenstein. Photo by Camilla Smith.

CHAPTER 27

604—Len Speier;
607—Michal Heron/Woodfin Camp & Assoc.;
608—From J.C. Armen, GAZELLE-BOY: A CHILD BROUGHT UP BY GAZELLES IN THE SAHARA DESERT, Universe Books, New York, 1974. Frank Mayo, artist;
609—After A. Schacter, THE PSYCHOLOGY OF AFFILIATION, Stanford University Press, 1959, p. 18;
610—(top) Neal Slavin;
610—(bottom) After I.R. Sarnoff and P.G. Zimbardo, "Anxiety, Fear, and Social Affiliation," JOURNAL OF ABNORMAL AND SOCIAL PSYCHOLOGY, 62, pp. 356-363, © 1961 by the American Psychological Association. Reprinted by permission;
611—Len Speier;
612—After Solomon Asch;
613—Don Rutledge/Black Star;
614—From S. Milgram, "Behavioral Study of Obedience," JOURNAL OF ABNORMAL AND SOCIAL PSYCHOLOGY, 67 (1963), pp. 371-378. © 1963 by the American Psychological Association. Reprinted by permission;
615—(bottom) Charles Gatewood/Magnum;
616—After S. Milgram, "Some Conditions of Obedience to Authority," HUMAN RELATIONS, 18 (1965), p. 63;
619—Marcia Resnick.

CHAPTER 28

622—"Good Morning II," by Alex Katz,

Courtesy, Marlborough Gallery, Inc.;
624—Buffon–Sygma;
626—Frank Mayo;
627—After K.R. Scherer, R.P. Abeles, and C.S. Fischer, HUMAN AGGRESSION AND CONFLICT: INTERDISCIPLINARY PERSPECTIVES (1975), p. 17. Reprinted by permission of Prentice-Hall, Inc., Englewood Cliffs, New Jersey. Harriet Phillips, artist;
628—(top) A. Bandura, D. Ross, and S.A. Ross, "Imitation of Film-Mediated Aggressive Models," JOURNAL OF ABNORMAL AND SOCIAL PSYCHOLOGY, 66, 3-11. © 1963 by the American Psychological Association. Reprinted by permission;
629—Frank Edwards/Photos International Pictorial Parade;
630—Anderson/Stock, Boston;
632—Owen Franken/Stock, Boston;
633—After J. M. Darley and B. Latane, "When Will People Help?" PSYCHOLOGY TODAY MAGAZINE, 2, p. 54, © 1968 Ziff-Davis Publishing Co. Frank Mayo, artist;
634—After I. Piliavin, J. Rodin, and J. A. Piliavin, "Good Samaritanism: An Underground Phenomenon?" JOURNAL OF PERSONALITY AND SOCIAL PSYCHOLOGY, 13:4, pp. 289-299, © 1969 by the American Psychological Association. Reprinted by permission;
635—(top) After I. Piliavin, J.A. Piliavin, and J. Rodin, "Costs, Diffusion, and the Stigmatized Victim," JOURNAL OF PERSONALITY AND SOCIAL PSYCHOLOGY, 32:3, 429-438, © 1975 by the American Psychological Association. Reprinted by permission;
635—(bottom) Charles Harbutt/Magnum;
636—After D.L. Rosehan, B. Underwood, and B. Moore, "Affect Moderates Self-Gratification and Altruism," JOURNAL OF PERSONALITY AND SOCIAL PSYCHOLOGY, 30:4, pp. 546-552, © 1974 by the American Psychological Association. Reprinted by permission;
637—Mary Jury Communications;
639—After M. Deutsch and R.M. Krauss, "The Effect of Threat Upon Interpersonal Bargaining," JOURNAL OF ABNORMAL AND SOCIAL PSYCHOLOGY, 61, pp. 181-189, © 1960 by the American Psychological Association. Reprinted by permission;
640—W. Ioors/Image Bank;
641—(top) After H. Wichman, "Effects of Isolation and Communication in a Two-Person Game," JOURNAL OF PERSONALITY AND SOCIAL PSYCHOLOGY, 16, pp. 114-120, © 1970 by the American Psychological Association. Reprinted by permission;
641—(bottom) After R.M. Dawes, J. McTavish, and H. Shaklee, "Behavior, Communication and Assumption About Other People's Behavior in a Common Dilemma Situation," JOURNAL OF PERSONALITY AND SOCIAL PSYCHOLOGY, 35:1, pp. 1-11, © 1977 by the American Psychological Association. Reprinted by permission.